THE PAPERS OF
General Nathanael Greene

*Nathanael Greene, 1742–1786; oil painting by Charles Willson Peale,
from which most later likenesses were copied or derived*
(Independence National Historical Park Collection)

THE PAPERS OF
General Nathanael Greene

VOLUME XIII
22 May 1783–13 June 1786,
with Additions to the Series

Roger N. Parks
EDITOR

Elizabeth C. Stevens
ASSOCIATE EDITOR

Dennis M. Conrad
CONTRIBUTING EDITOR

Assisted by Nathaniel N. Shipton

THE UNIVERSITY OF NORTH CAROLINA PRESS
Chapel Hill

Published for the
RHODE ISLAND HISTORICAL SOCIETY

© 2005 The University of North Carolina Press
All rights reserved
Manufactured in the United States of America

Publication of this work was assisted by a grant from the
National Historical Publications and Records Commission.

⊛ The paper in this book meets the guidelines for permanence
and durability of the Committee on Production Guidelines for
Book Longevity of the Council on Library Resources.

Library of Congress Cataloging-in-Publication Data
(Revised for vol. 10)

Greene, Nathanael, 1742–1786.
  The papers of General Nathanael Greene.
  Secondary editors vary.
  Vol. 13
  Includes bibliographical references and indexes.
  Contents: v. 1. December 1766–December 1776–
[etc.]—v. 11. 7 April–30 September 1782–v. 13. 22 May
1783–13 June 1786, with additions to the series.
    1. Greene, Nathanael, 1742–1786—Manuscripts.
  2. United States—History—Revolution, 1775–1783—
  Sources.   3. Manuscripts, American.   I. Showman,
  Richard K.   II. Rhode Island Historical Society.
  III. Title.
  E207.G9A3   1976   973.3'3'0924   76-20441
  ISBN 0-8078-1285-4 (v. 1)
  ISBN 0-8078-1384-2 (v. 2)
  ISBN 0-8078-1557-8 (v. 3)
  ISBN 0-8078-1668-X (v. 4)
  ISBN 0-8078-1817-8 (v. 5)
  ISBN 0-8078-1993-X (v. 6)
  ISBN 0-8078-2094-6 (v. 7)
  ISBN 0-8078-2212-4 (v. 8)
  ISBN 0-8078-2310-4 (v. 9)
  ISBN 0-8078-2419-4 (v. 10)
  ISBN 0-8078-2551-4 (v. 11)
  ISBN 0-8078-2713-4 (v. 12)
  ISBN 0-8078-2943-9 (v. 13)

09   08   07   06   05   5   4   3   2   1

TABLE OF CONTENTS

ILLUSTRATIONS

INTRODUCTION

After sending the last of his restive Southern Army troops home in July 1783, Nathanael Greene, with a few companions, set out from Charleston, South Carolina, in mid-August, traveling north by land to join his family in Rhode Island. After more than eight years of Revolutionary War service, beginning at the siege of Boston, Greene stood next to George Washington among American officers in terms of the military reputation and respect he had earned, and he had capped his career with successful campaigns in the South that had helped to turn the momentum of the war in favor of the Americans.

Along his way home—and later in Rhode Island—Greene received congratulations and thanks from the residents of a number of communities. At Richmond, Virginia, local officials expressed a hope that he would "possess in retirement, the generous confidence of a free people," that all of his "future days may be serene and happy," and that the "plaudit of future ages may follow the testimony of a living world in transmitting, to the latest posterity," the memory of his "Character and virtues." At Alexandria, Virginia, town officials informed Greene that his troops and he had shown the world that "circumstances of the greatest distress, and a Situation surrounded with danger and with difficulty can be nobly surmounted by brave Men, animated with the spirit of liberty, and under the command of wise, virtuous and persevering Leaders." The Alexandria officials hoped that Greene's future would be "attended with as much happiness" as his "command in the Army has been with glory and success."

In early October, Greene's arrival in Philadelphia was greeted by the ringing of bells. Later that month, at Princeton, New Jersey, Congress voted to give him two engraved cannon, captured from the British "at the Cowpens, Augusta or Eutaw," as "a public testimonial of the wisdom, fortitude & military skill which distinguished his Command in the Southern Department and of the eminent services which amidst complicated difficulties and dangers and against an Enemy greatly superior in numbers he has successfully performed for his Country." Congress also voted to allow him "a Clerk to copy into a Book or Books the papers or Letters in his possession relative to the Southern operations" and granted him leave to "visit his family at Rhode Island."

In late November, Greene arrived in Newport, where his wife, Catharine, and their children were living. During the next few years, his time with his family would be interrupted by frequent business trips, two of which were of considerable duration. Three more children would be born, only one of whom would survive. In late 1785, the family would leave Rhode Island to settle on Mulberry Grove, a rice plantation that the state of Georgia had given to Greene, but that move would take place little more than half a year before his untimely death in June 1786, at age forty-three.

The letters in this volume do not suggest that Greene experienced much serenity or happiness during his final years of life. Much of the correspondence deals with financial matters: with the settlement of various army accounts and of business partnership affairs, as well as with Greene's efforts to surmount an increasingly difficult burden of personal debt. In early August 1783, even before he left Charleston, he complained to Catharine, who had recently made some large purchases in Philadelphia during her own trip home from the South: "[Charles] Pettit writes . . . that he has got you a pair of horses to your liking, and a Phaeton and that a Chariot is making and that the amount of the whole will be upwards of 1400 Dollars. He adds also that he shall want the money the moment I arrive. How or where to get it god knows for I dont. Col [Jeremiah] Wadsworth informs me that all my stocks put into his hands have been lost; and that out of upwards of a thousand pounds put into his hands four years ago, I have not fifty left. This loss and those heavy losses with my brothers distresses my private affairs exceedingly. The demands upon me here are heavy and they will be more pressing as I go Northward. I had rather live in a cave than be under so much perplexity; and what adds to my vexation is I can not improve my Estate here without running still more in debt."

Greene, who had been given rice plantations by the states of South Carolina and Georgia (as well as a large grant of frontier land in what is now Tennessee from North Carolina officials), was determined to hold onto both of them and operate them profitably. To do so, he needed working capital. It was clear even before he left the army, however, that the businesses in which he had been essentially a silent partner during the war—the partnership with his former chief assistants in the Quartermaster Department, Pettit and John Cox; the Connecticut mercantile firm of Barnabas Deane & Company, in which Wadsworth, Deane, and he were partners; and his family's firm, Jacob Greene & Company—had not done well enough to be of much help to him. Between early 1784 and early 1786, Greene tried to obtain a loan in Europe to help him develop his properties. But in a troubled postwar economy and a political climate in which the Confederation government lacked power to fund and pay down the large public debt incurred during the war, Greene and many other American loan applicants were treated with great caution by European lenders. Robert Morris, the former superintendent of finance, who had corresponded with a Dutch firm on Greene's behalf, finally wrote him in January 1786 that he should no longer have any "expectations from that quarter" and that "an assiduous application to the Cultivation and Improvement of your Estates will be the surest Means of relieving you from the Weight of your engagements."

Greene made extended business trips between Rhode Island and the South during the summer and fall of 1784 and again during the winter and spring of 1785, but until the fall of 1785, when he moved his family to Mulberry Grove, near the city of Savannah on the river of the same name, he left the operation of both of his rice plantations almost entirely to others. He authorized the buying—on credit—of slaves and supplies, but poor crops each year and low market prices made it increasingly difficult to pay for those purchases. In a letter of 13 June 1786, just before he was taken fatally ill, a Charleston mercantile firm with which he had done business asked Greene not to "draw any further Bills upon us, for it will not be convenient, our entering into further advances."

As a plantation owner, Greene, a former Quaker, does not seem to have had any particular misgivings about slavery, although he did indicate on one occasion that he preferred to try to keep his slave families together. Nevertheless, in a June 1783 letter to his cousin Griffin Greene, who was in France trying to sell a ship for the family firm, he suggested that it might be better to load the vessel "for Guinea with French Brandy & some few dry goods." Then, "if the slave trade be opened here & the ship arrive at [Charleston] in April next I think she might make a profitable voyage."

Greene's most serious financial concerns were related to the guarantees he had signed in the early spring of 1783 for debts incurred by John Banks and others as contractors to the Southern Army. His reasons for making these assurances during the final months of the army's existence are discussed in Volume XII of this series. Even before Greene left Charleston in the summer of 1783, evidence had begun to emerge that Banks was not trustworthy and that Greene might be forced to honor the guarantees. By September 1784, facing strong demands from Banks's creditors, Greene had decided that Banks was "the greatest Monster and most finished vilian that this age has produced." The "vilian" was dead by the end of that month, and Greene afterward sought with little success to recover what funds he could from Banks's estate and to continue holding the creditors at bay. An appeal for help that he sent to Congress in August 1785 was unsuccessful, and in March 1786, one of the principal creditors, E. John Collett, again began to press Greene for a settlement. The two men finally met in Savannah on 12 and 13 June, at which time Greene signed new bonds to cover the amount owed to Collett. Greene became ill almost immediately after returning home from that meeting, and he died at Mulberry Grove on 19 June. Some years later, Catharine, with help from Secretary of the Treasury

Alexander Hamilton and others, was able to obtain relief from the federal government for the debts that Greene had guaranteed.

Before he was stricken, Greene had planned to spend part of the summer of 1786 on Cumberland Island, off the Georgia coast, just above the boundary with Spanish East Florida. He hoped to begin harvesting the rich timber resources on holdings he had acquired there and was corresponding with French officials about a contract to sell shipbuilding timber to that country's navy. Cumberland Island was one positive outcome of Greene's dealings with Banks et al., for he had obtained an indenture for a large, undivided half share of land there from Banks and one of Banks's partners, Greene's former aide Ichabod Burnet, as security against the financial guarantees he had signed for them. Burnet died a short time later, and after Banks's death, Greene sought and eventually obtained waivers of inheritance rights from the heirs of both. In addition to assuming responsibility for bonds that Banks and Burnet had given for these properties, Greene, who paid a visit to Cumberland Island and East Florida in the spring of 1785, tried to persuade others to join him in the investment. He seems to have had some hope that he could eventually realize enough profits from his rice plantations and Cumberland Island to extricate himself from his debts. Although Greene was unable to carry out his plan for Cumberland Island, Catharine did retain the holdings and eventually moved her family there.

Greene's untimely death left unanswered questions about the contributions he might have been able to make to the early development of the American republic. A strong nationalist during the war, he would undoubtedly have approved the efforts of the Constitutional Convention to construct a stronger central government. In a eulogy delivered three years after Greene's death, one of his wartime colleagues, Alexander Hamilton, remarked that it would have "required a longer life and still greater opportunities to have enabled [Greene] to exhibit in full day the vast, I had almost said the enormous powers of his mind." One of Greene's few political involvements after the war was an unsuccessful attempt, at Robert Morris's request, to persuade Rhode Island legislators to accept Congress's 1783 impost plan. On other occasions, citing personal reasons, Greene turned down a commission from Congress to participate in negotiations with Indian tribes and an appointment to a judgeship in Georgia. Nor did he take an active role in the controversial new organization of Revolutionary War officers, the Society of the Cincinnati, although the Rhode Island chapter had elected him its first president.

It seems unlikely that Greene would have become seriously involved in public service as long as he remained deeply in debt. His legacy, at any rate, is in his wartime services. These, as has been seen throughout this series of his papers, were important. According to Hamilton,

Greene's reputation as a soldier, though great in his lifetime, fell "far below his desert." (See Epilogue, at the end of the June 1786 documents.) A nineteenth-century historian of Georgia put it this way: "His fame was purely military; but, in that, he stood next to Washington. This fame he secured, not by victories, brilliant and important, but by a series of services, skilful maneuvres, and prudent, yet vigorous, generalship, which enabled him to secure, at length, advantages, greater perhaps than would have resulted from a few brilliant conquests." (Stevens, *History of Georgia*, 2: 373–74) Greene himself had once described his military achievements more succinctly: "We fight[,] get beat[,] rise and fight again." Although he won few battles, he unquestionably did play a significant role in winning the war.

At the end of this volume, we have included an Addenda section, consisting of forty-six documents found since the publication of volumes in which they ordinarily would have appeared. One of the most interesting of these, a letter of 9 April 1771 from Greene to Moses Brown, clearly establishes a fact that the editors of our first volume were unable to verify: that Greene served in the Rhode Island legislature before he entered military life. We have chosen not to include modern maps in this volume, but most of the American place-names mentioned here can be found in maps elsewhere in the series or in the period maps that are used as illustrations in this volume.

Providence, R.I.   ROGER N. PARKS, *Editor*
October 2004

ACKNOWLEDGMENTS

It has been our privilege, in completing our own long associations with the Greene Papers, to finish the work on the letterpress edition that the project's founding editor, the late Richard K. Showman, and his original staff began more than thirty years ago. Dennis M. Conrad, who devoted some eighteen years of full-time service to the Greene Papers, succeeded Showman as editor in 1993. While ably leading the project through the preparation of the important southern campaign volumes, he maintained and expanded upon the high editorial standards that Showman had established. Conrad left to accept another position shortly before the completion of Volume XII but has contributed his knowledge and editing skills to the work on Volume XIII.

Over the years, a number of other Greene Papers staff members, consultants, and interns have made valuable contributions to the project. We would like to mention in particular Robert E. McCarthy, Martha J. King, the late Margaret Cobb, the late Mary MacKechnie Showman, and Nathaniel N. Shipton.

Albert T. Klyberg initiated the project and gave it strong support during his long tenure as director of the Rhode Island Historical Society. Bernard Fishman, the present director, has likewise been supportive, as have many of the Society's other personnel, especially members of the library and business office staffs. For their help while we were working on the present volume, we would like to thank in particular library staff members Rick Statler, Peter Griswold, and Phoebe Simpson, controller Charmyne Goodfellow, and her assistants, Ann Dionne and Renata Luongo. The Society's trustees and its publications committee, the current members of which are listed on page iii, have also helped the project on many occasions.

Our ability to carry on and complete our work has been due in large part to the strong grant support we have long received from the National Historical Publications and Records Commission, the National Endowment for the Humanities, and the State of Rhode Island. We have also benefited from gifts from the Rhode Island chapters of the Society of the Cincinnati and the Sons of the Revolution and a number of other donors. Institutional sponsors are listed on page iii.

We have enjoyed a cordial relationship with the University of North Carolina Press throughout the publication of the series. Among the staff members who have been especially helpful are Ron Maner and Margaretta Yarborough.

For copies of some of the documents included in this volume, we thank Thomas E. Baker, Catherine Barnes, Robert F. Batchelder, David Coblentz, Bruce Gimelson, Robert Goldman, Thomas Casey Greene, Thomas Enoch Greene, Joseph Rubinfine, and Scott A. Winslow. We are grateful to Farris Cadle of Savannah, Ga., for his unflagging interest in the project and for the help he has given us with questions pertaining to Greene's tenure in Georgia. Other individuals who have helped with research questions or have helped us locate key materials include Jewell Anderson and Mandi Johnson of the Georgia Historical Society; Barbara Austen of the Connecticut Historical Society; Barbara J. Bair of the Library of Congress; Janet Bloom of the Clements Library, University of Michigan; Ellen McCallister Clark of Anderson House, Society of the Cincinnati; Steven Engerrand and Greg Jarrell of the Georgia State Archives; Sam Fore of the South Caroliniana Library, University of South Carolina; Alexandra Gressitt of the Library of Virginia; Lisa Gayle Hazirjian of the William R. Perkins Library, Duke University; Tom Hyry, William R. Massa, Jr., and Danielle Moon of the Yale University archives; Bertram Lippincott III of the Newport Historical Society; Rachel Onuf of the Historical Society of Pennsylvania; and Jan Slee of Newport, R.I. We are also grateful to John C. Dann, Thomas Casey Greene, Jr., Thomas Enoch Greene, and Robert Allen Greene for their continued assistance.

EDITORIAL METHOD

Arrangement of Materials

Letters and documents are arranged chronologically. Letters written over a span of several days have been placed at the last date indicated by the writer. If two or more related items are dated the same day, they are arranged in sequence; if unrelated to each other, they are arranged as follows:

1. Military orders and documents (as opposed to letters)
2. Letters from NG, alphabetically by recipient
3. Letters to NG, alphabetically by sender

Undated Items

If a date omitted by the author can be determined, it is printed in brackets, and the item takes its place chronologically. A doubtful conjecture is followed by a question mark.

If a precise day cannot be established, the shortest conjecturable time span is placed in brackets and the item arranged as follows:

Conjectured Time Span	Chronological Arrangement
[10–18 December 1779]	Placed at 18 December 1779
[April] 1780	Placed at end of April 1780
[November 1779–February 1780]	Placed at end of February 1780
[1780]	Placed at end of 1780
[1779–1781]	Placed at end of 1781
[before 12 June 1781]	Placed at end of 11 June documents
[after 20 July 1780]	Placed at end of 20 July documents

All such conjectures are explained in footnotes.

Misdated Items

If a correct date can be determined for a misdated item, it follows the incorrect date in brackets; if a date is suspected of being incorrect, a question mark in brackets follows.

Form of a Letter

The form of a letter is rendered as follows, regardless of the original:

1. Place and date are at top right.
2. Complimentary close is set continuously with the body.
3. Paragraphs are indented.
4. Author's interlineations or brief additions in the margin are incorporated into the text silently unless of unusual significance, in which case they are explained in a footnote.
5. Scored-out or erased passages are not included unless mentioned in a footnote.
6. Address sheet and docketing are normally omitted.
7. Words underlined in the text are normally italicized.

Calendared Items

Many less important items are calendared, with an abstract of the contents set within brackets. The item is arranged according to date. We often quote from a document, either to retain the flavor and characterize the author or because the quotation is more accurate than any paraphrase could be. The writer's original wording is set off by quotation marks, or if in a lengthy passage, by indentation.

MANUSCRIPT TEXTUAL POLICY

In earlier volumes, following the practice established by Julian Boyd, Leonard Labaree, and others, manuscripts were rendered in such a way as to be intelligible to the present-day reader while retaining the essential form and spirit of the writer. Beginning with Volume VII, the Greene Papers have moved closer to a literal rendering of the manuscripts, with the editors using brackets to indicate changes made to clarify the text. In a very few cases, spelled out below, the editors alter the text silently.

Spelling

Spelling is retained as written. If a misspelled word or name is not readily recognizable, the correct spelling follows in brackets. Names are correctly spelled in notes and index.

Inadvertent repetitions of words are corrected silently.

Capitalization

The author's capitalization is followed, including the eighteenth-century practice of capitalizing words within sentences, except where necessary to conform to the following rules:

1. All sentences begin with initial capitals.

2. Personal names and titles used with them, honorifics (such as "His Excellency"), geographical names, days of the week, and the names of months are capitalized.

Abbreviations and Contractions

1. Shortened word forms still in use or those that can easily be understood (as "t'was" or "twixt") are rendered as written.

2. Those no longer readily understood are treated thus: "cmsy [commissary]" or "warr[an]t."

3. Abbreviations of names or places—forms known only to the correspondents or their contemporaries—are also expanded in brackets, as in S[amuel] A[dams] or Chsn [Charleston].

Symbols Representing Letters and Words

When any of the following symbols are expanded they are done so silently:

1. The thorn, which by 1750 had been debased to "y" as in "ye," is expanded to "th." Such abbreviations as "ye," "y^t," or "y^m" are rendered as "the," "that," or "them."

2. The macron is replaced by the letter(s) it represents—as in com͠mission, which becomes commission, or hap͠en, which becomes happen.

3. The 𝓹 sign is expanded to the appropriate letters it represents (e.g., per, pre, or pro).

Punctuation

Where necessary, punctuation is changed to conform to the following rules:

1. A period or question mark is placed at the end of every sentence.

2. Dashes used in place of commas, semicolons, periods, or question marks are replaced with appropriate punctuation; dashes are retained when used to mark a suspension of the sense or to set off a change of thought.

3. No punctuation is used after a salutation.

Missing or Indecipherable Passages

If such passages cannot be conjectured, they are indicated by italicized editorial comments in brackets, such as [*mutilated*], [*indecipherable*], [*several words missing*], [*remainder of letter missing*].

If missing or indecipherable portions can be conjectured, they are treated in one of the following ways:

1. Any missing letters that are conjectured are inserted in brackets. If there is some doubt about the conjecture, it is followed by a question mark: Ch[arleston?].

2. If such portions can be supplied from a variant version of the manuscript, they are set in angle brackets: ⟨Washington⟩.

3. A blank left by the author is so depicted.

PRINTED MATERIAL

In reprinting documents from printed sources, the capitalization, spelling, punctuation, and paragraphing have been faithfully followed.

SOURCE NOTE

An unnumbered source note directly follows each document. For manuscript material it consists of a symbol describing the type of manuscript, followed by the symbol or name of the repository that owns the document, or the name of an individual owner. Pertinent facts or conjectures concerning the manuscript are added when required. Lists of manuscript symbols and of Library of Congress repository symbols follow the section on annotation below.

ANNOTATION

The editors have set several goals for themselves in annotating the documents. The most important of these is to explain a document sufficiently to make it intelligible to the modern reader who may be unfamiliar with the subject. In a sense, the editor puts the reader in the place of the eighteenth-century recipient of a document by alluding to facts that were unknown or unknowable to them. Another goal is the correction of errors in a document, since many a myth has found its source in "documentary evidence" that was false or inaccurate. Then, too, for the reader's convenience, the editor should relate the document at hand with other documents or notes in the series by the use of cross-references. And there is a final goal: to provide continuity and understanding to the reader by filling significant gaps in the documents.

A few procedural points need emphasis:

1. Identification of persons is usually made at the first appearance of their names and is not repeated. References to these biographical notes are found in the index. Identifications are omitted for such leading figures as Washington or Franklin, as well as for obscure persons who played an insignificant role in NG's career.

2. Cross-references to an earlier volume are designated by volume and page number, as in "See above, vol. 6: 418." Otherwise, cross-references to documents in the current volume are by date, as in "See above, NG to Washington, 11 January." If the document is from a different year, the year is also given, as in "See below, NG to Sumter, 9 February 1782."

3. When a page number does not appear in a citation, the reader can assume the work is in dictionary form.

DESCRIPTIVE SYMBOLS FOR MANUSCRIPTS

Following are the symbols employed in source notes to describe the kinds of manuscripts used in the texts.

AD	Autograph document
ADS	Autograph document signed
ADf	Autograph draft
ADfS	Autograph draft signed
AL	Autograph letter
ALS	Autograph letter signed
D	Document
DDf	Document draft
DS	Document signed
Df	Draft
DfS	Draft signed
L	Letter
LS	Letter signed
LB	Letter book copy
FC	File copy
Cy	Copy (made contemporaneously with original)
ACy	Autograph copy
ACyS	Autograph copy signed
RC	Recipient's copy
RCS	Recipient's copy signed
Tr	Transcript (later copy made for historical record)
[A]	Indicates some uncertainty about the autograph
[S]	Indicates signature has been cropped or obliterated

(No symbol is given to printed letters or documents.)

LIBRARY OF CONGRESS SYMBOLS OF REPOSITORIES

The following institutions have provided copies of manuscripts that are printed, calendared, or cited in Volume XIII:

CSmH	Henry E. Huntington Library, San Marino, Calif.
Ct	Connecticut State Library, Hartford, Conn.
CtHi	Connecticut Historical Society, Hartford, Conn.

CtY Yale University, New Haven, Conn.
DLC U.S. Library of Congress, Washington, D.C.
DNA U.S. National Archives and Records Service, National Archives Library, Washington, D.C.
DSoC Society of the Cincinnati, Washington, D.C.
G-Ar Georgia State Department of Archives and History, Atlanta, Ga.
GL-NHi Gilder Lehrman Collection, New-York Historical Society, New York, N.Y.
GU University of Georgia, Athens, Ga.
ICHi Chicago Historical Society, Chicago, Ill.
ICN Newberry Library, Chicago, Ill.
ICPRCU Polish Roman Catholic Union of America, Chicago, Ill.
MdAnMSA Maryland State Archives, Annapolis, Md.
MdHi Maryland Historical Society, Baltimore, Md.
MeHi Maine Historical Society, Portland, Me.
MH Harvard University, Cambridge, Mass.
MHi Massachusetts Historical Society, Boston, Mass.
MiU-C University of Michigan, William L. Clements Library, Ann Arbor, Mich.
MWA American Antiquarian Society, Worcester, Mass.
MWiW-C Williams College, Chapin Library, Williamstown, Mass.
Nc-Ar North Carolina State Department of Archives and History, Raleigh, N.C.
NcD Duke University, Durham, N.C.
NcU University of North Carolina, Chapel Hill, N.C.
NHi New-York Historical Society, New York, N.Y.
NIC Cornell University, Ithaca, N.Y.
NjGbS Rowan University, Glassboro, N.J.
NjHi New Jersey Historical Society, Newark, N.J.
NjMoHP Morristown National Historical Park, Morristown, N.J.
NjP Princeton University, Princeton, N.J.
NN New York Public Library, New York, N.Y.
NNC Columbia University, New York, N.Y.
NWM United States Military Academy, West Point, N.Y.
OclWHi Western Reserve Historical Society, Cleveland, Ohio
PHi Historical Society of Pennsylvania, Philadelphia, Pa.
PPIn Independence National Historical Park, Philadelphia, Pa.
PPRF Rosenbach Museum and Library, Philadelphia, Pa.
PVfHi Valley Forge Historical Society, Valley Forge, Pa.
PWacD David Library of the American Revolution, Washington Crossing, Pa.
R-Ar Rhode Island State Archives, Providence, R.I.
RHi Rhode Island Historical Society, Providence, R.I.

RNHi   Newport Historical Society, Newport, R.I.
RNR   Redwood Library and Athenaeum, Newport, R.I.
RP-Ar   Providence City Archives, Providence, R.I.
RPB   Brown University, Providence, R.I.
RPJCB   John Carter Brown Library, Providence, R.I.
ScCMu   Charleston Museum Library, Charleston, S.C.
ScCoAH   South Carolina Department of Archives and History, Columbia, S.C.
ScHi   South Carolina Historical Society, Charleston, S.C.
ScU   University of South Carolina, Columbia, S.C.
UkLPR   Public Record Office, Kew, Surry, England
Vi   Library of Virginia, Richmond, Va.
ViHi   Virginia Historical Society, Richmond, Va.

SHORT TITLES FOR WORKS FREQUENTLY CITED

Abernethy, *Western Lands*
　　Abernethy, Thomas Perkins. *Western Lands and the American Revolution.* New York: D. Appleton-Century Company, 1937.
American State Papers: Claims
　　http://hdl.loc.gov/loc.law/amlaw.lwsp
Annals of Congress
　　http://hdl.loc.gov/loc.law/amlaw.lwac
Arnold, *R.I.*
　　Arnold, Samuel Greene. *History of the State of Rhode Island and Providence Plantations.* 3d ed. 2 vols. New York and London, 1878.
Bagwell, *Rice Gold*
　　Bagwell, James E. *Rice Gold: James Hamilton Couper and Plantation Life on the Georgia Coast.* Macon, Ga.: Mercer University Press, 2000.
Banks, *Vindication*
　　Banks, Henry. *The Vindication of John Banks, of Virginia, against Foul Calumnies Published by Judge Johnson, of Charleston, South-Carolina, and Doctor Charles Caldwell, of Lexington, Kentucky. Also, the Vindication of General Henry Lee, of Virginia. With Sketches and Anecdotes of Many Revolutionary Patriots and Heroes.* Frankfort, Ky., 1826.
Bartlett, *Records of R.I.*
　　Records of the State of Rhode Island and Providence Plantations in New England. Edited by John Russell Bartlett. 10 vols. Providence, R.I., 1856–65.
Berkeley and Berkeley, *Alexander Garden*
　　Berkeley, Edmund, and Dorothy Smith Berkeley. *Dr. Alexander Garden of Charles Town.* Chapel Hill: University of North Carolina Press, 1969.

Biog. Dictionary of Md. Legislature
  A Biographical Dictionary of the Maryland Legislature, 1635–1789. Edited by Edward C. Papenfuse et al. 2 vols. Baltimore, Md.: The Johns Hopkins University Press, 1979–95.
Biog. Directory of S.C. House
  Biographical Directory of the South Carolina House of Representatives. Edited by Walter B. Edgar, N. Louise Bailey, et al. 4 vols. Columbia: University of South Carolina Press, 1977–84.
Biog. Dir. of Congress
  Biographical Directory of the United States Congress, 1774–Present. http://bioguide.congress.gov
Blount, *Papers*
  Blount, John Gray. *The John Gray Blount Papers.* Edited by Alice Barnwell Keith. 4 vols. Raleigh, N.C.: State Department of Archives and History, 1952–82.
Boatner, *Encyc.*
  Boatner, Mark Mayo, III. *Encyclopedia of the American Revolution.* New York: David McKay Company, 1974.
Boyd, *Jefferson Papers*
  Jefferson, Thomas. *The Papers of Thomas Jefferson.* Edited by Julian P. Boyd et al. Princeton, N.J.: Princeton University Press, 1950– .
Brunhouse, *Pennsylvania*
  Brunhouse, Robert Levere. *The Counter-revolution in Pennsylvania, 1776–1790.* Philadelphia: University of Pennsylvania Press, 1942.
Bullard, *Cumberland Island*
  Bullard, Mary R. *Cumberland Island: A History.* Athens: University of Georgia Press, 2003.
Bullard, "Uneasy Legacy"
  Bullard, Mary R. "Uneasy Legacy: The Lynch-Greene Partition on Cumberland Island, 1798–1802." *Georgia Historical Quarterly* 77 [1993]: 757–88.
Burnett, *Continental Congress*
  Burnett, Edmund C. *The Continental Congress.* New York: Macmillan Company, 1941.
Burnett, *Letters*
  Letters of Members of the Continental Congress. Edited by Edmund C. Burnett. 8 vols. Washington: Carnegie Institution of Washington, 1921–36.
Calendar of Va. State Papers
  Calendar of Virginia State Papers and Other Manuscripts, 1652–1781, Preserved in the Capitol at Richmond. Edited by William P. Palmer et al. 11 vols. Richmond, Va.,1875–93.
Callahan, *Knox*
  Callahan, North. *Henry Knox: General Washington's General.* New York: A. S. Barnes and Company, 1958.

Chesnutt, *Laurens Papers*
> *The Papers of Henry Laurens.* Edited by Philip Hamer, David R.
> Chesnutt, C. James Taylor, et al. 16 vols. Columbia: University of
> South Carolina Press, 1968–2003.

Clarke, *Greenes*
> Clarke, Louise Brownell. *The Greenes of Rhode Island, with Historical
> Records of English Ancestry, 1534–1902.* New York: Knickerbocker
> Press, 1903.

Clinton, *American Rebellion*
> Clinton, Henry. *The American Rebellion: Sir Henry Clinton's Narrative
> of His Campaigns, 1775–82.* Edited by William B. Willcox, with an
> appendix of original documents. New Haven, Conn.: Yale Univer-
> sity Press, 1954.

Coleman, *Revolution in Georgia*
> Coleman, Kenneth. *The American Revolution in Georgia, 1763–1789.*
> Athens: University of Georgia Press, 1958.

Columbia Encyc.
> *Columbia Encyclopedia.* 3d ed. Edited by William Bridgwater and
> Seymour Kurtz. New York: Columbia University Press, 1963.

Crane, *A Dependent People*
> Crane, Elaine Forman. *A Dependent People: Newport, Rhode Island,
> in the Revolutionary Era.* New York: Fordham University Press,
> 1985.

DAB
> *Dictionary of American Biography.* Edited by Allen Johnson and
> Dumas Malone. 21 vols. New York: Charles Scribner's Sons, 1928–
> 36. 5 supplements: 1944, 1958, 1973, 1974, and 1977.

Destler, "Wadsworth"
> Destler, Chester M. "Jeremiah Wadsworth." Unpublished biog-
> raphy.

Dexter, *Yale Graduates*
> *Biographical Sketches of the Graduates of Yale College.* Edited by Frank-
> lin Bowditch Dexter. 4 vols. New York: Henry Holt & Company,
> 1903.

Dictionary of Georgia Biography
> *Dictionary of Georgia Biography.* Edited by Kenneth Coleman and
> Stephen Gurr. 2 vols. Athens: University of Georgia Press, 1983.

DNB
> *The Dictionary of National Biography.* Edited by Sir Leslie Stephen
> and Sir Sidney Lee. 21 vols. London: Oxford University Press,
> 1937–38.

Doerflinger, *A Vigorous Spirit of Enterprise*
> Doerflinger, Thomas M. *A Vigorous Spirit of Enterprise: Merchants
> and Economic Development in Revolutionary Philadelphia.* Chapel Hill:
> University of North Carolina Press, 1986.

Fanning, *Narrative*
Fanning, David. *The Narrative of Col. David Fanning*. Edited by
Lindley S. Butler. Davidson, N.C.: Brierpath Press, 1981.
Ferguson, *Power of the Purse*
Ferguson, E. James. *The Power of the Purse: A History of American
Public Finance, 1776–1790*. Chapel Hill: University of North Caro-
lina Press, 1961.
A few salutary hints
"Cassius" [i.e., Burke, Aedanus]. *A few salutary hints, pointing out the
policy and consequences of admitting British subjects to engross our trade
and become our citizens; Addressed to those who either risqued or lost their
all to bring about the Revolution*. 1785. Reprint. New York, 1786.
Fitzpatrick, *GW*
Washington, George. *The Writings of George Washington, from the
Original Manuscript Sources, 1745–1799*. Edited by John C.
Fitzpatrick. 39 vols. Washington: U.S. Government Printing Office,
1931–44.
Flagg, *Genealogical Notes*
Flagg, Ernest. *Genealogical Notes on the Founding of New England*.
Hartford, Conn.: The Case, Lockwood & Brainard Company, 1926.
Flanders, *Plantation*
Flanders, Ralph Betts. *Plantation Slavery in Georgia*. Chapel Hill:
University of North Carolina Press, 1933.
Freeman, *GW*
Freeman, Douglas Southall. *George Washington*. 7 vols. Last volume
by John C. Alexander and Mary W. Ashworth. New York: Charles
Scribner's Sons, 1948–57.
Gordon, *History*
Gordon, William. *The History of the Rise, Progress, and Establishment
of the Independence of the United States of America*. 4 vols. London,
1788.
Granger, *Savannah River Plantations*
Savannah Writers' Project. *Savannah River Plantations*. Edited by
Mary Granger. Savannah: Georgia Historical Society, 1947.
Greene, *Greene*
Greene, George Washington. *The Life of Nathanael Greene, Major-
General in the Army of the Revolution*. 3 vols. New York, 1867–71.
Greene, *History of East Greenwich*
Greene, D. H. *History of the Town of East Greenwich and Adjacent Ter-
ritory*. Providence, R.I., 1877.
GW Diaries
The Diaries of George Washington. Edited by Donald Jackson and
Dorothy Twohig. 6 vols. Charlottesville: University Press of Vir-
ginia, 1967–79.

GWG Transcript
   George Washington Greene Transcript.
Haiman, *Kosciuszko*
   Haiman, Miecislaus. *Kosciuszko in the American Revolution*. New
   York: Polish Institute of Arts and Science in America, 1943.
Hattendorf, *History of Trinity Church*
   Hattendorf, John B. *Semper Eadem: A History of Trinity Church in
   Newport*. Newport, R.I.: Trinity Church, 2001.
Hedges, *Browns*
   Hedges, James B. *The Browns of Providence Plantations: Colonial
   Years*. Cambridge, Mass.: Harvard University Press, 1952.
Heitman, *Register*
   *Historical Register of Officers of the Continental Army during the War of
   the Revolution*. Compiled by Francis B. Heitman. 1914. Reprint.
   With addenda by Robert H. Kelby. Baltimore, Md.: Genealogical
   Publishing Company, 1967.
Hening, *Statutes*
   The Statues at Large; Being a Collection of All the Laws of Virginia
   [1619–1792]. Edited by William W. Hening. 13 vols. Richmond, Va.,
   1809–23.
Idzerda, *Lafayette Papers*
   Lafayette, Marquis de. *Lafayette in the Age of the American Revolution:
   Selected Letters and Papers, 1776–90*. Edited by Stanley J. Idzerda et
   al. 5 vols. Ithaca, N.Y.: Cornell University Press, 1977–83.
Iredell, *Papers*
   Iredell, James. *The Papers of James Iredell*. Edited by Don Higgin-
   botham. 2 vols. Raleigh, N.C.: Division of Archives and History,
   1976.
JCC
   Journals of the Continental Congress, 1774–1789. Edited by Worth-
   ington C. Ford et al. 34 vols. Washington: U.S. Government Print-
   ing Office, 1904–37.
Johnson, *Dictionary*
   Johnson, Samuel. *A Dictionary of the English Language*. 1755. Re-
   print. New York: Arno Press, 1979.
Johnson, *Greene*
   Johnson, William. *Life and Correspondence of Nathanael Greene, Major
   General of the Armies of the United States*. 2 vols. Charleston, S.C., 1822.
Jones, *History of Savannah*
   Jones, Charles C. *History of Savannah, Ga*. Syracuse, N.Y., 1890.
Jones, *Sketches of Delegates from Georgia*
   Jones, Charles C. *Biographical Sketches of the Delegates from Georgia to
   the Continental Congress*. 1891. Reprint. Spartanburg, S.C.: The Re-
   print Company, 1972.

Justice, *Warner Mifflin*
    Justice, Hilda, comp. *Life and Ancestry of Warner Mifflin*. Phila-
    delphia: Ferris & Leach, 1905.
Kohn, *Eagle and Sword*
    Kohn, Richard H. *Eagle and Sword: The Federalists and the Creation of
    the Military Establishment in America, 1783–1802*. New York: The
    Free Press, 1975.
Konigsberg, "Carrington"
    Konigsberg, Charles. "Edward Carrington, 1748–1810: 'Child of
    the Revolution': A Study of the Public Man in Young America."
    Ph.D. diss., Princeton University, 1966.
Kosciuszko Letters
    Autograph Letters of Thaddeus Kosciuszko in the American Revolution.
    Edited by Metchie J. E. Budka. Chicago: Polish Museum of Amer-
    ica, 1977.
Lambert, *South Carolina Loyalists*
    Lambert, Robert Stansbury. *South Carolina Loyalists in the American
    Revolution*. Columbia: University of South Carolina Press, 1987.
Lamplugh, *Politics on the Periphery*
    Lamplugh, George. *Politics on the Periphery: Factions and Parties
    in Georgia, 1783–1806*. Newark: University of Delaware Press,
    1986.
Livingston, *Papers*
    Livingston, William. *The Papers of William Livingston*. Edited by
    Carl E. Prince et al. 5 vols. Trenton: New Jersey Historical Commis-
    sion, 1979–88.
Lockey, *East Florida*
    Lockey, Joseph. *East Florida: 1783–1785*. Edited by John Walton
    Caughey. Berkeley: University of California Press, 1949.
Ludlum, *Early American Winters*
    Ludlum, David M. *Early American Winters, 1604–1820*. Boston,
    Mass.: American Meteorological Society, 1966.
Mackesy, *War*
    Mackesy, Piers. *The War for America, 1775–1783*. Cambridge, Mass.:
    Harvard University Press, 1964.
McPartland, *East Greenwich*
    McPartland, Martha R. *The History of East Greenwich, R.I., 1677–
    1960*. East Greenwich, R.I.: East Greenwich Free Library Associa-
    tion, 1960.
Madison, *Papers*
    Madison, James. *The Papers of James Madison*. Edited by William T.
    Hutchinson et al. Chicago: University of Chicago Press; Charlottes-
    ville: University Press of Virginia, 1962– . Publication by the Uni-
    versity Press of Virginia began with vol. 11.

Marietta, *American Quakerism*
Marietta, Jack D. *The Reformation of American Quakerism, 1748–1783.*
Philadelphia: University of Pennsylvania Press, 1984.
Mason, *Annals of Trinity Church*
Mason, George Champlin. *Annals of Trinity Church, Newport, Rhode
Island, 1698–1821.* Newport, R.I., 1890.
Masterson, *Blount*
Masterson, William H. *William Blount.* Baton Rouge: Louisiana
State University Press, 1954.
Mattern, *Benjamin Lincoln*
Mattern, David B. *Benjamin Lincoln and the American Revolution.* Co-
lumbia: University of South Carolina Press, 1995.
Meleney, *Aedanus Burke*
Meleney, John C. *The Public Life of Aedanus Burke: Revolutionary Re-
publican in Post-Revolutionary South Carolina.* Columbia: University
of South Carolina Press, 1989.
Morris, *Papers*
Morris, Robert. *The Papers of Robert Morris, 1781–1784.* 9 vols. Ed-
ited by E. James Ferguson et al. Pittsburgh: University of Pitts-
burgh Press, 1973–99.
Morris, *Peacemakers*
Morris, Richard D. *The Peacemakers: The Great Powers and American
Independence.* New York: Harper & Row, 1965.
Morrison, *Clarke Families*
Morrison, George Austin, Jr. *The "Clarke" Families of Rhode Island.*
New York: Press of the Evening Post Job Printing House, n.d.
Moss, *S.C. Patriots*
Moss, Bobby Gilmer. *Roster of South Carolina Patriots in the American
Revolution.* Baltimore, Md.: Genealogical Publishing Company,
1983.
Myers, *Liberty Without Anarchy*
Myers, Minor, Jr. *Liberty Without Anarchy: A History of the Society
of the Cincinnati.* Charlottesville: University Press of Virginia,
1983.
Nadelhaft, *Disorders of War*
Nadelhaft, Jerome J. *The Disorders of War: The Revolution in South
Carolina.* Orono: University of Maine Press, 1981.
N.C. Biographical Dictionary
Dictionary of North Carolina Biography. Edited by William S.
Powell. 6 vols. Chapel Hill: University of North Carolina Press,
1979–96.
NCSR
The State Records of North Carolina. Edited by Walter Clark. 26 vols.
Raleigh, N.C., 1886–1907.

Nelson, *Wayne*
  Nelson, Paul David. *Anthony Wayne: Soldier of the Early Republic.*
  Bloomington: Indiana University Press, 1985.
OED
  Oxford English Dictionary
Owen, *Eighteenth Century*
  Owen, John B. *The Eighteenth Century, 1714–1815.* New York: W. W.
  Norton, 1974.
Palmer, *Loyalists*
  Palmer, Gregory. *Biographical Sketches of Loyalists of the American
  Revolution.* Westport, Conn.: Meckler Publishing, 1984.
PCC
  Papers of the Continental Congress. Unless otherwise noted, all
  citations are from Record Group 360, M247, National Archives and
  Records Administration, Washington.
PMHB
  Pennsylvania Magazine of History and Biography
Rankin, *N.C. Continentals*
  Rankin, Hugh F. *The North Carolina Continentals.* Chapel Hill: Uni-
  versity of North Carolina Press, 1971.
Records of Georgia
  The Revolutionary Records of the State of Georgia. Compiled by
  Allen D. Candler. 3 vols. Atlanta, Ga.: Franklin-Turner Company,
  1908.
Reed, *Reed*
  Reed, William B. *Life and Correspondence of Joseph Reed.* 2 vols. Phila-
  delphia, 1847.
Remains of General Greene
  *The Remains of Major-General Nathanael Greene. A Report of the Joint
  Special Committee of the General Assembly of Rhode Island Appointed to
  Take Into Consideration the Desirability of Securing Within the State of
  Rhode Island a Permanent Resting-place for the Remains of General
  Nathanael Greene.* Providence, R.I.: E. L. Freeman & Sons, 1903.
Risch, *Supplying*
  Risch, Erna. *Supplying Washington's Army.* Washington: U.S. Gov-
  ernment Printing Office, 1981.
Rogers, *Evolution of a Federalist*
  Rogers, George C., Jr. *Evolution of a Federalist: William Loughton
  Smith of Charleston (1758–1812).* Columbia: University of South
  Carolina Press, 1962.
Rogers, *History of Georgetown*
  Rogers, George C., Jr. *The History of Georgetown County, South Caro-
  lina.* Columbia: University of South Carolina Press, 1970.

SCHGM
> *South Carolina Historical and Genealogical Magazine/South Carolina Historical Magazine*

S.C., House of Representatives, *Journals, 1783–84*
> South Carolina. General Assembly. House of Representatives. *Journals of the House of Representatives, 1783–1784*. Edited by Theodora J. Thompson and Rosa S. Lumpkin. Columbia: Published for the South Carolina Department of Archives and History by the University of South Carolina Press, 1977.

S.C., House of Representatives, *Journals, 1784–85*
> South Carolina. General Assembly. House of Representatives. *Journals of the House of Represenatives, 1784–1785*. Edited by Lark Emerson Adams and Rosa S. Lumpkin. Columbia: Published for the South Carolina Department of Archives and History by the University of South Carolina Press, 1979.

S.C., Privy Council, *Journals*
> South Carolina. Privy Council. *The State Records of South Carolina: Journals of the Privy Council, 1783–1789*. Edited by Adele S. Edwards. Columbia: University of South Carolina Press, 1971.

Siebert, *Loyalists in East Florida*
> Siebert, Wilbur H. *Loyalists in East Florida, 1774 to 1785*. 2 vols. Deland: Florida State Historical Society, 1929.

Smith, *Letters*
> *Letters of Delegates to Congress, 1774–1789*. Edited by Paul H. Smith et al. 26 vols. Washington: Library of Congress, 1976–2000.

Smith, *Slavery and Rice Culture*
> Smith, Julia Floyd. *Slavery and Rice Culture in Low Country Georgia, 1750–1860*. Knoxville: University of Tennessee Press, 1985.

Statutes of S.C.
> *Statutes at Large of South Carolina*. Edited by Thomas Cooper and David J. McCord. 10 vols. Columbia, S.C., 1836–41.

Stegeman, *Caty*
> Stegeman, John F., and Janet A. Stegeman. *Caty: A Biography of Catharine Littlefield Greene*. 1977. Reprint. Athens: University of Georgia Press, 1985.

Steuben Microfilm
> *The Papers of General Friedrich Wilhelm von Steuben*. Edited by Edith von Zemensky. 7 reels. Millwood, N.Y.: Kraus International Publications, 1982.

Stevens, *History of Georgia*
> Stevens, William B. *A History of Georgia*. 2 vols. 1859. Reprint. Savannah, Ga.: Beehive Press, 1972.

Stiles, *Diary*
> Stiles, Ezra. *The Literary Diary of Ezra Stiles*. Edited by Franklin Bowditch Dexter. 3 vols. New York: Charles Scribner's Sons, 1901.

Syrett, *Hamilton*
> Hamilton, Alexander. *The Papers of Alexander Hamilton*. Edited by Harold C. Syrett et al. 27 vols. New York: Columbia University Press, 1961–87.

Tanner, *Visit to St. Augustine*
> Tanner, Helen Hornbeck. *General Greene's Visit to St. Augustine in 1785*. Ann Arbor, Mich.: William L. Clements Library, 1964.

Thayer, *Morris County*
> Thayer, Theodore. *Colonial and Revolutionary Morris County*. N.p.: Morris County [N.J.] Heritage Commission, 1975.

Travels of Francisco de Miranda
> *Travels of Francisco de Miranda in the United States, 1783–84*. Edited by John S. Ezell. Norman: University of Oklahoma Press, 1963.

Turner, *Dictionary of Art*
> *The Dictionary of Art*. Edited by Jane Turner. 34 vols. London: Macmillan Publishers, 1996.

Updike, *Episcopal Church in Narragansett*
> Updike, Wilkins. *A History of the Episcopal Church in Narragansett, R.I. Including a History of Other Episcopal Churches in the State*. 2d ed. 2 vols. Boston, Mass.: D. B. Updike The Merrymount Press, 1907.

U.S. Statutes at Large
> http://memory.loc.gov/ammem/amlaw/lwsl.html

Virginia, House of Delegates, *Journal*
> *Journal of the House of Delegates of the Commonwealth of Virginia, 1781–86*. Richmond, Va., 1828.

Vital Records of Rhode Island
> Arnold, James N. *Vital Records of Rhode Island, 1636–1850. First Series. Births, Marriages, and Deaths: A Family Register for the People*. 21 vols. Providence, R.I.: Narragansett Historical Publishing Company, 1891–1912.

Waddell, *New Hanover County*
> Waddell, Alfred Moore. *A History of New Hanover County and the Lower Cape Fear Region,1723–1800*. 1901. Reprint. Bowie, Md.: Heritage Books, 1989.

Walsh, *Sons of Liberty*
> Walsh, Richard. *Charleston's Sons of Liberty: A Study of the Artisans, 1763–1789*. Columbia: University of South Carolina Press, 1959.

Ward, *Weedon*
> Ward, Harry M. *Duty, Honor or Country: General George Weedon and the American Revolution*. Philadelphia: American Philosophical Society, 1979.

Washington, *Papers*, Confederation Series
> Washington, George. *The Papers of George Washington*. Confederation Series. Edited by W. W. Abbot et al. Charlottesville: University Press of Virginia, 1992– .

Washington, *Papers*, Revolutionary War Series
> Washington, George. *The Papers of George Washington*. Revolutionary War Series. Edited by Philander Chase et al. Charlottesville: University Press of Virginia, 1988– .

Webster's
> *Webster's Third New International Dictionary of the English Language Unabridged*. Edited by Philip Babcock Gove. Springfield, Mass.: G. & C. Merriam Company, 1981.

Willcox, *Clinton*
> Willcox, William B. *Portrait of a General: Sir Henry Clinton in the War of Independence*. New York: Alfred A. Knopf, 1964.

Williams Calendar
> Works Project Administration. Division of Professional and Service Projects. Maryland Historical Records Survey Project. *Calendar of the General Otho Holland Williams Papers in the Maryland Historical Society*. Baltimore, Md., 1940.

WRMS
> War Department Collection of Revolutionary War Records, Record Group 93, National Archives and Records Administration, Washington, D.C.

Zahniser, *Pinckney*
> Zahniser, Marvin R. *Charles Cotesworth Pinckney*. Chapel Hill: University of North Carolina Press, 1967.

NAMES ABBREVIATED IN TEXT

NG   Nathanael Greene
CG   Catharine Littlefield Greene (NG's wife)

1783	3 June	NG writes Benjamin Lincoln, the secretary at war, that he has managed to avert a mutiny of Pennsylvania troops in the Southern Army over pay and rations.
	7 June	Catharine Greene [CG] leaves Charleston, S.C., for home in Rhode Island, sailing to Philadelphia on the brig *Christiana*.
	18 June	NG warns Lincoln that the delay in sending transports to carry troops to their home states could lead to large numbers of deaths and mutiny.
	21 June	In orders of this date—his last as commander in the South—NG prepares the troops remaining in Charleston for their evacuation and salutes their bravery and perseverance.
	26 June	Acting upon Congress's orders of 26 May, NG furloughs the Southern Army.
	11 July	NG writes Lincoln that the "greater part of the Troops" will embark on the transports that have finally arrived at Charleston.
	22 July	NG informs Governor Benjamin Guerard of South Carolina that his command in the South has ended.
	2 August	NG writes Lincoln that the "troops are all gone" and that the business of the Southern Army's staff departments is concluding.
	4 August	In a letter to CG, NG describes his financial problems and tells her that he will need capital to operate his plantations in the South.
	11 August	CG arrives in Newport, R.I., after visits in Philadelphia and New York.
	12 August	NG obtains an indenture from John Banks and Ichabod Burnet as security against the debts he guaranteed for them as army contractors. He will later use this "mortgage" to claim a large share of land on Cumberland Island, Ga.

	14 August	NG leaves Charleston to travel overland to Philadelphia. He is saluted along the way by the citizens of Richmond, Fredericksburg, and Alexandria, Va., and Annapolis and Baltimore, Md.
	4 October	NG arrives in Philadelphia.
	7 October	NG is in Princeton, N.J., where Congress is in session.
	15 October	Back in Philadelphia, NG receives news of the death of Burnet, his former aide and Banks's business partner.
	18 October	Congress votes to give NG two inscribed "pieces of field ordnance" in honor of his service. NG stays in Philadelphia for several weeks, trying to settle his wartime accounts.
	8 November	Charles Pettit agrees to purchase NG's share in their business partnership.
	24 November	NG is in New York City, preparing to sail to Newport.
	25 November	The British evacuate New York City; it is not known if NG is there when the Americans take possession.
	27 November	NG arrives in Newport and is reunited with his family.
	17 December	NG is notified that he has been elected president of the Rhode Island chapter of the Society of the Cincinnati.
1784	before 9 January	NG prepares a detailed estimate of his real estate holdings as he seeks an overseas loan to develop his plantations.
	after 21 January	Pettit writes NG about the complexity of NG's financial situation.
	after 22 February	NG presents his wartime account to the Rhode Island legislature; it is later settled to his satisfaction.
	4 March	Congress names NG to a commission to negotiate with Indians; he later declines to serve.
	9 March	NG continues his correspondence with James Milligan, the comptroller of the treasury, about the settlement of his army accounts.

	late March	NG entertains historian William Gordon and Gen. Thaddeus Kosciuszko at Newport.
	17 April	Louisa Catherine Greene, the Greenes' fifth child, is born in Newport.
	6 May	In a letter to Washington, NG declines to attend the annual meeting of the Society of the Cincinnati in Philadelphia.
	early–mid June	NG makes a short trip to Philadelphia and New York to attend to business matters.
	1 July	Rhode Island rejects the federal impost plan, for which NG has lobbied.
	12 July	NG sails from Newport for Charleston.
	1 August	NG arrives in Charleston to try to settle the "business of the [army] contractors."
	12 August	NG expresses despair over his financial difficulties; nine days later, he writes CG about the gravity of their situation.
	late September	NG leaves Charleston and arrives in Washington, N.C., to find that his nemesis, John Banks, has recently died.
	mid-November	On his way back to Newport, NG stops in Philadelphia on business matters.
	20 November	NG arrives in Newport.
	ca. 21 December	NG, in New York City, visits with the Marquis de Lafayette, who has completed his tour of the country.
	29 December	NG sells his share in Barnabas Deane & Company to Jeremiah Wadsworth.
1785	10 January	NG sails from Newport. He arrives in Charleston on the 28th, after a difficult voyage.
	ca. 23 February	NG is in Georgia.
	2 March	NG rejects a challenge to a duel by James Gunn, one of his former officers.
	10 March	NG leaves on a trip to East Florida and Cumberland Island.
	19 March	NG arrives in East Florida, where he is entertained at St. Augustine by the Spanish governor.
	ca. 26 March	NG visits Cumberland Island on his way back from East Florida.
	20 May	Washington writes NG that he approves the rejection of Gunn's challenge.

	25 June	NG arrives in Newport.
	8 July	Dutch investors decline to lend money to NG.
	early August	NG makes a business trip to New York City.
	18 August	NG returns to Newport, accompanied by Baron von Steuben.
	22 August	In a letter to the president of Congress, NG explains the financial problems he has incurred because of the guarantees he made on behalf of the army contractors and asks for help from Congress. He does not receive it.
	ca. August	NG's daughter Catharine is born in Newport but dies at the end of August.
	1 October	NG hires Phineas Miller to accompany his family to Georgia and serve as a tutor to the children.
	11 October	NG's will is signed and witnessed in Newport.
	14 October	NG and family leave Newport for Georgia on the *Dove*. They arrive in Savannah, Ga., on 30 October.
	ca. mid-November	NG and family take up residence at Mulberry Grove plantation, near Savannah.
1786	28 January	Robert Morris writes NG that there is no possibility of NG obtaining a loan in Holland.
	after 6 April	CG, who is pregnant again, falls and goes into premature labor; the baby dies.
	16 April	NG declines appointment to a Chatham County, Ga., judgeship.
	13 June	NG is stricken after returning home from Savannah, where he reached an agreement with one of his principal creditors, E. John Collett.
	19 June	NG dies at Mulberry Grove.
	20 June	NG is buried in Savannah after a military funeral.

From Major Joseph Eggleston, Jr.

Sir   Georgetown [S.C.] 22nd May 1783

You misapprehend me, when you suppose I think the Men less subject to Authority than formerly.[1] I only meant to inform you that they thought themselves so, & from a combination of Sentiments & Designs that the Infliction of Punishment, unless for immoral Acts, might produce very disagreeable Consequences. No Power of Reason or Argument could make them beleive they are not freed from their Enlistments; an Attempt to do so would raise a Flame that would not be easily allayed. They have in one Instance proceeded to a most unjustifiable Length, but were unexpectedly brought again to their Duty & a Sense of it without any fatal Consequences. I can retain them untill the 10th of June, but if they are not embarked or marched by that Time; I am informed they have determined on the most desperate Courses.[2] The Cavalry are much pleased at the Circumstance of being allowed to bid for their Horses; & the Infantry much mortified that they have no such Privilege.[3] Perhaps this Circumstance may produce a Division of Sentiment & Design, of which, if possible, I will take Advantage to retain each in their Duty. But after all that can or may be done, Officers are in a very disagreeable Situation, & I wish to be freed from it as soon as possible. I declare that I never before sacrificed so much to a Sense of Duty as I now do in continuing with the Troops, & I believe I am not singular in my Feelings.

Capt Armstrong mentioned Jacksonborough as the Place designed for the Sale of the Horses; I wo[uld] beg Leave to observe that this Place or Charlestown would be more eligible. For such is the suspicious Nature of the Soldiery, they would suppose some Duplicity or Detention intended, if they were ordered so far South, & probably would go off in a Body or desert in great Numbers. They might be marched to Charlestown with the Idea of embarking from thence, but I fear they could not be carried farther South. Forage too I suppose will be a consideration, we have enough here for twenty Days consumption.[4]

Colo Mentges will inform you of our Prospects for Provision, the Consequences of Want in this Respect would be immediately serious.[5]

I am sorry to take so much of your Time in reading so long a Letter, but my Intention & Situation must plead my Excuse. I wish, Sir, for a full Answer by the Bearer, & have the Honor to be, with the highest Respect & Esteem your most obedt humble Sert   JOS: EGGLESTON JR

RCS (Greene Papers: DLC).

1. See NG's letter of 17 May to Eggleston, the commanding officer of Lee's Legion, and Eggleston's to NG of 12 May, both above. (Vol. 12: 659–60, 652)

2. As seen at his letter to Gen. Benjamin Lincoln of 11 July, below, NG furloughed most of the dragoons in Lee's Legion, thereby averting the threat of "desperate Courses."

3. NG explained his decision to let dragoons bid on their horses in his second letter to Lincoln of 3 June, below.

4. The sale of the legion's horses was held in Charleston. (*South-Carolina Gazette*, 24 May)

5. The report from Francis Mentges, the Southern Army's inspector, is immediately below.

*   *   *

¶ [FROM COLONEL FRANCIS MENTGES, Georgetown, S.C., 22 May 1783. He arrived there on the 17th "to muster and inspect" Lee's Legion but had to wait until "yesterday" because several of the officers were absent. He found a "discontentment of the Soldiery[,] merely on account of their being detaind in the service," but has had "a long conversation" with the men, and they are "now willing to remain untill the 10 June."[1] Because of "the neglect of Mr Banks," though, they may disband sooner.[2] There are only "9 Barrels of pork and some Rum" in the commissary's stores, and the commissary has "no prospect of getting either Rice or Flour." Mentges will try to "procure Rice, that the Men shall have no reasons to complain." Banks seems to care "very little about the Contract," but Mentges will "make him pay" for the rice. Mentges plans to leave for "the Congary" the next day but has been informed that "the greatest part of the Reg^t is gone off under the Command of the Serg^t Major."[3] RCS (Greene Papers: DLC) 2 pp.]

1. On the unrest in Lee's Legion, see also Eggleston to NG, immediately above.

2. John Banks was the contractor responsible for supplying provisions to the Southern Army. (On the terms of the contract, see Edward Carrington to NG, 18 February, above [vol. 12: 458–59 and n].)

3. On the recent mutiny in, and large-scale desertion from, the First Continental Legionary Corps, which was stationed at the Congaree River, see NG to Gov. Benjamin Harrison, 21 May, above (vol. 12: 676 and n), and John Watts to NG, immediately below.

*   *   *

From Captain John Watts[1]

Dear sir   Howells Ferry [S.C.] 22^d May 1783

Nothing in the corse of Seven Years hard service ever gave me half ⟨the⟩ Concern, ⟨as⟩ the very extraordinary behaviour of the soldiers of the 1st Regiment have done, ⟨they have acted in⟩ such a manner as to reflect eternal Disgrace on themselves, and I fear, the Officers will not escape the censure of the Illiberal part of the world but I am convin⟨ced⟩ they all have the consolation to think, that they have acquitted themselves of their Duty to the Utmost power.

Lieut Meriweather will Deliver a Return of the Reg^t[,] such a one as I never expected to have been Mortified with the sight of.[2] He will be able to give you a St⟨ate of t⟩he Dispute between Maj^r ⟨Hort⟩ & Li⟨eut. Linton.⟩[3]

The men that remain seem to be perfectly satisfied on being informed that they are to be allowed to purchase their Horses.[4] M[r] [John] Banks has often amused us with a promise of our being better supplied but I see no prospect of it taking place shortly, provisions are hard to be Obtained here & they [i.e., the inhabitants] Part ⟨with it unw[ly]⟩ [i.e., unwillingly?].[5] I have the Honor to ⟨be Dear⟩ sir with the ⟨utmost Respect & Esteem Your Mot. H. Serv.   JOHN WATTS⟩

RC (Greene Papers: DLC). The manuscript is damaged; text in angle brackets is from a GWG Transcript (CSmH).

1. Watts commanded the detachment of the First Legionary Corps (formerly the First Continental Regiment of Light Dragoons) that was stationed on the Congaree River. About 100 of the men in his command had recently mutinied and deserted. (See NG to Gov. Benjamin Harrison, 21 May, above [vol. 12: 676 and n].)

2. The return that Lt. James Merriwether delivered to NG has not been found.

3. On the dispute between Maj. William Hort and Lt. John Linton, see NG to Watts, 15 May, above (vol. 12: 654).

4. On NG's plan to let the dragoons purchase their horses, see his second letter to Gen. Benjamin Lincoln of 3 June, below.

5. As a reason for deserting, the mutineers claimed that had they stayed in camp, they would have either starved or "Run the Risque of Being Ambuscaded and Shot" by area residents protecting their stocks of provisions from impressment. (PCC, item 788, vol. 17: 357, DNA)

From Ichabod Burnet[1]

Dear Sir   Philadelphia May 23[d] 1783.

After having made the necessary preparations for victualling the transports for the removal of the troops from C. Town I was not a little surprised to find M[r] Morris had contracted with M[r] Parker to furnish transports & victual them for the passage.[2] When it was surmised that we were under engagements to furnish the necessary provisions for that purpose he removed every difficulty with his wonted ease by saying we should be paid for that quantity at the price it cost us according to contract. I have yet said nothing to him of the matter, being persuaded you will secure to us the same price for the articles as if we issued them, agreeable to the verbal promise made me before my departure from Charles Town. It would be hard for us to be ordered expressly to provide such & such articles for certain purposes under the contract & then to be told another will furnish them cheaper therefore you shall not issue them, but recieve the first costs for them four months hence & that too in Bills which are very badly paid.

This conduct of M[r] Morris's amounts to breach of Contract. We were to furnish all provissions issuable by the United States in S. Carolina during the year eighty three at a fixed price and you were to ascertain the quantity to us. When I received the orders to procure the provisions you promissed to secure us the Contract price for them as I could not undertake to buy them on an uncertainty. We had contracted for more provisions at that time than would serve the troops, and it would have been unjust for us to be obliged to furnish those articles of provision necessary for a voyage & subject ourselves to havin[g] them thrown on our hands & be obliged to lay out of our money for several months. Provisions thus purchased cannot be considered as in the situation of that which by Contract we are to be paid only the first cost for.

You will readily see how ungenerous we should have been treated had we been altogether in their power. Your justice we shall fly to for security against their designs.[3]

I hope for the honor of seeing you in a few days in the mean time be assured I am with much respect & esteem Your Obed[t] Servant I. BURNET

RCS (MiU-C).

1. NG's former aide Burnet was now a business partner of John Banks, the contractor responsible for supplying provisions to the Southern Army. (For background, see note at NG to Gen. Henry Knox, 3 February, above [vol. 12: 412n].)

2. Unaware that NG had agreed to have Banks & Company purchase provisions for the troops who were returning to their home states on transports, Robert Morris, the super-intendent of finance, had contracted with Daniel Parker & Company to supply both the transport vessels and the provisions. (See Memorandum of an Agreement with Daniel Parker and Company, 16 May, Morris, *Papers*, vol. 8: 78–79.) As seen in the present letter, Morris proposed to solve that problem by having Parker & Company buy the provisions from Banks at cost.

3. The outcome of this dispute is not known. The editors of the Morris Papers believe the troops may have already used up the provisions purchased for the voyage by the time the transports arrived. (Morris, *Papers*, 8: 128n)

*   *   *

¶ [**FROM CHARLES PETTIT**, Philadelphia, 23 May 1783. He will reply only to NG's letter of 5 May, as he is "much thronged with other Matters, especially as Major Burnet is just returned from New York & some of his Business requires dispatch."[1] Pettit "did not hesitate to accept" NG's "Draught in fav[r] of M[r] Gervais," but he would not be treating NG "with the Candor & Confidence you have a Right to expect from me; if I did not intimate to you that it will occasion me some Difficulty."[2] If NG repays the money in "a Month or two," as he proposed, the problem will be eased. Pettit does not have time to explain more fully, but he trusts to NG's "good Nature & Friendship to give the most favour-able and friendly interpretation." Even if NG's "claim to draw on" him had been "much less," he would not have allowed the draft to be "dishonored," if he could in any way have prevented it, because he knows that NG would not impose on him "but on the best Reasons." When Mr. Clay delivered NG's letter, Pettit was preoccupied by "M[rs] Pettit's illness" and was "crowded with Busi-ness." He wanted to show "Civilities" to Clay, but although the latter promised to pay a visit, Pettit has not seen him again.[3] Pettit assures NG that he will take "Pleasure" in "attending" to NG's "Recommendations." He has been told that they may expect CG "every hour."[4] Adds: "George was well by the last Ac-counts from Princeton."[5] RCS (MiU-C) 2 pp.]

1. NG's friend Pettit, who had once been an assistant quartermaster general under NG, had agreed to serve as the Philadelphia representative of John Banks & Company, the firm in which Burnet was a partner. Burnet discussed some of his "Business" in the letter immediately above. As seen in his letter to NG of 23 July, below, Pettit soon found reasons to distrust some of Banks's and Burnet's business practices.

2. John Lewis Gervais served as a South Carolina delegate to Congress until 20 May, when he left Philadelphia to return home. (Smith, *Letters*, 20: xxii, 177n) In a letter of 12 April, Ralph Izard, another delegate, reported that Gervais was in distress because South Carolina had been slow in sending money to support its delegates. (Ibid., p. 177)

3. Joseph Clay, the former deputy paymaster for the Southern Department, may have gone to Philadelphia to settle his accounts. (See Robert Morris to Clay, 17 May, Morris, *Papers*, 8: 88.)

4. On CG's journey to Philadelphia from Charleston, S.C., see note at NG to Washington, 5 June, below.

5. NG's son George Washington Greene was staying with the family of Dr. John Witherspoon, near Princeton, N.J.

¶ [FROM JOHN WRIGHT STANLY, Philadelphia, 23 May 1783. According to John Banks & Company, NG wants to buy the certificates that the state of South Carolina granted to Stanly.[1] As he has not received NG's proposal on the subject, Stanly will have Mr. J. S. Cripps "treat with" NG and let him have the certificates "on terms which may be mutually Convenient."[2] Stanly is always "happy" to "promote the views" of NG and NG's "Friends," both in Philadelphia and in North Carolina.[3] Cy (MiU-C) 1 p. The word "Coppy" has been written at the top of the letter.]

1. Banks's partner Ichabod Burnet, who was in Philadelphia at this time, may have given this message to Stanly. (See also Edward Blake to NG, 3 May, above [vol. 12: 638].)

2. John Splatt Cripps was a "native-born merchant of immense influence in post-war Charleston." (Rogers, *Evolution of a Federalist*, p. 126) NG wrote Charles Pettit on 4 August, below: "Mr Stanley has bills on you for upwards of 2000 dollars which I was obliged to indorse before I could get my obligation out of the Treasury of the State."

3. Stanly had been involved in trade in both North Carolina and Philadelphia. (See Pettit to NG, 17 November 1782, above [vol. 12: 202], and Stanly to NG, 26 October, below.)

*   *   *

From General Anthony Wayne

Dear Sir   Augusta [Ga.] 23ʳᵈ May 1783

All prospects of a treaty ⟨with⟩ the Creeks ar⟨e⟩ vanished for ⟨the⟩ Present: the Talacy [Tallassee] King & head ⟨m⟩en of that Nation had a meeting in one of their principal towns, about three weeks since, & came into a resolution to send a talk in answer ⟨to the In⟩vitation of this State to ⟨hold⟩ a convention at this place on the 15ᵗʰ Instant, which Invitation they peremptorily decline on the following principals ie[,] they ⟨ca⟩nnot think of making a Cession of their hunting ground which is their only support & Natural Inheritance; that altho' they wish to live upon Amicable ter⟨ms⟩ w⟨ith⟩ the Americans yet hav⟨ing no surety⟩ for the safety ⟨of⟩ their horses & ⟨other⟩ property, & apprehensive of

⟨meetin⟩g with similar treatment to that they experienced at the last treaty, when not only all their horses were sto⟨le⟩ from them by the ⟨white⟩ people, ⟨but also⟩ the negroes & Cattle they were br⟨ing⟩ing in from the Nation to restore to their proper owners, in pursuance of their engagement with Govr Ma⟨rtin⟩ & my⟨self⟩ wh⟨ich⟩ reduced th⟨em to the fatiguing⟩ Necessity of walking home on foot, much poorer than they came.

I would wish for the honor of this ⟨Country⟩ that ther⟨e⟩ had not ⟨be⟩en ⟨too⟩ much cause g⟨ive⟩n for the latter complaint, ⟨by⟩ a set of Caitiffs permited to pass with Impunity from the relaxed & debilitated State of Civil Authority in Carolina & Georgia.[1]

As to the policy of publishing to ⟨the wor⟩ld an intention of demanding ⟨a Cession⟩ of Lands from the savages ⟨w⟩ill leave to others to determine. The Cherokees will be in, but as ⟨a⟩ll matters relating to peace, ⟨or war⟩ are vested in Congress nothing Legal or effectual can be done until that Honble body take up the Indian business on a General & broad basis. Which alone ⟨ca⟩n gi⟨ve⟩ Security to the Citi⟨zens⟩ & prevent the Clash⟨ing of⟩ different view⟨s &⟩ Interest among the States in their visionary claims ⟨to⟩ extensive teritory.[2]

I hope to have the pleasure of seeing you in Charlestown in ⟨the⟩ course of two weeks when I w⟨ill⟩ communicate viva voce ⟨such⟩ other observations as have or may occur.[3] Interim I am with sincere esteem Yours very Affectionately   ANT^Y WAYNE

My best & kindest wishes attend M^rs Gr⟨eene⟩ & the family.

RCS (Greene Papers: DLC). Some text is missing because of tears along the edges and the fold line in the middle. Most of the missing text has been found in an ADf at PHi and is enclosed in angle brackets here. The third paragraph is not in the draft, however, and the text missing there was taken from a GWG Transcript, CSmH.

1. The state of Georgia was seeking a cession of lands between the Oconee and Tugaloo rivers. The "last treaty" had been negotiated in September 1782, when "numbers" of Lower Creeks traveled to Augusta "in response to an invitation" from Gov. John Martin and Wayne. Martin invited a small delegation, headed by the Tallassee king of the Creeks, "to confer with him in Savannah." Historian James H. O'Donnell writes that promises made by Martin to the Creek leader in 1782 were "empty." (James H. O'Donnell, *Southern Indians in the American Revolution* [Knoxville: University of Tennessee Press, 1973], pp. 128–35) On Wayne's involvement in Georgia's efforts to negotiate with the Indians, see above, vol. 12: 523–24n.

2. As seen in Thomas Mifflin's letter to NG of 6 March 1784, below, Congress appointed commissioners, including NG, to negotiate with the Indians.

3. NG replied to Wayne on 26 June, below.

*   *   *

¶ [TO JEREMIAH WADSWORTH. From Charleston, S.C., 24 May 1783. NG's aide Capt. [William] Pierce and "Maj [Richard] Call," who "served their Country with reputation, have formed a house for the purpose of commerce in the

State of Georgia."[1] From "motives of friendship," and not because he has any "interest" in this firm, NG solicits Wadsworth's "friendly offices in their behalf in all matters of business, either in consignments, or other affairs you may have to negotiate in that State." Tr (CtHi) 1 p.]

1. Pierce and Call, the former commander of the Third Continental Regiment of Light Dragoons, were in partnership with Col. Anthony W. White, the former commander of the First Continental Regiment of Light Dragoons. (See also Morris to NG, immediately below, and NG to Morris, second letter of 4 June, below.)

¶ [FROM ROBERT MORRIS, SUPERINTENDENT OF FINANCE, Philadelphia, 24 May 1783. Encloses a letter for NG's "late Aid Major Pierce." NG will oblige Morris by "transmitting it" and "by any Informations" he can give "on his Subject."[1] RCS (CSmH) 1 p.]

1. In a letter of this date, Morris informed William Pierce, Jr., that the port of Havana would probably be closed soon and advised him to change his plan of going into business there. (Morris, *Papers*, 8: 116–17) As seen in NG to Wadsworth, immediately above, and in NG's reply to Morris, Pierce had already decided to establish his mercantile firm in Georgia. (NG to Morris, second letter of 4 June, below)

*   *   *

To Captain John Watts

Dear Sir   Head quarters Charles Town [S.C.] May 25th 1783.
Lieutenant [James] Merryweather made me this disagreeable report of the Mutiny among the Cavalry. I sent him immediately after the Men with propositions for their return; but dont expect they will listen to it. I informed them of the steps I had taken and should like to bring them to punishment if they persisted. I hope they may return but I fear they will not.[1] It was my intention to have given every Dragoon an opportunity to purchase his horse to be deducted out of his pay. Those of the Cavalry that remain subject to authority will have this priviledge.[2] If the insurgeants go on to Virginia there is no doubt of their being brought to punnishment.[3]

It is proposed to sell the Dragoon horses the 12th of next Month. Lt. Col Carrington will inform you of the plan and manner.[4] It was proposed to move your Corps to the lower Santee but Capt [Chitty] says you may be subsisted where you are and you will [study?] to keep the rest of the Men as quiet as possible; but I am afraid by a report of two divisions of the Cavalry being on their way to the Northward a second mutiny has taken place and that desertion will finally prove general.[5]

I have had some trouble with the Troops here; but nothing has taken place but a little desertion. One Regiment entered into a resolution to go off in a body; but the steps I took soon put them out of conceit of it. Let me hear from you as soon as you can with conveniency. I should have written you before this but for want of an opportunity. I am dear Sir Your Most Obed humble ser   N GREENE

ADfS (MiU-C).

1. On the mutiny among the dragoons of the First Continental Legionary Corps, see above, NG to Gov. Benjamin Harrison, 21 May (vol. 12: 676 and n), and John Watts to NG, 22 May. NG was correct in assuming that the deserters would not return.

2. As seen in NG to Lincoln, second letter of 3 June, below, the Southern Army's dragoons were allowed to purchase their mounts.

3. The mutineers were not punished. (See above, vol. 12: 677n.)

4. Col. Edward Carrington's letter to Watts has not been found; for the details of the sale, see note at NG to Lincoln, second letter of 3 June.

5. A "second mutiny" and general desertion did not take place.

*   *   *

¶ [FROM ROGER PARKER SAUNDERS, [near Boone's Barony, S.C.], 26 May 1783.[1] He was at NG's plantation "this day" and expects "a good Crop"; 130 acres of rice have "come up very well," and another twenty acres are "just planted." Saunders would have planted more if it had "not been so late," but "by planting [a] small Crop," NG will be able to get his land into "good order for another Year." The "Negroes" NG was going to send up have not arrived. Saunders wonders if NG is "sure of gitting Corn from Mr Banks," as there is no more than a month's supply left for his "people."[2] Mr. Ferguson is "out of Corn at his Ferry Plantation and is very Pressing" for NG to return 156 bushels of it there and 220 bushels in Charleston.[3] Mr. Croskey will also need repayment of the thirty-five bushels that he sent to NG. Saunders thinks corn "may be had at a dollar p^r Bushel Cash" but hopes NG can get "better terms" from Banks; if not, he should let Saunders know immediately.[4] Saunders asks NG to send "Seventy three pounds Seven Shillings and Six pence" by the bearer to pay for seed rice, potato seed, corn, and peas. He lists prices for oxen, cows, and calves; advises NG: "you will want oxen very much next Winter."[5] RCS (MiU-C) 3 pp.]

1. Saunders (d. 1795) lived in St. Paul Parish, S.C., and owned a house in Charleston. His properties included plantations "near Wallace's Ferry, on the Edisto River, and in Georgia." He had served as a captain in the First South Carolina Continental Regiment for several years during the war and was regularly elected to the South Carolina General Assembly during the 1770s and 1780s. (*Biog. Directory of S.C. House*, 3: 634) As seen in his correspondence with NG in this volume, Saunders helped to oversee the operation of NG's South Carolina plantation, Boone's Barony.

2. John Banks was the contractor responsible for provisioning the Southern Army. On his efforts to obtain corn for the work force at NG's plantation, see below, Saunders to NG, 20 June and 3 July.

3. Thomas Ferguson, one of the state commissioners who had purchased Boone's Barony for NG, was a large landholder and a member of the South Carolina Privy Council. (*Biog. Directory of S.C. House*, 2: 248–50)

4. Corn continued to be in short supply on the plantation. (See below, Saunders to NG, 20 June and 3 July.)

5. Saunders acknowledged NG's reply, which has not been found, and receipt of the money in a letter to NG to 7 June, below. On the livestock, see ibid. and Saunders to NG, 20 June, below.

*   *   *

To Colonel George Baylor

Dear Sir   [Charleston, S.C.] May 27th 1783

Inclosed I send you a copy of a letter written on the 21st of this instant giving you an account of a mutiny which had taken place in your regiment.[1] Lt. Merrywether [James Merriweather] is sent on to give you an account of the matter for fear my letters may miscarry and also to assist you in apprehending the mutineers. If the ring leaders are not brought to punishment the example will have the most disagreeable influence on service should there ever be occasion for soldiers again. Deserters being only received and forgiven in Maryland, who deserted from this army has had a very bad effect. Many have deserted from the presumption of being forgiven who would not have dared to have done it, had those been punished, who got home first. Reports of the kind soon get back to camp. I hope neither time or pains will be spared to apprehend the ring leaders, if the mutineers should have dispersed as I expect they have notwithstanding their threats of demanding their pay with their swords.[2] Mr. Merryweather can give you all further particulars necessary for your information. I am dear Sir Your most ob hble ser.

N. GREENE

Tr (GWG Transcript: CSmH).

1. See NG to Baylor, 21 May, above (vol. 12: 675–76). For more about the mutiny in the First Continental Legionary Corps, see also NG to Gov. Benjamin Harrison, 21 May (ibid., p. 676 and n), and John Watts to NG, 22 May, both above, and NG to Harrison, immediately below.

2. As seen above (vol. 12: 677n), these mutineers were never punished.

To Governor Benjamin Harrison of Virginia

Sir   Head Quarters Chs Town 27th May 1783[1]

For fear my letter of the 20th of this inst may not come to hand, and the mutineers of the first regiment of Cavalry misrepresent their conduct or leave government in some doubt how to take up the business, I have sent on Lieut Meriweather with a copy of my former letter on the sub⟨ject.⟩[2] The bad example of those men has already seduced several more to leave the army, and I fear the infantry will copy their example if orders do not immediately arrive for their being moved to the Northward.[3] I can but repeat my earnest wishes, that the ringleaders of this party, may be taken up and punished capitally as an example to deter others from a similar conduct. If this is not done I can readily foresee its baneful influence.

If the men should have dispersed and the horses sold, a bounty offered for the ringleaders & pardon for those who shall come in & deliver themselves up with their horses may put nearly the whole of them in our power. But as you are on the spot you can judge of the best mode to accomplish the business consistent with the dignity of government and the good of service. Never did a Corps forfeit a fairer reputation. The advisers deserve the Severest punishment.[4] I have the honor to be your Excellency's Most obedient, humble Servant   NATH GREENE

LS (Vi). The manuscript is faded; the text in angle brackets, unreadable in the LS, was taken from the ADfS at MiU-C.

    1. Although the "2" is readable in the date on the LS, the "7" is barely legible. A printed version of this letter gives the date as 27 May, as does the ADfS. (*Calendar of Va. State Papers*, 3: 493–94)

    2. Lt. James Merriwether carried a copy of NG's letter to Harrison of 21 May, above (vol. 12: 676). On the mutiny in the First Continental Legionary Corps, see also Watts to NG, 22 May, above, and NG to Baylor, immediately above.

    3. As seen in his second letter to Gen. Benjamin Lincoln of 3 June, below, NG was able to prevent a mutiny among the infantry regiments of the Southern Army.

    4. As seen above (vol. 12: 677n), the mutineers were never punished.

*   *   *

¶ **[FROM JOHN WIGFALL**, 27 May 1783.[1] He received NG's letter of 23 May [not found] "this day" and assures NG that he has "never seen your fellow March, Neither do I know where he is harbour'd or by whom."[2] Wigfall suspects, though, that "he has been Harbour'd by Some of my Negroes, as I was inform he was Seen in the Plantation, whilst I was Confin'd in Town."[3] Wigfall will do everything he can to "Get the Fellow" for NG; he has offered a "one Guinea Reward to any Person that will Take him, and at the same Time I Have Given Out, amongst the Negroes in Case any of 'em Shou'd See him, that your Honour will Give him a Pardon for his Parst offence, if he will Return to you."[4] RCS (MiU-C) 1 p.]

    1. Wigfall (1736–93) owned several plantations in St. Thomas & St. Dennis Parish, S.C. (*Biog. Directory of S.C. House*, 2: 710)

    2. "March" was presumably a slave belonging to NG.

    3. Wigfall had taken a commission in the Loyalist militia after Charleston fell to the British. Although he was subject to banishment and confiscation, "Neither action was carried out." (*Biog. Directory of S.C. House*, 2: 710; Lambert, *South Carolina Loyalists*, pp. 287, 292–93) It is not known under what circumstances he was "Confin'd" in Charleston.

    4. Roger Parker Saunders reported the death of the "Negroe fellow that was Wigfall's" in a letter to NG of 20 October, below.

¶ **[FROM DOCTOR NATHAN BROWNSON**, Charleston, S.C., 28 May 1783.[1] "Some time since," the deputy director approved an "abstract for Subsistence" for "officers of the prescriptive line of the hospital." Subsistance was drawn on that basis, and Brownson afterward made out an abstract "for the officers of the civil Staff of the Hospital" and signed it himself. He sent it to "M[r] [John S.] Dart," but Dart refused to approve it without the signature of the deputy director of the hospital department. Brownson made out a second abstract and sent it to the deputy director [Dr. David Olyphant], who replied "verbaly" that John Morris, who was listed as "Ward Mast[r]," was not entitled to provisions. Brownson then made out a third abstract, omitting Morris, and sent it to Olyphant, who this time replied "verbally" that he was unwilling "to sign distinct abstracts," but that if Brownson would prepare a return of "all the officers in the hospital department," he would sign it. Olyphant has "often" insisted that Brownson should prepare "general returns" of the hospital officers, but Brownson cannot do so because he is "not possesed of official Information necessary to Making such returns" and does not have the "power to compel such information." If he were to demand a return of officers of the "prescriptive line[,] distinguishing where & how each officer is employed[,] the date of the Order that destined them to such posts & duty[,] who are on furlow & the dates of such furlow," he supposes that Olyphant would find that action "very improper" and "refuse it." Such information is needed, however, for the sort of general return that Olyphant has mandated. The reasons for making separate returns for the "prescribing Line" and the "Civil Staff" are "very evident." The accounts of each are "kept distinct" and are sent to "diferent officers"—those of "The prescribing Line" to the "pay Master" and those of "the Civil Staff" to the purveyor. Moreover, "as Those Acc^{ts} are separately kept they must be supported by distinct Vouchers[;] the Abstracts are the Proper Vouchers to both but cannot be applied if not made distinct." Brownson does not want "to lodge a Complaint agains[t] any Officer," but he hopes that NG, knowing the "true State of the case," will tell him how to obtain subsistence "for Such officers as have a right to expect it through me."[2] RC (MiU-C) 2 pp. Brownson enclosed copies of two letters he had written to Olyphant, one undated and the other of 23 May. (MiU-C) 2 pp.]

1. Brownson was deputy purveyor for the hospital department in the South. (NG to John Habersham, 23 February, above [vol. 12: 472–73])

2. NG's reply has not been found.

¶ [FROM MAJOR SAMUEL FINLEY, [Camp, James Island, S.C.], 28 May 1783. "A few soldiers, who have connections on the way," have made "frequent application" to go to Virginia "by land" when the army leaves. Finley asks "whether such indulgence may be granted them or not." He believes they are "men that may be trusted."[1] RCS (MiU-C) 1 p.]

1. As seen in his letter to Gen. Benjamin Lincoln of 11 July, below, NG did allow Virginia troops to march home. (See also Lincoln to NG, 28 May, below.)

*   *   *

From General Benjamin Lincoln

Dear Sir   War-Office [Philadelphia] May 28th 1783

I was this morning honored with the receipt of your letter of the 17—instant.[1]

The Dragoons quartered here, refused in the first instance to give up their horses unless they could have a right to bid for them, and be debited for their value should they become purchasers. This conduct was considered a violation of order and discipline, and that it could not on that account be submitted to, nor could it be admitted in justice to other parts of the army. I was therefore induced to write a letter to Colonel Butler on the subject, of which the enclosed is a copy.[2]

Colonel Carrington will have received directions from the Q^r Mr Genl relative to the sale of the horses before this reaches you. I do not know whether his instructions will permit the Dragoons to buy or not.[3]

I lament exceedingly that, at the period of the war, any conduct in the Soldiers should tend to tarnish their well earned fame, and former good character, and to expose the United States to hazard and contempt. I will immediately make a full representation to the Governor of Virginia, that they may guard against insult, and be enabled to apprehend all delinquents, and bring them to justice, although, from the general temper of the people at this moment, I have little expectations of vigorous exertions.[4]

By the enclosed resolves of Congress you will learn that all the men engaged for the War, with a proportion of Officers, are to be furloughed.[5] If the Virginians will take their furloughs in Carolina, on being supplied with a sufficiency of provision to subsist them home, it will be a saving, for we shall find it difficult to procure Transports for the whole.

The North-Carolina troops, engaged for a term specified, are also to be furloughed, and I am directed to take measures with you to conduct them to their several homes. At this distance from you, I cannot render you any assistance in this business, and I do not know why I was mentioned. I can only in general say that I think the troops should be thrown into as many divisions as there are counties in which they reside, so that they may be marched under proper Officers to their respective homes. I think they should take what provisions they can well carry, and that a certain sum in cash, for mileage, should be given them to purchase supplies the remainder of the way. This I think would be a good mode for the Virginians should any of them incline to march before the transports arrive.[6] I am, Dear Sir, Your most obedient humble Servant   B LINCOLN

RCS (MiU-C).

1. NG's letter is above (vol. 12: 660).

2. Lincoln's letter to Col. Richard Butler of the Third Pennsylvania Continental Regiment has not been found. As seen in a letter to NG of 16 May, above, Robert Morris hoped that the sale of public property—including, presumably, dragoon horses—would raise enough cash to cover some of the Southern Army's expenses, including some pay for the troops. (Vol. 12: 657) Lincoln presumably had similar reasons for denying the dragoons in Philadelphia the opportunity to buy their horses.

3. Col. Timothy Pickering, the quartermaster general, gave instructions for the sale of Southern Army horses in a letter to Edward Carrington of 17 May but did not address the question of whether the dragoons could bid on them. (Pickering Papers, WRMS, vol. 86, p. 181, DNA) However, when Pickering himself conducted a sale of dragoon horses at the northern army's encampment at Newburg, N.Y., he did allow officers to purchase horses with credit against "the three months pay they are to receive." (Pickering to Morris, 27 May 1783, Morris, *Papers*, 8: 126)

4. Lincoln referred to the recent mutiny of dragoons of the First Continental Legionary

Corps. (See NG to Gov. Benjamin Harrison, 21 May, above [vol. 12: 676].) Lincoln traveled to Virginia soon after writing this letter, but as seen by the note at ibid., he could not persuade authorities there to arrest and punish the mutineers.

5. The resolution to which Lincoln referred was adopted on 26 May. (*JCC*, 24: 364)

6. As seen in his reply of 11 July, below, NG allowed the Virginia troops to march home. He was able to provide neither money nor adequate provisions to those troops or to the ones marching home to North Carolina, however. (Rankin, *N.C. Continentals*, pp. 390–91)

*   *   *

¶ [**FROM GOVERNOR BENJAMIN HARRISON OF VIRGINIA**, Richmond, Va., 30 May 1783. David Darden, "a Poor Man in this State," used a "great part of his fortune" to purchase a stud horse named Romulus. An officer of the Southern Army impressed the horse from him "in a very illegal Manner" and later traded it to Capt. Glasscock [Thomas Glascock], who took it to Georgia, where it "now stands as a covering Horse."[1] These actions are so contrary to NG's orders and "Sense of Justice" that Harrison is sure NG will do whatever he can to restore "the Property of the poor Sufferer." Even that will not compensate Darden for his losses, as the horse has been "two years out of his Possession and his greatest dependance for a support for himself & Family was on the Profits" from breeding the horse. The "offending Officer," whom Darden will identify, should be "called to the severest Account," for his conduct is not only contrary to NG's "express Orders," but is a "deviation from the common Principles of a Gentlemen and Man of Honor, and an intolerable abuse of Power."[2] LB (Vi) 2 pp.]

1. Harrison had previously written to NG about Darden and the horse on 24 December 1782, above (vol. 12: 341–42). As seen there, Romulus had been impressed by an officer of the Third Continental Regiment of Light Dragoons, had been returned to Darden as a result of NG's direct orders, but had been impressed again by Capt. James Gunn of the First Dragoons.

2. As seen in his response to the Findings of a Court of Inquiry, 3 June 1782, above (vol. 11: 286–87), NG had already called Gunn to "the severest Account." It is not known, however, whether Darden was able to recover the horse.

¶ [**FROM CAPTAIN JAMES NICHOLSON**, New York, 30 May 1783.[1] Encloses a copy of an agreement between the superintendent of finance [Robert Morris] and Daniel Parker & Company, under which "the latter are to procure 1500 Tons of Shipping for the purpose of bringing the Troops under [NG's] command to the Bay of Chesapeack."[2] Nicholson, who has been ordered to assist Parker in obtaining and forwarding the transports, adds: "It has been, & is still attended with difficulty to get the quantity of Tons Specified."[3] He believes that "without a great detention" they cannot get more than "13[00] or 1400 Tons." As he must stay in New York "a few days after the Sailing of this first Transport in order to froward the Remainder," he emphasizes "the necessity of puting as many Troops as can Stow with any conveniency in each Vessel so as not greatly to incommode the Men. At any Rate not less then one Man to each Ton of the Vessel."[4] To prevent "Demurrage,"[5] the transports should sail as soon as they are loaded, "without waiting for each other," and NG should so order the captains if Nicholson is not there. NG should also direct the officer commanding the troops on each transport to muster them and give the transport captain a certified copy of the muster, "which will determine the Pay of the Vessel agreeable to the Charter." No demurrage should be allowed, either, for "a Detention in Embarking & Debarking the Troops." In a postscript, Nicholson adds: "I expect the last Vessel will Sail in 4 or 5 days from this Date."[6] RC (MiU-C) 3 pp.]

1. Nicholson (ca. 1736–1804), a Marylander, was the senior officer in the Continental navy. (*DAB*)

2. The enclosure has not been found, but the agreement of 16 May between Morris and Daniel Parker & Company is printed in Morris, *Papers*, 8: 78–79. As seen there, the transports were to land Virginia troops at Williamsburg, Va., Marylanders at Annapolis, Md., and the rest of the army—i.e., troops from Pennsylvania—at Head of Elk, Md.

3. After signing the agreement with Morris, Daniel Parker went to New York to obtain transports to fulfill that and another contract that he had signed for supplying flour to British forces in New York and Nova Scotia. With the help of a Loyalist merchant and others, he engaged vessels to fulfill the transport contract; some of the same vessels would later be used to carry flour from Chesapeake Bay for the contract with the British. It was some time, however, before the vessels destined for South Carolina could be outfitted, provisioned, and sent on their way. (Morris, *Papers*, 8: 83–84, 85–86)

4. Because of desertion and furloughs, NG was able to fit the remaining troops into the available transports with no difficulty. (NG to Lincoln, 11 July, below)

5. By "Demurrage," Nicholson meant the fee that would have to be paid to Daniel Parker & Company if the transports remained at Charleston for more than twelve days. (Memorandum of an Agreement with Daniel Parker and Company, 16 May, Morris, *Papers*, 8: 79)

6. The vessels, which did not sail as soon as Nicholson expected, reached Charleston on 11 June. (NG to Lincoln, 11 July, below)

¶ [FROM RICHARD GRAHAM, Dumfries, Va., 31 May 1783. Asks for advice about "the Situation & produce of the Southern States of S° Carolina & Georgia for Trade," a subject he knows that NG is "well Acquainted with in general from a conversation we had at my House."[1] Now that the "great objects of Peace & independence" and "a free Trade" have been achieved, Graham is considering a move "either to Charles Town [S.C.] or Savanah in Georgia, having formed conections with some of the first Houses in all the Commercial States in Europe." Asks for NG's "Sentiments & advice on this Subject at a leasure hour."[2] Graham believes that commerce in Virginia "must decline fast." Merchants there are "so much despersed that they have no kind of Weight as a body with the Assembly," and the "principal Stapple Tobacco will soon leave" because the "Lands are wearing out, & the fresh Lands in the Western parts of Georgia & on the Ohio must soon produce a sufficient Quantity of that Article, & of a much Superior Quality." Virginia also has "but a poor chance to rival Pensylva[nia] in the Wheat & Flour Trade. So that upon the whole," he believes, "our Virginia Trade has seen its best days." He and Mrs. [Jane Brent] Graham "hope to have the pleasure of Seeing" NG and CG on their way "Northward in the course of this Summer."[3] RCS (MiU-C) 2 pp.]

1. The conversation may have taken place in November 1780, when NG traveled through Dumfries on his way to join the Southern Army. (See above, vol. 6: 456.)

2. NG's reply has not been found. Graham, a Scottish merchant, was still living at Dumfries at the time of his death in 1796. (*GW Diaries*, 6: 310, 336n)

3. CG traveled north by water in June. (NG to Washington, 5 June, below) NG passed through Dumfries on his way home in September, but it is not known whether he saw the Grahams then. (NG's Journal, 12 September, below)

¶ [FROM ROBERT MORRIS, SUPERINTENDENT OF FINANCE, Office of Finance [Philadelphia], 31 May 1783. Has NG's letter of 16 May; hopes "the Bills therein mentioned will be duly Paid as they fall due, for I put my self to inconvenience to supply the Money for which they were given."[1] Encloses two bills, "drawn by M[r] [John] Swanwick on M[r] James M[c]Call," which, Morris is sure, "will be duly Paid." McCall, "lately" a secretary in the Office of Finance, "is a most faithfull and Industrious Young Man, but has not been so amply rewarded for his Service as he ought or these Drafts would have been unnecessary[;] as the matter Stands he must pay them."[2] Morris's resignation, which he did not submit until he was "Confident of Peace," was "induced by a desire to serve the Army and other Public Creditors." When a committee of Congress, "previous to the Cessation of Hostilities," asked him to stay in office if the war continued, he replied that the same motives that first induced him to accept the position "would in that Case continue to operate."[3] He will be "extreamly happy" to see NG "here."[4] RCS (CSmH) 2 pp. Copies of the Swanwick and McCall "Drafts," dated 8 April and 31 May and totaling $662 42/90, are appended below Morris's signature.]

1. NG's letter of 16 May is above (vol. 12: 656). As seen there, NG feared that the Southern Army paymaster could not punctually pay the bills of exchange that Morris had forwarded.

2. McCall left Morris's office to become auditor general of South Carolina. When he left, Morris asked Congress to grant McCall $400 for extra service, but the request was not approved. (Morris to the President of Congress, 31 March, Morris, *Papers*, 7: 652 and n)

3. On Morris's resignation, see his letter to NG of 14 March, above (vol. 12: 514–15 and n).

4. It was not until early October that NG reached Philadelphia on his way home to Rhode Island. (See note at NG to Boudinot, 7 October, below.)

¶ [FROM MAJOR JOSEPH EGGLESTON, [Georgetown, S.C., May 1783].[1] Because of the "anxiety of a Number of the Soldiers to obtain their Discharges," he has given two of them permission to "wait on" NG "for themselves & some of the others. They are Men who have resided in the Carolinas, except three, who belong to the back Parts of Virginia." Eggleston encloses a list [not found], "specifying the States to which they belong." He cannot "detain these men on the Principles of Convenience" because they say they would be "farther from their Homes when at Richmond [Va.] than at Charlestown," S.C. RCS (MiU-C) 1 p.]

1. The month was conjectured from the contents. (See also Eggleston to NG, 22 May, above.) Lee's Legion, which Eggleston commanded, was stationed at Georgetown.

* * *

To General Benjamin Lincoln, Secretary at War

Dear Sir   Head quarters Charlestown [S.C.] June 3[d] 1783

I have been trying to possess my self of an exact account of the rations drawn by the officers in this Army in the year 1782 ever since you wrote me on the subject.[1] But Mr [John] Kean who acted as Commissary then is now out of office and lives near Beauford [i.e., Beaufort, S.C.] and has his papers with him and being under no obligation to furnish those papers and very busily engaged in his private affairs I find a difficulty in getting them. M^r [John M.] Verdier who was his Assistant has charge of the papers and did most of the executive part of the business is very tardy with Mr Kean in making out the accounts which renders it more difficult for Mr Kean to furnish them.

The delay has been so long and the officers here so discontented on the subject that I have been obliged to order a settlement with the Officers without their accounts from the Commissaries office. Before the Pensylvania Troops joined us it had been a rule for each officer to draw one Ration and there was little variation from it.[2] Some few officers at the heads of departments and commanding brigades had drawn more. In April 1782 from a representation from the Officers that the Northern Army had drawn two rations while at York and that it had been the practice of that Army I directed two rations to be issued to the officers here and from that time to the end of the year each Officer drew two rations when they could get them.[3] It is said the pay Master of the Northern Army have settled with the officers of that army who drew two rations as only drawing one[,] Congress having allowed the other gratis. On this information Mr Dart is settling with the officers here upon the same scale.[4] If these indulgences have not been granted the Northern Officers or the Officers here are not to have the same the pay master holds them accountable in the mode of settlement at a future day for all the rations each have drawn when the Commisaries Accounts shall be obtained.[5] All the Captains and Subalterns confined themselves to the number of rations specified in the General order. Some few field officers at the heads of departments and commanding brigades drew more. I believe the following are all that drew more than two from April and more than one except in the Pennsylvania line from the beginning of the year. Col Harrison and Col Mathews of Virginia[,] Col Harmar and Mengez of Pennsylvania[,] Col Adams and Stewart of Maryland[,] Colonel Murphy and Lyttle of North Carolinia. Col Baylor commanding the horse[,] Col Carrington at head of the quarter Master Genl Departments, and Col Kosciususko Chief engineer and Major De Brom Col Ternants inspector.[6] These with some few others on the Staff with whom we dont settle at present were all that drew more than two rations and if you settle the accounts with the officers on this scale the public will suffer no injury. But as soon as I can possess myself with the accounts they shall be forwarded without loss of time. I have made repeated applications; but have not been able to obtain them. The Moment the enemy left this Country every man flew to his own business and there has hardly been a possibility of drawing their attention from it for any consideration whatever. I repeated my application to Mr Kean a few days ago and he promised me if I would send up a man for the purpose of bring[ing] the Accounts down he would try to get them drawn off.[7]

You see my situation and I hope this will apologize for the disappointments I have felt much upon the occasion but have not had it in my power to redress my self.

If the settlement in the Northern Army has not been agreeable to what the pay Master has been informed here the sooner I can be advertized thereof the better. I am dear Sir Your Most Obedt humble Ser

N GREENE

ADfS (MiU-C).

1. Lincoln's request is in a letter to NG of 3 May, above (vol. 12: 640).

2. Troops of the Pennsylvania Continental line joined the Southern Army in January 1782. (See NG's Orders of 4 January 1782, above [vol. 10: 157].)

3. According to an undated chart in the Washington Papers, subalterns received two daily rations, captains three, and majors four. (Fitzpatrick, GW, 25: 490)

4. John S. Dart was the Southern Army's paymaster. (Vol. 11: 485–86, above)

5. Lincoln replied to this letter on 4 August, below.

6. The officers, in the order that NG listed them, were colonels Charles Harrison, George Mathews, Josiah Harmar, Francis Mentges, Peter Adams, John Steward, Hardy Murfree, Archibald Lytle, George Baylor, Edward Carrington, and Thaddeus Kosciuszko, Maj. Ferdinand de Brahm, and Col. Jean-Baptiste Ternant.

7. The earlier correspondence with Kean has not been found, but see NG's letter to him of 15 June, below. As seen in NG to Kean of 28 June, below, the accounts that Kean later sent were unacceptable.

To General Benjamin Lincoln, Secretary at War

Dear Sir   Head quarters Charlestown [S.C.] June 3ᵈ 1783¹

I have just got your letter of the 20th [and have] time enough to acknowledge the receipt of it by the return of Mʳ Lord.² From the great delay of the Express boat, the probability of her being lost[,] the uneasiness of the Troops I was advised unannimou[s]ly by the General and field officers to engage Shipping to carry home the Troops notwithstanding Shipping had been written for to the Northward[.] One Vessel was taken up and sailed before the arrival of your dispaches but by head winds was obliged to return. Another Vessel was engaged and ready to embark the Troops from which we could not disengage our selves without violating public faith; and as by the estimate of the Shipping engaged there will be a deficiency which render[s] our engagements not injurious,³ I was determined to delay engaging any farther as long as possible and am happy your dispaches have [*one or more pages missing?*]

The Troops for the war have been exceeding troublesome for their discharges. The Maryland Troops mutinied and were with great difficulty prevented from marching off. The Virginia Troops have been very insolant until I directed the Sergeants into confinement. The Pennsylvania Troops have murmured a good deal but by the address of the officers they have been kept quiet. The Legion has been very riotous and one half the first Regiment of Cavalry have mutinied and march[ed] off in a body for Virginia as I wrote you last week.⁴ I have sent an officer to apprehend if possible the ring leaders and if possible to get the public horses.[5] Such was the discontent of the Cavalry and such the advantages they had of going off in a body being at a great distance from the infantry that it was thought advisable and indeed the only chance the public had to bring the Cavalry horses to an open sale was to permit the Dragoons to bid to be deducted out of their pay. And to advertize the Cavalry for sale with out mentioning this in the advertizement would give all an opportunity to desert. What made the difficulty greater it seems the Cavalry officers promised the Dragoons at the close of the war they should have their horses. Major [John] Swan and others say they had orders to give the Men such assurances. I have never seen any such order of Congress or from the war office nor do I believe there ever was any. These assurances were given long before I came into this department and whether this notion was impressed upon the Troops to induce them to good care of their Cattle[6] or whether there ever was such an order from any authority I cannot tell but certain it is it had the same operation upon the mind[s] of the Troops as if it had been ever so well founded; and I believe had we attempted to sold the horses without priveledging the dragoons to bid they would have all gone off in a body and after wards dispersed in such a manner as to have rendered it difficult if not impracticable to have collected any considerable part of the Cavalry horses. How we shall manage the matter now I know not. I would wish to evade the Soldiers claim but can see no way without acting dishonorably. I am in hopes that by address to prevail with nearly the whole to forego their right founded on Col Carringtons advertizement; but if I cannot prevail on them it is thought by all those best acquainted with the matter the public will suffer less by indulging the Troops than rejecting their pretentions.[7] If the public could afford to make such large payments to particular Corps they would never do it on better terms than by letting the Cavalry purchase their own horses. Wed[d]ed to them by a long course of service[,] jealous of public faith and anxious to get some thing in hand they will bid very high for them. I have given you a short state of this business and would have been more explicit but am very ill with a fever attended with a violent head ache. I shall write you on the other parts of your letter in a day or two if my fever goes off and my head gets better. I am dear Sir Your Most Obed humble Ser   N GREENE

ADfS (MiU-C).

1. In his reply of 4 August, below, Lincoln acknowledged NG's letters of "the 2d 3d & 18th of June." This draft, though docketed "2d June," is clearly dated the third, as is the draft of the letter to Lincoln immediately above.

2. Lincoln's letter of 20 May is above (vol. 12: 674–75).

3. The two vessels were the brig *Adams*, which transported troops from Charleston to Annapolis, Md., and the brigantine *Christiana*, which carried CG and troops from Charleston to Philadelphia. (Treasury Waste Book D, p. 383, DNA)

4. The letter to Lincoln of "last week" has not been found. NG had also reported the unrest in Lee's Legion and the mutiny of dragoons of the First Continental Legionary Corps in a letter to Lincoln of 17 May, above (vol. 12: 660–61).

5. Lt. James Merriwether, whom NG sent to overtake the mutineers, was unable to persuade them to return. NG also sent his aide Nathaniel Pendleton to Virginia to meet with officials about apprehending and punishing the mutineers. As seen in Pendleton's letter of 17 July, below, the Virginia legislature was unwilling to take any action.

6. By "Cattle," NG meant livestock.

7. Edward Carrington's advertisement, which appeared in the *South-Carolina Gazette and General Advertiser* of 24 May, reads:

The sale of Public Property, advertised to be made at the Camp on James-Island, on Tuesday the 27th instant, will certainly take place on *Thursday* the 29th. When there will be exposed to sale, by Public Auction, upwards of seventy Waggons and Teams, with Gears compleat; a number of spare Waggons, Draught and Riding Horses, several Smiths Travelling Forges, a great variety of Artificers Tools for every branch of business, and many other very useful articles.

The following sales will also in like manner take place, viz. At Jacksonborough, on *Thursday* the 4th day of June, Fifty Waggons and Teams, and about 100 Dragoon Horses of the Legion. At Nelson's Ferry, on Santee, on *Thursday* the 11th of the same month, 200 Dragoon Horses of the first regiment, and a number of Waggons and Teams. At Charlestown, on *Thursday* the 18th of June, about 150 Dragoon Horses, the balance of those belonging to the Legion. At the above places will also be sold, the Saddles and Bridles in use with the Horses.

It is well known that all the above Dragoon Horses are of the first quality, and, having been for several months at rest and in good keeping, are now in high order. The Waggon Horses are also in point of age, size, and goodness, equal to any in the United States; as those that were old and poor, have, during the Winter, been selected and sold off; and the late situation of the army has afforded an opportunity to have them put in the best order for service. The Waggons and Gears have also been repaired during the Winter, so as to be nearly as good as if new.

Credit will be given until the first of January 1784, for all sums above One Hundred Dollars, on bond and approved security. And as the debts which will arise on these sales are to be fully and compleatly adjusted with the United States by myself, of the Quarter-Master General, the payments must be made in the most punctual and simple manner; and I hereby give Notice, as one of the terms of sale, that no Certificates whatever are to be received in payment, except that any dragoon purchasing a horse, will have the same set against his pay. For the payment of Certificates, other provision has, or will be made; and I am induced to take this precaution to avoid much unnecessary perplexity and inconvenience which I have experienced by having those that were neither authentic nor belonging to my department, opposed to my engagements merely as pretexts for delay.   EDWARD CARRINGTON
Charlestown, May 17.   DEP. Q M GEN

To Robert Morris, Superintendent of Finance

Sir   [Headquarters, Charleston, S.C., 3 June 1783][1]

I have receivd your several letters of the 16th of April and 16 & 17th of May.[2] Baron Glaubecks bills are the first and will be the last of the kind I will trouble you with.[3] I believe he is a Villian and an imposter. Major [Ichabod] Burnet informed me the Minister was acquainted with his family and knew him to be of noble extract and possessing a considerable fortune.[4] Congress gave him a commision from General [Daniel] Morgans report of his conduct at the battle of the Cowpens.[5] My situation precluded me from getting full information of his conduct and I am afraid I have given him a Certificate by which he may impose upon others as he has upon me. I am thinking to advertize him to prevent his availing him self of my Certificate. It will not be more indelicate than his conduct deserves. If he should be in Philadelphia which I dont expect altho he set out to go there I wish you could have him taken up on account of the bills protested and I will forward them to support the Action.

I am sorry my bills press you so hard. I was apprehensive of it and have drawn with as sparing a hand as possible. I was never so distressed in my life for Money nor so frequently called upon[.] After the enemy were gone nothing could be got but for cash or bills. Many debts that were contracted last winter was a year[6] for Clothing got by Col [John] Laurens & [Henry] Lee for the light Troops have been brought in Since the evacuation and this State from their having advanced pretty largely would not receive them. Those have swelled our bills and as the Merchants run great risques to oblige us in our greatest distress I could not refuse to do them some kind of justice.[7] I can assure you, you dont feel more pain at seeing my bills than I feel at signing them. Considering me as the signer and holding me responsible for acceptance and payment not only in my public but private charactor you may suppose with certainty I draw but from necessity and more especially for some time past since your continuance has been doubtful. I am made very happy by your determination to remain in office; and I hope time and a little more experience will produce a more enlightened policy among the States.[8] Opinions more favorable to Continental measures are gaining ground here dayly; but I even doubt now the adoption of the late plan for collecting a duty.[9] Many will support the measure but some powerful men will oppose it; and I must do them the justice to say I think they will do it from principle however erroneous their reasoning.

Money is so scarce in this Country that I fear was Col Carrington to attempt to sell the Cavalry horses for cash only[,] he could not get more than one half he can for six Months credit with good security.[10]

I have never been in a more perplexing situation than since the declaration for a cessation of hostilities. The Troops for the war have been so strongly impressed with an idea of their having a right to a discharge that it has been exceeding difficult to hold them subject to authority: one part of the Cavalry have mutinied and gone off to Virginia.[11] Several other Corps have been troublesome. The Cavalry lay at Congaree upwards of an hundred Miles from Head quarters.

I am very happy the Troops are going to their respective States; and the sooner they are disbanded the better. We shall contract every thing here upon as narrow a scale as possible. The secretary of war will inform you of our having engaged some shipping and our reasons for it.[12] I hope it will be no disadvantage as the Shipping you have engaged will not take all the Troops on board. The Troops will be held in readiness to embark the Moment the fleet arrives.[13]

I am very unwell or I would write you more fully on many matters.[14] I am Sir with esteem & regard Your most Obd't humble Ser   N GREENE

ADfS (MiU-C).

1. The date was taken from Morris's reply of 10 July, below; the place from other letters that NG wrote on 3 June.

2. The April letter, which was dated the 17th, and those of 16 and 17 May are all above (vol. 12: 616, 657–58, 661–62).

3. For background on Glaubeck and the bills that NG had given to him, see above, the note at NG's letter to the Chevalier de La Luzerne of 22 February (vol. 12: 469–70n).

4. The "Minister" was the French minister to the United States, La Luzerne.

5. Morgan's report on the battle of Cowpens is in his letter to NG of 19 January 1781, above (vol. 7: 152–55). Congress awarded Glaubeck the brevet rank of captain on 9 March 1781. (JCC, 19: 247) NG helped to obtain the brevet by writing to James M. Varnum, a delegate to Congress from Rhode Island, on Glaubeck's behalf. (NG to Varnum, 24 January 1781, above [vol. 7: 187])

6. NG presumably meant for the winter of 1781–82.

7. Arrangements had been made in the winter of 1782 to buy clothing for Lee's light troops from a Charleston merchant, Robert Powell. (See NG to Lee, 10 and 12 February 1782, above [vol. 10: 350 and n, 358 and n].) For a discussion of the clothing purchases that NG had arranged for the Southern Army, see NG to Gen. Benjamin Lincoln, 19 December 1782, above (vol. 12: 306–7 and n).

8. On Morris's decision to continue in office, see note at his letter to NG of 14 March, above (vol. 12: 515–16n).

9. As seen in the note at NG to Lincoln, 18 June, below, South Carolina effectively voted down Congress's 1783 impost proposal.

10. On Carrington's sale of the army's horses, see NG to Lincoln, second letter of 3 June, immediately above, and NG to Lincoln, 18 June, below. As seen in the note at the first of those letters, Carrington did allow purchases to be made on credit.

11. In the ADfS, this portion of the text is underlined and has a bracket around it. The editors believe these alterations were made by William Johnson, NG's first biographer, who also wrote a précis of the letter on the last sheet of the draft, below the docketing. For a discussion of the mutiny by dragoons of the First Continental Legionary Corps, see NG to Gov. Benjamin Harrison, 21 May, above (vol. 12: 676 and n).

12. The letter to Benjamin Lincoln in which NG discussed his decision to lease vessels to carry some of the troops of the Southern Army home is above, dated 20 May. (Vol. 12: 672)

13. The vessels that Morris had engaged in the North to transport Southern Army troops did not arrive in Charleston until 11 July. (NG to Lincoln, 11 July, below)

14. On NG's illness, see his letter to Washington of 5 June, below.

*   *   *

¶ [TO ROBERT MORRIS, SUPERINTENDENT OF FINANCE. From Headquarters, Charleston, S.C., 4 June 1783. Capt. William Pierce, Jr., "lately one of" NG's aides—and his secretary—will hand this letter to Morris.[1] NG has informed Morris that Pierce was "going to Hispannolia or the Havannah on a scheme of business," but Pierce has "droped that plan" and joined "Col White and Major Call in a scheme of business in Georgia."[2] They propose to operate stores in Savannah and Augusta, and NG thinks that they "will succeed well in business." Pierce needs "advice respecting the best mode for obtaining goods either in Europe or America[,] price and remittances taken into consideration." NG will be "exceedingly obliged" if Morris will "give him such advice and such letters as you may think will promote the interest of the concern."[3] NG asks this "not from motives of interest," for he has "no connection with the house," but from "principles of friendship." White, Call, and Pierce were all officers in the Southern Army, and NG wishes "their welfare," especially that of Pierce, who has been in his military family since NG came to the South. ADfS (MiU-C) 4 pp.]

1. Pierce visited Morris on 20 June. (Diary entry for 20 June, Morris, *Papers*, 8: 196)

2. NG had written to Morris about Pierce's plan to go to the West Indies on 16 February, but that letter has not been found. (See Morris to Pierce, 24 May, Morris, *Papers*, 8: 116.) On Pierce's partners, Richard Call and Anthony W. White, see note at NG to Wadsworth, 24 May, above.

3. In a diary entry for 17 July, Morris wrote: "Major Pierce aid De Camp to Genl. Greene for Letters in consequence of the Genls. recommendation of him &c." (Morris, *Papers*, 8: 298)

¶ [TO GOUVERNEUR MORRIS. From Headquarters, Charleston, S.C., 5 June 1783. CG, who "comes ready to answer all" of Morris's "accusations of silence or neglect," will hand this letter to him.[1] Although she is "in ill health," NG is sure she "will soon convince you, you cannot support the first what ever you may the last."[2] CG has "always professed a great regard" for Morris, and NG has "generally found her pretty candid. If the esteem is mutual the difference can have no long standing." NG is "heartily glad" that the troops will soon be evacuated; his "troubles have been greater" since the British left South Carolina "than before." Adds: "It was nothing more than I expected and foresaw, but people would not believe it possible for such changes to take place in so short a time." NG expects to see Morris "soon" and will be "silent" until then, as he is suffering from a fever.[3] ALS (NNC) 2 pp.]

1. See note at NG to Washington, immediately below.

2. Morris's letter accusing CG of "silence or neglect" has not been found.

3. NG did not arrive in Philadelphia until early October. (See note at NG's Journal, 15 August, below.) For more about his health, see the letter immediately below.

¶ [TO GEORGE WASHINGTON. From Charleston, S.C., 5 June 1783. NG is "now sick with a fever and almost blind with sore Eyes"; he writes only to "apologize for not writing." CG, who will deliver this letter, embarks "to day for Philadelphia."[1] Her health is "much improved," and NG is "anxious to get her to the Northward[,] notwithstanding" his own ill health. CG will bring a "Green silk embroidered pattern for a waiscoat," which a "Lady in the West Indies" sent to NG for Washington.[2] NG hopes to see Washington soon.[3] In a postscript, he sends regards to "Mrs Washington" and remarks that Washington's address to the army and letter to Congress are "universally admired."[4] LS (Washington Papers: DLC) 2 pp.]

1. CG was embarking on the brigantine *Christiana*, which was to carry troops to Philadelphia. The vessel apparently left Charleston harbor on 7 June. (*South-Carolina Weekly Gazette*, 7 June) According to a Philadelphia newspaper, it reached the Pennsyl-

vania city on the 14th. (*Pennsylvania Post and Daily Advertiser*, 21 June; see also Pierce to NG, 19 June, and Garden to NG, 20 June, both below.)

2. On the waistcoat pattern, see Richard Lushington to NG, 24 July 1782, above (vol. 11: 455).

3. NG did not arrive in the North until October. (See note at NG's Journal, 15 August, below.)

4. NG undoubtedly referred here to Washington's address to the army of 15 March, during the Newburgh Conspiracy crisis, and his letter to Congress of 18 March, spelling out the officers' grievances that had led to the conspiracy. (Fitzpatrick, *GW*, 26: 222–27, 229–32)

¶ [FROM ROGER PARKER SAUNDERS, [Charleston, S.C.], 7 June 1783. Acknowledges NG's letter "with the Money" [not found].¹ Agrees that the "Prices were extravagant," but they were the "best terms" available, "owing to the Scarsity of every thing in this part of the Country." Oxen are not available "at any price"; "young Steers" that can substitute for oxen cost "4 Guineas Cash"; cows and calves are also four guineas each. Furthermore, "no Credit can be got for Cattle."² Saunders wanted to plant twenty more acres of rice, "but the ground was so hard" that he could only get in "about five Acres"; NG now has "155 3/4 Acres Rice."³ Saunders wants NG to buy some "Negroes," whom Mr. Crouch bought from "Boons Esᵗ." They are "advertisd to be sold in Town" but are anxious to "live with" NG; Saunders believes they would "suit you b[etter] than any other Negroes."⁴ He and his wife send "respectful compᵗˢ" to CG and wish "she could have taken a ride up here."⁵ RCS (MiU-C) 2 pp.]

1. NG's letter was presumably a reply to Saunders's of 26 May, above.

2. Saunders wrote NG on 20 June, below, that he had purchased "Twelve Young Stear for oxen at 3 Guineas and drawn on you for the amoᵗ."

3. Heavy rains damaged the rice crop soon afterward. (Saunders to NG, 3 July, below)

4. The notice in the *South-Carolina Gazette and General Advertiser* of 3 June reads: "On Thursday the 12th June, 1783, will be sold at the Exchange, in Charlestown, precisely at 12 o'Clock, a number of valuable Negroes belonging to the estate of Henry Crouch, Esq; deceased." Crouch had been a Charleston merchant. (*Biog. Directory of S.C. House*, 3: 162–63) "Boon's Esᵗ" was the estate that had been confiscated from Thomas Boone, a former royal lieutenant governor of South Carolina. It included Boone's Barony, the plantation that the state of South Carolina had given to NG. (See Hugh Rutledge to NG, 26 February 1782, above [vol. 10: 411 and n].) For more about the sale, see Saunders to NG, 3 December, below.

5. As noted at NG to Washington, immediately above, CG sailed for Philadelphia from Charleston on the 7th.

¶ [FROM JOHN CARTER [i.e., JOHN BARKER CHURCH], Philadelphia, 9 June 1783. He has received Mr. [Francis] Kinloch's letter to NG of 22 March,¹ and more recently one from Kinloch of 9 April, stating that Kinloch's "Brother [Cleland Kinloch] would have Renewed the Bond" had NG "not ask'd compound Interest." Carter would have been "content to have the Bond Renewed at the legal Interest of the State, calculating only simple Interest." Carter will set out for Hartford, Conn., in a few hours to join [Jeremiah] Wadsworth, with whom he plans to travel to France.² As he will be "absent some Time," he asks NG to "transmit the Bond when Renewed" to his "Brother in Law," Col. Alexander Hamilton.³ Carter has paid two of NG's "Drafts on Wadsworth for 3000 dollars."⁴ He and his wife send "best Compliments" to CG. RCS (DLC) 1 p.]

1. See above, vol. 12: 542.

2. Carter and his business partner Wadsworth sailed for France on 27 July. (Wadsworth to NG, 26 July, below; Morris, *Papers*, 8: 342n)

3. Hamilton and Carter, whose real name was John Barker Church, were both married to daughters of Gen. Philip Schuyler of Albany, N.Y.—Hamilton to Elizabeth Schuyler and Carter to her sister Angelica. On the bond, see also Hamilton to NG, 10 June, below.

4. On the drafts, see also NG to Wadsworth, 21 April, above (vol. 12: 630), and Wadsworth to NG, 12–13 June, below.

*   *   *

To Griffin Greene

Dear Sir   Head quarters Charlestown [S.C.] June 9th 1783

If you should not be so happy as to see those persons to whom my particular letters of credit are addressed to; and your affairs in Europe require an advance any person giving you credit for fifteen or two thousand pounds may consider me as responsible for the amount and you may make use of this letter to obtain credit if it shou'd become necessary.[1] I am dear Sir Your most Obedient humble Servt

NATH GREENE

ALS (Ct).

1. NG's cousin Griffin was en route to France at this time on behalf of the family business, Jacob Greene & Company (See above, Griffin's letters to NG of 18 and 21 May [vol. 12: 662–64, 677–78].) In a letter to Griffin of 14 June, below, NG listed the recipients of his "particular letters of credit" and wrote that he had increased the amount that Griffin might draw. Griffin Greene replied to these letters on 1 October, below.

To Griffin Greene

Dear Sir   Head Quarters Charlestown [S.C.] June 10th 1783

Your favor dated the 18th May at East Greenwich [R.I.] was handed me a few days ago by Capt Pelig Greene.[1] I am sorry for your detail of misfortunes. It is not in the power of mortals to command success, all that they can do is to endeavor to deserve it. That you have done This I have no doubt. My disappointment is considerable, but I feel more for you than for myself. Thus my friendship will never forsake you nor shall your family want any blessings in my power to procure them. It is not my power to embark largely in business without hazarding more than I am willing. My landed property in this Country I am endeavoring to put in a way of improvement; which if I can effect, it will afford me a genteel Independence. To put this in the power of fortune may leave me in the decline of life, with a shattered constitution to struggle with difficulties painful to contemplate. But if hazarding something would give the concern any great advantages, I should be willing to run some risque.

I have no inclination to purchase any part of the *Flora* on my own account; but if you think a greater interest will or may be for the benefit of the company, I have no objection to your enlarging our interest in her.[2] But at the same time I will just observe that the comparative value of the *Flora*, upon a War [not?] Peace establishment is very great. Her fast sailing now is of little consequence & she will sail from her peculiar combination at almost double the expence that other vessels will carrying an equal burthen with her. Another reason against purchasing is the difficulty of getting freight, & the expence of laying still. If your stocks are principally engrossed in shipping, you will have nothing to load them. At Bourdeaux, I am told, the Merchants are enterprizing & adventurous. If the ship could be filled for Guinea with French Brandy & some few dry goods, & the slave trade be opened here & the ship arrive at this place in April next I think she might make a profitable voyage. But I candidly confess to you at the same time, it is all a matter of conjecture. The ship may also be employed in the Rice trade, but I think her too large for the Tobacco Trade. If you can obtain a credit on my being responsible for fifteen hundred or two thousand pounds, you may; but as trade is unsettled & remittances difficult, I wish you not to involve either yourself or me unless you can reap great advantage by it. I was talking with a British merchant today, of good information & great experience. He says that dry goods for a year to come, may be got in America on better terms than in England, owing to the large importations which will take place & the slow sale they will meet with here. I only hint these things for your information, & not to discourage you. As you will be in the channel of political[3] & commercial intelligence, you can form a much better judgement of matters & things than I can pretend to at this distance.

Mes^rs Banks & Hunter with whom Major Burnet is connected in business, may very probably gain in the purchase of a part of the ship *Flora*.[4] Mr Hunter is gone to Europe, & Mr Banks writes him by this opportunity. You will avail your self of Mr Hunters friendship as far as possible. I have some little acquaintance with him & have written him also.[5] He is an exceeding worthy character, sensible & judicious in his conduct. I have written to Mr Laurens also to aid & assist you as far as he may have it in his power.[6] I hope he will; but great men often think a letter of this sort is [totally?] complied with if they condescend to make two or three [bows?] on the occasion. I have also enclosed you a letter to the Marquis de la Fayette desiring him to advance for you one thousand pound sterling or to give you that credit if you should have occasion for it.[7] He made me an offer of this sort, some little time past but I am afraid he will leave Europe for America before you will see him, and if he should not He may think I have taken his offer in too strong a light. Courtiers are flowing in language but timid & cautious in conduct. I dont wish to do injustice to the Marquis's generous intentions; but I wish not to raise your expectations too high, lest it should prove a disadvantage to you.

If you should retain the present part you hold in the *Flora* and fit her, I think you should go in her. It is too great a property to be trusted to people who dont feel the effects of a dilatory conduct. I have only one thing more to observe; that is, you are in the vortex & whirlpool of pleasure and corruption. Avoid gameing at all events. Friendship will appear in many forms. Be wary of the man who upon a short acquaintance appears officious to oblige.

Mrs Greene sailed from this a day or two ago for Philadelphia. She has the same affection for you as ever she had. She had written you just before, was the reason for her not writing by the opportunity you mention. Let neither doubts or fears disturb your repose[;] our regards are too deep rooted to be shaken by the little strokes of adversity. I am in hopes to be in Rhode Island in August or Septem^r; but I am apt to think I shall return here this Winter. However this is uncertain & depends on many contingencies.[8]

We are waiting with no small degree of impatience for the definitive [peace] treaty; and while we are waiting for this the Soldiers are clamorous for their discharges. I shall write you by every opportunity; & I wish You would me; if it is but a single line, it will be matter of satisfaction, & may be of other [use?] to me.[9] I am   N GREENE

LS (Ct).

1. The letter is above (vol. 12: 662–64).

2. The Greene family business was a part owner of the *Flora*, a former British frigate that Griffin Greene had raised from the bottom of Newport Harbor in 1780. For more about the vessel and the family's investment in it, see ibid.

3. The word "information" is crossed through here.

4. On Ichabod Burnet's involvement in business with James Hunter and John Banks, see Statement of John Banks, 15 February, above (vol. 12: 445). No evidence has been found that they became investors in the *Flora*.

5. See NG to James Hunter, 14 June, below.

6. See NG to Henry Laurens, this date, below.

7. See NG to Lafayette, immediately below.

8. NG did not get back to Rhode Island until late November. (NG to Jacob Greene, 29 November, below) He returned to Charleston the following summer. (See note at NG to Hazlehurst, 26 June 1784, below.)

9. Griffin Greene replied to NG on 1 October, below.

*   *   *

¶ [**TO THE MARQUIS DE LAFAYETTE**. From Headquarters, Charleston, S.C., 10 June 1783. NG wrote to him "a few days ago by Mr Hunter of Virginia."[1] The present letter "goes inclosed to" NG's cousin Griffin Greene, with whom NG and his brothers "are concerned in trade." Griffin is "bound to Bordaeux to look after an interest we have laying there in the Ship *Flora* which by some mismanagement has been idle there for many months past." Should Griffin need a letter of credit for £1,000 or £1,200 sterling, NG will be much obliged if Lafayette will "give him this credit"; NG "will be responsible" for it. Lafayette's "polite letter from Nantz authorises this liberty," and NG hopes he will not "find it inconvenient."[2] NG will "say nothing upon politicks by this uncertain conveyance." ALS (NjGbS) 2 pp.]

1. The letter has not been found. As seen in NG to Griffin Greene, immediately above, James Hunter, a Virginia merchant and business partner of John Banks, had gone to France on business.

2. Lafayette's letter from Nantes, France, has not been found. In a letter from Cadiz, Spain, of 5 February 1783, however, Lafayette had asked NG to send him his commands and offered to introduce NG's business associates to the best commercial firms in France. (Vol. 12: 416, above) As seen in NG's letter to him of 24 March 1784, below, Lafayette offered to advance the money to Griffin Greene.

¶ [TO HENRY LAURENS. From Headquarters, Charleston, S.C., 10 June 1783. As he has never "received a line" from Laurens since arriving in the Southern Department, NG does not "know how far I may value my self on your friendship." Of course, Laurens's situation "has not been favorable for a correspondence most parts of the time."[1] NG would have written to him "long ago" but did not know where to "direct" a letter. NG wrote to Laurens "a few days past by Mr Hunter of Virginia."[2] The present letter will probably be delivered by NG's cousin Griffin Greene, who is going to Europe "on some business of a company with whom I am and was connected in trade before the war."[3] If Griffin has "occasion for a letter of Credit to the amount of a thousand pound Sterling," NG would be "much obliged" if Laurens could provide it; NG will be "responsible for the same." NG has advised Griffin to "consult" Laurens on "matters of business" and will be "under singular obligations" if Laurens will assist him.[4] He congratulates Laurens "upon the restoration of peace; and shall be happy to have the honor to take you by the hand in America."[5] ADfS (MiU-C) 2 pp.]

1. For much of the time during NG's command in the South, Laurens had been a prisoner of the British in the Tower of London. (See above, vol. 12: 149n.)

2. The letter to Laurens that NG sent with James Hunter has not been found.

3. See NG's letter to Griffin Greene, this date, above.

4. As seen in Laurens's reply of 26 August, below, Griffin did not contact him.

5. Laurens had been one of the American commissioners negotiating the peace treaty with Great Britain. (Vol. 12: 149n)

*　　　*　　　*

From Alexander Hamilton

D[r] General　　　　　　　　　　　　　Philadelphia June 10[h] 1783

I inclose you a couple of letters from M[r] Carter[:] one for yourself, the other for M[r] Kinloch.[1] There is nothing for me to add, except that I wish you when the business shall be transacted to transmit the bond to me under cover to General Schuyler at Albany.[2] I expect to leave this shortly for that place and to remain there 'till New York is evacuated; on which event I shall set down there seriously on the business of making my fortune. It has been hinted to me that you have some thoughts of making our state the place of your residence.[3] You will easily believe me sincere when I express my wishes that this may be the case, and when I add that I shall consider it as a valuable acquisition to the state.

There is so little disposition either in or out of Congress to give solidity to our national system that there is no motive to a man to lose his time in the public service, who has no other view than to promote its welfare. Experience must convince us that our present establishments are Utopian before we shall be ready to part with them for better.

I write in Congress and therefore can not enlarge;[4] but I need not assure you that no one will at all times have more pleasure in hearing from you than myself as no one is more warmly & sincerely Your friend than Dʳ Sir Yr Obed serv   A HAMILTON

RCS (Hamilton Papers: DLC).

1. In his letter to NG of 9 June, above, John Carter [i.e., John Barker Church] discussed his dealings with Francis Kinloch and the "bond" that is mentioned in Hamilton's next sentence.

2. See note at ibid.

3. NG did consider settling in New York City. (NG to Wadsworth, 4 November, below)

4. Hamilton was a delegate to Congress from New York at this time.

From the Marquis de Lafayette

My dear friend   Paris June the 10ᵗʰ 1783

I Have this long While Been Waiting for American Answers, and Answers from You are still Harder to Be Had than from Any Body Upon the Continent. My Vessel the *Triumph* is, I Hear, Arrived Safe, and from Her Return I expect a Good Cargoe of Intelligences.[1] I also Hope You will take Notice of what I Have Proposed, and Let it Be Major [Ichabod] Burnet or Any other friend of Yours, He May depend Upon Every thing that I Can either Command or influence.[2]

However Silent You Have Been, I felt no less Interested in Every thing that Might Concern You, and Since it Has been My Cursed fate, to Be, on public Account, long kept aWay from the Army, You Need not I Hope Be Assured that My Heart took a part in All your Motions and Circumstances. Some Newspapers Have Mentioned a Word Respecting the Affairs of the Army, and it plagues me to think the only part I now take in their Concerns is to feel for them in Reading Newspapers. I am Vexed at the idea, and wish to God Your Answers May Soon determine if it is Now, or when it is, that I May Hope to take you By the Hand. Unless Congress Have Any Immediate Occasion for me Here, I Shall immediately Embark, and tho it is late, I Hope, Before the fall, I may Challenge You to a Glass of Wine on Rhode Island.[3]

This is a Random letter I am Scribbling, for the Bearer of it is Going By

Way of England, and When I took the Penn, it Was With an Intention to Introduce Him to You. From the Beggining of the Contest I Have Known Him Both in England and in France, and He ever Appeared to me a Sensible and Warm friend to our Cause.[4]

Be So kind, My Good friend, as to Present My Best Respects to M[rs] Greene, Master George,[5] and all our friends, and Believe me What I Ever Have, and Ever Shall Be Your Affectionate friend   LAFAYETTE

RCS (MiU-C).

1. *Le Triomphe* was the French Navy frigate that the Comte d'Estaing had sent to America with letters from Lafayette, including one to Congress, reporting "the first tidings of a General Peace." (Lafayette to the President of Congress, 5 February, Idzerda, *Lafayette Papers*, 5: 85; see also Lafayette to NG, 5 February, above [vol. 12: 415–16].)

2. Lafayette had offered to assist NG's friends with introductions to the "Best" merchant firms in France. (Lafayette to NG, 5 February)

3. A short time after writing this letter, Lafayette received a request from Congress to try to obtain an alteration in the peace terms so that American merchants could have "three or four Years" to repay their debts to British and French creditors. (Elias Boudinot to Lafayette, 12 April, Smith, *Letters*, 20: 169–70)

4. It is clear from a letter that Lafayette wrote to Washington on this date that the bearer of the present letter was Dr. Edward Bancroft. Many years after Bancroft's death, it was learned that he had been a British double agent. (See Lafayette to Washington, 10 June, Idzerda, *Lafayette Papers*, 5: 132–33; Boatner, *Encyc.*)

5. "Master George" was NG's son George Washington Greene.

*   *   *

¶ [FROM JEREMIAH WADSWORTH, Hartford, Conn., 12–13 June 1783. He received NG's letter of 21 April at Philadelphia "two days before" leaving there.[1] With "sincerest pleasure," he returns NG's "congratulations on the return of peace & the establishment of American independence." Wadsworth has been "So very busy" that he "hardly had time to breath," but he assures NG of his "sincere friendship & attachment." Writing again on 13 June, he remarks that the intended bearer stayed "till this Morn[g]," giving him an opportunity to add to the letter. Since NG informed Wadsworth that he drew on him for $1,000, "M[r] Carter" has notified him that he paid $3,000 for "Your drafts on me."[2] All of "the French Bills are delayed payment for a Year," so Wadsworth is presently "imbarrassed" and will need all or part of the money as soon as possible after NG's arrival.[3] The Connecticut legislature "broke up last Week without doing any thing important[.] They came together against the half pay or commutation & fought hard & Adjourned." Wadsworth believes they will consider "half pay or commutation" again in their next session.[4] He fears "it will be some time before We have a regular system or tollerable legislation but as we are so far advanced in the Wrong we May begin to hope for a reformation." Below his signature, Wadsworth adds that he is going to France "soon" in regard to his firm's bills.[5] He adds that if NG is going to Newport, R.I., he would like to know it, "as I wish to see You."[6] RCS (CtHi) 2 pp.]

1. The letter is above (vol. 12: 629–30). Wadsworth was back in Philadelphia, preparing to sail to Europe, when he wrote NG again on 26 July, below.

2. John Barker Church, who used the alias John Carter, was a business partner of Wadsworth. On the drafts, see also Carter to NG, 9 June, above.

3. Wadsworth and Carter had served as purchasing agents for the French Expeditionary Force. They had "strained their resources" in this business and had overdrawn their account with John Chaloner, their agent in purchasing supplies for Washington's army. (Vol. 6: 11 and n, 63n, above) Robert Morris, the superintendent of finance, paid them in "hundred-day bills," made out in livres, which were accepted in France "on condition that payment of some of the large sum could be delayed." (Destler, "Wadsworth," pp. 171–73)

4. The issue of commutation, or half-pay for five years for officers of the Continental army (vol. 12: 557n, above), became a contentious one in Connecticut. It was not until January 1784 that the Connecticut legislature approved the 1783 federal impost proposal, the funds for which were to be used to finance commutation. (See Richard Buel, Jr., *Dear Liberty: Connecticut's Mobilization for the Revolutionary War* [Middletown, Conn.: Wesleyan University Press, 1980], pp. 297–319; the impost proposal is discussed at NG to Lincoln, 18 June, below.) The state's unhappiness over the half-pay plan, which was expressed in a protest that the legislature addressed to Congress in November, led Congress in April 1784 to pass a resolution stating that "where the pay has been secured by any State, the same shall not be again secured by the United States." (*JCC*, 26: 265–69; the quoted text is on p. 269.)

5. Wadsworth sailed for Europe in late July. (Wadsworth to NG, 26 July)

6. NG was still in South Carolina when Wadsworth left for Europe.

¶ [TO GRIFFIN GREENE. From Headquarters, Charleston, S.C., 14 June 1783. Griffin will see by NG's letters to "Mʳ Lawrens[,] the Marquis de la Fyette and to Mʳ Hunter" that NG has "written to give credit for a much larger amount" than he mentioned in his "first letter."[1] NG's "reasons for writing to so many and for a larger amount" is to give Griffin an "opportunity to obtain credit with some if others should fail or be from home." NG does not want to be "responsible for more than the two thousand pounds mentioned" in his "first letter" and asks Griffin not to request even that amount, "unless great advantage will result to the concern from it." He advises Griffin to use "dispach" in executing his business, "as being abroad must be expensive" and because "we can fix upon no decided plan of business" until Griffin returns.[2] ADfS (Ct) 2 pp.]

1. NG's letters to Henry Laurens and the Marquis de Lafayette are both above, dated 10 June; that to James Hunter is immediately below. NG's "first letter" to Griffin Greene is above, dated 9 June.

2. The "concern" was Jacob Greene & Company, in which NG and Griffin Greene were both involved. Griffin replied to NG on 1 October, below.

*   *   *

To James Hunter

Sir   Head quarters Charlestown [S.C.] June 14th 1783

The little opportunity I had to form an acquaintance with you would not authorise the liberty I am now about to take; but from the friendly connection I have with the other branches of your house. Mʳ Griffin [Greene] a Cousin of mine and with whom my brothers and my self are and have been connected in business both before and since the war is on a voyage to Europe for the purpose of selling or fitting the Ship *Flora* now at Bordauex.[1] She is a fine Vessel and I think would answer exceeding well for the Guinea or Rice trade. I have proposed to M[r] Banks to become a purchacer as three Eights is to be sold at all events. He writes you on the subject.[2] The object of this letter is to beg your advice and assistance to M[r] Greene to enable him to make the most of the Vessel whether you take a concern or not; and to take an interest in her if you can make it square with your other merchantile pursuits. M[r] Greene has never been abroad and therefore cannot be acquainted with all the finesse of business. Your friendly offices may be of singular service to him and I shall feel my self under particular obligations for them. Should he have occasion for credit and you can find it convenient to advance him to the amount of one thousand or twelve hundred pounds I will hold my self responsible for payment.[3] I am Sir with good wishes Your Most Obedt humble Ser[t]   NATH GREENE

ADfS (RHi).
    1. For background, see NG to Griffin Greene, 10 June, above.
    2. The letter to Hunter from his business partner John Banks has not been found.
    3. Hunter apparently left Europe for the West Indies before Griffin arrived. (See below, Griffin Greene to NG, 1 October, and Forsyth to NG, 24 February 1784.)

To John Kean

Dear Sir   Head Quarters Charles Town [S.C.] June 15th 1783
    I have no less than three letters from the board of war for the officer accounts of rations.[1] I must intreat you to forward them by this Express without fail. I can give no answer to the board until I hear from you; and I am unwilling to report that I am not able to obtain them. It will have a bad appearance. It will leave room to suspect the business has not been done with method or that it has not been conducted with propriety. As I am suree [i.e., sure] the contrary is the case I beg a state of the Accounts as early as possible.[2] I am dear Sir Your Most Obedt humble Ser[t]
                                                                    NATH[l] GREENE

ADfS (MiU-C).
    1. As seen in NG's first letter to Gen. Benjamin Lincoln of 3 June, above, the requests were from Lincoln, the secretary at war. NG explained there why Kean had not yet submitted the accounts.
    2. Kean replied on 4 July, below.

*   *   *

¶ [**TO GEORGE ABBOTT HALL**.[1] From Headquarters [Charleston, S.C.], 16 June 1783. "Capt Hambleton the clothier[,] in the settlement and [in?] receipts given" to Hall "for Mr Andrew Johnsons account[,] has included a number of Articles not belonging to his department."[2] This puts the accounts "in confusion." Hamilton has also "included a quantity of Rum and sugar never delivered by Mr Johnson to any public Officer." NG asks Hall to credit Hamilton's account for the amount of the rum and sugar included in Johnson's account "and let the matter be settled between Capt [John] Meals and M[r] Johnson in the Commisaries department to which account it properly belongs."[3] ADfS (MiU-C) 2 pp.]

1. Hall was the receiver of Continental taxes in South Carolina. (Vol. 12: 152n, above)

2. Lt. John Hamilton was the Southern Army's clothier. (Vol. 12: 27n, above) Andrew Johnston, a Georgetown merchant, had furnished some items to the Southern Army. (Johnston to NG, 18 December 1781, above [vol. 10: 73]; Rogers, *History of Georgetown*, pp. 150, 152–53)

3. Meals was the Southern Army's assistant commissary general of purchases.

*   *   *

To Jacob Greene

Dear Sir   Head Quarters Charlestown [S.C.] June 17. 1783

I have got your Letter of the 4[h] of May and am Very truly and Sincerely Sorry for your Misfortune.[1] But much more on your Account than my own although it will be an heavy Loss to me. My Expenses from a Variety of Causes have multiplied upon my Hand & press Hard upon Me. I was about to draw on you for about Four Hundred pounds Sterling before I Rec[d] your Letter. But shall not trouble you now, Let my Occasion be ever so pressing. Hearing nothing from you for more than a year left Me totally in the Dark as to your situation. Griffin I find is gone to England. I have forwarded him Letters to Several characters and have laid a Foundation.[2] I am in Hopes to give him a Credit for Two Thousand Pounds Sterling. I have also endeaverd to interest M[r] Hunter of Virginia in his Affairs who is gone to Europe on Business and is a Man of honor and Great Experience.[3] If Cousin Griffin happens to fall in with him it is probable he will take Part of the Ship and fit her immediately.[4] The connexion offerd him an Extension in Credit on M[r] [*illegible*]. Besides M[r] Hunter I have written to the Marquis de la Fayette and to Mr Laurens the Ambassador.[5] But these are great Folks and don't feel the Importance of Little concerns. However they may be of use to him. Don't send any vessels to this place until after next Crop. Everything is dull here and sells for less than the first Cost, come almost from what quarter it may. Little Business is done but at Vendues and the Difficulty of Selling to advantage at these you know as well as I do.

With unwearied Diligence & by bold Adventure and the good offices of some of my Friends in this Quarter I have got my Interest voted me by this state in a tollerable good Way. I am in hopes to raise this year 400 Casks of Rice and a Large Quantity of Provisions for the Plantation Use.[6] Next year I expect much more. I begin with this. My Interest in Georgia I am obliged to let out for a very Trifle not hav[in]g the means to improve it.[7] If I coud improve it it would neat [i.e., net] me a Thousand Sterling a Year. But for this is required an Advance of another Four Thousand Pounds and this I have not nor cannot command. Indeed I don't choose to run largely in Deb^t at this Time for any Advantages. My Plan of Living must be proportiond to my Income and I must be sure [of] Part of my Interest as I cannot conserve until a future day.

Mrs Greene is gone to Philadelphia and from thence she returns to Rhode Island. She thinks she can [live?] cheaper at Newport than anywhere else and I have written to Mr George Gibbs and also to Mr Nicholas Tillinghast to take a House for her, Two Rooms on a Floor with chambers and part of a Kitchen will be Sufficient for her Purpose.[8] Mr Garden one of my Aids accompanies her and I don't know wht [i.e., whether] Col^o Koscieusko will not.[9] They are particular Friends of mine to whom I beg your Invitations may be extended. Mr Thomas Farr also who carries this Letter I wish you to pay him some Attention, and introduce him to your Friends in Newport. I have given him Letters to a Number of my old Acquaintances in Newport, Providence & Boston.

I rejoice to hear your children are in such a happy Way. Education is the Foundation of all Business and the Corner Stone of Reason and Consequence in Life. I would rather have Education than Fortune. One is easier obtained than the other after you arrive to years of Maturity, but both may be got by great Application unless opposed by a current of Endless misfortune. Fortune often serves to hand, for natural Abilities come with the Advantages of a good Education.

It gives me singular Pleasure to hear Miss Polly begins to feel the Dignity of her own Standing and to judge properly between mere Pleasure and solid Improvement.[10] A just Task for the Polite Arts and more especially the polite Accomplishments gives a Relish for noble Prospects and such only as are ornamental to Human Nature. The best way of living is to mix Business and Pleasure. One sweetens the other and both add to the Happiness of human Life. I can give no opinion as to your scheme of putting Jabez to Study Physick. All depends upon the natural Bent of his Genius. If he has a Taste for it he may be eminent, without it he will only be a paltry Conjurer.[11] Tom will make a fine Fellow notwithstanding his Aversion to his Books. Age will redeem his Geniuss and as he enters into Life Pride will provide a Spur to his Industry. He appears to have a Generous Nature and I doubt not will be an eminent Character.[12]

Great changes have happend at Potowomut within the last year. Kitt I find is married again. Miss Polly I think will make him an Excellent Wife.[13] Nature has not been so bountiful in the Beauties of her Person, but for good Sense and a happy Disposition she has made her ample Amends. I had a Line from Kitt;[14] but none from either of the other Brothers; nor have I since I have been to the Southward. Aunt Greene and Col. Ward write me now and then or else I should have known little more of you than if you had all lived on the Moon.[15] I intend to be in Rhode Island in September if possable but it is yet uncertain, and will enter more particularly into your Future Plans for Life.[16]

I congratulate you on the happy Issues of the War. Every thing has terminated agreeable to our Wishes. It has been a doubtful Struggle: and I remember you entered upon it with Fear and Trembling. I was always persuaded[17] of a happy Issue if the People had but Virtue to Suffer and Courage to persivere. Of these I sometimes doubted; and cannot help thinking now how much has depended on the active Zeal of a few than on the generous Exertions of the great mass of the People. Be that as it may it is Sufficient for all that we gaind the Point and brought the Dispute to a happy Issue. The Army has much merit and many Citizens have no less and all may pride themselves on the Revolution as one of the most Glorious and most important that History affords.

Remember me affectionally to Sister Greene, Miss Polly & all the Family.[18] Be assured my Affection will never forsake you; and in every Situation in Life you may hope for every Aid in my Power to give for the Benefit of the family consistent with my other Duties & Calls in Life. I am dear sir with affectionate Esteem your most Obed[t] humble Servt

NATH. GREENE

Tr (Foster Transcript: RHi).

1. Jacob Greene's letter is above (vol. 12: [640–43]).

2. See NG to Griffin Greene, 10 June, above.

3. See NG to James Hunter, 14 June, above.

4. Griffin Greene was en route to Europe to sell "the Ship," the *Flora*. (Griffin Greene to NG, 18 May, above [vol. 12: 662–63]) Hunter apparently did not invest in the *Flora*.

5. NG's letters to the Marquis de Lafayette and to Henry Laurens, both dated 10 June, are above.

6. The plantation was Boone's Barony. On NG's efforts to secure the greatest advantage from the state's gift, see his letter to Hugh Rutledge of 26 February, above [vol. 12: 478]. The 1783 crops on the plantation turned out to be a disappointment. (Saunders to NG, 3 July and 20 October, below)

7. NG's "Interest in Georgia" was Mulberry Grove, the plantation that the state of Georgia had given to him. (Samuel Saltus to NG, 5 May 1782, above [vol. 11: 164 and n])

8. NG's letters to Tillinghast and Gibbs, both Newport merchants, have not been found. On Gibbs, see NG's letter to him of 17 August 1784, below; on Tillinghast, see Littlefield to NG, 25 April 1785, below.

9. Alexander Garden, NG's former aide, was suffering from the effects of malaria. (Garden to NG, 20 June, below) He accompanied CG when she left Philadelphia for Rhode Island in early August. (Garden to NG, 3 August, below) As noted at his letter to NG of 18 June, below, Thaddeus Kosciuszko did not visit Rhode Island until the spring of 1784.

10. Polly was Jacob's twenty-one-year-old daughter.

11. Jacob's son Jabez, who was born in 1770, did become a physician, but "at an early period engaged in business with his father." (Clarke, *Greenes*, p. 326)

12. The transcriber must have misread this name. As seen by Jacob's letter to NG of 4 May 1783, NG was referring here to Jacob Varnum "Jac" Greene, Jacob's ten-year-old son. As seen in the note at that letter, Jac did not become an "eminent Character." (Vol. 12: 644n)

13. NG's brother Christopher had married Deborah Ward, his recently deceased wife's sister. (See Griffin Greene to NG, 18 May, above [vol. 12: 664, 665n].)

14. See Christopher Greene to NG, 19 May, above (vol. 12: 669–70).

15. "Aunt Greene" was Catharine Ray Greene, CG's aunt and the wife of Gov. William Greene. "Col. Ward" was Col. Samuel Ward, Jr., NG's longtime friend. (See NG to Catharine Ray Greene, 5 December 1782, and NG to Ward, 21 December 1782, both above [vol. 12: 263–65, 327–28].)

16. NG did not return to Rhode Island until late November. (NG to Jacob Greene, 29 November, below)

17. It appears that the transcriber crossed through a word here.

18. "Sister Greene" was Jacob's wife, Margaret Greene Greene. As seen in note 8, above, "Miss Polly" was Jacob's daughter.

To General Benjamin Lincoln, Secretary at War

Dear Sir   Head quarters [Charleston, S.C.] June 18th 1783

The delay of the transports gives the most serious alarm to the troops.[1] They are suspicious all is a design to trick them. No assuran[c]es will convince them to the contrary. The fear of the Climate operates so powerfully that they will listen to nothing and are deserting in great numbers and I am really afraid if the Transports dont arrive in a few days they will all go off in a body.

The Dragoon horses are sold.[2] Many of the Soldiers have purchased. Nothing but this indulgence prevented their going off in a body or deserting by dozens. It was a disagreeable alternative but from mature deliberation it was considered as the most eligible mode for the good of the service. Lt Col Carrington will write a more full history of the affair.[3] We have done every thing in our power to accomodate the matter to the interest and views of Government and hope the measures will meet with approbation.

I have just got your letters of the 30th of April and 3ᵈ of May.[4] I will do every thing in my power to get the accounts you write for and have an Express now on that duty to urge Mʳ Kean to forward the Accounts.[5]

We hear various reports about the definitive treaty[,] the difficulties attending the business and the probability of its finally being rejected on the part of Great Britain. I cannot credit them. Reports prevail also respecting our flags having been insulted in New York and that Sir Guy Carlton has refused to deliver up the property which he advertized for the people to come and receive. I wish to be informed on all these matters. Is the peace establishment finally settled or not? Many are anxious to know what it is or will be.[6]

I am afraid from the best information I can get, the five per Cent duty now proposed by Congress will not be agreed to in this State.[7] The Assembly is called but it is uncertain whether they will meet so as to make a house.[8] I am dear Sir Your most Obed[t] humble Ser NATH GREENE

The Horses sold to the Dragoons averag'd between twenty & thirty pounds st[g] [i.e., sterling] And those sold to the Inhabitants, under twenty pounds.

ADfS (MiU-C).

1. The contract for the transports had been signed on 17 May, but the vessels did not reach Charleston until 11 July. (Robert Morris to James Nicholson, 17 May, Morris, *Papers*, 8: 82–86; NG to Lincoln, 11 July, below)

2. On the sale of the dragoon horses, see note at NG to Lincoln, second letter of 3 June, above.

3. The letter from Col. Edward Carrington to Lincoln has not been found.

4. These letters from Lincoln are above (vol. 12: 637, 640).

5. See NG to John Kean, 15 June, above.

6. Lincoln's reply has not been found, but the rumors about the treaty were false.

7. Following the recent defeat of its 1781 impost measure, Congress, in its 1783 revenue request, had asked the states for power to levy specific duties on a number of imported items, the revenues from which would be applied solely to the payment of interest and principal on "the debts contracted on the faith of the United States, for supporting the war." At the same time, the states were asked to institute measures of their own choosing to raise revenue for the payment of their "respective proportions" of $1.5 million to the federal government annually. A twenty-five-year limit was placed on both the import duties and state revenues designated for congressional use. The states, some of which had objected to congressional appointment of impost collectors under the earlier proposal, would also appoint the collectors themselves. (*JCC*, 24: 257–61; see also the note at NG to Morris, 3 July 1784, below.) In an August session, the South Carolina legislature refused to ratify the 1783 federal impost plan but did adopt a plan under which certain import duties imposed by the state would be used to pay South Carolina's quota of "the interest and principal of the debts contracted on the faith of the United States for supporting the war." (*Statutes of S.C.*, 4: 570) In March 1784, this act was repealed and a more comprehensive tax program was enacted in its place. (See note at Hutson to NG, 5 February 1784, below.)

8. As seen in the preceding note, the South Carolina legislature did "make a house" during the summer of 1783.

From Colonel Thaddeus Kosciuszko

Dear General   Philadelphia 18th June [1783]

The enxiety I have of going to my Country, as I will be of no farther service here by the Peace so happily obtained, induce me to request you the favor, wich will be perhaps the Last.[1]

In setling my accounts I forsee and aprehend will be tedious and difficult mater without your recomendation to the Financier and the President of Congress wich I would beg you was of such nature that they Could setled with me the Pay what is due, and what Congress resolv'd for half pay wich is five years pay in ready money if possible.[2] I pass the Land wich is now propos to Dispose of for the Officers in every State, been in the situation of the Izrealits.[3]

It gives me sensible pain that I am forced by unruly Chance of nature to write to you upon the subject, wich irrited even the disposition of thou[g]ht to the thing. Believe me Sir my feelings as they are they Strugle with wants Continualy even while I write this the Commotion of my heart is very great. Should I know for certainty of going strait to my Country I would not trouble you nor nobody else, but perhaps I will be oblidged to ramble one or two years more and this is my misfortune.

For fear I should go of[f] Sooner then you Come to Philadelphia give me Leave to present my thanks to you for all your kindness Shown to me while I live the memory of them will never Cease and the greatitude Shall die with me.[4] If you should be pleased to write to thos Gentilmen, I beg you would by the first Wessel going to Philadelphia. I am Sir with the perfect respect and Esteem your must Humble and must Ob^t Servant   THAD: KOSCIUSZKO

Mrs Greene is in perfect health.[5]

RC (ICPRCU).

1. Despite what he wrote here, Kosciuszko did not leave the United States for his native Poland until 15 July 1784. (Haiman, *Kosciuszko*, p. 165)

2. In his reply of 10 July, below, NG promised to write letters on Kosciuszko's behalf to Elias Boudinot, the president of Congress, and Robert Morris, the "Financier." Kosciuszko referred here to Congress's decision to commute its promise to Continental officers of half-pay pensions for life to five years' full salary. (Vol. 12: 557n, above)

3. In early June, Congress debated a motion by New York delegate Alexander Hamilton to "consider the best manner of carrying into execution the engagements of the United States for certain allowances of land at the conclusion of the war." (PCC, item 21, folio 354, DNA) That resolution was still under active consideration, as was another, introduced by Theodorick Bland of Virginia, to set aside a "tract of land" in the west for those who had served in the army. (PCC, item 186, folio 105, DNA) Kosciuszko presumably meant here that he would "pass" on this offer, which he believed would send officers into the wilderness, like the children of Israel in the book of Exodus.

4. Kosciuszko did see NG again, and in fact stayed with NG and his family at Newport, R.I., in the spring of 1784. (Littlefield to NG, 22 March 1784, below)

5. As noted at NG to Washington, 5 June, above, CG arrived in Philadelphia on 14 June. Kosciuszko had traveled there in the same party. (Pierce to NG, 19 June, below)

*   *   *

¶ [TO COLONEL EDWARD CARRINGTON. From Headquarters [Charleston, S.C.], 19 June 1783. Maj. [Joseph] Eggleston has certified that "Lt Jourdan [i.e., Cornet John Jordan] of the [Lee's] Legion has never received any gratuity for the extraordinary expence allowed to Cavalry officers in a resolution of Congress 27th of October 1778."[1] Jordan is "now possessed of a public horse which he supposes will be nearly of the value of the gratuity allowed" by the resolution. Carrington is to "have the horse valued and if his value don't exceed Mr Jourdans claim," he "should transfer the property" on his "records for the purposes aforesaid." If the horse is worth more than the value of the gratuity, Jordan should pay Carrington "the difference." Eggleston has also informed NG that "Lt [William] Winston has a horse due him from the public by a

Contract made with Maj. Rudolph [John Rudulph] in behalf of the public where in Lt. Winston put a horse into the Legionary service of superior quality and was to receive two of inferior [quality] in return." Winston now has both horses, "but the property has never been legally transfered." If Eggleston certifies that Winston's claim "appears to be just and well founded," and if Carrington is satisfied that the horse Winston now has "is not of greater value than the conditions of the Contract intitle him to," Carrington should "transfer the property of the horse" to Winston. ADfS (MiU-C) 3 pp.]

1. In its resolution, Congress directed that "the sum of five hundred dollars be allowed to the field officers, captains, subalterns, chaplain and surgeon of the light dragoons respectively, in the service of these United States, to compensate the extraordinary expence of his horse and equipment, beyond that of officers of the like rank in the infantry." (*JCC*, 12: 1067)

*   *   *

From William Pierce, Jr.

Dear General   Philadelphia, June 19th 1783.

Altho' we had a long passage it was an agreable one.[1] Our run from the Barr of Charles Town to Cape Henlopen [Del.] was only four Days; and had it not been for contrary Winds before we got to sea, and a disappointment in not procuring a Pilot for twenty four Hours after we arrived at the Cape, we should have made as good a passage as ever was known.[2] A fresh gale the whole way drove us along at the rate of seven knots an Hour. But the sea was not quiet enough to preserve us all from sickness. Mrs Greene, Col° [Thaddeus] Kosciuszko, Col° [Nicholas] Eveleigh, and myself were extremely indisposed, but we have all been capitally benefitted by it. [Alexander] Garden was preserved for a Land attack; ever since his arrival he has been horridly distressed with the Ague and fever, and is now very ill with it at Mrs Strictlands opposite the City Tavern.[3] The Troops all arrived safe and in good health; so did the Officers who commanded them.[4]

Congress with their usual benevolence have offered all the Troops for the War a furlough to go home untill called for.[5] But the Soldiers either from a suspicion of some unfair intention, or from an apprehension that they mean to get rid of them without paying them for their services, decline accepting their furlough, and speak in a language as if they were determined that their accounts should be adjusted before they would consent to retire from the Army.[6] I believe they would be induced to accept their discharges provided they could be final; but Congress being afraid to act untill the definitive treaty is settled they will not agree that they shall retire altogether.

The talk at the Court end of the Town is that there is to be a peace establishment of 6,000 Men, and that the Officers are to be elected. Four great Magazines are to be established on the Continent, one at Springfield [Mass.], another at Carlisle [Pa.], a third at Westham in Virginia, and a fourth at Camden in South Carolina. It is also said that 10,000 stand of Arms are to be deposited at each Magazine, with a compleat train of Artillery; and that a military Academy is to be erected for the instruction of the Officers.[7] General Lincoln set of[f] yesterday for the purpose of examining Westham.[8]

Our finances are still low, and appear as if they would long continue so. An offer is made the Army to pay them for the Months of February, March, and April, in Notes payable in 6 Months after date on the pay Master. This goes down because there is actually no Money in the Office for the purpose or at least because there is not enough to discharge the subsistance Bills now presented. M[r] [Robert] Morris appears industrious, and fame says he has arranged his system of finance very masterly. If the States will support Congress we may possibly have justice done us in the course of a few Years, and M[r] Morris may have the satisfaction to see his scheme succeed.[9]

M[rs] Greene has taken up her abode at Col[o] [Clement] Biddle's and is pestered to death with ceremony and civility.

In a few Days I expect to set off for New Jersey, where I may stay about 6 Days when I shall return and move instantly, (or as soon as I can meet with a passage) for South Carolina or Georgia.

I hope this Letter will meet you perfectly recovered, and in spirits sufficient to bear you to this Country where the Arms of every Person will be open to receive you.[10] With honor, and esteem I beg leave to subscribe myself very sincerely your Friend   W[M] PIERCE J[R]

This Letter being written in great haste must be excused for its inaccuracies.

RCS (MiU-C).

1. Pierce referred here to his voyage to Philadelphia on the *Christiana*. (NG to Washington, 5 June, above)

2. On Garden's condition, see his letter to NG of 20 June, below.

3. Mrs. "Strictlands" has not been further identified. City Tavern stood at 138 South Second Street, near Walnut Street in central Philadelphia.

4. The *Christiana* carried troops of the Pennsylvania Continental line. (See NG to Benjamin Lincoln, 20 May, above [vol. 12: 672].)

5. Congress's offer of a furlough for the troops was in a resolution of 26 May. (*JCC*, 24: 364–65)

6. Pierce referred here to a small mutiny on the part of Pennsylvania troops stationed in Philadelphia. These soldiers demanded their pay and threatened such " 'measures as would right themselves,' " including, it was widely rumored, an attack on the Bank of North America. (Morris, *Papers*, 8: 216–17) The mutiny was finally settled on 25 June, when a combination of cajolery and threatened force convinced the mutineers to submit to congressional authority. (On the mutiny, see Mary A. Y. Gallagher, "Reinterpreting the 'Very Trifling Mutiny' at Philadelphia in June 1783," *PMHB* 119 [1995]: 3–35.) As seen in President Elias Boudinot's proclamation and in a letter that he wrote to Washington, Congress subsequently removed to Princeton, N.J., from Philadelphia. The mutineers,

pressing their demands, had "surrounded" the "State House," where Congress was meeting, and delegates had become alarmed that the Pennsylvania government did not appear ready to call out militia to protect them. (Smith, *Letters*, 20: 367–69) Congress met in Princeton until adjournment in mid-November and then reconvened in Annapolis, Md., in December. (*JCC*, 25: 809)

7. On 18 June, a committee of Congress chaired by Alexander Hamilton submitted a "Report on a Military Peace Establishment." In this report, which Congress did not take up until October, the committee recommended the establishment of a peacetime army of 2,600 men and the establishment of five magazines, each containing enough supplies and munitions to outfit 6,000 men. The magazines were to be located at Springfield, Mass., "West Point & its dependencies," Carlisle, Pa., Camden, S.C., and at "Some convenient position on James River to be reconnoitered for that purpose." (Syrett, *Hamilton*, 3: 383, 384–87) Because of the expense, Hamilton did not recommend the establishment of a military academy, but he did make provision for professors to be attached to the artillery regiment, which he designated the Corps of Engineers, and he did not foreclose the possibility of an academy in the future. (Kohn, *Eagle and Sword*, p. 47)

8. Westham, Va., near Richmond, was presumably one of the sites under consideration for a federal magazine. (Mattern, *Benjamin Lincoln*, p. 144; on Lincoln's visit to Virginia, see also Pendleton to NG, 17 July, below.)

9. The "support" referred to here was for the proposed federal impost, which is discussed at NG to Lincoln, 18 June, above.

10. On NG's illness at the time of Pierce's departure from Charleston, S.C., see NG to Washington, 5 June, above.

From Baron Steuben

My Dear Friend   West Point [N.Y., after 19 June?] 1783.[1]

Notwithstanding I address you in official capacity I hope you will do me the justice to believe that Friendship would induce my writing to you had I no other motive.

I have the honor to inclose you the plan of a Society as therein mentioned, together with sundry resolutions, which have taken place, since its commencement.[2] You will see by the resolves of the 17th June, that his Excellency General Washington and other Gentlemen were chosen to fill the different Departments in the Society until a general meeting can take place; the absolute necessity of this measure will apologise for its being taken when the representation was not so full as could have been wished.[3]

In full confidence that this institution will meet your approbation, and assistance, I am my Dear friend, Your Obedient humble Servant

STEUBEN

LS (NWM).

1. The letter, which is undated, must have been written shortly after 19 June, the date of the resolutions mentioned here.

2. The enclosure, which has not been found, was Gen. Henry Knox's plan for the Society of the Cincinnati, which he envisioned as a national organization of former Continental army officers capable of exerting political pressure to protect the officers' interests. (The plan of the Society is printed in Myers, *Liberty Without Anarchy*, pp. 258–

62.) Steuben, who was serving as *de facto* president of the organization, probably also sent the minutes of meetings held on 10 and 13 May and 19 June to NG. (The minutes are printed in Edgar E. Hume, ed., *General Washington's Correspondence Concerning the Society of the Cincinnati* [Baltimore, Md.: Johns Hopkins University Press, 1941], pp. 1–15.)

3. The officers were: Washington, president; Knox, secretary general; and Gen. Alexander McDougall, treasurer. The elections were held in haste because orders had already been given to disband the army. (Myers, *Liberty Without Anarchy*, pp. 31–32) Although Steuben wrote "17th" here, the resolutions were passed on 19 June. (Ibid.)

*   *   *

¶ [TO DANIEL SMITH.[1] From Headquarters, Charleston, S.C., 20 June 1783. NG accepts his resignation, but Smith is "held in all respects to the full and final settlement" of his accounts "in the same manner as if in the full exercise" of his "Duty as Assistant Purveyor." ADfS (MiU-C) 1 p.]

1. Smith, a Virginian, had been assistant deputy purveyor in the Southern Department since September 1781. (Heitman, *Register*)

¶ [FROM ALEXANDER GARDEN, Philadelphia, 20 June 1783. The "severest attack of the Fever & Ague I ever experienced" keeps him from writing more fully, but he could not "let slip, the present opportunity of congratulating" NG "on the safe arrival of Mrs Greene in this city."[1] Garden hopes NG has "long before this recover'd the most perfect enjoyment" of his health.[2] In these and "all events which interest" NG, Garden's "heart is sensibly concern'd." He extends wishes for a "prosperous" journey northward. RCS (CtY) 1 p.]

1. Garden had accompanied CG to Philadelphia. (NG to Jacob Greene, 17 June, and Pierce to NG, 19 June, both above)

2. On NG's illness at the time that CG and Garden left him, see his letter to Washington of 5 June, above.

¶ [FROM ROGER PARKER SAUNDERS, [Charleston, S.C.], 20 June 1783. He has received NG's two letters, one "by Dr Geble" and the other "by the six Negroes."[1] As NG requests, Saunders will "return Your Taxable Property as soon as Mr Garnder one of the Collectors returns from Town." Saunders "should have done it sooner" but thought NG would "give it in," as "in Town there is no danger, of being doubly tax'd." He has "Purchas'd" twelve "Young Stear for oxen" for NG and believes that they, "with the Horses[,] will be sufficient for this Crop." He will also buy "12 Cows & Calves," which will "answer for the present," but recommends buying "150 or 200 head Good Cattle" as soon as it is "convenient." He adds: "Nothing is so profitable as Stock and your Lands afforde Good Pastures, and excellent Winter range."[2] Saunders advises NG to get "Hogs & Sheep," for if he is to live in South Carolina, he will "find a great Conveneance in haveing them sent down to Town." If NG does not decide to live there, "they can allways be sold to advantage."[3] The "Waggoner" is coming to Charleston to receive NG's "orders as there is nothing for him to do at the Plantation at present." They will "sometimes want the Waggon and Horses," but NG's "Negroe Fellow who is disabled by the wound he recd on the hand will answer as Well as a White Man and save the Expence."[4] Saunders was at NG's plantation "yesterday" and found "about 10 Acres of Rice last Planted is in a Critical situation the water is over it 5 or 6 inches." He is "affraid" the "Craw

Fish" will "destroy" the rice.[5] NG's "Crop in General is Good, the Corn is Injurd by the great Rains, but they are drawing up the beds." He hopes to see NG "in Town in a few days" and will give him "a particular acco[t] of every thing."[6] NG will need corn "in abo[t] a Month" for his "Negroes" and also some to return to "M[r] Croskey."[7] The "best Corn sells about here at 5/ and is very scarse." RCS (MiU-C) 4 pp.]

1. NG's letters, which have not been found, were presumably replies to Saunders's of 26 May and 7 June, above.

2. On the need for oxen and other cattle at NG's plantation, see ibid.

3. NG never lived on Boone's Barony, his South Carolina plantation; he moved his family from Newport, R.I., to Mulberry Grove, his Georgia plantation, in November 1785. (See NG to Ethan Clarke, 23 November 1785, below.)

4. The wagoner would have had to be paid for his labor; the "Negro Fellow," presumably a slave, would not.

5. See Saunders to NG, 3 July, below.

6. It does not appear that Saunders made this trip. (See ibid.)

7. See Saunders to NG, 26 May and 3 July.

*   *   *

General Greene's Orders

HEAD QUARTERS, Charlestown [S.C.], June 21, 1783. ONE of the transports for conveying the troops to the northward arrived this morning, and the rest are on their passage. The Quarter-Master General will examine the condition of the brig *Fortitude*, and inform the Captain how to fit her for the reception of the troops. The commanding officer of the Maryland regiment will hold the number of troops in readiness to embark, which the Quarter-Master General shall determine may go on board her. The transports come victualled for the number of troops they are to receive; nothing is to be drawn therefore from the Contractor for the men after they embark. The Director General will make the necessary arrangement in his department for the accomodation of the sick on the passage.

Hostilities having ceased, and a general peace almost concluded, it only remains to complete your character, that you retire from that field with Propriety, where you have acted with Glory. To review scenes that are past, and look over the incidents of the war, must be interesting to the feelings of every soldier. To call to mind a train of sufferings, and run over the many dangers we have passed in the pursuit of honor, and in the service of our country, affords a pleasing prospect for contemplation.

The General joined this army when it was in affliction, when its spirits were low, and its prospects gloomy. He now parts from it crowned with success, and in full triumph. We have trod the paths of adversity together, and have felt the sun-shine of better fortune. We found a people overwhelmed with distress, and a country groaning under oppression. It has been our happiness to relieve them—The occasion was pressing, the attempt noble, and the success answerable. In this it has been the General's good fortune to point the way, but you had the honor to accomplish the work. Your generous confidence, amidst surrounding difficulties; your persevering tempers, against the tide of misfortune; paved the way to success; and to these are the people indebted for the repose they now enjoy.

The progress of the Southern Army has been marked with peculiar difficulties. It has had to operate in a country wasted by war, and divided in politicks. It has had to contend with a very superior force well appointed, with inferior numbers destitute of every thing. It has been your lot to feel the sharpest suffering, from cold and hunger, but it has been the General's greatest misfortune to see, without being able to relieve, your wants. The suffering soldier has ever been the first object of his attention; but the Treasury exhausted and Public Credit annihilated, Congress could not afford sufficient to satisfy the claims of humanity, much less of justice. Nothing was left unattempted, no expedient untried to obtain relief; and tho' his measures for this purpose exposed him to low jealousies, and mean suspicions, he cannot but review them with a mixture of Pride and Pleasure, since they were dictated by good policy, and the feelings of humanity.

It is unnecessary, and might be deemed improper on this occasion, to enumerate the many trying scenes we have passed, or the sufferings you have sustained. It is sufficient for the General that they have subsided. It is his happiness that he has had the honor to command an army no less distinguished for its patience than bravery, and will add no small lustre to your character that you have rejected with abhorrence the practice of plundering, and the exercise of cruelty, altho' urged by your necessities to the first, and by the example of the enemy to the last. United by principle and cemented by affection, you have exhibited to the world a proof, that elevated souls and persevering tempers will triumph over every difficulty. The orders of government now separate us perhaps for ever. Our great object is answered; our first wish obtained. The same considerations which led us to the field, will now call upon us to retire. In whatever situation the General may be placed, it will afford him the highest pleasure to promote your interests; and it is among the first of his wishes to see you as happy as you have rendered millions of others.

The General cannot take leave of this subject without adding his strongest assurances to the army, that he is fully persuaded their country will do them ample justice, if not consider their merit with liberality.

Printed Extract (*South-Carolina Gazette and General Advertiser*, 2–6 September 1783). The newspaper printed this text under the heading "Extract from General Orders."

To Francis Tate

Sir   Head quarters [Charleston, S.C.] June 25th 1783
    In answer to your letter on the subject of bills I have to inform you
that I cannot draw upon the footing you mention.[1] If you mean them as
pay it would be granting an indulgence to you that necessity has
obliged me to refuse to others and subject me to a just censure of
unequal conduct. Or if you mean them generally for the use of your
department unless they are to discharge a special contract of which I
must be informed of the subject and amount, this would be more
objectionable than the other; and what I could not justify.[2] But besides
those reasons the financier writes me that my bills press hard upon him;
and begs me to draw as few as possible and none but upon the most
pressing occasions.[3] These reasons will convince you that it is not in my
power to comply with your request. I am Sir Your Most Obedt humble
Ser^t   NATH GREENE

ADfS (MiU-C).
    1. Tate's letter has not been found.
    2. Tate headed the Southern Army's commissary department. (See above, vol. 11: 289n.)
    3. See Robert Morris to NG, 16 May, above (vol. 12: 657–58).

                    *   *   *

¶ [TO GOVERNOR BENJAMIN GUERARD OF SOUTH CAROLINA. From
Headquarters [Charleston, S.C.], 26 June 1783. NG encloses a copy of a congressional resolution furloughing the army.[1] Orders have been given for this purpose, and as NG believes "the security of the magazines may require some necessary arrangements in consequence of the dismission of the regular Troops,"
he is informing Guerard by the "earliest opportunity." Photograph of LS (Steven
S. Raab Autographs, *Catalogue #37* [2001]) 1 p.]
    1. The resolution was undoubtedly that of 26 May. (*JCC*, 24: 364–65)

¶ [TO MAJOR JOHN HABERSHAM. From Headquarters, Charleston, S.C., 26
June 1783. The adjutant general is sending Habersham a copy of a general order
of Congress furloughing the army.[1] Habersham should execute this order with
his own troops "as early as possible."[2] He should deposit "all Military Stores"
now in his possession in the "State Magazine" and send a return to headquarters.[3] NG has written to the governor, "desiring him to receive" the stores.[4] If the
governor refuses, Habersham should "ship them" to Charleston, "directed to
Col Senf to be deposited in the Magazine of this State."[5] Senf will send instructions for disposing of the stores belonging to the Quartermaster Department.
NG sends his respects to Mrs. [Ann Sarah Camber] Habersham and "all friends
in Georgia." ADfS (NcD) 2 pp.]
    1. For the resolution, which was dated 26 May, see *JCC*, 24: 364–65.
    2. It appears from the wording of a 29 July resolution of the Georgia legislature that
the state's troops had not yet been furloughed. (*Records of Georgia*, 3: 389; see also the
next note.)
    3. On 29 July, the Georgia legislature ordered that "any Stores or Arms or Implements of

War whether belonging to the State or delivered over by the Officer Commanding the Continental Troops on his Furloughing his Men agreeable to the late Resolve of Congress . . . be lodged in a Magazine Subject to further order." (Ibid.) The return that was sent to NG has not been found.

4. See NG to Lyman Hall, immediately below.

5. As seen in note 3, above, the state accepted the stores. Christian Senf had been appointed to oversee the repair and storage of arms belonging to South Carolina. (S.C., Privy Council, *Journals*, p. 28)

¶ [TO GOVERNOR LYMAN HALL OF GEORGIA. From Headquarters, Charleston, S.C., 26 June 1783. NG encloses a copy of a resolution of Congress furloughing the army and informs Hall that "orders are gone out for this purpose."[1] The "regular troops" in Georgia are to be furloughed "immediately." NG is informing Hall by the "earliest opportunity" so that Hall can "take such measures" as may be "necessary upon the occasion." NG has directed Major [John] Habersham to ask Hall to receive "all Continental property," including "Military Stores and other things he may have in possession" when the furlough takes effect. NG asks Hall to deposit these stores in the "State Magazine" and to issue "such orders for their security" as may be needed.[2] The governor of South Carolina "does the same."[3] There is no news about the "definitive treaty," but NG believes "it must soon come to hand as it is impossible the enemy can retract after having gone thus far."[4] ADfS (NcD) 2 pp.]

1. The resolution ordering furloughs for the army was dated 26 May (*JCC*, 24: 364–65); for NG's orders concerning the furlough of troops in Georgia, see NG to Habersham, immediately above.

2. As seen in a note at the letter immediately above, Georgia did agree to take and store the "Continental property."

3. See NG to Benjamin Guerard, this date, above.

4. The "definitive" peace treaty ending the war did not reach America until November. (Thomas Mifflin to Certain States, 23 November 1783, Smith, *Letters*, 21: 162; on the treaty, see also the note at Lafayette to NG, 8 September, below.)

*　　　*　　　*

To General Anthony Wayne

Dear Sir　　　　　　Head quarters Charles Town [S.C.] June 26th 1783

I have had the pleasure of receiving two letters from you since you left this place one from Augusta the other from Savannah.[1] The grant of the Cherokees I imagine will be of but little consequence if the Creeks continue to disclaim their right of granting. An Indian war I expect will be the consequence and if Georgia is not aided by the neighbouring States or the force of the State greatly increased by new settlers the indians will contend upon no very unequal footing. I wish all these matters were to be settled by Commisioners from Congress. Both parties perhaps would be better satisfied. It is pretty certain there would be less reason for disputes.[2]

Congress have forwarded me a resolution for furloughing the army;

and orders are gone out for the purpose. Major Habersham has a copy of the orders and the resolution.[3] Transports are hourly expected to take the Northern Troops to the respective States to which they belong where both Men and Officers are to be furloughed until the signing the definitive treaty and then to be discharged.[4]

What has become of the Virginia Infantry you took with you? Have they gone to Virginia on the uper route or are they to join here again?[5]

Since you left us there has been great uneasiness among the Troops from an impatience to get home. The terrors of the climate and the discontent natural to idleness has produced great desertions; and near one half the 3[d] Regiment of Cavalry went off in a body.[6]

All our Waggons and public Stores in the Quarter Masters department are sold. Our Military Stores are depositing in the Magazine of this State and all our arrangements are drawing to a close. I expect to leave this place in less than a month for Philadelphia.[7] What can Governor Tonyn mean by his extraordinary conduct? It must be the effects of temper; and not the result of orders.[8] However Congress have remonstrated against the conduct of the british Generals in withholding the property of the people of the United States contrary to treaty.[9]

Dueling thrives apace here. Cap Pendleton and M[r] Waters have been out the latter got wounded the former not.[10] Col [John Skey] Eustace has been out with a M[r] Rule; but the matter was accomodated on the ground.[11] Disputes have run high among a number more; but the intervention of friends prevented a serious appeal to heaven.

Mrs Greene sailed for Philadelphia about [a] fortnight since and left her good wishes for you on your return.[12] How is Major Fishbourn? We hear he has been at deaths door and gave a soft tap but was not admitted.[13] Present me respectfully to all friends in Georgia and believe me to be with esteem and Affection your Most Obed[t] humble Ser[t]

NATH GREENE

ALS (PWacD).

1. Wayne's letter from Augusta, Ga., is above, dated 23 May; the one that he wrote to NG from Savannah has not been found.

2. See note at Wayne's letter to NG of 23 May, above.

3. See NG to John Habersham, this date, above.

4. NG's expectation was based on a letter from James Nicholson of 30 May, above. The transport vessels did not arrive until 11 July.

5. The Virginia troops had apparently marched for home.

6. On the mutiny by dragoons of the First Continental Legionary Corps, formerly the Third Continental Regiment of Light Dragoons, see NG to Benjamin Harrison, 21 May, above (vol. 12: 676 and n).

7. On the sale of the army's equipment, see note at NG to Lincoln, second letter of 3 June, above. NG did not leave Charleston until mid-August.

8. Patrick Tonyn was the royal governor of East Florida. The nature of his "extraordinary conduct" is not known, but this was a chaotic time in East Florida, as the British prepared to turn over control to the Spanish and to evacuate Loyalists, many of whom

had recently moved to East Florida from Georgia and South Carolina. (See J. Leitch Wright, Jr., *Florida in the American Revolution* [Gainesville: University Presses of Florida, 1975], pp. 125–43.)

9. No letter from Congress to Sir Guy Carleton, the British commander in America, or to any other British general concerning violations of the preliminary peace treaty, has been found. NG may have referred to a letter of 27 March from the South Carolina delegates to Carleton, calling for enforcement of the agreement "relative to the Restitution of Property to the Citizens" of South Carolina that was agreed to before the evacuation of Charleston. (South Carolina Delegates to Carleton, 27 March, Smith, *Letters*, 20: 118) Ralph Izard, one of the delegates who signed that letter, wrote Arthur Middleton on 30 May that although Congress realized the British had refused to return the property they had seized from many South Carolinians—"a most impudent evasion of the Treaty"—a majority of delegates "were afraid to make an express declaration that the British had violated it [i.e., the Treaty]. It was said that a renewal of hostilities might be the consequence of such declaration." (Ibid., p. 287)

10. For more about the duel between NG's former aide Nathaniel Pendleton and John Alleyne Walter, see below, NG to Williams, 2 July, and NG to CG, 7 August.

11. Nothing more is known about this incident.

12. CG sailed from Charleston on 7 June. (See note at NG to Morris, 5 June, above.)

13. Wayne's aide Benjamin Fishbourn, a native of Pennsylvania, recovered his health and settled in Georgia after the war. (Nelson, *Wayne*, pp. 199, 200; see also Gunn to NG, 2 March 1785, below.)

To John Kean

Dear Sir   Head quarters [Charleston, S.C.] June 28th 1783

I have got the returns you forwarded me; but they are not sufficiently explicit for the pay master to settle with the officers upon. Col Carringtons family account is blended with his of the department.[1] If it is possible I wish you to take your papers and Mr Verdier and come to Town that we may examin the matter and have the Accounts so stated as to enable the pay master to settle with the Officers.[2] Many are murmuring at not having it in their power to draw for their back rations which cannot take place until your Accounts are recievd and adjusted in the pay office. It is a matter of great consequence to the Officers and of some importance to the public, I wish you therefore to accomodate the business as early as possible. The Officers will be gone perhaps in less than ten days as the transports are hourly expected.[3]

Col Carrington writes you on his affairs.[4] Dont fail to put his matters to rights if it be possible to avoid it. I am dear Sir Your most Obedt humble Ser^t   NATH GREENE

ADfS (MiU-C).

1. Edward Carrington's "family" was his military family, including aides and assistants.

2. As seen in NG to Lincoln, first letter of 3 June, above, John M. Verdier had been Kean's assistant when Kean served as a commissary.

3. In his reply of 4 July, below, Kean refused to come to Charleston to meet with NG.

4. Carrington's letter to Kean has not been found.

To John S. Dart

Head-Quarters [Charleston, S.C.] June ye 30th 1783
To John Sandford Dart Esqr Dep^y Pay Master to the southern Army—
The situation of the Officers from the dissolution of the Army, is so truly mortifying and distressing, that not withstanding the reasons are great for not drawing more Bills on the Financier, I have concluded to draw for One Months pay for each Officer now with the Army, and you will issue them accordingly and this shall be your sufficient Warrant for so doing.[1] Given at Head-Quarters June ye 30th 1783— NATH GREENE

Cy (WRMS, Misc. Mss. #22330: DNA). This copy was enclosed in a letter of 30 July from Robert Morris to John Pierce, the paymaster of the army.
1. For more about NG's decision to pay the officers, see his letter to Robert Morris, the "Financier."

* * *

¶ [FROM OFFICERS OF THE VIRGINIA LINE, "Encampment near" Charleston, S.C., 30 June 1783. "Conformable to Genl Orders," they have considered the "Resolve of Congress" of 22 March and agree to accept the "commutation of the half pay voted the Officers" and to receive "five years full pay in lieu thereof."[1] The document is signed by ten officers: Samuel Finley, Clough Shelton, Alexander Parker, Nathaniel Darby, Robert Breckenridge, Joseph Conway, Charles Jones, Javan Miller, George Monro, and Nathan Smith. DS (DLC) 1 p.]
1. NG's orders have not been found. The congressional resolution is in JCC, 24: 207–10. (See also vol. 12: 557n, above, and the letter immediately below.)

¶ [FROM MAJOR EDMUND M. HYRNE, Charleston, S.C., 1 July 1783. "Agreable to the directions of Congress," he has polled the officers of the South Carolina line "now in service," and they "unanimously" desire "the commutation offered by Congress, in lieu of the half pay for life."[1] RCS (Greene Papers: DLC) 1 p.]
1. The South Carolina officers were responding to a congressional resolution of 22 March, offering five years of full pay to officers instead of a half-pay pension for life. (JCC, 24: 207–10; see also the preceding letter.)

* * *

To Otho H. Williams

Dear Sir Head quarters [Charleston, S.C.] July 2^d 1783
I was very happy to hear from you by your letter of the 20th of March.[1] It affords me great pleasure to hear your prospects are flattering in matrimony, and an easy competency in future life.[2] My satisfaction upon the occasion is increased from a recollection that I recommended your leaving the service and seeking a compensation for your Military services in some civil employments. Remember also that I recommended Matrimony in the strongest terms as necessary to domestic happiness.[3] All with out were but wild pleasures and unstable joys. It is

said you are courting a very agreeable Lady and I wish for both your sakes the issue may be favorable as the connection will be pleasing. You have good sense and a just taste which is an excellent foundation for matrimony. May many joys attend you is my sincere wish. Mrs Greene is gone to Philadelphia; and from thence goes to Rhode Island.[4] I expect to follow her in about a month. Capt Pearce has formed a connection in business with Col White and Major Call.[5] Capt Pendleton was studying the law—and was in a promising way; but by too intimate a connection at Doctor Olliphants he gave cause of suspicion to Mr Waters the Doctors son in law which obliges him to leave this Country.[6] Mr Fitzchugh [William F. Fitzhugh] will give you the particulars of the duel and the issue.[7] Morris is with his charmer and is quite the planter.[8] Burnet you know has been in business for some time.[9] Thus had I provided for all my family.[10] I forgot to mention to you that it is fully believed Capt Pearce is engaged to Miss Fenwick a very pretty young Lady.[11]

I thank you for your friendly hints respecting the reports propagated to my prejudice.[12] Perhaps some officers may harbour such suspicions as you mention; but it is impossible that others should unless they possess both hearts and principles far less candid and just than I am willing to think of them. M[r] Banks's officious conjecture in a letter to his partner, and Major Burnets connection in business gave rise to the report.[13] To remove any impressions which Mr Banks letter might give I made [him] go before a Magistrate and swear whether I had any connection with him in his business directly or indirectly.[14] And he declard upon oath that I had not. I got General Wayne and Lt Col Carrington to examin the whole transaction respecting the clothing I got M[r] Banks to engage for the Army and by authentic documents provd that all I did was by the order of the board of war and for the benefit of the Army; and I have the Secretary and Financiers letters of thanks for the steps I took to get clothing for the Army.[15] Never [damaged] benevolent transaction returned [damaged] ingratitude. It is impossible to govern vulgar prejudices but if the officers harbour any thing to my prejudice on that subject I despise their low suspicions and feel a conscious superiority. I defy all the World to tax me with justice, with doing any thing contrary to my duty or the public good. I expect to see you soon and will give you a full history of the affair. Mr Fitzchuch is waiting for this letter and the vessel for him and he cant stay for me to add or to read what I have written. Yours aff

AL (MdHi).

1. Williams's letter is above (vol. 12: 537–38).

2. As seen in Williams to NG, 14 January 1784, below, the romance did not lead to marriage. By "easy competency in future life," NG undoubtedly referred to Williams's acceptance of the post of customs collector for Maryland. (See Williams to NG, 20 February, and George Lux to NG, 24 January, both above [vol. 12: 467, 392].)

3. See NG's letter to Williams of 11 April 1783, above (vol. 12: 598).

4. CG sailed from Charleston for Philadelphia on 7 June. (NG to Washington, 5 June, above)

5. On William Pierce, Jr.'s, business partnership with Anthony W. White, and Richard Call, see NG to Wadsworth, 24 May, above.

6. On the duel between Pendleton and David Olyphant's son-in-law, John Alleyne Walter, see also NG to CG, 7 August, below. Pendleton wrote NG from Virginia on 17 July, below.

7. For more about this duel, see ibid. and NG to Wayne, 26 June, above.

8. The "charmer" was Lewis Morris, Jr.'s, wife, Ann-Barnett Elliott Morris, whose family's plantations had established Morris as "quite the planter."

9. Ichabod Burnet had gone into business with John Banks.

10. By his "family," NG meant his military family, or aides-de-camp.

11. Pierce married the heiress Charlotte Fenwick later that year. (Pendleton to NG, 4 December, below)

12. See Williams to NG, 20 March.

13. For a discussion of Banks's letter and his business connection with NG's former aide Burnet, see note at Benjamin Harrison to NG, 24 December 1782, above (vol. 12: 342–44).

14. See Statement of John Banks, 15 February, above (ibid., pp. 444–46).

15. See Statement of General Anthony Wayne and Colonel Edward Carrington, 15 February, above (vol. 12: 446–48).

*   *   *

¶ [FROM ROGER PARKER SAUNDERS, [Charleston, S.C.], 3 July 1783. The corn that NG bought "is wanted," and Saunders is sending a boat for it.[1] He asks NG to "send also a Barrel or two of Salt." The boat belongs to Saunders and the "Patroon";[2] the "Boat Negroes" are NG's. Asks NG to send them back "as soon as possible." NG now has "Carpenters and Coopers sufficient for Plantation use." The carpenters are not "us'd to Work in the Field," and as nothing had been "Saw'd" to repair NG's buildings, Saunders hired them out to Mʳ Haig "to make Indico [Indigo] Vatts"; he will use the money from this to purchase "Cows and Calves for Plantation use."[3] Since he last wrote, the "Crops of Rice" have "sufferd much by the great Rains." He thinks that "by Crawfish & Water," NG has "lost 14 or 15 Acres of the young Rice in the Chanel."[4] NG's "Corn is also hurt by Rain." Saunders is "very sorry" that NG has had "the Fever." He "may Come down to pay" his "Respects" when NG leaves South Carolina and give "a particular accoᵗ" of the plantation.[5] The woman who rented NG's land "has no Stock," and the "Rent will not be due before she disposes of the Crop now on the Land."[6] RCS (MiU-C) 3 pp.]

1. Saunders, who was overseeing the operations of NG's Boone's Barony plantation, had written on 20 June, above, that NG would need corn "in about a month" for his "Negroes."

2. A "patroon" was a "captain, master, or officer in charge of a boat." (*OED*)

3. As historian Julia Floyd Smith has observed, "slave hire," or the leasing of slaves to work on other plantations, was a common practice and could be a significant source of income for slave owners. (Smith, *Slavery and Rice Culture*, pp. 58–59) The rendering of indigo plants into dye was a "difficult process." The plants had to be "steeped in large vats of freshwater." (Bullard, *Cumberland Island*, p. 74) In his letter of 20 June, above, Saunders had advised NG that he needed to buy sufficient cattle for Boone's Barony.

4. Owners of rice plantations were vulnerable to the vagaries of weather. Too much rain could ruin a crop, and this turned out to be the case with NG's 1783 crop at Boone's Barony. (Saunders to NG, 20 October, below)

5. NG had been ill with a "fever" in early June. (NG to Washington, 5 June, above) NG set out for the North on 14 August. (See note at NG to Washington, 8 August, below.) It is not known if Saunders visited him before he left.

6. Nothing is known about the rental arrangement.

¶ [FROM JOHN KEAN, Beaufort, S.C., 4 July 1783. Is sorry that the returns are not "sufficiently explicit" but cannot "come to Charlestown & it does not suit Mr Verdier at this time," either.[1] Adds: "As to the murmuring of the officers it cannot with Justice fall on me. They ought to have been careful to have obtained certificates of what they did draw; their drawing in messes put it out of the power of the Brigade commissary to specify each particular officer & if the whole vouchers were now to be taken & a new set of books formed from them the number of rations drawn by each officer could not be ascertained." When Kean first joined the army, each officer drew one ration; sometime later—he believes at "the beginning of Feb^y"—NG ordered that they draw two rations each, "which they always drew."[2] The returns that Kean sent to Col. [Edward] Carrington are "in as explicit a form as it is possible."[3] NG may appoint anyone he pleases to inspect "the books & adjust them if they can." RCS (Greene Papers: DLC) 2 pp.]

1. See NG to Kean, 28 June, above. Kean had been commissary for the Southern Army. J. M. Verdier, his assistant, prepared the returns for Kean's department. (NG to Lincoln, first letter of 3 June, above)

2. On the rations, see also NG to Lincoln, first letter of 3 June.

3. In his letter to Kean of 28 June, NG had complained that Kean's returns combined the accounts of Carrington's military "family" with those of the Quartermaster Department. NG enclosed the returns he had received from Kean in a letter to Gen. Benjamin Lincoln of 2 August, below.

¶ [TO ELIAS BOUDINOT, PRESIDENT OF THE CONTINENTAL CONGRESS. From Headquarters, Charleston, S.C., 10 July 1783. Col. [Thaddeus] Kosciuszko, "who has been our chief engineer in the southern department, & with the northern army at the taking [of] Burgoyne;[1] and whose zeal & activity have been equaled by few, & exceeded by none; has it in contemplation to return to Europe." Kosciuszko wants to "close" his affairs in this country by collecting in "ready" money "such pay & emoluments, as he is entitled to" from his rank and from "the service he has performd for the accomplishing our independence." Because of Kosciuszko's "peculiar situation," NG hopes Congress will direct the "financier" to "settle & accomodate the matter." NG's friendship for Kosciuszko "must apologize for the singularity of this recommendation." NG is "warmly interested in his favor" but cannot "presume" to "judge of the difficulties attending the business."[2] LS (PCC, item 137, vol. 2: 757: DNA) 1 p.]

1. NG referred here to the capture of the British army commanded by Gen. John Burgoyne at Saratoga, N.Y., in 1777.

2. Congress referred this letter to Robert Morris, the "financier," on 26 July. (JCC, 24: 447) Morris reported on 1 August that "in the latter End of the Year 1781" his office had established a rule for the settlement of accounts of all foreign officers, under which they were to be paid one fifth of the balance owed them in cash "in Lieu of Depreciation," and were to receive interest-bearing notes for the rest. While conceding Kosciuszko's great

merit, Morris argued that only a "strict adherence to general Rules" could prevent "Complaints of Injustice which the Want of Pay to the Army in general has given but too much Ground for and which can alone be repressed by a Conviction that the Public have not ability to Discharge the whole and that there is an inviolable Determination of Government to make proportionate Distribution of what may be within their ability." (Morris, *Papers*, 8: 363–64) NG later wrote Morris directly on Kosciuszko's behalf. That letter has not been found, but Morris mentioned it in a diary entry for 12 November, adding that he had met with Kosciuszko, and "finding that he has not received the usual Consideration paid to foreign Officers for Depreciation," had arranged for a partial payment of £200 "untill the account can be finally settled." (Morris, *Papers*, 8: 751–52)

*   *   *

To Colonel Thaddeus Kosciuszko

Dear Sir   Head Quarters Charlestown [S.C.] July 10th 1783

I was happy to hear from you by your letter of the 18th of June. Mrs Greene says you had an agreeable passage and pleasing society.[1] Pearce also says all your health except Mr [Alexander] Garden[']s is bettered by the voyage.[2]

I have written to Congress and the Financier upon the subject of your pay and emoluments.[3] Inclosed are copies of my letters. I wish they may have the desired effect, but repeated application may obtain what no influence can effect. I know your modesty and feel your difficulty on this head, but unless you persist I am apprehensive nothing will be done in the matter. For once you must force nature and get the better of that independent pride which [is] our best support in many situations, and urge your suit from the necessity of the case, which may accomplish the business, and without which I have too much reason to apprehend a disappointment. Political bodies act not from feeling so much as policy, but if they find there is no other way of getting rid of an application which has become troublesome they will grant the thing altho against policy. I only offer these remarks to your consideration. Your own feelings must determine your conduct in the matter. In human life we are in a state of probation, and for the trial of our virtues mortification is sometimes necessary. Be not discouraged therefore because you dont succeed at once, nor drop your application from little obstacles. I expect to be in Philadelphia in six or eight weeks and if I can render you any farther services should you not have succeeded before my arrival it will afford me the greatest pleasure.[4] Should you be gone before my arrival my warmest wishes will attend you through all the thorny paths or pleasant fields where fortune may lead you.[5] It will add to my happiness to hear from you in whatever quarter of the world you are. I expect soon to become the peaceful citizen where your letters as your company will ever meet a hearty welcome. Permit me to return you my sincere thanks for the zeal with which you have served the public under my command and for your friendly disposition towards me. My warmest approbation is due to you as an officer and my particular acknowledgments as a friend. I am dear Sir your most hble serv.   N. GREENE

Tr (GWG Transcript: CSmH).

1. Kosciuszko's letter is above. CG's letter describing the voyage that she, Kosciuszko, and some of NG's other officers had recently made to Philadelphia has not been found.

2. See William Pierce, Jr., to NG, 19 June, above.

3. NG's letter to Congress is immediately above; the one to Robert Morris, the "Financier," has not been found.

4. As seen by the note at NG to Boudinot, immediately above, Kosciuszko did continue to pursue the matter, and NG assisted him by writing another letter to Morris.

5. Kosciuszko spent some time with NG and his family at Newport, R.I., during the spring of 1784. (See note at Littlefield to NG, 22 March 1784, below.)

*   *   *

¶ [FROM JOHN BANKS, Charleston, S.C., 10 July 1783. In closing their account with "Capt Hammleton the Clothier," Banks finds that his firm has been overpaid by some £2,000 "Carolina St[erlin]g."[1] This overpayment resulted from the following: Hamilton returning "many Articles he at first took up"; his not taking "Woollens" purchased by Bradford & Stewart—"a heavy burthen" on Banks's firm; and, "on the Expectation of Peace," the cancellation of an order for "shirts & Overalls." As it will be "impossible" for Hunter, Banks & Company to repay this amount before Hamilton's departure, Banks would be "glad to have Bills drawn on the Financier [Robert Morris] in the amt to be discounted from the Contract for the Subsistence of the S° Army."[2] Since his firm has "supported this Contract at an amasing inconvenience and have appropriated the first payments from [it]," Banks hopes "the Bills may not be less than ninety Days." RCS (Greene Papers: DLC) 1 p.]

1. Capt. John Hamilton was the Southern Army's clothier. For more about the contract with Hunter, Banks & Company to supply clothing to the Southern Army, see NG to Benjamin Lincoln, 19 December 1782, above (vol. 12: 306–7). In notes at that letter, the editors discuss the firm's financial problems in detail.

2. NG sent a copy of this letter with his to Robert Morris of 11 July, below. Morris reacted to Banks's proposal in his first letter to NG of 1 August and in another of 5 August, both below.

¶ [FROM ROBERT MORRIS, SUPERINTENDENT OF FINANCE, Philadelphia, 10 July 1783. Acknowledges NG's letter of 3 June and "that relating to Mr Corles Brig."[1] As NG "suspected," Baron Glaubeck was not in Philadelphia when NG's letter arrived.[2] Morris is "extreemly sorry to learn" that NG has "been so ill"; hopes his "Health is reestablished before the present moment."[3] Morris will "avoid replying fully" to NG's letters because he expects to see NG soon; he hopes, indeed, that NG will have left Charleston, S.C., before this letter arrives.[4] RCS (CSmH) 1 p.]

1. William Corlis was the owner of the brigantine Christiana, which NG had leased to carry troops from Charleston, S.C., to Philadelphia. (Morris, Papers, 8: 190–91) NG's letter to Morris concerning this arrangement has not been found, but it presumably was similar to what he wrote in his second letter to Benjamin Lincoln of 3 June, above.

2. NG discussed the "Villian" and "imposter" Baron Glaubeck in his letter to Morris of 3 June, above.

3. On NG's illness, see his letter to Washington of 5 June, above. By the time Morris wrote this letter, NG had recovered his health.

4. NG did not leave Charleston until 14 August. (See note at NG to Washington, 8 August, below.)

*   *   *

To General Benjamin Lincoln, Secretary at War

Dear Sir   H.Q. C[harles]. T[own]. [S.C.] July 11th 1783

Comodore Nicholson is arrivd and the greater part of the Troops will embark in a day or two but some of the transports have not arrivd and perhaps never will.[1] Agreeable to the resolution of Congress for furloughing the Troops of North Carolinia and those for the war I have issued the enclosed order.[2] The resolution of Congress mentions only the commander in Chief in the business; but as you direct the Virginians to be furloughed I considered it an explanation for me to give orders for furloughing the whole.[3] I hope the measures I have taken in the business will meet your and the Commander in chiefs approbation. The Military Stores are all deposited in this Town[.] The Commisary of Military Stor[es] is entering upon a Contract for keeping the Arms in repair.[4] The Quarter Master Generals Stores are nearly all disposed of and most or all the Agents will be dismissed in a few days. The hospital department will soon be closed. I have directed the Purveyor to sell such things as are not wanted for the sick now in the hospital. The North Carolinia Troops have all marched for their State in two divisions with provisions sufficient for twenty days. Col [Archibald] Lyttle and Col. [Edward] Carrington from a full enquiry into the matter prefered this mode; and I approved therof. Major [Edmund M.] Hyrne has furloughed the South Carolinians and I imagine before this all the Georgians are dismissed.[5]

I wrote you the 18th of last month that the Troops were very impatient for the arrival of the transports and that I apprehended great desertion or a general mutiny. There was great desertion but a mutiny was happily avoided. Most of the Cavalry who bought their horses went home on furlough.[6] The desertions which have taken place, those that went on furlough from the Cavalry and the infantry who have been furloughed since your letter has reduced our numbers considerably within the tonnage of the contract; but there is not shipping enough arrivd to take off even those that are remaining. However the Comodore says if the rest of the Vessels dont arrive in a day or two he will Charter a Vessel or two here. The Troops are geting sickly and very impatient to be gone.

Benjamin Lincoln, 1733–1810; oil painting by Charles Willson Peale
(Independence National Historical Park)

I am in hopes soon to bring the business of this department to a close. As soon as I have accomplished which I shall set out for Philadelphia unless you or the Commander in chief directs to the contrary.[7] I have the honor to be with great respect Your Most Obedt humble Ser[t] N GREENE

ADfS (MiU-C).

1. On the transports, see James Nicholson to NG, 30 May, above, and NG to Morris, immediately below.

2. On the order of Congress of 26 May furloughing the troops of the Southern Army, see Lincoln to NG, 28 May, above.

3. See ibid.

4. Christian Senf was—or had been until recently—the commissary of military stores. (Vol. 12: 675n, above; Mentges to NG, 6 August, below)

5. NG's order to Maj. John Habersham to furlough the Georgia troops is above, dated 26 June.

6. On the purchase of their horses by dragoons, see NG to Lincoln, 18 June, above.

7. NG left Charleston on 14 August. (See note at NG to Washington, 8 August, below.)

To Robert Morris, Superintendent of Finance

Sir   Headquarters Charles Town [S.C.] July 11th 1783

Comodore Nicholson is arrivd and part of the transports[,] but several are yet behind.[1] Most of the Troops remaining will embark in a day or two. Our numbers are so reduced by furloughs and desertion that something less Shipping than was contracted for will be sufficient. However there is not a sufficiency yet and if more dont arrive soon the Comodore proposes to engage a Vessel or two here.[2] It is pretty certain that one of the Transports is cast away upon Cape Hatterass.

The Mortifying situation of the Officers of this department on leaving this Country where every one had contracted debts and engagements of different kinds induced me to give the pay Master orders to issue bills for a months pay. The Troops have had no pay except the Legion who have had one Months. The amount of the Months pay for the officers is little more than four thousand dollars. These with some few bills drew for the quarter Masters and Purveyors department are all the bills I have drawn since I wrote you before.[3]

Inclosed is a copy of a letter from Mr John Banks respecting a ballance he owes to the Clothing department.[4] When the reports of peace began to prevail I directed the Clothier[5] to stop all heavy purchases in his department and to return all the goods he could. Mr Banks complains of this as a hardship. Altho I believe a considerable part of the ballance may have originated from the goods returned and others engaged and not receivd yet I am persuaded it has been partly owing to the Clothiers negligence and Mr Banks inattention in not comparing the payments with the amount of the goods receivd. Hambleton continued to draw on me until I was so fully persuaded that our payments exceeded the amount of the Clothing that I refused to sign any more bills until the Accounts were closed. Had I not put this check upon the Clothiers drafts perhaps the ballance might have been much greater. Mr Banks owes besides this ballance about four thousand dollars upon a sett of bills drew last Spring for 6000 dollars for which he was to advance me money occasionally to the whole amount by the time they became payable on these bills[.] He has advanced something less than 2000 dollars and the contract has so many demands upon him for money that I have no prospect of getting any more. I take this early opportunity therefore to report the state of the public demands upon him here that you and he may adjust the matter between you in the settlement of the business of the contract.[6]

I have sent home and furloughed all the Troops of the Three southern States[7] and shall soon have the whole department free from Continental expence or in a great degree. The Military Stores are deposited in the Magazine of this State and only one Agent will be left in charge of them. The quarter masters department will soon be dissolved and the hospital and Clothier business brought to a close. Such articles as remain on hand in the hospital department I shall order to be sold, and I believe those in the Clothing department also; but they will sell exceeding low from the great scarcity of cash and plenty of goods. But I think it best to sell them nevertheless as there will be a constant expence of storage and Agents that have them in charge. Please to give me your opinion in the matter.[8] I shall write to the Secretary of war on the subject.[9] The whole amount will be but triffling. I have the honor to be with great respect Your most Obedt humble Ser   N GREENE

ADfS (CSmH).

1. On James Nicholson's mission, see his letter to NG of 30 May, above.

2. If additional vessels were hired, Morris did not mention it in a diary note about a conversation that he later had with Nicholson in Philadelphia. (Diary entry for 11 August, Morris, *Papers*, 8: 413)

3. NG's orders for a month's pay to his officers are in a letter to John S. Dart of 30 June, above. The pay for the troops of Lee's Legion was authorized in May because of unrest in that unit. (See above, Joseph Eggleston to NG, 12 May, and NG to Eggleston, 17 May [vol. 12: 652, 659–60].) Morris replied that even the small sum of $4,000 was more than he knew "where to find or how to get at." (Morris to NG, first letter of 1 August, below)

4. This was undoubtedly a copy of John Banks's letter to NG of 10 July, above.

5. Capt. John Hamilton was the Southern Army's clothier. For more about the contract under which Hunter, Banks & Company supplied clothing to the Southern Army, see NG to Benjamin Lincoln, 19 December 1782, above (vol. 12: 306–7 and n).

6. Morris's initial reaction was that "Mr Banks having received £2500 Sterling of public Money more than he was entitled to proposes to receive £2500 Sterling more to repay the Officer from whom he received it." (Morris to NG, first letter of 1 August) A few days later, Morris modified his response. (Morris to NG, 5 August, below)

7. The three states were North Carolina, South Carolina, and Georgia. (On this, see also NG to Washington, immediately below.)

8. Morris approved NG's plan to sell supplies belonging to the Southern Army. (Morris to NG, first letter of 1 August)
9. See NG to Lincoln, immediately above.

To George Washington

Sir   Head Quarters Charles Town [S.C.] July 11ᵗʰ 1783
   I have received an order, since your Excellencys Letter of the 18ᵗʰ May from the War office, and a resolution of Congress for sending the troops to their respective states; and for furloughing them untill the definitive treaty is signed.[1] In consequence of which, I have sent home the North Carolinians, furloughed the troops of this State and Georgia, and expect to embark most of the rest in a few days, belonging to the States north of North Carolina.
   From an apprehension of the sickly season, and from an impatience to be discharged, a considerable number of the troops have deserted, and I have had great difficulty to prevent a general mutiny. The delay of the Transports, has been a source of great uneasiness.[2] As soon as the troops are gone, and I have got the Stores all in the deposits and the different Staff departments properly arranged, I shall avail myself of your Excellency's indulgence of coming to Philadelphia, where I hope to have the happiness of seeing you, and felicitating each other upon the happy close to all our difficulties.[3] I have the honor to be with great respect Your Excellencys Most obedient humble servant   NATH GREENE

LS (Washington Papers: DLC).
   1. Washington's letter of 18 May to NG is above (vol. 12: 667–68). The orders for furloughing the troops are in Lincoln to NG, 28 May, above. The congressional resolution was undoubtedly that of 26 May. (*JCC*, 24: 364–65)
   2. The transports, which were expected in early June, did not reach Charleston until 11 July. (See above, Nicholson to NG, 30 May, and NG to Lincoln, this date.)
   3. NG, who left Charleston in mid-August, arrived in Philadelphia in early October. (See note at NG to Boudinot, first letter of 7 October, below.)

                    *   *   *

¶ [FROM MAJOR EPHRAIM MITCHELL, [Charleston, S.C.], 11 July 1783.[1] The bearer, Joseph Turner, enlisted as a matross[2] in the artillery in January 1776 for a term of two years, for which he received a bounty of $16. In October 1777, he received a bounty of $30 "to Serve During the war." When his artillery regiment was disbanded, he was "Turnd Over to the Infantry" without receiving an additional bounty. While serving in the artillery he "Did his Duty as a good Soldier." As he did not receive a bounty when he joined the infantry—and "in Compensation for the Difference of pay"—Turner believes he should be paid the higher wages of a matross, as was promised when he enlisted, and asks NG to "Direct The paymaster Accordingly."[3] In a postscript, Mitchell adds that the pay of a matross is $8 ⅓ per month. RCS (MiU-C) 2 pp.]

1. Before his capture at Charleston in 1780, Mitchell was a major in the Fourth South Carolina Continental Regiment. When he returned to active duty in 1782–83, he served as captain and major in a Continental artillery regiment. (Moss, *S.C. Patriots*, p. 687)

2. A matross was an assistant to an artillery gunner.

3. Two Joseph Turners (probably the same person) are listed in Bobby Gilmer Moss's *Roster of S.C. Patriots*. The first by that name is said to have served as a matross in the Fourth South Carolina Continental Regiment throughout the war. The other began service in 1779 as a sergeant in the Second South Carolina Continental Regiment, was captured by the British at Charleston in 1780, and thereafter saw service in the militia. (Moss, *S.C. Patriots*, p. 943)

*   *   *

From Nathaniel Pendleton

My Dear General   Richmond [Va.] July 17th 1783

I arrived here two days since, after a passage of nine days to Hampton and four more to this place, in which we had every Opposition that Successive calms, and Storms could throw in our way.[1] When I came to Hampton I was informed General Lincoln was at this place, having been at the setting of the Assembly, and that he was to continue some time here for the purpose of distributing three months pay, which he had brought for the Southern Army; but he had been gone some time to Winchester where the troops of this State are quartered, and where they still remain unfurloughed. I cannot learn the cause of General Lincoln's visit to the Assembly.[2] It was probably to press the necessity of adopting the Resolution respecting the 5 per Ct.[3] Governor Harrison tells me, and it is the Sentiment of every Gentleman almost I have seen, that the Assembly will reject that plan unless General Washington's circular letter, which you will have seen before this reaches you, produces an alteration of the general Opinion. The last Assembly had formally rejected it, but I am told the Generals letter abovementioned, which was communicated to the Assembly Afterwards, appeared to have had a considerable effect, and the Governor who is an advocate for it, is not without hopes that the next Session may be wiser.[4] The Assembly rose about ten days since. They have directed the Accounts of their Officers and Soldiers to be settled and the depreciation made good til the 1t of January 1782 for the regular discharge of which a land and slave tax is appropriated. The interest on the ballance at the end of the Year 1781 is to be paid in Cash immediately to each Officer, and the principle is directed to be paid in the proportion of an eighth annually, together with the interest constantly accruing upon the ballance as it becomes less.[5]

Partial systems of policy prevail more in this State than, even in [South] Carolina. The interests of the Union seems to be forgotten, or lost in that of the State. If the nature and objects of the Union are not more known and attended to, the confederation in my opinion will soon exist no where but in idea. People talk, and measures are adopt[ed] here, as if the fate of the Union, of the whole thirteen States depended upon this State alone. It is the same in other States. A Demagogue in the Assembly here, thinks himself of more consequence, and speaks as though the fate of this Country depended more upon himself, than the finest Speaker in Congress would do.

In stead of punishing, the Assembly have rewarded the Desserters from the Cavalry. The Assembly were thrown into confusion, and hurried off General Morgan to meet them, give 'em some pay, and direct their route to Winchester, where they have been since furloughed by the advice of General Gates, and are now going about the Country and selling their horses. Dangerfield, I am informed is still there. If he remains so, upon my arrival I will have him tried and executed if I can.[6]

Governor Harrison appears quite asshamed of the conduct of Governm[t] which was most evidently dictated by timidity. He throws all the blame upon the Assembly who took the matter into their own hands, and upon the inefficacy of the executive powers.[7] He says the termination of the War, has annihilated the little Authority he had over the militia.

The people here [have] been informed that you have quarelled with every power, and every officer civil and military in the Southern Department. 'Tis strange what an aptitude mankind have to amplify. The Marvellous, is quite the Stile here. These things are brought into existance and expire in a day. They are unworthy a moments reflection, except as they afford new lights into the human Character.

I hope you have enjoyed your health since I left you, and I hope before this your embarrasments about the transports have subsided.[8] I shall expect the favor of a line as you pass through Virginia.[9] With the warmest Sentiments of grateful friendship I am Dear General Your Affectionate & Hbe Serv[t]   N PENDLETON

RCS (MiU-C).

1. Pendleton, a native of Virginia, had gone there after fighting a duel in South Carolina. (NG to Williams, 2 July, above)

2. According to his biographer, Benjamin Lincoln, the secretary at war, visited Virginia to "supervise the placement and construction of a powder magazine." Lincoln returned to Philadelphia on 17 July. (Mattern, *Benjamin Lincoln*, pp. 146–47)

3. For more about the fate of the congressional impost proposal of 1783 in the Virginia legislature, see the next note. (On the proposal, which included a five percent duty on imports, see also the note at NG to Lincoln, 18 June, above.)

4. Between 8 and 21 June, Washington addressed a long circular letter to the executive of each state. The copy that he sent to Gov. Benjamin Harrison of Virginia was dated 12 June. (Fitzpatrick, *GW*, 26: 483n) In the circular, Washington devoted a paragraph to the proposed impost as a means of restoring public credit. He wrote: "No real friend to the honor and Independency of America, can hesitate a single moment respecting the

propriety of complying with the just and honorable measures proposed . . . and that if it shall not be carried into immediate execution, a National Bankruptcy, with all its deplorable consequences will take place, before any different Plan can possibly be proposed and adopted; So pressing are the present circumstances! and such is the alternative now offered to the States!" (Fitzpatrick, *GW*, 26: 489) According to Joseph Jones, a member of the Assembly, the letter had a strong effect on the legislators but had not arrived until the session was nearly completed. Because of that, consideration of the proposal was postponed until the next session. (Joseph Jones to James Madison, Madison, *Papers*, 7: 197) In December, the legislature conditionally agreed to the impost, with a proviso that "each and every of the other states" must first enact similar legislation. (Hening, *Statutes*, 11: 350–52; see also the notes at NG to Washington, 26 September, and Weedon to NG, 2 December, both below.)

5. A bill to pay the money owed to Virginia Continental and state soldiers was passed on 24 June. A tax on imports of salt, wine, spirits, snuff, hemp, and cordage was also enacted, as well as an export duty of four shillings per hogshead of tobacco. If this combination of taxes proved inadequate to pay the interest and one-eighth of the principal on the certificates issued to the troops, the shortfall was to be covered by money derived from the state's poll tax on slaves. (Hening, *Statutes*, 11: 197, 202, 227–28)

6. Hoping to keep the mutineers from taking food from farmers along their route home, Governor Harrison requested that a commissary be dispatched to join the dragoons with money to feed them. He also recommended that Col. George Baylor, the former commander of these dragoons, be recalled to active duty. As Baylor was in poor health, however, the General Assembly asked instead that Daniel Morgan be sent with "such officers as he may think necessary, and a commissary," to take charge of these troops. (Virginia, House of Delegates, *Journal*, May 1783, pp. 25, 26) A short time later, Harrison received NG's letter of 21 May, above, demanding that the mutineers be arrested and punished. (Vol. 12: 676) Before Harrison could act, however, Arthur Lee apparently told him that Congress, on 24 April, had directed that the troops of the Southern Army, including the dragoons, be sent "back within their respective states." (Madison, *Papers*, 7: 98n; *JCC*, 24: 275) It was thus Congress that could be seen to have recommended the pardoning of these troops if they would surrender and "deliver up" their horses. (*JCC*, 24: 389n, 400–401; PCC, item 137, vol. 2: 557, DNA) Sgt. William Dangerfield, the leader of the mutineers, was never arrested.

7. As seen in the note immediately above, Harrison worked actively in the mutineers' behalf. He wrote the Virginia delegates to Congress on 31 May that he had "sharply reprimande[d]" the mutineers "for their conduct but promised in consideration of their past Services to overlook it as far as it related to me. They are really a band of heroes who have performed great & meritorious Services, and I am Satisfied would not have taken this rash Step if their Sufferings had not been very great." (Madison, *Papers*, 7: 97) Harrison's assertions to Pendleton thus appear to have been less than candid.

8. On NG's health, see his letter to Washington of 5 June, above. On the vessels that were to transport part of the Southern Army's troops, see NG to Morris, 11 July, above.

9. It appears from Pendleton's letter of 12 August, below, that he hoped to see NG while the latter was traveling through Virginia.

*   *   *

¶ [TO GOVERNOR BENJAMIN GUERARD OF SOUTH CAROLINA. From Charleston, S.C., 22 July 1783. In a letter similar to the one he wrote to Lyman Hall on 23 July, below, NG announces that his "command is now at a stop." He cannot leave, however, without offering his best wishes to the "good people of this State," who now enjoy "liberty and property where but a short time past nothing but oppression and tyranny prevailed."[1] Asks that the "suffering Soldier" receive some of "that benefit, which the community now enjoy from the blessings of peace and independence"; pledges his continued willingness to render the state "every service." ADfS (MiU-C) 2 pp.]

1. Guerard replied to this letter on 12 August, below. NG set out for the North on 14 August. (NG to Washington, 8 August, below)

*   *   *

To John Dickinson, President of the Pennsylvania Council

Sir   [Charleston, S.C.] July 23ᵈ 1783

The bearer of this Mʳ Clarke an Inhabitant of the City of Philadelphia in the fore part of this war, left it with the british Army in the spring of 78 in order to try to get from the Barack Master the rents of a considerable number of houses occupied by the british Army during their stay in the City. He failed in his plan and was detained so long in the attempt as to render his return both difficult and uncertain. I shall not pretend to apologize for Mr Clarkes misstep in leaving the City, nor will his conduct perhaps appear altogether excusable while the british Army was with you. All that can be said is that it is the lot of mortals to err and it is the mark of an enlightened policy to forgive where examples are not essential for the public good. I believe it will be found Mr Clarke has been inoffensive in his conduct since he left your State, and while there only aided the british Army in such matters as were necessary to mitigate the calamaties incident to the situation of the people. He appears to be a man of morality tho he had the misfortune to mistake his politicks. He was introduced to my Acquaintance and warmly recommended by Lt Col John Lawrens [i.e., Laurens], who engaged him to furnish us with intelligence from Charlestown. This he did both before and after Col Lawrens's death until the british Army evacuated the place. This and other friendly Acts towards many of our unfortunate prisoners claims the attention of Government and I beg leave to recommend him in the warmest manner to your consideration and forgiveness. I know nothing more of him than what Col Lawrens told me, nor have I a wish but from public obligations and the feelings of humanity.[1] I have the honor to be with great respect Your Excellencys Most Obedt humble Ser   N GREENE

ADfS (MiU-C).

1. Clarke has not been further identified. Col. John Laurens oversaw American intelligence service in the South before his death in battle on 27 August 1782. (Gregory D. Massey, *John Laurens and the American Revolution* [Columbia: University of South Carolina Press, 2000], pp. 213–14; On Laurens's death, see Mordecai Gist to NG, 27 August 1782, above [vol. 11: 579–81 and n].) The British evacuated Charleston on 14 December 1782. (Vol. 12: 290–92n, above) No reply from Dickinson has been found. NG also wrote to Washington on Clarke's behalf on this date, below.

To Governor Lyman Hall of Georgia

Sir   Chas Town [S.C.] July 23^d 1783

I am closing the business of my command in this department. Hostilities having ceased and the Army been furloughed until the signing of the definitive treaty, my services are no longer necessary in this quarter; but I cannot think of taking my leave of your State in my public charactor without offering my best wishes for your happiness and prosperity.[1] It affords me the most pleasing contemplation to see the happy difference betwixt the situation of the people now and when I first came into this Country. All I wish is that the suffering Soldier may partake from the hands of Government a part of those blessings which the people now enjoy.

I have reason to hope for it both from your justice and generosity; and that measures will be early taken to enable Congress to settle satisfactorily with the Army. I feel more than a wish to express upon this occasion having often pledged my self to the Army that Government would do them compleat justice if not reward their services with liberality.

However fortune may dispose of me I shall omit no opportunity of rendering your State every service in my power.[2] I have the honor to be with great respect your Most Obedt humble Ser^t N GREENE

ADfS (NcD).

1. On the order for furloughing the Georgia troops, see NG to Habersham, 26 June, above.

2. NG wrote a similar letter to Gov. Benjamin Guerard of South Carolina on 22 July, above.

*   *   *

¶ [TO GEORGE WASHINGTON. From Charleston, S.C., 23 July 1783. In a letter similar to the one that he wrote to John Dickinson on this date, above, NG introduces Mr. Clarke, a man of "education[,] a good Moral charactor and of an inoffensive disposition." ADfS (MiU-C) 2 pp.]

*   *   *

From Charles Pettit

My dear Sir   Philadelphia 23^d July 1783

Your Favor of the 12^h Instant affords me a fresh Opportunity of expressing my particular Thankfulness. The Attention you have shewn to my Request, which seems to have carried you so fully into my Views and to have pervaded every Part of the Business I suggested to you, is a most pleasing Mark of distinguished Friendship, and of the Concern you take in my Interests.[1]

My Negociations with & for Messrs Banks[,] Burnet & Co were undertaken entirely on Mercantile Principles, in which, views of Profit are always the leading Motive.[2] The Expectations of Profit are reciprocal, and so far as we reason on Mercantile Principles only, Friendship interferes no otherwise than in the Choice of Correspondents, and prefering those whose Interests we wish to promote. Thus far I am persuaded it operated with Burnet in giving me the Agency of their Business; in other Respects the Contract was confined within the Bounds of mercantile ideas, without an Expectation of more than ordinary Liberality on either side. The Expectations of Profit on my Part were unusually small in Proportion to the Amount of the Negociations in View; and the Stipulations were thus made on the express Consideration of the Simplicity of the Business and a perfect freedom from either Advances or Risk on my Part. I find myself, nevertheless, in an early Stage of the Business, deeply involved in Engagements which a long & profitable Connection would hardly have called for, and which, even under such Circumstances, not only the Custom of Merchants, but the Principles of Honor, would have justified me in declining. But perceiving how much the Reputation & Interests of their House depended on the Steps I have taken for their Support, and relying on their taking Instant Measures to relieve me at any Expence of Exertion, from a Burden so improperly rested on me, I let my personal Friendship for Major Burnet, and my Feelings for the Honor and Prospects of a rising House, so far suppress the Suggestions of selfish Prudence as to take this Burden upon me. This was the Situation of the Affairs when I wrote to you on the 20th of June,[3] when my Engagements subjected me to the Risk of advancing 6000 Dollars more than I had any Funds for, either present or remote. Some of these Engagements, it is true, were distant as far as the Middle of September, and I confidently hoped that the next Conveyance from Charleston [S.C.] would have brought me Remittances to rest upon, so that I should suffer no Inconvenience farther than in opposing my Front to the Enemy for a Time, & that they would completely relieve me before the Day of Attack. How great then must be my Astonishment to find them daily reinforcing the Enemy, without sending me any Succours, or comparatively triffling ones. And yet this is truly the Case. They have sent me a parcel of small Bills to the amount of about twelve hundred Dollars, the Payment of which, at any fixed Time is uncertain, & have advised me of fresh Draughts upon me to more than ten times the Amount. Most of these have been presented. The Conflict is painful, but the Risk of accepting them is too great, and I am obliged to yield to the Necessity of declining it, tho' I have softened the Refusal as far as possible by giving all the Expectations I fairly can that the Draughts will be paid as they become due. As far as the Amount of the former Engagements, it may be in my Power to advance on the strength of my own Credit, if their failure to furnish me should make it necessary; tho' I cannot suppose they will treat me so unkindly. But to have accepted this last Flight of Bills would have subjected me to the Hazard of total Ruin in Case their Resourses should fail to come in Season. The Consideration that they are safe at Bottom and would repay the Money at an after day, is not sufficient. An acceptance on my Part would bind me to payment at the Day, without any other alternative than the Loss of Credit which could never again be regained; and no Consideration at my time of Life, especially of the Mercantile kind, ought to induce me to run such a Risk, nor would any reasonable Correspondent expect or even desire it; nor would a friendly one accept it if offered without a moral Certainty of warding off the Danger.

The Conduct of these Gentlemen distresses me the more as it in effect arraigns either my Judgment & Discretion, or theirs, very highly. I need not explain to you how & by what Means; the Circumstances cannot fail to be apparent to you. It is true they promise remittances & Indemnifications, as well as grateful Compensations; but as yet these Promises are general both as to Time and Manner, as well as Amount. They talk of large Resources & great Command of Produce on the coming in of the next Crop; and the Return of Capt Finley from the Havanna. But these must in their Nature be contingent and remote, and avail Nothing towards the Payment of accepted Bills becoming due at a particular Day in the mean time. I doubt whether a premium of ten per Cent would procure them the Cash here on such Contingent Expectances, with the addition of Landed Security. How then can they possibly expect me to engage in the Hazard of being obliged to procure such Advances on any Consideration whatever, much less on such as have yet been held out to me. They may be & I hope are making Profits equal to these extraordinary pushes; but where the Profits are to Center, there also should the Risk, the Burden & the Inconvenience be sustained; it is at once unjust and ungenerous to roll either upon other Shoulders.

Thus far I have opened my Mind to you as a Friend, and I feel a Relief in it. I want at once to prepare you to give me such friendly Advice and Information as you may think requisite; and to combat any murmuring or discontent which may arise on their part from Disappointment, or from misunderstanding either my Conduct or their own. At the same time I know not that anything will be requisite to be done on your part. Delicacy & even Prudence may perhaps require that you should seem to know nothing of the Matter, and I wish to avoid the least unnecessary wound to their Feelings. But, to say the least, their Conduct appears to me strange, and as yet unaccountable on any other Ground than a want of Knowledge & Experience in the Business they have undertaken, and they may think me not entitled to suggest this Mode of accounting for it. As yet my Esteem for & Desire to serve them is not impaired & it is my earnest wish to understand satisfactorily what at present appears mysterious[.] When Major Burnet left me, their Affairs in my Hands were in good Condition.[4] He had not been long enough in Charleston when Capt [Matthew] Strong sailed, to be thoroughly informed of everything.[5] As soon as he gets such Knowledge, his Candor & his Friendship for me cannot fail to induce him, as well for his own sake as mine, to place our Concerns on a proper Footing. I tremble at the Consequence of a Number of their Bills returning protested; but I cannot risk my own Destruction to save them from, perhaps but a comparatively small Inconvenience.[6]

I commit myself on this Occasion to your Discretion in which I have at least as much Confidence as in my own. To say I have more would look like affected humility, though I believe I could say it with Truth. You will make no Disclosures without real Occasion, and then with that Delicacy & Discretion which marks your Conduct on all the Occasions I have seen toward equals & Inferiors. I say Nothing about Congress.[7]

I shall write to you again about some other Matters.[8]

I was near omitting to reply to a material part of your Letter. I mean the proposed Draught on me for £500 stirling payable in January next. Such a Draught would hardly be of any use.[9] The Bank will not advance Money ordinarily for more than 30 Days. It must be an Act of special Grace & Favour if they exceed it, & 60 Days is the outside. To obtain an Advance from them, there must be two Persons of good Credit in this Town or within their Reach, answerable for the Repayment as Drawers, Indorsers or Acceptors; and they consider anything more than 1000 Dollars to one Man, as a large Advance, be the Security ever so good. It is not therefore as a Thing of Course that Money can be taken up at the Bank, nor can individuals obtain it in very large Sums. And whenever it is obtained, Payment at the stipulated Day must be as certain as the Sun. Any Person who pushes for large Sums, or is found Shifty in getting Cash from the Bank by as many Channels as he can, will be marked & perhaps suspected. A Man who is tenacious of his Credit will therefore be cautious in this use of it.[10]

RC (MiU-C). As the manuscript ends without a complimentary closing or signature, it is likely that at least the final page is missing

1. NG's letter was probably in reply to one of 20 June that Pettit mentioned in the present letter. Neither has been found.

2. Pettit was representing John Banks and one of his partners, NG's former aide and Pettit's friend Ichabod Burnet, in their dealings with Robert Morris as contractors to the Southern Army. (See also Pettit to NG, 23 May, above, and Morris to NG, 5 August, below, as well as a letter on this subject that Pettit wrote to Jeremiah Wadsworth on 16 March 1788. [Syrett, *Hamilton*, 10: 455–58]) Entries in Morris's diary such as those for 31 May, 5 August, 1 and 4 September, 30 October, and 25 November help to trace Pettit's efforts on behalf of the partners—principally Banks, as it turned out, for Burnet died a few months after Pettit wrote the present letter. (Morris, *Papers*, 8: 136, 383, 480, 493, 679, 779, 780n; see

also Morris to NG, 5 August, and NG to Pierce, 15 October, both below.) As seen further in this paragraph, Pettit's involvement with the firm was probably due in part to his friendships with Burnet and NG. When last in Philadelphia, Burnet had been deeply disappointed by Morris's refusal to let Banks and him supply provisions to the fleet carrying Southern Army troops home on terms stipulated in Banks's contract with the army. (Burnet to NG, 23 May) As seen in note 4, below, Pettit apparently did not know at this time that NG was a guarantor for Banks's and Burnet's contract with the army. (On NG's role, see especially NG to Benjamin Lincoln, 19 December 1782, and Agreement between Hunter, Banks and Company and NG with Newcomen and Collett, 8 April, above [vol. 12: 306–7 and n, 591 and n] as well as NG to Lee, 22 August 1785, below.)

3. The letter of 20 June has not been found.

4. This was presumably in late May. (See Burnet to NG and Pettit to NG, both 23 May.) However, Burnet wrote one of his firm's creditors, James Warrington, from Philadelphia on 31 May: "It is to me a very disagreeable circumstance to mention that even [our?] reasonable expectation[s?] of making a speedy and considerable payment to you have failed." He assured Warrington that "the funds arising from" the provisions contract would be "appropriated to the fullfiling our engagements with you," and added: "Measures have been taken to place them in the hands of Mr Pettit with directions to hold them subject to your orders. There cannot I apprehend be any payment made before the 15th of July next." (MiU-C) In a meeting with Burnet and Pettit on 31 May, Morris had "told them to make themselves easy they might go and receive the Money for such [bills] as are already due and that I hope to pay the rest as they become due." (Diary entry for 31 May, Morris, *Papers*, 8: 136; see also the note at Morris to NG, 5 August, below.) In his letter to Wadsworth of 16 March 1788, Pettit wrote that Banks's and Burnet's

> "remittances to me, by other means, were considerable; but their drafts upon me greatly exceeded them; insomuch that I held some of their bills in suspense, after having accepted more than their funds in my hands, exclusive of the contract-money, would warrant. They urged me very pressingly to give a prompt acceptance to all their bills, promising ample resources to support them, and intimating, that the contract-money would be a security in my hands, if other resources should fail. It so happened, that I took up all their bills, which became due, in June and July, without breaking in upon the contract-money; and early in August, I paid to the British merchants, on account of their claims, twenty two thousand eight hundred and seventy five dollars, being all the contract money which had then come to my hands. Their drafts on me continued to increase, beyond their provision for the payment of them; and, in order to induce me to accept them, they gave me direct instructions, to apply the contract money to the payment of them, if I should find it necessary, intimating, that their contracts with the British merchants were not strictly payable till the first of November, and that, before that time, they should turn into my hands, six thousand pounds sterling from the Havannah, and ten thousand pounds sterling from Virginia, besides other remittances." (Syrett, *Hamilton*, 10: 456–57)

It was soon after that, when Pettit "found it necessary to apply some of the contract-money to other purposes," that he learned from one of the creditors, Warrington, that NG was "Banks's security for the money" and that failure to indemnify the merchants "would injure General Greene." (Ibid., p. 457) Pettit continued:

> "Out of the next instalment of the contract-money, I paid to the British merchants four thousand two hundred and twenty two dollars; the rest, I was obliged to apply to the payment of drafts which I had accepted. This last payment to the British merchants (which was the last they received from me) was in October 1783. Some time after which I understood, from several of Mr. Banks's letters to me, that they had ob-

tained other payments and securities, for the residue of their respective claims; but, in what manner, I was never particularly informed. I rested satisfied, however, that it was done, and that General Greene was made safe in the business, till some time after Mr. Banks had drawn the whole money out of my hands. He had drawn, indeed, for abundantly more, than he had any pretensions to, though I was lucky enough to decline acceptances, in time to save myself from going beyond my resources." (Ibid.)

5. Strong, who made frequent voyages between Philadelphia and Charleston, is known to have arrived in Charleston on 1 June and to have sailed from Philadelphia for Charleston on or about 27 July. (Finney, "Diary," p. 152; Pettit to NG, 27 July, below) As Burnet could not have left Philadelphia before 1 June at the earliest, Pettit most likely referred to a voyage that began later in June or earlier in July than the dates mentioned here.

6. NG wrote Pettit on 29 July, below, that Burnet "informs me to receive all the money due them upon the contract and that no more bills are to be drawn on you at any rate. This will leave you safe and at liberty to do justice to your interest." As seen in notes 2 and 4, above, Burnet died within the next few months, and additional bills were drawn on Pettit.

7. Pettit alluded here to NG's discretion—or lack thereof—in some of his past dealings with Congress. (See, for example, NG's letter of resignation as quartermaster general [NG to Samuel Huntington, 26 July 1780, above (vol. 6: 155–57)], and the headnote at that letter [ibid., pp. 150–55].)

8. See Pettit to NG, 26 July, below.

9. The purpose of the "proposed Draught" is not known.

10. According to historian E. James Ferguson, the primary purpose of the Bank of North America "was to make short-term loans to the government." (Ferguson, *Power of the Purse*, p. 137) The manuscript of Pettit's letter ends here. NG replied to Pettit on 4 August, below.

From Samuel A. Otis

Sir   Boston [Mass.] July 24 1783

I have no doubt of your wishes to do justice to all concern[d] in your negotiations, but the agency has turned out unfortunately, & haveing advanced all my stock I lay at the mercy of others, than which no situation can be more disagreeable.[1] I will not however distress you with my importunity assured you will do your utmost for my relief.

A glorious period indeed is put to the military career of those worthies whom providence has called forth to deliver their Country, But the people are not at present in a temper or indeed have they ability to compensate them. In my opinion however it will soon take place if prudence & good policy guide our councils.

I congratulate Col Morris upon his prospects[2] and am obliged to M[rs] G for her polite notice,[3] but your good constitution & younger life would put me out of all patience, Could such exalted merits be induced on my part as would make it less than presumption in me to aspire at the relief of General G, and therfore under these circumstances were it possible for the lady to have an imperfection, I should attribute her postscript to a cruel sporting with dispair, But am determined to evince a spec of magnanimity upon the occasion, at least that am not revengful, and assure her that it will constitute no small part of the happyness of my life, and that it is my sincerest wish, that you may glide happily thro life together, and if it were possible for so much vivacity to know old age, that it may be in its most advanced periods before either of you "take the leap in the dark."

You doubtless have heared that our friend Griffin is gone to Europe.[4] I hope a vixen who plays tricks with everybody will in future be more propitious.[5]

In hope I shall not make you regret a correspondence your permission of which does me honor & pleasure I am very sincerely your most humble Ser[t]   SAM A OTIS

RCS (MiU-C).

1. Otis, a Boston merchant, was a part-owner of the *Flora*, a vessel in which the Greene family partnership, Jacob Greene & Company, was heavily invested. (See Griffin Greene to NG, 8 October 1780, above [vol. 6: 357].) As seen in Jacob Greene's letter to NG of 4 May, above, the firm had been nearly ruined by its investment in the *Flora* and by the unwillingness of investors in Boston, whom Jacob called the "Eastern owners," to lay out money for additional expenses in fitting out the *Flora*. (Vol. 12: 641–42) NG presumably had asked Otis to increase his stake in the *Flora*.

2. On Col. Lewis Morris, Jr.'s, "prospects," see NG to Williams, 2 July, above.

3. CG's letter to Otis has not been found.

4. On Griffin Greene's trip to Europe, see his letter to NG of 18 May, above (vol. 12: 663).

5. The "vixen" was Dame Fortune.

*   *   *

¶ [FROM ALEXANDER GARDEN, Philadelphia, 25 July 1783. He has learned about NG's recovery with "particular pleasure" from Col. [Josiah] Harmar, who just arrived from South Carolina.[1] The "uneasiness" that NG's "friends experienced while they were uncertain" about his "health exists no longer." Garden hopes that "as the Seasoning, to which Strangers are ever subject is now over," NG will "never again experience any ill consequences from the climate." He is pleased to inform NG about CG's health. She is "no longer expecting" NG's "immediate arrival" in Philadelphia and "intends in a few days to go to New York, to embark from thence to Rhode Island."[2] Garden will go with her and "from time to time" will inform NG "of whatever occurs that may be interesting." He reports that in Philadelphia "for four days past the thermometer has stood at upwards of 90 degrees, during which time near sixty persons have perish'd on the streets. The water is so very cold, that it proves destructive to all who drink it when heated by exercise." RCS (NjMoHP) 2 pp.]

1. On NG's recent illness, see his letter to Washington of 5 June, above. Harmar had sailed with Pennsylvania Continental troops from Charleston, S.C., on 11 July. On the arrival of those troops in Philadelphia, see note at Morris to NG, first letter of 1 August, below.

2. CG was about to leave Philadelphia when Garden wrote NG on 3 August, below.

¶ [FROM CHARLES PETTIT, Philadelphia, 26 July 1783. He hoped to write "at more Leisure" but has had "much serious Business to prepare for this Conveyance" and must divide his attention between "the Ladies" and "the most urgent Calls of Business or distant Friends."[1] He adds that Capt. [Matthew]

Strong "will positively sail in the morning, it is now nine in the Evening, and I must yet write some other Letters." NG knows "what it is to write by Candle light in a warm Evening," and that should "form any Apology you may think this will stand in need of." CG "will tell her own Story, and if she tells the Truth & the whole Truth concerning herself, it will be so clever" that Pettit will not try "to embellish it."[2] As far as George is concerned, Pettit finds "some Occasion to be serious," as he thinks it "expedient to let him go with his Mamma, on her Promise that she will immediatly place him at a School, strongly recommended by Col [Jeremiah] Wadsworth, which I understand to be somewhere between Hartford [Conn.] & R[hode]. Island, about 60 miles from the latter."[3] Pettit will not discuss the reasons for this in detail but will "mention some of the heads":

> The Doctor's Demand, if persisted in, as it probably will be, would be sufficient of itself.[4] It is rendered more strikingly so by the small-ness of the extra Benefit the Child would probably receive by re-maining with him. This Probability is inferred from what I have heard since he has been there, and the various accounts I have heard respecting other Children, and the Opinions of divers of our Friends whose Information on the Subject is better than mine respecting the Doctor's Avocations & the little personal Attention they permit him to pay to those who are under his Care. This being the Case there seems to be no Choice but to let George go with his Mamma & per-mit the Doctor to form his own Opinions of her maternal Fondness, which he will probably fix upon as the moving Cause of what he will call our Folly. If I should keep him here, or send him to any other Place, the Doctor would be more likely to place an ill Picture of you in his Mind even though it should torment his Gizzard, and I am persuaded you would not wish his Enmity.[5]

Pettit is sending an account [not found], by which he finds his "engagements stand at upwards of 4500 Dol^s more than the Funds, but as the payments are not yet due I hope our Friends will enable me in due Time, not only to make these Payments but to take up the Bills for upwards of 14 M [i.e., thousand] which are not yet accepted, meanwhile I intend, in confidence of this, to pay what Contract Money I may receive as they have directed. If they should leave me subject to any advances I shall find Occasion for Exertion."[6] He has bought a pair of horses for CG at a cost, including that for a phaeton, of $733 ⅓. A chariot is also being built, which, "with some other matters," will cost about "as much more." Pettit mentions "these Disbursements" only because he may be financially "streight-ened in a Month or two."[7] He thinks he has informed NG that he was unable to get "the Payment for the Iron Works" and that he therefore "repurchased part of them last Winter."[8] Improvements there have been costly, "and the Peace puts a stop to present advantages besides striking dead a considerable Stock. In an-other Year they may again be worked to Advantage with a proper Capital, but they require more than I can command; in the mean Time they are such a constant Drain that they keep me constantly poor and needy." He now thinks "it best to sell out, & as M^r [Joseph] Ball will not hold nor manage them without me, we have advertized the whole for Sale. We expect for the Estate & Stock on hand about £12000 (32000 Dollars). To a Person who could employ about half as much more, as running Stock, they would be a good, and might be made a steady, profitable Interest, but though a business of that kind must be managed with Oeconomy, it will not bear to be starved; and to make it profitable it must be as well fed as your Horses."[9]

Believing it to be "in some Degree necessary," Pettit has "taken a Liberty" that NG probably "will not relish." When Maj. [Ichabod] Burnet was about to leave Philadelphia, he left NG's letter to Mr. Morris for Pettit to deliver. When Pettit found the letter, he decided not to give it to Morris.[10] He adds:

"You will readily believe I wish not to embezzle the Money; but in the Distress of the public Finances, undue Exercises of Power are too apt to be used to ease them, regardless of the private Injuries such measures may occasion. The Detention of this Money in my Hands is perfectly just in itself, and while it is not known to the Public Agents, even a supposed Injury is not felt. I do not know, nor can hardly suspect that M^r M[orris] would urge the Inconvenience I apprehend if he knew the whole; but it might be made a subject of disagreeable Discussion at least, by some others if not by him, under their present Difficulties, & therefore I wish it to remain for a while in Silence, especially while my Agency for the Contractors obliges me to negotiate Business at the Treasury.[11] These Reasons act powerfully on me. With respect to you these farther Considerations occur. I wish to be freed from the charge of suppressing your Letters. In every other Part I shall willingly take the whole on myself and avow it as far as shall be necessary at the proper Time. Mr M. professedly avoids paying any Debts contracted before his Administration; he ought therefore to leave the Funds of the same Period out of his Acc^{ts}. These Funds are of that kind, and the Bills I delivered up to him were cancelled, as he told me, instead of being sold to raise money. I therefore presume that he will be as well contented to know nothing of the Matter. If this Balance had arisen from Funds issued under his Administration, I should think differently of the Matter in point of Policy, tho' the Justice abstractedly as to myself would be the same. For these Reasons I do not apprehend your Honor so much concerned to make the Disclosure, as you have seemed to apprehend. But after all I must submit it to your Determination. I would wish to be as jealous of your Honour & Reputation as of my own; but perhaps the feelings of Interest may suggest a mode of Reasoning to me which I should not think so good in other Circumstances."[12]

The *Congress* reached Amsterdam and is probably on her return voyage now.[13] Wadsworth, who is just leaving for France, has left a letter for Pettit to forward to NG.[14] RC (MiU-C) 4 pp.]

1. "The Ladies" were presumably Pettit's wife and daughters.

2. CG apparently did not write to NG about her visit to Philadelphia. In a letter of 4 August, below, NG chided her for not writing and for the purchases that Pettit expressed concern about in the present letter. (See also NG to CG, 7 August, below.)

3. As seen by his letter to Pettit of 29 July, below, NG thought CG, on her way back to

Rhode Island, would remove their son George from Dr. John Witherspoon's school near Princeton, N.J. George was apparently enrolled in the Connecticut school recommended by Wadsworth the next year. (NG to Pettit, 23 June 1784, below)

4. Witherspoon had asked for 100 guineas per year for George's schooling. (Witherspoon to NG, 18 February, above [vol. 12: 462])

5. On this, see also Pettit to NG, 4 August, below. William Pierce, Jr., who had just returned to Charleston, S.C., from Philadelphia, wrote NG on 17 August, below: "You will be disappointed in seeing Mrs Greene at Philadelphia. She has long since taken her departure for Rhode Island, and carried with her her Son George."

6. "Our friends" were undoubtedly Southern Army contractors John Banks and Ichabod Burnet, who had retained Pettit as their agent. (Pettit to NG, 23 July, above) "Contract Money" was presumably money that the government owed them. Pettit hoped to use it to recover funds they had drawn on him. (Ibid.)

7. After learning about CG's purchases, which had been charged to his partnership account with Pettit, NG reproached her for adding to his financial problems. (NG to CG, 4 August)

8. As seen in Pettit's letter to NG of 19 August 1782, above, Joseph Ball, previously the manager of the Batsto Iron Works, had run into difficulties in attempting to purchase Pettit's and NG's shares in the business. (Vol. 11: 562)

9. The Batsto property was advertised in the Philadelphia *Independent Gazetteer* of 5 July. Failing to find a buyer, Pettit later decided to involve himself more directly in operating the iron works. (Pettit to NG, 13 March 1784, below)

10. The letter was most likely NG's to Morris of 21 April, above, suggesting that Morris and Pettit settle the dispute over bills of exchange on Morris that Burnet had left with Pettit by NG's order in late 1781. (Vol. 12: 629; for more about the bills, see Morris to NG, 7 November 1781 [vol. 9: 544 and n], and Burnet to Pettit, 12 April 1782 [vol. 11: 39, 41n], both above.) Wishing to hold the bills as surety for payments that the government owed him, Pettit had also declined to deliver an earlier letter on this subject, which NG wrote to Morris soon after the evacuation of Charleston. (See NG to Morris, 20 December 1782, and Pettit to NG, 8 February 1783, both above [vol. 12: 320 and n, 425].) For further developments, see Pettit to NG, after 21 January 1784, below.

11. As seen in note 6, above, and in his letter to NG of 23 July, Pettit was negotiating with Morris on behalf of Banks and Burnet as contractors to the Southern Army.

12. NG replied on 9 August, below.

13. Pettit and NG owned shares in the *Congress*. On the voyage, see also Pettit to NG, 8 and 26 February, above (vol. 12: 425–26, 479–80), and 4 August, below.

14. Wadsworth's letter is immediately below.

¶ [FROM JEREMIAH WADSWORTH, Philadelphia, 26 July 1783. He is "mortified" that he will not be able to see NG before sailing for Lorient, France, the next day; plans to be "at London in November, & return next Spring."[1] Encloses an "Estimate" of the "Stock" of Barnabas Deane & Company.[2] Has paid two bills drawn on him by NG, "amounting to three thousand dollars."[3] If it is "convenient" for NG to repay this amount when he gets to Philadelphia, Wadsworth asks him to "purchase Bank Shares," if they are "to be had at the original price." Wadsworth has "vested a considerable part" of his "fortune in the bank."[4] Asks in a postscript that NG write him in Paris "to the care of Messrs Lecouteal & C° Banquiers"; letters addressed to him in London should be directed to "[lay in?] the Post office till called for."[5] RCS (CtHi) 2 pp.]

1. According to the *DAB*, Wadsworth went to France to submit a report on his dealings as a supplier to the French army in America, and he later purchased merchandise in England and Ireland.

2. Wadsworth and NG were silent partners with Deane in Barnabas Deane & Company, which was formed in April 1779 to engage in trade and privateering. (See Articles of Partnership between NG, Wadsworth, and Deane, 4 April 1779, above [vol. 3: 377–79]; NG to Wadsworth, 14 April 1779 [ibid., p. 403]; and Destler, "Wadsworth," p. 113.) NG wrote CG on 4 August, below: "Col Wadsworth informs me that all my stocks put into his hands have been lost; and that out of upwards of a thousand pounds put into his hands four years ago, I have not fifty left." Deane sent a copy of the estimate to NG on 4 January 1784, below, commenting: "You will See by the inclos'd the Number of Heavy Losses we met Since Sep[r] 1781." (See also Deane to NG, 26 February 1784, below.) Under the 1779 articles of partnership, NG and Wadsworth were each to invest £10,000, and Deane, after an initial investment of £4,000, was to "pay Interest unto the Other Partners for the Partnership Untill he Shall furnish his Equal Proportion of Stock." (Vol. 3: 378) According to Wadsworth's biographer, though, "Wadsworth subscribed £17,333, Deane £14,707, and Greene £8,333 of which Wadsworth advanced £5,000. Wadsworth's investment had a specie value of £883." (Destler, "Wadsworth," p. 113)

3. On this debt, see also Wadsworth to NG, 13 June, above, and NG to Pettit, 4 August, below.

4. According to the editors of the Morris Papers, Wadsworth and his partner John Carter [i.e., John Barker Church] "eventually became the two largest stockholders under the first subscription to the Bank of North America," purchasing many of their shares from other investors at discounted prices. (Morris, *Papers*, 7: 308n)

5. NG's next known letter to Wadsworth is that of 4 November, below. Wadsworth replied to it from Paris on 21 December, below.

*   *   *

To Charles Pettit

Dear Sir   Head quarters Charles Town [S.C.] July 29th 1783.
    Since I wrote you before Major [Ichabod] Burnet informs me that they have shiped you for sale effects to a considerable amount to supply you with funds; but on the other hand [John] Banks has drawn on you to a large amount. However a power is sent you[,] the Major informs me[,] to receive all the money due them upon the contract and that no more bills are to be drawn on you at any rate. This will leave you safe and at liberty to do justice to your interest.[1] The Major is going to the West Indies [and] to the Havannah and perhaps less care will be taken to furnish you with funds after he is gone than now, it may not be amiss therefore to take a little care how you admit drafts on you contrary to the powers of appropriation given you for the contract monies.[2]
    All the Soldiers have embarked and sailed for their respective States; and I am left like Samson after Delilah cut his locks.[3] I am become quite like another Man. I am sorry to see such a spirit of mobing and Committee business going on through the Continent. It looks as if we were not satisfied with our Governments and hankered after another revolution. The spirit of Philadelphia has transplanted it self here. Doctor Fallen that Jesuit and disturber of all good Government is a busy Man in this business. It is happy for society he is a great coward or else he might do

much mischief having abilities well suited to the purp[ose].[4] We hear of Congress having fled to Prince Town and that the Soldiers had collected in great numbers in Philadelphia and held them prisoners some hours before they went off[.][5] Perhaps good may come out of evil. It may serve as a spur to the States for supplying their quota and laying a foundation for funding the public debts.[6] Fear will sometimes produce what justice cannot effect. At present we are very much in the dark in the history of this business, and impatient to hear further particulars; but I shall leave this so soon that unless I meet it on the road, I must remain in ignorance until I get to Philadelphia.

How did you and Mrs Greene manage the matter with Doctor Witherspoon? I hope for Georges stay; but the price and Mrs Greenes desire to take him home with her leave me little room to expect it.[7] I am also uncertain whether Mrs Greene has left Philadelphia as she seemed to hint at staying there until my arrival. If she is with you please to deliver her the inclosed letter; but if she is gone to Rhode Island forward it to her.[8] Present me affectionately to Mrs Pettit and the family and also to Governor Read.[9] I am dear Sir with esteem & affection yours sincerely

N GREENE

ALS (NHi).

1. As seen by Pettit's letters to NG of 23 and 26 July, above, the financial problems that Pettit had encountered as the agent in Philadelphia for Southern Army contractors Banks and Burnet—and that NG would continue to experience as a guarantor of their debts—had not been resolved. NG wrote Pettit about this again on 4 August, below.

2. Burnet died at Havana not long afterward. (Flagg to NG, 17 October, below)

3. On the troops' embarkation, see NG's letters to Benjamin Lincoln, Robert Morris and George Washington of 11 July, above.

4. On the sources of unrest in Charleston in the summers of both 1783 and 1784, see notes at Pendleton to NG, 18 April 1784, and second letter of 10 July 1784, both below. NG also mentioned the mob activity of 1783 in a letter to Washington, 8 August, below. Dr. James O'Fallon (or "Fallon"), who led public protests in Charleston during the summers of 1783 and 1784, was "a known rabble-rouser, in trouble with authority wherever he settled." (Meleney, *Aedanus Burke*, p. 108) O'Fallon, a native of Ireland, had served as a surgeon with the Pennsylvania Continental line and had set up a practice in Charleston after the war. He also served as secretary of the Anti-Britannic Society, of which Alexander Gillon was president. (John Carl Parish, "The Intrigues of Doctor James O'Fallon," *Mississippi Valley Historical Review* 17 [September 1930]: 230–35) In a letter of 17 July 1784, below, Lewis Morris, Jr., identified O'Fallon as a principal instigator of the Charleston mobs in the summer of 1784.

5. See note at William Pierce to NG, 19 June, above.

6. On the quotas that Congress had requested from each state that year, see *JCC*, 24: 231.

7. See Pettit to NG, 4 August, below.

8. As seen in ibid., CG left Philadelphia on 3 August.

9. Pettit's brother-in-law Joseph Reed had been the president of the Pennsylvania Executive Council, serving, in effect, as the governor of the state. (Vol. 2: 308n)

*   *   *

¶ [FROM ROGER PARKER SAUNDERS, [Charleston, S.C.], 29 July 1783. He "purchas'd a Grind Stone" for NG's plantation "at Mr Crouches Sale." Does not remember the amount but asks if NG will be "kind enough to settle it with M^r [Hext] McCall, one of the Executors."[1] RCS (MiU-C) 1 p.]

1. Saunders was handling NG's plantation affairs in South Carolina. In preparing rice for market, grinding stones were used in the "pounding process" to remove the kernels from the husks. (Bagwell, *Rice Gold*, p. 94) On the sale of Henry Crouch's estate, see Saunders to NG, 7 June, above. On McCall, an attorney in Charleston, see also Flagg to NG, 17 October, below.

*   *   *

From Robert Morris, Superintendent of Finance

Sir   Office of Finance [Philadelphia] 1st Augt 1783.

I have received your favor of the eleventh of last month and have the Pleasure to inform you that I hear the Troops are safely arrived in the Chesapeak[.][1] Of Course all Expences with you will have ceased before this Time. The situation of the Officers was undoubtedly of a Nature to excite every Sentiment in their favor but I am not certain that their Brethern will not feel somewhat hurt at what may be conceived a kind of Preference. One Thing I am certain of [is] that even so small a Sum as four thousand Dollars is four thousand Dollars more than I know where to find or how to get at.[2] That you may form a Judgment more easily on this subject I enclose a State of accounts up to the last Day of June.[3] The Information you give as to the Ballance due by M^r [John] Banks is (so far) very pleasing to me as it will lessen the Sum which they are about to press upon me for an account of the Continent.

I approve entirely of your Design to sell the Cloathing and Hospital stores for altho I am very well aware that these Things will go much under Value yet I am as well perswaded that to keep them would cost more than they would ever fetch.

Before I close this Letter I must mention a little mistake which Mr Banks seems to be under about the advance of Captn [i.e., Lt. John] Hamilton. Mr Banks having received £2500 Sterling of public Money more than he was entitled to proposes to receive £2500 Sterling more to repay the Officer from whom he received it.[4] I am Sir your most obed^t & humble Servant   ROB^T MORRIS

RCS (CSmH).

1. For more about the subjects discussed in this letter, see NG to Morris, 11 July, above, reporting Commodore James Nicholson's arrival in Charleston, S.C., with vessels to transport Southern Army troops to their home states. The *Pennsylvania Packet* of 26 July reported that "a detachment of the Pennsylvania line, commanded by Lieutenant Colonel [Josiah] Harmar," had arrived from Charleston on 24 July. The remaining Pennsylvania soldiers reached Philadelphia on Saturday, 2 August. (*Pennsylvania Packet*, 5 August; see also Reed to NG, 3 August, and Pettit to NG, 4 August, both below.)

2. See NG to Morris, 11 July.

3. The enclosure was undoubtedly "A State of the Receipt and Expenditures of the Super-intendent of Finance for January 1 to June 30, 1783," showing an excess of $1,074,153.67 in "Payments beyond the Receipts." The listed expenditures included $101,802.32 for "Major General Greene's drafts for the support of the Army in the Southern Department." (The statement is reproduced in Morris, *Papers*, 8: 240–41.)

4. See NG to Morris, 11 July.

*   *   *

¶ [FROM ROBERT MORRIS, SUPERINTENDENT OF FINANCE, Office of Finance [Philadelphia], 1 August 1783. In reply to NG's letter of 10 July about Col. [Thaddeus] Kosciuszko's affairs [not found], Kosciuszko's "acknowledged Merit and Services joined to [NG's] warm interposition in his favor" make Morris "Wish to render the adjustment of his Affairs equal to his most sanguine Expectations." NG's letter to Congress on this subject has also been referred to Morris, however, and, consistent with his duty, he has pointed out "the Danger of excepting Individuals out of the general Rules."[1] He adds that granting Kosciuszko's request "is a thing which I cannot do but Congress may. Should they think proper to make a special order I shall be very happy to carry it into Execution."[2] LB (DLC) 1 p.]

1. As seen above in NG's letter of 10 July to Elias Boudinot, the president of Congress, Kosciuszko planned to return to Europe and had asked to have his pay and other accounts "put upon such a footing as to enable him to reduce it all to ready money." (See also NG to Kosciuszko, 10 July, above. Kosciuszko's situation is discussed in Haiman, *Kosciuszko*, pp. 142–48.) Congress sent this request to Morris on 26 July. (*JCC*, 24: 447) In his report, dated 1 August, Morris referred to a rule adopted in 1781 that entitled foreigners who had served with the American armies—and, as they were not attached to any state line, were unable "to obtain a Recompence for the Depreciation of Pay actually received"—to one-fifth of their pay to the end of that year "in Lieu of Depreciation, and to place the remaining four fifths on Interest." This rule, according to Morris, had "been found satisfactory" and had placed the foreigners "on an equal footing with their Brethren who were Citizens of the United States." Experience, Morris added, had shown that only "strict adherence" to a general rule such as this could "prevent those Com-plaints of Injustice which the want of Pay to the Army in general has given but too much Ground for and which can alone be repressed by a Conviction that the public have not ability to Discharge the whole and that there is an inviolable Determination of Govern-ment to make proportionate Distribution of what may be within their ability." (The report is printed in Morris, *Papers*, 8: 363–64.) Despite Kosciuszko's merits, talent, and zeal, Morris argued, it would undoubtedly be necessary, if his request were granted, to comply with those of "other officers of Merit, Talents and Zeal." (The report is printed in *JCC*, 24: 488–89.)

2. In his report to Congress, Morris commented that it was "the Exclusive Priviledge of the Sovereign" to "mark and distinguish the Degrees of Activity, Knowledge, Ground and Enthusiasm which their Different Servants are endowed with" and to "declare the Rewards to be bestowed on the most eminent." He concluded, however, that "in Claims for Justice all must stand on equal Ground and distressed as they are [Congress] will naturally conceive that the duties of Justice must preceed those of Generosity." (*JCC*, 24: 489) Congress did not choose "Generosity" in Kosciuszko's case, and NG later tried again to intercede on his behalf. (See Morris to NG, 19 December, below.) When Kosciuszko left the United States in July 1784, he had received a brevet promotion to brigadier general but

had been paid with a "certificate for $12,280.49, bearing interest at six per cent, from January 1, 1784." (Haiman, *Kosciuszko*, pp. 153–54, 156–58, 161–65)

*   *   *

To General Benjamin Lincoln, Secretary at War

D[r] Sir   [Headquarters, Charleston, S.C., 2 August 1783]

I send you the Commisaries returns with copies of his letters and Certificates of the commanding office[r]s of Corps.[1] I wish the Commisary could have rendered a more perfect account; but it will not appear strange when it is considered that a great part of the time the Army had not paper to do the business much less to make seperate returns. After I took command of the army the officers drew only one ration until after the arrival of the Pennsylvania line and for some time after except that line but the officers of that line said the officers of the Northern Army drew two which induced me to give those to the Southward the same priviledge.[2]

The Commisary of Military Stores has deposited all the ordnance Arms and Military Stores in the Arsenal of this State and will forward a return to the war office and wait your further orders. He is getting the Arms cleaned and the Carriages painted.[3] The inspector is examining the business and will report upon it as well as the Clothiers and Purveyors departments[.] The Stores and clothing in both have been sold at public vendue and an account will be rendered of the Sales as soon as possible.[4] I thought it much better to sell the Articles than keep them on hand as there would be a constant waste and expence attending the business. I have been influenced from Motives of oconomy and hope it will meet your approbation.

The Troops are all gone and the business of every department will be closed in a few days. Most of the Agents in each department are already discharged; and I expect the rest will before I leave here which will be in Eight or ten days.[5] I am with great respect Your Most Obed humble Ser[t]

N GREENE

ADfS (MiU-C).

1. NG had found it difficult to obtain acceptable returns from the former commissary, John Kean. (See above, NG to Lincoln, first letter of 3 June, and 18 June; NG to Kean, 15 and 28 June; and Kean to NG, 4 July.)

2. See NG to Lincoln, 3 June, above.

3. The "Return of Military Stores at Charles Town" was dated 1 August. (WRMS) Col. Christian Senf had been the Southern Army's commissary of military stores until recently. (See, however, Mentges to NG, 6 August, below.)

4. See Mentges to NG, 6 August.

5. NG left Charleston to travel to the North on 14 August. (See note at NG to Washington, 8 August, below.)

*   *   *

¶ **FROM ALEXANDER GARDEN**, Philadelphia, 3 August 1783. He wrote NG "a few days" ago and now has "little to offer, more than the good wishes, which ever flow, from a heart bound by every tie of gratitude & affection to you." He will leave Philadelphia "in the space of an hour," for New York with Mrs. Greene. They will "embark for Rhode Island" from there.[1] Garden will inform NG about "Whatever occurs" that is of interest.[2] RCS (CtY) 1 p.]

1. CG arrived in Newport, R.I., on 11 August on the vessel *Good Intent* from New York. (*Newport Mercury*, 16 August)
2. No further letter from Garden has been found.

* * *

From Joseph Reed

My dear General   Philad^a Aug. 3. 1783

I could not let Major [William] Pierce go away without a Mark of my affectionate Remembrance. Having finished your military Tour with so much Advantage to your Country & Reputation to yourself & having securd an honourable Independance of Fortune your Friends may now sincerly & Justly congratulate you; among these I beg to claim an early Rank. Perhaps there is no one who can do it with equal Sensibility, as the Treatment I have met with enables me to form a truer Judgment of Mankind in this particular & to affix a proper Estimate to your Situation. I have not been disappointed in the Thing tho' I have in the Time, I allways expected the Return of Peace would remove the active Instruments of the War from their [*illegible*] Device of publick Estimation; but to be treated with Scurrility & Abuse & to be under a Species of political disability in Matters of Interest & Expectation was what I had not foreseen.[1]

It was no small Disappointment to your Friends here that you did not come this Summer. The Troops have all arrived & Mrs Green after a short Stay which we have endeavoured to make agreeable to her is on the point of setting off for Rhode Island.[2] I doubt you will not be an Exception to the old Adage that a Man receives less Honour in his own country than elsewhere. I think I have observed more Envy & Dissatisfaction on your Advancement of Fortune among them than any other Persons so that unless you have more powerful local Attachments than I suspect I am inclined to think your Residence will be more Southward.[3] I am perswaded you will do so much Justice to my Friendship & Attachment as to believe that your Views in this particular will have a governing Influence over mine to a very considerable Degree. I am therefore impatient to a Degree of Anxiety to learn your Sentiments on this interesting Subject. I was allways to a certain Degree a Citizen of the World. I find myself daily growing more so, & being single [i.e., widowed] can with less Difficulty execute a Plan in which the Society of valuable Friends without Regard to Place will be the capital Object.

After the great Scenes in which we have bustled I imagine we shall have little Temptation to embark again on the contracted Scale of publick Affairs which must [Give?] much to vex & little to gratify an extended mind. This is my present View & I think [printed?] in Principles not likely to change. As some previous Arrangements would be indispensable which will require Time to form & execute I was anxious to gather from Mrs Green what your Views were. Her Wishes she makes no Secret of, & they correspond very much with my Ideas on this Subject. In my present Situation I do not think it prudent to trust them to a Letter. Your coming is therefore a Matter of no small Importance to me & I hope to see you by October at farthest.[4] The British still are possessed of New York & will probably remain so till that time.[5] Congress having been grossly insulted by a few of the Pennsylvania Line (new Recruits) & no Exertion made by Governm^t for their Protection they have withdrawn to New Jersey from which at present there does not seem any Probability of their returning to this City as the Place of future Residence.[6] In short I am sorry to tell you my dear Friend that our Continental Governm^t wears a very sickly Aspect & we are not without serious Apprehensions of a second Paper Depreciation. [Robert] Morris's Notes are now at a Discount of 20 & even 25 per C^t, He has not had the Support to which he was intitled, for tho his own particular Emolument appears to be the first Object of his Concern, that of the publick is so blended with it that it would have been good Policy to have supported him at all Events.[7] Except this State there are no Receipts of Taxes in the Continental Treasury. Some States have not paid a Shilling since the Reform of our civil Establishments: others very little. At this Time the Payments of Pennsylvania exceed all the rest of the States united.[8] The submissive Patience of the Army with Respect to their Pay exceeds Belief, they get but a small Proportion of their Due, that paid in Paper at a heavy Discount, as they are obliged to pass it away immediately, & yet they seem satisfied or at least they do not complain.

I am at a Loss from any Thing I see at present to form a Judgment of the future, & upon the whole am rather inclined to think as well from the Extent of our new Empire as other concurrent causes that we shall find a radical Weakness pervading every Part making it very inefficient in some of those Particulars on which not only the Happiness but the Safety of the People essentially depend. The internal Governments as yet also want Energy, but I imagine Time & Necessity will produce it, unless the Manners of the People should counteract; for after all we can say, it is upon these & not upon Laws the Prosperity of a State depends.

I presume you have seen Gen. Washington's circular Letter. It is a masterly Performance full of good Sense & real Patriotism but I fear it will have the Fate of many an excellent Sermon to be admired & neglected.[9]

I cannot tell you by Letter why I wish your Journey Northward may not be protracted beyond October but if a little Time should make no material Difference to you I hope you will hasten it so as to [command?] that Period.[10]

As you know [We?] preserve you in the most affectionate Remembrance but none more cordially & sincerely than my dear General Your devoted & Obed[t]   J. REED

RCS (MiU-C).

1. On Reed's unhappy situation in Pennsylvania politics, see, for example, his letters to NG of 1 November 1781 and 14 March 1783, above. (Vol. 9: 514; vol. 12: 517–18 and n)

2. CG had visited in Philadelphia on her way home to Rhode Island from Charleston, S.C. (See note at NG to Gouverneur Morris, 5 June, above.) On the arrival of the troops in Philadelphia, see note at Robert Morris to NG, first letter of 1 August, above.

3. Reed referred to the plantations and land grant that NG had received from the states of South Carolina, Georgia, and North Carolina. (See above, Hugh Rutledge to NG, 26 February 1782 [vol. 10: 411 and n]; Samuel Saltus to NG, 5 May 1782 [vol. 11: 164 and n]; and Alexander Martin to NG, 24 May 1782 [ibid., pp. 239–40 and n].) Reed may have been suggesting here that Rhode Islanders of his acquaintance had expressed "Envy & Dissatisfaction" over these gifts.

4. As noted at his journal entry for 15 August, below, NG reached Philadelphia for an extended stay by 11 October.

5. On the evacuation of New York in November by the British, see note at To an Unknown Person, 24 November, below.

6. Because of the recent mutiny of some Pennsylvania troops in Philadelphia, Congress had relocated to Princeton, N.J. (See note at Pierce to NG, 19 June, above.)

7. See also Charles Pettit's comments on this subject in his letter to NG of 4 August, below.

8. On this, see also Pettit to NG, 4 August, below.

9. On Washington's circular letter to the states, see Pendleton to NG, 17 July, above.

10. Reed's desire to see NG by October was probably related to a trip to Europe that he was preparing to take. NG wrote Thomas Mifflin, the president of Congress, from Philadelphia on 12 November, below, that Reed was "going to Europe on private business, and intimates a wish to carry with him some testimony of Congress." As seen by the notes there, Reed's request was controversial.

*   *   *

¶ [TO JOHN GEYER.[1] From Headquarters, Charleston, S.C., 4 August 1783. NG certifies that Capt. [William] Wilmot "of the Maryland line was posted with a command upon the lines in the Campaign of 1782 and that in the fall of the year he made a seizure of a quantity of indigo that was being sent into town contrary to the laws of the State."[2] Under "Governor [John] Mathews proclamation," the indigo was forfeited, and Wilmot "and his party" were "intitled to the benefit of the seizure."[3] Wilmot sold the indigo to Geyer, a "Merchant on Johns Island." NG argues that Wilmot's "Executors ought to have the benefit of the sale," and because Wilmot "owed a considerable sum of money" to Geyer, the proceeds "ought to go to the payment of the ballance" on Wilmot's account, "the public having no claim upon it and the original owner having forfeited his property agreeable to the Laws of the State and practice prevailing at the time the seizure was made." ADS (MiU-C) 2 pp.]

1. Geyer was a "British merchant" who had remained in Charleston during the war. (Rogers, *Evolution of a Federalist*, p. 100)

2. On Wilmot's role in the southern campaign, see his biographical note, above (vol. 11: 56n). Wilmot was killed in the line of duty in November 1782. (Vol. 12: 190–91, above)

3. On the resolution to which NG presumably referred, see above, Mathews to NG, 13 February 1782 (vol. 10: 361 and n).

*   *   *

To Catharine Littlefield Greene

My dear   Charlestown [S.C.] August 4th 1783

I was disappointed and not a little hurt at not receiving a letter from you by Capt [Matthew] Strong until I saw a letter from Capt Pearce to Major Hyrne where in he writes that you was out of Town, upon a party of pleasure upon the Schoolkill.[1] Mr Garden writes me you are going immediately for Rhode Island by the way of New York and Col Pettit writes that you take George with you. I am not sorry if we can get off cleaverly with the old Doctor.[2] Pettit writes also that he has got you a pair of horses to your liking, and a Phaeton and that a Chariot is making and that the amount of the whole will be upwards of 1400 Dollars.[3] He adds also that he shall want the money the moment I arrive. How or where to get it god knows for I dont.[4] Col Wadsworth informs me that all my stocks put into his hands have been lost; and that out of upwards of a thousand pounds put into his hands four years ago, I have not fifty left.[5] This loss and those heavy losses with my brothers distresses my private affairs exceedingly.[6] The demands upon me here are heavy and they will be more pressing as I go Northward. I had rather live in a cave than be under so much perplexity; and what adds to my vexation is I can not improve my Estate here without running still more in debt.[7]

I shall leave this place next Monday or Tuesday; and should have set out sooner had it not been for Col Carrington who could not get ready before that time.[8] Mrs Washington is in bed with a daughter. The Col° is as proud upon the occasion as if he had got a roman triumph.[9] Adieu my dear Yours affectionately   N GREENE

ALS (MiU-C).

1. William Pierce, Jr.'s letter to Edmund M. Hyrne has not been found.

2. See Alexander Garden to NG, 25 July, and Charles Pettit to NG, 26 July, both above. CG left Philadelphia on 3 August, accompanied by Garden. (Garden to NG, 3 August, above, and Pettit to NG, 4 August, below) NG's and CG's son George had been living at the school operated by the "old Doctor," John Witherspoon, near Princeton, N.J. (See, for example, Witherspoon to NG, 18 February, above [vol. 12: 462].)

3. See Pettit to NG, 26 July.

4. NG apparently paid Pettit for most of these purchases in November, while he was in Philadelphia. (NG to Pettit, 22 April 1784, below) During that same month, NG also relinquished to Pettit the "Residue" of his unpaid commissions as quartermaster general and most of his holdings in his partnership with Pettit and John Cox. (Agreement between NG and Pettit, 8 November, below)

5. See Jeremiah Wadsworth to NG, 26 July, above. On NG's investment in his partnership with Wadsworth and Barnabas Deane, see the note there.

6. NG was also a partner in Jacob Greene & Company, the financial problems of which are reported in letters to him of 4 and 18 May, both above, from his brother Jacob and his cousin Griffin Greene. (Vol. 12: 641–43, 662–64)

7. NG's "Estate here" included Boone's Barony and Mulberry Grove, the plantations that the states of South Carolina and Georgia had given to him.

8. NG set out for the North on 14 August. (NG to Washington, 8 August, below) Carrington did not leave Charleston until about the 20th but caught up with NG along the way and traveled with him as far as Richmond, Va. (Hutson to NG, 19 August, below; see also NG's Journal entries for 16 August and 4 and 6 September, below.)

9. William and Jane Reily Elliott Washington named their first child Jane. (*Biog. Directory of S.C. House*, 3: 750)

To Charles Pettit

Dear Sir   Charlestown [S.C.] August 4th 1783

Capt [Matthew] Strong arrivd Night before last and deliver'd me your letters of the 26th of July.[1] I can readily conceive your embarassments respecting the bills drawn on you by Banks[,] Burnet & Comp and am clearly of opinion with you that you were under no obligation to hazard any thing.[2] M[r] [John] Banks felt his pride a little hurt in the affair but [Ichabod] Burnet did not. I had some conversation with Burnet on the business and all parties appear to be fully satisfied that you did nothing either dishonorable or ungenerous in the business. Banks is a sanguine young fellow and of an adventerous make; but Burnets caution will limit his enterprise. I wrote you in my last that the Company were making shipments to you and that a power was forwarded for you to receive all the contract Money.[3] Both these circumstances I hope will place you in perfect security. I wish to save Burnet but I would not wish to involve you and hope neither friendship or delicasy may lead you without the limits of prudence. I think the concern is worth a large sum of money; but the capital and debts of Merchants are difficult to be known. I am fully persuaded the company mean to act with honor; but they are but little acquainted with Mercantile propriety; however upon matters being fairly stated they embrace conviction and conform to reason.[4] Burnet sails to morrow for the Havannah from whence he expects to make you further remittances but these are precarious.[5] Mr Stanley has bills on you for upwards of 2000 dollars which I was obliged to indorse before I could get my obligation out of the Treasury of the State. I gave bills for this money to the Company on Col Wadsworth upwards of three Months ago; and my bonds was to have been immediately taken up; but demands on account of the contract here pressed them so hardly that they could not advance the money and therefore finally I was obliged to adopt the Negotiation with Stanly and get their bills on you for the amount.[6] Thus you see I have been a little embarassed with their affairs; but they in turn have assisted me in the last payments I have had to make, and are to take part of my coming crop.[7] It was Major Burnet who proposed my giving bills on you. I did not much admire the scheme but had no objection if it would have promoted your views.[8]

I wish not to give the old Doctor any just grounds of complaint and am glad to have the matter put on the footing you mention; but if the Child could have remained with him on reasonable terms and the old Gentlemen not too much ingaged in other business it would have been most agreeable to me.[9] However I am perfectly satisfied. On my arrival you may be assured I will do all in my power to replace your advances for me.[10] I did not think the horses and Carriage would have come to so large a sum. If Mrs Greene is but pleased I am happy. She is a little extravagant; but she spends money very good Naturedly.[11] Garden writes me she was going to leave you in a day or two.[12] She did not write at all; and Pearce gives as an apology that she was out of Town on the Schoolkill.[13] Remember me kindly to all the family. Yours affectionately

N GREENE

ALS (NHi).

1. NG undoubtedly referred to Pettit's letters of 23 and 26 July, both above.

2. See Pettit to NG, 23 July.

3. See NG to Pettit, 29 July, above.

4. Less than a year later, NG wrote concerning Banks: "I put no dependance on his promise." (NG to Saunders, 27 July 1784, below)

5. Burnet was probably still in Charleston when he wrote NG on 8 August, below. He died in Havana not long after his arrival there. (NG to Pierce, 15 October, below)

6. "The Company on Col Wadsworth" was Barnabas Deane & Company, in which Jeremiah Wadsworth, NG, and Deane were partners. On Wadsworth's and the firm's financial difficulties, see Wadsworth's letters to NG of 12–13 June and 26 July, both above. The "contract here" was with Banks and Burnet for provisioning the Southern Army. For more about NG's debt to Stanly for certificates on the state of South Carolina, see above, Edward Blake to NG, 3 May (vol. 12: 638), and John Wright Stanly to NG, 23 May.

7. NG referred here to Banks and his partners.

8. It is clear from his letters to NG of 23 and 26 July that Pettit did not consider himself to be in a position to accept these bills. His response is not known, but it appears that the matter of payment was not resolved immediately. In a letter to NG of 26 October, below, Stanly pressed for payment; Pettit wrote NG the following winter that he had accepted NG's "Draught on Mr Jacob Greene in fav^r of Mr Stanley." (Pettit to NG, 7 February 1784, below) Between those dates, NG and Pettit had reached an agreement concerning NG's debts to Pettit. (Agreement between NG and Pettit, 8 November, below)

9. As seen in Pettit's letter to NG of this date, below, CG was to take George Washington Greene home to Rhode Island and was to stop in Princeton, N.J., to remove him from Dr. John Witherspoon's school. (See also Pettit to NG, 26 July.)

10. See Agreement between NG and Pettit, 8 November.

11. On CG's purchases in Philadelphia, see Pettit to NG, 26 July, and NG to CG, this date, both above.

12. According to Pettit's letter of this date, CG "set out yesterday accompanied by Mr Garden." (See also Alexander Garden to NG, 25 July and 3 August, both above.)

13. On the information from William Pierce, Jr., see NG to CG, immediately above.

* * *

¶ [FROM GENERAL BENJAMIN LINCOLN, SECRETARY AT WAR, War Office [Philadelphia], 4 August 1783. Has NG's letters of 2, 3, and 18 June and 11 July, "with their several enclosures."[1] Would have written sooner but had "indulged the agreeable expectation of a personal interview so soon as to render any farther communication by letter unnecessary." Informs NG that "the allowance of two rations to the Officers was continued until the first day of January 1782 when it ceased."[2] A "Peace-establishment has been reported to Congress, and is now under consideration."[3] Refers NG to Maj. [William] Pierce "for the intelligence of the day."[4] RCS (MiU-C) 2 pp.]

1. These letters are all above, but the drafts of the two letters that NG wrote to Lincoln in early June are both dated 3 June instead of 2 and 3 June.

2. See NG's first letter to Lincoln of 3 June.

3. A committee of Congress had been appointed in the spring to "consider what arrangements it will be proper to adopt in the different departments with reference to a peace." Chaired by Alexander Hamilton, the committee had solicited Washington's views in April. (Smith, *Letters*, 20: 154; *JCC*, 25: 953–54) Washington wrote an extensive statement, "Sentiments on a Peace Establishment," which he enclosed in a letter to Hamilton of 2 May. (Fitzpatrick, *GW*, 26: 374–98) The committee submitted its findings to Congress in June. (Fitzpatrick, *GW*, 27: 140–44) On 7 August, Congress appointed another committee to confer with Washington in person. (*JCC*, 24: 494) This committee submitted Washington's lengthy observations to Congress on 10 September. (Ibid., 25: 549–51; Fitzpatrick, *GW*, 27: 140–45) A report was also submitted by the committee in October. (*JCC*, 25: 722–29)

4. As seen in his letter to NG of 17 August, below, Pierce returned to Charleston, S.C., from Philadelphia soon after NG left there for the North.

*   *   *

From Charles Pettit

My dear Sir   Philadelphia 4ᵗʰ August 1783

I will not intrude a long Letter upon you by every Conveyance. By Capᵗ [Matthew] Strong I sent you two full sheets, or 8 Pages in folio;[1] by this opportunity I expect to keep within 4 Quarto pages.

Mʳˢ Greene set out yesterday accompanied by Mʳ Garden. The Plan in Contemplation is to go to New York, & from thence by water if a good Opportunity should offer, if not to proceed by Land to the East End of Long Island. But Major Pierce can give you the Particulars more fully.[2]

Dʳ Witherspoon having been a long Time abroad, I have not seen him since Mʳˢ Greene's arrival from the Southward, and the Business respecting him remains as it did when I last wrote to you. I must confess that, considering all Circumstances, I find my Desire for George's continuance with him much abated, if not removed; at the same Time I wish the old Gentleman's mind to be free from censuring you on the Occasion. Mʳˢ Greene has no objection to his thinking what he pleases of her, and if that be not sufficient I would rather come next than let his Heart-burning extend to you. But Mʳˢ Greene's Tenderness (perhaps he will say Weakness) may be sufficient, & we have concluded that it is the best ground within our Reach to put it upon. Hitherto we discern no Benefit to the Child but what he would probably have derived from being placed in any reputable Family in the Country with the aid of a Common School, nor a Prospect of anything better for a year or two to come by his Continuance there. This Advantage Mrs Greene has premised to give him till you return to fix a Plan satisfactory to yourself. She has therefore taken him with her & proposed to call on the doctor in her way & put the Matter on as fair a Footing as she can. She is to let me know what passes at the Interview, and in the mean Time I decline writing to the Doctor, lest I should happen to miss, or thwart the turn their Conversation may take.[3]

I have this Day received Letters from my Son at Amsterdam, where he arrived the beginning of May, & I should not be Surprized to see the Ship *Congress* in a few days. Tho' his Letters being of early Dates (the 13 & 18th of May) do not propose a Time for her sailing. Her Voyage will not be a great one, tho' I hope a saving one. Tobacco was much fallen in Europe; the best being but 6 to 7 stivers P# in Amsterdam & subject to heavy Charges. In War time it was at least double that Price & generally more. At the same time European Goods had risen Considerably in Contemplation of the American Market, which in fact is already so glutted that the Importers of such Goods will lose rather than gain by such Importations. From these Considerations Andrew has wisely determined to be very sparing in shipping Goods this year on his Account & mine, at least till he shall receive farther Advices from me as he went away in war Time; and luckily he will find his Opinions confirmed by my Letters which have followed him. His attention to the Business committed to him, the Observations he makes & the Opinions he suggests, are thus far a pleasing Presage of his possessing suitable Talents for the Business he is pursuing, and flatter me with an Expectation that he will improve his Time to Advantage. Not being able on a Dividend of Stock to put him in possession of anything worth mention, I have proposed to him a general Partnership with me as the best I can do for us both. I shall therefore endeavour to extend the Establishment I have, as far as the Foundation will safely bear. The Principal Branch, on our own Account, will be the Importation of European Goods, the secondary Branch will be concerns in Vessels & the West India Trade as our Circumstances may admit; but we shall be open to the Commissions of our Friends from all Quarters, which I flatter myself we shall be able to execute equally with any House in this Place, and shall be thankful to our Friends whether in or out of Trade for their Recommendations of such Business to us. If the Public Debts were funded on such a Footing to become negociable I could manage business with more Ease & I should hope, with Satisfaction; in the mean Time I can only use my Part of them as a Fund for Credit, in which they may be of some use.[4]

Your Troops are arrived & were complimented by the Ringing of the Bells as a token of Joy, on their entering the Town and gratitude for their Services.[5] They, in common with the other Troops, will receive Notes, payable six Months hence, for three Months Pay, and be furlowed till called for or sine die. These Notes have been sold as low as 15 Per Cent Discount; but as there is a general Confidence that they will be paid at the Time specified, the Money-Managers are [*illegible*] them as an Object of Profit, & I believe they will not fall lower. For my Part, considering the low State of Public Credit for a long time Past, I consider it as a great Point gained that they are in so good a light as this.[6] The Collection of Taxes has [been?] shamefully neglected in all the States. Of the 8 millions of Dollars for 1782, above, 7 Millions are yet [deficient?] tho many of Individuals in this City have paid their full Proportion of the whole Sum. Of the Sum Collected, this State has paid more than one third, and yet she has not paid more than about a fifth of her Quota.[7] To the Idea of Peace many People in the Country seem to have annexed the Idea of freedom from Expence & thence infer that Taxes are no longer necessary. The great majority of the Representatives in every State are too ignorant of the affairs of Government and of the Principles of social Compact to comprehend & understand the Means and measures necessary to Political Happiness, and the accursed Idol Popularity leads too many to sacrifice every thing to that one object, and to obtain Votes they will not only Countenance and cherish, but absolutely generate and propagate Doctrines of the most pernicious Tendency to the Social Union.

I have great Hopes of good Effects from Gen[l] Washingtons Circular Letter.[8] The personal Respect which binds every [Individual?] to a Character at once so conspicuous & so much revered cannot fail to awaken Attention to his Reasoning & to inspire a kind of Truth in his decided Opinions where their Faculties cannot comprehend the Reasoning. But alas! His Opinions & his Reasonings will not, I fear, reach the Senses of a sufficient number of Individuals without the Aid of other Means than News Papers; and they must strike the Senses before they can reach the Mind. I would wish them to reach every Individual; and I was going to propose the Means of conveyance when the Bottom of my Paper put me in [mind?] that the Sheet was full & that I must go no farther. I should not have Room to say how much I am Dear sir yours

C. PETTIT

RCS (MiU-C).

1. Pettit had written long letters to NG on 23 and 26 July, above.

2. Alexander Garden was accompanying CG in her travels from Charleston, S.C., to Rhode Island by way of Philadelphia. (See above, Garden to NG, 20 June, 25 July, and 3 August.) William Pierce did not get back to Charleston from Philadelphia in time to see NG. (Pierce to NG, 17 August, below)

3. George Washington Greene, NG's son, had been placed in Dr. John Witherspoon's

school in Princeton, N.J., at Pettit's urging. (Pettit to NG, second letter of 14 June 1782, above [vol. 11: 332–33, 336n]; on the arrangements that were subsequently made, see the references to Witherspoon in the index to vol. 12, above.) CG did remove George from the school. (Pierce to NG, 17 August)

4. Pettit's son, Andrew, had sailed to Amsterdam on the *Congress* with a cargo of tobacco the previous spring. (Pettit to NG, 3 April, above [vol. 12: 569–70])

5. On the return to Philadelphia of Pennsylvania troops from the Southern Army, see note at Morris to NG, first letter of 1 August, above.

6. See also Reed to NG, 3 August, above.

7. A later statement of federal receipts against Congress's $8 million requisition on the states for 1782 showed slightly more than $6.5 million uncollected. Pennsylvania had paid $346,632.89 of the $1,486,511.64 that had been collected from all of the states but still owed $774,161. (The statement, dated 24 February 1784, is in Morris, *Papers*, 9: 138–39.)

8. On Washington's circular letter to the states, see Pendleton to NG, 17 July, above.

*   *   *

¶ [FROM ROBERT MORRIS, SUPERINTENDENT OF FINANCE, Office of Finance [Philadelphia], 5 August 1783. After further consideration of Mr. Banks's letter to NG, Morris has decided "not to deduct the Bills &c until the next Payment, and have therefore ordered the Amount of what is certified for the two first Months of the Contract to be paid to Mʳ Charles Pettit the Agent of the Contractors."¹ Morris has also "made an Exertion" to pay "what yet remains" of NG's bills, but the amount is so much greater than his "Expectations" that he has had to postpone the payment. Although "this has been Somewhat injurious" to NG's and his own credit, he assumes that NG has "drawn very little more than has already been presented" and believes "the Measures I am taking will retrieve both."² If he is mistaken in this, it could "plunge" him "into very dangerous Extremities." Hopes to hear from NG "very fully as to the Situation of the different accounts resulting from your drafts and the various Sums as well as total Amount" before NG leaves Charleston, S.C. This information will be needed "to open some Accounts and to check others."³ RCS (CSmH) 2 pp.]

1. NG had enclosed a copy of John Banks's letter of 10 July in his to Morris of 11 July, both above. Morris's initial response is in his first letter to NG of 1 August, above. On Pettit's role as agent for Banks and Ichabod Burnet, who had contracted to supply provisions to the Southern Army, see Pettit to NG, 23 July, above.

2. On the bills in question, see NG's letters to Morris of 19 December 1782 (vol. 12: 311–12), 2 February 1783 (ibid., p. 404), and 11 July 1783, all above. According to entries in his diary, Morris met with Pettit on 8 July and with James Warrington (one of Banks's creditors) on 25 July, both of whom requested payments against NG's drafts. In Pettit's case, Morris asked for a "Note for the Amount" of NG's drafts, "that I may get it discounted at the Bank and pay those bills"; Morris promised "to discharge the said Note when it falls due and also to pay the Discount[,] which [Pettit] agreed to." (Morris, *Papers*, 8: 257) Warrington informed Morris "amongst other Things . . . that part of the Supplies for which these bills were drawn had been used by the Southern Army in Janry. 1781. Upon this I immediately told Mr. Warrington that he gave me information which surprized me, that I had no Idea of Genl. Green paying Old Debts but that I had ever supposed his Drafts were for the Current expenditures of the Army under his Command, that I am at a Loss to know how Genl. Green can justify such drafts on me as I have no Money that can be appropriated to the payments of old debts and I declined paying these bills." (Morris, *Papers*, 8: 337–38)

3. It is unlikely that NG received this letter before he left Charleston, S.C., for the North. (See NG's Journal, 15 August, below.) Morris noted in his diary that he met with NG on 18 October "respecting his bills drawn on me whilst in Command at Carolina and respecting his Accounts[,] on which we had a long Conference." (Morris, *Papers*, 8: 629)

¶ [FROM COLONEL FRANCIS MENTGES, Charleston, S.C., 6 August 1783. In concluding his "Inspection of the several Departments in the southern Army," he has "strictly examined the Clothier Department" and finds that the "Vouches made from the several Reg^{ts} and Corps perfectly agree of the Issues made to them from the 8: of Novr 1782 to this Day." Clothing issued before that time "has not been so regularly accounted for owing to the situation of the Army." Col. [Henry] Lee obtained £2000 in goods "from Different Merchants of Charles Town," which he distributed to officers and soldiers, but only the "Issues to the Officers" have been properly documented. Lee's Legion therefore "stands Charged with upwards of 1300 Pounds Sterling," plus some £200 for "Detachments with the Legion."[1] The clothier has "now finished the accounts of the Issues of Cloathing to the Officers" and has submitted them to the paymaster general; the clothier will "render a General Account of his Transactions from the time of his Appointment to this Day for that purpose." Mentges has shown him the "Mode" in which to state his account.[2]

Mentges has "also careful[ly] examined the state of the Hospital and Purveyers Department" and finds it was "conducted in the most regular Manner." Dr. [Nathan] Brownson has shown him "the Monthly accounts of the Issues and expence of his Department," and Mentges is "convinced" that Brownson "acted with accuracy and oeconomy." The "Public interest" has been "preserved" because "the Derector and the purveyor" were always "at a Variance." As doctors "Oly[p]hant, Johnston & Flagg" were advanced "several sums of Money" that do not appear in Brownson's books, they should "render an account" to Brownson, "to enable him to render a general Account of the Expenditure of the stores and Monies received for his Department."[3]

Mentges reports that "Very little can be said in regard Of the Commissary of Millitary stores." Captain McClure was "but Latley apppointed and his bad state of health prevented him of puting the stores in such order as" Mentges "could wish them to be fixed."[4] Mentges examined the monthly returns and found "that by the moving of the stores from Cambden by Water the Boat Sunk and a great quantity of powder and Cartridges were lost and Damaged."[5]

Mentges "did not interfere" with the "Quarter Master General Department," as Col. [Edward] Carrington's "Knowledge, & attention to his Duty requiered no Inspection," other than in the "Branch of forage," which Mentges examined "from time to time." The "mode" that Carrington adopted for "the receiving and Issuing of forage had the greatest effect," saving "half of the expence" after Carrington's plan was "put in execution by a general Order in Octob[er] Last."[6]

In concluding his report of the "Inspectors Department," Mentges thanks NG for the "Appointment, Support, & Assistance you have Lend me from the beginning to the End." He hopes he executed his "Duties" to NG's and "the Publicks satisfaction" and that his "attention and Activity had not been wanted [i.e., wanting?] to promote the Public interest." The continuance of NG's friendship and "good Opinion" would be the "greatest reward" for his services.[7] RCS (MiU-C) 2 pp.]

1. The clothier, Lt. John Hamilton, had written the department's paymaster, John S. Dart, on 28 April that Lee "received great quantities of Goods from Charlestown in beginning of the Year 1782, his Accounts of the issues are very imperfect & if settled now, wou'd involve that gentleman in a heavy debt." (WRMS) NG commented about the "irregalarity with which the Legion soldiers were supplied" in a letter to Hamilton of 13 August, below, and later wrote to Lee about this matter. (NG to Lee, 27 October, below)

2. Hamilton's "General Account" has not been found.

3. Brownson returned to his post as purveyor for the hospital department in the South in June 1782, some six months after finishing a brief term as governor of Georgia. (Vol. 10: 172–73n, above) Dr. David Olyphant was the director of the department. On the disagreements between Brownson and Olyphant, see, for example, Brownson to NG, 28 May, above. Doctors Robert Johnston and Henry Collins Flagg had also served in the department.

4. "Captain McClure" has not been identified.

5. Camden, S.C., had been "the army's principal storage depot for clothing and foot-wear." (Vol. 11: 409n, above) NG gave orders for the removal of some of the stores from there by boat in a letter to Capt. William Ferguson of 11 May, above (vol. 12: 651).

6. Congress had adopted new regulations concerning forage rations in October 1782. (*JCC*, 23: 685–86) Mentges probably referred here to a plan that Carrington proposed to NG in March 1783, which he believed was better suited to existing conditions and prices of forage in South Carolina. (Carrington to NG, 14 March, above [vol. 12: 513–14 and n])

7. As seen in his letter of 6 October, below, Mentges had served in various administrative posts under NG. In his reply to Mentges of 8 August, below, NG thanked him for his "Zeal, & happy mode of conducting this business."

¶ [FROM HENRY PENDLETON, Culpeper County, Va., 6 August 1783. Although he does not know where to reach NG, Pendleton has heard from his brother that NG will travel through Fredericksburg, and he hopes this letter will be delivered there.[1] He decided to "postpone to some future summer" the "pleasure of drinking the fine Northern air" and went instead to Bethlehem, Pa., where he "recruited" his "Corporeal Oconomy"; should he have to "leave [South] Carolina again for the purposes of purification it shall be to Boston and Rhode Island." He "regretted" not seeing CG when she passed through Philadelphia on her way northward but hopes that she and NG will be in "Carolina next winter."[2] If NG should "brake any stay about Fred⁵burg," and can give him notice, Pendleton would be "very happy" to meet him, "it being not more than 35 miles, was it only for the pleasure of one afternoon."[3] His brother informs him that NG "will bring on a Gray horse and Sulkey of mine"; NG should leave them with Mr. James Hackley in Fredericksburg. If NG needs the sulky for the rest of his trip, Pendleton hopes he "will make no difficulty of doing so."[4] Sends "warmest wishes for your Happiness on all the articles of Interest Honour & Health." RCS (MiU-C) 1 p.]

1. Pendleton (d. 1788), a South Carolina judge, was the older brother of Nathaniel Pendleton, NG's former aide and close friend. (See vol. 11: 179n, above.) A native of Virginia, he had gone there on a visit, as had his brother. (See Nathaniel Pendleton's letter to NG of 12 August, below.) NG was about to travel overland from Charleston, S.C., on his way home to Rhode Island. (NG's Journal, 15 August, below)

2. CG, who sailed from Charleston in early June, spent some weeks in Philadelphia before heading home to Rhode Island in early August. (On her departure from Philadelphia, see Pettit to NG, 4 August, above.) CG did not return to the South until November 1785, when the Greene family left Newport, R.I., to settle on Mulberry Grove, their plantation in Georgia. (NG to Clarke, 23 November 1785, below)

3. As seen in his letter to NG of 12 October, below, Pendleton and NG did not see each other when NG traveled through Virginia.
4. See Pendleton's letters to NG of 12 and 22 October, below.

*   *   *

To Catharine Littlefield Greene

My dear Caty   Charles Town [S.C.] August the 7 1783
Notwithstanding all I wrote you the other day, I love you most affectionately and in saying this I speak not half what I feel. Some little things trouble me; but blessed with so good a wife such fine children and a decent fortune it is little less than ingratitude to be unhappy. In human life, every situation has its anxieties. Perhaps Providence in the order of creation has found it necessary. A happy mixture of dark and light shades forms the most pleasing picture. It is sometimes necessary to feel pain to relish pleasure. Fasting and exercise give us the keenest appetite and most pleasant repose. In this veiw of human life I am reconciled to many things painful in their nature; but to give pain unnecessarily is both cruel and unjust. I have not been pleased with my self ever since I wrote you my last letter and you know self reproach is a painful companion. In my present situation I wished you to be as economical as possible but at the same time I have no desire to deprive you of one rational amusement. My letter I am afraid was both indelicate and severe. I was much perplexed at the time I wrote and under no small mortification that I could not pay the little bills dayly presented. In this situation I am apprehensive nothing but pettulancy possessed the mind and the sentiments will always pertake of the temper. I know from the goodness of your heart you would forego many little pleasures rather than place me in so disagreeable a situation; but there is no recalling what is past.[1] All I wish is that you may feel as much interested in my happiness as I do in yours. My study has ever been to render you happy and when I have done or said any thing which may give you pain, I feel a double share of it my self. In matters of interest I have no wish independant of the family happiness; but as fortune is necessary to continue us upon a respectable footing in life as well as to educate our children properly, it is both our duty and our interest to limit our expences to our income. But besides these considerations which are of no small consequence the mortification of being in another mans power, or called upon for what one cannot pay, is not a little distressing to ones feelings. These reflections will mark my situation when I last wrote, and apologize for any thing that might be amiss. There was several little matters I was not pleased with which I will explain when we have the happiness of meeting.[2] You have naturally a generous disposition and perhaps a little vanity of being thought so, which renders you a prey to

the artful and designing; but I can but hope from your affection that no indulgence which gives me pain will give you pleasure. To gratify you in dress, in public and private diversions, is among the first of my wishes; and that your appearance may be answerable to your standing, I could wish for economy in little matters that you may display more splendor when your vanity is most interested.

I have been a little unwell with a return of the fever; but it is triffling. The weather since you left here, has been extreme hot, I have felt nothing like it since I have been to the Southward. The thermometer was up to 96 day after day. The profusion of perspiration was little short of dissolution; but all at once the weather changed and the thermometer fell from 96 to 68. This was pleasant to our feelings but trying to our constitutions. Being too inattentive to my dress I got a slight ague; but of short duration. Since I wrote you before I have been up to Goose Creek to see M^r [Arthur] Middleton and M^r [Joseph] Glover[;] both families desired their loves to you.[3] Miss Glov[e]r in a very particular Manner. Major Edwards is half in love with her; and it would have diverted you to have seen him figitting about her. He has not courage enough to tell what he wishes; nor do I believe he will have before he leaves the State. Is not this a hapless hopeless lover; and yet I think appearances were much in his favor.[4] Col Carrington has been playing round Mrs Harlston with more art than address, trying to find out her wishes; but he is so mechannical and she so skilled in coquetry that after a douzen visits he has still to guess at what he wishes to know.[5] Was the Colonel once married he would make a most excellent husband, but his formality in Courtship and his fear of a refusal will continue him on the bachelors list for a long time; until some Lady shall think more of merit than appearance; and offer him her hand in his own way.[6]

Mrs Butler who I wrote you lay so very ill in my last letter, contrary to every bodys expectation has got better and in a fair way of recovery.[7] Mrs Waters is still under a Cloud. Mr Waters has got over his wound; and the doctor has brought an action of defamation against Mr Marshall. The poor old fellow has been much distressed at the situation of his daughter.[8] Mrs Waters complains of you as neglecting her. She says she thinks she had as much right to expect a letter from your friendship as Mrs Harlston. I attempted no apology but that you had a great aversion to writing; and that it was very injurious to your health.

The Governor has been paying his addresses to me ever since you have been gone; and if I was not to leave the State soon, I dont see how I should avoid marrying him. He is sending after me day after day to dine with him and in the morning to inquire after my health[9]

AL (MiU-C). One or more pages are missing.
1. See NG to CG, 4 August, above.
2. It is not known what the "several little matters" were.

3. Arthur Middleton and Joseph Glover both had residences in St. James Goose Creek Parish. (*Biog. Directory of S.C. House*, 2: 280–81, 457) According to a biographical sketch, Glover died at his Goose Creek plantation on 4 August 1783. (Ibid., p. 281) It is not known how recently NG had made this visit, as further along in the present letter he referred to a "last letter" to CG that has not been found. (See note 7, below.)

4. Joseph Glover, to whom NG presumably referred here, was the father of three daughters. "Miss Glov[e]r" may have been the woman Edwards unsuccessfully began to court that fall, after traveling to Philadelphia with NG and returning to South Carolina. (See below, Pendleton to NG, 3 February and 18 April 1784, and Edwards to NG, 18 June 1784.)

5. Elizabeth Lynch Harleston was the widow of John Harleston, Jr., who apparently died in 1781 while serving with American forces in Virginia. (*Biog. Directory of S.C. House*, 3: 317) As noted at Pendleton to NG, 3 February 1784, below, she was married to Maj. James Hamilton the following June.

6. Carrington remain single until some years after the war. He married Eliza Ambler Brent, a sister-in-law of Virginia jurist John Marshall, in 1790. (*The Papers of John Marshall*, ed. Herbert A. Johnson et al. [Chapel Hill: University of North Carolina Press, 1974–], 1: 117n)

7. The letter in which NG referred to Mary Middleton Butler's health has not been found. She was the wife of Pierce Butler, who is identified at NG's letter to him of 9 September 1784, below.

8. Jane Olyphant Walter was the daughter of Dr. David Olyphant. Her husband, John Alleyne Walter, had been wounded in a duel with Nathaniel Pendleton after James Marshall, a lawyer, alleged that Pendleton was having an affair with her. (*Biog. Directory of S.C. House*, 2: 496; NG to Wayne, 26 June, and NG to Williams, 2 July, both above) Nothing more is known about Olyphant's lawsuit against Marshall, who died the following December. (Pendleton to NG, 4 December, below) Although NG and Pendleton consistently referred to Jane Olyphant and her husband as "Waters," their name was "Walter." (*SCHGM* 15 [1914]: 101; 18 [1917]: 184; 20 [1919]: 173)

9. The manuscript ends here. NG's relationship with Gov. Benjamin Guerard of South Carolina was obviously much more friendly at this time than it had been a few months earlier. (See above, vol. 12: xiii–xiv, and below, Guerard to NG, 12 August.)

*   *   *

¶ [CERTIFICATION OF FREDERICK PASCHKE. Charleston, S.C., 7 August 1783. Col. Edward Carrington certifies that Paschke, "having served with reputation in Count Pulaski's Legion Untill the reduction of that Corps, has, from his extraordinary zeal in the American Cause, continued ever since that event, to serve in the Staff departments and for near two years last past," under Carrington's "immediate direction." Paschke, who was first appointed "Brigade Quarter Master to the calvary" of the Southern Army by Col. [Timothy] Pickering, the quartermaster general, filled that post "with so much propriety, and managed with such capacity integrity & industry," that Carrington "in November last" recommended his appointment as "D. [Deputy] Quarter Master to the Army." Paschke served in that capacity until "the dissolution of the Army."[1] He has "so perfectly manifested" Carrington's "former opinions of him" that Carrington "cordially" provides this certificate and hopes "he will meet with every Countenance amongst those to whom he may become known, that his great Merits intitle him to." In a note below the certificate, NG adds: "After what has been said by Lt Col. Carrington in testimony of Capt Paskees merit and services,

it is unnecessary for me to add; but from my own observation I believe his Merit and services correspond strictly with Col Carringtons state of them." In a notation below NG's, dated 18 December at Philadelphia, Pickering affirms "the justness of the foregoing certificates" and adds that his "knowledge of Capt Paschke's worth & integrity induced" him to appoint Paschke to the Quartermaster Department. D (PCC, item 41, vol. 8: 201–3, DNA) 3 pp.]
    1. On this appointment, see Carrington to NG, 1 January, above (vol. 12: 366, 367n).

¶ [FROM JOSEPH WEST, Baltimore, Md., 7 August 1783. Encloses two letters, one to CG and the other from his father, recommending him to NG's "notice."[1] West had planned on "coming to So Carolina to settle" but has found it "more advantagious to establish an house" in Baltimore. If NG can provide an "introduction," based on the father's letter, West will be most grateful.[2] RCS (MiU-C) 1 p.]
    1. See Benjamin West to NG, 16 May, above (vol. 12: 659).
    2. West wrote another such request to NG on 3 July 1784, below.

¶ [FROM ICHABOD BURNET, [Charleston, S.C., before 8 August 1783?].[1] He writes: "Should it [be] proper to apply for any additional or extra pay for the extraordinary services of the Gentlemen of your family I am fully persuaded my claim will be held as equally good to any i[n]dulgence with the other Gentlemen."[2] RCS (MiU-C) 1 p.]
    1. Burnet, formerly NG's aide and now a business partner of John Banks's, presumably wrote this note sometime before he sailed from Charleston, S.C., in early August. (See NG to Pettit, 4 August, above, and Burnet to NG, 8 August, below.) He died at Havana not long afterward. (Flagg to NG, 17 October, below)
    2. "The Gentlemen of your family" were NG's former aides.

¶ [TO COLONEL FRANCIS MENTGES. From Headquarters, Charleston, S.C., 8 August 1783. NG has "just received" Mentges's "final report of the Inspection of the department" and will "report it to the board of War."[1] Mentges's "Zeal, & happy mode of conducting this business" claim NG's "warmest acknowled[g]ement." NG adds: "I only lament that I cannot make my approbation more public than by letter, but wish you to be fully perswaded of my favorable sentiments and disposition to serve you upon all occasion[s]." LS (WRMS, Misc. Mss. #8558, DNA) 1 p.]
    1. See Mentges to NG, 6 August, above. If NG forwarded Mentges's report to Gen. Benjamin Lincoln before he set out for Philadelphia on 14 August, the letter has not been found.

*   *   *

To George Washington

Dear Sir   Charlestown [S.C.] August 8th 1783
    When I wrote you last I did not expect to address you from this place again;[1] but Col [Edward] Carrington has detained me upwards of a week to complete the business of his department[.] On Thursday next we set off by land for the Northward.[2]
    The Assembly of this State have rejected the impost Act recommended by Congress. Had your circular letter been printed a fortnight

earlier I am persuaded it would have brought them in to the measure. On once reading in the house it produced an alteration of sentiment of more than one quarter of the Members. The force and affection with which it was written made everyone seem to embrace it with Avidity. You were admired before[;] you are little less than adored now. The recommendation of Congress had but a feeble influence until it was supported by yours. Altho the State did not come into the plan recommended by Congress they have laid a tax of five per cent under the Authority of the State to be solely for the Continental use. This I attribute entirely to your letter.[3] Its effects have been astonishing. I see by the papers the Northern Army dont choose to be furloughed.[4] The people have begin to be alarmed at it. I hope every thing will terminate both for the honor of the Army and satisfaction of the people notwithstanding. There has been several little mobs and riots lately in this town owing to the indiscretion of some of the british Merchants and to the violence of temper and private views of some of the Whig interest.[5] Tranquility now prevails and there is little probability of any further disturbances. I hope to be at Mount Vernon in about three Weeks but from all I can learn of the Northern affairs there is little probability of my having the pleasure of meeting your Excellency there.[6] Present me respectfully to Mrs Washington if with you and to all the family. I am with esteem & affection Your Most Obedient humble Serv[t]

NATH GREENE

ALS (Washington Papers: DLC).

1. See NG to Washington, 23 July, above.

2. NG did leave Charleston on "Thursday next," 14 August. (See *South-Carolina Weekly Gazette*, 16 August; NG's Journal, 15 August, and Pierce to NG, 17 August, both below.) Carrington did not leave with him but caught up with him along the way to Virginia. (NG's Journal, 4 September, below)

3. On Congress's 1783 impost proposal and the South Carolina legislature's action on it, see note at NG to Lincoln, 18 June, above. On Washington's circular letter to state executives in support of the impost, see Pendleton to NG, 17 July, above. Congress had agreed on 25 April to a lengthy "Address to the States," which recommended that the impost be approved as a means of providing revenue for the federal government to pay its debts. (*JCC*, 24: 277–83)

4. After Congress passed a resolution furloughing the soldiers and non-commissioned officers of the Continental Army in May, some troops refused to disband until adequate provision was made to pay them. In its issue of 9 August, the *South-Carolina Weekly Gazette* published the congressional resolution and a letter of 5 June from Gen. William Heath to Washington of 5 June, as well as Washington's reply to Heath of 6 June and a letter from Washington to the president of Congress on the matter.

5. See note at NG to Pettit, 29 July, above.

6. Washington, who was at his army's headquarters at Newburgh, N.Y., when NG wrote this letter, was staying near Princeton, N.J., where Congress was sitting, when NG visited Mount Vernon, Va., in mid-September. (Fitzpatrick, *GW*, 27: 86, 131; NG's Journal, 13 September, below)

*   *   *

¶ [FROM ICHABOD BURNET, [Charleston, S.C.?], 8 August 1783.[1] Asks NG to "make every essay to ingage Governor [Alexander] Martin and Willy [i.e., Willie] Jones Esq[r] in the business of securing the unlocated lands belonging to the Estate of the late Lord Grenville." An "acquaintance" of Burnet's is "confident he can obtain the right of the Heir" to the estate for the lands "for a trifling consideration" and will "give up two thirds of it, at first cost, if by any means it can be secured from confiscation." The estate is currently held by North Carolina "in a state of sequestration by a general law of the State."[2] Burnet believes "The policy of such Laws is too injurious not to furnish arguments sufficient to obtain a release" for at least part of the property. The "other property" is "immense but the prejudice of the people has it bound too fast for fear to admit a prospect of recovery." Burnet asks NG to write him "immediately after you see those Gentlemen," as Burnet must advise his acquaintance "whether to proceed in the business." This is "a matter of consequence" to Burnet, and he adds: "I pray your attention to it." He closes by wishing NG "an agreeable journey & every happiness you can desire."[3] RCS (MiU-C) 2 pp.]

1. The editors believe this letter was probably written from Charleston, where Burnet and NG had recently had some conversations about business matters. (NG to Pettit, 4 August, above) He was presumably about to sail for Havana when he wrote this letter. (Ibid.)

2. John Lord Carteret, later the Earl of Granville, was one of the "Lords Proprietors of Carolina" when the colony was established by charter in 1663. His extensive land holdings (roughly half of present-day North Carolina) were known as the Granville District. (Harry Roy Merrens, *Colonial North Carolina in the Eighteenth Century* [Chapel Hill: University of North Carolina Press, 1964], p. 24) In 1776, the state of North Carolina took over the rights to these lands. (Hugh T. Lefler and William S. Powell, *Colonial North Carolina: A History* [New York: Charles Scribner's Sons, 1973], p. 88n) "The late Lord" Granville was George Carteret, a descendant of the original proprietor; the Granville family later unsuccessfully sued the state to recover its property. (Smith, *Letters*, 20: 718, 765; Blackwell P. Robinson, *William R. Davie* [Chapel Hill: University of North Carolina Press, 1957], pp. 376–79)

3. NG saw Jones, but apparently not Martin, while traveling through North Carolina; it is not known whether he broached this subject with either of them. (See below, NG's Journal, 31 August and 1 September, and NG to Martin, 2 September.) News of Burnet's death in Havana reached NG in mid-October. (NG to Pierce, 15 October, below)

¶ [TO COLONEL EDWARD CARRINGTON. From Headquarters, Charleston, S.C., 9 August 1783. "Capt Smith" of the South Carolina line has a "note of hand against the public," signed by "Capt Neal" of Lee's Legion, "for a ballance due for a horse" that Neal bought "for the use of the Legion."[1] NG directs Carrington to give Smith credit "for the amount of the Note," in order to settle "for any purchases he may have made of public property in your department." ALS (Bruce Gimelson, 1979) 1 p.]

1. Smith was possibly Capt. John Carraway Smith of the Second South Carolina Continental Regiment; "Neal" was undoubtedly Capt. Ferdinand O'Neal (or "O'Neill"). (See vol. 10: 70n, above; Heitman, *Register*.)

*   *   *

To Charles Pettit

Charleston, [S.C.] August 9, 1783

"I send in charge of my steward my baggage and beg you will be kind enough to give it store room until my arrival. I set out the day after tomorrow.[1] I suppose Mrs Greene is gone before this. If not I think she may as well stay until my arrival unless she has got tired of the diversions of the City.[2]

I forgot to say anything in my last respecting the money in your hands. Major Burnet wrote me in Philadelphia on the subject, and I immediately forwarded another letter to Mr. Morris agreeable to what I understood was your wish;[3] and upon the whole I think it best. I would not choose to put myself in his power or give the world any handle against me. Envy is sufficiently loaded with misrepresentations without a shadow of cause. Give but occasion and it will burst on all sides. I shall see you soon and doubt not of getting the business accomodated to your wishes without exposing either to censure."[4]

Tr (Typescript: MiU-C).

1. As noted at his letter to Washington of 8 August, above, NG left Charleston on the 14th.

2. CG was already on her way home to Rhode Island from Philadelphia. (Garden to NG, 3 August, above)

3. In his letter to NG of 26 July, above, which NG had already received, Pettit discussed his reasons for not giving NG's letter "respecting the money" to Morris. That letter was presumably NG's to Morris of 21 April, a draft of which is printed in vol. 12: 629, above. It was the second such letter that NG had addressed to Morris and that Pettit had declined to deliver. (See note at Pettit to NG, 26 July.)

4. For further developments, see Pettit to NG, after 21 January 1784, below.

*   *   *

¶ [FROM GOVERNOR BENJAMIN GUERARD OF SOUTH CAROLINA, Government House, Charleston, S.C., 12 August 1783. He conveys to NG, "with the greatest Chearfulness & Pleasure," the legislature's "Resolve of this Day, to return you 'their Thanks for your eminent Exertions in the Field, & the many important Services you have rendered this State, during your Command in the Southern Department, & for your good Wishes for its Welfare, & the Tender of your Services in future,' expressed in your Letter to me, informing of your being about to close your Command & leave this State."[1] Guerard adds: "I feel a Singular Satisfaction in conveying to you this Vote of Thanks, I beg leave to add, that I heartily wish you a pleasant Journey, a happy Meeting with your Friends, after a very long Absence, & every Felicity this Life can afford." RCS (NcU) 2 pp.]

1. NG's letter to Guerard is above, dated 22 July. The legislative resolution of 12 August is printed in S.C., House of Representatives, *Journals, 1783–84*, p. 353.

*   *   *

From Nathaniel Pendleton

Dr General   Culpeper [Va.] August 12th 1783.

I find the Air of my Native place has had so happy an effect upon my constitution that it is unnecessary to go to Bath, where I had intended to remain the remaining part of this Summer.[1] I have declined the journey from another motive also, and that is the hopes of being informed when you arrive at Fredericksburg that I may have the pleasure of seeing you there. I have requested General [George] Weedon to be so good as to hire a man and send off immediately to let me know when you arrive, and my brother Henry, who is also here, and myself will come down immediately so that if you rest but one day at Fred^{ks}burg, we can arrive in time to see you.[2]

General Weedon will have informed you of the infamous Calumnies which have been propagated here respecting you. When I wrote to you from Fredericksburg by Maj^r [Robert] Forsythe I had no idea that these reports were of so black or so extensive a nature, and much less that the principal authors and propagators were officers who had served under you. I thought them only the insignificant effusions of some envious and malignant people, who wished to lessen that character they could not imitate. But I find many men of good Sense, some your friends, and indeed all except your most intimate ones, have either been deceived by these Reports, or compelled to be silent in your defence, against such a torrent of circumstances, anecdotes, pretended facts &^{ca} which must have required the invention of the Devil to frame them. The particulars of which you will here [i.e., hear?] from G. Weedon, if not before.[3]

I am extreemly anxious to hear from [South] Carolina, having had not one letter since my arrival here. If I should not be so fortunate as to meet you at Fredericksburg, I shall hope for a long letter, in which I shall beg you my Dear General to give me your advice respecting my return to Carolina, and the plan I hinted to you of going into some public employment.[4] You will know the public opinion respecting the affair with W—— and how far it will affect my plan and prospects, and whether it would be better to relinquish them or not. I wish sincerely he and his brother were gone from Ch^{s}Town, if he is still alive.[5] If you should have my horses [?] with you, and cannot stay one day I shall request you to leave them with some Gentleman, and let me know.[6] Genl Weedon can forward a letter any day. With Sentiments of the most gratefull affection I am Dr Sir your friend   N PENDLETON

RCS (MiU-C).

1. On Bath, in what is now West Virginia, as a health resort, see above, vol. 11: 452n. As seen in note 5, below, and in NG to Williams, 2 July, above, Pendleton had reasons in addition to that of his health for being away from South Carolina at this time.

2. See also Henry Pendleton to NG, 6 August, above. It is unlikely that NG saw either of the Pendletons while he was in the vicinity of Fredericksburg. (See below, Henry Pendleton's letter to NG of 12 October and NG's Journal entries for 9–11 September.)

3. Pendleton's only recent letter to NG from Virginia that has been found is that of 17 July, above, in which he reported from Richmond that "people here [have] been informed that you have quarelled with every power, and every officer civil and military in the Southern Department." In the present letter, Pendleton was undoubtedly referring to rumors, which had begun to circulate the previous winter, that NG was secretly involved in John Banks's business of selling supplies to the Southern Army. (On these rumors, see especially Benjamin Harrison to NG, 24 December 1782, above [vol. 12: 341–42 and n], and NG to Richard Henry Lee, 25 August 1785, below.) NG saw Weedon in Fredericksburg but did not mention anything in his travel journal about what they discussed. (See the entries for 9 and 10 September.)

4. The letter to NG in which Pendleton "hinted" at "going into some public employment" has not been found. However, when he wrote NG on 30 January 1784, below, he expressed at some length a wish to remain in the army on a "peace establishment." NG's replies to Pendleton's letters during this period have not been found.

5. Pendleton had quickly left South Carolina after fighting a duel with John Alleyne Walter in June. (See above, NG to Wayne, 26 June; NG to Williams, 2 July; and NG to CG, 7 August.) As seen in the letter to CG, Walter, whom NG and Pendleton called "Waters," had recovered from his wound. The identity of Walter's "brother" is not known. As will be seen later in this volume, Pendleton decided to practice law in Savannah, Ga.

6. See Henry Pendleton to NG, 6 August.

*   *   *

¶ [TO LIEUTENANT JOHN HAMILTON.[1] From Charleston, S.C., 13 August 1783. It is "impossible to find out" the amount of clothing that "each Soldier recievd" because of the "irregalarity with which the Legion soldiers were supplied," the "peculiar situation" that Col. [Henry] Lee "was in[,] being on the Advance of the Army," and "too much inattention to regular entries." Until Lee can give "a more perfect account of the business," Hamilton "must make the Legion chargeable for all the Goods which appears to have been deliverd to him not accounted for." Furthermore, "if no better mode of settlement can be had" when this business is concluded, "each individual must according to the numbers in service at the time, be charged with his equal dividend." NG adds in a postscript that "the rum & wine should be entered in the Commisaries department and until Lt Colo Lee can inform whether part or the whole was for public or private use it must stand that account."[2] ADfS (MiU-C) 2 pp.]

1. Hamilton was the deputy clothier general for the Southern Department.

2. Lee's Legion had been "on the Advance" of the Southern Army during the 1781 campaign. For more about this supply matter, see Mentges to NG, 6 August, above, and NG to Lee, 27 October, below.

*   *   *

NG's Journal

August 15, 1783[1]

We lodged this night at Colonel Horry's plantation on the Santee. His farm-house is one of the most spacious as well as convenient I have met with in my travels. The plantation is upon the Santee, and finely culti-vated. In front of the house is a beautiful pasture, over which is inter-spersed a great number of live oaks in natural order, which give it a very agreeable appearance. His plantation is large and fortune extensive, and it is said he has all the fears of poverty about him.[2] Our cavalry fared well, we indifferent, the keys and liquors not being to be had.[3]

Printed in Greene, *Greene*, 3: 496.
    1. This is the first known entry in a journal that NG kept while traveling north by land from Charleston, S.C. (As seen at NG to Washington, 8 August, above, NG left Charleston on 14 August.) The manuscript has not been found. The journal, as printed in Greene, *Greene*, 3: 496–511, follows NG as far as Baltimore, Md. (NG's Journal, 26 September, below) NG was in Princeton, N.J., where Congress was meeting, by 7 October, and in Philadelphia for an extended stay by 11 October. (See below, NG to Boudinot, 7 October, and NG to Martin, 11 October.)
    2. Col. Hugh Horry had been a partisan cavalry leader under Gen. Francis Marion. (Moss, *S.C. Patriots*) His plantation was on the North Santee River.
    3. NG's traveling companions included Maj. Evan Edwards, Maj. Edmund M. Hyrne, and (later) Col. Edward Carrington. (On Carrington, see note at NG to CG, 4 August, above.)

NG's Journal

16. [August 1783]

We passed the Santee, a long river with rich borders. It extends to the mountains, and when its northern borders is fully cultivated will afford produce almost sufficient for all the world. Rice, indigo, hemp, and indian corn are its great staples. The ferries and causeways over this river are a reproach to government. Nothing adds more to the reputa-tion and convenience of a people than good roads and well regulated ferries. Strangers pass with pleasure, and agriculture and commerce are promoted. Here the ferry-boats were in bad order, and the roads almost hedged up with bushes. We got to Georgetown [S.C.] about noon, and were very politely received and entertained by Mr. and Mrs. Tucker, who is Major Hyrne's sister.[1] We stayed here two days, waiting for Colonel Carrington to join us, but as he did not come agreeable to promise it was conjectured he had got another kind look from Mrs. Harlston,[2] and business furnished a pretense for a longer stay.

Printed in Greene, *Greene*, 3: 496–97.
    1. Daniel Tucker, a merchant, and his wife, Elizabeth, a sister of NG's aide and traveling companion Edmund M. Hyrne, lived on Litchfield plantation near Georgetown. (*Biog. Directory of S.C. House*, 3: 723–24)

2. On Edward Carrington and Mrs. Elizabeth Lynch Harleston, who later married another of NG's former officers, see also NG to CG, 7 August, above. Richard Hutson wrote NG on 19 August, below, that Carrington would leave Charleston the next morning. Carrington later caught up with NG's traveling party. (See NG's Journal, 4 September, below.)

From William Pierce, Jr.

My dear General   Charles Town, [S.C.] August 17ᵗʰ [17]83.

I arrived here too late by one Day to take you by the hand. Yesterday I was deposited in ChˢTown, after a boisterous passage of eleven Days from Philadelphia.[1]

I brought with me a number of Letters,[2] and had much to communicate to you on the score of friendship. Your Friends will be happy to see you, and I will undertake to say that the Philadelphia Papers will be more grateful to you than the Gazettes of this Country have been. There is, however, very little share of attention for military characters any where at present. I found myself more respected in a Citizens Coat than in a military garb, *even in the City of Philadelphia*.[3]

You have no doubt had reports of the arrival of the definitive treaty at New York. I can assure you they are all spurious. The reason given for its procrastination by the wise Men abroad, is that they mean to establish it upon such principles as to secure a long and lasting peace to Europe, to unfetter the prejudices of the People, and to spread more extensively the sails of commerce over the Globe. The great principle of trade seems to be the Line of policy at present: even France and Spain begin to respect the *Lex Mercatorio*.[4] You will be disappointed in seeing Mʳˢ Greene at Philadelphia. She has long since taken her departure for Rhode Island, and carried with her her Son George.[5]

As you pass through Virginia it will be in your power to render me material service. The Majority to the Artillery is rendered vacant by the death of old [Christian] Holmer, and Genˡ [Benjamin] Lincoln tells me that I shall fill it provided I can obtain a certificate from the State of Virginia. I wrote to Governor [Benjamin] Harrison upon the occasion, but he declined giving it to me upon a supposition that I had retired upon the half pay establishment. Now sir you know the circumstances relative to my situation, and I hope you will do me the justice to represent it to Governor Harrison. I consider myself as standing on the arrangement of the Army, and am justified in thinking so by the assurances you gave me. The Governor will shew you a Letter from me enclosing two Certificates, together with a Letter from Genˡ Lincoln informing him that no report had been made of my retiring, and untill that took place, he should consider me as a permanent Officer.[6]

I now sir take my leave of you with the strongest impressions of friendship and affection. May you retire into the bosom of private Life with this comfortable reflection, that you have done your duty, and deserve well of your Country. All that domestic happiness can give you I am sure you will have.

I beg Sir you will consider me as one of your best Friend[s], and believe that I would serve you with my Life. The follies of youth forgive, and my virtues remember. What sometimes may have appeared wrong, might perhaps have been imposed upon me by necessity, or urged by motives of the strictest propriety. I can assure you with great sincerety that I forget every unhappy feud, and look up to you as a Son would to a Father with veneration, love, and respect. Yours with sincerety

W^M PIERCE J^R

RCS (MiU-C).

1. NG left Charleston on Thursday, 14 August. (NG to Washington, 8 August, above) As seen at Richard Hutson's letter to NG of 19 August, below, Pierce arrived in Charleston on the 15th.

2. Among the letters that Pierce brought from Philadelphia were those to NG from Joseph Reed, 3 August, and Charles Pettit, 4 August, both above.

3. As seen in the note at NG's letter to Guerard of 8 March, above, NG's public support of the 1781 federal impost proposal in South Carolina had caused a storm of criticism against him in that state. (Vol. 12: 497n, above) NG's letter to Guerard of 9 March, above, in defense of the impressment of forage for the army horses, was equally unpopular. (Ibid., pp. 497–98) In the *South-Carolina Weekly Gazette* of 22 March, for example, "Hampden" asserted that NG's threat to impress forage, if South Carolina did not establish a method for providing it, was "a direct attack upon the unalienable rights of the people." "Hampden" argued that only the legislature could decide to allow impressments and suggested that if NG wanted to demonstrate that he "really has the cause of liberty at heart," he should take his request to the Assembly.

4. On the "definitive" peace treaty, see Lafayette to NG, 8 September, below. The *International Law Dictionary & Directory* (http:/august1.com/pubs.dict/'1.htm) defines *lex mercatoria* as "common commercial rules and procedures used throughout Europe in the Renaissance period."

5. See Pettit to NG, 4 August.

6. Christian Holmer, a Virginian, had been a major in the Continental artillery. (Heitman, *Register*) NG had previously recommended Pierce for promotion in a letter to Harrison of 7 September 1782, above. (Vol. 11: 632 and n) Harrison was not in Richmond, Va., when NG stopped there on his way north. (NG's Journal, 6 September, below) NG replied to Pierce on 15 October, below.

NG's Journal

19. [August 1783]

We left Georgetown [S.C.], which stands on a tongue or peninsula of land, formed by three great rivers, the Pedee, Black River, and the Waccamaw on one side, and a small river called Sampet Creek on the other. It was burnt by the enemy in 1781.[1] It is well situated for trade, and in time, will be a considerable place. Its situation is pleasant but rather unhealthy. Our horses had been sent up to Mr. Joseph Allston's the day before we left Georgetown, and Colonel Hamit was kind enough to furnish us with a fast sailing canoe to convey us up there by water; but he would not let us pass his plantation without taking a look at it.[2] He led us to his indigo works in all the pride of wealth, melting under the scorching sun, and almost suffocated with the disagreeable smell of the place. The business was agreeable to him who felt the profits, but to us it was a heavy tax, our curiosity having been satisfied before. [Evan] Edwards got out of all patience, and I was afraid would not preserve his good breeding. However we left the colonel in the most perfect good-humor. Our passage up to Mr. Allston's was pleasant and our arrival critical; for the moment we got into the house there came on a heavy shower. Mr. Allston gave us a cordial reception and regaled us with fine old wine. His fortune is ample and his heart is open. He is about fifty, with a fine open countenance and manly appearance, possessing an excellent judgment and supporting a good private character; but he has been rather too attentive to his interest to be popular among the people. He has a number of fine rich plantations laying upon the fertile borders of the Waccamaw, from which he has accumulated a prodigious fortune from the articles of rice and indigo.

Printed in Greene, *Greene*, 3: 497–98.

1. On the burning of Georgetown by the British in the summer of 1781, see above, NG to Thomas McKean, 25 August 1781 (vol. 9: 241, 243–44n).

2. "Colonel Hamit" was probably George Heriot, a business partner of Daniel Tucker, whom NG had visited near Georgetown. (See note at NG's Journal entry for 16 August, above.) On Allston, see *Biog. Directory of S.C. House*, 2: 35–37.

*   *   *

¶ [FROM RICHARD HUTSON,[1] Charleston, S.C., 19 August 1783. It gave him "infinite concern" that he was not at home when NG called "to bid adieu." NG "left no person in South Carolina, more sensible" of his "merit" than Hutson, "or more awake to the feelings of Gratitude" for his "distinguished exertions." Hutson writes: "May the peaceful Olive emulate the [Tree?] of the victorious Laurel in adorning your Brow. May Heaven prosper you in all your . . . undertakings and after a long protracted Life of Felicity here, crown you with the ineffable rewards which await the good, the virtuous and the brave." Col. [Edward] Carrington, who will leave "Tomorrow Morning," called on him "this evening," giving him the opportunity to send this "hasty line" and "give vent to the effusions of my heart." Hutson recommends to NG's "Notice and Patronage" his "Orphan Nephew Mr Isaac Hayne, who is studying Physics with Doctor Rush." NG must be "well acquainted with the affecting History" of Hayne's "worthy Father," whose "Estate is much involved."[2] Hutson is "straining every nerve to fulfill the ardent wish" of his "deceased Friend" Hayne "to have his Children qualified to figure on the Stage of Life, as useful Members of Society." He has sent two bills to Hayne, "one on the Financier, for One Hundred Dollars, another on the Paymaster for fifty ones." But according to a letter that arrived with Major Pierce, both bills have been rejected.[3] Hutson has already made so many disbursements, "in compliance with pressing demands," that he will not be able to provide "any farther supply before the next Boat comes in." Hayne must be "much embarrassed," and Hutson hopes that NG can help him "obtain payment of these draughts." NG's "services in this affair" will "lay an indissoluble obligation" on Hutson.[4] RCS (MiU-C) 2 pp.]

1. Hutson (1747–95), a lawyer and member of the General Assembly, had been the lieutenant governor of South Carolina and a delegate to the Continental Congress. He was also chosen to serve as the first intendant of the city of Charleston. (*Biog. Directory of S.C. House*, 3: 364–66; Hutson to NG, 5 February 1784, below)

2. Isaac Hayne (1745–81), a South Carolina militia officer and the husband of Hutson's sister Elizabeth, was executed by the British during the war. (Vol. 9: 251–52n, above) Hayne was the father of seven children, of whom Isaac (1766–1802) was the oldest. (*Biog. Directory of S.C. House*, 2: 310–11) The young man was studying with Dr. Benjamin Rush of Philadelphia, the most eminent physician in the country, who had served as physician general during the war. (Vol. 2: 68n, above)

3. Robert Morris was the "Financier"; John Pierce was the paymaster general. William Pierce had recently returned to Charleston from Philadelphia. (Pierce to NG, 17 August, above)

4. It is not known whether NG intervened on young Hayne's behalf.

*   *   *

NG's Journal

20. [August 1783]

We set out for Wilmington [N.C.], having poverty before us and leaving plenty behind us. This day would have been distressing both to man and beast but for Mr. [Joseph] Allston's ample provision for both. The roads were sandy, and the travelling heavy most part of the day, except in crossing Long Bay, where the beach is hard and the riding easy and delightful.[1] In crossing this we had a grandeur of incidents not common. It lays open to the sea, and is about sixteen miles long. While we were upon it there came up a heavy thunder-shower. To behold the sea rolling on one side upon the beach in all the majesty of the ocean, and on the other hand to see the forked lightning play, and hear the boisterous thunder roar, filled the mind with admiration, one of the most pleasing passions that can occupy the human soul. But we got a prodigious wetting by a heavy shower, and that soon banished all our philosophy and put us a little out of temper. We halted at one Varren's who looks as if he eat all his own provisions.[2] It is certain he had none for us, either for man or beast. In size he is little inferior to Sir Edward Bright[3]; in filthiness as dirty as imagination can form. It was our intention to put up here all night, but his poverty and appearance obliged us to ride twelve miles farther to a Mr. Bull's, where our situation was but little mended.[4] With great difficulty we got something for our horses, but nothing for ourselves. The house made a good appearance without, but had no furniture within excepting an ugly old woman and a dirty old man without principle or decency, whose want of modesty produced a bill four times as large as it ought to have been.

Printed in Greene, *Greene*, 3: 498.
1. On many eighteenth-century maps, Long Bay applies to a sixteen-mile stretch of sand called the Long Beach (now Myrtle Beach, S.C., and its vicinity).
2. Jeremiah Vareen, Sr., of All Saints Parish (now Horry County, S.C.), kept a public house "near the Long Bay, and a little out of the road." (*NCSR*, 15: 381)
3. Edward Bright of Essex, England, a legendary "fat man," weighed 616 pounds at the time of his death at age thirty in 1750. (E. Cobham Brewer, *Dictionary of Phrase and Fable* [Philadelphia: J.B. Lippincott Co., n.d.], p. 448)
4. Nothing more about Bull's tavern has been found.

NG's Journal

21. [August 1783]
We got to Mr. Russes.[1] The country through which we passed was very poor and the roads bad. A great extent of country in this quarter is too barren to afford any means of sustenance and will always remain uncultivated. At Mr. Russes everything had the appearance of poverty, but things were decent and clean, and the landlord and lady kind and obliging.

Printed in Greene, *Greene*, 3: 498–99.
1. Russ's tavern, some twenty-five miles south of Wilmington, N.C., on the road between Georgetown, S.C., and Wilmington, was operated by Francis, John, or Thomas Russ. (*GW Diaries*, 6: 121n)

NG's Journal

22. [August 1784]
We set off for Wilmington [N.C.] very early in the morning and rode sixteen miles to Learward's Ferry to breakfast.[1] And here again we had another of those scenes which are so disgusting to the eye and offensive to the smell. With much difficulty we got a little bread and milk, and this we were obliged to eat amidst the squalling of children. We got away from this place as soon as possible. The man was tenant to a gentleman who married one of General Howe's daughters.[2] [Evan] Edwards was taken with a fever, and [Edmund M.] Hyrne and he, between them, led us all in the party out of the way five or six miles.[3] The former was very sick and with difficulty got to Wilmington, where we found good quarters and better cheer than we had met with after leaving Mr. Allston's.[4] The roads the last day were intolerable, and the causeway at Wilmington very bad; but neither were as bad as Major Edwards had painted them. This kind of exaggeration has one good effect; bad as we

may find things we are pleased to find them better than we had expected. Wilmington is situated near the mouth of Cape Fear, formed by two branches which runs a great distance into the country, called northeast and northwest. The trade of this place will be considerable as agriculture increases. But Cross Creek [i.e., Fayetteville] will prevent its ever becoming very capital. The manners of the people are plain, and they made some show of rejoicing on our arrival by bonfires in the streets, firing of guns, and faint illuminations. The town lays partly under a hill, and is not very handsomely built or elegantly laid out. We were visited by all the principal people and our stay urged, but neither the pleasures of the place or the hospitality of the people could detain us more than a day. We dined with Mr. McCallister, who formerly led the advance party at the taking of Powley's Hook by Lieutenant-colonel Lee.[5] He put into this place by accident from Charleston, heard of a rich widow, boldly attacks her in the Hudibrastic style, and carried her off in triumph in a few weeks. She is an agreeable lady with a very pretty fortune,—a handsome reward for a bold enterprise. How many difficulties are got over if but boldly attempted, as well in the affairs of love as those of the field.

Printed in Greene, *Greene*, 3: 499–500.

1. "Learward's Ferry" has not been identified; it is possible that NG was referring to Lockwood's Folly, in central Brunswick County, near Wilmington.

2. The American general Robert Howe, who at one time commanded the Southern Department, lived in the vicinity of Brunswick, N.C., close to where NG was traveling. His plantation had been destroyed during a British invasion in 1776. (Boatner, *Encyc.*; Waddell, *New Hanover County*, p. 179)

3. Edwards and Hyrne were traveling with NG.

4. On Joseph Allston, see above, NG's Journal, 19 and 20 August.

5. On Henry Lee's attack on the British post at Paulus Hook, N.J., in August 1779, see above, NG to CG, 23 August 1779 (vol. 4: 333, 334n). Lt. Archibald McCallister's role in the attack is noted in Heitman, *Register*.

NG's Journal

23. [August 1783]

We continued at Wilmington [N.C.] and took lodgings at Mrs. Week's, a woman of a noble figure and agreeable manners; but she has a perfect Jerry for a husband. No pen can draw a character more perfect than this man answers to the character of Jerry Sneak.[1] The town was all illuminated this evening and made no bad appearance.

Printed in Greene, *Greene*, 3: 500.

1. According to *OED*, a "Jerry-sneak" was "a meansneaking fellow" or "a henpecked husband." This may have been Zachariah Weeks, who was listed as a property owner on the town's tax roles. (Donald R. Lennon and Ida B. Kellum, eds., *The Wilmington Town Book, 1743–1777* [Raleigh, N.C.: State Dept. of Archives and History, 1973], p. 83) His wife's name is not known.

NG's Journal

24. [August 1783]

We set off for General Lillington's,[1] and dined with Mr. Jones about twelve miles.[2] He gave us some excellent cider, and fine old cherry bounce; but he detained us so long for dinner that it was within night before we got to General Lillington's; the roads being very sandy, we found it heavy travelling.

Printed in Greene, *Greene*, 3: 500.

1. John Alexander Lillington, who usually went by his middle name, was a general in the North Carolina militia. Although he was an implacable foe to the British while they occupied Wilmington during much of 1781, local tradition holds that his impressive estate, Lillington Hall, in present-day Pender County, was saved from burning by the British through the intervention of local Loyalists who admired and respected him. (*N.C. Biographical Dictionary*, 4: 66–67)

2. This may have been William Jones, who lived on Long Creek, about twelve miles from Wilmington. He had been an active patriot during the Revolution. (Leora H. McEachern and Isabel M. Williams, eds., *Wilmington–New Hanover Safety Committee Minutes, 1774–1776* [Wilmington, N.C.: Wilmington–New Hanover American Revolution Bicentennial Association, 1974], p. 128)

NG's Journal

25. [August 1783]

We set off for Colonel Blount's, having the major, his son, for our pilot.[1] We rode five-and-forty miles this day, and lodged at one Winsett's, a very dirty place. We breakfasted the day before at Simmons', who told us the country had all been laid under water; for that it had rained forty days and forty nights. Major Blount entertained us with several curious anecdotes.

Printed in Greene, *Greene*, 3: 500.

1. This was Jacob Blount, the former paymaster of the North Carolina militia. His home, Blount Hall, was near Contentnea Creek, in the New Bern district (now Pitt County). (Blount, *Papers*, 1: xv, xvii) Maj. Reading Blount, his son, had served with NG, gaining distinction for bravery in the battles of Guilford Court House and Eutaw Springs. (*N.C. Biographical Dictionary*, 1: 178, 180–81)

NG's Journal

26. [August 1783]

We breakfasted with young General Caswell.[1] He has a pretty wife, and gave us a polite reception.[2] He was so liberal to our servants, and fed our horses so plentifully, that the first got drunk and the last got foundered. To-day we were to have dined with Colonel [Jacob] Blount, and should have got there in good season, but the major [Reading Blount], either from the effects of cherry bounce and morning bitters or from the charms of Mrs. Caswell, found his head so like uncle Toby's smoke-jack[3] that he missed the way where he was as well acquainted with it as with his bed-chamber, and led us at least seven miles out of the road, which prevented our arriving till within the evening. From this to Wilmington [N.C.] is about one hundred and eight miles; the country generally level and the soil sandy and poor; but there are spots of most excellent land. Colonel Blount gave us a most cordial reception and introduced us to his family.[4] His person and his manners appear with great dignity. He is very generous, polite, and hospitable; and all in that way which is most pleasing, being free from affectation and that troublesome civility of always teasing one to eat or drink or make free without leaving one at liberty to do either but by importunity. The colonel is no less marvelous than hospitable; he says a family in his neighborhood was excused from military duty from the amazing quantity of water they drank, each carrying a large tubful to bed with them. . . . This is related as a fact. So great was the aversion to the military service in this neighborhood that out of fifty-eight persons fifty-six were found to have artificial hernia. . . . This may appear extraordinary, but fear is ingenious to contrive modes of escape from approaching danger. Nothing can give a more striking proof of the danger of the southern service than this anecdote. . . . There is now in the neighborhood of Hillsborough a seventh son of a seventh son, who is said to cure only with the touch every species of complaint. Marvels in North Carolina thicken apace. Prodigies of every kind are propagated and believed. Hundreds of people are encamped round about this child, who is but eight years old, and will take nothing for the cures he performs. There are things in nature far above our comprehension. This may be one of them; but in this enlightened age, when science and philosophy have banished all those wonderful tales which formerly amused the world, I am not apt to be credulous.

Printed in Greene, *Greene*, 3: 500–501.

1. William Caswell, the son of former North Carolina governor Richard Caswell, was a general in the North Carolina militia. He had also served in the state legislature and in the Continental army as a captain. His plantation was in present-day Kinston, N.C. (*N.C. Biographical Dictionary*, 1: 344–45)

2. Gathra Mackilwea, known as Gatsey, had married Caswell, her cousin, in December 1782. (Ibid.; "Caswell Family Pages," www.freepages.genealogy.rootsweb.com)

3. The reference here is to Laurence Sterne's novel *Tristram Shandy*, which was a favorite of NG's.

4. On Jacob Blount, see note at NG's Journal entry for 25 August, immediately above.

From Henry Laurens

Sir   Bath [England] 26th Aug[t] 1783

I was yesterday honored by the receipt of your Letter of the 10th June, it came to me by the common Post & I have heard nothing from your Cousin M[r] Grif[fin] Greene. I shall to morrow write to a friend in London to make the necessary inquiry for him, with a tender of my best services, particularly in the article of procuring Mr Green a Credit for one thousand Pounds, in a word, nothing in my power shall be omited to assure you Sir, of my friendship & regard.[1]

Having obtained permission from Congress to return to America, I was actually taking proper measures for that purpose, my views for the present are defeated by an affecting call from the voice of a dying Brother to the south of France, whither I shall proceed in a few days, to take a last Leave of him & render my protection [to] a Widowed Sister & my youngest Daughter, hence I can entertain no hope of the pleasure of taking you by the hand, before the Spring of next Year.[2]

I sincerely rejoice with you Sir, on the happy return of Peace, but beleive me, we have much rough ground to go over before we shall reap solid fruits, true wisdom on our side, will nevertheless carry us safely through the rugged March with cheerfulness. I had a Letter to-day of the 21st Inst. from Doctor Franklin, nothing respecting new Treaties had then been concluded; dispatches from this side were then on the Road, which will probably, produce an eclaircissement for effecting, at least a temporary project for Commerce.[3] The Definitive is uncertain, indeed I may say every thing is so. I shall call at Paris in my way to the south, while I am in this Kingdom in pursuit of health, my time is not lost to my Country. I have the honor to be With very great Respect & Regard Sir Your obedient & most humble servant   HENRY LAURENS

RCS (NNC).

1. In his letter to Laurens of 10 June, above, NG had requested a letter of credit for Griffin Greene, who left for Europe about that time on business for the family firm. (See also NG to Griffin Greene, 10 June and 14 June, above.)

2. Laurens's brother James died in the south of France on 25 January 1784. (Chesnutt, *Laurens Papers*, 16: 373n) Laurens's daughter, Martha (Patsy) was staying with James and his wife, the former Mary Holland Crawford. (Ibid., p. 10n)

3. After his release from the Tower of London, Laurens had been appointed a peace commissioner to help negotiate a definitive treaty of peace in Paris. (Vol. 12: 149n, above) Congress had granted him permission to return to the United States in an April 1783 resolution (*JCC*, 24: 226). The original of Benjamin Franklin's letter is at the New York Public Library. (Chesnutt, *Laurens Papers*, 16: 817)

NG's Journal

27 and 28. [August 1783]
We remained at Colonel Blount's for the recovery of my horse. His house is agreeable situated near the river Contentment, which runs a great distance into the country.[1] His farm is large and fortune considerable.

Printed in Greene, *Greene*, 3: 502.

1. As noted at NG's Journal, 25 August, above, Jacob Blount's plantation was near Contentnea Creek, N.C.

NG's Journal

29. [August 1783]

We set out for Halifax [N.C.] and lodged at Colonel Hardy's an old gentleman who had lived with one wife upwards of fifty years, and near eighty years of age.[1]

Printed in Greene, *Greene*, 3: 502.
1. This may have been John Hardee, who had served as chairman of the Pitt County Committee of Safety in 1774 and helped to organize the county's militia regiment in 1773. (*NCSR*, 9: 696, 1079)

NG's Journal

30. [August 1783]

From this to Tarborough [N.C.] the country is hilly; generally pretty good land and very healthy. The people would take no money from us. We dined at Mr. Blount's in Tarborough, a small village situated on the banks of the river.[1] Our reception was polite and entertainment agreeable. We lodged this night at one Major Philips'.[2] He invited us home with him, but the poor man's heart seemed heavy; our retinue was so large as caused too great a consumption of corn.

Printed in Greene, *Greene*, 3: 502.
1. This was Thomas, another son of Jacob Blount. With his brothers William and John Gray Blount, Thomas had established and operated one of the largest mercantile establishments in North Carolina. The Blount enterprise had its principal base of operations in Washington, N.C., but had other establishments in the state, and Thomas operated the one at Tarboro, a small town along the Tar River. (*N.C. Biographical Dictionary*, 1: 182–83)
2. This was probably Ethelred Phillips, a member of the North Carolina General Assembly and a major in an Edgecombe district militia regiment raised in 1782. (*NCSR*, 16: 3; 19: 141, 145, 256)

NG's Journal

31. [August 1783]

At break of day we left this [i.e., Tarboro, N.C.] for Halifax, and breakfasted within eleven miles of it, at one ——, whose fondness for talking was a little less than the man's Horace complains of.[1] [Evan] Edwards and myself got each a book to avoid his impertinence, but having lived long in South Carolina, and being a good planter, he interested [Edmund M.] Hyrne pretty deeply in his conversation. We were met on the road by a number of officers and citizens and conducted to Colonel Ashe's, where we lodged during our stay in that quarter.[2] Halifax is a little village, containing about fifty or sixty houses, on the banks of the Roanoke, one hundred miles from the sea, and promises at some future day to be a considerable place. Mr. Wily Jones has the only costly seat in or about this place, and is one of its principal inhabitants.[3] Colonel Ashe and he married sisters, both agreeable women.[4]

Printed in Greene, *Greene*, 3: 502.

1. NG apparently had some familiarity with the writings of the Roman poet Horace (Quintus Horatius Flaccus, 65 B.C.–8 B.C.).

2. John Baptiste Ashe was from a prominent North Carolina family. As an officer in the North Carolina Continental line, he served in both Washington's army and with NG in the South, winning plaudits for the conduct of his command at the battle of Eutaw Springs in 1781. He later became an important politician in North Carolina and was elected governor in 1802 but died before he could assume office. (*N.C. Biographical Dictionary*, 1: 52–53)

3. Willie (pronounced Wyley) Jones was an important political leader in North Carolina. In the early 1760s, he inherited his family's home, "The Castle," three miles south of present-day Jackson, N.C. As Jones wanted to live in Halifax, he had the house dismantled and used many of its timbers, which were said to have come from England, in the construction of a new house, "The Groves," in the southern end of that town. Behind his home was one of the finest race tracks in North Carolina. (See also NG's Journal entry for 1 September, below.) During the Revolution, Jones served in a number of political offices, including delegate to Congress. (*N.C. Biographical Dictionary*, 3: 330–31; *DAB*)

4. John Baptiste Ashe had married Elizabeth Montfort; Jones, her older sister Mary. The Montfort sisters were daughters of Joseph Montfort of Halifax, N.C. (*N.C. Biographical Dictionary*, 1:53; *DAB*)

*   *   *

¶ [FROM GENERAL ISAAC HUGER, "South Carolina," August 1783.[1] "Agreeable to a resolution" of the South Carolina legislature, he will settle with the state for his pay as a brigadier general. Asks NG to determine the balance owed to him for the "five years pay voted by Congress to the officers of the Army." If NG finds "any prospect of pay to the officers," Huger asks him to "receive it for me." He also asks NG to "inquire of the best Coach maker the price of a Coach." If Huger can get his pay from Congress, he may ask NG to "engage" one for him.[2] Tr (Typescript: MiU-C) 1 p.]

1. On Huger, who had been the commander of the South Carolina Continental line, see above, vol. 6: 535–36n.

2. No reply has been found.

*   *   *

NG's Journal

Sept. 1. [1783]

We dined with Colonel [Willie] Jones, and was agreeable entertained with an account of his races, he being a great sportsman, and prostitutes most excellent talents to pleasure which should be employed in the service of his country.[1]

Printed in Greene, *Greene*, 3: 502–3.

1. On Jones, see also NG's Journal entry for 31 August, above.

To Governor Alexander Martin of North Carolina

Sir   Halifax [N.C.] Septem^r 2^d 1783
The bearer of this Thomas Moody, an old Gentleman represents his great sufferings by the enemy when they were in the neighborhood of Guilford. He was in our army in that action & piloted the Artillery, & no doubt was much exposed.[1] If any thing can be done for him in his distressed situation, it will be releiving the unfortunate, & rewarding the fidelity of an honest old man. Your Excellency is the best judge of the probability of interesting the Assembly in his affairs, and will advise the old Gentleman accordingly. I shall be happy if anything I can say will promote his wishes, as I beleive him to be an object of public charity, & meriting some attention.[2] I have the honor to be, with great respect, Your Excellencys most obedient humble servant   NATH GREENE

ALS (Nc-Ar).
1. On the battle of Guilford Court House, see NG to Samuel Huntington, 16 March 1781, above (vol. 7: 433–36 and n).
2. Martin's reply has not been found.

NG's Journal

2. [September 1783]
We dined with Colonel [Nicholas] Long, a character directly opposite to Mr. Jones'.[1] He has no taste for pleasure, but is remarkably industrious. He has been quartermaster-general to the States most part of the war. His mechanical ingenuity and great attention to business were admirably adapted to the wants and disposition of the people of that State.[2] This evening the officers and citizens [of Halifax, N.C.] gave a ball, and we were received at the assembly room with a discharge of twenty cannon. The notice of the ball had been so short, as our stay had been uncertain, the collection of ladies was not large, yet their numbers were considerable and the appearance tolerable. The room was very decent and the supper genteel. The company were in grand spirits, and all seemed to enjoy the amusements. [Evan] Edwards took himself to a gaming table and won most of his money back from Captain [Borruit?] which he had given him a few days before for a pair of fine bay horses well matched. The appearance of this officer the next morning after his losses, which amounted to near thirty guineas, was sufficient to disgust every man with gaming. The workings of his soul was visible in his countenance. If his feelings were painful to us, how must they have been to him. Nothing so distressing as self-reproach, and nothing so painful as to be author of one's own ruin. We have neither retreat or consolation to compose us. All is dark and horrible. Ruin lays before us, and madness and folly surround us. But to return to the ball, where the

sparkling ladies enlivened every soul and sweetened every pleasure. The evening closed agreeably, and the company parted in great good humor. Miss [Housen?], Miss Long,[3] Miss Taddy, and Miss [Gelahrick?] were the most celebrated for beauty.

Printed in Greene, *Greene*, 3: 503.
1. On Willie Jones's character, see NG's Journal entry for 1 September, above.
2. As NG noted here, Long had been the North Carolina state quartermaster. He had also served as a militia commander and was active in local and state politics. Next to Jones, he was the wealthiest man in Halifax. Long was married to the former Mary McKinne. (*N.C. Biographical Dictionary*, 4: 93)
3. Miss Long was presumably one of Nicholas Long's daughters, Martha or Mary.

NG's Journal

3. [September 1783]

We left Halifax [N.C.] accompanied by a number of both officers and citizens. During our stay at Halifax there had fallen a considerable body of rain and there was a remarkable change in the air. The thermometer fell from 90 degrees to 58. This made the riding cool and the roads delightful. Our passage through North Carolina had been rendered as agreeable as possible by the polite attention of the inhabitants. It will be a long time before this State will begin to feel its importance. Dissipation and idleness are too predominant for either law or reason to control. The people live too remote from each other to be animated by a principle of emulation. Where men live more contiguous they warm and rouse the passions of each other, and the desire of excelling inspires one common spirit of industry. What adds to the misfortunes of this State is, morality is at a low ebb and religion almost held in contempt, which are the great pillars of good government and sound policy. Where these evils prevail the laws will be treated with neglect and the magistrate with contempt. Patriotism will have little influence and government continues without dignity. We lodged this night at Hixes Ford, where we had a specimen of that worst of evils which can inflict the lower orders of people in any community, a general disposition for gaming.[1] It is the bane of all honest industry, and while it corrupts the morals it ruins the manners. Neither taste nor sentiment can prevail where this evil gets footing. Happily for the States the higher order of people have not catched the contagion so fully. Every vice is in the train of gaming, and ruin and disgrace will soon follow, if the example of the better order of people don't correct this folly. There will be neither spirit or union or principles of liberty to support our republican form of government. Ruin the morals and corrupt the manners of any people and they will soon become the fit instrument of tyranny and despotism. Great pains is taking to the southward to ruin the influence of what is called the aristocratic interest. It may appear strange, but I fear it will prove true the sooner their influence is lost the sooner monarchy under some form will begin. This order of men appear to be the only barrier to some enterprising spirit from rising up and putting down the republican fabric and building on its ruins monarchy if not tyranny. Sapping the powers of Congress and lessening their influence will also facilitate this business. With what avidity does people often embrace measures which gratify but for a moment and lay a train for their ruin.

Printed in Greene, *Greene*, 3: 503–5.

1. Hicksford, Va., near the North Carolina border and almost due south of Petersburg, was situated in what is now Emporia, the county seat of Greensville County. (http://www.rootsweb.com/~vagreens/)

NG's Journal

4. [September 1783]

We started early and breakfasted at Mr. Clevey's. This is a religious family and the happy fruits was visible in everything about them. He is one of Wesley's disciples and appears to be an honest man.[1] I could not help contrasting the happy prospects of this family with the wretched appearance of things at the place where we dined. In one there was neatness, plenty, and everything of the best kind; in the other noise, dirt, and all kind of filthiness prevailed. This man affects a general acquaintance with the British nobility, and says he knew the king [George III] when a boy, and that his appearance was always more like a shoeblack than a prince royal. At the former house [Evan] Edwards got to reading "Pilgrim's Progress," and got as far as Flash Lane and went to church.[2] He is remarkable for new doctrines as well as singular sentiments. [Edmund M.] Hyrne always opposed him. Before [Col. Edward] Carrington's arrival, Edwards always used to be boasting that he was sure of his [i.e., Carrington's] support, but they no sooner met than, like two game-cocks, they fell to fighting, and Hyrne and myself left quite at liberty to philosophize. We passed through Petersborough [i.e., Petersburg, Va.] and lodged at Mr. Bannister's.[3] He is a man of fortune and lives genteelly. Mrs. Bannister is not handsome, but sensible, and elegant in her manners.[4] This evening we went to Mr. Saint George Tucker's, who has a great turn for poetry.[5] His lady is a most elegant woman as well in her manners as her person, and she is as sociable as she is pleasing.[6] It is happy for her husband that he is a man of letters, and has a good natural genius, without which she must have felt a great superiority. We had a genteel supper and spent the evening sociably.

Printed in Greene, *Greene*, 3: 505–6.

1. "Mr. Clevey" has not been further identified. John Wesley was a founder of one of the main branches of the Methodist Church.

2. NG referred to John Bunyan's 17th-century work *Pilgrim's Progress from This World to That Which Is to Come.*

3. John Banister (1734–88), a Virginia military and political leader, had served as a lieutenant colonel in the militia, commanding a regiment of cavalry, and had also been a delegate to Congress in 1778–79, helping to draft the Articles of Confederation. His home, Battersea, was near Petersburg. It had suffered damage during the war, when it became a "convenient stopping-place" for the British during their 1781 invasion of Virginia. (*DAB*)

4. This was Banister's second wife, Anne Blair Banister. (*DAB*)

5. St. George Tucker (1752–1827) is best known as a jurist and legal scholar. According to the author of his profile in *DAB*, he also wrote "minor poetry of some charm."

6. Tucker married Frances Bland Randolph, a young widow, in 1778. They lived on her estate, "Matoax," in Cumberland County. (*DAB*)

NG's Journal

5. [September 1783]

We left Petersburg [Va.] for Richmond. This town is situated under a hill upon the river Apomatic [i.e., Appomatox]. Trade flourishes here, but the place is very sickly. Many families of distinction live in the neighborhood of this place, but few or none in it. A little below this town the Apomatic empties itself into James River. Tobacco and flour are the great staples of trade at this place. Mr. Bannister has one set of mills with which he manufactures sixty thousand bushels of wheat [flour] each year, that stands within a mile of this place. The profits are not less than £2,000 sterling. We intended to have dined to-day with Colonel Cary, but he was from home over James River at Mrs. Rastall's and we crossed the river and dined with her by especial invitation, and returned in the evening to Colonel Cary's.[1] The roads from Petersburg to this place are very uneven, not less so than the Northern States.

Printed in Greene, *Greene*, 3: 506.

1. Archibald Cary (1721–87) was a planter, businessman, and political leader who served as speaker of the Virginia Senate from 1776 through 1783. His estate, "Ampthill," was on the James River in Chesterfield County. He also owned a large and profitable flour mill. (*DAB*)

NG's Journal

6. [September 1783]

Colonel Cary being a[n] old bruiser, and swearing by God I should dine with him to-day, and doubling his fist at the same time, I did not care to contradict him for fear of a blow. He is one of patrician order and a man of great property, very liberal in his sentiments and hospitable in his disposition.[1] By a hint I gave him when he went to the southward, he told me he had saved the greater part of his property.[2] We went this evening to Richmond the capital of Virginia. The governor [Benjamin Harrison] was out of town, but the corporation met and presented me with a polite address, and an invitation to a public dinner.[3] The first I gave an answer to,[4] but the last I was obliged to decline as I was in a hurry to get forward. This city is agreeably situated upon the side of a large hill, little short of a mountain, about half a mile below the falls upon James River. It is a thriving place and bids fair to be a great place of trade. Here Colonel [Edward] Carrington parted with us, and here I had the pleasure of seeing Clairborne, [i.e. Richard Claiborne], formerly one of my family in the staff.[5] He was not altered, being as formal as ever.

Printed in Greene, *Greene*, 3: 506–7.
1. Archibald Cary was called "Old Bruiser" because of his compact and muscular build; his temperament has been described as "courteous, genial, and hospitable." (*DAB*)
2. NG had visited Cary in late 1780, while traveling through Virginia on his way to take command of the Southern Army. (NG to Washington, 19 November 1780, above [vol. 6: 488])
3. See From the Citizens of Richmond, 8 September, below.
4. See To the Citizens of Richmond, 9 September, below.
5. Maj. Richard Claiborne, most recently the deputy quartermaster for Virginia, had also been a deputy quartermaster general under NG. (See above, vol. 2: 515–16n.)

NG's Journal

7. [September 1783][1]
We were obliged to halt to get our horses shod and to receive and answer the address which was delivered by the mayor.[2]

Printed in Greene, *Greene*, 3: 507.
1. On the date, see note at From the Citizens of Richmond, 8 September, below.
2. As seen in ibid., John Beckley was the mayor of Richmond.

NG's Journal

8. [September 1783][1]
We set out for Fredericksburg [Va.] and lodged at Mr. John Baylor's, a man of considerable property, naturally very covetous and yet ostensibly generous. A great macaroni in dress, and was once the head of the Macaroni Club in London.[2] He possesses middling abilities and rather a morose temper. But what makes me have rather a disagreeable opinion of him is having treated his wife very ill, who is a very agreeable woman. [Evan] Edwards took a pleasure in mortifying him by exaggerating the South Carolina fortunes; comparing them with his, his appeared small. Before Edwards began on this subject, he [i.e., Baylor] was boasting of its extent, and he had not penetration enough to discover Edwards was a humming of him [i.e., joking].

Printed in Greene, *Greene*, 3: 507.
1. On the date, see note at From the Citizens of Richmond, 8 September, below.
2. Members of the "Macaroni Club in London" were foppish young men who affected a preference for Continental tastes. A "macaroni" was a "dandy." (*OED*)

*　　　*　　　*

¶ [FROM THE MARQUIS DE LAFAYETTE, Nancy [i.e., Nantes, France], 8 September 1783. Has NG's letter of 9 June but does not know "How, or Whence it Came." As soon as he sees Mr. Griffin Greene, Lafayette will do "Every thing that Can lay within My power" for him.[1] This letter will be sent by the recently established monthly packet, which also carries the "definitive treaty"; that document seems little different from the "preliminary Articles."[2] Lafayette warns that "A Great Storm is Now Gathering in the East ward": Russia has invaded the "Krimee," and the "Turk are Preparing to Repel" the invasion; "the Part Prussia will take is as Yet Unknown." A quarrel between "Despotes" would not normally be of concern, but "this May Hereafter Become interesting Both to France and Great Britain. The first on Account of Her Levant trade, the Second, not only for that, But Because She Has a Reverse interest in Every French Concern."[3] While Lafayette is in Europe—where he remains "on American Accounts[,] which Congress know"—he will inform NG of "Every Transaction."[4] He hopes that by "this time" the army has been "Satisfied, and Measures are taking to Consolidate the Faderal Union." Adds: "Upon these two Points I Have Been and Still am Very Uneasy. The Justice of the one, and the importance of the other So Clearly Appear to me, that My Heart is Most Warmly Interested in the Affair." Col. [Thaddeus] Ogden has been "Here," and Lafayette has "Connect[ed] Him with a Powerfull House."[5] Should NG have "that or Any other Command to Give," he "May depend Upon My Exertions." Lafayette remains at Nantes at the request of "Mr. Barkley Consul General."[6] That "Business" and orders from Congress, or the need for his presence in America, may "at Every hour alter" his plans. He hopes "By next Packet" to be able to give his "future Motions." As soon as he is "at liberty," he will "Most Certainly fly to the Wished for and Beloved Shores of America." Sends his respects to CG and to his friends in the Southern Army and in the "Country." Asks to hear from NG "often." Catalog excerpt (Phillips Catalog, 1983)]

1. See NG to Lafayette, 9 June, above.

2. The "definitive treaty" was virtually the same as the preliminary articles of peace. (Morris, *Peacemakers*, pp. 434–37) On the preliminary terms, see above, Robert Livingston to NG, 12 March (vol. 12: 507–8 and n).

3. In June, Russia initiated military action to annex the Crimea, which, under a treaty with the Ottoman Empire, was to have remained independent. This was part of an attempt by Russia to expel the Turks from Europe. The onset of winter kept the Turkish and Russian armies from going to war. Prussia, which was seeking to take the Polish port of Danzig, did not get involved in this dispute. (Idzerda, *Lafayette Papers*, 5: 133n, 165n)

4. Lafayette had stayed in France to attempt to negotiate an extension of the time in which American merchants were obliged to repay debts to their British counterparts. (See Lafayette to the Comte de Vergennes, 21 July, Idzerda, *Lafayette Papers*, 5: 144.)

5. Lafayette had written letters of introduction for Ogden to Vergennes and to Lefèvre d'Ormesson, the French minister of finance. He had also secured an invitation for Ogden to a reception for King Louis XVI. (Ibid., p. 140n)

6. Thomas Barclay wrote Robert Livingston that he had asked Lafayette to remain there because France seemed "determin'd on adopting some Commercial regulations respecting the Trade to be carried on between the United States and their [i.e., France's] West Indies Colonies." (Barclay to Livingston, 14 September, PCC, item 137, vol. 4: 309–10)

¶ [FROM SAMUEL A. OTIS, Boston, Mass., 8 September 1783. Introduces his son, "the bearer hereof," to NG's notice.[1] The younger Otis has "passed thro his accademical studies" and is "under the tuition of Judge Lowell," with whom he is making a "short excursion southward."[2] Otis hopes "the youth will continue to observe such a line of conduct as will intitle him to the protection of the wise [and] good." NG "intimated" in his last letter "some expectation of getting the old acc[t] settled"; nothing would please Otis more "than to attend you upon that occasion, as I should be happy to upon any other."[3] RCS (MiU-C) 1 p.]

1. Harrison Gray Otis, who had recently graduated from Harvard College, "read law" with John Lowell and was admitted to the Boston bar in 1786. (*DAB*)

2. Lowell, a lawyer from Newburyport and Boston, and a Massachusetts political leader, was appointed judge of Congress's Court of Appeals on Admiralty Cases in 1782. He later became judge of the United States Court for the District of Massachusetts. (*DAB*)

3. The "old acc[t]" was presumably NG's as quartermaster general. As a principal of the Boston firm of Otis & Henley, Otis had served as a purchaser for the Quartermaster Department under NG. He brought this subject up again in a letter to NG of 24 July, below.

¶ [FROM THE CITIZENS OF RICHMOND, VIRGINIA, Richmond, Va., 8 September 1783. The "Mayor, Recorder, Aldermen & Common Council" of the city "embrace" the occasion of NG's "passing thro" to offer a "tribute of gratitude" for his "military skill & abilities." They also pay tribute to the "gallant band of patriot citizens," that, under the "auspices of a gracious Providence" and NG's guidance, "rose superior to the pressure of misfortune" to produce "peace, liberty, and Independence" for their country. "The grateful citizens of America can never be unmindful of their sufferings, their merit, their services, or disappoint the generous confidence of the brave Soldier in meeting the just reward of his toilsome labours; but upon his return to the relative duties of civil life the Associate character of the soldier and the citizen, will, we trust, be remembered, approved, and rewarded." They hope that NG "may possess in retirement, the generous confidence of a free people," that all his "future days may be serene and happy," and that the "plaudit of future ages may follow the testimony of a living world in transmitting, to the latest posterity, The remembrance of your Character and virtues." The address is signed by the mayor, John Beckley. RCS (Greene Papers: DLC) 1 p. The letter is badly damaged; to help decipher the damaged parts, the editors have used a copy printed in the *Virginia Gazette* of 13 September. The newspaper copy was preceded by the following: "On Sunday last [7 September] arrived here from the Southward, the Honorable Major-General Greene and suite, and on Tuesday [9 September] proceeded from hence, on his way to the Northward. During his stay, the following Address of the Corporation of our City was presented to him."[1]]

1. It could be inferred from NG's Journal entries for 6, 7, and 8 September, above, that he arrived in Richmond on the evening of 6 September, received this address on the 7th, left the city on 8 September, and reached Fredericksburg on the 9th. However, in view of the present document and the letter that NG wrote to Gov. Benjamin Harrison from Richmond on 9 September, below, the dates given by the newspaper seem likely to be correct. NG's reply to the address is below, dated 9 September.

¶ [FROM WATSON, COPAIL & COMPANY, London, 8 September 1783. Griffin Greene "arrived some time since in the Brigg *Minerva* loaded with tobacco, for the purpose of establishing a regular correspondence for the negotiation of whatever business any branch of the concern may have in future in this quarter." The company is "happy to inform" NG that after "well acquainting himself as to the reputation of the several American houses" in London, Griffin has given them "the preference, by putting the Minervas cargo" in their hands. They hope their "exertions thus far, to promote his Interest," and their "future endeavour," will meet his and NG's "approbation."[1] They will be "proud to be charged with any particular commands" NG "may have either in France, or England." They enclose two circulars [not found]. In addition to their "European establishments," they are "particularly connected to the house of Smedly & C°" and "recommend" Mr. Smedly to NG's "particular notice." They would also be "extreemly gratefull for whatever services" NG's "influence in S° Carolina" might "render" them. They enclose several of their "last papers as well as a general Price Current" [not found]. In a postscript, they report that Griffin is "now at Bourdeaux about the *Flora*." They have taken "every means" in their "power to be serviceable" in this matter, but their exertions have had "no effect." They add: "Such ships are very unsaleable in the present moment, & we fear your expectations will be greatly frustrated, as she is only calculated for the East India trade."[2] RC (MiU-C) 2 pp.]

1. On Griffin Greene's business in Europe, see, for example, NG's letter to him of 10 June, above, and his to NG of 1 October, below.

2. Griffin still had no prospect for selling the *Flora* when he wrote NG on 1 October and again on 8 February 1784, both below.

*   *   *

NG's Journal

9. [September 1783][1]
We got to Fredericksburg [Va.], but dined by the way at General Sportwood's,[2] whose lady appeared to be an excellent breeder.[3] General Weedon received us with open arms, and would not let us go on the next day or the day after.[4]

Printed in Greene, *Greene*, 3: 507.

1. On the date, see From the Citizens of Richmond, 8 September, above.

2. Alexander Spotswood's plantation, "Nottingham," was in what is now Spotsylvania County, Va. (See Spotswood to NG, 30 December 1782, above [vol. 12: 358], and Map 1 in ibid.)

3. Alexander and Elizabeth Washington Spotswood had five daughters. (*GW Diaries*, 6: 313n)

4. NG's close friend George Weedon lived in Fredericksburg.

To Governor Benjamin Harrison of Virginia

Sir   Richmond [Va.] Sept 9th 1783
Having happily closed the business of my command in the Southern department, I am on my way to the Northward. It would have afforded me great pleasure to have seen and felicitated you upon the flattering prospects before us. I cannot contemplate the happy change in the Southern affairs without admiring the dispensations of Providence; nor can I review them but with sentiments of gratitude and veneration. In the hours of our deepest suffering and most critical situation I have

often found it necessary to give the Army the strongest assurances that Government would never fail to do them ample justice. It will give me the highest satisfaction to see at an early hour the suffering Soldier meet with a generous reward for all his toils dangers and hardships. Public confidence is the best foundation for political happiness and I cannot doubt but that a wise people will pursue a just policy. I have nothing to add but my best wishes for the glory and prosperity of the State and that you may have an honorable and pleasing Administration.[1] With Sentiments of respect and esteem I have the honor to be Your Excellencys most Obed[t] humble Ser   N GREENE

ADfS (MiU-C).
1. Harrison replied to NG on 11 October, below.

*   *   *

¶ [TO THE CITIZENS OF RICHMOND, VIRGINIA. From ⟨Richmond, Va., 9 September 1783⟩. "Fully sensible" of the "honor" of their "polite Address," NG feels "the most lively emotions" from their "flattering assurances of esteem and affection.[1] The compliment you have pai[d] to my Military charactor and the noble justice you have done to the merit and conduct of the Troops under my command are highly interesting to my feelings." The citizens' "generous wishes" for his "future happiness, and what concerns my reputation" warrant NG's "warmest acknowledgements. The approbation of good Men is my first wish and the happiness of Society my great object." He hopes that Richmond will enjoy "all the blessings flowing from peace and indep⟨e⟩ndence under the happy Governmen⟨t⟩ of the Corporation." ADfS (Greene Papers: DLC) 2 pp. The draft is torn along the margins, and portions are missing; the text in angle brackets, including place and date, was taken from a copy printed in the *Virginia Gazette* of 13 September.]
1. See From the Citizens of Richmond, 8 September, above.

*   *   *

NG's Journal

10. [September 1783]

We dined with the general and invisited Mr. Hunter's works.[1] They are a great curiosity to a mechanical genius. Fredericksburg stands near the falls upon the Rappahannock River. The rich borders upon this river, and the great extent of country to the southwest of it, will make it a place of some trade; but I think it will never answer the expectations of the inhabitants.

Printed in Greene, *Greene*, 3: 507.
1. The "general" was undoubtedly NG's friend George Weedon. James Hunter's ironworks in Fredericksburg had turned out most of the iron products used by NG's army. Shortly after NG visited Fredericksburg, Hunter went into bankruptcy, and the ironworks

ceased operations. (Kathleen Bruce, *Virginia Iron Manufacture in the Slave Era* [New York: The Century Co., 1930], pp. 67–78) Hunter, known as James Hunter, Sr., was an older cousin of the James Hunter who was John Banks's business partner. (Ward, *Weedon*, p. 236)

NG's Journal

11. [September 1783]
We had a public dinner and a very polite address, and we spent the day and evening sociably.[1]

Printed in Greene, *Greene*, 3: 507.
1. A Philadelphia newspaper reported that the citizens of Fredericksburg, Va., "presented a very polite and affectionate address to" NG on 12 September and that "a public dinner was also provided. The meritorious achievements of that gallant officer, while commanding in the southern department, impressed the citizens of this commonwealth with the warmest gratitude." (*Pennsylvania Packet*, 7 October 1783) The citizens' address is below, dated 12 September.

NG's Journal

12. [September 1783]
We set out for Mount Vernon, General Washington's seat. Within a few miles of Dumfries [Va.] I overset my carriage, broke the top and harness and bruised myself not a little, and if I had not lifted up the carriage and let it pass over me, it is probable I might have got killed or badly wounded, for the horse started upon a run and drawed the carriage after him until the harness gave way. I felt the hurt at first, but more afterwards. At Dumfries we got a little repaired, but was obliged to stay a night there, contrary to my intention. Colonel Grayson lives at this place, which stands upon a creek that empties into the Potomac.[1] We spent an agreeable evening. He was formerly of General Washington's family, and then in the Board of War, and is possessed of a pretty good history of the war.[2]

Printed in Greene, *Greene*, 3: 507–8.
1. Col. William Grayson (1736?–90), who lived in Dumfries, had served as a Continental officer (1776–79) and as a member of the Continental Board of War (1779–81). He later also served in the Virginia House of Delegates (1784–85 and 1788), in the Continental Congress (1785–87), and as a United States senator (1788–90). (*DAB*)
2. Grayson had once been an aide to Washington. (Heitman, *Register*)

*   *   *

¶ [FROM THE INHABITANTS OF FREDERICKSBURG, VIRGINIA, ⟨Fredericksburg, Va., 12 September 1783⟩. "Impressed" by the importance of NG's "singular services" to the country as commander of the Southern Department, they offer their "acknowledgments, as a grateful tho small tribute so justly due" to him for his "distinguished Character as a Soldier" and as a "friend to American Liberty." The "absence of the Mayor and other Offi⟨cials⟩" pre-

vents them from giving him a "token of gratitude in the stile of a corporation," but they do offer their "united thanks" for his "Zealous[,] important and Successful services in recovering the Southern States from our cruel Enemy and restoring peace, Liberty and safety to so great a part of our Country." They cannot "express" their "great joy" in having NG "once more amongst" them. "Langu⟨age⟩ is too faint to paint the contrast in the cause of Liberty since" NG last passed through Fredericksburg, en route "to take the command of the Southern Army." The citizens prefer to "pass over [that] gloomy moment and to participate in the pleasure" NG now enjoys "in the possession of the American Laurel⟨,⟩ a Crown as splendid as all the honors of a Roman Triumph." They hope he may "long enjoy uninterrupted under your own Vines all the happiness of that Peace Liberty & Safety for which you and your gallant Officers & Soldiers have so nobly fought and greatly conquered." This address is "Signed by order of the Inhabitants," by "Ch^s Mortimer, Chairman."[1] RCS (Greene Papers: DLC) 2 pp. The manuscript, which is undated, has several small holes, and parts of several words are missing. That text and the date were taken from a copy of the address printed in the *Virginia Gazette* of 27 September.]
   1. NG's reply is immediately below.

¶ [TO THE INHABITANTS OF FREDERICKSBURG, VIRGINIA. From ⟨Fredericksburg, Va., 12 September, 1783⟩. NG is "Highly flattered" by their "Address" and "no less hono⟨red⟩" by their "Sentiments." For their "hearty welcome" and their "good wishes" for his "future welfare," he feels "the overflowings of a grateful mind." He adds: "The noblest reward for the best of services is the favord opinion of our fellow Citizens. Happy in your assurances I shall feel myself amply rewarded if I have but the good wishes of my Country." ADfS (Greene Papers: DLC) 2 pp. The draft contains several holes and is torn along the right margin. Parts of a few words are missing; these and the place and date were taken from a copy of this letter that was printed in the *Virginia Gazette* of 27 September.]

*   *   *

NG's Journal

13. [September 1783]

   We dined at Mount Vernon [Va.], one of the most beautiful situations in the world. The house has more dignity than convenience in it. Nature never formed a finer landscape than may be seen at this seat. The Potomac River in full view, with several little bays and creeks. The plain and the hills, joined to the features on the waters, forms a most beautiful scene. Mr. Lund Washington, his lady, and Doctor [David] Stewart [i.e., Stuart] and Miss [Fanny] Basset, were at the seat. We stayed and dined and then set out for Alexandria. The evening I was taken very ill with a fever, after my arrival, which lasted me, with very little remission and no intermission, eight days. The constancy of the fever and the excess of the pain reduced me very low. Colonel [John] Fitzgerald was polite enough to have me removed from Lomexes [i.e., Lomax's] Tavern to his house, and he and his lady were exceeding kind. Dr. [William] Brown attended me. He was bred at Edinborough, and for a considerable time in the army. He is thought to be eminent in the practice of physic. I ate not a mouthful of anything for six days. The loss of appetite, want of sleep, and other causes, made me very faint.[1] The corporation presented me with a handsome address and provided a public dinner, but I was too sick to either receive their address or partake of their dinner. However, I was told they had a social time upon the occasion and all things terminated agreeably. R[ichard].H[enry]. Lee and many others came to see me, but I was too unwell to enjoy company, and most part of the time to see any. Timothy Richardson also came to see me, and being a very old acquaintance I was glad to see him. It was like meeting accidentally with one of my own family. Colonel [illegible] and his son William, an amiable youth, was to see me, and carried off Major [Edmund M.] Hyrne on a visit to Mr. [George?] Mason's, where one of the young ladies made a great impression on his heart. The day before I left this place I rode out to Mrs. [Eleanor Calvert] Custis' seat, near six miles from Alexandria, and beautifully situated on the river Potomac. From this seat you have a sight of George Town, the great river that runs up to Bladensburg [Md.], and extensive prospects with great variety of hills and dales up and down the Potomac. Mrs. Custis was not at home, and this left the plan incomplete.[2] The beauties without wanted the charm within. Alexandria stands upon the Potomac, happily situated for trade, having a large back country very fertile and growing in produce. If the Potomac should be made navigable above the falls this town will grow amazingly. It is regularly laid out and some good buildings in it, and more putting up. Shipping of almost any size can come up to this city. Tobacco, flour, corn, hemp and many other articles are exported from hence. This was the most favorable position for the enemy to have taken possession of for distressing the Southern operations, and Virginia in particular. They could have command from this to the ocean by their shipping, and, with their parties, from hence to the mountains. Virginia would have had no trade by land or water or got any supplies. Colonel Fitzgerald's gallantry in 1781 saved it from being burnt by the British. A party came up on purpose and paraded before the place, but the colonel made so good a display for the few men he could collect that the enemy were frightened and did not land, although they were five times the number of his men.[3] The colonel's lady is an amiable woman and he a very generous, hospitable, clever fellow. They live happily together and really deserve it: may many blessings attend them for their kindness to me.

Before I take my leave of Virginia I cannot help remarking that the ladies appear to be brought up and educated with habits of industry and attention to domestic affairs, while the gentlemen attend to little but pleasure and dissipation. This State is powerful in numbers, rich in revenue, and yet is weak and poor. Its extent is the great difficulty of governing it properly. There are many sensible men in it, but they all are interspersed throughout the State, they have no one general plan of policy, but each has his own scheme. A want of a spirit of union perplexes their politics and weakens their counsels. The democratic part of the community have got too much influence. The dignity of government or the faith of the nation has too little weight with this order of people. They are sacrificed to present advantages of interest of little consequence. Nothing ought to be more sacred with a people and yet nothing is more sported with.

Printed in Greene, *Greene*, 508–10.

1. On NG's illness at Alexandria, see also his letter to Washington of 26 September, below.

2. On Mrs. Custis, see also NG to Washington, 26 September, below.

3. For background, see Governor's Council of Maryland to the Marquis de Lafayette, 12 April 1781, Idzerda, *Lafayette Papers*, 4: 28.

* * *

¶ [FROM THE CITIZENS OF ALEXANDRIA, VIRGINIA, 16 September 1783. The "Mayor[,] Recorder and Common council" congratulate NG on his "safe return" from a war "glorious to yourself and honorable to your Country." He has proved to the world that "circumstances of the greatest distress, and a Situation surrounded with danger and with difficulty can be nobly surmounted by brave Men, animated with the spirit of liberty, and under the command of wise, virtuous and persevering Leaders." They hope NG's future "may be attended with as much happiness as your command in the Army has been with glory and success."[1] RCS (Greene Papers: DLC) 2 pp.]

1. NG's reply is immediately below.

* * *

To the Citizens of Alexandria, Virginia

Gentlemen   [after 16 September 1783?][1]

Permit me with a mind impressed with the deepest sinserity to acknowledge with all imaginable respect your kind congratulations upon my safe return, your grateful sentiments for my public services and benevolent wishes for my future life.

It is an honor to be employed by our Country; but it is a happiness to meet her approbation. The compliments bestowed by the corporation upon the conduct of the Southern Army are too flattering not to interest the feelings of every Soldier belonging to it. I have the honor to be Gentlemen Your most Obedient humble Servt   NATH GREENE

Cy (Greene Papers: DLC).

1. See the document immediately above.

* * *

¶ [FROM COLONEL EDWARD CARRINGTON, Richmond, Va., 21 September 1783. NG's wagon arrived there "last ev'ning"; Carrington made sure that "all the contents are safe" and sent it on to Philadelphia. He "exchanged one of the Horses & put a better in his place." Maj. [Evan] Edwards "has a trunk, & Johnsons lives of the Poets with some other books in a Box in the Waggon."[1] If NG has left Philadelphia, the wagoner is to leave the box "at the City Tavern" and "call on Colo [Charles] Pettit to direct him as to his farther route."[2] RCS (MiU-C) 2 pp.]

1. Samuel Johnson's *Lives of the English Poets; and a Criticism of Their Works* was originally published in ten small volumes between 1779 and 1781. (*Columbia Encyc.*)

2. The wagon arrived in Philadelphia in mid-October, during NG's visit there. (NG to Pierce, 15 October, below) Before he left the city, NG requisitioned another wagon for his trip home to Rhode Island. (Hodgdon to NG, 12 November, below)

*   *   *

NG's Journal

24 [September 1783].

We set out for Annapolis [Md.]; dined and lodged at Mr. Deggs'.[1] This is one of the most respectable families in Maryland; Governor Lee married his daughter, an only child.[2] She is one of the most agreeable women in the world. She has the most interesting countenance I ever saw. Nature seems to have formed her to animate and please. Governor Lee is little less engaging than she is. Mrs. Deggs is an elegant woman, Mr. Deggs a good country squire.[3] Economy his theme and censure his delight.

Printed in Greene, *Greene*, 3: 510.

1. Ignatius (Nacy) Digges (d. 1785) was a wealthy landowner in Prince George's County, Md. NG presumably stayed at "Melwood Park," Digges's plantation home. (*Biog. Dictionary of Md. Legislature*, 2: 52)

2. Mary Digges Lee, the wife of Thomas Sim Lee, who served as governor of Maryland from 1779 to early 1783, is remembered for her "warm support" of the Revolution and especially for her mobilization of Maryland women "for patriotic service." (*DAB*)

3. "Mrs. Deggs" was Elizabeth Parnham Craycroft Digges. (*Biog. Dictionary of Md. Legislature*, 2: 52)

NG's Journal

25. [September 1783]

We got to Annapolis and dined at the tavern.[1] Major Jennifer invited me to take lodgings with him.[2] The governor was out of town, but returned the next morning.[3] Here I had the pleasure of seeing the celebrated Mrs. Loyd.[4] She is a most elegant woman, but not so perfect a beauty as from some my imagination had formed her. The propriety of her conduct is not less remarkable than her beauty.

Printed in Greene, *Greene*, 3: 510–11.

1. This was presumably Mann's Tavern, near the Maryland State House. Washington sometimes stayed there. (*GW Diaries*, 6: 102n)

2. Daniel of St. Thomas Jenifer (1723–90) was an important political leader in Maryland. Although his home plantation was in Charles County, Jenifer was living in Annapolis, on Lot H, in 1783. The rank of major, probably honorific, was awarded to him in 1765. (*Biog. Dictionary of Md. Legislature*, 2: 485–86)

3. As seen in the Journal entry immediately below, NG afterward dined with Gov. William Paca.

4. This was the wife of Richard Bennett Lloyd. According to Baron Closen: "Madame Lloyd is surely one of the most beautiful women I have seen in America. She was born in London. Her husband is a rich native of Maryland, who, having been in England studying, begged her in marriage of her parents, and obtained her only on condition that he should spend two years in England while she remained in France. He agreed to this, and it is her stay in France which has given her so many graces and so many of the charming French manners that are hers to such perfection. In her home everything is French, and she dresses with a taste and a distinction which have fascinated us. She also speaks French and Italian perfectly. In a word, she is reputed to be *the* American beauty." The English painter Sir Joshua Reynolds was so taken with Mrs. Lloyd's beauty that he used her as the model for Shakespeare's Rosalind in one of his paintings. (Walter B. Norris, *Annapolis: Its Colonial and Naval Story* [New York: Thomas Y. Crowell Co., 1925], p. 182)

NG's Journal

26. [September 1783]

We dined with the governor, who is a very polite character and a great friend of the army.[1] He drank several toasts which were accompanied with the discharge of thirteen cannon. A ball was proposed; but the weather being good I excused myself and set up. Major [Edward M.] Hyrne was in the pouts all day, and would not go into Baltimore [Md.] that night. Before we left Annapolis the corporation presented us with an address expressive of their respect and affection.[2] I got into Baltimore about ten at night and put up at Mr. Grant's. Before I quit Annapolis I could not help observing this place is proposed for the fixed residence of Congress.[3] Its situation is both pleasant and healthy, but too much exposed in time of war for the purposes of deliberation. Baltimore is a most thriving place. Trade flourishes and the spirit of building exceeds belief. Not less than three hundred houses are put up in a year. Ground rents is little short of what they are in London. The inhabitants are all men of business. Here I had the pleasure of meeting two of my old officers, General [Otho H.] Williams and Colonel [John Eager] Howard. The pleasure of meeting is easier felt than described. The inhabitants detained me four days to pay me the compliments of an address and a public dinner. The affection of the inhabitants was pleasing and the attention of the people flattering. Hyrne got wounded here with a spear, and though it penetrated the heart he still survived.[4]

Printed in Greene, *Greene*, 3: 511.

1. This was Maryland governor William Paca.

2. See From the Corporation of Annapolis, Maryland, this date, below.

3. On Annapolis as one of the proposed sites for a "fixed residence of Congress," see also George Lux to NG, 23 November 1782, above (vol. 12: 213, 214n).

4. On the type of "wound" that Hyrne presumably suffered, see also NG's Journal entry for 13 September, above. This entry in NG's Journal clearly covers a few days after 26 September, as he was still in Annapolis when he replied to that city's Corporation on 27 September, below, and was the recipient of an address from the Citizens of Baltimore that is dated 30 September, below.

To George Washington

Dear Sir   Anapolis [Md.] Sept. 26ᵗʰ 1783.

I am this far on my way to the Northward and should have had the happiness of seeing you before this but have been sick with a fever at Alexandria [Va.]. I dined at Mount Vernon and went to Alexandria in the Evening and that night was taken with a fever which lasted me Nine days. For six days I had no intermission and but little remission.[1] My fever is gone but has left me exceeding weak. While it was on me I could help my self little better than a Child. My strength is now so exhausted that I am obliged to travel with care and shall make but slow progress for some days to come. I have the pleasure to hear your Excellency is in good health but I am sorry to hear Mrs Washington is otherwise.[2] Every thing is well at Mount Vernon and your friends universally are wishing to see you among them again. Virginia it is thought will grant the five per Cent duty agreeable to the requisition of Congress.[3] Present me most respectfully to Mrs Washington and the Gentlemen of your family. Reports say here that Mrs Custis is going to be married shortly to Doctor Stewart.[4] I am with esteem & affection Your Excellencys Most Obedᵗ humble Serᵗ   NATH GREENE

ALS (Washington Papers: DLC).

1. See also NG's Journal entry for 13 September, above.

2. Through the summer and fall of 1783, Martha Washington, in the words of her husband, suffered attacks of "Billious Fevers and Cholic's." (Washington to George William Fairfax, 10 July 1783, Fitzpatrick, *GW*, 27: 60; see also Washington to the President of Congress, 14 August; Washington to George Clinton, 11 September; and Washington to Henry Knox, 23 September, ibid., pp. 102, 148, 165.)

3. In December, the Virginia legislature provisionally approved the congressional impost plan of 1783. The Virginia act differed from Congress's proposal in that it required collectors for the state to be appointed by the Virginia "executive," limited the grant of authority to twenty-five years, and delayed implementation until all of the other states had passed the measure. (That never happened.) The act is in Hening, *Statutes*, 11: 247–49, 350–52; on the Virginia legislature's action, see also the notes at Pendleton to NG, 17 July, above, and Weedon to NG, 2 December, below. The impost as proposed by Congress is discussed at NG to Lincoln, 18 June, above.

4. Eleanor Calvert Custis, the widow of Washington's stepson, John Parke Custis, married Dr. David Stuart, a Fairfax County, Va., physician, in late 1783. In a letter of 20 September to his cousin Lund Washington, George expressed surprise that he and Martha had never heard anything about Eleanor Custis's "attachment to D.S." before they learned of her impending marriage. (Fitzpatrick, *GW*, 27: 157)

From the Corporation of Annapolis, Maryland

Sir   Anaˢ [i.e., Annapolis, Md.] 26 Sepᵗ 1783
    We the Mayor, Recorder, Aldermen, and Common Council of the City of Annapolis, impressed with the most grateful Feelings for the eminent Services rendered these United States, and the Cause of Liberty, by the Southern Army under your Command; beg permission to congratulate you on your Arrival in this City, and to testify, with the sincerest Respect and Regard; the lively Sense we entertain of the invaluable Blessings secured to us, by your Conduct and unremitted Assiduity, in the noblest Cause that ever graced a Soldiers' Sword.
    Justice would wear the Aspect of Adulation, were we to enumerate the many signal Endowments, which endear you to the Inhabitants of this City, and inspire us with the warmest and most respectful Gratitude. They are such as will ever engage our prayers to Divine providence, that you may long continue to possess the Affections of a generous Republic; to share the Sweets of Domestic Felicity; and to experience the happy Reward of your distinguished Virtues.
    This Address springs from the Heart, & we solicit your Acceptance of it, as the genuine Sentiments of a grateful people.[1] Signed by Order & in behalf of the Corporation   J[AMES] B[RICE]. MAYOR

D (PHi).
1. NG's reply is immediately below.

To the Corporation of Annapolis, Maryland

Gentlemen   Annapolis [Md.] Septemʳ 27ᵗʰ 1783
    It is with the highest satisfaction I receive your affectionate address,[1] & feel my bosom glow with gratitude upon the occasion. The happy termination of the war, affords the most pleasing field for contemplation, and while it promises the richest harvest to the good citizens of America, it gives the sweetest pleasure, and most desirable repose to the soldier. If the operations of the southern army have answered the expectations of the public, or have had any influence upon this great event, I shall consider it as one of the most happy employments of my life. And if to this I may venture to flatter myself that my conduct either merits, or meets, in the smallest degree, the approbation of the public, I shall be still more happy. The honor you have done me, and the troops,

under my command, are to[o] sensibly felt, to be fully expressed, or properly acknowledged. I beg leave to return my most sincere thanks to the corporation, for the interest they take in what concerns my future happiness, Peace, & Prosperity. I have the honor to be Gentlemen Your most obedient humble servant   NATH GREENE

LS (PHi).
  1. The address is immediately above.

To Governor William Paca of Maryland

Sir   Annapolis [Md.] Septem[r] 27th 1783.
  Having accomplished the purposes of my command in the Southern department, as far as in my power, and Peace and the dissolution of the army rendering my further stay unnecessary, I am now on my way to the Northward. The friendly attention which I have experienced from this State in the progress of the Southern war has just claim to every acknowledgement in my power. And altho I am fully sensible that a sentiment of gratitude from an individual addressed to a people, is of no significance, yet I cannot deny myself this peice of justice; which is due to my feelings. It affords me the highest Satisfaction to hear of the generous measures which this State is pursuing, for rewarding that band of Veterans who have been the greatest support of our southern operations in our most critical situation.[1] Nor should I do justice to their merit, not to add my highest approbation of their general conduct. Their patience & bravery have been equaled by few & exceeded by none. I contemplate the happy change in our affairs, since I had the pleasure of being in this City before with ineffable delight;[2] Nor can I view its future prospects but with equal Satisfaction. I beg leave to offer my best wishes for its prosperity, happiness and tranquillity, and that your Excellency may have a pleasing & satisfactory administration. I have the honor to be with great respect your Excellencys Most obedient humble servant
                                                              NATH GREENE

ALS (MdAnMSA).
  1. The Maryland legislature "had diverted funds requisitioned by Congress to advance five months' pay to the state's Continental line" at the beginning of June. Robert Morris had protested this action, and a congressional committee had supported Morris's position in a report given at the end of July. Action on the congressional report was "indefinitely postponed" in mid-August. It is likely that NG had heard about the state's efforts to pay its soldiers but not about the diversion of funds requested by Congress or the ensuing controversy. (Smith, *Letters*, 20: 516–17n; Morris, *Papers*, 8: 150–51n, 186, 197–99n)
  2. NG had spent several days in Annapolis in November 1780, while he was on his way to take command of the Southern Army. (See above, NG to Board of War, 7 November 1780, and NG to Thomas Sim Lee, 10 November 1780 [vol. 6: 468, 473].)

*   *   *

¶ [FROM THE CITIZENS OF BALTIMORE, MARYLAND, 30 September 1783. The "Inhabitants of Baltimore" are "strongly impressed with a grateful Sense of the important Services" that NG has "renderd" to his country and congratulate him on his "safe return" there.[1] They will "not attempt to recite the honors" of NG's "brilliant & successful Campaigns, already written in indelible Charactors on the hearts" of his "grateful Countrymen." They trust that his successes "will be faithfully transmitted to Posterity, in the brightest Pages of that History, which shall record the important Circumstances of the glorious Revolution" to which he has "so greatly contributed." The citizens feel "particular Satisfaction" when they "reflect, that the gallant Officers & Soldiers of this State have had so great a share in the brilliant Achievements" of NG's "successful Command." They close with "every Sentiment of Personal Respect for" him "& those brave Men, and wishing both a lasting enjoyment of Health Peace & Independence."[2] The letter is signed by Abraham VanBibber, William Smith, Samuel Smith, William Spear, and Samuel Purviance. RCS (Greene Papers: DLC) 1 p.]

1. On NG's "return" to Baltimore, see his Journal entry for 26 September, above. He may have passed through the city in November 1780, en route to take command of the Southern Army. A few days after he arrived in Baltimore, "an elegant entertainment was provided for" him "at Mr. Grant's tavern, by the citizens" of the town, "where a very numerous company spent the day with much cheerfulness and good humour, and with many agreeable reflections on the important revolution so lately accomplished; and in effecting [sic] which their illustrious guest acted so distinguished a part." This address from the citizens of Baltimore was presented to NG at the gathering. (Pennsylvania Packet, 7 October)

2. NG's reply is immediately below.

* * *

To the Citizens of Baltimore, Maryland

Gentlemen   [30 September 1783?][1]

Nothing can be more grateful to our feelings than repeated proofs of esteem and affection. And more especially when offered by those we hold in high estimation. Your polite Address flatters both my pride and friendship. It will always afford me matter of triumph to merit the confidence of a people so remarkable for private virtue and public zeal. Nor do I wish to suppress those lively emotions. I feel that my conduct is thought an honor to the State by the Inhabitants in general and my friends in particular. And it adds no less to my happiness that my small services have contributed to the safety of my friends than their having some consideration in this great Revolution, the blessings of which I hope we shall be as careful to preserve as zealous to obtain. I am Gentlemen with the greatest respect Your most Obedient humble Ser[t]

NATH GREENE

ALS (OClWHi).

1. This letter was in reply to the address immediately above.

* * *

¶ [**FROM V. & N. FRENCH & NEPHEW**, Bordeaux, France, 1 October 1783. At the recommendation of their friend Griffin Greene, who has been with them for "Some time," they report that "the definitive treaties between France, Spain & England are Just Signed."[1] Now, they believe, "a general Confidence will take place," and "the channels of Commerce" will "open with briskness and encourage to Speculation." Tobacco, rice, indigo, "furrs &c are in constant demand" in France, and the "consumption very Considerable." If NG would like to "commit any thing to our management," he can "assuredly confide in" their "best endeavours" for his "Interest & Satisfaction."[2] In a postscript, they refer him to Griffin Greene's letter regarding the *Flora*.[3] They also inform him that they are the "Correspondants" in Bordeaux for Robert Morris and "Mr Holker,"[4] who can give NG "Ev'ry Information & Satisfaction" about them. RCS (MiU-C) 1 p.]

1. NG's cousin Griffin Greene had sailed to France the previous May to try to sell the *Flora*, a vessel owned by Jacob Greene & Company, the family firm in which both NG and he had an interest. (Vol. 12: 662–64 and n, 677–78, above; see also NG to Griffin Greene, 10 June, above, and Griffin's letter immediately below.) On the "definitive treaties," see note at Lafayette to NG, 8 September, above.

2. French & Nephew did form a "connection" with Jacob Greene & Company (See NG's letter to French & Nephew, 7 January 1785, and theirs to him of 23 April 1785, both below.) It does not appear that NG personally conducted any business with the firm.

3. See the letter immediately below.

4. John (Jean) Holker had been the French consul general for the middle states and the French navy's principal agent in the United States. (Vol. 5: 322n, above) Holker, who arrived in America in 1778, "eventually shared in the provisioning of the Continental army under the contract system that Robert Morris instituted" as superintendent of finance. By the end of 1782, Holker was a "principal in the firm of Daniel Parker and Company, the major contractor for the Continental army in 1783 and the conduit for its pay." (Morris, *Papers*, 7: 276n, 277n) After the war, he was involved in a number of commercial enterprises and was closely connected with Morris.

¶ [**FROM GRIFFIN GREENE**, Bordeaux, France, 1 October 1783. Acknowledges NG's "obliging letters," to him of 11 June, and to Mr. James Hunter, a partner of "Messrs Banks Burnet & Co," who is "not at this place";[1] Griffin has written to Hunter "at all the places" NG thought he might be.[2] Griffin thanks NG for the letters of credit,[3] but he expects to "make no other use of them than to make myself of more consequence than I should have been without them. There is such a stagnation in all mercantile affairs that it is impossible to take advantage of any credit." He has had the vessel *Flora* "for Sale six weeks" and has "bid her off with all her stores at 20,000 Livres" but will "give the Original owners the opportunity of being Concerned again in the Ship if they please." As he will try to exchange the *Flora* "for a less[er ship?] & then if possible shall obtain a freight," he does not know when he will be able to return to America.[4] Hopes NG will consider him "as being upon business for the Company" and will be "content" with any plan for business that NG and Jacob Greene "may think for the good of the concern."[5] Although he is "exceedingly obliged" for NG's "advice against gaming," he assures NG that he never "had the least propensity to that vice."[6] Living expenses in France are "amazingly high[;] live as prudent as possible[,] you must spend near three times as much as it costs to live in America in the most genteel manner." He will "try to get as much knowledge of business done in different parts of the world as possible" while he is there, "that

Griffin Greene, 1749–1804; Anderson Lithograph
(Ohio Historical Society)

it may benifit us in future." Sends his love to CG; plans to write her a long letter about "the Customs and manners of England and France."[7] RCS (Ct) 3 pp.]

1. NG wrote to his cousin Griffin Greene on 9, 10, and 14 June, all above; NG's letter to John Banks's and Ichabod Burnet's partner James Hunter is also above, dated 14 June.

2. See NG to Griffin Greene, 10 June.

3. See NG's letters to the Marquis de Lafayette and Henry Laurens, both 10 June, and to Hunter, 14 June, all above.

4. Griffin Greene still had no prospect of selling the *Flora* when he wrote NG on 8 February 1784, below. Nor did he return to the United States until the summer of 1785. (NG to Gardoqui, 7 August 1785, below)

5. Griffin Greene and NG were partners with Jacob in Jacob Greene & Company.
6. See NG to Griffin Greene, 10 June.
7. If Griffin Greene wrote such a letter, it has not been found.

*   *   *

From Alexander Hamilton

Albany [N.Y.] October 1st 1783
By this time I presume My Dear General you have returned to your ancient residence.[1] I had the pleasure of seeing Mrs Greene at New York; and wa[s] induced by her to hope you would be prevailed upon to become a fellow citizen of ours.[2] I know you have long had a partiality for our state; but I have been afraid, and have not yet banished my apprehensions, that your new Mistress would detach you from your old. I could not indeed very much blame your inconstancy when I consider how much South Carolina has done to attach you to her.[3] Yet now you have revisited the ruddy and health-teeming countenance of our Northern lass, I am not without expectation that you may prefer it to the palefaced charms of the one you have left behind. I know besides that she will have a powerful advocate in one [i.e., CG] that will have a powerful influence with you.

Mr Carter sometime before he left this informed me that he had sent a Bond of Mr Kinlochs to you to be renewed by him, and which was to be transmitted to me by you. I have some confused idea that he afterwards mentioned something to me on the subject, which however I have forgotten. But I shall be glad to receive a line from you to inform me, whether the Bond has been received or not and what has been done with it.[4]

Let me assure you that no one interests himself more warmly in your health and happiness than myself, and request that you will present my affectionate complements to Mrs Greene. M^{rs} [Elizabeth Schuyler] Hamilton joins hers to you both Dr Sir y^r Affect^e & Obed ser   A HAMILTON

RCS (Hamilton Papers: DLC).
1. NG was still en route to Rhode Island from South Carolina at this time.
2. CG had recently stopped in New York on her way to Rhode Island. (Garden to NG, 3 August, above)
3. Hamilton referred to South Carolina's gift of Boone's Barony plantation to NG. (See Hugh Rutledge to NG, 26 February 1782, above [vol. 10: 411 and n].)
4. John Barker Church, a.k.a. John Carter, was Hamilton's brother-in-law. On Francis Kinloch's bond to him, see Hamilton to NG, 10 June, above. NG's reply has not been found.

From James Penman[1]

Sir   Charlestown [S.C.] October 1st 1783

Agreeable to my Promise I have now the honour to communicate to you the Return made to your Proposals for the Purchase of Negroes in Florida, and am sorry, to find it so much exceeds your Expectations. At some late Provost Marshals Sales which are for Cash common Field Negroes sold at St Augustine from £50 to £70 Sterling, and on Credit they sell of course much higher. The lowest Terms that any have been offerd at were £70 pr head for a Gang of 72, Viz. 25 Men, 24 Women & 23 Children, good Security to be given for the payment of the principal by Instalments; and the Interest to be regularly paid in London.

There are several other Gangs for Sale, but they expect higher Prices. General Grant has one of Seventy of which 50 are Workers, and the rest Children some of which are nearly fit for the Hoe; If a good Price is given for them, the Property well secured, and the Interest paid regularly, any reasonable length of time will be given for the payment.[2]

There is likewise a simular Gang belonging to Lady Egmont[3] and another belonging to a Mr Moss[4] for Sale, but the Terms of both will be high. In short none that are good Property are to be had at any thing near the price you have Limited; I therefore give you this Notice that you may provide Yourself elsewhere.[5]

The price of Negroes may probably fall in Florida at the Evacuation, But as there is no prospect of that taking Place this Winter, and on the contrary the people are Possessed with an Idea of it's being kept, while this is the Case there is no likelihood of their falling in Value.[6]

It is also incumbent upon me to tell you That although several Cargoes of Negroes have lately arrived here, the price still keeps up, good Men and Women selling from 70 to 80 Guineas and Boys and Girls in proportion, to be paid for out of the present Crop.[7]

I am exceedingly sorry to be under the necessity of acquainting you, That notwithstanding Mr [John S.] Darts repeated Promises, I have never yet received a Shilling of the Two hundred Guineas I advanced you upon leaving this Place, nor do I see the smallest Prospect of obtaining it, without your kind Interposition in my behalf, and as this Money is now become necessary to me, I must request the favour of you to take the first opportunity of pressing that Gentleman to an immediate payment.[8]

Doctor [Andrew] Turnbull joins me in most respectful Compliments to Mrs Green and the Gentlemen of your family, and in good wishes for the health and happiness of the whole.[9] I have the honour to remain with the most sincere Respect Sir Your much Obliged & Most Obedient Humble Servant   JAMES PENMAN

I beg to be particularly rememberd to my friend Garden if with you.[10]

RCS (NcD).

1. Penman had once been one of the principal merchants at St. Augustine, in the British colony of East Florida, where he settled before the war. During the war, he served as a volunteer in Col. [Lewis] Fuser's battalion of the British Sixtieth Regiment and provided financial support to the British garrison in East Florida. Sometime after the capture of Charleston in May 1780, Penman moved there with his friend Dr. Andrew Turnbull. He established a mercantile business in Charleston and stayed there after the British left the city. (Siebert, *Loyalists in East Florida*, 2: 17n, 319–20) In newspaper advertisements, he offered a variety of goods, including rum, sugar, salt, wine, paint, saddles, shoes, linens, snuff, coffee, and tea. (See, for example, *South-Carolina Gazette and General Advertiser*, 3 May 1783.)

2. Gen. James Grant (1720–1806), who played a prominent role militarily during the war, had been the governor of East Florida between 1764 and 1771 and had accumulated extensive land holdings there. (Siebert, *Loyalists in East Florida*, 2: 309–10)

3. Lady Catherine Egmont was the widow of John Perceval, the second earl of Egmont, who died in 1770. Egmont's estates in Florida included "lands on St. Johns River about seventy-five miles from St. Augustine and a large plantation on Amelia Island." (Siebert, *Loyalists in East Florida*, 2: 3n, 393)

4. "Mʳ Moss" was most likely William Moss, who had been a member of the "commons house" in the East Florida General Assembly. The "commons house" was made up of large landowners in the colony. Moss's plantation was a few miles outside St. Augustine. A return of British refugees who relocated to the Bahamas after the evacuation of East Florida listed him as arriving with eighty-one "Blacks." (Siebert, *Loyalists in East Florida*, 2: 100n, 244, 361)

5. NG's letter to Penman, stating what he was willing to pay for slaves, has not been found. In reply to the present letter, NG admitted that his instructions had been too restrictive. (NG to Penman, 25 October, below)

6. Under the terms of the preliminary peace treaty, East Florida was to be ceded to Spain, and British subjects who wished to leave were to be evacuated from the colony. Although some Loyalists believed that Great Britain would retain possession of the colony, transports evacuated provincial troops, Loyalists, and slaves from East Florida to England, Nova Scotia, the Bahamas, and the West Indies from the spring of 1783 until well after the Spanish took control in June 1784. The evacuation was completed in November 1785. (Siebert, *Loyalists in East Florida*, 1: 137–79)

7. See NG to Penman, 25 October.

8. On this, see also ibid. and Hyrne to NG, at 4 December, below. Dart was the Southern Army's paymaster.

9. Turnbull (ca. 1718–92), a Scot, had emigrated to East Florida in the 1760s and established a large indigo plantation, "New Smyrna," using indentured workers from Greece, Italy, and the Balearic Islands as laborers. This plantation experiment eventually failed, and Turnbull moved to Charleston during the British occupation of the city and assumed the medical practice of his friend Alexander Garden, Sr., the father of one of NG's aides. (Patricia C. Griffin, "Blue Gold: Andrew Turnbull's New Smyrna Plantation," in *Colonial Plantations and Economy in Florida*, ed. Jane G. Landers [Gainesville: University Press of Florida, 2000], pp. 39–69; Berkeley and Berkeley, *Alexander Garden*, pp. 214 and n, 289; Siebert, *Loyalists in East Florida*, 2: 325–27)

10. Alexander Garden, Jr., one of NG's aides, had accompanied CG from Charleston to Philadelphia in June. (See Garden to NG, 20 June, above.)

*   *   *

¶ [FROM COLONEL FRANCIS MENTGES, Philadelphia, 6 October 1783. Mentges, whom NG appointed "Inspector of Contracts for the southern army," has carried out his duties to NG's and "the public satisfaction."[1] He encloses a copy of an account of the pay that is owed him; he presented it to Mr. Robert Morris, who "referred it to the Comptrollers office."[2] According to the comptroller, "the account could not be settled, without a special resolve of Congress," because Mentges held two appointments.[3] Asks NG to "represent this matter" to Congress, "that I may receive the pay due me."[4] CyS (PCC, item 155, vol. 2: 647, DNA) 1 p.]

1. NG had appointed Mentges, an officer of the Pennsylvania Continental line, to the inspector general's department in November 1782 and had named him inspector of contracts in February 1783. (Vol. 12: 147–48, 151, 465, above; see also NG to Boudinot, second letter of 7 October, below.)

2. Morris noted in his diary on 22 August that Mentges had applied "for Pay as Inspector of Contracts" and that Morris "[d]esired him to exhibit his account to Mr. [James] Milligan," the comptroller. (Morris, *Papers*, 8: 447) In a diary entry for 29 September, Morris wrote that Mentges had again applied for his pay. (Morris, *Papers*, 8: 556)

3. A congressional resolution of 18 September 1776 barred officers from holding more than one commission or receiving pay in more than "one capacity at the same time." (*JCC*, 26: 232)

4. See NG to Boudinot, second letter of 7 October.

* * *

To Elias Boudinot, President of the Continental Congress

Sir   Princetown [N.J.] Octob 7th 1783

I beg leave to inform Congress that I have just arrivd from my Southern command, the business of which I hope has been closed agreeable to their intention in furloughing all the Soldiers and putting a stop to every Continental expence.[1] It is now going on Nine years since I have had an opportunity to visit my family or friends or pay the least attention to my private fortune. I wish therefore for the permision of Congress to return to Rhode Island having already obtained the consent of the Commander in Chief [Washington].[2] I have the honor to be with great respect Your Excellencys most Obed humble Se   N GREENE

ADfS (MiU-C).

1. According to the *Pennsylvania Evening Post & Daily Advertiser*, NG reached Philadelphia on 4 October. A typographical error in that newspaper read that his arrival was "announced by the ringing of the bills." (*Pennsylvania Evening Post & Daily Advertiser*, 4 October) After traveling on to Princeton, where Congress was in session, NG was back in Philadelphia by 11 October. (NG to Martin, 11 October, below)

2. For Congress's reply, see Thomson to NG, 18 October, below.

* * *

¶ [TO ELIAS BOUDINOT, PRESIDENT OF THE CONTINENTAL CONGRESS. From Princeton, N.J., 7 October 1783. NG encloses a copy of Col. Francis Mentges's letter "respecting some difficulty in obtaining payment for the services he performed as inspector of contracts for the Southern Army."[1] NG gave Mentges this appointment when "a Contract was made for the subsistence of the Army." At that time, Mentges also held the "Office of Inspector of the

Army," which "gave him an intimate knowledge of the number of the Troops."[2] NG believes "the exercise of both offices gave mutual checks and support to each other." NG could "get no other person to hold the office" who was "by any Means equal to" Mentges, and it was "necessary for public occoneny that the Office should be exercised by some body." At the time of the appointment, NG asked the secretary at war and the financier if there was "any impropriety" in Mentges's holding both posts.[3] "Neither ever made any objection," and Mentges "continued to perform the duties until the dissolution of the Army." NG adds that "the duties were hard" and that no one else "could have performed them more satisfactorily." He hopes that "Congress will give the necessary order in the business," so that Mentges can obtain "satisfaction in the matter represented which will require a special resolve for his being settled with as inspector of Contracts."[4] ADf (MiU-C) 2 pp.]

1. See Mentges to NG, 6 October, above.

2. On these appointments, see NG to Mentges, 5 November 1782, and NG to Robert Morris, 20 February 1783, both above. (Vol. 12: 147–48, 465)

3. NG wrote the "financier," Robert Morris, about Mentges's dual appointments on 20 February and asked Morris to "advise" him as to their propriety and to consult the secretary at war, Benjamin Lincoln, on the matter. (Vol. 12: 465; NG had informed Lincoln about Mentges's initial appointment as Southern Army inspector the previous December. [William Jackson to NG, 11 February, above (ibid., p. 431)])

4. This letter was read in Congress on 9 October and was referred to a committee consisting of William Ellery, James Madison, and James Duane. (JCC, 25: 664n) On 6 January 1784, their report was "recommitted" to Ellery, Arthur Lee, and Richard Dobbs Spaight (ibid.), who proposed on 6 April 1784 that Mentges be compensated for "His services, as inspector of contracts for the Southern army, in addition to his pay as an Officer in the line." A motion stating that Mentges had performed his duties by order of NG, "under the authority of the Superintendant of finance," and that he was entitled to "the sum of one hundred and sixty-six and two thirds dollars per month, for executing the duties of inspector of contracts to the Southern Army," was defeated at that time. (JCC, 26: 199–201) Ellery, Lee, and Spaight subsequently reported on 15 April 1784 that NG had informed both Lincoln and Morris of the dual appointment, "desiring them if there was any impropriety in Lieutenant Colonel Mentgez holding both Offices that they would inform him of it," and that neither Lincoln nor Morris had objected. They recommended that Mentges "be allowed as compensation for his services as inspector of Contracts for the Southern Army, in addition to his pay as an Officer in the line, the sum of one hundred and ten dollars per month, during the time he executed that Office." (JCC, 26: 232–33) Nothing more is known about the outcome of Mentges's claim.

¶ [FROM GOVERNOR WILLIAM PACA OF MARYLAND, Annapolis, Md., 10 October 1783. The "enclosed Address" [not found] is a "Duplicate." As no answer has been received to the "Original," they are "apprehensive" that it "did not get to Hand."[1] Extract (MdAnMSA) 1 p.]

1. It appears from NG's reply of 27 October, below, that the address was from the Maryland legislature—probably that of 15 January, above (vol. 12: 374).

¶ [FROM NATHANIEL TRACY, Newburyport, Mass., 10 October 1783.[1] In reply to NG's "very Polite Favour" of the previous May [not found], which he received "a few Days since," Tracy will be "ready at all Times to render the House of [William] Pierce, [Anthony W.] White and [Richard] Call every Service" in his power.[2] He adds: "On every Occasion they shall have my Influence in extending their Commercial Connections in this Country. A proper Attention to your Request demands my utmost exertions in their Favor, but in addition to that, their Services as Officers in the American Army, entitle them to every support from Gentlemen in the Mercantile Line." Tracy congratulates NG "on the return of Peace, which has been restored in a greater Measure by your Fortitude and Perseverance," and offers "warmest Wishes for a long & uninterrupted Enjoyment of Domestic Tranquillity which alone can repay you for the many Sacrifices you have made in the Service of our Country." Sends "Respectfull Compliments" to CG. RCS (MiU-C) 1 p.]

1. Tracy, a merchant, had supported the American cause through privateering and shipping ventures. Between 1775 and 1783, "he sent to sea twenty-four cruisers manned by 2800 men and captured 120 sail of vessels with 2225 prisoners of war." His merchant fleet of 110 vessels was decimated during hostilities, so that only thirteen remained by the war's end. (*DAB*)

2. NG's letter to Tracy on the firm's behalf was probably similar to the one he wrote to Jeremiah Wadsworth on 24 May, above.

¶ [TO GOVERNOR ALEXANDER MARTIN OF NORTH CAROLINA. From Philadelphia, 11 October 1783. "A Mr McNear," a former resident of North Carolina who is "now under the general denomination of a Refugee," was trying to return there in the hope of being "restored to the rights of Citizenship," but the "Capt of the Vessel in which he had agreed to take passage refused to carry him to the State for fear of giving offence."[1] McNear "has never been hostile; but on the contrary has done every good office to our suffering Prisoners." NG recommends him to Martin's "friendship" and hopes "his former good charactor[,] his future usefulness as a Merchant and his past good conduct to our prisoners will procure him a favorable reception among the people." ALS (MiU-C) 2 pp.]

1. This was Ralph McNair of Orange County, N.C., whose property had been confiscated because of his Loyalist inclinations. McNair traveled to Philadelphia in 1783 to seek redress. (Palmer, *Loyalists*, p. 572) Martin wrote McNair on 21 January 1784 that he had received this letter from NG, as well as one from McNair himself. He was "sorry to inform" McNair that "the Treason Law of this State prevents my granting you the passport & leave to return as you request . . . You have deserted the Country in which you say you wished to have spent your Days. What satisfaction can you have in returning to her in triumphant prosperity, when your late principal desire is frustrated which was to subjugate her to British depotism?" Martin added that he would "lay" NG's letter before the North Carolina legislature if McNair were to send a petition citing his "services" to "our prisoners on Long Island." He doubted, however, that redress would be granted. (*NCSR*, 17: 10)

*　　　*　　　*

To George Washington

Dear Sir   Philadelphia Octob 11th 1783

Several Officers belonging to the Southern Army have made application to me to use my interest with your Excellency for obtaining appointments in the peace establishment. Col Harmer was among the first and a better officer cannot be found; his whole soul is in pursuit of the

profession of Arms.[1] Col Mengez is also exceeding anxious to be put
upon the establishment both from his fondness for Arms and from his
having no other mode of obtaining a reputable lively hood. He is
certainly an excellent officer and has all those qualities which fits him
for the service that will be expected from him. He is a good diciplinarian
and an excellent economist.[2] Capt Singleton of Virginia belonging to the
Artillery is strongly recommended by Lt Col [Edward] Carrington for
the Artillery.[3] There is no better officer either for Action or Camp duty. I
have seen him proved in both charactors. Capt Armstrong of the Legion
is a brave good Officer without a fortune and desirous of being in
service. He has signallised himself in so many instances this war that
nothing more needs be said of his merit and pretentions.[4] Capt Zeigler
who formerly belonged to the old Riffle Regiment at Cambridge and
has been in the Army ever since in different charactors in every one of
which he has always discharged his duty with honor and integrity
wishes to be on the list. I feel my self interested for him from his peculiar
situation and hope your Excellency will have it in your power to serve
him.[5] The last person I have to mention is Capt Dyer of Maryland. To
give your Excellency a proper idea of his situation and wishes I inclose a
letter from General Williams to Capt Jackson of the board of War. His
family are in such a distressed condition that it will give me a particular
satisfaction if you can accomodate the measures to his wishes.[6] I hope
your Excellency will excuse the liberty I have taken in recommending
those Officers. I feel a friendship for them and could wish to serve them
and as you have always honored me with your confidence I presume
upon your indulgence.[7] I am with esteem & affection Your Excellencys
Most Obedt humble Ser^t   NATH GREENE

ALS (PCC, item 152, vol. 11: 549, DNA).
    1. Josiah Harmar of the Pennsylvania line had served under NG as the Southern
Army's deputy adjutant general and had taken temporary command of Col. Walter
Stewart's reorganized Pennsylvania regiment in March 1782. (See above, vol. 10: 182n,
291, 490n.) Harmar did serve, mainly on the frontier, in the "peacetime establishment" of
the army. He was breveted a brigadier general in July 1787 and later was appointed
"commander of the United States Army," a post that he held from September 1789 until
March 1791. He resigned from the army on 1 January 1792. (Heitman, *Register*; *DAB*)
    2. On Francis Mentges, who had commanded a regiment of the Pennsylvania line in the
Southern Army and had held staff positions under NG, see his letter to NG of 6 October
and NG to Boudinot, second letter of 7 October, both above. No evidence has been found
that Mentges served in the army after the war. (Heitman, *Register*)
    3. Anthony Singleton, a captain in the First Continental Regiment of Artillery, had
fought under NG at the battle of Hobkirk's Hill. (Vol. 7: 468n, 472–73 and n; vol. 8: 158n,
above) He does not appear to have served in the "peacetime establishment." (Heitman,
Register)
    4. Lt. James Armstrong of Lee's Legion had been taken prisoner at Dorchester, S.C., in
December 1781; he did not return to active service. (See vol. 7: 437n, above, and Heitman,
Register.)

5. Capt. David Zeigler of the Pennsylvania line began his service in the Continental army as a third lieutenant and adjutant of Thompson's Pennsylvania Rifle Battalion in June 1775, while the army was being organized at Cambridge, Mass. (Heitman, *Register*) He served under NG in the South, where he commanded a company of the First Pennsylvania Regiment. (Vol. 10: 566, above) Zeigler thanked NG for his recommendation to Washington in a letter of 20 October, below. He went on to serve in the "United States Infantry Regiment," beginning in August 1784, and attained the rank of major before resigning in September 1789. (Heitman, *Register*)

6. Edward Dyer had served in a Maryland Continental regiment in the Southern Army. Gen. Otho H. Williams wrote William Jackson, the assistant secretary at war, on 2 October about Dyer, describing him as a "plain, honest, poor man who has spent a great deal of his time in the service of the public and thereby very materially injured the circumstances of a large, and an amiable family." Because of his "Poverty," Dyer hoped to go to Detroit, where, Williams supposed, a garrison would be established and "a contractor, commissary, Quarter Master or some such officer may be wanting." Williams recommended him for such a post, hoping it would give him "an opportunity of improving his fortune." (PCC, item 152, vol. 11: 553, DNA) Dyer himself apparently delivered Williams's letter to Jackson, who promised to "present 'this gentleman' " [Dyer] to Washington and Benjamin Lincoln, the secretary at war. (Jackson to Williams, 6 October 1783, *Williams Calendar*, p. 87) It does not appear, however, that Dyer served in the "peacetime establishment." (Heitman, *Register*)

7. Washington replied to NG on 26 October, below, that he would "take pleasure in mentioning" these officers when the army's "Peace Establishment" was determined. In a letter to Congress of 21 December, when he was leaving the army, Washington recommended that a number of officers, including those named by NG in the present letter, be retained in the army "on any Peace Establishment that may take place." (Fitzpatrick, *GW*, 27: 279 and n)

From Governor Benjamin Harrison of Virginia

Sir   In Council [Richmond, Va.] Octo 11th 1783.

I was unfortunate in being absent from this place whilst you were here. I should have had much pleasure in participating with you the joy which our present prospects excite in the breast of every virtuous citizen.[1]

The event of the late war affords ample subject for the exercise of the grateful mind; and whilst I reflect on the happy effects which it must produce I cannot but possess the highest sentiments of those characters who have acted the most conspicuous parts in it. The sudden and glorious change of our affairs to the Southward formed an aera in which Virginia was too much interested to be unmindful of it. I can with safety assure you, sir, that she still preserves the most honorable testimonials of gratitude for him under whose auspices it was effected.

The Sufferings of the heroic troops which you have commanded are too well known to be forgotten. I flatter myself every exertion will be made to heal the wounds and administer comfort to the distresses which a long and active service cannot fail to bring. Government will unquestionably extend every nerve to comply with those engagements which have been made to the brave citizens who have fought its battles and iffused their blood in its support. I must hope you will do me the justice to believe that no body can experience an higher satisfaction than I shall in seeing this take place at an early hour.

I cannot bid you adieu without wishing you an undisturbed enjoyment of the tranquility which at present reigns and that you may for years continue to taste the blessings of that political freedom and independence which you have so long and so nobly struggled to support. I have the honor to be with every sentiment of esteem and respect, sir; Y^r most ob^t & most humble servant   B H.

LB (Vi).

1. NG had stopped in Richmond on his way north from Charleston, S.C. (See NG to the Citizens of Richmond, 9 September, above.) As seen in his letter to William Pierce of 15 October, below, NG had hoped to see Harrison while he was there.

*   *   *

¶ [FROM HENRY PENDLETON, Fredericksburg, Va., 12 October 1783. Two of his carriage horses have been "so lamed in shoeing" that he will have to leave them in Virginia and buy replacements.[1] He is therefore now forced to draw a "small bill" on NG for "Thirty Guineas" as partial payment for his "Chair & horse," which, he is happy to hear, "proved usefull to you in your Journey." Although he would have had "no concern" about punctual payment under other circumstances, Pendleton has written to ask Mr. [Charles] Pettit for the money in case NG has already left Philadelphia for Rhode Island.[2] He would have been "extremely happy to have seen you here in your passage" through Virginia, but the distance, Pendleton's "want of health," and NG's "rapid movements would not admit of it."[3] He hopes to see NG "in Carolina this Winter."[4] Does not have time to make this letter "amusive." Offers his "best" compliments to NG and CG. Will "write more particularly" when he gets back to Charleston, S.C., "the theatre in which we are both most interested."[5] RCS (MiU-C) 2 pp.]

1. As seen by his letter to NG of 6 August, above, Pendleton, a South Carolina judge and brother of NG's former aide Nathaniel Pendleton, was spending some time in his native state of Virginia after traveling farther north for reasons of health.

2. For more about the "Chair & horse," see ibid. and Pendleton to NG, 22 October, below.

3. In his letter of 6 August, Pendleton had expressed a hope of seeing NG in Virginia.

4. NG did not return to South Carolina until the summer of 1784.

5. The letter that Pendleton wrote to NG from Richmond, Va., on 22 October, is the only further correspondence between them that has been found.

¶ [FROM FELIX WARLEY, Charleston, S.C., 13 October 1783.[1] Lt. [John] Hamilton informed him "some weeks ago" that NG asked to have a bill drawn on himself "at Philadelphia at sight for the Amount" of his bond to Warley, which was due 28 July. Warley has therefore drawn on NG "this day" for "One hundred & seventeen pounds six Shillings Sterling at five days sight payable to the order of Captain Mathew Strong." This is the "amount of said Bond &

Interest up to the 12ᵗʰ November."² Warley will "deliver up" NG's bond to "any person here" at NG's direction.³ RCS (MiU-C) 1 p.]

1. Warley, who had been a captain in the South Carolina Continental line, was a merchant in Charleston. (Heitman, *Register*; Chesnutt, *Laurens Papers*, 16: 350n)

2. According to a notation "annexed" to this letter, the principal of this bond, dated 28 January 1783 and payable in six months at seven per cent interest, was £780, presumably in South Carolina currency. The interest to 12 November ("9 Months 12 days") amounted to £41.2, making the total due from NG £881.2, "Equal to" £117.6 sterling. The purpose of the bond is not stated in any known correspondence, but as noted above (vol. 12: 341n), NG had purchased slaves on 10 and 28 January 1783 in sales held by the South Carolina Commissioners of Confiscated Estates. As seen in Warley's letter to him of 7 April 1784, below, NG had also pledged a second bond to Warley on 28 January 1783, payable in one year.

3. In his letter of 7 April 1784, Warley thanked NG "for honoring my draught of the 13ᵗʰ October last" and enclosed "the Bond it paid off."

¶ [FROM ELIAS BOUDINOT, PRESIDENT OF THE CONTINENTAL CON-GRESS, Philadelphia, 14 October 1783. He expects "daily" to hear of "final orders for the evacuation of New York." There have been "Many and various" reports about "the enemys Intentions relative to this Measure." Orders were long since given to prepare for the evacuation, "but not to move till farther orders." Washington is "very uncertain as to the measures that will finally take place."¹ Catalog extract (Stan V. Henkels, *Catalogue #1005* [1909], p. 32)]

1. On the evacuation of New York, see note at To An Unknown Person, 24 November, below.

* * *

To William Pierce, Jr.

Dear Major   Philadelphia Octob 15th 1783.

I was very sorry I had not the pleasure of seeing you before I left Charleston.¹ Mrs. Greene wrote me you had a very agreeable journey into the Jerseys.² Doctor Draper left her about a fortnight since in Newport; but not much pleased with the situation. I intend to leave this and go there in about a fortnight.³ My journey from Charles Town was very agreeable except a fit of the fever which over took me at Alexandria [Va.]. Great politeness and attention was shewn me on the road and my reception here and at Congress and by the Commander in Chief were very flattering. I had many Addresses by the different Corporations on the road.⁴ At Richmond I had the misfortune not to see the Governor and as I had not my papers with me I could not refer to dates so particularly as I wished to write on the subject. My papers have arrivd to day, and I shall write to morrow; but Col Carrington promised to say the needful in the business from me to the Governor, until I could write him fully on the matter.⁵

Your assurances of friendship and esteem are very flattering to my feelings.⁶ It will always afford me the highest satisfaction to promote your interest. I wish you every possible success in trade but this will depend as I always told you very much upon the degree of application and attention which you pay to business. I have not time by this opportunity to write you so fully as I wish; but let me beg of you not to let your business get the command of you. As long as you can command that all things will go well; but once the business begins to push you, ruin will soon follow. Fix the charactor of your house, and your fortunes are made; Fail in that, and you fail in every thing.[7]

Before this I suppose you are in Hymens bonds. Nothing is so delicious to a generous nature as virtuous love. While you was absent I had the happiness to fall into company with Miss Charlotte several times, and was highly pleased with her person and manners. A letter you inclosed for her to Capt Pendleton I took the liberty of delivering as he had left Charles Town.[8] In borrowing opinions from others we are often imposed upon, which nothing but a more intimate acquaintance can correct. Please to present me to Miss Fenwick and all Mr Gibbs's family. Tell Mr Gibbs that the papers which I promised him respecting Col Fenwick shall be forwarded him by the first oppportunity.[9]

Congress are still at Princeton but have fixed their permanent residence at or near the falls of Trenton but their temporary residence is undecided upon.[10] The Dutch Minister has arrived and is a most agreeable man. His person and Manners are very engaging.[11] Yours most Affectionately   NATH GREENE

We have just got the Melancholy news of the death of poor Burnet.[12]

ALS (NjMoHP).

1. Pierce had accompanied CG to Philadelphia in June. (Pierce to NG, 19 June, above) He stayed there for a time to transact business and got back to Charleston, S.C., in mid-August, "too late by one Day" to see NG, who had just set out for the North. (Pierce to NG, 17 August, above)

2. CG's letter has not been found. In his letter of 19 June, Pierce informed NG that he expected to spend several days in New Jersey. CG had been in Newport, R.I., since 11 August. (*Newport Mercury*, 16 August)

3. CG, who had been ill the previous winter and spring (vol. 12: 471n, above), apparently had not recovered her strength before she left Charleston. It is not clear what her ailments were, but she was pregnant at this time; the child, Louisa Catharine, was born in April 1784. (NG to Pettit, 22 April 1784, below) George Draper of Virginia was a "Hospital Surgeon and Physician" who had served in the Continental army. (Heitman, *Register*)

4. On NG's overland trip from Charleston to Philadelphia, see the excerpts from his Journal, beginning 15 August and continuing at various dates through September, above. On the accolades he received en route, see: From the Citizens of Richmond [Va.], 8 September; From the Citizens of Fredericksburg, Md., 12 September; From the Citizens of Alexandria, Va., 16 September; From the Corporation of Annapolis, Md., 26 September; and From the Citizens of Baltimore, Md., 30 September, all above. On NG's illness at Alexandria, see his Journal entry for 13 September, above. A commendation from Congress was conveyed in a letter from Charles Thomson of 18 October, below.

5. In a letter of 11 October, above, Benjamin Harrison, the governor of Virginia, expressed regrets at missing NG, who stopped at Richmond on his way north. Pierce had

asked NG to intervene with Harrison in regard to a promotion that Pierce was seeking in a Virginia artillery unit. (Pierce to NG, 17 August)

6. In his letter of 17 August, Pierce strongly asserted his feelings for NG, concluding that "I look up to you as a Son would to a Father with veneration, love & respect."

7. Pierce had recently formed a mercantile concern with former cavalry officers Richard Call and Anthony W. White. (See above, To Whom It May Concern, 18 March [vol. 12: 536], and NG to Wadsworth, 24 May.)

8. Pierce married Charlotte Fenwick, a daughter of Edward and Mary Drayton Fenwick, in December. (*Biog. Directory of S.C. House*, 2: 243; Pendleton to NG, 4 December, below)

9. Col. Edward Fenwick of the British army, who had supplied intelligence to the Americans during the war, was a brother of Pierce's future wife. It is not known if NG forwarded papers on this subject to a Mr. Gibbs, but NG later did write to Gov. Benjamin Guerard of South Carolina on Fenwick's behalf. (NG to Guerard, 30 March 1784, below)

10. Congress had relocated to Princeton, N.J., at the end of June. (Morris, *Papers*, 8: 214; see also note at Pierce to NG, 19 June.) A vote was taken later in October to alternate meetings between Annapolis, Md., and Trenton, N.J. In January 1785, however, Congress began to meet in New York City until a "single federal town" could be built. (Morris, *Papers*, 8: 662–66)

11. Pieter J. Van Berckel, "the first Dutch minister to the U.S.," arrived in Philadelphia on 11 October but did not present his credentials in Congress until the 25th. (Morris, *Papers*, 8: 615n; *JCC*, 25: 748–49)

12. Ichabod Burnet, another of NG's former aides, had died suddenly at Havana. (See Flagg to NG, 17 October, and Banks to NG, 18 October, both below.) The news must have been distressing to NG. Burnet, who had served as his aide since 1777, had left the service in the winter of 1783 to form a business partnership with Southern Army contractor John Banks. (See above, vol. 12: 412n; a biographical note on Burnet can be found above in vol. 5: 110n.)

From Thomas FitzSimons[1]

Sir   Philad[a] 15 Oct[r] 1783

The Inclosed Letter[2] was given to me by the Sec[y] at Warr [Benjamin Lincoln] & when I Inclose it I take the Liberty of Mentioning to you a Circumstance which happened in Congress respecting you & I think created a Little delay in a business that all seemed disposed to forward. A Committee had reported that two feild P[s] [pieces] of Brass Ordinance should be presented you With the other testimonys intended for your Eminant service & it was Suggested by A Member that if you had taken any such during y[r] Command to the Southw[d] the Complem[t] would be greater if it was so Expressed but Neither the Members present or the Sec[y] at Warr Could Inform Congress whether any brass field pieces were taken in that Country, & it was tho[t] best to Let the Resolution Lay till the Circumstance was Inquired into.[3] You will [perceive?] the design is to make the Testimony as honorable as possible, & if you will please to Inform the Chairman of that Committee (M[r] Duane) how that Matter is, the Resolution will be Imm[y] passed.[4] With Great respect I am Sir Y[r] m[o] hble serv[t]   THO[s] FITZSIMONS

RCS (MiU-C).

1. FitzSimons was a delegate to Congress from Pennsylvania. (Smith, *Letters*, 21: xxiii)
2. The enclosure has not been found.
3. On the congressional resolution honoring NG, see Thomson to NG, 18 October, below.
4. NG wrote to James Duane on 16 October, immediately below.

To James Duane[1]

Sir   Philadelphia October 16th 1783
I received a letter from Mr Fitzsimmons, last evening, desiring me to inform you, whether any brass field peices had been taken from the enemy during my southern command.[2] We had the misfortune to lose several, but we took some. Two were taken at the Cowpens, two at Augusta and one at Eutaw.[3] I don't recollect anymore brass peices, but a considerable number of iron Ordnance were taken at the different fortifications. I have the honor to be with great respect Your most obedient Humble servant   NATH GREENE

LS (NHi).

1. Duane, a delegate to Congress from New York, was chairman of a committee appointed to consider NG's first letter to Elias Boudinot of 7 October, above, and to decide on a suitable testimonial for his services in the war. (See Thomson to NG, 18 October, below.)
2. Thomas FitzSimons's letter to NG is immediately above.
3. On the battle of Cowpens, the capture of Augusta, Ga., and the battle of Eutaw Springs, see above, Daniel Morgan to NG, 19 January 1781 (vol. 7: 152–55 and n); Andrew Pickens to NG, 25 May 1781, and Pickens and Henry Lee to NG, 5 June 1781 (vol. 8: 310–11 and n, 351–52 and n); and NG to Thomas McKean, 11 September 1781 (vol. 11: 328–33 and n).

From Doctor Henry Collins Flagg[1]

Dear General   Charleston [S.C.] 17 Octo 1783
I have been reliev'd from a great deal of anxiety on your account by Capt Carnes—that you wou'd be sick on the road was what I expected and am sincerely rejoic'd your illness has terminated so happily.[2]
Poor Burnet we are just inform'd died at the Havannah after a fever of three days. He was buried—but in the Sea—in a most splendid and honorable manner, for it seems he was denied "the charity their dogs enjoy." The Gov'r offer'd his sanction to his being inter'd on shore, but, such is the bigotry of the common people that they wou'd certainly have dug up his corps, and it was thought best to consign our friend over to the fishes, insted of the worms. I am very sensibly affected upon this occasion, for I can truly say I had a very sincere regard for him.[3]
There has been some alteration in our domestic policy since you left us. The town is incorporated and the Court of Wardens have pass'd

several ordinances which will have a very good effect in regulating this City, but these you will see in the papers.[4]

Great quantities of dutch goods have arriv'd as well as several english cargoes.[5] They sell very fast, but the most thriving business at present seems to be matrimony—R—ge & M^c—ll and some others of your acquaintance are lately married, and many more will soon light their torches at the altar of Hymen, and very probably some of them burn their fingers, you will say this is truly the old batchelor—so it is.[6]

The establishment of the Society of Cincinati has given umbrage to many people, in particular to Cassius, who has drawn his pen against it and has undertaken to prove that it will confer an hereditary nobility.[7] God help us, poor Nobles shall we be indeed. I will send you this peice soon, together with some of our by laws, one of which is, that no person who has taken protection from the British shall be admitted into the society.[8]

When shall I have the pleasure of seeing you here again? I have determin'd nothing about my Sister's coming for this reason, that I do not find that prospect I once thought so favorable, realized, but this entre nous.[9]

Shou'd a peace establishment take place and my former department be continu'd I shall be glad if it can be secur'd to me, unless the pay shou'd be reduc'd.[10]

You have heard of poor Hagan's death.[11] This season has been fatal to the country doctors[;] Gibb, and a Dr Hall have fell sacrifices to the fever of the season and a Dr Brown I think from Virginia was lately murder'd on the road.[12]

Mr N. Russel has arriv'd from England but unfortunately for him a few hours after the expiration of the term allow'd by our Assembly for the return of absentees. This was occasion'd by a passage of near twelve weeks. It is uncertain if he will be readmitted into this State. I have wrote to Govr Greene to request his sentiments respecting his admission into the State of Rhode Island and observ'd that before Mr Russel took protection he applied to the Gov: to be exchang'd. This was a mistake in me owing to M^r R's not being so explicit as he has been since. It was you, Sir, to whom he applied for an exchange, if you think proper I shall be oblig'd if you will write Govr Greene a few lines on this subject.[13]

I shall have the honor to write to you by the first opportunity to Rhd^e Island. In the mean time Sir I wish you a happy meeting with Mrs Greene and your relations there[14] and am with the most sincere regard Your affectionate friend and most obed^t hum. Servant

HENRY COLLINS FLAGG

Be so good as to present my best regards to Major Hyrne.[15] Will you excuse my troubling with the inclos'd to Aunt Greene and H: Ward.[16]

RCS (MiU-C).

1. Flagg, a Rhode Island–born physician who had served with the Southern Army, was a cousin of CG. (See above, vol. 11: 380n.)

2. On his trip north, NG had been detained by illness at Alexandria, Va. (See above, NG's Journal, 13 September.) Patrick Carnes, a native of Virginia, had been an officer in Lee's Legion. It is not known whether he traveled part of the way north with NG.

3. NG had already received news of the death of his former aide, and John Banks's business partner, Ichabod Burnet. (See above, NG to Pierce, 15 October.) According to a notice published in the *South-Carolina Gazette and General Advertiser* of 14–18 October, Burnet was "buried with great solemnity in the Sea; and a British Frigate being in the Harbour, the Captain manned his boat, and joined in the mournful Procession . . . As the Scholar, Citizen, and Soldier, Major Burnet was equalled by few—his loss will be long and deeply impressed on the hearts of those who served with him in the field."

4. The South Carolina legislature passed "An Act to incorporate Charleston" on 13 August. (S.C., House of Representatives, *Journals, 1783–84*, p. 370) Richard Hutson was elected "intendant" of Charleston, and the city was divided into wards, each of which elected a warden to the local governing body. Among the ordinances recently published in the *South-Carolina Gazette and General Advertiser* were "An Ordinance for imposing a Duty of Three pence per Ton on Vessels making Entry at the Custom-House of Charleston in the State of South-Carolina" and "An Ordinance to restrain the Exhibition of Theatrical Entertainments within the City of Charleston" (23–27 September); "An Ordinance to prevent the Killing of Cattle within the City of Charleston" (27–30 September); "An Ordinance for defining and ascertaining the duties of a Harbour Master for the Port of Charleston," "An Ordinance for governing Mariners and Seamen within the City of Charleston," and "An ordinance for appointing Constables in the several Wards of the City of Charleston" (4–7 October); "An Ordinance to continue the present Fire-masters, Commissioners of the Streets, and Commissioners of the Markets and Work-house, for the term therein mentioned" (7–11 October); and "An Ordinance for establishing and regulating A Nightly Guard and Watch, in Charleston" (11–14 October).

5. Advertisements in Charleston newspapers in September and October listed various goods "lately arrived" from Amsterdam and London. One firm, Lawson & Price, offered "European and East India Goods," including furniture, hats, cloth, tools, glassware, and leather goods. (*South-Carolina Weekly Gazette*, 13 September) Another merchant, Henry Smerdon, advertised "fine London porter" for sale. (*South-Carolina Gazette and General Advertiser*, 30 September–4 October) The firm of Ballantine & Warham listed toys, carpets, writing paper, window glass, tools, soap, candles, and medicine among its wares imported from Amsterdam. (*South-Carolina Gazette and General Advertiser*, 7–11 October) After years of wartime deprivation, many South Carolinians must have been glad to see the material goods that were now available.

6. Flagg undoubtedly referred here to the speaker of the South Carolina House, Hugh Rutledge, who had married Ann Smith on 9 October. (*Biog. Directory of S.C. House*, 3: 628) Hext McCall, Esq., was married to "the amiable and accomplished Miss Betsey Pickering" on 15 October. (*South-Carolina Weekly Gazette*, 18 October) Although Flagg claimed to be "truly the old batchelor," he, too, succumbed to matrimony the following year. (See below, note at NG to CG, 10 September 1784.)

7. The Society of the Cincinnati, a national organization of Continental officers, was officially formed the previous spring. (William Heath to NG, 20 May 1783 [vol. 12: 674 and n], above; Myers, *Liberty Without Anarchy*, pp. 1–25) Throughout the summer, officers had organized chapters in their home states. (Myers, *Liberty Without Anarchy*, pp. 38–44) In a letter from James M. Varnum of 17 December, below, NG was informed that he had been elected president of the Rhode Island Society. As information about the Society became known to the public in the early fall of 1783, the organization began to draw criticism.

There were fears that it might become powerful enough to threaten the authority of Congress and that it could create a hereditary aristocracy. Perhaps the Cincinnati's most noted critic was Aedanus Burke of South Carolina, an associate justice of the Court of Common Pleas and General Sessions, whose pamphlet, *Considerations on the Order of the Cincinnati*, published under the pseudonym "Cassius," was widely reprinted. (See *Biog. Directory of S.C. House*, 3: 105–7; Meleney, *Aedanus Burke*, pp. 84–98; Myers, *Liberty Without Anarchy*, pp. 49–51. Burke, also as "Cassius," had previously published a pamphlet criticizing South Carolina's policies of confiscation and amercement. [Vol. 12: 521n, above]) An advertisement in a Rhode Island newspaper claimed that Burke's pamphlet would demonstrate that the Society of the Cincinnati "creates a Race of Hereditary Patricians, or Nobility." (*Newport Mercury*, 14 February 1784) Despite Burke's hostility to the Society, he and NG were friends, and NG is known to have stayed with him in Charleston. In 1785, again as "Cassius," Burke authored a pamphlet opposing the "primacy" of British merchants in Charleston. In a letter, he claimed that NG was responsible for some of the opinions expressed there. (See McQueen to NG, 23 May 1785, and Burke's letters to NG of 4 July 1785 and 27 November 1785, all below.) As seen at NG's letter to Washington of 22 April 1784, below, opposition to the Society of the Cincinnati was especially strong in New England.

8. An "Extract for the Rules and Bye-Laws of the Society of the CINCINNATI, established in the State of South Carolina," was printed in the *South-Carolina Gazette and General Advertiser* of 20–23 September. It stated that the "State Society" agreed to the "Propositions and Rules" of the general organization, which had been given to Gen. William Moultrie the previous May and June. However, undoubtedly aware of the criticism that the Society had engendered, the members of the South Carolina chapter maintained that "if any of the said Propositions or Rules should by any construction be held obligatory on the Society to interfere in any shape whatsoever, with the Civil Polity of this, or any other of the United-States, or the United-States in general, this Society will not deem themselves bound thereby; they prizing too highly the Civil Liberties of this country, and their own Rights as Citizens; to consent that a Military Society should in any sense dictate to the Civil Authority." The second article in the printed extract also aimed to deflect criticism of the Society by asserting that the "principal end of the State Society is to maintain the indigent officers and their widows, and afford both maintenance and education to their indigent children, taking care to have the male children instructed in the mathematics and such sciences as officers should be acquainted with, that if this country should be ever again unhappily plunged in war, they may be the more readily qualified to defend those Rights and Liberties, their fathers were instrumental in establishing." (*South-Carolina Gazette and General Advertiser*, 20–23 September)

9. Flagg's sister Elizabeth, or "Betsy," was a close friend of NG and CG. (Vol. 11: 380n, above) It is not known what "prospect" Flagg had "once found so favorable."

10. Flagg apparently did not participate in the army's "peace establishment." (Heitman, *Register*)

11. Dr. Francis Hagan, who had served with Col. Moses Hazen's regiment, died in St. Stephen's Parish, S.C., in late August. (*JCC*, 22: 82; *South-Carolina Weekly Gazette*, 30 August)

12. Dr. Joseph Hall died in Christ Church Parish in late September. (*South-Carolina Weekly Gazette*, 27 September) "Dr Gibb" may have been Thomas Gibb, a physician who had served with the British army but had petitioned the South Carolina legislature in February 1783 "to be admitted to the rights and privileges of a citizen of this State." (S.C., House of Representatives, *Journals, 1783–84*, p. 128)

13. Nathaniel Russell (1738–1820) was a Rhode Islander who had begun doing business in Charleston in the mid-1760s. He eventually settled in South Carolina and became a prosperous merchant. Though a Whig supporter at the beginning of the war, Russell

moved to England after the capture of Charleston, and the confiscation of his property was ordered under a legislative act of March 1783. Russell returned to Charleston on 19 September but was "not allowed to disembark." He petitioned the legislature, however, and on 26 March 1784 received a "special exemption" from confiscation. During the postwar years, Russell served in the South Carolina legislature and held a number of other political posts. (*Biog. Directory of S.C. House*, 3: 624–25) Governor Greene was Gov. William Greene of Rhode Island. Nothing is known about NG's involvement in Russell's situation, and if NG contacted his kinsman the governor on Russell's behalf, the letter has not been found.

14. NG was reunited with his family in Newport, R.I., on 27 November 1783. (See below, NG to Jacob Greene, 29 November.)

15. Maj. Edmund M. Hyrne had accompanied NG from Charleston to Philadelphia. (See note at NG's Journal entry for 15 August, above.)

16. "Aunt Greene" was CG's and Flagg's aunt Catharine Ray Greene, the wife of the Rhode Island governor; "H: Ward" was Henry Ward, uncle of NG's close Rhode Island friend Samuel Ward, Jr. (Vol. 1: 19n, above)

From John Banks

Dear Sir   Charleston [S.C.] Oct[r] 18th 1783

Herewith you'l please receive Copy of my last Respects to you:[1] since which I have receiv'd the distressing Intelligence of the Death of Major Burnet at Havanna, from an intelligent [Passenger?] who attended his funeral and who was personally acquainted with him; as the Vessel was not destind for this Port and put in by Stress of weather there are no Letters by her for this place, from the Circumstance of my receiving no Letter from him in so long absence and from the precise Description the Gentleman gives of the Vessel Cap[t] and every other Circumstance relative to the Major I fear there is no doubt that his melancholy Fate is but too true;[2] I hope his genuine Merit is rewarded with celestial Happiness, which is the only consolation his distressed Friends can have for so irreparable a Loss. I shall have every Arrangement made for an imediate adjustment of his Affairs and shall hope [for?] your kind attention to a final Settlement when you return to this Country.[3] I am D[r] sir with the utmost Respect Your most Obedient Ser[t]   JOHN BANKS

RCS (MiU-C).

1. The enclosure has not been found.

2. On the death of NG's former aide and Banks's business partner Ichabod Burnet, see also NG to Pierce, 15 October, and Flagg to NG, 17 October, both above, and Forsyth to NG, immediately below.

3. Nearly a year later, long since angered by Banks's failures to settle debts he had guaranteed for Banks, NG set out from Charleston to find him but learned when he reached Washington, N.C., that Banks had recently died there. (See below, NG to Rutledge, after 30 September 1784, and NG to Forsyth, 2 October 1784.)

*   *   *

¶ [FROM ROBERT FORSYTH, Charleston, S.C., 18 October 1783. After receiving NG's letter from Georgetown [not found] "respecting Major Waties's demands," Forsyth immediately let Waties know he was "ready to attend to a settlement of his accounts."[1] Waties replied that he had "sent to Geo. Town for the necessary papers," but Forsyth has not heard from him again. "With pain," Forsyth relates news of "the unhappy Death of my respected & worthy Friend," Maj. [Ichabod] Burnet. The news gives him "heartfelt distress," and he is sure it will "give not less" to NG and Burnet's "Northern Friends." It came from "two Vessells bound from Havannah to Phil[a]," which "put in here in distress." There was no letter of confirmation, "but Circumstances are too manifest to admit of one hopeful doubt."[2] Forsyth will not write to Burnet's father "on this feeling subject," as Mr. [John] Banks "intends or has done it," and "the doleful Tale will reach him before this does Phil[a]."[3] RCS (MiU-C) 2 pp.]

1. NG had spent two days in Georgetown, S.C., on his way north from Charleston in mid-August. (NG's Journal, 16 August, above) John Waties, Jr., was a Georgetown merchant who had sold supplies to the Southern Army. (See, for example, vol. 11: 64n, above.) Waties wrote NG in September 1784 that he had given Forsyth vouchers and accounts relating to "my demands on the Public, for Stores purchased for the Army under your Command." As he was being harassed by creditors, Waties hoped NG would "point out some mode by which they may be satisfied." (Waties to NG, 27 September 1784, below) Nothing more is known about this matter.

2. NG already knew about the death of his former aide Ichabod Burnet. (NG to Pierce, 15 October; see also Flagg to NG, 17 October, and Banks to NG, 18 October, all above.)

3. Burnet's father, William Burnet, Sr., was a well-known physician in Newark, N.J. (Vol. 3: 339n, above) John Banks was a business partner of both Ichabod Burnet and Forsyth.

*　　　*　　　*

From Charles Thomson, Secretary of the Continental Congress

[Princeton, N.J.] October 18th 1783.

By The United States in Congress Assembled October 18th 1783. On the report of a Committee to whom was referred a Letter of the 7th from Major General Greene.[1]

Resolved That two pieces of the field Ordnance taken from the British Army at the Cowpens, Augusta or Eutaw be presented by the Commander in Chief of the Armies of the United States to Major General Greene as a public testimonial of the wisdom, fortitude & military skill which distinguished his Command in the Southern Department and of the eminent services which amidst complicated difficulties and dangers and against an Enemy greatly superior in numbers he has successfully performed for his Country; and that a Memorandum be engraved on the said pieces of Ordnance expressive of the substance of this Resolution.[2]

Resolved That the Commander in Chief be informed that Major General Greene hath the permission of Congress to visit his family at Rhode Island.[3]　　　　　　　CHA[S] THOMSON SEC[Y]

DS (PPRF).

1. See NG to Boudinot, first letter of 7 October, above. The members of the committee were William Ellery, James Madison, and James Duane. (*JCC*, 25: 701)

2. Congress apparently delayed official notification of this public testimonial to NG until it could learn whether there were any such pieces of field ordnance that had been captured from the British. In a letter of 15 October, above, delegate Thomas FitzSimons informed NG of Congress's intent and asked whether NG knew of any "brass" ordnance captured from the British during the southern campaign. NG responded to committee member James Duane on 16 October, above, that two field pieces each had been taken at Cowpens, S.C., and Augusta, Ga., and one at Eutaw Springs, S.C. Gen. Henry Knox, who succeeded Washington as army commander, was ultimately directed to find the cannon and supervise the engraving. (Knox to NG, 15 February 1784, below) In March 1784, presumably by Knox's order, Samuel Hodgdon, the commissary of military stores, asked Col. Timothy Pickering to "call on the Commandant at West-point for two pieces of Ordnance (Brass) six pounders with their Carriages compleat" and to arrange for "Mr Billings" to engrave them. The inscriptions were to read: "Taken from the Britons, and presented to Major General Green by order of Congress, as an illustrious monument of their high sense of his Military talents successfully displayed in the conduct of the southern Army, amidst complicated difficulties and dangers, against an enemy greatly superior in numbers." (Memorandum, 6 March 1784, WRMS) Knox wrote NG on 27 October 1785, below, that he had found the two field pieces and had an engraver set to work on them. (See also Knox to NG, 14–18 March 1784, below.) NG replied on 12 March 1786, below, that although he appreciated Knox's "polite attention" to "my public Trophies," he was so "embarrassed and perplexed" by financial reversals that he had "little spirit or pleasure on such subjects." NG did not receive the field pieces before his death in June 1786.

3. In his first letter to Boudinot of 7 October, NG, noting that it was "going on Nine years" since he had seen his family and friends, asked for permission to return to Rhode Island.

*   *   *

¶ [TO JOHN EAGER HOWARD.[1] From Philadelphia, 19 October 1783. Introduces Mr. Abraham Baldwin, "a young Gentleman of the State of Connecticut of a good charactor and liberal education who is traveling Southward with a view of settling in one of those States." Baldwin "has studied the law and been regularly introduced into practice." NG hopes he "will meet with a favorable reception where ever he may think proper to fix his residence."[2] ALS (MdHi) 1 p.]

1. Howard, an officer of the Maryland Continental line, had served under NG in the Southern Army.

2. Abraham Baldwin (1754–1807), a Yale graduate, and former chaplain in the army, was admitted to the Connecticut bar in April 1783. He probably solicited this letter of introduction from NG in Philadelphia, on his way south. Baldwin settled in Georgia, where he began to practice law in January 1784; he later served in the Georgia House of Assembly and Congress. While still a relative newcomer, Baldwin was the author of a charter for establishing a "complete educational system" in Georgia. For his involvement in the founding of the University of Georgia, he is known as "the Father" of that institution. He was a delegate to the Constitutional Convention from Georgia and is credited with bringing about a fundamental compromise between the large and small states that helped to pave the way for the adoption of the Constitution. (*DAB*)

¶ [FROM JOHN COX, Bloomsbury, N.J., 20 October 1783.[1] He is "greatly distressed" that he has not been able to meet NG in Philadelphia. "In less than twelve hours after parting with" NG,[2] he was "suddenly seized with a fever" and his "old Companion the Head-Ache," which have "confined me to my Bed ever since." This is the first day he has been able to "set up," but he does not expect even to leave his room "for several days." Asks NG "when we may expect the pleasure of your Company on your return to the Eastward."[3] RCS (MiU-C) 1 p.]

1. On Cox, who had been one of NG's two top assistants in the Quartermaster Department, see vol. 3: 85n, above.

2. NG had presumably seen Cox during his recent trip to Princeton, N.J., where Congress was meeting. (See above, NG's two letters to Elias Boudinot of 7 October.)

3. It is not known whether NG saw Cox again on his way home to Newport, R.I.

¶ [FROM JAMES DUANE, Princeton, N.J., 20 October 1783. NG's "Information came seasonably to notice," allowing Duane to "get the business Then in Contemplation perfected."[1] NG will be "apprised of it officially."[2] The "signal services" that NG has "performd" for his "Country in a most arduous & succesful Command intitle" him "to publick Honors and private Esteem, A sentiment which no Man feels in a higher Degree than" Duane. ADfS (NHi) 1 p.]

1. See NG to Duane, 16 October, above.

2. See Thomson to NG, 18 October, above.

¶ [FROM ROGER PARKER SAUNDERS, Charleston, S.C., 20 October 1783. He is "happy to hear" of NG's recovery from his illness and of his arrival in Philadelphia.[1] Saunders has "been so handled by the Fever" that he has not been able to take care of NG's business. He hopes NG's business affairs respecting the plantation have "sustaind no injury," as Mr. Croskeys was "kind enough" to visit the plantation "Frequently."[2] Saunders has just returned from a visit there and is "much hurt and disappointed at the present appearance" of the rice crop. The crop "sufferd Greatly from the Great Storm," and "the Rice Birds were so Numerous that they destroyd at least half of the Young Rice."[3] Saunders will "have the Rice to market as Soon as possible" and will "settle wth Capt Blake." The price will "not be under 14/76th," though, and "will in some Measure make up for a Short Crop." The "Negroe Fellow that was Wigfalls is dead,"[4] and "one of the Chesnut Horses died of Bots";[5] the other three horses "are in good order," but Saunders "cant dispose of them to advantage." NG's carriage "will not sel for any Price."[6] Saunders has heard nothing from NG since NG "left Carolina."[7] He sends "Respectful Comp[limen]^{ts}" to CG. RCS (MiU-C) 3 pp.]

1. NG had taken ill in Alexandria, Va., on his way north from Charleston. (See above, NG's Journal entry for 13 September.) He arrived in Philadelphia on 4 October. (See NG to Boudinot, first letter of 7 October, above.)

2. John Croskeys assisted in the running of NG's South Carolina plantation, Boone's Barony. (See his letter to NG of 10 August 1784, below.)

3. Edmund M. Hyrne described the storm as a "hurricane" and reported that he had lost twenty barrels of rice because of it. (Hyrne to NG, 26 November–4 December, below) The *South-Carolina Gazette and General Advertiser* of 4–7 October also reported on the "hurricane," which had caused extensive flooding in the vicinity of Charleston and damage to docks in the city. Historian Julia Floyd Smith has written that "among the many hazards to the growing rice were the eating habits of ducks and birds. The yellow and black bobolinks, called rice birds, could strip a field of sprouted rice and destroy it completely as they headed north in May, or do the same in August and September as they returned to South America. Slaves classified as 'bird-minders' used noisemakers such as clappers or muskets and built fires along the banks to protect the fields from these marauders." (Smith, *Slavery and Rice Culture*, p. 50) NG replied to Saunders that he was

"extremely unhappy at the failure of the Crops," as he had been "told from all quarters [that] crops were never better and my demands [were] never more pressing." (NG to Saunders, 4 January 1784, below)

4. "Wigfall" was probably John Wigfall, whose letter to NG of 27 May 1783 is above. Although he had been a member of the South Carolina legislature during the war, Wigfall joined a Loyalist militia unit after the fall of Charleston. The General Assembly voted to banish him and confiscate his estate, but these sanctions were never enforced. (*Biog. Directory of S.C. House*, 2: 710) In reply to the present letter, NG asked Saunders to investigate the report of the slave's death. As he had been told that Wigfall was dishonest, NG supposed he might have lied in order to keep the slave on his own plantation. (NG to Saunders, 4 January 1784; see also Wigfall to NG, 27 May.)

5. Bots is a disease in horses caused by the larvae of the botfly.

6. Saunders reported the following May that NG's carriage had been "Ruind by being exposd to the Weather." (Saunders to NG, 29 May 1784, below)

7. NG had left Charleston in mid-August.

¶ [FROM CAPTAIN DAVID ZEIGLER, 20 October [17]83. Thanks NG for "many Kindness[es]," especially for recommending Zeigler to "the Notice of His Excellen[cy] General Washington & the Honourable th[e] Congress to have a Command on the pease Establishment."[1] Zeigler will never be able to compensate NG, but his "thoughts will be directed to him, which is able to perform that with Prayer that he may Crown you her[e] in this world, & more in Eternity." RCS (MiU-C) 1 p.]

1. In a letter to Washington of 11 October, above, NG had mentioned Zeigler as one of several officers who wished to continue "on the pease Establishment." As noted there, Zeigler did serve in the peacetime army.

¶ [FROM DENNIS DE BERDT, London, 21 October 1783. He writes NG "by the permission & kind intimation" of his "affectionate friend & Brother Joseph Reed Esq[r]," who promised to "second my solicitation to be favoured with your commands in this Country." During the war, which "disgraced & impoverished this Nation," De Berdt "retired to a small Estate in the West of England," but he has now resumed his "former Mercantile connections with America," which he and his father carried on when his father was "Agent for the House of Assembly in Boston." De Berdt writes: "The caution I observed during the War in not prosecuting any views however apparently lucrative that I thought inimical to the Interest of America will I trust not go without some rewards from the discriminating & worthy Characters that now adorn that Country." He informs NG that "the field of commerical action is now opening fast, & will be extensive," although "there remains much yet to be done, to begin a good ground, & to draw the line of reciprocity of Interest." Parliament will "soon open," and it will then be clear "how far they encourage the American trade by Laws of liberality & moderate restrictions," to encourage Americans to become consumers of British manufactures. To make Americans pay excessively for British goods would be "neither politick nor wise." Few "American articles" have "as yet bore a price" in London, "except Rice." The "first consignment" of rice "of any consequence from Charles Town [S.C.] since the peace" came to De Berdt in the *Washington*, belonging to De Berdt's "friend George Henry Esq[r] of Philadelphia," who was introduced to De Berdt by Reed; De Berdt "cleared" Henry "above 100 per Cent." As NG will see by the "inclosed price Current" [not found], rice "still keeps up very high." De Berdt's price current "may be depended on, as more accurate than most printed ones of the kind, which in general are a mere pro forma." The price of Indigo has been "very steady for some time past & Tobacco very fluctuating," but De Berdt thinks "they have just taken a start of price," which "they will maintain thro' the Winter." De Berdt adds: "The great quantity of Goods imported since the Peace by the Northern States, the necessity of payment & the high price of all your produce, from so many foreign buyers, will make Bills of Exchange at a price far above Par, & will be a means of draining your Country of Specie to remit to England, which I should think will distress you much." De Berdt has "ever had a regard for the welfare & happiness of America" and hopes that "never will abate." He will always think it "an Honor, & a pleasure" to "serve its cause in general, or promote the Interest of its individuals." Whenever NG "may think proper" to lay his "commands" on De Berdt, they will be "most chearfully & faithfully obeyed."[1] CyS (MiU-C) 4 pp.]

1. NG later wrote Joseph Reed that he would be "happy to render" De Berdt, the brother of Reed's late wife, Esther, "any service in my power." (NG to Reed, 14 May 1784, below)

*　　　*　　　*

From Warner Mifflin[1]

Respected Friend Nath[l] Greene

Kent on Deleware [Del.] y[e] 21st of 10 m[o] 1783

The short interview we had with thee at Prince Town and open Caryage that appear'd with thee toward us induces me to Communicate some farther of my mind to thee than the time then would admit. I was very fearfull of intrudeing on thy Patience then, under the Perticular engagement that thou was.[2] I remarked to thee that I had left in Gen[l] [William] Smallwoods care a book that I presented thee for thy perusal on the Subjects of War and slavery seting forth the inconsistency thereof with the Spirit and precepts of the Gospel, thou then reply'd thy thoughts had been too much taken up other ways to attend to those subjects.[3] I then felt a desire, that inasmuch as it had pleased Divine Providence still to lengthen out thy day through a Series of time in a perilous enterprize, that thou might be thoughtfully concerned to lay to [heart?] what it will procure the[e], whither all the Honour thou can achieve to in that business will be likely to procure any treasure in Heaven laid up against the time to come, or whither it is not more likely that all thy great exploits will not be more likely to terminate in anguish of Soul, disappointment, and perplexity, this I do think is most likely from my apprehension of things, I hope I may speak my mind freely to thee without offence if I am not deceived in thee I believe thy disposition will bare it especially if thou believes it comes from one that really desires thy lasting wellbeing, which I doubt not thou will admit to be the case with me, and more especially as the Situation of things as to the outward at this time will not admit of the Jealosys and Surmises against an inofensive People that have been of their being Partizans.[4]

I was in measure led to admire the goodness mercy & Long forbareance of the Mercifull Creator of man in continueing the door of Mercy open to Rebellious and backslideing Creatures who have so deeply revolted from his Divine Laws, as I could not help thinking but was the case toward thee.[5] May I therefore be instrumental in puting thee on takeing a retrospective View of thy past life to examine whither thou cannot find wherein thou has gone contrary to the Manifestation of Grace in thy own mind, which thou wert made sensable was contrary to the will of thy Maker, and which brought thee under condemnation, and wherein thou had to discover that if thou yielded obedience to what was made known to be thy duty it would bring thee under the Necessity of takeing up the cross denying thy self of Thy beloved Lusts, this is what makes Quakerism reproachfull in the Eyes of the world, and in the Sight of those who give a Latitude to their sensual inclinations, but the obedient Humble Christian finds a perl of immense Value therein even an hundred fold of that Peace that the world nor all things in it cannot give, nor all the powers of the Earth take from them. This is a prize of much more Value than all the Honours that can be crowded on the greatest General that ever stood on the Earth by men. This I am confirmed in beyond all doubt in feeling the flowings forth of the Principles of Peace and good will to all men and a Concience clear that I had no party to Promote nor no scheme to cary forward but that of Universal Righteousness and Peace, I felt terror removed from me when from an Apprehension of duty to him who rules above the Kingdoms of men, I had to travel through the contending Armies and had to Observe the Brutal revenge that appeared in the countenances of the Soldirey against each other. I was not asshamed nor affraid at any time to Face the head General of Either Army and the time I was Named on the Committee to Present a Testimony to our Principles to the two Generals I thought indeed it was like takeing my Life in my hands when I went up to Perkiomen to General Washingtons Camp considering the Bloody Business the two armies had been at but Two day before,[6] and the exasperated situation of the minds of the American Army & the inveteracy that had been let in against our Society occasioned by some designing men, there was not much in prospect as to the outward but that our Necks must pay for it but I felt that to cover my mind that removed all fear of Man whoes breath is in his Narrow Norstrils, even a confidential trust in the Allmighty Arm of him at whoes angry Nod the Stoutest Monarchs are made to tremble, believing it was for his Name and Truth we were Called to appear on behalf of; and if even our Lives were to go for it, they could not be too much, and if I am not mistaken there was some present at that time that would like to have had the fingering of us in that way, but the innocency and uprightness of our movement appearing in such a manner I thought we were at last treated as Ambassadors from some Prince.[7]

So that I have to believe by our thus remaining firm to our principles the Powers of the Earth have to see that Swords, nor baygonets, fines nor imprisonments, can drive from the precious testimoney that we have to hold against the Spirit of AntiChrist that I am ready to conclude many who were bitter against us are now ready to judge more favourably, and to assent there must be more than mere whim among us, Yea I doubt not but some will be forced to assent that those people are peculiarly under the notice of him who preserved Daniel in the Lyons den if we are but faithfull to him I have no doubt but this will be more and more Visible.[8] May I then take the Liberty to ask thee what thou has done with thy share in this Principle and testimony as I understand thou was Educated among us has the Religion of thy Education never been the religion of thy Judgment, if this has never been the case thou might have been in an error to have continued it;[9] or has thou done as Easaw did sell thy birth right for a mess of Pottage[10] it is no harm for me to fear this has been the case which will turn out a Miserable exchange in the end if it should prove so. I would from a well grounded concern for thee at this time prevailing request thy impartial inspection therein I believe thou wilt one day find it to be a matter of greater concernment to thee as an Individual than all thy solicitude about the fate of America, what will all the vain Glory and Applause of Mortals do for thee when thou art arrested by the Awfull and undeniable Messenger that rides the Pale horse When the Pains of death which the greatest Ceasars must bend to,[11] have seized this Earthly house of thy Tabernicle and the Prospect of a never ending Eternity opens to thy View, then, O then, Nathaniel do thou let me intreat thee, do reflect what will all this do for thee; how does it last as thou passes a long, are they not all lying Vanities that perish with the Using, I mean all the Honours and applause of mortals. I did not when I took up my pen expect to have enlarged so much but I thought I felt love to increase toward thee and matters open that I thought might do no harm to throw before thy View I now wind up on that head and proceed to touch with thee on the subject of Slavery.[12]

I saw a letter thou wrote our friend Able Thomas or a Copy thereof which I thought contained a noble sentiment, and as thou mentioned a hope you should fix Liberty on so broad a basis that it would be lasting[13] tho' thou said nothing respecting Black People, yet as the Grand Strugle was for Liberty and thou took thy Commission from Congress who had in their Declaration set forth in such clear terms its being the Natural right of all men should thou after all by thy Conduct countenance slavery it would be a stigma to thy Character in the Annals of History if the Historians of the present day should do justice in transmiting to Posterity the transactions thereof.[14] I seem unsatisfyed in my mind in forming an Idea the part thou art likely to Act in regard to this matter thou expressed that thou united in sentiment somewhat with us on this Subject, but I did think before I saw thee and much since that the Part thou acts respecting the Estate I have been informed thou has had given thee in Carolina may do much in this Matter as I hinted to thee if thou Publickly should Protest against having the Labour of slaves thereon there might a degree of consistancy appear in thy contending for others to enjoy what thou holds so dear to thy self that is Liberty the odiousness of Slavery it would I should think appear almost an undervaluement to thee to attempt her[e] to paint it in its true Colours.[15]

If on the other hand thou should purchace a Number of slaves and place thereon, or if thou should tenant the same to those that are slave Holders and thou receive the Profits of the Slaves Labour their unreward[ed?] toil it would in its consequences tend to encourage the Petty Tyrants of America to hold on their Oppression, also to strengthen the infamous trade to Africa, and so to draw down renew'd displeasure from Heaven is my judgment thereof,[16] that if it is agreeable to thee I should be very glad to receive a few Lines from thee informing me more fully thy Sentiment on this Head which will be acceptable to thy real Friend and a Lover of mankind.[17]   WARNER MIFFLIN

P S I spoke to my Friend Dr Rush to present thee in my Name a small piece on slavery[18] also to Anthony Benezet[19] & if thou wert minded to send me a few Lines being directed to the care of either of those men might come safe to hand.   WM

RCS (NcU).

1. Mifflin (1745–98), a Quaker reformer and cousin of Thomas Mifflin, lived on a farm near Camden, Del. He had freed his slaves in 1774 and 1775 and was said to be " 'the first man in America to unconditionally' " do so. From the mid-1770s, Mifflin's "efforts to bring about emancipation were untiring." He traveled about the country, preaching antislavery doctrine to other Quakers, and, in addition to the address to Congress that is described in note 2, below, also gave a "Memorial to the President, the Senate and the House of Representatives of the United States" on the topic in 1791. (Sarah Mifflin Gay, "A Biographical Note on Warner Mifflin," in Justice, *Warner Mifflin*, pp. 38–40; *DAB*)

2. Mifflin was with a delegation of Quakers who presented an "address" to Congress, asking for the abolition of the slave trade, at Princeton, N.J., on 8 October, when NG was also there. The "deputation" presented its address "on behalf of the yearly meeting held in Philadelphia, for Pennsylvania, New Jersey, Delaware and the western parts of Maryland and Virginia." (*JCC*, 25: 654, 660 and n; PCC, item 43, p. 337, DNA) It is not clear what "particular engagement" NG was involved in when Mifflin encountered him at Princeton. (See above, NG's two letters of 7 October to Elias Boudinot, the president of Congress.)

3. The title of the book about war and slavery that Mifflin left with Smallwood is not known.

4. Mifflin and other Quakers considered themselves impartial in the war, but others

viewed them as "Partizans." According to his biographical sketch in the *DAB*, Mifflin "adhered to the Quaker peace principles" and "refused to have the least part in supporting the war, even to the use of Continental paper money." Consequently, "he was dubbed a Tory, and his patriot neighbors made serious threats against him." (*DAB*) According to one historian, Mifflin's "defiance and resignation to suffering may have outshone that of any other Friend in the Revolution." (Marietta, *American Quakerism*, p. 254)

5. One of the central tenets of the Society of Friends was its opposition to war. NG, who had been raised a Quaker, left the Society in 1777, some two years after he joined the Continental army. (Vol. 2: 104n, above) His involvement in the war would have rendered him "Rebellious" and "backslideing" in the eyes of devout Quakers.

6. After the battle of Germantown on 4 October 1777, GW had ordered his army to encamp "on the west bank of Perkiomen Creek (opposite Pennypackers) at Pawlings Mills." (Vol. 2: 179n, above; an account of the "bloody business" at Germantown can be found in ibid., pp. 171–77.) "Mifflin was one of a committee of six appointed by the Friends' Yearly Meeting" at that time "to visit both commanders-in-chief and present printed copies of the Quaker 'Testimonies' against participation in war." The committee members "went without passports through the lines of both armies and accomplished their mission." (See Mifflin sketch in *DAB* and Hector St. John De Crèvecoeur, "Anecdote of Warner Mifflin," in Justice, *Warner Mifflin*, pp. 41–63.)

7. As seen in note 4, above, some Quakers in the Philadelphia area, such as Mifflin, were seen as having allied themselves with the British and were thus considered enemies of the Americans. In a letter to his brother Jacob, written three weeks after the battle at Germantown, NG claimed that Quakers in Philadelphia had "voluntarily lent" the British general William Howe, "5,000 [£] sterling" after Howe's arrival in Philadelphia and that Howe had "laid" the Quakers "under the necessity of lending him 20,000 more." NG also reported in that letter that "A gentleman of undoubted truth sais he has heard several of the Friends say they wish G Washingtons army was cut [in] pieces that there might be peace." (NG to Jacob Greene, 27 October 1777 [vol. 2: 183–84, above])

8. In the Old Testament, Daniel was cast into a den of lions but survived because of God's protection. (*Daniel* 6)

9. As mentioned in note 5 above, NG had been raised as a Quaker.

10. In the Biblical account, Esau sold his birthright to his brother Jacob for "a mess of pottage." (*Genesis* 25)

11. Mifflin's Biblical reference was to the *Book of Revelation*, 6: 8. The "undeniable Messenger that rides the Pale horse" there is death itself.

12. Jack D. Marietta writes that there was a specific "link between the Revolution and Warner Mifflin's antislavery impulse" and notes that when Mifflin exposed himself to danger while crossing both armies' lines after the battle of Germantown (note 6, above), he felt sympathy "with our oppressed African Bretheren," who experienced similar risk of harm without any means of redress. (Marietta, *American Quakerism*, p. 275)

13. "Friend" Abel Thomas, a Quaker preacher from Pennsylvania, was in South Carolina while NG commanded the Southern Army there. Thomas wrote NG on 4 June 1781, above (vol. 8: 348), and NG replied to him on 7 June 1781, above, from his camp near Ninety Six. (Ibid., p. 358) In his letter to Thomas, NG acknowledged that the Quakers' "principles and professions are opposed to war" but noted that they were also "fond of both political and religious liberty." The Americans were "contending" for such liberties and, NG asserted, hoped to "establish them on such a broad basis as to put it out of the power of our enemies to shake its foundation." For this reason NG hoped "for the good wishes" of the Quakers, "as well for their own sakes as for ours who wishes to serve them upon all occasions not inconsistent with the public welfare." (Ibid.)

14. The Declaration of Independence had asserted the right of "life, liberty and the pursuit of happiness" to every human being. Clearly, though, the signers, some of whom were slave owners, did not intend to include African slaves in this statement. NG

responded that Mifflin was vastly overrating "my influence" on American attitudes toward slavery. (NG's reply to Mifflin is at the end of the November documents, below.)

15. The states of South Carolina and Georgia had each given NG an extensive plantation as a mark of gratitude for his role in the war in the South. Mifflin may have been referring here to NG's plantation in South Carolina, Boone's Barony.

16. NG was then purchasing slaves for his plantations. (See for example, Penman to NG, 1 October, above, and NG to Penman, 25 October, below.)

17. See NG's reply to Mifflin, at the end of the November documents.

18. The noted Philadelphia surgeon Benjamin Rush had served as surgeon general in the American army. (Vol. 2: 68n, above) An abolitionist, he had published *An Address to the Inhabitants of the British Settlements in America, upon Slave-keeping* in 1773, and in the following year he became a founder of the Pennsylvania Society for Promoting the Abolition of Slavery. (*DAB*) Rush was a prolific writer of essays and pamphlets, and it is not clear whether the "small piece on slavery" was one of his own writings.

19. Anthony Benezet (1713–84), a French Huguenot who converted to Quakerism at the age of fourteen while living in England, had moved with his family to Philadelphia in 1731. A teacher and writer, and a friend of Benjamin Rush, he had espoused the cause of antislavery since the 1750s. (*DAB*) After Benezet's death, Warner Mifflin became the "most vigorous antislavery Friend" in the country. (Marietta, *American Quakerism*, p. 275)

*   *   *

¶ [FROM HENRY PENDLETON, Richmond, Va., 22 October 1783. He has been told that "Maj Edward's Servant" was seen "at Susquehannah," en route to Virginia with a "Horse and Chaise for me"; he assumes that NG sent them. Pendleton delayed his departure from Culpeper and supposed he had "allowed full time for their Coming," but they never arrived. Because of the "accident" that befell two of his "Carriage horses," he has had to replace them, "not being able to wait" any longer "and having no expectation of the horse & Chair's coming on."[1] In making this purchase, he had to draw on NG for "20 Guineas." He is "much concerned at the acc^t of the horse and Chair's being on the way" but fears "some accident hath happened to the servant as it is now above a fortnight ago, and the servant might have come up before I set out." If the servant finds Pendleton gone and "is Judicious," he will return to Philadelphia with the horses. Pendleton comments in closing: "When this will reach you god knows."[2] RCS (MiU-C) 1 p.]

1. Evan Edwards had accompanied NG from Charleston, S.C., to Philadelphia. (See NG's Journal entries during August and September, above.) On the "horse and Chaise" that NG borrowed from Pendleton and the "accident" to Pendleton's own horses, see Pendleton's letters to NG of 6 August and 12 October, both above.

2. Pendleton drew on Charles Pettit to replace his horse and sulky. (See Pendleton to NG, 12 October, above, and Pettit to NG, 7 February 1784, below.)

¶ [FROM GENERAL BENJAMIN LINCOLN, SECRETARY AT WAR, War Office [Philadelphia], 24 October 1783. He forwards a "resolution of Congress which passed a few days since." Congratulates NG "on this very honerary testimony of the high sense your country entertain of your important services and on the means they have taken to perpetuate a remembrance of them."[1] Df (MHi) 1 p.]

1. For the congressional resolution honoring NG, see Thomson to NG, 18 October, above.

*   *   *

To William Ellery[1]

Philadelphia, 25 October 1783

"You have done me great honor by the resolution of Congress which you enclosed me; and I am very much indebted to the Committee for their polite report, and take this opportunity of returning you my thanks.[2]

"On the other subject which you wrote me, much will depend upon the nature of it, the time and place for meeting upon the business, the expense that will attend it, and the allowance that will be made for the service.[3] My affairs are now much deranged and I must attend first to my family, and then to my future. After which if the public claims my Service in a line in which I could do justice to them and to my Self without injury to my family or fortune I am in duty bound to serve them. But as I have spent great part of my life in the public Service and almost all that part which is most interesting (i.e., "the best years of my life") I think I may fairly claim an exemption from employment either prejudicial to my family happiness or private fortune. Having thus cordially stated to you my situation, sentiments & feelings, if after this you think my appointment will promote the public good & my own happiness I leave you at full liberty to act as you may think proper confiding in your judgement and friendship in the business."

Printed excerpt (Christies' "Kittyhawk" sale, 8 June 1990).
1. Ellery was a delegate to Congress from Rhode Island.
2. Ellery's letter to NG has not been found. For the Congressional resolution honoring NG for his wartime services, see Thomson to NG, 18 October, above.
3. In his letter, Ellery may have discussed the possibility of NG's serving on a commission to negotiate with Indians. NG was formally asked to be a member of such a commission in a letter from Thomas Mifflin of 6 March 1784, below.

To James Penman

Sir   Philadelphia October 25th 1783

I have this mor⟨ning⟩ got your letter of the 1ˢᵗ of this insta⟨nt.⟩ I am sorry you have it not in you⟨r⟩ power to procure me the Negroes ag⟨ree⟩able to the prices I proposed. Upon ⟨fur⟩ther reflection and from the conver⟨sation⟩ I have had with three or four Merch⟨ants⟩ of this place I am convinced Slav⟨es⟩ will not be to be had as low as I le⟨t⟩ you. My desire is great to put ⟨the⟩ plantation under cultivation in Geor⟨gia⟩ and Mr. William Gibbons my Att⟨orney⟩ in that State encourages me ⟨to⟩ give higher prices for Negroes than ⟨he had first proposed⟩ and thinks the cultivation will ⟨we⟩ll afford it.[1] From these considerations ⟨I⟩ have concluded to Purchase at higher rates and to solicit your friend⟨ly⟩ offices in Negotiating the business with ⟨G⟩eneral [James] Grant or any others you may find most reasonable on the best terms you ⟨ca⟩n not exceeding £70 a head and payments to be made by instalments and

⟨t⟩he interest to be paid annually in London; for ⟨w⟩hich I will get the first Merchants ⟨of⟩ this City Letters of credit on the sub⟨je⟩ct and for the principal I will give ⟨e⟩ither landed security or bondsmen for ⟨th⟩e payments to be made agreeable to ⟨t⟩he terms of the agreement. The Negroes ⟨m⟩ust be sound, not old, and the property unquestionable. I beg you will engage the Negroes as soon as possible and have them conveyed to my estate in Georgia without loss of time and reported to Mr Gibbons w⟨ho⟩ will receive receipt and provide for the⟨m.⟩ If any Agency should be necessary in ⟨the⟩ business my friend [Alexander] Garden I trust ⟨will⟩ do me the favor. Let your contract i⟨f possi⟩ble run for the Negroes to be delive⟨red⟩ at the plantation or some where ⟨in⟩ Georgia so that Mr Gibbons can take ⟨care⟩ of them. Get your payments as long ⟨as⟩ possible, Interest to be paid annually; b⟨ut⟩ if the payment of a thousand or fifteen hundred pounds down this fall or t⟨he⟩ beginning of Winter will favor th⟨e⟩ purchace greatly engage it, and I ⟨will⟩ provide the Money Accordingly; but do not e[n]gage this unless it should be absolutely ⟨necessa⟩ry for the purchase.

I am mortified at M^r [Dart] not having repaid you the money [*blank*] me. I have written him to do it ⟨without loss of time and⟩ pointed out the man[ner.]² Present me respectfully to Doctor [Andrew] Turnbulls family and believe me to be your Most Obedt humble Ser^t

NB. For Negotiating this business ⟨of⟩ the Negroes you will charge me what you may think reasonable and which I shall chearfully pay.

[N]B. I trust to your judgement or the person you may employ in the business as to the quality of the negroes: As much depends on the quality as the p[r]ice.³

ADf (MiU-C). The text in angle brackets was taken from a GWG Transcript (CSmH).

1. In his letter of 1 October, above, Penman reported that slaves were selling at higher prices than NG had proposed to pay. William Gibbons had acted as NG's agent in procuring slaves earlier in the year. (See NG to Gibbons, 25 February, above [vol. 12: 475–76].)

2. Penman had apparently advanced about 200 hundred guineas to NG, which John S. Dart, the paymaster, had not yet repaid. (Penman to NG, 1 October) NG's letter to Dart has not been found. For more about this debt, see Hyrne to NG, 26 November–4 December, and Penman's reply to NG, dated 4 December, below.

3. Roger Parker Saunders wrote NG on 25 November, below: "I have Just been with Mr Penman[;] he has the offer of 123 Negroes wch are now at [St.] Augustine," East Florida. (See also Penman to NG, 4 December.)

From Edward Carrington

Dr Genl   Richmond [Va.] Octo 26. 1783

Your Servant arrived here some weeks ago when I was out of Town, & being Still sick was obliged to remain under the direction of Doctor Foucher 'till now. I have paid his Physician & Tavern Bill being £9.0.6

Virg^a Money, also have furnished him with three pounds to go forward with, amounting in the whole to £12.0.6. This may remain between us untill I have the pleasure to see you or to transmit the former Acc^t on which there is a Balance due you.[1]

The assembly of this State is now convening. What may be the politics of that Body is hard to guess, a great degree of Madness with respect to the admission of the refugees, even to the total expulsion of Trade, has poisoned the good understandings of many conspicuous Characters. I am anxiously waiting to see what may be the result of the collective Wisdom of all, we at present may boast indeed an independancy as to Great Britain, but to my great Mortification we are dependent on, and greivously tributary to our sister states in the little Commerce we have.[2]

I hope you found Mrs Greene in perfe[ct] health.[3] When I have the pleasure to write you again I shall add a postscript or so for her. I am Dr Genl Y^{rs} affy   E CARRINGTON

RCS (MiU-C).

1. Carrington wrote NG on 29 November, below, that the servant, Tom, had arrived in Richmond "about the 10th of October and remained Sick untill the 27th," when Carrington advanced him $10 "to go on." Carrington anticipated that the servant would rejoin NG by the end of November, but Tom was "extreemly Ill" by the time he got to Fredericksburg, and NG's friend George Weedon doubted that he would survive. (Weedon to NG, 2 December, below; as noted there, however, he apparently did survive.) It is not known what was done with the account for medical care that Carrington sent with Tom from Richmond. (Carrington to NG, 29 November)

2. At its fall session, which convened on 20 October, the Virginia Assembly passed two bills that clarified the status of persons wishing to establish citizenship in the state. "An act for the admission of emigrants and declaring their right to citizenship" provided that "all persons other than alien enemies who shall migrate into this state" and who shall swear "fidelity to the Commonwealth" could become citizens. The second piece of legislation was "An act prohibiting the migration of certain persons to this commonwealth," which stipulated that persons who had "borne arms against the United States" or had owned a "privateer, or other armed vessel, cruising against the United States," or who had been members of the "Board of Refugee Commissioners at New-York," would not be allowed to be citizens of Virginia. All others who were "at present prohibited by law" from migrating to the state would be allowed to return and "enjoy all the rights of citizenship" but would not be allowed to hold office or vote for representatives to the legislature. This act repealed previous legislation that had prohibited British subjects from taking up residence in the state. (Hening, *Statutes*, 11: 299, 322–25)

3. The state of CG's health when NG reached Rhode Island at the end of November is not known. (See, however, NG to Pierce, 15 October, above.) CG was pregnant with her fifth child at this time.

*   *   *

¶ [FROM JOHN WRIGHT STANLY, New Bern, N.C., 26 October 1783. Acknowledges NG's letter of 22 September [not found]. Would have "waited on" NG in Alexandria but heard from Major "Horn [i.e., Edmund M. Hyrne?] that you were much Indisposed and confin'd to your Room."[1] Is glad to find that NG has "so far recovered as to be able to proceed" on his journey. Before Stanly left

Philadelphia, he put the "Bill forwarded to me by Capt Blake" into "the hands of My Agents to discharge in part my Engagements in that City and they count on it as Money when due."[2] If it were possible "by any Means," Stanly would "immediately give Orders" to have the bill "held untill it suited you to take it up." But he has been "so embarras'd by heavy Losses and disappointments about the time peace took place that I am obliged to call in every thing in my power to support my Credit & peace arrangments." Otherwise, he would have been "happy in an Oppertunity of Obliging you."[3] RCS (MiU-C) 2 pp.]

1. On NG's illness during his visit to Alexandria, Va., see NG's Journal entry for 13 September, above.

2. For more about this matter, see note at NG to Pettit, 4 August, above.

3. In his letter to Stanly of 22 September, NG had evidently asked for a delay of payment. It appears from Charles Pettit's letter to NG of 7 February 1784, below, that the issue of payment to Stanly was not resolved until the following winter.

¶ [FROM GEORGE WASHINGTON, Rocky Hill, N.J., 26 October 1783. It gives him "infinite satisfaction" to send NG an enclosed copy of the congressional resolution of 18 October.[1] "Perfectly coinciding with the sentiments which Congress have expressed on this occasion," Washington will "feel the greatest pleasure in complying with the Resolve"; however, he asks "where the pieces of Ordnance are to be found and to what place you would wish to have them sent."[2] In a postscript, he acknowledges NG's letter "with the names of several Officers who wish to remain in service on a Peace Establishment"; he will "take pleasure in mentioning them whenever such an Establishm^t takes place, at present it hangs in Suspense."[3] Df (Washington Papers: DLC) 1 p.]

1. On the congressional resolution, see Thomson to NG, 18 October, above.

2. Under the resolution, two pieces of ordnance that had been captured from the British were to be engraved and presented to NG. (Ibid.) NG replied to Washington on 3 November, below.

3. See NG to Washington, 11 October, above.

*   *   *

To Henry Lee, Jr.

Dear Sir   Philadelphia October 27th 1783.

Your letter from Alexandria [Va.] adds another proof to the list of human errors. It is evidently written in a spirit of discontent founded on an imaginary neglect and want of esteem and affection. In forming this opinion you only just take my place and place me in your situation. But how different is our calls in life. Remember I have a family whom I dearly love, A wife who I have not seen for upwards of six months, three Children that I never saw but once, and the oldest near seven years old, Brothers that I have not met for five years, and besides these all my former friends and relations and you may reasonably suppose my feelings were deeply interested in hastening my journey as fast as possible. Every moments delay was painful and every day brought fresh anxieties. I was sensible you would be disappointed at my passing without seeing you; but I had no conception that you would feel pointed mortification and much less that you would impute it to causes so different from facts. My heart is as warmly interested in your happiness as ever it was; but I could not indulge those feelings without doing greater violence to others. I can say with Socrates was my boosom glass you should see every wish of my soul.[1] At Alexandria I saw Mr Richard Henry Lee and was in hopes he would have got home [in] time enough to have given you an opportunity to have come up and seen me while I lay sick there. I staid there five days after he left the place.[2] Was I disposed to interpret the feelings of the heart from appearances I have greater reasons than you for apprehending a change in your sentiments and feelings than you have for mine. But I will never indulge opinions derogatory to friendship; but from the fullest conviction of intentional wrongs. It is now quite uncertain how fortune will dispose of me or whether I shall have the happiness of meeting you in this City next May.[3] The Army is disbanded and both duty and necessity will oblige me to attend to my family affairs. My circumstances is far from being easy and my family have not where to put their heads. They have been like the wandering jews all the war. It is men in my situation in the progress of this war who have had feelings which exceeds description. Alas few know what I have felt. My fondness for my family has increased my distress. Men of affluence have been in quite diff[erent] circumstances. Public virtue is best proved by private sacrafices. But enough of this. Your letter has thrown me into these disagreeable reflections.

I will say every thing I can to the Clothier respecting the Accounts you enclosed me; but too little allowances are made in the public offices to do justice to the situation of things in the Southern department.[4] Accounts and returns are expected with all the accuracy as if we had been doing business in a Counting house. My influence shall not be wanting to do you justice, and I hope I shall not fail. But I wish you could get a list of the Officers serving with Major Sneed who all had clothing which should go towards the ballance of your Account.[5]

It will be needless to apply for Mr Lees appointment as the Army is disbanded. Nor could it be obtained if I did.[6] Present me respectfully to M^{rs} [Matilda Lee] Lee and believe me to be Affectionately Yours

N GREENE

My public Accounts has kept me upon the [harrow?] here for a fortnight past and will keep me a week longer.[7]

ALS (CtY).
1. Lee's letter to NG has not been found. He and NG had been close friends and wartime comrades, but their relationship had become frayed in the recent past. (See, for example, Lee to NG, 26 January 1782, above [vol. 10: 264–65 and n], and subsequent correspondence between them in vol. 10.) Lee may have felt affronted by NG's failure to visit him on his way through Virginia.

2. Richard Henry Lee, an influential delegate to Congress, was a friend of NG's and a cousin of Henry's father. He lived near Henry's home, Stratford Hall, Va. (Vol. 11: 116–17n, above) NG had been ill in Alexandria for several days in September. (See NG's Journal entry for 13 September, above.)

3. NG may have referred here to the first general meeting of the Society of the Cincinnati, which was held in Philadelphia in May 1784. (Myers, *Liberty Without Anarchy*, p. 31) Henry Lee attended the meeting, but NG did not. (Ibid., p. 61; NG to Washington, 6 May 1784, below)

4. On Lee's accounts with the Southern Army clothier, see Mentges to NG, 8 August, above.

5. Smith Snead was an officer of the Virginia Continental line. (Heitman, *Register*)

6. Nothing is known about the proposed appointment.

7. NG had not yet left Philadelphia when he wrote to Thomas Mifflin on 12 November, below.

*   *   *

¶ [TO GENERAL BENJAMIN LINCOLN, SECRETARY AT WAR. From Philadelphia, 27 October 1783. NG acknowledges Lincoln's "polite letter accompanied by the very pleasing resolution of Congress." He adds: "A testimony so honorable to my conduct and so flattering to my feelings cannot fail to excite the Most lively Sentiments of gratitude & thankfulness." Asks Lincoln to "communicate to Congress my warmest acknowledgements for the distinguished honor done me and the high sense I entertain of its value."[1] ADfS (MiU-C) 1 p.]

1. See Lincoln to NG, 24 October, above. On the resolution of Congress honoring NG, see above, Thomson to NG, 18 October. No written communication from Lincoln to Congress on this subject has been found. Lincoln's resignation as secretary at war was accepted by Congress on 29 October, and he left office on 12 November. (*JCC*, 25: 753)

¶ [TO GOVERNOR WILLIAM PACA OF MARYLAND. From Philadelphia, 27 October 1783. NG has Paca's letter, "with the very honorable vote of thanks of your Senate & Assembly." He adds: "Major Junifer forwarded me the same Vote once before[,] to which I returned my humble acknowledgements and am sorry it never came to hand."[1] Asks Paca to "communicate to the Assembly the high Sense I entertained of the honor" and "to assure them that I shall always hold it in greateful remembrance." ADfS (MiU-C) 1 p.]

1. On the address, see above, Paca to NG, 10 October, and Daniel of St. Thomas Jenifer to NG, 21 January (vol. 12: 387–88 and n). NG's reply to Jenifer has not been found.

¶ [TO ELIAS BOUDINOT, PRESIDENT OF THE CONTINENTAL CONGRESS. From Philadelphia, 28 October 1783. NG writes in support of "Lt Fullerton of the Pennsylvania line," who is "about to prefer a petition to Congress praying for a brevet commision of Captancy." Of Fullerton, NG writes: "If merit can promote his wishes no man has higher pretentions. The several charactors in which he has served in the Army and the worthy manner in which he discharged his duty made him highly esteemd by every one who knew him." NG is not sure "whether what he sues for is practicable upon the principles which Congress have put this business," but "if it is," he hopes Fullerton "will meet with success equal to his merit and wishes."[1] ALS (PCC, item 42, vol. 3: 91, DNA) 1 p.]

1. Richard Fullerton had acted as assistant adjutant general under NG in the South. (Vol. 12: 669, above) Fullerton petitioned Congress for the promotion on 29 October. (PCC, item 42, vol. 3: 85, DNA) Anthony Wayne also wrote a letter to Congress in support of

Fullerton's petition. (PCC, item 42, vol. 3: 87, DNA) In a letter to Congress of 1 November, Benjamin Lincoln, the secretary at war, wrote favorably of Fullerton's petition while noting that if it were granted, a precedent might be established for other officers with "similar claims." Congress responded to Lincoln's letter by issuing "to Lieutenant Fullerton, the brevet commission of captain." (Lincoln's letter and the resolution are printed in *JCC*, 25: 789–90.)

¶ [FROM ROBERT MORRIS, SUPERINTENDENT OF FINANCE, [Philadelphia], 28 October 1783. "In Compliance with an Order of the United States in Congress assembled," he informs NG that "a public Audience will be given to the hon^ble Minister plenipotentiary of their high Mightinesses the States General of the United Provinces [of] the Netherlands." It will be held "in the Congress Room in Princeton [N.J.], on Friday next at Noon."[1] D (Morris Papers: DLC) 1 p.]
   1. The "Minister plenipotentiary" from the Netherlands was Pieter J. Van Berckel. NG mentioned his arrival in a letter to William Pierce of 15 October, above, but Van Berckel had apparently asked for "a postponement of his audience." (*JCC*, 25: 753 and n) He presented his commission to Congress on Friday, 31 October, in a ceremony in which he gave an address, "delivered" a letter from "their High Mightinesses the States General," and received a reply from the president of Congress. (*JCC*, 25: 780–86). Morris had been instructed by a congressional resolution of 25 October to "inform the Supreme Executives of New Jersey and Pensylvania, His Excellency the Commander in Chief, Honorable the Minister of France, and such civil and military Gentlemen as are in or near to Princeton of such intended audience." Benjamin Lincoln, the secretary at war, and Morris were asked by Congress to "perform on this occasion, the duties assigned to the Secretary for foreign affairs, in the ceremonial respecting foreign ministers." (*JCC*, 25: 749) It is not known whether NG attended the ceremony.

¶ [TO THOMAS BEE.[1] From Philadelphia, 29 October 1783. NG recommends "Count dal Verme a Nobleman of Milan on his travels through the United States" to Bee's "civilities." He has been "treated with great politeness and attention" in [Philadelphia].[2] ALS (PHi) 1 p.]
   1. Bee, a Charleston lawyer, had served in the South Carolina legislature and had been the state's lieutenant governor and one of its delegates to Congress. (*Biog. Directory of S.C. House*, 2: 69–72)
   2. Francisco dal Vermé (1758–1832) had arrived in New York from Milan in July 1783 with "letters of recommendation" from Benjamin Franklin, John Adams, and Henry Laurens. He spent several days in Philadelphia on three different occasions between 19 September and 24 October. (Morris, *Papers*, 8: 807n) According to the editors of the Morris Papers, dal Vermé left Philadelphia on 25 October. (Ibid.) If so, he could not have hand-carried this letter from NG dated 29 October. He apparently spent several weeks in Charleston, S.C., at the beginning of December before leaving for the West Indies. (Ibid.)

*   *   *

To Elias Boudinot, President of the Continental Congress

Sir   Princetown [N.J.] Nov 1st 1783
   The letters and misellaneous papers containing a history of the most material parts of the Southern operations may contain some things which Congress or their officers may hereafter have occasion to refer to. Loose files are easily disordered and where recourse is often had to them papers often get lost.

If Congress should think it an object worthy the expence and would indulge my wishes I should be glad to get the whole papers transcribed into bound books. Having taken the liberty of suggesting my wishes I shall be happy to take the trouble of directing the business if Congress will be at the expence of a Clerk to do the writing.[1] I have the honor to be with great respect Your Excellencys Most Obed^t humble Ser^t

NATH GREENE

ALS (PCC, item 155, vol. 2: 165: DNA).

1. This letter was read in Congress on 1 November. (*JCC*, 25: 788–89) In the Order immediately below, Congress directed its secretary, Charles Thomson, to provide a clerk to assist NG in organizing and transcribing his wartime papers. Thomson wrote NG, also on this date, below, in regard to arrangements for hiring and compensating the transcriber. As explained above in an essay on the history of NG's papers, the work of transcribing the papers into "bound books" had barely begun at the time of his death and was never systematically accomplished. (Vol. 1: xxvii–xxxiii)

Order of the Continental Congress

November 1st 1783.

A Letter of this day from Major General Greene was read stating that the Letters and Miscellaneous papers containing a history of the most material parts of the Southern operations may contain some things which Congress or their officers may hereafter have occasion to refer to, that if Congress should think it an object worthy the expence he would be glad to get the whole papers transcribed into bound Books and would take the trouble of directing the Business if Congress will be at the expence of a Clerk to do the writing, whereupon,

Ordered That the Secretary furnish General Greene with a Clerk to copy into a Book or Books the papers or Letters in his possession relative to the Southern operations and that the record thereof be lodged in the Secretary's Office.[1]   CHA^s THOMSON SEC^y

(PCC, item 19, vol. 2: 509, DNA).

1. As noted at the letters immediately above and immediately below, a clerk was never hired explicitly to transcribe NG's wartime letters into "bound Books." Thomson sent a copy of this order with his letter to NG immediately below.

From Charles Thomson,
Secretary of the Continental Congress

Sir   [Princeton, N.J., 1 November 1783?][1]

As the business above mentioned must be done under your Eye, I shall be obliged if you will look out for a proper person to undertake it and employ him. The Salary allowed at present to clerks in the office is at the rate of five hundred dollars a year. You will please to inform me of the name of the person you employ and the time when he enters on the service, that I may take measures to have him paid.[2] I am S[r] with much respect Your most obedient & most humble Serv[t]   CHA[S] THOMSON

RCS (NjMoHP).

1. On the date, see "Order of the Continental Congress," immediately above. Congress was meeting at Princeton at this time.

2. Congress had authorized NG to hire a clerk to transcribe his wartime papers in "bound Books." (See NG to Boudinot and Order of the Continental Congress, both of this date, above.) NG never formally employed a clerk to copy his papers. After he moved his family to Georgia in 1785, he apparently asked his children's tutor, Phineas Miller, to assist with the transcriptions, but NG's untimely death in June 1786 brought an end to the project.

To Thomas Mifflin, President of the Continental Congress[1]

Sir   Philadelphia Nov[r] 3[d] 1783

The Comptroller of Accounts, thinks a special resolution of Congress necessary for passing my accounts of money expended for travelling & family expences during my command to the southward, which amounts to two thousand five hundred and sixty four pounds eight shillings and four pence sterling. The particulars are stated from accounts kept by Major [William] Pierce, and Major [Edmund M.] Hyrne, while they were respectively Secretaries in my family, and both of them have given certified copies of all their payments stated from original entries accounting for all the moneys received, except, a sum stolen from Major Pierce, the public trunk being broken & robbed; To all which, he has made oath before the Governor of South Carolina. As this misfortune happened without any neglect of the Majors I hope Congress will not hesitate to make it a public loss. The sums here mentioned have been expended after my arrival to the Southern Army, besides what were drawn through the medium of the Commissary but the last nine months he furnished nothing.[2]

The paper money which was drawn here to defray my travelling expences to the southward was received by Major [Ichabod] Burnet, one of my Aids, & the account of the expenditure kept by him, which account is among his private papers.[3] Part was given to Baron Steuben on our parting in Virginia, part was expended on the road, and the remainder paid into the hands of the Paymaster General of the southern Army.[4]

Major Hyrne who will have the honor to deliver this can explain any matters which Congress may wish further in the business.

I am much indisposed & extremely anxious to get to my family, & beg the decision of Congress as speedily as possible.[5] I have the honor to be with great respect Your Excellency's most obedient humble servant

NATH GREENE

LS (PCC, item 155, vol. 2: 672–74: DNA).

1. Mifflin was elected president of Congress the day this letter was written. (*JCC*, 25: 799)

2. NG had met with Robert Morris on 18, 23, and 29 October "respecting his [i.e., NG's] Accounts, want of Money &c." (Morris, *Papers*, 8: 629, 657, 676; quote from p. 676) James Milligan, the comptroller of the treasury, was comptroller of accounts. (See NG's letter to him of 10 November, below.) In the first sentence of this letter, NG referred both to his expenses while traveling south in the fall of 1780 to take command of the Southern Army and to the expenses of his military family—i.e., his aides—during his southern command; the rest of this paragraph deals with the "family expences." A copy of Pierce's and Hyrne's statements of accounts, which NG presumably enclosed with this letter, is in PCC, item 155, vol. 2: 676–77, DNA. (See also NG's Statement of Accounts, 8 November, below.) According to an affidavit dated 6 March 1783 and signed by Gov. Benjamin Guerard of South Carolina, Pierce had "the most positive proof that Thomas [Guerney?], and the most circumstantial evidence that Lewis, a servant of Major [John] Habershams, were the Persons who stole" £329.6.3 from the public trunk. (A copy of the affidavit is in PCC, item 155, vol. 2: 680, DNA; see also note 3, below.)

3. On the papers of the recently deceased Ichabod Burnet, see also note 5, below, as well as NG's Statement of Accounts, 8 November, and Hyrne to NG, 26 November–4 December, also below.

4. NG's aides Burnet and Col. Lewis Morris, Jr., had traveled south with NG, accompanied by Baron Steuben as far as Virginia. (Their itinerary can be traced through documents in Vol. 6, above.) The Southern Army's deputy paymaster general at that time was Joseph Clay. As seen in Hyrne to NG, 26 November–4 December, Clay's successor, John S. Dart, was now holding part of the travel money.

5. This letter was referred to a congressional committee consisting of Hugh Williamson, Thomas Jefferson, and Jacob Read. Replying to a query from Williamson, Milligan reported on 1 January 1784 that the sum mentioned in the present letter "agrees neither with the Total Amount of Expences, or with that of the balance; this, I attribute to its having been taken from the different Accounts, in a hasty manner by Major Hyrne, by which, it is highly probable, this inaccuracy happened." (PCC, item 155, vol. 2: 688, DNA) Meanwhile, NG had again urged the settlement of these accounts in a letter to Milligan of 7 December, below. (See also Milligan to NG, 9 February 1784, below.) The congressional committee's report was first read on 13 January 1784 and was acted upon by Congress on 6 April 1784. (PCC, item 155, vol. 2: 675, DNA; *JCC*, 26: 198–99 and n) According to the report, NG had exceeded by $4,045 16/90 his allowance of $5,972 20/90 for "extra expences" as commander of a "separate Department." However, "in consideration of the high price of all the necessaries of life in the southern states" during his command there, Congress adopted a resolution that, in the words of delegate Arthur Lee, allowed NG his "Expences as stated." (*JCC*, 26: 199; Lee to NG, 6 April 1784, below) The expense items specifically approved of in the resolution included £329.6.3, "Virginia currency," which, it appeared from Pierce's affidavit, had been stolen from his trunk "while the public money was in his custody." (*JCC*, 26: 199; see also note 1, above.) However, NG was still awaiting reimbursement for some of his travel expenses when he wrote to Milligan on 6 June 1784, below, and he wrote Samuel A. Otis on 24 July 1784, below, that he had been "compelled to Account for every shilling" expended during his southern command "without the least allowance for my expences altho I spent above five Weeks in Philadelphia on the business and [was] obliged to go there no less than three times on it." In addition to his stay in Philadelphia in October and November 1783, NG also traveled there in June and November 1784.

To George Washington

Sir   Philadelphia Nov[r] 3[d] 1783

I return your Excellency many thanks for your polite letter accompanying the resolution of Congress, complementing me with a couple of Cannon.[1] I am not very certain where those Cannon are, but I believe two are in Virginia & three in S° Carolina, and it is no less difficult for me to determine where I would wish those sent which are made choice of for me. If those in S° Carolina should be fixed upon, I would wish them to remain in Charleston. But if those in Virginia should be appropriated for this purpose, if agreable, let them be sent to Newport.[2] Should anything happen before this business is executed, which should enable me to be more explicit on the subject I shall take the earliest opportunity of signifying to your Excellency, my further wishes in the matter. I am with the highest respect and greatest esteem Your Excellencys most obedient humble servant   NATH GREENE

ADfS (MiU-C).

1. Washington's letter is above, dated 26 October. Congress had recently voted to award two engraved cannons to NG in commemoration of his wartime services. (Thomson to NG, 18 October, above)

2. It is not known where the cannons were ultimately found. Henry Knox wrote NG on 15 February 1784, below, that he had obtained them and was making arrangements to have them engraved. Knox wrote NG again on 27 October 1785, below, that the engraver was ready to begin work. No evidence has been found that the cannons were sent to NG before his death in June 1786. (See NG to Knox, 12 March 1786, below.)

To Jeremiah Wadsworth

Dear Colonel   Philadelphia Nov 4th 1783

I have but a moment [to wr]ite you. Many changes of sentiment[,] wishes and opinions happen in human life from a change of circumstances. You may remember it was once our agreement to enter into business at New York after the war was over. How your mind may now stand in this business I know not; but as you have not hinted any thing of the kind I am led to suppose you have forgot it or have other wishes. I am far from wishing to urge it contrary to your inclination. I have not fully determined upon my plan of future life and only wait to see or hear from you to fix upon my ultimate determination.[1] The Army is now disbanded and I at liberty to pur[sue] my own inclination. I shall say no more only that I wish to hear from you as early as possible. I am my dear Col your most Obed[t] humble Ser   NATH GREENE
Present me respectfully to M[r] Carter.[2]

ALS (CtHi).

1. As noted at Wadsworth's letter to NG of 12 December 1782, above, it is not known when NG and Wadsworth discussed the possibility of going into business together in

New York after the war. (Vol. 12: 288n) Wadsworth's reply to the present letter is below, dated 21 December.

2. Wadsworth's business partner John Barker Church went by the alias "John Carter." (See note at Carter [i.e., Church] to NG, 9 June, above.)

*   *   *

¶ [TO THE COMTE D'ESTAING.[1] From Philadelphia, 5 November 1783. "General [Joseph] Reed late Governor of the State of Pennsylvania who is going to Europe and purposes spending some time in France," will hand this letter to d'Estaing. Of Reed, NG writes: "The distinguished part he has acted in the late revolution endears him to America and I hope will procure him a polite reception in Europe."[2] NG recommends him, as "one of my most intimate friends," to d'Estaing's "civilities during his stay in France."[3] He also offers "complements of congratulation upon the signing of the definitive treaty and upon the compleat establishment of that revolution for the success of which you gave such early and interesting proofs."[4] ACyS (PHi) 3 pp.]

1. Charles Hector, comte d'Estaing, a French admiral, had commanded the French fleet off Newport during the battle of Rhode Island in 1778. NG met him at that time. (For a brief biographical note on d'Estaing, see above, vol. 2: 457n.)

2. Reed, the former chief executive of Pennsylvania, left for London in late December. (See below, Pettit to NG, after 21 January 1784.)

3. Although Reed planned to visit France during his trip abroad, illness kept him from going there. (Reed, *Reed*, 2: 400) NG wrote similar letters of introduction for him to the Marquis de Lafayette and the Comte de Rochambeau on 9 November, below. (See also NG to Mifflin, 12 November, below.)

4. On the "definitive treaty" of peace, see note at Lafayette to NG, 8 September, above.

¶ [FROM JACOB BAYLEY, West Point, N.Y., 7 November 1783. He has "waited on" Mr. Denning concerning his quartermaster accounts but cannot obtain a settlement without the vouchers he returned to NG's office at "the Beginning of the year 1780."[1] He supposes those and "the Recepts for moneys Recd" are in NG's hands and asks NG to have "the whole of vouchers" sent to Denning.[2] Bayley will also ask Col. [Moses] Hazen to close his accounts "with the Comission," and he asks NG to "Certify my Pay."[3] Bayley served under NG "one year and nine months[,] Received no Subsistance from the publick," and has taken "three Journeys 240 miles for Settlement." Asks NG for advice; he has been "at this Time as far as Princetown," but as he has never had "the Small pox," he does not dare to go Philadelphia, where he understands NG is staying.[4] RCS (Benson Ford Research Center at The Henry Ford Museum, Dearborn, Mich.) 1 p.]

1. Bayley had served under NG during part of his tenure as deputy quartermaster at Co'os, N.H., during the war. In a letter to Congress of 29 October 1783, Benjamin Lincoln, the secretary at war, described Bayley's contributions "since the capture of General Burgoyne" in 1777 as "gaining intelligence of the situation and designs of the Enemy in Canada, and of the Savages in their service; in supplying the friendly tribes which came within our lines and a company of them formed by the direction of Congress; and in supplying also our prisoners in their return from captivity." (*JCC*, 25: 761; a biographical note on Bayley is in vol. 4: 420n, above.) William Denning, the "Commissioner to the Quartermaster Generals Department," was responsible for determining the validity of claims by officers in that department. (Story to NG, 9 December, below)

2. Neither NG's reply to this letter nor any voucher that NG may have provided for Bayley has been found. Washington had written to Denning on Bayley's behalf in July, asserting that "[t]his Gentleman has performed, to my knowledge, several beneficial Services for the U States, for which he deserves a just and reasonable Reward." (Fitz-patrick, *GW*, 27: 44–45)

3. Col. Moses Hazen's regiment had been sent to Co'os, N.H., in March 1779 (vol. 3: 370n, above) and had undoubtedly incurred expenses from Bayley's department. Whether NG provided a certificate for Bayley's pay is not known.

4. Congress was then meeting at Princeton, N.J. Although the extent of a smallpox infection in Philadelphia at this time is not known, at least one delegate to Congress, Abiel Foster of New Hampshire, was "detained at Philadelphia more than three weeks by the smallpox." (Smith, *Letters*, 21: 205) In his letter to Congress about Bayley, Lincoln noted that the "several duties in which he has been employed" would require Bayley to settle his accounts "at different offices, unless he obtains the particular order of Congress directing some one of the departments to close his accounts. A direction of this kind would in my opinion unite the two desirable objects, a saving to the public and ease to an individual." Congress responded by directing the "commissioner for settling the accounts of the quartermaster's department" to settle Bayley's accounts "for money advanced, supplies given, and services rendered by him." (*JCC*, 25: 761)

* * *

Agreement between NG and Charles Pettit

[Philadelphia] 8 November 1783

Whereas divers Sums of money have [arisen?] and become due to Nathaniel Greene Major General in the Armies of the United States as Quarter Master General, and to John Cox and Charles Pettit as Assistants to the said Quarter Master General by way of Commissions or reward for their Executing the said Office of Quarter Master General under the appointment of the United States in Congress assembled.

And Whereas the said Nathaniel Greene, John Cox and Charles Pettit have at divers Times drawn from the Cash and Effects put into their Hands for the Use of the Department of Quarter Master General several Sums of Money on Account of the said Commissions which stand charged to their respective Acco^ts in the Books of the said Department kept under the care and direction of the said Charles Pettit, on which account of the said Nathaniel Greene there appears to be a Balance for Monies appropriated to his use over and besides the monies placed to the Credit of his said account of One hundred and seventy five thousand six hundred and sixty one Continental Dollars or thereabouts,[1]

And Whereas also divers sums of Money have been drawn from the same Source by the said Charles Pettit for and on the joint account of the said Nathaniel Greene, John Cox and Charles Pettit to be invested in Trade and Merchandize, which stand charged to the Account of the Quarter Master General and his Assistants in the aforesaid Books, and it is supposed that farther Sums yet remain due to the said Quarter Master General and his assistants from the United States for Commissions as aforesaid, And Whereas the said Nathaniel Greene stands indebted to the said Charles Pettit, on private or separate accounts between them, in the Sum of twelve hundred Pounds Specie and upwards,[2]

Now be it known to all whom it may concern that I the said Nathaniel Greene, for and in consideration of the said last mentioned Sum of Money due from me to the said Charles Pettit, and of the Release and acquittal of the same and of all other private or separate Demands by the said Charles Pettit to me, have sold, assigned, transferred and set over and by these Presents do fully and amply sell, assign[,] transfer and set over to the said Charles Pettit & to his assigns my full share and Proportion, that is to say all my Estate, Right, Title, Property, Claim and Demand of, in and to the said Commissions and other Reward which have or shall become due to the Quarter Master General and his assistants in Manner aforesaid as well such Balance as shall be found due to me on a Liquidation of the Sums already drawn by the said John Cox, Charles Pettit and myself severally, and jointly as aforesaid, as my Proportion of what may yet remain to be drawn from the United States on the said account excepting the aforesaid Balance of Monies by me received amounting to one hundred and seventy five thousand six hundred and sixty one Continental Dollars or thereabouts, which is to remain to me without farther account.

Also all my Share and Proportion of and in the said Stock in Trade under the care and management of the said Charles Pettit,[3] including all Vessels, Shares of Vessels, Adventures, Merchandize, Cash, Profits, Debts due to the said Company and the Debts and produce arisen or to arise on the sale of my one sixth Part of the Iron Works and Estate known by the Name of Batsto and its appendages, he the said Charles Pettit freeing and indemnifying me from all Debts due from the said Trading Company and from the said Batsto Estate.[4]

In Witness whereof I the said Nathaniel Greene have hereunto set my hand and Seal the 8th Day of November in the Year of Our Lord one thousand seven hundred and Eighty three.   NATH GREENE

Sealed & delivered in Presence of (The Words "Stock in Trade under the Care & Management of the said" being first interlined between the 13th & 14th Lines of this Page)[5]   JOHN DUFFIELD

JOHN WHITE

Explanatory Notes agreed upon by the Parties to the foregoing Instrument

1st Respecting the Commission Accounts in the concerns of the Quarter Master's Department, the Sums charged to General Greene in the Quarter Master's Books, are to remain to him without farther account, the Residue only of General Greene's share thereof being conveyed to the said Charles Pettit subject to the Incumbrances of Family [i.e., military family] Expences in Camp and the allowance intended to be made to the said Charles Pettit for his Extra Expences in Philadelphia, and such other Expences as have been understood by the Parties to be Deductions from the said Commissions down to the present Time. And the said Charles Pettit is to indemnify the said Nathaniel Greene against all such future Expences in settling the accounts of the Quarter Master's Department as would become a proper charge against the Quarter Master General and his assistants out of the said Commissions, Provided that if such Expences shall be of such a Nature and so extensive as that the said Charles Pettit shall not choose to take on himself the share thereof of the said Nathaniel Greene, it shall be in his Power to avoid such undertaking by relinquishing to the said Nathaniel Greene his original one third Part of the Commissions arising or to arise on the Debts now due from the Quarter Master's Department as an Equivalent for his Proportion of such Expences,

And it is also agreed and understood that if on a Liquidation of the accounts the sums of Money already drawn by the Quarter Master General and his assistants jointly and severally as beforementioned, shall exceed the amount of their Commissions so that any part of the Sums drawn are to be refunded, such Refund, so far as it relates to the Part of the said Nathaniel Greene shall be made by the said Charles Pettit.

2^d It is also agreed and understood that the Balance which may be found due from Mr John Cox to the said Nathaniel Greene on account of the Prize Ship *Venus* and other Privateering Concerns at Eggharbour [i.e., Egg Harbor, N.J.], is not to be considered as transferred to the said Charles Pettit, but remains the Property of the said Nathaniel Greene.[6]

NATH GREENE
CHA^S PETTIT

Witness JOHN DUFFIELD JOHN WHITE

DS (NjP).

1. Pettit and Cox had been NG's assistant quartermasters general while he headed the Quartermaster Department, from March 1778 until the summer of 1780. Congress had authorized the three to share a commission of one percent on all of the department's purchases, and NG, Pettit, and Cox had agreed among themselves to divide this amount equally. (NG also retained his salary as a major general.) As noted in an earlier volume, "Pettit was to keep track of 'Cash and Accounts.'" (See above, vol. 2: 310–11n; quote on p. 311.)

2. NG and his two assistants had formed a partnership, managed by Pettit, as a vehicle for investing their commissions. (As noted above [vol. 5: 43n], the terms of the partnership have not been found.) As seen most recently in Pettit to NG, 26 July, above, the partnership had not done well financially. For more about NG's indebtedness to his quartermaster and partnership accounts and to Pettit, see ibid., Pettit's letters to NG of 23 May and 23 July, and NG to CG, 4 August, all above.

3. As seen under NG's signature to this agreement, the words beginning with "Stock in Trade" and ending with "of the said" were noted as being an interlineation.

4. For more about the troubled affairs of the Batsto Iron Works, see, for example, the notes at Pettit to NG, 26 July.

5. See note 3, above.

6. On Cox's role in the partners' privateering investments at Egg Harbor, N.J., see Pettit to NG, first letter of 5 January 1780 and 11 June 1780, both above. (Vol. 5: 241 and n; vol. 6: 12 and n) For further developments, see Pettit's letters to NG of 7 February, 6 March, 22 April, and 18 May 1784, all below.

NG's Statement of Accounts

Philadelphia Novem[r] 8th 1783

Account of the Money drawn in October & November 1780 of M[r] Thomas Smith, and which now stands Charged to me in the Pay Master Generals Accounts, and was to defray mine and the Baron Stubens expences to the Southern Army.[1] The Amount of the Money drawn for this service was, One Hundred and Eighty thousand Continental dollars of the Old Emission, then passing for 120 for one here and at much greater depreciation to the southward. This money was deposited in the hands of Major [Ichabod] Burnet, who acted as secretary, until Major [William] Pierce's appointment, and a particular account of all the expenditures, kept by him, reference being had to his papers, will fully appear; But generally the expenditures were as follows. "Advances to Baron Stuben," expences on the road, Advances to officers for different services, after our arrival at the southern Army, and the balance paid into the hands of the Deputy Pay Master General of the Southern Army (M[r] Dart) after the Money ceased to have a Currency.[2] The foregoing is a[s] particular [a] State of the expenditure of the above money as I can give, without being possess'd of Major Burnets papers, which I believe are now in Charleston [S.C.] in the hands of M[r] John Banks.[3]   NATH GREENE

Cy (PCC, item 155, vol. 2: 686: DNA).

1. It appears from NG's letter to James Milligan of 10 November, below, that this statement was submitted to substantiate the claim to travel expenses that NG reported in his letter to Thomas Mifflin of 3 November, above. Thomas Smith was commissioner of the Pennsylvania loan office when NG left Philadelphia to join the Southern Army in the fall of 1780. (JCC, 18: 1119, 1266) As noted at NG to Mifflin, 3 November, Steuben had accompanied NG as far as Virginia.

2. On the papers of Burnet, who had recently died, see Hyrne to NG, 26 November–4 December, below, as well as NG to Mifflin, 3 November. John S. Dart, the Southern Army's deputy paymaster general, had thus far refused to release the balance to James Penman, who had loaned money to NG for his return trip to the North. (Hyrne to NG, 26 November–4 December)

3. On Burnet's business partner, Banks, and the papers in question, see ibid.

To the Marquis de Lafayette

Dear Marquis   Philadelphia Nov 9th 1783

This will be handed you by my good friend Governor Reed whose merit and active zeal you are perfectly well acquainted with.[1] Nor can you be ignorant of the ungenerous measures which have been taken here to lessen his public estimation. Every man who has the pleasure of his acquaintance must feel an honest indignation at the unmerited treatment he has met with; and a pleasing satisfaction that his abilities will triumph over party and faction.[2]

He is going to Europe and has in contemplation to spend some time in France. I am persuaded you will take a pleasure in rendering every thing as agreeable to him as possible. And as he is perfectly well acquainted with the politicks of America I beg leave to refer you to him for every thing of this sort on this side of the water.[3]

Present me most respectfully to all my friends in France and believe me to be with esteem and affection Your Most Obed[t] humble Ser[t]

NATH GREENE

ALS (NHi).

1. Joseph Reed, the former chief executive of Pennsylvania, left for London in late December. (See below, Pettit to NG, after 21 January 1784.)

2. On Reed's "unmerited treatment," see his letter to NG of 3 August, above.

3. As noted at NG's letter to the Comte d'Estaing of 5 November, above, Reed was unable to visit France during his trip abroad. NG also wrote letters of introduction for Reed to d'Estaing (ibid.) and the Comte de Rochambeau, immediately below. (See also NG to Mifflin, 12 November, below.)

* * *

¶ [TO THE COMTE DE ROCHAMBEAU.[1] From [Philadelphia, 9 November 1783].[2] Introduces Joseph Reed, who is traveling to France.[3] Reed's "great abilities and early zeal have justly endeared him to every friend to the revolution in America," and NG has the "happiness to be one of his most intimate friends." NG offers Rochambeau his "compliments of congratulation upon the signing of the definitive treaty and upon the complete establishment of our independance; for which America is so highly indebted to your Excellency for your seasonable and eminent services."[4] AL (NHi) 2 pp.]

1. Jean Baptiste Donatien de Vimeur, comte de Rochambeau, had commanded the French expeditionary force in America.

2. The place and date were taken from the address sheet.

3. NG wrote similar letters of introduction for Reed, the former chief executive of the state of Pennsylvania, to the Comte d'Estaing, 5 November, above, and to Marquis de Lafayette, immediately above. (See also NG to Mifflin, 12 November, below.) As noted at the letter to d'Estaing, Reed did not go to France.

4. On the "definitive treaty" of peace, see note at Lafayette to NG, 8 September, above.

¶ [TO JAMES MILLIGAN, COMPTROLLER OF THE TREASURY. From Philadelphia, 10 November 1783. In his "report to Congress of the Money expended for my family and traveling expences in the Southern command," NG "added Sixty five pounds sterling to my expences here while I have been upon the business and to pay my own and my Secretary's expences home."[1] Of this amount, £40 were for NG's own expenses and £25 for his secretary's "bills in town" and "passage and provision for the voyage." Asks Milligan to "add those sums to the foot of my account given into your office[,] that when Congress shall decide on the business of the aggregate sum given into them the two may agree."[2] ADfS (MiU-C) 2 pp.]

1. NG presumably referred to his Statement of Accounts, dated 8 November, above. Edmund M. Hyrne was NG's secretary at this time.

2. The account submitted to Milligan has not been found. NG wrote Milligan again about his travel expenses on 7 December, below. It appears from NG's letter to Samuel A. Otis of 24 July 1785, below, that he was not reimbursed for his expenses in Philadelphia while trying to get his accounts settled.

¶ [FROM JOHN BANKS, Charleston, S.C., 11 November 1783. Acknowledges NG's letter of 25 October and encloses a copy of one that he wrote on 20 October, in reply to NG's letter of the 15th of that month.[1] Adds: "I can only appeal to the event of Time to administer to the Wounds of my Feelings, with strong confidence, that it will at last place me on the Permanent Basis of Propriety & rectitude which I find only a conscious good disposition is unequal to."[2] RCS (MiU-C) 1 p.]

1. None of the letters mentioned here has been found, but it appears from Banks's comments here that NG had criticized him for financial practices.

2. NG's reply has not been found.

¶ [TO THOMAS MIFFLIN, PRESIDENT OF THE CONTINENTAL CONGRESS. From Philadelphia, 12 November 1783. Gen. [Joseph] Reed, who is going to Europe "on private business," would like "to carry with him some testimony of Congress."[1] Reed has "just claim to this distinction" because of "his general conduct and active zeal in both the civil and Military departments in the progress of this war"; his request should also be honored, moreover, because of his "special services in the darkest hours of our affairs." NG cites the risks that Reed took to render these services, and their importance to the army, as giving him "just claim to a generous acknowledgement from his Country."[2] NG speaks from his "own observation, being in the confidence of his Excellency [Washington], and acquainted with the secrets and operations of the Army." If NG's "wishes can have any influence, and Congress discovers no political impropriety," he would be "highly gratified if M[r] Reed could travel under the[ir] patronage]."[3] ALS (NHi) 3 pp.]

1. For other letters that NG wrote in behalf of his friend Reed, who at different times had been an aide to Washington, adjutant general, and president of the Pennsylvania Council, see those to the Comte d'Estaing of 5 November and to the Marquis de Lafayette and the Comte de Rochambeau of 9 November, all above. Reed himself wrote to Mifflin— a political opponent of his, and a former quartermaster general with whom NG had some differences—to request the "testimony of Congress" referred to here. (Reed to Mifflin, 13 December, PCC, item 78, vol. 19: 459, DNA; on Reed's and NG's differences with Mifflin, see especially Reed to NG, 5 November 1778, above [vol. 3: 41–42, 46n].)

2. These services included Reed's role in the court-martialing of Gen. Benedict Arnold in 1779 for Arnold's conduct as commandant at Philadelphia and Reed's negotiations with the mutinous soldiers of the Pennsylvania Continental line during the winter of 1781. (See above, vol. 3: 197–98n, and vol. 7: 117–18n.) Reed, however, had been em-

broiled in controversy for some time over both his political and military services. (See, for example, Charles Pettit to NG, 8 February, and Reed to NG, 14 March [vol. 12: 425–26, 516–18 and n], as well as Reed to NG, 3 August, all above.)

3. Reed left for Europe in late December. (Pettit to NG, after 21 January 1784, below) This request was never acted upon, although a congressional committee to which a letter from Reed of 13 December was referred did offer the following resolution on 30 January 1784: "That Congress always entertained a high sense of the zeal, abilities and activity in the public service manifested by Joseph Reed, Esquire, formerly Adjutant General in the service of the United States, and late President of the State of Pennsylvania." (*JCC*, 26: 60; see also ibid., 27: 399, 529, 585.) On 5 May 1784, Massachusetts delegate Elbridge Gerry wrote Reed, who was then in England: "A Report was made on your Application for a Certificate, & having brot on the Matter I found that it was considered by some Members as an Interference in a personal Dispute, & that the Question could not be carried, but would probably be negatived by the Yeas & Nays; for which Reason, it is dropped." (Smith, *Letters*, 21: 584)

¶ [FROM SAMUEL HODGDON, Philadelphia, 12 November 1783. Had he been "present" when NG first requested a wagon, NG would have had it "before this time," although wagons "are now with difficulty obtain'd." Hodgdon has "a prospect of getting a very fine team" for NG's purpose and will "know for certain in about an hour." If he can get the wagon, it will "attend you immediately." If not, Hodgdon will try to "procure some other in the course of the day" and will notify NG.[1] LB (WRMS, vol. 93: 160: DNA) 1 p.]

1. Hodgdon, the commissary general of military stores, wrote quartermaster general Timothy Pickering on 13 November that he had "furnished and sent off" a wagon "loaded with General Green's baggage, and bound for Rhode Island." (WRMS, vol. 93: 166, DNA) It is not known when NG himself left Philadelphia, but as seen in the two letters immediately below, he was in Newark, N.J., on 20 November and in New York City on 24 November.

*   *   *

To Jacob Van Waggonen[1]

Sir   Newark [N.J.] Nov 20th 1783

I have been making a settlement with Mr William Burnet jun for the produce of my plantation and for the taxes paid upon it.[2] I flatter myself you will not hesitate to allow me for your proportion of the tax[es] agreeable to the division of the produce of the place. The whole amount of the taxes paid since you have been on it is £34.8.2. Your dividend of this is £22.18.8.[3] It appears very clearly you have fallen far short of the conditions upon which you entered the place if any were made. The finishing the dam and bringing on manure upon the place in the terms proposed were capital articles [a]nd in both of which you have failed. Doctor Burnet says you mentioned these matters to him as part of the conditions and I remember perfectly well I made them so in the conversation we had on the subject.[4] The Meadow is ruined since you have been on the place and even supposing you mistook my intentions which was not possible you have failed upon your own plan; for you have neither finished the uper dam or kept in repair the lower one. The terms upon which you pretend you was to have the place will leave me no rent after paying the taxes & I flatter myself you cannot think this reasonable. Young Doctor Burnet will shew you a state on which I think a settlement ought to be made;[5] and if you act with honor and are willing to do justice you can not refuse to comply with the demands he will state to you. And even if you should allow more than I ask the conditions on my part will be very hard. But if you should refuse to do me justice he is authorised to submit the whole matter to some good honest Men to determin[e] what is right between us. This you cannot refuse. The farm ought to rent for 130 Dollars a year and if the Meadows were as good as when you went on it the [hay?] would be good on [i.e., for?] the present settlement propos[d]. My profits even if you comply with the greatest extent of my demands will hardly amount to one half this Sum. As to ⅓ of the grain being a consideration for the rent of the place it is idle to urge it. Any body with out living upon the farm would be glad to plant the Lands on those terms which leaves the house rent[,] fire wood[,] pasture &c &c to be accounted for.

　　As you are going to leave the farm early in the Spring it is unnecessary for me to say any thing about the future conditions. But if you should stay I shall expect 120 dollars rent for the next year and you pay the taxes and cut up all the Hassocks in the Meadow and that the Meadow may be restored to its former state I have desird Doctor Burnet to have the Dam finished early in the Spring at my expence. Nor would I let the farm for less than $150 dollars if the Meadow was in good order.[6] I give you this early notice that you may not deceive your self in your future expectations. I am Sir Your humble Ser^t　　NATH GREENE

　　NB Any person living on the farm are to cut the salt hay on the two lots and have it foddered on the farm.

ADfS (NcD).

　　1. As noted at NG's letter to him of 17 July 1780, above, Van Waggonen was the tenant on a farm that NG had obtained as confiscated property from the state of New Jersey at "Second River in the Township of Newark" in 1779. (Vol. 6: 119 and n)

　　2. Dr. William Burnet, Sr., had purchased the farm at auction for NG. (Ichabod Burnet to NG, 10 March 1779, above [vol. 3: 338–39])

　　3. By "dividend," NG meant Van Waggonen's share.

　　4. When this conversation took place is not known.

　　5. NG's proposed terms of settlement with Van Waggonen have not been found.

　　6. NG later estimated the farm's value "at about a thousand pounds Sterling rather more than less." (See below, Estimate of NG's Estate, [before 9 January 1784].) On 26 March 1785, below, NG gave Jeremiah Wadsworth a power of attorney to sell this property.

　　　　　　*　　　　*　　　　*

¶ [TO AN UNKNOWN PERSON. From New York, 24 November 1783.[1] Samuel Bowne, "a friend and old Acquaintance" of NG, is "apprehensive that from the confusion of the Night after the entry of [the American] troops, he may be insulted."[2] As NG knows Bowne's "charactor" and is "convinced of his being of a good disposition," he will "esteem it a favor" to have Bowne "protected from insult should any confusion arise which I don't expect."[3] ALS (MiU-C) 1 p.]

1. The recipient may have been Gen. Henry Knox, whose detachment led the American entry into New York City the next day. (See note 3, below.)

2. Despite NG's assertion that Bowne was "a friend and old Acquaintance," nothing is known about him. He may have been related, though, to Loyalist Obadiah Bowne of Monmouth County, N.J., several of whose sons were in New York when the British evacuated the city. (Palmer, *Loyalists*, p. 84)

3. The transition from British occupation to American possession of New York City was orderly. Washington informed Thomas Mifflin, the president of Congress, on 3 December that although the British had planned to leave the city on 23 November, they stayed until the 25th because of bad weather. A detachment of Washington's army marched into the city that day. According to Washington, "The Civil Power was immediately put in possession," and "perfect regularity and good order have prevailed ever since." (Fitzpatrick, *GW*, 27: 255) Washington himself left West Point on 20 November to stay at a tavern in the village of Harlem, five miles north of the city. In the afternoon of the 25th, Gen. Henry Knox and his detachment marched into New York while Washington and Gov. George Clinton of New York proceeded toward the city from Harlem. After Knox and his men had established an orderly takeover, Washington and Clinton, both riding "magnificent" steeds and escorted by crowds of cheering civilians, headed a procession into the city. At Cape's Tavern, his destination, the commander-in-chief "received the usual addresses" from soldiers and citizens, and the American standard was raised at Fort George. Days of celebrations, fireworks, and encomiums to Washington ensued, culminating in his tearful farewell to his officers at Fraunces Tavern on 4 December, after which he left for Philadelphia. (Freeman, *GW*, 5: 458–68) It is not known when NG left New York to sail home to Rhode Island or whether he was present at the Americans' triumphal entry into New York. (He did have a reunion with his good friend Knox while he was there. [NG to Knox, 4 March 1784, below]) NG arrived in Newport, R.I., on 27 November. (NG to Jacob Greene, 29 November, below)

¶ [**FROM JOHN HUGHES**, Carlisle, Pa., 24 November 1783. NG appointed Hughes quartermaster to Gen. [Anthony] Wayne's brigade in December 1778, for which service he was to receive "the accustomed pay."[1] He "Serve[d] with Every Care and atention" until NG "Ceast acting as" quartermaster general but was paid "only one Thousand Continental Doll[s] amounting to about five Pounds."[2] Although he received an order for "fourteen Hundred and fifty three Do[llars]" from George Olney on John Story, the paymaster, dated 22 August [17]80, Hughes cannot determine "how or where such accounts was to be Settl[d]."[3] He would be "verry Much oblig[d]" if NG would let him know "by the first oppertunity" where to "apply for settlement."[4] RCS (MiU-C) 1 p.]

1. Hughes had been the quartermaster of the First Pennsylvania Continental Brigade. (Heitman, *Register*)

2. NG resigned from his post as quartermaster general in July 1780. (NG to Samuel Huntington, 26 July 1780, above [vol. 6: 155–57])

3. Olney had been auditor of the Quartermaster Department during NG's tenure there (vol. 3: 79n, above); on Story, the departmental paymaster, see above, vol. 4: 52n.

4. NG's reply has not been found.

*   *   *

From Roger Parker Saunders

Dear Sir   [Charleston, S.C.] 25 Novr 1783

I wrote you the 20th October since wch have Your favr^s of the 15th Oc^r and 2^d Novr to wch this is an answer.[1]

The letter you wrote from Waccammaw I never rec^d and never heard a word from Mr Allston of the Stock he was to get you.[2]

Your Negroes unfortunately got the Measles among them wch I prevented from spreading Generally but It has been a hindrance to the work but you have lost none, I have not been able to get the slaves without neglecting other things of Greater Consequence but will get as many as possible after Christmas.[3] I shall not draw on Mr Pettit for your Tax as I borrowd Money from a Friend to pay It.[4] It will take you 60 hands or 65 to Cultivate your Georgia Land to Advantage. It is Impossible to hire Negroes. New Negroes sel here for £70 the Pick and there is a riske in purchasing at this Season.[5]

I shal Ship You 2 casks rice by the Very first opp^y that offers for New Port [i.e., Newport, R.I.].

I have Just been with Mr Penman he has the offer of 123 Negroes wch are now at [St.] Augustine[.] They are Clitherals[,] I know them perfectly, and think them inferior to no Gang at that Number in the State. I have advised him to purchase if they can be had at £70 but as much lower as possible[.] They will suit you and Genl Wayne and If there is too Many for you two I would be glad to take 20 [as?] our Commission, we will not lay violent hands on them when I bring them here. I will willingly go to Augustine If I can serve you by It but at pres^t Mr Penman thinks It would not be proper.[6] The Negroes are 45 Men 34 Women & 44 Children[.] All under 15 years old are calld Children[;] 8 or 10 under that denomination will be fit for Work in two years[.] There is among them 16 Sawyers Two Coopers 1 Carpenter, 2 Tanners Farriers Cooks Seamstresses &^{ca}.[7] Mrs Saunders Joins me in best Wishes for yours & Mrs Greenes happiness I am wth respect Dr Sir y^r Hbl^e St R^R PARKER SAUNDERS

RCS (MiU-C).

1. Saunders's letter of 20 October is above; NG's letters to him of 15 October and 2 November have not been found.

2. Early in his trip north in August 1783, NG had stopped at Joseph Allston's plantation on the Waccamaw River and had written to Saunders from there. (NG's Journal, 19 August, above; NG to Saunders, 4 January 1784, below) It is not known what "Stock" Allston was to obtain for NG.

3. Julia Floyd Smith, writing about the health of slaves on Georgia plantations, observes that "Life in the slave community was a breeding ground for several year-round diseases that were contracted through respiratory secretions." Among those were measles, whooping cough, chicken pox, and mumps. (Smith, *Slavery and Rice Culture*, p. 139n)

4. This was presumably the property tax on NG's South Carolina plantation, Boone's Barony. (See Saunders to NG, 20 June, above.)

5. In a letter of 25 October, above, NG asked James Penman to pay no more than £70

"per head" for slaves in East Florida, an amount he had previously thought too great. The large amount of capital needed to operate a rice plantation such as Mulberry Grove included the cost of purchasing slaves. NG wrote Penman on 4 January 1784, below: "The earlier the Negroes are got on the plantation the better."

6. Penman was trying to buy slaves for NG from Loyalists in East Florida. (See above, Penman to NG, 1 October, and NG to Penman, 25 October.) On Dr. James Clitherall's slaves, see also Penman to NG, 4 December, and NG to Penman, 4 January 1784, both below. Richmond, the rice plantation given to Anthony Wayne by the state of Georgia, was on the Savannah River near Mulberry Grove. (Nelson, *Wayne*, p. 200) NG wrote Penman on 4 January 1784 that the number of slaves available from Clitherall's property "is greater than I can venture upon. But this will be no objection as General Wayne and Mr Saunders are both in want and we can divide them."

7. The value of slaves was often derived from specialized skills they possessed. (Smith, *Slavery and Rice Culture*, p. 57; Flanders, *Plantation*, p. 189)

*   *   *

¶ [EDMUND M. HYRNE TO JOSEPH CLAY. From Charleston, S.C., 26 November 1783. Mr. [Edward] Lloyd is bringing "a mortgage, by way of security," to Clay. NG "entrusted" this document to Hyrne in Philadelphia and wants to have it recorded. If Clay will do "what may be necessary" with it, he will "very much oblige" NG and Hyrne.[1] ADfS (MiU-C) 1 p.]

1. The "mortgage" was an indenture—i.e., written document—from John Banks and Ichabod Burnet to NG, secured by a number of pieces of real estate. These included two lots in Brunswick, Ga.; a 2,000-acre tract "on the Head branch of Crooked Creek" in St. Mary's Parish, S.C.; and, most notably, an undivided half-share ownership of nine tracts of land on two timber-rich sea islands—Great Cumberland and Little Cumberland—off the coast of Georgia near the mouth of the St. Marys River, the boundary between Georgia and what was then the colony of East Florida. In this volume, we term the Great Cumberland and Little Cumberland properties, which are an important topic in NG's 1785 and 1786 correspondence, "Cumberland Island."

On 12 August 1783, just before he left Charleston to travel to the North, NG had obtained the indenture from Banks and Burnet, some of whose debts as Southern Army contractors he had earlier guaranteed. (On NG's role as guarantor, see especially NG to Benjamin Lincoln, 19 December 1782, and Agreement between Hunter, Banks & Company and NG with Newcomen & Collett, 8 April, above [vol. 12: 306–7 and n, 591 and n]; and NG to Lee, 22 August 1785, below.) As noted by Mary R. Bullard in her history of Cumberland Island, "The indenture came in two parts, as was customary: a deed of lease and a deed of release." (Bullard, *Cumberland Island*, p. 88) As seen in Hyrne's letter to NG of 26 November–4 December, below, the document that Hyrne referred to here and that he sent to Clay was the "release." That document, which Clay recorded in Savannah on 28 December, is in Colonial Conveyance Book BBB, pp. 134–41, G-Ar.

Under the terms of the release, Banks and Burnet, who were purchasing the properties from John McQueen, were indebted to NG "in the penal Sum of Ten thousand Guineas of the Lawfull Coin of the Realm of England" for a series of twelve bonds to McQueen that he had, in effect, guaranteed for them. These debts were to fall due, with interest, on 1 December of each year between 1784 and 1787. (Colonial Conveyance Book BBB, pp. 134–37, G-Ar) Banks and Burnet were to keep NG "harmless" by making these payments to McQueen themselves; if they defaulted, he would become liable for the payments and could take possession of the properties, which are described in some detail in the indenture. (Ibid., pp. 141–43)

By 12 August, when he made this agreement with Banks and Burnet, NG was probably aware of the danger that they might default on the financial obligations he had guaranteed for them as army contractors. Charles Pettit's letter to him of 23 July, above, certainly must have caused him some concern, and NG also had a chance to discuss the partners' financial situation with his former aide Burnet before the latter left for Cuba. (NG to Pettit, 4 August, above; it appears from the indenture, in which Banks acted as Burnet's attorney, that Burnet had left Charleston by 12 August.) It seems probable, therefore, that NG, knowing the potential value of the timber-rich Cumberland Island properties, took this indenture as security against possible losses on the guarantees he had earlier made for Banks and Burnet. (Cumberland Island's resources are described in NG to Marbois, 15 April 1785, below.) While he was in Philadelphia, NG learned that Burnet was dead. (NG to Pierce, 15 October, above) Moreover, the conversations that he had with Pettit and Robert Morris while he was in Philadelphia are unlikely to have added to NG's confidence that Banks would fulfill his obligations. (See notes at Pettit to NG, 23 July.) So when Hyrne, who had traveled with him to Philadelphia, returned to Charleston, NG probably felt some urgency to get the indenture into Clay's hands for recording in Georgia.

By September 1784, NG had come to consider Banks "the greatest Monster and most finished vilian that this age has produced." (NG to CG, 8 September 1784, below) Banks died before the end of that month (NG to Rutledge, after 30 September 1784, below), and not long afterward, NG began to turn his attention to Cumberland Island. As the deaths of Burnet and Banks did not negate their heirs' rights of inheritance to the properties listed in the indenture, it became one of NG's priorities to obtain waivers of those rights as partial compensation for Burnet's and Banks's obligations to him. This does not appear to have been a problem in the case of Burnet's heirs, but Banks's brother Henry did not give up his rights as easily. (See below, William Burnet to NG, 13 August 1785, and Samuel Ward, Jr., to NG, 11 November 1785.) Meanwhile, NG tried, without success, to find investors who could help him to meet the payment schedule for the properties and harvest the live oak timber on Cumberland Island in profitable quantities. (See, for example, NG to Wadsworth, 3 and 17 February 1785; Wadsworth to NG, 23 February 1785 and 4 March 1785; and NG to Marbois, 15 April 1785, all below.) Although NG visited Cumberland Island during a trip to East Florida in the spring of 1785 (NG to CG, 14 April 1785, below), he had not managed to do much with the properties there by the time of his death in June 1786. Cumberland Island, however, proved to be one of his most lasting, tangible legacies to his family. CG, who would spend the rest of her life there, no longer owned either Mulberry Grove or Boone's Barony plantation when she moved her family to Cumberland Island in 1800. (Stegeman, *Caty*, p. 174; see also Bullard, *Cumberland Island*, pp. 125–27, and Bullard, "Uneasy Legacy.")

¶ [FROM ROGER PARKER SAUNDERS, Charleston, S.C., 27 November 1783. Since he last wrote, he has purchased "1200 Acres Prime Swamp Land on Ely [i.e., Isla] Island in Georgia directly opposite to Mulberry Grove." This land is "inferior to none in Carolina or Georgia." The price, 10,000 guineas, is "lookd on by the best Judges to be a very great Bargain indeed," as the land should be worth twice that much in five years. This "purchase is too great" for Saunders's "Fortune," though, for he "can Cultivate but a Small proportion of the Land." He plans to keep 400 acres for himself, has "ingag'd" 600 acres to friends, including 150 acres for [Edmund M.] Hyrne, and will reserve 200 acres "directly opposite" NG's house until he learns whether NG wants it.[1] "Col° Wilkinson" will take this land if NG does not want it, but Saunders thinks NG should buy it "by all means."[2] He has been "inform'd the Land is far superior to yours, indeed Island Land is Generally best." "Mr Williamson" recommended that NG buy land there when NG was at Williamson's house.[3] A London firm, Higginson &

Greenwood, owned part of the island, but their holdings were confiscated and later sold to Jacob Read for what Saunders thinks was eighteen guineas per acre.[4] Saunders is asking nine guineas per acre, with "5 years Credit wch bearly Pays me for the trouble and Expence I shall be at in dividing the Land." His "Brother Mr Hewet" will take 200 acres and "means to reside in Georgia." Saunders would be "much oblig'd" if Hewet could use NG's house, for which he would pay rent and "undertake the Care of your Negroes." Hewet is "a Very industrus young Man, and a Good Planter."[5] Saunders also hopes that NG will "send the Sheep as soon as possible" and give him "an Immediate answer to this Letter."[6] Sends his compliments to CG. RCS (NcD) 4 pp.]

1. Saunders's most recent letter to NG was undoubtedly that of 25 November, above. NG replied on 4 January 1784, below, that he would be "glad to take" the 200 acres "if I can accomodate the payment." He added that he planned to see Saunders again in "less than two Months" and would make arrangements then to purchase the land. NG did not return to the South until summer; Saunders wrote him in July 1784: "You can have what Quantity you please of the Island I wrote you abo^t some time agoe opposite your Land." (Saunders to NG, before 17 July 1784, below)

2. Col. Morton Wilkinson (1745?–90), who served under Gen. Andrew Pickens during the war, had been one of the South Carolina commissioners who purchased Boone's Barony for NG. (*Biog. Directory of S.C. House*, 2: 715)

3. "Mr. Williamson" was probably William Williamson, Sr. (d. 1785), who owned "two major plantations on the Stono and Savannah Rivers, and on the Ogeechee River in Georgia." (*Biog. Directory of S.C. House*, 2: 720–22)

4. Jacob Read (1752–1816), a prominent attorney and politician, served at different times in the South Carolina legislature, in the Continental Congress, and eventually in the United States Senate. He owned properties in South Carolina, Georgia, and Newport, R.I. (*Biog. Directory of S.C. House*, 3: 597–99) In regard to his friendship with NG, see his letter to NG of 30 July 1784, below.

5. "Hewet," whom Saunders referred to here as his "brother," may have been a descendant of Andrew Hewatt, the second husband of Catherine Brisbane, whose first husband, Joseph Elliott, had been a brother of Saunders's grandmother Ann Elliott. (*Biog. Directory of S.C. House*, 2: 99, 224) NG replied that it would be "perfectly agreeable" for "Hewet" to live at Mulberry Grove and "manage the place" if Saunders could recommend him as "a good planter and one that I can confide in." (NG to Saunders, 4 January 1784)

6. See ibid.

*　　　*　　　*

To Jacob Greene

Dear Sir　　　　　　　　　　　　　　　　　Newport [R.I., 29][1] Novr 1783.

I arrived here night before last but have not determd where to spend the winter. Indeed I have not been out of the House since I came to it. Our present Quarters will not answer well for the Winter and we shall have others to seek. Tomorrow I intend to begin to make Enquiry and if I can find a House which pleases me I purpose to stay the Winter here.[2] It will be hardly possible for me to be at Greenwich before the sitting of the Assembly there.[3] If you have Business at this Place I shall be glad to see you sooner. Tell George I will come and see him soon.[4] Present me affectionately to Sister Greene and all Friends at Coventry and Greenwich.[5] Yours affectionately   NATH[i] GREENE

Tr (Foster Transcript: RHi).

1. According to the *Newport Mercury* of 29 November, NG arrived there "Last Tuesday." That was 25 November, but the editors of this volume believe that date is incorrect. In his letter to William Greene, immediately below, which he dated 29 November, NG wrote, as he did here, that he arrived "night before last," i.e., the 27th.

2. The address at which NG's family was living at this time is not known, but it was in the "Point" section of Newport, near the water; sometime later, they moved to a house at a higher elevation in the city. (William Littlefield to NG, 25 April 1785, below) NG remained in Newport most of the time until July 1784, when he sailed for Charleston, S.C., to deal with personal business matters. (See note at NG to Griffin Greene, 8 July 1784, below.)

3. The Rhode Island General Assembly convened in East Greenwich "on the fourth Monday in December, 1783." (Bartlett, *Records of R.I.*, 9: 734)

4. NG's seven-year-old son, George Washington Greene, may have been staying with Jacob at this time.

5. "Sister Greene" was Jacob's wife, Margaret Greene Greene, a sister of his and NG's cousin Griffin Greene. (Vol. 1: 38n, above)

To Governor William Greene of Rhode Island

Dear Sir   Newport [R.I.] Nov[r] 29[h] 1783[1]

I arrived at this place night before last and am happy to set my foot once more on the land of my nativity.

When I left Philadelphia I was requested by M[r] Ellery to inform you that your Delegates were without money & could not go on to Anapolis, to which place Congress have adjourned, until they heard from you & got a new supply of cash.[2]

I congratulate you upon the arrival of the definitive treaty and upon a happy close to all our troubles.[3] Present me affectionately to M[rs] [Catharine Ray] Greene & all your family. I am dear Sir Your most obedient humble Serv[t]   NATH GREENE

Tr (Burnett Transcript: DLC).

1. On the date of NG's arrival in Newport, see note at NG to Jacob Greene, immediately above.

2. Traveling overland from Charleston, S.C., NG had arrived in Philadelphia in early October and had left there for Rhode Island in mid-November. On William Ellery, a delegate to Congress from Rhode Island, see above, vol. 1: 233n. In its December session, the Rhode Island General Assembly voted to pay Ellery and David Howell £120 "out of the general treasury" and to provide cash compensation "for services" to two other delegates, John Collins and Jonathan Arnold. (Bartlett, *Records of R.I.*, 9: 746; see also William Greene to NG, 7 December, below.) Congress, which had adjourned at Princeton, N.J., on 4 November, began to assemble again at Annapolis, Md., on 26 November but did not achieve a quorum until 13 December. (*JCC*, 25: 807, 809) Ellery and Howell were both present on that date. (Ibid., p. 810)

3. On the "definitive treaty" of peace, see note at Lafayette to NG, 8 September, above.

From the Citizens of Newport, Rhode Island

Sir [Newport, R.I., 29 November 1783][1]

Amidst the general Applause which has been testified for your meritorious Services, we flatter ourselves the grateful Acknowledgements and cordial Congratulations of the Citizens of this Metropolis will not be unacceptable. We review with pleasing Horror, the vastly variegated Scenes of a Calamitous War, & imbrace with exultation the glorious Certainty of Peace and Independance. In this mighty Revolution which regards the Rights of Humanity for it's Basis, we feel a Pride, peculiarly interesting to our Felicity that a Citizen of this State has brighten'd the Paths of Glory which display the Greatness of our illustrious Commander in Chief. May you continue Sir, to deserve the most unfeignd Esteem, & may your future Happiness be equalled only by your Magnanimity & Virtue.[2] We have the Honour to be, &c^t &c^t

Cy (MiU-C).

1. This address was printed in the *Newport Mercury* of 29 November, where it was dated "November 29."

2. NG's reply is immediately below.

To John Malbone, William Channing and Henry Goodwin[1]

Gentlemen Newport [R.I.] 29th Novr 1783

My arrival in the Metropolis of my native State affords me a peculiar happiness, and the cordial reception of its good Citizens sweetens the pleasure.[2] To see a happy close to all the horrors of war, and my country triumphing in her Independence is no less flattering to my pride than interesting to my humanity. Nor will I attempt to suppress the satisfaction I feel that my Military conduct thro' all the Vicissitudes of war is thought by my fellow Citizens deserving of that political confidence which first plac'd me in public life.

Your kind wishes for my future happiness claim every return from a generous Nature; and it will afford me the highest felicity to see this town enjoying all the blessings flowing from Peace, Independence & a flourishing Commerce. I am Gentlemen with the greatest respect Your most Obed^t humble Servt NATH GREENE

Cy (MiU-C).

1. It was undoubtedly Malbone, Channing, and Goodwin who had delivered the address from the Citizens of Newport, immediately above.

2. As noted at his letter to Jacob Greene of this date, above, NG arrived in Newport on 27 November.

* * *

¶ [FROM EDWARD CARRINGTON, Richmond, Va., 29 November 1783. Has NG's letter of 12 November [not found] and is glad that NG is on his way to see his family; "congratulates" him "in terms of sincere friendship." Nothing has been said about "the motion of [Col. William] Grayson & [George] Weedon" there "by either of them"; Carrington's "most zealous wishes were with them." He believes that NG's "observations as to the season are just, and perhaps would have been thought so by others." The "several instances which have happened to the Southward are considerable, but at the same time proper." Had Carrington attempted a similar act in Virginia, it might have been thought, from his "intimacy" with NG, that the "principal had urged me to it."[1] The officers are afraid that "the Tracts allotted for them will be bearly sufficient for their purpose & some of those idle jealousies which have existed might have been revived."[2] The "Back country" of Virginia is "in a most deplorable situation"; a "Mr Pomeroy from Pensylvania" has traveled to "the Kentucky," telling people that "Congress have passed a resolution which declares that Virg^a had no powers to grant lands beyond the Allegeny Mountains, and that those Bodies of lands held by People not resident in the settlement, ought to be taken possession of by others." Pomeroy's fabrication has "inspired such a spirit of licentiousness that the most alarming convulsions are to be apprehended." In "some instances," people have already begun to "mark off, on divisions, the large monopolized Tracts." It is not known how the governor of Viriginia will act in this situation. The "tranquillity of" the western area of the state was "far from being secure," even before Pomeroy's reports, because of the "loose manner in which most of the locations were made." Many land titles have been in dispute, and Carrington thinks that "adventuring at present in that Country is by no means eligible"; no "valuable tracts in this side of the Ohio except what have been allotted for Military Bounties can now be taken up." Obtaining titles to these lands will require "greater hazards" than "the immediate object can justify," but "some years hence the order of the society will be regulated & quiet and the Titles will be secure, and as the large monopolizers will no doubt, be compelled from the good policy of whatever Government exists, to sell out, Lands cannot become very high." Carrington plans to write again on this subject.[3] He has seen "the Attack of the Worthy judge of South Carolina on the Cincinnati. It is specious, but by no means just."[4] Is "sorry" that the "state society" of South Carolina has "intimated that a latent design, Mischevous to the Community, lurks under the present countenance of the establishment." NG has seen "an extract conveyed to the Attack"; Carrington agrees with him that "if it cannot go to effect without creating extensive alarms it ought to be dropped," but he doubts "that will be the case."[5] NG's servant Tom arrived in Richmond "about the 10th of October and remained Sick untill the 27th," when Carrington "advanced him ten dollars to go on." Carrington thought he should have arrived by the date of NG's letter but is "still in hopes he has before this come up with you. He has with him a State of the sums I advanced for his Physicians Bill &^{c}."[6] RCS (MiU-C) 4 pp.]

1. Nothing is known about the "motion" by William Grayson, formerly an aide to Washington, and Gen. George Weedon, a friend of NG's, but it is possible that it may have concerned a proposal to commemorate NG's wartime contributions with a grant of land by the state of Virginia. In a letter to NG of 12 June 1782, above, Weedon had discussed his

lobbying efforts as he tried to persuade the Virginia General Assembly to reward the soldiers of the state's Continental line with land bounties. In that letter, Weedon also referred NG to Carrington and "Major Forsythe [Robert Forsyth]," concerning "what prospects You may have from this State." (Vol. 11: 322, 323n) The "several instances . . . to the Southward" that Carrington mentioned seem likely to have been the plantations and lands that the governments of South Carolina, Georgia, and North Carolina had given to NG. No written "observations as to the season" have been found, but they may have been made in conversations between NG and Carrington while they traveled north together in August and September. Such conversations might have included the possibility of NG receiving a grant from Virginia—which, like the Carolinas and Georgia, was part of the Southern Department—and, as Carrington implied later in this letter, of NG investing in that state's western lands.

2. The Virginia officers had sent several memorials to the Virginia Assembly the previous spring. One "noted the 'insufficiency' of an act of 5 January 1782 which had set aside for them and their men 'all that tract of land included within the rivers Mississippi, Ohio, and Tenissee, and the Carolina boundary line.'" (Madison, *Papers*, 7: 79n) The House of Delegates delayed acting on these memorials until after the matter of Virginia's cession of lands to the federal government could be settled. (Ibid., p. 195) As noted at David Howell's letter to NG of 5 November 1782, above, Virginia had offered to cede its extensive "western lands" to the federal government in return for certain concessions. (Vol. 12: 149) After some months of debate in Congress and the Virginia Assembly about the conditions for this cession, the Assembly agreed to Congress's terms in December, and Congress ratified the agreement the following March. (Abernethy, *Western Lands*, pp. 258–73) Soon after settling the cession question with Congress, the Virginia legislators passed "An Act for surveying the lands given by law to the officers and soldiers on continental and state establishments and for other purposes" and appointed a "deputation of officers" to oversee the verification of veterans' land claims. (Hening, *Statutes*, 11: 309; *Virginia Gazette*, 20 December 1783)

3. The identity of "Mr Pomeroy" from Pennsylvania is not known. The chaotic situation concerning land claims in the Virginia "Back country" had existed for some time. The editors of the Madison Papers have observed:

> "From 23 October 1779, when [Thomas] Jefferson signed the first warrant until [September 1783], the Virginia land office issued warrants or patents for many thousands of acres in spite of early protests both from Congress and from Washington. The boundaries of these grants often overlapped not only in an area such as Kentucky, undoubtedly owned by Virginia, but, much more seriously for promoting discord among the states, in acreage claimed by Maryland or Pennsylvania or by land speculators resident therein. By 1780 the patents and especially the warrants issued by the Virginia land office, had become a 'source of constant speculation,' often by purchasers fated to discover that the validity of their titles could be contested by other claimants to the same acreage. With the close of the war greatly accelerating the westward movement of settlers and the issuance of transferable military-bounty land warrants to needy Virginia veterans, who often had little choice but to sell them for a pittance, the pace and amount of speculation, centering chiefly at Philadelphia, rapidly increased."

(Madison, *Papers*, 7: 310n) No further correspondence between Carrington and NG about speculation in Virginia's western lands has been found.

4. On Aedanus Burke's treatise criticizing the Society of the Cincinnati, see note at Flagg to NG, 17 October, above.

5. On the South Carolina chapter of the Society of the Cincinnati, see ibid.

6. Tom was "extreemly ill" by the time he reached George Weedon's home in Fred-

ericksburg, but as noted at Weedon's letter to NG of 2 December, below, he apparently did recover.

*   *   *

From Michel-Guillaume St. John de Crèvecoeur[1]

Sir   New York 30th Nov[re] 1783
    Pushed by an Irresistible Impulse, I cannot refrain from recalling myself To the Memory of your Excellency. I was in New York Just Landed from on board the French Pacquet, and detained by a Severe Indisposition, when Your Excellency was in New York; I Shou'd be Angry against my Fate for depriving me of the Singular Pleasure of Waiting on You, if I was not in hopes of repairing this disappointement at your return Through this City; & if I did not flatter myself you'd receive this Letter with kindness. It is dictated by the warm effusions of an hornest [i.e., honest] Heart.[2]
    I was in France during your most Glorious & arduous Campaigns; there the Citizen & the Military follow'd you on the Map with Equal admiration & Surprise; Impressed with the Same Sentiments; they have Seen you Terminating, your Military Labours, which at Last have made us a Free & an Independent People.
    Permit an antient Cytisen of America, an acquaintance of Some date, as well as the Man & the French Consul for the States of New York, New Jersey & Connecticut[3] to offer you his feeble but Sincere Tribute of Thanks & Praise, for the virtue & the Military Talents your Excellency has displayed, as well as for the benefit of the astonishing revolution which your Excellency has So greatly Contributed to bring about; The Most Consolatary & usefull one which Mankind has ever beheld. I have the Honor To be with the Most Sincere Respect & Esteem Your Excellency's Most obedient & Most Humble Ser   S[T] JOHN

RCS (ScCMu).
    1. It is not known when or under what circumstances the well-known essayist Crève-coeur (1735–1813) had become acquainted with NG. This is the only correspondence between them that has been found. A native of France, he settled in America by the 1760s, married an American woman, and lived on a farm in Orange County, N.Y. He went back to France in 1780 but had returned to America earlier in November 1783 to find that his home had been burned, his wife was dead, and his children had disappeared, all as the result of an Indian raid. (He later found the children.) Crèvecoeur, who became the French consul at New York at this time, returned to France again in 1790 and spent the rest of his life there. (*DAB*)
    2. The only date on which the editors are certain that NG was in New York was 24 November. (See NG to an Unknown Person, 24 November, above.)
    3. On Crèvecoeur's role as consul, see also note 1, above, and Wadsworth to NG, 6 May 1785, below.

To Warner Mifflin

Sir   [November 1783][1]

I have just received yours of the 21st of last month; and as it breathes nothing but a spirit of good-will, it cannot be offensive. The subject of it demands a fuller answer than I have time to give it.[2] Mortals have limited capacities, and can comprehend but a small part of universal Providence. Whether wars originate from the constitution of human nature, or from lusts which creep into the soul in the progress of human life, is difficult to determine. Customs have their influence, and habits have their force; but passions and appetites have their origin in nature, or how could they operate. We feel in ourselves strong affections and resentments, forcible sympathies and powerful antipathies; and all these inhabit the same soul, and have their operation upon our conduct; they form the dark and light shades of human life, and like the alternate seasons of day and night, may have their use. To say more, would be presumption; and to say less, would be to draw into question the perfection and plan of universal government. To me war was ever a business of necessity. Not that I have a doubt of its being fully authorized from nature and reason, nay necessity, and unavoidable from the plans of our creation; but I am averse to it from its being opposite to my temper and feelings. Nature has linked us together, into different societies, from a social principle; and where the happiness of one is disturbed by the inroads of another, opposition becomes both just and necessary. To submit tamely to imposition, either in private or public life, is to invite oppression and entail slavery. The feeble voice of justice and humanity, affords but little security against power, under the direction of ambition and resentment. Nor will the light of the Gospel, or the lamp of reason, check its rage or control its force. Nature has armed all creation, more or less, with weapons of defence; and when the temper and means are so admirably suited to this end as in man, it is difficult to suppose it was not in the original order of creation. Good and evil, both moral and physical in the plan of human life, are inseparable; and how far they may operate, by their different influence, to promote the great work of universal Providence, is not for me to say. He must be a fool indeed, who will not allow, that, in this wonderful system, the hand of God is visible in all its parts. The progress of reason is slow, and the light of our moral nature is dim, without great cultivation. The business of human life is not to avoid all evils, for this is impossible; but to shun the greatest, and such as will entail the most lasting misfortunes upon ourselves, and upon mankind. War has its calamities; but whether it contributes more, in its consequence, or less, to human happiness and the plan of Providence, is not easy to determine, without a more comprehensive knowledge of all the counter parts of creation than we possess. It is pretty certain the propensity grows up with us; nor can universal benevolence prevail while the present mixture of passions continues to influence human life. Those who feel themselves under religious restraints, have just claims to every political indulgence not opposed to the safety of the people, or the happiness of society. And whether those feelings originate from principle or enthusiasm, it matters not; the obligation from reason and policy is the same. Persecution never pulls down, but often establishes doctrines that have no foundation either on religion or morality. It excites the pity and sympathy of others, and gives an air of merit and confidence to ourselves. From my knowledge of the principles of your society,[3] my influence has never been wanting to soften their sufferings. But it must be confessed, while many of you have acted from principle, there are others whose conduct has been directed by policy. It is such as those who have given birth to suspicions against the whole order; and where it is difficult to discriminate, resentment becomes common. From this cause you have suffered more persecution than from any other; and though it was bad policy from those in power, yet the misconduct of some furnished the pretence. I esteem the people, and admire their moral system; but I think they have many religious prejudices, not suited to the constitution of human life, and by no means adapted to political liberty.[4] On the subject of slavery, nothing can be said in its defence. But you are much mistaken respecting my influence in this business.[5] With all the address I was master of, I could not obtain the liberty of a small number, even for the defence of the country; and though the necessity stood confessed, yet the motion was rejected.[6] The generosity of the southern states has placed an interest of this sort in my hands, and I trust their condition will not be worse but better. They are, generally, as much attached to a plantation as a man is to his family; and to remove them from one to another is their great punishment.[7] "I am," &c.

Printed in Johnson, *Greene*, 2: 451–52.

1. The exact date of this letter is not known, but NG indicated here that he was replying to Mifflin's letter "of the 21st of last month." That letter is above, dated 21 October.

2. In his letter, Mifflin, a devout Quaker, had expressed strong opinions on the subjects of war and slavery.

3. By "your society," NG meant "The Society of Friends," or Quakers.

4. As noted at Mifflin's letter of 21 October, some Quakers were seen as enemies of the American cause because of their stance of neutrality during the war.

5. Mifflin had suggested that NG, because of his prominence, could set an example by refusing to have any involvement with slavery. (Ibid.)

6. Late in the war, NG had urged the states of South Carolina and Georgia to recruit troops from the slave population, but his proposals had been rejected. (See above, NG to Gov. John Rutledge of South Carolina, 9 December 1781 and 21 January 1782 [vol. 10: 22–23, 228–29 and n], as well as NG to Gov. John Martin of Georgia, 2 February 1782, and Martin's reply of 15 March 1782 [ibid., pp. 304, 506–7, 508n].)

7. Boone's Barony and Mulberry Grove, the rice plantations that the states of South

Carolina and Georgia had given to NG in recognition of his wartime services, were large, working plantations that employed numbers of slaves, whom NG purchased through various agents. (See, for example, Penman to NG, 1 October, above; and below, NG to Saunders, 4 January 1784, and Saunders to NG, 29 May 1784.) As noted at NG to Washington, 13 July 1780, above (vol. 6: 96n), slave owning on a small scale was still common in Rhode Island, where NG had spent his formative years, and he does not seem to have been greatly troubled by it. NG does appear to have wanted his plantation slaves to be well-treated, and he wrote his South Carolina agent, Roger Parker Saunders, on 4 January 1784: "Don't fail to find [i.e., feed] and cloth the Negroes well." Writing about his Georgia plantation in August 1784, NG similarly asked William Gibbons to "take care to have the Negroes well clothed and properly fed." (29 August 1784, below) In a letter to NG of 25 November, above, Saunders promised he would "not lay violent hands on" a group of slaves he was purchasing for NG, and Gervais & Owens, a firm that had brokered sales of slaves to NG, reported in a letter to Saunders of 7 September 1784 that they had "divided the slaves [purchased for NG] into lots by families." (MiU-C; see also the note at NG to Gibbons, 29 August 1784, below. As seen in Clegg to NG, 9 March 1784, below, it appears that NG wanted to keep the married couples among his slaves together.) Although NG asserted here that "nothing could be said" in defense of slavery, he nevertheless hoped that profits derived from the labor of slaves on his plantations would enable him to settle debts he had incurred during the war and insure his family's financial stability. He also appears to have had no objection to the possibility of improving his and his family's fortunes by participating in the Atlantic slave trade, as he suggested in a letter to his cousin Griffin Greene of 10 June, above. As implied in William Gordon's letter to him of 26 September 1785, below, NG may have given some thought to a more humane system of plantation labor, by which slaves could be admitted "to the rights of copy-holders." (Gordon, like Mifflin, wanted NG to lend his prominence and national stature to the effort to end slave labor in the South. [Ibid.])

From William R. Davie[1]

Dear Sir   Halifax, N° Carolina, December 2ᵈ 1783.

I sincerely regret that your arrival and departure were both announced to me by your letter.[2] I should have felt a similar satisfaction indeed on seeing you at "the close of all our troubles" after the many anxious hours We have been together. I have it also to regret, that I had not an opportunity to assist in doing the Honours of my country to the man, he [to?] whom of all others we are principally indebted.

We have nothing now to do, but to give strength and permanancy [to] the common union; this will be a difficult task with our young republicks whose views are all local and limited, and whose councils cannot yet be illuminated with the truest principles of policy.

As to the report referred to in your Letter, it was dropt by some of the discontented of the Army, passing thro' this Country. Very little is wanting to make calumny successful against the absent, only the means of opening the mind to suspicion, the people are always easily alarmed in money matters, and the slightest circumstances readily received as confirmation. Banks's letter, the mode of its discovery, his character, conduct and communication with you, served all the purposes of envy and malice.[3]

I had brought with me from the Superior Court at Salisbury the Deposition of Banks, with the attestation of General Wayne and Col. Carrington and with this indeavoured to controvert the malicious attacks of your Enemies, but to this they answered it was but an equivocal state of facts at best, that Mr Banks had confessed even in this instrument, so little attachment to principle, that his affidavit deserved little credit.[4] I was not possessed of the whole circumstances and therefore had it not in my power to do you the Justice every public character deserves. I had some thoughts of writing to you for a copy of the document you mentioned, but when I reflected that reason and gratitude had already generally effaced those impressions, that your friends never did believe it, and that your enemies would not receive conviction, I concluded it was unnecessary. However if you think it might at some time be of any service, inclose it by the post.[5]

You have a handsome Territory in our Western Country[.] I am desired to inquire whether you would dispose of all, or one half of it, or &ca &ca.[6]

I was from the first of January to the 1st of June in the imployment of the Continent, at your particular instance my Freind you know, I forgot, when I parted with you, to ask for a certificate of those services; but it will do as well now, and you can tell me How I shall get my money.[7] I have also a few small credits to give the Continent, which, as I am an Honest Fellow, I wish to know how to do.

I have already in my own mind taken leave of you, as one of my friends I shall never see again, for public business will scarcely ever jostle us together hereafter; but I wish to know where you intend to live, that should I ever be in your neighbourhood, I may call upon you and see what kind of quarters you keep in time of peace. With every wish for your Happiness, I am Sir with sincere respect and esteem your mo. obedient   WILLIAM R. DAVIE

PS. Doctor Burke is dead. This public loss needs no comment.[8]

RCS (NcU).

1. Davie, a militia officer and North Carolina's former state commissary general, had served as commissary to the Southern Army during the winter and spring of 1781. (See NG to Davie, 11 December 1780, above [vol. 6: 561–62 and n].)

2. The letter has not been found. On NG's visit to Halifax, see his Journal entries for 31 August and 1–3 September, above.

3. Davie referred to rumors that NG had been involved in John Banks's business of supplying the Southern Army. (See Benjamin Harrison to NG, 24 December 1782, above [vol. 12: 341–42 and n], and NG to Lee, 22 August 1785, below; on Banks's letter to his partner James Hunter, see ibid. For a discussion of the "discontented" officers of NG's army, see especially vol. 12: xvi–xvii, above.)

4. See Statement of John Banks and Statement of General Anthony Wayne and Colonel Edward Carrington, both 15 February, above (vol. 12: 444–48).

5. It is not known what document NG had mentioned, nor does it appear that he re-

plied to the present letter. (See Davie to NG, 27 June 1784 and 4 December 1785, and Mountflorence to NG, 23 April 1786, all below.)

6. On the tract of land that North Carolina had granted to NG in what is now Maury County, Tenn., see Alexander Martin to NG, 24 May 1782, above (vol. 11: 239–40 and n). Davie wrote NG on 27 June 1784 that "some designing and powerful" individuals had instigated encroachments on that land.

7. Davie referred to his service as commissary to the Southern Army in 1781. (See note 1, above.) He repeated this request in his letters to NG of 27 June 1784 and 4 December 1785.

8. As Thomas Burke, the former governor of North Carolina, died on this date at his home near Hillsborough, Davie probably added this postscript after 2 December. (John Sayle Watterson, *Thomas Burke: Restless Revolutionary* [Washington, D.C.: University Press of America, 1980], p. 213)

*　　　*　　　*

¶ [FROM HEWES & ANTHONY, Philadelphia, 2 December 1783.[1] They have drawn on NG "this day" for £232.5.4 "in favour of Mr George Gibbs."[2] That is the amount of NG's order "in favour of Captain [Matthew] Strong" and also the amount "we gave you a Check upon the Bank for."[3] It is now past "the four or five weeks" that NG asked for "before the bill became due, but if it is then paid to Mr Gibbs, the Loan of it will be of no disadvantage to us."[4] RCS (MiU-C) 1 p.]

1. The partners in this Philadelphia concern were probably Josiah Hewes (see Morris, *Papers*, 8: 538) and certainly Joseph Anthony, whose letter to NG of 1 January 1784 is below.

2. On NG's business dealings with Gibbs, a Newport, R.I., merchant, see also NG to Jacob Greene, 17 June, above, and NG to Gibbs, 17 and 22 August 1784 and 3 February 1785, all below.

3. For more about NG's dealings with Hewes & Anthony, see Anthony to NG, 1 January 1784; Hewes & Anthony to NG, 12 March 1784; Wightman to NG, 13 March 1784; Warley to NG, 13 July 1784, and Anthony to NG, 15 July 1784, all below.

4. NG's reply has not been found.

¶ [FROM GEORGE WEEDON, Fredricksburg, Va., 2 December 1783. Upon his "return to Virginia," he spoke with Gen. [Alexander] Spotswood "respecting his Negroes."[1] Spotswood declines to sell any, but "the Ideas of this Gentleman changes with the wind," and "in all Proberbility" he will eventually sell the slaves. If he does, NG will be informed about the terms of sale.[2] NG's servant Tom has been with Weedon "near six weeks extreemly ill"; Weedon believes "the Odds are greatly against his ever getting over it." Although "Every care has been taken," and "a Doctor has constantly Attended him," Tom has "six or Eight fitts of a day and is at this moment as bad as a person can be to live." When he arrived in Fredericksburg, the "poor fellow" was "Naked, and almost eaten up with the Moth," and his horse had "an ugly rupture in one of his thighs." Weedon can give NG only "small encouragement of ever seeing either of them again," but "every Attention shall be paid to them."[3] He hopes this letter finds NG "in the range of Domestic life enjoying the Sweets of Your own Fireside, with Madam on the Right, and the small Fry covering Your left." He has no news about "the Deliberations of our wise heads" at Richmond, except that "they have adopted the impost agreeable to the Ideas of Congress in the fullest latitude."[4] The "Citizens Bill" has provoked "warm Debates," but Weedon thinks it "will be agreed to with very few Discriminations." He finds that "resentment seems to Subside and give way to Sound Policy" and wishes this would "prevail through out the whole Union, as a few Disagreeable Charactors can make but little Differance when mixed with the community at large and are certainly below the Consideration of Civil Authority."[5] Sends "affectionate love to Mrs Greene" and asks NG to tell her that she "did not behave Cl[e]aver in passing us."[6] RCS (MiU-C) 3 pp.]

1. It is not known where Weedon had recently been outside Virginia. NG had visited both Spotswood and Weedon at Fredericksburg in September, while he was traveling through Virginia. (NG's Journal, 9 September, above)

2. Nothing more is known about this matter.

3. In regard to Tom, see also Carrington to NG, 26 October and 29 November, above. It appears that Tom did survive, for William Washington wrote NG the following summer that his letter would be handed to NG by "your Man Thomas, who came with me from Virginia under expectation of meeting with you at" Charleston, S.C. (William Washington to NG, 8 July 1784, below)

4. On the 1783 federal impost proposal, see note at NG to Lincoln, 18 June, above. As seen in the note at NG to Washington, 26 September, above, Virginia did not approve the congressional proposal "in the fullest latitude." Robert Morris, who considered the congressional plan inadequate, wrote George Webb, Virginia's receiver of Continental taxes, on 23 December: "It gives me Pleasure to learn that the Impost Act is passed with you but this Pleasure is somewhat allayed by the Commutation of your Taxes for Articles of Produce." (Morris, *Papers*, 8: 836 and n; see also Pendleton to NG, 17 July, above.) Although every state eventually ratified the 1783 impost in one form or another, it had become clear by the time of the Constitutional Convention in 1787 that the unanimity required under the Articles of Confederation would never be achieved. (Ferguson, *Power of the Purse*, pp. 239–42)

5. On the "Citizens Bill" that was passed by the Virginia legislature, see note at Carrington to NG, 26 October, above.

6. In traveling by water from Charleston, S.C., to Philadelphia in June, CG had missed a visit with the Weedons.

¶ [FROM ROGER PARKER SAUNDERS, [Charleston, S.C.], 3 December 1783. Refers NG to Saunders's letter of 27 November, above. Dr. [David] Olyphant "has offered" to sell "the Driver and his Family wch he purchased at Boones Sale."[1] There are ten slaves in all, including five workers "priced £100 Sterling," available at two years' credit. Saunders considers the price "great but not More than they would Fetch at any Vendue.[2] The Fellow is Equal to any driver in Carolina[;][3] his Wife a Remarkable fine wench and very ancious to live with you." Col. [Morton] Wilkinson recently "purchas'd 28 Negroes" for "£100 Round." Saunders "consulted M^r [Thomas] Ferguson" about that sale, and Ferguson thought "the Negroes worth the Money," but Saunders "did not chuse to make the Purchase without" directions from NG.[4] He asks NG, "as a fav^r," to spare Mr. James [Ladson?] "100 Acres of Timber Land" if it can be done "without injury to yourself." Ladson will give a "Generous Price," and NG has "More timber Land than is Necessary."[5] Saunders also asks NG to spare "me a Small Quantity of high Land in the Lower part of your Tract" in Georgia as a "Settlement to suit the 400 Acres I have reservd for Myself on Ely [i.e. Isla] Island as It is disagreable Liveing intirely in the Swamp and I purpose being a great part of my time in Georgia, being convens'd no Land will be Equal to river Swamp in Value."[6] RCS (MiU-C) 3 pp.]

1. Dr. David Olyphant had been the director of hospitals in the Southern Department under NG. On "Boone's sale," see note at Saunders to NG, 7 June, above.

2. Saunders apparently did make this purchase, paying £1000 for the slaves. (Pendleton to NG, 30 January 1784, below)

3. Historian Julia Floyd Smith has written:

> "Drivers were foremen who directed the work of field laborers; they were also middlemen who represented management and were responsible for the successful production of crops. The mode of crop production along the rice coast and the prevailing task system of labor demanded that there be a supervisor to set work loads and to measure the performance of laborers through each successive stage of the growing process. Drivers possessed certain talents that qualified them for leadership and were selected from among the slave population upon that basis. They were usually tall, strong men, competent and reliable, able to display fair judgment in carrying out their duties. They helped get the slave gang out in the mornings, assigned tasks, set the work pace, and, at the end of the day's work, examined the quality of the work performed. Their authority was not limited to directing labor in the field. They were responsible for the general conduct of slaves. They had to keep order in the settlement and had authority to discipline slaves and punish them. They also helped issue rations and clothing and, on occasion, when the overseer and owner were absent from the plantation, they had sole responsibility for plantation operation." (Smith, *Slavery and Rice Culture*, pp. 66–67)

4. Ferguson and Wilkinson had both been members of the South Carolina commission that purchased Boone's Barony for NG. (*Biog. Directory of S.C. House*, 2: 248–51, 715) NG replied to Saunders on 4 January 1784, below.

5. For more about this land, which was presumably on Boone's Barony, see NG to Saunders, 4 January 1784.

6. In the letter immediately below, Edmund M. Hyrne reported that Saunders had "engaged to purchase 1200 Acres of Swamp land on Ely [i.e., Isla] Island, immediately opposite" NG's Georgia plantation, Mulberry Grove, and had "desired me to inform you he had reserved 200 acres of it for you, as he imagines it would complete that place." (See also Saunders to NG, 27 November, and NG to Saunders, 4 January 1784.)

*   *   *

From Edmund M. Hyrne

Dear General   Charleston [S.C.] Novr 26th[–4 December] 1783[1] Immediately on my arrival here [John] Banks told me he had examin'd [Ichabod] Burnets papers but could find nothing relative to the business I wrote to him about; & that he had inform'd me of it by letter, which perhaps you may have received; but not satisfied I requested to search them myself; I quickly found the originals of the enclosed which I hope will be all that are necessary.[2] There was an acco^t also of bills drawn in favor of Col^l [Charles] Pettit[,] Col^l Laureans [John Laurens] & Haym Solomon with certificates of their application, but I imagined they were accounted for in the register of Bills.[3] I have directed duplicates of the inclosed, by Capt [Matthew] Strong, to M^r [James] Milligan to whom I have sent the receip^t from M^r [John S.] Dart for 15074 Con^l

dollars.[4] M^r Ed[ward]: Lloyd an officer formerly of the Georgia line I found just going to Savannah. By him I wrote to M^r [Joseph] Clay & inclosed the release, requesting that he would have it recorded & sent back to me as quickly as possible.[5] I scarce know what to inform you on the subject of M^r B^s [i.e., Banks's] credit, but I think the complexion of it is not favorable. I know of a considerable bond of his, in a lawyers hands. M^r [James] Penman ask'd me to inform him what you meant by "unquestionable property." It was a matter that I could not absolutely determine, as the legislature had not decided whether confiscated property, removed out of the state Should be considered as legal capture or no. Yet as I had heard many say there would be great risque in making purchase of such property & as I did not think you wished to run any hazard, I told him I beleived you did not mean to be concerned in that species of property & advised him to give orders accordingly.[6] He said he would & had no doubt of accomplishing the business. [Roger Parker] Saunders I beleive wishd him to purchase such for the Georgia plantation That is such as were confiscated here.[7] I am sorry I can not send you very favorable accounts of your Carolina crop. Mr Ferguson says it suffered much and that he beleives you will make but little more than 200 barrels. Saunders is not in Town. Should I see him before [Capt. Matthew] Strongs departure I will write further on the subject. I lost 20 acres of rice in the hurricane.

Since the above Capt Saunders has been in Town he confirmed what Mr Ferguson said, & told me the loss had been sustaind in the hurricane.[8] Capt Saunders lately engaged to purchase 1200 Acres of Swamp land on Ely [i.e., Isla] Island, immediately opposite to your Georgia plantation, and he desired me to inform you he had reserved 200 acres of it for you, as he imagines it would complete that place. He begs to have your answer upon it soon, as he has promised it (should you decline the purchase) to M^r [Morton] Wilkinson.[9] I have taken some of it, from character, for I never saw the land; and have thought of cultivating it immediately. He offers it to you at the same he has engag'd it to others that is nine guineas per acre.

We had a very excellent passage in Capt Strong, only six days from the City.[10] I wish you may have as good a one on your return here. I congratulate you General on your release from the anxiety, and painful confinement of a military life, & on your restoration to your friends— may your happiness continue complete. I beg the favor of you Sir to make my compliments to Mrs Greene. I wish her every happiness I wish you, and shall rejoice with a number of others to find her accompany you here this Winter.[11] I claim the honor to be Dear General Your most obed^t humble servant   EDM^D M^D HYRNE

Mr Davis rece^t for the Con^l money I have sent to Mr Milligan amo^g to 15074.[12] Decem 4th I postpon'd closing my Letter untill the last moment in hopes I should be able to inform you that Mr Penmans acco^t was settled, But I am sorry I can not. On my first arrival, I spoke to Mr Dart about it. He said he had sold the bills, before he received the orders you gave him by my letter, to Mr Banks on his promise, to take up the note immediately, which bills he disposed of a month agoe, and not a farthing of the money is yet paid. I then apply'd to Mr Banks, & told him how uneasy you would be on hearing Mr Penman remain'd unsettled with. He made many shuffling excuses & evasions, & promised from time to time, but always broke his promises. I call'd on Mr Penman this morning, he told me Mr Banks had just promis'd him he shou'd be satisfied in a few days & M^r B told me, presently after, that Mr Penman was perfectly content, but to my judgement he appeared to have no kind of reliance on a promise so frequently broken. At one time M^r B declar'd it sh^d be closed in a day or two, at another that M^r P was at that time receiv^g rice for it, when upon enquiry the rice was for payment of an old contract. At another time the Note should certainly be taken up before Strong sailed; how ever, Strong sails this day & the Note remains. I am sorry to give you this acco^t as I am sure it must vex you much. Mr Penman I suppose will write to you further on the Subject.[13] He shew'd me a list of negroes, which by the description, I think a very good parcel, whether you will think the property questionable or no, I can't tell. Policy & the law of Nations, & common reason, I think, paints them, as unquestionable.[14] I am Dr General Your most obed^t   EDM^D M^D HYRNE

RCS (MiU-C).

1. As seen in the paragraph below his signature, Hyrne completed this letter on 4 December.

2. Hyrne, who traveled with NG from Charleston to Philadelphia the previous summer, had recently returned to Charleston. The enclosure was a copy of a statement by Burnet, certified on 7 August 1782 by Southern Army auditor of accounts John S. Dart, and notarized by Dart as the army's paymaster on 2 December 1783, which showed that of $180,000 in Continental money that NG received from Congress in late 1780 for travel expenses to join the Southern Army, $10,033 ⅔ had been expended on NG's private account, $27,656 had been turned over to NG's aide William Pierce, Jr., and Burnet had "turned in" $141,409 ⅓ on 20 July 1781. (PCC, item 155, vol. 2: 682, DNA; see also NG to Mifflin, 3 November, and NG's Statement of Accounts, 8 November, both above.) As seen in NG to Pierce, 15 October, above, Burnet had recently died.

3. The account of these bills has not been found.

4. Milligan was the comptroller of the Treasury.

5. On the "release," see Hyrne to Clay, 26 November, above.

6. See NG to Penman, 25 October, above, and Penman to NG, 4 December, below. Penman had been looking into the purchase of slaves for NG from Loyalists and other British subjects living in East Florida. (Penman to NG, 1 October, above, and 4 December) According to Penman, "the greatest part of the Negroes in Florida" were considered to be confiscated property. (Penman to NG, 4 December)

7. See Saunders to NG, 25 November, above.

8. On the damage to NG's South Carolina rice crop, see also Saunders to NG, 20 October, above.

9. See Saunders to NG, 25 November and 3 December, above, and NG to Saunders, 4 January 1784, below.

10. "The City" was Philadelphia.

11. CG did not travel to South Carolina with NG the following summer. Meanwhile, Hyrne died suddenly about a week after finishing the present letter. (See Pendleton to NG, 30 January, below.)

12. The receipt has not been found. "Davis" was presumably Col. William Davies, the former Virginia commissioner of war, whose letter to NG of 25 October 1784 is below.

13. The debt in question was for money that Penman had advanced to NG for travel expenses from Charleston the previous summer. (For more, see Penman to NG, 1 October, and NG's Statement of Accounts, 8 November, both above, and Penman to NG, 4 December, and NG to Penman, 4 January 1784, both below.)

14. See Penman to NG, 4 December.

*   *   *

¶ [FROM NATHANIEL PENDLETON, Charleston, S.C., 4 December 1783.[1] In a brief note enclosed in "Hyrne's Letter," he sends "affectionate respects" to NG and CG.[2] Hyrne has probably given "all the news public and private from this quarter," but Pendleton reports that Marshal has "relieved the World as well as myself" by dying "two days ago by a fit consistant with his life."[3] Pierce will be married "next Thursday."[4] RCS (MiU-C) 1 p.]

1. Pendleton had returned to Charleston since writing NG from Virginia on 12 August, above.

2. The letter from Edmund M. Hyrne is immediately above.

3. On James Marshall, see especially NG to CG, 7 August, above, and Pendleton to NG, 30 January 1784, below. Marshall died on 1 December. (*South Carolina Weekly Gazette*, 5 December)

4. As noted at NG to Williams, 2 July, above, NG's former aide William Pierce, Jr., married Charlotte Fenwick. "Next Thursday" was 11 December. On the wedding, see also Pendleton to NG, 30 January 1784.

*   *   *

From James Penman

Sir   Charleston [S.C.] 4th Decemr 1783

I had the honor on the 4th Ulto of receiving your letter of the 25th October, and immediately communicated the Contents to my Attorney at St Augustine; who writes me in return, that General [James] Grants Manager cannot conclude a Bargain for his Negroes before he hears farther from him.[1]

From the Terms you now authorize me to give I have not a doubt of succeeding in the purchase of the Number you mention, but I regrete your not being more explicit with respect to Confiscated property, the greatest part of the Negroes in Florida coming under that description, who from the peculiar Situation of their Owners might be purchased upon much easier Terms than the other.[2]

As the Negroes you mean to Purchase are intended for your Estate in Georgia, I recommended the enclosed List of Negroes to Mr Saunders's attention for two Reasons, First because I knew he must be personally well acquainted with the Quality of the Negroes, and secondly That giving the utmost extent to the Confiscation Law of this State, it could not possibly operate to your Prejudice in Georgia.[3]

These Negroes are at present the property of Major Tho[s] Fraser, but formerly belonged to D[r] Clitherall, and as such fall under the Confiscation Law of this State. I think they may be got for the Terms you mention, and M[r] Saunders considering them a Valuable Gang has wrote to Major Fraser respecting the purchase of them, and my Correspondent at S[t] Augustine has likewise been directed to Treat with him.[4]

Should the Number exceed your Wants M[r] Saunders will either take the overplus, or you can spare them to General Wayne.[5]

I inclose you two letters from M[r] Saunders and one from M[r] Laurens which I received two days ago from M[r] Drayton.[6]

I am sorry to be under the necessity of adding that M[r] Dart has not yet taken up Major Hyrnes Draft for 200 Guineas owing to some disappointment from M[r] Banks.[7]

Doctor [Andrew] Turnbulls Family request of me to present their best respects to you and M[rs] Green. I beg also to subjoin mine, and have the honor to remain with much Respect Sir Your much Obliged and Most Obedient Hum[ble] servant   JAMES PENMAN

RCS (NcD).

1. NG had engaged Penman to attempt to buy slaves in East Florida for NG's Mulberry Grove, Ga., plantation. (See above, Penman to NG, 1 October.)

2. NG had informed Penman that he would be willing to pay more for slaves than he had originally planned. Slaves who had previously belonged to Loyalists or British citizens in the United States were considered "confiscated property," however, and NG was undoubtedly concerned about the legal status of any purchase he might make of such slaves in East Florida. (NG to Penman, 25 October, above)

3. Roger Parker Saunders was also helping NG to obtain slaves. (Saunders to NG, 3 December, above)

4. Maj. Thomas Fraser of the South Carolina Royalists had gone to St. Augustine with his regiment after the evacuation of Charleston. Dr. James Clitherall, a surgeon with the same regiment, had also accompanied it to St. Augustine. While he was in East Florida, Clitherall "tried to assist inhabitants of Georgia and South Carolina, whose estates had been sequestered by the British authorities, in recovering their plundered Negroes, but he was prevented from doing so by Governor [Patrick] Tonyn and part of his council." (Siebert, *Loyalists in East Florida*, 2: 208–9n, 209, 351; see also Saunders to NG, 25 November, above, and NG's reply to Penman of 4 January 1784, below.)

5. Anthony Wayne's plantation, Richmond, was on the Savannah River near NG's Mulberry Grove.

6. Saunders's letters may have been those of 27 November and 3 December, both above; the only recent letter from Henry Laurens to NG that has been found is that of 26 August, above, written from England. It is not clear which of several Draytons forwarded the letters.

7. Edmund M. Hyrne discussed this matter in greater detail in his letter to NG at 4 December, above.

To Governor William Greene of Rhode Island

Dear Sir   Newport [R.I.] Decem 5th 1783

The inclosed is a letter from a M^r [Moses] Badger a Clergyman of the Church of England. He was an Inhabitant of Massachusets state formerly and on the evacuation of Boston went with the enemy. His political principles were in favor of Great Britain but I am told he has conducted himself with great moderation and kindness towards our people in distress.[1] His moral charactor is good and his social temper agreeable. In a word he is an inoffensive charactor and is in great distress and wishes to remain in the state for the winter if he can get your permision.[2] He is a perfect stranger to me. I never saw him until I came passenger with him from New York. After I found he was coming in the same Vessel that I was I took some pains to find out his charactor and had the pleasure to hear it from my friends in New York as I have before related it.[3] Mrs Greene had letters also respecting the family from New York recommending them to her good offices. This was before I came home.[4] Mrs Badger has been in Newport for some time. If you can grant permission to Mr Badger agreeable to his request it will contribute to the relief of a distressed family and from principles of humanity I shall rejoice upon the occasion. I am dear Sir Your most Obed^t humble Servt NATH GREENE

ALS (RHi).

1. Badger, an Anglican minister, had served as a chaplain to De Lancey's Second Battalion. (Sabine, *Biographical Sketches of Loyalists*, 1: 201) He was originally from Massachusetts but at this time was living "temporarily" in Newport, where the vestry of Trinity Church invited him to "officiate occasionally." (Hattendorf, *History of Trinity Church*, p. 143; Frederick Lewis Weis, *The Colonial Clergy and the Colonial Churches of New England* [Lancaster, Mass., 1936], p. 24) Badger officiated at the marriage of CG's brother, William Littlefield, and Elizabeth Brinley there in 1785. (Mason, *Annals of Trinity Church*, p. 170; Littlefield to NG, 25 April 1785, below)

2. William Greene replied on 7 December, below, that he did not have authority to let Badger stay in Rhode Island for the winter but would lay the request before the legislature when it met at the end of December. No evidence has been found that the General Assembly took any action at that time in regard to Badger, but he did stay in Rhode Island and became the rector of King's Chapel, Providence. (Bartlett, *Records of R.I.*, 9: 734–46; Sabine, *Biographical Sketches of Loyalists*, 1: 201)

3. As noted at his letter to Jacob Greene of 29 November, above, NG arrived in Newport from New York on 27 November. It is not known who in New York had vouched for Badger.

4. The letters that CG received attesting to Badger's character have not been found.

*   *   *

¶ [FROM PIETER J. VAN BERCKEL, Philadelphia, 6 December 1783.[1] Has NG's letter of 19 November [not found], "by which you put it in my power to give proves of the value I sett upon the friendship of General Green." Adds: "Whatever I can do for Mr Biddle, you may be sure, it will be done."[2] Offers "hearty thanks for the good opinion, you seem to entertain of me." RCS (MiU-C) 1 p.]

1. Van Berckel, the newly appointed minister from the Netherlands, presumably had met NG in Princeton, N.J., or Philadelphia in October, shortly after he arrived in the United States. (See Morris to NG, 28 October, above.)

2. Van Berckel undoubtedly referred to NG's friend Clement Biddle, who had advanced money for NG's travel expenses home from Philadelphia. (See the next letter.) Biddle probably was hoping to obtain a loan from Holland and later may also have tried to help NG negotiate one there. (Pettit to NG, first letter of 8 March 1784, below)

¶ [TO JAMES MILLIGAN, COMPTROLLER OF THE TREASURY. From Newport, R.I., 7 December 1783. NG asks for "every information respecting my public accounts under your examination." If "the loss Captain Pierce reported is less than he mentions," Milligan should report it to Congress.[1] NG also asks whether Milligan has any bills that were "not included in my list and in whose favor they were drawn and to what department they belong." If there is a "ballance agreeable" to the one in NG's "last letter" to Milligan, NG requests a "warrant for the Money," as he "borrowed to that amount of Col [Clement] Biddle to bring me home and would be glad to have it replacd in this way."[2] NG would be "exceedingly obliged" if Milligan could bring "my affairs to a close as soon as possible."[3] ADfS (MiU-C) 2 pp.]

1. On the "loss," see NG to Mifflin, 3 November, above. As seen there and in NG to Milligan, 10 November, above, the accounts in question were for "money expended for travelling & [military] family expences during my command to the southward."

2. See above, NG to Milligan, 10 November, and the letter from Biddle that the editors have tentatively dated at before 4 June 1784.

3. Milligan replied to NG on 9 February 1784, below. NG was still trying to obtain reimbursement for the travel money that Biddle had advanced to him when he wrote to Milligan on 4 June 1784.

¶ [FROM GOVERNOR WILLIAM GREENE OF RHODE ISLAND, Warwick, R.I., 7 December 1783. Acknowledges NG's letters of 29 November and 5 December and congratulates him on his "safe arrival into this State." Hopes NG can now enjoy "the fruits of the important services so compleatly performed in the defence of our distressed Country." He is "unhappyly disqualifyed to communicate to you my Ideas upon the Occasion[,] although gratitude demands the highest expressions." The Rhode Island delegates "have drawn a Bill of exchange upon [Deputy] Gov' [Jabez] Bowen, and have gone on to Congress."[1] As for "M' Badger and family," the legislature "have not thought fit to place any power of the kind in the Executive Authority," so the governor will lay NG's and Badger's "letters respecting Him" before that body when it convenes on the fourth Monday of this month.[2] Having heard that NG plans to come "here in a few Days," William Greene hopes he will bring CG with him so that "w[e] may have an oppertunity of conversing together as [in] Days of old."[3] Offers his and Mrs. Greene's "sincere regards to y[ou] all." RCS (CtY) 2 pp.]

1. See also NG to William Greene, 29 November, above.

2. On Moses Badger and his family, see NG to William Greene, 5 December, above.

3. CG had grown up—and married NG—in the home of William and Catharine Ray Greene, her aunt. (NG to Samuel Ward, Jr., 10 July 1774, above [vol. 1: 64–65 and n]) NG probably saw the William Greenes while he was visiting in the vicinity of Warwick in late December. (See Rhode Island General Assembly to NG, 26 December, below.)

¶ [FROM SAMUEL A. OTIS, Boston, Mass., 8[–9] December 1783. According to a brief note dated 8 December, he has not heard from NG since NG's "arrival in Philadelphia." He now renews his "solicitations upon a Subject of the utmost importance" and hopes NG will "find it agreeable" to visit him in Boston "in the course of the Winter."[1] At the bottom of the page, Otis appends a note dated 9 December, stating that "before the above was sent to the office," he received NG's letter of 29 November [not found], "in which you intimate your expectation of comeing to Boston and determination of projecting some experiment to bring on a settlement." Otis is anxiously waiting to see NG.[2] RCS (MiU-C) 1 p.]

1. For background, see above, Otis's letters to NG of 24 July and 8 September.

2. NG's reply has not been found. (See, however, Otis to NG, 21 December 1784, and NG to Otis, 24 July 1785, both below.)

¶ [FROM JOHN STORY,[1] New York, 9 December 1783. He was disappointed by not seeing NG "here."[2] When he "returned from Camp last winter," Story "applied to the State of Massachusetts for a settlement of the depreciation" of his pay. A decision was "put off untill last October," when the committee of accounts "refused to settle" with him until he could show a certificate from NG "that I was not indebted to the Public." Although the committee "supposed" that Story was "accountable for public Stores," he was never in charge of any, and his accounts had all been "examined in Colonel [Charles] Pettit's office and the Vouchers left with him." Story encloses "such a Certificate as will procure a settlement of my depreciation to January 1780"; asks NG to sign it.[3] He supposes that the pay owed to him since then will be settled by Mr. [William] Denning, "the Commissioner to the Quarter Master Generals Department," who plans to open an office in New York.[4] In the certificate that he encloses, Story "mentioned the time of service and the Pay agreeable to a Resolve of Congress in May 1777, when the department was first Arranged, and agreeable to a former Certificate" from NG, specifying the pay he was "intitled to" from 17 October 1777.[5] As of 15 August 1781, Story "relinquished the settlement of the Old Accounts."[6] He also encloses a copy [not found] of "General [John] Glovers Certificate" showing "when I was appointed Quarter Master to his Brigade."[7] Story flatters himself that NG "will not see any impropriety in signing" the certificate; asks him to send it to "my father William Story, Esq[r] at Boston who will transact the business for me in my absence." Story would not have "troubled" NG with this if he were not on his way to Philadelphia. He is "riding for my health which I have been deprived of for Nine Months."[8] The lack of pay for five years has obliged him "to apply the little Interest I had, for my support, that my whole dependance is from what the public owes me, and if I can get my depreciation settled by the State [i.e., Massachusetts], I shall receive immediate releif as one fourth will be paid by the Treasurer and for the remainder I shall have State security which is more valuable than that of the United States." He congratulates NG that "America is blessed with so honorable a peace and ranks with the Nations of the earth"[9] and that NG has "returned from the field of honor and may now enjoy the sweets of a private life."[10] Sends his "Regards" to CG and hopes NG's "future days may be as happy as your former ones have been honorable and successfull."[11] RCS (MiU-C) 3 pp.]

1. Story had served as a paymaster in the Quartermaster Department and as a deputy quartermaster. (Vol. 4: 52n, above)

2. NG had stopped briefly in New York on his way home to Newport, R.I., from Philadelphia. (To an Unknown Person, 24 November, above)

3. The certificate that Story enclosed was no doubt identical to the one that he sent to NG the following March, commenting that he had not received a reply to the present letter. (See note 5, below.)

4. Pettit, as "late" assistant quartermaster general, wrote Story on 17 January 1784 that because Story had kept the "Account of Disbursements in Camp in the Quarter Master General office under General Greene," he should "lay that Account, together with the one which arose in like manner before that time," before Denning, "the Commissioner Appointed for settling such Accounts, for Examination and Allowance." Pettit asked Story to "give such attendance and assistance in the Examination and Explanation of the said Accounts as may be Necessary on the part of the Quarter Master General" and to "consult with" Denning "as early as may be as to the practicability of pursuing this business with Expedition." In that letter, Pettit also enclosed a certificate, "To Whom It May Concern," stating that Story was appointed quartermaster to "General [John] Glover[']s brigade" on 1 June 1777 and that on 17 October of that year he was appointed deputy quartermaster and "is intitled to the pay as such to the 15th of August 1781"—$40 per month as brigade quartermaster and $75 per month as deputy quartermaster. Pettit added that Story was "not Indebted to the United States and is intitled to the depreciation of his pay from the Commonwealth of Massachusetts on the same principles as the Officers of the Line." (MiU-C)

5. On the arrangement of the Quartermaster Department in May 1777, see above, vol. 2: 313n. NG's certificate stating that Story was appointed deputy quartermaster general on 17 October 1777, and that he was entitled to "pay and rations" from that date, is above, dated 19 February 1780. (Vol. 5: 402) As noted there, Story enclosed that document in his letter to NG of 12 March 1784 and asked NG to sign it.

6. It is not clear what Story meant by "the Old Accounts."

7. See note 5, above.

8. Story wrote NG on 12 March 1784 that he was "detained for more than two months" in Philadelphia "by indisposition." On the outcome of his negotiations with Denning, see Story to NG, 19 November 1784, below.

9. On the definitive peace treaty, see note at Lafayette to NG, 8 September, above.

10. NG had returned to Rhode Island at the end of November. (NG to Jacob Greene, 29 November, above)

11. NG's reply, if any, has not been found. Story wrote him again on 12 March 1784, enclosing a "duplicate" of this letter, "lest it should not have reached you."

¶ **[FROM WELCOME ARNOLD**, Providence, R.I., 10 December 1783.[1] Acknowledges NG's letter of 5 December [not found] and congratulates him on returning to his "agreeable Family, & this State." Arnold has "one of the Set of bills Referrd to"; it was forwarded to him by "Mr Stanly with a Request that I would apply to your Brother [Jacob Greene] and get it accepted payable at Some house in Philadelphia agreeable to the Tenor of the Bill."[2] Arnold sent the bill to Jacob "for acceptance with an Intention to have Inclosed it Immediately back to Mr Stanly," but Jacob asked him to retain it until NG returned. Arnold informed Stanly that the bill would be "accepted" as soon as NG came back to Rhode Island. Now that NG is there, Arnold has sent the bill to Jacob but has not "had any Returns yet." It would give him "particular pleasure to Render Mrs Greene any Friend[dly] Offices," and he would be "very glad" to see NG and CG "at Providence."[3] RCS (CSmH) 2 pp.]

1. On Arnold, a Providence merchant and Rhode Island politician, see above, vol. 1: 54n.

2. On the "bills Referrd to," see above, Edward Blake to NG, 3 May (vol. 12: 638); John Wright Stanly's letters to NG of 23 May and 26 October; and NG to Pettit, 4 August.

3. NG's reply has not been found.

¶ [FROM CHARLES PETTIT, Philadelphia, 12 December 1783. Asks NG to excuse the "Shortness and other Marks of haste in this Letter." Pettit's "Brethren of the Mercantile Line" have put him "in Front on an Entertainment given by them to Gen[l] Washington on this Day."[1] In the middle of his preparations for the entertainment, Capt. [Matthew] Strong arrived "this Morning" with "a Volume of Letters from Charleston," S.C.; some of these were "covering Letters" for NG, "with a particular request of speedy Conveyance."[2] Pettit is forwarding them by post, which should be the "most speedy as well as most safe" mode. He sends "best Respects to M[rs] Greene and George."[3] RCS (CtY) 1 p.]

1. After an emotional farewell to his officers at Fraunces Tavern in New York on 4 December, Washington made his way to Philadelphia by way of New Brunswick and Trenton, N.J. He arrived in Philadelphia on 8 December. (Freeman, GW, 5: 465–69) The city's merchants sent him an "address" on 9 December, to which he replied the same day. (Washington Papers, DLC) The "entertainment" that Pettit was organizing must have been a "dinner at the City Tavern" that the merchants gave for Washington on this date. (Fitzpatrick, GW, 27: 262n)

2. Strong sailed regularly between Philadelphia and Charleston. (See, for example, Pettit to NG, 4 August, above.) It is not known what letters he had brought for NG.

3. Pettit had previously taken care of NG's son George Washington Greene and had been involved in decisions regarding his schooling. (See above, vol. 10: 199n, and Pettit to NG, second letter of 14 June 1782 [vol. 11: 332–33, 336n].)

¶ [FROM ROBERT L. HOOPER, Trenton, N.J., 16 December 1783. He has received one letter from NG since NG left Trenton, containing the "agreeable intelligence" that NG is in better health than when he was there.[1] As soon as CG's "favourite Horse was in condition to travel," Hooper ordered it to his stable and "this day" sent it on "by Post, to the care of Doct[r] [William] Burnet at Newark."[2] He hopes Burnet will "take more care" of this horse than he has "of the Mare and sulkey, neither of which have I been able to get possession of 'till yesterday. What has made the good Gentleman so crusty I can't tell, he has not, on this occasion, vouchsafed an answer to any of my Letters."[3] NG's "Filley" is being cared for by "Josiah Furman near this place" and will be "well managed during the Winter." RCS (MiU-C) 1 p.]

1. NG must have passed through Trenton on his way to New York en route to Newport, R.I., in November. NG's letter to Hooper, one of his former deputies in the Quartermaster Department, has not been found. (On Hooper, see above, vol. 2: 331n.)

2. Burnet was the father of NG's former aide Ichabod Burnet, who had recently died in Cuba. (See above, vol. 3: 339n, and Pierce to NG, 15 October.)

3. Nothing more is known about CG's "favourite Horse" or "the Mare and sulkey."

*   *   *

From James M. Varnum[1]

Sir   Providence [R.I.] 17th December 1783.
I have the Honor of inclosing the unanimous Vote of the Society of Cincinnati for the State of Rhode Island, appointing you their President 'till the next Election; And am peculiarly happy in joining my own to their Request, that you will honor them with an Acceptance of their Appointment.[2] I have the honor of being Sir, with unfeigned Esteem, your very obed[t] & most humble Serv[t]   J M VARNUM

RCS (DSoC).
1. On NG's friend Varnum, a former brigadier general in the Continental army and delegate to Congress, see above, vol. 1: 14. Varnum was elected vice president of the Rhode Island Society of the Cincinnati at the same meeting at which NG was named president. (Myers, *Liberty Without Anarchy*, p. 39)
2. According to historian Minor Myers, NG had been informally named president of the Rhode Island Society at a meeting of Rhode Island officers at the Saratoga Barracks in Schuylerville, N.Y., on 24 June. (Myers, *Liberty Without Anarchy*, p. 39) The formal election took place at the first meeting of the Rhode Island Society, on 17 December. (Ibid., 47n) NG supported the aims of the Society of the Cincinnati but never took a very active role in it, partly because of financial and health concerns, which occupied much of his time until his death in 1786, and also because he divided much of that time between Rhode Island and the South. He wrote Washington on 22 April 1784, below, that he had paid little attention to the Society until a "clamour" began to be raised against it; he added: "It was uninteresting to me before. Assuming honors hurt my delicacy; but persecution bannishes the influence." Despite the urging of the former commander-in-chief, NG was unable to attend the Society's first general meeting, at Philadelphia in May 1784. (See below, NG to Olney, 15 April 1784; Washington to NG, 20 and 27 March 1784; and NG to Reed, 14 May 1784.)

*   *   *

¶ [FROM ROBERT MORRIS, SUPERINTENDENT OF FINANCE, Philadelphia, 19 December 1787 [i.e., 1783].[1] He supposes that Colonel Kosciuszko informed NG "how desirous I was to comply with your request in his behalf."[2] Morris hopes NG "may have interest sufficient to induce your little state to join in measures for the relief of him & all other public creditors."[3] Catalog excerpt (Anderson Galleries, 1927), p. 38]
1. The catalog excerpt is dated "1787." Since NG replied to this letter on 9 January 1784, the editors have dated it at "1783."
2. On the "request," see also NG to Thaddeus Kosciuszko, 10 July, and Morris to NG, 1 August, both above.
3. As seen in NG's reply of 9 January 1784, below, Morris was asking him to help persuade the Rhode Island legislature to support Congress's current funding proposal, which included a federal duty on imports and additional taxes to be collected by the states but pledged to Congress. (On the proposal, which was initially rejected by Rhode Island and never was adopted, see in particular the note at NG to Lincoln, 18 June, above, as well as Morris to NG, 19 May 1784; NG to Morris, 3 July 1784; and Morris to NG, 17 July 1784, all below; and Ferguson, *Power of the Purse*, pp. 220–27. On Morris's efforts to obtain NG's help, see also Gouverneur Morris to Robert Morris, 22 November [Morris, *Papers*, 8: 776, 778n].) It appears from John Brown's letter to NG of 10 March 1784, below, that NG did attempt to use his influence on behalf of the impost proposal.

¶ [FROM JEREMIAH WADSWORTH, Paris, [21 December 1783].[1] He received NG's letter to him of 4 November from "M[r] L'Enfant."[2] When Wadsworth "agreed to set down in New York," he felt it was "tolerably certain" that the stock of their company "woud so prosper us to make it a Capital for great business"; he still hopes "it will neat us a fund for a tollerable Establishment," and New York is where he would plan to live if he were to move from Hartford, Conn. Although "Many changes of Sentiment wishes & opinions happen in human life" because of alterations in "circum[stances]," he has "never lost sight" of the plan he formed when they "began business—to Wit to live at N York," but, he writes, "my circumstances have happily changed for y[e] better since that time, and I have no intention to make my selfe a Slave to business [*damaged*] future unless changes for the Worse shou'd arise."[3] He and Mr. Carter have "acquird a considerable fortune, but not one half what the World talks of, they judge from what appears but know not that appearances in this instance are wide of the truth." He and Carter have "resolved with our Stock to establish a bank at N York," but this will not "interfere" with any other business dealings.[4] NG has been "silent on the subject of American Polliticks," as have all of Wadsworth's "friends in America," but the "intelligence" he has obtained from others who hear from friends in America is "unpromising" and leads Wadsworth to understand that "the Citty of N York will be at least for some Years, Governed by Men under whose direction or influence I shoud not chuse to reside."[5] He adds: "America in General is looked on in Europe as in a Critical situation & tho' brought 'to the birth has not Strength to bring forth' any thing like a Tollerable featured Government, and I who am obligded to judge from such evidence as I get second hand am apt to fear we shall not soon be tollerable Governed." He has supposed that NG, with his southern estates, would not be interested in pursuing "a life of business," for NG has "certainly been too long indureing a life of care & anxiety not to want rest." Wadsworth's own "inclination & consti[tu]tion" require him to "live peacably & carefully."[6] He finds himself, at forty—"an old Man" who is "Skateing fast down the Hill of human life tho chearfull and without the least Evidence of Spleen or Melancholy." He has a "kind of forebodeing" that he will not live long.[7] He plans to return to the United States "in the Summer," and "next to imbraceing" his "own family," Wadsworth plans on "imbraceing" NG and his family.[8] General Chastellux "often talks of Nancy Vernon" and has written to her, but his letter has not been sent. Wadsworth asks NG to give her his own "compliments" and to "kiss her very cordially" for him.[9] RCS (CtHi) 4 pp.]

1. Only the month this letter was written is legible. However, the letter has been docketed with a date that appears to be "[D]ecem 21 1784." Since it is certainly a reply to NG's letter to Wadsworth of 4 November 1783, and because Wadsworth was in Paris in December 1783 but not December 1784, the editors have dated the letter at 21 December 1783.

2. Pierre-Charles L'Enfant, the French architect and engineer best known for his plan for Washington, D.C., had served with the American army since 1777. (Heitman, *Register*) In the summer of 1783, he designed the insignia for the Society of the Cincinnati, and, in October, Washington gave him leave to return to France and have orders and medals for the Society produced there. (Fitzpatrick, *GW*, 27: 194–96; Myers, *Liberty Without Anarchy*, pp. 33–34)

3. Wadsworth and NG were partners with Barnabas Deane in Barnabas Deane &

Company, a firm they had established in 1779. (See Deane to NG, 5 January 1784, below. Wadsworth would buy out NG's share in December 1784. [NG to Wadsworth, 29 December 1784, below]) In his letter to Wadsworth of 4 November, above, NG recalled that they had once agreed to go into business together in New York. NG wrote there that he had not yet "fully determined upon his plan of future life" and wondered what Wadsworth's intentions were. A year earlier, Wadsworth, assuming that NG would settle on one of his southern plantations, had lamented that NG and CG were to become "S Carolinians." (Wadsworth to NG, 12 December 1782, above [vol. 12: 286]) Although Wadsworth never moved his principal residence from Hartford, after his return from France he did spend extended periods of time for business and social purposes in New York, especially during his tenure as board member and president of the Bank of New York. (See notes 4 and 5, below.) During his visits there he was a frequent guest in the home of his friend Aaron Burr. (Destler, "Wadsworth," pp. 249–51)

4. John Barker Church, a.k.a. John Carter, was one of Wadsworth's principal business partners. (See his letter to NG of 9 June, above.) Wadsworth and Church later became shareholders in the Bank of New York, which was organized while Wadsworth was abroad. Wadsworth became a director of the bank in 1785 and was elected its president shortly thereafter. According to his biographer, he served in that post for about a year before resigning in May 1786. (Destler, "Wadsworth," pp. 248–50)

5. As seen in the previous two notes, Wadsworth spent significant amounts of time in New York after he returned from Europe.

6. Although NG may have wanted "rest," he would be troubled with financial problems for the remaining two and a half years of his life.

7. Wadsworth had turned forty the previous July; he lived another twenty years, dying in 1804. (*DAB*, 10: 309–10)

8. Wadsworth returned to the United States in September 1784. (Wadsworth to NG, 28 September 1784, below) As seen in ibid. and in NG's letter to Wadsworth of 12 November 1784, a disagreement over financial matters brought a temporary cooling to their friendship. They met at NG's home in Newport, R.I., in December 1784, at which time Wadsworth bought out NG's share in Barnabas Deane & Company. (NG to Wadsworth, 29 December 1784; Wadsworth also visited CG in Newport in May 1785, while NG was in the South. [Wadsworth to NG, 6 May 1785, below]) Thereafter they remained in close correspondence for the rest of NG's life, and Wadsworth later served as an executor of NG's estate.

9. On Nancy (Ann) Vernon of Newport, a longtime friend of NG's and CG's, see vol. 6: 481n, above. François-Jean de Beauvoir, Chevalier de Chastellux, was a major general in Rochambeau's expeditionary force, who arrived in Newport in July 1780 and lived there "until the start of the Yorktown Campaign." (Boatner, *Encyc*.) Vernon, known as " 'one of the sprightliest wits of Newport colonial society,' " undoubtedly charmed Chastellux during his stay there. (*Biog. Directory of S.C. House*, 2: 496; see also vol. 6: 481 and vol. 9: 37, above.) She married David Olyphant in October 1785. (Thomas Farr to NG, 10 December 1785, below)

¶ [FROM A COMMITTEE OF THE TOWN OF COVENTRY, RHODE IS-LAND, Coventry, R.I., 22 December 1783. While "justly merited" commendations "are resounding from State to State" for "the very essential Services" that NG rendered throughout "the glorious struggle for Liberty and Independence," the residents of Coventry, where he formerly lived,[1] "wish to participate in the general Joy" and congratulate him "on the happy Restoration of Peace, with its attendant Blessings." In taking a "retrospective View of the important Contest," they "cannot but admire the steady Patriotism, enterprizing Spirit, and most undaunted Bravery" that he exhibited "in every Vicissitude of the War." They express "Satisfaction" that he has returned to his native state, "crowned with Honor and Glory." They conclude: "As you have now exchanged the Toils of a military Life for the Enjoyment of domestic Felicity, we most cordially wish that your well-earned Renown may be as perpetual as your Services have been useful to the United States, that unintermitted Pleasures may ever await you through the variegated Scenes of Life, and finally that you may receive the Rewards appropriated to the Virtuous in the blissful Regions of Futurity."[2] Excerpt from *Providence Gazette*, 31 January 1784]

1. NG had moved to a new house near his family's Coventry mills and forge in the summer of 1770. He and CG lived there after their marriage in 1774, and she continued to make the house her residence for some time after he left for the army the next year. (Vol. 1: 8–9n; 83n, above) NG visited her there in July 1778 and again in September 1778, after the battle of Rhode Island, when he took a brief leave, awaiting the birth of their daughter Cornelia. (See, for example, vol. 2: 476n, above, and NG to John Brown, 6 September 1778 [ibid., p. 507].) Those were the last times he lived in the Coventry house.

2. NG's reply is immediately below.

*   *   *

To the Committee of the Town of Coventry, Rhode Island

Gentlemen   [after 22 December 1783?]

The polite compliments and flattering sentiments of the patriotic Inhabitants of Cov[entry] cannot fail to make the most pleasing impression on a Mind which recollects its former Connections and early Attachments with singular satisfaction.[1]

In reviewing this wonderful Revolution nothing gives me more pleasure than to find the people at the Close in the full enjoyment of those blessings which they had in Contemplation at the beginning. Nor will anything add more to my happiness than to have the advantages rendered as lasting as they are diffusive.

Your generous wishes for my present and future felicity claim the acknowledgments of a grateful Mind which I wish could be as powerfully expressed as felt. I am Gentlemen Your most obed[t] humble serv[t]

NATH[l] GREENE

Cy (Thomas Enoch Greene, North Providence, R.I.).

1. NG was replying here to the address immediately above.

*   *   *

¶ [FROM THE CITIZENS OF EAST GREENWICH, RHODE ISLAND, East Greenwich, R.I., 26 December 1783. They meet NG "at the happy Moment" of his "Return from the Field of Glory with all the Joy that affectionate Hearts can feel and with more Satisfaction than their Language can express." They remember "with the greatest Felicity, the pleasing Hours in which many of them," with NG, "first essayed the military Science, guided only by the Love of Liberty."[1] They "expected the important Events which have since rescued this Country from the oppression of Great Britain," and they "now feel their Happiness increase, that in obtaining the inestimable objects of their Wishes," NG has "invariably deserved the Sublime Character which Time itself must Leave unsullied." They wish "to be Considered In the Number of your warmest Friends, & cannot be more happy than in your future Prosperity."[2] Signed by J[ames]. M. Varnum, A[rchibald]. Crary, and T[homas]. Tillinghast. DS (Varnum House Museum, East Greenwich, R.I.) 1 p.]

    1. Although NG was born and grew up at Potowomut, which is within the boundaries of Warwick, East Greenwich was the nearest town to his family's farm. It was there that NG joined in the formation of the "Military Independent Company of East Greenwich" (later the Kentish Guards) in August 1774. He and other members of the company first learned "the military Science" by practicing rudimentary drilling with two veterans of the British army. (Vol. 1: 69n, above)

    2. NG's reply is below, dated after 26 December.

*   *   *

From the Rhode Island General Assembly

Sir   [East Greenwich, R.I. 26 December 1783][1]

    The Governor[2] and Company, in general Assembly convened, present to you their sincerest Congratulations upon your happy Return to this, your native State. When they appointed you to the most honorable Office in the Service of your Country, they anticipated the great Events, which have more than justified their Expectations. Your Military Conduct and Atchievements, so brilliant through[t] the whole Revolution, have excited an unabating Affection in the Breasts of all those, who are friendly to the Rights of Mankind. The Citizens of this State in particular will hold you dear while the Tribute of Praise is rendered only to the claims of Virtue. May the same divine Beneficence, which has secured to this State the blessings of Peace and Independence, continue to you every Felicity that worthy Actions, estimated by Gratitude and Affection, deserve.[3]

    We are Sir, with every Sentiment of Friendship and Esteem, your very obd[t] & most humble Serv[ts]

Df (R-Ar).

    1. The Assembly convened in East Greenwich on the fourth Monday in December. (Bartlett, *Records of R.I.*, 9: 734) The editors have dated this document 26 December because the Assembly resolution on that date approved the "Draught of an Address to Major General Greene" and requested that "a fair copy thereof" be made and presented to NG by the governor and speaker. (R-Ar) The exact date of the "fair copy" is not known. NG's response is below, tentatively dated 27 December.

    2. NG's distant kinsman William Greene was the governor of Rhode Island.

    3. The Assembly had "voted and resolved" that a committee of three—Archibald Crary, Rouse J. Helme, and James M. Varnum—be appointed to "draft an address to the Hon. Major General Greene, on his return to this state, and that they lay the same before this Assembly." (Bartlett, *Records of R.I.*, 9: 737–38)

To the Citizens of East Greenwich, Rhode Island

Gentlemen　　　　　　　　　　　　　　　[after 26 December 1783?][1]

Was my heart of a colder make or my affections less interested your kind and pleasing address could not fail to kindle them into life. I embrace with lively emotions your generous welcome and rejoice with you in our common triumph. If my conduct in the progress of this war has any claim to approbation your steady patriotism merits the highest applause. A recollection of our infant essay in the science of War affords a double satisfaction that the conduct of each has been such as to continue an unabating affection and growing esteem. Connected with the place and the people from early youth I wish their happiness as my own. Nor can I express what I feel or how sensible I am of the honor done me.[2] I am Gentlemen Your Most Obedient humble Servant

NATH GREENE

ALS (The Current Company, 1978).

1. This letter was in response to an address from the residents of East Greenwich, dated 26 December, above.

2. NG's reply and the address from the residents of East Greenwich were printed in the *Newport Mercury* of 3 January 1784. A note in the newspaper reads: "We hear that last Monday Evening [29 December], at the hall in East-Greenwich, a very splendid Ball was given by General [James M.] Varnum, in Consequence of the Arrival of the Hon. Major-General Greene at that Place."

To the Governor and Assembly of Rhode Island

Gentlemen　　　　　　　　　　[Newport, R.I., 27 December 1783?][1]

My bosom is warm with Gratitude from your kind and affectionate Address.[2] As it has ever been my Pride to deserve your good Opinion, so it is my highest Gratification to meet your Approbation. I feel myself weded to the Interest and happiness of this State, from the earliest attachments. It will ever give me the most pleasing Satisfaction to promote its interest and welfare.

Permit me to return you my most respectful acknowledgments for the honor you have done me, and for the interest you take in my present and future happiness. I have the honor to be Gentlemen with all possible respect, your Most Obd^t Humble Servant　　　　　NATH GREENE

ADS (R-Ar).

1. This letter, the date of which was taken from the docketing, was in reply to the General Assembly's address to NG, dated 26 December, above. It was printed in both the *Providence Gazette* and the *Newport Mercury* of 3 January 1784.

2. See Rhode Island General Assembly to NG, 26 December.

*　　　*　　　*

¶ [FROM GEORGE WASHINGTON, Mount Vernon, Va., 28 December 1783. In a circular letter, he informs the presidents of the state chapters of the Society of the Cincinnati that a general meeting of the Society will be held in Phila-

delphia on "the first Monday in May next, agreeably to the original Institution."[1] The "punctual attendance" of delegates from the state societies "will be
expected at the time and place beforementioned."[2] Washington thinks it will be
better for the presidents to "give the necessary notice to your Delegates by
Letter, rather than by a public Notification," and he urges that "measures be
taken to prevent a possibility of failure in the communication."[3] In a postscript,
he asks the recipient to acknowledge "receipt of this Letter."[4] LS (Rhode Island
Society of the Cincinnati Records, on deposit, RHi) 3 pp.]

1. This copy of the circular letter was sent to "The President of the State Society of
Cincinnati in Rhode Island"; NG had officially been elected president of the Rhode Island
chapter earlier in the month. (Varnum to NG, 17 December, above) The "original institution" of the Society, which had been drawn up the previous May, called for an annual
"general meeting" of representatives of the state societies. ("Institution of the Order of the
Cincinnati," 13 May 1783, Society of the Cincinnati Records, on deposit, RHi)

2. For reasons of CG's and his own health—and the press of personal business—NG was
unable to attend the meeting, despite subsequent requests from Washington to attend.
(See Washington's letters to NG of 20 March and 27 March 1784, and NG's to Washington
of 22 April and 6 May 1784, all below.) Only one Rhode Island officer, Colonel Samuel
Ward, Jr., is known to have attended, and he apparently arrived too late to participate in
most of the discussions. (Pettit to NG, 18 May 1784, below)

3. No letter about the general meeting from NG to members of the Rhode Island Society
of the Cincinnati has been found.

4. NG replied to this letter on 16 February 1784, below.

¶ [FROM JOSEPH AND WILLIAM RUSSELL, Providence, R.I., 29 December
1783. They are sorry to report that they have a letter from "Messrs Lacasc. &
Mallet" [i.e., James La Caze and Michael Mallet] of Philadelphia, enclosing a
protested bill of exchange endorsed by NG. The Russells enclose an extract of
that letter and an account in the amount of £331.3.11, which they have made out
in behalf of La Caze and Mallet.[1] They hope NG can "Recover" that amount
from "the Drawer," and they request an answer that will allow them write to La
Caze and Mallet "by Next Tuesdays post."[2] Their "best wishes have attended"
NG "through the whole progress of the Warr," and they "Sincerley Congratetu-
late" him on his "Safe Return from the Feild of Glory" to his "Native state." RCS
(MiU-C) 1 p.]

1. According to the enclosure, dated 3 December, the protested bill was a bill of
exchange for "£5040, tournois drawn by the Baron Glusbeck [i.e., Glaubeck] at Charlestown [S.C.] the 18th Feby 1783 on Mr Jean Jacques Boyer at Bourdeaux [France] & indorsed
by his Excellency General Greene. As we are informed that his Excellency is now in Your
State, be pleased to have the said Protest presented to him for Payment of the Value &
remit us the same as soon as possible in good Bills." (MiU-C) "Tournois" was "money
coined at Tours [France], one-fifth less in value than that coined at Paris." (OED) On the
bill drawn by Glaubeck, see especially NG to Glaubeck, 16 February (vol. 12: 449); ibid.,
pp. 469–70n; and NG to Morris, 3 June, all above.

2. "Next Tuesday" was 6 January 1784. NG replied to the Russells on 4 January 1784 and
wrote to La Caze and Mallet about this matter on 14 January 1784, both below. (See also
NG to Lafayette, 24 March 1784, and NG to Washington, 29 August 1784, both below.)

¶ [FROM JOSEPH ANTHONY, Philadelphia, 1 January 1784.[1] Acknowledges
NG's "Esteemed favour" of 5 December [not found] "by Captain Wightman."[2]
Is "happy to heare" of NG's safe arrival in Newport and is pleased that NG "met
Such a Cordial Reception" there.[3] Anthony could "easily Believe that you found

Newport in Tears," for he knows that the town "wants Comforting." Its "present Distressd Situation is certainly owing to the Mistaken Policy of a few wrongheaded people who have taken the Lead there," and "it would have been fortunate" if NG "had been fixed there at an Earlier Period"; hopes NG is "yet in time to be of Service." He adds: "I can assure you Sir it affords me a pleasure I cant Express to find you so well Disposed towards that Delightsome Spot where I drew my first Breath." NG's "Influence at this time will be of Real Service, and perhaps be a means of saving" the town "from total Destruction." Newport has "long wanted a friend who dare Speak to help them out of the Distracted State in which they have been Involv'd for Some years past." There was once a "Sett of Hospitable Inhabitants & agreeable Society" there, and Anthony is "Heartily Dispos'd, to lend them Every aid in my Power."[4] The pig iron that NG wrote about "is Not to be had." Mr. [George] Gibbs asked NG's brother [Jacob] for some, "but there has not been one Brought from Durham in Some months," and Col. [Charles] Pettit will not have any from Batsto "this winter."[5] Anthony has also made inquiries about "the Chairs" but finds it "Difficult to get them mad[e]"; he hopes they can be "done in time to Send by Captain Wightm[an]," who has been "detain'd by the Severity of the weather."[6] Sends "Compliments of the Season added to Every other Blessing" to NG and CG.[7] RCS (MiU-C) 2 pp.]

1. Anthony, a native of Newport, R.I., was a partner in the Philadelphia mercantile firm of Hewes & Anthony and had a "GOLD and SILVERSMITHS business" in the city. (RNHi; Smith, *Letters*, 18: 598; Hewes & Anthony to NG, 13 March, below; advertisement in *Pennsylvania Packet*, 21 October 1783)

2. Valentine Wightman was the master of the schooner *Victory*. (Wightman to NG, 13 March, below)

3. NG, who returned to Newport on 27 November 1783, had been hailed almost immediately by the town's residents. (From the Citizens of Newport, 29 November 1783, above)

4. Newport, formerly a thriving mercantile center, had been nearly eviscerated by the war. Many houses had been destroyed, and the population in the postwar era was half of what it had been previously. J. P. Brissot de Warville, who visited Newport about this time, found "an empty place, peopled only by groups of men who spend the whole day on corners. Most of the houses are in disrepair; the shops are miserably stocked and offer for sale only coarse cloth, packets of matches, and other cheap goods. Grass is growing in the public square in front of the State House; the streets are badly paved and muddy; rags hang from windows; and tatters cover the hideous women, the emaciated children, and the pale, thin men, whose sunken eyes and shifty looks put the observer ill at ease." (J. P. Brissot de Warville, *New Travels in the United States of America, 1788*, ed. Durand Echeverria [Cambridge, Mass.: Harvard University Press, 1964], p. 128) NG apparently also commented about the "deserted" nature of the town in a letter that he wrote about this time to another Newport native, Henry Collins Flagg. (Flagg to NG, 5 May, below)

5. On Gibbs, see NG's letter to him of 17 August, below. The Batsto works in southern New Jersey, in which NG had recently sold his interest, were being managed by Pettit, one of his former partners in the business. (See above, Pettit to NG, 26 July 1783, and Agreement between NG and Pettit, 8 November 1783.) Pettit wrote NG on 13 March, below, that he could supply "pigs" for the Greene family's ironworks.

6. The chairs were not sent until March. (See Hewes & Anthony to NG, 12 March, and Wightman to NG, 13 March.)

7. New Year's Day was traditionally a time of celebration.

*   *   *

To James Penman

Dear Sir   Newport [R.I.] January 4th 1784

I have just got your favor of the 4th of December inclosing a list of Doctor [James] Clitharells Negroes. Their number is greater than I can venture upon. But this will be no objection as General Wayne and M[r] Saunders are both in want and we can divide them.[1] Their being confiscated property is an objection to me as I would rather have property out of dispute.[2] But I beg you to consult our friend M[r] Edward Rutledge and M[r] [Thomas] Ferguson and if they advise to it I will venture upon the purchase.[3]

You will get the terms as low and the payments as long as possible altho I am in hopes to Negotiate for the payment of the greater part of mine in less than a year.[4] The earlier the Negroes are got on the plantation the better. Mrs Greenes situation prevents my return to South Carolinia as early as I expected which obliges me to be more solicitous about the business.[5] It gives me pain to hear M[r] [John S.] Dart has not replaced the Money borrowed of you and the more so as I directed him to sell bills for cash only. I beg you will reduce the matter to a certainty and let me know by the next opportunity what you have to expect. If you are not likely to get the money immediately I will have it remitted through some other channel.[6]

Mrs Greene joins me in respectful complements to you and Doctor [Andrew] Turnbull[']s family. I am dear Sir Your Most Obed humble Ser[t]   N GREENE

ADfS (CtY).

1. The state of Georgia had given plantations on the Savannah River to both Anthony Wayne and NG. On Roger Parker Saunders, a South Carolinian who owned plantations in that state and Georgia, see note at Saunders to NG, 26 May 1783, above, and the letter immediately below. Penman was trying to purchase slaves for NG in East Florida. (See above, Penman to NG, 4 December 1783.)

2. See ibid.

3. Edward Rutledge (1749–1800) had been a delegate to Congress from South Carolina and a signer of the Declaration of Independence. He had also been a captain of artillery during the war and had been captured and imprisoned by the British after the fall of Charleston. While serving in the South Carolina legislature (1782–83), Rutledge "drew up the bill which ordered the confiscation of property of loyalists." (*Biog. Directory of S.C. House*, 2: 573–76; Heitman, *Register*) NG turned to Rutledge for legal advice from time to time, and it was Rutledge who drafted NG's will in 1785. (The will is below, dated 11 October 1785.) On Ferguson, see note at Saunders to NG, 26 May 1783. It is not known whether Penman purchased these slaves for NG.

4. On the terms under which NG hoped to buy the slaves, see also NG to Penman, 25 October 1783, above, and NG to Robert Morris, 9 January, below.

5. CG was pregnant with the Greenes' fifth child, Louisa Catharine, who was born the following spring. (NG to Pettit, 22 April, below)

6. On the 200 guineas that NG had borrowed from Penman—and the problems he had encountered in trying to pay that loan—see especially Hyrne to NG, 26 November–4 December 1783, above.

*   *   *

¶ [TO JOSEPH AND WILLIAM RUSSELL. From Newport, R.I., 4 January 1784. NG has their letter "with an account of the protested bill."[1] He expects to be in Providence "in a little time" and will give them an "answer on the subject" then. Thanks them for their "polite and obliging congratulations on my safe return." ADfS (MiU-C) 1 p.]
  1. See the Russells' letter to NG of 29 December 1783, above.

*   *   *

To Roger Parker Saunders

Dear Sir   Newport [R.I.] January 4th 1784
  I have recievd your several letters of the 20th of October 25th & 27th of November and 3d of December.[1] I am exceeding unhappy at the fortune of the Crops and the moreso as I was told from all quarters crops were never better[,] and my demands never more pressing. Nor can I but hope it will exceed your expectation from the slight view you took of it.[2] I could wish you to make particular enquiry respecting the Negroe said to be dead formerly belonging to [John] Wigfall. It is not impossible he may give out he is dead with an intention to keep him on his own plantation. I am told he is a charactor of this stamp.[3] If Doctor Olliphant will take an hundred pounds a head for the Negroes he got from my plantation and give two years credit, without interest take them. Otherwise I think them too high.[4] I am willing to spare Mr Ladsdon either one or two hundred Acres of Land if it will not injure the plantation; but I expect to be with you so soon I should not choose to sell before I see it. At Present I know so little about the upland of my plantation in Georgia that I can give you no answer only that I have every disposition to oblige you.[5] It will be perfectly agreeable to me for Mr Hewet to live in my house on the Savannah and to manage the place if you can recommend him for a good planter and one that I can confide in. And the terms for the house &c shall be made agreeable.[6] I should be glad to take the two hundred Acres you mention; if I can accomodate the payment on my arrival which will be in less than two Months we will adjust the matter.[7] I like the charactor of Doctor Clitharells Negroes. General [Anthony] Wayne you and my self shall want the whole.[8] But I have my fears respecting the confiscating Law. Not that It has a legal operation upon a just and liberal construction; but what interpretation the State may give it is impossible for us to tell. If you think the terms are good both as to price and time of payment consult Mr Ed[war]d Rutledge and Colo [Charles C.] Pinkney and Mr [Thomas] Ferguson and if those Gentlemen give it as their opinion the purchase is good close a bargain, Unless you should meet with a better offer from another quarter.[9]
  I am surprisd you have never receivd a letter from me since I left

Charleston. I wrote you from Philadelphia that Col [Walter] Stewarts father had refused payment upon your order; but if you still wished to have the Sheep they should be shiped. Please to say fully on this head in your next and write to Capt William Littlefield who I will get to ship them[;] fix the number, you will have and they shall be got at the best kind.[10] I am sorry you did not get my letter from Aulstons.[11] Remember the Negroes I have with M[r] Banks.[12] I hope you will be able to get out some Staves and bark to make up for a short crop.[13] Dont fail to find & cloth the Negroes well.[14]

Mrs Greene joins me in respecful complements to you & Mrs Saunders. I am dear Sir Your Most Obedt humble Sert   N GREENE

ADfS (MiU-C).
1. These letters are all above.
2. NG's autumn crop had fallen far short of expectations. (See above, Saunders to NG, 20 October 1783, and Hyrne to NG, 26 November–4 December 1783.)
3. See Saunders to NG, 20 October 1783.
4. On David Olyphant's slaves, see also Saunders to NG, 3 December 1783, above, and Pendleton to NG, 30 January, below.
5. In his letter of 3 December 1783, Saunders had suggested that NG sell off several parcels of land from his South Carolina plantation, including one to James Ladson.
6. Saunders had asked NG to let "my brother M[r] Hewet," who was buying land near NG's Mulberry Grove plantation in Georgia, rent NG's house there and "undertake the Care" of NG's slaves. (Saunders to NG, 27 November 1783, above)
7. On the land that Saunders had offered to NG on Isla Island, "directly opposite to Mulberry Grove," see ibid.
8. Dr. James Clitherall, a Loyalist refugee from South Carolina, was then in East Florida. (Saunders to NG, 25 November 1783, and NG to Penman, 4 January, above)
9. As noted at NG to Penman, 4 January, it is not known whether Clitherall's slaves were purchased for NG. Saunders later bought fifty-eight slaves for NG from the firm of Gervais & Owen. (Saunders to NG, 29 May, below)
10. Nothing more is known about the matters mentioned here.
11. NG had stayed at Joseph Allston's South Carolina plantation while he was traveling north the previous August. (NG's Journal, 19 August 1783, above)
12. Nothing more is known about "the Negroes" NG had "with M[r] [John] Banks."
13. NG hoped that income from the production of pipe staves and "bark" could offset some of his losses from the rice crop. (See also NG to Saunders, 6 June, below.)
14. NG was directing Saunders here to provide adequate food and clothing for the slaves.

*   *   *

¶ [FROM BARNABAS DEANE, Hartford, Conn., 5 January 1784. Encloses a detailed "Estimate of B. Deane & C[o] Affairs," dated 30 June 1783.[1] Col. [Jeremiah] Wadsworth carried a copy of this estimate to Philadelphia, where he expected to see NG and inform him about the company's "State of Affairs" before he left for France. NG will see by the enclosure "the Number of Heavy Losses we met Since Sep[r] 1781."[2] As Wadsworth directed him "To Continue the Buissness as Usual untill Further Orders," Deane has carried on as "Before the Term of Our Partnership Expired." Stills have been "Purchas'd in London" and will be "out this Winter"; he has also "Sent a Large Brig to Surinam for Molasses" and plans "Next Season to begin to make Rum." Asks if NG approves of "the Continuance of the Partnership Since last July (the Time by Agreement which it was to Expire)" and if NG will consent to "the Continuance of it to any Future Time."[3] RCS (MiU-C) 2 pp.]

    1. On the "estimate" of the company's affairs, see note at Wadsworth to NG, 26 July 1783, above. Wadsworth and NG were Deane's partners in the company.

    2. See note at ibid.

    3. Under the terms agreed to on 4 April 1779, the partnership was to "Continue for the Term of Four Years from the Day of its Commencement." (Vol. 3: 378, above) In a letter to NG of 26 February, below, Deane acknowledged NG's reply, which has not been found. Wadsworth bought NG's share in the partnership at the end of 1784. (NG to Wadsworth, 29 December, below)

¶ [FROM THOMAS SHUBRICK, Charleston, S.C., 7 January 1784.[1] Has NG's letter [not found], enclosing "my commission"; thanks NG "for the trouble you have had with it." Shubrick was appointed "a Major Brigade to Gen[l] Howe" on 24 October 1777 "and acted as such for a considerable time which then gave me the rank of Major.[2] When Congress pass'd the resolution respecting the rank of Aid de Camps & Majors of Brigade that they should have none but what they held in the line," Shubrick understood that "they excepted those which were appointed prior to that resolution[,] by which I conceive I have a right to the rank."[3] If NG agrees, he would "for ever oblige" Shubrick by submitting this matter to the secretary at war.[4] Shubrick has "taken the liberty of shewing that paragraph" of NG's letter concerning "M[rs] E. to her[,] who was much surprised at it." He adds: "As she is one of those wives who is unfashionably fond of her husband she took what you said as a compliment unless as she says she did not understand what you meant and that you intended to offend her which she could not suppose and which I undertook to declare was not the case."[5] Mrs. [Mary Branford] Shubrick gave birth to a son on "the last day of the last year," and both are well. She joins Shubrick in asking to be "Affectionately remembered" to NG and CG. RCS (MiU-C) 2 pp.]

    1. On Shubrick, one of NG's aides in the South, see above, vol. 9: 271n.

    2. Shubrick was brigade major to Robert Howe from 24 May 1777 to September 1778. (Heitman, *Register*)

    3. The resolution passed on 27 May 1778. (*JCC*, 11: 543)

    4. If NG wrote to Gen. Benjamin Lincoln on Shubrick's behalf, the letter has not been found.

    5. "M[rs] E." has not been identified.

¶ [TO JACOB GREENE. From Newport, R.I., 8 January 1784. "Cousin Charles Greene" says that Jacob lost his "Anchor Shop in the late great Flood"; NG asks for more information.[1] He comments that fortune seems "to pursue you to the last Stage of Ruin" and that "Brother Kitt has suffered also."[2] CG has been "ill with a Coliquy complaint" but is better now. Asks what Jacob has "concluded respecting the Brigg."[3] Adds: "The winter is setting in so cold. Nothing new from abroad." Tr (Foster Transcript: RHi) 1 p.]

    1. NG's and Jacob's cousin Charles Greene lived in East Greenwich, R.I. (Vol. 1: 66n, above) On the damage to Jacob Greene's "Anchor shop," dam, and forge, see NG to Griffin Greene, 8 July, below. The bitter cold of the winter of 1783–84 had been interrupted by "a complete thaw . . . toward the end of the first week of January," which melted large

amounts of snow and caused extensive flooding and damage to bridges, dams, and other structures in New England. (Ludlum, *Early American Winters*, p. 65) That winter is considered one of the coldest on record. (Ibid., pp. 64–67; see also Pettit to NG, 13 March, below.)

2. Nothing is known about the problems of NG's and Jacob's brother Christopher ("Kitt") Greene.

3. On the brigantine that Jacob Greene sent to the West Indies and Charleston, S.C., to obtain a cargo for Europe, see his letter to NG of 11 June; NG's to Robert Hazlehurst of 26 June; and NG's to Jacob Greene of 5 July, all below.

*   *   *

Estimate of NG's Estate

[Newport, R.I., before 9 January 1784?][1]

Half barony in South Carolinia laying upon Edisto River navigable waters up to the plantation and is not more than from twenty five to thirty miles from Charleston. It consists of from seven to ten thousand acres with proper buildings on it. Ther[e] is from six to eight hundred acres of Rice ground under cultivation[,] Between three and four hundred more may be made for Rice. But besides the Rice ground there is a considerable quantity fit for Indigo and a great plenty of Corn land to raise provisions for the Negroes and a large quantity of good timber Land now loaded with timber fit for Lumber of all kinds. This Plantation was formerly owned by Governor Boon [Thomas Boone] and produced annually from Seven hundred to a thousand Casks of Rice and kept not less than three hundred head of Cattle. He had on it upwards of two hundred Negroes and valued the Plantation and Negroes to upwards of thirty thousand pounds Sterling. I have on it not more than one hundred and twenty Negroes. The land was estimated to me at nine thousand Sterling and the Negroes that I have on it at the rates they are now selling for cash or the best of security will amount to upwards of Eight thousand pound. It was the intention of the Legislature of the State of South Carolinia that I should have the interest voted me at its full value in solid property and the estimation of the Land was generally thought far short of its value.[2] The hands that are now on the Plantation can raise five hundred Casks of Rice yearly and raise their own Provisions if the seasons are but tolerable.[3] The Rice at Market is worth two and half guineas [per cask] which will amount to twelve hundred and fifty Guineas, but of this there is the Negroes to cloth[e,] salt and Tools to provide and the overseer and Superintendant to pay which will amount to one hundred and fifty Guineas. This will leave Eleven hundred guineas good. But not to overcalculate I will reduce it to a thousand pounds Sterling. And throw in all the profits of the Stock and sale of lumber which is considerable in a year. There is carpenters and Coopers on the Plantation to do all the work necessary for the place.

My Georgia Plantation lays upon the Savannah River eleven Miles from the Capital of the State and all Vessels that can come over the bar of the River at the Mouth can come along side of the Plantation which saves all the expence of sending the Crops to market.[4] There is on the place a fine large dwelling house[,] an excellent Garden[,] two large Barns with complete Machinery for getting out the Rice besides the necessary building for out houses. There is under cultivation completely damed two hundred & forty acres of fine River Swamp which will bear planting a thousand years running and it is of a most excellent quality and produces three barrels to the acre.

The plantation consists of about two and twenty hundred acres and upwards. There is considerable inland swamp which may be fitted for Rice ground but it is much less profitable than the River swamp. The plantation is covered with timber fit for Lumber which the situation of the place renders valuable. The plantation formerly belonged to Lt Governor Grayham [John Graham]. It was bought for me at Seven thousand Guineas and thought a good purchace but as the grant of the State to me was only five thousand guineas the Commissioners laid the matter before the Legislature and they threw in the ballance.[5] It is a very valuable Plantation and from its fertility and situation I believe would fetch from five to Eight thousand guineas. It will produce annually five hundred Casks of Rice which will amount to twelve hundred & fifty guineas.[6] Less than one hundred Negroes including big and little will cultivate this place. The produce will pay the interest of the money necessary to stock & improve the plantation and leave a ballance upon the most Moderate computation of Seven hundred pounds Sterling to pay off the principle advancd for stocking it.

The grant that was made me by North Carolinia consists of twenty five thousand Acres, it is located upon Tennessee River not far from Cumberland River both of which communicates with the Ohio.[7] The Land is all surveyed and plot[t]ed and is of an excellent quallity as I am informed by those that have been upon it. I can give little information of the real value of this property. But from the great number of Settlers crouding back it is very growing property. Land is sold now in that neighbourhood from one to three dollars an acre. But the value of back lands will greatly depend upon the Government which finally prevails in America. I am confident I could sell it at this time for half a dollar an acre for the best security and upon interest.

I have a plantation laying upon the Pasaick [i.e., Passaic] River near Newark [N.J.] with some Wood and Salt Meadow Lots belonging to it, the whole of which is estimated at about a thousand pounds Sterling rather more than less. The plantation formerly belonged to Mr Booth.[8] Upon the borders of the North [i.e., Hudson] River directly opposite to Claverack [N.Y.] I have about three thousand acres of Land which[,] as Land was sold at the same place and of the same kind last year[,] it is worth upwards of one thousand pounds Sterling.[9] Besides these I have a plantation in Rhode Island worth from one thousand to fifteen hundred pounds Sterling including the Stock upon it.[10] The United States owes me from Sixteen to eighteen thousand dollars for pay & commutation. There is owing me on Bond about nine thousand pound Sterling.[11] Besides these I have some stocks in trade. They are now of no great value tho once considerable.[12] Out of these I owe Eight thousand Dollars. The far greater part of which was for purchases made last year for my Southern estate.[13]

ADf (David Coblentz, 1973).

1. This document, or a portion of it, was probably the "inventory of my little fortune" that NG enclosed with his letter to Robert Morris of 9 January, immediately below. (In a letter to NG of 19 May, however, Morris described the enclosure as "the Estimate of your Southern Estate.")

2. On South Carolina's gift of Boone's Barony plantation to NG, see especially Hugh Rutledge to NG, 26 February 1782, above (vol. 10: 411 and n).

3. As seen in Saunders to NG, 20 October 1783, above, the plantation's 1783 crop had been disappointing.

4. On the state of Georgia's gift of Mulberry Grove plantation to NG, see especially Samuel Saltus to NG, 5 May 1782, above (vol. 11: 164 and n).

5. NG's letter to the Georgia commissioners is above, dated 16 January 1783 (vol. 12: 375). On the legislature's subsequent action, see ibid., p. 376n.

6. The value of the 1784 rice crop at Mulberry Grove was "very little more than £200." (Pierce to NG, 13 May 1785, below)

7. On North Carolina's grant of land to NG in what is now Tennessee, see Alexander Martin to NG, 24 May 1782, above (vol. 11: 239–40 and n).

8. For more about this property, see NG to Van Waggonen, 20 November 1783, above, and Power of Attorney to Jeremiah Wadsworth, 26 March 1785, below. In the summer of 1785, a prospective buyer decided that this property was overpriced at "one thousand pounds Sterling." (See NG to Wadsworth, 13 July 1785, and Wadsworth to NG, 28 July 1785, both below.)

9. As seen by the note at Power of Attorney to Wadsworth, 26 March 1785, this included land that NG owned in common with Clement Biddle.

10. On the property in Westerly, R.I., see also Christopher Greene to NG, 26 March, below.

11. This was presumably the indenture for an undivided half share of Cumberland Island, Ga., which NG had obtained from John Banks and Ichabod Burnet the previous summer. (See note at Hyrne to Clay, 26 November 1783, above.)

12. NG referred here to his partnership with Charles Pettit and John Cox and to his shares in Barnabas Deane & Company and Jacob Greene & Company.

13. On the slaves that NG had purchased for his plantations in South Carolina and Georgia, see note at Warley to NG, 13 October 1783, above.

To Robert Morris, Superintendent of Finance

Dear Sir   Newport [R.I.] Janu[y] 9th 1784

I am favored with your letter of the 19th of December with an inclosed copy of a letter Addressed to Mess[rs] Wilhem & [Jan] Willink on the subject of a loan for me.[1] Agreeable to your desire I have enclosed you as exact an inventory of my little fortune as I can.[2] In doing this you must be sensible I speak more from information than experience of the value and produce of my Southern estate.[3] But the information I have is from good authority. It is from those who have had the interest under their Management. I wish not [to] deceive you or my self. My object is not to get credit for to live with splendor but to improve and increase my fortune. If I did not think my prospects were good to pay both principle and interest I would not venture upon the measure.

Since I left Philadelphia I have got letters from my Agent in Charleston [S.C.] and I find I can get my Georgia plantation stocked with good Gangs of Negroes at about £70 a head and the payments made mostly by installments if not all and those for a considerable length of time.[4]

I thought I had perfectly understood you on the subject of a loan. You advised me to contract for the Negroes and you would support me. My payments were to be made by installments and at as long periods as possible. You said you thought it was probable the Money might be had of Col Wadsworth and promised to write him without loss of time. But I did not understand that you meant [to] limit my contract to that resource alone. This would have placed the business upon such a precarious footing as would have rendered my engagements both dangerous to my self and injurious to those with whom I might contract. What I meant from what I wrote you from the City Tavern was to know how far I might value my self upon your friendship with regard to some particular directions I gave respecting the purchase of the Negroes I wanted, which was to engage a thousand or fifteen hundred pounds Sterling payable in three Months if it would make a material odds in the condition of the contract. If not to get as long payments as possible with the priviledge of paying them at any time when I might b[e] in cash. As you said nothing of an immediate advance, I thought it necessary to know how far you could assist me if the contract should be made on the special conditions I had written upon that I might be provided from some other quarter if it should be inconvenient to you.[5] I am much obliged to you[r] favorable sentiments you entertain of my principles and conduct and hope I shall never give you reason to alter them. I shall try all possible measures to bring this State into the general plan of finance but it will take time and in order to bring the thing about I believe it will be necessary to get it to pass the Assembly under a quallified sense which will be the ground work of its finally passing agreeable to the plan of Congress. Nothing more can be done than this and to urge it will defeat the whole.[6]

ADf (MiU-C). The following note was added at the foot of the draft: "Not an exact copy of this sent but in essence the same."

1. The catalog extract of Morris's letter to NG of 19 December 1783, above, does not contain the information referred to here. The enclosure—Morris's letter of that date to the Dutch firm of Wilhem and Jan Willink—reads in part:

"... the Honble Major Genl. Nathl. Greene who drove the British Troops from the Carolina's and Georgia was presented by the Government of South Carolina with some valuable Estates in that Country in reward for his faithful Services. These Estates he is now in possession of, but he wants hands to work them and has given Directions for the Purchase of a Gang of negroes for this purpose, the payments for which he expects must be made by installments or Gales at certain periods of time to be fixed in the Contract of purchase. The amount of this purchase will probably be Five thousand pounds Sterling and the first payment in part of that sum may be £1000 or £1500 Sterling and to be made within a pretty short space of time, the other payments at distant periods. I know it will be necessary that you should be informed of the value of the Estate and negroes to be given in Security, the quantity of produce to be raised annually and the exact periods and Quantum of each payment, all these shall follow. The present Letter is intended to ask, whether it will suit you to advance the Sum wanted by paying bills to be drawn upon you when necessary; provided the Plantation and Negroes are of Double the value or more than Double; and that the Rice and Indico made annually on the Estate is shipped to your address untill the principal and Interest shall be fully replaced or paid. The Interest to be six per Cent per annum and the usual Commissions on the Sales of the Goods consigned to you. Genl. Greene is a brave Soldier, but that is no great recommendation in many matters, but Gentlemen he is an Honest, Prudent, active and Sensible man who is very desirous of improving his Fortune for the benefit of his Family and whose utmost Industry will be stimulated to pay the Debt the soonest that is possible in order that he may enjoy the Fruits of the Estate himself, and even when the Debt is paid, you will probably continue to receive the consignments as I am persuaded that your Management will entitle you to his Friendship. You may impower any Person you think proper to take the Securities and see that they are of sufficient Value and as your Attorney, to see that the crops are annually Shipped to your address. If you are not particularly connected in Charles Town the House of Robert Hazelhurst & Co. in which I am interested will be ready to serve you, and I hope and expect that whatever that House may undertake will be executed most faithfully. When you reflect that your money will be safe, the Interest 6 percent and the Commission on the Sales as well as on any supplies you may send out for the Estate will be considerable, I think you will find this object worthy of your Attention because I am told that money may be obtained in Holland on Security like yours on the Spot; at three to four percent. I believe that Genl. Greene's Estate was valued at Ten Thousand Guineas during the war and the value is much enhanced by the Peace to this will be added the value of the negroes, these you may say are liable to Mortality which is true, but I believe Negroes on these Estates encrease by natural population faster than"

The incomplete copy of this letter (probably the copy that Morris sent to NG) ends with "than." (MiU-C; the letter is also printed in Morris, *Papers*, 8: 824–25.) Morris discussed the status of his request to the Willinks in letters to NG of 19 May and 12 and 17 July, all below. Portions of their reply are printed in a note at the letter of 12 July. NG was not able to obtain a loan from the Dutch firm. (Ibid.)

2. The "inventory" is immediately above.

3. In the draft, the words from "I speak" through "experience" are an interlineation.

4. See above, Penman to NG, 1 October 1783 and 4 December 1783.

5. As noted at NG to Mifflin, 3 November 1783, above, NG met with Morris several times about financial matters while he was in Philadelphia. Neither NG's letter to Morris from City Tavern in Philadelphia nor any letter from Morris to Jeremiah Wadsworth about this matter has been found. For the terms that Morris had suggested to the Willinks, see note 1, above.

6. For background, see Morris to NG, 19 December 1783. On the Rhode Island legislature's rejection of the congressional revenue proposal, see NG to Morris, 3 July, below.

To La Caze & Mallet

Gentlemen   Providence [R.I.] January 14th 1784

Mess[rs] Joseph & William Rusel of this place presented me with a protest made on a set of bills drew by Baron Glaubeck in Charleston [S.C.] and said to be indorsed by me.[1] I did indorse a sett of bills but whether these are the same I am not yet certain. At the time the Baron was represented to me as a man of family and property but I found afterwards he was a great vilian.[2] And I believe it was an agreement between him and the drawer to defraud me of the money for the drawer did not give one half the sum of the bills.[3] But whether I have any remedy is uncertain. However as I indorsed the bills without fee or reward I am persuaded you will not think it either just or generous to exact either damages or interest and if time can be had [for] any further relief I must beg your interposition. As I have no prospects of ever getting a farthing of the drawer I think the drawer ought not to have more than he actually advanced and the interest thereon and what will pay him for the trouble he has been at in the business. Permit me to solicit your kind offices in the matter to relieve me as far as possible from this embarassing affair.[4] I am Gentlemen Your Most Obed[t] humble Ser[t]   N GREENE

ADfS (MiU-C).

1. See Joseph and William Russell to NG, 29 December 1783, and NG's reply of 4 January, both above.

2. See above, NG to Glaubeck, 16 February 1783 (vol. 12: 449), and NG to Morris, 3 June 1783.

3. As noted at the Russells' letter to NG of 29 December 1783, the "drawer" was Jean Jacques Boyer, a French merchant.

4. It appears from NG's letter to the Marquis de Lafayette of 24 March, below, that the Philadelphia firm of La Caze & Mallet did allow NG to pursue this matter. However, NG wrote Washington on 29 August, below, that he expected "to loose a thousand dollars having endorsed his [i.e., Glaubeck's] bills and had them to settle."

*   *   *

¶ [FROM OTHO H. WILLIAMS, Baltimore, Md., 14 January 1784.[1] He writes about "an affair, which when we last parted, lay nearest to my Heart."[2] NG had "commanded" him not to report "any thing desponding" in regard to this matter, but although Williams believed that the young woman's "persevering unequivocal attachment," her "public declarations, never to be the wife of any other man," and their "private interviews, clandestine correspondence and personal endearments" were "incontestible proofs of a sincere affection," he was mistaken. He continues: "The apostacy of the fascinating Sophia astonishes every body, even her obdurate, malevolent, mother hardly yet relaxes her tyranical severity lest her daughter may be practising a deception, at which she is the most accomplished of any Girl in the World; Perhaps no age or Country every [i.e., ever] produced so singular an instance of infidelity." Recounting at length the painful tale of his rejection, Williams asserts: "Nothing can compensate for the wretchedness to which I have been wantonly exposed. I have suffered the extremity of mental misery and am convinced that the smallest exaggeration of my distress would have produced a sort of insane felicity 'which none but madmen know.' " Although "the capricious Girl is universally condemned for her unparalleled conduct," that is "no consolation" to him.[3] He asks NG to "Tell my good M^{rs} G not to pity me."[4] He does not "think less favorably" of women than he did before this disastrous affair, but he wonders if "Kosciuszko will be petrified at all this if he hears it." Kosciuszko promised to be in Baltimore "a month ago" but has not been seen there yet.[5] Williams wishes NG and his family "happy lives and a glorious immortality." ADfS (MdHi) 5 pp.]

1. Williams apparently did not send this letter until mid-March. (Williams to NG, 15 March, below)

2. NG had seen Williams in Baltimore in September 1783. (NG's Journal, 26 September 1783, above)

3. "The fascinating Sophia" has not been identified. Concerning his rejection, Williams later wrote NG that he was "exercising all my philosophy to recover that happy indifference which used to set me at ease with all the World." (Williams to NG, 15 March)

4. Williams again remarked about CG's opinion in ibid.

5. Williams and others had teased Thaddeus Kosciuszko about his aversion to marriage. According to his biographer, Kosciuszko decided to visit NG in Rhode Island at this time rather than go to Baltimore. (See Haiman, *Kosciuszko*, p. 160, and Littlefield to NG, 22 March, below.)

¶ [TO GOVERNOR WILLIAM GREENE OF RHODE ISLAND.[1] From Providence, R.I., 19 January 1784. NG offers him, "with no small pleasure," an honorary membership in the Rhode Island Society of the Cincinnati. The governor's acceptance will "give pleasure to every officer; and to no one more than to my self." Asks him to reply "when it is convenient."[2] ALS (RHi) 2 pp.]

1. Similar letters, also dated 19 January, were apparently sent to Jabez Bowen, William Bradford, and Henry Ward. (MiU-C; transcript incorrectly dated 19 June) Their replies have not been found.

2. NG was president of the Rhode Island chapter of the Society of the Cincinnati. (Varnum to NG, 17 December 1783, above) The Continental officers who founded the Society made provision for admitting "honorary members" who did not otherwise qualify for membership. Those selected were to be "eminent for their abilities and patriotism, whose views may be directed to the same laudable objects with those of the Cincinnati." Honorary members were admitted "for their own lives only" and could not pass membership to their sons. ("The Original Institution of the Cincinnati as Signed by the Members of the Rhode Island State Society," Society of the Cincinnati records, on deposit, RHi) William Greene's reply is below, dated 1 March.

* * *

From the Freemen of the Town of Providence, Rhode Island[1]

Sir   Providence [R.I.] Jany 21. 1784.
The Address made you by the General Assembly, at their First Session after your Arrival within this your Native State, afforded us a very Sensible Pleasure, as it expressed the Just and grateful Sentiments we entertain of the Eminent and very essential service You have Rendered your Country, during the Course of a Long and arduous War: in which its most important Interests were so deeply involved and which has Terminated so Gloriously to the United States.

Although Represented in the General Assembly and of Course included in that Address we cannot resist the Inclination we feel, on this First Visit with which you have honored us, of expressing the Peculiar Pride and satisfaction we feel from the High Rank in Military Fame which the World in Justice to your superior Talents has placed a person who was born among us and whose First Military Appointed was born in this State.

We Beg Leave to Renew with great Sincerity the Tribute of Gratitude, and of the most affectionate Regard which ha[s] lately been paid you through our Representatives.

By the Unanimous Order, and in Behalf of the Freemen of the Town of Providence legally assembled in Town Meeting, at the State House on Wednesday, January 21. 1784.[2]   THEODORE FOSTER[3]

Cy (RP-Ar).
1. The Rhode Island General Assembly's address to NG is above, dated 26 December 1783.
2. The "Freemen" of the "Town of Providence" had named "Colonel William Russell, John Innes Clark, Esq; Colonel Joseph Nightingale, Colonel John Mathewson, Colonel William Barton, and Theodore Foster, Esq" a committee to present this address to NG "in Behalf of the Town." (*Providence Gazette*, 24 January)
3. Foster was the town clerk. (Vol. 1: 93n, above)

To the Freemen of the Town of Providence, Rhode Island

Gentlemen   [Newport, R.I., between 21 and 24 January 1784][1]
Nothing can be more grateful to our Feelings than Repeated Proofs of Esteem and Affection; and mo⟨re⟩ Especially when offered by those we hold in High Estimation. Yo⟨ur⟩ Polite Address Flatters both my Pride and Friendship. It wi⟨ll⟩ always afford Me Matter of Triumph to Meet the Confidence of a People so remarkable for Private Virtue and Public Zeal.

Nor do I wish to Suppress those Lively Emotions I feel that my Conduct is thought an Honor to the State, by the Inhabitants in General and my Friends in particular. And it adds no less to my Happine⟨ss⟩ that my Small Services have contributed to the Safety of my Friends than their having some consideration in this great Revolution, the bless⟨ings⟩ of which I hope we shall be as Careful to preserve as Zealous to obtain. I am Gentlemen with the Greatest Respect your Most Obedient Humble Servant NATH^l GREENE

Cy (RP-Ar). The text in angle brackets was taken from the *Providence Gazette,* 24 January.

1. The Address of the Freemen of the Town of Providence to NG, immediately above, was written on 21 January. NG's undated reply was printed in the *Providence Gazette* of 24 January.

From Charles Pettit

Dear Sir [Philadelphia, after 21 January 1784][1]
    The Captain who brought me your Favour of the 5th of December, being alarmed by the appearances of Winter, hastened away sooner than he gave me Reason to expect, & without giving me Notice, which is the Reason I must assign for neglecting to write to you by him.[2] I had previously found however that he could not take the Carriage otherwise than on Deck, & my Judgment concurred with Mr Quarrier's that the Body must not by any means be trusted to the Dangers of such a Situation. Since that, no Opportunity has been in my Power. Mr Quarrier tells me it has been for some Time so nearly ready that he requires no farther Time on any Call than a Day or two to case it properly; but it will require a Hatchway of at least 4 feet 9 Inches to take it in.[3]
    I have had much serious Negociation with [Robert] Morris on the Subject of the Balance stated to be in my Hands on Acc^t of the Bills rec^d from you by Major Burnet. The whole of that Bal^l is £3229.12. The balance due to me on the Shot & Shells which he agrees to pay, will be about £1200. This I have proposed to deduct from the former & that the residue, wch will be about £2000, shall be charged to Genl Greene as QMG to be accounted for, as was usual in monies granted to the Department. But the Officers of the Treasury have charged the whole Balance of £3229.12 together with Int[eres]^t from Octr 1781, to the Acc^t of Mr Banks as Contractor. I have positively objected to any Charge whatever against Mr Banks on this Account.[4] Much of our Negociation has been in writing, and were it not for the Expence of Postage I would send you Copies of the whole; I mean however to inclose a Copy of one of my letters wch will shew you fully the Footing I have rested the Dispute upon, and it is Ground I mean to adhere to.[5] Mr Morris's personal Behaviour has seemed to wear a friendly appearance, & his writing, all Circumstances considered, is at least civil as to the Manner & Expression tho' it carries some Sentiments farther than I have thought necessary on his Part. To the letter I now send you a Copy of, he proposes to

furnish me with the money in dispute if I will give him a Note payable in three Months, then apply to Congress for their Decision & if that should be in my favor, the Note to be given up, if not that I pay the money. This I have refused as it would place me on a worse Footing than I stand at present, & have again requested a Settlement of Mr Banks's Acc^t free from any Connection with this Business—and there it rests at present.[6]

I wrote to Mr Morris on the 1st & 18th of November, stating what I thought legal Claims & mentioning also various other Considerations which I thought deserved Notice & might have weight in some way or other. He invited me to a Conferance in which he perceived I was so deeply affected with some Circumstances that it touched his Feelings & he seemed willing to comply with my Desire if the Business were solely in his Hands; but the Auditors & Comptroller were to make the Report, & he could not undertake to *direct* them, tho' he recommended to me to apply to the Comptroller & promised himself to speak to him. In the Course of this Conversation he intimated that perhaps the surest way would be for you to take the Matter on yourself, & at once say that the Money was transferred to the Quarter Master's Department & boldly [hold?] it for that purpose, & intimated that he would do so were it his Case. I told him (& so I afterwards told the Comptroller) that I was authorised to say you would assent to it's being charged as I had desired; but that I had wished to keep you otherwise out of sight in the Business, for that neither you nor Major Burnet had the least Knowledge of any Intention to make this Appropriation till long after the Transaction which put the Money into my Hands; but that I was fixed in my Determination to hold the Money even if it should oblige me to lean more on you than I wished in order to [do] it. Matters being thus Circumstanced I must request of you to bear me out in the Determination I have expressed if your Aid should be necessary. I shall keep the Water smooth if possible, but I must hold my anchoring Ground if possible however hard the Wind may blow.[7]

I communicated your letter to Col. Cox respecting the Egharbour Concerns. At first he was unwilling to allow that any money rested in his Hands on that Account. After getting him & M^r [Joseph] Ball together & talking the Matter over, I convinced him there was a considerable Sum. For my own Part, however, I saw Reasons which induced me to reduce the Claim considerably, but told him I could not answer for your coming into the same Opinion. It appears that he has not benefited by all that we have lost in that Business & therefore I was willing to reduce my Claim to what he had actually received. He desired me to settle the Matter at what I should think right on the whole; but I told him I could not give up for you as much as I would for myself without your Consent, & there it now rests. I imagine there may be 600 or £700 due to each of us on the Plan I should agree to, but I have not made the Calculations exactly.[8]

Our Navigation has been stopped since about Christmas; but a Thaw is now at work which bids fair to open it.[9]

My Affectionate Regards with those of the Family, attend you & M[rs] Greene, with a particular Regard to George, who I hope is gaining due Improvement.[10] M[r] Reed left the Capes for England the 21st of December.[11] Believe me, Dear Sir, affectionately Your most hum[b] Serv[t]

CHA[S] PETTIT

RCS (MiU-C).

1. The docketing reads: "M[r] Pettit 1784"; above that, someone has added, presumably at a later time: "say 6th March." This letter, however, is clearly the recent one that Pettit briefly recapitulated in his to NG of 9 February, below. In the present letter, Pettit enclosed a copy of one he had written to Robert Morris on 20 January, and he also referred to Morris's reply, which was dated 22 January. (The copy of Pettit's letter to Morris is at MiU-C; that letter and Morris's reply to Pettit are also printed in Morris, *Papers*, 9: 43–46, 53–54.) The present letter, then, cannot have been written before 22 January and obviously was written before 9 February.

2. NG's letter to Pettit of 5 December 1783 has not been found.

3. The "Carriage" was a chariot that CG had ordered while she was in Philadelphia the previous summer. (Pettit to NG, 26 July 1783, and NG to CG, 4 August 1783, both above) A vessel suitable for transporting the chariot could not be found until June. (Pettit to NG, 26 June, below) Quarrier, whose first name is not known, was apparently a carriage-maker in Philadelphia. (Smith, *Letters*, 20: 438–39)

4. NG had ordered the now-deceased Burnet to leave the bills of exchange with Pettit in late 1781, instead of turning them over to Morris. (See note at Pettit to NG, 26 July 1783, above.) In addition to the two letters referred to in note 1, above, the correspondence on this subject that has been found includes a letter from Morris to Pettit of 15 January. (Morris, *Papers*, 9: 31–33; see also Morris's diary entries for 31 May 1783, 19 September 1783, 14 and 25 November 1783, and 15 January 1784. [Ibid., vol. 8: 136, 531, 762, 779; vol. 9: 30]) The "Shot & Shells" were produced for the government at the Batsto Iron Works, the owners of which had included the partnership of Pettit, NG, and John Cox. NG, however, had recently assigned to Pettit his interest in the Batsto business and most of the compensation that was still owed him for his services as quartermaster general. (NG's agreement with Pettit is above, dated 8 November 1783.) Morris, in his letter to Pettit of 22 January, appears to have given conditional approval to Pettit to deduct the amount owed to him for shot and shells from the bills that Burnet had given him, if Pettit would agree to apply the remaining balance, at least temporarily, against the amount still owed to the government by Pettit's client John Banks. (Morris, *Papers*, 9: 53–54 and n) Morris had previously explained to Pettit his reasoning in regard to Banks and the bills:

"Bills of Exchange were remitted to the Paymaster of the Southern Department *for the current Service*. The Paymaster delivered some of these Bills to Major Burnett *for the same Service*. Major Burnett placed these Bills in your Hands *to be sold*. Upon your Account of the Sales there remains a Balance of eight thousand six hundred and twelve Dollars and twenty four ninetieths. You retain this Ballance alledging *that the Public owe you Money for Services and Expenditures under Quarter Master General Greene whose accounts are yet unsettled*, and you desire that the Balance in your Hands be passed to account of that Quarter Master General. But as you was agent of Majr. Burnett in selling the Bills and are now Attorney to Mr. Banks the Contractor for supplying Rations in South Carolina and Georgia, in which Contract Major Burnett was interested, the Officers of the Treasury have carried that Balance to the Debit of the Contract by which Means there appears a Balance still due to the United States as is above mentioned [$2,715 88/90]. It must be remembered that the Bills in question were paid in Europe out of Funds expressly granted to the United States for the current Expenditures."

(Morris to Pettit, 15 January, Morris, *Papers*, 9: 31–32) Replying to Morris in the letter of 20 January that he enclosed with the present one to NG, Pettit reiterated his own claim to, and need for, the balance and argued that Burnet, in conveying the bills of exchange to him, had been acting as "the Servant of General Greene." Thus, he maintained, the disposition of the bills had been subject only to NG's orders. (Morris, *Papers*, 9: 45) Morris responded: "You desire that a certain sum of Money in your hands be passed to your Credit and to the Debit of General Greene as Quarter Master General. I do not think I can with Propriety order this to be done. You say that an application to Congress will not do[,] for that their Order would come too late to save you from Bills which are soon to fall due. I will do all which I can for your releif. If therefore you will give your Note with a sufficient Indorser payable in three Months for the Sum now due [from John Banks] after deducting the amount of the Shot and Shells and pay the Discount at the Bank I will get it discounted and you shall have the Money." Pettit could then apply to Congress for "the Sum in Question," and if he succeeded in obtaining an order for it, Morris would "pay the Note[,] and if not you must provide for it." (Morris to Pettit, 22 January, Morris, *Papers*, 9: 53–54) As seen in the present letter, Pettit rejected this proposal, and Morris continued to treat the balance in Pettit's hands as a charge against Banks's account. (Pettit to NG, 6 May, below; as seen there, Morris issued warrants to Pettit for the "Iron" account but would not allow him "to apply them to a reduction of the Balance stated.")

5. See notes 1 and 4, above.

6. This request to Morris has not been found.

7. Neither letter has been found. According to an entry in his diary for 25 November 1783, Morris "sent for Mr. Pettit in consequence of his Letter of the 18th Instant and told him that I will enable Mr. Hodgdon to compleat his [i.e., Pettit's] Iron Contract, but that the Comptroller having deducted the Sum of £3,200 from Mr. Bank[s]'s account I cannot pay more than the Balance which he has Certified, that if he consents to alter the Certificate and thinks proper to Charge the £3,200 to Genl. Greene whom I think accountable for it I shall be content and promise to speak with the Comptroller on the Subject. I also promised him payments of the Money due as fast as possible." (Morris, *Papers*, 8: 779; see also note 4, above.) Samuel Hodgdon was the commissary of military stores. As a charge against NG as quartermaster general, the £3,200 would have been deducted from the amount of NG's compensation as quartermaster general that Pettit was seeking to retain.

8. On Cox's role in the partnership's privateering investments at Egg Harbor, N.J., see Pettit to NG, first letter of 5 January 1780 and 11 June 1780, both above. (Vol. 5: 241 and n; vol. 6: 12 and n) In his agreement with Pettit of 8 November 1783, NG had retained his interest in the Egg Harbor "Concerns." For further developments, see NG to Pettit, 22 April, and Pettit to NG, 18 May, both below.

9. As seen in Pettit to NG, 8 March, below, the Delaware River continued to be frozen. As noted there and at NG to Jacob Greene, 8 January, above, the winter of 1783–84 was one of the coldest on record. Other correspondents of NG's also mentioned the severe conditions. (See, for example, Pendleton to NG, immediately below.)

10. George was NG's and CG's son George Washington Greene.

11. "The Capes" were the capes of the Delaware River. On Joseph Reed's trip abroad, see also NG to Mifflin, 12 November 1783, above.

*   *   *

¶ [FROM NATHANIEL PENDLETON, Charleston, S.C., 30 January 1784. Has not heard from NG "since your letter to my brother."[1] Assumes that NG has been "long since" with his family; wishes him "a joy infinitely more grateful and lasting, in an Affectionate heart, than the glory of Conquest, or the Admiration of the Multitude." Congratulates NG "on the late public events, not so much on account of the distinguished part you had in producing them, as on account of the approbation of your country."[2] Pendleton has "seen so many instances, wherein ingratitude and even reproaches have been the retribution of public Services," that he considers "that man to be uncommonly Fortunate, who meets with tolerable justice in the public estimation." He has heard that "Mrs Greene has not entirely recovered her health," but he hopes she will "accompany" NG to the South.[3] The "Ladies" in Charleston "are led to believe she has paid them high encomiums to the Northward, and that she speaks warmly in favor of Carolina"; although Pendleton believes that "pride, rather than Vanity," is their "ruling passion," they "appear to be highly flattered" by this. Mr. Marshall's "exit," which NG has probably heard about, has put an end to Pendleton's "Apprehension of being embroiled again account of M^{rs} W–," whom he has not seen since his return to Charleston. "Mrs Marshall and M^{rs} W– are now the most intimate friends immaginable—Confidants; and this Circumstance has opperated so much in favor of the latter, that she goes to public places and is almost intirely restored to her former glory." Pendleton has "only to regret, in that whole Affair, the report circulated by Marshall, & which had made unfavorable impressions in many places where I wished it should not," but he hopes that "a little time will efface them."[4]

The legislature is now "sitting," but remarkably cold weather and "floods of rain" have "made the Members so backward in coming down from the back Country that they have but just made a house." They have not taken any action, and "What they may do is uncertain,[5] but as Maj^r B.–r is at the head of the Committee of ways and means; and as he has been for some time studying the *Wealth of Nations*, we may expect the *budget* will produce money; but whether it will be for the benefit of the United States, this State, or individuals," Pendleton leaves it for NG "to determine from your knowledge of the people in general, & that Gentleman in particular."[6] There is now "a rage for all kinds of reformation, particularly, in the System of jurisprudence. One Committee are to be Appointed to digest the Laws, and form the whole into one general Code, and to report in two years, while others are appointed to frame such Laws as are immediately necessary, particularly an Alien-Bill."[7] In regard to the alien bill, Pendleton's brother and "M^r E: Rutledge," who are usually "like oyl and water," are "in the same vessel."[8] Pendleton has been informed that NG will have "less than 300 Barrells of Rice" from his plantation; he does not know whether [Roger Parker] Saunders "has sold any or whether he may not have informed" NG about this. The price of rice "is from 13 & Six, 14 & Sixpence a hundred," and "Indigo is low."[9] Saunders has "bought ten Negroes from Doct^r Olyphant of Boons gang, for which he gave £1000 Sterling" on NG's account.[10] Pendleton adds: "Negroes sell most amazingly high." NG has "no doubt" heard of "the death of poor Major Hyrne," who "indiscreetly fatigued himself by run[n]ing to Seven places on the Morning of Maj^r Pierce's wedding & just as he was going to embark for John's Island, he was seized with a kind of Apoplexy & died in four hours, without having uttered above one or two words." Hyrne "was much lamented by every body" in Charleston, and Pendleton knows that NG will "regret the loss of a friend, & a man of honor and Virtue." As "Poor Burnet too, had scarsely fixed himself at the Havannah, before he went off," there have been "serious changes among the Gentlemen who composed your family." Pendleton remarks. "To what different fates were two of them reserved! One to die by a fit, & the other [i.e., Pierce] to be married in the same day."[11]

Pendleton has "very much withdrawn" himself "from Company, in order to attend the Law more closely," but he is "almost tempted sometimes to despair of succeeding in the practice in this Country. Those Gentlemen of that profession who have established themselves, are secured no less by the influence of their extensive commissions than by their abilities, and their popularity; so that a stranger, labouring under many accidental disadvantages, tho' of tolerable genius, would find innumerable difficulties to encounter, & many mortifications to feel, so that it would be a considerable time probably not til the present Lawyers had retired from the business, before he would find even a small compensation for his labor and expence." These difficulties have "not prevented but rather increased my application," though they have caused him "much pain."[12] He wishes "most ardently" to see NG and "avail" himself of NG's "Advice," which he has "found so just, and received so kindly on all occasions."[13] He has thought that if he could "retain a place in the Army," in the grade to which he was recently promoted by a resolution of Congress, he could "enjoy more real happiness, because [of] more independence than I have at present."[14] He adds: "I prize personal Independence at so high a rate, that I would exchange any thing for it. The value of this like all other Advantages can only be ascertained by the loss of it. I would not feel the pain I have lately felt on this account, to acquire the fame of Cicero; and I see no other probable period for its termination, but by an Appointment in the Army to be kept on foot." He is "already much indebted to your goodness," but if NG could arrange a suitable appointment for him—one that would be "preferable to the uncertain consequence of depending upon the Law"—he asks NG to "secure it." If, "after some time," Pendleton should discover his "prospects" in South Carolina to be "more agreeable," he could then resign the appointment to anyone whom NG wished. If an appointment such as this cannot be secured now, "it will be impossible hereafter." A "Military Appointment, in time of peace would afford much leisure for those kinds of Study which most delight" Pendleton, and if an "honorable Staff Appointment were added" to his "Commission, it would afford ease, plenty, and independence." However, if NG is "of a contrary opinion," or "cannot make any solicitation," except to someone to whom he "would not wish to be obliged," he should be "silent." Pendleton is not sure about the "propriety" of obtaining an appointment, nor would he "accept of any benefit, to which the dignity of your character would in the smallest degree be a sacrifice."[15] He asks NG to "present me most Cordially and affectionately" to CG and hopes "she will remember every thing of me but my faults." For NG, he wishes "health & quiet" and that "honor will attend you without my prayer tho' none would pray for their increase with more Ardour or sincerity." In a postscript, he reports: "M͏ʳ Daniel Huger has parted with his wife (for which cause I know not). She lives with her mother, and he has become a factor to sell rice & supply Country Gentlemen with goods, upon Commission. He is more Capricious than an old maid."[16] RCS (MiU-C) 6 pp.]

1. NG's letter to Henry Pendleton has not been found.

2. In his comments congratulating NG, Pendleton was referring to the definitive peace treaty (see note at Lafayette to NG, 8 September, above) and to the resolution of Congress praising NG for his contributions to the American victory. (Thomson to NG, 18 October 1783, above)

3. Since returning to Newport, R.I., from South Carolina the previous August, CG had suffered from several health complaints that may or may not have been related to her pregnancy.

4. James Marshall had died suddenly "of a fit." (Pendleton to NG, 4 December 1783, above) "Mrs. W–" was Jane Olyphant Walter, whom Marshall had accused of having an extramarital affair with Pendleton. (On the subsequent duel between her husband and Pendleton, see above, NG to Wayne, 26 June 1783; NG to Williams, 2 July 1783; and NG to CG, 7 August 1783.) By April 1784, Pendleton believed he was close to becoming engaged to "the madman's widow," as he referred to Mrs. Marshall in a postscript to his letter to NG of 18 April, below. However, in a letter of 10 July, below, he explained at some length that she had broken off their relationship. In the late summer or early fall of 1785, Pendleton married Susan Bard, the daughter of Dr. John and Susannah Vakelleau Bard, in Savannah, Ga. (SCHGM 19 [1918]: 175; http://www.geocities.com/janet_ariciu/Pendleton.html; see also Pendleton to NG, 23 September 1785, below.)

5. The South Carolina legislature convened on 27 January. (S.C., House of Representatives, Journals, 1783–84, p. 376) On its activities during that session, see also Pendleton to NG, 3 February, below.

6. Pierce Butler had been named to head the lower house's ways and means committee. Butler took an active interest in economic policy, both in the legislature and later in the Constitutional Convention. (Biog Directory of S.C. House, 3: 110–11; S.C., House of Representatives, Journals, 1783–84, p. 378) Adam Smith's An Inquiry Into the Nature and Causes of the Wealth of Nations was first published in 1776. (Columbia Encyc.)

7. A committee appointed in February 1783 "to Consider and report to the House the most proper method they can Devise to be pursued in Order to obtain as speedily as is consistant with the importance of the subject, a proper digest of the Laws necessary for the good government of this State, and reduced as far as practicable to as small a Compass as the Happiness and Convenience of the People . . . may require," reported to the legislature on 29 January. (S.C. House of Representatives, Journals, 1783–84, pp. 139, 391; see also Pendleton to NG, 3 February.) On the "alien bill" and other legislation taken up or passed by the legislature, see Pendleton to NG, 18 April, below.

8. The members of the committee appointed on 28 January "to revise the Acts of Assembly respecting making Aliens Citizens of the State" were Pendleton's brother Henry, Edward Rutledge, and Charles C. Pinckney. (S.C., House of Representatives, Journals, 1783–84, p. 381)

9. On the shortfall in NG's rice crop at Boone's Barony plantation, see above, Saunders to NG, 20 October 1783, and Hyrne to NG, 26 November–4 December 1783.

10. In a letter to NG of 3 December 1783, above, Saunders had reported that David Olyphant was willing to sell these slaves.

11. The men who served as aides to NG were his military "family." Edmund M. Hyrne had been deputy adjutant general and commissary of prisoners in the Southern Department, as well as an aide, and had traveled to Philadelphia with NG the previous summer. (For a biographical note on Hyrne, see above, vol. 6: 594–95n.) Only in his mid-thirties at the time of his death, he had suffered an apparent stroke in late 1781. (Hyrne to NG, 6 December 1781, above [vol. 10: 9]) Another of NG's aides, William Pierce, was married on

11 December. (Pendleton to NG, 4 December 1783) Former aide Ichabot Burnet had recently died in Cuba. (NG to Pierce, 15 October 1783, above)

12. Pendleton, who was originally from Virginia, soon decided to establish a law practice in Savannah, telling NG in a letter of 18 April, below, that it would have taken two years to be "admitted to practice" in South Carolina. His initial reception by members of the Georgia bar was not encouraging, however, and he returned to Virginia and gained admission to the bar there before moving to Georgia in "the Fall" of 1784. (Pendleton to NG, 10 July, below)

13. Before NG returned to Charleston in the summer, Pendleton wrote him to express regrets that he would not be able to see him "till September or October." (Ibid.)

14. In a resolution of 30 September, Congress had extended to all army officers under the rank of major general "a brevet commission one grade higher than their present rank, having respect to their seniority." (*JCC*, 25: 633) Pendleton, a captain, had thus been promoted to the brevet rank of major.

15. It is not known whether NG attempted to "secure a military appointment" for Pendleton, who asked again, in his letter of 3 February, for "Advice on the Subject of an establishment in the Army." By April, Pendleton had made up his mind to become a lawyer—unless his idea of a military appointment should meet with NG's "approbation & be practicable." (Pendleton to NG, 18 April)

16. Daniel Huger (1742–99) owned a plantation in the parish of St. Thomas & St. Dennis and a house in Charleston, as well as a large tract of land in Craven County. He had served in the South Carolina legislature during the war, and on the privy council. His wife, whom he married in 1772, was the former Sabina Elliott. Nothing is known about the separation that Pendleton reported here, but the *Biographical Directory of the South Carolina House of Representatives* notes that "[t]hroughout his life Huger had a reputation as a hothead. In 1785 he fought and wounded Charles Cotesworth Pinckney in a duel." (*Biog. Directory of S.C. House*, 2: 340–41)

¶ [FROM THE REVEREND WILLIAM GORDON, Jamaica Plain, Mass., 31 January, 1784.[1] He did not go with "Col Henley" to Newport, R.I., because there would have been no "supply for my pulpit in case of staying[,] together with the uncertainty of the snow's continuing to assis[t] us upon our return."[2] He hopes to visit NG "within a month, unless unexpectedly prevented." Asks if NG will "remain upon the present spot till April"; if so, Gordon may delay the trip "rather longer to prevent any inconvenience that may otherwise offer."[3] Gen. [Henry] Knox "& family" were all well when Gordon dined with them, and he hopes that NG and his family "are in the like happy circumstances."[4] Sends his respects to CG. RCS (MiU-C) 1 p.]

1. On Gordon, who was writing a history of the war and had asked NG for assistance, see above, vol. 10: 439n.

2. David Henley was a partner with Samuel A. Otis in the Boston firm of Otis & Henley. (Vol. 4: 13n, above) On business matters that were probably discussed during his visit with NG, see Henley to NG, 10 April, below. It appears from what Gordon wrote here that there had been enough snow on the ground for sleighing.

3. Gordon visited NG in Newport in March. (Knox to NG, 14–18 March, and NG to Knox, 25 March, both below)

4. Knox and his wife, the former Lucy Flucker, lived in Dorchester, near Boston. (See note at Knox to NG, 15 February, below.)

¶ [FROM NATHANIEL PENDLETON, [Charleston, S.C., January 1784?].[1] Major [Robert] Forsyth is expected there shortly, and Pendleton "will get him to give a State of what he knows."[2] He will "also write to Captain [John] Meals."[3]

Mr. [James?] Miller "was in Town at Christmas," but Pendleton did not see him and "cant therefore say anything particularly of the Crop."[4] RCS (MiU-C) 1 p.]

1. The place, month, and year were conjectured from the contents.

2. See Forsyth to NG, 24 February, below.

3. On NG's concerns with Meals, formerly the Southern Army's assistant commissary general of purchases, see Meals to NG, 30 September, below.

4. "The Crop" was probably NG's rice crop at Boone's Barony plantation. Henry Collins Flagg wrote NG on 7 February, below, that Mr. Miller had sent "some papers" to NG.

* * *

From Nathaniel Pendleton

Dear General   [Charleston, S.C.] February 3[d] 1784.[1]

Captain Allebone's delaying a day or two Affords me an opportunity of giving you some farther accounts of the proceedings of the Assembly & other matters, which I think may be interesting to you.[2] Since writing that letter Your Letter of the 10th Ultimo to M[r] Penman has arrived, which robs me of all hope of seeing you soon.[3] From the Affection I feel, as well as the circumstances mentioned in my other Letter you will easily conceive how greatly I regret this circumstance. I must intreat you, my Dear General to give me your Advice on the Subject of an establishment in the Army, and that you will act on the occasion, as tho I had already determined to pursue it; as on this occasion I am determined to yield myself entirely to what you recommend. I Will thank you to inclose Your Letter to some of your friends, with a request they would deliver it into my own hand. My motive for this request will be obvious to you.[4]

The Little Governor met both Houses of Assembly two days ago, and delivered them an oration commonly Called a Speech, which, as it is not yet printed, I am sorry I cannot Send you. No possible description can give you any idea of the Original, One half of it at least is taken up in abuse of the Society of the Cincinnati, who in his humble Opinion will more probably "deserve a halter than a badge of Merit." He concludes his speach with the same Words that Hamlet begins his Soliloquy with; which it resembles only in being something in the Soliloquial Stile. In short he is ridiculous, tho still spoken well of, which I can account for, upon no other principal, than that as triffling abilities do not excite envy, so they do not excite any resentment. We are disposed to laugh at folly and impertenance; but the vindictive passions rise upon [i.e., up?] against pride Crimes.[5]

Three persons by a vote of Yesterday are to be appointed to revise & digest the whole System of Jurisprudence. It is determined to reduce all the Common Law into one Code, so that it may have the Sanction of an Act of Assembly, instead of immemorial usage. You, who know how much more powerfull Custom is than any written precept, will regret this Arrangement, which in my humble Opinion will introduce all that Confusion, Contention, and incertainty, which it seems expected to prevent. The persons to whom the care of this business is to be committed, are to be appointed either today, or Tomorrow, with a fee of 1800£ Sterling each, & they are to compleat the business in two Years, which will then require 12 Months constant sitting & Attention of the Assembly to examine & read three times, before it can come into use; & which I think therefore it never will.[6]

Mr J. Rutledge has just taken his Seat in the house. His abilities will procure him influence any where. Some, who envy him, think he meanly courts popularity.[7] I do not think the removal of the Seat of Government will be agitated this session.[8] All those persons whose cases of Consfiscation, were reported favorably upon, before your Departure, are to be reconsidered, by which some persons may perhaps suffer, who did not expect it.[9] M. Simons is in the Assembly.[10] Nothing has been done in favor of those who are precluded the rights of Citizenship at Elections &ca by which McQueen is more mortified than ever. He has taken a house at one Corner of the State house, where he retails Turtle & good wine with great liberality, so I leave you to guess what will be his situation before the end of the Session. He has Sold Horse Savannah for about 10,000 Guins.[11] Hamilton will Shortly be married tho the Opposition still Continues.[12] Mr Redwards [i.e., Edwards] has been dancing attendance ever since November. He is now more swainish than any Gentleman in Charleston. I think he will probably succeed.[13] Yours most truely & Affecty   PENDLETON

RCS (MiU-C).

1. Although the letter is clearly dated "February 3d," Pendleton referred in it to the South Carolina governor's speech (of 2 February) as having been given "two days ago." In a later paragraph, he also mentioned "a vote of yesterday" to appoint a legislative committee to consider a digest of the laws. That vote was taken on 4 February. Pendleton may have misdated the letter, or he may have begun it on 3 February and continued it later without indicating the dates.

2. Pendleton had also written to NG on 30 January, above. Charles Pettit wrote NG on 8 March, below, that William Allibone sailed from Charleston on 8 February. Allibone, the captain of the brig *Charleston Packet*, made frequent trips between Charleston and Philadelphia. (Saunders to NG, before 17 July 1784, below)

3. NG's letter of 10 January to James Penman has not been found. (See, however, NG to Penman, 4 January, above.)

4. In his letter of 30 January, Pendleton had asked NG for advice and / or help in regard to an appointment in the peacetime army. (See also Pendleton to NG, 18 April, below.)

5. On the speech in which Benjamin Guerard, the "Little Governor," denounced the Society of the Cincinnati, see note at Knox to NG, 10 April, below. Guerard concluded his speech with these words: "In short, upon the present Sessions entirely depends that serious question, whether, we are to be or not to be," paraphrasing the opening lines in Hamlet's well-known soliloquy, " 'To be, or not to be,' that is the 'question.' " (S.C., House of Representatives, *Journals, 1783–84*, p. 406; William Shakespeare, *Hamlet*, Act III, Scene 1, lines 56–57)

6. On the committee to digest the laws of South Carolina, see also Pendleton to NG, 30 January. The members reported on 4 February that "the Multiplicity and Confusion of the Laws" under which South Carolina was then "Governed require in the highest degree the attention of the Legislature, and that it is Essentially necessary to the future Happiness of the People, that there should be formed as speedily as possible a concise and Accurate System of Laws, founded in Principles of Liberty and Humanity, wherein public wrongs, the Rights of Persons, and the rights of things, shall be clearly, and with as much Brevity as the nature of such a work will admit of ascertained, and determined." The committee recommended "that three Gentlemen be chosen by the joint Ballot of the Senate and House of Representatives, who shall have access to all Public Records and shall within the space of Two years at farthest Compose and form such system of Laws." For their "Trouble in the Completion of this important and necessary work," the committee recommended that the three men be paid "Eighteen hundred pound Sterling each." Their "necessary expences" would also be paid by the government. (S.C., House of Representatives, *Journals, 1783–84*, p. 417) These recommendations were approved by the Assembly (ibid., p. 418), and in 1785 an act was passed "to effect a Revisal, Digest, and Publication of the Laws of the State." (*Statutes of S.C.*, 4: 659–60) A compendium—*The Public Laws of South Carolina*—was published in 1790. (Nadelhaft, *Disorders of War*, p. 112)

7. A biographical note on John Rutledge, the former delegate to Congress and governor of South Carolina, is above, vol. 10: 33–34n.

8. The "removal" of the capital from Charleston to "a more central part of the state" was first proposed at the Assembly's February 1783 session. The proposal was defeated then but was passed in 1786, and the legislature moved to Columbia in 1790. (Nadelhaft, *Disorders of War*, pp. 136–38)

9. On the February 1782 act authorizing the state of South Carolina to seize Loyalist properties, see above, vol. 10: 415n, 459n, 584–85n. The legislature voted on 31 January 1784 to empower "[t]he Committee Appointed on the Petitions of those whose Estates have been Confiscated and their persons Banished, and those Persons whose Estates have been Amerced," to "reconsider the Cases of Persons whose Petitions were heretofore favourably reported upon in either House, where they have not been finally determined upon by the Legislature." (S.C., House of Representatives, *Journals, 1783–84*, p. 395) Richard Hutson wrote NG on 5 February, immediately below: "A spirit of Clemency and Forgive[ness] towards our Political Delinquents prevails in a high degree." During the winter 1784 session, the legislature considered the petitions of scores of former Loyalists who had petitioned to have their confiscated property and their rights of citizenship restored. An act "for restoring to certain persons, therein mentioned, their estates, both real and personal, and for permitting the said persons to return to this State" was passed at the end of March. (*Statutes of S.C.*, 4: 624–26) Historian Robert Lambert has written that "[a]ltogether in that session the General Assembly removed 122 persons from the confiscation law, relieving thirty of all future penalties, amercing the estates of sixty-two at 12 percent, and amercing and disqualifying thirty others from voting or holding office for seven years. In addition, forty-seven persons were dropped from the Amercement Act." (Lambert, *South Carolina Loyalists*, p. 293)

10. Maurice Simons (1744–85) was a factor and merchant in Charleston. (*Biog. Directory of S.C. House*, 3: 652–54)

11. On John McQueen, the British-educated land speculator who had spied for the Americans during the war but was also suspected of being a Loyalist, see, for example, vol. 10: 570n, and vol. 11: 75n, above, as well as *Biog. Directory of S.C. House*, 3: 464–66. It is not known if he had been denied the right to vote when the South Carolina legislature restricted the rights of adherents to the British cause and of suspected British sympathizers, at its Jacksonborough session in February 1782. In any event, no action was taken on McQueen by name at this legislative session, although he may have been

covered by the legislation described in note 9, above; nothing more is known about his mercantile affairs in Charleston at this time. He moved to Georgia later in 1784 to pursue the timber business. (McQueen to NG, 23 May 1785, below; Chesnutt, *Laurens Papers*, 16: 593n) McQueen owned a plantation at Horse Savannah, S.C., where Henry Lee had once taken post during the war. (Vol. 10: 13n, above)

12. Maj. James Hamilton married Elisabeth Harleston in June. (*South-Carolina Gazette and General Advertiser*, 5–9 June) The reasons for the "Opposition" are not known.

13. On Evan Edwards's unsuccessful courtship of a South Carolina woman, see above, NG to CG, 17 August 1783; and below, Pendleton to NG, 18 April, and Edwards to NG, 8 June.

*   *   *

¶ [FROM RICHARD HUTSON, Charleston, S.C., 5 February 1784. Encloses "the Act incorporating Charleston," which NG requested in his letter of 5 January [not found].[1] Adds: "Our Legislature met and proceeded Business, on Tuesday f'nnight past.[2] I am much pleased with [the] present complecion of our Affairs. A spirit of Clemency and Forgive[ness] towards our Political Delinquents prevails in a high degree, although [it] does not come up entirely to my Wishes."[3] Committee reports from "last Winter's session" will be considered at the present sitting. "The Restoration of our public Credit seems at length to [ha]ve engaged our Serious attention. A foreign Loan, an additio[n]al duty on the importation of Slaves, and a heavy Tax, payable [m]ostly in Treasury Indents and partly in Specie, are the great outlines of the System, at present under the deliberation of our Committee of Finance."[4] Hutson hopes NG "will soon return and long continue to participate with us in the rich profusion of gratification and enjoyments, which you have been so instrumental under heaven in securing to us."[5] RCS (MiU-C) 1 p.]

1. It was Henry Collins Flagg who forwarded the act of incorporation to NG. (Flagg to NG, immediately below; the act is discussed at Flagg to NG, 17 October 1783, above.) It is not known why NG wanted this document.

2. As noted at Pendleton to NG, 30 January, above, the South Carolina legislature achieved a quorum on 27 January.

3. On the "spirit of Clemency and Forgive[ness]" in the South Carolina legislature, see also Pendleton to NG, immediately above.

4. A comprehensive "Act for Levying and collecting certain Duties and Imposts therein mentioned, in aid of the public Revenue," was passed by the legislature at the end of March. Among its many provisions were a tax on liquor licenses, a duty on the importation of slaves, liquors and wines, molasses, playing cards, sugar, cocoa, tea, and coffee. In addition, a duty of 2.5 percent was imposed on all imported "goods, wares and merchandises" not specifically named. This act repealed an earlier one of 13 August 1783. (*Statutes of S.C.*, 4: 607–16; see also the note at NG to Lincoln, 18 June 1783, above.) A broad tax bill also passed at the same session. The tax covered lands, buildings, and slaves and authorized the state's treasurers to "receive, by way of discount, as far as one year's interest, due on indents, in discharge of any of the taxes." The extensive bill named tax collectors and assessors for the various parishes and districts. (Ibid., pp. 627–37) In addition, the legislature passed "An Ordinance to encourage subjects of Foreign States to lend money at interest on real estates within this State." (Ibid., pp. 642–43)

5. NG returned to South Carolina in midsummer.

¶ [FROM DOCTOR HENRY COLLINS FLAGG, Charleston, S.C., 7 February 1784. "His Honor the Intendant" asked Flagg to forward to NG the "Act for incorporating the City of Charleston with all the Ordonances the Corporation have issued since their creation."[1] Flagg also forwards "the Governor's speech at the opening of the Sessions," noting that "Our poor nobility seem to have rais'd his ire to a tremendous degree. Indeed we receive very little quarter here."[2] Flagg has read the address that his "countrymen presented" to NG. He observes: "It is just like themselves. They have an excellent knack at saying an handsome thing, but a much better at paying left handed Compliments. They grudge even the cheap reward of praise without some drawback. I on my part grudge them your company and think the time tedious till I have the pleasure of seeing you again."[3] He offers to "render" NG "any services." Mr. Miller, who has sent "some papers" to NG, asks Flagg to "present his very respectful Compliments."[4] RCS (MiU-C) 2 pp.]

1. On the act incorporating Charleston as a city, see note at Flagg to NG, 17 October 1783, above. Richard Hutson, whose letter to NG is immediately above, was the city's first intendant.

2. In his recent address to the South Carolina legislature, Gov. Benjamin Guerard had been highly critical of the Society of the Cincinnati. (See Pendleton to NG, 3 February, above, and note at Knox to NG, 10 April, below.)

3. Flagg, a native of Newport, R.I., probably referred to the Newport residents' address to NG of 29 November 1783, above, which was published in the *Newport Mercury* of that date. The address, which praised Greene's wartime contribution, appears to have been written with some restraint. It proclaimed "a Pride peculiarly interesting to our Felicity, that a Citizen of this State [NG] has brightened the Paths of Glory which display the Greatness of our illustrious Commander in Chief." The Newport address appears tepid in comparison with those of the residents of East Greenwich, R.I., and the R.I. General Assembly, both 26 December 1783, above, which were both effusive in their praise of NG's wartime contributions.

4. This was probably James Miller, on whom see above, Pendleton to NG (at the end of the January documents), and below, Pettit to NG, 27 April, and NG to Henry Banks, after 11 November.

¶ [FROM CHARLES PETTIT, Philadelphia, 7 February 1784. He wrote NG "lately" about "my negociations with Mr [Robert] Morris respecting the Balance in my Hands on the Bills of Exchange." After "deducting the Sum" that Morris "agrees to allow" on the "Iron Contract," there will be about £2000 left. Having put the earlier letter "into the Office Post paid," Pettit trusts in "its safe Passage to you" and will "therefore recapitulate the less of it" here, "nor did I keep a Copy." In that letter, he acknowledged NG's of 5 December [not found] and "mentioned a conversation with Mr [John] Cox on its contents." He "also accounted for not having sent the Carriage[,] which has hitherto been impracticable."[1] NG's "Draught on Mr Jacob Greene in favr of Mr Stanley [John Wright Stanly] for £300 Sterling, payable 9 Months after the 12th of Augt 1783," has been presented to Pettit. It was "indorsed by Jacob & G[riffin]. Greene accepted," payable at Pettit's firm. Stanly's partner wanted to "negociate the Bill" and asked Pettit to "subscribe the Acceptance." Having had "no Advice of it" from either NG or "the Acceptors," Pettit was "at some loss." As the partner urged him, however, he "signed the Acceptance, supposing I should thereby conform to your Wishes."[2] Pettit has made "an Estimate of the Egg Harbour [N.J.] Concerns on the Plan" that he supposes Cox "will assent to." There are "about £2000 in his [i.e., Cox's] Hands[,] of which we are each intitled to one third Part;"

but Pettit is not sure whether Cox "will consent to pay this or contend that it shall remain to be settled at the Close of our other Concerns." Pettit is sure that Cox also has "at least a full Proportion of what has been appropriated by us all, or any of us, even admitting his Mode of Accounting for what he early took to his own Use. He must not therefore at any Rate draw on me for your Proportion of this Sum, whatever he may do as to withholding my Proportion." NG knows "the Considerations which induce me to yield in many Points rather than risk a Breach" of Cox's friendship. Of Cox, he adds: "The Sense of former Obligations are not easily to be erased from a grateful Mind, and however his Opinions may be biased by self interest to which Humanity is always liable, I have the fullest Confidence that he means to do what is right."[3] In regard to one of their other business arrangements with Cox—the "purchased Share of the Prize"—Cox claims losses that should have been shared among all three but that he has kept in "his own Account."[4] Pettit received a letter some time ago from Mr. [Henry] Pendleton, "appologizing for drawing on you (or on me on your Account) for 20 or 30 Guineas for a Sulky you had of him.[5] I expected in consequence to have had such Draught presented, which I should have paid without hesitation, but it has not appeared." RCS (MiU-C) 2 pp.]

1. For more about the matters mentioned here, see Pettit to NG, after 21 January, above.

2. On NG's debt to Stanly, see NG to Pettit, 4 August 1783; Stanly to NG, 26 October 1783, and the note immediately below.

3. NG's partners Cox and Pettit had been his two chief assistants in the Quartermaster Department. The "Considerations" to which Pettit referred probably included his connection with Cox through Joseph Reed, who was Pettit's brother-in-law and Cox's nephew. (Vol. 3: 85n, above) For more about Cox and the Egg Harbor concerns, see Agreement between NG and Pettit, 8 November 1783, and Pettit to NG, after 21 January, both above; and Pettit to NG, 8 March; NG to Pettit, 22 April; and Pettit to NG, 18 May, all below. In the last of those letters, Pettit reported that he had obtained the money that NG owed to Stanly out of Egg Harbor profits that Cox owed to NG. (See also note 2, above.)

4. On the prize vessel *Venus*, see Agreement between NG and Pettit, 8 November 1783.

5. See Henry Pendleton to NG, 22 October 1783, above.

¶ [FROM GRIFFIN GREENE, Paris, 8 February 1784. He does not know when he will have "any better prospect" than he did when he wrote to NG in December 1783.[1] After the Marquis de Lafayette "urged it two & half Months," the "Minnister of France" finally gave Griffin a permit to send the vessel to the East Indies.[2] But after Griffin "wrote to Bordeaux," he learned that "the Acc^{ts} from India is such that the merchants will not be conserned in a voyage their[,] The Peace having caused the fall of all European Goods . . . in that Country." Someone is now trying "to get the Ship a voyage to Guinea," and Griffin should know how that turns out in "ten or twelve days."[3] He will then go to Bordeaux, decide what to do, and inform NG "by the first oppertunity."[4] Lafayette has "don every thing in his powar to assist me[,] & his friendship for you is such as has caused him to be verry polite & kind to me." RCS (MiU-C) 2 pp.]

1. The December letter has not been found. Griffin Greene had sailed to France the previous spring to sell the vessel *Flora*, in which the Greene family partnership owned a part interest. (See above, Griffin Greene to NG, 18 May 1783 [vol. 12: 662–63].)

2. The "Minnister of France" was the Marquis de Castries, the naval minister. (See NG's letter to him of 1 June 1785, below.) In a letter to NG of 8 September 1783, above, Lafayette had promised to do "Every thing" in his power to help Griffin Greene.

3. The *Flora* was not sent on a voyage to Guinea.

4. Griffin Greene wrote NG from Bordeaux on 6 April, below.

¶ [FROM JAMES MILLIGAN, COMPTROLLER OF THE TREASURY, Philadelphia, 9 February 1784. Acknowledges NG's letters of 7 December 1783 and
3 January;[1] has waited until now to reply to the former in the hope of giving a
more satisfactory answer than he "can yet do." He also received a letter of 24
December 1783 from Hugh Williamson, the chairman of the congressional
committee to which NG's request concerning the allowance for his military
family during his southern command was referred. Williamson asked for more
explicit information about the request, and Milligan replied to him on 1 January,
summarizing NG's account of expenses and "Showing the total Amount of
family expences, the Amount of your allowance for that purpose, as a Major
General commanding in a Separate department, and the Sum that your expenditures exceeded your allowance, which Sum I observed must be the object of your
requisition."[2] Milligan also sent Williamson a notarized copy of the "Settlement
made by M[r] [John S.] Dart," which Maj. [Edmund M.] Hyrne sent from Charleston.[3] He informed Williamson about NG's letter of 7 December 1783, "Urging a
final Settlement," and expressed a wish "that the determination of Congress
might be obtained as soon as possible."[4] He is "in daily expectation" of learning
the result of NG's "application." If the loss of money reported by Capt. [William]
Pierce turns out to be "less than he mentions," Milligan will be pleased to comply
with NG's request.[5] He finds that the amount of NG's bills "paid and presented
for payment" is $185,521 77/90, but "the amount drawn for by your Accounts
rendered, is only" $173,971 41/90. That leaves a difference of $11,550 36/90. NG
"will probably be able to ascertain" the reasons: e.g., some bills may not yet have
been presented. Milligan adds: "As the Accounts are not yet Stated, it is not in
my power to be more particular at present." If he does not hear from Congress
soon, he will write to Williamson again.[6] RCS (MiU-C) 3 pp.]

1. Only the letter of 7 December 1783 has been found.

2. NG's letter to Thomas Mifflin, the president of Congress, is above, dated 3 November
1783. On the correspondence between Williamson and Milligan, see note at that letter.

3. On the documents sent by Hyrne, see his letter to NG of 26 November–4 December
1783, above.

4. See Milligan to Williamson, 1 January, PCC, item 155, vol. 2: 688, DNA.

5. For more about the "loss of money" by Pierce, see NG to Mifflin, 3 November 1783.

6. As noted at NG to Mifflin, 3 November 1783, Williamson's committee presented its
report on 13 January, and Congress acted upon it on 6 April. The terms of the settlement
are also noted there. NG replied to Milligan on 9 March, below.

¶ [FROM CLARKE & NIGHTINGALE, Providence, R.I., 10 February 1784.[1]
They ask NG for letters of recommendation to "some Gentlemen" in Virginia for
"John Murray, a Gentleman of this Town who formerly lived with us." Murray
plans to settle in "some part of Virginia," where he is an "intire Stranger." They
vouch for his "Integrity & Abilities" and assure NG that he "will not abuse any
trust you may please to repose in him."[2] RCS (MiU-C) 1 p.]

1. Clarke & Nightingale was a mercantile partnership in Providence. (Vol. 1: 204n, above)

2. Murray has not been identified. In his reply, which has not been found, NG evidently
asked where in Virginia Murray planned to settle. (See Clarke & Nightingale to NG, 26
February, below.) No letter of introduction from NG for Murray has been found.

¶ [FROM SAMUEL PARTRIDGE, Boston, Mass., 10 February 1784. He is the executor of the estate of John Gooch, who died about "six weaks" ago, but is "Not Acquainted" with Gooch's accounts, which a "long Indisposition kept him" from recording "in the best, Ordor."[1] Gooch "did send forward his Acco^ts And Vouchers for which, He has a Receipt from y[e] 'Comis^r Genl of forrages' offis, Excepting the last two months." Partridge asks how he can settle the accounts for which there are no "Receipts" and to whom he should apply "for Aney farther Adjustment." He believes there is "money due" to the estate but needs NG's help to calculate the amount. Asks for a reply "As soon As you Can Make it Convenant, which Will in Sum degree Releave the good Mrs Gooch, who was Taught by her husband to beleve that you would do her every Kindness that you had in your power."[2] RCS (MiU-C) 1 p.]

1. Gooch had served under NG as an assistant deputy quartermaster general for Massachusetts. (Vol. 2: 8n, above)

2. NG's reply has not been found.

*　　　*　　　*

From Joseph Reed

My Dear General   London Feb 12th 1784

I arrived safe after a tolerable Passage and tho' I have not enjoyed that perfect health I could have wished, I hope I shall soon have Reason to speak more favorably.[1]

The Affairs of this Country are so connected with ours that whatever we may wish or feel towards them they must affect us. I find we have flattered ourselves too much in the Belief of returning Cordiality and also indulged too much Vanity in supposing that our Conduct in the War and final Success had created Sentiments of Respect and Esteem. It is not so, the War was a popular War and only ceased to be so when all hope of final success ceased. Of course the real Sentiments of the People are no otherwise changed than as some partial Interests of Commerce and very particular Connexions may operate favourably to America. But the Court and it's Party, the Army, the Navy, Clergy and in short the general class of Gentry find the Pride of old England so mortified by the Issues of the War that they cannot speak of the Country and it's Inhabitants in any other Dialect than that of Rebellion, False Reports of our Disunion, ill Treatment of their Adherents and in short every other unfavourable Sentiment.

Their own Affairs are in great Confusion and if they should bring about a Dissolution of the Parliament it is hard to say where and how it may end. Rising up and laying down we ought to congratulate ourselves on our Separation[.] We can now at a Distance contemplate these Objects as Matters of Speculation, which we must have Shared as of intimate Concern.[2]

In Matters of Peace they seem to be determined on their Principles to treat us fully as a foreign Nation and it will happen in this, as the War, that nothing but feeling and dire necessity will convince them of their Error. In the mean time Goods are going out to a very great extent far, far beyond our Necessities or Means of Payment.[3] Should Mr Pitt continue[,] which at present seems most probable it will be happy for both Countries, his Sentiments are liberal and views extensive.[4] We stand very low in France and not very high in Holland: almost all the French Merchants connected with America are ruined and they speak of us all with very great Freedom. I find few of our People go there and those who do come back much disgusted. Our Intercourse with them declines daily.

I am impatient to hear from America on the Return of Mr Morris's Bills bottom'd on the Dutch Loan which meets with unexpected Difficulties. It is a prevailing opinion throughout Europe that our Governments and publick Affairs are in very great Confusion. Would you suppose the Riot at Philad. last Summer had a very great indeed a most capital Effect upon our Affairs here—but the Fact is certainly so and if the Dutch Loan should fail we must ascribe it in some Degree to that Event. I observe I have spoken of Mr M^s Bills as returned[.] I should perhaps have said noted; tho' I think the Fact is that some of the Bills of that Connexion have been returned, founded on the Dutch Loan. This is a Matter of so delicate a Nature and coming from me that I must commit it to your well known prudence.[5] In consequence of a Hint from you I sounded some Persons here on the Probability of procuring some advance of Money on improving American Estates in Carolina but it was such a cold Scent I found it would not do[.] Reasons political and commercial were staited without Number.[6] After what I have said you will suppose I do not find this Country very agreable. The Character of an American Officer either in civil or Military line is far from drawing Respect: the latter would as well to have his Uniform behind him and the other his official Distinction. The two Officers who came here on Acc^t of the Mutiny wearing their Uniforms were insulted in the Streets. This did not happen from their particular Conduct, because it could not be known to the mixt Multitude, but merely from what was called their Presumption in wearing a Rebel Coat.[7]

I shall be happy to hear from you directed under cover to Denys D. Berdt Esqr Broadstreet Buildings[8] and if Mrs Greene is with you I pray you to say every thing to her that great and sincere Regard will suggest. To other friends proportional attentions and beleive me my Dear Friend, very Affectionately and Sincerly Yours   J. REED

Since the above a Compromise has taken Place between Messrs Pitt and Fox at the Expence of Ld North who retires with a good grace probably with a Title and Pension.[9]

Cy (NHi).

1. Reed, who left for England in late December 1783, had arrived in London in January. (Pettit to NG, after 21 January, above; Reed, *Reed*, 2: 400) Despite the hopes he expressed here, Reed continued to experience ill health in London. He returned to America in September and died in March 1785. (Reed, *Reed*, 2: 415; on Reed's death, see also Eyre to NG, 7 March 1785, below.)

2. John B. Owen has described the years 1782 to 1784 as especially "chaotic" in British politics. Controversy over India beginning in December 1782 led to a long and bitter power struggle that resulted in the dissolution of Parliament in March 1784. (Owen, *Eighteenth Century*, pp. 235–52)

3. On the postwar influx of European goods into American markets, see, for example, Pettit to NG, 4 August 1783, above.

4. William Pitt the Younger, who had become prime minister in 1783, was a liberal Tory who favored, among other measures, lower import duties. The parliamentary election of 1784 sustained Pitt in power, and he continued as prime minister until 1801. (Owen, *Eighteenth Century*, pp. 235–69)

5. On the problems with the "Bills bottom'd on the Dutch Loan," see Robert Morris to NG, 19 May, below. The "Riot at Philad. last Summer" involved troops of the Pennsylvania Continental line. (See note at Pierce to NG, 19 June 1783, above.)

6. NG had apparently asked Reed to make inquiries in London about a loan for the support of his two plantations in the South. (NG to Reed, 14 May, below)

7. Reed probably referred here to the mutiny that had taken place among Pennsylvania troops in Philadelphia the previous year. (See note at Pierce to NG, 19 June 1783.)

8. As noted at his letter to NG of 21 October 1783, above, Dennis De Berdt, a London businessman, was the brother of Reed's late wife.

9. Political enemies Charles James Fox and Frederick, Lord North, had forged a coalition in Parliament during the previous year. In the politically tumultuous months of January, February and March 1784, Fox eventually broke with North and allied himself with Pitt. (Glyn Williams and John Ramsden, *Ruling Britannia: A Political History of Britain, 1688–1988* [London: Longman, 1990], pp. 124–28)

*   *   *

¶ [FROM LUIS DE UNZAGA, Havana, Cuba, 12 February 1784.[1] He has not had time to answer NG's letter of 24 July [not found], recommending Major [Ichabod] Burnet. He now has the "displeasure" of notifying NG of Burnet's death "a few days after his arrival." Burnet's "baggage was collected by someone he trusted and sent to his mother." According to the "laws and orders" that apply there, Unzaga cannot allow entrance to any vessel or foreigner unless the vessel is in distress and its passengers in danger of perishing.[2] RCS (MiU-C) pp. In Spanish.]

1. Luis de Unzaga y Amenzaga was captain-general of Cuba from 1782–85. (Lockey, *East Florida*, p. 112n)

2. Burnet had sailed to Havana on business the previous August. (See NG to Pettit, 4 August 1783, above.) On the death of Burnet, NG's former aide, see NG to Pierce, 15 October 1783, and Flagg to NG, 17 October 1783, both above.

*   *   *

From General Henry Knox

Dorchester Near Boston [Mass.] 15 Feby 1784

I have apololgies ennumerable to make you for not having written since my arrival here,[1] such of the whole catalogue; a diminution of affection is not of the number. It was my hope that some particular matters which I have with the government here would have been adjusted in such time as to have admitted of my making a Journey to Newport for the sole purpose of gratifying those sensations [*illegible*] you and Mrs Greene that will ever be my pride and happiness to entertain. I am now rather apprehensive that I shall not be able to come by reason of the flurry of business, but if it is possible I shall [*illegible*] for me.[2] If you & Mrs Greene Could make it convenient to come this way you will find besides your friend, a people who will rejoice to shew you how much they esteem you.[3] Indeed Our friend the Genl and you absorb the whole praise of our republick.[4]

I hope you are deeply interested in our society of the Cincinnati[.] Mr Burkes pamphlett has created here & as far [as] I can learn throughout Ne[w] England jealousies of our infant institution—Jealousies [unmeritted?] by the conduct of the Army, or their [*illegible*]. Perhaps among you Carolinians the matter may be different, in consequence of the [i]nequalities of Fortune. Whatever may be the fears of the honest part of the community, I assure my self they will subside when experience (of the officers & especialy of Citizens) shall have more matured their judgements.[5]

I intended to have had your Cannon engraved at West Point, & engaged a man to execute the inscription & emblems, [but?] unfortunately he found upon examination that all the Cannon there were engraved already.[6] I have written since I came here to Mr Hodgdon at Philadelphia to have two of those at that place engraved with the enclosed inscription, which I hope will be agreable to you. If it should not give me the hint & I will have it put in some other form. He will let me know his progress in the business which I will communicate to you.[7]

We have taken a house at Dorchester about 5 ½ miles from the town, where my Lucy and I will be happy indeed to receive you & Mrs Greene. It is but forty minutes ride from town and this permits as you mentioned ye light Dragoon you would ride it comming & returning.[8] We both beg you to present our perfect respect & affection to Mrs Greene. I am my Dear friend y^r truly affectionate   H KNOX

ADf (GL-NHi).

1. Knox had gone home to Massachusetts from West Point in January. (Callahan, *Knox*, pp. 209, 227)

2. The "matters with the government" that kept Knox from visiting NG and CG in

Newport, R.I., were presumably related to an inquiry into the Society of the Cincinnati by a committee of the Massachusetts legislature. (Myers, *Liberty Without Anarchy*, p. 51) Knox commented on the legislative report in a letter to NG of 10 April, below.

3. NG replied on 4 March, below, that CG's imminent confinement and his own business concerns in the South would keep them from visiting the Knoxes.

4. In his reply of 4 March, below, NG modestly asserted that "whatever credit may be given to General Washington and myself there are others no less deserving."

5. As noted at Flagg to NG, 17 October 1783, above, Judge Aedanus Burke of South Carolina had written a widely circulated pamphlet the previous fall that was highly critical of the Society of the Cincinnati. (See also Myers, *Liberty Without Anarchy*, pp. 49–52.) In his reply to Knox, NG suggested that the controversy might subside if the Society simply let its critics vent their wrath. (NG to Knox, 4 March) Opposition to the Society of the Cincinnati was highly pronounced in New England at this time. (NG to Washington, 22 April, below) Elsewhere, critics of the Society included, for example, the governor of South Carolina, who had attacked it in an address to his legislature in early February. (See Pendleton to NG, 3 February, above, and note at Knox to NG, 10 April.)

6. Congress had voted to award the cannons to NG several months earlier. (NG to Washington, 3 November 1783, above) In December, while at West Point, Knox asked Maj. Andrew Billings of Poughkeepsie, N.Y., to do the engraving. (Knox to Billings, 23 December 1783, MHi)

7. In a letter to NG of 14–18 March, below, Knox again sent the proposed inscription for NG's approval, adding that the project had been "put into train of execution" and that NG should call on Samuel Hodgdon if he were in Philadelphia. NG replied that the inscription was acceptable, "if you think it is not so remote from truth as to make it ridicule in disguise." (NG to Knox, 25 March 1784, below; the text of the inscription is in a note at Charles Thomson to NG, 18 October 1783, above.) Knox wrote again in October 1785 that he had the cannons and that the engraver was ready to work on them. (Knox to NG, 27 October 1785, below) NG later replied that because of his financial problems he could find "but little spirit or pleasure" in commemorations of his wartime achievements. (NG to Knox, 12 March 1786, below)

8. Knox and his wife, Lucy, had moved to a "picturesque and comfortable" home in Dorchester, which is now a part of Boston but was then a town between Boston and Milton. According to Knox's biographer, the house was the "property of the Welles family, Boston and Paris bankers." (Callahan, *Knox*, p. 227)

To George Washington

Dear Sir   Newport [R.I.] Feb 16 1784

I had the pleasure of receiving your letter of the 28th of December past; and having had the honor of being appointed President of the Cincinnati of Rhode Island I embrace the earliest opportunity of giving you an Answer.[1] General [James M.] Varnum[,] Major [Daniel] Lyman and my self are in the appointment to attend the annual general meeting of the order. It is not expected more than one will attend the Meeting. I intend to be in South Carolina before that time.[2] General Varnum or Major Lyman will attend;[3] and I have the pleasure to communicate to your Excellency that the measures necessary for the establishment of the order is fully gone into and all the officers appointed agreeably to the insitution[.] With esteem & affection I am dear Sir Your Most Obe^d humble Ser   NATH GREENE

ADfS (Rhode Island Society of the Cincinnati Records, on deposit, RHi).
1. A copy of Washington's circular letter of 28 December 1783 to the presidents of the state societies of the Cincinnati is above. NG had been elected president of the Rhode Island Society in December. (Varnum to NG, 17 December 1783, above) NG's copy of the letter had apparently been sent to Providence, where Jeremiah Olney forwarded it to him "by Some Gentleman" traveling to Newport in January. (Olney to NG, 10 April, below)
2. NG's return to South Carolina was delayed by CG's pregnancy and problems with his own health in the spring of 1784. (NG to Washington, 22 April, below) In letters of 20 and 27 March, below, Washington, concerned that a critical number of officers would not be present, urged NG to attend the meeting. When it became clear that he would still be in the North at the time of the Philadelphia meeting, NG wrote Washington that he would make every effort to be there. (NG to Washington, 22 April, below) Ultimately, health problems kept him from attending. (NG to Washington, 6 May, below) NG did travel to Philadelphia on personal business soon afterward, however. (See NG to Milligan, 4 June, below.)
3. Apparently neither Varnum nor Lyman attended the meeting. NG wrote Washington on 6 May that Col. Samuel Ward, Jr., had agreed to be Rhode Island's representative.

* * *

¶ [FROM JEREMIAH WADSWORTH, Paris, 20 February 1784. Encloses a "Copy of my friend Mon^s Dcorneys memorial to obtain Admission into the order of the Cincinatus." NG will remember him [Dominique-Louis Ethis de Corny] from "Morris Town."[1] Wadsworth believes that de Corny's claims are "so well founded that he may obtain" membership, though opposition may arise; he begs NG "to remove any objection," as de Corny "will do honor to any order."[2] Describes him as "a Man of letters, deep understanding a real friend to America: particularly the American officers[;] is amiable in private life, as he is able in public, his wit and humour enlivens the Society of his friends, and he is altogether such a Man as you my friend admire." If NG ever goes to France, he "woud derive much pleasure from the acquaintance" of de Corny and his wife, as "they are both possessed of those talents & accomplishments that are sure to please & instruct." Wadsworth hopes to see NG "in America in the Summer." He will write "a very long letter" to CG from England "& make attonement for past neglect."[3] RCS (CtHi) 2 pp.]

1. De Corny, a member of the French commissary service, served in America during the war. As quartermaster general, NG had dealings with him at Morristown, N.J., in 1780. (Vol. 5: 581n, above) De Corny's "memorial to obtain Admission" into the Society of the Cincinnati has not been found, but he was admitted to the Virginia chapter in 1785. (Washington, *Papers*, Confederation Series, 3: 52–53n, 65–66, 145–46 and n)
2. It is not known whether NG acted in de Corny's behalf.
3. If Wadsworth wrote such a letter to CG, it has not been found. He returned to the United States in late September but did not see NG until the end of the year. (See below, Wadsworth to NG, 28 September and 3 December, and NG to Wadsworth, 29 December.)

¶ [NG'S ACCOUNT WITH THE STATE OF RHODE ISLAND, [after 22 February 1784].[1] This is a statement of NG's wages while he was in the Continental service from 1 January 1777 to 1 August 1780. At the bottom of the account, a Rhode Island legislative committee notes that it "adjusted the depreciation account of Major General Nathanael Greene" and found a "balance due thereon from the United States" to him of "one thousand seven hundred and thirty pounds sixteen shillings and threepence, lawful money."[2] Printed in Bartlett, *Records of R.I.*, 10: 17.]

1. NG's undated account with the state was entered into the proceedings of the session that began on the "last Monday in February 1784," which was 23 February. (Bartlett, *Records of R.I.*, 10: 3)

2. The legislature voted to pay NG with a promissory note. (William Greene to NG, 1 March, below)

*　　　*　　　*

To Samuel Ward, Jr.[1]

Dear Sir　　　　　　　　　　　　　　　Newport [R.I.] Feb 24th 1784

Caty's situation forbids my being at the assembly. My own private business calls me there, and my wishes for the public would urge my attention; but I must not forget what is due to humanity and the voice of Affection. It is unfortunate but it must be submited to.[2] This sessions is one of the most important of the year; and the affairs of the Continent at large, and the business of the State at home will render it more peculiarly so. It is probable the impost Act will come under consideration. If it cannot be adopted in full I hope it will be in part. The Reputation of the State demand[s] its attention. To treat the subject with neglect is treating the Continent with contempt. It is my firm opinion it is the interest of the State to adopt the Resolution in form; but as the Sentiments of the people are against it nothing remains to be done but to take it up under certain qualifications. This will manifest a good disposition and remove a charge of obstinacy. It is of importance to the United States and may be more particularly so for this to have this business acted upon this assembly.[3]

You know my esteem for the Governor and you cannot doubt my good wishes for his happiness. If what I am going to say should be new dont reject it without some consideration. The Governor has served with great reputation and given universal satisfaction. He has now an opportunity of retiring with the highest honor and applause. Perhaps a like opportunity may never ⟨again⟩ offer. The ambition of some and the ⟨love of⟩ novelty of others may not be always equally silent. To retire from the troubled ocean and secure a port before a storm is always prudent and sometimes necessary to our safety. I dont think the Governor will meet with any opposition this year but I could not promise for another. To retire from choice will be a triumph; but from necessity mortifying and disgraceful. The door is now open[;] the Governor can withdraw and the people will regret his loss. Another year the case will be otherwise if I may venture to form any opinion from the little enquiries I have heard made.[4] I dont expect to be in the State and if I was you know I will hold no office what ever.[5] I have never heard a person so much as hinted for his successor but I have heard it suggested that the constitutions of this States provided against one persons holding an office too long. You will make your own reflections upon these circumstances and act as you may think the honor and interest of the family is concerned. The subject is delicate and you will be cautious.[6] I rely on your friendship and confidence. Nothing but affection for the Governor would induce me to say any thing; but after all I may be quite mistaken. Yours affectionately   NATH GREENE

ALS (RHi).

1. On NG's longtime friend Ward, see above, vol. 1: 19–20n.

2. CG was pregnant with the couple's fifth child. Although they anticipated that she would give birth at any time, the baby was not born until April. (NG to Pettit, 22 April, below) NG's "private business" was the settlement of his Continental army accounts with the legislature. (See the document immediately above.)

3. As seen in NG to Morris, 3 July, below, the Rhode Island legislature later rejected Congress's 1783 impost proposal.

4. William Greene, CG's uncle by marriage and a distant kinsman of NG's, had been governor of Rhode Island since 1778. (Vol. 1: 10n, above; Ward, the son of a former governor, was a nephew by marriage to William Greene and a cousin of CG. [Ibid., p. 19n]) In his *History of the State of Rhode Island*, Samuel Arnold wrote that the winter of 1784 saw the "formation of new political parties and the revival of old ones" in the state. Arnold noted that the supporters of the Confederation, the State Rights party, were the farmers who formed a majority in Rhode Island; mercantile interests "favored the Union," or a stronger central government. In addition to this philosophical difference, Arnold observed that "another element was added to embitter the hostility of the rival parties"—the retirement of the state's debt. "This debt was chiefly in the hands of the commercial class," Arnold wrote. "The farmers owed the traders. Paper money was the ready and often tried expedient for paying an old debt, by contracting a new one. Hence the strife between paper and specie parties was now revived." This dispute would "bring the State to the very verge of civil war." (Arnold, *R.I.*, 2: 505) NG no doubt referred in this letter to the revival of these divisions; the paper money party gradually gained the ascendancy and swept into office in the election of May 1786, when William Greene was defeated by John Collins. (Ibid., p. 520)

5. In late 1785, NG moved his family to Mulberry Grove, his rice plantation in Georgia. (See below, NG to Ethan Clarke, 23 November 1785.)

6. It is not known if Ward took any action in response to this request.

*   *   *

¶ [FROM ROBERT FORSYTH, Charleston, S.C., 24 February 1784. He received NG's letter of 14 January, enclosing letters to Mr. [John] Banks, Mr. [Roger Parker] Saunders, and Mr. [William] Gibbons, on 13 February.[1] In answer to NG's letter of 9 January, Forsyth sent NG "a Line" he had written to Col. [Charles] Pettit, "acquainting you fully of the situation of the Debts which you guaranteed the payment of."[2] Since then, Mr. James Hunter and Forsyth's brother "have arrived in safety from St Kitts."[3] There has been no word from Mr. [E. John] Collett "since his arival in Virginia." Forsyth considers this is a positive sign, and he gains "further hopes" every day that Collett will succeed, "as Mr Banks continues to make & extend his purchases of dry Goods &c."[4] Forsyth also believes the "other two Debts are in such a situation as to remove fully every uneasiness" from NG's mind.[5] NG has asked about "the price of Rice, the Freight to England & the probability of a Briggs [i.e., brig's] geting loaded in Feb[y] of a hundred & Twenty Ton." Forsyth believes "there is no doubt but she would get a load, for but a small proportion of the Crop is yet to Markett. The number of shiping & great scarcity of River Craft has in a great measure kept up the price of Rice." He gives an estimate of specific prices for rice and shipping. Indigo "continues a very dull sale indeed." Thanks NG for his "enquiry respect-ing the Packet"; if Forsyth were "unembarrassed," he would be "happy to have an interest" in it with NG's brother, "not so much from an expectation of emolument therefrom as an introduction to further Business."[6] The legislature is in session and has "appointed General [William] Moultrie L[t] Governor." For-syth believes "there is not a doubt but the wishes of Congress will be complied with & the 5 per C[ent] duties fully adopted."[7] Maj. [James] Hamilton "is shortly to be united to the divine M[rs] Earleston" [i.e., Elisabeth Harleston].[8] RCS (MiU-C) 3 pp.]

1. NG's letter to Saunders may have been that of 4 January, above; none of the other correspondence, including NG's letter to Forsyth, has been found.

2. The correspondence referred to here has not been found. However, Pettit wrote NG on 27 April, below, that Forsyth, who was in partnership with Banks, "writes to me in February that there is an Apparent Profit on the Business & that he is aiming to get the Partnership affairs settled & the Debts paid, but seems to be far from satisfied with M[r] Banks's conduct, & to think that he [i.e., Banks] Counts more largely than justly on the Profits." As the attorney for Banks in the latter's capacity as contractor to the Southern Army, Pettit was holding a number of Banks's unpaid bills of exchange. (See Pettit to NG, 23 July 1783, above; the note at Pettit's letter dated after 21 January, above; and Pettit to NG, 27 April.) In addition, NG had first advanced bills to Banks to purchase clothing for the army and then later guaranteed debts that Banks had acquired while carrying out that contract. (NG to Benjamin Lincoln, 19 December 1782, and Agreement between Hunter, Banks and Company and NG with Newcomen and Collett, 8 April 1783, both above [vol. 12: 306–7 and n, 591 and n; see also note 4, below, and NG to Lee, 22 August 1785, below.])

3. Hunter was another of Banks's partners.

4. Under the terms of the agreement that Banks and NG, as his guarantor, had signed in April 1783 with the Charleston firm of Newcomen and Collett, Banks had the options of either paying in specie or "good Bills of Exchange" by 10 November 1783, or, by that date, of delivering enough "James River Merchantable Tobacco" to cover the debt. (Agreement between Hunter, Banks & Company, NG, and Newcomen and Collett, 8 April 1783) As seen in Pettit's letters to NG of 13 March and 27 April, below, Collett had gone to Virginia to try to collect tobacco from merchants indebted to Banks. In his letter of 27 April, Pettit quoted from one he had received from Collett: " 'My Stay here [in Virginia] will be much longer than I could have expected as I have been much disappointed in the Payments which were promised to me by M[r] Banks, and I am afraid I shall at last be obliged to have Recourse to our Rhode Island Friend [NG].' " In letters of 23 June and 8 August, below, NG sought, unsuccessfully, to dissuade Collett from having "Recourse" to him.

5. On the status of the debts to which Forsyth referred, see notes 2 and 4, above.

6. The vessel referred to here was probably the sloop *Charleston Packet*, on which see note at Hazlehurst to NG, 26 June, below. (As noted at Pendleton to NG, 3 February, above, a brig operating between Philadelphia and Charleston was also named the *Charles-ton Packet*.)

7. For more about the South Carolina General Assembly's session, see above, Pendleton to NG, 30 January and 3 February, and Hutson to NG, 5 February.

8. See Pendleton to NG, 3 February, above.

¶ [FROM CLARKE & NIGHTINGALE, Providence, R.I., 26 February 1784. They have NG's letter of 24 February [not found]. Concerning his offer to write letters of introduction for Mr. [John] Murray, they reply that Murray is "uncertain in what part of Virginia he may settle" and that he would like "letters to Gen¹ Washington, and other of your Freinds upon or near the Rappahannock, York or James Rivers, such as York Town[,] Petersburg, Richmond or in the Vicinity of those towns." Murray thinks he will most likely "fix on James River" and leaves it to NG "to whom it will be most proper for a man of Bussiness to be introduc'd." As he will leave Providence "in two or three days" and "sail from Boston in less than a fortnight," NG should "send on the letters as soon as convenient."¹ RCS (MiU-C) 1 p.]

    1. In a letter of 10 February, above, Clarke & Nightingale had asked NG to write letters of introduction for Murray. As noted there, no letter from NG on Murray's behalf has been found.

¶ [FROM BARNABAS DEANE, Hartford, Conn., 26 February 1784. Acknowledges NG's letter of 3 February [not found],¹ "in which you observed [that] by the Stateing of Our Company Stock there Appears to be about Seven Thousand pounds Still remaining." However, "Debts Due from the Company," as well as for Deane's "Services for Transacting the Buisness were not deducted from the Seven Thousand pounds," and therefore the amount is much less. The firm was "uncommonly unfortunate the Last Year of the warr"; otherwise, it "Should have made Something handsome" by its "Connexion in Buisness."² When Col. [Jeremiah] Wadsworth returns in June, they will be able to determine "the time of our Concern in Buisness."³ Deane adds: "I once flatter'd my Self of Doing Something Clever for our Concern but the fortune of War Swept it away." The partnership lost "a Considerable Sum the first year" because Deane had "too much faith in Continental money and being unwilling to give the Very high prices for goods which Others did."⁴ RCS (MiU-C) 2 pp.]

    1. NG's letter of 3 February was presumably a reply to Deane's of 5 January, above.

    2. On the firm's recent losses, see note at Wadsworth to NG, 26 July 1783, above.

    3. Wadsworth did not return to the United States from Europe until late September. (Wadsworth to NG, 28 September, below) Concerning "the time of our Concern in Buisness," see note at Deane to NG, 5 January.

    4. NG replied to Deane on 13 March, but the letter has not been found. (Deane to NG, 30 March, below) On NG's settlement with the partnership, see NG to Wadsworth, 29 December 1784, and Wadsworth to NG, 5 September 1785, both below.

¶ [FROM SAMUEL OGDEN, Boonton, N.J., 29 February 1784. He is "Settling the Cutting Mill Company Accounts" but cannot "compleat" them without the accounts of "several of the deputies" who acted under NG in the Quartermaster Department.¹ He submitted his accounts to Col. [Timothy] Pickering, as NG suggested, but Pickering "has done nothing thereto."² Ogden would be "happy to have a conferance" with NG, and if NG is going to visit "the Western States" in the near future, he would like to be notified so that they could meet; this would "prevent the Necessity of my making the jaunt to Rhoad Island."³ Ogden will move to New York "On the first of May," and "go into Business" there. He will be "very happy to receive, and execute, any Commands" from NG or any of NG's friends. He would also be "very thankfull for any Consignments." Adds: "I expect a pretty General Assortment of dry Goods, Immediately from the place of their Manufactory in Europe."[4] While he is in New York, Odgen's estate in New Jersey and his "Works" will be overseen by his friend [John Jacob] Faesh.[5] They are "establishing a Number of Trip Hammers." Asks if "any good Workmen who Understand the plating of Scythes &c &c" could be "procured" from Rhode Island.[6] RCS (NjHi) 2 pp.]

1. Ogden's Boonton ironworks in Morris County, N.J., had supplied everything from camp kettles to cannon for the Continental army. During NG's tenure as quartermaster general, Ogden had also acted as an agent for the Quartermaster Department. (Vol. 2: 370n, above; Thayer, *Morris County*, pp. 56, 63, 209; *DAB*) NG wrote his former deputy James Abeel on 8 August 1785, below, that he had looked over papers relating to Ogden's contract for camp kettles and that they appeared to be in order.

2. Pickering was NG's successor as quartermaster general.

3. It is not known if Ogden and NG later conferred.

4. The name of Ogden's mercantile establishment in New York is not known. Several years after the war, Ogden engaged in major land purchases in northern New York State, and the city of Ogdensburg is named after him. (*DAB*)

5. Faesh owned the Mount Hope Furnace in Morris County. (Vol. 3: 152n, above)

6. NG's reply has not been found.

¶ [FROM GOVERNOR WILLIAM GREENE OF RHODE ISLAND, Warwick, R.I., 1 March 1784. Thanks NG "and the other Gentlemen of the Cincinnati" for their "polite invitation to become a Member of that Society" but declines because "the Honor conferrd" would cease at his death. He and his "Posterity" would thus not have "equal standing" with other members.[1] Hopes NG approves the Assembly's settlement of his account. Would have been "much happier had there been money in the Treasury to have paid off a debt so dearly earned," but as "that is not the case," he is sure that NG "will consider those proceedings as the best in the power of the Assembly."[2] Asks to be remembered "very affectionately" to CG. RCS (RHi) 1 p.]

1. The invitation is in NG to William Greene, 19 January, above. As noted there, regular memberships in the Society of the Cincinnati—held by former officers in the Continental army—could be passed along to offspring, but honorary memberships could not.

2. In its February session, the Rhode Island legislature, acting upon a committee report that showed a balance of £1,730.16.3 due to NG "for the depreciation of his wages," directed the general treasurer to give him a "promissory note" for that amount, "payable on demand, with interest." (Bartlett, *Records of R.I.*, 10: 17; see also Bourne to NG, 20 March, below.) NG's account with the state is calendared above, dated after 22 February.

*   *   *

To General Henry Knox

Dear Sir   Newport [R.I.] March 4 1784

Mrs Greene situation has prevented my visiting Boston this Winter. I expect her to be put to bed every hour.[1] To provide for my little flock and arrange my private concerns has found me employment for some months past. My feelings are more flattered by domestic duties than public bustle. However the hearty welcome I meet at home and the approbation of friends abroad are highly interesting to a mind ever sensible of the partiality of my friends. What ever credit may be given to

General Washington and my self there are others no less deserving. If it were possible it would give me pleasure to see the veil drawn and a just history of facts displayed from the beginning to the end of the war; but this can never happen and Merit in many instances will lay buried in the confusion of incidents. I wish to see you but do not expect it before I go to the Southward.[2] The meeting of friends is rather tender than joyous and your observation at our meeting on York Island that you was rather affected than joyful was highly flattering to my feelings.[3] My esteem and affection for you has never suffered dimunition and to merit and preserve your friendship and esteem is one of the first wishes of my heart.

The Cincinnati is a subject of much conversation. Jealosies are awake and discontent perhaps will shew her head; but the less there is said on the subject and the less anxiety Members shew upon the occasion the sooner they will dye.[4]

I have heard nothing further of the peace establishment. I wish you was at the head of it.[5] It has been hinted to me that I have been in nomination for the War department and that the Marine and that were to be United. Is it not my interest to reject it if I should have an offer of the kind; and perhaps that is not probable? Give me your opinion on the matter.[6]

If you and Lucy could make it convenient to pay us a Visit we will try to render it as agreeable as possible.[7] Mrs Greene joins me in kind compliments to you and Mrs Knox and others of our intimate acquaintance. Yours affectionately   NATH GREENE

ALS (GL-NHi).

1. CG was still waiting for the birth of their fifth child when NG wrote Knox again on 25 March, below.

2. NG did not travel to South Carolina until summer.

3. Knox had commanded the American troops who marched into New York when the British evacuated the city on 25 November 1783. (Callahan, *Knox*, pp. 206–7; Freeman, *GW*, 5: 461) NG, on his way home to Rhode Island, presumably saw him there briefly at that time. (NG's letter to an unknown recipient of 24 November 1783, above, was datelined "New York," and as noted there, it is possible that Knox was the recipient. By 27 November 1783, NG was home in Newport, R.I. [NG to William Greene, 29 November 1783, above])

4. In his letter to NG of 15 February, above, Knox had expressed concern about widespread opposition to the Society of the Cincinnati. (See also Knox to NG, 10 April, below.)

5. Knox had become the commander-in-chief after Washington left the army in December 1783. (Freeman, *GW*, 465; Fitzpatrick, *GW*, 27: 256–58)

6. No "hint" of this sort has been found in NG's correspondence. In a letter to NG of 14–18 March, below, Knox urged him to accept a combined post if it were offered. Knox himself was appointed secretary at war in March 1785. (*JCC*, 28: 129)

7. It is likely that Knox visited NG when he passed through Newport in April, on his way to Philadelphia for the general meeting of the Society of the Cincinnati. It is not known whether Lucy Knox accompanied him. (See note at Knox to NG, 10 April.)

From Thomas Mifflin,
President of the Continental Congress

Sir   Annapolis [Md.] March 6ᵗʰ 1784

I have the honor to inform you, that Congress have appointed you a Commissioner for holding a Treaty with the Indians, "and that as it is the wish of Congress that the Negotiations should commence as soon as possible, the Commissioners are desired to meet at New York on the 10ᵗʰ day of April next, to fix upon the Times and Places of holding the Treaties with the different Nations and Tribes of Indians; and give them respectively the speediest information of the Time and Place determined on, inviting them to meet accordingly."[1]

The Gentlemen appointed to act with you are Mʳ George Rogers Clarke,[2] Mʳ Oliver Wolcott,[3] Mʳ Richard Butler[4] and Mʳ Stephen Higgenson.[5] I request the favor of your answer by the Express who will deliver this letter.[6]

I have the honor to be with the greatest Respect & Esteem Sir your most Obedient & humble Servant   THOMAS MIFFLIN

RCS (MiU-C).

1. Congress elected the five commissioners on 4 March and the next day directed Mifflin to "immediately inform the gentlemen elected commissioners for holding a treaty with the Indians, of the said election." (*JCC*, 26: 124–25) As seen in Mifflin's letter of 22 March, below, the commissioners were empowered to negotiate with the Indians "in the northern and middle departments."

2. For several years before the war, George Rogers Clark (1752–1818) had explored lands on the western frontier. As a militia major during the war, Clark organized his men in defense of lands west of the Allegheny. After the war, he often served as the chairman of commissioners negotiating with Indians and continued to lead military expeditions on the frontier. (*DAB*)

3. Wolcott (1726–97), a signer of the Declaration of Independence and a future governor of Connecticut, was one of the commissioners who negotiated a treaty with the Six Nations at Fort Stanwix, N.Y., in 1784. (*DAB*)

4. Butler (1743–91), a lieutenant-colonel in the Pennsylvania Continental line, had been an Indian agent before the war. He participated in commissions that negotiated treaties with the Iroquois in 1784, the Wyandot, Delaware, Chippewa, and Ottawa tribes in 1786, and the Shawnees in 1786. (*DAB*)

5. Higginson (1743–1828) had served in the Massachusetts legislature and in Congress. (*DAB*)

6. NG wrote Mifflin on 28 March, below, that his family situation and "engagements to the Southward" made it impossible for him to take part "in this business."

*   *   *

¶ [FROM CHARLES PETTIT, [Philadelphia, 6 March 1784?].[1] In a two-page "memorandum" about the political situation in Philadelphia, Pettit reports that "Another great Revolution in Politics has taken Place in this Town." Although he cannot describe the causes or "secret Springs which have moved it in the Operation," there are now "two Great parties which have alternately governed—one as favourers of the present Constitution; the other as wishing it altered."[2] The latter party, "with an Appearance of Liberality, had obtained the weight & Influence of the Neutrals & Tories, & seemed to be very secure in the command of this auxiliary Aid. These were also the principal Proprietors & Directors of the Bank. This Institution was supposed to be much under the Influence of one Man, whose Dependants were supposed to Rule all its affairs, & much murmuring was heard (whether justly or not) of partiality & undue preferences in Accomodation." A plan was therefore "set on foot for a new Bank, which for a Time was understood to be supported by Quakers, neutrals & Tories chiefly; but on the Subscription being opened, it was found that their opposite extreme, the constitutional, or high Whigs, exerted their strength in it, & in a few days 1000 Shares were subscribed for."[3] The Whigs then submitted a petition to the Assembly "for taking off the Tests & restoring the Tories to all the Rights of Citizenship." This "unnatural Connection" can only be "accounted for" as "Nothing short of that Party Spirit which for a Time reconciles extremes of any kind."[4] The proponents of the "old Bank (who early called themselves Republicans in Opposition to the Constitution)" supported "the Petition to repeal the Test," but they also "remonstrated to the Assembly" against "a Charter to the new Bank, called a meeting of their Stock holders, opened the Door to 4000 new Shares, reduced the Price of new Subscriptions to the Old Standard, & proposed such alteration in their Constitution as to meet the Objections raised against it." Pettit adds that "Public Hearings have been had before the House & the Matter yet remains *sub judice*, whether the New Bank shall have a Charter or not. Mean Time the Partizans are as warm as Cayenne Pepper & the Conversation of the Town is much engrossed by the Subject."[5] D (MiU-C) 2 pp.]

1. According to a note (not in Pettit or NG's hand) on the second page of this otherwise undated document, it was written on "6 March 1784."

2. The Radicals, or "Constitutionalists," had controlled the Pennsylvania government from the time the state constitution was adopted in 1776 until 1780, when a "counter-revolution" gave the Republicans, or "Anti-Constitutionalists," the ascendancy. "Quakers, neutrals and Tories" were allies of the Republicans. By the time that Pettit wrote this letter, the Radicals, also known as Whigs, were poised to take control of the state government once again. (Brunhouse, *Pennsylvania*, passim)

3. Republicans and their supporters—neutrals and Tories—had organized the Bank of North America in Philadelphia in November 1781. (Ibid., p. 111) Radicals made plans to incorporate another bank during the winter of 1783–84 and applied to the Assembly for a charter. They claimed that the Bank of North America represented a "monopoly" under the control of Robert Morris, the superintendent of finance. (Ibid., pp. 150–51)

4. The "Tests"—oaths of allegiance—were prerequisites for obtaining voting rights under the Pennsylvania constitution. Republicans and their allies had strongly objected to the "tests," while Whigs (Radicals) had fiercely supported them. (Brunhouse, *Pennsylvania*, pp. 16, 40) The "unnatural connection" between Whigs/Radicals and "Quakers, neutrals & tories" in this matter was thus remarkable. (Ibid., p. 151)

5. In a move to undercut the initiative for a new bank, the directors of the Bank of North America issued a number of new shares and made other changes, thereby giving their political enemies, the Radicals, greater access to the established bank. As a result, the Radicals withdrew their petition for a new bank. One observer wrote of these happenings: " 'You might have seen the violent whig, the bitter tory & the moderate man laying their heads together with the earnestness & freedom of friendship: the Constitutionalist and Republican were arm in arm: & the Quaker and Presbyterian forgot their religious antipathies in this coalition of interests.' " (Brunhouse, *Pennsylvania*, p. 151)

¶ [TO GOVERNOR WILLIAM GREENE OF RHODE ISLAND. From Newport, R.I., 8 March 1784. NG has had an "interview" with Gen. [James M.] Varnum about a letter that Mr. Ray Sands sent to the governor.[1] Varnum thinks that he and the governor "can negotiate the business" to the governor's satisfaction.[2] Varnum "can pay in a short time the greater part of the debt" and will give "ample security for the remainder." NG "has no connection with this business but as security," and Varnum, who wants to "disengage" him from that, "can render your property perfectly safe without my Agency." NG adds: "Perhaps fortune may place me where it may be less convenient for you to settle with me than with General Varnum. I shall be glad to know your determination on the matter; and cannot but persuade my self you will relinquish your demand on me unless you see a probable loss may ensue."[3] ALS (Varnum House Museum, East Greenwich, R.I.) 2 pp.]

1. The letter has not been found. Sands was the husband of CG's sister (and William Greene's niece by marriage), Phebe Littlefield Sands, who had helped to take care of NG's and CG's children at times during the war. (See William Littlefield to NG, 12 March 1780, above [vol. 5: 456–57], and Stegeman, *Caty*, p. 179.) Sands, who owned property on Block Island but lived in South Kingstown, had also represented the town of New Shoreham (Block Island) in the Rhode Island General Assembly's June 1783 session. The Assembly, noting that New Shoreham's "insular situation" often made it "impracticable" for its deputies to attend legislative sessions, voted at that time to allow the town's freemen to choose as their representative "any person, being a freeman of any town in the state, who is seized in his own right of a freehold estate" there. (Bartlett, *Records of R.I.*, 9: 706–7) A number of years after NG's death, Sands and his family took up residence with CG on Cumberland Island, Ga. (Stegeman, *Caty*, pp. 179–80)

2. The details concerning this debt that NG and William Greene had apparently both guaranteed are not known.

3. William Greene replied to NG on 15 March, below.

¶ [FROM CHARLES PETTIT, Philadelphia, 8 March 1784. He has delayed an answer to NG's letter of 14 January [not found] "in hopes of Intelligence from the Southward, but the [ice?] Bridge over the Delaware is yet firm & we have had little Information from Charleston [S.C.] since December."[1] Captain [William] Allibone, who left "Carolina" on 8 February, has "arrived on the Coast" but has left his passengers at Cape May [N.J.] and "sent up no Letters." Pettit has "suffered several of M[r] Banks's heavy Dr[af][ts] to be protested," for although Banks claims to have sent "funds to take them up," Pettit has not received any since NG's "Departure from hence."[2] It may be, though, that the funds are in Allibone's "Vessel."[3] [Captain Matthew] Strong has been "shut up" in Philadelphia this winter.[4] Pettit hears that "A Brother of Major Burnets" is in Charleston, and that may account for "my hearing nothing farther from the Doctor on that Business."[5] After he received NG's letter of 14 January, Pettit wrote "a serious letter to Bloomsbury," and he has been told "that Provision will be made for taking up" NG's "Draught of £300 Sterl[g]."[6] He "cannot but congratulate" NG "on the Marks of Attention you receive from the People of your native Country. They at once evince the good Judgment & Candor of those People and afford the highest Evidence of your deserving the Respect they shew you."[7] As he presumes that Col. [Clement] Biddle has written to NG about "your obtaining an Accomodation" through Biddle's friend, Pettit mentions it here only to inform him "that a Dutchman gets high Interest at 5 or 6 per Cent, especially with good

Security and ascertaining an annual Commission on Business."[8] Pettit has received a bill for £36.10 for "rich silver Orrice[,] Ground Gold & Colours Brocades," purchased by CG, and a "Taylor" has mentioned a "Bill for some Cloathing for George last summer."[9] Pettit is "paying pretty dear for the Honor conferred on me as Chairman of the standing Committee of Merchants; as much Draughting & a deal of Correspondence falls to my Share in Consequence of it." The committee has "a flattering hope" of "doing some Good to the Nation as well as to the commerce" of Pennsylvania. They have received "answers from all the Eastern States except Rh. Island, all expressing a strong Desire of strengthening the federal Union as the only effectual Means of obtaining an equality in Commerce with the Nations in Europe." Several of the southern states, "indeed all whose answers are received, tend to the same Point."[10] He hopes Rhode Island "may distinguish itself by other Means than by shewing it's Power of frustrating the Plans of Congress."[11] Adds in a postscript that Mr. [Joseph] Reed "sailed from the Capes [of Delaware Bay]" on 19 December and that NG's carriage "will go by the first Vessel I can get to take it in a proper Manner."[12] RCS (MiU-C) 3 pp.]

1. In his letter to NG dated after 21 January, above, Pettit had reported: "Our Navigation has been stopped since about Christmas; but a Thaw is now at work which bids fair to open it." The winter of 1783–84 is considered one of the three most extreme winters of the eighteenth century. It was remarkable for unusually cold temperatures and heavy snowfall, which resumed after a thaw in January. In his book on meterological conditions in America, David M. Ludlum has written that "1784 would long remain in the memories of mariners as their toughest ice season. . . The Delaware River at Philadelphia stopped [i.e., froze over] on 26 December and remained so until March 12th." (Ludlum, *Early American Winters*, p. 65)

2. As Banks's attorney, Pettit was being pressed for payment of a number of unpaid bills of exchange that he was holding for Banks. (See Robert Morris to Pettit, 15 January, Morris, *Papers*, 9: 31–32, an extract from which is printed in a note at Pettit to NG, after 21 January.)

3. No evidence has been found that this was the case.

4. This was undoubtedly due to the ice on the Delaware River.

5. As seen in Pettit to NG, 27 April, below, John Burnet was representing the interests of his late brother Ichabod, who had been Banks's partner in the contract to supply provisions to the Southern Army. NG, who had left Philadelphia in mid-November 1783, replied to Pettit on 22 April, below: "Doctor [William] Burnet writes me that I am in a fair way to get disentangled from Mr Banks's affairs." (Burnet's letter has not been found.) NG's optimism proved to be misplaced. (See Saunders to NG, before 17 July, below.) For more on Pettit's problems with Banks, see his letter to NG of 26 July, below.

6. Bloomsbury was the New Jersey home of Pettit's and NG's partner John Cox. As seen in Pettit's letters to NG of after 21 January and 7 February, above, NG was concerned about his share of profits from the partnership's "Egg Harbor" concerns, which Cox controlled. NG commented further on this matter in his letter to Pettit of 22 April. On NG's "Draught of £300 Sterl⁸," see Pettit to NG, 7 February.

7. See, for example, Rhode Island General Assembly to NG, 26 December 1783, above.

8. No letter from Biddle to NG on this subject has been found. Pettit wrote NG on 27 April that from a recent conversation with Biddle he "could find no Room to hope for" a loan.

9. On CG's purchases in Philadelphia the previous summer, see Pettit to NG, 26 July 1783, and NG to CG, 4 August 1783, both above. Orris is "a name given to lace in various patterns of gold or silver; embroidery made of gold lace." (*OED*) George was the Greenes'

son George Washington Greene, whom CG had removed from Dr. John Witherspoon's school in New Jersey on her way home to Rhode Island that summer. In his letter to Pettit of 22 April, NG questioned his responsibility for these bills.

10. Pettit had mentioned his involvement with other public creditors in a letter to NG of 17 November 1782, above. (Vol. 12: 199–200, 203–4n)

11. On Rhode Island's action in regard to the federal impost proposal of 1783, see NG to Morris, 3 July, below.

12. In an earlier letter to NG, Pettit gave the date of Joseph Reed's departure for England as 21 December. (Pettit to NG, after 21 January) It was not until June that Pettit found a vessel to accommodate the chariot that CG had ordered in Philadelphia. (Pettit to NG, 26 June, below)

*   *   *

To Thomas Mifflin,
President of the Continental Congress

Sir   Newport [R.I.] March 9th 1784
By Major [Edmund M.] Hyrne when I was in Philadelphia last fall on my return from the Southward I addressed a short letter to Congress on the subject of my family expences during my command in the Southern department[,] refering to the major who was perfectly acquainted with the history of the matter for further particulars.[1] The Comptroler of Accts said a Vote of Congress was necessary to justify his passing whatever Amount the expences might exceed what formerly had been fixed as an Allowance for a Major General on a seperate command. The Comptroler now writes me there is some difficulty in the matter.[2] I am persuaded Congress cannot wish to oppress an individual. The circumstances of the Country and the nature of the command created heavy charges. Was I to be subject to the additional expences attending the service it wou'd prove a grievous tax upon my little fortune and distressing both to me and my family. When I was appointed to that command I wrote to Congress (copy of the letter inclos'd) that I expected they would bear my family expences;[3] and I appeal to those conversant with the affairs to the Southward for the unavoidable expences attending a command there in the situation the Country was in. It is impossible to regulate the expences of a military family upon a scale of domestic oeconomy. The changes and revolutions of Persons and things which attends one prevents the order and regularity which might be established in the other. I have in my plan of living studiously avoided ostentation and meanness. I wished not to burthen the public or dishonor the appointment. No person could be more careful to curtail expences in the General arrangment of the Army or those of my family. Congress has done me the honour to approve of my conduct; and I persuade myself they will not load me with a heavy debt incured in their service. I kept a detail of the expences and lodged it in the

Comptrolers Office. But besides all that I have charged to the public my private expences have been great.[4]

The money mentioned to be lost by Capt. [William] Pierce was one of those accidents there is no guarding against and it would be a hardship upon him to loose it being only cash keeper for the Public[,] there being no paymaster with the Army the far greater part of the time I held the command there[,] and had it been lost in his hands it must have been a public loss, and to hold me responsible for this money would be still harder who had no immediate agency in the Matter. I hope Congress will therefore consider of the matter with its attendant circumstances and relieve me from the present anxiety which I feel upon the occasion.[5] I have the honour to be with great respect your Excellency's most Ob[dt] humble Serv[t]   NATH GREENE

LS (PCC, item 155, vol. 2: 692, DNA).
1. See NG to Mifflin, 3 November 1783, above. By "family," NG meant his aides, or military family.
2. See James Milligan to NG, 9 February, above, and NG's reply to Milligan, immediately below.
3. The enclosure was undoubtedly a copy of NG's second letter to Samuel Huntington of 3 November 1780, above (vol. 6: 461).
4. The outcome of this matter is noted at NG to Mifflin, 3 November 1783.
5. See note at ibid.

To James Milligan, Comptroller of the Treasury

Sir   Newport [R.I.] March 9th 1784
    I am favored with your letter of the 9th of February. I am sorry to find that any difficulty or delay should happen in Congress to the passing my accounts. I have written them again on the subject and hope you will soon receive their final determination.[1]
    I am at a loss to account how the bills paid should so far exceed the amount of the charges made for the drafts.[2] My Secretary must have omitted some entries. And I know of no way of finding them out but by comparing the original bills with the entries made and note such as are omitted. After which they may be placed to the proper departments to account for them. I never drew a bill for any private purpose what ever. The accounts therefore should square. I beg you will get M[r] Swannington to make the examination as soon as possible. He promised me that he would take this trouble if it should become necessary to place the business on a proper footing.[3] I left every paper with you respecting the matter.[4] Such bills as you may find omitted please to transmit me a list of them[,] the amount[,] the persons name in whose favor they were drawn[,] and the date of the bills and I will tell you how to charge them. Let me intreat your kind attention to this business as early as possible. It will remain a heavy load upon my mind until I have the matter properly

explained and get a discharge from the affair.⁵ I am Sir with esteem Your most obed^t humble Ser   NATH GREENE

ADfS (CSmH).

1. See NG to Mifflin, immediately above.

2. See Mifflin to NG, 9 February, above, and note at NG to Mifflin, 3 November 1783, above.

3. NG may have referred here to John Swanwick, Robert Morris's "partner, unofficial cashier to the Office of Finance, and federal tax receiver for the state of Pennsylvania." (Ferguson, *Power of the Purse*, p. 136)

4. As noted at NG to Mifflin, 10 November 1783, above, the accounts that NG submitted have not been found.

5. The outcome of this matter is noted at ibid.

*   *   *

¶ [TO JEREMIAH OLNEY.¹ From Newport, R.I., 9 March 1784. NG asks him to "interpose" in a dispute involving two soldiers in Olney's regiment. George Townsend "complains of being wronged by Lt Wheaton."² Townsend "is poor & in distress and his mother is also in want, both are objects of charity and require the kind offices of some friend." Olney is "a friend to the Soldier," and NG will be "happy" if he will assist "George."³ ALS (RHi) 2 pp.]

1. On Olney, who had been breveted a colonel in the Rhode Island Continental line at the end of the war, see above, vol. 1: 153n.

2. Townsend, "a soldier in the Rhode Island Regiment," had "lost all the toes off his feet" in the "attempt upon Oswego." (NG to William Greene, 10 March, below) Joseph Wheaton served in Olney's regiment from 1781 to 1783. (Heitman, *Register*)

3. For more about the dispute between Townsend and Wheaton, see also NG to William Greene, 10 March, below.

*   *   *

From Samuel Clegg¹

Sir   South Carolina March 9. 1784

By an Advertisement of yours in the News papers I found their was a Negro wench of mine in your possession.² Mr Benjamin Porter³ a son in law of mine informd me he made application to you for the S^d wench & she was sent off to the Northward[,] that a Negro Fellow of yours had her for a wife and as they ware fond of Each Other you ware not wiling to part them,⁴ that you would [have] Gladly paid him for the wench, but he was against Seling her without my Consent, which I partly Blame him for[,] Knowing my Situation was a good Deel Distresing Occationd by the Brittish[.] A few Circumstances I will mention that will Leave no Doupt but that the wench is mine Viz, the wench was Raised mine. She has Two Sisters now with me by name Judy & Nanncy. She has a Daughter now living with my Daug[hter? M]^rs Town [*illegible*] by Name Hager. She [has a?] Husband by Name Dick[.] She [has?] two Nephews went of[f with?] the Brittish, with Several Others, by Name Tom &

George[.] I had all my Building Burnt with Every thing in them by the Brittish. I Lived on Waccamaw Point opposit George Town Commonly caled the Barony which Name She Knows.[5] She has Lost some of her fore Teeth, her proper Name is Hannah[.] If She will be Honest Enough to Acknowledge the Truth these are Sufficient to prove her mine. I am wiling to part with her, as money is Lowe with me Owing my misfortunes[.] My price is one Hundred Guinies which I hope your Honour will not think is out of the way.[6] Please Remit the money to Roger Smith Esq[r] in Charleston or M[r] John Cogdell in George Town[7] which is most Convenient to you. I am Sir your most Hble Serv[t]   SAMUEL CLEGG

RCS (MiU-C).
1. Clegg, a planter in Prince Frederick Parish, S.C., owned some 3,000 acres "of the old Hobcaw Barony on Waccamaw Neck." (*Biog. Directory of S.C. House*, 2: 155)
2. NG's "Advertisement" had appeared in the *South-Carolina Gazette and General Advertiser* the previous May in the form of a notice placed by "John Sandford Dart, J.P." It read: "The Hon. Major General Greene informs me of a Negroe wench, named Lucy, about 50 years of age, who says she belongs to Mr. Samuel Cleg, at Wacamaw, and has been absent from home about two years, being now at Head Quarters. The owner is desired to prove his property to the above described wench within six months from the date hereof, agreeable to an act of the general Assembly, past the 12th of March last." (*South-Carolina Gazette and General Advertiser*, 3 May 1783) The South Carolina General Assembly had passed "An Act to Oblige persons having Negroes or other Effects not their own Property in their possession, to render an account thereof and to punish such as shall embezzle, conceal or neglect to render an Account of the same . . ." on 12 March 1783. (S.C., House of Representatives, *Journals, 1783–84*, p. 261)
3. Benjamin Porter, like Clegg, was a large landowner in Prince Frederick Parish. (*Biog. Directory of S.C. House*, 3: 572–73)
4. On NG's practices as a slave owner, see note at his letter to Warner Mifflin, at the end of the November 1783 documents.
5. The British had set fire to many of the buildings in Georgetown, across the bay from Waccamaw Neck, in the summer of 1781. (NG to Thomas McKean, 25 August 1781, above [vol. 9: 241]) It is not known when Clegg's buildings were destroyed, but the British had made frequent raiding parties and attacks in the vicinity of Georgetown during the war. (Rogers, *History of Georgetown*, 122, 129, 143, 155–56)
6. Roger Parker Saunders had recently paid £1,000 for ten slaves on NG's behalf. (Pendleton to NG, 30 January, above)
7. Smith (1745–1804) was a Charleston merchant; Cogdell (1729–1807), a planter and merchant, owned a plantation on Waccamaw Neck. (*Biog. Directory of S.C. House*, 2: 635–36; 3: 144–45) NG's reply has not been found.

To Governor William Greene of Rhode Island

Dear Sir   Newport [R.I.] March 10th 1784
George Townsend a soldier in the Rhode Island Regiment complains of his being wronged by Lt Wheaton. He was one of the unfortunate sufferers in the attempt upon Oswego and has lost all the Toes off his feet.[1] He lay confined many Months and while in the Hospital and in distress Lt Wheaton applied to him to purchace his wages and the fel-

low says took advantage of his ignorance in the contract and got a power from him to receive his wages for the consideration of only twenty dollars paid in goods taken up at the Store of Mr Cumston[,] Merchant in Albany [N.Y.]. George says his agreement was to have twenty dollars for each years pay due him from the State and he has receivd only twenty dollars in the whole and can get nothing more. The first contract was a great imposition but the second is much worse than the first. How far the fellow states facts I cannot say but if he tells the truth I think Mr Wheaton ought not to be permitted to receive his wages until he has given some satisfactory history of the transaction. It is not good policy in general for Magistrates to interfere in civil contracts but there are cases where both justice and human[it]y claim it.[2] The fellow is in distress[,] his mother is poor and helpless[,] and both have occasion for more than is their due to keep them from suffering. They came to me to represent their situation to you and Col Olney and I have written the latter on the subject;[3] and I beg your kind attention to the sufferings of a poor unfortunate soldier ignorant and incapable of obtaining his right without the interposition of some friend. I know nothing of Mr Wheaton; but he must be of an unfeeling make to take advantage of one who he ought to protect. Perhaps George may not have given a right state of the matter and Mr Wheaton is not to blame. I wish for the honor of human Nature it may be so; but I should be glad he would satisfy you that no injustice is done the fellow.[4] I am dear Sir with great respect Your Most Obed humble Ser^t NATH GREENE

ALS (RHi).

1. In "a mid-winter advance on snowshoes," Col. Marinus Willett had led an unsuccessful raid on the British post at Oswego, on Lake Ontario, in February 1783. (Boatner, *Encyc.*, p. 1208) The raiding party consisted of "a part of the Rhode Island Regiment and the State Troops of New York." (Fitzpatrick, *GW*, 26: 165) Townsend was a private in the Rhode Island Regiment under Jeremiah Olney. (See NG to Olney, 9 March, above.) His "disability and the reasons that occasioned it" were described in an official list of war invalids as "Loss of all the toes from the right foot, and the left foot and toes very much injured, by reason of severe frost when on the Oswego expedition." (Bartlett, *Records of R.I.*, 10: 163)

2. It is not known if William Greene intervened in this matter. At its May 1784 session, the Rhode Island legislature voted to enroll Townsend and several other soldiers "on the list of invalids; and that they receive their pay quarterly as other invalids." (Bartlett, *Records of R.I.*, 10: 38) As of February 1786, Townsend was on the official "List of Invalids resident in the State of Rhode Island, who have been disabled in the service of the United States during the late war, and are in consequence thereof entitled to receive a monthly pension during life." The invalids' pensions were to be "a compensation proportionate to their respective disabilities and sufferings while in the service of the United States." Townsend was awarded $3.75 per month. (Ibid., pp. 162–63)

3. See NG to Olney, 9 March.

4. The outcome of the dispute between Townsend and Wheaton is not known.

*   *   *

¶ [FROM JOHN BROWN, Providence, R.I., 10 March 1784.[1] Acknowledges NG's letter of 24 February [not found]. Informs him that there was "but Very Little or no Difficulty in your Acc^{ts} passing the House."[2] Would be "Exceeding sorry if any Accident should Happen" during NG's "Intended absence" that would "prevent" his "speedy Return" to Rhode Island; hopes NG "will by and by sett down amoung us and take a Leading part in Government."[3] Adds: "The publick Debt most Certainly ought to be One of the First & principle Objects of Government. The Resources of our Country Unitedly and Juditiously apply'd I am Fully Convinced in my Own mind is Quite sufficent to Discharge the whole Debt of the War in the same number of years or but few more than it has been in the accumulation, but I believe it will be as wise to take double the time for the utter Demolition, as to do it in a less time Grant^g it to be in our power, but that the Interest and part of the principal ought to be paid Annually." Brown approves "the plan Offerd Congress by Mr Morris," but he cannot condone keeping "only one Quarter" of it and eliminating "all the Rest," as Congress has done. If they would "adopt the whole," Brown has no doubt that Rhode Island would be "Induced to Join the Measure." However, "the amaising high Sallerys Granted by Congress should be reduced to Reason and the number Curtaild to due bounds." If, as is said, "the back Lands will Reddily Sell for Enough to pay the Whole Continentelle Debt," Rhode Island should be able to pay its debt "in seven years both principal and Interest, besides the sound Expense of Government dureing the Term." Brown does not believe that "adopting the Requisition for the Importation will Reach the Object," though. He will "not be in the house the insuing year," but he believes the legislature would pass the measure "if Mr Morris should think it Would answer a good purpose for this State to Comply, so far with the Requissition as to adopt the 5 per C^t on Condition That the Money Raised theirby should be apply'd by the Loan Office here to first Discharge the Interest of all Continentell Debts Due to the Inhabitants of this State before any part be Remitted to the Continentell Treasury."[4] When NG returns to Rhode Island, Brown assumes he will "Take a seat in Government."[5] RCS (MiU-C) 2 pp.]

1. On Brown, a merchant and leading citizen of Rhode Island, see above, vol. 1: 84n.

2. NG's account with the state of Rhode Island is calendared at after 22 February, above.

3. NG was planning to travel to the South on personal business, but he did not leave Rhode Island until summer. Although Brown apparently thought NG's absence would be temporary, and that he would live in Rhode Island and "Take a seat in Government," NG later decided to settle in the South.

4. As noted at his letter of 19 December 1783, above, Robert Morris had asked NG for help in persuading the Rhode Island legislature to ratify the 1783 impost proposal of Congress. For details of the congressional plan, see note at NG to Lincoln, 18 June 1783, above. NG wrote Morris on 3 July, below, that the legislature had rejected the proposal "by so great a Majority and from such false reasoning that I begin to despair of their coming into the measure at all."

5. See note 3, above.

¶ [FROM HEWES & ANTHONY, Philadelphia, 12 March 1784. They enclose a bill of lading for "Eight Chairs on board Captain Wightman."[1] They hope the chairs, which were made by their "best work man" (who has also made chairs for "M^rs [Robert] Morris and at the Same price"), will "please your good Lady."[2] NG can "pay the money" to Mr. George Gibbs. D (CtY) 1 p.]

1. Joseph Anthony, a partner in the firm, had written NG on 1 January, above, that he was having trouble getting the chairs made but would send them with Capt. Valentine Wightman, who had been "detain'd by the severity of the weather." On the bill of lading, see Wightman to NG, 13 March 1784, below.

2. The chairs were evidently among the items that CG had ordered while she was in Philadelphia the previous summer. (See above, Pettit to NG, 26 July 1783, and NG to CG, 4 and 7 August 1783.)

¶ [FROM JOHN STORY, New York, 12 March 1784. In case the original has gone astray, he encloses a duplicate of his letter to NG of 9 December 1783. He arrived in New York "a few day's since," after being "unfortunately detained" in Philadelphia "for more than two months by Indisposition." He had gone to Philadelphia to settle his "Accounts and Vouchers, which have passed one examination by Colonel [Charles] Pettit." At the latter's request, Story has taken additional "Accounts that originated in Camp," before he joined NG in November 1778, for examination by Mr. Denning in New York.[1] Although Denning promised to examine the accounts as soon as he received them, Story finds, to his "disappointment," that they "have not been entered upon." Denning is "not in Town" but is "daily expected"; when he arrives, Story will use his "Utmost endeavors to have all the Accounts Examined."[2] It has been Story's "earnest wish," since NG "intrusted" the accounts to him, "to obtain a final settlement of them." He informed NG about his "situation" in August 1781 but has not had "the honor of" an answer.[3] Since that time, he has "made two journey's from Camp to Philadelphia and the last from Boston was to compleat this business if possible." His expenses in trying to get the accounts settled amount to about £200, none of which has been "paid by the public"; in fact, he has not received "any Cash since the year 1781," as seen by the enclosed account. He has "accounted for all the Cash" that he was "charged with," and NG will note that "the public is in my debt." He encloses other accounts proving the "disagreeable situation" that he is in from not having his accounts settled or receiving the depreciation of his pay.[4] Story is the "only person from the State of Massachusetts whose duty has been in the field" who has "not had the depreciation made good"; Mr. Whiting, who was in a similar situation, has recieved his depreciated pay.[5] Had Story made application sooner, all might have been resolved; the current objection by the committee of accounts is that they do not know whether he is "Accountable for public Stores." He hopes NG will "pardon the liberty I have taken in troubling you and soliciting the Certificate." Obtaining the certificate "will cause justice to take place"; without it, he will "be undone in point of Interest," as the "whole of my private Interest is in the hands of the public."[6] Story has been "obliged to hire Money to defray the Expences which have Occur'd on public Account." If he should "obtain a Certificate from Mr Denning," it will "not command [as] much Cash" as Story has "advanced to obtain a settlement of the public Accounts," but if he could get the depreciation of his pay "settled by the State," he would "receive more Cash than all the other security will fetch."[7] He submits these facts for NG's "consideration with a hope that, no objection will Arrise" and that NG "will grant a Compliance" with his request. Story has "The Books of the department" in his possession and would be glad to supply any information that NG may need. He hopes to "effect an Examination of the Cash accounts (in Camp)" of NG's department, and if Denning will consider them, Story "will attend untill the business is Compleated."[8] He adds in a postscript that he would be "happy in receiving an Answer"; gives his address in New York.[9] RCS (MiU-C) 4 pp.]

1. William Denning had been appointed a commissioner to settle quartermaster accounts. (See Bayley to NG, 7 November 1783, above.) A copy of Pettit's letter to Story of 17 January, asking him to present his accounts to Denning and to bring them to Pettit for examination, is at MiU-C.

2. Story wrote NG on 2–5 April, below, that Denning had still not arrived in New York. Denning ultimately did inspect Story's accounts, concluding his examination in July, "greatly to my disadvantage." (Story to NG, 19 November, below)

3. Story's letter of 27 August 1781 is above (vol. 9: 263–64). As noted there, no reply from NG has been found.

4. The accounts that Story enclosed with this letter are at MiU-C.

5. Timothy Whiting had been an assistant deputy quartermaster at West Point. (NG to Udny Hay, 21 October 1779, above [vol. 4: 488, 489n]; Heitman, *Register*)

6. On the certificate requested by Story, see note at his letter to NG, 9 December 1783, above.

7. According to Story, Denning did not accept NG's "Certificate," did not allow the depreciation of Story's pay, and did not reimburse him for expenses incurred "while settling the public accounts." (Story to NG, 19 November)

8. By November, Story was confident that his "farther exertion" had made possible "a settlement of the Advances made to the Deputies and Agents" and that NG would "receive a Certificate for what is due, and obtain a discharge for the Money's charged" to him. (Ibid.)

9. NG's reply, dated 21 March, has not been found. Story responded to it on 2–5 April. NG eventually wrote to Congress on Story's behalf. (See below, NG to Lee, 2 January 1785.)

*   *   *

From Charles Pettit

Dear Sir   Philadelphia 13th March 1784

If the Uncertainty of your being at R. Island be too great to write to you, I shall nevertheless write at you, and if the Letter should miss the male half, it may hit the female, & do equal Execution. If you retain due respect for Congress, & are not so selfish as to prefer the cultivation of your private Interest to the national Concerns they have assigned you, as joint Ambassador to many Nations, you will be consulting with your Brethren at New York; but if the Crops of Rice and Indigo should be uppermost in your Mind, you may be gliding along the Coast to the Southward.[1] Your other Affairs in the Southern Country, are, I believe, mending their Situation. M[r] [John] Banks, I believe, does not imagine that I know anything of your Concern in them, but from what he tells me & from the Information I derive from other Quarters, the Business is negociating chiefly in Virginia; M[r] Warington & M[r] Collett are both in that Country collecting Tobacco, & with a Prospect of Success, tho' subject to some Delay.[2]

I have taken the necessary Pains to find an Opportunity of forwarding Mrs Greene's Carriage, & have had the Hatchway of every Vessel I could find bound to R. Island measured; but not one can be found that will admit it under Deck, nor do I think it likely one will be found. The Carriage has been ready for some time past & I wish to get it forward. Perhaps it may go safely on Deck, being Cased, a Month or two hence, but I am unwilling to send it in that way without special Directions.[3]

Col Mentges spoke to me t'day about Baron Glaubeck. He says he is well ascertained that he is of good Family & of adequate Estate to pay his Debts; that he thinks it unnecessary to write to the Marquis about him as you desired, as the Marquis is expected in this Country in May. I have advised Col Mentges to write to you at N York & promised to mention these Circumstances in my Letter to R Island.[4]

The Captain by whom I mean to send this, tells me that he lives in your Neighbourhood—that M^rs G looked very stout when he came away and expected every Day to be taken to pieces.[5] I hope by this Time she is recovering a desirable Situation, taking it for granted that after the stateliness she has lately assumed she must have been taken down; tho' I hope she will not be so humbled as to prevent her from assuming as good an appearance again as ever; for I see not why the braceing Climate & good Living of Rhode Island should be less likely to excite stateliness than the debilitating air of Ogechee & Charleston; and surely it is a Land of equal Liberty where people may enjoy the use of their Faculties with due Freedom. Be pleased however to tell her that her growing Pride has cost Mrs P. a dozen of Gloves in a Bet with L[or]^d Bloomsbury on the Fruitfulness of Carolina Cultivation. In this Bet I am blamed, for he had read your Letter of the 5th of December but she had not and confided merely in the meek appearance of Mrs G. when here supposing that if she had then possessed the means of figuring away as she has since done she would not have kept the matter so profound a Secret from so intimate an acquaintance.[6]

I mentioned in a former Letter the departure of Mr Reed for England on the 19th of December; on the 28th of Jany there was no account of his arrival; but we daily expect later Accounts.[7]

This Winter has been uncommonly severe, & continues later than any within my Remembrance. We have yet scarcely a Vestige of Vegetation, nor the appearance of a Blossom or a Bud on a Fruit Tree in an exposed Situation. The Length of Winter & the Delay of arrivals has distressed the Merchants.[8] The Attempt at a new Bank, tho' it has blown over, unhinged the Course of Circulation, and the drain of Specie to Europe, China, Charleston & Virginia has rendered it so scarce, that when the Channels of Circulation were again opened, the Fountain was too near dry to afford more than very scanty Streams.[9] Trade of course is much embarrassed, and credit severely tried, every one feels a Difficulty & some must stagger under it. Foreseeing the Cloud I guarded against it as far as possible and as yet feel it in a less Degree than most of my Neighbours, tho' I perceive it's pressure on stronger Backs than mine. It will work some good Effects as to reducing Prices to a proper Standard, introducing Oeconnomy &c, tho' some People will be crushed in the Operation.

I am yet obliged to continue an Owner of Batsto, but in order to have a better chance of selling as well as to avail ourselves of a better year than we may meet with again, we are preparing for a vigorous Blast of 12 or 18 Months; we expect to begin to blow in June & shall make chiefly Pigs & hollow ware. Pigs are now in Demand at £10 per Ton & towards fall we expect [to] have a Stock beyond the Demand. Mr Jacob Greene once mentioned a desire of having some of our Pigs, I therefore mention these Circumstances that he may have an Opportunity of getting them if he should then want.[10] Hollow ware we have the vanity to think we make perferable to any other Works from the excellency of our Patterns as well as of the Metal, but this kind of Ware I believe is also made in your Neighborhood.[11]

Pray mention me with affectionate attention to Mrs Greene & to George, & be pleased to remember that I claim some Interest in the latter, at least so far as to be desirous of knowing how he thrives, in accomplishments as well as in Person.[12] Yours with great Sincerity.

CHA^S PETTIT

RCS (MiU-C).

1. Citing personal reasons, NG rejected his appointment by Congress to a commission to negotiate with Indian tribes. (NG to Mifflin, 28 March, below) It was not until summer, however, that he was able to travel to South Carolina on personal business.

2. On John Collett's and James Warrington's efforts to obtain tobacco in Virginia as reimbursement for debts that Banks owed them and that NG had guaranteed, see above, Pettit to NG, 24 February, as well as Robert Forsyth's letters to NG of 18 February, above, and 18 June, below.

3. The carriage that CG had ordered in Philadelphia the previous summer was finally sent at the end of June. (Pettit to NG, 26 June, below)

4. NG wrote the Marquis de Lafayette about his problems with Glaubeck on 24 March, below. Lafayette arrived in the United States in early August. (See note at Griffin Greene to NG, 12 June, below.) No letter from Col. Francis Mentges to NG in regard to Glaubeck has been found.

5. CG was pregnant with the couple's fifth child, Louisa Catharine, who was born on 17 April. (See note at NG to Pettit, 22 April, below.)

6. CG had visited the Pettits in Philadelphia the previous summer, on her way home from South Carolina. Based on NG's letter to Pettit of 5 December 1783, which has not been found, John Cox ("Lord Bloomsbury") had evidently bet Pettit's wife, Sarah, that CG was pregnant.

7. Reed was in London by 12 February. (See his letter to NG of that date, above.)

8. On the extreme winter of 1783–84, see also the note at Pettit to NG, 8 March, above.

9. On the new bank in Philadelphia, see Pettit to NG, 6 March, above.

10. NG had recently assigned his own share in the Batsto Iron Works to his partner

Pettit. (See above, vol. 3: 356n, and Agreement between NG and Pettit, 8 November 1783.) In June, Jacob Greene asked NG to have Pettit ship him four or five tons of pig iron. (Jacob Greene to NG, 11 June, below)

11. "Hollow ware" included cups, bowls, and other containers.

12. NG's son George Washington Greene had lived with the Pettits for a time, and Pettit had placed him in Dr. John Witherspoon's school in New Jersey. (Pettit to NG, second letter of 14 June 1782, above [vol. 11: 332–33])

*   *   *

¶ [FROM CAPTAIN VALENTINE WIGHTMAN, Philadelphia, 13 March 1784. He certifies that eight chairs, "Shipped in good Order and well conditioned" by Hewes & Anthony, are aboard his "Good Schooner" *Victory*, "now lying in the River Delaware and bound for Newport Rhode Island." The chairs are to be delivered "in the like good Order and well conditioned" to NG or his "Assigns" at Newport "(the Danger of the Seas only excepted)." The cost of freight will be "Two Shillings Lawfull Money per Chair with Primage and Average accustomed."[1] DS (MiU-C) 1 p.]

1. On this shipment, see also Hewes & Anthony to NG, 12 March, above.

¶ [FROM GOVERNOR WILLIAM GREENE OF RHODE ISLAND, Warwick, R.I., 15 March 1784. Gen. [James M.] Varnum brought NG's letter of 8 March to him and "made some proposals respecting his [i.e., Varnum's?] affair in which" William Greene and NG "are connected."[1] William Greene is "very sorry" that the proposals "were such as could not discharge the security" NG mentioned "so as to relieve us, but as they rather tended for me to raise a very considerable part of the debt and to be security therefor I am under the disagreeable necessity to inform you that it is out of my power to comply with this request without injureing my Creditors." However, "as the matter is now taken up," he thinks, from what Varnum has told him, that if Varnum "meets with good success in his arrangements and Mr [Ray] Sands can be Patient where he is so as to allow a proper time that we may yet escape the effects which very often happens to those of our undertaking."[2] Asks NG in a postscript "to excuse my erasements &c as I am from Home and scant of paper." RCS (MiU-C) 2 pp.]

1. As seen by NG's letter to William Greene of 8 March, above, little is known about the "affair," except that it involved a debt owed by or to CG's brother-in-law—and the governor's nephew by marriage—Ray Sands.

2. Varnum had proposed to relieve NG of his responsibility as surety for the debt. (Ibid.) Nothing more is known about this matter.

¶ [FROM OTHO H. WILLIAMS, Baltimore, Md., 15 March 1784. Explains why NG has not heard from him: He left Baltimore "about the middle of January" to visit friends "in the Western part of the state," intending to return in two or three weeks, but the unusual severity of the Winter and the prodigious depth of Snow (which in the back parts of Maryland, and indeed almost all over the western shore exceed any thing in the memory of our oldest men)[,][1] the pleasure of sleying, snowballing and balls of a more agreeable composition detained me 'till two days ago." He got home to find "a letter which I intended to go by post, and these are the reasons why you have not heard from me." Upon "reperusal," he finds nothing in his "former letter" that "requires alteration," unless, "for decency sake, I should take the trouble of writing it over again,"[2] but as NG "some times" displays "examples of negligence in writing"—which Williams considers "an obliging familiarity"—he assumes that NG will excuse the same deficits in him. He has "not had a toll to my mill since Christmas" because Chesapeake Bay has been frozen, but as "it has been raining and thawing for a week past," he now expects that "Merchantmen from all parts of the world will be glideing into this port." Williams's "finances have been considerably embarrassed" by this, but he hopes soon to "repair the injuries my fortune has sustained."[3] Although he does not know how long it will take to "repair an injury of a more delicate nature," he has been "exercising all my philosophy to recover that happy indifference which used to set me at ease with all the World."[4] He knows that CG wishes him "success," even though she has been "cruel enough to think the severity of my Chastisement was not *altogether* unmerited."[5] He asks if NG will be at the meeting of the Cincinnati in Philadelphia "the first Monday in May next."[6] CG has "a permanent place" in his "affections." RCS (DSoC) 3 pp.]

1. On the unusually cold and snowy winter of 1784, see also the note at Pettit to NG, 8 March, above.

2. See Williams's letter to NG of 14 January, above, in which he lamented his rejection by a "capricious Girl" with whom he had been enamored.

3. Williams held the potentially lucrative state post of "Comptroller of the customs." (Williams to NG, 20 February 1783, above [vol. 12: 467]; see also George Lux to NG, 24 January 1783 [ibid., p. 392].)

4. Williams married Mary Smith, the daughter of a wealthy Baltimore merchant, in 1786. (*DAB*)

5. See Williams to NG, 14 January.

6. NG did not attend the general meeting of the Society of the Cincinnati. (NG to Washington, 6 May, below)

¶ [**FROM BENJAMIN BOURNE**, Providence, R.I., 17 March 1784.[1] He has just received NG's letter of "yesterday" [not found]. Cannot send NG's "Securities" by Mr. [Ethan] Clarke, who is "leaving Town immediately," but Mr. [William] Channing, who is there "attending the Superior Court," will bring them.[2] NG's "Approbation of my Services in the settlement of your Account is extremely satisfactory" to Bourne.[3] He was "very unhappy" that "Business" kept him from accepting NG's "Invitation while at Newport." RCS (MiU-C) 1 p.]

1. Bourne, formerly the assistant deputy quartermaster general for Rhode Island, was a member of the legislative committee that had recently recommended payment of NG's "depreciation of his wages." (Bartlett, *Records of R.I.*, 9: 500; 10: 17; see also William Greene to NG, 1 March, above.)

2. For more about the securities, see Bourne to NG, 20 March, below.

3. On the settlement of NG's account with the state of Rhode Island, see note 1, above, and the note at William Greene to NG, 1 March.

*   *   *

From General Henry Knox

My dear friend   Dorchester [Mass.] 14[–18] March 1784

I wrote you on the 15th of last month, and I am to suppose by not having received an answer that it did not reach you.[1] Doctor Gordon informs me that he shall set out in a day or two, for Newport, in order to examine your papers, and to receive verbal information for his history of the War.[2] I cannot omit so certain an occasion, again to repeat to you, that neither time, nor distance, have in the least degree, diminished that respect and affection which were imbibed in an hour, when our political sun, glimmer'd dimly through the Shade. I confess I feel not a little mortified, that a friendship, which I flatter myself was always reciprocal and will be durable, should not through the course of this Winter have produced any letters, but one on my part.[3] In this observation, it is my intention to censure myself, more severely than I do you, as my present and retrospective affairs, are much less important than yours. I have no excuse, but Such as I ought to be ashamed of producing, which is an indolence in writing. I will however if you reply to this, promise amendment.[4]

I mentioned to you that all the Cannon, at West Point were already engraved, and therefore I had written to Mr Hodgdon at Philadelphia, to have two of those at that place engraved, agreeably to an inscription, which I forwarded to him, a copy of which I also enclosed to you, with a request, that if you wished any alteration, that you would communicate a hint to me and I would conform to it. Least you should not have received the other letter [I] enclose you the inscription.[5]

Present Mrs Knox's Love and mine to Mrs Greene. Let me know your destination. I wish ardently to see you, but I am afraid I shall not have the opportunity. I shall go to Philadelphia, the latter end of April.[6] I am your truly affectionate   H KNOX

Genl Greene   Dorchester March 18th [17]84
I intended the above to go by Doctor Gordon butt he had set out before my letter reached his house.[7] I have recieved a letter from our friend the General who is excedingly anxious that you should be at the general meeting of the Cincinnati in May next at Philadelphia and he has desired me to intimate the same to you. I beg you to go.[8] I have received your esteamed favor of the 4th which cancels the [balance?] of this respecting not having written.[9] As you mention nothing of receiving mine of the 15th last month, I think it necessary to send you this concerning the Cannon which Mr Hodgdon writes me are put into train of execution. If you go to Philadelphia call upon him.[10] God send Mrs Greene a happy deliverance.[11] Your affectionate   H KNOX
Genl Greene
I sin[c]erely hope that if they offer you the War department, blended with the marine that you will accept them. The Country wants your services in those respects, and I pray that you may find it convenient to let it have the benefit of your talents.[12]   KNOX

RCS (MiU-C).
1. NG's letter of 4 March, above, may have been a reply to Knox's of 15 February, also above, although NG did not explicitly acknowledge receipt of that letter. In the letter of

4 March, NG did not answer one of Knox's 15 February queries—the one concerning the proposed inscription on the cannons that Congress had voted to give him.

2. William Gordon, who was writing a history of the war, had hoped to visit NG earlier in the winter but had had to postpone his trip. (Gordon to NG, 31 January, above) He spent time with NG in Newport sometime between 14 March, when Knox hoped to have him carry the first part of this letter to NG, and 25 March, when NG had him carry a letter to Knox. (NG to Knox, 25 March, below) The visit is discussed in ibid. and in Gordon to NG, 5 April, below.

3. Knox had written NG on 15 February. He had not yet received NG's letter to him of 4 March but acknowledged it in the portion of the present letter that he dated 18 March.

4. See below, NG to Knox, 25 March, and Knox's reply of 10 April.

5. Knox had sent the proposed inscriptions to NG in his letter of 15 February; NG replied to Knox's query in his letter of 25 March.

6. Members of the Society of the Cincinnati were to hold their first general meeting in Philadelphia at the beginning of May. (See above, Washington to NG, 28 December 1783, and NG to Washington, 16 February.)

7. On the timing of Gordon's visit, see note 2, above.

8. In a letter to Knox of 20 February, Washington had written: "I hope Genl Greene will be in the Delegation from Rhode Island—and that we shall see him at the Genl meeting of the Cincinnati—will you intimate this to him." (Washington, *Papers*, Confederation Series, 1: 138) Washington also wrote to NG directly, urging him to attend the meeting. (See below, Washington to NG, 20 and 27 March.)

9. In the portion of this letter dated 14 March, Knox had lamented the lack of correspondence between NG and himself. (See notes 3 and 4, above.)

10. See Knox to NG, 15 February, and NG to Knox, 25 March.

11. CG gave birth to Louisa Catharine, the couple's fifth child, on or about 17 April. (See note at NG to Pettit, 22 April, below.)

12. As noted at NG's letter to him of 25 March, Knox himself was later appointed to head the War Department.

*   *   *

¶ [FROM BENJAMIN BOURNE, Providence, R.I., 20 March 1784. NG's "Business has been negotiated at the Treasury," as requested.[1] Bourne has received "several State Notes" for the "Ballance" of NG's "depreciation account," which will be delivered by Mr. Channing, "the Bearer."[2] "By an Act of Assembly," NG is entitled "to an order from the Treasurer on any Collector of Impost for one years Interest" on his "Securities." Because orders such as these are plentiful in Providence, "and the offices of Impost being destitute of Cash," they "sell a little under par" there and would probably "sell better" in Newport. Bourne will "apply to the Treasurer for an order on M[r] [Robert?] Crooke at Newport for one years Interest" and send it to NG. RCS (CSmH) 1 p.]

1. NG's request has not been found. For background on the present letter, see Bourne to NG, 17 March, above.

2. For more about NG's pay account with the state of Rhode Island, see William Greene to NG, 1 March, above.

¶ [FROM WINTHROP SARGENT,[1] Boston, Mass., 20 March 1784. He sends NG and CG "a Poem on a very *unpopular* Institution." It was "written by a Lady" from Massachusetts who would "deem herself highly honor'd by their Approbation." Their approval of the poem would "add much much" to his happiness, and he is "anxiously interested in its Reception."[2] He adds in a postscript that he has been "injoin'd to permit no Copy of this Poem." RCS (MiU-C) 1 p.]

1. Sargent had been an aide to Gen. Robert Howe. (Heitman, *Register*)

2. The enclosure, which has not been found, was presumably the same 300-line poem that Sargent sent to Washington on 20 February, commenting: "Desirous of contributing to the Amusement of your Excellency I do myself the honor to Transmit you a Poem of Eulogy on the Institution of The Society of Cincinnati." It was written by a "fair Poetess," whom the editors of the Washington Papers have identified as Sargent's sister, Judith Sargent Stevens. (Washington, *Papers*, Confederation Series, 1: 140 and n) No reply to the present letter has been found. (Stevens, widowed in 1787, later was married to NG's friend John Murray, the noted Universalist minister. [Sheila L. Skemp, *Judith Sargent Murray: A Brief Biography with Documents* (Boston and New York: Bedford Books, 1998), pp. 49, 51])

*   *   *

From George Washington

My D[r] Sir   Mount Vernon [Va.] 20th March 1784

From the purport of your Letter dated Feb[y] 16th at New-port (which only came to my hands yesterday) I have little expectation that this reply to it will find you in the State of Rhode Island. If however the case be otherwise it is to express an earnest wish that you might make it convenient to take the Gen[l] Meeting of the Cincinnati in your way to S[o] Carolina.[1]

I was concerned to hear you say, only one Delegate from your State would be there.[2] It were to be wished on many accounts, that the ensuing Meeting might not only be full in Representation, but that the best abilities of the Society might also be present. There are, in my opinion very important reasons for this, & I cannot avoid expressing an earnest wish, that yours may be among them. I would add more were I not apprehensive that this will not meet you in time. I have received Letters from France on this subject which, with the sentiments which many seem disposed to entertain of the tendency of the Society, makes it, I repeat it again, indispensably necessary that the first meeting shou'd be full & respectable.[3]

As there is time (supposing this letter gets to your hand in Rhode Island) to give me an acknowledgment of it, let me entreat an answer.[4] My best wishes attend M[rs] Greene, yourself & Family, in which M[rs] Washington joins, and I am very sincerely & affectionately Yours &c[a] &c

GO: WASHINGTON

Cy (DLC).

1. As noted at NG's letter to Washington of 16 February, above, his return to the South had been delayed by CG's imminent confinement and his own ill health. NG did not leave Rhode Island for South Carolina until July.

2. In ibid., NG reported that he, James M. Varnum, and Daniel Lyman had been "appointed" to attend the general meeting in Philadelphia, but that only one of them was likely to go. In a letter to Gen. Henry Knox of this date, Washington also expressed dismay that "it is not expected that more than one" Rhode Island representative would attend the

meeting. "I wish this could be otherwise," he added, "& that General Greene would attend—private interest, or convenience may be a plea for many, & the Meeting thereby be thin & unfit for the purpose of its institution." (Washington, *Papers,* Confederation Series, 1: 229; see also Knox to NG, 14–18 March, above, and 10 April, below.)

3. Washington's concern was undoubtedly related to the public criticism that was then being directed at the Society. (See, for example, Flagg to NG, 17 October 1783, above, and Knox to NG, 10 April.) On the "Letters from France on this subject," see also Washington to NG, 27 March, below. NG's health problems ultimately kept him from attending the general meeting. (NG to Washington, 6 May, below)

4. NG replied to Washington on 22 April, below.

*　　*　　*

¶ [FROM WILLIAM LITTLEFIELD, Block Island, R.I., 22 March 1784.[1] He hopes that "before this M[rs] Greene is safe in bed with another fine son or perhaps daughter"; her friends are "all equally anxious to hear of her welfair."[2] Littlefield reached Block Island safely, and the business that brought him there "will terminate" as he expected. The "*Old Gentleman*" is "Very infirm," and "his prejudices increase with his infirmities. He will not move but is willing that I shou'd let my part of the farm which I think will detain me a fortnight or three weeks longer upon the Island."[3] Littlefield plans on "being very industrious" while he is there, and "if possible to replace all the fencing stuffe which is missing in stone wall." He has "partly agreed to let" the property, and if he fences it, "there will be no difficulty in the terms." He informs NG that "Nat is the greatest Pet in the world. He is in perfect health, as ragged as is necessary and Master of the whole House. He drinks his dram every morn[g] with his Grand Papa & when I attempt to hinder him he says he wishes uncle Bill was gone home he don't love him."[4] Littlefield knows that NG is "very desirous" to see his son, and if NG thinks best, he will bring Nat back with him, "provided his Grand Papa will consent." Littlefield will "Return again to the Island in May when the weather will be warm," and Nat could then "be brough[ht] back without any difficulty." Littlefield has been asked to represent Block Island at the "May Sessions," but he has not decided whether to do so. If he thought it would advance his "affair[s] which will then be brought forward," he would not "hesitate to Accept."[5] Asks to be remembered to "Miss *B* and Genera[l] Ko [i.e., Kosciuszko]."[6] He would "be glad to hear from the family by the return of the Bote." RCS (MiU-C) 4 pp.]

1. Littlefield was CG's brother.

2. As seen in NG to Knox, 25 March, below, CG had not yet given birth to the Greenes' fifth child.

3. As seen in this letter, the "*Old Gentleman*" was presumably Littlefield's and CG's father, John Littlefield. (See also Stegeman, *Caty,* p. 1.)

4. Nat—NG's four-year-old son, Nathanael Ray Greene—was staying at his grand-father's while CG was waiting to give birth. His morning "dram" was probably of hard cider.

5. New Shoreham (Block Island) was not represented in the session of the Rhode Island General Assembly that convened at Newport on 5 May. (Bartlett, *Records of R.I.,* 10: 20) In a June session, also at Newport, the Assembly granted a request from Littlefield to revoke a 1781 resolution—based on "a malicious and false report" that he had planned "to carry on a trade with the enemy"—ordering him to "remain upon Block Island, and be incapable of receiving the balance due for the depreciation of his wages" as a Continental officer. Littlefield stated in his petition that, "conscious of his own innocence, and of having

served with the reputation becoming a good officer, he took the earliest opportunity of applying for liberty to appear before the General Assembly for a hearing, which was granted; but that his petition hath laid upon the board ever since, without any further proceedings thereon." (Ibid., p. 45)

6. Thaddeus Kosciuszko, who had been breveted to brigadier general in September 1783, was visiting the Greenes in Newport. (*JCC*, 25: 673; Haiman, *Kosciuszko*, p. 160; Gordon to NG, 5 April, below) "Miss *B*" may have been Elizabeth ("Betsy") Brinley of Newport, whom Littlefield married in 1785. (See Littlefield to NG, 25 April 1785, below.)

*   *   *

From Thomas Mifflin, President of the Continental Congress

The Honorable George Rogers Clarke, Oliver Wolcott, Nathaniel Greene, Richard Butler, and Stephen Higginson Esq[rs] Commissioners at New York

Gentlemen   Annapolis [Md.] March 22[d] 1784

I have the honor to transmit to you a Commission under the seal of the United States authorizing you to treat with the Indians within the boundaries of the United States of America, in the northern and middle departments; comprehending the whole of the Indians known by the name of the Six Nations; and all to the northward and westward of them, and as far South as the Cherokees exclusive; for the purpose of receiving them into the favour and protection of the United States, and of establishing boundary lines of Property for seperating and dividing the settlements of the Citizens of the United States of America, from the Indian Villages and hunting grounds, and thereby extinguishing as far as possible all Occasions of future Animosities, disquiet and Vexation.[1]

I also transmit to you the several Acts of Congress of the 15[h] of October 1783 the 3[d], 4th, 5th and 19th of March 1784 on that subject.[2] I have the honor to be with the greatest respect and esteem Gentlemen Your Most Obedient Servant   THOMAS MIFFLIN

Cy (PCC, item 16, p. 295: DNA).

1. Mifflin had informed NG of his appointment as a commissioner in a letter of 6 March, above. NG replied on 28 March, below, that he would not be able to serve.

2. See *JCC*, 25: 680–95, 26: 123, 124, 125, 152–55.

To the Marquis de Lafayette

My dear Marquis   Newport [R.I.] March 24th 1784

I have to thank you for your kind offer of advance and assistance to M[r] Griffin Greene; but I am happy to learn from him that he should have no occasion to draw on you.[1] I am the more happy upon the occasion as I am under the necessity to draw on you for two hundred & sixteen pounds fifteen shillings which falls upon me for indorsing a sett of bills for Baron Glaubeck the same mentioned by General [Daniel] Morgan and honored by a Brevet commision by Congress for his conduct in the Action at the Cowpens.[2] He is certainly a Vilian and I fear an imposter. He claims the rank of Nobility but his conduct little merits the distinction. He being in distress in Charleston [the] Winter before this last I endorsed a sett of bills for five thousand Livers on Mr Jean Jaques Boyer at Bourdeaux which he promised should be covered in case of protest at the Chevalier de la Lucerne [i.e., La Luzerne,] Minister of France. The bills have returned protested and the Baron has left America without giving the least cover to the Bills.[3] Nor can I tell where to find him or his family if he has any. But it is possible you may find out him or them and by your influence obtain repayment. If you cannot recover the money for me I will remit you the amount of the bills next fall and thank you for your friendly offices in the business. The fellow must be the greatest of vilians to commit such a breach of honor in an act of friendship.[4] I am my dear Marquis Your Most Obed^t humble Ser^t NATH GREENE

Mess[.] Lacase & Mallet will forward the necessary papers for you to proceed upon.[5] This is the substance of the letter sent but not an exact copy.[6]

ACyS (CtY).

1. See Lafayette to NG, 8 September 1783, and Griffin Greene to NG, 1 October 1783, both above. Griffin Greene wrote NG from Paris on 8 February, above, that Lafayette had "don every thing in his powar to assist me."

2. On Glaubeck's role in the battle of Cowpens and the brevet rank that Congress awarded him, see Morgan to NG, 19 January 1781, above (vol. 7: 155, 161n).

3. For more about the protested bills of exchange that NG had given to Glaubeck, see NG to Morris, 3 June 1783; Joseph and William Russell to NG, 29 December 1783; and NG to La Caze & Mallet, 14 January, all above. Francis Mentges had recently suggested that NG not write to Lafayette about Glaubeck. (Pettit to NG, 13 March, above)

4. No reply has been found. Lafayette would have had little or no time to pursue this matter before he sailed for America in June. (Lafayette to the Comte de Vergennes, 28 June, Idzerda, *Lafayette Papers*, 5: 232) NG wrote Washington on 29 August, below: "I expect to loose a thousand dollars having endorsed his [i.e., Glaubeck's] bills and had them to settle."

5. See NG to La Caze & Mallet, 14 January.

6. The document transcribed here is a copy that NG presumably made sometime after sending the original to Lafayette.

To General Henry Knox

Dear General   Newport [R.I.] March 25th 1784

I have just got your kind and obliging letter time enough to give it an acknowledgement by the return of Doctor Gordon.[1] This opportunity only affords me time to say my heart is warm in your interest and my esteem and affection unabated. The pleasures of your freindship has been a constant source of happiness to me during the war; and I should esteem it one of the greatest blessings of my life to be placed where we could indulge a more social intercourse. Nothing could be more grateful to my feelings or more flattering to my wishes. But I know too little of your intentions and [am] too undecided in my own affairs to indulge the pleasing hope that fortune will mingle our future life. You recommended my acceptation of the war department; but is it not too great a sacrafice of private happiness to public utility? After the fatigues and hardships I have undergone have I not a right to indulge the natural bent of my mind which is reading and retirement? The public have great demands upon every individual but we owe something to our selves and more to our family. What ever I may determin concerning the war department I hope to see you at the head of the peace establishment.[2] I should be happy to meet General Washington in Philadelphia if my private business would permit; but I am obliged to go to the Southward in April.[3]

Doctor Gordon has been here collecting materials for a history of the war. I gave him a full opportunity to see every thing which made for and against us.[4] If we have many faults we have some merit. I wish not to shine in borrowed clothes and tho I may be less amiable I shall be nearer truth and candor.

I thank you for your flattering inscription for the Cannon. It is highly complimentary and no less pleasing, if you think it is not so remote from truth, as to make it ridicule in disguise.[5] For you know this is Popes sentiment where Praise exceeds merit.[6]

Mrs Greene is not yet in bed but in hourly expectation.[7] My little flock engross my attention and the little prattlers find some new avenues to the heart every day. Mrs Greene joins me in affectionate compliments to you and Mrs K[nox] accompanied with our best wishes for your future happiness. Yours sincerely   N GREENE

ALS (MeHi).

1. Knox's letter of 14–18 March is above. As seen in the present letter, the Reverend William Gordon, who was writing a history of the Revolutionary War, had visited NG in Newport.

2. In his letter of 14–18 March, Knox wrote that he hoped NG would accept an appointment as head of the War Department if it were offered to him. In 1781, when the department was established, Gouverneur Morris had urged NG to consider the position, but NG had replied at that time that he was not interested. (Gouverneur Morris to NG, 10 September 1781, and NG to Gouverneur Morris, 21 November 1781, above [vol. 9: 313–15 and n, 599–601]) It does not appear that NG was considered for a position in the postwar government; Knox himself was appointed secretary at war in March 1785. (*JCC*, 28: 129)

3. NG was not able to go to Philadelphia for the first general meeting of the Society of the Cincinnati. (NG to Washington, 6 May, below) He did not leave for the South until July.

4. Gordon's four-volume history of the war was first published in 1788. (Vol. 10: 439n, above)

5. On the inscriptions, see above, Knox to NG, 15 February and 14–18 March.

6. NG was referring to eighteenth-century poet Alexander Pope's line, "Praise undeserv'd is scandal in disguise." (Imitations of Horace: Epistles, Bk. II, epis. 1, l. 413 [1733])

7. CG gave birth to the couple's fifth child, Louisa Catharine, on 17 April. (See note at NG to Pettit, 22 April, below.)

*   *   *

¶ [FROM BENJAMIN BOURNE, Providence, R.I., 25 March 1784. Encloses NG's "State Notes together with the order for one years Interest." If "Mᵣ [Robert?] Crooke has not left Town," Bourne will "deliver him" this cover letter "and its enclosures."¹ RCS (MiU-C) 1 p.]

1. For background, see above, William Greene to NG, 1 March, and Bourne's letters to NG of 17 and 20 March.

¶ [FROM WANTON CASEY, Warwick, R.I., 26 March 1784. Has NG's letter of the previous day [not found]. As NG requested, he is forwarding £71.15.8, "the ballance that was due to Capᵗ Littlefield." Is "very sorry Mᵣ Tom Greene refused paying the order when it was presented"; hopes NG will "excuse me, as I could not suppose but he would have paid it at sight." Casey is sending the money in cash with NG's servant.¹ RCS (MiU-C) 1 p.]

1. On the money for William Littlefield, CG's brother, see also Ward to NG, 27 March, below. Littlefield was on Block Island at this time. (Littlefield to NG, 22 March, above)

¶ [FROM CHRISTOPHER GREENE, Potowomut, R.I. [26 March 1784].¹ After "Looking over and Viewing" the "Plantation" in Westerly, he came to some "Conditions" with "[Nathan] Potter and [Samuel] Burlinggame," who wish to rent the property for two years at $200 per year, "with the same Stock[,] farming Tools and, other articles, as when Jacob [Greene] & Griffin [Greene] rented the Place, with this addition": NG is to "Put on one thousand of [fence] Rails this spring and one scow this Summer" and "find all the hay seed that is used on the farm."² In three paragraphs, Christopher Greene lists other conditions of the tenancy. The tenants say these conditions are "harder than" NG's, and they wish they had taken NG up on his "offer at Newport." NG is "not bound to the bargain," but Christopher thinks he should "let them have it[,] all Circumstances Considered." NG should let them know his decision by "the earliest oppertunity." Christopher has not obtained "the lease nor memorandum of the articles of Jacob"³ but will send them as soon as he does. Asks NG to pay "Brother Elihu" only for "my exspences going and Coming from Westerly"; "my services you are welcome to." An undated list of "Conditions on which Potter & Burlingame are to have the farm," in NG's hand, is appended below Christopher's signature: "To give 200 dollars each year. To Cart in 400 load of Rebend Sea Weed in the two years as much as six oxen can draw. To have firewood and Stock & Tools. The Hay seed to be found between us. To plant forty acres and have a Scow built and 1000 Cedar Rails put on the Farm. The orchard to be trimed and the Walls to be put in order." In an undated paragraph below this list, NG later adds: "The forgoing was written to Potter & Burlingame and all agreed to except the furnishing half the hay seed. Make a Lease for one year binding them to put on the 400 Load of Sea Weed including what they have got on since brother Kitt [i.e., Christopher] made the contract. Settle the rent for the year 1783, 150 Dollars and charge interest for deficient payments and give Credit for any payments made before hand. In the Lease specify the Stock Tools and every thing as in the former Lease. Bind the Tenants to trim the Orchard."[4] RCS (MiU-C) 3 pp.]

1. Christopher Greene was one of NG's brothers.

2. The farm in Westerly, which NG's brothers bought with assets from their father's estate, became NG's share when the estate was divided in 1779. The Greene brothers had purchased the 380-acre property from the estate of Gov. Samuel Ward, Sr., the father of Christopher Greene's first and second wives and of NG's friend Samuel Ward, Jr. (See above, Division of the Estate of Nathanael Greene, Sr., 10 June 1779 [vol. 4: 136–37 and n].) It is not known when NG's brother Jacob and his cousin Griffin Greene rented the farm, but CG had lived there for a time during NG's absence with the army. (See NG to CG, 18 July 1781, and James M. Varnum to NG, 17 September 1781, both above [vol. 9: 36, 368].)

3. The "articles of Jacob" were presumably items that Jacob Greene had left on the farm.

4. See also Burllinggame and Potter to NG, 30 March, below.

¶ [FROM SAMUEL WARD, JR., Warwick, R.I., 27 March 1784. "Mess[rs] Carry [i.e., Casey?] & Company have paid the Money." The amount is £71.15.8, for which Ward has "Cap[t] [William] Littlefields order to take a recp[t]." Ward is "extremely sorry my acceptance of an order was a disappointment to to you. They assured me it should be paid at sight and I knew you would not leave the state in several weeks."[1] RCS (MiU-C) 1 p.]

1. On the subject of this letter, see also Casey to NG, 26 March, above.

*   *   *

From George Washington

My dear Sir   Mount Vernon [Va.] March 27th [1784]

A few days ago, by the Post (on when of late their seems to be no dependance) I wrote you a few lines expressive of an earnest wish that you could make it convenient to be at the General meeting of the Society of Cincinnati, before you took your departure for S° Carolina.[1] I did not then, nor can I now, assign all my reasons for it; but to me it should seem indispensable, that the meeting in May next should not only be full, but composed of the best abilities of the representation. The temper of the New England States in particular, respecting this Society, the growing jealousies of it,[2] a letter from the Marq[s], & other considerations point strongly to wise determination at this time.[3] If then private interest or convenience with hold the first characters from the meeting, what may be the consequence? 'Tis *easier*, & perhaps *better* to be conceived than expressed. At any rate a *bear* representation will bring the Society into disrepute, and unfit it, perhaps, for the decision of the weighty matters which may be brought on. Besides, such excuses as I have suggested, may be offered by one man as m[u]ch as another, & none I am sure could urge them with more truth than my self.[4]

I would add more, but that I fear this letter will not reach you in time, and because I am detaining a Country man of yours (who is to be the

Society of the Cincinnati insignia; Greene/Andrews Eagle, ca. 1784–91
(Anderson House, Society of the Cincinnati)

bearer of it) with a fair wind, who is in as bad a situation as a Man on tenter hooks would be, from his eagerness to embrace it. Adieu. I am sincerely & Affect[ly] Y[rs]   GO: WASHINGTON

RCS (Anonymous).

    1. See Washington to NG, 20 March, above. As noted there, NG was unable to attend the meeting but did not leave for the South until July. NG replied to that letter and the present one on 22 April, below.

2. See NG to Washington, 22 April and 6 May, below.

3. Lafayette wrote Washington on 25 December 1783 that "claims are Raising" in France for the admission to the Society of the Cincinnati of officers who had been captains in the navy. He also reported that the king of France had granted permission to some French officers who had served in America to wear the Society's badge on their uniforms. (Idzerda, *Lafayette Papers*, 5: 179–80 and n) In a letter to NG of 10 April, below, Henry Knox predicted that this royal permission would "operate against the society in America, prejudiced as the people are against us." Lafayette also wrote Washington on 10 January and 9 March about the claims of French officers wishing to be admitted to the Society. (Idzerda, *Lafayette Papers*, 5: 191–93, 205–7)

4. Forty-five delegates from twelve states were present when the meetings began in Philadelphia on 4 May. (Myers, *Liberty Without Anarchy*, p. 58) Rhode Island's only representative, Samuel Ward, Jr., arrived late and missed most of the deliberations. (See note at NG to Washington, 6 May.)

To Thomas Mifflin,
President of the Continental Congress

Sir   Newport [R.I.] March 28th 1784

Your Excellency's favor of March the 6th I had the honor of receiving last evening and embrace the earliest moment to give it an answer. The situation of my family forbids my leaving home immediately and my engagements to the Southward claim my attention. It would give me pleasure to comply with the wishes of Congress; but it will not be in my power to answer their expectations in this business. I am too sensible of the honor intended me by Congress to omit so favorable an opportunity of making my warmest acknowledgements upon the occasion.[1] I have the honor to be with great respect Your Excellency's Most Obedient humble Servant   NATH GREENE

ALS (PCC, item 155, vol. 2: 698, DNA).

1. Congress had asked NG to be one of five commissioners to negotiate with Indian tribes. (See above, Mifflin's letters to NG of 6 and 22 March.)

*   *   *

¶ [TO GOVERNOR BENJAMIN GUERARD OF SOUTH CAROLINA. From Newport, R.I., 30 March 1784. NG certifies that "Col Fenwick continued to give intelligence until the British Army left Charleston since which I have not heard from him." In view of Fenwick's services to the army, NG recommends him "to the Legislature agreeable to promise as highly deserving their forgiveness and entitled to their consideration." NG would have made this recommendation "at an earlier day but he being with the British Army I thought he might fall a sacrafice in consequence of it."[1] DS (ScCoAH) Incomplete.]

1. Edward Fenwick of the South Carolina Loyal Militia had served as a spy for the Americans before the British left Charleston. (Vol. 11: 181–82n, above) In August 1782, NG had also certified that Fenwick was providing intelligence and had written: "Upon [Fenwick's] performing this duty faithfully I do promise to use all my influence with the State of South Carolinia to restore him to all his fortunes and the rights and priviledges of

a Citizen." (See "To Whom It May Concern," 14 August 1782, above [vol. 11: 545].) NG wrote to Guerard again on Fenwick's behalf on 19 September, below.

¶ [FROM SAMUEL BURLLINGGAME AND NATHAN POTTER, Westerly, R.I., 30 March 1784. They briefly clarify specifics of their agreement with NG as tenants on his farm there: "You to find the hay seed and the fire wood for the youse of ous; two fires[,] to Plant 30 acors [i.e., acres] a Bove the house and teen [i.e., ten] acor⁵ Beloe the house ware we are a moynty to Plow it and all Beloe the Next Year and all the 30 acor⁵ a Bove the house to Soe with Rye this faul."¹ RCS (MiU-C) 1 p.]
1. For more about the agreement, see Christopher Greene to NG, 26 March, above.

¶ [FROM BARNABAS DEANE, Hartford, Conn., 30 March 1784. Has NG's letter of 13 March [not found]. Deane has never set a price on his services in "Transacting the Companies Buisness," his "Design" having been to let NG and Col. [Jeremiah] Wadsworth decide what they were worth.¹ The business has been "Verry unfortunate Indeed" and "will Illy Aford any Considerable Sum" for his services.² Despite the losses, though, the "Service of Managing" the firm has "been as great as if Ever so Successfull, and much more Disagreeable." The "Losses & Disappointments Often Embarrased" Deane greatly; for he gave up his "Private Buisness on the Commencement of Our Partnership." As he had no clerk, there has been "no Expence" to the company "for any Service Except my Own." He is aware that "Every Person Should fix a price on their own Service," and if NG and Wadsworth will not do so, he will "Set one that Shall not be tho't unreasonable."³ RCS (MiU-C) 1 p.]
1. In a letter to NG of 26 February, above, Deane pointed out that "Debts Due from the Company & my Services for Transacting the Buisness" had not yet been "Deducted from the Seven Thousand pound[s]" that NG thought Barnabas Deane & Company had earned.
2. On the partnership's losses, see Wadsworth to NG, 26 July 1783, above.
3. In late 1784, Wadsworth bought NG's share in the company. (NG to Wadsworth, 29 December, below) In September 1785, when paperwork was being completed for closing out the partnership, Deane again raised the issue of his compensation. (Deane to NG, 4 September 1785, below)

*   *   *

From the Reverend John Murray

Dear Sir   Gloucester [Mass.] March 30ᵗʰ 1784

Some years agone I had the happiness to be acquainted with, and to conceive very warm affection for, a most excellent Person, of the then Province, now State of Rhode Island. The tumults which brought on the calamities so happily terminated in the conclusion of the War, tho they drew my most excellent freind into public life, yet in the midst of the busy scences by which he was continually surrounded, and in which he was unavoidably engaged, he still continued for a long season, to distinguish, by his partial regard, his highly honoured Friend.

Repeated opportunities of meeting this amiable Man, served to convince me that, how dissimiler soever our circumstances, our affections were reciprocal. Yet, accustomed to view Human nature in its ruins, my heart frequently sunk in the prospect of what I conceived may take place; and once, I remember, from the abundance of a heart that told me I could not patiently bear the loss of such a Treasure, I hinted my fear of losing the *Freind* in the *Commander* of an Army, but the generous Man made me blush by asking if I had ever discovered any thing in his conduct that justified such a fear. With strict truth I could declare I never had.

That Being who not only fixes the bounds of our Habitation, but openeth his bo[u]nteous hand, supplying us with just as much and in just such a way as he pleases, had, in the course of his Providence called me to act in a dependant sphere: but, that my spirits may not be too much depressed by this, to some minds, so humiliating a consideration, he enables me first to view my dependance primarily on himself, and secondly, for the most part, graciously made use of such Instruments to do his work, in supplying my wants, as tended rather to sooth than sink my spirits. The Gentleman I am speaking of was peculierly distinguished in this respect, he frequently rather prevented, than relieved my wants, and that with so much ease, and so good a grace that I only seemed sensible of it: Thus he always made me for a while lose sight of the Gift, in beholding the Giver. But his gifts were the genuine offspring of true Freindship, and a numerous progeny they were. How oft have I reposed in his Tent! And fed with appetite at his hospitable Board! My spirits has been raisd by the temperate distribution of his circulating glass, but much more exhilarated by the "Feast of reason and the flow of Soul"[1] which never failed to accompany it. Through his favours I have frequently been received with more than respectful civility, with generous condescending familiarity by the deliverer of his Country, and placed at the Table, near the person, and honoured by the friendly notice of the first of Men. But the current of his kindness stoped not here—he followed me with the flattering proofs of his regard to my present retirement, and at the close of each Campaign, put a period to a state of torturing suspence, and apprehension, by leting me see in his own hand that, under the divine Panoply the "Patriot Hero Freind" was still preserved to all America and me.

But when the distressed Inhabitants of the Southeren States called the right hand of his Excellency to their aid, where fame stood on tiptoe to record his matchless achievements he left his Freind behind! and, pressing forward in pursuit of Glory, well earn'd Glory he has got, happy that through all his meanderings, the fickle goddess has never been able (and in this instance, I am perswaded not willing) to elude his grasp. He is now, I understand (after reaping a plentiful harvest of Laurels, which will perpetually retain their verdure on the page of [his?] History) retired to that little (tho' greatly, and deservedly distinguished) Land of

Liberty[,] honouring the Capital thereof with his abiding residence. There, rich in the affections of the grateful part of his country, the plaudit of his own heart, (the never failing reward of the virtuous and the brave), and peculierly so, in the injoyment of one of the best and most amiable of her Sex, surrounded by her smiling offspring, he injoys that happiness, the prospect of which so often tended to brace his nerves, renew his strength, and sweeten all his toils—and O, may no untoward accident ever dash the Cup of Domestic felicity which a person of his disposition must enjoy with such a zest! and quaff with ineffable delight! May he live thus blessing and blest, till he shall see his Childrens Children and peace upon Israel.

But, say, dear Sir, are you acquainted with this excellent Man "All knowledge centres there." If so you know whither he still honours me with his regard, and whither, if I should be able to prosecute my present purpose, next Summer, in passing through Rhod Island, I shall have the happiness of seeing this greatly valued Freind there, or if not there, where? One line of information respecting how, and where, directed to the care of Captn Prentiss near Doctor Coopers Meeting, Boston, will very much oblige dear Sir Your ever faithful[,] oft obliged[,] most obedient, Humble servant[2]   JOHN MURRAY

RCS (MiU-C).
   1. "There St. John mingles with friendly bowl / The feast of reason and the flow of soul." (Alexander Pope, *Imitations of Horace: Satires*, bk. 2, satire 1, lines 126–27 [1732])
   2. Murray, the founder of Universalism in America, had once been a chaplain in NG's Continental brigade. (Vol. 1: 81n, above) NG was a friend and defender of the radical cleric. (See "To Whom It May Concern," 27 May 1777, above [vol. 2: 96].) Although none of NG's wartime letters to him are extant, several of Murray's to NG have been found. (See above, vol. 3: 135–38; vol. 4: 9–10; vol. 5: 298–300.) It is not known if Murray visited NG in Newport, R.I., that summer; NG left for Charleston, S.C., in July.

*   *   *

¶ [FROM JACOB GREENE, Coventry, R.I., 3 April 1784. Acknowledges NG's letter [not found], "Covering one from Griffin" Greene. It is the "old Story from the *Flora*[:] A Wasteing untill She Comes to Nothing."[1] Is sure the vessel "Will be A Charg[e] upon the owners." Before receiving the letters, Jacob obtained "the Determination of the Whole of the owners At the Eastward," and they have decided to "Hold their Parts of the Ship Except Smith & [Isaac] Sears who Abide the Sail [i.e., sale] which Was Agreable To their First orders."[2] Jacob thinks "Fourtune[,] bad Judgment Want of Capassity and want of foursight will Bring us with our Familys To Want and Misery."[3] He is surprised that Griffin "Had not Made A french Bottom of the Ship and brought out A freight to the West Indias Where he Might have Taken the Neat Profeits of the Freight in West India Goods And Loaded the Ship with Salt and Saved Himself[.][4] Now I think A total Loss will take Plase with a Larger bill of Expences in the bargain[.]" Griffin will probably be disappointed in a plan to go to London and bring out "Spring Goods," as his "Merchant is broke and Creadit Will be Hard to be obtained

Without Proper Creadentals."[5] It seems as if "the Devil Has his Clovren foot AGainst us upon Every Side." Jacob has "About" $5,000 due him on the first of April but has called upon "Severreal Persons with Little Success," for they offer "Fair Promises but no Money." He is afraid he will be "Disapp[oint]ed in Collecting" money for NG to take to "Carrolina" but will do everything he can to "Lodge as Large A Sume" as possible in NG's hands "by the Time the brig Arrives" there.[6] Hopes CG is "Well in bed" before this letter arrives; her confinement will release NG "from one Great Ansity [i.e., anxiety]," as "She has Amost Perswaded you that She will not Live."[7] Hopes "Polly behaves with Propriety in your Family and At the Assembly."[8] RCS (CtY) 3 pp.]

1. Jacob may have referred here to Griffin Greene's letter to NG of 1 October 1783, reporting on his thus-far unsuccessful efforts to sell the *Flora* in France. (See also Griffin Greene to NG, 8 February, above, and 16 May, below.)

2. In his letter of 1 October 1783, Griffin Greene wrote that he had "bid off" the *Flora* "with all her stores at 20,000 Livres but I shall give the Original owners the opportunity of being Concerned again in the Ship if they please." David Henley wrote NG on 10 April, below, that the vessel's owners "all agree to hold her (and have subscrib'd for that purpose) except Sears & Smith who settle for her at her sales." NG had suggested a trading voyage—to Africa—in a letter to Griffin of 10 June 1783, above. (See also Griffin Greene to NG, 8 February.) Concerning the "first orders" for selling the *Flora*, see above, Jacob Greene to NG, 4 May 1783, and Griffin Greene to NG, 18 May 1783 (vol. 12: 641–43, 644n, 662–63).

3. Jacob had expressed similar concerns in his letter to NG of 4 May 1783. NG commented on Jacob's pessimism in a letter to him of 8 July, below. (See also NG to Griffin Greene, 8 July, below.)

4. By "french bottom," Jacob presumably meant loading the *Flora* in France for a trading voyage such as he outlined here. (As it turned out, the condition of the *Flora*'s "bottom" later complicated the vessel's sale. [Griffin Greene to NG, 14 December, below]) The British merchants Watson Copail & Company had advised NG in a letter of 10 September 1783, above, that the *Flora* was "only calculated for the East India trade."

5. As seen in his letter to NG of 8 April, Griffin Greene had purchased £2,000 worth of goods.

6. See also Jacob Greene to NG, 11 June, below.

7. For more about NG's anxieties in regard to CG's pregnancy, see his letter to Charles Pettit of 22 April, below.

8. Jacob's twenty-two-year-old daughter Polly, in whom CG had taken a special interest, was apparently staying with CG and NG at this time. (On Polly, see also Jacob's letter to NG of 4 May 1783.)

¶ [FROM FRANCIS GROOME, Newport, R.I., 3 April 1784. Has NG's letter of 21 March [not found] "Respecting M[rs] Aveys ac[coun]t." The horse that NG "Left was Burnt in the Stable [in] the Great Fire in 76 where M[rs] Avey and Family only ascap[t] with their Lives" and lost everything they owned. She has "allweis Expresst" NG's "Goodness to her and Kindness." She has "met with So many Losses" that Groome believes she is "a Good [d]eale Distresst." Groome will send NG a list of more accounts; if NG would be "kind a nough" to inform him "where those Gentlemen Recide," it will be a "Perticular Favour for the Widow." At the bottom of the letter, Groome lists amounts for "Genl Greens ac[coun]t" and those of two other officers. RCS (MiU-C) 1 p.]

*   *   *

From the Reverend William Gordon

Dear General   Jamaica Plain [Mass.] Ap^r 5. 1784
I have not yet had the pleasure of hearing that your family is happily increased, but hope that event will have taken place before the receipt of this.[1]
I have a grateful sense of your kindness when I was at Newport,[2] & that I believe in your [professions?] shall convince you by these presents[.] Pray you to inform me[:][3]
Who accompanied You when reconnoitring for a position upon the landing of Genl Howe.[4]
How far the Cross Roads were from him.[5]
What was the name of the place the army occupied at the back of Wilmington.[6]
What was the particular spot You would have chosen on the other side of the Schuylkill instead of crossing it, in hopes that Genl Howe would have fought you ere he attempted passing it & going on for Philadelphia?[7]
My best regards to your Lady & Genl Kuskiasco.[8] You have the sincere wishes for a pleasant & safe [*damaged*] or passage to the southward.[9] Your affectionate Friend & humble Servant   WILLIAM GORDON

RCS (MiU-C).

1. CG was pregnant with their fifth child, a girl, who was born on or about 17 April. (NG to Pettit, 22 April, below)

2. Gordon, who was writing a history of the American Revolution, had visited NG in Newport, R.I., the previous month. (NG to Knox, 25 March, above)

3. Gordon's questions in this letter concerned decisions that were made before the battles of Brandywine and Germantown during the summer of 1777. (This period is covered above in vol. 2: 126–71.) Although NG's reply to the present letter has not been found, it appears from Gordon's narrative, as related below, that NG did respond to Gordon's queries. (See notes 4–7, below, and Gordon, *History*, 2: 492–518.)

4. Gordon asserted that after the British commander William Howe landed at Head of Elk, Md., "Gen. Greene attended with gen. [George] Weedon was sent to reconnoitre and find out an eligible spot for their encampment." (Gordon, *History*, 2: 494)

5. According to Gordon, NG "pitched upon" the site at "the Cross Roads near six miles distant from the royal army." (Ibid.)

6. Although NG wrote Washington "acquainting him with the spot he had chosen," Gordon asserted, the letter arrived after "a Council of war had determined . . . to take a position upon Red-Clay Neck, about half way between Wilmington and Christiana, alias Christeen." (Gordon, *History*, 2: 495)

7. According to Gordon, NG and Washington's aide Tench Tilghman "reconnoitred for a position and fixed upon the range of mountains from Valley Forge, toward the Yellow Spring." NG "considered the ground as strong, difficult of access, and yet allowing of an easy descent; and as favorable for partial actions without 'admitting of any very decisive.' " (Gordon, *History*, 2: 516) Gordon wrote that because Gen. Anthony Wayne "was in the rear of Sir William Howe," NG "concluded that the position would bring all the American force partly upon Sir William's flank and rear, and within striking distance of him, if he attempted crossing the Schuylkill, and would oblige him to fight the Americans on their

own terms." According to Gordon, NG "thought also, that the position would afford them the possibility of beating him; or at least so crippling him, that he would not venture to possess himself of Philadelphia; and that in case of their being beaten, it would afford them a safe retreat." (Ibid.) Gordon noted that before NG's letter conveying his opinions could be transmitted to Washington, NG was informed that a council of war had determined "to cross the Schuylkill above French-creek and take a position in front of gen. Howe." (Ibid.)

8. Thaddeus Kosciuszko stayed with NG and CG in Newport at about this time. The dates of his visit are not known, but Gordon's stay with the Greenes probably took place while Kosciuszko was there. (See Littlefield to NG, 22 March, above.)

9. NG left for the South in July. (See note at NG to Hazlehurst, 26 June, below.)

*   *   *

¶ [FROM JOHN STORY, New York, 2–5 April 1784. Acknowledges NG's letter of 21 March [not found]; thanks NG "for your kind offer to render me assistance, in obtaining justice, which I deem a New Mark of your friendship."[1] He hopes to obtain the "Necessary Certificate" from Col. [Charles] Pettit and will then send it to NG.[2] Encloses NG's "account as it stands in the Camp Books" and the "Account of Jacob Greene Esq[r]." According to Pettit, "there appeared a Charge against" Jacob Greene of $56,000, which NG "thought was an error." No such charge appears in the "Camp books," and Story thinks "the mistake must have been in the Books at Philadelphia."[3] He still hopes that Mr. [William] Denning, who has "not yet come to Town," will arrive soon to help "complete a settlement of the Camp Accounts."[4] Story will be happy to "render you any service." According to a postscript, dated 5 April, Mr. [John] Pierce has informed him that "you had wrote for your accounts to be settled." Pierce will "settle them with any person" NG may "please to Authorise," but either that person or NG himself must be "present."[5] Pierce has moved his office to Philadelphia. If NG does not expect to be in New York soon, Story will do himself "the honor of waiting on" NG at Newport, R.I.[6] RCS (MiU-C) 2 pp.]

1. NG's letter was undoubtedly a reply to Story's of 12 March, above. (See also Story to NG, 9 December 1783, above, and note 2, below.)

2. As seen in his letters to NG of 9 December 1783 and 12 March, Story needed the certificate in order to obtain a settlement with the state of Massachusetts for the depreciation of his pay. He enclosed with the second of those letters a copy of the desired certificate with a copy of a letter that Pettit had written to him on 17 January. (MiU-C) NG's docketing on that enclosure reads: "Answered the 21st of March and refered to M[r] Pettit for a Certificate with a promise to Counter Sign it and address a letter to the Legislature of Massachusetts to obtain his [i.e., Story's] depreciation." For more about Story's efforts to obtain the settlement, see his letter to NG of 19 November, below.

3. Story had kept "the Account of Disbursements in Camp in the Quarter Master Generals Office under General Greene" from 10 November 1778 "to the closing of that Office." (Pettit to Story, 17 January, MiU-C) Nothing is known about the sum charged to Jacob Greene.

4. Denning was in New York by early June and settled the accounts—but not to Story's satisfaction—in early July. (See Denning to NG, 9 June, below, and Story to NG, 19 November.)

5. On these accounts, see above, NG's letters to Thomas Mifflin and James Milligan of 9 March. As seen in Lee to NG, 6 April, below, Congress approved the settlement of these accounts. John Pierce was the paymaster general. It is not known whether NG appointed someone to represent him.

6. Story traveled through Newport in early August, after NG left for South Carolina. (Lutterloh to NG, 3 August, and Story to NG, 19 November, below)

* * *

From Griffin Greene

Dear General   Bordeaux [France] April 6. 1784
   Had you no more consequence in the World, than I, or the Americans, in general, I must have returned home, after spending eight or nine Months, in attempts which would [have] ended in disappointments & vexation[.] But your well deserved respect & esteem has procured me a markett for my Ship. Your sinsear friend, and that Friend of all the American[s] that have the least pretentions, The Marquis de La Fayette, after many attempts in vain passiveared untill he had procured me a sale for the Ship. His Excellence the Minnister of France as a compliment to you, & that he would oblige the Marquis, has consented to buy her, and has appointed the Major of Marien [i.e., Marine?], at this place, [to] Estimate her Value, which he has don. I had a letter to him from the Marquis & it appears to me that he is disposed to serve you so far as he can consistant with Honour[.] How much longer I shall be hear upon this bussiness is unseartain, but as I know the Marquis will urge the finishing stroake I hope it will not be very long.[1] After a long suspence I have at last determined to make use of your cradit to procure me Goods to the amount of two Thousand pounds payable in one Year from the delivery.[2] I hope to be able so to conduct, as not to give you any trouble on this head. I have Ordered Twelve hundred pounds from England for Rhode Island on my own cradit to be Shipped this Spring.[3] I sent out seventeen hundred pounds last August from England all of which I have & shall Insure. I have Established corispondance in all parts of Europe which I hope will be of service in futer. I shall go to New York or Philadelphia but I am apt to think the latter as I am obliged to procure a full freight or not be able to get my own shipped & I am not sure of one to New York.[4] The Goods that I take from France, is Brandy[,] Wines of different sorts, Silks, &c which I am in hopes will give us a profit.[5] As quick as possiable I shall finish my affairs & imbarke for America, where I hope to have the happiness of seeing you, & the advantage of hearing, your good a[d]vice for my futer conduct.[6] Give my Love to Caty, & tel her I hope the time is ⟨not⟩ far of[f], when we shall be happy in one neighbourhood, & when this period arives, She will, entertain me with her Sothern Voyage;[7] & I will when nothing more worthy of her notice, give a history of my Europian one. I am with a most hearty wish for both your wellfare your friend.
                                                              GRIFFIN GREENE

Cy (MiU-C). The word in angle brackets is from a copy at MWA.

1. Even with help from the Marquis de Lafayette, the sale of the *Flora* to the French government took a considerable time to close. (See, for example, Griffin's letters to NG of 16 May, 12 June, end of September, 2 November, and 14 December, all below.) The "Minnister of France" was the Marquis de Castries, the naval minister. (See NG's letter to him of 1 June 1785, below.) According to Griffin's letter at the end of the September documents, the name of the man who was appointed to do the valuation was "Tirol." As seen there and in Griffin's letters of 16 May and 12 June, a second valuation was required.

2. On the credit referred to here, see NG to Griffin Greene, 9 June 1783, above. Griffin apparently drew on Jeremiah Wadsworth for this amount, but NG refused to accept the bills, not realizing that Wadsworth had "any agency in the business" that Griffin reported here. (NG to Wadsworth, 12 November, below; on NG's refusal, see ibid. and Pettit to NG, 19 June; NG to Griffin Greene, 8 July; and Wadsworth to NG, 28 September and 1 November, all below.)

3. See also Jacob Greene to NG, 3 April, above.

4. See note 6, below.

5. NG replied to this letter on 8 July, below.

6. Griffin did not return to the United States for another year. (See French & Nephew to NG, 23 April 1785, and NG to Gardoqui, 8 August 1785, both below.)

7. CG had been with NG in the South from April 1782 to June 1783.

From Arthur Lee[1]

Dear Sir   Annapolis [Md.] April 6th 1784

I have the pleasure of informing you that the resolutions for allowing your Expences as stated, & the loss of Money by Major Peirce [William Pierce, Jr.] passd this day unanimously.[2] I hope you will attend the Indian Treaty, which I think will be of infinite importance to our Country. Genl. Clarke [George Rogers Clark] is gone to the western Country & I much doubt whether he can attend.[3] It is probable that Congress will adjourn toward the end of May, leaving a Committee of the States.[4] But if you are so fortunate as to finish the treaty with the Indians soon,[5] by which a determinate territory may be securd in our disposal, it will be but justice to our Creditors to apply the Lands therein as speedily as possible to the payment of their demands; which Congress alone can execute.

The very uncommon severity of the winter, has been extremely injurious to all manner of Stock, & greatly embarrassd the People in general in preparing for their crops. Commerce & trade have also sufferd much from the same cause. I am therefore apprehensive that the product of taxes will be very small. This will render a recourse to the western lands more necessary, & I cannot but hope, that this fund will contribute largely to the abolition of our public debt.[6]

I shall be exceedingly rejoic'd to hear from yourself, of your having engag'd in the indian negociation & likely to bring it to a speedy & happy conclusion.[7]

I have the honor to be, with very great esteem, Dear Sir yr most Obed Servt   ARTHUR LEE

RCS (Papers of the Custis-Lee Families: DLC).

1. Lee, an old acquaintance of NG, was a delegate to Congress from Virginia.

2. For background on this congressional resolution, see especially the note at NG to Mifflin, 3 November 1783, above.

3. On NG's appointment to a commission to negotiate with Indian tribes, see Mifflin to NG, 6 and 22 March, both above. NG had already declined the appointment in a letter to Mifflin of 28 March, above. Clark, who would later serve as an Indian commissioner, was unable to do so at this time. Only two of the members appeared at New York on the appointed date, and when a rescheduled meeting was held in August, the commission consisted of Richard Butler, Oliver Wolcott, and Arthur Lee, who had resigned from Congress to accept the appointment. (Robert Morris to the Commissioners of Indian Affairs, 18 August, Morris, *Papers*, 9: 495–96n)

4. Congress adjourned at Annapolis on 3 June and began to reassemble at Trenton, N.J., on 1 November. It was not able to proceed to business until 29 November, however, when a sufficient number of states was finally represented. (*JCC*, 27: 556, 641) For a little more than two months after the adjournment, some routine business was occasionally transacted at Annapolis by the Committee of the States, a body authorized under Article 9 of the Articles of Confederation, elected from among the delegates, and given "all the powers which may be exercised by seven states in Congress assembled." (*JCC*, 27: 474; on this body's specific powers and membership, see ibid., 474–77. Its journal from 4 June to 13 August is in *JCC*, 27: 561–638.) The committee was effectively dissolved in August, when the departure of several members left only six states represented. (Burnett, *Continental Congress*, p. 609)

5. The Indian commissioners appointed by Congress did conclude treaties with the "principal western tribes." (Abernethy, *Western Lands*, p. 309)

6. The editors of the Morris Papers note that "on April 30 Congress paved the way for revenues from land sales by adopting another grand committee report urging the states to complete their cession of western lands to the Continental government." (Morris, *Papers*, 9: 143n) It was stipulated in that resolution that proceeds from the sale of western lands would be "applied to the sinking such part of the principal of the national debt as Congress shall from time to time direct, and to no other purpose whatsoever." (*JCC*, 26: 329)

7. NG's reply has not been found.

*   *   *

¶ [FROM NICHOLAS HOFFMAN, New York, N.Y., 7 April 1784.[1] In NG's letter of 9 March [not found], which just arrived "last Evening," he asked Hoffman "to be Explicet" about "the moneys Advenc'd for you." Hoffman replies "that itt has been no disappointment to me as yet, but I am under the Necessity of making a Considerable payment on the fir't of May Next, at which time wish to be reimburced if you can make it convenient."[2] Hoffman's wife "& boys" join him in sending compliments to NG and CG. RCS (MiU-C) 1 p.]

1. This is the first of a number of letters between Hoffman, a New York businessman, and NG that has been found. NG, who lodged in Hoffman's home in Morristown, N.J., during the winter of 1777, described him at that time as "a very good-natured, doubtful [i.e., potentially Loyalist] gentleman." (See NG to CG, 1 February 1777, in the Addenda section of this volume, below; Thayer, *Morris County*, p. 194.) Hoffman "fled to the British in New York" soon after that, and New Jersey officials later confiscated his property holdings in that state. (Thayer, *Morris County*, p. 194; on Hoffman, see also Syrett, *Hamilton*, 3: 497, 498n; 17: 481 and n.)

2. NG sent £86:11.7 to Hoffman with a letter of 18 April, which has not been found.

(Hoffman to NG, 26 April, below) Nothing more is known about the money that Hoffman had "Advenc'd for" him.

¶ [FROM FELIX WARLEY, Charleston, S.C., 7 April 1784. Thanks NG for honoring "my draught of the 13ᵗʰ October last"; encloses "the Bond it paid off."[1] Since then, NG's "other Bond has become due," and as Warley is "very much pressed for money," he has drawn "a Bill of this date" on NG, "payable at Ten days sight to the order of Captain Matthew Strong." Below his signature, Warley notes that the second bond was for £356.13.4, was dated 28 January 1783, and was payable one year later. Including interest at seven per cent, the amount due, as of 28 April, is £387.17.2, "equal to Sterling £55.8.2."[2] RCS (MiU-C) 1 p.]

1. On the terms of this bond, see Warley to NG, 13 October 1783, above.

2. As noted at ibid., NG purchased slaves at about the time these bonds were pledged to Warley. For more about the second bond, see Warley to NG, 13 July, below.

*   *   *

To Hugh Wallace[1]

Sir   Newport [R.I.] April 10th 1784.

I[n] consequence of your polite offer and some propositions I made to you by Mr. [Nicholas] Hoffman I have taken the liberty to give a sett of bills on you for seven hundred dollars. If it should not finally be agreeable to you to advance the money which I wanted to settle my Georgia plantation and which Mr. Hoffman said you could not certainly determine until your arrival in London I wish you to honor those bills not with standing and I will repay the amount at any time and place most agreeable to you.[2] And you may rely upon it that I will not disappoint you. My present demand arose from a small concern I took in navigation to promote the views of one of my brothers.[3] And being just ready to set out for Charleston [S.C.] and having no time to collect the money here and the gentlemen in whose favor I draw preferring the bills to the money I have ventured upon your politeness so far as to give a draft on you and hope my expectations may be fully gratified.[4] In complying with which you will oblige me and I shall be happy to render you any good office in my power. I am Sir Your most ob hble ser.

NATH. GREENE

Tr (GWG Transcript: CSmH).

1. As seen in his reply, dated 1 July, below, Wallace, who had been banished from New York, was now a merchant in England. He had been known to NG since early in the war, his name appearing on a list of "principal Tories" in the New York City area that NG forwarded to Washington in August 1776. (Vol. 1: 276, above) NG wrote Nicholas Hoffman on 9 March 1785, below, that he had given a letter of credit to a relative of Wallace "in the beginning of the war" at Wallace's request.

2. As seen in ibid. and in Hoffman to NG, 26 April, below, Wallace was unable to arrange a loan. Mulberry Grove was NG's "Georgia plantation."

3. On the brigantine that NG's brother Jacob sent to the West Indies and Charleston to

obtain a cargo for Europe, see below, Jacob Greene to NG, 11 June; NG to Robert Hazlehurst, 26 June; and NG to Jacob Greene, 5 July.

4. NG did not leave for Charleston until July. (See note at NG to Hazlehurst, 26 June, below.)

* * *

¶ [FROM DAVID HENLEY, Boston, Mass., 10 April 1784.[1] Has NG's letter of 29 March [not found] and is "oblig'd to you for your kind expressions towards my affairs. Your influence will serve me greatly." Henley thought that "Mess [Leonard] Jarvis & Russell" had written to Jacob Greene "and sent the papers compleat in regard to the *Flora* last post." He finds, though, that he was "misinform'd" about this and that the owners "all agree to hold her (and have subscrib'd for that purpose) except [Isaac] Sears & Smith who settle for her at her sales."[2] Henley will bring "the Papers" to NG "this week on my way to the Southward."[3] RCS (MiU-C) 1 p.]

1. On Henley, see note at Gordon to NG, 31 March, above.

2. On the various partners' positions on Griffin Greene's attempts to sell the *Flora* in France, see also Jacob Greene to NG, 3 April, above.

3. As seen in NG's letters to Charles Pettit, 22 April, and to Washington, 6 May, both below, Henley carried correspondence for him "to the Southward."

* * *

From General Henry Knox

My dear Sir   Dorchester [Mass.] 10 April 1784

I thank you for your affectionate favor by Doctor Gordon.[1] I shall now only say a word or two respecting the Cincinnati. You have seen the report of the Committee of the Legislature of this State, but the wrath and indignation of the *respectable public* are upon a much higher key and think the opinion of the Legislature too mild.[2] Nothing less than disfranchisment, ought to have been the penalty for so high a transgression, and it is not improbable that this may be the case at the next Legislature, especially as they are now strengthned by the thundering denunciation of wrath from your friend the Governor of South Carolina as published in the papers of last thursday, and which you will receive by this post.[3]

Our friend the Marquis de la Fayette, in his zeal of Love, has rendered the order too effulgent in France, so that every body who has the least claim and endevering to render it valid. He with some formalities obtained the permission of the King & his ministers that the officers who had served in the American Army and those under Count de Rochambeau might wear *the illustrious order of the bald eagle*. This will operate against the society in America, prejudiced as the people are against us.[4]

I have received a letter from Genl Washington of the 20th of last month in which he states the uproar that has been raised and the probability of its encrease,[5] and in consideration of it, presses with great anxiety a general attendance of all the members chosen from the respective States, and particularly he exceedingly wishes you to be there. Speaking of your intentions further Southward, he says "I wish this *could* be otherwise, and that Gen[l] Greene *would* attend."[6] I beg therefore my dear friend, if it is possible that you will so arrange matters as to go from Philadelphia by Water, instead of Rhode Island, provided it is your intention to take a water passage. If you go by land two or three days will be nothing to halt at Philadelphia.[7]

I shall set out from hence by the 20th and shall if possible call at Newport, as it is my intention to go by Water to New York from Providence.[8] I am my dear friend your truly affectionate   H KNOX

RCS (DSoC).

1. The Reverend William Gordon, who had visited NG in Newport, carried NG's letter to Knox of 25 March, above.

2. Popular opposition to the Society of the Cincinnati in Massachusetts had been growing for some time. The Massachusetts legislature began a formal inquiry in February 1784 and presented a report in March terming the Society of the Cincinnati "a threat to the 'peace, liberty and safety of the United States in general, and this Commonwealth in particular.' " (Myers, *Liberty Without Anarchy*, p. 52) On public resistance to the Society in New England more generally, see NG to Washington, 22 April, below.

3. Gov. Benjamin Guerard had denounced the Society of the Cincinnati in a speech before the South Carolina legislature in February. Excerpts of his critical remarks were printed in newspapers throughout the country; they appeared in the *Newport Mercury* of 17 April, reprinted from a Boston source, dated 8 April. Guerard considered the Society an "alarming institution," which threatened the leveling effects of democracy. By excluding state militia and navy from their ranks, the Society "will most certainly be generative of Suspicion, Jealousy, division and domestic discord," he warned, "if not ultimately open a vein, and deluge us in blood." Its assumption of "the self-made [power] of creating Orders descendible to the Oldest male posterity" created a dangerous "precedent," and its honorary memberships, which created hierarchies within its own ranks, ran counter to the spirit in which the Revolutionary War was fought. Guerard charged that "design, ambition, Vanity and mischief" were the Society's true purpose, and he questioned whether there was "any safety or Security to person or property" when "this and that body of men" could "whenever they please, assume a power coeval with that of Legislation, the Bulwark of a Commonwealth, and Palladium of Liberty." Guerard found it "really too humiliating in Officers of the justly far famed American Army, to copy [their "foe"] in extravagancy, luxury, voluptuousness and effeminancy and envy their paltry badges and dignities—what have ever been the Source of all their Country's evils, and what ultimately will be the cause of its downfall." It was also "incompatible with magnanimity, modesty and sense and having rather an aspect of weakness and vanity, for an intrepid illustrious band of heroes themselves to undertake to sing their own praises and perpetuate their merits and achievements." Guerard cautioned that "wise and great men always patiently and diffidently wait for the sound of the Trumpet of fame, and the eulogium of the historic page—a Contrary conduct in this instance, will furnish pretext to say that, vanity and a thirst after dignities, gewgaws and bawbles were the Objects of the late contention, and not merely Liberty, freedom and patriotism." (S.C., House of Representatives, *Journals, 1783–84*, pp. 403–5)

4. After receiving word of the formation of the Society of the Cincinnati in December, the Marquis de Lafayette had been assessing the claims of many French officers who asked to be admitted to the Society based on their service in America. (Lafayette to the Comte de Vergennes, 16 December 1783, and Lafayette to Washington, 25 December 1783, Idzerda, *Lafayette Papers*, 5: 176–78, 179–80) French army officers had not been allowed to wear the insignia of foreign countries on their uniforms, but Lafayette interceded with the king of France to gain special permission for those who had served in America to wear the badge of the Society of the Cincinnati—a gold eagle—with their formal military regalia. Lafayette wrote Washington the previous December that he had received this permission. (Lafayette to Washington, 25 December 1783, Idzerda, *Lafayette Papers*, 5: 179–80 and n) The Comte de Rochambeau had commanded the French expeditionary force in America during the war.

5. On the "uproar" raised by the formation of the Society of the Cincinnati, see also Flagg to NG, 17 October 1783, above, and NG to Washington, 22 April and 6 May, both below.

6. Knox did not repeat the second half of Washington's sentence, which read: "private interest, or convenience may be a plea for many, & the Meeting thereby be thin & unfit for the purpose of its institution." (Washington, *Papers*, Confederation Series, 1: 229) NG had also received letters from Washington of 20 and 27 March, above, urging him to attend the general meeting of the Society of Cincinnati in early May in Philadelphia. NG was unable to attend. (NG to Washington, 6 May)

7. Knox and Washington believed that NG might be on his way to South Carolina at the time of the meeting, as NG had informed both of them that urgent financial matters there would keep him from attending. (NG to Knox, 25 March, and NG to Washington, 16 February, both above) CG's recent confinement and his own health problems kept NG from leaving Newport at that time. (NG to Washington, 6 May, below)

8. Knox passed through Newport on his way from Boston to Philadelphia on 23 April. (*Newport Mercury*, 24 April 1784) It is not known if he visited NG at that time, but his desire to see NG, as expressed in this and other letters written during the winter and spring of 1784, suggests that Knox may have purposely routed his trip through Newport to see NG. (See, for example, Knox to NG, 15 February, above.)

* * *

¶ [FROM JEREMIAH OLNEY,[1] Providence, R.I., 10 April 1784. Encloses "a Copy of Col° Walkers Letter," which he just received. Walker refers "to a Circular Letter" that Washington sent the previous December to "the President of the State Societys of the Cincinnati."[2] Olney forwarded Washington's letter to NG in January "by Some Gentleman going from Hence to Newport"; in case NG has not received it, Olney "thought proper to Transmitt the Inclosed Copay of Colo Walkers Letter."[3] RCS (DSoC) 1 p.]

1. Olney had been elected treasurer of the Rhode Island Society of the Cincinnati in December 1783. (Arnold, *R.I.*, 2: 500)

2. The enclosure has not been found. Col. Benjamin Walker of New York had been an aide-de-camp to Washington. (Heitman, *Register*; Fitzpatrick, *GW*, 23: 375n) Walker seems to have been involved in disseminating Washington's circular letter of 28 December 1783, above, one version of which contains a postscript in Walker's hand. (Fitzpatrick, *GW*, 27: 287 and n) Washington wrote him on 24 March: "I have obtained no answers yet to the circular Letters you took with you for New Jersey, New York & New Hampshire—the two first certainly must have got to hand; but it may not be amiss nevertheless for you to enquire (by a line) of the Presidents of those two (State) Societies, whether they have or have not got them—accompanying the enquiry with information of the time & place of

the Genl Meeting." (Washington, *Papers*, Confederation Series, 1: 233–34) Given the content of the present letter, it is likely that Walker's letter to NG as president of the Rhode Island Society of the Cincinnati was similar to what Washington had asked him to write to chapter presidents in the other states.

3. NG's reply to Washington's circular letter of 28 December 1783 is above, dated 16 February; Washington received it on 19 March. (Washington to NG, 20 March above) NG replied to Olney on 15 April, below.

*   *   *

To Jeremiah Olney

Dear Sir   Newport [R.I.] April 15th 1784
    I wrote General Washington in Feb[r]uary who were appointed to attend the Meeting of the Cincinnati at Philadelphia and thought that a full answer to his Circular letter.[1] But to leave him without any impression of disrespect or neglect either with you or me I will send him a letter of apology assigning the reasons of that letters not being more particularly attended to.[2] I am sorry there is likely to be such a puzzle about our representation. Indeed I fear we shall have none unless you can go.[3] Mrs Greene is in such a situation as utterly forbids my going at present if at all.[4] And besides which I am under such engagements to go to the Southward it is next to impossible for me to attend. Was my engagements all concerning my self I would dispense with them but I am under some for my brother very interesting to him.[5] I wish it was possible for you to go; but I can not urge it in your present situation. Popular opinion has no weight with me if I could accomodate my other means to the measures. I am dear Sir Your Most Obed humble Ser

NATH GREENE

ALS (RHi).
    1. This letter is a reply to Olney's of 10 April, above. NG had responded to Washington's circular letter of 28 December 1783, above, on 16 February, above, reporting that either James M. Varnum or Daniel Lyman would represent the Rhode Island chapter of the Society of the Cincinnati at the general meeting in Philadelphia in May. Washington received NG's response on 19 March and replied to him the following day. (Washington to NG, 20 March, above)
    2. NG's next letter to Washington about the Society's general meeting is below, dated 22 April.
    3. Varnum and Lyman must have decided against going to the meeting. (See note 1, above.) Washington had been urging NG to attend and to bring a full delegation from Rhode Island. (See Washington to NG, 20 March and 27 March, and Knox to NG, 10 April, all above.) As it turned out, Samuel Ward, Jr., was the only Rhode Island member who attended the meeting. (NG to Washington, 6 May below)
    4. On the birth of the Greenes' fifth child, see NG to Pettit, 22 April, below.
    5. On NG's "engagements to the Southward," see his letter to Washington of 22 April.

*   *   *

¶ [FROM NATHANIEL PENDLETON, Charleston, S.C., 18 April 1784. NG's friends there have "flattered themselves with the hope of seeing you before the Spring," but Pendleton now despairs of this, because NG is "again called from Domestic Concerns into public business." He does not know, however, if NG has accepted "the troublesome honor of a Commissioner to treat with the Indians."[1] He reports some news from the South Carolina legislature: "They Settled the mode of admitting Aliens into the Country.[2] They settled a Land tax at 1 per C^t Ad Valorem,[3] & they repealed the Confiscation Law with respect to many persons, some of whom were among the most obnoxious Characters." There was "much talk" about repealing the confiscation law "generally with an exception only of a few Characters," and Pendleton thinks that will be done "at the next meeting."[4] John Rutledge was "Challenged to fight a Duel, by Mr Thompson The keeper of the City Tavern"; Rutledge "complained to the house, who in some heat ordered Thompson to beg pardon of the House, and of Mr Rutledge at the Bar and give Security for his good behaviour."[5] Pendleton remarks that "Mrs Greene's interesting situation" kept NG from leaving for the South as soon as he "originally intended"; hopes CG has "recovered."[6] Some of CG's friends "are in high expectation of seeing her in Carolina," and none wishes it "more ardently" than Pendleton. Because it will be "impossible" for him to be "admitted to practice" in South Carolina, he has decided to go to Georgia and "make an Essay there for a year or two." His plans could change if the scheme he mentioned in a previous letter should meet NG's "approbation & be practicable"; he fears that Georgia will not "suit" his "Constitution," as he has "already had a slight touch of the fever."[7] He supposes that "Mr Sanders [Roger Parker Saunders]" writes to NG "regularly" about NG's "private Concerns." Saunders has "made a most advantageous purchase of Slaves" for NG.[8] Major [William] Pierce has "removed to Savanna," and Pendleton proposes to "follow him in the Fall." He believes that Pierce's "Concern" will "succeed better than we expected."[9] Pendleton sends his "most affectionate and respectfull good wishes" to CG; he plans to "take an opportunity soon of giving her a history of some little anecdotes, among her acquaintance" in South Carolina, "which may perhaps afford her Some amusement." In a postscript, he reports that he has "been on the point of an Engagement with Mrs Marshall, the Madman's widow, but there is a slight interruption at present," and he does not know "how it may opperate."[10] In addition, "Mrs Harlston" is soon to be married, and "Poor Edwards has a Dismission."[11] RCS (ScHi) 4 pp. The manuscript is damaged.]

1. NG had recently turned down an appointment by Congress to a commission that was to negotiate with Indian tribes. (NG to Mifflin, 28 March, above) Although he had planned to leave for the South by this time, CG's confinement and his own ill health kept him from going until July. (See NG to Washington, 6 May, and note at NG to Hazlehurst, 26 June, below.)

2. "An Act to Confer the Rights of Citizenship on Aliens" had been ratified on 26 March, the last day of the legislature's winter session. (S.C., House of Representatives, *Journals, 1783–84*, p. 629)

3. The legislature voted to enact the real estate tax on 4 March. (Ibid., p. 521)

4. An "act for restoring to certain persons" their "estates both real and personal and for

permitting the said persons to return to this state" was passed on the final day of the legislative session. (*Statutes of S.C.*, 4: 624–26)

5. William Thompson, a former captain in the South Carolina Continental line, was the proprietor of the City Tavern in Charleston. His adversary, Rutledge, the former governor of South Carolina, was now a member of the General Assembly. They gave differing accounts of how the controversy began. Rutledge claimed to have sent a verbal message for the Sons of St. Patrick to Thompson via a slave woman, but Thompson later denied that he had received the message. Summoned to Rutledge's house to explain his conduct, Thompson apparently erupted in anger over Rutledge's acceptance of his slave's version of the incident—i.e., that the message had been properly delivered. Thompson then wrote to Rutledge, demanding an apology. Despite Pendleton's report here that Thompson challenged Rutledge to a duel, historian Michael Stevens asserts that Thompson made it "clear that he was not proposing" one. After receiving Thompson's letter, Rutledge also demanded an apology, which was not forthcoming. On 19 March, Rutledge laid his and Thompson's letters before the legislature, arguing that as he was a legislator, Thompson's "threats" to him constituted a "breach of privilege." According to English law and tradition, threatening behavior toward a legislator was considered an unjust interference with his ability to perform his duties. Summoned before a legislative committee on privileges and elections, Thompson was denied the right to counsel and was ordered to apologize to Rutledge and the South Carolina House of Representatives or be jailed. Although he agreed to apologize to the House, he refused to do so to Rutledge and was jailed for the "remaining week of the session." (Michael E. Stevens, "Legislative Privilege in Post-Revolutionary South Carolina," *William and Mary Quarterly* 3rd Series 46 [January 1989]: 71–79) This controversy took place within a context of larger tensions between radical, egalitarian members of the Anti-Britannic Society of Charleston, of which Thompson was a member, and aristocrats such as Rutledge, who were seen as being allied with British merchants and Loyalists. Those tensions had led to social unrest and riots in the city the previous summer and would do so again during the summer of 1784. (See NG to Washington, 8 August 1783, above; William Washington to NG, 8 July, and Pendleton to NG, second letter of 10 July, both below.)

6. CG's advanced pregnancy was one of the reasons NG had delayed leaving for the South. She gave birth to the Greenes' fifth child, Louisa Catharine, on or about 17 April. (NG to Pettit, immediately below)

7. In a letter of 30 January, above, Pendleton had discussed the problems he was encountering in trying to establish himself as a lawyer in South Carolina. After settling in Savannah, Pendleton became a judge and served as a delegate from Georgia to the Constitutional Convention. (See above, vol. 7: 308n.) The "scheme" he had mentioned in a "previous letter" was to take a commission in the peacetime army instead of pursuing a career in law. (Pendleton to NG, 30 January, above)

8. On Saunders's "advantagious purchase" of slaves for NG, see note at Pettit to NG, 27 April, below, and Saunders to NG, 29 May.

9. For more about Pierce's business firm, see, for example, NG to Wadsworth, 24 May 1783, above.

10. On Pendleton's relationship with Mrs. Marshall, see his letters to NG of 30 January, above, and 10 July, below.

11. On Elizabeth Harleston's marriage to James Hamilton and Evan Edwards's failed courtship of a Charleston woman, see also Pendleton to NG, 3 February, above.

*   *   *

To Charles Pettit

My dear Sir   Newport [R.I.] April 22[d] 1784

I imagine you will be equally surprised to find me here as not having heard from me before. Mrs Greenes not getting to bed as early as she expected prevented my setting out for the Southward[,][1] and a very disagreeable complaint in my breast has forbid my writing. Its symtoms are alarming and its progress more so. It arose from a sprain I got in Providence last winter in a slippery season by a violent exertion to save my self from a fall. I hurt the vessels of the stomach and about three weeks since I was seized with a deadly pain which attends me night and day. Feeling my self a little better to day and a good opportunity to write by Col Henly [David Henley] offering I have hazarded the use of the pen against the advice of my Physician. M[rs] Greene is in bed and in a good way of recovery. I expect she will be about house in ten days or a fortnight. If my complaint gets well enough for me to travel I shall pay a visit to Philadelphia on my way to the Southward.[2]

I hope you and [Robert] Morris have brought your affairs to a close without any farther appeals. My situation you know is delicate in that business. I hope you will not place me therefore in any disagreeable point of view if you can avoid it, but I mean to stand or fall with you in the matter.[3]

I cannot dictate a settlement with Col [John] Cox. His fortune is extensive, mine is limitted, and much embarassed. I am not willing therefore to give up any just claims nor do I wish any thing more than justice[.] On this principle you will settle the matter. What ever may appear to you to be right between me and the Col agree to and I shall be satisfied. I am glad he is making provisions to take up my bills. It will relieve me from great difficulty.[4]

I think you must have forgot respecting M[rs] Greens bills. In your Account you charge all the payments made which was done the day before I left Philadelphia and then write at the bottom of the Account thus "Assumed to pay for a Chariot not yet finished and some bills for Mrs Greene not yet settled the amount of which are uncertain but are supposed to be £250 or £260." This is an exact extract from the Account word for word. But besides this I remember perfectly well there was sundry outstanding bills of hers which I thought you took upon you to discharge even if they exceeded our calculation. But if you are not satisfied with the terms of our agreement I shall not insist, but it was so understood at the time. You will please to settle the bills and we will talk the matter more fully at our next meeting. But in settling the bill for the Silk Mrs Greene says she agreed with Col [Clement] Biddle for a Guinea a yard and the charge is much higher. Dont settle it at any other rate than Mrs Greene agreed. And send the Carriage by the first good opportunity.[5]

Doctor [William] Burnet writes me that I am in a fair way to get disentangled from Mr Banks's affairs. If I get clear of this it will be difficult to draw me into engagements of the like nature again. But I hope you will still keep your eye upon his affairs for not withstanding all the Doctor says I can not help having my fears.[6]

Mrs Greene joins me in affectionate compliments to you and Mrs [Sarah Reed] Pettit and all the family. Yours sincerely   NATH GREENE

ALS (NHi).

1. Although NG had expected the baby to be born "any hour" since the beginning of March (NG to Knox, 4 March, above), CG did not give birth to their fifth child, Louisa Catharine, until on or about 17 April, according to the daybook of Isaac Senter, the Greene family physician. (Senter Daybook, RHi) This birth, which took place more than ten months after CG left NG at Charleston, S.C., in early June 1783, may have contributed to rumors of infidelity on CG's part. Jeremiah Wadsworth wrote Washington in 1786, soon after NG's death, that one such rumor had caused "much pain to the Generals, & her friends," but, Wadsworth believed, had "never reachd [NG's] Ears: if it did he certainly never gave the least credit to it—as imedeately after it was circulated and believed here (that they had parted), they came together to my House and I never saw more unaffected fondness and attachment than existed between them at that time." (Wadsworth to Washington, 1 October 1786, Washington, *Papers*, Confederation Series, 4: 282) In regard to rumors about CG's conduct—and NG's alleged unhappiness with her—see also Isaac Briggs to Joseph Thomas, 23 November 1785, *Georgia Historical Quarterly* 12 [1928]: 179–82. The beautiful and vivacious "Caty" appears to have had many prominent, male admirers, and her biographers suggest that after NG's death she may have had more-than-flirtatious relationships with several married men, including Wadsworth. (Stegeman, *Caty*, pp. 133ff)

2. NG paid a brief visit to Philadelphia in early June, but not on his "way to the Southward." (See note at NG to Washington, 6 May, below.) He sailed to Charleston, S.C., from Newport in July. (See note at NG to Hazlehurst, 26 June, below.)

3. See Pettit's letters to NG of after 21 January and 7 February, both above. Pettit replied on 6 May, below: "You are very obliging in your Determination to support me as far as lies with you, but I have (& intend to go on so) taken the Matter on myself."

4. On NG's claim against his and Pettit's partner, John Cox, see Pettit's letters to NG of after 21 January and 7 February, above, and 18 May, below.

5. Pettit, who had mentioned the bills in his first letter to NG of 8 March, above, discussed the matter further in his reply of 6 May. NG and Pettit had signed a financial agreement on 8 November 1783, above, while NG was in Philadelphia; the statement quoted here has not been found, however. Pettit had still not found a vessel that could accommodate the vehicle when he wrote NG on 13 March, above, but he was finally able to report on 26 June, below, that it had been loaded onto a sloop bound for Newport.

6. William Burnet was the father of Banks's deceased business partner--and NG's former aide—Ichabod Burnet. His letter to NG on this subject has not been found. Pettit replied to NG on 6 May that he saw some reason to hope "your Entanglement on the Suretyship [with Banks] is in a better way of Extrication than I had supposed"—or than would prove to be the case. (See also Pettit to NG, 27 April, below.)

To George Washington

Dear Sir   Newport [R.I.] April 22[d] 1784

Your two letters of the 20th and 27th of March both came safe to hand. My indisposition is such I fear it will not be in my power to comply with your wishes if there was no other obstacle. I have a constant pain in my breast and am now so weak as to be incapable of bearing the fatigues of a Journey. Besides which the Doctor thinks it would be dangerous to go by water for fear I might burst a blood vessel as I am very subject to sea sickness and the Vessels of the stomach are exceedingly uncoated. And he thinks it equally dangerous to ride for fear of the same evil. My complaint arose from a strain I got in Providence last Winter in making a violent exertion to save my self from a fall.[1]

It was my intention to have been in South Carolina before this; but M[rs] Greene not being put to bed as early as I expected I continued my stay until my own complaints forbids my going.[2] But was I well enough to travel I would certainly go by the way of Philadelphia notwithstanding it would be attended with no small injury to my private affairs; and my necessities on this head are far different from yours. In addition to my own embarassments on this subject I am under such engagements to provide a Cargo for a vessel of my brothers expected in Charlesto[n] that I should be at a loss how to accomodate that matter even if I had no calls of my own and what makes me more anxious on this subject he has been unfortunate in trade at the close of the year which renders my obligation to fulfill my engagements the greater[.][3] You never felt embarrasments in matters of interest and god grant you never may[.] No body can feel but those that experience [it]. It sinks the spirits and depresses the mind.

The uproar that is raised against the Cincinnati makes me more anxious to [be] at the Meeting than I ever expected to feel. It was uninteresting to me before. Assuming honors hurt my delicasy; but persecution bannishes the influence. The subject is important and it may be equally dangerous to recede or push forward; but I am decided in my opinion not to abolish the order from the prevailing clamours against it. If this is done away the whole tide of abuse will run against the commutation.[4] The public seem to want somthing in New England to quarrel with the officers about, remove one thing and they will soon find another. It is in the temper of the people not in the matters complained of.[5] I hope the meeting will not be hasty in their determination or in too great a hurry to seperate. It is yet uncertain what the politicks of America will lead to if they are not influenced by some collateral cause. It is necessary to create a jealosy in the people to bind them together. If they are not afraid of the Cincinnati[,] local policy will influence every measure.[6] If Congress is silent on the subject as I hope they will it will be a convincing proof they both see and feel its advantages.[7] I am confident the tranquility of the public can only be preserved but by the continuance of the order. If I can come I will but whether I do or not I am for continuing the institution with out alteration: To make any alteration in the present hour will be premature, injure its influence, and defeat all the good that may be expected from continuing it an object of public attention.[8] My breast pains me so much that I cannot add only my good wishes for your health and happiness. Mrs Greene joins me in kind compliments to Mrs Washington and all the branches of the Family. I am dear Sir with esteem and affection Your Most Obedt humble Sert   NATH GREENE

ALS (Washington Papers: DLC).

1. NG described the origin of his physical complaint in his letter to Charles Pettit of this date, immediately above. The injury was so debilitating, NG wrote Washington on 6 May, below, that he would not be able to attend the general meeting of the Society of the Cincinnati in Philadelphia, as Washington had urged in letters to him of 20 and 27 March, above. The pain "hung about" him for "upwards of two months," but, he wrote Washington on 29 August, below, "by the use of" balsam of fir, he was finally able to relieve it.

2. CG had recently given birth to a daughter, Louisa Catharine. (NG to Pettit, this date) NG had hoped to return to South Carolina on personal business by this time.

3. NG's "embarassments on this subject" were presumably the financial problems resulting from the suretyship he had signed for John Banks. (See also NG to Pettit, immediately above, and NG to Lee, 22 August 1785, below.) On the brigantine that NG's brother Jacob sent to the West Indies and Charleston to obtain a cargo for Europe, see below, Jacob Greene to NG, 11 June; NG to Robert Hazlehurst, 26 June; and NG to Jacob Greene, 5 July.

4. On the "uproar" against the Society of the Cincinnati, see, for example, Flagg to NG, 17 October 1783, above. The issue of commutation of officers' retirement pay is noted at Wadsworth to NG, 12–13 June 1783, above. The question of funding for this pay was especially contentious, and there was strong opposition to Congress's impost proposal of 1783 as a means of obtaining the necessary revenue. (On the impost, see especially the note at NG to Lincoln, 18 June 1783, above.) The "order"—i.e., Society of the Cincinnati— had been founded, at least in part, to agitate for officers' commutation rights. (Myers, *Liberty Without Anarchy*, pp. 1–19)

5. In his monograph on the Society of the Cincinnati, Minor Myers writes that the "outcry" against commutation "was severe in New England." He notes that two "representative meetings" in Middletown, Conn., during the fall of 1783 had called for that state's legislature to "investigate Congress's power to grant commutation," although "only in one instance was commutation linked with the Cincinnati." After Aedanus Burke of South Carolina published his pamphlet criticizing the Cincinnati in October 1783 (Flagg to NG, 17 October 1783), the Middletown convention called for a "permanent committee to communicate with critics of commutation throughout the nation." Protests against the Cincinnati also erupted in Massachusetts, where the legislature held a "formal inquiry" into the Society's legitimacy in February 1784. Rhode Island had vocal critics of the Cincinnati, but its legislature did not vote to investigate or condemn the Society. (Myers, *Liberty Without Anarchy*, pp. 49–52; on the Massachusetts legislative hearings, see above, Knox to NG, 10 April. For a detailed discussion of opposition to the Cincinnati in New England, see also Wallace Evan Davies, "The Society of the Cincinnati in New

England, 1783–1800," *William and Mary Quarterly*, 3rd series 5 [1948]: 3–15.) NG wrote Washington on 6 May that the "clamour" against the Society in the New England states was increasing.

6. The delegates to the Society of the Cincinnati's general meeting convened in Philadelphia on 4 May. On the results of the meeting, see note at NG to Washington, 6 May.

7. According to Minor Myers, two resolutions adopted by Congress during the winter and spring of 1784 were seen as taking "indirect aim" at the Society. One of these forbade a select group of American officers from wearing the insignia of a similar Polish organization. The other resolution prohibited any federal official from holding a "'hereditary Title.'" (Myers, *Liberty Without Anarchy*, pp. 52–53) Although Congress did not address the subject directly, some delegates were highly critical of the Society. (See, for example, Elbridge Gerry to John Adams, 23 November 1783, Smith, *Letters*, 21: 161.)

8. Although NG was in favor of maintaining the Society's "institution," the delegates to the May meeting altered the organization's regulations and requirements. (See note at NG to Washington, 6 May.) Of the changes, NG later admitted to Washington: "I am happy you did not listen to my advice. The measures you took seemed to silence all jealosies on the subject." (NG to Washington, 29 August) As seen in note 1, above, NG was unable to attend the meeting.

* * *

¶ [FROM NICHOLAS HOFFMAN, New York, 26 April 1784. Acknowledges NG's letter of 18 April [not found] "this morning by Capt Read with £86:11.7."[1] Hoffman forwarded NG's letter for "Doctor [William] Burnett" by a "carefull hand," and Burnet should have it "this day."[2] Has a letter from "M[r] Hugh Wallace dated London the 6th March," in which Wallace sends his compliments to his "friend Gen[l] Green" and asks Hoffman to let NG know that he has inquired "about procuring the money" but finds that people in London "do not think Affairs" there or in America are "settled, and are in such an unsettled Situation that they will not at present Lend mon'y." Indeed, everyone there complains "for want of" money; "the Funds are low and Vast sums wanting to pay of[f] the Expences of the warr." As matters stand, Wallace has "no hopes of procuring the money as Every thing is in the utmost confution."[3] Hoffman is "sorry" that NG "will meet with a disappointment." Gen. [Henry] Knox, who is "now with us," joins Hoffman and his wife in compliments to NG and CG.[4] RCS (MiU-C) 1 p.]

1. This letter and the remittance were undoubtedly in response to Hoffman's request of 7 April, above.

2. NG's letter to Burnet has not been found.

3. See also NG to Wallace, 10 April, above, and Wallace to NG, 1 July, below.

4. Knox wrote NG on 10 April, above, that he planned to travel from Boston to New York by way of Rhode Island.

* * *

From Charles Pettit

Dear Sir   Philadelphia 27th April 1784

By Cap[t] [Matthew] Strong, who left Charleston [S.C.] the 8th or 9th Instant, I have a Letter from M[r] R[oge][r] Parker Saunders of the 28th of March of which you will receive a Copy herewith. This Communication of it's Contents appears to be the more necessary on my Part, as he mentions that he does not write to you, expecting that you may be on the Way to Carolina.[1]

Knowing of some Negociations through Col. Biddle about Funds in Europe I applied to him to know whether the Business was in such forwardness as that any Assistance could be obtained from it on the present Occasion; but I could find no Room to hope for it.[2] I am much grieved to find that it is not in my Power to give the Aid I would wish to give: but I have so far exhausted myself in preparing the Furnace for a Blast, that all the means I can use are scarcely sufficient to keep Pace with absolute Engagements besides leaving some Matters to the chance of uncertain Resources & leaning more on Credit than is by any means pleasant.[3] I hope however that you are otherwise provided to answer this Demand of Mr Saunders.[4] The great Drains of Specie from hence to Carolina & Virginia, and, above all, in Remittances to Europe, have rendered Cash extremely Scarce in this Town. The Bank [of North America] has also diminished the Quantity of Circulation, by contracting its Discounts latterly, and many People, depending perhaps too much on that mode of Payment, are greatly distressed for Means to make good their Engagements, insomuch that 3, 4, & 5 per cent per Month are given for ready Money, & I have heard of Instances of 10.[5] I mention these to shew the Difficulty of the Times in this Place, and tho' I feel it only for others in its direct operation, it's Influence is too general to permit any one to escape wholly the Effect of its Consequences.

Some time ago you desired me to inform you particularly about certain Affairs in Carolina in which you are Interested. At that Time I perceived nothing of Consequence more than that those Affairs seemed to gradually increase in labouring & at the same Time they were gradually diminishing in Size, so that on the whole I thought they were drawing to a Close that would dissolve your Obligations. That may yet be the Case for aught I know; but Appearances in that View are not now so pleasing as they have been. I have heretofore informed you that the Draughts on me exceeded the Funds in my Hands. The Promises of Remittances to answer them have generally proved delusive as you seemed to expect they would be.[6] I therefore guarded against actual Acceptances, but gave such Expectations as I was enabled to give, to the Holders. Some of the Bills were protested; others were recalled; but still a Number remained on the Strength of those Expectations, and I intended to pay them as I should be enabled. But by Capt Strong came an Order signed by M^r [John] Banks to pay whatever Balance might be in my Hands to Mr James Miller, together with a short Letter signed by Messrs [Robert] Forsyth, [James] Hunter & Jno Burnet expressing their Approbation of the Order, but not a Line from Mr Banks other than the Order itself on the Back of an Account.[7] These Papers were bro^t by M^r

[Robert] Morris who is now here. He tells me that he has obtained assignments & Paper Securities of one Kind and another, which he hopes will in the End Satisfy his Demand, but that he cannot release you till the Payment shall be actually made.[8] Mr Collet & Mr Warington got Orders on the Virginia Concerns & posted thither to negociate them into Tobacco.[9] I have Letters from them both complaining of the Difficulties & Delays they meet with. Mr Collet in a Letter of the 8th Ins^t expresses himself as follows. "My Stay here will be much longer than I could have expected as I have been much disappointed in the Payments which were promised to me by Mr Banks, and I am afraid I shall at last be obliged to have Recourse to our Rhode Island Friend [i.e., NG]. Perhaps Funds of B. B. [i.e., Banks, Burnet?] & Co[mpany], or of J[ohn]. B[anks] may be remaining in your Hands unappropriated, and that you can put me in a way of accomodating Matters more agreeably than troubling the General. Can you with Propriety my dear Sir answer this Question?"[10]

Mr Forsyth writes to me in February that there is an Apparent Profit on the Business & that he is aiming to get the Partnership affairs settled & the Debts paid, but seems to be far from satisfied with Mr Banks's conduct, & to think that he Counts more largely than justly on the Profits.[11]

From this State of Appearances you will form your Own opinions. I have not a shilling in Hand on Acc^t of that [i.e., Banks's] Concern, but am in Advance on Actual Payments, tho' I have means in my Hands that I expect will leave about 3000 Dollars for the general order above mentioned, when I can receive the Money from the Treasury, but Bills to a larger Am^t must go back protested.[12] I believe a considerable Sum remains at the Havanna, and that large Sums are due to the House from Planters in Carolina, but what Appropriations may have been made of them I am uninformed. Having now given you all the Information that I am possessed of, it is unnecessary for me to make any Observations on it, as your former Knowledge of those Affairs was superior to mine.[13] With the purest Esteem, I am, Dear Sir, Your Friend & most humble Servant   CHA^S PETTIT

RCS (MiU-C).
1. In the enclosure, which was extracted from a letter to Pettit of 28 March, Saunders wrote: "I have lately purchased for our Friend Genl Greene fifty Negroes from Messrs Jervay & Owin [i.e., Gervais & Owen] to settle the General's Plantn in the St[a]te of Georgia, which he wrote me to do at all Events. I was obliged to engage six hundred Guineas Cash wch is out of my Power to get here, I must therefore request your Assistance to inable me to comply with my Engagement—I don't write Genl Greene as I expect he is on his way to Carolina." (MiU-C; NG did not travel to South Carolina until July.) For more about this matter, see note 4 below.
2. On Clement Biddle's efforts to help NG obtain a loan in Europe, see also Pettit to NG, 8 March, above.

3. Pettit wrote NG on 13 March, above, that he was "preparing for a vigorous Blast of 12 or 18 Months" at the Batsto Furnace in New Jersey.

4. During a brief visit to Philadelphia in early June, NG obtained a letter of credit for the 600 guineas from Robert Morris. (See NG to Morris, 5 June, and NG to Saunders, 6 June, both below. A guinea was worth twenty-one shillings, or one shilling more than a pound. [OED]) After returning home, NG received further word from Saunders about the terms of the sale: "£700 to be Cash and the Ballance in 3 Years." (Saunders to NG, 29 May, below)

5. According to the editors of the Morris Papers, at about this time "specie drains resulting from payments for heavy importations of goods from Europe caused the bank to turn down many who wished to borrow." (Morris, *Papers*, 9: 639n)

6. Pettit was discussing here NG's and his own problems with the continuing indebtedness and financial manipulations of John Banks & Company, for whom NG was serving as a surety and Pettit as an attorney. (See also, for example, Pettit to NG, after 21 January, above.) In a letter to Pettit of 22 April, above, NG expressed some hope that these problems would be resolved.

7. In a statement dated 7 April, Banks appointed James Miller his assignee, "in and to what money and other profit which shall be found due to me upon the result of final adjusting and settlement" of Banks's account with Pettit. (*Annals of Congress* [Fifth Congress, 1797–99], p. 3655) According to a letter written by Pettit on 16 January 1798, Banks had claimed that Pettit owed him a balance of $16,119.11. (Ibid., p. 3656) The letter to Pettit from Forsyth, Hunter, and Burnet has not been found.

8. Pettit meant that Morris would not release NG from his obligation for advances that NG had made to Banks until Banks's debts to the Office of Finance were paid. (See also Pettit to NG, 8 May, below.)

9. On E. John Collett's and James Warrington's efforts to obtain tobacco in Virginia as reimbursement for debts that Banks owed them, see also Forsyth to NG, 18 February, and Pettit to NG, 24 February and 13 March, all above; Forsyth to NG, 18 June, below.

10. Pettit wrote NG in a more optimistic vein on 8 May that he now thought "your Entanglement on the Suretyship is in a better way of Extrication than I had supposed." (He based that conclusion on a conversation with John Burnet, who is mentioned in connection with Banks earlier in the present letter.) As seen in NG's letters to Collett of 23 June and 8 August, below, Collett did seek "Recourse" from NG. As noted at Forsyth to NG, 18 June, this issue was not fully resolved until some years after NG's death.

11. The letter to Pettit from Forsyth, one of Banks's partners, has not been found. Forsyth had written NG on 18 February that he believed the firm's debts were "in such a situation as to remove fully every uneasiness from your mind." He was less optimistic, though, in his letter to NG of 18 June.

12. As Banks's attorney and former agent, Pettit was also responsible for advances he had paid on Banks's behalf. (See, for example, Pettit to NG, 8 March.) For more about this, see Pettit to NG, 6 May.

13. For further developments, see Pettit to NG, 10 June, below.

*   *   *

¶ [FROM DOCTOR HENRY COLLINS FLAGG, Charleston, S.C., 5 May 1784. He is "sincerely oblig'd by" NG's letter of 8 March [not found]; adds: "every instance of your regard calls up my affections in the most sensible manner." NG is "very good to take the trouble to inform" him about his relatives, and Flagg is pleased with NG's "account of them all but that of my Cousin Nancy. What Devil influences the family on the Hill I cannot conceive. I wish my fair Cousin was in other hands, she is a lovely Girl and I am vex'd with myself for having been precipitated into a foolish resentment that has deprived me of the pleasure of a social correspondence with her." If he were to visit his "native Country," Flagg would like to "cultivate her esteem."[1] NG gives "a striking description of a deserted Town, and I cannot help being affected with the distress of my Countrymen."[2] Despite NG's disapproval of his comments about "the address," Flagg still thinks "it might have been concluded in a more pleasing stile."[3] He is "exceedingly anxious to know" how CG is faring.[4] On another subject, he informs NG: "I have taken your lecture upon matrimony into serious considera- tion, and after turning and twisting all you say upon the subject together with all the arguments I cou'd recollect pro and con and taking some examples which have fallen under my observation into the account, the result is that I am too unsex'd, fickle, poor and proud to take a Wife."[5] There has been "some degree of confusion" in Charleston because of a "hand bill which has appear'd ordering a number of those persons who have lately return'd from banishment by permis- sion of the legislature to quit this State in ten days." This has "produc'd a proclamation," for which he refers NG to the newspapers. Flagg thinks that the "mischief arises" from "a certain jesuitical medicin" and "about half a dozen more miscreants."[6] He hopes their actions "will be attend[ed] with no ill conse- quences" and trusts that NG will "soon be inform'd upon the spot" about "all these things and the noise made by Thomson Master of the City Tavern."[7] NG will have "heard of M[rs] Waters's death, her youngest daughter Polly has fol- low'd her and the other three children lay dangerously ill with a putrid sore Throat and scarlet fever.[8] Hamilton is soon to be married."[9] RCS (CtY) 4 pp.]

1. As noted at his letter to NG of 17 October 1783, above, Flagg, a Rhode Islander, was a cousin of CG. His "Cousin Nancy" was NG's and CG's close friend Ann "Nancy" Vernon, whose mother was a sister of Flagg's mother. The Samuel Vernon family lived on Church Street, "on the hill" in Newport, R.I. (Flagg, *Genealogical Notes*, p. 151; *Genealogies of R.I. Families*, 2:276; see also vol. 2: 8n and vol. 6: 481 and n, above.) Dr. David Olyphant, whose recently deceased daughter, Jane Olyphant Walter, is mentioned in this letter, later mar- ried Nancy Vernon. (Farr to NG, 10 December 1785, below)

2. On postwar conditions in Newport, R.I., see the note at Anthony to NG, 1 January, above.

3. See Flagg to NG, 7 February, above.

4. As NG had written to him on 8 March, Flagg must have known about CG's advanced pregnancy. (NG to Pettit, 22 April, above)

5. Flagg was married in September 1784. (NG to CG, 10 September, below)

6. Members of the Anti-Britannic Society had issued a handbill demanding the depar- ture from the state "in ten days, under the heaviest of denunciations and threats," of twelve named Loyalists who had recently been "restored by their Country to their property and rights of citizenship" and of a British subject who had been allowed to return to "settle his affairs." (See note at Pendleton to NG, 18 April, above.) In response, Gov. Benjamin Guerard issued a proclamation condemning the perpetrators of the hand- bill and offering a reward of $1,000 to persons who would "give evidence against, and prosecute to conviction, the offender or offenders thus impiously daring to insult the Sovereignty, Dignity, Laws, and Peace of the State, by issuing and ordering to be posted up the said most flagitious Mandate." (*South Carolina Gazette & General Advertiser*, 27–29 April) The "jesuitical medicin" was presumably Dr. James O'Fallon, on whom see NG to Pettit, 29 July 1783, above.

7. On the "noise made by" William Thompson, who operated the City Tavern, see Pendleton to NG, 18 April, above.

8. Jane Olyphant Walter died in March "after an illness of only two days, in the bloom of

life." (*SCHGM* 18 [1917]: 184) A son of hers was also reported to have died "of Sore-throat" in early May. (Ibid., p. 187) Jane Olyphant Walter's husband had fought a duel with Nathaniel Pendleton the previous year because of rumors that Pendleton was having an affair with her. (See note at NG to CG, 4 August 1783, above.)

9. On the marriage of James Hamilton and Elizabeth Harleston, see Pendleton to NG, 3 February, above.

*   *   *

To George Washington

Dear Sir   Newport [R.I.] May 6th 1784

Since I wrote you by Col [David] Henley I took a ride to Boston to try my strength and see how traveling would affect me. It increased my complaint but not so much as to discourage my attempting to be at the Cincinnati had not my complaint increased since my return. The Doctor thinks my life would be endangered by attempting to cross the Water and my pain in my stomach increased by riding by land.[1] In this situation prudence forbids my coming; but that the Society may not be unrepresented Col Ward has agreed to go altho not on the original appointment. He is sensible and prudent and deserves every degree of confidence you may think proper to repose in him. He is a young Gentleman of a liberal education and great observation.[2]

The clamour against the order rather increases in Massachusets and Connecticut States. In this [i.e., Rhode Island] little is said about it but in one County. Many sensible people are anxious for the continuance of the order.[3] Many more wish the Herad[a]tory part loped off as the most exceptionable part of the whole institution. Others again are offended at the Heradatory part on account of the French officers. It is thought it may lead to an improper influence in our National affairs.[4] But what ever objections are raised against the order it is evidently paving the way for the commutation. People begin to say they should have no objection to paying the commutation but for the dangerous combination of the Cincinnati. Drop the Cincinnati and the old question will revive; but continue the order and I am confident the commutation will go down. It is the wish of many that the order should be altered and admit no honorary members and terminate with the present Genera-tion.[5] But I fear any alteration in the present state of things would go far to defeat its influence up[on?] the federal connection and the business of the commutation. It is worthy some consideration to attempt giving reasonable satisfaction to the apprehensions of the people; but I am at a loss to determin what will effect it.[6] I hope the Meeting will not rise hastily and the Moment my health will permit I shall leave this for Philadelphia. My brea[st?] will not permit me to write more and I have written in much pain already.[7] I am dear Sir with esteem & affection Your Most Obed humble Ser   N GREENE

ALS (Washington Papers: DLC).

1. NG had written Washington on 22 April, above, that a severe pain in his chest might keep him from traveling to Philadelphia to represent Rhode Island at the first general meeting of the Society of the Cincinnati in early May.

2. NG, James M. Varnum, and Daniel Lyman had originally been chosen to represent Rhode Island at the meeting. (NG to Washington, 16 February, above) Col. Samuel Ward, Jr., an old friend of NG's, had served in the First Rhode Island Regiment. (Vol. 1: 19n, above; Heitman, *Register*) The meetings were nearly concluded when Ward arrived in Philadelphia. (Pettit to NG, 18 May, below)

3. On opposition to the Society of the Cincinnati in New England, see NG to Washington, 22 April.

4. Membership in the Society was to be passed down to the "eldest male posterity" of the original members. Some of the original members were French officers who had served in the American Revolution. (Myers, *Liberty Without Anarchy*, p. 259) For many Americans, the hereditary provision of the Society's institution was antithetical to the aims of the Revolution.

5. On the issue of the commutation of retirement pay for Continental officers—five year's full pay instead of half-pay for life—see also NG to Washington, 22 April, and the note at Wadsworth to NG, 12–13 June 1783, above.

6. Although NG recommended here that the first general meeting not tamper with the regulations of the Society of the Cincinnati, a number of revisions were approved at the meetings in Philadelphia. Hereditary provisions were modified, and states were given more control over the Society's charters and funds. State militia officers were qualified for membership, and the Society voted to include French officers only of certain ranks and to accept donations only from American sources. (Myers, *Liberty Without Anarchy*, pp. 58–62; Washington, *Papers*, Confederation Series, 1: 328–64) As noted at his letter to Washington of 22 April, NG later conceded that he had erred in recommending that the Society's regulations not be changed.

7. The Society of the Cincinnati meetings took place over a two-week period. By 19 May, the members were "dispersing." (Morris to NG, 19 May, below) NG was not able to travel to Philadelphia for the meetings, but he did go there for a short time on personal business soon afterward. (See note at NG to Reed, 14 May, below.) The pain in his chest subsided after treatments with balsam of fir. (NG to Washington, 29 August, below)

From Charles Pettit

Dear Sir   Philadelphia 6ᵗʰ May 1784

Since writing to you by Post last Week, I have seen Mʳ Jnᵒ Burnet on his way from [South] Carolina, and on conversing with him I am induced to believe that your Entanglement on the Suretyship is in a better way of Extrication than I had supposed.[1] He seems to be confident that Mʳ Harris has got enough to afford him Satisfaction,[2] that Mʳ B—ks is coming forward to Virgᵃ where he will probably settle finally with Mʳ Warington & Mʳ Collett,[3] that Majʳ [Robert] Forsyth has a good deal in his Hands, which he is determined to hold for these Purposes till they shall be settled, that Mʳ B—ks is undertaking new Engagemᵗˢ on fresh Credit, & particularly expects large Importations from Europe w[hi]ch will fill his Hands & enable him to discharge the old affairs with ease, whatever may become of newer ones, that Mʳ Forsyth is very attentive to your Concern in those Affairs & spares no Pains to get your

Obligations discharged.[4] I hasten forward this Information lest what I wrote you before should give you unnecessary anxiety & perhaps run you into Inconveniencies.

M[r] [Robert] Morris persists in the Charge ag[t] M[r] Banks on Acc[t] of the Bills in a Manner I did not expect, & I am determined to stand it out also. I have stated the whole Matter to Banks & propose to transfer his Power to some one else to contest the Matter.[5] If I am not deceived in my Conjecture these Difficulties owe their Support to M[r] G. M.[6] You are very obliging in your Determination to support me as far as lies with you, but I have (& intend to go on so) taken the Matter on myself, making no other Use of your Name than to assert that I have your Authority to have the Am[t] charged to your Acc[t] as Q.M. Gen[l].[7] M[r] M[orris]. has given me War[rants][ts] for the [Batsto] Iron Acc[t] w[hi]ch will reduce the Bal[l] to near £2000 if he will permit me to apply them to a reduction of the Balance stated; but as yet the Treasury Officers have refused to alter their Entries.[8]

I have rec[d] your Fav[r] per Col. Henly, before which I had heard of your Indisposition & one Reason for charging you with the Postage of this is in hopes of saving you from taking Measures incompatible with your Health, which my last might have alarmed you into.[9]

With respect to the Acc[t] for Silk, it is not an Object for Uneasiness between us, fall which way it will. The Note you allude to at the Foot of the Acc[t] was intended for divers little Bills w[hi]ch M[rs] G[reene]. had desired me to pay & which I had promised, but I neither knew nor had the most distant Idea of the one in Question. However we can discuss this at more Leisure.[10] The Carriage has long been ready, but I see little Chance of getting it under Deck, I will therefore try to get the best Vessel I can to take it on Deck, at present there is none here from R. Island.[11]

I have Letters from M[r] Reed ab[t] 2 Months old. His health is improved, he expects to sail about June for America.[12]

The weight of getting the Furnace in Blast presses me hard, but I hope I shall not have many more calls till we begin to reap some Produce.[13] Believe me Dear Sir sincerely Yours   CHA[s] PETTIT

RCS (MiU-C).

1. John Burnet was a brother of Banks's late partner—and NG's former aide—Ichabod Burnet. In earlier letters, including that to NG of 27 April, above, Pettit had been less optimistic about resolving the matter of NG's "Suretyship" for John Banks. As it turned out, his optimism here was misplaced. (See, for example, NG to Jacob Greene, 12 August, below.)

2. As noted above (vol. 12: 309n), the firm of [Michael J.] Harris & [Joseph] Blachford was one of the creditors to whom NG had guaranteed debts incurred by Banks and his partners in supplying clothing to the Southern Army. As seen in Pettit to NG, 18 May, below, Harris traveled to Virginia in what turned out to be an unsuccessful effort to obtain "Satisfaction" from Banks. Later, he sought relief from NG as Banks's guarantor. (For more about this, see especially Pendleton to NG, 10 November, below.)

3. Banks did not make good on his obligations to James Warrington or E. John Collett.

(Forsyth to NG, 18 June, and NG to Collett, 23 June, both below) On the eventual resolution of Collett's demand, for which NG was finally responsible, see note at NG to Collett, 8 August, below.

4. Forsyth, NG's former commissary of purchases, was another partner of Banks. For more on his efforts to protect NG from the creditors, see Forsyth to NG, 18 June.

5. In regard to Robert Morris's demands on Pettit, see notes at Pettit to NG, after 21 January, above.

6. "Mr G. M." was presumably Gouverneur Morris, Robert Morris's assistant in the Office of Finance. The reason for Pettit's conjecture here is not known.

7. NG had written Pettit on 22 April, above: "I mean to stand or fall with you in the matter." On NG's part in this issue, see also the notes at Pettit to NG, after 21 January.

8. For more about the settlement of the Batsto Iron Works account, see note at ibid.

9. Col. David Henley had been the bearer of NG's letter to Pettit of 22 April. Pettit's "last" to NG was his letter of 27 April.

10. The "Acc^t for Silk" is discussed in Pettit to NG, first letter of 8 March, above, and in NG to Pettit, 22 April.

11. Pettit wrote NG on 26 June, below, that the carriage, which he had ordered for CG while she was in Philadelphia the previous summer, had finally been loaded onto a sloop bound for Newport, R.I.

12. Joseph Reed, NG's friend and Pettit's brother-in-law, was traveling in Europe. (See, for example, NG to Mifflin, 12 November 1783, and Pettit to NG, 13 March 1784, both above.) As noted at NG's letter to him of 14 May, below, Reed returned to Philadelphia in ill health in September and died the next winter.

13. As seen in his letters to NG of 13 March and 27 April, Pettit was now actively involved in the management of the Batsto Iron Works.

*   *   *

¶ [FROM JOSHUA UPHAM, London, 10 May 1784.[1] Based on his "slight Acquaintance" with NG "at New York" and NG's "established Reputation as a Man of liberal Principles," Upham recommends to his attention "the Case and Wishes of Mr Vassel a Gentleman of Fortune & unblemished Character," who is now in America. Upham believes that NG must be acquainted with Vassall's "History," which Vassall will "communicate" his "Views &c" on, in a letter in which the present one will be enclosed. Upham adds, "as mere matter of opinion," in which he "can have no interest," that a "Gentleman of Mr Vassals Character & Fortune, circumstanced as he is & situated as his Fortune is must be an Acquisition to any Country & particularly to yours." Asks "your Forgiveness of this Liberty"; sends "respectful Compliments" to CG.[2] RCS (MiU-C) 2 pp.]

1. Upham, a lawyer from Worcester, Mass., had joined the British army in Rhode Island in 1778. He served as an inspector of military claims, major in the King's American Dragoons, and an aide to Sir Guy Carleton in 1781. (Palmer, *Loyalists*, p. 879) NG's and Upham's paths may have crossed while NG was in New York the previous fall on his way to Rhode Island.

2. William Vassall, a Loyalist from Massachusetts, owned an estate in Bristol, R.I., that had been confiscated in 1776; other property belonging to him in Rhode Island was also seized by the state during the war. (Bartlett, *Records of R.I.*, 8: 66, 261, 471; William Greene to NG, 2 October 1785, below; Howard W. Preston, "Point Pleasant: William Vassall's Confiscated Estate," *Rhode Island Historical Society Collections* 18 [January 1925]: 3–5) Later, after receiving a letter from Vassall, NG wrote to Gov. William Greene of Rhode Island on his behalf. (The letter is below, dated 22 August 1785.)

*   *   *

From Evan Edwards

Dr Gener^l 12th May 1784[1]

On my arival in this place I wrote you a few lines in a hurry.[2] I am now from circumstances Colon^l [Charles] Petit will transmit to you inducd to explain the matter relative to the business containd in his Letter.

[John] Banks's situation with respect to his affairs in Charles Town was reducd to such a situation as obligd him to put his accomp^{ts} in the hands of an attorney as well to recover them as to be a security to his Creditors.

He informd Roger Saunders he should sue without discrimination and sent him in Your Accomp^{ts}. Saunders to prevent your being class'd in the Number drew Bills on Colon^l Pettit for the amount, he [i.e., Banks] desird Mr Saunders to draw the bills in my favor—what this was for I never knew; as he did not owe me the Money.[3]

You will see by the two Letters I gave Colon^l Pettit to inclose you, that in the first, Saunders requests me not to part with the Bills. I then wrote him I had nothing to do with them; they were not for me, and should of course certainly not deliver them to Banks without his farther order but should tear them up. Upon a seccond application from Banks backd by the Assurances You will see, Saunders in his seccond Letter directed me to give Them up without restriction.[4]

I have Thus explaind the matter to you, as far as respects myself, as although my name appears in the Bills it's a thing I have nothing to do with.

Banks disposed of them and receivd the Cash for them, and omitted forwarding a Letter to Colon^l Pettit from Saunders praying him to accept them with the reasons, as, if he did not & they were disposd of the People in whose hands they are would instantly come on him for the amount & damages. Yours Very sinc   E EDWARDS

NB. Banks has orderd Gener^l [William] Moultrie Gener^l [Isaac] Huger Colon^l [William] Washington and in fact every body to be suid [i.e., sued] unless they make instant payment, and has put their accomp^s in an attorneys hands.[5]   E E

RCS (MiU-C).

1. Edwards, who had traveled north with NG the previous summer, did not give his location but was presumably in or near Charleston, S.C., where he seems to have spent the winter and early spring months. (See Shubrick to NG, 7 January, and Pendleton to NG, 3 February and 18 April, all above.) He returned to Philadelphia in early June. (Edwards to NG, 8 June, below)

2. On Edwards's location, see the preceding note. The letter has not been found.

3. For more about this matter, see Saunders to NG, 29 May, and Pettit to NG, 10 and 19 June, all below. According to Banks's partner Robert Forsyth, Banks drew these bills "to forward Mr Colletts payment." (Forsyth to NG, 18 June, below) As seen in Forsyth to NG, 24 February, above, E. John Collett had been in Virginia for several months to try to collect money that Banks owed him. As seen in NG's letters to Collett of 23 June and 8 August,

below, Collett was also seeking recourse from NG as Banks's guarantor. (On the eventual resolution of this matter, see note at NG's letter to Collett of 8 August.)

4. On the letters from Saunders to Edwards, see Pettit to NG, 10 June.

5. Edwards wrote NG on 8 June that he was afraid Banks "is in a bad way. I hope not ruind intirely in purse; but I am apprehensive too much so in Character as a Merch[t]."

*   *   *

¶ [FROM GIDEON MUMFORD AND ANDREW BOYD, East Greenwich, R.I., 12 May 1784. They are "Commissioners, to receive and settle the claims against the Estate of Doctor [Joseph] Joslyn Deceased."[1] The "Creditors demands a Dividend to be Struck," and Mrs. [Hope Campbell] Joslyn has sent NG "the Doctors account from his Book." If NG has "any account against the Doctor," he should "send it up by the first opportunity," and if he objects "to any of the Doctors charges," Mumford and Boyd will "leave it to Doctor Peter Turner to adjust."[2] As soon as NG's "account is Settled," they will "proceed to make a Dividend." LS (MiU-C) 1 p.]

1. Joslyn (also spelled "Jocelyn"), of East Greenwich, had once been NG's family physician. (See vol. 1: 57n, above; Greene, *History of East Greenwich*, p. 160, McPartland, *East Greenwich*, p. 123.)

2. As seen in his letter to NG of 31 May, below, Turner did examine "the Doctors charges."

*   *   *

To Joseph Reed

Dear Sir   Newport [R.I.] May 14th 1784

My plan and intentions have been so altered since we parted at Philadelphia that I have not had it in my power to go where I expected and where you wished to hear from me.[1] On my return home last fall I found M[rs] Greene far advanced in a state of pregnancy.[2] That and the severity of the weather which has exceeded any thing known since my time has prevented my going to the Southward. So little communication was there between this and Philadelphia that I did not hear of your sailing until the Middle of February.[3] Since Mrs Greene has been in bed I have been too unwell to travel. My breast is constantly affected with a disagreeable pain.[4] Within a few days past I have got a little better and intend to go to Philadelphia in a few days and to Charleston in about a month or a little more. Where I hope to have the pleasure of meeting you.[5]

Since you left America I think the spirit and temper of her politicks are mending. In New England there has been great commotions respecting the commutation. That is now subsiding and the current of publick prejudice is directed against the Cincinnati. The people in the Northern States are much enraged against it. General Washington is much alarmed at it.[6] The order is now sitting at Philadelphia[;] what will be the result of their meeting I know not. Many wish an alteration of the order but more a dissolution.[7] Honorary Members are much objected to and the hereditary descent more so.[8] Burkes Address has sounded the alarm and the order how ever innocent the plan and benevolent the design is thought to contain dangerous designs, pregnant with mischief and may be ruinous to the people.[9] General Washington wanted me to be at the Meeting and sent letter after letter; but my health prevented my going.[10] Congress has said nothing on the subject but they are not less displeased with the order than other Citizens.[11]

I had a letter from your brother in law M[r] Dennis De Ber[d]t and shall be happy to render him every service in my power.[12] I could wish to hear from you on the subject of a loan if you are not likely to be in America soon. But I am afraid our public affairs are unfavorable to private Loans.[13] Property will be thought unsafe in the hands of people pretty much out of the reach of Law: Most of the States have agreed to the impost and this State will come into it at their next meeting.[14] New York has been much convulsed by faction but it is dying away.[15] Congress have laid out a great number of new States[16] and M[r] Morris has or will resign.[17] These are the great political matters on our side of the water. I am with esteem Dear Sir Yours   N GREENE

ALS (NHi).
1. NG had last seen Reed in Philadelphia in November 1783.
2. NG arrived in Newport at the end of November 1783; CG did not give birth to their fifth child until mid-April. (NG to Pettit, 22 April, above)
3. The winter of 1783–84 in the Northeast was one of the most bitter on record, with unusually low temperatures and heavy snowfalls. (Ludlum, *Early American Winters*, pp. 64–67) Reed, who sailed for London in December 1783, arrived there in January. (Reed to NG, 12 February, above)
4. On NG's physical complaint, see his letter to Washington of 22 April, above.
5. NG wrote Baron Steuben from New York on 9 June, below, that he had "left Philadelphia yesterday, and Newport ten days ago; and expect to get home in less than a fortnight from the time I left it." He was in Philadelphia by at least 4 June. (See his letter to James Milligan of that date, below.) He did not leave for the South until 12 July. (See note at NG to Hazlehurst, 26 June, below.) If NG saw Reed again, it must have been in November, when NG stopped in Philadelphia again on his way back to Rhode Island. (See, for example, NG to Saunders, 12 November, below.) Reed, who had returned to Philadelphia in ill health on 29 September, died there on 5 March 1785, at age forty-four. (Reed, *Reed*, 2: 415; Eyre to NG, 7 March 1785, below)
6. On "public prejudice" in New England against the Society of the Cincinnati and the commutation of officers' pay, see note at NG to Washington, 22 April, above. In a letter of 27 March, above, Washington had urged NG to attend the general meeting of the Society in Philadelphia at the beginning of May, citing the "temper of the New England states in particular" and "growing jealousies" against the Society.
7. On changes in the Society's regulations during the meetings in Philadelphia, see note at NG to Washington, 6 May.
8. As noted at ibid., the hereditary provisions of the Society's "institution" were modified at the May meetings. Honorary memberships were also eliminated, unless they were accepted by "the government of the state involved." (Myers, *Liberty Without Anarchy*, p. 62; on the provision for honorary memberships in the Society, see NG to William Greene, 19 January, above.)

9. Aedanus Burke, a South Carolina judge, had denounced the Society of the Cincinnati in a widely disseminated pamphlet published the previous October. (Flagg to NG, 17 October 1783, above)

10. In letters of 16 February, 20 March, and 27 March, all above, Washington had urged NG to attend the general meeting of the Society of the Cincinnati. On NG's health problems, see his letters to Washington of 22 April and 6 May.

11. As noted at NG to Washington, 22 April, Congress took no direct action against the Cincinnati, but two resolutions that it adopted after the Cincinnati's inception were thought to contain oblique criticism of the Society.

12. De Berdt, Reed's brother-in-law, had written to NG on 21 October 1783, above, requesting help in obtaining business in the United States. NG later asked De Berdt for help, as well. (See NG to De Berdt, 9 March 1785, below, and later correspondence between them.)

13. Reed wrote NG on 12 February that he had made discreet inquiries about a loan for NG but had met with refusals. On the effects of "our public affairs" on Americans' ability to obtain credit from European lenders, see also Morris to NG, 19 May, below.

14. On the congressional impost proposal of 1783, see especially the note at NG to Lincoln, 18 June 1783, above. As seen in NG to Morris, 3 July, below, the Rhode Island legislature rejected the proposal.

15. Controversy had simmered in New York with the introduction of anti-Loyalist legislation in the Assembly in March 1784. The bill was opposed by Alexander Hamilton, who argued against its passage in "Second Letter from Phocion," published in April. (Syrett, *Hamilton*, 3: 530–31n) According to one historian, "the crisis climaxed on 12 May, when the legislature passed an act that disenfranchised all but a few specially-excepted loyalists." (John P. Kaminski, *George Clinton: Yeoman Politician of the New Republic* [Madison, Wis.: Madison House, 1993], p. 80)

16. A committee appointed to "prepare a plan for the temporary government of the western territory" had presented its report to Congress in March. After some debate, an amended version of the proposed plan for organizing the western territory into states was adopted on 23 April. (*JCC*, 26: 118–20; 275–79)

17. Robert Morris had submitted a letter of resignation in January 1783 but had continued to function as superintendent of finance since then at the request of Congress. (Vol. 12: 515–16n, above) On his departure from office later in 1784, see note at NG to Morris, 13 November, below.

* * *

¶ [FROM GRIFFIN GREENE, Bordeaux, France, 16 May 1784. When he wrote to NG "last month," he thought his "bussiness in France was nearly finished."[1] He has since learned, though, that "Minnisters of State, don't always act up to their contracts more than private men." The *Flora* was valued by a man chosen by the buyer, who, for "some reason," changed his mind and "ordered the estimate to be taken anew." As Griffin has no "alternative," he "will submit to" the buyer's "terms with a good Grace."[2] He is afraid he has "worn out the patience" of their "Good friend the Marquis de la Fayette" with frequent letters on the subject; has written to him three times and has yet to receive a reply, but Lafayette may have already left for America. The Marquis is "one of the best men in the world, & if any man acts disinterestedly it is he."[3] If Griffin has been "intolerably troublesome" to Lafayette, he begs NG to "make him satisfaction as it is not in my powar."[4] Hopes his "unavoidable stay" in France will not give NG "any unfavorable impressions" of his conduct. If it does, Griffin will be "doubly punished" by NG's "sensure" and "the state of suspence I am held in." He has already informed NG that he has used NG's letters to obtain "cradit for two thousand pounds payable in one year." He will "have the amount Inssured" and will "indevor the pay shall be made" in such a way as to give NG no "farther trouble."[5] Sends his "Love to Caty [i.e., CG] & all Friends." Adds in a postscript: "The first valuation of the Ship was 82,000 Livers the second not known but I fear much short."[6] RCS (MiU-C) 3 pp.]

1. On Griffin's errand to France to sell the *Flora*, see especially his letter to NG of 18 May 1783, above (vol. 12: 662–63). His letter to NG of "last month" is also above, dated 6 April.

2. The buyer was undoubtedly the French naval minister, De Castries, who had appointed "One Tirol" to do the valuation. (See Griffin's letter to NG at the end of the September documents, below.) In his letter to NG of 6 April, Griffin reported that Lafayette had arranged for the French government to purchase the vessel. Jeremiah Wadsworth wrote NG on 28 September, below, that "the indefatigable Marquis de Lafayette has persuaded the French government to take the ship at 100,000 livres."

3. Lafayette, who was about to sail to the United States, was the bearer of Griffin's letter to NG of 12 June, below. Griffin informed NG in that letter that Lafayette "has taken as much pains to serve us, as if the whole bussiness had been his own." On Lafayette's trip to America, see note at his letter to NG of 25 August, below.

4. In a letter of 24 March, above, NG had thanked Lafayette for helping Griffin. As noted at Lafayette to NG, 25 August, NG saw Lafayette in New York in December, shortly before the latter returned to France.

5. See NG to Griffin Greene, 8 July, below.

6. In his letter to NG of 12 June, Griffin wrote that the "first Valuation upon the Ship was 82,000 livers, & the second was much higher," but that he would be "happy" to accept the first in order to conclude the sale. (See also note 2, above, and Griffin's letter to NG at the end of the September documents, below.)

¶ [FROM CHARLES PETTIT, Philadelphia, 18 May 1784. Thanks NG "for the Pleasure of Colonel Ward's Acquaintance." Is sorry that neither he nor Ward has "had sufficient Leisure, during his short continuance in Town," to become better acquainted. Ward will inform NG about the "Business of the Cincinnati," which was "nearly matured" by the time he arrived.[1] As to Ward's "private Business," Pettit offered "any Assistance in my Power," but Ward "seemed to think no Aid of the kind necessary, and communicated but little to me on the Subject."[2] NG's bill for "£300 sterling" has been "passed to my Debit at the Bank where I had lodged Funds for the Purpose." Pettit is not sure about the amount to be paid, but taking into account the exchange rate and the common par, he believes it will be an "even £500," and he has Mr. [John] Cox's "Consent to extract it from his Funds & consider it as a Payment from him on Acc[ts]" of NG's "Claim on the Eggharbour Concerns."[3] Pettit was "apprehensive" that the letter he wrote "some Posts ago would give you some alarm about your Engagements in Carolina."[4] After speaking with Mr. [John] Burnet, Pettit wrote NG again to "soften the Matter."[5] He has "conversed farther with M[r] [Michael J.] Harris" since then and thinks "pretty favourably" of NG's "Prospects of getting safely through that Business."[6] Pettit also sent NG a copy of Mr. Saunders's letter requesting 600 guineas for NG's "Use"—a request that he could not comply with—and has heard "nothing farther of that business."[7] He is "much concerned" about NG's "want of Health." Adds: "Laying aside the Idea of danger to Life, the being incapacitated to pursue the Establishment of a Fortune for your Family which you have so fairly earned, and which you seem to have a good Foundation laid for, would be mortifying."[8] Pettit believes that "we must allow something for the Enthusiasm of Gentlemen who are turning their Attention to the Western Country, but after making such Allowance, I cannot but conceive an high Idea of your Lands in North Carolina from the Description given by Col. [Jacob] Blount and some others, tho' it will hardly be in our Day that they will produce much Revenue.[9] The Margins of the Rivers Mississippi and Ohio are settling with great Rapidity and must become a very rich Country." RCS (MiU-C) 2 pp.]

1. NG, who had written a letter of introduction to Robert Morris for his friend Samuel Ward, Jr., presumably wrote one to Pettit, as well. Neither letter has been found. (See, however, Morris to NG, immediately below.) Ward was in Philadelphia at this time to represent Rhode Island at the general meeting of the Society of the Cincinnati. (NG to Washington, 6 May, above; on the results of the meeting, see the notes at that letter and at NG to Washington, 29 August, below.) NG left for Philadelphia the day that Ward got back to Rhode Island. (Ibid.)

2. In the letter immediately below, Morris said he had offered to help Ward in "any business in which he could find me likely to be usefull."

3. On the bill for "£300 sterling," see Pettit to NG, 7 February and first letter of 8 March, both above. NG's "claim on the Eggharbour Concerns" is discussed in those letters and in Pettit to NG, after 21 January, above.

4. See Pettit to NG, 27 April, above.

5. The letter referred to here is Pettit to NG, 6 May, above.

6. On Harris, see also Pettit to NG, 6 May.

7. Pettit sent a copy of Roger Parker Saunders's request with his letter to NG of 27 April. (See also Saunders to NG, 29 May, below.) NG was able to obtain a letter of credit for the 600 guineas through Robert Morris during a visit to Philadelphia in early June. (See below, NG to Morris, 5 June, and NG to Saunders, 6 June.)

8. NG had written Pettit about his "want of Health" on 22 April, above. He was well enough soon after Pettit wrote this letter to travel to Philadelphia, where he conducted some financial transactions with Pettit and others. (See, for example, Agreement between Charles Pettit and NG, 7 June, and NG to Saunders, 6 June, both below.)

9. Pettit referred here to the 25,000 acres of land in what is now Tennessee that the state of North Carolina had given to NG. (Alexander Martin to NG, 24 May 1782, above [vol. 11: 239–40 and n])

*　　　*　　　*

From Robert Morris, Superintendent of Finance

Dear Sir　　　　　　　　　　　　　　　　　Philad[a] May 19th 1784

As the Society of the Cincinati have finished the business on which they met, & are now dispersing on their Return home, I despair of seeing you here at this time.[1] It is needless to tell you how much pleasure I lose by the disapointment & I shall proceed to acknowledge the Receipt of your letters of the 9th Jan[y] & 6th Ins[t].[2] In Compliance with the intent of the latter, I assured Col[o] Ward of my promptitude to assist or advise him in any business in which he could find me likely to be usefull. I thank you for this Gentlemans acquaintance and hope to enjoy more of his Company than his & my own engagements have yet permitted.[3] I did entertain hopes that your Legislature would have passed the Impost before they Adjourned but my last letter from M[r] Olney mentions their having broke up without mentioning the Subject. I dont know what is to become of the Public Creditors nor indeed of the National Character & Credit of the United States if that business is suffered to linger on in the way we are going.[4]

Soon after the Receipt of your letter of the 9th Jan[y] I received the most alarming advices from Holland where our Credit recd Such a Shock, that the Public Loan came at once to Stand Still & the Commissioners of that Loan found themselves under a Necessity to protest (for Non-Acceptance) the bills which I had drawn to Compleat the payment made to the Army. This step injured not only the Public Credit of the Country but the Individual Credit of its Citizens. When I drew the Bills, the measure was Sanctioned by advices from M[r] [John] Adams & from the Commissioners so that I had not a doubt of the Money being ready before the bills could become due; but the translation into the Dutch Newspapers of our disputes, Quarrells, refusal to grant compliance to the Requisitions of Congress &c &c it is said, spread the Alarm amongst the Capitalists in Holland, & instead of continuing to lend they begun to sell those obligations of M[r] Adams under Parr.[5] This continued untill some advices from home begun to operate a little differently & the Commissioners taking advantage of the Changes shut the old Loan unfinished & Opened a New One on terms more advantageous to the lenders by which means they had secured part & hoped to obtain the whole that was necessary to discharge the bills which I had drawn upon them,[6] but as to any thing more, we need not look for it untill we establish Funds for the discharge of the Interest annually & of the principal at the periods Stipulated. In this State of things I have been obliged to involve myself in heavy engagements to keep things going and my Mind has been far from easy.[7] You must not wonder then if my attention could not be turned so much as perhaps it ought to considerations of a private Nature. I shall be very sorry indeed if you & I have misunderstood each other. The encouragement which I gave You to make engagements for Stocking your Estate could go no farther than that dependance which could be had on my assurance that I would assist You in borrowing, because I told you expressly that my own Situation & engagements did not admit of my being a lender;[8] In pursuance of my promise I not only wrote the letter to Mess[rs] Wilhem & Jan Willink of which you have a Copy,[9] but in various modes I have been trying other people both in England & Holland, the result hitherto has been heavy Complaints of the Scarcity of Money throughout Europe (in which there is Truth)[,] of the Number of Loans attempted by Sovereign Powers on terms more advantageous than private persons dare propose, and only one House did agree to borrow the Sum of £10,000 Sterl[g] on Landed Security in this Country but so Transmitted that I refused without hesitation to comply with the terms. I have not yet heard from Mess[rs] Wilhem & Jan Willink in Answer but am in daily expectation of their reply when you Shall hear from me again.[10]

When you can ascertain the engagements that have been made for You let me know and if the periods of payment are distant & the Sum of each seperate one, not too heavy I still hope notwithstanding present discouragement that the Money may be obtained either in America or Europe, for I think the distresses which have been felt from the Scarcity will operate a plenty in each Country, by compelling People to limit their Views so that less will be actually wanted. I do not transmit the Estimate of your Southern Estate to Mess[rs] Willink & C[o] untill I receive their Answer to my letter & if that is favorable as I hope it may then the Estimate shall be sent forward & probably you will have no farther to look for Money.[11] Shou'd their answer be unfavourable I will persevere in my endeavours to assist you & hope that our joint endeavours will finally be Crowned with Success. I Shall be anxious to learn the reestablishment of your Health for which you have my best wishes in which I am joined by M[rs] [Mary White] Morris as also in compliments to M[rs] Greene. I am Dr Sir Your Obed[t] hble serv[t]   ROB[T] MORRIS

RCS (Greene Papers: DLC).

1. On the meeting of the Society of the Cincinnati, see especially the notes at NG's letters to Washington of 6 May, above, and 29 August, below. Morris did see NG in Philadelphia not long afterward. (See his diary entry for 4 June [Morris, *Papers*, 9: 376], and NG to Morris, 5 June, below.)

2. NG's letter to Morris of 6 May has not been found.

3. NG's friend Samuel Ward, Jr., who represented Rhode Island at the meeting of the Society of the Cincinnati, had also met with Charles Pettit about personal business matters while he was in Philadelphia. (Pettit to NG, immediately above)

4. George Olney was the receiver of Continental taxes in Rhode Island. (Morris, *Papers*, 9: 436–37) His letter to Morris has not been found. Morris had enlisted NG's help to promote ratification of the impost proposal of 1783 in Rhode Island. (Morris to NG, 19 December 1783, and NG to Morris, 9 January, both above) According to his diary entry for 4 June, Morris met with "Genl. Greene from Rhodes Island with whom a Conversation took Place on the Temper and Politics of that State. He is of Opinion they will adopt the Plan of Congress for funding the public Debts." (Morris, *Papers*, 9: 376) As seen in NG to Morris, 3 July, below, the Rhode Island legislature rejected the impost during its next session.

5. Morris wrote the president of Congress, Thomas Mifflin, on 17 March:

"Permit me thro your Excellency to call the Attention of the United States to the Situation of my Department. During the last Year, Engagements were made to a very considerable Amount for Payment of the Army. This Payment was effected by Notes which fell due the End of last Year and Commencement of this. The funds at my Disposal were unequal to the Discharge of them. I was therefore under the Necessity of drawing Bills on the Credit of the Loan in Holland. The Informations I had received from the Gentlemen who had the Management of it gave me Hopes that Funds sufficient to discharge those Bills were in their Hands for in the Months of

April, May, June and July [1783] they had received on distributed Obligations One Million, one hundred and thirty six thousand current florins. But from Causes which will readily suggest themselves to Congress that Loan which had taken a rapid Start at the Peace began to decline in August and stood still during all November. It has happened therefore that Bills to the Amount of One Million three hundred and twenty five thousand current florins equal at the current Exchange to five hundred and thirty thousand Dollars are protested for Non Acceptance. Should they come back protested for Non Payment the Consequences will be easily imagined." (Morris, *Papers*, 9: 190)

6. For details of the new loan negotiated with Dutch bankers in early 1784, see Morris to Mifflin, 4 May, Morris, *Papers*, 9: 313–14 and n, and the headnote to that letter (ibid., pp. 307–13).

7. Morris and some of his associates had pledged personal funds in order to redeem protested public drafts. (Morris, *Papers*, 9: 307–8)

8. For background, see above, NG to Morris, 9 January.

9. See note at ibid.

10. Morris enclosed extracts of the Willinks' reply in letters to NG of 12 and 17 July, below.

11. See Estimate of NG's Estate, before 9 January, above. An extract of the Willinks' reply is printed in a note at Morris to NG, 12 July, below. As noted there, NG was unable to obtain a loan from them.

*   *   *

¶ [**TO WELCOME ARNOLD**. From Newport, R.I., 22 May 1784. NG asks him to buy and send "a ferken of hogs Lard," which should "be good[,] as it is for family use." ALS (CSmH) 1 p.]

*   *   *

From Roger Parker Saunders

Dear Sir   [Charleston, S.C.] 29th May 1784

I have not done Myself the pleasure of writing you for some time Past as I expected You every hour in Carolina.[1]

I lately purchasd for You from Messrs Jervay and Owen Fifty Eight Negroes wch I sent to Mr Gibbons.[2] They have planted you a Crop wch I hope will turn out well. I am to give abot 64 Guineas Round for the Negroes £700 to be Cash and the Ballance in 3 Years. I think the Bargain a Good one. I Consulted your Friends who I knew were Judges before I made the Purchase.[3] I wrote Colo Pettit requesting he would If possible send me the Money or an order on some punctual House here but I am greatly disappointed at Colo Pettits not being able to comply with My Request. He writes me he had sent on the Letter to You & I am in hopes to be inabled by You to Comply with the engagement.[4] Mr Jervay presses me hard he is so Circumstansd he cant doe without the £700, as he is only an agent for Mr Oswald of London, he desires I will give him up the Negroes If I cant pay the Money. This will put you to a great

Inconveniance, Negroes cant be had on so Good terms and you must loose y^r Crop. I know not what to doe I can't Borrow the Money here at any rate. Previous to the Rec^t of Col^o Pettits ans^r I was compeld by Mr Banks to draw for the Amo^t of Your Acco^t. He told me he positively would put Your Acco^t in Suit Immediately wch he was compeld to doe by his Creditors that the most of y^r Acco^t was for Money lent &c^a[.] Rather than let an action be commenc'd against You, I consented to draw at 30 days Sight after Mr Banks giveing me his honor Verbally he would find means should the Bills not be Honor'd to prevent their being protested and return them to me in a private way. He afterwards gave It from under his hand he [said] he only ment them to ans^r a tempory Purpose and I might rely on his Honor[.] If he fails in his promise I must intreat you will not let the Bills be protested. I cant possibly pay them. I would not have drawn but was affraid your Credit would be injurd.[5] You have in General a Good prospect of a Crop, you will make double what you did last Year, unless something unforeseen happens.

You have been very unfortunate in y^r Horses. The Bays are both dead of the Farcy and one of the Chestnuts of the Bots.[6] Your Carriage is Ruind by being exposd to the Weather, you never Left me a Memorandum what you had done with It. The Coach Maker went away to Philadelphia left y^r Carriage exposd when I got It I would not [sell?]. I got leave from Col^o [William] Washington to let It in the Carriage House where It has remaind ever Since. I will write you again should any opp^y offer for Rhode Island. I am with Respectful Comp^{ts} to Mrs Greene Dr Sir with regard y^r Very Hum Se^t R^R PARKER SAUNDERS

NB Messrs Jervay & Owen propose If It will suit you better to take a Bill on London for £400 Sterling at 30 days Sight the £300 will be wanted in Cash but an Order on Some Punctual House here at ten or 15 days or even 20 days may doe.[7]   R. P. S.

RCS (MiU-C).

1. In a letter to Saunders of 6 June, below, NG explained why he had been detained in Rhode Island. (NG did not get to Charleston until mid-summer. The first extant letter that he wrote there in 1784 was to Hewson & Edwards, 6 August, below.)

2. John Lewis Gervais (1741?–1798), a "planter-merchant" and politician, had been president of the South Carolina Senate and a delegate to Congress during the war. He was in partnership with John Owen, a Charleston merchant. (*Biog. Directory of S.C. House*, 3: 256–58, 529–30) William Gibbons, NG's attorney in Georgia, was handling NG's affairs in that state. (See above, vol. 12: 475 and n.) As seen in his letter to Gibbons of 29 August, below, NG later had some reservations about the sale.

3. NG had encouraged Saunders to discuss the prices with Edward Rutledge, Charles C. Pinckney, and Thomas Ferguson. (NG to Saunders, 4 January, above)

4. Saunders wrote Pettit on 28 March that when NG left the South the previous summer he directed Saunders to draw on Pettit if he had "occasion for money," and that NG had "lately" informed Saunders that he was "about establishing a Fund in Europe," presumably to help support the capital needs of his plantations. Saunders informed Pettit that if

he would send "a Bill on some punctual House in Cha[s]ton[;] it will answer as well as the Cash." Pettit's reply to Saunders has not been found, but Pettit wrote NG at the end of April, enclosing Saunders's letter and saying that he hoped NG was "otherwise provided to answer this Demand of M[r] Saunders." (Pettit to NG, 27 April, above) In a letter of 5 June, below, NG asked for and received a "bill of exchange" for 600 Guineas from Robert Morris to send to Saunders. (See also NG to Saunders, 6 June, and Morris to NG, 17 July, both below.)

5. NG discussed this matter in his letters to Saunders of 6 and 26 June. (See also the note at Edwards to NG, 12 May, above.)

6. "Farcy" was another name for glanders, a "highly contagious and very destructive disease of horses and other equines." (*Webster's*) NG had lost another "chestnut" horse to "bots" the previous fall. (Saunders to NG, 20 October 1783, above)

7. Evan Edwards forwarded this letter from Philadelphia with his to NG of 8 June, below. NG, who left there on the same date, could not have learned about its contents until after he returned home. (See also Pettit to NG, 10 June, below.) As seen in note 4, above, NG did make arrangements while he was in Philadelphia to have 600 guineas (the amount mentioned in Pettit's letter of 27 April as a necessary, initial payment for the slaves) sent to Saunders. (See, however, the note at NG to Morris, 5 June.)

*   *   *

¶ [FROM JOHN BROWN, Providence, R.I., 30 May 1784. Acknowledges NG's letter of 20 May [not found], which, along with many others, arrived while Brown was at his farm; otherwise, he would have replied to it sooner. Has had "Repeeted Drafts" on him "for Money towords the Deficienceys" of his cargoes that were "Sent to Verginnia & Baltimore." Tobacco is "So Very high," and his cargoes are "Selling So Extreemley Low"—with many "Articals" not selling at all—that he must "Send a person on purpose with all the Money I Can Raise in the month of June, to Compleat their Cargoes of Tobacco." Is "Extreemly Sorry" that it is out of his "power to Supply" NG with "Aney Money," for he finds "new Demands" on him from "allmost Every Quarter."[1] RCS (MiU-C) 1 p.]
1. NG presumably had asked Brown for a loan.

¶ [FROM DOCTOR PETER TURNER, East Greenwich, R.I., 31 May 1784.[1] "In obedience" to NG's letter of 14 May, he has "inspected the Charges of D[r] [Joseph] Joslyn against" NG and has not been able to find any "vouchers but his Ledger for the Charges of 1775, 6 & 7," totaling £8.6.0.[2] As Joslyn's "Visits make the greater part of the Sum"—and Turner is "unable to determine where they were made, & the species & quantity of medicine are entirely unknown"—he cannot "form any Judgment of the propriety of the Charge." He has copied Joslyn's account as Joslyn's "Book has it, so far," and thinks anyone can judge it as he does. Turner has taken the rest of the account from the doctor's "Day Books," where the entries were made in "depreciated Continental Charges," and has "affixed such sums" as he "supposed were adequate to their value, at the time, in real money." Hopes this is "acceptable" and is "sorry" that he could not "find the Original Entries of the other part," which Mrs. [Hope Campbell] Joslyn "begs" NG "to consider & do with as may seem right." She "only Acts as Administrator to the Estate" and hopes that NG "will adopt such a Conduct in this affair as may shield her from the censure of the Creditors."[3] RCS (MiU-C) 2 pp.]

1. Turner (1751–1822), a surgeon, served with the First Rhode Island Regiment between 1777 and 1781. After the war, he established a practice in East Greenwich. He was a brother-in-law of General James M. Varnum. (Heitman, *Register*; Greene, *History of East Greenwich*, pp. 161–63) As noted in the Epilogue below, Turner's son later became the second husband of NG's oldest daughter, Martha ("Patty").

2. For background, see Mumford and Boyd to NG, 12 May, above.

3. On Joslyn, see note at ibid. Joslyn died at age forty-four, apparently from the effects of alcoholism. (Greene, *History of East Greenwich*, p. 160)

¶ [FROM BARBARA BENTLY, East Greenwich, R.I., 1 June 1784.[1] Acting on NG's advice, she "applied to a Gentleman here that understands acc^{ts} to Examine the Settlement Made Between y^r Self and Me." This person found that the settlement was "all Very right," except for "the Article of £ 8.6.4 Charged in Mr Jacob Greens acc^t paid Charles Green[,] which is twice Charged." NG will see that this is so if he compares the two accounts Charles Greene prepared, which she encloses [not found]. When Charles presented his first account to Jacob Greene, Jacob asked him "to make out his aco^t ag^t me according to the old fashion Prices which he accordingly Did and that the amount thereof in that way was £8.2:1. And which Sum he Says is all that I ought to Stand Charged with on his aco^t" She asks NG "Pleas to right it by remitting" the £8.6:4.[2] RCS (MiU-C) 1 p.]

1. Bently had apparently been taking care of one of NG's children, possibly as a wet-nurse for his infant daughter, Louisa Catharine. She was anxious to settle her bill before NG left for the South. (Bently to NG, 4 July, below)

2. On this matter, see also Bently's letter to NG at the end of the June documents, below. Charles Greene may have been NG's and Jacob's first cousin Charles, on whom see vol. 12: 664n, above.

¶ [FROM CLEMENT BIDDLE, [Philadelphia, before 4 June 1784?].[1] "The sums lent were £52.10, & £75."[2] Biddle has "sent Mr Whitehead in Search of money to make up the rest in which he was disappointed in yesterday." Biddle has also spoken with his partner, who believes "a loan in Holland" can be "Obtaind." They will "enquire the usual Conditions & Requsites" from "a Gentleman here who is versed in those Affairs."[3] Biddle will write NG "fully" if he cannot get this information before NG leaves.[4] RCS (MiU-C) 1 p.]

1. The editors believe that Biddle probably wrote this letter during NG's visit to Philadelphia in June. In the letter immediately below, NG asked James Milligan for payment of money mentioned here, which Biddle had loaned him for travel expenses. (See also NG to Milligan, 8 November 1783 and 7 December 1783, both above.)

2. See the preceding note.

3. For background, see above, Pettit to NG, 8 March and 27 April.

4. No further correspondence on this matter has been found.

¶ [TO JAMES MILLIGAN. From Philadelphia, 4 June 1784.[1] As Col. [Clement] Biddle was "so Obliging" as to advance money "to defray" NG's travel expenses "Comeing here & returning home from my s^o Com^d," NG asks Milligan to "give the utmost dispatch" to settling the accounts "lodged with you for that Service." Asks him to give Biddle "a Certificate to receive the ballance" from the superintendent of finance [Robert Morris].[2] Df (MiU-C) 1 p.]

1. This is the first letter written by NG during a short visit to Philadelphia that has been found. NG wrote Samuel A. Otis on 24 July 1785, below, that he had gone "no less than three times" to Philadelphia, "dancing attendance" on officials there to try to get his army

accounts settled. This was the second such visit; the others took place in October–November 1783 and November 1784.

2. On the loan and NG's efforts to repay Biddle, see NG to Milligan, 7 December 1783, and the letter immediately above. On the reimbursement for travel expenses that NG was still awaiting, see above, NG to Mifflin, 3 November 1783, and Lee to NG, 6 April. As seen in Milligan to NG, 30 August, below, complications may have arisen after it was found that a balance was due from NG for bills of exchange that he had drawn during his southern campaign.

¶ [TO ROBERT MORRIS, SUPERINTENDENT OF FINANCE. From Philadelphia, 5 June 1784.[1] NG requests "a bill of exchange" for 600 guineas on Morris's "agent in Charleston," in favor of Roger Parker Saunders, NG's "Attorney in the State of South Carolina." NG will be "accountable" for the bill and asks that it be "drawn on as short sight as you can render convenient[,] as the time will make a material difference to me in the value."[2] ALS (CSmH) 1 p.]

1. According to his diary, Morris met with NG on 4 June. (Morris, *Papers*, 9: 376)

2. This money was needed as an initial, cash payment for slaves that Saunders had purchased for NG's plantation in Georgia. (See Pettit to NG, 27 April, above.) In the letter immediately below, NG wrote Saunders that he was sending "a letter of credit for the Money on M[r] Robert Hazlehurst," a Charleston, S.C., merchant. After returning to Rhode Island, NG received Saunders's letter of 29 May, above, stating the terms of the sale as "£700 to be Cash and the Ballance in 3 Years." NG wrote Morris again on 25 June, below, expressing the hope "not to distress you but little more whether you obtain the loan for me or not." (As noted at his letter to NG of 12 July, below, Morris's efforts to arrange a loan for NG in Europe were unsuccessful.)

*   *   *

To Roger Parker Saunders

Dear Sir   Philadelphia June 6th [17]84

M[r] Pettit wrote me some little time ago that you had written to him for 600 Guineas on my account to complete a contract you had made for improving my Georgia plantation.[1] I now send you a letter of credit for the Money on M[r] Robert Hazlehurst which you will apply for and pay according as your contract may run.[2] I hope you have taken Care to make your purchaces on good terms as the conditions are in part for ready Money.[3]

I have had a complaint in my breast which has prevented my being in South Carolinia at an earlier period. M[rs] Greene's situation fi[r]st prevented my coming. On her recovery I was immediately attacked with this disorder.[4] I am now better and shall return to Newport [R.I.] on Monday in hopes to get through the impost law.[5] After which I shall immediately set out for South Carolinia by water.[6] But in the meantime I beg you will acknowledge this letter and the receipt of the money as soon as obtained.[7] I also beg you to give me the particulars of the purchase you have made, the Sales of my last years crop and what prospects for the next both in South Carolinia and Georgia. Please to inform me also whether you made the purchase of Doctor Olliphants

Negroes. In a word give me a short history of all my affairs in that Country and whether you got any pipe Staves or bark.[8] Give my compliments to Mrs [Amarinthia Lowndes] Saunders and the family and believe me to be I am dear Sir Your Most obed[t] humble Ser NATH GREENE

ADfS (MiU-C).

1. See Charles Pettit to NG, 27 April, above.

2. As seen in the letter immediately above, NG had obtained the letter of credit through Robert Morris.

3. NG's understanding of the terms of the purchase was based on information in Pettit's letter of 27 April. (See also Pettit to NG, 18 May, above.) As seen in Saunders's letter of 29 May, above, which NG had not yet received, the terms included £700 in cash.

4. NG was being treated by a Newport, R.I., physician for a persistent pain in his chest. (See his letters to Charles Pettit and Washington of 22 April, both above.) CG had given birth to a daughter, Louisa Catharine, in April. (NG to Pettit, 22 April, above)

5. Monday was the following day, 7 June; NG left Philadelphia on the 8th. (Edwards to NG, 8 June, and NG to Steuben, 9 June, both below) On the Rhode Island legislature's rejection of the federal impost proposal of 1783, see NG to Morris, 3 July, below.

6. NG did not arrive in South Carolina until 1 August. (*South Carolina Gazette & Public Advertiser*, 31 July–4 August)

7. Lewis Morris, Jr., wrote NG on 17 July, below, that Saunders had received the bills.

8. Saunders included some of the information requested here with his letter to NG dated before 17 July, below. Nothing more is known about the purchase of slaves from Dr. David Olyphant, which Saunders had earlier discussed and reportedly made for NG, or about stave and bark production, which NG had suggested as a means to offset some of his losses from the previous year's disappointing rice crop. (See Saunders to NG, 3 December 1783; Pendleton to NG, 30 January; and NG to Saunders, 4 January, all above.)

Agreement between NG and Charles Pettit

[Philadelphia] June 7th 1784

It is agreed by & between Nathaniel Greene Esq[r] of Rhode Island & Charles Pettit Merch[t] in Philadelphia that the said Charles Pettit shall purchase for the joint Account and Risk of the said Parties such and so many Certificates of Debts due from the United States bearing Interest as he in his Discretion shall think proper, and at such Rates as he can agree for, keeping a fair Account of his Transactions and Purchases, and rendering such Acc[t] to the said Nath[l] Greene from Time to Time when required. The Interest and other Profits arising to be considered as an Increase of the Stock & laid out in farther Purchases unless either Party shall choose to divide them. The Extent of Purchases to be as large as four thousand Dollars will accomplish as early as may be, and afterwards to be increased or not according to Circumstances on a farther Communication of Sentiments.[1]   NATH GREENE
                                                                    CHA[S] PETTIT

DS (NjP).

1. For more about this agreement, see Pettit to NG, 10 and 26 June, both below.

To Jeremiah Wadsworth

Dear Sir Philadelphia June 7th 1784

I wrote you from Newport a little time past that I apprehended I should have some pressing necessity to draw on you for two thousand dollars.[1] Accordingly I have drawn in favor of Mr Charles Pettit. If I have mistaken your politeness for sentiments of kindness it will lead me into some mistakes that may prove injurious. Be that as it may I have drawn and rest the matter with your feelings.[2] I am dear Sir with esteem & affection your Most Obedt huml Sert NATH GREENE

ALS (CtHi).

1. The letter referred to here has not been found.

2. The purpose of this transaction is not known. This letter was sent to Wadsworth, who was then in England, in care of a Liverpool merchant. It did not arrive before Wadsworth left England, however, and had to be forwarded to him in America. In a letter of 1 November, below, Wadsworth informed NG that he had returned the bill, which was in favor of Charles Pettit and his son, Andrew, unpaid, to the person "to whom it was indorsed." He added that it would "not be convenient" for him "to accept any more Bills" from NG.

* * *

¶ [**FROM JOHN CRUDEN**, St. Augustine, East Florida, 8 June 1784.[1] Encloses a "duplicate of a letter to Major [Ichabod] Burnet."[2] News of Burnet's death gives him "much Concern."[3] Asks NG not to be "Surprized at any story you hear or at any Shape I may assume," for it is his "Ardent wish" to "realize Evry part of the within Scheme[,] but the ice must be broke[,] for I know your Character so well that I feel a Certain Confidence when I think of you and am firmly persuaded that it must be the wish of your heart to make the Country that already owes So much to you happy." If NG could lend a sum of money to a person he names, Cruden would be "very happy indeed and then I should rejoice in giveing you that insight into my plans which Can not be done Safely in any other Way, and be assured that nothing would give me greater pleasure than to have the honor to Act under your Command."[4] RCS (MiU-C) 2 pp.]

1. As noted above (vol. 10: 221n), Cruden, a native of North Carolina, had been the British commissioner for confiscated estates in South Carolina. As a Loyalist refugee in East Florida, he had led opposition to the transfer of control of that colony to Spain. (Chesnutt, *Laurens Papers*, 16: 258n)

2. In a letter of 7 November 1783 to Burnet, who was then already deceased, Cruden intimated a scheme to unite East Florida with the United States under another form of government, or, failing that, to join East Florida with Georgia and the Carolinas in a presumably British-controlled "Kingdom" under "the command" of Burnet's "friend" [NG]. The letter stated in part:

> "I fear America is not to be happy, and I am very sorry for it, for I must Confess I love the Country and lament the Cause of Separation. As I wrote you before, I do know that your friend [NG] is highly respected here at the fountain head. His abilities and his tenderness to the distressd has gained him the affection of all Ranks of people in this Country, which with a desire to render our purchase Valuable, permenant & lasting, to be again a Member of your Community, and to Establish a

Government, in such a footing as would give real freedom to the inhabitants, which ought to be the Object of Evry man[,] I was led to a train of thinking, which was partly occasioned by the Strange infatuation of the diffrent states Respecting the Loyalists."

Cruden added that as he had

"gained Certain information that France was labouring to place the power of the Continent in the hands of G[eorge]- W[ashington]- whom they have guessed more firmly in their intrest, I thought if it Could be So managed that the Loyalists and the disbanded Troops of both Armies Could be brought to act together in the So Provinces, We might be able to form Georgia, N° & So Carolina into a Kingdom, under the Command of your friend, and in order to bring forth the Loy[alis]ts and British troops disbanded of Col [John] Hamilton & myself to Step out and act under his Command our Strength united with those Still disposed for Monarchy in the So Province would be too powerful for GW [i.e., Washington] and such of his adherents as Could not be gained over[,] These forces after being digested in my Mind and on Mature deliberation appearing not only feasable but if put in Execution Such as would Effectually permit the happiness of the people at large, Counteract France, and make your Friend the greatest of the Humane Race, the Saviour of a Country."

If this "plan were to take place, a Constitution similar to that of Ireland would be granted," and Cruden could "assure" Burnet that NG would be commander-in-chief, and "the first Military Appointments will be to himself, his friends will be first provided for, that he will have any Title he pleases." Cruden, who enclosed a cypher for Burnet's use, hoped to hear from him "very soon" and looked "forward with pleasure to that day that will make him [NG] far greater than any Prince on Earth." (MiU-C)

3. On Burnet's death, see Flagg to NG, 17 October 1783, above.

4. On the "plan," see note 2, above. There was presumably no further correspondence between NG and Cruden. NG commented on ideas such as this in a letter to Washington of 29 August, below.

¶ [FROM EVAN EDWARDS, [Philadelphia,] 8 June 1784. It was "truly unfortunate" that he arrived in Philadelphia the day that NG left, for he had "a thousand things" to tell NG "beyond the bounds of a letter."[1] He is forwarding "a Letter from R Saunders," which, he supposes, relates the "situation of your affairs."[2] Edwards would like to travel to Rhode Island, if his "finances will admit," but is "apprehensive I shant have the pleasure"; he would think himself "fully compensated" if he could see NG for "an hour or two."[3] Expects to "return to [South] Carolina in the fall, not to be married."[4] Is afraid that [John] Banks "is in a bad way. I hope not ruind intirely in purse; but I am apprehensive too much so in Character as a Mercht."[5] [James] Hamilton "was married this night Week to Mrs Horrleston [Elisabeth Harleston]," and "Mrs Thoms Bee and Mrs Coatsworth Pinckney are dead, both in child bed."[6] Adds: "Politicks and every thing else I must defer 'till I am more composed." It would be a "great pleasure" to hear from NG; a letter "directed" to Edwards in Philadelphia would reach him.[7] Hopes CG "is well. No person on Earth I wish better." RCS (MiU-C) 3 pp.]

1. As seen in his letter to Baron Steuben, immediately below, NG left Philadelphia on the 8th. Evans undoubtedly arrived from Charleston, S.C., that day on Capt. Matthew Strong's vessel. (See Pettit to NG, 10 June, below.) For some of the news that Evans brought with him but did not relate here, see ibid. and Evans's letter to NG of 12 May, above.

2. See Roger Parker Saunders to NG, 29 May, above.

3. No evidence has been found that Edwards visited NG in Newport.

4. On Edwards's failed courtship of a Charleston woman, see Pendleton to NG, 18 April, above.

5. Saunders wrote NG before 17 July, below, that Banks had left Charleston with "upwards of 20 Suits and Several Judgments" against him there. (See also Pettit to NG, 10 June.)

6. On the Hamilton-Harleston wedding, see also Forsyth to NG, 24 February, above. Sarah Smith Bee, the second wife of former congressional delegate Thomas Bee, died in childbirth on 1 June. (*Biog. Directory of S.C. House*, 2: 70) Sarah Middleton Pinckney died on 8 May. (Zahniser, *Pinckney*, p. 80n) The *South Carolina Gazette & Public Advertiser* of 5–8 May reported that she died "in the bloom of life, after enduring a long and tedious illness with christian patience and resignation."

7. No further correspondence between Edwards and NG has been found.

¶ [TO BARON STEUBEN. From New York, 9 June 1784.[1] A "short stay" in New York will keep NG from "the pleasure of seeing" Steuben. NG "came into Town" that morning and will leave the next morning for Newport, R.I. He "got a Carriage and horse to come out and see" Steuben but had to give up that plan because of "the rain increasing and the horse proving bad." The visit, he adds, "would have given me great pleasure," and he would be "happy" to see Steuben at Newport.[2] "Congress have adjourned, the remaining Troops are disbanded and a sett of commissioners appointed to succeed Mr Morris in the finance office."[3] This is "all the news" NG has heard. He "left Philadelphia yesterday, and Newport ten days ago; and expect to get home in less than a fortnight from the time I left it." ALS (NHi) 2 pp.]

1. As seen in this letter, NG made a brief stop in New York on his way home to Newport from Philadelphia.

2. Steuben visited NG at Newport during the summer of 1785. (NG to Ellery, 23 August 1785, below)

3. Congress adjourned its session at Annapolis, Md., on 3 June. (*JCC*, 27: 556) As noted at NG to Morris, 13 November, below, a Board of Treasury was to serve in Robert Morris's place after he concluded his duties as superintendent of finance later that year. Before its adjournment, Congress named William Denning, Oliver Ellsworth, and Daniel of St. Thomas Jenifer to serve as commissioners. (*JCC*, 27: 546–47) None of them accepted the appointment, and Congress, meeting in New York the following January, elected John Lewis Gervais, Samuel Osgood, and Walter Livingston to the posts. (*JCC*, 28: 18)

¶ [FROM WILLIAM DENNING, New York, 9 June 1784.[1] Introduces the bearer, who is "on the business of Settling the Accounts of Mr Oates of Boston while acting under your appointment."[2] RCS (MiU-C) 1 p.]

1. On Denning, the commissioner of accounts for the Quartermaster Department, see also Story to NG, 12 March, above.

2. "Oates" was presumably Samuel A. Otis, whose letters to NG of 25 July, 8 September, and 7–9 December 1783 on the subject of his accounts are above.

*   *   *

From Charles Pettit

Dear   Philad[a] 10th June 1784

Tuesday Afternoon Cap[t] [Matthew] Strong arrived from Charleston [S.C.].[1] I was shortly after saluted by a Draught of M[r] [Roger Parker] Saunders for upwards of 500 Dollars & another for 300 at thirty Days sight & expressed to be on your Account, but I had no Letter of Advice.[2] Observing that the Bills were in fav[r] of Major [Evan] Edwards & hearing that he was in Town, I sought Information from him.[3] He tells me M[r] [John] Banks being hard pushed put all his Accounts & Specialties indiscriminately into an Attorney's Hands to be prosecuted, among them an Acc[t] against you for upw[ds] of £300 Sterling, that M[r] Saunders, desirous to save you from a Suit, agreed to draw Bills for the Am[t] on me, & put them into Major Edwards's Hands on the Footing ment[d] in the Letter N[o] 1 herewith[;] that M[r] Banks afterwards demanded the Bills, which he refused to give him without orders from M[r] Saunders, that M[r] Banks & he both wrote to M[r] Saunders, & on receiving the letter N[o] 2 he delivered the Bills to M[r] Banks, who has sold or paid them away, two of them have been presented as abovement[d], the third has not yet appeared. Maj[r] Edwards adds that M[r] Saunders wrote to me on the Subject & committed the Letter to M[r] Banks, who set out for Virginia ab[t] a Month ago, that M[r] Saunders's Letter to you was forwarded on Tuesday Evening & he hopes it will overtake you at N York.[4]

As these Bills have been negociated & M[r] Saunders is at all Events a[n]swerable for the Payment, I presume it will be your Desire to pay them, but they yet remain unaccepted & I may have Time to hear from you before they become due, rather than you should be baulked in such Desire I will take up the Bills on knowing it to be your wish, on my own Strength; but if you can provide the Funds in Time it will be the more convenient to me; however, I would not have it distress you, but you must give me Notice as early as possible.[5] The two Letters from M[r] Saunders to Major Edwards of which the Copies are herewith were lent me for this Purpose this Morning.[6]

I have contracted for the Pay Master's Certificates at 1/5th as far as will cost about 1600. Dollars, these are confined to the Jersey Line wch at present appear preferable; Penns[a] I consider next; then perhaps N York, promiscuous Cert[s] may be had lower & I may take some for that Reason.[7] Pray advise me respecting the several States northward of N York. I have got a Key by which I can know those of Jersey by their Numbers, & expect one for Pennsylvania. I should like to have a Key for each State if I could get it in a proper way, but at present it is difficult to distinguish those of one State from those of another.[8] I am affectionately, D[r] Sir Your most obed[t] Serv[t]   CHA[S] PETTIT

RCS (MiU-C).

1. Tuesday was 8 June. NG had left Philadelphia that same day. (NG to Steuben, 9 June, above)

2. For background, see Edwards to NG, 12 May, and Saunders to NG, 29 May, above.

3. Edwards arrived in Philadelphia from Charleston on 8 June, undoubtedly on Strong's vessel. (Edwards to NG, 8 June, above) On the bills drawn in favor of Edwards, see also his letter to NG of 12 May and Saunders's to NG of 29 May.

4. Saunders's letter to NG was that of 29 May. As NG was in New York for only a day, it is unlikely that he received it there. (NG to Steuben, 9 June, above)

5. NG replied to Pettit on 23 June, below.

6. The enclosed copies of letters from Saunders to Edwards are at MiU-C.

7. As seen in his agreement with NG of 7 June, above, Pettit was speculating in paymaster receipts and other "Certificates of Debts due from the United States" for NG and himself.

8. When NG replied to Pettit on 23 June, he was unable to provide the requested information.

*   *   *

¶ [FROM JACOB GREENE, Coventry, R.I., 11 June 1784. Tells NG: "You never wrote me whether you intended going to [South] Carolina or not, upon your return from Philadelphia."[1] Hopes NG will be there "early in July," when Jacob expects that Captain Pierce will also be there. If NG does not go, Jacob asks him to write to some of his friends there and ask them to give Pierce "all the assistance in their Power in procureing a Cargo of rice upon Purchase, and freight."[2] He also asks NG to "Draw on some Person there for two thousand Dollars and I will answer the money to you here, or you may Direct them to Draw on you for that sum here.[3] I have more than Double that sum due here and a Considerable Part in good hands, so that I am shure of Collecting to that amount as I would not wish to imbarrass you." Jacob's "motives for Doing this is to make the Capitol as large as possible in the Brig." Otherwise, "She might loose the stock," and it might not be "worth his Pursueing the voyage to Europe." Adds: "his orders admit of Selling the Brig in Carolina which I should Choose he might do."[4] Jacob would "be very happy" if NG could procure for "Tommy" a "small consignment of Fifty or Eighty casks of rice by way of encouragement under the directions of" Pierce; if the "Brig should go to Europe," the "commission" would be an "inducement for him to pursue the voyage."[5] Jacob also asks NG to have Col. [Charles] Pettit "ship me four or five Tons of Pig Iron" as a trial; he will pay Pettit in "three Months Which is the Conditions I can have from New York."[6] The "Repairs of the Works" have turned out to be "much greater than" Jacob expected, "from there being rotten."[7] There is no recent news from Griffin Greene.[8] CG and the children "were well but had not moved" the last time Jacob heard from them.[9] He meant to be in Newport before this but is "so ingaged" that he "cannot stir from home"; is also "very unwell and almost wore out with Fatigue." RCS (MiU-C) 2 pp.]

1. On NG's return to Newport from Philadelphia, see note at NG to Steuben, 9 June, above.

2. NG left for the South on 12 July and arrived on 1 August. (See note at NG to Robert Hazlehurst, 26 June, below.) On Benjamin Pierce's business in Charleston, see NG's letters to Hazlehurst and Roger Parker Saunders, both 26 June, and Jacob Greene's letter to NG of 5 July, all below. Pierce commanded the *Minerva*, a brigantine constructed under the

auspices of Jacob and Griffin Greene and completed in 1780. (Vol. 5: 481 and n, above; Jacob Read to NG, 30 July, below)

3. NG asked Hazlehurst to advance $2,000 to Pierce in cash or rice, for which NG would be responsible. (NG to Hazlehurst, 26 June)

4. As seen in Jacob's letter to NG of 5 July, Pierce rejected a favorable offer to sell the *Minerva*. (See also NG to Griffin Greene, 8 July, below.)

5. "Tommy"—most likely Jacob's seventeen-year-old son, Thomas—apparently had sailed with Pierce on the *Minerva*. (Clarke, *Greenes*, p. 200; Jacob Greene to NG, 5 July)

6. Pettit had mentioned the possibility of supplying pig iron to Jacob in a letter to NG of 30 March, above.

7. Jacob's "anchor shop" had been destroyed, and his forge rendered "useless," in a flood the previous winter. (NG to Jacob Greene, 8 January, above; NG to Griffin Greene, 8 July)

8. Griffin Greene wrote NG from France on 12 June, immediately below.

9. CG and the children later moved from "the Point" neighborhood of Newport, which was near the harbor, to a house on "the Hill." (Littlefield to NG, 25 April 1785, below)

¶ [FROM GRIFFIN GREENE, Bordeaux, France, 12 June 1784. He hopes the Marquis de Lafayette, who is reportedly leaving soon for America, will deliver this letter to NG.[1] Lafayette, he writes, "has taken as much pains to serve us, as if the whole bussiness had been his own."[2] Although Griffin has "been in great doubt, of late whether all has not been don[e] in vain," he now has "hopes." Mr. James Price, "an American Gentleman, at Paris," has written to the firm of V. & P. French & Nephew, "my friends, at this place," relaying a message from Lafayette that Griffin "might make him self, intirely easy that all would be settled relative" to the *Flora*.[3] Griffin adds: "The great length of time, I have been upon this bussiness, & the disagreable scituation I have been in, on account of troubleing other people that was not conserned, has tryed my patience to the bottom." He wishes he were "so happy as to write it was all finished," but that is not the case, and he fears he must "stay much [lon]ger yet."[4] The "first Valuation" of the ship was for "82,000 livers"; the "second was much higher." Griffin would be "Happy, to have the first, rather than be held any longer in suspence, & possiabilly not get any thing finnaly."[5] He asks NG to inform Jacob Greene what he has written and to let his family know that he is well.[6] RCS (MiU-C) 3 pp.]

1. Lafayette embarked on the *Courrier de New York* on 28 June and was supposed to sail for New York the following day. (Idzerda, *Lafayette Papers*, 5: 231) He arrived in August and spent some five months in America. (See note at his letter to NG of 25 August, below.) It is not known when or how NG received this letter, as he was in South Carolina by the time Lafayette reached New York.

2. On Lafayette's help in trying to sell the *Flora* in France, see also Griffin's letter to NG of 6 April, above.

3. In a letter at the end of the September documents, below, Griffin identified Price as "the Honorable Gentleman that had the thanks of Congress for his assistance at Quebeck."

4. Griffin had sailed for France in May 1783. (Vol. 12: 662–64 and n, above) As noted at his letter to NG of 6 April, he did not return to the United States until 1785.

5. On the second valuation of the *Flora*, see Griffin's letter to NG at the end of the September documents. The sale was not finalized until April 1785. (NG to CG, 14 April 1785, below)

6. No letter from NG to his brother Jacob or to Griffin's family about this news has been found.

¶ [FROM ROBERT FORSYTH, Charleston, S.C., 18 June 1784. He wrote NG on 27 April after receiving NG's letter of 9 March; since then, he has been "in daily expectation" of seeing NG in South Carolina.[1] Has received "a line" from Mr. [E. John] Collett, "who continues to be disapointed in Virginia." Collett reports that he "has not yet received even enough to clear his Expences" and that he has written to NG "on this very disagreable subject."[2] Forsyth informs NG: "As the presence of M[r] [John] Banks in Virginia apeared to me to be the only thing that coud forward his payment, I have strained every Nerve to effect his departure from hence." Banks left Charleston "some Weeks ago" for Virginia, intending first to spend some time in New Bern [N.C.] to collect "some old Funds due Hunter, Banks & C[o]" and to "send something" to "relieve my ingagements in becoming his Bail &c &c."[3] Forsyth was obliged to post bail for him, as Banks "cou'd not have departed" otherwise. Banks was "under the necessity" of using NG's "Accounts" in order to "procure Money," and Forsyth believes that Banks "has got Bills" on Col. [Charles] Pettit from Mr. [Roger Parker] Saunders for $1,325.[4] Concerning Banks's use of NG's accounts, Forsyth writes: "This was with my knowledge[,] and circumstances were such as to put it out of my power to prevent and as it was done to forward M[r] Colletts payment I hope you may excuse it."[5] Before Banks left, Forsyth let him take "Acc[ts] &c to amount of £2000 St[g] [i.e., sterling] to lodge for a Debt" that Banks owed "here." Forsyth agreed to this only because of "a promise from Cap[t] [Erasmus] Gill that M[r] Collett shoud receive an equal amount from the proceeds of a shipment of Goods then shiping for Petersburg."[6] In letting Banks take these accounts, Forsyth believed he was guaranteeing a sum to Collett and at the same time allowing Banks to use accounts that "coud be turned into nothing that woud answer the purposes of M[r] Collet." When Banks left, he took with him "a survey of 100,000 Acres of Lands in the back Country of Virg[a] which he received from his Brother," who, Forsyth understood, was "half owner." Forsyth hopes the lands "may be apropriated as to aid M[r] Colletts paym[en]t and give him an Ultimate certainty of receiving his Debt without having recourse" to NG.[7] Forsyth has sent Collett "a copy of the Receipt" given by Banks for the accounts worth £2000, which certifies that Banks obtained the accounts in "consequence of his having Credit for M[r] Colletts Debt to be paid by him in Virg[a]."

In his last letter [not found], Forsyth wrote that the "settlem[t] of the Ch[s]ton speculation" between Banks and Mr. John Ferrie, by which profits equal to £7200 sterling had been assigned to Ferrie, was "under Arbitration," which has since been "determined" in Forsyth's favor.[8]

> "That is, That the Settlement is eronious[,] that M[r] Banks had no exclusive right or authority to allow the same and that it is not binding on the other partners concerned in the said purchase. And further that the said John Ferrie hath no claim or demand against the said Rob[t] Forsyth, James Hunter and Ichabod Burnett excepting only his due proportion of what may be fairly deemed the profits arising from the Sale of such Goods Wares & Merchandise in which he the said John Ferrie was interested & that only when the whole payments are made and further that John Banks is accountable unto Rob[t] Forsyth & Co or John Banks & C[o] for such Sum of money as

may be retained from them or either of their respective Firms by
Pierce, White & Call by Virtue of their possessing the said John
Banks acceptance in favor of the said John Ferrie for the above mentioned Sum of £7200 Sterling Money of this State. Respecting the
Contract, the profits of which Mr Banks claimed for himself, They
have determined That it was for the mutual benefit of the Company
viz Hunter, Banks & C° one half & Robt Forsyth & Ichabod Burnett
the other half."

"Soon after" this determination was made, Ferrie left "for Georgia, very sud-
denly," before Forsyth "coud have a bill in Chancery filed ag[ains]^t him."
However, "a M^r McWhann one of the Gentlemen who sold part of the Spec.
Goods am^t £2700 yet owing him, has set out for Savannah with Instructions from
M^r [Hugh?] Rutledge." Forsyth hopes McWhann can keep Ferrie from "leaving
the Country & finally recover his paym^t from him." Ferrie's one-third share of
the profit "will not be £2500[,] and each of the other parties will not have a
Thousand each." This will render Forsyth unable to "discharge" his "Engage-
ments" in November and January, as he had expected to use "the profit on this
Speculation" to do so, and "it will turn out a Nothing when the Debts are paid."
Rice is up to eighteen pence per hundred weight and is expected to go up to
twenty "in a few Days." The "very small proportion of the Crop on Hand and
the number of Vessells wanting Loads has occasioned the very uncommon
price."[9] Mrs. Harleston has been "married sometime to Maj^r Hamilton," and
Mrs. Bee and Mrs. Pinckney "are both dead."[10] Forsyth sends his respects to CG
and family. RCS (MiU-C) 6 pp.]

1. Neither letter has been found. NG left for South Carolina on 12 July.

2. Collett, a British merchant in Charleston from whom John Banks had purchased
clothing for the Southern Army, had been in Virginia since at least February, trying to
recover money that Banks owed him for those purchases and for which NG was a
guarantor. (See Forsyth to NG, 24 February, and Agreement between Hunter, Banks &
Company, NG, and Newcomen and Collett, 8 April 1783 [vol. 12: 591], both above.) On 23
June, below, NG replied to two letters from Collett, neither of which has been found.

3. Evan Edwards wrote NG on 12 May, above, that Banks had left Charleston and gone
to Virginia after giving his accounts due—NG's among them—to an attorney.

4. See preceding note and Pettit's letters to NG of 10 June, above, and 19 June, immediately below. As seen in Pettit's letters, the bills drawn on him by Saunders were to cover the
amount that Banks claimed NG owed him. (See also NG to Pettit, 23 June, below.)

5. NG wrote Pettit on 15 August: "Mr Collett has receivd partial payments and upon the
whole I am not with out hopes of getting off without loss." As seen by the note at NG to
Collett, 8 August, below, this did not prove to be the case. (On the "partial payments," see
Pendleton to NG, 10 November, below.)

6. Gill, a former cavalry officer, had become a merchant in Petersburg, Va. (Banks,
Vindication, pp. 20, 21) On Gill's "promise," see also NG to Forsyth, 5 June 1785, below.

7. In a letter of 8 August, below, NG urged Collett to place attachments on lands
belonging to Banks and Banks's brother Henry.

8. The Charleston "speculation" had undoubtedly been in the supplies of clothing that
Banks and his partners procured for the Southern Army. On Ferrie's involvement, see
also Pierce to NG, 24 September, and Call to NG, 30 September, both below. After NG got
to Charleston, he sought to attach property belonging to Ferrie and to claim the profits of
at least one of the other partners in the speculation, to whom he wrote on 28 August,

below: "It is not your misfortune that I became a guarantee for the Company[,] which never would have happened but from their being contractors for [the] army, it is mine to be perplexed with the affair." (NG to Richard Lushington, 28 August, below; see also NG to Collett, 8 August, and NG to Pettit, 15 August, below.) William Pierce, Jr., wrote NG on 24 September, below, that he believed Ferrie had "so secured" his property in Georgia "that it will be impossible to reach it." After NG's death, however, his estate won a "recovery" in South Carolina from Ferrie, "one of the partners in the House of Hunter, Banks and Company." (See note at NG to Collett, 8 August, below, and Alexander Hamilton, "Report on the Petition of Catharine Greene," 26 December 1791, Syrett, *Hamilton*, 10: 416.) In a statement dated 2 November 1790, Charles C. Pinckney, who had represented Ferrie in the South Carolina suit, wrote that Ferrie "assisted Banks, in the purchase of the goods, and had been instrumental in his obtaining credit. He [i.e., Ferrie] had kept the books of the Company. He appeared to me, to have known all the concerns of the Company, most intimately and minutely." (Pinckney's statement is printed in ibid., pp. 465–67; quoted text is on p. 466.)

9. On prices earlier in the year, see Forsyth to NG, 24 February.

10. On this news from Charleston, see also Edwards to NG, 8 June, above.

¶ [FROM CHARLES PETTIT, Philadelphia, 19 June 1784. He wrote NG "last Week" about some bills that Mr. [Roger Parker] Saunders drew "on me in fav^r of Major [Evan] Edwards amounting to about £300 Sterling"; since then, he has heard nothing more about this matter.[1] He also gave as much information about the transaction in that letter as he could get from Edwards: that Edwards's name was "only borrowed, the Bills being to pay a Demand of Banks against" NG, "which with other Claims of his had been promiscuously put into the Hands of an Attorney to recover."[2] Pettit also asked NG for "Directions whether to pay the Bills or not, holding them in Suspence in the mean Time"; they are "at 30 days sight."[3] Since writing that letter, Pettit has been informed by "M^r [John] Chaloner" that Chaloner has received bills on NG "to the Amount of about £2000. Sterling, drawn by M^r [Griffin] Greene in France payable at 12 Months after date (February last)."[4] Pettit presumes that Chaloner has written to NG, because Chaloner "took up a Letter" for NG, "which he supposed to be from Col. Wadsworth & to contain Advice of the Bills, in order to forward it" to NG. That letter was directed to Pettit's care and came to him from the post office, but he does not know how it got there.[5] Pettit thinks that Chaloner mentioned "these Bills to me on a Supposition of my acquaintance with your Affairs; and the Business is not farther known in this Town that I know of, nor is it perhaps material whether it be or not. It is material however that you should know it, & therefore I mention it to apprize you of it in Case it should not otherwise have reached you." Two "R. Island Sloops" are now in Philadelphia, and Mr. Quarrier "has promised to get the Carriage on board one of them."[6] Pettit gave Mr. [John] Story permission to "draw on" him for $100, but before Story received the letter, he had already drawn for £100. Pettit comments: "If all the Accounts are to be proportionately expensive in the Settlement, it will require many such Estates as mine to accomplish it."[7] Having heard that "a Sloop is to sail in the morning," he has "run over" this letter "in Haste for the Opportunity." RCS (MiU-C) 2 pp.]

1. See Pettit to NG, 10 June, above, and NG's reply to that letter, dated 23 June, below.

2. For more about this matter, see above, Edwards to NG, 12 May, and Saunders to NG, 29 May.

3. See NG to Pettit, 23 June.

4. Chaloner, a Philadelphia merchant, had been an agent for Jeremiah Wadsworth and John Carter as contractors to Washington's army. (Morris, *Papers*, 7: 46n) NG wrote Griffin Greene on 8 July, below: "A sett of bills was presented me some little time past for two thousand pounds in favor of Col Wadsworth. I did not accept them nor can I imagine for what purpose they were drawn." For more about the bills and NG's refusal to accept them, see note at Griffin Greene to NG, 6 April, above. As seen in his letter to Wadsworth of 12 November, below, NG had misunderstood the purpose of the bills and Wadsworth's "agency in the business."

5. Joseph Anthony informed NG in a letter of 15 July that Chaloner had written to NG on this subject, but neither that letter nor the one presumed to be from Wadsworth has been found. (See, however, the preceding note.)

6. CG had ordered the carriage in Philadelphia the previous summer. (Pettit to NG, 23 July 1783, above) Quarrier appears to have owned a shop in Philadelphia where carriages were sold and repaired. (Smith, *Letters*, 20: 438) Pettit wrote NG on 26 June, below, that the vehicle had been loaded onto the sloop *Delaware*.

7. Story's reason for drawing this money is not known.

* * *

To E. John Collett

Sir   Newport [R.I.] June 23. 1784.

I have just got your letter of the 28th of May, the one you wrote in april come to hand Some time ago, and I should have answered it at an earlier day, but had such assurances from Charleston that Mr Banks would accomodate our demands to your satisfaction that I thought a Letter by post would only tax you without profit and I am now assured by Major Edwards who has just come from Charleston, that Mr Banks sett out for Virginia some time since, & must have been with you long ago.[1] From the expectation of this, I would not write now, did I not apprehend you may put improper constructions upon my conduct.

Mr Banks cannot treat you with more Cruelty than he does me in neglecting you. Inclosed I send you a Copy of his counter Security.[2] I had such assurances from him of Speady payment, & the feeding the Army so connected with his Credit, that I consented to guarantee your & some other debts.[3] You will see the Cruelty of my situation, and as I am persuaded with you that Mr Banks has funds in Virginia & elsewhere abundantly Sufficient to satisfy all your demands, I hope you will not think of troubling me on the Subject. Besides which I am largely in debt & my property given in pledge for Security. After this information I hope you will not turn your thoughts to me; it is true you have it in your power to distress me, but without benefiting youself. I have made use of every argument in my power to induce Mr Banks to settle & pay you, & have told him that he & I would not live long in the same World if he brought me into difficulties in the matter, and I will follow him to the Ends of the Earth for Satisfaction.[4] I am now going to Charleston and shall be glad to hear from you there.

I do not understand you on the subject of demurrage, I hope you do not think me answerable for any after Contracts you & M[r] Banks may enter upon to negotiate payment.[5] This is a matter intirely between you & him. M[r] Mills wrote me in February last that the extent of your demand, principal & Intrest did not exceed £7000. You in your first letter make it more than ten. M[r] Mills also mentions a dividend you had received of M[r] [Charles] Pettit upon those Bonds. It is unne[ce]ssary to add on the subject.[6] M[r] Banks has it in his power to satisfy you, & your debt has never been render'd less safe by my Guarantee, and it will be cruel in you to distress me, as I have no Interest in the matter, and I tell you with candour I will sooner go to goal [i.e., jail] than pay anything, but will do every thing in my power to obtain for you justice & satisfaction from the interested parties.[7] I am Sir your mo[t] obed. humble Servant   NATH: GREENE

PS. Please forward the letter of [i.e., to?] M[r] Harris wherever he may be.[8]

Cy (MiU-C).

1. Neither of Collett's letters has been found. As seen at Forsyth to NG, 24 February and 18 June, above, Collett had been in Virginia for some time, trying to recover debts that John Banks owed him and for which NG was the guarantor. Evan Edwards, who arrived in Philadelphia on 8 June, wrote NG on 12 May, above, that Banks had left Charleston, S.C., and gone to Virginia. (See also Edwards to NG, 8 June, above.)

2. This document has not been found.

3. See Agreement between Hunter, Banks & Company, NG, and Newcomen and Collett, 8 April 1783, above (vol. 12: 591), and NG to Lee, 22 August 1785, below. NG was the guarantor for Banks's unpaid debts to Newcomen and Collett for clothing that he purchased from them for the Southern Army during the fall of 1782. (On Banks's financial difficulties, see also vol. 12: 308–9n; on the contract that Banks agreed to in February 1783 to supply provisions to the army, see Edward Carrington to NG, 18 February 1783, above [vol. 12: 458–59 and n].)

4. NG set out for North Carolina and Virginia early that fall to try to find Banks, only to learn that Banks was "dead & buried." (NG to Rutledge, after 30 September, below)

5. NG presumably referred here to any additional, time-related charges for which he might be liable if he were required to satisfy Collett's demand against Banks.

6. The letter from Mills has not been found.

7. Collett continued to press his demands on NG. (See NG to Collett, 8 August, below.) On the eventual resolution of this matter, see note at ibid.

8. NG wrote Charles Pettit on this date, immediately below: "I have forwarded letters to Harris and Collet and wish you to send them on as soon as possible." As seen in Pettit to NG, 18 May, above, Michael J. Harris, to whom Banks was in debt—and to whom NG, as Banks's guarantor, was ultimately responsible—had also gone to Virginia, presumably on a mission similar to Collett's. (See also NG to Collett, 8 August.)

To Charles Pettit

Dear Sir   Newport [R.I.] June 23[d] 1784
    Your letter of the 10th did not find me until last Evening. I got home the third day after I left Philadelphia and went into Connecticut to put George to School where both his education and morals are strictly

attended to. And for his boarding schooling working and lodging I give only Sixty five dollars a year.[1] On my return from Connecticut I found your letter. I am sorry Mr Saunders interfered in the matter. I would rather have suffered a suit than drawn bills or negotiated payment in any other way.[2] I told Mr Banks that I would discharge those demands the moment he took up my guarantee Bonds and not before.[3] Mr Saunders drawing those bills leaves me no security for any damages I may sustain. But besides this objection the draft is for a much greater sum than I once knew. I have his Account signed at the time of my leaving Charleston [S.C.] which amounts to only 272.12 And I left a Negroe in his service and which I wrote him he might keep afterwards which cost £80 Sterling. So that there will remain only a ballance of about £192 and the drafts it seems is for upwards of three hundred. I am loth Mr Saunders should suffer; and therefore I shall be greatly oblige to you to take up the bills. I will go for Charleston immediately and take measures for taking up the bills. I wish you to write Saunders that you have taken up the bills on his Account.[4] This will leave me at liberty to assume the payment or not. I will be ultimately answerable to you but I wish to leave any disputes if there should be any between Saunders and Banks for them to settle between themselves. If I pay the bills without reserve I shall have to look to Banks for the Ballance and this I am not willing to.

I know not the Key for the final settlement Notes of this State or any other. Mr Pearce [John Pierce] the pay master doubtless can inform you. He and M^r [William] Denning can give you the best information. I will try to learn the [Rates?] of this State and Boston and let you know before I go to the Southward.[5] I have forwarded letters to [Michael J.] Harris and [E. John] Collet and wish you to send them on as soon as possible.[6] Mrs Greene joins me in kind compliments to Mrs [Sarah Reed] Pettit and the family.   N GREENE

ADfS (MiU-C).

1. NG left Philadelphia on 8 June. (NG to Steuben, 9 June, above) The Connecticut boarding school in which NG enrolled his son George was presumably the one mentioned in Pettit to NG, 26 July 1783, above. As noted at ibid., Dr. John Witherspoon, from whose school in New Jersey CG removed George the previous summer, had asked NG for 100 guineas a year.

2. See Pettit to NG, 10 June, and Roger Parker Saunders to NG, 29 May, both above.

3. As guarantor for certain debts that John Banks had incurred in supplying clothing to the Southern Army, NG was now being pressed for relief by merchants who had been unable to collect from Banks. (See, for example, Agreement between Hunter, Banks & Company, NG, and Newcomen and Collett, 8 April 1783 [vol. 12: 591], above; NG's letters to E. John Collett of 23 June, immediately above, and 8 August, below; and NG to Lee, 22 August 1785, below.)

4. Pettit wrote NG on 26 July, below, that he had asked Saunders to replace "the Amount of his Draughts on me for your Account." NG's reply to that statement is below, dated 15 August.

5. Pettit had asked NG for this information in his letter of 10 June.

6. On these letters, see also NG to Collett, immediately above.

From William Pierce, Jr.

My dear General Green   Savannah [Ga.] June 24th 1784

The Days of youthful gaiety have passed away, and my follies are thrown into the crusible of reflection. I shall be a poor chymist indeed if I do not derive or extract some profit from them.

Benedicted and ornamented with the domestic trappings of matrimony, I cannot look back at single life without feeling the greatest degree of pleasure in the change. My ambition has made a pause, not to stop forever, but to look around for a worthy pursuit, before I put it again in motion.[1]

Your Letter of the 20th March will contribute not a little towards the support of a prudential conduct.[2] I begin to be of opinion that tranquility is the only state of happiness we ought to aim at, for if we progress beyond it we are often obliged to stoop to some low or bad action, before we venture to look up, and when we have reached the utmost summit our reflections hurry us back to experience perhaps the height of wretchedness and pain.

I have, as it were, but just entered into Life, and, as yet, have scarcely had time enough to digest a plan for the support of it. Seven or eight years have passed away with no other advantages but the tinsel ornaments of a Soldiers fortune. I have given way to dissipation, and to some wild pursuits that hurt me on reflection; but I have never yet lost sight of that great object which supports a Gentleman in every situation.[3]

Human life is chequered by a prodigious variety of fortune, a croud of incidents pass along with it, and make our calculations very dubious and uncertain. These are the suggestions of a mind in retirement. Matrimony involves a Man in reflection, and makes him look at his condition with a measured pursuit of caution. It ties down his views to domestic life, and calls home his dissipated spirits to settle in the narrow circle of his Family and Friends. When he is at ease, he looks back and speculates on what has past, laughs at others, and moralizes upon his own actions.

I still trudge on in the dull path of business, but as yet I cannot tell what my fortune will be. I must be industrious, and work myself into success. Nature like fortune is totally unacquainted with distributive justice. I am suspicious (perhaps it is nothing more) that other Men have more talents and more reward for their labor than myself. Don't take it for granted that I mean to complain, for I assure you I do not.[4]

Mr Gibbons who conducts your Estate in this Country, has very often called upon me for assistance, I shall with chearfulness supply him with every thing he may want, and I believe cheaper and at a better rate than any Merchant in this place can.[5]

I have furnished him from time to time with Corn, Rice, & Cash for the purposes of the plantation, and shall continue to render him every service in my power during his Stewardship. He is, I am told, a very good Planter, and will make you a tolerable good crop of Rice.[6]

I understand you do not intend visiting this part of the World untill October, when you mean to take up your residence altogether in Carolina. I hope you will bring health enough with you to last several Years.[7]

M[rs] Pierce joins me in her best respects to you and M[rs] Greene.

The Thermometer is up at 90, my blood is as warm as my friendship.

W[M] PIERCE

RCS (MiU-C).

1. Pierce had married Charlotte Fenwick the previous December. (Pendleton to NG, 4 December 1783, above) *OED* defines "benedicted" as "blessed," and a "benedict" as "a newly married man, esp. a confirmed bachelor who marries."

2. NG's letter to Pierce of 20 March has not been found.

3. Pierce, who entered the army in 1776 as a captain of artillery, became NG's aide in December 1780 and served until March 1783. (See above, vol. 6: 523n; vol. 12: 536 and n.)

4. Pierce had left the army to go into business with Richard Call and Anthony W. White. (NG to Wadsworth, 24 May 1783, above)

5. William Gibbons was supervising NG's plantation in Georgia, Mulberry Grove. (See NG to Gibbons, 29 August, below.)

6. As seen at ibid., NG was grateful for Pierce's assistance to Gibbons.

7. NG returned to South Carolina in July; he apparently did not go to Georgia during that visit. He took up permanent residence in Georgia in November 1785. (NG to Ethan Clarke, 23 November 1785, below)

To Robert Morris, Superintendent of Finance

Dear Sir   Newport [R.I.] June 25th 1784

On my arrival here I found your kind and obliging letter of May the 19th. Impressed with your goodness and flattered by your assurances I find it difficult to express my feelings nor shall I attempt it upon the occasion being persuaded you are too generous to wish to make me feel a greater weight of obligation than is consistent with my own delicasy and your dignity. I hope always to manifest a greatful temper and flatter my self with a continuance of your confidence and esteem.[1]

I have got letters from M[r] Saunders my Agent to the Southward since I left Philadelphia. He is not explicit but says he has made a purchase of 58 Negroes at about £64 Sterling round. Seven hundred pounds to be paid down the remainder in three years.[2] I have written for a more explicit state of the matter when it comes to hand you shall have it.[3] If I have understood him properly I am in hopes not to distress you but little more whether you obtain the loan for me or not.[4] However while my Crops are growing and my stocks all out of my hands I feel my self distressed for little matters. People here are poor and Money difficult to be got on any terms. I have from the difficulty I meet with taken the liberty to draw on you for 250 Dollars and if you can with any tolerable conveniency pay this and allow me to draw for 250 More It will place me in a less disagreeable situation. These sums I will replace this fall whether I obtain a loan or not unless some very great accident attends my affairs.[5]

M[rs] Greene joins me in respectful complements to you and Mrs [Mary White] Morris accompanied with our best wishes for your healths and happiness. Next week you shall hear from me on the impost.[6] I am dear Sir with esteem & regard Your Most Obed[t] humble Ser   NATH GREENE

ADfS (CSmH).

1. NG had not received Morris's letter of 19 May, above, before he left for a brief visit to Philadelphia, but had met with Morris while he was there. (See note at NG to Morris, 5 June, above.)

2. In response to information from Charles Pettit about the purchase of slaves by Saunders, NG, during his visit to Philadelphia in early June, had requested and received an advance of 600 guineas against that expense from Morris. (See Pettit to NG, 27 April; NG to Morris, 5 June; and NG to Saunders, 6 June, all above.) After he returned to Newport, NG received Saunders's letter of 29 May, above, containing the further details about the purchase that he reported here.

3. NG's reply to Saunders's letter of 29 May has not been found.

4. As noted at Morris to NG, 12 July, below, Morris's efforts to arrange a loan for NG in Europe were ultimately unsuccessful.

5. Morris replied on 12 July: "Your draft for 250 Doll[rs] is honoured & I will do the same by another for the same amount as you desire."

6. See NG to Morris, 3 July, below.

*   *   *

¶ [TO ROBERT HAZLEHURST. From Newport, R.I., 26 June 1784. NG's brother Jacob "expects a brigantine commanded by Capt Benjamin Pearce [i.e., Pierce] to arrive at Charleston [S.C.] in a few days to take in a Cargo for Gottenberg in Europe."[1] That vessel is currently in the West Indies, and if she goes to Europe, Jacob wants "to add to her Cargo." NG therefore asks Hazlehurst "to advance to Capt Pearce to the amount of two thousand dollars for which you may draw bills and depend on their payment and for which I pledge my self to be accountable." Rice would probably suit him "as well as the Money." NG will be under "particular obligation" to Hazlehurst for his "advice and aid in procuring Capt Pearce freight and giving dispach to his business."[2] NG is "concerned in a Paquet building at this place" and hopes to "embark for Charleston" in it in a "fortnight."[3] Asks to be remembered to "Mr Tom Morris." ADfS (MiU-C) 3 pp.]

1. See Jacob Greene to NG, 11 June, above.

2. In the letter immediately below, NG also asked Roger Parker Saunders to help Pierce. On the *Minerva* and its cargo, see also Jacob Greene to NG, 11 June, above, and 5 July, below, as well as NG to Griffin Greene, 8 July, below.

3. The vessel was the sloop *Charleston Packet*, not to be confused with the brig of the same name that is mentioned in a note at Pendleton to NG, 3 February, above. NG sailed from Newport in the new vessel on 12 July and arrived in Charleston on 1 August. (*Newport Mercury*, 17 July; *South Carolina Gazette & Public Advertiser*, 31 July–4 August)

¶ [TO ROGER PARKER SAUNDERS. From Newport, R.I., 26 June 1784. In a letter similar to the one immediately above, NG tells Saunders that he has asked Mr. Hazlehurst to advance "two thousand Dollars in cash or Rice suitable for" the market in Europe to the captain of a brigantine owned by NG's brother Jacob. If the captain, Benjamin Pierce, cannot obtain the money or rice from Hazlehurst, NG asks Saunders to make the advance and "draw on my brother for the money." NG will be "accountable" and will be greatly obliged if Saunders can render "any services in obtaining freight or giving dispach" to the "business." NG plans to leave for Charleston, S.C., in a "fortnight" on a "Paquet" in which he is concerned that is now being built at Newport.[1] ADfS (MiU-C) 3 pp.]

1. On the contents of this letter, see notes at NG to Robert Hazlehurst, immediately above.

¶ [FROM CHARLES PETTIT, Philadelphia, 26 June 1784. He has received "an Official Report that the Chariot & it's appurtenances are on Board the Sloop *Delaware*, Israel Ambrose Master bound for New-Port," R.I. The "Packing & Stowing" were done by Mr. Quarrier and the "Captain," Pettit judging it "better & safer to leave it wholly to them than to interfere in it" himself. He has been "several Times informed" that "so difficult & troublesome a Job as the Captain finds or thinks he finds this to be, would not have been undertaken for any Person but General Greene." Pettit has "noted that the same Motives which admitted the Carriage on board, would also protect it from Injury with all possible Care." He is afraid that the vehicle's "Springs may want new gilding as they are much exposed to the friction of Ropes &c," but "Quarrier thought they would be safer in this Way than covered, as he apprehends that the covering, by preserving the Wetness they would be apt to receive, would be fatal to the gilding & perhaps contract Rust." Pettit believes "the best is done that could be under the attending circumstances." He expresses wishes for the carriage's "Safety and that it may be pleasing to Mrs Greene." He has "not stipulated the Freight of the Carriage, which must be settled on the Arrival."[1] Pettit notes that "Noaille has taken his Passage in the same Vessel, being anxiously desirous to throw himself at the Feet of his Mistress & implore her Pardon for the anxiety he gave her by his Desertion."[2] In a letter of 31 May, Maj. [Robert] Forsyth "mentions the Bills drawn by M^r [Roger Parker] Saunders on me." Forsyth knew about this transaction, but although it was "much against his wish," he "could not positively object to it as it was to enable Mr Banks to proceed to Virg^a to complete a payment" for which NG is "engaged." M^r [E. John] Collett "complains exceedingly," and Forsyth is "'fearful he may not be able to procure Satisfaction.'" Forsyth adds: "'I have wrote him pressingly to use his best Exertions to get his Demand and not to rely on any thing in this Quarter.'"[3] Pettit has bought almost $10,000 worth of "Jersey Cert^s of final Settlement at ⅕." He will "wait for" certificates from Pennsylvania, which "will be out in a few Days & will probably be lower." The "Promiscuous ones are yet at ⅖ to ⅔ but rather inclining to rise, but the Flood that will be issued in a short Time will be a check for a while during which I shall make some gathering."[4] RCS (MiU-C) 2 pp.]

1. Pettit wrote NG on 19 June, above, that he had finally found a vessel to accommodate the vehicle that CG ordered in Philadelphia the previous summer. (For more about CG's chariot and the problems of finding transportation for it, see Pettit to NG, 26 July 1783; after 21 January, 8 and 13 March, 22 April, and 6 May 1784; and NG to CG, 4 August 1783, all above.)

2. The Vicomte de Noailles, brother-in-law to the Marquis de Lafayette, had become fond of Mary ("Molly") Robinson of Newport while he was stationed there with the French expeditionary force and had corresponded with her after leaving Newport. (Anna Wharton Wood, "The Robinson Family and their Correspondence with the Vicomte and Vicomtesse de Noailles," *Bulletin of the Newport Historical Society* No. 42 [1922]: 7, 10–35)

3. See also Forsyth to NG, 18 June, and NG to Collett, 23 June, both above.

4. As seen in his agreement with NG of 7 June, above, Pettit was speculating in paymaster receipts and other "Certificates of Debts due from the United States" for NG and himself.

¶ [FROM WILLIAM R. DAVIE, Halifax, N.C., 27 June 1784. As his letter to NG of December 1783 has never been answered, he thinks it must have "miscarried."[1] He regrets that NG "left Halifax before I recieved your letter: it would have given me singular pleasure to have shared in doing the Honors of my Country to the person [to whom] I think we are principally indebted." Adds: "Gratitude and reflection have perfectly effaced the malicious impressions of the report you alluded to in your letter, and the conduct of our assembly last month will be satisfactory testimony of the high esteem with which they regard your character and services."[2] In a damaged portion of the letter, Davie discusses recent legislation by the North Carolina Assembly concerning NG's "Western lands."[3] He also reports that "We have done every thing consistent with the interest of the State to strengthen the Hands of Congress, the internal Tax was the most difficult and unpopular, and cost me a great deal of Labour in the House."[4] When he left NG at Ninety Six [S.C.], Davie forgot to "apply to" NG for certification of his employment in the Continental service from "first of January to the first of June." Asks NG to send a certificate and let him know how he will be paid.[5] Davie also has "a few small credits to give the Continent," which, as an "Honest man," he does not "wish to deprive her of." In another damaged portion, he asks where NG plans to live and says that if he should "ever be in your neighbour[hood] shall do myself the pleasure to beat up your Quarters."[6] RCS (NcU) 3 pp. The manuscript is damaged.]

1. See above, Davie to NG, 2 December 1783.

2. On NG's visit to Halifax, see his Journal entries for 31 August–3 September 1783, above. The letter that NG wrote to Davie at that time has not been found.

3. On North Carolina's grant of land to NG in what is now Tennessee, see Alexander Martin to NG, 24 May 1782, above (vol. 12: 239–40 and n). During its spring 1784 session, the North Carolina legislature passed "An Act to describe the lands granted to Major General Nathaniel Greene, and to confirm the Title thereof in the said Nathaniel Greene, his Heirs and Assigns forever." (*NCSR*, 24: 569–70)

4. Proceeds from a tax voted by the legislature during its spring session were to be applied to the state's share of the war debt incurred by Congress. (*NCSR*, 24: 557–59)

5. On the siege of Ninety-Six, see NG to Samuel Huntington, 20 June 1781, above (vol. 8: 419–22 and n). On Davie's Continental services, see note at his letter to NG of 2 December 1783.

6. NG's reply has not been found. Davie wrote him again on 4 December 1785, below: "I have sent letters to you in every quarter of the Continent, and indeed it seems more difficult to get a letter to you now; than when you was surrounded by your enemies." It is unlikely that they saw each other again.

¶ [FROM BARBARA BENTLY, [East Greenwich, R.I., June 1784].[1] Adds details about the account in question, hoping to convince NG that the £8.6.4 is a "wrong

Charge."[2] If NG needs more information, she asks him "to Let me know by a Line from y[r] Self and I Shall Endeavour to Procure it."[3] RCS (MiU-C) 1 p.]

1. The year is from the docketing; the place and month are conjectured from Bently's letters to NG of 1 June, above, and 4 July, below.

2. For background, see Bently to NG, 1 June.

3. NG's reply has not been found, but in her letter of 4 July Bently asked him, as he had informed her that he was about to leave for the South, to send "what is Due on your Childs acount."

¶ [FROM NICHOLAS HOFFMAN, New York, 1 July 1784. He received NG's "favour with the Sundry Letters for" Charleston, S.C., "yesterday," and will forward them on the "schooner *Polly*," which is to sail for Charleston "Tomorrow."[1] RCS (MiU-C) 1 p.]

1. NG's letter to Hoffman has not been found, nor is it known what letters Hoffman forwarded to Charleston. As seen in the note at his letter to NG of 4 October 1785, below, Hoffman paid £14.11.6 for "Sundrys" for NG on 3 July 1784.

¶ [FROM HUGH WALLACE, Liverpool, England, 1 July 1784. NG's letter of 10 April was forwarded to him from London to Liverpool, where he is visiting. He informs NG: "The cruel & undeserved ill Treatment I have met with at New York has intirely ruined me & Family and put it out of my Power to serve myself or Friends."[1] He has the "firmest Relyance" on NG's "honor & Integrity" and would have been "happy to accommodate" NG with the amount of money that Mr. [Nicholas] Hoffman mentioned. But as Wallace's property has been "confiscated and sold at New York," and he has been "proscribed and banished from that Province," he cannot do so.[2] He has directed a friend to pay NG's "Bill on me" for £150 sterling and has promised to repay this amount "immediately with Interest."[3] As this will keep the bill from "being returned with Damages," he hopes that NG will "remit a Bill for said Sum" to him in care of a firm of London merchants" as soon as possible."[4] CyS (MiU-C) 1 p.]

1. As noted at NG's letter to him of 10 April, above, Wallace, a Loyalist, had been banished from New York.

2. On Wallace's decision not to help NG obtain a loan, see also Hoffman to NG, 26 April, above.

3. In regard to the bill that NG had drawn on him, see NG to Wallace, 10 April.

4. As seen in NG to Hoffman, 9 March 1785, and Wallace to NG, 18 September 1785, both below, NG had trouble paying the bill.

¶ [FROM JOHN FREEBODY,[1] [Newport, R.I., after 2 July 1784].[2] He is "extremely distress'd" to find himself "under the Necessity of Addressing" NG "in this familiar manner" but is "happy" that NG, "thro the Extensive Concerns of Publick Business," has not "Lost every Recollection of me or my Family."[3] In a "Conversation some time past" with a mutual acquaintance, NG said he would be "happy to render me or my Family any assistance in your power." Freebody hopes his confidence in the "Benevolent Attention" that NG has "ever manifested to the Distressed" will "apologize for my useing this Freedom." For "Six Weeks previous to the Enemys Evacuating Rhode Island," Freebody was "upon Long Island, upon a small Estate belonging" to his family; he then "embrac'd the first Opportunity" to go back to Newport, "expecting to be Received and to Reside there as I was conscious I had never Acted any Hostile or Inimical part against my Country." To his "great mortification," he found he was "not permitted to Land."[4] Ever since the British evacuated Newport, he has been "Soliciting for an Enquiry" into his "conduct but without effect until the Last Session of Assembly," when the Rhode Island legislature ordered that his property and "Rights and Privalages of a Citizen" be "Restor'd."[5] Because he was not "permitted to return sooner to Newport, a Small Plantation in N° Carolina" belonging to his brother, four sisters, and himself "has been Confiscated" and was sold on 31 December 1783. Freebody asserts that in this sale "The Publick gave a Long Credit to enhance the Price," and the buyers have not yet made a payment.[6] If NG would ask the governor of North Carolina to have the plantation "Restor'd," it would "ever greatfully be remember'd as a singular favour" and would be "the means of Relieving a very Distress'd Family who's Situations a few Years since ware in easy Circumstances" but are "now far otherwise";[7] but "to recite my misfortunes wou'd to your Excellency be an unpleasing Narative." RCS (MiU-C) 2 pp.]

1. Freebody, a ship's captain, was a member of a prominent Newport family. (NG to Caswell, 8 July 1785, below; the Rhode Island legislative committee that met to determine Freebody's fate referred to him as a "mariner." (Bartlett, *Records of R.I.*, 10: 46)

2. This letter has been dated after 2 July 1784 because Freebody mentioned in it the restoration of his civil rights in Rhode Island, which took place by a vote of the legislature in response to a committee report of 2 July. (Bartlett, *Records of R.I.*, 10: 46–47)

3. In a letter of 8 July 1785, below, to Gov. Richard Caswell of North Carolina, NG wrote that he had been "intimately acquainted with the father who is dead and feel a regard for his Children."

4. The British evacuated "Rhode Island"—i.e., Aquidneck Island, on which Newport is situated—on 25 October 1779. (Vol. 4: 498–99n, above) The Rhode Island legislature, in its July 1780 session, ordered that Freebody and other named individuals who had "left this state, or either of the United States of America, and joined the enemy; or who have joined the enemy in this state," be forbidden to enter the state, under penalty of confinement or banishment. (Bartlett, *Records of R.I.*, 9: 139–41) In a petition to the legislature in October 1783, Freebody's wife, Rebecca, asserted that during the British occupation of Newport, her husband "endeavored to support his family in such a manner as became a peaceable man, by bringing wood and other freight from Long Island." She claimed that when he learned the British had left Newport, he returned "in the first flag, in order to get admission into the state as a citizen thereof, but was not, for reasons unknown, admitted." (Ibid., pp. 730–31)

5. In response to Rebecca Freebody's October 1783 petition, the General Assembly allowed John Freebody to "come within this state, in order to have a trial at the next session of this Assembly, on the merits of the application for his right of permanent residence within this state." (Bartlett, *Records of R.I.*, 9: 730–31) Freebody himself petitioned the legislature in June 1784, "setting forth the reasons and circumstances of his being at Long Island at the time the enemy evacuated Rhode Island; that he had never borne arms against the United States, or was inimical thereto." (Ibid., 10: 46) After hearing a committee report relating to his financial affairs, the legislature voted to make Freebody "a free citizen of this state" and to restore his confiscated property. (Ibid., p. 47)

6. In his June 1784 petition to the legislature, Freebody stated that he had "an estate in North Carolina, which has been confiscated, in consequence of his having been deemed an absentee in this state [i.e., Rhode Island]; and which, he is fully assured, if he was restored to the rights and privileges of a citizen of this state, would be delivered to him again." (Bartlett, *Records of R.I.*, 10: 46)

7. See NG to Caswell, 8 July 1785.

*   *   *

To Robert Morris, Superintendent of Finance

Dear Sir   Newport [R.I.] July 3ᵈ 1784

The Legislature of this State have again rejected the impost and by so great a Majority and from such false reasoning that I begin to despair of their coming into the measure at all or at least in season to save us either from convulsions or bankruptcy.[1] At the opening of the Sessions public opinion seemed to promise the most favorable issue nor would there have been the least difficulty but from the art and the insinuations of Mʳ Howel and Mʳ Ellery. Mʳ Howel under took to prove that the State by adopting the impost would loose four fifths of its revenue collected upon it. This argument was conclusive with far the greater part of the Members who could not enter into the sophistory of his Arguments. To this he added that there was little expectation in Congress that the State would ever come into the measure and that it was not the wish of the most sensible of that body that they should. He insisted upon the credit of the United States standing fair in Europe and that the bills noted for protest in Holland was from the scarcity of Money from the numerious applications and not from any apprehension of our funds.[2] I produced your letter to the contrary but all to no effect.[3] Mʳ Ellery went upon the common danger of altering the constitution and frightened the people with the loss of liberty.[4] Many arguments were used by General [James M.] Varnum and Mʳ Merchant [Henry Marchant] to remove these prejudices but to little purpose. The General [i.e., Varnum] spoke two hours and half, his arguments were learned[,] sensible and conclusive but they were unavailing. The truth of the matter is a large Majority of the Members are incompetent judges of so complicated a question. Influenced by present prospects of interest and frightened with the future loss of liberty, they are ignorantly led into measures unjust to many and must be fatal to themselves. The people have much less wickedness than ignorance but the later is equally fatal to a just policy. What is to become of us or of our National honor god only knows. No people ever had brighter prospects shaded so unexpectedly.[5]

The Assembly have adjourned to August. A liquidation of public securities is talked of. That is the possessors shall receive no more than they gave for them. Many of the holders begin to be frightened and to soften down respecting the impost. If the impost is not adopted I am sure this will take place. And the apprehensions from this quarter may gain it a majority. But this is uncertain nor am I sanguine on the subject.

I go for South Carolinia in a few days and shall return before the sitting of the next assembly.[6] I beg my compliments and those of Mʳˢ Greene to Mrs. Morris and to Mʳ Gouverneur [Morris]. I am dear Sir with esteem you[rs]   NATH GRE[ENE]

ADfS (MiU-C).

1. "Us," as NG used it in this sentence, was the United States. On 1 July, in a session held at Newport, the Rhode Island legislature took up the federal impost resolution of 18 April 1783, which recommended "a mode to the several legislatures of ascertaining the proportions of the several states of the public expenditures, in lieu of the mode pointed out in the eighth article of confederation." (On the congressional proposal, see note at NG to Lincoln, 18 June 1783, above.) By a vote of fifty-two to twelve, the Rhode Island legislators adopted a resolution "that the mode pointed out in the said article of confederation is more just and equal than that recommended" by Congress "and that this Assembly therefore adhere to the rule already established in the said article of confederation." (Bartlett, *Records of R.I.*, 10: 44–45; Morris, *Papers*, 9: 437n) Under Article 8 of the Articles of Confederation, a state's share of the annual general expenses was to be determined "in proportion to the value of all land within each State." The congressional impost proposal of 1783 included a request to repeal that provision and adopt in its place a system based on population—i.e., "the whole number of white and other free citizens" and "three-fifths of all other persons," except Indians. (*JCC*, 24: 260) Although it was undoubtedly an advantage to Rhode Island, a small state with no western land claims, to leave Article 8 unchanged, other issues were involved, as seen in this letter.

On the Rhode Island legislature's rejection of an earlier federal impost proposal, see above, David Howell to NG, 18 October 1782. (Vol. 12: 82–83, 85n) Morris had asked NG to promote the 1783 impost proposal in Rhode Island, and NG had told him during a visit to Philadelphia in June that he thought the measure would pass. (Morris to NG, 19 December 1783, and NG to Morris, 9 January, both above; see also Morris's diary entry for 4 June in Morris, *Papers*, 9: 376.) The extent of NG's involvement in the ratification effort is not known, but he wrote Roger Parker Saunders on 6 June, above, that he hoped to "get through the impost law" in Rhode Island before he left for South Carolina.

2. David Howell and William Ellery, outspoken opponents of the impost, were Rhode Island delegates to Congress, which had been in recess since 3 June. (*JCC*, 27: 566) In a letter to Deputy Governor Jabez Bowen of 31 May, Howell outlined plans for traveling home after the recess. (Smith, *Letters*, 21: 654) Ellery was a member of the Committee of the States, which conducted business during the recess, but he does not appear to have been present after the committee's initial meeting on 4 June, and he, too, returned to Rhode Island. (*JCC*, 27: 561–638; Ellery to Samuel Dick, 2 August, Burnett, *Letters*, 7: 579) Howell and Ellery, then, were probably both present to make their arguments when the legislature took up the question of the impost. For more about Howell's opposition to the measure, see his letters to Bowen of 23 March, 12 and 19 April, and 31 May. (Smith, *Letters*, 21: 453–55, 513–15, 530–31, 651–55)

3. NG presumably referred here to Morris's letter to him of 19 May, above, which read in part: "The Translation into the Dutch Newspapers of our disputes, Quarrells, refusal to grant compliance to the Requisitions of Congress &c &c it is said, spread the Alarm amongst the Capitalists in Holland."

4. On the legislature's response to "altering the constitution," see note 1, above. Ellery had informed a correspondent on 3 April: "Our State did not so much as look at the [impost] recommendation at their [last] Session, and I think will never admit it." (Ellery to Benjamin Huntington, 3 April, Smith, *Letters*, 21: 484)

5. Morris's reply is below, dated 17 July. For more about Rhode Island's rejection of the impost, see Morris, *Papers*, 9: 434–39n.

6. NG left for South Carolina on 12 July but did not get back to Rhode Island until late November. (See note at NG to Hazlehurst, 26 June, above, and NG to Gibbons, 29 November, below.)

*   *   *

¶ [FROM JOSEPH WEST, Baltimore, Md., 3 July 1784. He "sett out from Providence [R.I.] for South Carolina" in May 1783 to establish a business in Charleston but had to "put into the Chesepeake" because of "adverse winds" during the voyage. He decided to stay in Baltimore and has established a business, known as "Blakeley & West," with Josiah Blakeley, who is from New Haven, Conn. Asks NG for introductions to "the principle Merchants in S° Carolina" and to "Col. John E[ager] Howard" of Baltimore, with whom he understands NG is "acquainted." He takes this "liberty" of writing to NG "by virtue of a letter" from his father, "Mʳ Benjᵃ West of the State of Rhode Island," which he forwarded to NG from Baltimore in May 1783.[1] NG can check on Blakeley's "Character" with a firm in Philadelphia.[2] RCS (MiU-C) 1 p.]

1. Benjamin West's letter to NG of 16 May 1783, above, was a letter of introduction for his son Joseph. (Vol. 12: 659; see also Joseph West to NG, 7 August 1783, above.)
2. NG's reply has not been found.

¶ [FROM BARBARA BENTLY, East Greenwich, R.I., 4 July 1784. She has NG's letter [not found] informing her that he is leaving for "Carolina." As NG may be "Detaind" in the South longer than he expects, she would be "Very Glad if you will send me what is Due on your Childs acount as I want it very much."[1] RCS (MiU-C) 1 p.]

1. For background, see Bently's letters to NG of 1 June and at the end of June, both above. For more on the services she provided to NG and his family, see Bently to NG, 1 September 1785, below. NG did not return from South Carolina until late November. (NG to Gibbons, 29 November, below)

¶ [FROM JACOB GREENE, Coventry, R.I., 5 July 1784. Encloses "Capᵗ Peirces orders" concerning the brig. Jacob did not know whether Pierce would "go to Carolina or return home," as "it was left for him to govern as Circumstances might Direct With full power to Deviate from his orders for the interest of the concerned." Jacob told him "Verbally," though, that he should not "let any literal Construction or nice Distinctions in his orders destroy any advantages that might turn up in favor of the owners."[1] Jacob does not know "What envious Demon" could cause him "not to take the price offered for the Brig," because "he knew our Circumstances Required her being sold." As Jacob is "intirely at loss" as to what "Directions" he should give NG in case the vessel is in South Carolina when NG gets there, NG should do as he thinks best: "Either to sell the Brig, Sent her home? Or freight her from Georgia? Turn Peirce out? Or let him Continue."[2] The brig "is a good vessel for Carrying Lumber and small stock from Georgia Provided she was commanded by a prudent Industrious Master." If she could make "one or two good Freights to the West Indias with the Capitol she now has," she should be "able nearly to Load with rice by new Crop."[3] Jacob leaves "Tommy" to NG's care but supposes "he will be for Comeing home[;] as he never was a Broad Before his attachment for home must be overcome by Degrees."[4] As Pierce will probably leave Charleston before NG gets there, Jacob asks for NG's opinion as to whether "he can be prosecuted with a prospect of Success."[5] RC (MiU-C) 2 pp.]

1. Jacob Greene & Company owned an interest in the brig *Minerva*, commanded by Captain Benjamin Pierce, who had sailed it from Barbadoes to Charleston, S.C. Jacob Greene had asked NG for help in procuring a cargo in South Carolina for a voyage to

Europe. (See above, Jacob Greene to NG, 11 June; NG to Robert Hazlehurst, 26 June; and NG to Roger Parker Saunders, 26 June.)

2. NG wrote Griffin Greene on 8 July, below, that Jacob was "angry" over Pierce's failure to sell the brig "but cant help himself."

3. The *Minerva* soon afterward sailed for Rhode Island. (Jacob Read to NG, 30 July, below)

4. On "Tommy," see note at Jacob Greene to NG, 11 June.

5. Nothing more is known about this matter.

¶ [FROM NICHOLAS HOFFMAN, New York, 6 July 1784. He received NG's letter of 27 June [not found] "this morning" and, "in consequ[ence]," is shipping ten mattresses "of a Good Quallity covered with Ticking." He could have bought some "of an inferior Quallity at a much less price." In a postscript, he gives the total cost of the mattresses—"with a pillow to Each" and including the cost of cartage—as £14.11.6. RCS (MiU-C) 1 p.]

*   *   *

To Griffin Greene

Dear Sir   Newport [R.I.] July 8th 1784

By your letter of the 6th of April I think it highly probable you will be in Philadelphia before I get back from Charleston to which place I am going this moment.[1] A sett of bills was presented me some little time past for two thousand pounds in favor of Col [Jeremiah] Wadsworth. I did not accept them nor can I imagine for what purpose they were drawn. None of your letters mentions them and you say in your last that you had concluded to make use of the Credit I meant to give you [and?] had concluded to bring out a quantity of Brandy Wine & Silks. This renders the bills a Mistery.[2] But besides these difficulties I had other reasons for letting the matter remain until it is better explained. I have paid dearly for indorsing bills and am afraid I shall suffer more. Pressed on every side I find caution to be necessary or ruin will attend me.[3]

Jacob has met with heavy losses this Winter, The Anchor shop was totally Swept way with all the Tools, the Dam broke and carried off, and the forge rendered useless the whole season, besides suffering great damages.[4] The brigg is gone to South Carolinia from Barbadoes. Pearce had a good offer for her but would not sell for fear of getting out of business. Jacob is angry but cant help himself.[5] Upon the whole your affairs are in a deranged State.[6]

I think your Brandy if you bring out any quantity will sell well in Boston but not to the Southward. I have desird brother Bill to get of M[r] Gibbs a price current and send you.[7]

Sally is well but very impatient to see you.[8] My stay will be short to the Southward but if you have a good oppertunity to write to Charleston, write me how you sold the *Flora* and what goods you have brought out. Many of the owners of the *Flora* have abided the Sale you first made.[9] Yours affy   N GREENE

ALS (Ct).

1. In his letter of 6 April, above, Griffin had written that he was hoping to conclude the sale of the *Flora* and return to New York or Philadelphia from France "as soon as possiable." As noted there, he did not return to the United States for another year.

2. See note at Griffin Greene to NG, 6 April, and Pettit to NG, 19 June, above. As seen in his letter to Wadsworth of 12 November, below, NG had misunderstood Wadsworth's "agency in the business."

3. See, for example, Edwards to NG, 12 May, and Saunders to NG, 29 May, above; Saunders to NG, before 17 July, below.

4. The damage had occurred in a flood in January. (NG to Jacob Greene, 8 January, above) In September, the firm of "Jacob & Griffin Greene" announced that they had "thoroughly repaired their Forge, at Coventry, which was destroyed by the rapid Floods last Winter," and had resumed their anchor business. (*Newport Mercury*, 4 September)

5. See Jacob Greene to NG, 5 July, above.

6. NG referred here to the financial affairs of Jacob Greene & Company, in which Griffin was a partner.

7. "Brother Bill" was NG's brother William; George Gibbs is identified at NG's letter to him of 17 August, below.

8. Griffin's wife "Sally" (Sarah Greene Greene) had not seen her husband since his departure for France in May 1783.

9. NG sailed for Charleston on 12 July and returned to Newport at the end of November. As seen in Griffin's letter to NG at the end of the September documents, below, the sale of the *Flora* was delayed.

To the Citizens of North Carolina

Newport [R.I.] July 8th 1784

The bearer of this is M[rs] Balfour the unfortunate Widow of the late Col Balfour who was killed by the Tories in Randolf County in North Carolinia. She Vissits North Carolinia to see after her husbands affairs and being a Lady of a good reputation and having drank deeply of the cup of bitterness from the calamities of war I beg leave to recommend her to all the good people of Your State as deserving their notice civilities and protection. This recommendation can only be necessary from her not being known, and it is from that consideration I give her this open letter of Address.[1]   NATH GREENE

ADfS (MiU-C).

1. Andrew Balfour, a Scottish merchant, had settled in New England in 1772. In 1777, he moved to Charleston, S.C., and from thence to North Carolina, where he acquired a large plantation near Salisbury. By 1781, he was a colonel in the Randolph County militia. He was murdered at his plantation, with his family present, by Loyalist Col. David Fanning on 11 March 1782. Balfour's sister and daughter were also assaulted by Loyalists at the time of his death. (Fanning, *Narrative*, pp. 37n, 71n; see also vol. 11: 24n, above.)

From William Washington

Dear General   Charleston [S.C.] July 8ᵗʰ [17]84

This will be handed you by your Man Thomas, who came with me from Virginia under expectation of meeting with you at this Place, but as it is uncertain when we shall have the Pleasure of seeing you I have imbrac'd the first opportunity of sending him to you.[1]

The Repose of the peaceable Citizens of Charleston has been disturb'd for three Nights past by Mobs; but as they are contemptable in Number & Quality, and our Intendant conducts himself with firmness & resolution in Opposition to them I'm in hopes we shall have no more of them. Perhaps an Example or two made the Evening before last may have a good effect. Mʳ [Henry] Peronneau one of the most respectable favorers of the Mob was knock'd down in the Street by one of the Supporters of Government; & one of their Body who had the Assurance to ware a Standard was cut with a Horse-Man's Sword in the Head & Arm & the Standard taken from him. At the request of the Intendant I met him last night at the State-House with about 30 volunteer Horse determin'd to carry his Orders into execution; but the Town appear'd to be in perfect peace & quietness. Such is the Situation of Charleston.[2]

When shall we have the pleasure of seeing you & Mʳˢ Greene in this Quarter.[3] Mʳˢ Washington desires her love to Mʳˢ Greene[4] & beli[e]ve me to be with much Esteem Yʳ Very obedᵗ Servᵗ   Wᴹ WASHINGTON

RCS (MiU-C).

1. NG's servant Tom had been gravely ill in Virginia the previous autumn. (Weedon to NG, 2 December 1783, above)

2. On the mobs in Charleston, and William Washington's involvement in helping to quell the unrest, see also Pendleton to NG, second letter of 10 July, below.

3. As noted at NG to Hazlehurst, 26 June, above, NG arrived in Charleston on 1 August. CG did not go with him to the South until the fall of 1785, when they left Rhode Island to settle in Georgia. (NG to Clarke, 23 November 1785, below)

4. Jane Reily Elliott Washington had become acquainted with CG when she accompanied her new husband to Kiawah Island, where CG was recuperating from malaria, in September 1782. (vol. 11: 660, 661n, above)

*   *   *

¶ [FROM NATHANIEL PENDLETON, [Charleston, S.C.], 10 July 1784. The arrival of Colonel Morris "releived" Pendleton "from a very painful anxiety," for he had heard that NG "met with an unfortunate accident" that was of "dangerous consequence" to his health.[1] Pendleton adds: "This is always the Case. Every thing relative to men, who have made a considerable figure in the World is magnified beyond the truth; from that universal weakness of mankind, which inclines them to the marvellous on all occasions." Pendleton regrets that he will not see NG until "September or October." He traveled to Georgia with a plan of going into "practice" there but met "so much opposition, from the Bar, and so ill a reception from the Chief Justice Walton," that he would not "undergo the Fatigue and Expense of a journey to Augusta, where the assembly were currently meeting," to "make an Application for admission."[2] Instead, he is stopping in Charleston on his way to Virginia, where he can "obtain an Admission" that will "open" his way "into Georgia in the Fall." Georgia offers Pendleton the "best prospects," and if, "after two or three years" there, he wishes to return to Charleston, there "will be no obstacle."[3] However, "several little cross accidents" have occurred, which make Charleston a less agreeable place for him now than before. He relates: "M[rs] W—'s affair made many persons look on me with an ill eye, whose esteem I highly valued; and this hurt me so much the more, as it originated from M[r] Marshall's false representation; but still it is irremediable."[4] NG will also be informed "of another affair respecting M[rs] M— which has made me more enemies and given a subject of malice to the old."[5] He adds: "She is a woman void of honor or delicacy, and I can only regret I did not know her sooner." Pendleton discusses some of the details of his estrangement from her and writes: "the low Company she kept and dissipated life she lives, I believe will make the disappointment no loss to me, upon the whole. Those of my friends who know me, I trust will vindicate me as far as they can. I am Conscious of never have [i.e., having] done a dishonorable action designedly, but perhaps I have not been sufficiently cautious to guard myself from Susp[i]cion; this I will do hereafter." RCS (NcD) 4 pp.]

1. Lewis Morris, Jr., wrote NG from Charleston on 17 July, below. NG had been suffering from a "pain in his breast" that resulted from a near fall he took the previous winter. His ill health kept him from attending the general meeting of the Society of the Cincinnati in Philadelphia in May, but he had recovered by June. (See NG to Washington, and NG to Pettit, both 22 April, above.) Morris, who had been in the North, would have heard rumors about NG's condition at that time.

2. Pendleton had decided to seek admission to the bar in Georgia because he thought the process there would be easier than in South Carolina. (As explained below in this letter, he also had personal reasons for hesitating to settle in Charleston. [See also his letters to NG of 30 January and 18 April, both above.]) George Walton had served in Congress, in the militia, and as governor of Georgia before being named chief justice in 1783. (*Dictionary of Georgia Biography*, 2: 1030–31)

3. Pendleton did settle in Savannah, where he practiced law for some time, but he eventually relocated to New York. (See above, his biographical note in vol. 7: 308n.)

4. On Pendleton's involvement with "Mrs. W" (Jane Olyphant Walter) and Mrs. Marshall, see his letter to NG of 30 January.

5. On 18 April, above, Pendleton had written NG that he was "on the point of an engagement" with Mrs. Marshall. Nothing is known about the other "affair respecting Mrs. M."

*   *   *

From Nathaniel Pendleton

D[r] General   Ch[arle][s]ton [S.C.] July 10th 1784.

I wrote the inclosed Letter, with an Intention to leave it here till your arrival, but hearing there is a vessel going immediately to Rhode Island I have sent it on.[1]

I said Nothing of the commotions which have arisen again here, respecting the persons who have been permitted to return from banishment. This Town is now in dismal alarms. The persons, who composed the Anti britannic Society, at least a great part of them, have so wrought upon the passions of the people, by inflamatory publications and discourses, that for two Nights before the last, there was a large mob assembled, who went to the Houses of the obnoxious persons, in a tumultuary manner and sought for them, in order to compel them as they said to leave the State. They did not get any.

The first night which was on the 7th Inst their numbers were few, and as they appeared early in the evening, they soon retired, but on the Next evening, which was the night before last, they came out in greater numbers and assumed a more threatening appearance. They consisted of more than two hundred, cheifly tradesmen, Sailors &ca. They displayed a flag, and marched from the State House about Sun set, along broad Street to the corner of King Street where they broke the windows of one of the obnoxious Persons. Then they went up King Street to the Green, and down to Cooper River to the Bay, and so to the Exchange, & from there towards the State House. Before they reached the State House, the Intendant and Wardens, and a great concourse of People had met at the State House, but there was neither Order or regularity and None of the Multitude had Arms. Several Gentlemen had got on horse back with their Swords which seemed to me to be all the military force Government chose to use. In this Situation when they [i.e., the] mob arrived to the Opening of the market, in direct March for the State House where all the City Magistrates, and Officers of Government were convened, the Horse men rode in among them, caught some and dispersed the rest; Then the Magistrates gave arms to all who chose it, tho they refused it before; & very soon there was 100 men armed and, in order under the militia officers.[2]

It was expected there would have been a more formidable party last evening & [William] Washington had about 30 men armed in Cavalier who paraded at dark; but there was no appearance of any Necessity to use them.[3]

A Mr [Henry] Peronneau a young lawyer, in conjunction with Mr [James O']Fallon, was supposed to have been the Cause of these Commotions. Fallon has not at all appeared lately. I beleive he is frightened; but the Other avows his determination, and behaved with great insolence in his examination. "What you call a mob, Says he, I call an assembly of the People." He was this day examined at the exchange before the City Council, in the presence of a vast concourse of people, & is bound to appear at the Court of Sessions, for a rioteer.[4]

Other circumstances will be communicated to you by the Ladies and Gentlemen, who go passangers to New Port. Mrs Shubrick is one of them. Poor Tom Shubrick is in a dangerous way.[5] My most Cordial good wishes & respectful Complements attend Mrs Greene. I Congratulate

both her and yourself upon the birth of a Daughter, & her recovery. Is
she to be named Carolina?[6] Yours Unalterably N PENDLETON

RCS (MiU-C).

1. The enclosure was undoubtedly Pendleton's first letter to NG of this date, immediately above.

2. The Marine Anti-Britannic Society, an "anti-aristocrat" faction led by Alexander
Gillon and consisting primarily of artisans and mechanics, strongly supported South
Carolina's 1782 legislation banning scores of Loyalists from the state and resented the
more lenient treatment that the legislature had recently given to a number of individuals
who had previously been banished or had had their property confiscated or amerced.
American merchants whose trade was threatened by remaining and returning British
merchants also supported the Anti-Britannic Society. Mobs instigated by the Society's
inflammatory rhetoric had roamed the streets of Charleston in July 1783, attacking
individuals whom they considered to be Loyalists or British sympathizers. (See NG to
Washington, 8 August 1783, above.) The controversy between tavern keeper William
Thompson and John Rutledge in March 1784 (Pendleton to NG, 18 April, above) was a
more recent outgrowth of the same tensions. Rioting in Charleston in July 1784 apparently followed the "spirited celebrations of independence" in the city's streets. In his book
on the artisans of Charleston, Richard Walsh has written that "street battles ensued
between the magistracy with their supporters, the Aristocrats, against the Marine Anti-
Britannics and mechanics, the Democrats. . . . Heated accusations filled the gazettes. . . .
The Democrats accused the magistracy of senseless and provocative behavior bringing on
terror. For more than a month, Charleston continually existed in such hot-headed confusion." The September election, in which the Charleston city intendant, Richard Hutson,
soundly defeated his challenger, Gillon, seemed to signal a decline in the influence of the
Anti-Britannic Society. However, in a concession to that faction, the "aristocratic" leaders
of the South Carolina General Assembly passed legislation in March 1785 placing greater
restrictions on exiles and banishing some persons who were then living in the state.
(Walsh, *Sons of Liberty*, pp. 111–24; quotes from pp. 120–21; Meleney, *Aedanus Burke*, pp.
102–12; the anti-Loyalist legislation of 1782 is discussed above in vol. 10: 415n.) Unhappiness over the status of Loyalists and British merchants continued to simmer in South
Carolina, as seen in the note at Burke to NG, 27 November 1785, below.

3. William Washington, one of NG's former cavalry commanders, wrote NG on 8 July,
above, about his efforts to restore order.

4. Henry Peronneau, a leader of the Anti-Britannic Society, apparently claimed that the
leader of a "mounted band" had "picked on the Whigs." This charge culminated in a
challenge to a duel, which Peronneau declined. (Walsh, *Sons of Liberty*, pp. 120–21)
According to historian John C. Meleney, the estate of Peronneau's father had been
amerced because of the father's Loyalist sympathies, and the son had joined the Anti-
Britannic Society to demonstrate his family's adherence to the American cause. (Meleney,
Aedanus Burke, p. 108 and n) On Dr. James O'Fallon, see also NG to Pettit, 29 July 1783,
above. Lewis Morris, Jr.'s, letter to NG of 17 July, below, identifies O'Fallon as a principal
instigator of the mob.

5. NG's former aide Thomas Shubrick was still ailing when NG arrived in Charleston; it
was Mary Branford Shubrick, his wife, who traveled to Newport. (NG to CG, 8 September, below) Shubrick, who recovered from his ailments, lived until 1810. (*Biog. Directory of
S.C. House*, 3: 643–44)

6. CG had given birth to a daughter, Louisa Catharine, in April. (NG to Pettit, 22 April,
above)

* * *

¶ **[FROM ROBERT MORRIS, SUPERINTENDENT OF FINANCE**, Philadelphia, 12 July 1784. Encloses "the Extract of a letter from Messrs Wilhelm & Jan Willink of Amsterdam respecting the Loan of Five Thousand Pounds Sterling" that NG wants.[1] If NG complies "with the Forms and Terms they have prescribed," Morris believes he will be successful.[2] NG should let Morris know if he needs any more assistance. Morris has just received NG's letter of 25 June. NG's draft for $250 "is honoured," and Morris will "do the same by another for the same amount."[3] LS (CSmH) 1 p.]

1. For background, see NG to Morris, 9 January, above. An extract of the Willinks' letter to Morris is printed in Morris, *Papers*, 9: 211–13, and reads as follows:

"We observe your application in favor of the Honorable Major Genl. Nathl. Greene who would be desirous to find 5000£ giving for Security his Estate presented to him by the State of South Carolina with Negroes, &ca. in purchase of which he'd lay out said money to work his Land, that he shall want 1000£ and 1500£ in a short while and the remainder afterwards, of which he'd Pay six percent Interest and be obliged to consign us the produces of Rice and Indigo 'till Capital and interest is redeemed.

"Similar proposals are already made here, but as far as we know all declined by the repugnance of every one of lending money on plantations &Ca. since of the immence sums borrowd in that way for Suriname [i.e., Surinam] and all our other Islands prove very fatal and leave all them to loose considerably. This will be a great obsticle; the more as our People are naturally cautious in which respects however we suppose full Satisfaction should be given as for Instance[:]

"A Testimonium of two reputed Lawyers that according to the Laws of the Country such a debt is preferent to any else, even if the State or Widowers or Orphans in other cases preferent Debts had any demands upon the borrower such money lenders on an Estate have an Exclusive preference and right to be registrated by Government that it becomes never liable to any dispute nor discussion, nor is contrary to any Law or Custom.

"A sworn valuation of such an Estate, a legal Document that no money is borrowed on the same and She [i.e., the estate] is clear of any Demands.

"The Borrower may not borrow any more on her 'till this Capital is entirely redeemed and that by a power of attorney he qualifies the House to borrow said Sum for his Account for which he engages all his property and binds chiefly such an Estate in the manner required in conformity of the Laws of the Place renouncing of every exception as usual.

"Our desire to be of Service to such a worthy man as Genl. Greene protected by you is the strongest recommendation to exert all our endeavors for him but we should wish to do this by way of a Loan for the following reasons.

"To endeavor to remove the prejudices of our money men and to accustom them again to such placings of their Capital which will prove very convenient for Americans and become beneficial to us, which we cannot effectuate by furnishing the money underhand and besides that we prefer rather to employ it several ways. We have preferred to take a handsome share in the Continental Loan, than to accept other offers, and we flatter ourselves Mr. [John] Adams, Mr. [William] Bingham, [and] Gilmore [i.e., Robert Gilmor] will readily convince you, if our House has contributed his Share in its success, our delicacy doth not permit to say any thing nor to manifest the displeasure the refusal of acceptance of Congress drafts, occasioned to us.

"The Borrower [i.e., NG] should be obliged to submit to every thing Mr [Robert] Hazlehurst should find necessary to perform in whom we have Confidence to Trust every Examination to, and in case your Freind will permit to borrow the Sum in the mentioned way, and the Terms of redeeming are regularly Stipulated and documents in order we beleive it will be a matter to do to his Satisfaction as we enjoy enough Confidence that our People rely on our precaution and regularity to take of it, but every Document wants to be in good order as we think ourselves liable never to abuse of public Confidence for any private benefit. Mr. Greene moreover should be obliged to allow 4 percent for the Charges and Commissions on the Transaction, and further the usual Commission on the Sale of Goods, which produces we rely should regularly and fidelely be shipt, and the Character he bore and your assurance of his Honor and integrity will not permit any doubt with us on this head.

"Your following letter will give us more illucidations and in case he will venture to empower us, we shall directly in return mention the event, and however this money is than at once bearing interest we suppose by paying sooner than the Stipulated terms for his Negroes, he can enjoy a Correspondent discount, but the documents mentioned shall always be required, and we hope you'll justify our intention to prefer this way to raise money for your Friend by supplying it previously to him, not for his sake in particular but such applications in general."

2. On the prescribed terms, see the paragraphs beginning with "A Testimonium of two reputed Lawyers," in the extract immediately above.

3. In a letter to NG of 17 July, below, Morris sent another copy of the extract and replied more fully to NG's letter of 25 June, above. On 15 March 1785, below, Morris wrote that he was sending NG "the form of a power of Attorney such as has Been sent to Holland on similar Occasions[;] you will have one filled up in the same way and forward it to Messʳˢ Willinks." Morris added, though, that while the Willinks' "letters mention a probability of their obtaining the Loan, yet we know that every Application hitherto made has proved ineffectual." Morris wrote NG on 28 June 1785, below, that he had just "received letters from Amsterdam which put an end to the expectation of Loans from that quarter." NG wrote to the Willinks in April 1785 [letter not found], requesting a loan, and wrote to them again on 7 January 1786, below, after he had taken up residence on his Georgia plantation. No reply to either letter has been found, and it is unlikely that NG pursued this matter again during the months before his death in June 1786.

¶ [FROM JOHN-JOSEPH SOUERBADER DE GIMAT,[1] "Port Royal," 12 July 1784. Introduces a "Mr. Du beauchamp, a deserving officer as ever was among the engeoners of the french army and the most amiable gentleman in the society," who followed NG's "Successful campaings through South Carolina" with "pleasure." Gimat will be "obliged" for any "favors" NG may "confer" on this gentleman. If Gimat can be of service to NG, he asks NG to "command" him. In a postscript, he presents his "respectful compliments" to CG. RCS (NNPM) 2 pp.]

1. Gimat had been a colonel in the Continental army and an aide to the Marquis de Lafayette. (Vol. 6: 478n, above)

¶ [FROM FELIX WARLEY, Charleston, S.C., 13 July 1784. Since writing to NG on 7 April, he has received NG's "kind favor" of 6 June [not found]. Is sorry that Capt. [Matthew] Strong did not know NG "had left directions with Capt. Joseph Anthony for payment of the Bill" that Warley drew on NG.[1] Warley will be "sati[s]fied with the money" upon Strong's return and in the meantime has "drawn an order" for $242 dollars on Strong, whose "Receipt shall be a full discharge of your bond." The "above mentᵈ Bill will not be presented." Below his signature, he states the terms of NG's "bond due this day": £356.13.4 principal, plus 36.11.8 interest at seven percent for the past eighteen months, for a total of £393.5, "equal to 242 Dollars."[2] On the reverse side of the letter, Warley has written: "Received 4th September 1784 of General Green Fifty Pounds Sterling in part of his Bond."³ RCS (MiU-C) 1 p.]

1. For background, see Warley's letters to NG of 13 October 1783 and 7 April 1784, both above.

2. As seen in Warley to NG, 7 April, the bond, dated 28 January 1783, was originally to have been paid in one year. In that letter, Warley gave the total amount due as of 28 April as £387.17.2, "equal to Sterling £55.8.2."

3. NG, who was in Charleston at that time, presumably had Warley write the receipt on the back of this letter.

*   *   *

From Thaddeus Kosciuszko

My Dear General   New York 14th July [1784]

The events are uncertain, a Parson amidst the most glaring prospects; may find at Last nothing but a fantom, or only a Light Like in Looking glace, which will never be a possesion for injoyement.

Drawing the tickets in the lottery of chance for So many Years, I am too well acquainted to depend upon probabilities where even certainties are so often doubtfull.

To put myself upon less precarious footing, I must contaract all possible accidents, that can befal me, and this by over sight am capable of. I am going to embark to morow for France.¹ I beg you hoever if Congress should adopt a Peace establishement, you will please to interest your self in the apointement as a cheif Ingenieer with the rank of Briggadier General if it possible, this will be a proviso in case I should be bafled in my expectations at home.²

The principle of propryety inculcated in my early age, have to[o] strong hold of my feelings, that, to act against invard Conviction make me very unhappy indead. As I must part, give me Leave to present [sincere?] thanks to you both, for so generous hospitality I experienced in your house, for so much interesting yourself in my favor, and for your friendship for me, your delicat feelings forbids me to express of my Greatitude, and the wishes of my heart. I Leave to the stragle of my invard emotion; and the practice, to time; whenever uportunity will presents its self without knowkledge to you.³

The Seperation must be very sensible to a Person of susceptible mind and more so when the affection with Esteem Link's to the persons of Merit.

I expect hoever that you will do me the honour to write me, it will be the only satisfaction I may [y]et enjoy by absence, and sure you will not deny me that.⁴

In your Letters I hope you will not forget of your and your famillys health, which I am So much interested; as to the information of public nature here, you will be pleased to give me very minute in acount, as by

Long staying here I have forme[d] a partiality for this Country and for its Inhabitants, and would equally [estheam ?] where ever I should be. I feel the Sentyment of good Patriot upon every occasion. Fare well my dear General once more farewell be as happy as my bosoom will [*illegible*] for you, Let me Shook here you by the hand by my delusive Imagination, as you Should be present in Person, and Seal our friendship for each other for ever. Your^s   THAD^s KOSCIUSZKO

Pleas to inclose the Letters for me a Monsieur Gerard. Have arive a[t] Paris. He will send to me where ever I should be.

RCS (ICPRCU).

1. Kosciuszko had stayed in the United States until this time to settle his accounts with Congress. (NG to Kosciuszko, 10 July 1783, and Morris to NG, 1 August 1783, both above) He sailed from New York on 15 July. (Haiman, *Kosciuszko*, p. 165)

2. Kosciuszko was not offered an appointment in the peacetime American army.

3. As seen at Littlefield to NG, 22 March, and Gordon to NG, 5 April, both above, Kosciuszko had been a house guest of the Greenes in Newport.

4. Kosciuszko wrote NG on 20 January 1786, below, that he had not heard from him since leaving the United States.

*   *   *

¶ [FROM JOSEPH ANTHONY, Philadelphia, 15 July 1784. Acknowledges NG's letter of 26 June. Has spoken with Mr. Chaloner about the bills, and Chaloner has written to NG on this subject.[1] These bills are for "a Serious Sum," and NG is "Certainly Justifiable in not medling with them without the most Satisfactory advice." Anthony did not understand that he "was to call on Captain [Matthew] Strong to Enquire for those bills, but in case he [i.e., Strong] call'd upon us, you Desir'd we would take them up." They have "heard Not a word" from Strong, who has since "Return'd to Charleston." Anthony would be "Happy in Rendering" NG "Every Service." RCS (MiU-C) 1 p.]

1. Neither NG's letter to Anthony nor John Chaloner's to NG has been found. In regard to these bills, see above, Pettit to NG, 19 June; and below, Wadsworth to NG, 28 September and 1 November, and NG to Wadsworth, 12 November.

*   *   *

From Roger Parker Saunders

Dear Sir   [Charleston, S.C., before 17 July 1784?][1]

Your favr^s of the 14 and 16th June I Rec^d but the letter you mention to have wrote me from Philadelphia enclosing me a Bill on Mr Hazelhurst is not come to hand. I am affraid It is on board a Brigg wch is Missing.[2] Cap^{ts} Strong and Alebone are ariv'd and this Vessel saild before them.[3]

M^r [John] Banks has behavd in a most Base manner[.] Soon after I gave him the Bill [under?] the Conditions I wrote You he left the State and It is thought will never return[.] He inform'd me he had setle'd every matter with You and gave me from under his hand he w^d pay the

Bills himself as he had Money in Col° Pettits hands, but from his Conduct since I put no dependance on his promise. I am very sorry I gave him the Bills but thought I was serving You. Banks swore unless I setled with him he would arrest me on Your Acco[un]ᵗ as Your Attʸ. The half of Your Acoᵗ he said was Cash lent and his Necessitys compeld him to Commenc[e] an action much against his inclination &Cᵃ. This I knew would injure Your Credit greatly, he refusd giveing me time to write You. I knew you were Security for Mʳ Banks but thought he had Secured You but even If he had not he could Compel me to settle[.] Your being Bound for him could not be allowd in discount.⁴ If the Bills come back protested I shal be injurd greatly, I have now no Idea of Banks paying the Bills[;] upwards of 20 Suits and Several Judgments are against him[;] he has I fear ruind Capᵗ Carnes by seling him Negroes under Mortgage and geting him to become his Security[;] he has deseav'd Col° [William] Washington & Joe Brown and injurd them Greatly[;] they are arrested on his accoᵗ. Carnes is going to the Northward after him.⁵

Inclosed is an Accoᵗ of Your last Years Crop the Number of Negroes I purchas'd for You amoᵗ and terms of Payment.⁶ I expected you here every hour or should have [been?] some Moore particular[.] I will send You an Accoᵗ Current of every thing I have transacted for you in the Money way next oppʸ would send It now but My Accoᵗˢ are in the Country.⁷

I have purchas'd 600 Bushels Corn for Your Negroes at 3/ and am in want of Money to pay for It. The Merchᵗˢ press me greatly for Amoᵗ of your Accoᵗ for Negroe Cloth &Cᵃ. If you should not come here soon please enable me to discharge the accoᵗˢ.⁸

You have aboᵗ 250 Acres of Rice planted in Carolina & Georgia, the rice in this State is injur'd greatly by the drie weather but I think you will make near double the quantity You did last Year exclusive of what you plant in Georgia, I have been lately to Mulberry Grove[.] Your prospect there is not Extraordinary, but hope It will be a [saveing?] Crop.⁹ I send by Capᵗ Pearse a Negroe Wench that has for some time been in a bad state of health. She is a great Favourite with her Mistress and is a Faithful Servant. I will take It as a particular favʳ If you will get her to some Farm, or Proper place for health where she can get every thing Necessary, and leave directions If you leave Rhode Island for her to be sent Back here in about two Months any expence attending It shal be paid with thanks.¹⁰ I think on your Comeing here If you can dispose of Your Lands here and purchase in Georgia, a place wᶜʰ I will inform You of It will double Your Interest.¹¹ I have made a very advantageous purchase in Georgia and intend removing all My Negroes there in the Spring. You can have what Quantity you please of the Island I wrote you aboᵗ some time agoe opposite your Land.¹²

Mrs [Amarinthia Lowndes] Saunders Joins me in kind Comp^{ts} to Mrs Greene. I am Dear Sir with Great Respect Your Very hum Servt

ROGER PARKER SAUNDERS

RCS (MiU-C).

1. This letter is docketed 27 July, but the editors believe it was written before the one immediately below, in which Lewis Morris, Jr., reported on 17 July that Saunders had received bills from NG that had not yet "come to hand" when Saunders wrote the present letter.

2. As seen in the preceding note, Saunders soon afterward received NG's letter with the "Bill on M^r [Robert] Hazelhurst." (NG to Saunders, 6 June, above) NG's letters to Saunders of 14 and 16 June have not been found.

3. Capt. Matthew Strong's vessel, the *Philadelphia*, reached Charleston on 6 July, and the brig *Charleston Packet*, captained by William Allibone, arrived the next day, both from Philadelphia. (*South Carolina Gazette & Public Advertiser*, 3–7 July)

4. On the bills that Saunders had given to Banks—and on Banks's departure from South Carolina—see above, Saunders to NG, 29 May; Charles Pettit to NG, 10 June; and NG to Pettit, 23 June. Hoping to confront Banks, NG traveled to Virginia at the end of the summer but learned when he reached Washington, N.C., that Banks was "dead & buried." (NG to Forsyth, 2 October, below) On NG's role as "Security for Mr Banks," see vol. 12: 308–9n and Agreement between Hunter, Banks & Company, NG, and Newcomen and Collett, 8 April 1783 (ibid., p. 591 and n), above; and NG to Lee, 22 August 1785, below. Some questions regarding NG's liability as guarantor for Banks remained unresolved as long as a decade after NG's death in June 1786. (See below, the notes at NG to Collett, 8 August, and at Pendleton to NG, 10 November, as well as NG to Lee, 22 August 1785.)

5. Patrick Carnes was a former officer in Lee's Legion. William Washington, one of NG's former cavalry commanders, had become a large landowner in South Carolina by virtue of his marriage to Jane Reily Elliott. (Vol. 11: 294n, above; see also *Biog. Directory of S.C. House*, 2: 220–21, 3: 749–752.) Joseph Brown's wife, the former Harriet Lowndes, was a sister of Saunders's wife, Amarinthia. (*Biog. Directory of S.C. House*, 2: 415–17) On Carnes's and John McQueen's dealings with Banks, which also affected NG, see especially Pettit to NG, 26 July; Penman to NG, 12 August; NG to Pettit, 15 August; and Pendleton to NG, 10 November, all below.

6. The enclosure has not been found. On NG's 1783 crop at Boone's Barony plantation, S.C., see above, Saunders to NG, 20 October 1783, and Hyrne to NG, 26 November–4 December 1783. On the slaves that Saunders had purchased for NG, see Pettit to NG, 27 April, and Saunders to NG, 29 May, both above.

7. Saunders's "Acco^t Current" has not been found.

8. As noted at NG to Hazlehurst, 26 June, above, NG arrived in Charleston on 1 August.

9. Mulberry Grove was NG's Georgia plantation. As seen in NG's letter to George Gibbs of 3 February 1785, below, the 1784 crops also fell "far short of our expectation being much injured in the harvest by the heavy Rains."

10. The African American woman whom Saunders sent to Rhode Island was undoubtedly a slave belonging to Saunders and his wife. Benjamin Pierce was the captain of Jacob Greene & Company's vessel the *Minerva*. (Jacob Greene to NG, 11 June, above)

11. On 4 April 1786, below, a little more than two months before he died, NG wrote Samuel Ward, Jr., that he was "determined" to sell his "property in South Carolina"— Boone's Barony. (He did not do so.) It is not known what property in Georgia Saunders had in mind.

12. This was Isla Island, Ga., in the Savannah River opposite Mulberry Grove. (See above, Saunders to NG, 27 November 1783.) NG had written Saunders on 4 January,

above, that he was interested in buying the 200 acres Saunders had offered him there, "if I can accomodate the payment on my arrival."

From Lewis Morris, Jr.

Dear Sir   Charleston [S.C.] July 17ᵗʰ 1784
    Before this can reach Rhode Island, I apprehend that you will be on your way to Carolina;[1] but as it is possible you may not, to convince you that I bear your request in remembrance, I shall endeaver to give you as particular an account of your affairs as my information will permit. Your last year's crop, by what I can learn, is far short of your expectations, not more, if that, than two hundred barrels. But this years prospect [is] more flattering. In Georgia you have about forty working hands, in South Carolina upwards of sixty, and in both States you have upwards of three hundred acres planted in rice, which upon a moral certainty may yeild you seven hundred barrels, or five hundred neat, for the market tho' at [Boun's?--i.e., Boone's Barony, S.C.] like the rest of your Neighbours you have suffered by the drought in corn as well as rice. About [illegible] acres of the latter will not turn out from the appearance above an half a crop but the [corn?] since the last rain has much improved, and perhaps there will be sufficient for provision.[2] The Gentleman who has the charge of your affairs has too much to attend to, I am afraid, to do you justice. He is I am persuaded, well disposed and no doubt very capable; but his business is so extensive that it is impossible for him to pay that particular attention to yours that you could wish.[3] He has received the Bills which you sent to him from Philadelphia and therefore will be able to comply with the condition of the late purchase he made for you unless the person who sold the negroes wishes to retract.[4] I do not know how many slaves were delivered to Mʳ Banks and Company last winter.[5] Mʳ Banks has gone to Virginia and Mʳ Forsythe is in North Carolina.[6] Money is very difficult to be obtained. I am told that 5.0 and 10 per Cᵗ has been given for it and there is yet a material difference between cash and credit. Great quantities of money have been shipped to the Africa traders and some to the British merchants instead of rice and other produce. Negroes still [keep?] up at an exorbitant price seventy pounds for males, sixty for women and fifty for children are given at a years credit.[7]
    Your taxes will fall heavy upon you this year. I presume you have no indents from the State, the interest upon which are received in payment for taxes,[8] and therefore you will be obliged to make your payment in case the negroes are rated at two dollars pʳ head, and all your real property at one per cᵗ ad valorem.
    We have been in some confusion since I arrived here. The Anti Brittanic sec[t] wishes to give laws to the people, to destroy what they

call the family compact to level the spirit of Aristocracy and to extirpate the people who were permitted to return by the last Assembly from the Country. Or in other words to establish a dutch monopoly and prevent all commercial intercourse with Great Brittain. The good conduct of the Citizens has put a stop to the confusion at present but how long we shall continue in peace depends in a great measure upon Doctor [James O']Fallon and others.[9] M[rs] Morris and all this family[10] join me in best respects to you and M[rs] Greene and beleive me to be Dear Sir, your sincere friend and very Hum[l] Serv[t]   L M

RC (MiU-C).

1. NG was en route from Rhode Island to South Carolina at this time. (See note at NG to Hazlehurst, 26 June, above.)

2. A hurricane and other problems had left NG's rice crop of the previous year far short of expectations. (Saunders to NG, 20 October 1783, and Hyrne to NG, 26 November–4 December 1783, above) NG's 1784 crops also fell short of expectations. (NG to Gibbs, 3 February 1785, below)

3. The "gentleman" in charge of Boone's Barony, NG's South Carolina plantation, was Roger Parker Saunders, who gave a more detailed report on NG's "affairs" in both that state and Georgia in the letter immediately above.

4. On the slaves that Saunders had purchased for NG, see above, Pettit to NG, 27 April; Saunders to NG, 29 May; and NG to Morris, 25 June. On the bills that NG sent to Saunders in partial payment for this purchase, see NG to Morris, 5 June, and NG to Saunders, 6 June, both above. When Saunders wrote the letter immediately above, he had not yet received the bills.

5. On the slaves mentioned here, see also Saunders to NG, immediately above, and Pettit to NG, 26 July; Saunders to NG, 27 July; Penman to NG, 12 August; and Pendleton to NG, 10 November, all below.

6. Charles Pettit had reported Banks's departure from South Carolina for Virginia in his letter to NG of 10 June, above. (See also Forsyth to NG, 18 June, and Saunders to NG, before 17 July, above.) NG wrote Pettit on 15 August, below, that Banks's partner Robert Forsyth had gone "in persuit" of Banks.

7. On the "exorbitant" prices of slaves, see also, for example, Penman to NG, 1 October 1783; NG to Penman, 25 October 1783; and Pendleton to NG, 30 January 1784, all above.

8. Indents were public-debt certificates.

9. On the Anti-Britannic faction and Dr. James O'Fallon, see also William Washington to NG, 8 July, and Nathaniel Pendleton's second letter to NG of 10 July, both above.

10. Morris, one of NG's former aides, had married Ann-Barnett Elliott, a South Carolina heiress, the previous February. (Vol. 12: 390n, 574n, above)

From Robert Morris, Superintendent of Finance

Dear Sir   Philad[a] July 17th 1784

A few days since I sent you an extract of the letter which I have received from Mess[rs] Wilhem & Jan Willink of Amsterd[m] respecting the Loan proposed to them on Your behalf & herein (for fear of accident) you will find another Copy.[1] You can now open a Correspondance with them on the Subject & from what they say, I am satisfied that by pursueing the Steps they have pointed out you will obtain the money.[2]

Your letters of the 25th June & [3]d July are now before me, your draft for 250 Dollrs is paid & so shall another for the same Sum, these advances as well as the Credit on Mr Hazlehurst can be replaced when you obtain the Loan or otherwise find it convenient.[3]

I think Mr Saunders has made a good bargain for You and hope you will find resources to put your Estates instantly upon a Respectable footing.[4]

I lament the Conduct of Rhode Island exceedingly, that State will lament it, for we must be Honest, the Public Debts must be paid, & if we persist in the practice of Injustice, I shall not be Surprized to see, that we shall in the Hands of an Over ruling Providence soon be made the Instruments to Chastise each other for the Neglect of Public Justice.[5] I shall not however Consume Your time or my own with foreboding Evils. I had much rather employ myself & so would you in taking timely measures to prevent them. I am Dear Sir Your most Obedient & humble Servant   ROBT MORRIS

RCS (NjP).

1. The extract is printed in a note at Morris to NG, 12 July, above.

2. On NG's correspondence with the Dutch firm, see note at ibid. and his letter to the Willinks of 7 January 1786, below. As noted at Morris to NG, 12 July, NG was not able to obtain the loan.

3. NG discussed the draft in his letter to Morris of 25 June, above. In regard to the "Credit" on Charleston merchant Robert Hazlehurst, see NG to Morris, 5 June, and NG to Saunders, 6 June, both above.

4. Roger Parker Saunders had purchased slaves for NG. (See Pettit to NG, 27 April; NG to Morris, 25 June; and Saunders to NG, 29 May, all above.)

5. On "the Conduct of Rhode Island," see NG to Morris, 3 July, above.

*   *   *

¶ [FROM CHARLES PETTIT, Philadelphia, 26 July 1784. As he assumes that NG left soon afterward for Charleston, Pettit has not written since receiving NG's letter of 4 July [not found].[1] Mr. [Roger Parker] Saunders will probably show NG a letter to him "by this Conveyance," in which Pettit expresses "the fullest Confidence in his replacing in my Hands the Amount of his Draughts on me for your Account.[2] This reimbursement is the more necessary on Account of the unusual Difficulties" in Philadelphia. Pettit explains:

"It has long been apprehended that there was more Glitter than Gold among some of our Merchants and Traders, and that when the Storm should begin it would be extensive in it's Effects. Messrs Sluyter & Co, and Messrs Basse & Soyer, two high-aiming Dutch Houses, who had made a Glare in Gaiety and large Purchases, suddenly fell, & involved many in Difficulty who had taken their Bills or otherwise given them Credit. Van Vleck & Barton were pulled down with them. Some in a smaller way soon after tottered & fell. Suspicion broke loose & roamed at large like an untamed Colt, & there were not wanting heedless & even malicious People who either directed or encouraged it's course to the Doors of many who could not expell it wholly unhurt tho' they afforded it no Harbour. But so feeble is the Poiso[n] of this mischievous Being, that it infects wherever it app[ears] and People of weak Nerves, tho' otherwise of good Constitutions, frequently receive irreparable Injury from its merely playing about the Door. A violent Attempt was made on the Credit of our Friend Col. Biddle in the midst of the Storm; but luckily his Situation was such as resisted the Shock, tho' he may yet feel that he is injured by it. The Bank very handsomely declared their full Confidence in him, and did all they could to wipe away the Stain which had become so vizible as to induce Mr Biddle & his Friends to make public Declarations at the Coffee House, which occasioned the promoters of the Mischief to shrink into Concealment. He is now endeavouring to find an Object on whom to fix a charge for legal Discussion. But it may be impossible for him to extend the Antidote to every Point which the Slander may reach; and tho' he may strengthen his Root in the Scuffle it may take some Time before all his Branches recover due Vigor. A Merchant's, like a Woman's Fame, once tainted, never recovers perfect Purity in every Eye."

Mr. Abel James "has actually called a parley with his Creditors," and Pettit believes James's "Family will have something handsome left." He adds: "In Times like these you will readily suppose that a command of Cash, laying aside Prospects of immediate Profit, is a necessary Weapon of Defence."[3]

Pettit has had two letters from [John] Banks since Banks's arrival at New Bern, N.C.[4] The first was "accompanied with a sweeping Draught" on Pettit for $400 dollars, although Banks, before he left Charleston, had already "given a Draught on me for the Ballance in my hands, be the same more or less." In his other letter, dated 17 July, Banks asked Pettit to "pay Capt Tinker £800 on the Acc^t of his Purchase of part of a Brig^e [i.e., brigantine] to assist the Captain in the Outfit of the Vessel on a new Voyage, & to pay for & forward a Carriage for a Friend of his." Banks requested these drafts "with so much Ease & Confidence," accompanied by "such Assurances of a Remittance" in three weeks, "that you would hardly suppose they would not be complied with." The "Contract for the Vessel is not understood a like by the Parties," and whatever might be Pettit's "Disposition, that Bargain will probably fail." He will make an inquiry about the carriage, which "may also be under some Embarrassment."[5] Mr. [Michael J.] Harris, who will be leaving for London "in a Day or two," showed Pettit a letter from Mr [Joseph] Blatchford, "mentioning that some Negros, purchased by M^r [John] McQueen & Capt [Patrick] Carnes for which they had given Bonds, were under a prior Incumbrance, & that they had declared their Intention of refusing Payment of their Bonds." Harris says the bonds, worth "upwards of £5000 Sterling," were assigned to him by "M^r B[anks]." Pettit adds: "You will perceive how far you are interested in them."[6]

The "Certificates from the Pay Office for the Line of this State & southward, are not yet issued," but contracts are being made for them at the land office, which is "open within certain Limits." Pettit does not think the demand will be "very great till after the Indian Treaty when a new Purchase of Territory is expected to be opened." In a damaged portion of the letter, he further discusses the certificates and his plans "for taking Care of Penns^a Paper."[7] Adds: "I am far from being discouraged at the Measures of your State. If, as I am told, they are disposed to contribute their Quota in another Way I shall be disposed to meet them in that Way.[8] My Views are nevertheless to take our Measures in such Manner as to admit of their being at any time wrought into any such reasonable continental Plan as may be formed, but in the mean Time to give temporary Relief to the Public Creditors in Pennsylvania." He finds that "similar Sentiments are taking Place in Virginia, and that public Paper [is rising?] in Value there." Asks NG "what may be expected from the Carolinas & Georgia."[9] The Pennsylvania legislature, which was to have met on the 20th, does not yet have "a House," but "we expect it today"; as Pettit has to "attend" the legislature, "you may suppose I have something to do." RCS (MiU-C) 4 pp.]

1. As noted at his letter to Robert Hazlehurst of 26 June, above, NG left Newport, R.I., for Charleston, S.C., on 12 July.

2. For background, see Pettit to NG, 10, 19, and 26 June, all above. NG replied to Pettit on 15 August, below: "Capt Saunders has not shewn me your letter but I shall urge him to replace the Money and from present appearances he must see the impropriety of his interfering in the matter." In a letter of 12 November, below, NG asked Saunders to pay Pettit "1000 or 1200" dollars.

3. Historian Thomas M. Doerflinger has written of this period: "The headlong rush of merchants, merchandise and money into Philadelphia briefly created a frenetic speculative atmosphere in which fortunes were won and lost in a few months." By 1784, an oversupply of goods led merchants to "sell off their inventories" in New York, Charleston, and elsewhere. According to Doerflinger, "careers as well as commerce collapsed in this speculative maelstrom; Philadelphia firms went bankrupt at the rate of over one per month during the year ending in June 1785." Doerflinger cites a series of letters by Stephen Collins, a Philadelphia merchant, cataloging the bankruptcies much as Pettit did here: "Among the first to fall was a man named Sluyter, and he was soon followed by the reckless French firm of Basse and Soyer . . . Next to fall were Vanuleck and Barton, who were followed by 'a poor pettyfoging Dutch shopkeeper in Market Street' and a French merchant." Abel James was "a venerable Philadelphia Friend [i.e., Quaker] whose name had been synonymous with prudence and propriety for over four decades." James "speculated wildly in urban real estate in 1783 and 1784," and, when finally called in, "his debts amounted to seventy-five thousand pounds." (Doerflinger, *A Vigorous Spirit of Enterprise*, pp. 245–47) Clement Biddle's financial problems, which Pettit mentioned here, later became much worse. (See, for example, Pettit to NG, 23 March 1785, below.)

4. As seen in Forsyth to NG, 18 June, above, Banks had stopped in New Bern on his way to Virginia from Charleston.

5. Pettit, who had long since tired of honoring drafts that Banks did not repay, undoubtedly refused these requests. (For background, see above, Pettit to NG, 23 July 1783 and after 21 January 1784.)

6. As seen in Pendleton to NG, 10 November, below, Carnes's and McQueen's refusals did have ramifications for NG. (See also Saunders to NG, before 17 July, above, and NG to Collett, 8 August; Penman to NG, 12 August; and NG to Pettit, 15 August, all below.)

7. As seen in his agreement with NG of 7 June, above, Pettit was speculating in certificates of public debt for NG and himself. In his reply of 15 August, NG was unable to provide this information.

8. Rhode Island had recently rejected the 1783 impost proposal of Congress. (NG to Morris, 3 July, above)

9. NG replied to Pettit on 15 August, below.

*   *   *

From Jacob Read

Sir   Annapolis [Md.] 30th July 1784

My Letters from Charles Town of the 14th Ins^t inform me that My Mother Mrs Rebecca Read and Sister Eliza were at that time embarked & on the point of Sailing for Your Island in the Brigantine *Minerva* Capt [Benjamin] Pierce.[1] I trust that after a Safe and agreeable passage these very dear friends are Long Since Safely Landed in New Port. As the Ladies are unaccompanied by either of my Brothers they will Stand in great Need of your Kind Attentions and advice with respect to a proper residence &c^a. I hope I do not take too great Liberty when I request for them every Service that you can render without inconvenience to Yourself. The Obligation will be considered as most weighty by me and I Shall be always happy in an opportunity of testifying my gratitude.[2]

Had the State of the Committee of the States been Such as woud have permitted my absence, I Shoud have been in Your State much Sooner than this Letter possibly can but as the absence of a Single Member woud dissolve the Committee at this time I am obliged to wait till I may be relievd by my Colleague Mr Pinckney who is at Philadelphia.[3]

I shall however hasten to meet my friends when I hope the pleasure of seeing yourself & Lady well. Your State has once more dampd our hopes & thrown things into Confusion. The Consequences will I fear be fatal in Europe. What the public Creditors will do in this Country I cannot forsee but I fear a Scene of Anarchy will take place from Which I turn my Eyes with horrour. God bid Some Change of Sentiment may take place in Your Councils![4] Without it we are lost. Do me the honour to present my most respectful Compliments to Mrs Greene. I am with great esteem & regard Sir Your Most Obedient & most Hum^l Servt JACOB READ

PS. By Tuesdays post I wrote to my Brother Master James Bond Read & sent him orders to proceed immediately from Prince Town to Rhode Island to be & for a Short time attend his Mamma. I request Your Countenance of him & any Assistance he may Stand in need of.[5] J READ

The present post carries letters for my Mother addressed to your care to which I request your Attention.

7 Oclk PM This days post brot us Letters from our Minister abroad. The Ratification of the Definitive Treaty was [exchanged?] at Pasey by the Respective Plenepot^s [i.e., plenipotentiaries] on 12th May last.[6]

RCS (MiU-C).

1. On Read, see note at Saunders to NG, 27 November 1783, above. As seen there, he owned property at Newport, Aquidneck Island, R.I. His mother was Rebecca Bond Read; his sister, "Eliza" Read, later married Thomas Simons. (*Biog. Directory of S.C. House*, 3: 597, 654–55) The brigantine *Minerva*, captained by Benjamin Pierce, was owned by Jacob Greene & Company. (Jacob Greene to NG, 11 June and 8 July, above)

2. NG was en route to Charleston, S.C., at this time. (Note at NG to Hazlehurst, 26 June, above) Thus, he would not have been able to extend hospitality to the members of Jacob

Read's family when they arrived in Newport; it is not known if CG, who remained in Newport, entertained them.

3. On the "Committee of the States," which was to sit while Congress was in recess, see note at Lee to NG, 6 April, above. Read's colleague from South Carolina was Charles Pinckney, Jr. (1757–1824), who served as a delegate to Congress from 1784 until 1787. (*Biog. Directory of S.C. House*, 3: 555–58)

4. The Rhode Island legislature had recently rejected the federal impost proposal. (See above, NG to Morris, 3 July.)

5. The age of Read's younger brother, James Bond Read, is not known, but he was still "underage" when Rebecca Bond Read, their mother, died in 1786. (*SCHGM* 25 [1924]: 9)

6. On the "definitive treaty" of peace, see note at Lafayette to NG, 8 September 1783, above. Writing to the president of Congress from Passy, France, on 12 May, Benjamin Franklin, the American minister to France, had enclosed a copy of "the ratification of the Definitive Treaty of Peace" with Great Britain. (*JCC*, 27: 615–16; the text of the treaty is printed in ibid., pp. 617–25.)

*   *   *

¶ [FROM HENRY LUTTERLOH, New York, 3 August 1784.[1] As Maj. [John] Story is "going to you," Lutterloh asks NG if the "proposall about the recovery of the Eng.[l] Debts, has met with any Success" in Rhode Island. "From Every state a Gentleman is to go, who can receive his Money which will be recovered and we shall only expect Two Sixth for our share & trouble, to which the other States have agreed."[2] Congress passed a resolution "in May last to Instruct our Ministres abroad to Solicit the Demands of the Crown,"[3] but Lutterloh knows "by Experience & Three years Solicitation after the last [i.e., French and Indian?] War That it will end in the same Unsuccessfull manner." He adds: "The Crown has No Right to pay the greatest part of the Claims, Tho just in their nature, therefore I made this our Plan to come directly to the [right?] Debtors. One State alone could not do it without delays & great Expences." Lutterloh wants to "join the whole in a Solid Claim." He is "certain of" success and would be "extreamly happy to be an Instrument to do Justice to our Claimants in General." He is going to North and South Carolina and would be "much obliged" if NG would "honour" him with "a Letter either to the Gover.[r] or any other Gentleman."[4] RCS (MiU-C) 3 pp.]

1. Lutterloh had been a deputy quartermaster and commissary of forage during the war. (Vol. 6: 229n, above)

2. Nothing more is known about the "proposall" than what Lutterloh wrote in this letter.

3. In an earlier resolution, dated 30 May 1783, Congress had called upon the states to "remove all obstructions which may interpose in the way of the entire and faithful execution" of the preliminary articles of peace. One of those articles, to which the resolution referred specifically, stipulated "that creditors on either side shall meet with no lawful impediment to the recovery of the full value in sterling money of all *bona fide* debts heretofore contracted." (*JCC*, 24: 370–71) The resolution to which Lutterloh referred here was dated 11 May 1784. In it, Congress directed its ministers to foreign nations to use "perseverance" in carrying out the instructions in the earlier resolution "relative to British debts." The ministers were also to "require with firmness and decision, full satisfaction for all slaves and other property belonging to citizens of these states taken and carried away in violation of the preliminary and definitive articles of peace." Congress, on its part, was to furnish "necessary facts and documents" to the ministers. (*JCC*, 27: 368)

4. No evidence has been found that NG wrote to anyone on Lutterloh's behalf.

¶ [FROM PEYTON SKIPWITH,[1] Charleston, S.C., [4 August 1784].[2] He supposes, from their names, that the witnesses to "the Deeds put into my hands" are South Carolina residents. If it is necessary for NG's "security" to have these deeds recorded, Skipwith believes the "want of Witnesses" will put it out of his power to do so.[3] He thinks that not only Virginia law, but that of "all the other States requires that Deeds of every kind when delivered in to be recorded shall be proved by one or more witnesses." If he is wrong about this, he asks "to be set right"; if he is correct, "it wou'd be a very easy matter for M[r] [James] Hunter to acknowledge the Deeds before me and a M[r] Blair who is going in the same Vessell to Virginia." Skipwith adds: "I wish to act as will be compatible wth your interest, and without the power of doing so, I shall be disappointed."[4] RCS (MiU-C) 2 pp.]

1. The writer was Peyton Skipwith, Sr. (1740–1805), whose then-small child Peyton, Jr. (1780–1808), "a member of a prominent Virginia family," would marry NG's daughter Cornelia in 1802. (Stegeman, *Caty*, p. 177; www.mindspring.com/~kandiandi/skipwith.htm; Clarke, *Greenes*, p. 239) Louise Brownell Clarke identified Peyton, Sr., as "Sir Peyton Skipwith, Baronet," of "'Prestwould,'" in Mecklenburg County, Va., and noted that his father, "Sir William Skipwith, sixth baronet, was of royal descent." (Clarke, *Greenes*, p. 329) Peyton, Sr., had recently sailed to Charleston from Newport, R.I., with NG. (*South Carolina Gazette & Public Advertiser*, 31 July–4 August; see also NG to Skipwith, 19 August, and Skipwith's reply of 20 August, both below.)
2. The date was taken from the docketing.
3. On the "Deeds," see the note immediately below.
4. Skipwith was apparently still in South Carolina when NG and he exchanged letters on 19 and 20 August. The "Deeds" have not been found, but in an indenture signed before two witnesses at Charleston on 11 September, John Banks's partner Hunter, "late of the Commonwealth of Virginia, but now of the state of South Carolina," pledged to NG his title to certain properties in Fredericksburg and Portsmouth, Va., as security against a promise to "save harmless and indemnify" NG from damages that might result from NG's being "bound unto divers[e] persons in considerable sums of money for goods, wares and merchandises sold by them to Robert Forsyth and Company." (A copy of the indenture is at ViHi. Forsyth had been a partner of Banks and Hunter. On the debts that NG had guaranteed for them, see especially NG to Benjamin Lincoln, 19 December 1782, and Agreement between Hunter, Banks and Company and NG with Newcomen and Collett, 8 April 1783, both above [vol. 12: 306–7 and n, 591 and n]; and NG to Lee, 22 August 1785, below.) Not long afterward, NG expressed doubts to Forsyth about Hunter's integrity in making this pledge. (NG to Forsyth, 2 October, below) For further developments, see Hunter to NG, 1 June 1785, and NG's reply of 29 August 1785, both below.

¶ [TO HOWSON, EDWARDS & COMPANY. From Charleston, S.C., 6 August 1784.[1] NG has agreed to send them "the produce of my plantations in this Country on Account of Doctor John Sentor Physician in Newport [R.I.] to the amount of six hundred dollars which he says you have agreed to sell without commision." NG is still "uncertain whether it will come in Rice or Indigo," so if this letter has "an early arrival," he asks them to let him know "which Article promises the most ready and beneficial sale." He will return to Newport "in a few days" and asks them to send a "price current" to him there. He adds: "I am a stranger to you but having been long in the Army in the late revolution in America and commanding the Troops in the Southern States you may not be altogether unacquainted with my charactor. Upon this presumption I take the liberty to recommend Doctor Sentor to your good Offices, who is a particular friend of mine. The Doctor is a man of good sense[,] emminent in the practice of physick attentive to his business, economical in his living and thriving in his circumstances." NG hopes they will find Senter "both an agreeable and useful correspondent."[2] ADfS (MiU-C) 3 pp.]

1. This letter is the first that NG is known to have written after his arrival in Charleston on 1 August. As seen by their letters to NG of 27 June 1785, below, Howson, Edwards & Company were London merchants.

2. NG was undoubtedly referring here to his friend and family physician, Dr. Isaac Senter, who, in addition to his medical practice, owned a shop "on the South Side of the Parade" in Newport, where he sold pharmaceutical preparations imported from London. (*Newport Mercury*, 13 December 1783) On Senter, see also vol. 1: 250n and the note at NG to Pettit, 22 April, both above. Howson, Edwards & Company replied to NG on 16 October, below, that they were "perfectly Satisfyd with the Character of M[r] Sentor but not with his way of dealing."

*   *   *

To E. John Collett

Sir   Charleston [S.C.] Aug 8th 1784

I am sorry to find on my arrival at this place letters from you of the same import of those you wrote me while I was in Newport [R.I.] and I am still more distressd upon the occasion to find M[r] [John] Banks's affairs in the most disagreeable Situation.[1]

M[r] [James] Hunter wrote you by the last post of my arrival & distress at the Situation of your demands.[2] M[r] Banks has behaved in so extraordinary a manner respecting Harris & Blachfords affairs that I have much more to apprehend than I expected.[3] I am reduced to worse than beggary unless you can get hold of property to cover your demands.[4] Let me therefore beg of you to leave no stone unturn'd to secure your property, & if it is not of the kind you wish, cover the debt notwithstanding, & this difficulty may be got over by Negotiation. I wish you to attach to the amount of your whole demands in the hands of M[r] Henry Banks who I believe can be brought to account for what may extinguish your debt. It is said & I believe with truth that he has got surveys of a very large landed property in the back Country, not less than 150,000 Acres, which must & will be valuable.[5] Besides this Step if the greater part of your dues is not paid I wish you to levy an attachment upon a square of Lotts in Richmond, which Hunter Banks & Co bought some time since of M[r] Ross, & which M[r] Henry Banks has been selling without sufficient authority to give a title. If either of the Banks's give you a mortgage of Lands or other property let them first make oath that the property has not been previously mortgaged to some other person. This precaution is necessary from what has happen'd between Harris & Blachford & Banks.[6]

Once more let me repeat my earnest wishes, nay let me beg it as a favor that you get hold of every kind of property you can, and trust nothing to Mr Banks's promises. We shall take every measure in our power here to get hold of Mr Ferries property but I fear it is so circumstanced that little can be got. However a Bill is filing in Chancery & the Lawyers make no doubt of its taking full effect.[7] I have nothing to add, but that you will consider my ruinous situation, & give me every possible relief from this Load of anxiety which is truly insupportable.[8] I am Sir Your humble Servant   Sign'd NATH^l GREEN^E

Cy (MiU-C).

1. Collett was seeking redress from NG for unpaid debts that NG had guaranteed for John Banks and his partners as contractors to the Southern Army. (Agreement between Hunter, Banks and Company, NG, and Newcomen and Collett, 8 April 1783 [vol. 12: 591 and n], above; for further background, see ibid., pp. 308–9n, and NG to Lee, 22 August 1785, below.) The letters from Collett have not been found. (See, however, NG to Collett, 23 June, above.)

2. The letter to Collett from James Hunter, one of Banks's partners, has not been found.

3. For more about NG's situation with the mercantile firm of Harris & Blachford, to whom he had also guaranteed some debts for Banks and his partners, see Pendleton to NG, 10 November, below.

4. Collett had been in Virginia for some time to try to "get hold of" assets belonging to Banks. (See note at Forsyth to NG, 24 February, above.)

5. On the back country lands belonging to John Banks and his brother Henry, see also Forsyth to NG, 18 June, above, and notes at NG to Rutledge, after 30 September, and at Henry Banks to NG, 7 October, both below.

6. On the reasons for "this precaution," see Pettit to NG, 26 July, above, and Pendleton to NG, 10 November.

7. As noted at Forsyth to NG, 18 June, the suit against John Ferrie was not settled until after NG's death. For more about efforts to attach property belonging to Ferrie, see especially NG to Pettit, 15 August; Pierce to NG, 24 September; Call to NG, 30 September; and NG to Rutledge, after 30 September, all below. William Pierce, Jr., wrote NG on 24 September that he believed Ferrie had "so secured" his Georgia property "that it will be impossible to reach it."

8. NG wrote Charles Pettit on 15 August that Collett had obtained "partial payments and upon the whole I am not with out hopes of getting off without loss." As it turned out, Collett continued to seek restitution from NG until just before NG's death on 19 June 1786. (See, for example his letters to NG of 6 and 24 March 1786, 8 and 10 May 1786, and 9 and 13 June 1786, all below.) According to NG's attorney Nathaniel Pendleton, NG and Collett met in Pendleton's house in Savannah, Ga., "on the Tuesday [i.e., 13 June 1786] before the death of General Greene" and reached a settlement in which NG "executed bonds for, I believe, about six thousand pounds sterling, payable at different periods, and delivered them, in my presence, to Collet, who gave him, also, in my presence, the bond, the General had signed, as guarantee." Pendleton's statement, dated 21 June 1790, was submitted in support of a petition to Congress by CG on 4 March 1790 and is printed in Syrett, *Hamilton*, 10: 458–64; the portions quoted here are on p. 463. (See also Collett to NG, 13 June 1786.)

CG's petition, submitted during the second session of the First Congress under the United States Constitution, was "founded" on the request for indemnification that NG made to the Continental Congress in August 1785. (See NG to Lee, 22 August 1785, below.) CG's petition reads in part:

"That it will appear by the said Representation, that it was the intention of her late husband, to have ascertained the loss on the transaction therein stated, previously to his making application to the United States for indemnification; and, in pursuit of this intention, he instituted suits for the recovery of the bonds and mortgages by him received of Messrs. Banks and Company, as collateral securities; but his designs in this and all other earthly respects were frustrated by his untimely death [in June 1786].

"That the Suits for the recovery of the said bonds and other collateral securities have been protracted by the death of the debtors, and various other circumstances entirely without the controul of your petitioner.

"That while the recovery of the said bonds and other collateral securities is placed at a future distant period, and their amount uncertain, not only the estates conferred on her late husband, by the munificent gratitude of the States of South Carolina and Georgia, but his paternal estate will be legally wrested from your petitioner and her children, in order to satisfy those obligations, which her late husband was constrained to enter into, for the public service, whereby your petitioner and her helpless children will be exposed to all the bitter effects of poverty.

"That your petitioner thus brings forward her situation and that of her children, with the firmest hope and expectation, that the United States will, after a full examination into the transaction stated in her late husband's representation, grant her effectual relief, by assuming the payment of the said obligations, entered into for the benefit of the United States, or, in such other manner, save her and her children's estate from impending ruin, as in the judgment of Congress, shall appear meet and proper." (Syrett, *Hamilton*, 10: 407–8n)

On 30 July 1790, the House of Representatives referred a committee report, "favorable to the prayer of the petition," to NG's and CG's friend Alexander Hamilton, the secretary of the treasury. (*Annals of Congress*, 2: 1758) More than a year later, in a report dated 26 December 1791, Hamilton discussed the merits of the request and produced evidence to refute two of three objections that had been raised against it: "Want of authority from the government to enter into the suretyship in question" and "a personal or private interest [on NG's part] in doing what was done foreign to the duties and relations of a commanding officer." (Syrett, *Hamilton*, 10: 412–19; quotes from pp. 412, 413) As for the third objection—"omission of notice to the government, at, or about the time of the transaction, that the suretyship in question had been entered into"—Hamilton speculated "that General Greene was naturally led to imagine, that all hazard in the affair was obviated by the measures which had been taken to secure, as he supposed, an application of the monies to be received from the public, on account of the contract, to the payment of the debts, for which he had become surety; and, therefore, omitted a communication to the government, as not necessary to his safety." (Ibid., pp. 419–20) Declining to state his own opinion in regard to the third objection, Hamilton left it to Congress to decide whether NG's "omission" was "a sufficient ground for dispensing with the observance of a precaution, which, as a general rule, would be proper to be made a condition of indemnification; or how far, the peculiar merit of the officer, or the peculiar hardship and misfortune of the case, may render advisable a deviation from that rule." Hamilton concluded his report by expressing the hope that he was "justified by the occasion" in observing "that strong and extraordinary motives of national gratitude for the very signal and very important services, rendered by General Greene to his country, must serve to give a keener sting to the regret, which ought ever to attend the necessity of a strict adherence to maxims of public policy, in opposition to claims, founded on useful acts of zeal for the public service, if no means of protecting from indigence and penury, the family of that most meritorious officer, shall, upon examination, be found inadmissible." (Syrett, *Hamilton*, 10: 420; the full report, with documents submitted in support of CG's petition, is printed in ibid., pp. 406–68.)

On 10 January 1792, the House of Representatives took up consideration of Hamilton's report and CG's petition. In a lengthy debate, representatives Jeremiah Wadsworth and Anthony Wayne, both close friends of NG and CG, spoke strongly in favor of indemnification; those opposed included Thomas Sumter, the former South Carolina militia commander with whom NG had differences during the war. In concluding his remarks, Sumter called statements by NG about the South Carolina militia and the patriotism of South Carolinians, as quoted in William Gordon's history of the Revolution, "gross calumnies on, and misrepresentations of the character of that people." (See *Annals of Congress*, 3: 318–27; quote from p. 327.)

On 4 April 1792, by a vote of twenty-nine to twenty-six, the House voted in favor of a resolution pertaining to NG's bond for £8,743.15.6 to "Newcomen and Collett, merchants in Charleston," as surety for John Banks & Company. According to that resolution, the United States was to reimburse NG's estate for that amount, plus interest, "or for such sum" as treasury officers might determine

> "that neither General Greene nor his executors shall have received any payment or compensation for: Provided, The executors of the said General Greene shall account for a sum, being about two thousand pounds, be the same more or less, recovered by John Ferrie, one of the partners of the said Banks and Company, to be in part of the indemnification aforesaid. And, also, shall make over for the use of the United States, all mortgages, bonds, covenants, or other counter-securities whatsoever, now due, which were obtained by the said General Greene, in his life-time, from the said Banks and Company, on account of his being surety for them as aforesaid, to be sued in the name of the said executors, for the use of the United States." (*Annals of Congress*, 3: 561)

On 11 April 1792, by a vote of thirty-three to twenty-four, the House approved a bill based on this resolution. (Ibid., p. 574; on the progress of the indemnification proposal through the House, see also *Annals of Congress* 3 [1834]: 330–31, 424, 427–28, 454–55, 536–38, 540.) The act of indemnification, which became law on 27 April 1792, is printed in *U.S. Statutes at Large* 1 [1845]: 258. Not included under the terms of this act was the debt to the firm of Harris & Blachford that NG had also incurred as surety for Banks and his partners. As seen in a note at Pendleton to NG, 10 November, that issue was not settled by Congress until 1796.

From John Croskeys[1]

D[r] Sir   10 August [17]84
   I Send you a list of all the negros on your Plantations with 2 that is absent one has been gon Sinse Last winter the other this Summer[.][2] I donte [*damaged*] besides the Carpenters drivers & drivers wifes thi [the] 2 absent is not reckned with The warkers[.] The wench mentioned in the List not Sold has 2 Children[.] She is a Crippel has not warkt for Some years past. A feller—Sipeau by name that Cap[t] Saunders bought of Boons Estate had that wench for a wife & all so has one of yours he is now in the woods & has ben all the yeare.[3] I [t]hink you had beter give out that youe have bought him that he may Com in, weather you by him or not as he must be a determent To youe by being about the plantations[.] He is a very good fell[er] for wark Should youe get him D[r] Sir your humble S[t]   JOHN CROSKEYS

RCS (MiU-C).

1. As seen at his letter to NG of 16 February 1786, below, Croskeys was the manager of NG's South Carolina plantation, Boone's Barony.

2. The list has not been found.

3. Roger Parker Saunders had purchased slaves for NG at "Boone's sale" the previous year. (See note at Saunders to NG, 7 June 1783, above.)

To Jacob Greene

Charleston [S.C.], *August* 12*th* 1784.

"My heart is too full, and my situation too distressing, to write much; but from a wish that you may not feel more inconvenience than is unavoidable, I embrace the earliest opportunity to make you acquainted with my situation. You may remember I told you last winter of some heavy embarrassments which hung over me from becoming security for Banks, Hunter & Company.[1] They being public contractors, and the feeding of the army depending upon supporting their credit, I was obliged to guarantee sundry of their debts.[2] But that I might be secure, they engaged that all the contract money should go to the discharge of my guarantee bonds. This they have found means to avoid; and their affairs have grown desperate, and I am and shall be involved in heavy and unavoidable losses. And although it will not reduce me to a state of poverty, yet it will put it out of my power to do any thing for you and Griffin.[3] Indeed, it will oblige me to sell considerable part of my estate. My situation is truly afflicting! to be reduced from independence to want, and from the power of obliging my friends, to a situation claiming their aid. You and Griffin must do the best you can, and God grant you better fortune! My heart faints within me when I think of my family. I have only one consolation—it is not the fruits of extravagance."

Extract, printed in Johnson, *Greene*, 2: 411.

1. Since his recent arrival in Charleston, NG had learned that the financial problems stemming from the guarantee he had provided for John Banks and Banks's partners as Southern Army contractors were worse than he had supposed. (See also NG to Collett, 8 August, above, and NG to Pettit, 15 August; NG to Arnold, 17 August; and NG to Gibbs, 17 August, all below.)

2. For the guarantee, see Agreement between Hunter, Banks and Company, NG, and Newcomen and Collett, 8 April 1783 (vol. 12: 591 and n). For further background, see ibid., pp. 308–9n, and NG to Lee, 22 August 1785, below.

3. NG was a partner with his brother Jacob and cousin Griffin Greene in Jacob Greene & Company. In a letter of 8 July, above, NG informed Griffin, who was in France trying to complete the sale of a vessel in which the company owned an interest, that Jacob had suffered heavy recent losses and "Upon the whole your affairs are in a deranged State."

*   *   *

¶ [FROM EDWARD PENMAN, [Charleston, S.C.?], 12 August 1784.[1] "Two parcels of Negroes" were sold by "J & E. P. Where Mr Banks was concerned."[2] The first group was "secured by Bond by Capt Carnes & Mr Banks"; the second was secured by "Mr Banks Col. Washington & Mr Brown." In both cases, "Mortgages" were taken. Penman informs NG that Carnes "Signed the Mortgage of the first parcel with Mr Banks, consequently knew of it." Carnes had "no concern in the Second Purchase," and Penman does not know if Carnes was aware that "the Negroes were Mortgaged"; Washington did know, as Banks "inform^d him of it, previous to his becoming security in the Bonds." Penman was "ignorant" of Banks's "Subsequent transactions with Mr McQueen" and cannot say whether McQueen "knew any thing of those Mortgages."[3] Cy (MiU-C) 1 p.]

1. Penman was a cousin of Charleston merchant James Penman, who had acted as an agent for NG in procuring slaves in East Florida. (See James Penman to NG, 1 October 1783, above; Nelson, *Wayne*, p. 201.) Edward Penman seems to have gone into business with his cousin in Charleston after the war. By the summer of 1783, their advertisements were signed "James & Edw. Penman." (See, for example, *South-Carolina Gazette & General Advertiser*, 26 July 1783.)

2. "J. & E. P." was the firm of James and Edward Penman.

3. On the involvement of Patrick Carnes, William Washington, Joseph Brown, and John McQueen in Banks's financial affairs, see Saunders to NG, before 17 July, and Pettit to NG, 26 July, both above; NG to Pettit, 15 August, immediately below.

* * *

To Charles Pettit

Dear Sir   Charleston [S.C.] Augt 15th 1784

I got your letter five days ago dated the 26th of July. I have been in great distress from an apprehension of heavy losses in M^r [John] Banks affairs. Major [Robert] Forsyth wrote [that] Mr [Michael J.] Harris & [Joseph] Blachfords affairs were all settled and that none but Collettes remained.[1] Mr Banks had deceivd both Harris & the Major by giving in to the hands of Mr Harris securities arising from property sold previously under Mortgage. This discovery was a terrible blow which had been but a few days before my arrival.[2] Banks was gone to Virginia and Forsyth in persuit of him nor have I heard from either since.[3] But I shall be able to get hold of property of Mr Ferries to the full amount of this deficiency.[4] Mr Collett has receivd partial payments and upon the whole I am not with out hopes of getting off without loss.[5] But Mr. Banks is a great vilian and deserves nothing short of hanging however this is in confidence until I get out of his clutches. I expect to be here for some time as I am determined not to quit the business until I am secure or see their is no possibility of being so.[6] Capt [Roger Parker] Saunders has not shewn me your letter but I shall urge him to replace the Money and from present appearances he must see the impropriety of his interfering in the matter.[7]

On Paper funds I can say nothing. Those of this State are selling at 6 and 7 for one and the funds provided for their payment are not inferior to any in the United States.[8] Yours aff   NATH GREENE

ADfS (MiU-C).

1. Forsyth's letter has not been found. On the debt to E. John Collett that NG had guaranteed for Banks, see especially NG to Collett, 8 August, as well as vol. 12: 308–9n, and Agreement between Hunter, Banks & Company, NG, and Newcomen and Collett, 8 April 1783 (ibid., p. 591 and n), all above.

2. As seen above in Saunders to NG, before 17 July, and Pettit to NG, 26 July, Banks, in partial payment of debts that NG had guaranteed for him, had turned over to Harris some bonds that he had obtained from the sale of a number of slaves. Some of the purchasers, after learning that the slaves Banks had sold them were "under a prior Incumbrance," were refusing payment on these bonds. (See also Penman to NG, 12 August, above, and Pendleton to NG, 10 November, below; for background on the debts to Harris & Blachford that NG had guaranteed for Banks and his partners, see note at Pettit to NG, 6 May, above.)

3. On Banks's departure for Virginia, see Pettit to NG, 10 June; Forsyth to NG, 18 June; and Saunders to NG, before 17 July, all above. Forsyth apparently returned to South Carolina by late September. (Meals to NG, 30 September, below)

4. On NG's plan to attach property belonging to John Ferrie, see above, Forsyth to NG, 18 June, and NG to Collett, 8 August.

5. As seen by the note at NG's letter to him of 8 August, Collett continued to press NG for payment of debts that NG had guaranteed for Banks until just before NG's death.

6. NG set out for North Carolina and Virginia at the end of the summer to confront Banks but learned when he reached Washington, N.C., that Banks was dead. (NG to Rutledge, after 30 September, below)

7. On the money that Pettit wanted Saunders to replace, see Pettit to NG, 26 July. In a letter of 12 November, below, NG asked Saunders to pay Pettit "1000 or 1200" dollars. NG tried to make a partial payment against this debt by sending a bill of exchange to creditors of Pettit's in London in March 1785. (NG to De Berdt, 9 March 1785, below) As noted there, the bill, backed by a credit that NG had received in advance of what turned out to be a disappointing rice crop, was rejected.

8. In his letter to NG of 26 July, Pettit, who was speculating in public debt certificates for NG and himself, had asked about the prices of South Carolina and Georgia certificates.

To Welcome Arnold

Dear Sir   Charleston [S.C.] Augt 17th 1784

I have been under no small apprehensions of heavy losses from some debts which I guaranteed for the Contractors of the Southern Army about a year and a half ago. The funds of the Contract was to have gone to the discharge of those debts and powers given accordingly for my better security. But not withstanding this they found means to divert them into other channels and left me still responsible. This was the situation I heard of the business being in, before I left home and so I found it on my arrival.[1] I have taken decided measures for my security and as I have several persons as counter security, I can but hope I shall finally Meet with no loss.[2]

Mr Bartlet the young Gentleman you have planted here appears to be a man of business and a very steady charactor and I doubt not will succeed well in business. Perry and he has done business together and Perry seems to be much pleased with him.[3] But for this disagreeable business which brought me here my Mind would be much at ease, my crops are promising and business in a good way. If no misfortune unforeseen attends my crops I think I shall make upwards of fifteen hundred pounds sterling.[4]

This letter will be handed you by Mr Gadsden son of the Generals, M[r] Brown a Gentleman of fortune and Doctor Stewart. I beg leave to recommend them to your civilities and my complements to your Lady.[5] I am dear Sir with sincere regard Your most Obedt humble Serv[t]

NATH GREENE

ALS (MiU-C).

1. On the financial problems resulting from NG's guarantee of certain debts of Hunter, Banks & Company, see also his letters to Jacob Greene, 12 August, and Charles Pettit, 15 August, both above, and to George Gibbs, immediately below.

2. In letters above to E. John Collett, 8 August, and Charles Pettit, 15 August, NG discussed some of the measures he was taking for his security. As seen below in his letter of 22 August 1785 to Richard Henry Lee, the president of Congress, NG was disappointed in his hope of meeting with "no loss," and he eventually turned to Congress in search of relief.

3. Perry was NG's brother Perry Greene. (See also NG to CG, 17 and 21 August, below.)

4. NG's 1784 crops did not meet his expectations. (NG to Gibbs, 3 February 1785, below)

5. Gen. Christopher Gadsden was the father of three sons, Christopher, Thomas, and Philip. (*Biog. Directory of S.C. House*, 2: 262) Young Gadsden and his companions were apparently traveling to Rhode Island. (See also NG to Gibbs, immediately below.)

To George Gibbs

Dear Sir   Charleston [S.C.] August 17th 1784

The business which hurried me to Charleston at this season was sundry debts which I guaranteed for the Contractors of the Army while it was in this Country and which ought to have been discharged from the funds arising from the contract money. This was stipulated at the time but the funds were converted to other purposes and my guarantee bonds left unpaid and the companies affairs in a bad if·not in a ruinous situation. This was the account I had before I left home and on my arrival I found matters rather worse than better.[1] However upon looking into the business and the Counter securities I possess I can but hope I shall be able to get sufficient to secure my self from loss; but it has given me much pain and still is a load upon my mind. My crops are promising and but for this affair my mind would be much at ease. I think my Crop will neat me fifteen hundred pounds rather more than less.[2] If you should advance any Money for me and it will be agreeable to you to remit the amount from this in the fall & Winter, I will gladly do it. Please to write me by the first opportunity as it is more than probable I shall remain here until your answer can arrive.[3]

This letter will be hand[ed] you by three young Gentlemen from this Country Mr Gadsden M[r] Brown and Doctor Stewart who I beg leave to recommend to your civilities.[4] I beg my complements to Mrs Gibbs and am dear Sir Your Most Obedt humble Ser[t]   NATH GREENE

ADfS (MiU-C).

1. See also NG's letters to Jacob Greene of 12 August, Charles Pettit of 15 August, and Welcome Arnold of 17 August, all above.

2. See notes at NG to Arnold, immediately above.

3. It appears from NG's letter to Gibbs of 3 February 1785, below, that Gibbs did advance money to him.

4. See also NG to Arnold, immediately above.

To Catharine Littlefield Greene

My dear Angel   Charleston [S.C.] Aug[st] 17 1784

I have sent you curtain trimming but the price is enormous the whole cost amounts to upwards of £16 sterling as Per the inclosed bill. If there is more than is wanted, the woman has agreed to take what remains, or if it dont please you I can return the whole. It is thought to be very good and the quantity little more than is used here for two beds. White fringe and trimming is all the mode for any coloured curtains.[1]

I have met with no Jerandoes[2] or Pickals [i.e., pickles?] but will make further inquiry when I get more time. Perry has conducted his business with great cleaverness and I can but hope will succeed in the plan.[3] I have got nothing new to communicate on M[r] Banks's affairs.[4] Two Vessels have arrivd from Newport [R.I.] and not a word from any of our friends. I imagine you must have been still with your friends on Block Island.[5] I have heard nothing from Lucy's master since we arrived. Such additional servants as you may want it will be best to hire.[6] Ham is fond of the sea and I think it will be best to continue him on board of the Sloop but do as you please.[7] I have sent you a cask of Rice and if you can spare half of it to Maxwell I wish you would or a less quantity if you think proper.[8] My stay I fear will be longer than I wish or you expect; but I shall not feel happy for a moment until I embrace you.[9] Kiss all the Children and tell them I am well, and long to hear them prattle. Yours aff   N GREENE

ALS (MiU-C).

1. The "enclosed bill," which NG copied on the last page of this letter, was a list of the bed-trimming items, including "16 Tassels," twelve dozen "fringe," and four gross of "bed lace," and their prices. (MiU-C)

2. It is possible that NG meant girandole, an "ornamental branched candle holder." (*Webster's*; see also NG to CG, 21 August, below.)

3. NG's brother Perry Greene had presumably sailed on the same vessel that brought NG to Charleston. (See also NG to Arnold, 17 August, above; NG to Skipwith, 19 August, and NG to CG, 21 August, both below.)

4. As NG wrote CG on 21 August that he had discussed the "disagreeable situation" he was in with respect to John Banks in a letter to her three days earlier, it is possible that he wrote to CG again on 18 August. If so, the letter has not been found.

5. CG had spent her early life on Block Island, R.I. (Vol. 1: 66n, above)

6. Lucy was undoubtedly the "Negro wench" about whom Samuel Clegg had inquired in his letter to NG of 9 March, above. NG wrote CG on 8 September, below, that he still had Lucy with him and had "got no news" from her master, Clegg.

7. In a letter dated after 8 September 1785, below, NG's brother Christopher Greene acknowledged receipt of a letter that Ham, a servant, had brought to him from NG, who was then at home in Rhode Island.

8. Adam Maxwell had once been NG's tutor. (Vol. 1: 14n, above) William Littlefield wrote NG on 15 May 1786, below, that Maxwell and his family were "very needy" and "very much on Charity."

9. NG did not return to Rhode Island until late November. (NG to Gibbons, 29 November, below)

To Francis Tate

Sir   [Charleston, S.C., 17 August 1784][1]

I find by Major [Robert] Forsyths books and M^r [James] Hunters information that you are indebted to that company upwards of £600 pounds sterling. You know how this company have been oppressed and how this debt arose. I am persuaded it is unnecessary to use arguments to urge you to take proper measures to secure them. Both justice and generosity claim it but besides these reasons you have more to expect from them than from those who have pushed you so hardly of late. In securing them you will benefit me as I have guaranteed sundry of the company Debts while they were contractors for the Army.[2] If now or here after I can be of any service to your affairs I shall gladly exert my self to serve you. I wish you to come down to the Quarter House and send in your Servant[,] and Mr Hunter and my self will attend you. Please to give me an immediate answer to this letter.[3] I am Sir Your humble Ser^t NATH GREENE

ADfS (MiU-C).

1. The date was taken from the docketing; the place from other letters that NG wrote on this date.

2. On NG's efforts at this time to secure himself against debts he had incurred in consequence of serving as a guarantor for Hunter, Banks & Company, see also his letters to E. John Collett of 8 August, Charles Pettit of 15 August, and Welcome Arnold and George Gibbs of 17 August, all above.

3. Tate replied to NG on 24 August, below.

*   *   *

¶ [TO PEYTON SKIPWITH. From Charleston, S.C., 19 August 1784. NG's brother left "the inclosed Account which he has charged to me and desird me to settle the matter with" Skipwith.[1] NG's brother claimed that Skipwith "had been spoke to but had waved the subject." NG was "also concerned" to hear that Skipwith was "dissatisfied with the price" of his "passage being higher than the Jews and particularly in being obliged to pay for" his servant's passage. NG can "hardly think" this was "more than a banter for Sir Payton would never wish to be put upon the footing with insignificant Jews where thier poverty obliged them to contract under the terms settled for a Gentleman." Nor should Skipwith think "that passages from Newport can be at a lower rate than from Philadelphia," which is "20 dollars for the Master and 10 for the servant." NG quotes these prices, even though he has "an interest in the Vessel."[2] He adds: "If you was serious I wish to set you right in the matter; but if it was a banter and nothing more I wish to be set right my self." If the account had been "originally mine," he would have been "silent on the subject," nor would he "charge any thing for the Cyder claret Geese turnips and several other things which I sent on board." NG requests: "If you will add this bill and your bill together and half it between us it will be what I wish and my brother expects."[3] ADfS (MiU-C) 3 pp.]

1. NG's brother Perry Greene left Charleston about this time to return to Rhode Island. (NG to CG, 21 August, below) On Skipwith, see his letter to NG of 4 August, above. The account has not been found.

2. NG owned an interest in the sloop *Charleston Packet*, the vessel that had brought Skipwith and him to Charleston from Newport, R.I. (See above, NG to Hazlehurst, 26 June, and Skipwith to NG, 4 August.) As noted at the Skipwith letter, "Sir Payton" was a baronet.

3. Skipwith's reply is immediately below.

¶ [FROM PEYTON SKIPWITH, [Charleston, S.C.], 20 August 1784. Encloses "Mr Greens receipt for Passage" for NG's "satisfaction." Also encloses a "state of the supply acct," hoping that "upon an examination," NG will think, as Skipwith does, "that Mr Green did me great injustice when he insinuated to you, that I was backward in doing what Justice directed at the time I paid my Passage."[1] Col. [Nicholas] Eveleigh witnessed the exchange and will attest that Skipwith did not dispute the bill and "paid it with readiness."[2] ALS (MiU-C) 1 p.]

1. This letter was undoubtedly a reply to NG's of 19 August, immediately above. The enclosures have not been found. "Mr Green" was presumably NG's brother Perry.

2. No further correspondence between Skipwith and NG has been found.

*   *   *

To Catharine Littlefield Greene

My dear Caty   Charleston [S.C.] Augt 21st 1784

I wrote you three days ago by Perry a full Account of the very disagreeable situation I was in respecting Mr Banks's affair and I wish I had something more pleasing to say on the matter but I have not.[1] Major [Robert] Forsyth is still in North Carolinia and from his long stay I can but hope he is getting hold of considerable property and I am the more inclined to indulge this opinion from being informed that Mr Banks had made large purchaces there.[2] Some say to the amount of ten or twenty thousand pounds sterling. I have taken such steps here as I am in hopes will secure the greater part if not all my guarantee bonds if nothing is got in North Carolinia.[3] But as matters of this nature depend upon contingencies after every precaution, it hangs over my head like a heavy

Cloud. I am determined to pursue it until I bring it to a crisis.[4] From this you will see the uncertainty of my return; but nothing shall detain me a moment longer than is necessary for the happiness of my family.[5] My affliction is aggravated from the distress it will give you, and I tremble for the effect it may have upon your health. It is impossible for you not to feel but I hope sorrow will not triumph. In every situation we have something to hope nor shall the posions [i.e., poisons] of fortune relax my exertions to render you happy to promote which is one of the greatest pleasures of my life.

Before I left home I wrote to Kosciuzko a letter concerning your and his Tickets. If he has written any answer follow his directions. I told him I would follow his directions in the matter. Brother Perry told me that there was but one Class of the parade Lottery. If so you'll get the ballance of your Tickets without loss of time.[6] If M[r] Samuel Vernon should want the Money I borrowed of him and would wish to have this discounted let it be done and I will replace it in your hands from hence. Write me on the subject. But if he dont want the money or it suits M[r] George Gibbs to pay it, and have a remittance made from hence to his Merchant in London, in either of those cases you will draw the ballance from the Lottery and do with it as you please.[7]

By Capt Philips I have sent you the 7/2 lbs of best green powder Tea.[8] My reasons for sending you so much at once is, I have it at the wholesale price and that I think is low being one dollar & three quarters a pound.

I have this moment got a very agreeable piece of information from Mr [John] M[c]Queen which will take off a heavy part of my guarantee.[9] I am much less unhappy upon the business than I have been but I cannot feel easy until I am free from it. I have met with no Jerondoes Chairs or Pickles but perhaps I may by the next opportunity.[10] Give my love to M[r] [Francis] Brindley's family[,] to Mrs [Sarah Pope] Redwood and my compliments to all friends.[11] Yours aff   N GREENE

NB The South Carolinia people write their friends that the people of Newport [R.I.] are not sociable. I hope this charge wont lay against you. Try to shew them every mark of respect and attention.[12]

ALS (MiU-C).

1. If NG wrote CG on 18 August with "a full Account" of his financial situation vis-à-vis John Banks, the letter has not been found. In his letter to her of 17 August, above, he wrote only that he had "nothing new to communicate on Mr Banks's affairs." As seen at ibid., Perry was Perry Greene, one of NG's brothers.

2. Forsyth, one of Banks's business partners, was en route to Virginia, "in persuit" of Banks. (NG to Pettit, 15 August, above)

3. On NG's efforts to secure himself against the liability he had incurred as a guarantor for Banks, see, for example, NG to Collett, 8 August; NG to Pettit, 15 August; and NG to Tate, 17 August; all above, as well as NG to Lushington, before 28 August and 28 August, both below.

4. The matter of NG's liability as a guarantor for Banks was still unsettled at the time of

NG's death in June 1786, almost a year after he appealed unsuccessfully to Congress for financial relief. (See below, Rutledge to NG, 20 May 1786, and NG to Lee, 22 August 1785.)

5. NG returned home to Newport, R.I., in late November but was back in Charleston by the beginning of February 1785. (NG to Gibbons, 29 November 1784, and NG to Gibbs, 3 February 1785, both below)

6. On the lottery tickets, see Thaddeus Kosciuszko to NG, 14 July, above.

7. NG had borrowed $400 from Vernon. (NG to Gibbs, immediately below) CG's reply has not been found.

8. J. Phillips, captain of the sloop *Dove*, had reportedly arrived in Newport from South Carolina by 4 September. (*Newport Mercury*, 4 September)

9. The "agreeable piece of information" from John McQueen has not been found. For background, see Pettit to NG, 26 July, and Penman to NG, 12 August, both above. As seen in Penman to NG, 10 November, below, this information presumably did not turn out to be as agreeable as NG expected.

10. On the "Jerondoes Chairs or Pickles," see also NG to CG, 17 August.

11. On Francis Brinley, see below, Littlefield to NG, 11 December 1785. Sarah Pope Redwood (1742–1819) was the widow of the recently deceased William Redwood, a prosperous Newport merchant. His father, Abraham Redwood, was the founder of the Redwood Library. (Bertram Lippincott III, "Redwood Genealogy," unpublished manuscript, RNHi; *Newport Mercury*, 22 May)

12. Newport was a longtime summer destination for wealthy South Carolinians, three of whom are mentioned in NG's letters to Welcome Arnold and George Gibbs of 17 August, above. NG mentioned the South Carolina people in Newport again in a letter to CG of 8 September, below.

*   *   *

¶ [**TO GEORGE GIBBS**. From Charleston, S.C., 22 August 1784. NG's "prospects are mended with respect to Mr Banks affairs," but he is "still apprehensive of losses."[1] His stay in Charleston will be "much longer" than he planned.[2] Asks to hear from Gibbs "on the subject of remittance" from Charleston to "your Merchant in London for what you may have advanced for me." NG wants to "discharge" three debts: $400 "borrowed of Capt Sam Vernon if he wants the money if not let it lay, about 80 dollars to Mrs [Ficks?] & 50 to Mr John Townsend." The "two last" should not be paid until NG remits the amount of Gibbs's "advances" to the "Merchant, which will be in the beginning of Winter," as per their agreement. Asks to hear from Gibbs "as soon as possible."[3] ADfS (MiU-C) 1 p.]

1. The matter of NG's liability as guarantor for John Banks was still unsettled at the time of NG's death, almost a year after he appealed to Congress for financial relief in August 1785. (See note at NG to Collett, 8 August, above, and NG to Lee, 22 August 1785, below.)

2. NG returned home to Newport, R.I., in late November. (NG to Gibbons, 29 November, below)

3. It was not until the following winter, when he returned to Charleston, that NG read Gibbs's "letter of last summer," which has not been found. (NG to Gibbs, 3 February 1785, below)

¶ [**FROM FRANCIS TATE**, "Georgia," 24 August 1784. He is "extremely Sorry" that he cannot "wait on" NG "immediately" about the business NG mentioned in the letter he received the previous day.[1] It would be "useless" to do anything now, unless Mr. [John] Banks or Maj. [Robert] Forsyth were present, as it is "Clear" from NG's "account of the sum due" that Tate has not been given all of the credits that are due him. When a "settlement Can be effected" by either Forsyth or Banks, Tate will "wait on" NG at Charleston, S.C., or another place of NG's choosing. Tate has "disposed of" his property in Virginia "on a long Credit," but when the amount he owes the "Concern" is settled, he will "have the debt Secured to them by some means or other." He adds that the manner in which he has been "harrass'd" for a debt he "had no hand in Contracting has put it intirely out of my power to attempt any business on my own Account since Jany last[;] this has rendered impossible for me to make payments which otherwise I should have done some time ago." He thanks NG for the "obliging offer to Serve me in my affairs which are realy in a bad way, but I hope I shall be able to extricate myself without Troubling You with Them." RCS (NcD) 3 pp.]

1. See NG to Tate, 17 August, above.

¶ [FROM THE MARQUIS DE LAFAYETTE, Mount Vernon, Va., 25 August 1784. He was " 'much mortified,' " after arriving in New York, to learn that NG " 'had sailed to South Carolina.' "[1] Adds: " 'While I am enjoying the Happy light of this Beloved Country, where Confusion and destruction have given way to Peace and Plenty, while I am happy in seeing again my numerous friends and my dear Brother Officers, what pleasure it will be for me to embrace my Good Friend, General Greene.' "[2] Lafayette now has only " 'the very agreeable business to visit these States and their inhabitants.' " He would have come a year sooner had not " 'American concerns' " kept him in Europe.[3] He reports on NG's business in Bordeaux, France, and sends compliments to friends in Charleston, S.C.[4] Concludes the letter by reporting the opening of four ports in France " 'to favour American Commerce' " and the reduction of duties on American goods. As this information is contained in letters from the French " 'Administration,' " Lafayette asks NG not to print this news until the letters have been forwarded.[5] Catalog Extract (Chapel Hill Rare Books, Catalog #100 [November 1995]) 2 pp.]

1. Lafayette arrived in New York at the beginning of August and traveled from there by land to Washington's Mount Vernon home, stopping along the way for receptions and honors in New Jersey and Philadelphia. (Idzerda, *Lafayette Papers*, 5: 232–38) He reached Mount Vernon on 17 August. (Washington, *Papers*, Confederation Series, 2: 48) After a visit of about two weeks there, he set off for Baltimore, Philadelphia, and New York before traveling to the "Territory of the Six Nations" and a meeting with representatives of Indian tribes in early October. Before sailing back to France in December, he also spent several weeks in the northeastern states—at Hartford, Conn., Albany, N.Y., and Boston, Mass.—and made return trips to Philadelphia and Virginia before calling on Washington again at Mount Vernon. (On his second visit to Mount Vernon, see note at NG to Carrington, 10 November, below.) In December, Lafayette addressed Congress, which had offered him an affectionate tribute in a resolution of 9 December. (On Lafayette's 1784 visit to the United States, see especially Idzerda, *Lafayette Papers*, 5: xxiv–xxv, 233–90.)

2. NG saw Lafayette in New York in December, shortly before Lafayette's return to France. There is no mention of this meeting in any of NG's known correspondence, but Lafayette wrote Washington from his ship in New York harbor on 21 December that NG had traveled from Hartford to see him and that "I Had the pleasure to Spend Some days with Him." (Washington, *Papers*, Confederation Series, 2: 227) The *Newport Mercury* of 25 December noted that NG had returned there "from New York" the previous Thursday [23 December] and that Lafayette had "sailed from New York for France" the previous Wednesday. Lafayette also visited Newport, R.I., in October, at least in part to pay his respects to CG. Arriving by water from Providence on the evening of 24 October, he was

"waited upon by the Mayor, Aldermen, and several other of the principal Gentlemen" and was afterward "conducted" to "the House of the Hon. Major-General Greene, where he lodged that night." He left the "next Morning about 11 o'clock" to return to Boston by way of Providence. According to a report in the *Newport Mercury*, Lafayette's visit to Newport was "unexpected." (*Newport Mercury*, 30 October)

3. The "American concerns" to which Lafayette referred included his successful efforts to persuade the French government to adopt policies beneficial to American trade. (Idzerda, *Lafayette Papers*, 5: 109–10) He had also been active on behalf of the Society of the Cincinnati in France. (See above, Washington to NG, 27 March.)

4. NG's "business in Bordeaux" involved his cousin Griffin Greene's efforts to sell the vessel *Flora*. (See, for example, Griffin Greene to NG, 12 June, above.)

5. The letters from France were undoubtedly some that Robert Morris presented to Congress on 30 September, noting that Lafayette's "unexampled Attention to every American Interest . . . cannot fail to excite the strongest Emotions in his favor." (Idzerda, *Lafayette Papers*, 5: 254–55)

¶ [TO RICHARD LUSHINGTON. "At Major [Robert] Forsyths," [Charleston, S.C.,] "Saturday" [28 August 1784?].[1] NG wants to see him "on some business" regarding "your speculation in Charleston with John Banks[,] Robert Forsyth and others."[2] NG "guaranteed those debts" while Banks was "contractor for the Army," and as the bonds are "still unsatisfied," NG now calls upon "the part[n]ers for Counter security in case I should suffer any loss. This you will find to be your safest and best Mode and the only thing that can save you from a suit as a common partner and held responsible for the whole of the debts unpaid."[3] ALS (GU) 2 pp.]

1. As seen at NG's letter to him of 26 June 1782, above (vol. 11: 373 and n), Lushington, a former militia officer, was a Charleston merchant. The editors believe this letter preceded the one of 28 August, immediately below; 28 August was a Saturday.

2. On the "Charleston speculation," as NG termed it in the next letter, see Forsyth to NG, 18 June, above.

3. See also the letter immediately below.

¶ [TO RICHARD LUSHINGTON. From Charleston, S.C., 28 August 1784.[1] NG encloses a copy of Lushington's "original agreement in the Charleston speculation," by which Lushington is "jointly and severally bound."[2] Adds: "It is unnecessary to make any comment upon the subject. No man can be firmer bound to all the consequences than you are. It is not your misfortune that I became a guarantee for the Company which never would have happened but from their being contractors for [the] army, it is mine to be perplexed with the affair."[3] Lushington "was bound originally," and "nothing could release" him but "the payment of the compan[y's] debts for the speculation or getting discharges from the original Creditors. All I want is not to suffer. You see your situation and if you act wisely you will do what I recommended." NG's role as "guarantee" puts Lushington "neither in a worse or better situation as to the final claims of the original Creditors."[4] ALS (Joseph Rubinfine, 1991) 2 pp.]

1. The editors believe this letter was written after the meeting with Lushington that NG requested in the letter immediately above.

2. On the "Charleston speculation," see also the preceding letter and Forsyth to NG, 18 June, above. The agreement has not been found.

3. On NG's role as a guarantor for the firm of Hunter, Banks & Company, see vol. 12:

308–9n, and Agreement between Hunter, Banks & Company, NG, and Newcomen and Collett, 8 April 1783 (ibid., p. 591 and n), both above; NG to Lee, 22 August 1785, below.

4. NG wrote Robert Forsyth on 2 October, below: "Desire Mr Rutledge to press Lushington to an agreement or bring forward the Action if he continues to refuse to give a bond of indemnity." (See also NG to Hugh Rutledge, 2 October, below.)

* * *

To William Gibbons, Jr.[1]

Dear Sir   Charleston [S.C.] Augt 29th 1784

Your letter of the 17th I have had the pleasure to receive.[2] I have made enquiry respecting the negroes and find good judges are of opinion that they are a good gang tho many are small as you write. It is certain they were not the refuse tho they may not be equal to some gangs.[3] I have no doubt you have done the best you could for me, tho I was in hopes the Crop would have amounted to two hundred and fifty barrels.[4] I am much obliged to Major Pearce for supplying you with Provisions. And wish to have cash or good bills on London for the ballance of such parts of the Crop as he may take being obliged to remit a considerable sum there this Winter. Sell the crop if you can to be delivered at the landing on the place.[5]

Planters in this Country think oxen better than horses to beat out Rice tho slower in the business are more profitable in the end. If they are so, you will buy oxen, instead of horses but of this I am no judge, and confide implicitly in you; and therefore leave you at full liberty to purchase which you please, persuaded you will do the best for me.

I thank you for the precaution you took to prevent Mr Gibbons from getting possession of part of my property; and I wish you to forward me the title by the first safe conveyance. And I hope Mr Stark will have them so worded as to prevent Mr Gibbons from prosecuting his ungenerous intention.[6]

You will take care to have the Negroes well clothed and properly fed for all which you must draw upon the Crop having no other resource and being hard pressed to accommodate payments to the demands upon me. I can but hope your Crop will yet prove larger than you expect tho I would not wish to be deceived.[7] It is my intention to spend next winter with you and I want to return to Rhode Island soon which I believe will induce me to pospone my visit to Georgia until then; but I am not fully determined yet.[8]

I have been in much perplexity with the affairs of the Contractors of the Army. Thier funds being unequal to the business I was obliged to strengthen their credit and guarantee some of their Debts from which I have apprehended great loss; nor am I yet without my fears, tho the Gentlemen of the Bar, tell me I am in no danger of finally loosing any thing.[9]

I dont wish to have my Negroes worked too hard; but cannot they get out considerable lumber and make up the Pitch Knots without injury to other business in the course of the Winter? I am dear Sir Your most Obedt hum Ser   N GREENE

ALS (MHi).

1. Gibbons, whom NG called his "attorney in Georgia," was handling affairs related to NG's plantation there. (See above, NG to Penman, 25 October 1783, and vol. 12: 475–76n.)

2. This letter has not been found.

3. Fifty-eight slaves, purchased for NG from the firm of Gervais & Owen, had been sent to Roger Parker Saunders and "forwarded" by him to Gibbons. (Saunders to NG, 29 May, above) In reply to a question that Saunders had raised about the "[di]vision of" these slaves among NG, Thomas Ferguson, and himself, Gervais & Owen assured Saunders in a letter of 7 September that "the greatest exactness & propriety was observed in making [*damaged*] the Division, because it had been suggested that [slaves] allotted to him [i.e., NG] were the refuse of a Gang." Instead, they asserted, the slaves were divided into lots by families "as nearly as possible," and NG's "division" was "Superior in Value." (MiU-C)

4. As seen in NG's letter to Dennis De Berdt of 9 March 1785, below, the rice crops on both of his plantations fell "far short of" expectations.

5. William Pierce, Jr., NG's former aide, was acting as a broker for NG's rice crop and was supplying NG's plantation in Georgia with necessary provisions, including corn. NG later obtained a credit from Pierce, using an overestimated value for his fall rice crop. (See below, Pierce to NG, 13 May 1785, and NG to Pierce, 17 May 1785.)

6. On the claim of William Gibbons, Sr., to part of NG's Mulberry Grove property in Georgia, see NG's letter to him of 8 March 1785 and Pendleton to NG, 23 September 1785, both below.

7. On the disappointing rice crop that year, see notes 4 and 5, above.

8. NG, who was back in Newport, R.I., by late November, returned to the South in January 1785 and soon afterward visited Georgia. (See NG to CG, 14 April 1785, below.)

9. For background, see, for example, NG to Pettit, 15 August, above.

To George Washington

Dear Sir   Charleston [S.C.] Augt 29th 1784

My ill health and the distressing situation of my private affairs for some time past has claimed too much of my Attention to afford me either time or inclination to attend to any thing else. At the time of the meeting of the Cincinnati in Philadelphia I had a dangerous and dis-agree[able] pain in my breast. It had hung about me then upwards of two months; but by the use of balsam of fur [i.e., fir] soon after I wrote you from Newport I got better of it.[1] And the very day that Col° Ward returned from the Meeting I set sail for Philadelphia upon some matters very interesting to my Southern affairs and was in hopes to have arrivd in time to have had the pleasure of seeing you.[2] On my return from Philadelphia[,] and my stay was short[,] I got information that my fortune was much exposed from the situation of sundry debts which I had guaranteed for the Contractors of the Southern Army while I had the command in this Country. The amount of the debts and the situation of the Contractors affairs made it seriously alarming and brought me to this Country without a moments hesitation notwithstanding the season and climate. I have been under great apprehensions of heavy losses; but I have now got matters in so happy a train that I have little to fear but from partial inconveniencies. It has given me much pain and preyed heavily upon my spirits.[3] My stay I expected would have been short in this Country; but from the peculiar situation of my concerns it will be protracted to a much greater length than I wish or expected.[4]

After the war I was in hopes of repose, but fortune will not allow me what I most wish for. Some good natured Acts done for individuals and the low state of public credit [of] this Country has drawn me into many inconveniencies and some heavy losses. By Baron Glaubeck whom Congress noticed for his conduct in Morgans affair. I expect to loose a thousand dollars having endorsed his bills and had them to settle.[5] And if I suffer no loss by the Contractors; the uncertainty will hang over me like a Cloud until the whole affair is closed.[6]

While I feel much for my self I feel for you. You have had your troubles since you left public life. The clamour raised against the Cincinnati was far more extensive than I expected. I had no conception that it was so universal. I thought it had been confined to New England alone, but I found afterwards our Ministers abroad and all the Inhabitants in general throughout the United States were opposed to the order.[7] I am happy you did not listen to my advice.[8] The measures you took seemed to silence all jealosies on the subject; but I wish the seeds of discontent may not break out under some other form.[9]

However, it is hardly to be expected that perfect tranquility can return at once after so great a revolution: where the Minds of the people have been so long accustomed to conflicts and subjects of agitation. In this Country [i.e., the South] many discontents prevail; Committees are formed and correspondences going on, if not of a treasonable nature highly derogatory to the dignity of Government as well as subversive of the tranquility of the people. And I wish they may not break out into acts of violence and open rebellion against the Authority of the State.[10] Nor am I without some apprehensions that the situation of our public credit at home and abroad and the general discontent of the public creditors may plunge us into new troubles.[11] The obstinacy of Rhode Island and the tardiness of some other States seem to presage more Mischief.[12] However I can but hope the good sense of the populace will correct our policy in time to avoid new convulsions. But many people secretly wish that every State should be completely independant; and that as soon as our public debts are liquidated that Congress should be no more. A plan that would be as fatal to our interest at home as ruinous to it abroad.

I see by the Northern Papers that the Marquis de la Fyette had arrived at New York and set out for Mount Vernon [Va.]. Doubtless you will have a happy meeting. "It will be the feast of reason and the flow of soul."[13] Present him my respectful compliments of congratulations upon his safe arrival in America and my affectionate regards to Mrs [Martha] Washington. I am dear Sir with esteem & affection Your Most Obed humble Ser[t]   NATH GREENE

ALS (Washington Papers: DLC).

1. Washington had urged NG to attend the general meeting of the Society of the Cincinnati in Philadelphia at the beginning of May. (Washington to NG, 28 December 1783, and 20 March 1784, both above) NG, who was unable to be at the meeting because of ill health, had written to Washington about his malady on 6 May, above.

2. Samuel Ward, Jr., had been the sole delegate from Rhode Island at the general meeting of the Society of the Cincinnati. NG's trip to Philadelphia on personal business took place in late May and early June. (See note at NG to Washington, 6 May, above.) On the "Southern affairs" that he dealt with there, see especially his letters to Robert Morris, 5 June, and Roger Parker Saunders, 6 June, above.

3. For background on NG's decision to travel to South Carolina at this time, see especially Saunders to NG, 26 May; Pettit to NG, 10 June; Forsyth to NG, 18 June; and NG's letters to Charles Pettit of 23 June and 15 August, above. Even after appealing to Congress for financial relief in August 1785, NG still had not extricated himself from the financial problems resulting from his guarantee of debts owed by army contractors Hunter, Banks & Company by the time of his death in June 1786. (See below, NG to Lee, 22 August 1785, and Rutledge to NG, 20 May 1786.)

4. NG had been in Charleston since 1 August. He left South Carolina in late September, traveling first to North Carolina in the hope of confronting John Banks, the former army contractor, and then to Virginia. He arrived home in Newport, R.I., in late November. (See note at NG to Hazlehurst, 26 June, above, and NG's letters to Robert Forsyth, 2 October, and Williams Gibbons, 29 November, below.)

5. In addition to the debts he had guaranteed for Hunter, Banks & Company in the spring of 1783, NG's ill-fated, "good natured Acts" included an advance of money to Baron Glaubeck when Glaubeck, whom he later found to be "a Villian and an imposter," left the army. (See especially NG to Glaubeck, 16 February 1783 [vol. 12: 449], and NG to Morris, 3 June 1783, both above. On Glaubeck's role in the battle of Cowpens and the brevet rank of captain that Congress had given him, see Gen. Daniel Morgan's report to NG of 19 January 1781, above [vol. 7: 155, 161n].)

6. As seen in note 3, above, NG's "uncertainty" in these matters continued for the rest of his life.

7. NG had informed Washington about the strong protests against the Society of the Cincinnati in New England. (NG to Washington, 6 May) Gov. Benjamin Guerard of South Carolina was also a harsh critic of the society, and one of the most vocal opponents, Aedanus Burke, was also a South Carolinian. (Knox to NG, 10 April 1784, and Flagg to NG, 17 October 1783, both above) Members of the society encountered opposition when they ran for office in Virginia in the spring of 1784, and, historian Minor Myers has written that American diplomats in Europe, including John Jay, John Adams, and Benjamin Franklin, "were almost uniformly critical of the society." (Myers, *Liberty Without Anarchy*, pp. 52–55; quote from p. 53)

8. In his letter of 6 May, NG had advised Washington that the society should not make any significant changes in its "institution" at the general meeting. As noted there, the delegates did alter the organization considerably.

9. In ibid., NG expressed an opinion that if public attention were not as focused against

the Cincinnati, it might be directed more favorably to issues such as the commutation of officers' retirement pay.

10. NG himself was the recipient of one such "correspondence." (See note at Cruden to NG, 8 June, above.)

11. On the "situation of our public credit at home and abroad," see Morris to NG, 19 May, above.

12. Rhode Island had rejected the federal impost. (See above, NG to Morris, 3 July.)

13. On the Marquis de Lafayette's visit to the United States, see his letter to NG of 25 August, above. The quote is from Alexander Pope. (See note at Murray to NG, 30 March, above.)

*   *   *

¶ [FROM JAMES MILLIGAN, Comptrollers Office, Philadelphia, 30 August 1784. Encloses copies of "an Arrangement of the Bills of Exchange" that NG drew while he "Commanded the Southern Army" and of a "General Statement" of NG's account "during that period, as Stated upon examination at the Treasury."[1] NG appears to owe about $6,229. Milligan adds: "Much labour and pain have been exerted in Arrang[ing] and Stating these Accounts, and I believ[e] they are as accurately done, as the nature of the materials presented would admit of." He believes it would be "useful and satisfactory," before the accounts are "finally passed and Entered in the Treasury Books," to let NG examine "the whole," point out "Errors, if there are any," and make any objections he may have "to this mode of Statement."[2] "Subjoined" to the "General State" are "a Number of Notes and observations" regarding orders drawn by NG "for monies of the Old and new Emissions, and Orders on the States of Maryland and Virginia, for all which the parties receiving are held Accountable."[3] A "State of the old Emissions received at Philadelphia," when NG was on his "way to the Southward," is also appended.[4] RCS (MiU-C) 2 pp.]

1. The enclosures have not been found. (See, however, NG's reply to Milligan, dated 6 February 1785, below.)

2. It is not known how the issue of these expenses was resolved. As seen in the note at NG to Mifflin, 3 November 1783, above, Congress had previously approved some of the expenses—for his own travel and the maintenance of his military family—that NG incurred as Southern Army commander.

3. The "Notes and observations" have not been found.

4. On the money that NG received at Philadelphia, see above, NG to Samuel Huntington, 3 November 1780 (vol. 6: 461 and n).

*   *   *

To An Unknown Person[1]

[Charleston, S.C., August 1784?][2]

"Since my arrival here I have written you nothing but the most melancholy accounts.[3] I wish I had less reason than I have to dwell on the same subject still. However, I am not as apprehensive as I have been. But it is a painful situation, to be held responsible for heavy debts, subject to all contingencies, and have your redress to look for from different people, and from various kinds of property. This will be my situation for some time to come.[4] The gentlemen of the bar tell me I am safe, yet I cannot feel easy, nor ever shall, until I get entirely disengaged from this business. My wishes are very strong to be helpful to all branches of the family, and if I am not distressed in the infancy of my affairs, I hope I shall have it in my power to serve you. But at present I seem to be in the dark; nay, I am in deep distress, and know not how to accommodate payments to the many demands upon me. I shall not return to the northward until I can get myself in a securer situation, respecting these guarantees.[5] My own matters would be easy, were I not perplexed with other people's."

Excerpt, printed in Johnson, *Greene*, 2: 412–13.

1. Although the recipient of this letter is not identified, the editors believe, from internal evidence, that it may have been NG's brother Jacob Greene.

2. The place and date have been conjectured from the contents. This letter was most likely written while NG was in Charleston during the summer of 1784, and in writing to William Gibbons, Jr., on 29 August, above, NG used a phrase—"The gentlemen of the bar tell me I am safe"—that is identical to wording in this letter.

3. If Jacob Greene was the recipient of this letter, NG had indeed written him a "melancholy account" of his financial situation on 12 August, above.

4. In ibid., NG had termed it "truly afflicting! to be reduced from independence to want, and from the power of obliging my friends, to a situation claiming their aid."

5. During his lifetime, NG was unable to "get entirely disengaged" from the problems associated with his guarantee of debts for army contractors John Banks et al. (See especially the notes at NG to Collett, 8 August, above, and at Pendleton to NG, 10 November, below.) NG returned "to the northward" in November.

To Catharine Littlefield Greene

Dear Caty   Charleston [S.C.] Sept 8th 1784

I wish I had more welcome news to write than I have but I am still much perplexed with this business of the Contractors.[1] However I am getting every thing into my hands necessary for my security which can be got hold of; and the Gentleman of the barr tells me I am ⟨in⟩ no danger of loosing. However I am far from feeling easy upon the matter. I can get no news from Virginia. It is more difficult to get intelligence from Virginia than from London. If matters go well there I am in hopes to get rid of the business without loss or much more trouble. But Banks has been such a peculiar curse to me that I am almost led to beleive that Providence has designed him for a scourge for some of my evil deeds. That he is an instrument of the Devil is certain and tho he may not act from Authority under Providence it amounts to the same thing for he is permitted to torment Mankind. He has got hundreds into difficulties and some families will be inevitably ruined. He is cursed from Dan to Barsheba and I verily believe if I was to meet him I should put him to death.[2] He is the greatest Monster and most finished vilian that this age has produced. There is no crime but murder that he has not committed. Even forgery has not escaped him. It is after all but a poor consolation to rail at such a rascal and this the only return you can have for all the painful moments he causes.

I begin to feel anxious about the little Girls. We must contrive to get a master in the family. Desire Billy to write to Doctor Stiles to recommend a good young Man and get his terms.[3] Methinks this mode will be little more expensive than boarding the Girls abroad or sending them to school and they will be better taught at home, than from home, and thier morals and manners much more attended to. What think you my dear. Give me your opinion. I am so much in the dark as to the ultimate situation of matters here that I can fix upon nothing at all. It will be necessary on my return to fix upon our final plan of life.[4] In this you have an equal voice, our happiness must be the same or neither will be satisfactory. I confess I am much divided in my own Mind. On my return you shall have an exact state of all our prospects and we will unite our wishes in forming a decision. Interest demands attention but without health where is its value. Here is the Labyrinth in which we are placed. I am not anxious to be rich, but wish to be independant. For I agree perfectly with Lord Littleton that he that cannot pay his Taylors bill is a dependent charactor even tho a Lord.[5] To have a decent income is much to be wished; but to be free from debt more so. I never owned so much property as now, and yet never felt so poor and unhappy. But if I was free from others peoples affairs I should have little to fear. The people here are very polite and my own matters go on well. Write me how you are supplyed with Money and if you are in want of any thing. The South Carolinia people say they admire Newport but the people are unsocial. When these letters came away you were not in town. Pray shew them all the respect and attention in your power.[6] You must hire or buy such Servants as you want. Lucy and Charles are with me yet. I have got no news from Lucy's Master. If Ham is wanted at home take him.[7] Accomodate your self as well as you can. Capt Shubrick is very poorly. Give my love to Mrs Shubrick. I am sorry I am not at home to enjoy her society.[8] Remember me to all friends.   ⟨N GREENE⟩

You see I have written in haste for I have posponed writing to the last Moment. Did you get the Rice and Tea I sent you and also respecting the bed furniture[:] If it suits dont send it back tho too dear.[9]

AL (MiU-C). The text in angle brackets was taken from a Foster Transcript (RHi.).

1. NG had been in Charleston since the beginning of August on the "business of the Contractors"—John Banks and his partners, for whom he had guaranteed some unpaid debts. For other recent letters on this subject, see especially NG to Collett, 8 August; NG to Jacob Greene, 12 August; and NG to Pettit, 15 August, all above. On the guarantee, see above, vol. 12: 308–9n; Agreement between Hunter, Banks and Company, NG,

and Newcomen and Collett, 8 April 1783 (ibid., p. 591 and n); and below, NG to Lee, 22 August 1785.

2. Dan and Beersheba were near the northern and southern extremities of biblical Israel. (*Columbia Encyc.*) NG set out for North Carolina and Virginia soon afterward in the hope of confronting Banks, but he learned at Washington, N.C., that Banks had recently died there. (NG to Rutledge, after 30 September, below)

3. "Billy" was William Littlefield, CG's brother; NG's friend Ezra Stiles, formerly a Congregational minister in Newport, R.I., was the president of Yale College. CG's reply has not been found, but Stiles did find a tutor for the children shortly before NG took his family to live on Mulberry Grove plantation, Ga. (NG to Wadsworth, 1 October 1785, below)

4. As seen in the preceding note, NG's "final plan of life" included settling his family on Mulberry Grove plantation.

5. Sir Thomas Littleton's fifteenth-century work *Tenures* was "the standard text on property law" at this time. (*Columbia Encyc.*)

6. On the South Carolinians in Newport, R.I., see also NG to CG, 21 August, above. It is not clear what NG meant by "these letters."

7. These were all presumably African-American servants. On Lucy and Ham, see NG to CG, 17 August, above.

8. On Thomas Shubrick's illness and the visit of his wife, the former Mary Branford, to Newport, see also Pendleton to NG, second letter of 10 July, above.

9. See above, NG to CG, 17 and 21 August. NG wrote to CG again on 10 September, below.

*   *   *

¶ [FROM WILLIAM PIERCE, JR., Savannah, Ga., 8 September 1784. As he had been on a trip to St. Augustine [East Florida], he only received NG's letter [not found] "yesterday." Cannot give "much information about [John] Ferrie's property" yet but believes he can soon. Thinks the land that Ferrie "had of Maj[r] [Richard] Call" is "made over to a M[r] [Leonard?] Cecil here."[1] Will send more information "hereafter."[2] Pierce's wife sends "her particular respects." RCS (MiU-C) 2 pp.]

1. For background, see above, Forsyth to NG, 18 June; NG to Collett, 8 August; and NG to Pettit, 15 August.

2. For more about efforts to attach property belonging to Ferrie, see note at Pierce to NG, 24 September, below.

*   *   *

To Pierce Butler[1]

Dear Sir   Charleston [S.C.] Sept 9th 1784

Comodore Gillon will write you fully on a plan of business which he and I have in contemplation; and in which we wish to interest you. My right in Cumberland Island which is to be the basis of the business is at present precarious. I have a mortgage which can be foreclosed after the first of December, if the first payments are not Made, and there is little probability of their being made, from the ruinous situation of M[r] John Banks's affairs, from whom I took the Mortgage, from being bound to M[r] [John] McQueen for the purchace Money. The Comodore will give you a full history of the plan and you will see that it is extensive and he thinks may be made profitable.[2] Public affairs here have been in some confusion, Mobs and riots have prevailed, and factions and disputes still continues; but more moderate than they have been.[3] General [Christopher] Gadsden and the Comodore are engaged in a long and abusive paper war. They are both wrong. General Gadsden began and is on this account blameable. Their strictures on each other are severe and generally illiberal.[4] Congressional measures are much the same as when you left America except the business of finance which is put into Commision and M[r] Morris retires.[5] Rhode Island still continues to oppose the five per Cent act and have rejected every other matter recommended by Congress.[6] In a word our public affairs are not in my opinion in the most promising train. Public credit is at a low ebb, Public creditors much discontented and no plan to be found on which they can lean with confidence and security. However taxes are going on briskly, from which, and the State imposts, considerable revenue will be collected, to strengthen the hands of Government.

I had the pleasure to see Mrs [Mary Middleton] Butler a few day[s] ago, who was well and the rest of the family. I shall be happy to hear from you with such observations upon the politicks and commerce of Europe as you may think proper to favor me with.[7] Crops of Rice are promising if not injured by the heavy rains which prevail now.[8] Indigo has suffered greatly upon the Rivers. Most of the Crops are lost upon the Congaree Wataree and Santee. Those Rivers have been higher than was ever known at this season. I am dear Sir with esteem & regard Your Most obedient humble Ser[t]   NATH GREENE

ALS (PHi).
1. Butler (1744–1822), once an Irish officer in the British army, had married Mary Middleton, a South Carolina heiress, during a tour of duty in the colonies and had settled in South Carolina before the war. Through his advantageous marriage and successful business dealings, he became one of the largest landowners in South Carolina and eventually "one of the wealthiest planters in the United States." During the war he served as South Carolina's adjutant general and in various other capacities. Although he held the rank of brigadier general in the South Carolina militia, he preferred to be known by his British army rank of "Major." Butler was in England at this time, having traveled there in April to "secure a personal loan and to obtain a minister for St. Michael Parish." He returned to the United States during the fall of 1785. (*Biog. Directory of S.C. House*, 3: 108–13; see also Pendleton to NG, 30 January, above.)
2. On NG's "right in Cumberland Island," Ga., and the mortgage he had taken from Banks in conjunction with it, see note at Hyrne to Clay, 25 November 1783, above, and NG to Bowman, immediately below. On Alexander Gillon, who had served in the South Carolina State Navy during the war, see vol. 12: 602–3n, above. NG later asked other individuals to join him in financing the development of the island's timber-rich resources. (See, for example, NG to Wadsworth, 3 February 1785, below.) Butler replied to NG on 23 December, below.

3. See note at Pendleton to NG, second letter of 10 July, above, and William Washington to NG, 8 July, above.

4. On Gillon's role in the Marine Anti-Britannic Society at Charleston, see note at Pendleton to NG, second letter of 10 July. His "fiery newspaper duel" with Gadsden, who "spoke for the Nabobs at this time," is discussed in Walsh, *Sons of Liberty*, p. 116. (See also Burke to NG, 27 November 1785, below.)

5. On Robert Morris's departure from the post of superintendent of finance and the appointment of a Board of Treasury to replace him, see note at NG to Morris, 13 November, below.

6. Rhode Island's rejection of the 1783 impost proposal is discussed at NG to Morris, 3 July, above.

7. See Butler to NG, 23 December.

8. NG's 1784 crops fell short of his expectations. (NG to Gibbs, 3 February 1785, below)

*   *   *

¶ [TO JOHN BOWMAN. From Charleston, S.C., 10 September 1784. NG has been told that Bowman has "an interest in Cumberland Island in Georgia."[1] He has also heard that "A party of Refugees to the number of two or three hundred . . . are cutting down the timber, and four or five Vessels are loading with it."[2] Adds: "If some measures are not immediately taken to put a stop to these depredations the Island will soon be rendered of little value."[3] NG has "a Mortgage of one half of the Island" and has "too much reason to believe" he will be "obliged to pay the purchace and hold the property."[4] He wishes, "in conjunction with the owners of the other half to take some measures without loss of time for the preservation of the Timber." If Bowman has any business in Charleston, NG would be happy to see him "on the subject."[5] NG is staying at Mr. [Thomas?] Ferguson's. ALS (MiU-C) 2 pp.]

1. Bowman (1746–1807), a South Carolina planter, owned extensive properties along and near the Santee River. (*Biog. Directory of S.C. House*, 3: 82–83) Through marriage to Sabina Lynch, daughter of wealthy landowner Thomas Lynch, Bowman, a lawyer, had also become the administrator of Lynch's estate, which included a large, undivided half-share of properties on Cumberland Island. (Bullard, *Cumberland Island*, p. 75) As noted at Hyrne to Clay, 26 November 1783, above, NG came to own the other undivided half-share. He visited Cumberland Island during his next trip to the South and described the island and its timber-rich resources in a letter to the Marquis de Barbé-Marbois of 15 April 1785, below.

2. Cumberland Island was close to East Florida, a former British colony that had been ceded to Spain in the recent peace treaty. (See NG to Zéspedes, 26 March 1785, below.) After the evacuation of Charleston and the end of hostilities in America, Loyalist refugees from South Carolina and Georgia had fled to East Florida in large numbers.

3. NG also wrote to John Houstoun, the governor of Georgia, to request intervention in this matter. (The letter is below, dated 12 September.)

4. On the "Mortgage," see note at Hyrne to Clay, 26 November 1783.

5. Bowman apparently met with NG to discuss this matter the following day. (See Bowman to NG, 12 September, below.)

*   *   *

To Catharine Littlefield Greene

Dear Caty Charleston [S.C.] Sept 10th 1784

I wrote you by Capt Fry a few days past who was to go by the way of New York.[1] Whether those or this letter will get to you first is uncertain. In those letters by Capt Fry I gave a short state of matters which oblige my stay in this Country. I wish my prospects were more promising for a speedy return. [John] Banks writes M^r [James] Hunter his former partner that his brother [Henry Banks] has made an arrangement with Mr [E. John] Collette to his satisfaction and that he was gone to England; but I can give but little credit to it, he is such a monstrous liar and besides Mr Collette must have written me, if this had taken place. I am rather inclind to think Mr Banks wants to slaken my indeavors to get hold of his property here and coming from England. And writes Mr Hunter that Mr Collette was settled with on that account. But I shall be duped by no such artifice. I am still in hopes to free my self from this affair without loss. If Collette is really settled with[,] the matter will be easy. I expect accounts hourly from Virginia on the subject.[2] In the mean time I am laying hold of every circumstance to secure my self here. I have got Mortgages and suits which the Gentlemen of the Law say cannot fail, to the full amount of all I am bound for and more.[3] It is vexatious to be perplexed with other peoples affairs and had not my public situation imposed the necessity I could never forgive my self. And even under that if I could have foreseen the risque and difficulty I should have let matters [go?] to ruin rather than ruin my self.[4] If I get clear, it will be a lesson to be careful how I engage for others in future. But besides the vexation attending the business upon the subject of losses, it is cruel to be so long from ones family. While my apprehensions were very great I felt this inconvenience light; but as my danger grows less, the other increases. And what makes it more painful to me, I cannot fix upon the happy moment for my return with any degree of certainty.[5] If my stay could be made agreeable by the politeness of the people I should be happy. I am commonly ingaged a week aforehand to dine.[6] But my mind being tortured with painful anxiety I have but little satisfaction from the civilities shewn me. However I am in pretty good health and have never been in the Country. Not that Charleston is free from disorders. The yellow fever and throat disorder prevails. Many dye and more lay dangerously ill. I dont go where it is and am little exposed to its malignant influence. Doctor Flagg is certainly courting a Widow Awlston, and I think will certainly marry her. The Widow is willing, the Parents are opposed to it, which I think the most likely circumstance to continue the Doctor steady in his attachment. If his conquest was too easy he might get out of [conceit?] of it. She is said [to] be a fine Woman, has a good fortune; but there are three ready made Children, and this is not a pleasing part of the inventory.[7]

Rachel Moore Allston Flagg, 1755?–1839; oil painting by Henry Benbridge
(Museum of Early Southern Decorative Arts, Old Salem, Inc.)

It is now almost two Months since we parted and no accounts from
you.[8] The time is long and the suspense painful. My love to the Children
and all friends. Yours aff   N GREENE

ALS (MiU-C).

1. NG's most recent letter to CG that has been found is that of 8 September, above.

2. For background, see especially NG to Collett, 8 August, above. Henry Banks had not
reached an agreement with Collett, and, as noted at ibid., Collett, to whom NG had guaranteed certain debts of Hunter and John Banks, was still seeking a settlement with NG
until just before NG's death. As seen by NG's letter to Hugh Rutledge, after 30 September,
below, NG traveled to North Carolina and Virginia in the hope of confronting Banks but
learned when he reached Washington, N.C., that Banks was "dead & buried."

3. On NG's efforts to "secure" himself, see above, his letters to Collett, 8 August; to Charles Pettit, 15 August; to Francis Tate, 17 August; and to Richard Lushington, before 28 August and 28 August, as well as Pierce to NG, 8 September, above, and 24 September, below.

4. See above, Forsyth to NG, 24 February; Agreement between Hunter, Banks and Company, NG, and Newcomen and Collett, 8 April 1783 [vol. 12: 591 and n]; and ibid., pp. 308–9n.

5. NG reached his home in Newport, R.I., in late November. (NG to Gibbons, 29 November, below)

6. On a separate page of his draft letter to George Gibbs of 22 August, above, NG listed his dining engagements for several days: "Pearsol Wednesday, Izard Thursday, Hugh Rutledge Saturday, Hext McCall Monday, Mr Jervey [Gervais] Fryday, Col [Lewis] Morris Wednesday."

7. CG's cousin Dr. Henry Collins Flagg married Mrs. Rachel Moore Allston (b. 1757) on 5 December 1784, despite her parents' opposition. She was the daughter of John Moore, a wealthy planter, and his wife, Elizabeth, and was the widow of Capt. Richard Allston, whom she had married in 1775. The children from Rachel Moore Allston's first marriage were Mary Allston (b. 1778), Washington Allston, the noted American painter (b. 1779); and William Allston (b. 1781). (*South-Carolina Gazette & General Advertiser*, 6 December; Flagg, *Genealogical Notes*, pp. 138, 143; *Biog. Directory of S.C. House*, 2: 471; John R. Welsh, "Washington Allston: Expatriate South Carolinian," *SCHGM* 67 [April 1966]: 84; see also NG to CG, 25 May 1785, below.)

8. On NG's departure from Newport, see note at his letter to Robert Hazlehurst of 26 June, above.

*　　　　*　　　　*

¶ [TO WILLIAM GIBBONS, JR. From Charleston, S.C., 12 September 1784. As in his letter to John Bowman of 10 September, above, NG expresses concern about the cutting of timber by refugees on Cumberland Island, Ga., of which NG expects to become a part owner.[1] NG has also written to the governor and "claimed the protection of the State." If "legal process is only necessary," he has "desird" the governor to "put it into the hands of his brother."[2] NG asks Gibbons to "put the business in some train for the preservation of our property" and to inform him as soon as possible what steps have been taken. Gibbons has not informed NG whether anyone else is planting at Mulberry Grove. He has been told that "the lower field was all planted." Inquires about the price of rice in Georgia, adding: "Most people think the difference of price betwixt this and Savannah will be greater than the freight. The first to market will be the highest."[3] NG wrote Gibbons "about a fortnight since in answer to your letter conserning horses."[4] ACyS (NcD) 4 pp.]

1. On NG's part-ownership of Cumberland Island, see note at Hyrne to Clay, 26 November 1783, above.

2. See NG to Houstoun, immediately below.

3. No reply has been found.

4. See NG to Gibbons, 29 August, above.

¶ [TO GOVERNOR JOHN HOUSTOUN OF GEORGIA.[1] From [Charleston, S.C.], 12 September 1784.[2] NG writes on behalf of Mr. Bowman and "others who hold an interest in Cumberland Island" regarding the "large number of Refugees said to amount to two or three hundred" who are purportedly "cutting down and shipping the Timber from that Island." If they are "permitted to proceed," the refugees will "soon strip" the island "of its most valuable prop-erty."[3] The owners "claim the protection of the State," but if Houstoun thinks "a procecution at common law only necessary," NG would like him to ask his brother "to bring such actions upon the occasion as may recover damages for what is past and prevent any future depredations."[4] The "business is of the highest importance" to the owners of the Island, "being a valuable interest with the Timber but of little or no value without it." NG asks for a reply "as early as possible."[5] ADfS (NcD) 3 pp.]

1. Houstoun (1744–96), elected governor in 1784, had previously been elected to that post in 1778. An early leader of the American independence movement in Georgia, he had also served as a delegate to Congress. (*DAB*; *Dictionary of Georgia Biography*, 1: 478–79)

2. The place was taken from other letters that NG wrote at this time.

3. See also NG to Bowman, 10 September, above. On Cumberland Island's timber-rich resources, see NG to Marbois, 15 April 1785, below.

4. Houstoun's brother William was a lawyer in Savannah. (Jones, *Sketches of Delegates from Georgia*, pp. 118–19) No evidence has been found that he became involved in this matter.

5. See Houstoun to NG, 12 November, below.

¶ [FROM JOHN BOWMAN. "Haddril's," S.C., 12 September 1784. "On a farther consideration of the Subject" that he and NG "conversed upon yester-day," Bowman proposes that "a Person be procured to go to Cumberland in the feigned character of a Refugee" to gather "Evidence respecting the Freebooters, the Names of the Vessels on board which Timber has or shall be shipped, & their destination." He and NG could then have the timber "attached" when it reached market. "A Person fit for such an Undertaking is not to be found every where," but because of his military connections, NG might be able to suggest someone who would "suit the purpose."[1] Bowman does not expect to have any "Redress by legal Measures within the State of Georgia, in its present Situation," and believes that "Nothing perhaps would sooner dislodge the gang in question than finding the fruit of their unlawful labors snatched from their Mouths." Bowman's and NG's "own Interest & the safety of the person to be employed, demand secrecy." Bowman adds: "Our Claim of the Protection of the State & Our desire that Suits be commenced against the Offenders can do no harm even should we execute the other scheme." RCS (MiU-C) 3 pp.]

1. See NG to Bowman, 10 September, above. No evidence has been found that the idea of sending an undercover investigator to Cumberland Island was implemented. In March 1785, Benjamin Eyre suggested that the timber, which had been cut under the auspices of a Philadelphia merchant, be impounded when it reached that city. (Eyre to NG, 7 March 1785, below)

¶ [TO GOVERNOR BENJAMIN GUERARD OF SOUTH CAROLINA. From Charleston, S.C., 19 September 1784. NG "addressed" him and the South Caro-lina legislature "last Spring in behalf of Colo Edward Fenwick of the british army" concerning "a contract," made between Capt. [William] Wilmot and Fenwick, and "confirmed" by NG, "for obtaining intelligence of the motions and intentions of the british forces while they were in possession of Charles-ton."[1] The "conditions of the contract" were specified in the papers enclosed in NG's previous letter, to which was appended NG's "recommendation on the subject."[2] Since he arrived in South Carolina, NG has received a letter from

Fenwick, which he encloses;[3] it contains a paragraph that "seemed to cancel all his claim upon the contract as having acted with the knowledge and consent of the british commander." Since writing the letter, Fenwick has arrived in Charleston in person and has "explained away" the paragraph, but NG feels "bound to lay the letter before the Legislature that they may judge for themselves from all the circumstances of the merit of" Fenwick's conduct. Fenwick alleges that "the british commander advised him to make his peace with his Country; but that he never had the most distant hint of the mode he adopted to effect it, either at the time or since." Fenwick "is here and subject to such interrogatives" as Guerard or the legislature "may think necessary for the discovery of truth or to do him justice."[4] ALS (ScCoAH) 4 pp.]

1. NG wrote Guerard about Fenwick on 30 March, above.

2. At least one of the papers enclosed with his letter to Guerard of 30 March was undoubtedly NG's certificate stating Fenwick's role as a spy for the Americans and NG's promise to petition the S.C. legislature to restore Fenwick's full rights as a citizen of the state after the war. It was written on 14 August 1782. The ACyS of that document, which is printed above (vol. 11: 545), bears the signed, but undated, notation: "A true copy from the original files of the papers in my possession" and is almost certainly the copy that NG enclosed with his letter to Guerard of 30 March, above.

3. Fenwick's letters to NG have not been found. The only extant letter from Fenwick to NG is dated 5 December 1785, below.

4. On 24 January 1785, Guerard presented some "letters" to the Assembly that NG had sent him during "his late visit" to Charleston. In them, NG "recommended a delicate mention of Mr. Fenwicke's predicament and Situation." Guerard agreed that the "Nature of the Subject unfolded in the Letters will naturally point Out the Propriety of the recommendation." (S.C., House of Representatives, *Journals, 1784–85*, p. 15) Fenwick's petition was presented to the House on 27 January. In it, he admitted having "unhappily engaged in the service" of Great Britain and "that the Resentment of his Countrymen hath been justly shewn against him." Fenwick pleaded that "while he continued in the British Service he endeavor to lessen the horrors of war by every office of Humanity and attention towards the Persons and property of those who fell within his Power." Because he was "extremely desirous of becoming a Citizen" of South Carolina, Fenwick wrote, "he throws himself upon their Mercy hopes for their Pardon and requests that he once more may be received as a Son of America." His petition was referred to a committee. (Ibid., p. 24) Additional letters on Fenwick's case from NG and Henry Laurens were referred to the committee on 9 February 1785. (Ibid., p. 73; see also NG to Guerard, 4 February 1785, below.) On 10 March 1785, the House voted to restore Fenwick's property. (S.C., House of Representatives, *Journals, 1784–85*, p. 212) It was not until March 1786, however, that Fenwick's citizenship was restored by the South Carolina legislature, "for the Special reasons offered by General Greene." This was done after NG interceded with Gov. William Moultrie at the behest of Fenwick and Thomas Gadsden, Fenwick's brother-in-law. (See ibid., p. 499, as well as Fenwick to NG, 5 December 1785; Gadsden to NG, 9 February, 1786, and NG to Moultrie, 12 February 1786, all below.)

¶ [FROM MINOR WINN, "Martins," S.C., [before 20 September 1784?].[1] He has made "Several propositions" to a "Mr Smith" about the "the Business I mentiond to you." Smith "will not Acceed to any of them Untill Colonel [Henry?] Hampton comes & Settles the whole of their Concern." Winn is "about to prepare" a letter informing Hampton of the "impractacability" of "negociating the Busin[ess] for him." Winn has "no doubt" that when Hampton receives the letter "three Days hinse," he "will Loose no time in fixing Some practacable method" by which NG may receive "the amt of Col. Cook's notes" before NG leaves the state. Winn is "convinced" that Hampton will be "truly Distress^d" to find that Smith "does not answer as paymental [liability?]," and he flatters himself that "the matter will in a Short time be settle agreeable to your wish."[2] RCS (MiU-C) 1 p.]

1. Winn (b. 1759), the owner of extensive land holdings in the Camden and Ninety-Six districts, served in the South Carolina General Assembly in the years immediately following the war. (*Biog. Directory of S.C. House*, 3: 778–79) The letter is docketed "1784"; if this is correct, the editors believe that it probably was written sometime during NG's visit to South Carolina in August and September. The last date on which NG is known to have been in Charleston is 19 September. (See the letter immediately above.)

2. Nothing more is known about this matter.

¶ [FROM WILLIAM PIERCE, JR., Savannah, Ga., 24 September 1784. He has NG's letter [not found]; would like to visit NG in Charleston but is entirely "taken up in making arrangements for the present Crop" and cannot go to South Carolina until late December.[1] In regard to the "timely precaution" that NG hinted at, Pierce thinks himself "doubly secure against any thing that can happen."[2] He explains: "When the first of January arrives the whole of [John] Banks's acceptances will become due, and then Major [Richard] Call (to whom I have sold out) will demand a settlement with Major [Robert] Forsyth, who we considered at the time we made a purchase of the Goods, as one of the concern of Jn° Banks & C° from whom the Goods were purchased. Should this be refused the right must be contested. It would indeed be very hard if the concern of Pierce White & Call was to suffer." When Banks's debt "against the House" is "liquidated, there will be a balance in our favor to the amount of 15, or £16,00 sterling," although Forsyth is now setting up claims against them for the goods they purchased, "under a pretence that they were the property of Robt Forsyth & Co." Pierce and his partners did not contract with Forsyth & Company, but with Banks & Company, "and all the World knows that Robt Forsyth & C° were only the retailers of Jn° Banks & C°, so that the claim is founded upon a principle [that], if granted, would drive justice out of the Country." Forsyth "consented to" a settlement when Pierce first proposed it, but he later changed his mind. Pierce and his partners "rece[ive]d the acceptances as a debt of Banks & C° to balance the Account of that company against the House of P,W, & C [Pierce, White and Call], and came by the debt with a fair purchase, not by collusion, or any mean or unjustifiable art." As "we were innocently engaged in this matter, it would be extremely cruel to make us the sufferers. If Law is in favor of Major Forsyth, equity will surely establish our right." Pierce has explained this matter "at large" so that NG "may clearly understand it" and to prove "that there is no necessity for any steps of precaution" on his part. If Forsyth & Company do establish their claim, Pierce will still be "saved harmless by Major Call, who is under a penalty of £50000, in case I suffer; but as I am under no apprehensions of that sort, I shall rest satisfied of my safety. To prove that the purchase was not made of Robt Forsyth & C° we have Letters and other documents to attest it; these Papers will be carefully preserved and arranged, as I foresee no settlement will take place without a Law suit."[3]

Pierce is sorry "for the predicament" in which Banks has placed NG and wishes he could give "such hints of [John] Ferrie's property" as would enable

NG "in some measure to seek a relief." But he thinks Ferrie "has so secured" his property "that it will be impossible to reach it." A merchant in Savannah, Mr. [Leonard?] Cecil, "has charge of" Ferrie's property, and it is Pierce's understanding that Cecil has had "Deeds for all the Land made out in his name."[4] Pierce believes that "Ferrie was taught by Banks the art of finesse and cunning." He adds: "These troubles General are the sweet effects of credit. I believe more evils may be traced from it than from any other circumstance that can intrude itself on a Country. It evidently destroys the morals of the People, and holds out an object of temptation, that leads Men imperceptibly out of their depths. All this is as fully exemplified in Georgia, as, perhaps, in any other Country in the World."

If NG visits Georgia, Pierce will show him "all the civilities in my power. All that a plain hospitality can afford you shall have." Mr. [William] Gibbons has told him that NG wants to sell his rice "at the Landing."[5] If NG is "authorized, from a knowledge of its situation to sell it for Cash paid down imediately, or for Bills on London," he should let Pierce know his terms. If Pierce likes them, he will "instantly pay either down" to NG or Gibbons. Asks for a reply "as soon as possible."[6] If NG does visit Georgia, he should bring Colonel Fenwick, who will "meet a better treatment in Georgia when he comes again."[7] Pierce sends his wife's and his own "affectionate respects" and adds in a postscript: "My little Son is a fine rosey-cheek'd fellow." RCS (MiU-C) 8 pp.]

1. NG had also asked Pierce's former business partner Richard Call to meet with him in Charleston. (Call to NG, 30 September, below)

2. NG's "timely precaution" to Pierce can be deduced from the discussion in the rest of this paragraph.

3. For more about Forsyth's demand against Pierce, White & Call, see Forsyth to NG, 18 June, above, and Pendleton to NG, 10 November, below.

4. On NG's efforts to attach property belonging to Ferrie, see ibid. and NG to Collett, 8 August, above. (As seen in the note at Forsyth to NG, 18 June, NG's estate eventually won a suit against Ferrie in South Carolina.) Ferrie had acquired the Georgia land that Pierce referred to here in payment of a debt from Call and his partners. (Pierce to NG, 8 September, above, and Call to NG, 30 September) According to an undated and unsigned "Memorandum re Banks affair" at MiU-C: "Ferrie obtains Banks's Acceptances as per State with Mr Rutle[d]ge. Ferrie, the Day after Forsyth arrives in Charleston, goes to Georgia purchases Land of Peirce, White & Call, pays them those Acceptances or pledges them to be regularly transferred by Banks for a Debt which P W & Call owed the Company[,] they arrive in Charles Town to execute those Transfers; Forsyth gets Intimation of the Affair, and prior to their being assignd by Banks, warns Ferry, P W & Call & Banks that the Company would not abide by the Transaction, they persisted & Banks assigned them."

5. See NG to Gibbons, 29 August, above.

6. On the complications that developed from Pierce's sale of NG's rice crop, see below Pierce & Company to NG, 8 April 1785 and 13 May 1785, and NG to Pierce, 17 May 1785.

7. Edward Fenwick, a Loyalist who had acted as an American spy, was the brother of Pierce's wife, Charlotte Fenwick Pierce. (Vol. 11: 596n, above) On Fenwick's efforts to regain his citizenship in South Carolina, see NG's letters to Benjamin Guerard of 30 March and 19 September, both above.

¶ [FROM JOHN WATIES, JR.,[1] Santee, S.C., 27 September 1784. After NG left South Carolina "last Summer," Waties received a request from Maj. [Edmund M.] Hyrne to "make out a fair state of my demands on the Public, for

Stores purchased for the Army under" NG's command and give them to Maj [Robert] Forsyth, to whom NG also wrote "on the subject."² Waties complied with Hyrne's request "and produced such Vouchers for the delivery of the Stores as met with the Majors approbation." Waties's papers are now in Forsyth's hands, and NG may review them if he wishes.³ As he is "frequently threatned by the Creditors, with prosecutions," Waties "will be happy if you will point out some mode by which they may be satisfied." Otherwise, he "cannot tell how long they [i.e., his creditors] will forbear."⁴ RCS (MiU-C) 1 p.]

1. NG had authorized Waties to act as a "special Agent for the post of George Town" to purchase supplies for the Southern Army during the war. (Vol. 10: 104 and n, above)

2. NG's former aide Hyrne, who accompanied him to Philadelphia in the late summer and early fall of 1783, died in December 1783. (Pendleton to NG, 30 January, above) Forsyth had written NG about Waties's "demands" on 18 October 1783, above.

3. It is not known whether NG reviewed Waties's "papers."

4. The outcome of this matter is not known.

*   *   *

From Jeremiah Wadsworth

Dear Sir   Philadelphia 28 Sepʳ [1784]
    I arrived here the 26th instant from Europe and was surprised to find you had refused to accept Griffin Greens bills in my favor.¹ I indorsed them in consequence of your letter now in my possession which you authorise him to make use of to obtain Credit.² I had no interest in the matter but to serve you & him, he was critically [si]tuated & distressed & promised not to make use of them without he was obligded to. In June I being in London ready to set out for Ireland & America was informed that he had paid the Bills to my friends Dumousse frers [i.e., Dumoussay et Frères] at Paris for Merchandize & that the Ship was not sold. I flew to Paris, found the indefatigable Marquis de Lafayette had persuaded Government to take her at about 100,000 livres to be paid at different periods.³ Mʳ Greene was then at Bordeaux [France]. I desired his freind Mʳ Price to Write him and press him to come immediately to Pari[s], he [i.e., Price] did so. No answer had arrived when I was forced to leave Paris or miss my Passage in our Ship from Ireland which I did at last. I was detanied [i.e., detained] till the 7 of August & had but an indifferent Ship to come home in. I do not know what will be the consequence of the non acceptance but non payment will be prejudicial to my Character. Your sentiments on this Subject will greatly oblidge Dʳ Sir Your Hum seʳ⁴   JERE WADSWORTH

RCS (CtHi).
    1. According to his biographer, Wadsworth returned home soon afterward "to a seriously depressed Connecticut in an equally unprosperous United States. Despite his wish to retire from trade, his large, varied interests would keep him active for years to come." (Destler, "Wadsworth," p. 244) For background on NG's refusal, see especially the

note at Griffin Greene to NG, 8 April; Pettit to NG, 19 June; and NG to Griffin Greene, 8 July, all above. As seen in his letter to Wadsworth of 12 November, below, NG had misunderstood the purpose of the bills and Wadsworth's "agency in the business."

2. The letter in question has not been found, but NG is known to have sent letters of credit for Griffin Greene to several other individuals and to have authorized him to draw on them for a total of "fifteen or two thousand pounds" while trying to sell the vessel *Flora* in France. (See above, NG to Griffin, 9, 10, and 14 June 1783; NG to Lafayette and NG to Laurens, both 10 June 1783; and NG to James Hunter, 14 June 1783.) Griffin Greene wrote NG on 6 April, above, that he had used NG's credit to purchase "Goods to the amount of two Thousand pounds payable in one Year from the delivery."

3. On Lafayette's efforts to promote the sale of the *Flora* to French authorities for NG and Griffin Greene, see above, Griffin Greene to NG, 6 April, 16 May, and 12 June, and Lafayette to NG, 25 August. The sale had still not been completed. (See Griffin Greene's letter to NG at the end of the September documents, below.)

4. Wadsworth again asked NG to explain "the non acceptance" in a letter of 1 November, below. (See also note 1, above.)

*　　*　　*

¶ [FROM RICHARD CALL, Augusta, Ga., 30 September 1784. In reply to NG's letter of 23 August [not found], Call is sorry that he cannot "attend at Ch[arle]s-ton" [S.C.] as soon as NG would like, but he plans to go there during the next month and will be "happy to act in such manner as will be most conducive to your and my interest."[1] The land that "Mr Ferrie received in payment of our Debt was one tract in Ogeeche near the Ferry, which we purchased of Capt [James] Gunn, the other six Hundred Acres in So Carolina nearly opposite the Town of Savannah called [Nelville?]." These, Call writes, are "two very valuable Plantations," and "nothing but an anxious desire of geting clear of a large Debt which I knew could not be done from the sales of the Goods [John] Banks put on us ever wou'd have induced me to have parted with the Lands I did."[2] Ferrie "really got a great bargain in them," and these lands, if sold now, "woud fetch 50 P C [i.e., percent] more than he" paid. RCS (MiU-C) 2 pp.]

1. NG had also asked Call's former business partner William Pierce, Jr., to meet with him in Charleston. (Pierce to NG, 24 September, above) By the time Call wrote the present letter, NG had left Charleston, traveling first to North Carolina and Virginia and later returning home to Rhode Island. (NG to Rutledge, after 30 September, and NG to Gibbons, 29 December, both below)

2. NG was hoping to attach land belonging to Ferrie. (NG to Collett, 8 August, and NG to Pettit, 15 August, above; NG to Rutledge, after 30 September, and NG to Forsyth, 2 October, below) On the involvement of Call and his former partners Pierce and Anthony White in dealings with Banks and Ferrie, see also Forsyth to NG, 18 June, and Pierce to NG, 24 September, above; Forsyth to NG, 18 November, below.

¶ [FROM JOHN MEALS, Augusta, Ga., 30 September 1784. Maj. [Robert] Forsyth's return from North Carolina "renders a compliance" with NG's "requisition unnecessary," but Meals, to "be but polite," acknowledges NG's letter "by Mr [Richard] Call" [not found] and assures him that "when an opportunity is given me to do you any acceptable Service, I shall ever receive much pleasure."[1] Meals wrote "a long Letter" [not found] to NG the previous December, giving "every information then in my power, respecting the Business that has occasioned you so much uneasiness and distress." As he has not had a reply to that letter, Meals is afraid it "miscarried" and is sorry if it did, for it would have given NG the "small satisfaction" of knowing that Mr. [James] Warrington's bond had been canceled and would also have convinced NG that "I have been more than barely professional."[2] Hopes CG and the rest of NG's family are well. RCS (MiU-C) 2 pp.]

1. On Forsyth's reasons for going to North Carolina, see his letter to NG of 18 June and NG's to Charles Pettit of 15 August, both above. The "requisition" has not been found. Meals, who had been an assistant deputy commissary of purchases under Forsyth, appears to have left the Southern Army soon after Forsyth resigned his commissary post to become a business partner of John Banks. (Meals to NG, 14 December 1782, above [vol. 12: 292]) Meals and Francis Tate, Forsyth's successor in the commissary department, wrote NG on 8 May 1783, above, that Forsyth had instructed them "Not to go further into a settlement" of commissary accounts "during his Agency, than has already been done, our being out of Office, & no prospect of a compensation for trouble &c." (Vol. 12: 650)

2. NG's "uneasiness and distress" were "occasioned" by unpaid debts he had guaranteed for John Banks in the latter's capacity as a supplier to the army. Warrington, one of the creditors of Banks and his partners, had encountered difficulties in the summer of 1783 in trying to obtain payment from Robert Morris for bills of exchange that NG had advanced to Banks and others for army purchases. (See notes at Pettit to NG, 23 July 1783, and Morris to NG, 5 August 1783, above.) Pettit wrote NG on 27 April, above, that E. John Collett and Warrington were continuing to encounter difficulties in their efforts to obtain control of Banks's assets in Virginia. On the resolution of Collett's remaining claims years after NG's death, see note at NG to Collett, 8 August, above. In 1798, a congressional committee reported that Warrington, as a creditor to Banks and agent for others, eventually obtained $27,000 in treasury payments authorized by Pettit as Banks's agent. (*Annals of Congress*, 5th Congress [1797–99], p. 3650)

¶ [FROM ROBERT MORRIS, SUPERINTENDENT OF FINANCE, Philadelphia, 30 September 1784. Encloses a "Bill of Exchange drawn upon the late Governor [John] Mathews by his wife" in NG's "Favor for two hundred and sixty six Dollars and two thirds."[1] This bill "stands to" NG's "Debit in the Treasury Books." Advises NG that "it will be proper to take Measures for obtaining the Payment or else for having the usual Protests made so that you may be discharged." RCS (CSmH) 2 pp.]

1. On Mathews (1744–1802), whose one-year term as governor of South Carolina had ended in early 1783, see above, vol. 6: 336n. His wife was the former Mary Wragg. (*Biog. Directory of S.C. House*, 2: 439)

¶ [FROM GRIFFIN GREENE, Bordeaux, France, September 1784.[1] Hopes NG "will not draw any unfavorable conclutions, on accompt of my long stay in France"; if NG does, Griffin will be "doubly punnished, firstly in not being able to get away, & secondly with your displeasure."[2] He came to Bordeaux "from Paris, with written orders, from the Minnister, such as I suppose, must finish the whole bussiness respecting the sail of the *Flora*."[3] To facilitate the sale of the vessel, the minister appointed "One Tirol," a "man seeking after promoshen." This is the "same person, that caused a second valuation upon the Ship, by representing to the Minnister, that the first valuation was partial"; the "second valuation was raised near 50,000 livers from the first."[4] Griffin observes: "This man sticks at nothing, to gain his ends." Griffin relates in detail his frustrations in dealing with Tirol, who assured him that he would facilitate the sale of the vessel but was not capable of doing so. At one point, Griffin enlisted the assistance of "Mr James Price, the Honorable Gentleman that had the thanks of Congress for his assistance at Quebeck, & who was with me" for the first valuation.[5] Griffin has now given the "minnister" some "information" about how Tirol has "deseved" him. Griffin may have to go to Paris "once or twice more on this bussiness before I have finished it so that God only knows how long it will be before it is don."[6] Sends his love to CG "& your little Family." RCS (MiU-C) 4 pp.]

1. Only the month and year are recorded in the dateline.

2. On Griffin Greene's trip to France, see above, vol. 12: 662–64 and n, and earlier correspondence between NG and him in this volume.

3. In his letter to NG of 6 April, above, Griffin Greene had expressed optimism that the intervention of the French naval minister, De Castries, would smooth the way to a successful completion of the sale of the *Flora*.

4. As seen in Griffin Greene to NG, 6 April, Tirol was presumably the "Major of Marien [i.e., Marine?]" at Bordeaux. On the valuations of the *Flora*, see ibid. and Griffin Greene's letters to NG of 16 May and 12 June, both above.

5. On James Price, see also Griffin Greene to NG, 12 June.

6. By 14 December, Griffin Greene was back in Paris, attempting to conclude the sale of the *Flora* to the French navy. (See his letter to NG of that date, below.) As noted at his letter to NG of 6 April, above, he did not return to the United States for another year.

*   *   *

To Hugh Rutledge

Dear Sir   [Washington, N.C., after 30 September 1784][1]

John Banks is dead and buryed. He was buryed two days before my arrival. My prospects are now worse than ever.[2] My hopes are all upon you. I have stated to Nash & McClaren the funds relinquished by M[r] [Michael J.] Harris and they are both of opinion a chancery suit will releive me to the amount of those funds.[3] Harris can certainly make himself whole from the Lands of Ferrie and funds with Lushington; and if so he ought not to push me even if I am in his power.[4] I wish Collett's suit may be forwarded against the Company and the execution levied upon Ferr[i]es Lands.[5] M[r] Cooper[6] will pay his bill to M[r] [Edward] Pennman and I wish all those matters could rest until our return. I mean the parties concerned in the issue. I have not seen Capt Carnes but expect to see him tomorrow.[7]

AL (MiU-C).

1. The place and approximate date were determined from the letter of similar content immediately below, in which NG reported that he "arrivd here yesterday [1 October] and found John Banks dead & buryed." Washington, which is near the coast in Beaufort County, N.C., was originally known as "Forks of Tar River." (William S. Powell, *The North Carolina Gazetteer* [Chapel Hill: University of North Carolina Press, 1968], p. 518)

2. It is clear from his correspondence at Charleston in August and September (and at Newport, R.I., before he left for Charleston) that financial problems resulting from Banks's failure to pay the debts that NG had guaranteed for him had become an overriding concern for NG. It is also clear that NG went to North Carolina and Virginia to find

and confront Banks and to try—unsuccessfully, as it turned out—to gain control over those problems. He wrote Robert Forsyth from Richmond on 25 October, below: "I leave this place with a heavy heart, the business which brought me here hangs still over my head like a threatning Cloud which embitters every moment of my life."

It is not known when NG left Charleston, S.C., for North Carolina and Virginia, but his last letter from Charleston that has been found is dated 19 September. (NG to Guerard, 19 September, above) It is likely that in traveling from Charleston to Washington, NG went by water as far as Wilmington, N.C. (See NG to Blount, 25 October, below.) From Washington, where he borrowed a horse and saddle, NG went on to Petersburg, Va., where he stayed about ten days. (Ibid.; NG to Blount, 15 October, below) Then, after a brief stop in Richmond, where he met with both Edward Carrington, his "Attorney" in Virginia, and Banks's brother Henry, he continued northward, reaching Philadelphia by mid-November and his home in Newport, R.I., by the end of that month. (See below, note at Henry Banks to NG, 7 October; NG to Blount, 24 October; NG to Saunders, 12 November; and NG to Gibbons, 29 November.)

3. NG was asking Rutledge to initiate a suit in South Carolina. As noted at Pettit to NG, 6 May, above, Harris & Blachford was one of the firms to which NG had guaranteed debts incurred by John Banks and his partners in supplying clothing to the Southern Army. On Harris & Blachford's relinquishment, see also NG to Forsyth, immediately below, and Pendleton to NG, 10 November, below. As noted at the Pendleton letter, a settlement between NG's estate and Joseph Blachford, the surviving partner, was finally achieved a decade after NG's death.

4. On the efforts to attach property belonging to John Ferrie, see especially the note at Forsyth to NG, 18 June, above. As seen there, NG's estate eventually won a suit against Ferrie in South Carolina. On Harris, see also the preceding note; on Richard Lushington, see above, NG's letters to him of before 28 August and 28 August.

5. See also NG to Forsyth, immediately below.

6. On Cooper, see also ibid.

7. Patrick Carnes, as well as NG, had financial issues with Banks. (See above, Saunders to NG, before 17 July; Pettit to NG, 26 July; and Penman to NG, 12 August.) NG wrote William Blount on 15 October, below: "Capt Carnes is well but the guarantee hangs heavy on his Spirits." Nathaniel Pendleton wrote NG on 10 November, below, that the relinquishment of bonds that Carnes and John McQueen had given to Banks "will not be of an advantage to you." In a letter of 2 November 1785, below, Henry Banks informed NG: "I have setled with Maj. Carns for the whole amo^t of my Securityship by giving up Kentucky Lands to be valued. I expect to arrange with the other demandants upon me in the same way this fall."

To Robert Forsyth

Dear Sir   Washington [N.C.] Octo 2^d 1784

I arrivd here yesterday and found John Banks dead & buried.[1] His papers are in the hands of Mr Cooper of this place and from the little I have seen of them am convinced you ought to come here without loss of time.[2] Henry Banks's letters give information of consequence and lay a good foundation for our future security. I shall do all I can to get matters in the best possible train until your arrival.[3] Part of your old funds in this State I believe are not done away but this is not certain. Pray bring an Account of the funds which Harris & Blachford relinquished. The Lawyers of this State tell me a Court of chancery will relieve me to the amount of what ever they relinquished.[4] Tell M^r

[Joseph] Blachford to urge his suit against [John] Ferrie[5] and desire M[r] [Hugh?] Rutledge to press Lushington to an agreement or bring forward the Action if he continues to refuse to give a bond of indemnity.[6] I pray you to give to M[r] [Nicholas?] Primerose[,] M[r] [E. John] Colletts attorney an assignment of all the remaining funds for outstanding Debts upon the books.[7] I am ruined if you do not exert your self to save me. M[r] Cooper says M[r] [James] Hunters Portsmouth [Va.] estate has been sold at public Vendue and by M[r] Hunters order about the time he was conveying it to me as counter security and that it is bought & held for him by M[r] Minor.[8] If the fact is so, which I will not credit yet it will give me an ill opinion of Mr Hunters intentions or integrity. If Mr Hunter could come with you he may profit by it.[9] Henry Banks letters may be of consequence to him not only in his late concerns with John Banks but their former.[10] Yours Affe[ctionately]   N GREENE

ADfS (MiU-C).

1. See also NG to Rutledge, immediately above.

2. Edward Carrington wrote NG on 27 February 1785, below: "Neither [James] Hunter nor Forsythe have yet come to Virginia." (See also NG to Forsyth, 5 June 1785, below.)

3. The letters referred to have not been found. (See, however, Hunter to NG, 1 June 1785, below.) On the involvement of Henry Banks in his brother's financial affairs, see above, Forsyth to NG, 18 June, and NG to Collett, 8 August. Henry Banks, in his reply of 7 October, immediately below, to a letter from NG that has not been found, complained about NG's "Expressions and Sentaments equally dictatorial and illeberal and devoid of what ought to have been their fundamental Source[:] Good Information." However, NG was able to obtain an indenture from Henry Banks in late October. (See note at ibid.)

4. See also the note at NG to Rutledge, immediately above.

5. See also ibid.

6. In regard to Richard Lushington, see NG's letters to him of before 28 August and 28 August, above.

7. NG presumably referred to the business records of Robert Forsyth & Company, in which John Banks and Forsyth had been partners. (On this, see also NG to Rutledge, immediately above.)

8. On the "counter security" that Hunter had given NG, see note at Skipwith to NG, 4 August, above. As seen below in Hunter to NG, 1 June 1785, and NG to Hunter, 29 August 1785, the claims of Hunter's creditors to his property did take precedence over NG's claims.

9. NG wrote Forsyth on 25 October, below: "I beg you will take every step in your power for my relief. Hunter and you had better sell your property in this Sta[te] [Virginia] as there appears little probability of extinguishing Collett's demands in any other way." (See also note 2, above.) On the eventual settlement with Collett, see note at NG to Collett, 8 August.

10. See note 3, above.

From Henry Banks

Sir   Richmond [Va.] Octo 7: 1784.

The more I reflect the more am I astonished at your late unexampled Letter couched in Expressions and Sentaments equally dictatorial and illeberal and devoid of what ought to have been their fundamental Source[:] Good Information.[1]

To have received such a letter from a man of your personal Consequence would with Two thirds of Mankind be full implication of Guilt, and I have not a doubt but full that proportion of those to whom the Circumstance has or may be made known will admit no other Construction. This Consequence you have no doubt surmised, and in proportion as your Momentary Impulses swayed, so do I stand in the Opinion of a Strange Multitude.

Altho I am well assured that the mind will ex Semitapso[2] be wrought into a competent State of determination, where a counteracting Power does not exist, and that therefore I have met your Censure, still I hope that your feelings as a Man have withheld a publication of those reproachful Surmises, which are linked through the Whole of your Letter. Because as that will leave it necessary for me to attempt a personal Vindication. Because the Event may terminate contrary to what has been advanced and Because the result may be that General Green has prematurely and undeservedly injured the Character of a Young Man, with whom he neither ever had personal dealings or personal knowledge, and ag[t] whom the only complaint surmise, What trouble a Bussiness of this kind may Occasion, I leave to your own determination.[3]

But to return to the purpose after enumerating your Services to my Brother and his want of Gratitude and proper attention for your Indemnification,[4] you conclude by saying that so far as respects me no Evasion shall be taken to obviate the reembursement of large shipments undoubtedly made to me from Charleston [S.C.], as incontestable proof will invalidate any testimonials which I may adduce, and to enforce which, the Court of Chancery or the Legislature will be appealed to.[5] The warmth of your disposition may sometime carry you beyond the sound doctrine of an able Lawyer or the peaceful Manner of a freeborn Citizen; not reflecting that the Liberties of the elective and legislative Bodies are one and the same thing, and that a Native Son of Virginia, enjoying and contributing to the freedom of his Country cannot be treated with the Dictatorial Command, of an Officer on Duty, or the Monarchichal Dictates of an absolute Government, besides when Equity is in quest, is there not an equal demand of an Injured Defendant, born down by the immediate Power of the plaintiff to seek redress for a vexatious Suit or injured Character, as for a common Prosecution at Law.

Supposing however that you have so far proceeded on your way to Richmond, I concieve it unnecessary to mention Particularly the Situations now and heretofore of myself with the Parties ag[t] whom you complain. Being confident of full ability to evince the [propriety?] of my every transaction therein, when the Parties themselves will require a further explication than they have had, from whose Conduct with you I am sorry to become a party in a dispute whose Merits and Demerits

I only know from contradictory Circumstances, and can therefore have no other opinion than that a general Concurrence of fault has made a general Rupture among Friends.

When we meet you may personally discover how anxious I am to expunge from my Memory the remembrance of those Events, to convince you and all Mankind of the good Intention of my own Conduct and be reinstated, as a Stranger, in your fr^dship and good opinion.

Provided M^r [James] Hunter and my Brother will seriously ingage in the Settlem^t of their transactions I will take some Steps which may tend to their advantage, if they do not I shall certainly avoid every further aid to them.[6] The enclosed Letter for your Perusal I beg to be deliverd and that the Gentleman may be no longer induced to act in such a line as to entail disagreeable Disputes on him.[7] I am sir Yr mo Hum Ser^t

HENRY BANKS

RCS (MiU-C).

1. NG's letter has not been found. (For background, see above, NG to Collett, 8 August, and NG to Forsyth, 2 October.) As it is clear from the present letter that Henry Banks did not yet know about his brother John's death, NG probably had written to him before learning that fact himself. (On NG's knowledge of John Banks's death, see his letter to Hugh Rutledge, after 30 September, above.)

2. Banks may have meant "ex semilapsu," i.e., "from its half-error."

3. In 1826, after most of those involved in the affairs of John Banks were dead, Henry Banks published a pamphlet vilifying NG and portraying his brother—"the saviour of the southern army"—and himself as victims of manipulation and fraud by NG and others. (Banks, *Vindication*; quote on p. 5) His allegations against NG in that publication included an "opinion" that NG had been present when John Banks died and, indeed, that either NG or his servant had strangled John Banks to death. (Ibid., p. 34) In his letter dated after 30 September, NG told Hugh Rutledge that John Banks "was buryed two days before my arrival."

4. For discussions of NG's "Services" to John Banks and the latter's "want of Gratitude," see especially vol. 12: 308–9n, above; Benjamin Harrison to NG, 24 December 1782 (ibid., pp. 341–42 and n); and NG to Lee, 22 August 1785, below. In a letter to CG of 8 September, above, NG had written of John Banks: "I verily believe if I was to meet him I should put him to death. He is the greatest Monster and most finished vilian that this age has produced." (As seen in the preceding note, Henry Banks alleged long afterward that NG had been responsible for his brother's death.)

5. NG presumably had threatened a suit to prove that Henry Banks had been one of his brother John's partners and that he therefore shared in his brother's liability for the debts that NG had guaranteed. (On the guarantee, see especially Agreement between Hunter, Banks & Company and NG with Newcomen and Collett, 8 April 1783, above [vol. 12: 591 and n], and NG to Lee, 22 August 1785.)

6. As seen in notes 1 and 3, above, John Banks was already dead. NG met Henry Banks in Richmond in late October and obtained from him, as security for Henry's agreement to "save" him from obligations incurred in guaranteeing John Banks's bonds to the firms of Harris & Blachford and Newcomen & Collett, an indenture for Henry's share of a 100,000 acre tract of western land in Jefferson County, in the area of present-day Louisville, Ky. Henry declared that under the terms of the bonds, he was "personally bound" to NG for £24,000, "current money of Virginia." (The indenture, dated 30 October, is at CSmH.) NG's issues with Henry Banks were by no means ended by this indenture. (See especially

NG to Banks, after 16 November; the six letters from Banks to NG between 13 July 1785 and 13 January 1786; and NG to Ward, 4 April 1786, all below.)
    7. It is not known to whom the enclosure was addressed.

To William Blount[1]

Dear Sir   Petersburgh [Va.] Octo 15th 1784
    M^r [E. John] Collettes Attorney Mr Cambell of this place has sent on a Copy of the Bond of Hunter Banks Forsyth & Company[,] to which I became guaranter[,] Addressed to General [Richard] Caswell desiring him to sue the Administrator of John Banks in North Carolinia.[2] You will please to confess judgment to the amount of the property you may obtain of his [i.e., Banks's]. I will write you again in a few days.[3] We arrivd here only an hour since & push off an Express without loss of time lest any Attempt should be made to circumvent me in the object of the Administration. John Banks's death had not reached this place.[4] Capt Carnes is well but the guarantee hangs heavy on his Spirits.[5] Give my compliments to the family and beleive me to be with esteem & regard Your Most Obed humble ser^t6   NATH GREENE

ACyS (NjMoHP).
    1. Blount, a former army officer and delegate to Congress, was a partner at this time with his brothers John Gray Blount and Thomas Blount in a business that "became one of the largest mercantile concerns" in North Carolina. (Blount, *Papers*, 1: xxi) NG had stayed at William Blount's home while traveling north in the summer of 1783. (See above, NG's Journal entries for 25, 26, and 27–28 August 1783.)
    2. It appears from this and subsequent correspondence that Blount was representing NG in North Carolina in NG's efforts to free himself from obligations incurred in guaranteeing bonds for army contractor John Banks and Banks's partners. (On the bond referred to here, see Agreement between Hunter, Banks and Company and NG with Newcomen and Collett, 8 April 1783, above [vol. 12: 591 and n], and NG to Lee, 22 August 1785, below.) As seen in NG to Rutledge, after 30 September, above, Banks had recently died.
    3. See NG to Blount, 24 October, below.
    4. On this, see also the note at Henry Banks to NG, immediately above.
    5. In regard to Patrick Carnes, see NG to Rutledge, after 30 September.
    6. Blount replied to this letter from New Bern, N.C., on 26 October, below.

                    *   *   *

¶ [FROM HOWSON, EDWARDS & COMPANY, London, 16 October 1784. They received NG's letter of 6 August "yesterday" and enclose him "the price Currant," which is based on accounts from their "Corespondents at Charles Town," S.C.[1] They inform NG that "Rice will by no means answer, for this Markett owing to the heavy loss upon it," and there is "but little Sale" of indigo because of "the Great quantitys in hand." They add: "The Importers will find thers been heavy losses this year." If NG ships indigo, he should "let it be a Bright Copper Large Shape & perfectly dry." They explain what they meant by "charging no Commission": "Where we have Sent out Goods, to the Amount of the Goods remitted us we charge nothing for our trouble." They think NG "could procure us a good Bill which would answer our purposes much better." They know there are "good Bills to be got at Charles Town" because they have had "large remittances from there per Bills."[2] They are "perfectly Satisfyd with the Character of M[r] Sentor [i.e., Isaac Senter?] but not with his way of dealing."[3] RCS (MiU-C) 1 p.]

1. For background on this letter, see NG to Howson, Edwards & Company, 6 August, above.

2. NG apparently complied with this request. (Howson, Edwards & Company to NG, 27 June 1785, below)

3. Howson, Edwards & Company replied to another letter from NG on 27 June 1785: "From the Good Character you gave M[r] Senter we have immediately Ship'd him more Goods."

¶ [TO WHOM IT MAY CONCERN, 21 October 1784.[1] NG certifies "that Nathaniel Pendleton my Aid de Camp was on extraordinary Service out of Camp by my Order Twenty one days" from 11 April to 2 May 1781, and "again Twenty three days in December 1781."[2] LS (WRMS, Misc. Mss. #28826, DNA) 1 p.]

1. Pendleton prepared this certificate for NG's signature and sent it from Richmond, Va., with a letter to NG of 22 October, below. (NG was still at Petersburg at this time. [See his reply to Petersburg officials of 22 October, below.])

2. On Pendleton's missions from South Carolina to Virginia at those times, see NG's letters to him of 11 April 1781 and 21 November 1781, both above. (Vol. 8: 82; vol. 9: 603)

*   *   *

From the Mayor, [Recorder],
Aldermen and Common Council of Petersburg, Virginia

[Petersburg, Virginia, before 22 October 1784?][1]

"SIR: We, the Mayor, Aldermen and Common Council of the town of Petersburg, beg leave to testify our happiness in your arrival at this place, and in having an opportunity of expressing our grateful sense of the signal services you have rendered to America in general, and to this State in particular. Your military character and honorable perseverance, during a long war, merit the highest applause from a people to whose independence you have so ably contributed. By your exertions in the South, the inhabitants were relieved from the calamities of a cruel war, and the enemy, who had ravaged in all quarters, were with a small force confined within the limits of a town. While we look back to this happy period of the war, we contemplate with admiration the events that led to it, the difficulties you surmounted, and the resources you created. Sensible as we are of the great talents that form your character as a soldier, we are no less pleased with your social virtues and agreeable manners, than with your moderation of justice to all parties.

"To your abilities and eminent services we trust the affectionate gratitude of your fellow citizens will be ever mindful, and that the faithful historian will transmit them with honor to all posterity. Finally, we implore the Supreme Being, who has conducted you through so many dangers, to hold you in his protection during a long and happy life."[2]

Printed letter (*Historical Magazine* 2: [1858]: 275).
1. This letter, as printed in the *Historical Magazine*, has no date.
2. NG's reply, dated 22 October, is immediately below. (NG had been in Petersburg since at least 15 October. [See his letter to William Blount of that date, above.])

To the Mayor, Recorder, Aldermen and Common Council of the Town of Petersburg, Virginia

Petersburg, Va., 22 October 1784

"GENTLEMEN: This instance of your politeness is the more pleasing, as it was unexpected.[1] The war being at an end and my command extinct this address seems not to be matter of form, but a mark of esteem. The flattering terms in which you express yourselves of my public conduct displays both your justice and your generosity. In reviewing the calamities that are past, and contemplating the pleasures to come, I feel a happiness in distress. For though I am oppressed with difficulties created by public necessity, and though I have too much reason to think they will cloud, if not embitter future life, yet as they have contributed to public happiness, it serves to soften private misfortune.[2]

"The compliment you pay to my social character and the solicitude you express for my future protection, merit every acknowledgment which a generous nature can feel, or a grateful temper return, and such I wish to offer. I am, gentlemen with the highest esteem your most obedient humble servant   "NATHANIEL GREENE"
"PETERSBURG, Oct. 22, 1784"

Printed letter (*Historical Magazine* 2 [1858]: 275).
1. NG was in Petersburg at this time, on his way north from Charleston, S.C. He was replying here to the proclamation printed immediately above.
2. On the personal, financial difficulties to which he alluded here, see note at NG to Rutledge, after 30 September, above.

*   *   *

¶ [FROM NATHANIEL PENDLETON, [Richmond, Va.], 22 October 1784. He takes "the liberty to trouble" NG with a letter, "Inclosing my Account settled here, to the Paymaster General."[1] Pendleton has been told by the paymaster's "Agent" that he "pays Six months pay" (which Pendleton has "credited the public for here") and his "subsistence for 82 & 83 in cash."[2] Pendleton has drawn an order in NG's "favor to receive the Money." He writes: "I would not have put so troublesome a Commission into your [han]ds, but from the great Convenience the Mo[ney] will be to me this Winter, & the difficulty of getting another opportunity."[3] If he does not get the money, he will "feel all the embarrasments from which the hope of getting It has releieved" him. Asks NG to "sign the inclosed certificate and stick it in the Letter."[4] He adds: "I remember the days perfectly well," and closes: "Yours Unalterably." RCS (MiU-C) 1 p.]

1. Pendleton undoubtedly knew that NG, who was on his way home from Charleston, S.C., would be stopping in Philadelphia and could deliver this account in person to John Pierce, the paymaster general.

2. Pendleton had "lodged" his accounts with A. W. Dunscomb, the paymaster's agent in Richmond. A copy, dated 20 October 1784, is in WRMS, Misc. Mss. #16701, DNA.

3. A copy of Pendleton's order indicates that it was drawn on Pierce and that it asked him to pay NG "the Balance due" to Pendleton "from the United States as Capt and Aid de Camp." (WRMS, Misc. Mss. #17382, DNA)

4. For the "inclosed certificate," see To Whom It May Concern, 21 October, above.

¶ [FROM JOHN MACKENZEY, Wilmington, N.C., 23 October 1784. He sends a "Packet" that he just received "under cover from Major [Robert] Forsyth," who asked to have it "immediately forwarded" to NG by express.[1] The bearer will wait for NG's "commands." Forsyth is hoping for "an answer by the Pacquet," but as it is to sail "on Tuesday or Wednesday next," MacKenzey is afraid the express will not be able "to return [in?] that time."[2] If he can be of "the smallest service" in forwarding NG's "Dispatches," MacKenzey hopes NG will "freely dispose" of him. RCS (MiU-C) 1 p.]

1. It is not known what the "Packet" contained. NG had not received this letter when he wrote to Forsyth from Richmond, Va., on 25 October, below.

2. As MacKenzey wrote this letter on a Saturday, "Tuesday or Wednesday next" was presumably 26 or 27 October. The "Packet" mentioned in this letter was a packet of letters or other documents; the "Pacquet" was a sailing vessel.

*   *   *

To William Blount

Dear Sir   Petersburgh [Va.] Octo 24th 1784

Before this you will have receivd my letter from this place on my first arrival here.[1] And with which I hope you got Mr Cambells letter [in answer?] to General [Richard] Caswells letter with an order to sue John Banks's administrator.[2] The Lawyers think Mr Cambell has done wrong in giving the order[,] for if the suit is commenced and you confess judgment for any given sum he can never recover any thing more of me. I wish this doctrine was true and that judgment was made up before General Caswell gets contrary orders[,] which you may expect in four or five days at farthest.[3] I find on my arrival here that Mr Collette [E. John Collett] has forced Mr Banks to a settlement at the time he was here and obliged him to pay a great part of his penal bonds; from which I am cut off of the benefit of £2000 sterling which had been paid him [i.e., Collett] under every disadvantage.[4] Could I get hold of a circumstance to redress my self no man could tax me with injustice or dishonor. Should Mr Cambell countermand his order to General Casswell you must contrive some other mode to cover the property should any body else lay claim to it; and if you can do no better let Mr [Thomas?] Ogden bring suit; but I hope you will not be reduced to this necessity.[5] After you have got from the books and papers of John Banks all that is necessary to close the Administration or secure for my benefit all his property I beg you to forward them to Colonel [Edward] Carrington of Richmond with whom I wish you to correspond he being my Attorney in this State [i.e., Virginia]. Capt [Patrick] Carnes will tell you of our desperate situation and the little I have to depend on with certainty but what you have under your care and management. And should Capt Carnes prevail on McWhan to bring a suit against you for Banks's property and Cambell countermand his order you will confess judgment for him he having promised to be finally accountable to me for the amount.[6]

ADf (MiU-C).
1. See NG to Blount, 15 October, above.
2. See ibid.
3. NG wrote Blount on 26 October, below: "This doctrine as I expected has no foundation."
4. It is not known when this payment was made to Collett.
5. NG wrote Blount again on 26 October. In a letter of 10 July 1785, below, Blount informed NG that he had instituted several suits but had not yet "got into my Hands a Single Shillings worth of Banks's Property" and did not expect he could get hold of more than $1,000 worth.
6. On "McWhan," or "McWhann," see also Robert Forsyth to NG, 18 June, above. It appears from NG's letter to Forsyth of 25 October that it was James Campbel who had "promised to be finally accountable."

*   *   *

¶ [TO JOHN GRAY BLOUNT.[1] From Petersburg, Va., 25 October 1784. As Capt. [Patrick] Carnes is returning to South Carolina "by the uper Road," NG must send his own servant "back with Mr Cooper horse." NG has borrowed a saddle from Thomas Ogden and has instructed his servant to leave the saddle with Blount, who should "convey" it to New Bern [N.C.] by "the first opportunity." As NG's servant is "apt to drink," NG will "give him only Money sufficient to carry him from Stage to Stage." The servant will travel from Washington to Wilmington "on foot." NG asks Blount to let the servant have "two or three dollars or what may be necessary to bear his expences from Washington to Wilmington where he is to embark from by water for Charleston," S.C. Blount's brother [William?] could "minute" this expense in his "bill of disbursements." NG is en route to Philadelphia and Newport [R.I.] but intends to be back in Charleston "by the 10th of December."[2] Printed in Blount, Papers, 1: 179–80.]
1. As noted at NG to William Blount, 15 October, above, John Gray Blount was a partner with his brothers Thomas and William in a large mercantile firm. It appears from the contents of the present letter that John Gray Blount was at Washington, N.C., where the firm had its main store. (See also Blount, Papers, 1: xxii.)
2. NG returned to Charleston in late January 1785. (NG to Gibbs, 3 February 1785, below)

*   *   *

To Robert Forsyth

Dear Sir   Richmond [Va.] Octo 25th 1784

I leave this place with a heavy heart, the business which brought me here hangs still over my head like a threatning Cloud which embitters every moment of my life.[1] I beg you will take every step in your power for my relief. [James] Hunter and you had better sell your property in this Sta[te] as there appears little probability of extinguishing [E. John] Collett's demands in any other way. And I trust you will not oblige me to go to Gaol [i.e., jail] or sell my property until you have parted with you[rs?] which you have given in trust for this purpose.[2] M[r] [Henry] Banks seems disposed to settle with M[r] Hunter upon friendly terms and upon just princip[es.][3] Such funds as the old Company have drawn from the new the former must be accountable to the latter for. But it will be best to consult the Lawyers on the subject. Bradwine & Smith are accountable in my opinion as a part of the old Company.[4]

Cambell has agreed to bring an Action against [Robert] Patton; but whether this will produce any thing for our relief is uncertain.[5] Collette and John Banks have made a settlement and swallowed up all the payments in the penal bonds. I shall dispute the matter.[6] If you will get me free[7]

AL (MiU-C). The manuscript is incomplete.

1. On the purpose of NG's unsuccessful trip to North Carolina and Virginia, see note at NG to Rutledge, after 30 September, above.

2. Forsyth and Hunter were business partners of the recently deceased John Banks. (On Banks's death, see ibid.) Debts that NG had guaranteed for them as contractors to the Southern Army remained unpaid, and creditors such as Collett were now seeking recourse from NG. (See Agreement between Hunter, Banks & Company and NG with Newcomen & Collett, 8 April 1783 [vol. 12: 591 and n], and NG to Collett, 8 August 1784, both above, and NG to Lee, 22 August 1785, below.) For more about NG's request to Forsyth, see especially Pendleton to NG, 10 November; Hunter to NG, 1 June 1785; and NG to Forsyth, 5 June 1785, all below. NG wrote Edward Carrington on 29 September 1785, below: "I did all I could to get Forsyth to Virginia but could not."

3. On NG's recent meeting with John Banks's brother Henry, see note at Henry Banks to NG, 7 October, above. Hunter wrote NG on 1 June 1785 that Henry Banks "endeavoured to exculpate himself, and threw an Odium on me."

4. NG wrote Forsyth on 5 June 1785: "Those gentlemen have been pushing Henry Banks to get all the property of the old house [Hunter, Banks & Company] into their hands and have got a great deal."

5. James Campbel of Petersburg, Va., was an attorney employed by Collett. (NG to Blount, 15 October, above) Patton, a merchant who had been another of Banks's partners in the business of supplying clothing to NG's army, is named in the 8 April 1783 Agreement between Hunter, Banks & Company, NG, and Newcomen & Collett. John Banks, Patton, and Hunter had signed a statement on 7 May 1783, indicating that NG had no involvement in that business and pledging "to release and exonerate the said General Greene, from the principal or damages, should any arise, of or from [NG] being security for us" in that agreement. (Syrett, *Hamilton*, 10: 444) In a letter written after 16 November, below, NG told Henry Banks: "Every man who has seen the state of the matter think

Collett bound both in honor and justice to obtain all he can of Patton before he distresses me as he [i.e., Patton] was first bound." Edward Carrington wrote NG on 23 March 1785, below: "Mr Campbell [attorney James Campbel] has not yet sued Patton[,] for which he has alledged a Variety of reasons."

6. On the settlement between Collett and Banks, see also NG to Blount, 24 October, above.

7. The manuscript ends here, about one-third of the way from the bottom of the second page.

*   *   *

¶ [FROM WILLIAM DAVIES, Prince George, Va., 25 October 1784.[1] He "cannot sufficiently express my chagrin at losing the opportunity of paying my personal acknowledgements of respect and obligation" to NG. Had hoped to dine with him "in public" on Wednesday, but NG's "arrival was not soon enough and the corporation did not meet." On Thursday and Friday, "the distressful indisposition" of Davies's family "confined" him. On Saturday, Davies had the "disappointment" to discover that NG was "out of town," and the day he wrote the letter, although he "called very early at Col. Banister's," Davies found that NG "had set out."[2] He writes: "To merit and distinction like yours any tribute of my respect must be unequal, and lost amidst the joyful acclamations of my countrymen, whose gratitude I know is ever warm towards you and who have long called you the protector of the southern states." Davies's "feelings" alone would lead him to express "veneration" for NG's "character"; his "interest" would have made it "still more incumbent" on him, as he seeks NG's "friendly aid" in obtaining the "rights and privileges" due to him in his capacity as an officer. He reminds NG that he was appointed "commissioner of war" in Virginia at the beginning of 1781. Worried that acceptance of the post would compromise his "rights and rank as an officer," Davies consulted Steuben and NG "for direction" at that time. Davies recalls that NG not only gave his "permission," but that he also asked Davies to "act in the department."[3] As he was "Unwilling" to "do any thing which might give any umbrage," Davies never took "any of the oaths of office," conceiving himself to be an "officer on furlow or command." Similarly, Captain Young, "with permission," served in the Quartermaster Department, and Captain Pryor acted "in the Military stores."[4] Davies assumes they all "met with and merited the approbation of the commanding generals." Lately, however, "an objection has been started that it is contrary to the resolutions of Congress that we should exercise *civil* appointments and retain our rank in the army." Davies asks NG "for a testimonial how far I had your approbation and direction in the conduct I adopted, in undertaking the business of the war office, which I do not conceive a civil office. It would be hard too, if I should be deprived of any of my rights for acting in that difficult department, when many officers were at home doing nothing, and yet have no objections made to their claims." Young obtained "letters on the subject" from Davies, "which satisfied every person who had an objection," but he never returned those letters to Davies, who is now "obliged to have recourse to your goodness for such a testimonial on this subject as may be sufficient and proper."[5] RCS (MiU-C) 3 pp.]

1. On Davies, a Continental officer who had served as Virginia's commissioner of war, see above, vol. 6: 483–84n.

2. Davies lived in Prince George, near Petersburg, where NG had stopped for about ten days during his trip north from Charleston, S.C., to Rhode Island. NG left Petersburg for Richmond the day before this letter was written. (See NG to John Gray Blount and NG to Robert Forsyth, both 25 October, above.) On Col. John Banister, see NG's Journal entry for 4 September 1783, above.

3. Davies had served as commander of the Continental depot at Chesterfield Court House, Va., after he accepted the appointment as state commissioner of war. According to Davies, Steuben at that time "strenuously" urged "the necessity" of his continuing in both posts; Steuben informed NG on 30 March 1781, above, that Davies would do so. (Vol. 8: 15 and n) When, in a letter of 2 April 1781, Steuben asked NG to reconcile Davies's appointment with the "System laid down by Congress," NG replied that the rules of Congress permitted the holding of a state and a Continental office simultaneously but prohibited the holding of "two offices under Congress" at the same time. (Vol. 8: 30–31, 99 and n, above) Although he did not explicitly say so, NG's letter to Davies of 11 April 1781, above, appeared to support Davies's right to hold both offices at the same time and undoubtedly constituted a "request" in Davies's mind that he remain in the Continental service while holding a state office. (Vol. 8: 80–81)

4. Capt. Henry Young had served as state quartermaster general for Virginia while holding a Continental commission. Capt. John Pryor had been field commissary of military stores for the Southern Army. (See above, vol. 8: 27 and n, 243.)

5. If NG provided a "testimonial" for Davies on this matter, it has not been found.

* * *

To William Blount

Dear Sir   Richmond [Va.] Octo 26 1784

I wrote you by my Servant that Mr Cambell had got alarmed respecting the suit he ordered against the Administrator of John Banks; And that it was the opinion of some of the Lawyers here that a suit commenced and judgment entered up that the judgment could operate no farther t[han?] the amount of Banks property and that he could have no further remedy against me.[1] This doctrine as I expected has no foundation. Mr Randolph and Baker advise your pleading [E. John] Colletts bond in bar to any suit which may be commenced and so pay the Money into Mr Colletts hands as fast as recovered.[2] And this mode I wish you now to pursue notwithstanding all has been written before.[3] You will apply to General Casswell [Richard Caswell] and get the Bond or desire the General to plead it in bar to any Action which may be commenced. I am dear Sir with esteem Your Most Obed^t humble Ser

NATH GREENE

ADfS (MiU-C).

1. See NG to William Blount, 24 October, above. On NG's servant, see NG to John Gray Blount, 25 October, above.

2. On Collett's bond, see especially Agreement between Hunter, Banks & Company and NG with Newcomen and Collett, 8 April 1783, above (vol. 12: 591 and n), and NG to Lee, 22 August 1785, below.

3. In the letter immediately below, Blount wrote: "I fear that the Property I shall get will hardly pay for the Trouble of collecting it." (See also Blount to NG, 10 July 1785, below.)

From William Blount

Dear Sir   New Bern [N.C.] October 26th 1784
    I am favoured with your's of the 15th Ins[t] and shall observe the Contents.[1]
    I fear but very little of John Banks Property will be found. Evans and Jones Write and say they owe but a small Balance on their Bond that bond is in the Hands of Cap[t] Shute who promises me to deliver it in a few days. The Sloop at Beaufort commanded by youn[g] Easton sailed before our letters got down for Charleston [S.C.] or your old Friend his Father would have detained her.[2] I have not yet got the Brig's Salt into Possession nor is the little Sloop that was at Sea yet arrived and when She does the Cargoe will probably be salt and he (Banks) was only half Owner.
    In short I fear that the Property I shall get will hardly pay for the Trouble of collecting it.[3] Herewith you will receive a letter that was yesterday handed me by Express from Charleston.[4] Cap[t] Howell declining to purchase a Horse [from?] Cap[t] [Erasmus] Gill's Servant, I purchased one at forty Dollars, please get the Mony for me.[5] A House of Assembly was formed last Evening.[6] Please present my compliments to Carns [Patrick Carnes] and believe me with the highest Esteem, Your most Obedient Humble Servant   W[M] BLOUNT

RCS (MiU-C).
    1. See also NG to Blount, 24 and 26 October, above.
    2. The father was presumably John Easton, who mentioned in a letter to NG of 14 May 1782 from Beaufort, N.C., that he had once stayed with NG's family in Rhode Island. (Vol. 11: 193, above)
    3. See also Blount to NG, 10 July 1785, below.
    4. It is not known what letter Blount forwarded to NG.
    5. Blount apparently purchased the horse for NG.
    6. The North Carolina General Assembly had convened at New Bern on 22 October. (NCSR, 24: 650)

                    *   *   *

¶ [FROM CASEY SON & GREENE, East Greenwich, R.I., 26 October 1784. The Bell, which Jacob and Griffin Greene "are concerned in," will be ready to sail "by the last of November." She is "a very fine Strong Vessel of ab[t] 300 tons burthen." Casey Son & Greene want to send her "to Ireland with a Load of Flaxseed," but they fear they will not be able to "procure enough of that article to Load her." The Bell "woud stow 18 hundred Casks," and they ask NG to "enquire, whether it is probable she could procure a full freight at Charles Town [S.C.] for Europe & the price given per ton." If they could "procure a freight," they would not "hesitate a moment in sending her for that purpose." They ask NG for "the earliest information" about their proposal.[1] RC (MiU-C) 1 p.]

1. NG apparently tried to help, but Wanton Casey wrote him from Charleston on 25 July 1785, below: "As to the business I came upon[,] nothing has succeeded to my wishes or expectations, & the only alternative left is to send the Ship after a Load [of] Salt." Later that year, Griffin Greene sailed on the *Bell* to Charleston, hoping to procure a cargo for Europe. (Griffin Greene to NG, 16 December 1785, below)

¶ [FROM RICHARD CASWELL, New Bern, N.C., 26 October 1784. Has NG's letter of the 15th, "together with a Letter from [M]ʳ Campbell [i.e., James Campbel] & a Copy of Mʳ [John] Banks &c Bond [to?] [E. John] Collett & Company." As NG directed, a suit "will be instituted on this Bond to the Superior Court of this District on the 15ᵗʰ of next Month. Notice will be given to Colᵒ [William] Blount & if no defence is made a Judgement will probably be entered this Court."[1] RCS (MiU-C) 1 p.]

　　1. The enclosures have not been found. (See, however, Agreement between Hunter, Banks & Company and NG with Newcomen and Collett, 8 April 1783, above [vol. 12: 591 and n], and NG to Lee, 22 August 1785, below.) For background on the present letter, see also NG's letters to Blount of 15, 24, and 26 October, above. There was further correspondence between NG and Caswell on the subject of Banks's estate, but it has not been found. (Blount to NG, 10 July 1785, below)

¶ [FROM WILLIAM FINNIE, Richmond, Va., 28 October 1784. Asks NG for help in obtaining "relief against sundry Suits commenced, and some of them actually carried into Execution, for Debts due from the United States," that Finnie contracted while acting under NG "in the character of a public Servant." The suits have been "individually injurious, and a dishonour of public Justice."[1] Finnie complains bitterly of his "unmerited treatment" in this matter. His former assistants are "daily looking up" to him for "their just Rights," but their "Depreciation" has been "long withheld from them."[2] Finnie has "never realized a single Shilling, or rec[eiv]ed any compensation" for his services. He has applied to Congress and the state of Virginia "for relief" but finds himself "still neglected and exposed to the Suits of every public Creditor in the State."[3] As he does not wish to "trespass" on NG's "Time, and Goodness," He will "only State a few Cases for your Consideration and opinion, to enable you to plead my Cause with Congress."

　　First, he asks NG "to solicit from Congress an order for the final Settlement of all my Accounts," so that he and his assistants can be compensated for their services.[4] He believes his assistants deserve "as much the notice of Congress as any men in the Department of the Quarter Master General." One of them in particular, who joined the department "early in the war," is "clogged and burthened with a large Family." Secondly, Gilbert's judgment "for a quantity of Boots for the Cavalry to the Southward has actually been levied on my Property, which obliged me to dispose of some Certificates for my Pay as Quarter Master General for this State, at an enormous discount, and a valuable Negro, to save my Person from the horrors of a Prison."[5] Finnie refers NG to "the honᵇˡᵉ Samˡ Hardy, Chairman to the States for Information, and Papers" to support his claims.[6] Finnie believes the Assembly wanted to "relieve" him but did not know how; "If they could have been assured any advances made to me would have been allowed as discounts in the Requisition of Congress" on Virginia, Finnie is "confident they would have done it."[7] In conclusion, he asks NG to "employ your utmost Assistance" in promoting his cause at "the Seat of Congress."[8] RCS (MiU-C) 2 pp.]

1. Finnie had served as deputy quartermaster for Virginia. (Vol. 2: 312n, and vol. 3: 83n, both above)

2. Finnie referred here to compensation for the depreciation of his assistants' pay because of monetary inflation.

3. Finnie had petitioned the Committee of the States, then acting in place of Congress, the previous summer, but the Committee had decided it lacked authority and had referred the matter to the next meeting of Congress. (JCC, 27: 587) In a memorial to Congress of 6 December, Finnie again asked for relief from debts he had incurred on behalf of the United States. (PCC, item 41, vol. 3: 286, DNA)

4. NG wrote a brief, eloquent letter to Richard Henry Lee, the president of Congress, on 3 January 1785, below, pleading Finnie's cause. (See also JCC, 28: 19n.)

5. In his summer 1784 memorial to Congress, Finnie included "several authentic documents" and explained that in August 1780 he had been called upon to supply boots for "Col. [Anthony W.] White's and [Col. George] Baylor's dragoons then on their march to join the Southern army." When he asked Robert Gilbert of Williamsburg to provide the boots, Gilbert "refused to deliver them unless the said Finnie would *personally* undertake to pay him £180 per pr." Afterward, Finnie's memorial stated, Gilbert "instituted a suit in the Court of Hustings for the city of Williamsburg" against him and "recovered a Judgement against him for £197 Specie." (JCC, 27: 587)

6. Samuel Hardy was a delegate to Congress from Virginia.

7. According to a congressional report of 24 February 1785, a Virginia legislative committee had recommended that Finnie be "relieved" of Gilbert's suit against him, but the Assembly had rejected the report "because the state of Virginia could receive no Credit for such an Advance in the Annual requisition from Congress without an order of Congress authorizing the same." (JCC, 28: 100)

8. See NG to Lee, 3 January 1785. A committee, including Samuel Hardy, to whom Finnie had referred NG for particulars on his case, reported the facts of Gilbert's lawsuit against Finnie on 24 February 1785, and Congress resolved on that date that Finnie should be reimbursed "the sum of six hundred and fifty six dollars and two thirds of a dollar, the amount of a Judgement obtained against him by Robert Gilbert," and for his legal fees. In a further resolution of that day, Congress voted that the "commissioners of the treasury" should settle Finnie's accounts by paying him what was due him, "or such part thereof as the state of the finances will admit, without giving him any undue preference to other creditors." (JCC, 28: 100–01) Finnie continued to encounter difficulties in obtaining reimbursement for his services to the United States. (JCC, 31: 688–89, 739, 746)

¶ [FROM WILLIAM FINNIE, New Kent Court House, Va., 29 October 1784. "Mʳ [Patrick?] Henry" has promised to use his influence concerning Finnie's "bounty of lands &c." Finnie thinks "a few lines" from NG "respecting my conduct while in Office under you; would put the matter out of doubt."[1] Asks NG to leave a certificate with Henry.[2] RCS (MiU-C) 1 p.]

1. Officers who retired from the Continental army at the rank of colonel were entitled to grants of land at the close of the war. Finnie, however, had to establish that he was entitled to that rank. (JCC, 29: 637n) After looking into the matter, Henry Knox, the secretary at war, decided that because Finnie had been appointed to the Quartermaster Department in 1776, before Congress bestowed the rank of colonel on deputy quartermasters, he was not entitled to the privileges of that rank. Knox's report was ratified by Congress in February 1786. (The report, dated 15 September 1785, is in PCC, item 151, p. 107; see also JCC, 30: 40–41.)

2. In his decision on Finnie, Knox took into account a "certificate," dated 2 November 1784, in which NG wrote that Finnie "possesses an unquestionable claim upon the public" for the rank he sought. (PCC, item 151, p. 108; JCC, 29: 637n) The certificate has not been

found. NG's letter to Richard Henry Lee of 3 January 1785, below, was also read in Congress to bolster Finnie's claim. (*JCC*, 30: 26n)

* * *

From Jeremiah Wadsworth

Dear Sir   Hartford [Conn.] Nov 1. 1784

Your letter of Nov[r] 4th 1783 is the only one I received from you in Europe. That of the 7th June 1784 accompanying your Bill in fav[r] of Charles & And[w] Pettit for four hundred & fifty pounds sterling reached me here the 30th ulta[o] under cover of a letter from M[r] [John?] Lawrence to whom it was indorsed and was intended to have reached me at Liverpool,[1] but I was in Ireland & left it before any letters from England cou'd reach me. I now return the Bill to M[r] Lawrence supposing by this he may be returned to Phil[a]. The doubt You express of the sincerity of my sentiments of kindness[2] surprizes me after haveing pay'd your several Bills for more than three thousand dollars drawn on me without any advise except in one instance. I cannot well account for Your makeing use of such expressions in Your letter. If the Bill had arrived before I left England I certainly should have paid it tho I had appropriated all my Money and taken some Credit, but how you cou'd Venture, to draw on me when I was every moment expected in America I know not & It must certainly injure your Credit and my own to have the Bill returned, but to prevent any further mistakes it will not be convenient for me to accept any more Bills.[3]

I wrote you on my arrival at Phil[a] respecting Griffin Greenes Bill which wait your reply[.] The account of its non acceptance has reached Europe, and I need not observe to you that every person who has thier name on it must suffer in thier Credit. If I am left to pay that Bill I shall be greatly injured. I am certain I shou'd have accepted the Bill had I been in your situation and You in mine.[4] I am D Sir Your very Hum Ser[t]

JERE WADSWORTH

RCS (CtHi).

1. NG's letters to Wadsworth of 4 November 1783 and 7 June 1784 are both above.

2. See NG to Wadsworth, 7 June 1784.

3. Wadsworth's mood at this time was no doubt influenced by what his biographer has described as "the unprecedented business contraction" he had found upon his return from Europe.

"A drastic decline of prices, precipitated by the great export of specie to Europe, was intensified by the catastrophic effect of the closing of the British, Spanish, and most of the French West Indies to American ships upon the prices of farm produce, livestock, lumber, and small vessels. Excessive imports precipitated intense competition between merchants. The closing of the Mediterranean to American ships by the Barbary Pirates denied its market for fish and flour to American merchants. Mercantilist restrictions limited entry of American ships into English and Portuguese ports.

Independence had greatly curtailed outlets formerly enjoyed by American trade. The deepening depression would culminate early in 1785 in a business panic producing numerous bankruptcies. This crisis and business problems of the depression would tax Wadsworth's entrepreneurial skill as he extricated his affairs from a seriously unliquid condition." (Destler, "Wadsworth," pp. 244–45; see also Wadsworth to NG, 16 November, below.)

4. Wadsworth's letter to NG is above, dated 28 September. On NG's refusal to honor the the "Bill," see especially the note at Griffin Greene to NG, 6 April, as well as Pettit to NG, 19 June, and NG to Griffin Greene, 8 July, all above. Griffin Greene also discussed this matter in the letter immediately below. As seen in his reply to Wadsworth of 12 November, below, NG had misunderstood the purpose of the bills and Wadsworth's "agency in the business." It appears from NG's letters to Wadsworth of 24 April 1785, 13 May 1785, and 13 July 1785, all below, that an agreement was later reached to pay for the bills of exchange with proceeds from the sale of the vessel *Flora* by Griffin Greene. NG replied to the present letter on 12 November.

From Griffin Greene

Dear General   Bordeaux [France] Novr 2 1784

I fear the length of time I have been in this Country, has caused some jealoussy in your mind, respecting the prudence of my conduct, or that some part of the management of bussiness, has not met your approbation.[1] I know that you are just, in your determinations, & that you seldome condemn unheard, without their is proof so possitive as not to admit of any doubt. By the bulk of mankind the unsuccessful are always condemned, but I am sure you dont dwell upon the surface, neither do you go with curent oppinnion; it is your desire to take up all matters that come before you, without prejiduce [i.e., prejudice]. Their is a secrate influence in interest that is apt to sway the mind, that it is almost impossiable for humane nature not to feel its force, how ever I am of the oppinnion, if any man escapes its influ[en]ce you are that happy being. You have been home in my absence, & have seen that I have not been one of the number of the Sons of Fortune. Hear may some doubts, arise in your mind, how to account for my ill success, You are acquainted, & was before you left private life with my capacity to manage bussiness, & if I have not acted with prudence and good judgement, you are accessary in the fault, by setting me afloat in a Ship that I was unable to manage, you being an able Seaman, & capable of determining what Vessil I could manage, or was worthy to command, That I have not been industerious, or that I have meant to be unjust, I defy the sons of Adam to make out, to convince you that I intend to do what is right, I will leave all to your desision, and that I will abide. A man is courted or neglected as he meets success in the world. Your standing, has deservedly gained you many sutors; & they will all desire to be first in your sentiments, to gain that end they will not always stricttly attend to justice, it is not uncommon amongst men, that pay their coarte to the great, to have a little invey mixed in their charecters, & this possiabelty may make them once think of me in my absence, knowing the friendship, that has always subsisted betwen us, they may a little indulge by trying to undermine me, hopeing to rise on my fall. If I deserve not to stand, may I mete my just reward. I wrote you last winter, and gave the Letter to Col° [Jeremiah] Wadsworth to have forwarded which he told me he did,[2] I then Informed you, that I had taken goods to the amount Two Thousand pounds on your cradit.[3] These goods I had of Aug^te Dumoussay, freres [i.e., brothers],[4] Rue, d'Anjou, and Marais, N° 19 a Paris for the payment of which, I drew bills, on you payable in one Year, But had Contract, with the above Gentlemen, that the Bills, [w]ould not be protested; if not paid untill one year, the time of the goods being delivered which was principally in the Month of April following. I have been so unhappy, as not to get these goods, Shipped untill the Month of Augt hoping, to have took the[m] home my self. The Goods, was Shiped, by Cap^tn Edmun[d] Roberts bound for Boston. I have inclosed four Bills of Lading, to Jacob [Greene] by different Ships. They are ordred to be delivered Wm Gooch, of that place, & I h[ave] wrote him to weight [i.e., wait] Jacobs orders, respecting them[.] I have made Insurance, upon the Goods, at 4 ¼ p^r C['].[5] I am trying to get a credit lengthned Six, Mont[hs] longer, if I cannot, will pay for them out of the proseeds of the Ship *Flora*. The Bills are indorsed by Col. [Jeremiah] Wadsworth. I have made a contract, with the Messrs Dumoussay's to continue this cradit, as long as you are security, & we make punctual payment, that is they will advance, that sum so often as the first sum is paid, I conceived this to be advantageous, as the goods are bou^t at the cash price, so that we have the money for six P: C.[percent] p^r year, it was not in my powar to send the Invoice with the Goods. The Merchants not having furnished me with one, I now send them [to] Jacob, by Different Vessels. Pray rest easey, about this bussiness, as I will asuredly pay for them before I leave France, or will git the payment one year from now.[6] When at Paris last I was made very unhappy respecting these goods, Messrs Dumousay's having received a letter, from one Mr Chandler of Conecticut that the Bills had been presented you, & you had not accepted them saying that you did not know by what authority I undertook to draw on you, I have frequently informed you by letter, tha[t] I should make use of your letters of Cradit.[7] I have also wrote Jacob, from time to time, & informed that I had entred into contract; for Goods to the amount of two thousand pounds, on your cradit. The principal cause of my pain, in this affair is this, that you should suppose, that I had run you in debt to so large amount, & that I had not made any provision for the payment, hear I think you supposed that I had fell into the vice, you warned me against, that of gameing, but be assured I never in the whole time of my absence, ever gaimed for two

Coppers.⁸ I have wrote Jacob, a long letter, in which I have given him a history, how I have been imployed, & as I am, not acquainted, whare you are at Rhode Island, or at Carolina, have desired if at the latter place, he will send you a Copy. I see a French Man, that said you was at Rhode Island in june, whch is all that I know.⁹ It is very unhappy, for me to be so long, upon the Bussiness, of the Ship, especially as I have been so unfortunate, heartofore, but I live in hopes that you will point out some Chanel, through which I may do better with industry.

The General Opinnion is, that a War, betwe[e]n the Emperor [Joseph II of Austria], & the States General [rulers of Holland], is unavoidable, he having published a manifesto, that he would look upon it as a declareration (by the Duch if they fired upon his flag) of War, He previously, having given them information, that he should send a Vessel, from Anttwerp, to Hamburg down the River Scheldt. The Dutch not only fired upon theis Vessel, but took & condemned her, he send a second & they served her in like manner. The Emperor has surounded many of the Dutch settlements with his troops, & it is expected that hostillityes will soon commence. It is expected that this will involve all Europe, in a War.¹⁰ The French have opend their portes in the West Indieas, to all Nations, this is a matter that gives great uneasiness with the French Merchants, & espessially in this place.¹¹ I recievd a letter from the Che^y La Lusearne, wharein he speeks in the highest terms his Words, I shall be happy to do any thing in my powar, to serve General Greene, for I love him, for his sivel Virtues, & millitary tallents. I had applied to him to assist me, in gitting my bussiness finished & this appli[c]ation was made by informing him that it was to serve you,¹² & this way I have always taken to git the King to buy the Ship, The Owners are intebted [i.e., indebted] to your name that I get any thing considerable for her, without whch I could not ge[t] twenty thousand livers.¹³ I hope that you will not be offend[ed] at the above liberty, when you consider that I am not with out some reason for so doing, & not only so, cant see that it can possiably be of any disadvantage to your Charrecter, and it has given me the oppe[r]tunity of having the pleasure to know how you are regarded across the Atlantick & even by the great & brillient Coart of France. I hav[e] been told by the M[a]rquis de Casteries many times that the King took the Ship mearly to serve you.¹⁴ I fear I shall be Obliged to go again to Paris to get my bussiness of the Ship *Flora* through however I have taken every method to prevent it as I shall be ab[le] to convince you & every other reasonable person.¹⁵ So that I cannot tel any thing about the time that I shall be able to imbarke for America, but be assured that their is not any thing that I more ardiently wish than this period.¹⁶ You know my love for home & how domestick I am in my Ideaes, theirfore I am not much in fear that you will judge unfavorable tho I dont think that ever poor man was in

surcumstances that admitted more reasons for suspicion that was inno-
sent. My Love to Caty, I hope that she has not yet forfetted the wager,
little did I think when I parted with her that two years & half would
elaps towards five without my knowing who was likely to be the gainer
by the bett, if she should be intitled to the prize, at the conclution of the
appointed time, I am sure that many you[n]ge Women would give half
of all that they ever expect to receive to obtain the mistry however I fear
I have won the wager & that she has seen the tim[e] when her expectation has failed.[17] My best respects to all friends & be assured I am & ever
will be your sensear friend   GRIFFIN GREENE

RCS (MiU-C).
1. Griffin had expressed a similar fear in his letter to NG at the end of the September
documents, above. NG's letter to him of 8 July, above, as well as the difficulties he had
encountered in trying to sell the vessel *Flora* in France, were undoubtedly among the
causes of Griffin's concern. (See, for example, his letter to NG at the end of the September
documents.)
2. See Griffin Greene to NG, 8 February, above.
3. See Griffin Greene to NG, 6 April, above. NG had authorized Griffin to draw on him
for as much as £2,000 in France if necessary. (NG to Griffin Greene, 9 June 1783; see also
NG to Griffin Greene, 14 June 1783, both above.) Griffin had reported in his letter to NG of
6 April, above, that he was making use of this credit, but NG had afterward rejected the
bills he received, misunderstanding their purpose and Jeremiah Wadsworth's "agency in
the business." (See note at ibid.; NG to Griffin Greene, 8 July, above; and NG to Wadsworth, 12 November, below.) Griffin commented on NG's rejection of the bills in the
present letter and in one that he wrote to NG on 14 December, below. On the eventual
means of payment for the bills, see note at Wadsworth to NG, immediately above.
4. On this firm, see also Wadsworth to NG, 28 September, above.
5. The bills of lading have not been found. On William Gooch, see above, vol. 2: 8n.
6. On the results of Griffin's efforts to get his credit extended, see NG to Wadsworth, 13
July 1785, below. The invoices have not been found.
7. NG's rejection of the bills is discussed in note 3, above. "Chandler"—John Chaloner—
was a Philadelphia merchant. (Pettit to NG, 19 June, above)
8. NG had warned Griffin about gambling in a letter of 10 June 1783, above.
9. Griffin's letter to NG's brother Jacob has not been found. NG, who had left Rhode
Island in July to attend to business in South Carolina, returned home in late November.
(NG to Gibbons, 29 November, below)
10. On the threat of war in Europe, see note at Butler to NG, 23 December, below.
11. See note at Wadsworth to NG, 1 November, above.
12. Griffin referred here to the Chevalier de La Luzerne, who had been the French
minister to the United States during the war.
13. As seen in Griffin's letter to NG of 6 April, the French government had tentatively
agreed to buy the *Flora* at a price yet to be determined. The intervention of friends of NG,
including the Marquis de Lafayette, had apparently been important in moving negotiations to that point. (Griffin Greene to NG, 12 June, and Wadsworth to NG, 28 September,
both above) The vessel had already been valued twice. (Griffin Greene to NG, 16 May and
end of September, above) Griffin wrote NG on 14 December that the price had again been
adjusted because of "the Bottom of the Ship proving bad and unsound."
14. The Marquis de Castries was the French naval minister.
15. As seen in his letter of 14 December, Griffin did return to Paris because of the
problems with the "Bottom of the Ship."

16. Griffin did not return to the United States until the summer of 1785. (Wadsworth to NG, 10 July 1785, below) NG discussed receiving this letter from Griffin in a letter to CG of 14 April 1785, below.

17. The nature of Griffin's long-standing wager with CG is not known, but Griffin, if he won, would apparently be entitled to a suit of clothes. The wager was still unsettled the following April. (Vol. 12: 665n, above; NG to CG, 14 April 1785, below)

To Edward Carrrington

My dear Col   Mount Vernon [Va.] Nov 10th 1784
  My own happiness the fate of my family and every thing that is interesting to me depend so much upon the issue of the business you have in charge that I cannot omit this favorable opportunity by General Washington of soliciting again your special attention to the matter.[1] Those Richmond Lots I beg you to find out if possible and engage Harry to appropriate them for my release from my present engagements. I wrote to old Mr Banks near Fredricksburgh and can but hope now Harry is ingaged for the consequences that he will do some thing for his relief as he offered his brother £2000 for his [i.e., John Banks's lots] before his death.[2] If my importunity is troublesome let my situation serve as an apology for it. The loss of property is nothing to the distress of a family. To have those involved in ruin is a tryal almost too severe for phylosophy it self. Dont fail to spur on Cambell to bring forward his suit against [Robert] Patton and when [Robert] Forsyth and [James] Hunter arrive urge them to turn all the property Mortgaged to me into pay-ments to Collette and let them settle the matter with Harry as to the proportion which he or they ought to pay.[3] It is unreasonable to oblige me to sell my property and with hold theirs and this must take place or I go to Goal [i.e., jail] unless they accomodate payments in this way. I see no prospect of any other mode. God bless you with better health and may fortune be more propitious to you than to me is the wish of your sincere friend   NATH GREENE
  If Cambell could be made to believe that Collette will loose part of his Debt if he dont pursue Patton his interest will oblige him to it. I am much in debt and will pay my own Creditors first either by mortgages or other modes.[4]

ACyS (NNPM).
  1. "The business" concerned NG's efforts to free himself from debts to E. John Collett and others that he had guaranteed for the late John Banks; Carrington was serving as NG's attorney in Virginia. (NG to Blount, 24 October, above) The "favorable opportunity" to write to Carrington, whom NG had seen during a recent stop in Richmond, was undoubtedly a visit there that Washington, NG's host at Mount Vernon, was about to make in order to meet the touring Marquis de Lafayette and escort him back to Mount Vernon. Washington arrived in Richmond on 14 November, a few days before Lafayette. (Washington, *Papers*, Confederation Series, 2: 135–36n, 144)
  2. "Harry" was John Banks's brother Henry. On the "Richmond Lots," which Henry

was believed to have owned with his brother, see above, NG to Collett, 8 August, and below, NG to Henry Banks, after 11 November. NG probably obtained information about the lots from correspondence of Henry's that he had seen, as well as from word of mouth. (See NG to Forsyth, 2 October, above; NG to Banks, after 11 November, and Hunter to NG, 1 June 1785, both below.) NG's letter to "Old Mᴿ Banks"—John's and Henry's father, Gerard—has not been found. In a letter of 27 February 1785, below, Carrington advised NG: "I fear indeed that you are badly circumstanced with respect to any property which may have been connected with J[ohn]. B[anks]."

3. "Cambell" was James Campbel, an attorney for Collett in Virginia. (NG to Blount, 15 October, above) Patton, Forsyth, and Hunter had all been connected with John Banks in the business transactions that NG guaranteed. In his letter to NG of 27 February 1785, Carrington reported: "As to Patton I can give you no flattering prospects from that quarter, no Suit has yet been brought, at least there was not a few weeks ago, you know it is dependent on others and they alledge that circumstances are not yet favourable for such a Measure." As seen, for example, in Hunter's letter to NG of 1 June 1785, Hunter and Henry Banks reached a legal impasse. NG wrote Carrington on 29 September 1785, below: "I did all I could to get Forsyth to Virginia but could not."

4. On the proposed suit against Patton, see the preceding note.

From Nathaniel Pendleton

My Dear General   Charleston [S.C.] Novᴿ 10ᵗʰ 1784.

As soon as I arrived, I set myself to make the enquiries and execute the Commission you gave me.[1] There has been an inconvenience arising from the Bond given to Collett being in the hands of a Gentleman in Virginia, and not in this State. This circumstance has prevented Mᴿ Rutledge from laying hold of [John] Ferrie's Lands on account of that Debt, but he has thought it best not to delay the matter, and has fixed an Attachment on them, on the Bond to Harris and Blachford.[2] As you are equally bound to pay both those Debts I imagined it would be better to secure the Lands on Harris and Blachford's account than to wait a Month or two till Collett's Bond could be obtained from Virginia: And I believe one Debt is as desperate as the other. The Lands in Georgia will remain till Colletts Bond comes, whereas if it had been here, I intended to have issued an attachment against them immediately.[3] Mᴿ [Nicholas?] Prim[e]rose[,] Colletts agent has sent to Virginia for the papers, & I hope they will arrive before the time of your return here. I have examined into the relinquished funds of Harris & Blachford and the true State of that case seems to be this—the Ballance of a settlement due to H.& B. was about £14000. They took two Bonds from Carnes and McQueen which reduced it to £7624. On the same day Forsyth & Cᵒ assigned over to them by a seperate Deed of Assignment Debts to the amount of this 7624£ in which Deed those Bonds of Carnes & McQueen's were not included, being taken only for the ballance due, after deducting them as so much paid. Afterwards H & B relinquished this last Assig[n]ment, and took about 3000£ in Maryland Certificates, with other assignments of Debts to the amount of the £7624. Now you will observe that this assignment which was relinquished, was subsequent to the assignment of Carnes's & McQueen's Bonds, and they being considered as payments, which now prove to be bad, they leave so much of the Bond due, as they were intended to pay. I am of opinion therefore with Mr Rutledge that the relinquishment of the Assignment will not be of an advantage to you, or hurt to H & B.[4]

With respect to [William] Pierce, [Anthony W.] White, and [Richard] Call, I go to Georgia on Sunday next, and will interest myself in the business. Call is in Town, but I can't find out the date of the Deeds, to know whether Pierce had notice of the fraud at the time of their being made. I shall endeavor to induce them by all means to concur with you in Charging Ferrie's property as the only way to secure themselves. Call would be glad to have back the Lands and pay the Debt due to the Company, and this I think would be equitable, and might be effected with the concurrence of all the parties. It would be cruel, if it were practicable to take away the Lands, and oblige them to pay the Debt too, whereas by their concurrence the Debt might be paid to Banks & Co's Creditors, and Ferrie be compelled to Deliver up Conveyances which were obtained upon a fraudulent suggestion. I beg you to think of this plan, and see if any thing like it can be done, and I will endeavor to prepare our friends in Georgia against your arrival.[5]

Forsyth tells me he had written you a Letter relative to the assignment of the remaining Debts, which he hopes you have received. He declines making any farther Assignments until all the accounts shall be Settled. He hopes you will not think him wrong in this, as those Debts are all he has to depend upon to keep between him and the other Creditors, whose Debts being smaller are more Clamorous, than the other[s].

[James] Hunter left Town, about an hour after my arrival, but I saw Forsyth, who saw him before he went. I requested Forsyth to ask him to go with me before his departure, and add another Witness to the Deeds, but he said he would do nothing more in the business either as to Settlements or Securities, before he consulted his Lawyer in Virginia. Forsythe declines also adding another Witness to his Deeds, and says he thinks it unnecessary, and indeed I think so too, if what he says is true, that he had never had deeds for the Lot mortgaged, but only a bond for Conveyance; and he says Hunter's is the same. A Bond to Convey an Estate, does not give Such an Estate, as is capable of being Mortgaged, therefore you have only such an agreement by the mortgage, as Equity will compel them to perform specifically, which is inferior to a mortgage in this, that a Mortgage is such a tie upon the Land, that the prior one will always take place; wherefore if they were to have Conveyances made, & then mortgage the same lands, the latter would take place before your agreement, even tho' it had twenty Witnesses. The best thing you can do is to get them to have Deeds made to them, and then take a proper Mortgage. This distinction in Law arises from the difference between a Contract absolutely executed, and one which is only made but not executed.[6]

I have now said every thing, I think will contribute to give you a satisfactory account of the State of this perplexing affair from which I most cordially wish you were entirely free. With Activity I hope the worst thing attending it, will be the trouble, and anxiety, which are great, and very mortifying.

I hope you will receive this letter, before you leave New Port [i.e., Newport, R.I.].[7] Colonel [Lewis] Morris [Jr.] has promised to inclose it to a Gentleman in New York, to whom it will set off on Saturday, by a Sloop going there; On which day also I set out to Savannah. I am told they are quarrelling with each other about Lands there, and Lawyers much sought for.[8] What a profession is ours that can never thrive but by the frequent rascallity of mankind! We first foment their differences, that we may have an opportunity to be paid for composing them again.

There are several matrimonial plans in agitation here. And among the rest Brooke Roberts to Miss Van Bram. The young Lady being extreemly sick, she informed her father no medecine could cure her but his consent to marry her Lover. She pined, he refused. She grew worse, he grew angry; When some of those good Divinities, who interest themselves in the affairs of lovers interposed in her favor took away all his other four Children, and reducing her to the brink of the Grave, threatened to leave him childless. Whereupon the old Gentleman gave his consent to save his Child, and Hymen is to crown the matter, as soon as she recovers so much fire in her half extinguished eyes as is necessary to light his torch.[9] This story is for M[rs] Greene, to whom I beg to be presented in the most respectfull & Affectionate manner. I will not tell you my Dear General, how gratefully I remember all your kindnesses to me, nor the value I set upon the friendship that prompted them. Time only can shew. Adieu adieu   NATH[l] PENDLETON

RCS (NcD).
1. NG apparently had seen Pendleton in Virginia on his way north. (See To Whom It May Concern, 21 October, and Pendleton to NG, 22 October, both above.) As seen in the present letter, Pendleton, who was about to move to Savannah, Ga., was handling some of NG's legal affairs in Charleston.
2. For background, see above, NG to Hugh Rutledge, after 30 September, and NG to Robert Forsyth, 2 October. On the "Bond given to [E. John] Collett," see above, Agreement between Hunter, Banks & Company and NG with Newcomen and Collett, 8 April 1783 (vol. 12: 591 and n). NG was the guarantor of that agreement and of one that the now-deceased John Banks and his partners had made with the firm of Harris & Blachford. (See also NG to Collett, 8 August, above.)
3. On Ferrie's involvement with Banks and on efforts to attach property belonging to Ferrie, see especially Forsyth to NG, 18 June, above. As noted there, NG's estate eventually won a suit against Ferrie in South Carolina.
4. NG was hoping to obtain relief for the amount of Banks's debt that Harris &

Blachford had relinquished. (NG to Rutledge, after 30 September, and NG to Forsyth, 2 October) On the bonds that Patrick Carnes and John McQueen had given to Banks, see above, Saunders to NG, before 17 July; Pettit to NG, 26 July, and Penman to NG, 12 August. In a sworn statement, Pendleton wrote in 1790: "The House of Robert Forsyth and Company made an assignment of debts to a very considerable amount, (I cannot recollect, how much) to Harris and Blackford, which I drew, and they were, then, generally considered, as good debts. These, I believe, were afterwards, relinquished by Harris and Blackford, for some bonds, which bonds, I understood, are disputed; and I am informed, a suit in Chancery is still depending concerning that affair." (Pendleton's statement, dated 4 June 1790, is printed in Syrett, *Hamilton*, 10: 458–64; quote from p. 460.) The issue of NG's obligation to Harris & Blachford was not finally resolved until a decade after NG's death. Edward Rutledge, writing from Charleston on 27 May 1795, informed Alexander Hamilton, the secretary of the treasury, about the outcome of a civil suit there: "The Cause of the Execs of General [Greene] vs. Harris & Blackford, has been decided; & we have lost it: The Argument lasted for three days, & I exerted every Faculty in favor of our Friend [NG]: but it was all in vain; & we shall have the enormous Sum of 11000 Sterling to pay in this unfortunate Business. Mrs: Greene, (as well she might) relies implicitly on your Friendship for assistance. She means to make an application to Congress for Relief, & is sanguine in her expectation." (Syrett, *Hamilton*, 18: 353) In response to a memorial submitted by CG on 14 March 1796, Congress voted in June of that year to indemnify NG's estate for £11,297.9.8 "on a certain bond given by" NG "to Harris and Blachford" on 8 April 1783 "as surety for John Banks and partners; and the interest thereon: *Provided*, it shall appear, upon due investigation by the officers of the Treasury, that the said General Greene, in his life-time, or his executors since his decease, have not already been indemnified, or compensated for the same: *And provided*, the said executors shall make over to the United States all property, mortgages, bonds, covenants, or other counter securities whatever, if any such there are, which were obtained by General Greene in his life-time, from the said John Banks and partners, or either of them; and all causes of action on account of his being surety for them as aforesaid, to be sued for, in the name of the said executors, for the use of the United States." Payment was to be made to the executors by the U.S. Treasury with "money not otherwise appropriated" and was to be accounted for "as part of the said estate." (*U.S. Statutes at Large* 6 [1846]: 28) As noted at NG to Collett, 8 August, Congress had previously indemnified NG's estate for certain other obligations, including one to Newcomen & Collett. According to the report of a House of Representatives committee in 1798, the two acts "in discharge of the debts originally contracted by Hunter, Banks, & Co., for which General Greene became surety," had resulted in payments to NG's estate of $47,504.15, including $27,504.15 "Under the first act [1792]" and $20,000 "Under the second [1796]." (*American State Papers: Claims* 1 [1834]: 212) In the 1798 report, a resolution was offered that had been sought in Blachford's behalf several times since 1792: To change a debit of $9,768 80/90 that Robert Morris had charged against Banks's account in 1783 into a credit to his estate, payable to its creditors, including Blachford. Under this resolution, which apparently was never enacted, that amount would have been drawn from Treasury funds still owed to NG's estate. (Ibid.)

5. For background, see above, Forsyth to NG, 18 June; Pierce to NG, 24 September; and Call to NG, 30 September.

6. Forsyth's letter to NG has not been found. (See, however, NG to Forsyth, 2 October) On 2 September, Forsyth had assigned to NG two bonds in his possession that were backed by land holdings in Virginia. (Syrett, *Hamilton*, 10: 444–46) As seen in NG's letter to Forsyth of 2 October, NG was under the impression that Hunter, another of Banks's business partners, had sold land in Virginia "about the time he was conveying it to me as counter security." This was apparently not true. (Hunter to NG, 1 June 1785, below)

7. NG's reply, if any, has not been found. When Pendleton wrote NG from Savannah on 25 April 1785, below, it appears that he had recently seen NG there.

8. According to his statement of 4 June 1790, Pendleton took up residence in Georgia about this time. (Syrett, *Hamilton*, 10: 460–61n)

9. Roberts was Richard Brooke Roberts, a former Continental officer, whose father, Owen, also a Continental officer and a former legislator, had been killed in the line of duty in 1779. (*Biog. Directory of S.C. House*, 3: 612; Heitman, *Register*) He married Everarda-Catharine-Sophia Van Braam Houckgeest, daughter of A. E. Van Braam Houckgeest, of Charleston, in January 1785. (*SCHGM* 19 [1918]: 137)

To Henry Banks

Sir   [after 11 November 1784][1]
The evening I left Richmond I was told by a person who said he knew it to be a fact that there was sundry Lots in Richmond the property of Hunter Banks & Company unappropriated. I desird Col [Edward] Carrington to speak to you on the subject and if it was as I was told to get it deposited in the hands of Colletts attorney.[2] I hope you will have no objection to this as it will release so much of your other property and greatly oblige me.[3] And I assure you I find my distresses hourly increasing from the alarm which my own creditors have taken.

On my arrival here I find it is made a question by a Gentleman of the Law whether the ballance due upon the contract from M[r] [Robert] Morris can be recoverd by M[r] [James] Miller who had I am told a power and order to receive it. If M[r] Miller has got an assignment from your brother it will be good but if only a power [of attorney] it ceases from the death of your brother. And should that be the case who ever Administers on your brothers effects will have the right of appropriation[,] for your brother being mentioned in the contract alone[,] none but his Administrator ever gave an assignment. M[r] Miller will no doubt claim it.[4] If you Administer you will do as you thing [i.e., think] your honor [*several lines deleted*] While at Fredericksburgh [Va.] I wrote your father and solicited his aid as you had become engaged and I can but hope he will as he made an offer to this effect to your brother.[5] Dont fail to press Cambell to bring forward his suit against [Robert] Patton. Every man who has seen the state of the matter think Collett bound both in honor and justice to obtain all he can of Patton before he distresses me as he was first bound.[6] I am Sir Your humble Ser

NATH GREENE

ADfS (MiU-C).

1. This letter was most likely written after NG's to Edward Carrington of 10 November, above, probably from Philadelphia, where NG is known to have spent at least two days: 12 and 13 November. (See his letters of those dates, below.)

2. NG was in Richmond, Va., in late October. (NG to Forsyth, 25 October, and NG to Blount, 26 October, above) On the "Lots in Richmond" and the involvement of E. John Collett's attorney, see especially NG to Carrington, 10 November.

3. Carrington wrote NG on 27 February 1785, below: "Your affairs with Hen. Banks I fear will e'er long wear but a bad aspect, and although nothing authorizes my declaring that it will be out of his power to give you any indemnification on your sufferring by J[ohn].B[anks].⁵ Creditors, yet I cannot forbear to Warn you that such a circumstance from present appearances is too probable."

4. For background, see Pettit to NG, 27 April, above. The contract referred to here was that of Henry Banks's late brother John for supplying provisions to the Southern Army. (On the contract, see Carrington to NG, 19 February 1783, above [vol. 12: 463 and n].) Law.com Dictionary (http://dictionary.law.com) defines assignment as "the act of transferring an interest in property or some right (such as contract benefits) to another." As noted at Pettit to NG, 27 April, Miller had received an assignment from John Banks for contract money owed to Banks.

5. As noted at NG to Carrington, 10 November, the letter to Banks's father, Gerard, has not been found.

6. On the proposed suit against Patton, see ibid. "Cambell" was Collett's attorney James Campbel.

*   *   *

¶ [TO ROGER PARKER SAUNDERS. From Philadelphia, 12 November 1784. NG has "only time to tell" Saunders that he is "here and well" and that he is "going from this to Newport [R.I.] and from thence to Charleston," S.C.¹ He is "still in great jeopardy as to [John] Banks's affairs" but has "added som[e] little security from the measures" he has taken.² Asks Saunders for "attention to my Crop" and to make the payments that NG instructed by letter from North Carolina: "Pay Nat Russel £50, the London Druggist 600 Dollars,³ Mʳ [Charles] Pettit 1000 or 1200,"⁴ and, if possible, 100 guineas to CG. Saunders is to pay "the several Account[s] against" NG in Charleston "for supplies to the Plantation"; he should also retain the "rest of the Crop" until NG returns "and pray see that it is not wasted." At the foot of the letter, NG lists the amounts, totaling $2,930, that are to be paid to the persons and accounts mentioned here.⁵ ADfS (NjP) 2 pp.]

1. NG wrote Samuel A. Otis on 24 July 1785, below, that he had gone "no less than three times" to Philadelphia, "dancing attendance" on officials there to try to get his army accounts settled. This was the third such visit, the others having taken place in October–November 1783 and June 1784. NG was in Newport by the end of November and in Charleston by the beginning of February. (NG to Gibbons, 29 November, and NG to Gibbs, 3 February 1785, below)

2. The "measures" NG had taken to try to secure himself against liabilities he had assumed in guaranteeing debts for Banks are discussed in many of the letters he wrote in August, September, and October, above, while he was in the South.

3. NG's letter to Saunders from North Carolina has not been found. (He was there in early October.) Nothing is known about the debt to Nathaniel Russell. The "London Druggist" was presumably either Dr. Isaac Senter of Newport, whom NG included in his list of creditors at the foot of this letter, or an English exporter from whom Senter had obtained pharmaceuticals for his store. (See note at NG to Howson, Edwards & Company, 6 August, above.)

4. See above, Pettit to NG, 26 July, and NG to Pettit, 15 August.

5. NG wrote Dennis De Berdt on 9 March 1785, below, that he was sending £180 sterling on Pettit's account but added: "My Crops in South Carolinia and Georgia fell so far short of my expectation from the heavy Rains which prevailed in harvest time that I cannot

fulfill my engagements. I was to have remitted about thirteen hundred Dollars for Mr Pettit and shall still try to get another bill to complete my engagement. But I am not certain it will be in my power to accomplish it."

*　　　*　　　*

To Jeremiah Wadsworth

Dear Sir   Philadelphia Nov 12th 1784

For so I will address you notwithstanding the line of formality you have drawn between us.[1] Warm attachments are ever susceptible of fears of a want of returning affection from those we esteem. If my letters betrayed any thing different from this the language has not corresponded with my feelings. If I have injured you in friendship, if I have done any thing inconsistent with the laws of honor or principles of justice let me suffer without alleviation. My distress from a variety of misfortunes imposed upon me from public necessity was sufficiently oppressive before I got your letters which weakened a keener sensibility. I will open to you my bosom, if I have been guilty of an impropriety much less an intentional wrong bury a dager in that heart which ever wished you well.

You say had you been in my situation and I in yours, you certainly should have accepted the bills.[2] Nor should I have hesitated for a moment had I known the circumstances. But at the time they were presented I got a letter from Mr Griffin Greene who wrote that he had mortgaged my letter of credit for sundry merchandize without mentioning a syllable of your having any agency in the business.[3] This made it all a mystery to me. Bills drawn for £2000 in your favor and my letter mortgaged for £2000 more. The sum was serious and the consequence might be fatal. Griffin, a young man, little acquainted with the world, I could not tell what folly or extravagance had given birth to such heavy drafts. His draft and letter arriving at the same moment, and no reference from one to the other left me all in the dark and being then under lash of similar misfortunes from acceptance of bills rendered some precaution necessary. All I desird was to be informed of the object and intention of the draft and the reason and cause of it. It was upon my letter of credit I held myself bound both in honor and conscience but if other wise I did not. Griffin was to blame in not stating facts and the more so as you had ingaged in the business from motives of kindness. Had you been in my situation and I in yours your prudence would not have been less precautious. And what served to increase my perplexity, Griffin had written me but a little while before that he should have no occasion to make use of my letter.[4] If my conduct towards you in this business has been either improper or ungenerous as you seem to hint in your letter it has proceeded from ignorance and not intention. And had

Jeremiah Wadsworth, 1743–1804, and his son Daniel, 1771–1848;
oil painting by John Trumbull
(Wadsworth Atheneum)

you known the facts I am persuaded you would have been less cold and severe in your strictures. I was transported with the news of your arrival and promised myself great happiness from our meeting. My distresses were lessened from the contemplation of having a friend to lean upon. Think what were my feelings on finding you offended and reproaching me with folly, presumption and ingratitude. To struggle manfully with adversity adds dignity to human nature; but I never wish to be the cause, I had rather be the sufferer. My misfortunes may have led me to exceed the bounds of merchantile propriety nor did I consider this as a rule of conduct between you and me. I mean not to complain. You have obliged upon former occasions. I acknowledge it with all the frankness due to friendship. I will not say that I ever had or ever shall have it in my power to oblige you. I can assure you I never wanted a disposition. I am going from this to Newport and soon to the Southward.[5] But before I go it would give me pleasure to have an opportunity to place my conduct in a proper light. It is not from motives of interest that I wish it but from principles of delicacy. I should be exceeding glad to see you at Newport, but if you can not come I would visit you at Hartford altho it will be inconvenient.[6] I am dear Sir with sentiments of esteem & regard Your Most Obed & humble Ser   NATH GREENE

ALS (CtHi).
1. See Wadsworth to NG, 1 November, above.
2. On NG's rejection of the bills that Wadsworth had endorsed for Griffin Greene, see especially the note at Griffin Greene to NG, 6 April; Pettit to NG, 19 June, and NG to Griffin Greene, 8 July, all above.
3. See Griffin Greene to NG, 6 April.
4. The letter referred to here is Griffin Greene's to NG of 1 October 1783, above.
5. NG returned to Newport, R.I., in late November and was back in Charleston, S.C., by early February 1785. (NG to Gibbons, 29 November, and NG to Gibbs, 3 February 1785, both below)
6. Wadsworth replied to this letter on 16 November, below. He visited NG at Newport in late December. (NG to Wadsworth, 29 December, below)

*   *   *

¶ [FROM GOVERNOR JOHN HOUSTOUN OF GEORGIA, Savannah, Ga., 12 November 1784. He received NG's letter of 12 September "whilst at Augusta."[1] When he returned to Savannah, he "took the earliest opportunity" of writing to the "Spanish Governor, and the late British Governor" regarding the "Subject Matter" of NG's letter. He has not yet heard from either man but expects to "soon" and will inform NG of the "result."[2] He is "really at a Loss how to proceed against these lawless People. Their conduct in many particulars is such as would justify any Steps whatever, And their Insolence so great as would render it unsafe for any but a pretty strong force to go amongst them. However, it's possible my application may produce the intended Effect."[3] As his brother is in Philadelphia, Houstoun could not "put the Business" into "his Hands."[4] RCS (NcD) 2 pp.]
1. The Georgia government assembled alternately at Augusta and at Savannah during this period.
2. Houstoun wrote Vicente Manuel de Zéspedes, the Spanish governor of East Florida, on 27 October: "It having been represented to me by the Proprietors of the Island of Cumberland, that certain British subjects at present in your Province make a Practice of cutting and shipping Live Oak and other timber from that Island to the West-Indies; I take the liberty of mentioning the same to your Excellency in order that, so far as the British

shipping in St Marys River may be subject to the Controul of His Catholic Majesty's Officers, a Conduct so unjustifiable may be prevented in future." (Lockey, *East Florida*, pp. 300–301) Zéspedes replied on 28 November that "since the last treaty of peace concedes eighteen months for the British to evacuate this province without molestation, I cannot, during that term, disturb their transports on the St. Marys River, nor can I at any time take cognizance of the excesses committed by subjects of another sovereign on territory not under my sovereign's jurisdiction." (Ibid., p. 315; a translation of an extract of Zéspedes's letter to Houstoun, dated 12 December, is at MiU-C.) On the transition from British to Spanish rule in East Florida, see NG to Zéspedes, 26 March 1785, and NG to CG, 14 April 1785, both below. Houstoun's letter of 27 October to Patrick Tonyn, the British governor of East Florida, who was organizing the evacuation of Loyalist refugees from the province, has not been found, but a copy of Tonyn's reply, dated 6 December, is also at MiU-C. Tonyn wrote there that if Houstoun's "Information" about the "Trespasses said to be committed by the British subjects" on NG's and John Bowman's property on Cumberland Island should "prove to be well founded," such deeds were committed "intirely without my Knowledge and contrary to orders." He had written to the "agent of the British Transports Shipping at St Marys to make particular Inquiry therein," asking the agent to send him "a Circumstantial report of the Damages said to be done and by whom," and had given the agent "Strict Injunctions That all depredations whatsoever may be carefully avoided by British Subjects." (MiU-C; Tonyn's letter is appended to the translation of Zéspedes's that is mentioned in this note.) No further correspondence on this matter between Houstoun and Tonyn has been found.

3. Many of the refugees had left Cumberland Island by the following spring, when the evacuation of British subjects and Loyalists from nearby East Florida was nearly completed. (See note at Osborne to NG, 23 April 1785, below.) By then, NG was hoping to induce some of them to stay and form a permanent settlement on the island. (Fatio to NG, 6 April 1785; NG to CG, 14 April 1785; and NG to Marbois, 15 April 1785, all below) Cumberland, however, continued to attract refugees from the mainland during the mid-1780s and later. Historian Mary Bullard notes that "in 1788 a traveling Frenchman saw many *habitations* (little houses)" there, "built, he said, by refugees from the depredations of Creek Indians." (Bullard, *Cumberland Island*, p. 110)

4. On Houstoun's brother William, see NG to John Houstoun, 12 September, above.

¶ [TO ROBERT MORRIS.[1] From Philadelphia, 13 November, 1784. In a promissory note, NG agrees to pay Morris 3,229 "Dollars of Mexico or other Coin equivalent, being for Value advanced by him for my use." Payment will be made on 14 July 1785 "in the National Bank of N^o America at Philadelphia."[2] DS (Ct) 1 p.]

1. Morris, who submitted his resignation as superintendent of finance in January 1783, had continued to serve through 1783 and most of 1784 at the request of Congress. (Morris to NG, 14 March 1783, above [vol. 12: 514–15 and n]) On 30 September, he notified the Board of Treasury that he would "terminate" his "Operations" on that date. (Morris, *Papers*, 9: 548) According to the editors of his papers, Morris did not "completely 'cease to act'" as superintendent until the Board of Treasury actually convened, but he did close "the official accounts of his administration" on 30 September. (Ibid., p. 548n; see also Wadsworth to NG, 15 February 1785, below.) Charles Thomson, the secretary of Congress, wrote Daniel of St. Thomas Jenifer, one of the board members, on 19 October that Morris closed "his transactions with the end of last Month and though he continues to discharge the Engagements he had made, he contracts no new ones. So that business is partly at a stand until the board meets." (Smith, *Letters*, 21: 814; for more about the Board of Treasury, see Wadsworth to NG, 15 February 1785, below.)

2. For more about this loan, see Morris to NG, 28 January 1786, below.

¶ [FROM GRIFFIN GREENE, Bordeaux, France, 14 November 1784. According to "Mr James Price at Paris," Dumoussay et Frères have received a letter from "a Mr Chandler [i.e., John Chaloner] of Philadelphia" stating that NG "had avoided going through that place" and "would not come to an explanation."[1] Griffin writes: "what ever you have don in this matter I dare say you had good Reason. I only wish that I could recall the Bills without this publick noise."[2] As Griffin will "pay for the Goods," NG "may rest easey."[3] In a postscript, he adds that "War is absolutely declared betwen the Emperor & the Dutch."[4] Griffin is "obliged to go once more to Paris" but is afraid he will "not meet success."[5] RCS (MiU-C) 1 p.]

    1. See also Griffin Greene to NG, 2 November, above; NG to CG, 14 April 1785, and Wadsworth to NG, 10 July 1785, both below. On the reasons for NG's rejection of the bills of exchange that Griffin had drawn on him, see NG to Wadsworth, 12 November, and Wadsworth to NG, 16 November, immediately below. By happenstance, NG was in Philadelphia at about the same time that Griffin wrote this letter. (See NG to Wadsworth, 12 November, and NG to Morris, 13 November, above.)

    2. On the "publick noise" that had resulted from NG's rejection of the bills, see also Wadsworth to NG, immediately below.

    3. See also Griffin Greene to NG, 2 November, above, and 14 December, below.

    4. On the political situation in Europe at this time, see Butler to NG, 23 December, below.

    5. See Griffin Greene to NG, 14 December.

*   *   *

From Jeremiah Wadsworth

Dear Sir   Hartford [Conn.] November 16th 1784
    Your letter of the 15th reached me yesterday that of y[e] 12th today.[1] I am sorry any thing in my letter shoud give you pain and I was possibly mistaken in saying had you been in my situation & I in yours I wou'd have accepted G.G.ˢ [i.e., Griffin Greene's] Bills, but I had then no doubt G. Greene had been particular in his advise respecting those Bills as I cou'd not have guessed any Man coud be otherwise on so important a Subject & when I indorsed them, I injoined it upon him to advise you & not to press them without absolute necessity.[2] I also told him how impossible it wou'd be for you [to] pay them if not early apprised of them. I coud wish the people to Whom he passed them have given him at that time yᵉ same or a greater Credit without those Bills, & I confess I was not a little vexed at finding them so disposed of as to charging you with folly presumption & ingratitude. I cannot think such expressions escaped me, if any thing that coud be so construed was in my letter I am excedingly sorry for I do not believe it possible for me to be so angry at a Man I esteem more than any of my male friends, nor can I be persuaded I coud so far forget my self. On my arrival at Philadelphia Mʳ [Charles] Pettit told me he had forwarded your Bill for £450 Sterling. I told him I had heard nothing of it & that it woud not be paid as I had no Money in Europe. On the day of the date of my letter I had receᵈ a letter from

England with that Bill inclosed & requesting my acceptance of it payable in London, the letter derected to me at Liverpool where I was supposed to be but where I never went. Your letter which accompanied it had these words, Viz, If I have mistaken your politeness for sentiments of kindness it will lead me into some mistake.[3] I felt my selfe hurt at such language as it implied a doubt of my sincerity of which I felt their ought to be none. I had whilst abroad advanced a large Sum for ye unfortunate partnership of B[arnabas] D[eane] & C° which they were utterly unable to pay me[,][4] and I found my selfe surrounded with debts & demands occured by my willingness to serve my friends & instead of large sums which I had a right to expect to receive, I found I had large ones to pay, and tho I left Europe with sanguine expectations of going extensively into the Banking business at N York I found I coud not do any business at all my sto[c]k being in the hands of others & out of my reach, my goods Shiped from Europe unsold or worse sold where no pay coud be obtained. Of many thousands in Shiping when I left America the greatest part lost or so circumstanced that not even accounts coud be obtained, & of three thousand pounds Credit taken in Europe I coud find no means to remit one. Pressed with these circumstan[c]es so untoward & finding my Credit woud suffer in France and perhaps in England by having bills come on me and no care taken to have them taken up for nobody thus woud suppose they were drawn without my knowledge. I may have been warm but be assured no Man had ever such hold of my Affections as you and nothing cou'd be farther from my thoughts than to give you pain but I felt it necessary to explain to You my inabillity to remain liable to be drawn on without the least advice & under such embarrassing circumstances. If in doing it I have been ungarded and hasty my appology must be that I was in a trying situation & perhaps misapprehended your letter. I will not dwell on this disagreeable Subject but conclude with assuring you of my esteem & attachment. You have observed in your letter that you never had it in your power to oblidge me & perhaps never shoud[.][5] Had not your letter of a later date arrived I shoud have supposed this was reminding me of my obligations to You.[6] But I now will [illegible] those expressions to your goodness of heart but will here with pleasu[re] acknowledge myself under Many obligations to you and be assured have ever felt the force of them & ever shall. Present me affectionately to Mrs Greene & all my N Port [i.e., Newport, R.I.] friends. I will if possible come to see you at N Port but as my affairs are in such a wretched train I do not know that it will be possible. My intention is to set out in the first days of december but perhaps it may be later if I am prevented. I wish to hear when I shall see you here or at N York where I must shortly go & on to Phil^a.[7] I am Dr Sir With every sentiment of esteem & regard Your Sincere friend & very Hum Servant   JERE WADSWORTH

RCS (CtHi).

1. The letter to Wadsworth of 12 November is above; the other has not been found.

2. See above, Wadsworth to NG, 28 September and 1 November. On NG's refusal to honor Griffin Greene's bills, see especially the note at Griffin Greene to NG, 6 April; Pettit to NG, 19 June; NG to Griffin Greene, 8 July, and NG to Wadsworth, 12 November, all above.

3. Regarding the bill that Wadsworth had returned, see NG to Wadsworth, 7 June, above, and Wadsworth to NG, 1 November.

4. Wadsworth and NG were partners in Barnabas Deane & Company. According to Wadsworth's biographer, the advance was for the purchase of stills. (Destler, "Wadsworth," p. 245) Wadsworth soon afterward purchased NG's "Stock in trade" in the company. (NG to Wadsworth, 29 December, below)

5. See NG to Wadsworth, 12 November.

6. This was presumably the now-missing letter referred to in Wadsworth's first sentence, above.

7. Wadsworth visited NG at Newport in late December. (NG to Wadsworth, 29 December)

*   *   *

¶ [FROM JOHN STORY, Boston, Mass., 19 November 1784. His stay in New York was much longer than he expected, for he was "violently seized with the Reumatism in my Stomack, which brought me to Deaths door."[1] He recovered in time to leave the city on 11 August and hoped to see NG at "New Port" en route to Boston, but NG "had been gone, some day's to the southward."[2] Story "finished the settlement of the public Accounts" with Mr. Denning, as far as he was able, on 8 July. However, the accounts were finalized "greatly to my disadvantage" because Denning "did not allow any depreciation on my pay &c to the 4th of August 1780." Denning has settled with him "by more than two years" what Story believes he is entitled to; he did not consider NG's certificate, by which Story continued in office after NG resigned as quartermaster general, "to be a sufficient Voucher."[3] Nor has he "allowed me any thing while settling the public accounts." Story is therefore "left in a disagreeeble situation," and unless NG can "interpose" in his behalf, he does not know how he "can obtain justice."[4] He thought NG's "desire and Certificate" would be "sufficient to entitle me to pay untill the Accounts were settled," but as it is "not so for the Commissioner," it is "necessary application should be made to Congress before I can obtain justice."[5] If NG will let him know when he arrives at Newport, Story will "wait upon" him there as soon as possible.[6] He is "determined to persevere untill I obtain a final settlement with the public."[7] His persistence, "although attended with great Expence," has not been "ineffectual"; he has brought about "a settlement of the Expenditures in Camp"—not only what he himself paid, but also payments that were made before he joined the department. He is sure that "by a farther exertion" a "settlement of the Advances made to the Deputies and Agents may be effected." When that is "Accomplished," NG may receive "a Certificate for what is due and Obtain a discharge for the Money's charged" to him. When they meet, Story will show NG the "Accounts settled with Mr Denning and give you fa[r]ther information respecting them."[8] RCS (MiU-C) 3 pp.]

1. Story had been ill the previous spring. (Story to NG, 12 March, above)

2. NG had left Newport, R.I., for Charleston, S.C., in July.

3. On Story's settlement of his accounts with Mr. Denning, the commissioner appointed to resolve Quartermaster Department accounts, see Story's letters to NG of 12 March, and 2–5 April, above. Story's status had changed when NG left the post of quartermaster general in August 1780, and he was then entrusted with settling NG's accounts. In November 1780, NG had certified that Story should receive pay and rations as a deputy quartermaster general from 4 August 1780 until NG's accounts as quartermaster general were settled. (See above, vol. 6: 462 and n.)

4. NG interposed on Story's behalf by writing to Richard Henry Lee, the president of Congress, on 2 January 1785, below.

5. Story's memorial to Congress, "praying for a depreciation of his pay," was read in Congress on 8 February 1785 and referred to a committee, which reported on 27 April that under a resolution of 24 July 1781, Story was "entitled to the same pay and rations for his services from the time of General Green's resignation as Quarter Master General, until the 21st day of April last [i.e., April 1781] which he received or was entitled to receive when acting immediately under" NG. However, the committee further reported that on 15 August 1781, "Congress Resolved that John Story be informed that Congress, do, at his request, dispense with his further services." For this reason, the committee decided that Story's claim to pay after the 15 August 1781 resolution was "not well founded." (*JCC*, 28: 47n, 313; Story's February 1785 memorial is discussed in depth in a 1 February 1788 report of the Treasury Board concerning his claims. [*JCC*, 34: 16–18]) In response to the committee's report, Congress resolved on 7 June 1785 that "the commissioners" who had been "appointed under the resolution of 27 February 1782, in settling the Accounts of their respective departments," would "have recourse to the resolutions of June 3, 1784, so far as they may apply." (*JCC*, 28: 434) Those resolutions, which set guidelines for settling claims against the United States incurred during the war, included the following paragraph, which seems to apply to Story's situation: "That if bills of credit advanced to any State or person to be expended for the use of the United States, shall have depreciated before the same were so applied, the receiver shall not be charged with the depreciation, if satisfactory evidence be given to the Commissioner by such receiver, that such bills had not been applied to any other use, (and were applied to the purpose designed, as soon as occasion required); otherwise such receiver will be chargeable with such bills at their value when received, or at such lesser value as the Commissioner, on consideration of all circumstances attending the case, shall judge equitable." Other parts of the resolution concerned compensation for the use of buildings and stores and the use of wood and forage. The commissioners were "instructed to proceed in the business of settling accounts [with] all possible despatch." (*JCC*, 27: 541, 543)

6. No evidence has been found that Story visited NG in Newport.

7. In a February 1788 report on Story's 1785 memorial to Congress (note 5, above), the Board of Treasury termed his claims "inadmissable." (*JCC*, 34: 16–18) Story again petitioned Congress on 20 March 1788, and it appears that his case was finally settled in a resolution of 5 September 1788, allowing him "the sum of six hundred and three dollars and twenty five ninetieths in full consideration of all his past services and claims." (*JCC*, 34:500)

8. See note 6, above.

¶ [TO WILLIAM GIBBONS, JR. From Newport, R.I., 29 November 1784.[1] Since writing Gibbons in Charleston, S.C., that he wanted bills,[2] NG has decided "to get them through other channels" and therefore asks him "to sell my Crop for cash only[,] having heavy demands upon me for this Article." Gibbons should "Give Capt Pearce [William Pierce, Jr.] the refusal and if he don't take the Crops pay all his demands upon the Plantation."[3] As he expects to see Gibbons "in little more than a month," NG will "say nothing more at present."[4] ALS (NN) 2 pp.]

1. This letter and the one to Nicholas Hoffman, immediately below, are the first that NG is known to have written after returning to Newport on 20 November. (On his arrival, see *Newport Mercury*, 27 November.)

2. See NG to Gibbons, 29 August, above.

3. See below, Pierce & Company to NG, 8 April 1785, and Pierce to NG, 13 May 1785.

4. NG was back in Charleston by early February. (NG to Gibbs, 3 February 1785, below)

¶ [TO NICHOLAS HOFFMAN. From Newport, R.I., 29 November 1784. "Iron is selling at 48/ [New] York currency here and but little on hand." Hoffman could "sell Eight or ten tun" at Newport and "have the remittances made in a couple of Months." If he does send any iron, he could consign it to "Messrs Joseph and Daniel Rogers of Newport Merchants." Commissions are five percent for retail and two and a half percent, wholesale. NG has been informed that his brothers need "three or four tun"; he has not seen his brothers since his return to Newport, but if it is "agreeable," Hoffman could "Ship for Elihue & Christopher Greene three tuns of your largest square Iron." The remittances will be made "in two Months at farthest." By sending directly to NG's brothers, Hoffman could "save the commision," for they will receive the iron "directly out of the Vessel if it is shipped by Capt Fairbanks," who is to "call on you upon the subject." ALS (MiU-C) 2 pp.]

* * *

To George Washington

Dear Sir   Newport [R.I.] Decem 2^d 1784

M^r [Elkanah] Watson by whom this will be handed you having some things for you brought with him from England and having it in contemplation to call at Mount Vernon it gives me an opportunity to inform you of my safe arrival with my family. I found Mrs Greene and the children all in good health.[1]

I hope the Marquis arrivd safe in Virginia. A report prevails here that his Frigate is cast away near the [Sandy?] Hook; but this must have happened if true since the Marquis landed in Virginia. I wish to se[e] him before he returns to Franc[e] and would meet him in New York if he embarks from that place. I hope he will return [to] France well pleasd with the r[e]ception he has met with in America and advocate our cause tho we little deserve it in many respects.[2] Congress are dilatory in meeting and I fear little will be done to restore public credit.[3] I have not been at home long enough to learn the present temper of the people of this State. Many begin to be alarmed at the proposition of Connecticut; and I can but hope if Congress persist in the Plan of finance it will finally succeed.[4] However we are such a heterogeneous body that it is difficult to draw conclusions from any general principles which influence human conduct.

Mrs Greene joins m[e in a]ffectionate compliments to you and Mrs Washington to Doctor Steward [i.e., David Stuart] and his Lady. I am dear Sir with esteem & regard Your most Obed^t humble Ser^t

NATH GREENE

ALS (Washington Papers: DLC).

1. Watson, a merchant in France since 1779, had recently returned home to Rhode Island and was traveling to Mount Vernon "to discuss with Washington the feasibility of a system of" canals in the United States—a subject in which he had developed an interest while in Europe. (*DAB*) He delivered NG's letter to Washington on 19 January 1785. (Washington, *Papers*, Confederation Series, 2: 162n) On the other papers that he brought to Washington, see ibid. NG had recently visited Washington at Mount Vernon, on his way home to Rhode Island from South Carolina. (NG to Carrington, 10 November, above)

2. The Marquis de Lafayette, who was preparing to leave after a four-month visit to the United States, had recently stayed with Washington in Virginia. (Note at NG to Carrington, 10 November; see also Lafayette to NG, 25 August, above.) Lafayette and NG were able to meet in New York before Lafayette's departure for France. (See note at Lafayette to NG, 25 August.) The French frigate *Nymphe*, on which Lafayette returned to France, was still seaworthy after running aground en route from Virginia to New York. (Lafayette to Samuel Adams, 19 December, Idzerda, *Lafayette Papers*, 5: 288–89 and n)

3. As noted at Pierce to NG, 26 October 1783, above, Congress, which had been in adjournment since early June 1784, finally assembled at New York in January 1785.

4. On Connecticut's position in regard to the federal impost proposal of 1783 and the commutation of Continental army officers' pay, see note at Wadsworth to NG, 12–13 June 1783, above. Rhode Island had rejected the impost in July. (NG to Morris, 3 July, above)

*   *   *

¶ [FROM JEREMIAH WADSWORTH, Hartford, Conn., 3 December 1784. He wrote NG "per last post" that he expected to set out "soon" for Newport, R.I.[1] "Some new difficulties have arisen" in his business, however, which have kept him from going "yet."[2] He still hopes to leave in "a few days," but if he cannot—and if NG cannot go to Hartford—he would like to meet in New York, where he will stop on his way to Philadelphia. So that they will not "Miss each other on ye road," Wadsworth will travel to Newport by way of Lebanon and Norwich [Conn.] and Little Rest and Connanicut [Island, R.I.] "&c."[3] RCS (CtHi) 1 p.]

1. Wadsworth wrote NG on 16 November, above, that he expected "to set out in the first days of December."

2. On the kinds of business difficulties with which Wadsworth was likely dealing, see his letter to NG of 16 November and the note at Wadsworth to NG, 1 November, both above.

3. Wadsworth visited NG at Newport in late December. (NG to Wadsworth, 29 December, below)

*   *   *

From Griffin Greene

Dear Sir   Paris Decr 14. 1784

No doubt you will think it strange to receive a letter from me dated at the above place as I dare say you think I am on my passage for America before this, but you will think it unaccountable, when I tel you I now have to jorney through France, on the Bussiness of that hated Name, of the Ship *Flora*, half the distance to you, before I can get it [deseved?].[1] I wrote you last mon[th] that I was obliged to come hear [i.e., here] on acc^t

of the Bottom of the Ship proving bad and unsound[.]² On my arivel vissited the Marᵉ de Casteries & got an Order with which I am to go to Rochforte to give a new Bill of Sail for Eighty two thousand livers [i.e., livres] the other being for One hundred & two thousand. I have given a formal requittal of the deduction of twenty thousand livers & have got the Chevʳ la Luzearn to use his influence for the Bussiness to be negociated hear but in vain,³ I shall have to return hear for my security after this & then shall have to go again to some Sea Porte to imbarke, by the time I have don this, I shall wride near half way to America, have I reason for corage & passeverience or not, I have wrod 4,000 Mile[s] already, my cradit is low my few friends are tired of my story, the pavements has freted out my Cloaths, added to all this I am unacquainted whether any one person that I used to love and expect friendship from be still living or not, all that I know is that I have forfitted your confidence & this I know only by your protesting the Bills I drew on you, what ever you may have heard or what ever judgement you have formed respecting my conduct I declare to God, if it is unfavorable to my friendly intentions to you, is unjust & of this I will convince you if ever I live to see you, I shall take care that you have not any trouble respecting the above Bills & you may rest easey on that accᵗ. I wrote you lengthy from Bordeaux & as the way I send this letter is unsartain shall only say if it shall so happen that I never see you more I hearby impowar you to settle the accᵗˢ betwen us as you think right to your self & my family, having full confidence that you will do them justice.⁴ I feel my heart full of love & friendship for you and be assured that their is not the man on the face of the Globe, that can give that cutting pain to me as you do by doubting my conduct on accᵗ of the letters of cradit you gave me. Mʳ Chandler [i.e., John Chaloner] writes that you was informed that I had taken goods for the amount of the Bills but would not believe it to be true theirfore you must suppose I had spent the money.⁵

Pray see that my Children are kept to School as this is the first thing I desire, good acts never go unrewarded. My Love to Caty & all friends. Adue   GRIFFIN GREENE

RCS (MiU-C).

1. On Griffin Greene's stay in France while trying to sell the *Flora*, a vessel owned by the Greene family firm, see his letters to NG of 1 October 1783 and 8 February, 6 April, 16 May, 12 June, end of September, and 2 November 1784, all above.

2. Griffin had written NG on 2 November that he might be "obliged" to go to Paris to complete the sale.

3. The Marquis de Castries was the French naval minister and the official with whom Griffin was arranging for the sale of the *Flora* to the French navy. (Griffin to NG, 6 April) The vessel had previously been valued twice. (Griffin Greene to NG, 16 May and end of September)

4. On NG's rejection of bills that Griffin had drawn on him, see especially the note at Griffin Greene to NG, 6 April; NG to Griffin Greene, 8 July; and NG to Wadsworth,

12 November, all above. In his letters to NG of 2 and 14 November, above, Griffin had promised to make good on the payments for the bills. His "lengthy" letter from Bordeaux is that of 2 November.

5. On the information that Griffin had received from Chaloner, see also Griffin's letters to NG of 2 and 14 November. Griffin was back in the United States by July 1785. (Wadsworth to NG, 10 July 1785, below)

*   *   *

¶ [FROM BENJAMIN EYRE, Philadelphia, 19 December 1784.[1] He is "exceedingly Oblig'd" to NG for the "kind offer you made me in regard to joining you in the Isleand of Live Oak." Although he declines the offer, he will "allways think my self happy in haveing it in my power of serveing you by night or day." NG can "command me freely for vessails[,] moulds[,] men or any thing else" he may want.[2] "Captain Steward [i.e., James Stewart], who has come from that part lately," told Eyre that there are people "now on your land Cutting without your leave."[3] Eyre asks NG to write him when he gets there; hopes to join NG "this summer."[4] RCS (MiU-C) 1 p.]

1. Eyre, who had been a superintendent of the boat department during the war, was in the shipbuilding business in Philadelphia. (Vol. 2: 476n, above; Eyre to NG, 7 March 1785, below)

2. See NG to Butler, 9 September, above. The offer to Eyre has not been found, but NG was trying to find investors to join him in developing the timber resources of Cumberland Island, Ga. (See, for example, Butler to NG, 23 December, and NG to Wadsworth, 3 February 1785, both below; on NG's involvement in the island, see especially the note at Hyrne to Clay, 26 November 1783, above.)

3. On the cutting of timber on Cumberland Island by Loyalist refugees, see, for example, NG to Bowman, 10 September, above, and Eyre to NG, 7 March 1785, below.

4. NG's reply, which was dated 9 February 1785, has not been found. (Eyre to NG, 7 March 1785)

¶ [FROM SAMUEL A. OTIS, Boston, Mass., 21 December 1784. Encloses his "account current made up to the present day." Asks NG, if he agrees with the amount, to remit the balance of £48.9.6 to him.[1] RCS (Ct) 1 p.]

1. For background, see Otis's letters to NG of 24 July 1783, 8 September 1783, and 8–9 December 1783, all above. Differences between NG and Otis over the account continued. (NG to Otis, 24 July 1785, below)

*   *   *

From Pierce Butler

Dear Sir   London y[e] 23[d] of December 1784

Your favour of the 9th of September did not reach my hand till last Monday. It gives me sincere pleasure to know that You have returnd to add to the number of good Citizens in S[o] Carolina, where I hope You may be induced to take up Your Residence. It is certainly a Country if well Governd, and its resources properly manag'd, that must take a distinguish'd Rank in the Confederacy.[1]

I have well attended to what You and Comodore [Alexander] Gillon

write, respecting Cumberland Island.[2] It woud be exceedingly agreeable to me, to have a Connection with You in any plan that wou'd
promise advantage or even a saving return to Us; but my good Sir, it is
too late in the day for me, to Enter on so distant a One as that respecting
Cumberland Island, which coud not be immediately under our own
Care.[3] I will chearfully take a Concern with You in any other plan that
You will please to point out. You may rest assured of my giving the
same attention to promote the success of Your Scheme respecting Ship
Building, as if I was a party concernd in the business. I have already
made several inquiries and a proposal to one of the first Ship Yards in
England; to which I am to have an answer shortly, which shall be sent to
You. I must observe to You, that Shipping are Cheap all over Europe at
this time; that private Yards prefer the White Oak to Live Oak, from the
difficulty of working it. So that in England I fear We shall be able to do
nothing, except with Government, and they are too poor to pay punc-
tualy. If I return to Holland, I will certainly make the necessary enquirey
there. I think for the present till there is a War between some of the
Maratime powars of Europe that other plans may be fallen on more
advantagious. I have mentioned one respecting the Establishment of a
Bank in Carolina, to Commodore Gillon; which may not be unworthy
Your attention. I beg leave to refer You to my letter to Him on the
Subject; And to assure You that You may Command me in any way I can
render You service.[4]

I am now to thank You for the information of the State of things in
America. I lament, sincerely lament that factions and Mobs, so truely
disgraceful to good Gover[t] Shoud raise their heads among Us.[5] It be-
hoves the Independent thinking part of the Community to Crush such
shameful proceedings in the bud. The State of public affairs still demands the attention of the [wisest?] among Us. Unless the Confederation is Religiously adhered to, and the Laws in general more respected,
We have still much to apprehend. This Country [i.e., Great Britain] be
assured is still Inimical to Us; and Seizes every oppertunity of representing America to the Powers of Europe, as a factious, turbulent Un-
governable People; overtur[n]ing the very Constitutions & Laws that
they framed themselves; that Our Confederacy is a farce; that We are at
varience with each other; and that the Country will soon experience the
miseries of Civil discord. Tho totaly unfounded all this, yet it has the
effect that our Enemies wish. It checks Emigration, which otherwise
woud be Considerable; and Injures the Creditt of America amazingly.
Here the Creditt of the States is very low. It is low all through Europe.
The Agents of Congress in Holland have been under the wretched
Necessity of Negociating a New Loan just to pay the Interest of the Old;
this is a ruinous measure, and must, if known in Europe, stab Our
Creditt; yet nothing else coud be done. Nor can any blame be lay'd to

the Office of Finance tho the Loan appears on terms not favourable.[6] Nothing can raise and Establish Our Creditt but substantial proofs of Our determination to Establish a proper fund, by Taxation, and Revennue Laws, for the Sinking the Principal and Interest. I have been asked the question by the first House in Europe; and I have good reason to believe, if that was Once Establishd and proper persons appointed to make the application, that Congress may get any Sum they have occasion for on moderate terms. And surely my good Sir it woud be wise to do so, to sink on such advantagious terms as it may be done, part of the heavy Load of paper among Us; and be an Act of justice that We owe to the Citizens in America; many of whom have trusted their all to the faith of Congress.[7] The State of S° Carolina may get three Million of Florrins if She inclines to extricate Herself.

It is to be regretted that the States do not send all their Representatives, Men of Weight and Knowledge in Money Transactions, to Congress; that some effectual plan may timely be fallen on; to rescue the Creditt and reputation of the States from a Stain. At the distance You are, You can scarcely conceive the effect the late reports of an Engagement between the People of Connecticut & Pennsilvenia had on the minds of all ranks of Men here, and on the Continent where I was at the time it arrived.[8] Such is the folly and ignorance of some Men here that it revived a hope of part of America throwing itself on Britain for protection and can You Creditt it, tho it realy is so, induced some foolish Men to lay fresh plans before the K— of E g—d for the recovery of part of America which from the wickedness of His heart, & the weakness of His head, He attended to with eagerness.

The Politicks of the Continent appear to stand thus—The Emperor [Joseph II of Austria] obstinate in His Claim on the free Navigation of the Scheldt, the Dutch not disposed to comply with it, the French are supposed to favour the Dutch, The King of Prussia determined to support the Dutch, Russia friendly to the Emperor, the Turks wishing for a favourable occasion to humble the House of Austria. Much depends on the determinations of the Courts of Versails & Berlin, to prevent a destructive War. They with Britain are Mediators on the Occasion; but report says that the Emperor is obstinate. Be that as it may, it is certain that a large Austrian Army are on their March for the Netherlands; and that Magazines are forming there. A large French Army are under orders, to be in readiness to March on the shortest Notice, all their Troops are filing off from the South and to the Nord. While I was in Lisle part of the Garrison recd Marching Orders. It is a pitty that so Rich, so fertile, so beautiful and well cultivated a Country as Austrian Netherlands, shoud be made, the Theatre of War. The Inhabitants are so much alarmd, that vast Numbers of them woud go to

America if they coud get off, but the Emperor who is extremely Arbitrary, not only forbids their quitting the Country, but absolutely prohibits their sending a Yard of Linnen or any other of their Manufactures out of the Country. The Inhabitants tremble at the Storm that is gathering. I visited the Banks of the Maise and the Mayne, the two Rivers where the Armies are to Encamp.[9] Holland appears no way alarmd. Shoud the War break out, America may derive much advantage from it. Amsterdam, and indeed all the Provinces, appear to wish for a Trade with America. We may carry on an Advantageous Trade with Germany, by way of the Rhyne. A great deal of Our Rice & Tobacco is Consumed in Germany, and in return their Linnens, Osnabrigs and Wines woud answer very well at Our Markett. Our Indigo Commands no price on the Continent. The Dutch, and indeed the English, have lately Imported large Quantities of Indigo from India, and much superior to Ours. I saw while at Amsterdam, a Large Quantity disposed of at publick sale, some as High as 14/Sterling a pound. Some of Our low priced Indigo will sell in Germany for dyeing their Coarse Wollens.

My fingers are so cold I can scarce hold a pen. The Winter has sett in very severe. I am with great regard and Esteem Dear General Yr Most Obed.^t Servant P BUTLER

When You see Cap^{tn} [Roger Parker] Saunders will You be so kind to tell Him that I have wrote to Him by this opp[ortunit]y and sent Him the Necessary papers? PB

RCS (MiU-C).

1. NG eventually settled in Georgia. (NG to Clarke, 23 November 1785, below)

2. As noted at Benjamin Eyre's letter to him of 19 December, above, NG was trying to find investors to join him in developing the timber resources of Cumberland Island, Ga.

3. As seen by the note at Hyrne to Clay, 26 November 1783, above, NG did not yet have a clear title to the undivided half share of land of Cumberland Island; his claim at this time was based on an indenture that he had received in the summer of 1783 from the since-deceased John Banks and Ichabod Burnet.

4. Butler's letter to Gillon has not been found.

5. On the mobs and unrest in Charleston, S.C., see above, Pendleton to NG, 18 April and second letter of 10 July, and William Washington to NG, 10 July.

6. For details of the new loan negotiated with Dutch bankers in early 1784, see Robert Morris to Thomas Mifflin, 4 May, Morris, *Papers*, 9: 313–14 and n, and the headnote to that letter (ibid., pp. 307–13). For background, see Morris to NG, 19 May, above.

7. On the confounding of efforts to establish revenue for "Sinking the Principal and Interest" of the federal debt, see in particular the notes at NG to Lincoln, 18 June 1783, and Weedon to NG, 2 December 1783, both above.

8. On the longstanding dispute between Connecticut and Pennsylvania over jurisdiction in the Wyoming Valley, see above, vol. 12: 205n.

9. Joseph II, the Austrian emperor, had taken "strenuous efforts to force the opening of the River Scheldt to non-Dutch shipping" in order to "revive the economic prosperity of the Austrian Netherlands." Although it then appeared that war between Austria and Holland was imminent, France supported the Dutch, and "Joseph was forced to abandon

his scheme." (Derek McKay and H. M. Scott, *The Rise of the Great Powers, 1648–1815* [New York: Longman, 1983], p. 233; see also Idzerda, *Lafayette Papers,* 5: 295n.) However, as seen below in letters from the Marquis de Lafayette to NG of 16 March 1785 and 16 April 1785, the threat of war continued for a time.

*   *   *

¶ [TO JEREMIAH WADSWORTH. From Newport, R.I., 29 December 1784. NG acknowledges receipt of "One hundred, twenty three pounds, Sixteen Shillings Lawfull Money" from Wadsworth "on Account of my Stock in trade with Barnabas Deane & C° which the Said Wadsworth has bought my Share of & to be conveyed by deeds of Sale When the Ballance due me is ascertaind & paid me."[1] DS (Bruce Gimelson, 1979) 1 p.]

    1. NG and Wadsworth had been partners with Deane in the business. Wadsworth wrote NG on 16 November, above, that he had "advanced a large Sum" for the firm, "which they were utterly unable to pay me." As seen in To Whom It May Concern, 7 September 1785, below, NG received £960.9.4. in the final settlement—a profit of "232% on his original investment," according to Wadsworth's biographer. (Destler, "Wadsworth," p. 245) Wadsworth, now the owner of three-fifths of the company, retained Deane as its manager. (Ibid., p. 258)

*   *   *

To Richard Henry Lee,
President of the Continental Congress

Sir   Newport [R.I.] January 2d 1785.
    Mr John Story formerly paymaster to the Quartermaster Generals department in Camp Addresses Congress for a compensation for his services since the expiration of my appointment. Many transactions were unsettled when I went out of office which were no less interesting to the public than to individuals. To bring these to a close and effect a final settlement of Money transactions rendered Mr Storys continuance in office unavoidable. He has zealously pursued the business[,] effected a settlement with Mr Denning the commisioner of accounts and obtained a certificate of the faithful discharge of his duty. The Commissioner of Accounts altho convinced of his merit and the expence to which he has been subject in transacting the business conceives he has no power to allow any compensation. Mr Story has done his duty with so much fidelity and devoted so much time in accomplishing it, I can but hope Congress will do him that justice to which he has a good claim.[1] I have the honor to be with Great respect Your Excellencys Most Obedt humble Servt   NATH GREENE

Cy (PCC, item 41, vol. 9: 301, DNA).
    1. For background and further information, see Story to NG, 19 November 1784, above.

To Richard Henry Lee,
President of the Continental Congress

Sir   Newport [R.I.] January 3ᵈ 1785

Inclos'd I send a copy of a letter from Col° Finny late Deputy quarter Master General in the State of Virginia.[1] The facts therein stated are so notorious and the cruelty of his situation so great that I conceive it to be unnecessary to offer arguments upon the subject. In great public commotions incident to revolutions there are hours when justice is perverted and the Voice of distress is heard without pity. We have happily emerged from this situation and I hope Congress will save from ruin a family the head of which from long and faithful services merits justice if not liberality.[2] I have the honor to be with Great respect your Excellency's most Obdᵗ humble Servᵗ   NATH GREENE

ALS (PCC, item 155, vol. 2: 702, DNA).
1. See William Finnie's letter to NG of 28 October 1784, above.
2. On Finnie's claims and Congress's response, see ibid.

*   *   *

¶ [FROM GEORGE SHEFFIELD, Stonington, Conn., 3 January 1785. Acknowledges NG's letter [not found]. Is "under the greatest Obligation" to Colonel [Samuel] Ward for his "generous Recommendation of My Carector" to NG. Sheffield would be "happy" to work for NG, but the "Notice is so short" that he is "under Some Disadvantage to give a Direct answer"; will try to do so "Within the time" that NG specified. Would "take it as a great favʳ" to hear again from NG. Would find it difficult to "go to Georgia this Winter[,] as My Mind Now Stands Consistent With My Present Ingagements." Would like to know the "time & terms" of NG's "Request as fully as Possably Can Be Concievd." While he waits to hear again from NG, he will, "If Possable Consistent With My Present Ingagements Prepare My Self for yʳ Exelencyˢ Service."[1] RCS (MiU-C) 1 p.]
1. It is not known what kind of employment NG had offered Sheffield. No further correspondence between them has been found.

¶ [FROM JEREMIAH WADSWORTH, Hartford, Conn., 5 January 1784 [i.e., 1785].[1] He has been offered "a Bond payable in Charlestown South Carolina against Nath Russel & Tho [Newell?]," the former of whom "was once of" Newport, R.I. Asks whether NG is "acquainted" with them "& whether they are safe."[2] The "Pork Season is over," so Wadsworth "can not obtain the Hams" that NG wanted. The "Negro Boy," who will be there "tomorrow," apparently has "some complaint that unfits him for hard labor"; Wadsworth will be careful not to buy "an invalid" for NG. He plans to "set out for New York on Monday" if the "Weather holds good."[3] Will take his "old Cypher" with him so that he can correspond with NG "in case of need with Secrecy." Wonders when NG will leave Newport; asks him to write from "Charles Town."[4] RCS (CtHi) 1 p.]
1. This letter, although it is docketed "1784," was definitely written in 1785. (See Wadsworth to NG, 21 February, below.)

2. In ibid., Wadsworth wrote that he had found "they are good men."
3. Monday was 10 January.
4. See NG to Wadsworth, 3 February, below.

¶ [TO V. & N. FRENCH & NEPHEW.[1] From Newport, R.I., 7 January 1785. NG sees by their letters to him and to "the house of Mess[rs] Jacob and Griffin Greene" that French & Nephew have "formed a connection in business" with Jacob's and Griffin's establishment. NG is related to Jacob and Griffin and is "very much interested in their happiness." He hopes that French & Nephew "will have every reason to be pleased with their conduct." His "intimate connection" with the Greenes "forbids" his saying more, but he would be happy to render "every service" in his power to either firm. He concludes: "I am little in the way of commerce but so far as I have influence I shall make it a point to promote your joint interest."[2] ADfS (MiU-C) 2 pp.]

1. In his letter to NG of 12 June 1784, above, Griffin Greene referred to the mercantile firm of French & Nephew as friends of his at Bordeaux, France.
2. French & Nephew replied to this letter on 23 April, below.

¶ [TO GEORGE GIBBS. From Charleston, S.C., 3 February 1785. On his arrival there,[1] NG asked his brother about "the ballance due on the Rum" and learned that "he is unable to discharge it without defeating his future plan for a voyage."[2] NG cannot remit "the whole" now and still "fulfill" his "other engagements," but he has sent Gibbs a "bill for 150 Dollars."[3] He adds: "If Captain Littlefield should not be able to discharge the ballance from the interest due on my public securities I will try to forward the remainder by the time you set. He will let you know and me also."[4] The crops "fall far short of our expectation being much injured in the harvest by the heavy Rains," but NG still hopes to have enough "to fulfill all of my engagements to the Northward."[5] Since his arrival, he has received Gibbs's letter of "last summer." As "I was then under peculiar circumstances from common opinion," Gibbs's "sentiments of kindness were the more pleasing."[6] ALS (MiU-C) 2 pp.]

1. NG had sailed from Newport, R.I., on 10 January aboard the *Union* and had arrived in Charleston on 28 January. (*Newport Mercury*, 15 January; *South-Carolina Gazette & Weekly Advertiser*, 31 January–2 February) On the voyage, see NG to Wadsworth, immediately below.
2. This was most likely NG's brother Perry, who appears to have made trading voyages to Charleston from time to time. (See NG to Arnold, 17 August 1784, and NG to CG, 17 and 21 August 1784, all above; Clarke to NG, 15 March; and NG to CG, 29 May, both below.)
3. For background, see NG to Gibbs, 22 August 1784, above.
4. As seen in William Littlefield's letter to NG of 25 April, below, no interest was due on NG's Rhode Island state notes until March 1786.
5. NG had written Gibbs on 17 August 1784 that the crops on his southern plantations were "promising."
6. Gibbs's letter, which has not been found, was undoubtedly a reply to NG's letters to him of 17 and 22 August 1784, above.

*   *   *

To Jeremiah Wadsworth

My dear Sir   Charleston [S.C.] February 3rd 1785

My passage to this place was terrible. We just escaped destruction and that is all.[1] On my arrival I find my self in more distress than I expected to accomodate payments.[2] One of the payments for Cumberland Island on which I have a Mortgage is due and the parties press me for a part if not the whole.[3] If you have not paid the money for the redemption of my note in the Bank I wish you to hold it in reserve until you hear from me. If you have paid it I wish you to lodge the Note herewith enclosed in the Bank upon the same principles and footing the former was there. If the form of the Note is not proper send me a form and I will send you another. In the meantime if necessity should oblige me to draw on you I beg you to deposit your Note until I can send one to take it up.[4]

If it was or could be made consistent with your interest it would make me very happy if you would [take?] part of Cumberland Island. I think it a good purchace but I am unable to hold it. If you and Seagrove would take each a share I am confident you cannot vest your Money in better property. The purchace is five thousand Guineas. There is upwards of 7000 Acres of land, most of which is fit for planting and the whole as full of Ship timber of live oak as it can stand. It is estimated by those best acquainted with the property that the timber alone as it formerly sold and is now selling in Philadelphia paying the freight and cutting out of the Sales would amount to forty thousand pounds. Did I not owe Money I would not wish to sell any part of it. If you will take part of it I am so confident of its value that I will engage to indemnify you from loss. Payments are as follow that [is?] £1250 Guineas in December 1784, £1250 Guineas in December 1785, 1250 Guineas in December 1786 and 1200 Guineas in December 1787. Interest on [the] whole from December 1783. Speak to Seagrove on the subject and let us all engage in the Spanish trade. If in Seagroves opinion it may be more profitable. Be assured whatever interest you take in my affair you shall not suffer by it.[5] I am with esteem & affection Dear Sir Yours sincerely

NATH GREENE

ALS (CtY).

1. As noted at the letter immediately above, NG had recently arrived in Charleston from Newport, R.I. According to a report printed in the *Newport Mercury* of 26 February, the vessel *Union*, on which NG was a passenger, reached Charleston "very much damaged in her Masts, Spars, &c. In a few Days after she sailed from hence she met with such an extreme severe Gale of Wind, as to overset—washed the Captain with such force against the Chains as to dislocate his Leg, and greatly injured the first Mate—During this critical Juncture, and while the Ship was on her Beam-ends, the Hon. Major-General Greene, who was a Passenger on board, by an Exertion and presence of Mind peculiar to himself, was greatly instrumental in extricating themselves from the impending Destruction which seemed immediately to hover over them."

2. As seen in the letter immediately above, one of the reasons for NG's greater "distress" was that his 1784 crops had fallen "far short of our expectation."

3. In regard to the "Mortgage" on Cumberland Island, Ga., see note at Hyrne to Clay, 26 November 1783, above. On the payment then due, see also NG to Wadsworth, 17 February, below.

4. The enclosure was a note, dated 3 February, in which NG promised "to pay into the Bank of Philadelphia on or before the last of January next five hundred pounds sterling with interest until paid value received." (CtY) Wadsworth replied on 21 February, below.

5. On the possibility of Wadsworth and James Seagrove becoming investors in Cumberland Island, see their letters to NG of 23 February, both below. Seagrove's interest in the "Spanish trade" is discussed in his letter to NG of that date. NG did retain his holdings in the island, and CG and her family took up residence there in 1800. (Stegeman, *Caty*, p. 173)

To Governor Benjamin Guerard of South Carolina

Sir   Charleston [S.C.] Feb 4th 1785[1]

M[r] Fenwicks extremes anxiety for his fate from his peculear situation solicits this Letter of Address.[2] I hope the occasion and the Agency I had in the affair will apologize for the liberty I take in the business. I wish not to urge any thing either prejudicial to the honor or interest of the State but Subjects of this sort are of an extreme delicate nature and claim tenderness and indulgence.[3] In Parlimentary debates in Great Britain matters of intelligence are held sacred and where public faith is engaged National honor is held responsible. Objects of this kind in the hours of tranquility lose much of their force but they are not unimportant. Not to have an eye to future evils would be wide of the mark of a just policy. Intelligence to an Army is like the soul to the body it directs all its motions. To obtain this with the greatest certainty and to have an opportunity of comparing different accounts created a necessity for employing a number [of] persons in this service. Among whom M[r] Fenwicks intelligence was accurate & seasonable.[4] We had timely information from him to counteract several British detachments. All the Country can witness from their perpetual alarms how necessary this was for their Safety. Nor could either thier lives or property had any security without it. This may happen to be our situation at some future day. Should we wound public confidence from too nice an examination into the motives and conduct of people employed for such purposes many calamities may follow which might be avoided. Mr Fenwicks claims will no doubt have a just consideration and to forgive those we have in our power discovers greatness of soul and generosity of temper. Under the influence of this opinion I am persuaded I shall never have to reproach my self of having betrayed a man into a situation fatal to himself and ruinous to his family.[5] ⟨I have the honor to be with due respect your Excellencys Most obedient humble Servant

NATH GREENE⟩

ADf (MiU-C).

1. A contemporary copy at ScCoAH, from which the text in angle brackets was taken, is dated 5 February.

2. On the case of Col. Edward Fenwick, a British officer who had served as an American spy in Charleston during the latter stages of the war, see also NG to Guerard, 19 September 1784, above.

3. In exchange for Fenwick's services during the war, NG had promised to intercede with the South Carolina government on his behalf after the war. (Vol. 11: 545, above)

4. As noted at William Wilmot to NG, 10 May 1782, above, the South Carolina legislature was reluctant to assist Fenwick because much of the intelligence he provided " 'was available to Greene from other sources.' " (Vol. 11: 182n)

5. Fenwick was removed from the confiscation list in 1785 but did not receive "his right of Citizenship & being permitted to remain in the Country" until March 1786. (See note at NG to Guerard, 19 September 1784.)

*   *   *

¶ [FROM RICHARD CHAMPION, Queen Street [Charleston, S.C.], 5 February 1785.[1] Sends NG "some Considerations which I drew up" concerning "the Situation of the United States of America and Great Britain, with a view to their future Connections." Adds: "A very strong desire to testify the Respect which I have always felt for your Charactor, has induced me to give you this Trouble, and to tell you that I shall be highly gratified by your Acceptance of it."[2] RCS (MiU-C) 1 p.]

1. Champion (1743–91), who had recently left his native England to settle in South Carolina, was a "Quaker ceramist and planter." He had been the "manager and partner of William Cookworthy, the earliest manufacturer of true porcelain," while still in his twenties and had formed his own company in the 1770s, eventually selling his patents to Staffordshire potters. An active participant in British politics, he had "long favored the American cause." After moving to South Carolina in late 1784, he again became politically active and served in the South Carolina General Assembly and other political offices. (*Biog. Directory of S.C. House*, 3: 136–37)

2. The "considerations" that Champion sent to NG were undoubtedly those contained in his anonymously published thirty-six-page pamphlet, *Considerations on the Present Situation of Great Britain and the United States of North America* (2d ed.; London, 1784), which argued for free trade between the two countries. NG's reply has not been found.

*   *   *

To James Milligan

Sir   Charleston [S.C.] Feb 6th 1785

Upon examining the Account and arrangement of the public bills drawn in this department and stated in your Office, I find some errors and some omisions.[1] Under the head of bills drawn and not paid, I find two setts charged and included in the sum total of my Account. They are both drawn in favor of John Banks. One sett is for 995 18/90 Dollars, The other sett is for 270 70/90 Dollars. One is dated the 9th of June the other the 9th of July 1783. These ought not to be included in my general

Account having never been paid; and in all probability will never appear. But if they are they must be charged to Banks & Comp. To include them in my Account and not charge them against Banks will be doing the greatest injustice to me. The bill for 995 18/90 Dollar, I think is double charged. One to the same amount is charged to Robert Forsyth & Company which was the firm of the house at one time. The sums agreeing tho the dates are different inclines me to think they are the same bills. It is certain John Banks's account should be charged with the bill which are charged to Robert Forsyth & Company. Otherwise Forsyth will be unjustly a sufferer.

The next mistake is a bill charged under the head of bills sold for cash. It was drawn in favor of John Banks for 428 51/90 Dollars. This bill should be charged to Banks's Account he having never bought any bills of me for which he paid cash except what he advanced towards the bills for 6000 Dollars which I drew in his favor. I left a sett in the hands of Col Dart to sell of 800 Dollars which Banks bought, but it was after I left the Country.[2] Those two were the only bills he ever advanced Money for. You will please therefore to have that bill of 428 51/90 placed to his Account before M[r] [Robert] Morris brings his account to a final close. I must beg your attention to it as it so nearly affects me.

The next error is Col Blaines charge of 500 Dollars. This was upon a special order of Congress; and Col Blaine says he never meant to bring it in as a charge against me; and promised to wait on you and place the matter on a right footing.[3]

The last thing is the omision of credit for cash advanced the clothing Department paid to John Banks by Robert Forsyth one of the company and receipted for by him and entered against Banks & Company by Capt John Hambleton Clotheir General.[4] This Money I receivd of M[r] Abbot Hall the amount was 5597 67/90 Dollars as appears by M[r] Halls list of the different species of Money.[5] I deliverd this Account to M[r] Morris at the same time that I left my books and papers with you. But by applying to Capt Hambleton he will satisfy you of the Justice of the charge.

Inclosed is a state of the account with the errors corrected and the omisions added, by which you will see there is a ballance due to me of 1563 18/90 Dollars which I beg you will please to report upon and obtain me an order to recieve; for no man on Earth wants it more. I shall continue some time in this Country and shall be happy to hear from you by the next Paquet.[6] I am Sir with respect Your Most Obed humble Ser[t]

NATH GREENE

ADfS (MiU-C).

1. See Milligan to NG, 30 August 1784, above.

2. NG had presumably turned these bills over to John S. Dart, the Southern Army's paymaster, before leaving Charleston in August 1783.

3. Ephraim Blaine had been the commissary general of purchases.

4. John Hamilton had been the Southern Army's clothier general.

5. On the money that NG had received from George Abbott Hall for the purchase of clothing supplies, see above, NG to Robert Morris, 19 December 1782 (vol. 12: 312).

6. NG's "state of the account" has not been found. Nor has Milligan's reply, but he referred the present letter to auditor John D. Mercier, who wrote the following report to Milligan on 15 April:

"I have examined an account Major Gen' Nathaniel Greene, against The United States adjusted by Ramsey & Nixon Clerks. And Report

"That from the state of said account, adjusted the 7th of July 1784 there appears, a balance due from Nathaniel Greene to the United States, of Six thousand two hundred & twenty nine dollars, fifteen & three quarter Ninetieths.............................. Dollars...6229.15 3 / 4

That bills of exchange to the amount of Eight hundred Dollars, received from Joseph Clay Deputy paymaster General, southern Department remained unaccounted for................................Dollars.....800.

In the above state of account, there is passed to General Greene's credit the sum of 4957.48 / 90th dollars, said to be a balance due from John Banks & C° on bills of exchange sold them, for which no Voucher appears, therefore ought not to have been allowed.

In an account inclosed in Gen' Greene's letter, dated the 5th February last, he further charges J Banks & C° with the Sum of 5597.67 / 90 dollars, Cash paid them for which no Receipt appears, therefore cannot be allowed.

He also charges J Banks & C° with a bill of exchange for 428. 51 / 90th Dollars, which appears to have been included in the bills sold them for Cash, and for which they are charged, in the balance due on said bills, however an acknowledgement from them will be suffecient to pass it to Gen' Greene's Credit.

As Gen' Greene resides in the same place with the House of John Banks & C° it is easy to remove these difficulties by getting an acknowledgement of the sums they ought to be charged with, otherwise the accounts cannot be settled without bringing him greatly in debt.

The charge of 587.37 / 90th dollars, being stores purchased for the use of his family ought to be allowed.

The two bills, the one for 995. 18 / 90th dollars, the other for 270. 70 / 90 dollars, which were charged, & have never appeared; were drawn for the use of his family, included in the calculation of those expences, allowed him by Congress, in the sum of 4045. 16 / 90th Dollars, & balance each other, he being first debited & then credited with said Bills, and Gen' Greene can have no claim, in case those bills should never appear."

The above is from a copy of Mercier's report (MiU-C), which undoubtedly was sent to NG. Sometime later, NG wrote a rebuttal and presumably sent it to Milligan. (See Answers to the Auditor's Report, after 15 April, below.)

*　　　*　　　*

¶ [FROM WILLIAM DRAYTON, [South Carolina], 7 February 1785. He has "consider'd the several Cases" that NG "laid before" him "the other day," and if the enclosed papers [not found] contain "a proper State" of the cases, Drayton's "opinion is annex'd to each."[1] RCS (ScHi) 1 p.]

1. Drayton was serving as "a Judge of the state's Vice-Admiralty Court." (*Biog. Directory of S.C. House*, 2: 206) The nature of the "Cases" is not known.

¶ [FROM THE MARQUIS DE LAFAYETTE, Versailles, France, 9 February 1785. He has been in Paris for only "a few days" and is therefore "a Short and Less interesting Correspondant."[1] Has sent the "News" that he has been able to "gather" in a letter to "Mr Jay," a copy of which he encloses. Adds: "In this Note of Uncertainty I thought I ought at least to write what public reports and my own politics Could Make up."[2] NG's cousin [Griffin Greene] is "either at Bordeaux or is gone to America. I am Waiting for intelligences on the subject." The frigate has been sold for "some what Under 100,000 livres."[3] Will write "a longer letter" the next time.[4] RCS (OClWHi) 1 p.]

1. Lafayette had just returned from a tour of America. (See above, his letter to NG of 25 August 1784, and NG to Washington, 2 December 1784.)

2. In a letter of 8 February to John Jay, the American secretary of foreign affairs, Lafayette discussed the current political situation in Europe and expressed the hope that favorable trade policies between the United States and France would ultimately prevail. (Idzerda, *Lafayette Papers*, 5: 293–95) The copy of this letter that Lafayette sent to NG has not been found.

3. On the sale of the frigate *Flora* to the French government, see especially Griffin Greene to NG, 2 November 1784, 14 November 1784, and 14 December 1784, all above. Griffin was presumably in Bordeaux at this time. (French & Nephew to NG, 23 April, below)

4. Lafayette's next letter to NG was presumably that of 16 March, below.

*   *   *

From Jeremiah Wadsworth

Dear Sir   Philadelphia Feb[y] 15. 1785
    In New York I conversed with [James] Seagrove on the subject of the Iseland [i.e., Cumberland Island, Ga.], trade, building Ships &c. He had no settled plan & his affairs are so deranged that he can not meddle indeed he is I beleive nearly ruined.[1] I have had this day a long conversation with Robert Morris, he declines any concern in any business as he finds enough to settle his old matters.[2] I have not taken up your Note as I find money not plenty.[3] Col Pettit is so busy in the Assembly that I have only just seen him. Party rages as violent as ever & I see no end to it in this Citty.[4] General Reed is in such ill health that his life is despaired of but his party does not decline with him.[5] Many Merchants here are in a very critical situation indeed I fear their will be very great losses by bankrupts, of which losses our W & C Partnership will feel some disadvantages.[6] I shall leave this Citty tomorrow & return to N York Where Congress are siting.[7] They have appointed a Board of treasury in the place of M[r] Morris the Members are M[r] Osgood of Boston M[r] Walter Livingston New York M[r] Jervies [i.e., John Lewis Gervais] S[o] Carolina. I fear they want such abillities as are necessa[ry?] to give Vigor & Credit to an Empty Treasury.[8] I had some thoughts of being concerned in the Southern business since I saw you but I am under the Necessity of

giveing over every Idea of extending my concerns & must contract them.[9] I am D[r] Sir sincerely your freind & Hum Servant

JERE WADSWORTH

RCS (CtHi).

1. On the prospect of James Seagrove becoming an investor in Cumberland Island—and on the other financial propositions mentioned here—see Seagrove's and Wadsworth's letters to NG of 23 February, both below.

2. NG presumably had hoped that Morris would invest in Cumberland Island. (NG to Wadsworth, 17 February, immediately below)

3. In regard to the note, see NG to Wadsworth, 3 February, above.

4. On Charles Pettit's activities in the Pennsylvania legislature, see his letter to NG of 23 March, below. On party factions in Philadelphia and Pennsylvania, see, for example, Pettit to NG, 6 March 1784, above.

5. Joseph Reed, who had returned from a trip to England gravely ill, died in early March. (Eyre to NG, 7 March, below)

6. On the recent financial problems of many Philadelphia merchants, see note at Pettit to NG, 26 July 1784, above. Wadsworth undoubtedly referred here to his business partnership with John Barker Church, a.k.a. John Carter.

7. Congress convened in New York on 11 January. (JCC, 28: 1) Wadsworth wrote NG on 21 February, below, that he had arrived in New York on the 18th.

8. On 25 January, Congress elected Samuel Osgood, Livingston, and Gervais "Commissioners to constitute a board of Treasury." (Ibid., p. 18; concerning the board, see also NG to Morris, 13 November 1784, above.)

9. Wadsworth asked more about the "Southern business"—Cumberland Island—in his letter to NG of 21 February.

*   *   *

¶ [TO JEREMIAH WADSWORTH. From Charleston, S.C., 17 February 1785. Since writing to Wadsworth about Cumberland Island, Ga.,[1] NG finds he can "improve the purchace." He has been offered "the bonds of the last payment for twenty per cent discount" and believes "the party will give thirty [percent] for the last if not for the three last [payments]."[2] NG has asked Mr. [Robert] Morris "to negotiate the Loan" for £5,000, but he adds: "In the mean time if I can get the money or any part of it I would wish to take up the Bonds." Asks Wadsworth to "be good enough to make enquiry" and to write to him.[3] As "the Vessel is just going," NG cannot write more.[4] ALS (CtY) 1 p.]

1. See NG to Wadsworth, 3 February, above.

2. A payment was then due on NG's Cumberland Island "purchace." (Ibid.)

3. NG's request to Morris has not been found. (See, however, Morris to NG, 15 March, and Pendleton to NG, 25 April, both below.) Wadsworth could not offer much help in attracting investors. (See his letters to NG of 15 February, above, and 21 February and 4 March, both below.) As seen below in NG to Shattuck, 23 August, and Crafts to NG, 27 January 1786, NG was later pressed for payment by at least one Cumberland Island bondholder.

4. NG was about to leave for Georgia. (See note at his letter to James Gunn of 23 February, below.)

*   *   *

From Jeremiah Wadsworth

My dear Sir　　　　　　　　　　　　　New York Feb[y] 21. 1785

I returned here the 18th from Philadelphia. I left a letter there for you informing you I had not paid your Note.[1] I this day received your favor of the 3[d] instant. Am glad you escaped, I never was fond of these winter Voyages.[2] I was not able to obtain a Single Shilling in Philadelphia except my dividend at the Bank about Eighteen hundred dollars.[3] My affairs like every bodys in Philadelphia are in a bad way yet I here [i.e., hear] not so bad as most peoples. I do not know five People there whose Bills I woud buy, and every one is pressed for Money you can have no Idea of the distress & want of confidence in that Citty.[4] M[r] [Robert] Morris says he cannot meddle in any new matters till he has got through his old ones.[5] Seagrove can not do any thing[;] I found by acident he is greatly involved. I beleive beyon[d] the power of recovery. He dont know that I know this & I believe it is very little known, but I have read his letter to his Creditors in Phila[a] and I am persuaded he is deeply diped in misfortune.[6]

I proposed a purchase of part of Cumberland Iseland to Marbois, he wishes to be concerned but bid me not mention his name to any body.[7] He wants to know the Size of the Timber on y[e] Iseland the quantity[,] the extent[,] number of Acres & the harbors, its Vicinity to the Main Land in a Word he wants a Minute description of the Whole Iseland.[8] This known he will determine, & I promised to obtain it for him, by your conversation I supposed your Mortgage only extended to one half the Iseland but by your letter I shoud suppose you meant the whole[.] Explain this matter to me and let me know if half is meant whether their is a division to be made with the other owners. If the whole Iseland is not alike if a division is made the chance of an equal division to absent owners is not great, and to hold in common & enter into a concern with strangers will scare Marbois. He will be pleased with a concern with you but must be well informed and know minutely every thing about it. He is a Frenchman and must know more about it than woud satisfy two Americans.[9]

I wrote you from Hartford [Conn.] respecting a Mr Russel & somebody else whose Bond we had for about a thousand dollars. This letter went by the Post & ought to have reached you before you sailed, but as you dont notice it I presume you did not receve it. This might (as I find they are good men) serve as a remittance to pay your debts in part at Charlestown.[10] I shall be as prepared as possible for your drafts but do not draw on Sight or exceed the sum of your note on the Bank as I have very little prospect of being in Cash. Advise me by every opportunity & let me know your situation. I will do every thing in my power to aid You. I shall not use your note for five hundred pounds sterling payable to ye Bank of Philadelphia, indeed I beleive no body but Robert Morris coud borrow of that Bank for a longer time than two Months, so that any support from thence can not be expected.[11] I have heared once from Mrs Greene since you left her she had been indisposed but was recovered.[12]

Marbois Idea is to supply the Marine of France with timber but he fears this of Cumberland Iseland is not big enough[;] the size therefore is material[.][13] Is their not common Oak on the Neighboring Mainland large [enough?] for Knees &c.[14] He I believe expects to be recalled to France soon & wishes to be informed as soon as possible of every thing that relates to ye Iseland. You will therefore loose no time in giving the information, if you can see the Isel^d Yourselfe it will be best.[15] After all I am not sanguine about his purchase as Frenchmen are generally Warmest at first but as the Minister of Marine has Wrote him on the Subject of Timber I think it the best possible chance.[16] I am sincerly & affectionately my dear Sir Your very Hum Servant   JERE WADSWORTH

I leave this in 8 or ten days for Hartford & shall go to attend a suit at Providence [R.I.] in March, if possible will Visit Mrs Greene.[17]

RCS (CtHi).

1. Wadsworth presumably left his letter to NG of 15 February, above, in Philadelphia in order to have it sent on the next vessel to Charleston, S.C.

2. In his letter to Wadsworth of 3 February, above, NG reported that his passage to Charleston had been "terrible" and that "we just escaped destruction."

3. Six months earlier, the dividend on Wadsworth's holdings in the Bank of North America had been $4,354. The bank's president had then predicted "a 9% dividend for years to come," and Wadsworth, through an associate, had acquired "seven more shares." Since August, however, shares had fallen from "$525 to par of $400." (Destler, "Wadsworth," pp. 245–46)

4. Wadsworth's financial problems in Philadelphia at this time are discussed in ibid., pp. 244–48. (See also Wadsworth to NG, 4 March, below.)

5. See also Wadsworth to NG, 15 February.

6. In ibid., Wadsworth informed NG that James Seagrove was "nearly ruined." On Seagrove's financial affairs, see also his and Wadsworth's letters to NG of 23 February and Wadsworth's to NG of 4 March, all below.

7. The Marquis de Barbé-Marbois was the French chargé d'affaires in the United States.

8. See note 15, below.

9. In his letter to Wadsworth of 3 February, NG reported that he was being pressed for "a part if not the whole" of the payment then due on his Cumberland Island mortgage. (NG's holdings on the island—he held an indenture for an undivided half share—are discussed at Hyrne to Clay, 26 November 1783, above.)

10. Wadsworth had asked about Nathaniel Russell and Thomas [Newell?] in a letter to NG of 5 January, above.

11. On the note for £5,000, see NG to Wadsworth, 3 February.

12. NG did not hear from CG for some weeks and was relieved to have this bit of news from Wadsworth. (NG to CG, 14 April, below). The nature of CG's indisposition is not known, but she was pregnant. (See note at NG to Wadsworth, 30 August, below.)

13. On Marbois's plans for supplying the French navy with timber from Cumberland Island, see NG's letter to him of 15 April, below.

14. A "knee" is a "piece of timber naturally or artificially bent for use in supporting structures coming together at an angle (as the framing and deck beams of a ship)." (*Webster's*)

15. NG visited Cumberland Island in the early spring and gave a detailed description of its resources in a letter to the Marquis de Barbé-Marbois of 15 April, below.

16. The Marquis de Castries was the French "Minister of Marine." (See NG's letter to him of 1 June, below.)

17. The nature of the lawsuit that Wadsworth was to "attend" in Providence is not known. Wadsworth visited CG in Newport in May. (Wadsworth to NG, 6 May, below)

From James Gunn

Sir   [Savannah, Ga.?][1] Feb[y] 23[d] 1785

This being the first leisure moment I have had from publick business since your arrival I am sincerely sorry I am under the necessity of seizing it for a demand of reparation for the injuries I received whilst under your command in the Southern department. I beg you sir not to believe any thing in this letter, alludes to your duty as an Officer.[2]

Permit me sir to remind you of the personal abuse I received from you at M[r] Warings,[3] the ungenerous letter you wrote the president of the Court Martial[4] and the letter of abuse I received after being acquitted by that Court, the last complained of as cruel ungenerous and unjust by your greatest Friends.[5]

My situation as a subordinate Officer compelled me at that period to pocket those repeated insults and to forbear reply till the hour should arrive to place us on an equal footing. I mean the ending of that glorious revolution we were engaged in.[6]

That hour is now come and the military command is lost in the Citizen, the persecution has been such the delay of satisfaction would betray a want of that spirit every officer & Gentleman should feel. I flatter myself one moments reflection to a man of your nice sensibility will convince you that such injustice and violence offered my reputation cannot be passed over.

Col [James] Jackson who will be the bearer of this will wait your answer which I expect will be in writing.[7] I am sir with the highest respect yr most Obed[t] servt   JAMES GUNN

RCS (MiU-C).

1. Gunn, whose exact whereabouts are not known, may have been at his plantation, Clifton, near Savannah. (See note at Gunn to NG, 2 March, below.) At any rate, he and NG were in close proximity, as Gunn's letters to NG of this date and of 2 March, below, were both answered on those dates, and it appears that NG had recently arrived in Savannah. (See NG's letter to Gunn of this date, below.)

2. Gunn, a former cavalry captain, had resumed the practice of law in Georgia after the war. (Jones, *Sketches of Delegates from Georgia*, p. 44) In the spring of 1782, NG accused him of appropriating a horse that belonged to the army and exchanging it with another officer. A court of inquiry cleared Gunn of any misdoing in the matter, but NG rejected the court's

finding and obtained a resolution from Congress in support of his action. (See above, Ichabod Burnet to Gunn, 13 May 1782; Findings of a Court of Inquiry and NG's Response, 3 June 1782; and NG to Benjamin Lincoln, 22 June 1782. [Vol. 11: 187 and n, 286–87 and n, and 358–59 and n])

3. The Southern Army had camped near the home of John Smith Waring during the spring and early summer of 1782. (Vol. 11: 477n, above) Gunn had been summoned there for an interview with NG about his dealings with public property and Gunn had presumably interpreted something that NG said at that time as constituting "personal abuse." (NG commented on that meeting in his letter to James Jackson of 28 February, below.)

4. For NG's response to the court of inquiry's findings, see vol. 11: 287.

5. The "letter of abuse" was undoubtedly NG's to Gunn of 9 June 1782, above (vol. 11: 310–11).

6. It can be inferred from Gunn's reply to ibid. that he might well have challenged NG to a duel at that time under other, non-military circumstances. (Gunn to NG, 16 June 1782, above [vol. 11: 338–39]) He did so in a letter to NG of 24 February, below.

7. NG's reply is immediately below. (See also NG to Jackson, 28 February.)

To James Gunn

Sir   [Savannah, Ga., 23 February 1785][1]
I have just got your letter of this day deliverd me by Major [James] Jackson.[2] Conscious of having done nothing respecting you or any other officer while in command but what my public duty imposed upon me I can not think my self accountable to every individual who may put a different interpretation upon it. The delicasy which I preserved towards all the officers will acquit me from a charge [of] offering any personal abuse to any. You must have confounded the action with the person to give my sentiments such an interpretation. It is as much below the dignity of an Officer as it was foreign from my intention to offer you or any other Officer an insult or to say more than my duty requird.[3] I am Sir your humble Ser   NATH GREENE

ADfS (MiU-C).
1. The date was determined from Gunn's letter "of this day," immediately above, to which NG referred here. It is not clear when NG arrived in Savannah from Charleston, S.C., but he was undoubtedly there by this date.
2. Gunn's letter is immediately above.
3. Gunn's reply is below, dated 24 February.

*   *   *

¶ [FROM JAMES SEAGROVE, New York, 23 February 1785.[1] Acknowledges NG's "favour, without date [not found], relative to our intended visit to the Southward." Seagrove "fully intended to have been in Carolina and Georgia" by now, but the settling of his "Havana transactions" has detained him "unavoidably."[2] He is "determined," though, to go "very soon upon the plan" that he and NG "conversed on" in New York. Adds: "I am every day more convinced that great advantage may be had from a proper Commercial establishment on St Mary's River or thereabouts." With his "acquaintance & connections in the Havana as well as Florida," Seagrove could "draw there as much Business" as he wished. He is "determined to try it" and would be happy to give NG "a preference."[3] The purchase of Cumberland Island is a "weighty matter," and Seagrove cannot make a decision "until its know[n] in which situation stands the Timber, Soil, Harbours, situation &ᶜ &ᶜ." NG will be "able to judge," and if the conditions are acceptable, Seagrove will "have no objection of holding a part" with him.[4] Seagrove is "determined to fix" himself "in the superintending of any matters to the Southward" and thinks that "in a few years something handsom may be done as well in the way of Business, as in forming a settlement in that Country."[5] When he travels to the South, he can bring with him "a person who will be a great acquisition in our Spanish Concerns."[6] Seagrove has had "very favourable Letters from Havana." His friend "Coppinger" had "his Petition granted by the Court of Spain for a very extensive Trade" from the United States, all of which will be under Seagrove's direction and would be "favourable" to the plan at St. Marys.[7] Seagrove has written to Coppinger about the "Banks[,] Burnet & Cᵒ affairs in his hands," and Coppinger wants NG to give him "Orders which he will attend to." The letter should be sent to "Don Cornelio Coppinger in Havana," enclosed to "Jesse Fish Esqʳ in Sᵗ Augustine," who will forward it.[8] Col. [Jeremiah] Wadsworth was with Seagrove the previous evening, and they "conversed fully on our intended plan." Wadsworth "sees it in the same light as I do," and Seagrove refers NG to Wadsworth's letter, which will be sent by the same vessel.[9] "Genˡ Webb" is in New York and is well.[10] Seagrove has "No news [in] particular. Trade exceeding dul & must be worse. Shoals of Protested Bills returning Dayly, no knowing who to trust, all commercial confidence seems lost. Matters wors[e] in Philᵃ if possible."[11] Hopes to see NG in three weeks.[12] RCS (MiU-C) 3 pp.]

1. Seagrove, a merchant, had furnished supplies to the Continental army during the war. (Syrett, *Hamilton*, 15: 400n)

2. Seagrove's mercantile activities included dealings with merchants in Havana, Cuba, where he had been based for a time. (*Travels of Francisco de Miranda*, p. 19)

3. Details of what NG and Seagrove discussed in New York are not known, but the "plan" was clearly concerned with NG's interest in Cumberland Island, Ga., near at the mouth of the St. Marys River, the boundary between Georgia and what had recently become the Spanish colony of East Florida. Seagrove apparently hoped to establish a base in southern Georgia for trade between the United States and the Spanish colonies of Cuba and East Florida. (See note at NG to CG, 14 April, below.) Helen Hornbeck Tanner has written that Seagrove assisted Francisco Miranda, the "famous precurser of the independence movement in South America, to escape from Havana to Charleston [S.C.] in 1784." After founding the town of St. Marys, Ga., on the border with East Florida, in 1790, Seagrove also "served briefly as Indian superintendent, endeavoring to diminish Spanish influence among the Creeks, and later as collector of the port of St. Marys. From this strategic location, he supported a series of projects, some with secret federal government support, to foment uprisings in Spanish East Florida in order to provide an excuse for American occupation of the province." Tanner speculates that in "view of Seagrove's later career," his "plans" with NG could have had more sinister implications. (Tanner, *Visit to St. Augustine*, pp. 4–5)

4. NG had been trying to attract investors to the property on Cumberland Island in which he had an interest. (See, for example, Eyre to NG, 19 December 1784, and NG to Wadsworth, 3 February, both above.) NG visited the island several weeks after Seagrove wrote the present letter and later wrote a detailed précis of its natural resources. (NG to

Marbois, 15 April, below) Wadsworth wrote NG on 21 February, above, that Seagrove was in trouble financially. As Wadsworth observed in his letter to NG of this date, immediately below, Seagrove's financial "imbarrasments" were such as to preclude his becoming an investor in Cumberland Island.

5. Seagrove and his brother Robert eventually established a trading post at Coleraine in southern Georgia. (Syrett, *Hamilton*, 15: 400n)

6. It is not known whom Seagrove proposed to bring with him to the South.

7. As discussed at NG to CG, 14 April, below, trade between Spanish colonies and the United States had been restricted. Coppinger has not been identified.

8. Nothing is known about Coppinger's involvement in "Banks Burnet & Cº affairs," nor has an "order" from NG to Coppinger been found. Jesse Fish was a landowner in St. Augustine. (Siebert, *Loyalists in East Florida*, 2: 365) According to Tanner, Fish, a merchant, "had served as principal intermediary in real estate transactions between British and Spaniards in East Florida since 1764." (Tanner, *Visit to St. Augustine*, p. 4)

9. Wadsworth's letter is immediately below.

10. Samuel B. Webb of Connecticut was the stepson of NG's former business partner Silas Deane and a good friend of NG's. (Vol. 1: 258n, above) He had been breveted to the rank of brigadier general in September 1783. (Heitman, *Register*)

11. In his letter to NG of 15 February, Wadsworth had reported numerous bankruptcies in Philadelphia. Charles Pettit also informed NG about the economic conditions there in a letter of 26 July 1784, above.

12. NG wrote Wadsworth on 24 April, below, that he was waiting for Seagrove to make an "appearance." Seagrove apparently was in Georgia by January 1786, as seen in his letter to NG at the end of the documents for that month, below.

¶ [FROM JEREMIAH WADSWORTH, New York, 23 February 1785. [James] Seagrove, with whom he spent the previous evening, has received "letters from the Havannah which give him great hopes that he shall soon be in trade with that Country." Seagrove thinks "an establishment on Cumberland Iseland will be very profitable if only for the trade with the Spaniards." Wadsworth previously "observed" to NG that "acc[i]dent had brought me acquainted with his [i.e., Seagrove's] imbarrasments." Although Seagrove has not "communicated any thing on this subject himselfe," Wadsworth is "well assured that he can do nothing where any advance is required" and that "nothing can be expected from him at present."[1] Wadsworth asks for more information about the "Iseland[:] the quantity & quallity of the Land, the Size of the timber[,] the quantity & different species, the harbors, the distance from the Continent, the climate &c. Is their any game & of what Sort[;] are their any Cattle or Horses or can they subsist if put on." He also wonders whether the "whole Iseland" can be "obtained." Asks for a "complete description," including whether there are any inhabitants and whether there are "fish in or about it."[2] Mr. Marbois is the only person Wadsworth has found "who Seems inclined to be concerned" in the island;[3] "indeed every body is poor. Money scarce & universal distrust prevailing."[4] Wadsworth's letter of 23 [i.e., 21] February is a reply to NG's letter "respecting the Note" that NG enclosed; Wadsworth does not "find it Possable" to become "a purchaser" himself. He adds: "I am so greatly disappointed in every expectation of Money & find so many new & unexpected demands that I can not at present venture in any new purchase."[5] He has asked about the value of NG's lands "up this River," but his inquiries "have not been very usefull," and he has received various opinions as to "its Value."[6] In any case, "Money is no where to be found for Land." The state of New York seems presently to have "as little Vigor & decision as any one in the union," and Wadsworth is afraid it will "head in the Steps of Rh^d Island respecting the impost."[7] He comments that the legislature is now "siting but they appear to me to be more concerned about secureing to them selves a good share of their new Lands than to Legislate." Wadsworth, who has been "detained" in New York to "compleate a settlement of several Accounts," comments: "a settlement is all I hope[,] for payment is out of the question."[8] RCS (CtHi) 3 pp.]

1. See Wadsworth to NG, 21 February, above, and Seagrove to NG, this date, immediately above.

2. After a visit there at the end of March, NG wrote a "complete description" of Cumberland Island, Ga., for potential investors. (See below, NG to CG, 14 April, and NG to Marbois, 15 April.) NG's interest in the island is described in a note at Hyrne to Clay, 26 November 1783, above.

3. The Marquis de Barbé-Marbois, the French chargé d'affaires, was interested in obtaining high-quality timber from the live oak trees on Cumberland Island for the French navy. (See Wadsworth to NG, 15 February, above and NG to Marbois, 15 April.) Although Wadsworth decided not to invest in the island, he continued to communicate with Marbois on NG's behalf. (Wadsworth to NG, 10 April, below)

4. In his letters to NG of 15 and 21 February, Wadsworth had discussed the precarious financial situations of many businessmen in Philadelphia and New York.

5. On "the note," see NG to Wadsworth, 3 February, above.

6. On 26 March, below, NG gave Wadsworth a power of attorney to try to sell the land that NG owned along the Hudson River in New York and the Passaic River in New Jersey.

7. On Rhode Island's rejection of the federal impost measure of 1783, see NG to Morris, 3 July 1784, above. Wadsworth wrote NG on 10 May, below: "New York have rejected ye impost and we are now all afloat." The New York legislature, "under heavy pressure," finally "granted the impost" in 1786, but added stipulations that Congress found unacceptable. (Ferguson, *Power of the Purse*, p. 240; see also *JCC*, 31: 554–61.) For later developments in Rhode Island, see note at Pettit to NG, 23 March, below.

8. "On Manhattan Island," according to his biographer, "Wadsworth could not even collect money on newly settled accounts. Universal distrust prevailed." (Destler, "Wadsworth," p. 246)

*   *   *

From James Gunn

Sir   [Savannah, Ga.?] Feby 24th 1785[1]

I have just received your answer to my letter delivered by Col [James] Jackson and must express a surprize at your attempt to justify the abuse complained of under a Cloak of command.[2] Whatever may be your idea of interpretation permit me sir to assure you I cannot have mistaken. The three heads of insult were not only the complaints of myself but those of every Officer acquainted with them.[3] Whether or not you are accountable to every Individual is not for me to determine more than on the delicacy wherewith every Officer under your command has been treated. Let others judge for themselves my feelings are my own and so widely do I differ with you that however sorry I may be for the occasion

I am compelled to call on you for the apology of a Gentleman or an information when & where I may meet that redress the laws of Honor demand.[4] I am sir yr most Obed[t] servt   JAMES GUNN

RCS (MiU-C).
1. On Gunn's location at this time, see note at Gunn to NG, 23 February, above.
2. NG's letter is above, dated 23 February. For background, see Gunn to NG, 23 February.
3. See Gunn to NG, 23 February.
4. Dissatisfied with NG's response, Gunn formally challenged him to a duel. (See NG to Jackson, 28 February, and Gunn to NG, 2 March, both below.)

From Edward Carrington

D[r] General   Richmond [Va.] Feb[y] 27. 1785
    I had the pleasure to write you by favor of the Marquis [de Lafayette] in Dec[r] which no doubt you have rec[d].[1] Your affairs with Hen[ry]. Banks I fear will e'er long wear but a bad aspect, and although nothing authorizes my declaring that it will be out of his power to give you any indemnification on your sufferring by J.B.[s] [i.e., John Banks's] Creditors, yet I cannot forbear to Warn you that such a circumstance from present appearances is too probable. His [i.e., Henry Banks's] Creditors are pushing him hard and although he affects to carry a good countenance I apprehend he must fall.[2]
    I would therefore by no means recommend your declining any Step which may possibly releive you otherwise. I fear indeed that you are badly circumstanced with respect to any property which may have been connected with J.B., because as Several are still living in this Country who have been connected with him in business, they will not bring their affairs with him to a close until they have perhaps diverted every Shilling which might arise from them to other purposes, and of those perhaps H.B [i.e., Henry Banks] may be found to be one. He sometime ago talked of depositing in my hands Sundry Debts due to H.B. & C[o] to be collected and the money reserved under certain conditions for the indemnification of yourself & [Patrick] Carnes, but upon my having Signified an inclination to undertake the business, he is off the measure, alledging that the other partners will not consent to it, so that I think it is much to be apprehended that amongst them, the property, if any, will slide out of the reach of either you or Carnes.[3] Under these circumstances and appearances I must recommend that you have the Debts you are security for put to their final issue as soon as possible, that you may be authorised to persue the property of the Company wherever you can find it, and indeed to force an adjustment of all the concerns with which John Banks was connected. Of this you cannot however judge accurately without coming to Virginia and looking somewhat into the State of them. As to [Robert] Patton I can give you no flattering

prospects from that quarter, no Suit has yet been brought, at least there was not a few weeks ago, you know it is dependent on others and they alledge that circumstances are not yet favourable for such a Measure, Mr Baker who is warmly your freind has several times spoken with me to this effect.[4]

Neither [James] Hunter nor [Robert] Forsythe have yet come to Virginia, the Former, they say, is in Burmudas and will be here in a few Months: when he arrives I will see him, and if the conveyance of the Lotts from [George?] Mathews can be brought about, it shall be done. How Hunter & Mathews may agree as to the consideration Money being fully paid I do not know, but H Banks & Mathews differ widely, the one alledging that he Suffers much for want of it, and the other that it is more than paid.[5] Inclosed is a letter covering an Inventory of John Banks's property in North Carolina which has been transmitted to me by Col. [William] Blount, you find that the debts which appeared to be due there are likely to be explained away to very little indeed.[6]

You must not neglect to have Hunters Mortgage transmitted to me as early as possible proved by three Witnesses whose proof thereof must be properly certified under the Seal of the State of South Carolina where, no doubt, they all live, as it is necessary that it be committed to Record here, in eight months after it was executed.[7] You will recollect too that you have never sent me a power of Attorney, which if it should at any time be in my power to serve you, will be absolutely necessary, you may be assured that with the utmost zeal I shall be ready to embrace any opportunity to be of Service. Having lately had the misfortune to lose both my Father and mother for whom I had a most tender Affection, I have been much from Town, and having his Affairs now to Manage must retire to the Country altogether.[8] When you come to Virginia you will much oblige me by Staying with me as long as you can, my residence is about fifty Miles from Town, in the mean time your letters will regularly come to hand, being Sent to Richmond p^r post,[9] and I remain, with the greatest Affection, Dr Sir your Most Ob^t Servt

ED. CARRINGTON

NB. About June I shall go to Phil^a.

RCS (MiU-C).

1. This letter has not been found.

2. In a letter of 10 November 1784, above, NG had asked Carrington to pay "special attention to the matter" of attaching property and funds belonging to John Banks's estate in Virginia.

3. See also Carrington to NG, 23 March, and Hunter to NG, 1 June, both below.

4. NG had urged Carrington in his letter of 10 November 1784 "to spur on Cambell to bring forward his suit against [Robert] Patton."

5. Hunter did go to Virginia. (Hunter to NG, 1 June) NG wrote Carrington on 29 September, below: "I did all I could to get Forsyth to Virginia but could not." Nothing is known about "the conveyance of the Lotts."

6. The inventory has not been found.

7. NG did send Hunter's mortgage, but Carrington reported in his letter of 23 March that the documentation was defective.

8. Carrington was the eighth of eleven children of Col. George and Mrs. Anne Mayo Carrington of Boston Hill in Cumberland County, Va., both of whom had died earlier in February. (Konigsberg, "Carrington," pp. 3–4; http:/aut.ancestry.com)

9. Carrington was in Richmond when he wrote NG on 23 March.

To James Jackson[1]

Dear Sir   Savannah [Ga.] Feb 28th 1785.

Having always felt for you from our earliest acquaintance a sentiment of esteem and friendship and having ever flattered myself both from your public and private conduct that you were impressed with similar sentiments I cannot omit to satisfy you that my conduct is influenced by just principles respecting Capt. [James] Gunn's.[2] And this I think the more necessary as you have become connected with the subject.[3] To do this nothing more is wanting than to give a short history of the affair which I will do as well as the distance of time from memory will enable me, confident at the same time that the document among my public Papers will confirm every part of it. Some time in the spring or the forepart of the summer of 1782 complaint was made at head quarters that Capt. Gunn had been selling public property. I wrote to the commanding officer of his corps to send him to head Quars to answer to the charge.[4] He came and I was so far from wishing to treat the matter with severity that I consulted with him on the mode he would prefer for establishing the fact & the nature & tendency of the thing.[5] A court of enquiry was agreed on and a board of officers appointed accordingly. That the board might not mistake the thing with respect to my public duty I stated the subject fully to them both as to its effects on the discipline and the obligation I should be under of transmitting the proceedings to Congress, should they authorize the precedent.[6] It was both my wish and intention to get the precedent condemned without bringing Capt Gunn before a court martial for a breach of the rules & articles of war which must have been fatal to him. But strange as it may appear the board of officers reported that Capt Gunn had a right to sell public property. This was placing the matter in a most serious and alarming light. It was little less than a death warrant to the army. I condemned their proceedings as subversive of the discipline of the army destructive of public interest and ruinous to all military operations. If an officer have a right to sell public property so have a soldier. A precedent so dangerous and which was increased by the distresses of the army made it justly to be dreaded.[7] In this situation of things Capt Gunn demanded a confirmation of the proceedings of the board in justification of his conduct. At first I could hardly suppose him serious, but finding him persist in [the] thing I was obliged to give him my sentiments on the subject however unpleasant to his feelings or opposite to his wishes. But no man ever heard me use language disgraceful to a gentleman. My sense of the act was that it was criminal and altogether unwarrantable. He then wrote me a letter claiming it as a matter of right to have the proceedings of the board confirmed.[8] Finding there was both a wish and intention to try to get the precedent established, I gave his letter a pointed answer stating the impropriety of his conduct in the first act and then reprobating the disposition he discovered for establishing a precedent for his justification which would be the highest breach of duty in me to comply with. This is the letter he complained of as out of the line of my duty.[9] To have been silent and given countenance to an opinion so fatal in its nature and operation would have rendered my conduct less excuseaable than his. Those who are acquainted with the proceedings of Court martials and Courts of inquiry know that they have no operation but by the approbation of the commanding officer and that he makes himself responsible to his sovereign if he authorizes any thing contrary to the rules & articles of war or injurious to the discipline of the army. Impressed with these sentiments I sent all the papers to Congress as well the letter to the board of Officers as the letter to Capt Gunn which he complains of. I recieved their full approbation of every step I had taken in the matter, a confirmation of my sentiments to the board of Officers with a pointed resolve condemning Capt Gunns conduct and the sense of the board of officers upon it. Accompanied with an order to call Capt Gunn to account for the horse, the property sold.[10] Had I been disposed to have persecuted him I could have prosecuted him by a court martial by which he must have lost his commission.[11] I was at first charitably disposed to think Capt. Gunn was ignorant of the nature and tendency of the act he had committted and his not comprehending the line of my responsibility had I confirmed proceedings which were improper might have led him to suppose there was something personal in the business. But when I assured him that I meant him no insult and was not conscious of treating him with indelicacy to ask further satisfaction was inconsistent with that degree of delicacy which is due to a gentleman. If Capt Gunn has a right to mark out the line of my duty and to determine upon my conduct by his feelings and to discriminate between what I did from a sense of duty, and from personal resentment, nothing remains for me to say. But to demands so unreasonable I would disdain a reply. If my conduct had nothing personal in it Capt Gunn was not injured. This I assured him was the case in my first letter.[12] If his feelings were hurt 'twas his misfortune not my fault in placing himself in the situation he did.[13] I am dear Sir your most Obedient humble Servant

NATH GREENE

Cy (GU). A heavily edited ADf is at MiU-C.

1. Jackson was one of the leading men in Georgia during the twenty years following the Revolutionary War. As a colonel of Georgia dragoons, he had been designated by Gen. Anthony Wayne to lead the party that marched into Savannah when the British evacuated the city in July 1782, and for his wartime services he was awarded a house in Savannah. (Vol. 11: 441n, above; *DAB*) After the war, he became a lawyer, served in Congress, and was elected governor of Georgia in 1798. Jackson, who was serving at this time as the aggrieved James Gunn's intermediary with NG, was himself known for a willingness to "fight at the drop of a hat." He had killed the lieutenant governor of Georgia in a duel in 1780 and is said to have eventually died from the wounds he "received in the last of his many duels." (On Jackson, see *DAB*; *Dictionary of Georgia Biography*; William Omer Foster, Sr., *James Jackson: Duelist and Militant Statesman, 1757–1806* [Athens: University of Georgia Press, 1960].)

2. For background, see Gunn's letters to NG of 23 and 24 February, both above.

3. It was Jackson who had delivered both of Gunn's letters to NG. (Ibid.)

4. See NG's letter to Col. Anthony W. White of 13 May 1782, above (vol. 11: 188).

5. Gunn had felt aggrieved from his interview with NG at camp. (Gunn to NG, 23 February)

6. See Instructions to a Court of Inquiry, 3 June 1782, above (vol. 11: 285–86).

7. See Findings of the Court of Inquiry and NG's Response, 3 June 1782, above (vol. 11: 286–87).

8. Nothing more is known about the exchanges referred to here.

9. See NG to Gunn, 9 June 1782, above (vol. 11: 310–11).

10. NG enclosed the papers relating to Gunn's case in a letter of 22 June 1782 to Gen. Benjamin Lincoln, the secretary at war. (Vol. 11: 358–59, above) The resolution of Congress is noted at ibid.

11. Gunn had declined NG's offer to submit the matter to a court-martial. (Gunn to NG, 16 June 1782, above [vol. 11: 338]; the offer is in NG's letter to Gunn of 9 June 1782.)

12. See NG to Gunn, 23 February.

13. Gunn responded to this letter by challenging NG to a duel. (Gunn to NG, 2 March, below)

*   *   *

¶ **[FROM NATHANIEL SHALER**, New York, 28 February 1785.[1] Has NG's letter of 4 February [not found] and has "forwarded by a special messenger" the letters "for the Burnetts at Newark [N.J.] acquainting them of the opertunities that [are?] presented" for NG's "place should answers be required."[2] The "other Letter," which is for CG [not found], has been "forwarded," and NG need not have apologized for these requests; Shaler will be pleased to serve him in the future. RCS (MiU-C) 1 p.]

1. Shaler was a friend and business associate of Jeremiah Wadsworth. (NG to Wadsworth, 13 May, below)

2. NG's letters for the family of his late aide Ichabod Burnet have not been found but may have concerned a possible sale of the land that NG owned near them in New Jersey. (See, for example, Power of Attorney to Wadsworth, 26 March, and NG to Wadsworth, 13 July, both below.)

*   *   *

From James Gunn

Sir   Savannah [Ga.] Mar. 2^d 1785

Your letter to Colonel Jackson, I have now before me, and sorry I am to observe, there appears a want of that attention to consistency, You wo^d willingly wish the World believe you possess.[1] However its fortunate for me, there are some few now here, who recollects every circumstance respecting the matter in Question and who can & will put it in my Power, to do *Justice*; altho it has been denied me; by a partial representation to Congress of my Conduct:[2] My present situation puts it out of your power to do me an Injury notwithstanding you may feal a disposition to do so. Consequently as I feal myself equally Independent with you: there Can be no acceptation taken:[3] nor can you object to meeting me with your friend, provided with Arms necessary on those occations, at 4. oClo. this afternoon, on Mr Campbells plantation opposite to Savannah, to render that satisfaction, which is due to Injured reputation.[4]

I have been Informed, that the Sheriff has Interfered on your part, I have therefore recommended, the opposite shore as the most eligable, for the scene of action as I wo^d not wish to Committ a breach, on the laws of the State.[5]

Colo. Jackson being necessarily engaged, wth the present Court,[6] and I being under the necessity of leaving town this even^g. Major [Benjamin] Fishbourn my friend on this occation will convey from you, any answer you may have for me.[7] I am Sir Y^r hble Servt JAMES GUNN

RCS (MiU-C).

1. See NG to James Jackson, 28 February, above.

2. For background, see Gunn to NG, 23 and 24 February, above. "A partial representation to Congress" was presumably NG's request to that body to uphold his reversal of a court of inquiry's findings in regard to Gunn's conduct. (See NG to Benjamin Lincoln, 22 June 1782, above [vol. 11: 358–59 and n].)

3. Gunn meant that as neither he nor NG was now acting in a military capacity, NG could no longer treat him as a subordinate. Although nearly three years had passed since his original dispute with NG, Gunn may have been provoked to renew the quarrel by NG's presence in the state. Gunn, who would later serve in Congress as a representative and senator and would also become "implicated in the Yazoo [land] speculations," has been described as "violent, aggressive, addicted to extravagant statement and profane swearing, overbearing, disposed to pander to the lowest prejudices of the populace, unscrupulous in the means employed for the accomplishment of his ambition, vain, boastful, negligent of public duty when intent on schemes of personal advantage, and intolerant of opposition." (Jones, *Sketches of Delegates from Georgia*, pp. 44–47; see also NG's comments about him in letters to Jeremiah Wadsworth, 8 March, and Washington, 25 April, both below.)

4. Gunn was formally challenging NG to a duel. The plantation of McCartan Campbell, where Gunn suggested they meet, was on the South Carolina side of the Savannah River. (Granger, *Savannah River Plantations*, p. 202)

5. Nothing is known about the sheriff's possible involvement in this matter. As seen in the preceding note, the site that Gunn suggested for a duel was in South Carolina, outside the jurisdiction of any Georgia official.

6. As noted at NG's letter to him of 28 February, Jackson was an attorney.

7. Gen. Anthony's Wayne's former aide Benjamin Fishbourn had settled in Georgia. (See Nelson, *Wayne*, pp. 199, 200.) NG's reply is immediately below.

To James Gunn

Sir [Savannah, Ga.] Wednesday [2 March 1785][1]
I have just got your letter by Major Fishburn [Benjamin Fishbourn]. Having written you fully on that subject by Col Jackson in answer to your first letter,[2] I have noth[ing] to add and shall only repeat that having never injurd you out of the line of my duty nor done any thing respecting you but in support of the dicipline of the Army, I have nothing more to say on the subject, only that I will never establish a precedent for subjecting superio[r officers] to the call of inferior officers for what the former have done in the execution of their public duty.[3]

N. GREENE

ADfS (MiU-C).
1. This letter, which is a reply to Gunn's, immediately above, was presumably written on the same date as Gunn's—2 March.
2. See NG to Jackson, 28 February, and Gunn to NG, 23 February, both above.
3. NG wrote Jeremiah Wadsworth on 8 March, below, that he had "rejected the proposition" of a duel with Gunn "with contempt," adding: "He has threatned to insult me, if he should he may take a sudden leap for I keep a good pistol in my pocket." NG later asked for Washington's opinion of his conduct in this matter. "If I thought my honor or reputation might suffer in the opinion of the World and more especially with the Military Gentlemen," NG wrote, "I value life too little to hesitate a moment to answer the challenge." He believed, however, that accepting it would set a harmful precedent. (NG to Washington, 25 April, below) In a reply dated 20 May, below, Washington agreed that NG had acted appropriately in refusing to accept Gunn's challenge.

* * *

¶ [FROM JEREMIAH WADSWORTH, New York, 4 March 1784 [i.e., 1785].[1] He has written to NG several times from New York since receiving NG's letter from Charleston, S.C.[2] Mr. Marbois, the "only person who seems likely to be a purchaser of Cumberland Island," wants to know "every particular" about it, including "harbors bays inlets streams produce size of timber stock if any if not if there is grass for stock," and "its distance from y[e] Continent." Wadsworth asks for a "Minute" description of the island, as "a french man can ask ten questions to an Americans one." Although Marbois is interested, "he is changeable as a frenchman & no time shoud be lost."[3] Wadsworth has yet not paid NG's "note in y[e] Bank" but will do so.[4] "Money is extremely scarce and a universal distrust prevails, our friend C[lement] Biddle has stoped payment for large Sums. Every body seems alarmed & I find it impossible to get paid any thing."[5] The only money that Wadsworth received in Philadelphia was his "dividend on Bank Stock," and he is now "discouraged from any attempts in trade." He has informed NG that Seagrove is in a "disagreeable situation respecting his Havannah Matter." Although Seagrove is now "Sanguine & hopes every thing," Wadsworth is afraid that "his affairs are worse than I guessed."[6] RCS (CtHi) 2 pp.]

1. The year was determined from the contents.

2. See Wadsworth to NG, 15, 21, and 23 February, as well as NG to Wadsworth, 3 February, all above.

3. On the Marquis de Barbé-Marbois's interest in the timber on Cumberland Island, Ga., where NG claimed a part ownership, see Wadsworth's letters to NG of 21 and 23 February. NG gave a detailed description of the island's resources in a letter to Marbois of 15 April, below.

4. In his letter of 3 February, NG had asked Wadsworth to pay a note for him in Philadelphia.

5. On the financial distress that was spreading among merchants in New York and Philadelphia, see Wadsworth to NG, 15 February and Pettit to NG, 26 July 1784, both above. On Biddle's situation, see also the Pettit letter and Eyre to NG, 7 March, immediately below.

6. Wadsworth mentioned New York merchant James Seagrove's financial problems in his letters to NG of 15, 21, and 23 February. Seagrove wrote NG on 23 February, above, that he had been preoccupied with settling his "Havana transactions."

¶ [FROM BENJAMIN EYRE, Philadelphia, 7 March 1785. He received NG's letter of 9 February [not found] on 3 March and was pleased to hear of NG's "safe arrival."[1] It "is now intirely out of" his power to "wait upon" NG, because "business" is "very dul" in Philadelphia, and his "vessails" are "both unsold"; there are "fifteen new vessails on the stocks unsold some of them Liveoak." The "Last cargo of Liveoak" that came to Philadelphia is "unsold and times are so dul at presant that liveoak will not Command Cash." As soon as "there is a demand for it," Eyre will give NG "the Earlyest advice." He encloses "the prices of liveoak when in demand."[2] He has inquired about the timber that has been cut on NG's land, and NG's "information" is "perfectly true";[3] Capt. William "Sample" [i.e., Semple], a merchant from Philadelphia, "owns the Vessail & Captain [Alexander] Cain Commanded her."[4] Eyre received this information from "Mr James Stewart" of Philadelphia, who "has men now Cutting liveoak at Sappalow." Stewart has written to "General [Lachlan] Macintosh" about this for "farther information."[5] Col. Thomas "Casdrop," a Philadelphia shipbuilder, "sold the timber for them" and informed Eyre "yesterday that the timber was Cut upon Cumberland Isleand."[6] Eyre reports that "General Reed is dead & Buryed yesterday. The most respectfull burial that we ever had in this City. The Toreys & the disappointed party broke the poor mans hart."[7] Col. [Clement] Biddle has "Broke up Stock & Fluke to the amount of" £38,000, and a "great number of his Freinds are taken in considerablely with him. It has Surprised every person of his acquaintance."[8] Col. [Charles] Pettit is "poorly at present."[9] Eyre asks NG to "Command me freely upon all Ocasions."[10] RCS (MiU-C) 2 pp.]

1. On NG's "safe arrival" at Charleston, S.C., see NG to Wadsworth, 3 February, above.

2. NG presumably had asked Eyre, a shipbuilder, if he would be interested in buying live oak timber from NG's holdings on Cumberland Island, Ga. (See Eyre to NG, 19 December 1784, above.) The enclosure that Eyre sent with the present letter is at MiU-C, dated 7 March.

3. Loyalist refugees had apparently been cutting timber on Cumberland Island since at least sometime in the previous year. (See above, NG to Bowman, 10 September 1784; Bowman to NG, 12 September 1784, and Houstoun to NG, 12 November 1784.)

4. See also Eyre to NG, 14 May, below.

5. On Sapelo Island, off the Georgia coast, about fifty miles above Cumberland Island, see also Pendleton to NG, 23 September, below.

6. "Casdrop" presumably had sold the timber for Semple and Cain.

7. Joseph Reed, a close friend of NG, died on Friday, 5 March, and was buried two days later. Gen. Richard Butler wrote: "I believe there never was so great a number of people at one funeral in America." (Reed, *Reed*, 2: 415 and n; for a biographical note on Reed, see above, vol. 2: 307–8n. On Reed's death, see also Pettit to NG, 23 March, below.) Reed had been a member of the Radical faction in Pennsylvania politics, which had long feuded bitterly with the Republicans. The latter were now "the disappointed party," having lost control of the Pennsylvania legislature the previous year. The Tories, or British sympathizers, were often aligned with the Republicans. (Pettit to NG, 6 March 1784, above)

8. On Biddle's financial misfortune, see also Wadsworth to NG, immediately above, and Pettit to NG, 23 March.

9. On Pettit's health problems, see his letter to NG of 23 March.

10. NG apparently replied to Eyre on 11 April. (Eyre to NG, 14 May, below)

*   *   *

To William Gibbons, Sr.[1]

Sir Savannah [Ga.] March 8th 1785

M[r] William Gibbons Jr wrote me sometime last Summer that you set up a claim to a part of the estate granted me by Georgia. Nothing would give me greater pain than to have to defend by Law what had been granted me by the Legislature. You was one of the house at the time if I remember right and cannot but be sensible it was the intention of the Legislature to put me in possession of all Grayhams [i.e., John Graham's] property joining Mulberry Grove which he had purchaced at different times and from different people. My Deed from the Commisioners include them.[2] The honor of the State is opposed on one hand and the Laws on the other to your claim. I hope therefore you will not trouble me. My engagements for the Contractors of the Army in this Country has exposed me to heavy losses and subjected me to endless difficulties. The deplorable situation of our finances and the distresses of the Army for want of provisions obliged me to comply to save the Country from farther calamities. But it has been a terrible misfortune and engrosses all my time and attention.[3] Under these circumstances I am sure your humanity will forbid your detaining me. While others are enjoying the blessings of peace I am perplexed with the consequences of the war.[4] I wish to have seen and conversed with you on the subject but am now going to [St.] Augustine.[5] I beg my respectful compliments to your Lady. And am Sir with esteem your Most Obed humble Ser[t] NATH GREENE

ADfS (MiU-C).

1. William Gibbons, Sr., was the father of NG's attorney in Georgia. (On Gibbons, Jr., see above, vol. 12: 475n.)

2. In a letter of 29 August 1784, above, NG had thanked William Gibbons, Jr., "for the precaution" he had taken "to prevent Mr Gibbons from getting possession of part of" the Mulberry Grove property given to him by the state of Georgia. (On Georgia's gift to NG, see above, vol. 11: 494–95n.)

3. On the guarantees that NG had provided for army contractors John Banks and his partners near the end of the war, see especially NG to Benjamin Lincoln, 19 December 1782, and Agreement between Hunter, Banks and Company and NG with Newcomen and Collett, 8 April 1783, both above (vol. 12: 306–7 and n, 591 and n); and NG to Lee, 22 August 1785, below. On matters as they currently stood, see, for example, Carrington to NG, 27 February, above, and 23 March, below.

4. As seen in Pendleton to NG, 23 September, below, Gibbons pursued his claim to the property.

5. On NG's trip to Cumberland Island and East Florida, see his letter to CG of 14 April 1785, below.

To Jeremiah Wadsworth

Dear Sir   Savannah [Ga.] March 8th 1785

I wrote you from Charleston [S.C.] concerning Money matters and on the subject of Cumberland Island [Ga.]. I am in hopes to get your answer on my return to Charleston.[1] The more I enquire into the value of the property of Cumberland Island the more I wish to interest you in it as well for your sake as mine. Doctor [Nathan] Brownson formerly a Member of Congress has given me several calculations founded on experiment of the value of stock and Lumber and the profit is immence.[2] But besides it is one of the best stands for Trade in this Country.[3] A Capt Sample [i.e., Semple] of Philadelphia has opened a store on the Island and sells a bundance of goods for great profit and all cash.[4] It is so contiguous to [St.] Augustine it can always supply that place with flour. I am confident you may increase your own fortune and serve your friends in taking a concern. We can supply all the Northern States with live oak and Ship a great deal to Europe. But besides selling timber a large stroke of ship building can be drove at the place and lumber of all sorts may be got in any quantity and it is constantly a cash article.[5]

My prospects of getting clear of the engagements made for the Contractors of the Army are not worse but better than when I last saw you.[6] Present me to all friends. Yours affectionately   NATH GREENE

I am just going to Cumberland Island and Augustine.[7] A Capt Gunn of this State wants me to fight him for calling him to an account for selling public property while I had the command in this Country. It being a matter of duty and of a public nature and Gunn little better than a mad man I rejected the proposition with contempt. He has threatned to insult me, if he should he may take a sudden leap for I keep a good pistol in my pocket. I should have more fighting after the war than before if every officer who had undergone a tryal was to call on me for satisfaction.[8]

ALS (CtHi).

1. See NG's letters to Wadsworth of 3 February and 15 February, above. Wadsworth wrote NG on these topics on 15, 17, 21, and 23 February, and 4 March, all above.

2. For a biographical note on Brownson, see above, vol. 10: 26n. His "calculations" on the value of the timber on Cumberland Island have not been found.

3. Cumberland Island, at the mouth of the St. Marys River, is near what was considered one of the finest harbors in North America. (See note at NG to Wadsworth, 24 April below.)

4. Alexander Semple kept a store "in the Crown reserve of Fort St. Andrews," on the island's north end. According to historian Mary Bullard, Semple had "for several years conducted a booming trade in contraband, even attracting Spanish officers from St. Augustine." (Bullard, *Cumberland Island*, p. 110) On Semple's dealings with NG, see Osborne to NG, 23 April, below.

5. Wadsworth wrote NG on 23 February, above, that his financial situation would preclude him from investing in Cumberland Island.

6. It is not known why NG believed his prospects had improved for "getting clear" of the debts he had guaranteed for John Banks and associates. (See, for example, Carrington to NG, 27 February, above, and 23 March, below.)

7. On NG's trip to Cumberland Island and St. Augustine, see his letters to Vicente Manuel de Zéspedes, 26 March, and to CG, 14 April, both below.

8. For NG's rejection of the challenge, see his letter to James Gunn of 2 March, above.

*   *   *

¶ [FROM ROBERT WALTON, [Savannah, Ga.?], 8 March 1785.[1] Asks NG to "write the Assembly of Georgia that I have your Draught on the State of Virginia for one hundred & twenty Six thousand weight of Tob° (protested) which was owing to a representation of Co[l] [Edward] Carrington[']s then D.Q. M. Gen[l] being misconstrued by the Governor & Council of Virginia." Walton explains the situation to NG: "the State of Virginia had a demand from the financier which was to be paid imediantly, Co[l] Carrington was Caled on to Know if this Draught was Accepted if it would be allowd in the present demand, he informed the Council it would not, in consequence of which your Draught was protested." Walton wants NG to fully explain this matter in a letter to the Georgia Assembly and ask them "to take the Draught up"; asks for NG's "Oppinion whether it will answer part payment of their Continental demand or not." In a postscript, he urges NG to "do this business" before he leaves "town" [i.e., Savannah]. He may not see NG "this summer again"; will be going to Virginia as soon as he returns to Augusta, "and your multiplicitty of business will perhaps put it out of your mind to Serve me."[2] RCS (NcD) 2 pp.]

1. The location was taken from Walton's reference in this letter to NG's leaving "town." NG was in Savannah at this time.

2. NG provided a certificate for Walton on 11 March 1786, below.

*   *   *

To Dennis De Berdt

Sir   Savannah [Ga.] March 9th 1785

I herewith inclose you a bill for one hundred and Eighty pounds Sterling on account of M[r] Charles Pettit. I am sorry it is not for a greater sum. My Crops in South Carolinia and Georgia fell so far short of my expectation from the heavy Rains which prevailed in harvest time that I cannot fulfill my engagements. I was to have remitted about thirteen hundred Dollars for Mr Pettit and shall still try to get another bill to complete my engagement. But I am not certain it will be in my power to accomplish it.[1]

I am proprietor of one half of Cumberland Island [Ga.], on which there is very great quantities of live oak. I wish to know the value of it in London and what quantity may be sold annually.[2]

The british transports employed to take off the Inhabitants of East Florida cut and carried off great quantities of live oak and bay timber from Cumberland Island. If you can find out the Capt and owners so as to make them account for it you will render me an essential service. I imagine the Ships must have arrivd in England some time last fall or the latter part of Summer. On my return to Charleston [S.C.] I mean to forward you powers for calling them to account. Perhaps the matter may be best settled by composition.[3] I am Sir with great respect Your most Obed^t humble Ser^t NATH^l GREENE

ADfS (MiU-C).

1. De Berdt, a London merchant, and Pettit had both been brothers-in-law of the recently deceased Joseph Reed, on whose death see Eyre to NG, 7 March, above, and Pettit to NG, 23 March, below. On the debt, which amounted to £300 sterling, see above, the note at NG to Pettit, 15 August 1784, above, and Pettit to NG, 23 March and 21 September, below. NG wrote to De Berdt about this matter again on 3 and 13 April, both below. On the shortfall in the rice crop, see also NG to Gibbs, 3 February, above; NG to Hoffman, 9 March; Pierce & Company to NG, 8 April; and NG to Gibbons, 26 April, all below. De Berdt wrote NG on 21 July, below: "The Bill [for] £180 on Strahan Mackenzie & Co is Noted & as they say not Likely to be paid." NG had supposed this bill was secured by a credit he had received from Pierce & Company against his rice crop. (See note at NG to Pettit, 15 August 1784; Pierce & Company to NG, 8 April; Pierce to NG, 13 May; and NG to Pierce, 17 May.) As noted at the last of those letters, the issue was not quickly resolved.

2. On NG's proprietorship on Cumberland Island, Ga., see especially the note at Hyrne to Clay, 26 November 1783 above.

3. NG had been concerned for months about British refugees cutting timber on Cumberland Island. (NG to Bowman, 10 September 1784, above) Following the transfer of East Florida from Great Britain to Spain in the recent peace settlement, an evacuation of British residents and Loyalist refugees from the colony took place over a two-year period. British transports carried the residents and refugees to various British-governed places, including islands in the West Indies, the Bahamas, England, and Nova Scotia. (See note at NG to CG, 14 April, below.) Benjamin Eyre wrote NG on 7 March, above, that timber illegally cut on Cumberland Island was also being shipped to Philadelphia by a merchant on the island. "By composition," as NG used the term here, presumably meant by "mutual settlement or agreement." (*Webster's*) De Berdt's reply has not been found, but James Penman provided information about timber imports and sales in England in a letter to NG of 6 February 1786, below.

To Nicholas Hoffman

Dear Sir   Savannah [Ga.] March 9ʰ 1785
My crop has fallen so far short of my expectations at this place that
I find my self unable to fulfill my engagements.[1] I intended to have
remitted you the amount of Mʳ Wallaces demand for my bill but the
crop will hardly pay the bills against the plantation. I am the more
distressd at the disappointment from the nature of my obligation to Mʳ
Wallace. I have some hopes of getting the Money in another way but
should I fail in that I will hire the money at any expence rather than
leave the money unpaid.[2]
I gave a relation of Mʳ Wallaces in the beginning of the war a letter of
credit on Messrs Clarke & Nightingale in Providence at Mʳ Wallaces
request. Those Gentlemen mentioned the matter to me a little time past
that they had been disappointed in getting the Money advanced and
should hold me responsible. What shall I do in the business.[3] Give my
complements to Mrs Hoffman and believe me to be   N GREENE
NB I lost by the fall pick by the rise of Savannah River near one
hundred barrels of Rice at my plantation.

ADfS (MiU-C).
   1. NG wrote George Gibbs on 3 February, above, that "heavy rains" had ruined his crop.
(See also NG's statement at the end of the present letter.)
   2. Hugh Wallace, an expatriate Loyalist, had loaned £150 sterling to NG. (Wallace to
NG, 1 July 1784, above) Hoffman sent the present letter to Wallace in England. Wallace's
reply to NG is below, dated 18 September.
   3. Wallace stated in ibid. that he had previously repaid the £50 that NG advanced to a
"Mr. Wallace," who was a "naval prisoner." Clarke & Nightingale were Providence, R.I.,
merchants. (Vol. 1: 204n, above)

*   *   *

¶ [FROM PETER BARD, Savannah, Ga., 9 March 1785.[1] Encloses a "Sketch of
the terms" on which he would like to "purchase a gang of Negroes." He had
"Concluded" a bargain with "Doctʳ Houstoun," but it has "fallen through."[2] If
NG wants to be "Concerned," Bard will "ingage to make the first payment."
One of the "gangs" offered by Houstoun is said to have belonged to Lady
Egmont;[3] Mr. Osburn can give NG the names of others "who proposed Selling."[4] Encloses a letter to Mr. Turnbull, who "has a Small gang" at Savannah that
Bard would like to hire, if he does not buy them. He has asked Turnbull to give
NG "his proposals in Writing"; if NG wants to buy Turnbull's gang, he should
let Bard know as soon as possible.[5] RCS (MiU-C) 1 p.]
   1. Bard represented Chatham County, in which NG's Mulberry Grove plantation was
located, in the Georgia legislature. (*Records of Georgia*, 3: 446) In March 1784, he had been
appointed a state commissioner to meet with Gov. Patrick Tonyn of East Florida in an
attempt to recover slaves and property believed to have been taken to that colony from
Georgia. (Ibid., 2: 608–9)
   2. Dr. James Houstoun was a brother of Gov. John Houstoun of Georgia. (See above, vol.
11: 227n.)

3. On Lady Egmont, see Penman to NG, 1 October 1783, above.

4. "Mr. Osburn" was probably Col. Adlai Osborn, originally from North Carolina, who had served as "Register of Probates for Chatham County." (*Records of Georgia*, 2: 371–72)

5. On the Loyalist Dr. Andrew Turnbull, who was also a friend of NG's, see note at Penman to NG, 1 October 1783.

¶ [FROM ETHAN CLARKE, Newport, R.I., 15 March 1785.[1] He politely declines to take part in a business deal proposed by NG in a letter of 9 February [not found]. Adds: "My Present Engagements (and Having a Vessel missing) Forbids my making the Purchase Refer[d] to, on any Reasonable Terms whatever."[2] Clarke is determined not to "anticipa[te] A broad or at home, untill Trade is better Regulated, and Remittances more Certain and Easy." He has told NG's brother Perry, that should Perry have "Orders to Sell Mess[rs] Rogers Part and Could Sell to a Good Concern in Charleston," Clarke would take NG's "Part," if they could agree on terms.[3] RC (MiU-C) 1 p. Incomplete.]

1. Clarke (1745–1833), a Newport merchant, "amassed a fortune" in the West India trade through business conducted by his firm, Clarke & Hammond. He was married to Samuel Ward, Jr.'s, sister—and CG's cousin—Anna Ward, with whom NG had been infatuated before his marriage to CG. (Vol. 1: 20n, above) The Clarkes' daughter Anna Maria married NG's son Nathanael Ray Greene in 1808. (Morrison, *Clarke Families*, p. 68; see also vol. 1: 20n, above.)

2. NG had presumably asked Clarke to become an investor in Cumberland Island, Ga. (See, for example, NG to Wadsworth, 3 February, above.)

3. Nothing more is known about this matter.

¶ [FROM ROBERT MORRIS, Philadelphia, 15 March 1785. Acknowledges NG's letter of 9 February.[1] Encloses "A Case, and Querie arising thereon [not found]" and asks NG to "procure the best opinions[,] applying the same to the State of Carolina instead of Pennsylvania."[2] Morris also encloses "the form of a power of Attorney such as has Been sent to Holland on similar Occasions"; asks NG to "have one filled up in the same way" and send it to "Mess[rs] Willinks."[3] He does not think NG should send "the Mortgage Vouchers &c[a]" at this time, for although the Willinks "mention a probability of their obtaining the Loan," thus far "every Application" has "proved ineffectual." NG can forward his power of attorney to the Willinks, and when they give him "Positive Assurances that they can negotiate the Loan," it will then be "time enough to execute the Mortgage & other papers, which may be delivered to Such Attorney as they may appoint to receive the same."[4] Morris advises NG to communicate with the Willinks directly. He has "already advised" them that NG has "renewed his application" through him, and he will forward NG's letter to them "by the first Conveyance."[5] Morris regrets that "the prospect of War with the Emperor had prevented [the Willinks's] Success in another instance"; he is starting to think "they take example from their Neighbours and are getting afraid to trust us."[6] Gen. [Anthony] Wayne has "actually sent over his Mortgage and all papers agreeable to the form recommended by Messrs Willinks[;] therefore we shall know if he succeeds what to depend on."[7] RCS (CSmH) 2 pp.]

1. The letter has not been found. (See, however, note 4, below.)

2. The nature of the "Case, and Querie" is not known, but in a reply of 28 June, below, to one from NG of 20 May that has not been found, Morris mentioned that NG had enclosed "an ordinance for encourageing Foreigners to lend Money."

3. On the power of attorney requested by the Dutch firm of Wilhem & Jan Willink, see also the note at Morris to NG, 12 July 1784, above.

4. NG had asked Morris to help him negotiate a loan from the Willinks, using his Georgia plantation, Mulberry Grove, as collateral. (NG to Wadsworth, 17 February, above, and Willinks to NG, 8 July, below; on the request for a loan, see also Pendleton to NG, 25 April, below.) It appears that NG may have hoped to use the loan, at least in part, to "improve the purchace" of an undivided half share of Cumberland Island, Ga. (NG to Wadsworth, 17 February; on NG's interest in the island, see especially the note at Hyrne to Clay, 26 November 1783, above.)

5. In reply to a letter from NG of 27 April that has not been found, the Willinks wrote him on 8 July: "We See you are determined to borrow from 2000 to 4000£ on your Plantation in the State of Georgia, and that you will Send the Necessary vouchers for the purpose. We are Sorry to inform you of the impossibility to perform it [i.e., make the loan] at present." They added, however, that they might be in a position to offer a loan at some future date but would first have to examine and approve NG's "Vouchers." As noted at Morris to NG, 12 July 1784, above, the Willinks had also rejected an earlier request from NG for a loan. In a letter to the Willinks of 7 January 1786, below, NG again inquired about the possibility of obtaining a loan.

6. On the likelihood of war between Austria, led by Emperor Joseph II, and Holland, see note at Butler to NG, 23 December 1784, above.

7. Wayne, like NG, had received a Savannah River plantation from the state of Georgia. (See above, vol. 11: 164n.) He had asked the Willinks in January for a loan worth about 5,000 guineas to use as operating capital but finally learned in the fall of 1785 that this, as well as several other loan requests of his, had been denied. (Nelson, *Wayne*, pp. 199–202)

¶ [FROM THE MARQUIS DE LAFAYETTE, Paris, 16 March 1785. He is "not yet" able to "Execute" NG's "Commands" concerning the tutor.[1] In Europe, "War is not begun, or is peace made." Encloses a "declaration printed in the Leyden Gazete," so that NG can "see what part France has taken." An account of "an Intended Surprise against Mastreik [i.e., Maastricht]" has been "Mentionned in the Hague Gazette," but although "warlike preparations are going on," negotiations have not been "one instance interrupted." The Dutch are "divided into two parties, and being Warm on Both Sides, the patriots are decidedly Attached to France"; the emperor's plan to give the Austrian Low Countries to the Elector of Bavaria "Has Been opposed by the Elector's nephew and Heir." Lafayette thinks it "will End quietly terminated."[2] NG asked for his opinion about "the Effect that Would Result in Europe, in Case Congress Have powers to Regulate trade, and Measures are taken to Restore public Credit." Lafayette believes the effect "would be greater than Can be Imagined"; he wishes that those who "oppose those Measures Could Come to this side of the Atlantic" and "Hear what is said of the probable divisions among the States, or the Neglect that is likely to take place" in many aspects of civic life. He adds: "altho' those Bad omens, are, Thank God, ill founded, altho' American patriotism, Virtue and Wisdom Cannot but being Roused to Every thing that is good and great, provided you give the people time to Consider and judge their own faults, Yet I Cannot Hear those ideas spocken, without Heartly wishing no time may Be lost in Insuring the Consequence and prosperity of the American Confederation." He briefly discusses a controversy about the "Admission of foreigners in the West Indias."[3] Sends his "best respects" to CG and asks to be remembered "affectionately to our friends in Rhode Island, Carolina, and where ever you go." He adds in a postscript that he is enclosing an extract of a book by "M. Necker," which, although it "makes great deal of noise and produces much Exageration," is "a great Book indeed."[4] RCS (MiU-C) 3 pp.]

1. On NG's plan to have his son tutored in France under Lafayette's guidance, see Lafayette to NG, 16 April, below.

2. As noted at Butler to NG, 23 December 1784, above, despite tensions and threats by Emperor Joseph II of Austria, war did not ensue, and, as Lafayette predicted, the affair was "quietly terminated."

3. The controversy was undoubtedly over the trade policies of European powers in their West Indies holdings.

4. Jacques Necker had been the French "director general of finances" during the American Revolution. Lafayette undoubtedly referred here to Necker's *Traité de l'administration des finances de la France* (1784). (*Columbia Encyc.*)

* * *

From Edward Carrington

D[r] General Richmond [Va.] March 23[d] 1785

Your favour of the 3[d] of February came to hand not until last Saturday, such is the irregularity of the southern post.[1] The papers inclosed are safely received. Hunters Mortgage is intirely defective, not only in point of having too few Witnesses, but manner of authenticating their proof of the deeds.[2] Three Witnesses are requisite to a deed for Conveying lands in this Country, nor can it be admitted to record with less, these must each swear for himself, one proving that he saw another sign as a Witness will not do, and the Authority under which the proof must be established to give it force here, will appear from the inclosed extract from the Act in that case made, which passed in the year 1776.[3] Had Hunter yet arrived here I should immediately go to him & get deeds effactually executed. However, what has been done gives you an equitable Estate in the Lands, which must be established[:] a legal one by the Court of Chancery, for which purpose I have Commenced a Suit under the auspices of the Attorney General, but in the mean time the Deeds as they are executed must be proved in the proper Manner as the Law directs so as to establish the equity of the case on the best possible ground. For this purpose I am directed by the Attorney to inclose them to you. You will therefore be good enough to have the proof of the two Witnesses Authenticated as the extract directs, and if both are still in being let each swear for himself, if not you may let the other swear that he saw him Subscribe as a Witness, and have it certified that he is dead. You will be good enough to have this done and transmitted to me as early as you can that there may be no inconvenience with respect to the Suit.[4]

You will before this Arrives, have received my letters advising you of the bad prospect of your indemnification by H.B. [i.e., Henry Banks] and that it would be best for you and [Patrick] Carnes to come to Virginia and take some decisive Steps towards the administration of

J.B.ˢ [i.e., John Banks's] affairs so as to bring forward the property which, if any thing, will be getting further and further from your reach the longer it is delayed.⁵ You have Still my advice to this purpose. I have now had a further conversation with him H.B. on these subjects. He says he wishes you to administer and writes you the inclosed letter [not found]. I have applied to him for the relinquishment you are advised to get of the lands on Cumberland Island. He refuses to give one alledging that he had rather go to the southward sometime hence and make the most of it that he can if you do not foreclose his Equity of Redemption. I think you had better forclose and bring the Matter to an issue as soon as you can. Indeed perhaps his power of attorney which you have may authorise you to sell without forclosing, but of this take advice. There can however be no doubt of your having a power to effect the business by the former method.⁶

Mʳ Campbell [i.e., James Campbel] has not yet sued [Robert] Patton for which he has alledged a Variety of reasons, amongst which were his having been disappointed in receiving the money you engaged to have paid from the administration in Nᵒ Carolina which he had apprehended might be devoted to some other Debt. He has now upon my assuring him that no money has yet been received there, and also writing him a letter assuring him for you that whatever shall arise from that administration shall be paid towards Collets debt, agreed that he will immediately commence the Suit. Copies of his letter and mine on the subject are inclosed by which you will see the engagement I have made for you—and I hope he will accordingly bring the Suit notwithstanding my answer falls short in some degree per his request—from Colᵒ Blounts invoice of the effects which I transmitted to you sometime ago I think there can no great sum arise from thence.⁷

I observe the transaction with Colᵒ [John S.] Dart for 150 dollars which I had Creditted him as pᵈ to Mʳ Cochran and also for 30 Dolˢ Settled with you for, pᵈ for printing work and on the certificate sent, have so applied them in my Accounts as to Credit you for the full amount 180 dols. of the 200 advanced you last fall. When I get the Recᵗ from the Doctor at Fredericksbᵍ or the Bill from you which you pᵈ that Sum shall also be carried to your Credit.⁸ I am Dʳ Genˡ with great Affection yʳ Mᵒ Obdᵗ Sᵗ ED CARRINGTON

RCS (MiU-C).

1. "Last Saturday" was 19 March. The letter has not been found.

2. James Hunter, who had been a business partner of the late John Banks, was liable for debts that NG had guaranteed for Banks and him. (On the mortgage, see also Carrington to NG, 27 February, above, and Hunter to NG, 1 June, below.)

3. The "inclosed extract" of the act has not been found. During a time when "deeds for conveying land, slaves, or other estates" had not been recorded in many places because of the temporary "suspension of government," the Virginia General Assembly had passed

an act in 1776 requiring the signature of "three witnesses" to make a deed legally binding. (Hening, *Statutes*, 9: 214–15)

4. NG wrote Carrington on 29 September, below: "I wrote you the 29th of April [letter not found] and inclosed you sundry papers relative to Hunters matters."

5. See Carrington to NG, 27 February. Henry Banks wrote NG on 2 September, below, that he had reached a settlement with Carnes. In the same letter, he expressed a wish that NG "Would come to Virginia, that you w[ould] be both satisfied of my Innocence of things spoken to my prejudice and the readiness I ever have to do what is right."

6. As noted at Hyrne to Clay, 26 November 1783, above, NG had laid claim to sizable land holdings on Cumberland Island, Ga., on the basis of an indenture he had received from John Banks. Before he could obtain clear title to those lands, however, NG needed a relinquishment of Henry Banks's claim to that property as his brother's heir. Banks wrote NG on 2 September: "Cumberland Island is represented to me as being exceedingly more valuable than £10,000 St^g," i.e., the value of the indenture. But as seen in a letter to Samuel Ward of 4 April 1786, below, NG did eventually obtain a "Deed of relinquishment." (See also Banks to NG, 13 January 1786, below.)

7. For background, see note at NG to Forsyth, 25 October 1784, above. The "administration in N° Carolina" was of John Banks's estate there. The enclosures, copies of a letter of 22 March from Campbel to Carrington and of Carrington's reply of 23 March, are at MiU-C. Campbel, who represented John Banks's—and thereby NG's—creditor E. John Collett, asked Carrington to make sure that "the produce of [John] Banks Effects in North Carolina, that is to say, what can be got possession of, in consequence of the administration, shall, without loss of time, be put into money and paid into my hands for Mr Collet, or some Sum of Money nearly equivalent, say £1500 Sterl^g, and the Suit shall forthwith be commenced against Mr Patton. Upon your Answer to the purport [of what] I wish I will give Patton & Ferries [i.e., John Ferrie] to Mr Baker to prosecute." (On Ferrie, see note at Forsyth to NG, 18 June 1784, above.) Carrington replied: "I am certain that General Greene never intended the monies which might arise from his administration on the Effects of John Banks in North Carolina, for any other debt than that of Mr Collet, in case of your prosecuting, effectually, a Suit against Mr Patton on his and Ferries engagement for that debt. I do therefore hereby engage for the General, that in case of your so prosecuting such Suit, to be commenced in a short time from hence, so as to be returnable to the ensuing Genl Court, all the monies which Shall arise on the Said Administration in North Carolina, shall be paid into your hands towards Mr Collets debt—no doubt the business of this administration will be passed to a conclusion as quickly as possible." Nothing more about the proposed lawsuit has been found. William Blount wrote NG from Wilmington, N.C., on 10 July, below: "As yet I have not got into my Hands a Single Shillings worth of Banks's Property. I have several Suits depending from which I expect something will be got."

8. Nothing more is known about this matter.

From Charles Pettit

Dear Sir   Philadelphia 23^d March 1785

When I received your Favour from Carolina (I cannot now lay my Hands on it nor mention the Date, but it is the only one I have had from you since your arrival there)[,]^1 The Copy of the Assignment you allude to could not be found. It has lately, however been found in the Hands of M^r [Jared?] Ingersoll, where it had been lodged by Mr Skewell in Behalf of M^r [Michael J.] Harris to defend him against a Claim of Scarborough & Cooke on a protested Bill of Mr Banks's. Herewith you will receive a

Charles Pettit, 1736–1806; oil painting by Charles Willson Peale
(Worcester Art Museum)

Copy of it according to your Desire; but to avail yourself of any Use from it I imagine you must have recourse to the Original or to the Record of it, which I imagine are to be found in Charleston, What was here being only a certified Copy. That Copy will now be returned to M^r [Joseph] Blachford by this Conveyance, he having wrote for it for some use in Carolina; and if he had not it would have been sent back to be far-ther authenticated before it could be given in Evidence in our Courts.[2]

I hope that ere this M[r] [Roger Parker] Saunders has remitted the £300 Sterling to M[r] DeBerdt in London either in Bills or in Rice, as I have relied much on it & shall be much hurt if it be not done. If it yet remains to be done I hope no Time will be lost in doing it, as the Return of some Bills protested leaves me unexpectedly in Arrears where I was warmly desirous for particular Reasons, to be rather beforehand.[3]

I have had one of the severest Winters I ever experienced. Having got into the Vortex of Politics, I had a Task difficult enough on my Hands in that way.[4] M[r] [Joseph] Reed's Situation added much to the Calls upon me. His Disorder returned upon him early in November, in December it had evidently seized on his Lungs & operated something in a Dropsical way. About the first of January his Case became at best doubtful, but his Strength of Constitution resisted till the 4th Instant when it surrendered. My attendance was useful & pleasing to him & I could not withhold it tho' oppressed with a load of public Cares during his Illness.[5] Ten Days after his Funeral we had to attend that of his Sister Polly who had been long decaying in my House.[6] These complicated Afflictions you may suppose were deeply distressing to my Family; my own Health was much injured by it & brought on a smart attack of the Gout from which I am now but rising & yet Lame. In the midst of these Difficulties our Friend M[r] [Clement] Biddle has added something to my Troubles. His Failure saddles me with the Payment of 1500 Dollars having indorsed one of his Notes for that Sum to oblige him. People in his Situation always incur Blame. His greatest Fault appears to have been in dabbling with Usurers by which he has sunk Six or £8000 in extraordinary Discounts, & at length has stopped £36,000, in Debt by his Estimate, about £20,000 of which is on Notes discounted in which many of his Friends are taken in as I am.[7] He shews an Estimate of Property to the Amount of £37,000, but much of it is in Kentucke[y?] Lands, Officers Rights Land in N. Jersey, N York &c. About 8 or £10,000 perhaps may be got otherwise; the Rest depends on these Lands & Rights which will be slow in their production. I am made one of his Assignees which I accepted chiefly with a View to soften & accomodate for his Benefit, as I really regard & wish to serve him tho' I am thus injured. By the way, I observe you are concerned with him in the N York Lands. What will you do with your Share?[8]

Let this for the present suffice for the gloomy Part of my Communication. In the midst of my Troubles I have had the Pleasure to succeed in my funding Plan nearly, tho' not Quite according to the Scheme I had proposed. I intended to have embraced the whole of our part of the Debt of every kind, but have been obliged to exclude such of the Army Certificates (both Final Settlements & Depreciation Notes) as have been alienated by the original Holders; but as our Land Office is now opening at £30 per 100 Acres & these Certificates are receivable there in common with others & with Specie, I hope to get the greater part if not all of these excluded Certificates into the State Treasury in a short Time. I have met with great Opposition & some Abuse, but by steady perseverence & a Confidence that we were right we were at length gratified by a Majority of 52 to 18 in passing the Law. The President & Council gave their whole Weight to the Opposition & took extraordinary Pains to propagate their opinions by argumentative Messages. Genl Wayne was the Hero of the Opposition in the House & 'tis likely will take some Pains to reprobate our Measures in the southern States; but I am so confident they will be attended with beneficial Effects in this State, & indeed be usefully influential in other States, that I cannot but rejoice in what we have done.[9] The Papers tell us that R. Island has in a degree acceded to the Continental Plan of Revenue, & that Georgia has or is about it also. Our Measures are so calculated that whenever Congress pronounce their ability to proceed, we can take a wheel from our Carriage & annex it to theirs, without impeding the Machin[e].[10] I shall inclose you a Paper containing the Act for your Satisfaction.[11]

M[r] [John] Cox is now here in as good health as he ever enjoyed. Believe me Dear Sir, Affectionately yours   CHA[s] PETTIT

RCS (MiU-C).
    1. NG's letter to Pettit, which was probably written sometime in February, has not been found.
    2. This may have been the deed of assignment from Robert Forsyth & Company to Harris & Blachford that is noted at Pendleton to NG, 10 November 1784, above. The copy has not been found.
    3. As seen at NG to De Berdt, 9 March, above, the note for partial payment of the debt was later rejected. (See also De Bert to NG, 21 July, and Pettit to NG, 21 September, below.)
    4. As seen in Wadsworth to NG, 15 February, above, Pettit had been serving in the Pennsylvania legislature.
    5. On the recent death of Pettit's brother-in-law and NG's friend Reed, see also Eyre to NG, 7 March, above.
    6. Pettit's wife, Sarah, was a sister of both Joseph and Polly Reed.
    7. On Biddle's financial troubles, see also Wadsworth to NG, 4 March, and Eyre to NG, 7 March, above.
    8. NG gave Jeremiah Wadsworth a power of attorney to sell the lands he held in common with Biddle. (NG to Wadsworth, 24 April, below; see also the document immediately below, as well as Pettit to NG, 30 June; Wadsworth to NG, 2 October; NG to Wadsworth, 12 October, and Wadsworth to NG, 8 April 1786, all below.)
    9. Pettit was speculating in various government certificates for himself and NG. (Agreement between NG and Pettit, 7 June 1784, above) According to historian Robert Brunhouse, the legislative struggle was over a plan by the Radical faction (to which Pettit belonged) to have the state pay interest on all federal and state certificates held by Pennsylvania citizens. The interest would be paid

    "by a combination of revenue from the sale of public lands, a general tax, and an issue of paper money. President [John] Dickinson took exception to the plan. He asserted there should be a discrimination between original holders of certificates and dealers in certificates. Collection of the arrearages of back taxes, he thought, would provide sufficient specie to pay off the interest to original holders who were the most deserving group; the back lands could be sold at a fixed price per acre in payment of which the holders of alienated certificates might redeem their investments. Stripped of all verbiage which flowed between Council and assembly over the problem, the crucial struggle was between speculators in depreciated public certificates and property owners who would be called on for additional taxes to fund these certificates." (Brunhouse, *Pennsylvania*, p. 170)

It was rumored that Pettit, "the head of the plan," stood to earn £6,000 per year in interest on the certificates he owned if this legislation were enacted. Indeed, according to Brunhouse, Pettit "took such a personal interest in seeing the act passed that privately he referred to it as 'My funding Plan.' " (Ibid., pp. 170–71) The Republican opponents of the law as it was finally passed complained "that the State thus assumed the burden of paying interest on over one-third of the total amount of loan office certificates issued by the United States government whereas actually Pennsylvania had always been rated as only one-eighth of the Confederation." Merchants also objected to the issuing of paper money in the form of bills of credit. (Ibid., p. 171)

On Anthony Wayne's involvement in the politics of his home state at this time, see Nelson, *Wayne*, pp. 188–97. Wayne, who had been elected to the Pennsylvania legislature in the fall of 1784, was a member of the Republican faction, which opposed the funding plan.

10. Although the Rhode Island legislature in July 1784 had refused to ratify the federal impost proposal of 1783 (NG to Morris, 3 July 1784, above), Rhode Island merchants had since found that their trading ventures were being hurt by the various state taxes on imports that the federal proposal would have eliminated. (Patrick T. Conley, *Democracy in Decline: Rhode Island's Constitutional Development, 1776–1841* [Providence: Rhode Island Historical Society, 1977], pp. 78–79) Thus, at its February 1785 session, Rhode Island adopted a measure incorporating portions of the 1783 proposal. (Bartlett, *Records of R.I.*, 10: 87–88) The secretary of Congress, reporting on 4 January 1786 about the extent to which various states had complied with the 1783 proposal, summarized the Rhode Island measure as follows:

"Rhode Island, in the session of their legislature in the spring of 1785, passed an Act for levying the duties pointed out by Congress, but have therein enacted that the Collectors shall be appointed by and amenable to the General Assembly, and that of the money arising from the duties a certain sum, viz. 8,000 dollars, shall be appropriated in their treasury for the payment of the Interest of that State's proportion of the foreign debt of the United States, and paid to the order of Congress, and that the surplus of the duties and the amount of other taxes ordered by the said Act, shall be appropriated to the payment of the Interest of the internal debt of the United States due within that State. This Act to take effect, when the other States in the Union agree to the said Impost to the Acceptation of Congress, and have provided other adequate funds for compleating their quota of 1,500,000 dollars, according to the requisition of Congress of 18ᵗʰ April, 1783; but with this proviso and upon this express condition, 'that no duties shall be collected upon articles imported into any State upon which the said duties have been paid in any other State and that no duty shall be imposed by any one State upon the citizens of another State, either upon imported Articles having paid the duties aforesaid, or upon any articles of the growth, produce, or manufacture of the United States.' " (*JCC*, 30: 8)

In addition, the Rhode Island act, "on the condition above set forth," provided for an annual tax of "one spanish silver milled dollar" per 100 acres of land, "upon every male poll in the State of 21 Years of Age, and upon every horse or mare of two years old and upwards," the proceeds of which would be "appropriated to the payment of the Interest" owed by the state for the "internal debt of the United States." (Ibid., p. 9) The Georgia legislature, which had failed to take action on either the 1781 or 1783 proposals for a federal impost, finally enacted a measure in 1786 that included giving Congress the right to levy a five percent tax on imports. (Coleman, *Revolution in Georgia*, p. 255)

11. The enclosure has not been found, but the "Act for furnishing the Quota of this state towards paying the annual Interest of the Debts of the United States; and for funding and paying the Interest of the Public Debts of this state" was printed in the *Pennsylvania Packet and Daily Advertiser* of 18 March.

* * *

¶ [POWER OF ATTORNEY TO JEREMIAH WADSWORTH. From Charleston, S.C., 26 March 1785.[1] NG gives Wadsworth a power of attorney to sell "to any person or persons he may think proper all my Lands laying upon the Pas[s]aic River in the State of New Jersey and also all my Lands in the State of New York ne[ar] the North [i.e., Hudson] River laying opposite to Claverack[,] none held with Clemment Biddle Esqr of Philadelphia and formerly purchaced of M[r] Abraham Lott of New York[,] for such price and consideration as he or my said Attorney may think the property is worth."[2] DS (CtY) 4 pp.]

1. Although this document, witnessed by Aedanus Burke, is dated 26 March at Charleston, it is almost certain that NG was not there on that date. He was still in Georgia when he wrote to Dennis De Berdt on 3 April, below.

2. NG also later gave Wadsworth powers of attorney to sell the land that he owned with Biddle. (Powers of Attorney to Wadsworth, 24 April and 12 October, below; see also Pettit to NG, immediately above, and 30 June, below.) In October 1780, just before he left the North to take command of the Southern Army, NG had sent CG "a deed for about 3000 Acres of land which I have in company with Col. Biddle." (NG to CG, 21 October 1780, above [vol. 6: 416]) On NG's land holdings in New Jersey and New York, see also Estimate of NG's Estate, before 9 January 1784, as well as NG to Van Waggonen, 20 November 1783, both above.

* * *

To Governor Vicente Manuel de Zéspedes y Velasco of East Florida

Sir ⟨Cumberland Island [Ga.] March 26, 1785⟩

I am at a loss which to admire most in Your Excellencys appointment to the Government of East Florida the wisdom of Spain in the choice or the good fortune of the United States from your Administration.[1] The happy disposition which you possess and the polite attention of all those under your command cannot fail to cultivate right[,] lasting good understanding. National policy directed by liberal principles which evidently mark every part of your Excellency's conduct will inspire esteem & affection, and secure the confidences of the Inhabitants of the United States. I am happy in having it in my power to tell them how much your conduct corresponds with their wishes. And that if we may venture to interpret the intentions of the Court of Spain from the polite attention of those acting under her orders the prospect is as pleasing as the policy will become interesting to the happiness of the subjects of both Countrys.[2] Impressed with these sentiments I have only to acknowledge my personal obligation to your Excellency and family for your very polite attention during our stay in the Province; and in particular for the good company of Colonel Fernandes on our return.[3] Nor can I omit to mention the politeness of the Commodore Don Pedro Basquez where we receivd every mark of respect and attention.[4] I beg your Excellency will do me the honor to present my most respectful compliments to your Lady and family and to the officers and Gentlemen of the Garrison.[5] ⟨And have only to add my wishes to serve M[r] Flemming and Doctor Quin the Gentlemen where we lodged; and for which purpose I beg leave to recommend them to your Excellencys good offices.[6] I have the honor to be with the most profound respect Your Excellency's Most obedient Humble Servant[7]   NATH GREENE⟩

ADf (MiU-C). The text in angle brackets was taken from Lockey, *East Florida*, pp. 492–93.

1. Zéspedes had been appointed to "the governorship and captaincy-general of the city of St. Augustine and the provinces of Florida" by the king of Spain in October 1783, after Spain assumed control of the colonies of East and West Florida. (José de Gálvez to Zéspedes, 31 October 1783, Lockey, *East Florida*, p. 174 and n) He did not arrive in St. Augustine to take up his duties until the following summer, however. (Zéspedes to Bernardo de Gálvez, 16 July 1784, ibid., p. 230)

2. As noted at NG to CG, 14 April, below, relations between East Florida and the United States were in a formative stage when NG wrote this letter.

3. On NG's recent visit to St. Augustine, see ibid. Col. Antonio Fernández commanded a troop of mounted dragoons who maintained order in the province during the transition from British to Spanish rule. (Zéspedes to Bernardo de Gálvez, 9 August 1784, Lockey, *East Florida*, p. 247) Fernández had accompanied NG on his return trip from St. Augustine to Cumberland Island. (NG to CG, 14 April)

4. Don Pedro Vásquez commanded a convoy that had provided transport for the Spanish troops who were sent to maintain the garrison in East Florida. (Zéspedes to Bernardo de Gálvez, 16 July 1784, Lockey, *East Florida*, p. 223) NG had visited with Vásquez aboard the latter's ship in the harbor at St. Marys on his way back to Cumberland Island from St. Augustine. (NG to CG, 14 April)

5. On Zéspedes's family, see ibid.

6. NG had stayed with George Fleming, a "Dublin-born Irishman and former resident of South Carolina," who later married Sophia, a daughter of Francis Phillip Fatio, with whom NG visited during his trip. NG's traveling companion, Benjamin Hawkins, stayed with a "Dr. Quin." (Tanner, *Visit to St. Augustine*, p. 16n; Fatio to NG, 6 April, below; on Hawkins, see note at NG to CG, 14 April.)

7. Zéspedes was apparently uneasy about NG's motives for visiting St. Augustine. (See note at NG to CG, 14 April.) He wrote Bernardo de Gálvez, who had been governor of Louisiana and was about to become the viceroy of Mexico, that he found this letter from NG and one from NG's traveling companion, Hawkins, to be "courteous to the point of flattery, but they [i.e., the letters] seem ominous also." (Lockey, *East Florida*, p. 490)

*   *   *

¶ [TO DENNIS DE BERDT. From Savannah, Ga., 3 April 1785. NG wrote to him from Savannah "about a month since," enclosing "a bill on Messrs James

Strackan[,] James MacKensie & company Merchants London for one hundred & Eighty pounds Sterling to be placed to the credit of M\u02b3 Charles Pettit of Phila-delphia Merchant." NG reported in that letter that he would have "remitted a larger bill" if his crops had not "fallen so much short" of expectations because of "heavy rai[n.]" He also informed De Berdt that "Money is so scarce here and the demands so great that it is utterly impossible to borrow or hire."[1] NG hopes to send the rest of the money upon his "return to the Northward."[2] As "part owner" of Cumberland Island, Ga., "on which there is large quantities of live oak and red bay," he asks "what these articles will sell at." This timber "is of the first quality in Ameri[c]a and perhaps in the World for ship building"; dealing in it "may lay a foundation for an extensive branch of business."[3] Asks De Berdt to write him at Newport, R.I., where he will soon be going.[4] Also asks for "a pair of good Eighteen Inch Globes of the newest kind," if this will not cause "any inconvenience." ADf (MiU-C) 2 pp.]

1. See NG to De Berdt, 9 March, above, and note 4, below.

2. See below, NG to De Berdt, 13 April.

3. As owner of a large, undivided half share of land on Cumberland Island, Ga., NG hoped to profit from the sale of valuable timber there. He was also trying to encourage other investors to join him in his Cumberland Island venture. (See, for example, NG to Wadsworth, 3 February, above, and NG to Marbois, 15 April, below.) He had asked De Berdt in the letter of 9 March for information about timber prices in Europe. Now, having just returned from a visit to the island, NG was presumably even more interested in the potential for timber sales.

4. NG sent another payment with a letter to De Berdt of 13 April, below. De Berdt wrote NG on 21 July, below: "The Bill [for] £180 on Strahan Mackenzie & Co is Noted & as they say not Likely to be paid." As noted at NG to Pierce, 17 May, below, this issue was not quickly resolved.

*　　*　　*

From Francis Phillip Fatio[1]

Sir   S\u1d57 Augustin [East Florida], 6\u02b0 April 1785

By the return of L Col: Fernandez I received the honour of your letter of the 27\u02b0 Instant March last.[2] Your kind expressions put me to the Blush. Terrible that it was out of my power to receive you in this wreched town, as I would wish. It was a lucky circumstance that brought me to the honour of your Acquaintance, I shall do my best to cultivate it & improve it.[3]

Since your departure I have had no Opportunity to write you at Savannah which I presume you will have left before this date.[4] I have now to inform you Sir, that the Comte de Galvez has made new ar-rangements in regard of the commerce of this Province, with the States of America.[5] A small vessel arrived from the Havannah two days ago. Report that we shall have a free trade with Spanish Bottoms, unluckily the vessel who has the dispatches, carried away his main mast in the Gulph & put back at the Matanzas, Cuba. In such case we could easily carry in execution the plan you [were] kind enough to sketch in my garden; American provisions of all kind will be permitted from hence to the Havannah, tho' it is said, yet I can't believe Dry goods will be admitted to Spanish Settlements.[6] I shall have the particulars as soon as the treasurer (who is likewise the minister of the Custom house) receive them. I can flatter myself I am upon the best terms with him, he is realy a worthy & honest man with more Sincerity than generaly found with his overpolite contrymen. As yet he is dependant of the Governor who is the real intendant. As this, is realy a very Good man to the utmost extent of the meaning, we shall be well enough. Corn & provisions begin to be Scarce, corn sell at 1 ½ dollars, flour is raised to 9 ½ at 10 Drs Philadelphia; rice 20 dollars per bar^l. I have leave to bring, direct, to St John a Cargo of Corn for my plantation, with a few articles of dry goods. Under this I understand that my vessel will not be searched or inquired for.[7] If you had any opportunity to introduce me to some friends of yours to the northward, if you are not fixed in Bussiness; Sundry articles would answer very well. Cash in plenty is arrived at the Havannah, 2 million 600 d^{rs} of which poor 50/m are only to come here besides the arrear & the pay of the troops. I will call it 80/2 dollars. The right plan would be to have a vessel of a small draft of water, & roomy. I would fill it with Lumber & naval Stores, for the Havannah, leaving room for flour, holland stripes, be in printed linnens, Light french Silks, fine thread Stockings. No cotton goods of any kinds. The vessel may be made my property, & turn a Spaniard as well as myself.[8]

The only objection I have to open bussiness as a Merchant is, purchasing at second hands, merchants in General have not corrected their Invoice, & keep their War price. Unless I sell my negroes here & my Stocks in England I have not a large capital of cash, having speculated upon houses, with all these nevertheless I could easily realise a capital to beg credit upon it. We had very little time to talk this matter. On your return from the Northward I will do myself the honour to wait upon you at Cumberland, or Georgia & receive what proposals you may have digested, upon that Bussiness.[9]

The Indians & the few wretched devils that cant emigrate, eat me fairly up, and I shall want corn to keep 'em in good humour & avoid quarrelling. These last would be no incumbrances at Cumberland, as they are only permitted to Stay for another Crop. They are harboured at or near New Switzerland.[10] I should take it as a real piece of service if you could send me a small cargo of Corn either from North Carolina or Virginia on my own Account. Spanish milled Dollars shall be the return either by the Vessel or paid to any of your friends either at Savannah or Charlestown.[11] And as you may want some of 'em to begin your new Settlement it may serve you as a remittance towards gathering your necessaries. I have had time, to ruminate on your grand Scheme Selling lots, either town or Country, will not be so encouraging as leasing.[12] But great number will resort to you, with their families, if you receive rent in produce, pigs, fowls, corn &c. As for those that intend to get Lumber, I don't suppose 10 per c^t will be refused. Cash will not be introduced but by you[,] & our indolent floridians, will be glad to receive from your Island, all kind of produce that will cost 'em no other troubles but putting their hands in their pockets, most of 'em receiving King's Pay they don't know the full price of cash.[13] An act of Assembly, for indulgence, a few years free of taxes, or any kind of Douceurs that cannot be well refused to you by your friends of Georgia. The limit of a letter can't admit of full particulars.[14]

There is 200 p C^t difference in having Cumberland or Amelia well settled. Let it be as a farmer, a merchant or a politician.[15] Mrs Fatio & Sophia begs to be remembered, & present you their most respectfull Compliments.[16] I have the honour to be respectfully Sir, Your most obedient & most humble Servant   F P FATIO

RCS (Greene Papers: DLC).

1. Fatio (1724–1811), a native of Switzerland, had lived in England before moving his family to St. Augustine in 1771. A merchant and planter there, he had been appointed a justice of the peace by the Spanish governor, Vicente Manuel de Zéspedes, to adjudicate disputes among the British refugees who were awaiting transport to Great Britain or British colonies from East Florida. Fatio remained in the colony after the British evacuation as a Spanish subject. (Lockey, *East Florida*, p. 265n; Zéspedes to Bernardo de Gálvez, 28 February, ibid., pp. 461–62; "Memorial of Francis Phillip Fatio," 23 February, ibid., p. 464) According to historian Wilbert H. Siebert, British residents complained that Fatio sometimes overstepped his authority and decided cases by "whim and caprice." (Siebert, *Loyalists in East Florida*, 1: 162)

2. NG's letter to Fatio of 27 March has not been found. Col. Antonio Fernández is identified at NG to Zéspedes, 26 March, above.

3. It is not known what "lucky circumstance" brought NG and Fatio together during NG's recent visit to St. Augustine. On NG's trip to East Florida, see his letter to CG of 14 April, below.

4. NG was back in Charleston, S.C., by 13 April. (See his letter to Dennis De Berdt of that date, below.

5. Bernardo de Gálvez had recently been appointed viceroy of Mexico. (See note at Zéspedes to NG, 26 March.)

6. The plan that NG "sketched" in Fatio's garden presumably involved trade with the Spanish colonies of Cuba and East Florida. The financial motives behind NG's trip to East Florida are discussed in a note at NG to CG, 14 April. (See also note 8, below.)

7. Gonzalo Zamorano was the colony's treasurer. (Lockey, *East Florida*, p. 34); Zéspedes was the governor. Fatio had a plantation on the St. Johns River, near St. Johns Bluff. (Fatio to NG, 5 December, below; on the town of St. Johns, see NG to CG, 14 April.) He had provided an invaluable service to the Spanish by "supplying the ordinary rations to the detachments stationed on the banks of the St. Johns River," at a time when those troops lacked supplies and cash. (Zéspedes to Gálvez, 28 February, Lockey, *East Florida*, pp. 461–62)

8. NG may have suggested that he could provide a vessel or vessels with which Fatio could conduct trade with Cuba. No evidence has been found that NG and Fatio joined in any commercial venture. By "turn a Spaniard as well as myself," Fatio referred to his own decision to petition East Florida authorities for Spanish citizenship. ("Memorial of Francis Phillip Fatio," 23 February, Lockey, *East Florida*, p. 464)

9. NG returned to Georgia to settle on Mulberry Grove plantation in November 1785. (NG to Clarke, 23 November, below) He died the following June, without seeing Cumberland Island again. Fatio wrote NG on 5 December, below, that personal matters would keep him from visiting the island that winter. (Fatio to NG, 5 December)

10. As part of his duties as liaison between the Spanish authorities and the British subjects in East Florida, Fatio seems to have been responsible for provisioning the "Indians and the few wretched devils that cant emigrate." (Siebert, *Loyalists in East Florida*, 1: 168) Although most of the British in East Florida—those who had settled there before the war and Loyalists who had fled there from the United States—left the colony by the fall of 1785, a few remained. (Lockey, *East Florida*, p. 11) Some British subjects had been living on Cumberland Island, which was near the border between Georgia and East Florida. (NG to Bowman, 10 September 1784, above) It is not known where New Switzerland was located.

11. No indication has been found that NG sent corn to Fatio.

12. According to his letter to the Marquis de Barbé-Marbois of 15 April, below, NG planned to "lay out a town towards the south end of Great Cumberland; and many people have spoke for lotts." He had undoubtedly asked Fatio for advice about getting refugees or others to settle there.

13. Fatio may have been referring to the pensions and allowances that the British government paid to Loyalist refugees who had lost property, possessions, and income as a result of the war. (Palmer, *Loyalists*, pp. x–xxv)

14. No evidence has been found that NG solicited or received favors from friends in the Georgia legislature that could have helped him establish a settlement on Cumberland Island.

15. Amelia Island, off the coast of what was then East Florida, is on the opposite side of the mouth of the St. Marys River from Cumberland Island. Similar to Cumberland Island in topography, it was also rich in timber and other resources. ("Letter and Report of Nicolás Grenier," 10 November 1784, Lockey, *East Florida*, pp. 306–11)

16. Sophia was Fatio's daughter. (See note at NG to Zéspedes, 26 March.)

*   *   *

¶ **[FROM WILLIAM PIERCE & COMPANY**, Savannah, Ga., 8 April 178[5].[1] Their clerk, who has "just returned from Mulberry Grove," reports that only seventeen barrels of rice are "ready for Market," and "only three or four more [are] expected to be beat out." To date, they have received only fifty-two barrels, and "from the appearances of the [Savannah] River," they have "no hopes of receiving any more."[2] They therefore ask NG to return the bills they gave him "on London," as what they "have in hand" will not be "sufficient to discharge" their "store debt" and what they have "engaged to pay" for NG. If, after receiving all of the rice, the firm is found to owe NG a balance, they will honor his draft "at sight."[3] Their "friends in Augusta" hope they can "procure the Corn"; Pierce will set off for there in a few days and will "do all in his power to get it."[4] RCS (MiU-C) 2 pp.]

1. The last digit of the year is too faded to decipher; "5" was taken from the docketing.

2. Pierce & Company had contracted to sell the rice harvest from NG's Mulberry Grove plantation and had given him a credit against the expected proceeds. (See Pierce to NG, 24 September 1784, above; Pierce to NG, 13 May, and NG to Pierce, 17 May, both below.) On the disappointing rice harvest, see, for example, NG to Gibbs, 3 February, above.

3. On the bills that NG had sent to London, see NG to De Berdt, 9 March, above, as well as the correspondence between Pierce and NG in May. Pierce & Company wrote NG on 9 July, below, that they had drawn on him for £60.

4. NG was attempting to purchase corn for use at Mulberry Grove. The "friends in Augusta" undoubtedly included Edward Telfair, who wrote NG about this matter on 16 April, below.

¶ [FROM JEREMIAH WADSWORTH, Hartford, Conn., 10 April 1785. Wadsworth, who has just received NG's letter of 8 March from Savannah, Ga., wrote NG "largely" from Philadelphia.[1] It is impossible for him to "enter on any new speculations" because of his financial circumstances, but he would like a "particular account" of Cumberland Island, as he has had "many applications" for information about the island and thinks he can "interest the French nation" in it to NG's "advantage."[2] Wadsworth plans to send a vessel to Charleston, S.C., in the near future, and he will write again at that time.[3] In a postscript, he comments that NG's "conduct respecting Gunn Is perfectly right." If NG were to fight every man he offended in doing his duty, there would be "more fighting now than in yᵉ Warr."[4] RCS (CtHi) 2 pp. The manuscript is damaged.]
    1. See NG to Wadsworth, 8 March, and Wadsworth to NG, 15 February, both above.
    2. NG had been trying to persuade Wadsworth to invest in Cumberland Island, Ga. Wadsworth, whose financial situation precluded such an undertaking at this time, was communicating with the Marquis de Barbé-Marbois on NG's behalf. (See above, Wadsworth's letters of NG of 15, 21, and 23 February and 4 March, and NG's to Wadsworth of 3 and 17 February and 8 March.) NG wrote a description of the island's resources for Marbois on 15 April, below.
    3. See Wadsworth to NG, 6 May, below.
    4. NG had rejected James Gunn's challenge to a duel. (NG to Gunn, 2 March, above)

¶ [TO DENNIS DE BERDT. From Charleston, S.C., 13 April 1785. NG wrote to him on 3 April, enclosing "the second bill of a sett drawn by William Pierce & Company Merchants at Savannah on James Starker and James McKensie Merchants London"; the bills, "when paid," are to be "placed to Account of Charles Pettit Merchant Philadelphia."[1] For "fear of accidents," NG now encloses the third set of bills.[2] CyS (MiU-C) 1 p.]
    1. For background, see NG to De Berdt, 3 April, above, and note at NG's letter enclosing the first set of bills. (NG to De Berdt, 9 March, above)
    2. De Berdt's reply has not been found. (See, however, his letter to NG of 21 July and the note at NG to Pierce, 17 May, both below.)

*　　　*　　　*

To Catharine Littlefield Greene

My dear Caty   Charleston [S.C.] April 14th 1785

I am disappointed and mortified. On my arrival here I expected to meet your letters but can hear of none. It is now three Months and upwards since I left home and no accounts from my family. I should have been much alarmed but for a letter I got from Colonel Wadsworth. He wrote me that he had lately heard from you that you had been unwell but was now perfectly recovered. God grant it may be true.[1] I long to be with you but when it will happen I cannot tell. My stay here will be longer than I intended and from this I go to North Carolina & Virginia and at the last place I expect to be detained a long time as I am determined to bring [John] Banks's affairs to a close if possible. At least to know on what ground I stand in the business.[2]

My last letter was from Savannah, in that I informed you that I was going to Cumberland Island and Augustine.[3] Was I to attempt to give you a full account of our voyages, travels, shift of scenes and change of charactors it would require a Volum. But not to leave you entirely in the dark I will just give you a hint of some of the most interesting parts of our expedition. M[r] [Benjamin] Hawkins was my companion. I believe you are not acquainted with him. He is a Gentleman of property in North Carolina and formerly a Member of Congress. He is very agreeable, sensible, social and generous.[4] We embarked in a large Canoe and went the inland passage. This navigation is formed by a range of Islands which are seperated from the main by a narrow channel of about three quarters of a Mile wide and they extend almost from Charleston to Augustine. There is little or no sea except in crossing from one Island to the other where the outlets of the great Rivers are. At those places there is sometimes a considerable swell; but not dangerous and of short duration. By this navigation we avoid sea sickness and all stress of weather as you are always in a secure harbour and may go on shore at any time you please. And as most of the Islands are inhabited you may get many conveniencies. We had an awning to our Canoe and matresses to sleep on. In every other respect we liv'd like an Army on the March. The passage was pleasant and the weather favorable. We visited all the Islands particularly Cumberland in which I am interested. I find it a very valuable property and had I funds to improve it to advantage it might be made one of the first commercial objects on the Continent. The Island is twenty odd Miles long and great part of it excellent for Indigo. The situation is favorable for trade, the place healthy and the prospects delightful. On the seaside there is a beach Eighteen Miles long as level as a floor and as hard as a Rock. It is the pleasantest Ride I ever saw. There is an excellent harbour and seven capital Rivers empty themselves opposite the Island and at the outlets upon each end.[5]

From Cumberland we went to [St.] Augustine, as far as St Johns by water, and from thence by land which is about forty Miles. At St Johns we found a Spanish guard. The officer treated us with great politeness; but the place for poverty beggars all description. Some few refugees were still there but most of them gone. Those remaining carried every mark of wretchedness in countenance and appearance. But under this veil of missery there is all the bitterness of party and malevolence of disappointment. They eyed us as a Beast of prey survey an object they wish to devour.[6]

It was with difficulty we got horses to carry us from St Johns to Augustine and the Cavalry and people were much alike. Our Journey was disagreeable, the roads bad indeed it was nothing but a foot path.

The whole distance is one continued range of pine barrens. Not one enlivening object to be seen the whole way. Nor is there any thing to be got for Man or beast. We arrivd in the Night and the darkness servd to cover the shabby appearance of the horses and savd us from some little mortification of entering the Town like state criminals. Tho we had kept our voyage as secret as possible report had got a head of us and a party came out seven Miles to meet us but returned before we came up.[7] The Governor sent us a Lieutenant Generals guard and paid us every possible mark of respect and attention.[8] We were introduced to his Lady and daughters and compliments flew from side to side like a shuttle cock in the hands of good players. You know I am not very excellent at fine speeches. My stock was soon exhausted; but what I lacked in conversation, I made up in bowing. The Governnante is about fifty five, as chearful as a Girl of sixteen, and enters with spirit and pleasure into all the amusements of the young people. She is sister to the Vice Roy of Mexico and highly respected both from her family and pleasing manners.[9] The daughters are not hansome, their complexion is rather tawny, but they have got sweet languishing Eyes. They look as if they could love with great violence. They sang and played upon the Harpsicord and did every thing to please if not to inspire softer emotions. Hawkins professed himself smitten.[10] The old Lady unluckily asked me if I was married and in so unexpected a manner that I had no chance to evade the enquiry. This limitted my gallantry or perhaps I might have got in love too. The Governor who is rather corpulent has a good share of natural benevolence and is more remarkable for politeness than understanding gave us an entertainment. It was the first he had given since his arrival. The people told us the british were not a little vexed, they had given several dinners to the Spannish Governor and he had made no return of their civilities. And to compliment us in so extraordinary a manner added not a little to their mortification.[11] The dinner was truly elegant and I believe in my soul there was from one hundred and fifty to two hundred dishes of different kinds servd up in seven courses. French cookery prevails with the Spannish. I was posted by the Governnante and Mr Hawkins by the Young Ladies. Dinner lasted five hours and as I was obliged to taste most of the dishes from the attention of the Governnante I was not unlike a stuffed pig and almost in the condition of the Country tenant who said he had rather fight than eat any more. We had a variety of Spannish, and some good French Wines. We spent the Evening at Cards and retird about ten at night.[12] Next Morning the Governnante sent us a large basket of Cakes and fruit curiously ornamented with flowers and cut paper. And among other things there was a large box of guaber Jelley. This I left to be forwarded to you. It has not arrivd here yet but I am in hopes it will. It will come directed to M^r [Robert] Hazlehurst. We staid four days in Augustine. The town is larger than I expected but the houses are huddled together not unlike one of our winter encampments. The buildings make but a mean appearance; but the orange trees which are interspersed among them give the whole a pleasant air. The place is exceeding healthy and the houses are built of a kind of concretion of shells which forms a substance not unlike free stone.[13] The fortifications I did not visit for fear of exciting Jealosy.[14] The spannish Ladies are very free and it is said will admit more freedoms than most Ladies think either decent or reputable. Our stay was too short to try experiments. The Governor sent a guard with us a Col of light horse and a party of Dragoons to escort us clear into the State of Georgia and directed the Comodore of the Ship in St Maries River to pay us all the honors due to Lt General of Spain. We had salute upon salute and the Comodore gave us a genteel entertainment.[15] Here the british were mortified again for there lay not less than twenty sail in the harbour of the british transports employed in the public service removing the Inhabitants of East Florida to Noviscotia [i.e., Nova Scotia] and the Bahama Islands. They considered the complements paid us little less than an insult to them.[16] We spent four days on our return examining Cumberland Island, the quantity of timber on it is immence and the best in the World for ship building.[17] From Cumberland we embarked for Savannah and arrivd there in two days having a fine free wind all the way. I visited my plantation and sett all my affairs in as good a train as possible;[18] and embarked for this place and had a disagreeable passage of five days, pent up in a little Cabbin with a noisy Irishman, an impudent Scotchman and a Nasty Dutch woman with a bawling brat of a child. God deliver me from another such a passage. A little distance from Charleston bar we carried away our bowsprit.

The players are at this place and the people half mad to see them act altho they perform wretchedly. The house is crowded by five in the afternoon and from that time until Eleven at Night they are stewing and mixing together like a dish of chowder.[19] I have been to no place of amusement since I left home. My heart is too heavy to enjoy it. I had tickets sent me both here and Savannah; but declined going.

Mrs Morris has got a son and Mrs Hambleton also.[20] Mrs Huger has recovered a very hansome provision from her husband. She is universally respected and he as much despisd.[21] I have just got a long and serious letter from Griffin. He says I may make my self perfectly easy respecting the bills that he will pay them out of the product of the *Flora*. He adds that the owners of the *Flora* will be indebted to me for what ever they get for her, the Duke of D Casters having often informed him that the King took the Ship entirely to serve me. Griffin seems a little mortified that the bills has made so much noise.[22] Mr Challenor gave an unfavorable impression from misrepresenting the matter; but before this all will be set to rights.[23] Merchants are breaking in every part of America. Our friend Colonel Biddle has failed for forty thousand pounds. It astonishes every body. I am still in hopes he has more property than will pay his debts; and that his stopping payment has been only from the scarcity of cash.[24] I tremble at my own situation when I think of the enormous sums I owe and the great difficulty of obtaining Money. I seem to be doomed to a life of slavery and anxiety, but if I can render you happy it will console me. I have many things to say and propose; but as I am yet too much in the dark to form a proper judgment I must wait until matters ripen more. God bless and preserve you and the children in good health until my return.

A dieu my dear; and remember me affectionately to all friends upon the hill and upon Block Island.[25] Tell Mrs Redwood I have never met with so sprightly a genius, nor one so agreeable in a l—— l—— as herself since I left home.[26] Griffin enquires about his wager upon the secret and wishes to know if it has not failed.[27]   N GREENE

Mrs Turnbull and abundance of the Ladies enquire after you very affectionately.[28]

ALS (MiU-C).

1. See Jeremiah Wadsworth to NG, 21 February, above.

2. Instead of traveling to North Carolina and Virginia, NG sailed home in June from Charleston, arriving in Newport, R.I., on 25 June. (See note at NG to CG, 25 May, below.)

3. Cumberland Island, in which NG held a substantial interest, is near the mouth of the St. Marys River, the border between Georgia and what was then East Florida. (On NG's interest in the island, see note at Hyrne to Clay, 26 November 1783, above; for a further description of the island, see NG to Marbois, 15 April, below.) St. Augustine was the capital of East Florida, which had recently passed from British to Spanish control. British subjects there, many of whom were Loyalist refugees from Georgia, South Carolina, and other states, were supposed to leave by 19 March 1785, but the evacuation was not completed until November. Patrick Tonyn, the former British governor, stayed in East Florida until then, creating an uneasy situation with Zéspedes. (Lockey, *East Florida*, pp. 13–15) During the transition from British to Spanish rule, civil unrest broke out, and Loyalist "banditti" preyed on plantations across the border in Georgia. (Ibid., pp. 14–15)

The reasons for NG's trip to East Florida are not fully known. One purpose was undoubtedly related to Cumberland Island, where he wanted to assess the situation and the possibilities for settlement. Loyalist refugees had been cutting timber there, and NG may have hoped to get the East Florida government's help in ending the practice. (See NG to Bowman, 10 September 1784, and Tanner, *Visit to St. Augustine*, pp. 6–7.) James Seagrove, a New York merchant with whom NG met the previous winter, had also suggested that a "proper Commercial establishment on St. Mary's River" could allow investors in Cumberland Island to take advantage of Seagrove's trade connections with East Florida and Cuba. Seagrove was hoping to travel to East Florida himself and ascertain the possibilities for a "plan" that he and NG had discussed in New York. (Seagrove to NG, 23 February, above; see also Wadsworth to NG, 23 February, above.) Helen Hornbeck Tanner, who asserts that NG "was cautiously searching for methods to circumvent . . . Spanish trade restrictions," also suggests that Seagrove—who later, as a founder of the border town of St. Marys, Ga., attempted to "foment uprisings in Spanish East Florida in order to provide an excuse for American occupation of the province"—might have given NG more than purely trade and financial reasons for his visit to

St. Augustine. (Tanner, *Visit to St. Augustine*, pp. 4–5) Clearly, NG did use this trip to make contacts that could have later involved him in trade with East Florida and Cuba. (See Francis Phillip Fatio's letters to NG of 6 April, above, and end of June documents, below.) Given his own financial worries at this time, though, it can be presumed that immediate, financial considerations were uppermost in his mind.

Zéspedes, the governor, was suspicious of NG's visit, which had been preceded several months earlier by a trip to East Florida by William Pierce, NG's former aide, who brought a letter from Gov. John Houstoun of Georgia expressing hope in a "Mutuality of Good-offices" between the two governments. (Houstoun to Zéspedes, 10 August 1784, Lockey, *East Florida*, pp. 250–51) Pierce wrote letters of introduction to Zéspedes for NG and his traveling companion, Hawkins, before they left for St. Augustine in March, as did Samuel Elbert, Houstoun's predecessor as governor of Georgia. Concerning the purpose of NG's visit, Elbert wrote that "the general has a valuable estate on Cumberland Island, which he is going to look over, and he has it in mind to visit Your Excellency's province before he returns." (Ibid., p. 472) Pierce informed Zéspedes that NG was visiting St. Augustine "on some business of a private nature." (Ibid., pp. 476–77)

As the most notable American to have visited East Florida since Zéspedes became governor, NG may have appeared to him to be an unofficial representative of the state of Georgia, if not of the United States government. (Tanner, *Visit to St. Augustine*, p. 1) Zéspedes may have been concerned that Americans wanted to gather intelligence in the event that Georgia or the United States should wish to annex the province. (As noted at NG to Gardoqui, 7 August, below, the boundaries between the United States and East Florida were not firmly established at this time.) As an example of the mistrust that existed between the Spanish colonial government and its neighbor, Georgia, Zéspedes considered a June 1785 resolution by the Georgia legislature for fixing the boundaries of the state to be evidence of their "ambitious and usurpative, though still impotent, designs" toward East Florida. (Zéspedes to José de Gálvez, 19 June 1785, Lockey, *East Florida*, p. 561) NG implicitly acknowledged the delicacy of relations with East Florida when he wrote further in the present letter that he did not visit the fortifications at St. Augustine, "for fear of exciting Jealosy." After NG and Hawkins concluded their visit, Zéspedes wrote that "As curiosity was undoubtedly not the sole cause of their coming, I confess that their visit was not altogether acceptable to me." He added that he had "discovered that independently of the idea of seeing the country, he [i.e., NG] came perhaps to invite certain British families to settle on the aforementioned island [Cumberland], which up to the present has been uninhabited." (Ibid., p. 489) After he received effusive thank-you notes from NG and Hawkins following their brief stay in St. Augustine, the Spanish governor expressed unease in a letter to his superior. (See NG to Zéspedes, 26 March; Zéspedes to Gálvez, 1 April, Lockey, *East Florida*, p. 490.) The military escort that accompanied NG and Hawkins back to Georgia may therefore have been sent to keep an eye on them. NG's letter informing CG of his impending trip has not been found. He and Hawkins left Savannah on 10 March and arrived in East Florida on the 19th; they had left the Spanish colony by 26 March, when NG wrote Zéspedes from Cumberland Island. (See also *New Hampshire Gazette*, 10 June, in Greene, *Greene*, 3: 530.)

4. Hawkins (1754–1818), who accompanied NG to Cumberland Island and East Florida, had served as an interpreter on Washington's staff during the war and was a North Carolina delegate to Congress from 1781 to 1784. On 21 March 1785, he was appointed a commissioner to negotiate with Cherokee and other southern Indians, a commission he may not have known about before he left for East Florida with NG. (PCC, item 186, p. 34, DNA) He was later instrumental in negotiating several key treaties with southern Indians, and he also served in the United States Senate from North Carolina before receiving an appointment as "agent to the Creeks and general superintendent of all Indian tribes south of the Ohio," a post that he held for many years. (*DAB*)

5. NG also described Cumberland Island in his letter to the Marquis de Barbé-Marbois, immediately below. On the harbor at St. Marys, see NG to Wadsworth, 24 April, below. CG moved to Cumberland Island in 1800 and lived there until her death. (Stegeman, *Caty*, p. 174)

6. The town of St. Johns Bluff, or St. Johns, as it came to be called, was six or seven miles from the mouth of the St. Johns River. It had become a thriving settlement with the infusion of refugees from Georgia and South Carolina in 1782 and was expected to become a bustling trade center because the entrance to its harbor had greater depth than that at St. Augustine and because many of the most successful plantations in the province were located along the St. Johns River. However, when news of the cession of East Florida to Spain reached St. Johns in 1783, "the favorable prospects of the flourishing village vanished," and by late 1785 it was "a deserted place." (Siebert, *Loyalists in East Florida*, 1: 117–18, 177)

7. It is not clear why NG would have wished to "keep his voyage as secret as possible." (On his motives for traveling to East Florida, see note 3, above.) Samuel Elbert's letter of introduction for NG to the governor of East Florida was written on 8 March; it is not known if it was sent ahead or if NG carried it. (Ibid.)

8. Zéspedes was the governor of East Florida.

9. The "Governnante" was Zéspedes's wife, Maria Concepción Aróstegui. She belonged to a "prominent merchant family in Havana" but was not a sister of the viceroy of Mexico. (Tanner, *Visit to St. Augustine*, p. 14n)

10. The daughters were named Maria Dominga and Maria Josepha. Two months after NG's visit, Maria Dominga eloped with a Spanish officer. (Tanner, *Visit to St. Augustine*, pp. 14–15n; Zéspedes to José de Gálvez, 3 June, in Lockey, *East Florida*, pp. 549–52)

11. According to Tanner, it was not until May that Zéspedes gave a dinner and ball in honor of the former British governor, Patrick Tonyn. It was during that affair that Zéspedes's daughter eloped with the Spanish officer. (Tanner, *Visit to St. Augustine*, p. 15n; see also the preceding note.)

12. A contemporary newspaper account of NG's visit to St. Augustine relates that "every mark of politeness and attention, and every military honor was paid the General worthy so great a character. A captain and fifty men were sent to his quarters as his guard, which the general modestly refused accepting, as being no longer in a military character. Sentinels were placed at his quarters and the different guards of the garrison paid him the same honor as they do a lieutenant-general of their own nation." (*New Hampshire Gazette*, 10 June, in Greene, *Greene*, 3: 530–31n) In reply to Samuel Elbert's letter of introduction for NG, Zéspedes wrote that he regretted "the limited opportunities of this place have not permitted me to entertain him [i.e., NG] as he merited and I desired." (Zéspedes to Elbert, 22 March, Lockey, *East Florida*, p. 483)

13. Tanner writes that "St Augustine's narrow streets were bordered by solid lines of walls and garden fences, with wooden balconies projecting over the roadways." At the time of NG's visit, "Only about half of the 250 houses were in good condition." She notes that "Coquina rock, composed of layers of marine shells compressed below the surface of the earth, was used for the more substantial buildings in St. Augustine. Coquina was quarried on Anastasia Island, across Matanzas bay, and brought to the town by barge." (Tanner, *Visit to St. Augustine*, pp. 16n, 17n)

14. See note 3, above.

15. NG and Hawkins were escorted by Col. Antonio Fernández. (See NG to Zéspedes, 26 March, above.) The fleet of Commodore Don Pedro Vásquez was anchored in the harbor at the mouth of the St. Marys River. (Lockey, *East Florida*, p. 226) NG and Hawkins "lodged" aboard the commander's brigantine on the night of 25 March. (Hawkins to Zéspedes, 26 March, Lockey, *East Florida*, pp. 493–94) NG was reportedly greeted "by the discharge of thirteen cannon. After partaking of an elegant entertainment which the

commodore had provided for the occasion, he [i.e., NG] was attended by the commodore in his barge (and again saluted by thirteen cannon) to Cumberland island in the State of Georgia." (*New Hampshire Gazette*, 10 June, in Greene, *Greene*, 3: 531n)

16. On the evacuation of British subjects from East Florida, see note 3, above. They sailed from St. Marys to settle in Nova Scotia, the Bahamas, the West Indies, Bermuda, England, and, as restrictions on former Loyalists began to be relaxed in Georgia and other states, in the United States. (Siebert, *Loyalists in East Florida*, 1: 137–59, 182–210; see also vol. 12: 616n, above.) The tributes that the Spanish paid to NG, as the former American commander in the South and as a symbol of the victorious American cause, would have been regarded as an "insult" by the British subjects waiting to leave.

17. In his letter to Marbois, immediately below, NG described at greater length the timber and other natural resources of Cumberland Island.

18. NG's Georgia plantation, Mulberry Grove, was near Savannah.

19. "The American Company of Comedians" had been performing in Charleston since March, at "The Theatre, in the City *Exchange*." (*Columbian Herald* [South Carolina], 28 March) They were to perform "She stoops to Conquer, Or, the Mistakes of a Night," on 14 April, and another "entertainment, call'd The Citizen," the following evening. A newspaper notice advised "Ladies and Gentlemen" to "send their servants to keep places as soon as the doors are opened [at 5 P.M.], with positive orders not to quit the box for which they hold tickets on any account; without this is done, the manager cannot possibly prevent a continuance of the disappointments that have lately happened, and which he is very sorry it was not in his power to remedy." In order to "prevent confusion," patrons, according to the location of their seats, were also advised to have their servants drop them off at specific locations in the street outside the theater. (*Columbian Herald* [South Carolina], 14 April)

20. Ann-Barnett Elliott Morris was the wife of NG's former aide, Lewis Morris. Elisabeth Harleston had married James Hamilton the previous June. (Forsyth to NG, 24 February 1784, above)

21. Sabina Elliot Huger was the wife of Daniel Huger and a sister of Ann-Barnett Elliott Morris. On the couple's marital difficulties, see Pendleton to NG, 30 January 1784, above.

22. See Griffin Greene to NG, 2 November 1784, above. The Marquis de Castries was the French naval minister.

23. Griffin Greene expressed his distress about the "publick" nature of NG's protest of the bills in a letter to NG of 14 November 1784, above. On John Chaloner, see note at Charles Pettit to NG, 19 June 1784, above.

24. On the financial problems of Clement Biddle, a former associate of NG's in the Quartermaster Department, see above, Eyre to NG, 7 March, and Pettit to NG, 23 March.

25. NG and CG had lived until recently in the "Point" neighborhood of Newport, near the harbor; CG moved to a higher elevation, on the "hill," sometime in the spring of 1785. (Littlefield to NG, 25 April, below) CG, who grew up on Block Island, still had relatives and friends there.

26. On Sarah Pope Redwood, see above, NG to CG, 21 August 1784.

27. On the long-standing "wager" between Griffin and CG, see Griffin's letter to NG of 2 November 1784, above.

28. "Mrs. Turnbull" was presumably the wife of Dr. Andrew Turnbull. (See Penman to NG, 1 October 1783, above.)

To the Marquis de Barbé-Marbois[1]

Sir   Charleston [S.C.] April 15th 1785

I am told by my friend Col Wadsworth that you have some inclination to be interested in Cumberland Island in the State of Georgia. And want a description of it and the conditions on which it may be had.[2] The following is the most accurate I can give you. Mr Hawkins formerly a Member of Congress was with me and from both our enquiries and observations these were the result.[3]

The Island forms one part of the Harbour of St Marys, into which there is an easy entrance and twenty four feet water on the bar. Shipping when in are perfectly secure from all stress of weather.[4] There is a confluence and communication of Seven Rivers at this place St Johns Nassau St Marys Crooked River Great & little Santella and Turtle River. And all of them Navigable a considerable distance into the Country and several of them a very great distance. Great Cumberland Island runs paralel with the main and the sound between them is about one Mile wide and the Island is said to be upwards of twenty miles long and in many places more than three miles wide and not less than two upon an average. The Shore is bold, vessels of any burthen may lay close to the banks of the Island in almost every part of it. There has been some few settlements formerly on the Island; but the war coming on they were broken up.[5] The Soil is excellent for Indigo and the greater part of the Island fit for planting. The whole of it except a few old fields is covered with the best of live oak and red bay timber. Both of which are of the best quality for Ship building. The size of the oak is fit for the first rate line of battle Ships. Towards the North end there is some good pine timber. The Island is healthy, abounds with good water, the prospect delightful and the Situation cool, the tail of the trade winds reaching as far as this place. Scale and skill fish are to be got in abundance in all parts of this Island. The quantity of Mast or Acorns which grow upon the live oak afford food for any number of hogs which neat a prodigious profit to those that will attend to it. Horses thrive admirably on the Island; but horn Cattle not so well. There is now on the Island not less than two hundred horse & some Mules. It is an excellent place for breeding either. Near one half of the horses and Mules belong to the purchace. Nothing can be more favorable than the situation for a spannish commerce or Lumber trade. Nor is it less convenient for an Indian trade up St Marys and with the settlements on the Rivers of the Southern parts of Georgia.[6] The surveys which have been made on this Island specify only about twelve thousand acres more or less; but from the length and width of it there cannot be less than twenty thousand Acres in it. It is estimated to contain forty square Miles and upwards.[7]

Little Cumberland lays North of great Cumberland and is parted from it only by a narrow Creek. It is full of timber but the soil is not good. It is good for stock being surrounded with marshes, and contains upwards of two thousand acres. The half of great Cumberland except three small surveys and the one half of little Cumberland and upwards of two thousand Acres upon Crooked River upon Crooked Creek about Six miles from Cumberland on the main belongs to my pu[r]chace.[8] The

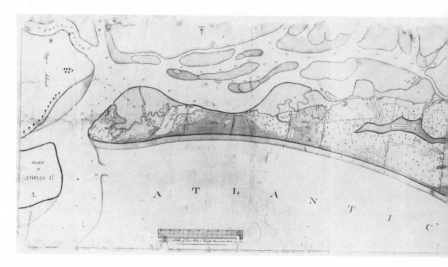

Map of Great and Little Cumberland Islands, Georgia, by John McKinnon, 1802
(Georgia Archives)

lands upon Crooked River is excellent for indigo and for provisions of all kind and full of timber. No difficulty will attend a division of any part of the property. I am going to lay out a town towards the south end of Great Cumberland; and many people have spoke for lotts.[9] For the whole of this property I gave five thousand Guineas which has been on interest from last December twelve Months. Twelve hundred and fifty Guineas was due last December twelve hundred and fifty more will be due next December and twelve hundred & fifty more the December following and the last payment of twelve hundred and fifty Guineas a year after.[10]

There is about twenty families settled on the Island since the war. There is multitudes of Deer and wild fowl to be got on the Island and green turtle in great numbers at some seasons of the year.

I have several offers for this purchase, but wish to secure the best payments. Was I not involved from my engagements for the public in the Southern Department I would not sell any part of it.[11] I am Sir with great respect Your most Obedt humble Servt   NATH GREENE

ACyS (CtY).

1. François, Marquis de Barbé-Marbois (1745–1837) had served as secretary to the Chevalier de La Luzerne, the French minister to the United States, during the war. He also acted at times between 1783 and 1785 as French chargé d'affaires in America. (See vol. 6: 407n, above, and Idzerda, *Lafayette Papers*, 5: 447.)

2. Jeremiah Wadsworth, who was communicating for NG with possible investors in Cumberland Island, had identified Marbois as the most likely prospect. Marbois, as French chargé d'affaires, was interested in supplying timber to the French navy. (Wads-

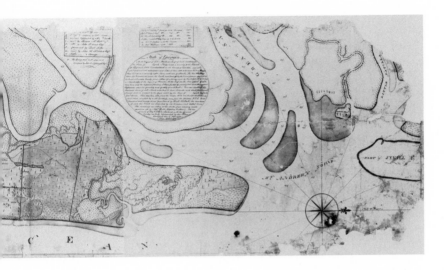

worth to NG, 21 February and 4 March, both above) Wadsworth asked NG to send Marbois a "Minute description" of Cumberland Island and its resources in his letter of 21 February and repeated the request in his letters to NG of 23 February and 4 March. In the letter of 4 March, he wrote that Marbois wanted "every particular" respecting the island, adding that the description should be "Minute[,] as a french man can ask ten questions to an Americans one." (On Marbois's interest in Cumberland Island, see also his letter to NG of 18 May, below.)

3. Benjamin Hawkins and NG had recently returned from a trip to Cumberland Island and East Florida. (NG to Zéspedes, 26 March, and NG to CG, 14 April, both above)

4. The harbor at the mouth of the St. Marys River was considered one of the best on the continent. (See note at NG to Wadsworth, 24 April, below.)

5. On pre-war settlement on Cumberland Island, see Bullard, *Cumberland Island*, pp. 41–63, 108.

6. NG had been in communication with New York businessman James Seagrove about the possibility of using Cumberland Island as a center for commerce with the Spanish colonies of Cuba and East Florida, as well as with settlements in Georgia. (See Seagrove to NG, 23 February, above) NG had also met with East Florida merchant Phillip Francis Fatio about the commercial possibilities for settling the island and making it a profitable endeavour. (Fatio to NG, 6 April, above)

7. According to the National Park Service, which administers the Cumberland Island National Seashore, [Great] Cumberland Island is "17.5 miles long and totals 36,415 acres of which 16,850 are marsh, mud flats, and tidal creeks." (www.nps.gov / cuis /)

8. For background concerning NG's "pu[r]chace" on Cumberland Island, see note at Hyrne to Clay, 26 November 1783, above.

9. On NG's plan for laying out a town on Cumberland Island, see also Fatio to NG, 6 April. Fatio suggested in that letter that it would be better to lease lots than to sell them.

10. See also NG to Wadsworth, 3 February, above, and note at Hyrne to Clay, 26 November 1783.

11. Alexander Semple was presumably one of the potential investors to whom NG

referred. (See NG to William Semple, 4 June, below.) By his "engagements for the public in the Southern Department," NG meant the financial burden he had incurred as the American commander there from guaranteeing debts of Southern Army contractors John Banks et al. Marbois replied to this letter on 18 May.

Answers to the Auditors' Report

[after 15 April 1785][1]

1. M^r [Joseph] Clay deliverd all the bills to Major [Ichabod] Burnet. The one for 800 dollars he sold to pay his expences at Philadelphia[,] the account of which he audited at Col Darts [i.e., John S. Dart's] office as per Col Darts state of the matter[.] What discount the Major sold the bill or how his account stands respecting the ballance I know not. All that I know of the matter is he did sell the bill and his account must be answerable.

2. This objection is surprising when in the Controlers office John Banks is charged with the ballance of the bills in a state of his account between him and M^r [Robert] Morris on the Contractors account. And I will give my oath that I deliverd to Mr Morris a state of the balance of the bills made out and acknowledged by John Banks himself. And from that Account the charge was made by Mr Morris against the Contractors in the Comptrolers office. What right they have to charge Banks without giving me credit remains to be explained. But Mr Morris knows the charge is right & proper and Mr Gouverneur Morris went to the office in my hearing & told M^r [James] Milligan to give my account credit for the ballance of the bills. [B]ut still those objections are created—

3. To support this charge I now send Robert Forsyths Recept for Eleven hundred and twenty three pounds three shillings sterling dollars at 4/6. These payments being made before the Law of South Carolinia fixed them at 4/8. M^r [George] Abbot[t] Hall furnished 5597 67/90. The whole of which I thought had been paid to John Banks & [Company] Capt [Nathaniel] Pendleton receivd the first parcel of Money of Mr Hall for which I gave my Recept some time afterward and Major Pearce the last and recepted for it; but how the difference has happened I cannot tell; but it must have been owing to the irregular[i]ty of Major Pearces [i.e., William Pierce, Jr.'s] entries which have involved me in much perplexity. But as I cannot establish only the £1197=3 I must suffer the loss of the rest.

4. This bill charged in my account of bills sold for cash should be charged to John Banks & Comp on Account unless it makes a part of the account of the bills on whic[h] the ballan[ce] of 4957 48/90 due from John Banks & Comp. If it makes a part of that amou[nt] it will stand right in my cash Account but I am confident it does not. Referenc[e] being had to that Account will explain the matter. That Account in-

cludes all the cash I ever had of Banks for bills and if that amount is in the Comptrolers office it is a little surprising that so many objections have been raised to the charge of the ballance for it must be I think the same Account deliverd Mr Morris.

5. It is not so easy for me to get the necessary Vouchers. The books & papers of John Banks & company since Banks's death are dispersed in so many hands, and I have been at much expence and trouble already in the business. And having no allowance for all the risque trouble and expence which I have [been] exposed to I cannot but consider it a cruel hardship.

7th The bill for 995 18/90 Dollars is double charged in the account of bills against me. It is first charged to Robert Forsyth & Comp and then to John Banks & Comp. They were all the same Company only under different names. The charge in my Account was given for supplies had from Robert Forsyths store for the family. And it ought to be taken out of his Commisaries Account and placed to John Banks & com debit. And my Account must be credited for it. The bill for 270 Dollars must have happened in the same way for I am confident there is no charge in my Account but that was well founded; but the irregular manner in which Major Pearce made his entries may have involved the matter in some perplexity. And as I left all the original papers in the Comptrolers office I cannot without them explain the matter. But let the mistake be as it may the Allowance by Congress is for a given sum without any regard to the Account and was for a far less sum than I ought to have had to have done me the least justice exclusive of all the trouble and expence I have been at in bringing the Accounts to a close. I shall insist therefore that my Account be credited for the full Allowance and that all the bills double charged be credited for.

ADf (MiU-C).

1. This undated draft was written to refute auditor John D. Mercier's report of 15 April to James Milligan, the comptroller of the treasury, concerning NG's account "against The United States." Mercier's report is printed in a note at NG to Milligan, 6 February, above. NG presumably sent a final version of this rebuttal to Mercier or Milligan, but no further correspondence has been found.

From the Marquis de Lafayette

My dear Greene   S[t] Germain near Paris 1785 April the 16[th]
    Your letter [of] January the 7[th] Came Very late to Hand,[1] and as the post is just Going I have only time to tell you, that Your kind Sentiments do me honor. Your George along with mine Makes me Extremely Happy. I Beg You to present my most affectionate thanks to Mrs Gre[e]ne. She may depend upon my warmest Care.[2] By the next opportunity I will write to you Every particulars Concerning it. The

tutor is not an Easy matter to obtain. Musicians, particularly in large Citty are not very orderly people. But more of this when I write upon our two Georges.[3] There will be no war, at least this year, unless the Emperor [Joseph II of Austria] makes a Very unexpected political move. But I dont think it will be the Case.[4] The more I see, the more I believe, the more I am Impressed with the Necessity to give Congress powers to Regulate trade. Adieu Yours   LAFAYETTE

RCS (MiU-C).

1. The letter has not been found.

2. Lafayette had suggested that NG's son George Washington Greene, who was then nine years old, come to live with him in France. Lafayette's son George-Washington-Louis-Gilbert du Motier de Lafayette, born in 1779, was three years younger than George Washington Greene. (Idzerda, *Lafayette Papers*, 5: 457) In his letter to Lafayette of 7 January, NG must have expressed CG's approval of such an arrangement. Lafayette wrote Alexander Hamilton on 13 April that NG had consented to the proposal for educating his son. (Idzerda, *Lafayette Papers*, 5: 317)

3. Lafayette wrote NG again about plans for the education of their sons on 12 June, below.

4. On the political situation in Europe, see Lafayette to NG, 16 March; Griffin Greene to NG, 2 November 1784, and Butler to NG, 23 December 1784, all above.

*   *   *

¶ [FROM EDWARD TELFAIR,[1] Augusta, Ga., 16 April 1785. He has NG's letter of 6 April [not found] and "can readily procure the quantity of Corn" that NG mentions, "If conveyance can be had to send it down to your place. The season of planting being now on hand prevents other Craft going so as to procure freight." Telfair will "keep in view your present necessity," but if NG obtains a supply from another source before "one from" him, it would not cause any "inconveniency," as Mr. [Joseph] Clay could "dispose of" Telfair's corn at Savannah.[2] Telfair would be pleased to see NG in Augusta and to render "every ser[vice]" in his power. RCS (NjP) 1 p.]

1. Telfair (1735–1807), a merchant, had been a member of the Georgia legislature and a delegate to Congress. He would later serve several terms as governor of Georgia between 1786 and 1793. Although he was "headquartered" in Savannah, he owned land in the Georgia back country and spent much of his time in Augusta. (*Dictionary of Georgia Biography*, 2: 965–66)

2. NG's letter of 6 April has not been found. Corn, a staple in the diet of slaves on every Georgia coastal plantation, was ground into meal by the slaves themselves. (Smith, *Slavery and Rice Culture*, pp. 113–14) William Pierce, who wrote NG on 8 April, above, that he thought their "friends in Augusta" could supply corn, may have had Telfair in mind. Robert Forsyth wrote NG from Augusta on 22 April, below, that he was unable to supply corn to NG and that he doubted that Telfair could, either. By 12 May, NG forwarded "fifty bushels" of corn to William Gibbons for use at Mulberry Grove plantation. (NG to Gibbons, 12 May, below) He may have obtained that supply in Charleston, S.C. (See Saunders to NG, 22 June, below.)

¶ [FROM NATHANIEL RUSSELL, [Charleston, S.C., after 20 April 1785?].[1] He does not have "fifty Guineas in the house," but if NG is "not in immediate want," Russell can "oblige" him "with that Sum by Saturday next at farthest."

In the meantime, if "Twenty will be of Service," Russell will send them. RCS (MiU-C) 1 p.]

1. On Russell, see Flagg to NG, 17 October 1783, above. Russell dated this letter only "Wednesday morn^g." The editors have given it the above, tentative date because NG, writing to Jeremiah Wadsworth on 24 April, below, acknowledged receipt "a few days past" of Wadsworth's letter of 21 February, above, suggesting that NG approach Russell for a loan.

¶ [FROM ROBERT FORSYTH, Augusta, Ga., 22 April 1785. NG's letter of 6 April [not found] did not arrive until the 15th, and this is Forsyth's first opportunity to respond. He is so "distressed" by his own situation that it will be "impossible" for him to accompany NG to Virginia as soon as NG wishes; neither he nor the "Major" could set out before "late in May," and even then there is "no certain prospect" of having enough money for the journey. However, he does "wish and desire to go to Virginia and make a final close in the business, if possible." He adds: "being fully sensible of your kindnesses to me I consider myself bound to do every thing I can in order to ease y^r present distressing situation."[1] He has received a letter of 14 February from Mr. [James] Hunter, who "was then at Bermudas, having been blown off the Coast on his way f^m Ch^{s}ton [i.e., Charleston, S.C.,] & he got to Dominica after experiencing great distress[;] he afterwards was obliged to put into Bermudas from whence he intended sailing for Baltimore [Md.] the Day after the Date of his Letter."[2] Forsyth cannot "engage" the corn for NG; it is "extremely scarce" and expensive. He fears that Mr. [Edward] Telfair will not be able to buy any, either, and advises NG to buy it at Charleston. Forsyth does not have "five Bushels nor a Bushel engaged" at this time and does not "know where to get a supply."[3] Is "anxious" to hear from NG. RCS (NcD) 3 pp.]

1. In his letter of 6 April, NG must have urged Forsyth, as one of the late John Banks's business partners, to go to Virginia and help Banks's creditors obtain the proceeds from Banks's estate there. (For background, see above, NG to Carrington, 10 November 1784, and Carrington to NG, 27 February and 23 March.) NG wrote Carrington on 29 September, below: "I did all I could to get Forsyth to Virginia but could not." The "Major" was presumably Patrick Carnes, on whom see also Carrington to NG, 27 February and 23 March, and Penman to NG, immediately below.

2. Banks's and Forsyth's partner Hunter was in Virginia before June. (Hunter to NG, 1 June, below)

3. On the corn, see note at Telfair to NG, 16 April, above.

¶ [FROM EDWARD PENMAN, Charleston, S.C., 22 April 1785. He has been trying to remember when he informed Mr. [Michael J.] Harris about the mortgage that Mr. [John] Banks gave "to us" for "the Negroes sold Cap^{tn} [Patrick] Carnes & him" but cannot "fix it to a day." Is "very certain" that he did inform Harris and Mr. James Miller as soon as he heard about their plan to buy "those Negroes"; knows he informed Miller as soon as he heard about their intention and cannot believe that Miller did not inform Harris, as they "lived in the same house." Adds: "It would seem they considered the situation of Mr Bank's affairs such at that period, that Messrs Harris & [Joseph] Blachford founded an agreement, even under that disadvantage." Penman, however, considers this "a matter of no sort of consequence," as giving the information to either Miller or Harris was "an act of friendship, not of right because as the Mortgage was recorded immediately after it was given it was their business, as it is of every person who makes such purchases to see that they are clear of such incumbrances. Otherwise they must abide all Consequences." Penman can prove that Mr. [John] McQueen "knew of this Mortgage." He concludes: "Indeed from the perplexed State of Mr Banks' affairs which was generally known *at that time* every person must have considered us void of every Idea of common Prudence to invest him with so valuable a property payable at a distant Day without the fullest Security."[1] Cy (MiU-C) 2 pp.]

1. For background and a discussion of NG's connection with this matter, see especially Pendleton to NG, 10 November 1784, above. NG's reply has not been found.

¶ [FROM V. & N. FRENCH & NEPHEW, Bordeaux, France, 23 April 1785. They have just received NG's letter of 7 January "by the New York Packett," are "highly obligated" to him "for the contents," and will be happy "if Ever you put it in our way of Convincing you the weight your recommendation bears with us." The "affectionate & obliging manner" in which NG expresses himself about his brother's and cousin's "house is a sufficient reason for our availing of Ev'ry opportunity of seeking a connection with these friends."[1] This letter will be delivered by their "friend" Griffin Greene, who can provide "all p'ticulars" regarding their firm; "nobody" can be more "intimately acquainted" with them, and they hold the "highest opinion of his friendship & regard."[2] Griffin is leaving with their friend Mr. [James] Price.[3] French & Nephew hope NG "may be p'suaded that in Bordeaux you have friends no where more Sincerely devoted to you" than they are. Cy (MiU-C) 2 pp.]

1. In his brief letter of 7 January, above, NG had stressed his connection with Jacob Greene & Company, his brother Jacob's and cousin Griffin Greene's firm.

2. Griffin Greene, who had been in France since the summer of 1783, was back in the United States by early summer of 1785. (Wadsworth to NG, 10 July, below)

3. On Price, see note at Griffin Greene to NG, 12 June 1784, above.

¶ [FROM HENRY OSBORNE, Savannah, Ga., 23 April 1785.[1] According to two men who arrived the day before from St. Marys, expecting to see NG, the "people are very uneasy to know your final determination respecting the settlement of Cumberland." If NG wants to pursue the plans he "had in contemplation when at Cumberland[,] no time ought to be lost."[2] The transports will "soon sail from St Mary's," and the refugees will "go on board if not assured of a settlement on Cumberland."[3] Osborne will be happy to go there on NG's behalf if it will "contribute to" NG's "interest."[4] Mr. Houstoun advertises 500 acres on Cumberland for sale; Osborne encloses a "paper" with that information.[5] Colonel Hawkins and Major Pierce have been at Augusta "these two weeks past."[6] In a postscript, Osborne notes that "Gov[r] [James Edward] Powel of the Bahamas has by Proclaim dismissed the American flag from those Islands after the 17th of May next."[7] RCS (MiU-C) 2 pp.]

1. Osborne, who has been described as "an ambitious Irish lawyer intent on feathering his nest in Georgia," had moved to "the St. Marys area" and by June 1785 owned "nearly all the public land at South Point" on Cumberland Island. Mary R. Bullard writes that Osborne and Alexander Semple both "sought to ingratiate themselves with" NG "when he visited Cumberland in 1785, and Osborne even traveled with the general to St. Augustine." (Bullard, *Cumberland Island*, pp. 109–10; on Semple, see NG to Wadsworth, 8 March, above. In a letter describing his recent visit to St. Augustine, East

Florida, NG mentioned only Benjamin Hawkins as his traveling companion. [NG to CG, 14 April, above])

2. NG, who was trying to organize a settlement on Cumberland Island, had visited there recently. (Fatio to NG, 6 April; NG to CG, 14 April; and NG to Marbois, 15 April, all above)

3. British transports were removing British subjects from East Florida at this time. (See NG to CG, 14 April, above.) Osborne apparently did not receive NG's reply until late July, by which time some refugees had moved from Cumberland Island to the mainland. (Osborne to NG, 30 August, below)

4. As seen in his letter of 30 August, Osborne did travel to Cumberland Island. Benjamin Hawkins wrote NG on 24 June, below, that Osborne had taken possession of about 1,000 acres on the island. (See also Bullard, *Cumberland Island*, p. 109.)

5. John Houstoun McIntosh was six years old when he inherited his parents' "vast holdings" in Georgia, including land on Cumberland Island, in 1779. His mother, the former Priscilla Houstoun, was from "one of the most powerful" families in Georgia, and his guardians were two of his maternal uncles, Sir Patrick and George Houstoun. (Bullard, *Cumberland Island*, pp. 58–59) Osborne was presumably referring here to one of the uncles.

6. Hawkins had traveled to Cumberland Island and East Florida with NG. (See note at NG to CG, 14 April.) William Pierce, Jr., a former aide to NG, was a merchant in Savannah.

7. The proclamation concerning American shipping in the Bahamas has not been found.

* * *

To Jeremiah Wadsworth

My dear Sir   Charleston [S.C.] April 24th 1785

I had the pleasure a few days past to receive four letters from you, one dated the 15th of Febu^y in Philadelphia one the 21st and another of the 23^d of Feb and one of the 4th of March at New York.

I thank you for your kind indulgence respecting the bills which I may have occasion to draw on you.[1] But I am sorry your affairs forbid your being interested in Cumberland. Inclosed is a copy of a letter to Marbois.[2] It is a good purchace, you may depend on it. I cannot help considering it a very great commercial object. I had not half so good an opinion of it before I went to see it as I have now.

I went from Cumberland to [St.] Augustine[.] The Spannish Governor treated us with great politeness. Little less respect was shewn us than is paid to Crowned heads.[3] While we were at Augustine I learned that the Spannish Court had it in contemplation to form the Capitol of East Florida at St Marys. Should they do that Cumberland will become of double value.[4] At any rate the Spannish will have a post there. Supplies for which will be no small object. One Semple from Philadelphia has a store on the Island and sells abundance of Goods.[5]

I must get you to assume some debts for me to cover my property here with a Mortgage. You will see the payments are at distant periods except for a part of Cumberland which I expect to Negotiate from the sale. At any rate you shall suffer no inconvenience from it.[6] I send you a power to sell my plantation on the Pasaic near Second River New Jersy; and my lands up the North River held with Colonel Biddle. You will dispose of them if you have an opportunity either for cash or good securities as you may think best either for my interest or your own convenience.[7] All I mean by the Mortgage is to cover my property against [John] Banks's creditors. If they can get at it they will look no farther for payment; but if I can cover it they will seek farther rather than put me to Goal [i.e., jail].[8]

If I could get twelve or fourteen hundred Guineas I am confident I could buy up the bonds for the two last payments of Cumberland at a very great discount. If you could hire this amount for me it would afford me a great advantage. One half the benefit of which should result to you. But to procure me this advantage I dont wish to subject you to any inconvenience. I only hint the matter[;] act as your interest and inclinations may dictate.[9]

[James] Seagrove has not yet made his appearance. I thank you for the hint you gave me. I wish his affairs had been otherwise he might have been useful.[10] If Mrs Greene was willing I should like to live a few years at Cumberland.[11] A great plan of business might be struck out there.

M[r] Griffin Greene has written me that the Sales of the *Flora* is not yet compleated; but all things are in a good train, and that out of the product he means to pay the bills by you indorsed. But for fear he should not I mean to include them in the Mortgage.[12]

My stay in this Country will be longer than I expected or intended. I must beg your kind attention to Mrs Greene. I have every reason to hope I shall get rid of one of the principal demands on me by Banks's creditors from some papers I lately got at. My Attorneys tell me all will go well. But while I am in this situation people will be cautious of lending her any assistance by which there is a possibility of suffering.[13] Present me respectfully to your family and beleive me to be Affectionately Your friend   NATH GREENE

Debts to be assumed

3000 Guineas due to Jervey [i.e., Gervais] & Owens payable in two years from last March[14]

5000 Guineas payable as by the letter you may see to Marbois for Cumberland Island &c[15]

1500 pounds Sterling due you for my bills already drawn in the year 1783 and those you authorise me to draw now.

2000 pounds for the bills you indorsed for Griffin Greene[16]

1000 pounds payable to Doctor Olliphant ⅓ now due ⅓ due next fall and the other third 6 Months after.[17]

<u>600</u> due to Blake & Stanley[18]

13,100

ALS (Ct).

1. The letters are all above; in that of 21 February, Wadsworth had offered to do anything in his power to help NG deal with his financial problems

2. Wadsworth informed NG in his letter of 23 February that he was unable to invest in Cumberland Island, Ga., and that the Marquis de Barbé-Marbois was the only person he knew of who might be willing to do so. In several recent letters, Wadsworth had urged NG to send a detailed description of the island and its resources to Marbois and him. (Wadsworth to NG, 21 February, 23 February, and 4 March, all above) The description is in NG to Marbois, 15 April, above. (See also note 15, below.)

3. On NG's visit to East Florida, see especially his letter to CG of 14 April, above.

4. The harbor at the mouth of the St. Marys River, adjacent to Cumberland Island, was a better natural port than the one at St. Augustine, where vessels were sometimes wrecked on a treacherous sandbar. The governor of East Florida, Vicente Manuel de Zéspedes, claimed that the harbor at the mouth of the St. Marys was, "according to all accounts, the deepest and easiest to enter on the whole North American coast between Mexico and New York." (Zéspedes to Gálvez, 29 July, Lockey, *East Florida*, p. 571) In the letter immediately below, Francis Phillip Fatio wrote that Zéspedes was planning to move the capital of East Florida to Amelia Island, adjacent to St. Marys and Cumberland Island. The transfer of the colonial capital from St. Augustine never took place.

5. On Alexander Semple, see above, Eyre to NG, 7 March, and NG to Wadsworth, 8 March.

6. On the loan that NG was hoping to obtain in Holland, using his Georgia plantation, Mulberry Grove, as collateral, see Morris to NG, 15 March, above, and 28 June, below. The debts that NG wanted Wadsworth to cover are listed at the end of the present letter. As noted at Morris to NG, 12 July 1784, above, NG did not obtain the loan.

7. On 26 March, above, NG had sent Wadsworth a power of attorney to sell NG's properties in New York and New Jersey, except for those that he owned jointly with Clement Biddle. Wadsworth reported in his letter to NG of 4 March that Biddle was in trouble financially. Wadsworth wrote NG on 3 July, below: "I never had it in my power to take any measures to sell your Lands in N York [or?] New Jersey, nor do I believe it will be possible for me to do it as it will be necessary to Visit each place." NG assigned another power of attorney to Wadsworth on 16 August, below.

8. As noted at Hyrne to Clay, 26 November 1783, above, NG's claim to an undivided half share of much of the land on Cumberland Island was based on an unredeemed indenture that he had received in August 1783 from John Banks and Ichabod Burnet.

9. The "twelve or fourteen hundred Guineas" presumably were meant to cover most or all of the "Debts to be assumed" that NG listed at the end of this letter. Wadsworth's reply has not been found, and no indication has been found that he tried to obtain such an amount for NG.

10. See Wadsworth to NG, 15 and 23 February.

11. NG, who died less than fourteen months after writing this letter, never lived on Cumberland Island. (As noted at his letter to her of 14 April, above, however, CG later did.)

12. NG's cousin Griffin Greene had been in France for some time, attempting to sell the vessel *Flora*. On the mortgage to which NG presumably referred here, see note at his letter to Wadsworth of 13 July, below.

13. It was not until years after NG's death that CG, as his widow, was able to obtain relief from Congress for the debts he had guaranteed for Banks et al. (See especially the notes at NG to Collett, 8 August 1784, and Pendleton to NG, 10 November 1784, both above.)

14. This was presumably for slaves previously purchased for NG from the firm of Gervais & Owen. (Saunders to NG, 29 May 1784, above)

15. Marbois replied on 18 May, below, to NG's letter of 15 April, that he had been incorrect in thinking the French government "might purchase the whole Island or a part of it" as a source of timber for its navy.

16. On the bills that Wadsworth had endorsed for Griffin Greene, see especially the note at Griffin Greene to NG, 6 April 1784, above, and Wadsworth to NG, 10 July, below.

17. This was money owed for slaves purchased for NG from David Olyphant. (Pendleton to NG, 30 January 1784, above) NG wrote William Price on 12 August, below, that he had learned "you was about to put my bond in suit given to Doctor Olliphant." (See also Wadsworth to NG, 10 July, below.)

18. See above, Pettit to NG, 19 February 1784, and note 9 of the present letter.

*   *   *

¶ [FROM FRANCIS PHILLIP FATIO, [St. Augustine, East Florida, after 24 April 1785.][1] He received NG's letter of 24 April [not found] "somewhat late," from "by Mr Lewis Newhouse instead of Mr Borel." Thanks NG "for having brought me to his acquaintance"; hopes to "have some good bussiness" with him.[2] Fatio reports: "We are still without money & of course all Dull—man, women, & all kind of Bussiness. I won't enlarge on this distressfull topic, you can't form too bad an Idea of our present Situation." He feels very much "for the Chicanes d'Allemand" with which NG's "ungratefull countrymen have plagued" him.[3] Adds: "If I had not been on the other side of the question I could or would have devoted them to some infernal duties. It would ill become me to give them some of Tristram Shandy's elegant curses as extracted from the Roman Breviary. But that don't prevent my sharing with you part of your just ressentment—no more about it."[4] They are "still in the dark" about "this province"; the "Dispatches from Madrid are all gone to Count Galvez at Mexico—even those for E Florida."[5] Fatio writes that "by the quickness of the Spanish motions, we may expect in the year & day the promulgation of all those fine priviledges granted in August 1784 to their new acquired provinces E & W Florida." If "trade is once reinstated" there "by the arrival of the dollars," and Havana is "set at work again," Fatio believes "a great deal of good bussiness can & may be done, by vessels of our own." He has purchased "a large Sloop" but considers it "too small." This vessel has a "British register," though, which "will suit if we touch at Jamaica." He believes Cumberland Island "will be a propitious harbour in some critical moment," but there are people there now who destroy NG's "timber near at hand" and "encroach" on his rights.[6] After the British fleet leaves, Fatio will "visit St Mary" on business; if NG is also there, they can view NG's "Dukedom with some good designs.[7] There will be some works on our [i.e., the Spanish] side very soon, and a marine establishment, a frigate, some Gallies, & gun boats. They are granted but not arrived."[8] The governor is also pressuring his "court" to "make on Amelia a Capital Settlement & to give up St Augustin for a state prison." This should "Suit" NG, and "Any friend or friends you shall recomand me, will be received well with an addition for the great regard I have for what merit they carry in mentioning to me, such pleasing remembrance-our unexpected Acquaintance.[9] You Sir a Great General & the second Saviour of his Country and I, an Atom—vegetating in the desert of Florida and of no consequence in the World." Fatio's family was happy to read "the paragraph" in which NG mentioned "their names so kindly"; they send their "best wishes" and hope to see NG "extricated" from his "undesserved embarrassments."[10] Mr. Fleming, "our dear doctor," also wishes to be remembered to NG. He is now "a Merchant & a Physician of great renown at the Havannah."[11] Fatio, who has written to him "fully on both capacitys, with a few straggled words of Latin," is now "going to answer one of the most curious production[s] of genius—in his [i.e., Fleming's] way, which I have received a few days ago from the Havannah, which he describe[s as] gloomy & far from inviting. The characters that he delineate[s] are unpleasing and please God— untrue or too much Outré, No Confidence, no trust—very little honour—no money, no business and a great deal of Cheat & trumpery. Yet he does very well, is well suported as well recomanded & has obtained all he petitioned." Fatio has two letters "in hand" for "Mr George Crimen," who, he hears, has "gone to Mexico with Count Galvez"; will send them to Havana for forwarding to NG's "friend" in Mexico.[12] If any letters arrive for NG from Havana, Fatio will take care of them. RCS (NcD) 3pp.]

1. This letter, which is docketed "1785," is a reply to one that NG wrote to Fatio on 24 April.

2. Newhouse, to whom Fatio presumably referred here, has not been identified. NG had discussed the possibility of commercial ventures with Fatio, a resident of East Florida, during his trip to St. Augustine in March. (NG to Fatio, 6 April, above)

3. The source of the phrase, meaning German chicanery, that Fatio used here is not known.

4. *Tristram Shandy*, by Laurence Sterne, was NG's favorite book. (Vol. 4: 345n, above)

5. Bernardo de Gálvez, had recently been appointed viceroy of Mexico. (See NG to Zéspedes, 26 March, above.)

6. On the cutting of timber on Cumberland Island by Loyalist refugees, see NG to Bowman, 10 September 1784, above.

7. NG died in June 1786, before he could visit Cumberland Island again.

8. The St. Marys River was the boundary between the United States and East Florida. The Spanish provincial government evidently planned to erect fortifications on its side of the river and to station additional naval defenses there.

9. On Amelia Island, directly opposite Cumberland Island, on what was then the East Florida side of the mouth of the St. Marys River, see also Fatio to NG, 6 April; NG to CG, 14 April; and NG to Wadsworth, 24 April, all above. In the letter to Jeremiah Wadsworth, NG also mentioned—incorrectly—that the colonial capital might be moved to Amelia Island from St. Augustine.

10. Fatio's immediate family apparently consisted of his wife and a daughter, Sophia. (Fatio to NG, 6 April and 5 December, below)

11. NG had stayed with Dr. George Fleming during his visit to St. Augustine. As noted at NG to Zéspedes, 26 March, Fleming eventually married Fatio's daughter.

12. Nothing is known about "George Crimen" or NG's "friend" in Mexico.

*　　　*　　　*

To George Washington

Dear Sir　　　　　　　　　　　　　　　　　Charleston April 25th 1785

Some little time ago Capt. Gunn formerly an officer in the horse sent me a challenge to fight him upon the footing of equality as Citizens. His reasons for it are he says I injured him in a tryal while I was in command in this Country. He sold a public horse and was called to account for it. To avoid breaking him I refered the matter to a board of Officers in preference to a Court Martial. I was at the time charitably disposd to think he had done the thing partly through ignorance. His pretence was that the public owed him a horse and that he thought he had a right to sell their property to pay himself. Such a precedent in our service would have given a fatal stab to the very existence of the Army, for soldiers might with the same propriety sell their Arms as Officers their horses. But to my very great surprise the Board of Officers reported that Captain Gunn had a right to sell a public horse. I disapproved of the opinion of the board in General Orders and refered the matter to Congress. They also condemned the proceedings of the board, confirmed my sentiments on the subject, and pointedly censured Capt Gunn and directed him to return the horse. Capt Gunn thought himself injured because I did not confirm the opinion of the board of officers and urged it very indecently both by letter and language for which I gave him a reprimand. It is for this he says he thinks himself entitled to satisfaction affecting to discriminate what was in the line of my duty as an officer and what was other wise. I refused to give him any satisfaction having done nothing more than my public duty imposed upon me in support of the dicipline of the Army. If a commanding Officer is bound to give satisfaction to every Officer who may pretend he is injured and this pretence would not be wanting to try to wipe off the disgrace of a public tryal and condemnation, it places him in a much more disagreeable situation than ever had occured to me before. But as I may have mistaken the line of responsibility of a commanding officer I wish for your sentiments on the subject. It is possible you may be placed by the ignorance of sum or the impudence of others in the same predicament tho I believe few will be hardy enough to try such an experiment. If I thought my honor or reputation might suffer in the opinion of the World and more especially with the Military Gentlemen I value life too little to hesitate a moment to answer the challenge. But when I consider the nature of the precedent and the extent of the mischief it may produce I have felt a necessity to reject it. Thus far I have offered nothing but my public reasons; but the man is without reputation or principle. Indeed he is little better than a public nuisance being always engaged in riots and drunken [flaunts?]. I do not wish these circumstances to have any influence upon your Opinion. Because if they were the only objections I would fight him immediately.[1]

I am still embarased with Banks [i.e., John Banks's] affairs and God knows when I shall be other wise. Present me affectionately to Mrs Washington and the family. I am dear Sir with esteem & affection Your Most Obed^t humble Ser^t   NATH GREENE

ALS (Washington Papers: DLC).

1. See James Gunn to NG, 23 February, 24 February, and 2 March; NG to Gunn, 24 February and 2 March, and NG to Jackson, 28 February, all above. In a nineteenth-century treatise on the practice of dueling, Lorenzo Sabine wrote of NG's letter to Washington: "The affair with Gunn evidently gave [NG] much disquiet. His courage had never been doubted. But he dared not act definitely and finally without the assurance of the most illustrious man in history [i.e., Washington], that his 'honor,' his 'reputation,' would not suffer by disregarding the call." Sabine used this example to illustrate how difficult it was for even a "gentleman of Greene's lofty character and standing, in every sense," to reject a challenge, once it had been made. (Lorenzo Sabine, *Notes on Duels and Duelling* [3d ed.; Boston, 1859], p. 190) Washington replied on 20 May, below.

From William Littlefield

Dear General   Newport [R.I.] 25th April 1785

I recd your kind Letter of the 15th of April and am happy to find that you have once more set your face to the Northward and return'd to Charlestown. May fortune favor all your concerns and enable you soon to return with safety to your family & friends at Newport.[1] Mrs Greenes & the Childrens health is a matter of no small weight upon your mind; but permit me to assure you that they all enjoy perfect health.

The Air upon the Hill has been more efficacious than a multitude of Physicians and had she not mov'd from the Point am sure she cou'd not have existed much longer and the whole family was much in the same situation. I suppose e'er this you have heard of her being mov'd into Tillinghast's House.[2] The rent is higher than where she movd from but the situations dont admit of a comparison—the diffirence of rent is 85 dollars which perhaps may appear high at first sight; but when you settle with the Physicians am confident you will more than save that money in Six months.[3] I am every day with Mrs Greene [i.e., CG] but have chang'd my Lodgins since the 10th of March which I presume you have heard of before this. Betsy is in perfect health and loves you dearly. I gave her your Letter—she read it; but not without tears of Gratitude.[4] I thank you ten thousand times for your Good advice. The Letter is laid up amongst Betsys choisest treasures and we are determin'd it shall be our Oracle. I shall not fix upon any plan of business until I see you.[5] Trade wears a Gloomy aspect in this part of the Country and the Merchants are every day failing from some cause or other. The Great scarcity of money I believe is the Great cause. I Lett your farm to Mr [Samuel] Burlinggame agreeably to your directions but have not been able to get any money from him. There was none due for the year 1783, and upon settleing the amt found a small ballance in his favr. He then agree'd to send a hundred dollars to Mrs Greene by the 25th of March which was the time that the rent became due and the other hundred dollars to be laid out in building a Scow agreeably to your directions

House on Mill Street, Newport, Rhode Island, leased to Greene family in 1785
(*Reproduced from* The Remains of Major-General Nathanael Greene
[Providence, R.I.: E. L. Freeman & Sons, 1903])

which will be finished some time in June, but the money has not yet come to hand.[6] The interest which you expected to receive from your State Notes has also failed for when I took them to the Gen[l] Treasurer found the interest paid up to the first day of March 1785, so that you can't receive any thing on their acc[t] until the 1st day of March 1786.[7] M[rs] Greene has rec[d] part of the money left in Jacobs Greenes hands and I have been able to supply her with a little which I rec[d] out of the Gen[l] Treasurer and which dont exceed Ten or Twelve pounds or there abouts and have not borrowed a dollar of any body else. Doct[r] [Isaac] Senter was kind enough to offer her Ten or Twelve Guineas the other day which I beleive she must accept and which I am in hopes will suffice her un[t]il your return.[8] There is some considerable bills against her but beleive no body will press very hard for their money until your return.[9]

There is no news worth communicating. We are all in prefect [i.e., perfect] peace and quietness no body troubles their heads about politics. Gen[l] Election is near & the Prox stands as usual[10] except the Delegates for Congress which are as follows Viz[t] M[r] John Brown[,] M[r] Paul Mumford[,] M[r] Ge[o] Champlin[,] M[r] Peter Phillips.[11]

M[rs] Littlefield joins in presenting her love & beleive me to be D[r] Gen[l] your Ob[dt] hbl Serv[t]   W: LITTLEFIELD

RCS (CtY).

1. NG's letter of 15 April to Littlefield, CG's brother, has not been found. NG had returned to Charleston, S.C., from Georgia and East Florida when he wrote that letter. (NG to CG, 14 April, above) He arrived in Newport in late June. (See note at NG to CG, 25 May, below.)

2. When she moved to Newport in the late summer of 1783, CG had rented a house in the Point neighborhood, near the harbor. (NG to Jacob Greene, 17 June and 27 November 1783, both above) The house to which she moved ca. March 1785 was a "fine Georgian house" that had been the home of John Tillinghast, "a wealthy merchant and shipowner who became heavily involved in privateering." It was located on Mill Street on the "Hill," overlooking the town. ("Historic Hill Architectural Survey," RNHi)

3. The additional rent was presumably per year. Littlefield meant here that the new location was healthier and that there should therefore be fewer physicians' bills to pay.

4. Littlefield had married Elizabeth Brinley of Newport on 11 March 1785. (Mason, *Annals of Trinity Church*, p. 170; see also Littlefield to NG, 11 December, below.)

5. Littlefield was still pondering his "plan of business" after NG left Newport to settle in Georgia. (See his letter to NG of 11 December, below.)

6. On the leasing of NG's farm in Westerley, R.I., see Christopher Greene to NG, 26 March 1784, above. It is not known whether the scow was completed.

7. For background, see Bourne to NG, 20 March 1784, above.

8. Senter was the Greene family physician.

9. As an example of someone "pressing" for the payment of bills after NG's return to Newport, see Barbara Bently to NG, 1 September, below.

10. In Rhode Island elections, a prox was originally the paper on which the names of the candidates voted for were listed. In time, the term came to be applied to the list of candidates put forward by different political parties. (Arnold, *R.I.*, 2: 560–61n) For a list of candidates elected to statewide posts in the 1785 election, see *Providence Gazette*, 7 May. NG's kinsman William Greene was again elected governor. (Ibid.)

11. During its May session, the Rhode Island legislature elected these four men to represent the state in Congress. (Bartlett, *Records of R.I.*, 10: 94)

From Nathaniel Pendleton

D[r] General   Savannah [Ga.] April 25th 1785.

I was much disappointed when upon my return from the Circuit I found you had passed on to Charleston [S.C.].[1] I wished to have the pleasure of seeing you again before your return to y[e] Northward, and I also wished for farther instructions relative to the mortgage you proposed for the Holland loan; and also the business of fixing the property of Cumberland Island.[2]

The Conversation we had upon the subject of the mortgage for the loan, having been so slight, just before your Departure, & not receiving any letter from you, upon my arrival has induced me to suppose you have either changed, or perhaps relinquished your plan, and in that case the trouble and expence of getting the necessary certificates, and writings properly authenticated, might be saved; I have therefore postponed it till I hear farther from you.[3] I was much pleased with the idea of the loan; I know of nothing that could be more beneficial to this Country, or to the individuals concerned, and I was, as you may remember, perfectly convinced it was practicable. This opinion is now confirmed by letters from Major [Pierce] Butler. He has written to M^r [John] McQueen, in the strongest terms to go to Holland, and that he will certainly succeed to the utmost of his wishes, upon the terms he mentions, and he advises McQueen by all means, if possible to join with several landed Gentlemen upon the same plan. M^r McQueen has shewn me Butler's letter and informs me he has determined to make the Experiment. I mentioned to him the offer you had received of a loan, and, that you meant to accept it, and advised him, as the surest means of success to both, to join your views and interest, and to associate Eight, or ten other Gentlemen of this State and Carolina who might be desirous of a similar plan.

From what you said when here, I was of opinion this scheme was what you wished to have adopted, and if so, this is the fairest occasion that will perhaps ever again present itself, to carry it into Execution. It will interfere very little with your other S[c]hemes to remain two or three weeks longer, which would be time, fully sufficient to compleat the business; and McQueen is so anxious that he proposes, and is in hopes he shall be ready, to Sail in a month. He is determined at any rate to go himself, and writes to you, and has requested me also to mention it, that if you have it in view to obtain a loan he will either join you, or negociate yours seperately as you think fit. He makes this offer he says, because he hopes you are of opinion his friendship for you would induce him to be more Zealous for you, than Brokers, whom he supposes you mean to employ. I am convinced he would exert himself as much in your interest as he would in his own. You will judge whether this Offer is not too advantageous to be rejected, and if so, you will not hesitate I imagine to return here for a few days, in which time the business might be compleated. If you should think proper to come into this plan, it would probably be well to speak to three or four Gentlemen in Carolina, of whom there are I dare say several who would be desireous of such a plan. Authenticated certificates from both States, would give weight and consequence to the proposals; and Butler advises that Commodore [Alexander] Gillon and Bourdeaux be engaged to facilitate the plan, and be of the number of the appraisers. This plan will certainly make the fortune of all who engage in it. McQueen means to mortgage his whole estate, and strongly recommends your doing the same. You are the best Judge.[4]

I feel much embarrassed to know in what manner to come at the absolute Estate of Cumberland Island. Our Cheif Justice [George Walton] has decided that under the Constitution, no proceedings in Chancery can be admitted, so that, we have no established mode to proceed in, to foreclose the Equity of Redemption on Mortgages. The Strong reason of the thing will certainly find out a mode sooner or later, but as yet we have none. It is my Opinion the safest method would be take the Debt, upon yourself and get a release from Banks of the equity of Redemption.[5]

Health & Happiness attend you my Dear General & best friend. Should I not see you again, give my Affectionate respects to M[rs] Green. Tell her I am very desireous of giving her an Opportunity to laugh at me, for my former follies.[6] Yours ever NATH[l] PENDLETON

RCS (NcD).

1. Pendleton, who was now a lawyer, had presumably been on a "Circuit" of Georgia courts. On NG's return to Charleston, S.C., from Savannah, see note at Fatio to NG, 6 April, above.

2. NG wrote to the Dutch firm of Wilhem & Jan Willink about this time, expressing an interest in using his Mulberry Grove, Ga., plantation as collateral for a loan and indicating that he would send "the Necessary vouchers for the purpose." (See Willinks to NG, 8 July, below.) It appears from NG's letter to Jeremiah Wadsworth of 17 February, above, that he hoped to use the loan, at least in part, to "improve the purchace" he was making of an undivided half share of much of Cumberland Island, Ga. (See also Morris to NG, 15 March, above.) Near the end of the present letter, Pendleton advised NG to "take the Debt" for Cumberland Island upon himself "and get a release from [Henry] Banks of the equity of Redemption." (For background on NG's Cumberland Island claim, see note at Hyrne to Clay, 26 November 1783, above; as noted there, NG did obtain a release from Banks.)

3. NG's reply has not been found, but he did have Pendleton work on getting the necessary papers together. (Pendleton to NG, 23 September, below) Meanwhile, the Willinks wrote NG on 8 July that because of current financial conditions they were unable to offer a loan at that time but might be able to consider one in the future after examining and approving NG's "Vouchers." NG wrote to them again on this subject on 7 January 1786, below. As noted at Morris to NG, 12 July 1784, above, NG did not obtain a loan from the Willinks.

4. Pendleton wrote NG on 23 September: "M[r] M[c]Queen is preparing and will go to New York in two or three Weeks, and from there to England, or rather to France." On McQueen's purposes in going to Europe, see ibid., as well as McQueen to NG, 23 May, and NG's letters of 1 June to Thomas Jefferson and the Marquis de Lafayette, all below.) As seen in McQueen's letter, NG did not take part in a joint effort to obtain a loan. The "offer" that Pendleton referred to here may have been the suggestion in Robert Morris's letter of 15 March about the possibility of NG's obtaining a loan from the Willinks.

5. See note 2, above.

6. On Pendleton's "former follies," see, for example, the note at his letter to NG of 30 January 1784, above.

To William Gibbons, Jr.

Dear Sir   Charleston [S.C.] April 26th 1785

When I left Savannah I expected I had provided for the payment of M[r] Clays [i.e., Joseph Clay's?] and M[r] Roberts accounts.[1] But by a letter I got a few days ago from the house of William Pearce and Company I find the conditions of the sales of my crop has been so mistaken between us that I am obliged to re[qu]est M[r] Clay and M[r] Roberts to let their ballances stand until my next Crop and for which indulgence I will allow them the interest and they shall be paid out of the first of the Crop.[2] If this is not agreeable to one or both of them please to advise me and I will try to negotiate some other mode of payment. The mistake between me and the house of Pearce & Comp involves me in much perplexity; but I had rather subject my self to any inconvenience than have any dispute on the subject.[3]

The more I have thought on the crop at Mulberry Grove falling so much short of your expectation who is so good a judge the more I am convinced of the necessity of inq[uiring] into the matter. If Mr Rob[erts] has sufferd the Rice to be stolen away or wasted it in any improper manner he ought to be accountable. He certainly cannot be intitled to his wages unless he performs the duty expected from him. To say the Negroes stole the Rice only proves inattention in him. But I wish not to judge hardly of the man and only mean for you to satisfy your self that all is right; of which I have my doubts.[4] Please to let me hear from you as soon as possible. I am dear Sir with esteem & regard Your Most Obed[t] humble Serv[t]   NATH GREENE

ALS (CSmH).
1. On NG's departure from Savannah, see note at Fatio to NG, 6 April, above. It appears from Pierce to NG, 13 May, and NG to Pierce, 17 May, both below, that Roberts was the overseer of Mulberry Grove, NG's Georgia plantation.
2. The firm of NG's former aide William Pierce, Jr., was handling the sale of the rice crop from NG's Mulberry Grove plantation. On 8 April, above, Pierce & Company had written NG that the crop there was so meager that they were unable to "discharge our store debt, and what we have engaged to pay for you."
3. For more about the "mistake" between NG and Pierce's firm, see below, Pierce to NG, 13 May, and NG to Pierce, 17 May.
4. No reply to the present letter has been found. Pierce wrote NG on 13 May: "Instead of the 160 Bar[l s] which Roberts had promised that there was no lik[e]lihood of getting more than 60 or 70."

*   *   *

¶ [FROM JOSEPH WEBB, Wethersfield, Conn., 2 May 1785. Following up on a letter about "Hides" [not found] that he wrote soon after NG was there, Webb adds that "Two thousand Pensicola Hides woud be a most capital affair to my family."[1] He wishes that NG could ship him "Three or four Hundred or Even a thousand" of them during the summer "on my Acc[t] Risque," for which Webb will remit some "Cargo" or send cash; the latter must be "raised by sending some Cargo abroad," as "there is no Cash left in this part of the world." Adds: "Our little cursed small Beer people have so arranged & discour[a]ged Trade Liberality together with Every other bad management that the times through out N England are wretched. Congress have no power, something must be done upon the broader base." If NG can ship the hides, he will "render me more real service than all Congress can do." [Jeremiah] Wadsworth is "at Home & well" and reports that "All friends are well" at Newport, R.I. Webb would like "a line" from NG but would be happy just to hear that "a Quanity of Hides was already Shipt or Bargain^d for." Asks for particulars as to the size of vessel needed for shipping them.[2] RCS (CtY) 2 pp.]

1. It is not known when NG visited Webb. On Webb's tannery at Wethersfield, see his letter to NG of 17 November 1779, above (vol. 5: 94).

2. NG's reply has not been found.

¶ [FROM JEREMIAH WADSWORTH, Hartford, Conn., 6 May 1785. Since his last letter to NG—in reply to NG's from Savannah, Ga.[1]—Wadsworth has spent a day at Newport, R.I., where he found CG "in a good House pleasantly Situated" and "in tollerable health, much better than when at ye point."[2] He is sending this letter "by a Vessel which comes to Charlestown [S.C.] with a Cargo of fine fat Cattle & a few Horses"; would like to sell the vessel, as well as the cargo, because his "trade is so Cramped" that he does not "want Vessels."[3] He and [John Barker] Church, who are about to "close our matters," have had "many disagreeable losses and doubtfull debts."[4] The affair with Mason & Malbone in Newport remains as Wadsworth left it the previous fall, and "Reeds & Adams at Providence [R.I.] & Uxbridge [Mass.] owe £1200." Wadsworth adds: "Adams broke[,] ye Reeds have convey'd away their Estate, in a word Credit here is all gone." It will thus be difficult for him to pay NG's draft, "but if it comes," he "will do it."[5] B[arnabas] D[eane] & Company "will suffer a loss in ye Debt of Reynoldses[;] Of about ¾ of ye whole debt the rest of the Stock will turn out nearly as formerly Estimated." There has been a "severe flood" in "the Distillery," but he hopes no "material injury" will result. He considers the partnership with Deane to have been terminated at the time he assumed NG's share; supposes that NG is in agreement. Adds: "I mention this that in case of accident In that business & You or I shoud drop away, their may be no dispute." The distillery would be "a tollerable business" if they could sell the rum, but there is "a poor Market" for it, and it is now difficult to "buy ordinary Horses with it for ye French Market."[6] Wadsworth has just received a letter from St. John, the French consul, "who has obtained leave to go to France for Six Months." St. John is "sanguine" about the live oak on Cumberland Island, Ga., and "from his industry & assiduity," Wadsworth has no doubt that he will obtain orders from the French court "to Contract for quantities"; NG should therefore provide particulars about "Size quantity &c," as well as information about "ye Water Harbors & Size of ye Timber" on the island.[7] Wadsworth does not doubt that with Lafayette's assistance, "something very important will be done."[8] He reiterates that he wants to sell the vessel that carries this letter; if it cannot be sold, he expects it to go to Turks Island for salt, and it might also "do for ye timber trade from Cumber^d Iseland." If NG can use the vessel, "she will be Cheep as we want to be rid of her."[9] Wadsworth concludes: "New York have rejected ye impost and we are now all afloat. I am in our [i.e., the Connecticut] legislature and foresee much trouble."[10] RCS (CtHi) 4 pp.]

1. See above, NG to Wadsworth, 8 March, and Wadsworth to NG, 10 April.

2. On CG's move from "the Point" section of Newport to a house at a higher elevation, see Littlefield to NG, 25 April, above.

3. According to his biographer, Wadsworth did continue to buy and sell vessels at this time. (Destler, "Wadsworth," pp. 258–59)

4. On Church, a longtime business partner of Wadsworth's, see also Wadsworth to NG, 21 December 1783, above. Wadsworth wrote NG on 3 July, below, that he expected to close their affairs the next week.

5. Mason & Malbone were merchants in Newport. (*Newport Mercury*, 7 May); nothing is known about the situation of "Reeds & Adams." In a letter of 12 May, below, NG informed Wadsworth that he had drawn on him for $300.

6. NG, who had been a partner with Wadsworth and Deane in this firm, sold his share to Wadsworth at the end of 1784. (NG to Wadsworth, 29 December 1784, above; the results of the settlement are noted there. For more about the partnership, see, for example, Deane to NG, 5 January 1784, above.) On 5 September, below, Wadsworth sent NG "the Papers necessary for closeing [*damaged*] the Barnabas Deane & Co concern." Although the partnership was dissolved as far as NG's involvement in it was concerned, Barnabas Deane & Company remained in business, with Wadsworth as three-fifths owner and Deane as manager. (Destler, "Wadsworth," p. 258) The rum distillery was in Hartford. (Deane to NG, 7 November 1781 [vol. 9: 542–43], and 5 January 1784) The "French Market" was in the West Indies, where the company's vessels brought livestock, produce, and other items to exchange for products including the molasses used in making rum. (Destler, "Wadsworth," pp. 257–58) In his letter to NG of 5 September, Wadsworth reported that the distillery was worth less then than when it was built during the war.

7. On Michel-Guillaume St. John Crèvecoeur, the French consul at New York, see note at his letter to NG of 30 November 1783, above. It is not known whether he tried to obtain any orders at the French court for live oak from NG's holdings on Cumberland Island. Wadsworth had not yet received his copy of NG's letter to the Marquis de Barbé-Marbois, giving detailed information about the island's resources. (The letter to Marbois is above, dated 15 April; see also NG to Wadsworth, 24 April, above.)

8. For an example of the Marquis de Lafayette's efforts to assist with sales of Cumberland Island timber in France, see his letter to NG at the end of the May documents.

9. No information has been found as to what was done with the vessel.

10. The New York Senate, which in March had rejected the federal impost proposal of 1783, did so again in April "by a greater Majority than before." (William Hindman to William Paca, 18 April, Burnett, *Letters*, 8: 99) It was not until 1786, "[u]nder heavy pressure," that New York "at last granted the impost, but with unacceptable conditions." (Ferguson, *Power of the Purse*, p. 240)

¶ [FROM PETER BARD, Savannah, Ga., 8 May 1785. Since writing to NG "a few weeks ago," he has received "Several verry interesting pieces of information from the Southward" and has decided to visit Cumberland Island; will "Set out in four or five days for the purpose of making Some Observations on the Situation and trade which may be Carried on there."[1] The "Distress" they have endured "by the Universal failure of the Contracts of our Customers" has obliged them to "look around for Some Spot to Vend the Goods" that they expect from England so as to "discharge the debt" they have contracted "without injury" to their credit. If the "prospects at Cumberland any ways answer the accounts" he has heard, Bard will "undoubtedly make a beginning there."[2] There is reason to believe that Mr. Semple "will not long be Capable of doing business," and if there is an opening, they would like to take advantage of it. They will be happy if NG approves of their plan, and if he has the "least inclination" to be part of the venture, it will always be in his "Power" to do so.[3] Mr. Osborne left Savannah the day before without hearing from NG and has been "verry impatient." If NG's "commands for him arrive" before Bard leaves Savannah, Bard will "Convey them" to Osborne.[4] RCS (MiU-C) 2 pp.]

1. Bard wrote to NG on 9 March, above. The information he had received "from the Southward" since then apparently pertained in some way to Cumberland Island.

2. Bard and others purchased about 4,000 acres "on Crooked River" and began a "trading scheme" with Indians. (Hawkins to NG, 24 June, below) The Crooked River, in southern Georgia, empties into the ocean near Cumberland Island.

3. Alexander Semple had opened a "store" on Cumberland Island. (NG to Wadsworth, 8 March, above)

4. Henry Osborne had written NG on 23 April, above, to inquire about NG's plans for the settlement of Cumberland Island. NG wrote to Osborne on 9 June, but the letter has not been found. (Osborne to NG, 30 August, below)

¶ [TO JEREMIAH WADSWORTH. From "Plantation near Parkers Ferry," S.C., 11 May 1785.[1] NG received Wadsworth's letter "by Captain Tinker just before I left Town."[2] As the captain was planning to "sail again next Thursday," NG writes "only a line of acknowledgement."[3] He has sent a "description of Cumberland to Marbois" and has enclosed a copy of it to Wadsworth.[4] He comments: "If I can dispose of my Northern property and get free from Banks [i.e., John Banks's] creditors without great loss I am not very anxious about selling more than one quarter more than I have good offers for here."[5] He expects to see Wadsworth soon and will tell him "more about the matter."[6] ALS (CtY) 1 p.]

1. NG was at Boone's Barony, his plantation in South Carolina. (NG to Wadsworth, 13 May, below)

2. This was most likely Wadsworth's letter of 10 April, above. It is not known when NG left "Town," i.e., Charleston. His most recent letter that has been found was to William Gibbons, 26 April, above, written from Charleston, and he was back there on 12 May. (See the letter immediately below.)

3. A note on the outside of this letter reads: "To be put on board of Capt Tinker bound for New York." By "next Thursday," NG probably meant the next day, 12 May. (See NG to Wadsworth, 13 May, below.)

4. In his letter of 10 April, Wadsworth had asked for a "particular Account" of Cumberland Island, Ga. (See also Wadsworth to NG, 21 and 23 February and 4 March, all above.) NG wrote his "description of Cumberland" for the Marquis de Barbé-Marbois on 15 April and sent a copy of it with his letter to Wadsworth of 24 April. (Both letters are above.)

5. NG wrote Marbois on 15 April that he would gladly keep as much property on Cumberland Island as he could. As noted at NG to Collett, 8 August 1784, and Pendleton to NG, 10 November 1784, both above, NG did not "get free from Banks creditors" during his lifetime. On the "Northern property" that he hoped Wadsworth could sell for him, see the powers of attorney that NG gave Wadsworth on 26 March, above, and 16 August, below. It is not known who made the "good offers" to invest in Cumberland Island, but NG had also informed Marbois that he had "several offers for this purchase." (NG to Marbois, 15 April)

6. It does not appear that NG saw Wadsworth again.

¶ [TO GOVERNOR GEORGE CLINTON OF NEW YORK. From Charleston, S.C., 12 May 1785. Introduces the bearer, a "Mr Philips a Gentleman of fortune and a Planter upon the Island of St Kitts." During the war, Philips was "a British American being originally a Native of Virginia." NG recommends him to Clinton's "Civilities." ALS (ICHi) 1 p.]

¶ [TO WILLIAM GIBBONS, JR. From Charleston, S.C., 12 May 1785. NG has been told that Gibbons is "reduced to the necessity of borrowing Corn for the use of the plantation" and is "mortified to think you are put to this trouble." NG has sent fifty bushels and asks Gibbons to let him know "the least you can do with"; will send it from Charleston if Gibbons is uncertain of getting it in Georgia.[1] NG is also sending $50 "for fear that you should be subject to inconveniences"; asks "if more will be necessary."[2] Also asks him not to "let the matter between me & Gibbons come on until my return which will be in October or November."[3] NG is hoping for a good crop "and that the Carpenters will put the buildings in good order as I expect to occupy them this Winter with my family."[4] ALS (RHi) 2 pp.]

1. On NG's efforts to procure corn for his Georgia plantation, see Telfair to NG, 16 April, and Forsyth to NG, 22 April, both above.

2. No further communication between Gibbons and NG about the corn has been found.

3. NG referred here to the property dispute between William Gibbons, Sr., and himself. (See above, NG to Gibbons, Sr., 8 March.)

4. NG returned to Georgia with his family the following November to take up residence on Mulberry Grove plantation. (See below, NG to Clarke, 23 November.)

¶ [TO JEREMIAH WADSWORTH. From Charleston, S.C., 12 May 1785.[1] "Agreeable to your permisson," NG has drawn on him "for three hundred Dollars in favor of the honble John Kean esquire Member of Congress."[2] Asks Wadsworth to "honor the draft agreeable to the tenor of the bills."[3] ALS (CtY) 1 p.]

1. A note on the cover indicates that Wadsworth's friend Nathaniel Shaler should open the letter in case of Wadsworth's absence. (See also the letter immediately below.)

2. NG presumably referred to a statement in Wadsworth's letter to him of 4 March, above. Kean, a former commissary with NG's army, was then a delegate to Congress from South Carolina. (*Biog. Directory of S.C. House*, 3: 393)

3. NG mentioned this draft again in the letter immediately below. Wadsworth's reply has not been found.

¶ [TO JEREMIAH WADSWORTH. From Charleston, S.C., 13 May 1785. NG wrote to him "a few days ago" from his plantation but does not know if that letter "got on board the Ship."[1] Since then, NG has heard again from Griffin Greene, who tells him to "rest assured the bills shall be paid." The "Sale of the Ship" [i.e., the *Flora*] has not yet been completed, and the vessel is "reducd in her valuation." NG wishes that Griffin would "compleat her sale even at her present valuation which is 82,000 Livers."[2] Wadsworth "will see the extent and value of the property" from a copy of the letter that NG sent to Marbois.[3] NG's return to the North will be "so much sooner" than he expected that he will not elaborate on that subject until he sees Wadsworth, probably in about a month.[4] NG has drawn a bill on Wadsworth for "three hundred Dollars in favor of the honble John Kean, delagate from this State."[5] He also wrote a note to Wadsworth's friend Mr. [Nathaniel] Shaler "on the letter of Advice," asking him to open that letter if Wadsworth were away.[6] NG adds: "These are the first and only bills I have drawn on you. I fear I shall have to add some more but I am in hopes not many."[7] ALS (CtY) 2 pp.]

1. See NG to Wadsworth, 11 May, above. NG had been at Boone's Barony, his South Carolina plantation.

2. As seen in Wadsworth to NG, 11 July, and NG's reply of 13 July, both below, problems persisted with bills that Griffin Greene had drawn in France. The letter that NG referred to here was presumably Griffin's of 14 December 1784, above. The Marquis de Lafayette wrote NG on 9 February, above, that the "frigat is Sold" to the French government, "some what Under 100,000 livres."

3. On "the extent and value of the property" that NG owned on Cumberland Island,

Ga., see his letter to the Marquis de Barbé-Marbois of 15 April, above. NG sent a copy of that letter with his to Wadsworth of 24 April, above.

4. It does not appear that NG saw Wadsworth again.

5. See also NG to Wadsworth, immediately above.

6. The "letter of Advice" is immediately above.

7. No indication has been found that NG drew bills on Wadsworth again.

* * *

From William Pierce, Jr.

Dr Genl May 13 1785[1]

Your sending our Bills on London, and getting Mr Auldjo without our permission, to credit them, is what I could not have expected. You have done us an injury with our correspondents by it that will require a great deal of explanation to do it away; indeed I know not what will be the consequence. Nothing can exceed my uneasiness upon the occasion.[2]

I shall write you fully when I get to Savannah, but I very much fear we shall be under the necessity of insisting upon your sending another Bill to London to replace it.[3]

Your Rice will amount to very little more than £200, and I have also to inform you that the disappointment [*damaged*] upon us, really has made it, the dearest Rice we have purchased in the State; besides putting us to the expence of sending a Vessel, he did not let us have the last parcel untill the *William* was ten Days on demurrage.[4]

Remember General I told you to the last not to send the Bills before I sent you a Bill of lading. I had heard that instead of the 160 Bar^{l s} which Roberts had promised that there was no lik[e]lihood of getting more than 60 or 70; that circumstances made me press your not sending the Bills before the Bills of lading were signed.[5] I am D^r sir, with much respect Your very ob^t serv^t W^M PIERCE

RCS (MiU-C).

1. As seen in this letter, Pierce was not in Savannah, Ga., his home and place of business.

2. In a letter of 8 April, above, William Pierce & Company informed NG that his rice crop had been a disappointment and asked him "to r[e]turn us the Bills we gave you on London, as what we have in hand will not be sufficient to discharge our store debt and what we have engaged to pay for you."

3. If Pierce wrote such a letter, it has not been found.

4. A vessel on demurrage was one that had overstayed the time allotted for its loading and had thereby incurred a charge to be paid by those responsible for the delay.

5. On Roberts, who was apparently NG's overseer at Mulberry Grove, see also NG to Gibbons, 26 April, above, and NG to Pierce, 17 May, below. The bill of lading, signed by the captain of the vessel, would have attested to the exact amount of rice shipped from NG's plantation. By drawing a sum based on the quantity of rice that he or his overseer expected the plantation to produce, NG would have risked overextending Pierce & Company's credit. In reply to Pierce on 17 May, below, NG denied that he had done so.

* * *

¶ [FROM BENJAMIN EYRE, Philadelphia, 14 May 1785. Acknowledges NG's letter of [11?] April;[1] has been to "Captain Samples [i.e., Semple's] store to settle your business respecting the timber Captain [Alexander] Cain brought here with him." Has seen Cain and "made the demand for the whole of the timber." Cain claimed "he did not know that the timber that was cut belonged to you but would meet me with Mr Sample and settle for it." Col. Thomas "Casdrop," who sold the timber, has promised to give an "account of the amount of sales"; whenever payment can be obtained, Eyre will send the money to Nicholas Hoffman "of New York." If NG has "any account of the Number of pieces of timber or feet," he should send it on "by the first opportunity." NG "may rest assurd" of receiving justice in this matter.[2] Eyre will let NG know when timber can be shipped from Cumberland Island to Philadelphia to NG's "advantage," but "at this present time it will not do."[3] He concludes: "By the papers you will see the Commotions that has arrisen at Boston and the w[h]igs here are determind to support them."[4] RCS (NjP) 2 pp.]

1. NG's letter, which has not been found, was most likely a reply to Eyre's of 7 March, above.

2. In his letter of 7 March, Eyre informed NG that Capt. William Semple had been supervising the cutting of timber on NG's land and that Semple was shipping the lumber to Philadelphia in care of Cain. NG must have asked Eyre, in his reply, to apprehend Semple and Cain and demand restitution for his losses. On Thomas "Casdrop," or Casdorp, see Eyre to NG, 7 March. NG's reply to the present letter has not been found. Hoffman wrote him on 20 October, below, that he had not heard from either Cain or Eyre.

3. In his letter to NG of 7 March, Eyre had written that there was no market for live oak in Philadelphia.

4. In mid-April, Boston merchants published "resolves" in local newspapers regarding "a threatened monopoly of trade by British merchants, agents, and factors, with large importations of British goods." (Burnett, *Letters*, 8: 108n) Rufus King wrote Elbridge Gerry from New York on 1 May: "The resolves of Boston have reached us, and the flame will communicate from State to State. There is a report this evening that a ship is coming up the harbour, which has fled from Boston; if so I believe she will not better her condition. [T]he Whig merchants will make opposition to the landing of her goods." (Ibid., p. 108)

*   *   *

To William Pierce, Jr.

[Charleston, S.C.] May 17th 1785

I have just got your note and am as much surprisd at it as you say you are of my sending the bills. I wish you had been so candid as to have told me before I left Savannah [Ga.] that you meant to stop the bills unless the Rice came up to your former expectation. I could not imagine what you meant by sending me the bill of Lading unless it was to procure the bills acceptance should my letters get to England before yours. And Mr Aldjo writing on the subject I thought was answering all your wishes.[1] My contract with you was expressly this[:] you was to pay sundry accounts and give me a bill for a thousand Dollars and take the crop of Rice at the plantation for 12/6 a hundred. I knew less about the Crop than you did but let it be more or less those were the terms.[2]

Agreeable to your letter of last summer that you would take the Crop if we could agree on terms, I made you the offer on my arrival at Savannah before I had been up to the place. So we agreed and so I calculated.[3] But finding the Crops likely to fall short of both our expectations and knowing how obliging you had been I lessened the bills two hundred Dollars and paid one of the cash Accounts.[4] If you had intended the bills should have depended on the quantity of Rice why did you give them before the Crop was in. You must Naturally have supposed that I should count on those bills and forward letters of Advice. I did so to Mr Pettit that I had sold your house my Crop of Rice and should forward a bill of 800 Dollars. If I had had the most distant Idea that the bills depended on the quantity of Rice I should not have sent letters on the subject.[5] All that you can have any pretence to demand of me is the ballance due you upon the bills and your Original Account supposing the contract out of the question. I am sorry the first contract we ever made we should have so widely mistaken each other. I trust you know me too well to suppose I would seek any mean or pitiful advantages. As it has been a mistake you may put it on any footing you please; but my claim upon the contract is what I have stated and I declare upon my honor that you never gave the most distant hint that the bills were to go forward or not according to the quantity of Rice. If the bills were to depend on the quantity of Rice they ought never to have been given. [From] Your knowing the quantity you had reason to expect and desiring me not to forward the bills without the bill of lading I concluded nothing more could be intended than to procure them Acceptance. Whether the Rice has been dear or cheap is out of the question. The Rice was good and I think the price low. The over seer disappointing you does not make me chargeable. I am not a little vexed with him as well as you.[6] I wish you had been explicit on my return from [St.] Augustine on the bills[;] it would have saved me much Mortification and you no small trouble.[7] Letters are poor things to bring matters to an explanation, I wished to have seen you before you left Johns Island [S.C.].[8] But you must be greatly mistaken about the quantity of Rice. Your letters say 72 Casks and the Casks were upwards of Six hundred neat that at 12/6 and the price of the Casks at 2/ will amount to near three hundred pounds. Let me know your final determination. I will have no dispute on the subject however disagreeable the consequences may be to me.[9]   N GREENE

ADfS (MiU-C).
    1. See Pierce to NG, 13 May, above.
    2. No written contract between Pierce and NG regarding the rice crop from Mulberry Grove plantation in Georgia has been found.
    3. Pierce had written NG on 24 September 1784, above, that he would be interested in NG's "terms" for selling the Mulberry Grove rice crop. If he liked the terms, Pierce wrote,

he would "instantly" pay cash or "Bills on London" for the crop. NG, who left Charleston about the time Pierce wrote that letter, reached an agreement with him in Savannah in February 1785.

4. On NG's disappointing rice crop and its effects on debt payments he had planned to make, see above, his letters of 9 March to Dennis De Berdt and Nicholas Hoffman and of 3 April to De Berdt.

5. NG's letter to Pettit regarding the sale of the rice crop to Pierce & Company has not been found. (See, however, NG to De Berdt, 9 March and 3 April.)

6. On NG's overseer, a Mr. Roberts, see also NG to Gibbons, 26 April, and Pierce to NG, 13 May.

7. NG had returned from a trip to Cumberland Island, Ga., and East Florida in mid-April. (See his letter to CG of 14 April, above.)

8. It is not known when Pierce was at Johns Island.

9. Pierce & Company wrote NG on 9 July, below, that they had drawn on him for £60. Two letters written by Henry Laurens in the late winter and early spring of 1786 indicate that problems resulting from NG's use of the bills he had received from Pierce & Company continued for some time. In one, which Laurens wrote to Pierce & Company from Charleston on 25 February 1786, he reported that he had "lately received" their "Draught dated 7ᵗʰ March 1785 on Messʳˢ James Strachan, James McKenzie and Co: London, payable at sixty days sight, to Nathaniel Green Esqʳ, [on?] order, One hundred and eighty Pounds Sterlᵍ endorsed by NG to Mʳ Dennis Debert, together with an Acct of Protest for Nonpayment, the Amount with charge of Protest, damage & Interest to be adjusted, I presume according to the Custom of your State, for which my Friend requests me to recover an Equivalent, by informing me in what Manner you propose to render Satisfaction, whether by a new Draught which will be most acceptable . . ." (Laurens Papers, ScHi)

In the second letter, dated 20 April 1786, Laurens complained to William Bell that he had received a letter from Pierce & Company "respecting their Protested Bill, containᵍ not a syllable to any good Effect." He had asked them "to inform me in what manner they proposed to render Satisfaction, whether by a new Draught which would be most acceptable to you, or otherwise to which they give as kind of answer, they content themselves with sending me a long Copy of a Letter to their Correspondent in London, tending to prove that a breach of Promise by General Greene, the Endorser of the bill, was the Cause of the Protest." (Ibid.; see also Chesnutt, *Laurens Papers*, 16: 609–10n.)

From the Marquis de Barbé-Marbois

Sir   New York May 18ʰ 1785.
I received the favour of your letter dated the 15ᵗʰ of last month. I am much obliged for the confidential & Satisfactory information it containd, & Shall answer with equal candor.[1] When I applied to Col Wadsworth, I had in contemplations that the King might purchase the whole Island or a part of it for the use of his navy on acccount of the excellent timbers I have heard it produced. Yet by a late instruction from his Maj.'s minister, I am inforem'd that Governement will not adopt the plan. However they will in all probability want timber's from the Island, & especially the live oack.[2] Mʳ De La Fore[s]t the King's Vice-Consul has received directions to transmit full information to the Court as to the quality & price of these timbers, & I Shall be much obliged to you, sir, if you'll let him Know any thing which could pave the way to a

Contract.³ I would have been very glad to be a Joined tenant with you sir; but had my private circumstances allowed it, you'll now conceive there would have been an impropriety in case the Contract Should have been concluded. I have the honour to be with great respect Sir, Your most obᵗ hᵇˡᵉ servant   DE MARBOIS

RCS (MiU-C).

1. At the behest of Jeremiah Wadsworth, NG had sent Marbois a detailed description of Cumberland Island, Ga., and its resources. (NG to Marbois, 15 April, above)

2. The live oak and other timber on Cumberland Island produced superior lumber for shipbuilding. (Ibid.) The king's minister was the French naval minister, the Marquis de Castries. (See NG to Castries, 1 June, below.)

3. On the Chevalier de la Foreste, see note at his letter to NG of 16 December, below. For more about NG's dealings with the French government in regard to the live oak timber on Cumberland Island, see ibid.

From George Washington

My Dʳ Sir   Mount Vernon [Va] 20ᵗʰ May 1785.

After a long & boisterous passage, my nephew G[eorge]. A[ugustine]. Washington returned to this place a few days since & delivered me your letter of the 25ᵗʰ of April.¹

Under the state of the case between you & Capt. Gun[n], I give it as my decided opinion that your honor and reputation will not only stand perfectly acquited for the non-acceptance of his challenge, but that your prudence & judgment would have been condemnable for accepting of it, in the eyes of the world, because if a commanding officer is amenable to private calls for the discharge of public duty, he has a dagger always at his breast, & can turn neither to the right nor to the left without meeting its point. In a word, he is no longer a free Agent in office, as there are few military decisions which are not offensive to one party or the other.

However just Capt. Guns claim upon the public might have been, the mode adopted by him (according to your accoᵗ) to obtain it was to the last degree dangerous. A precedent of the sort once established in the army, would no doubt have been followed, & in that case would unquestionably have produced a revolution, but of a very different kind from that which, happily for America, has prevailed.²

It gives me real concern to find by your letter that you are still embarrassed with the affairs of [John] Banks. I should be glad to hear that the evil is likely to be temporary only, ultimately that you will not suffer. From my Nephews account this man has participated of the qualities of Pandora's box & has spread as many mischiefs. How came so many to be taken in by him? If I recollect right, when I had the pleasure to see you last, you said an offer had been made you of backlands as security or payment in part for your demand. I then advised you to accept it. I now repeat it, you cannot suffer by doing this, altho' the lands may be high rated. If they are good I would almost pledge myself that you will gain more in ten years by the rise in the price, than you could by accumulation of interest.[3]

The Marq[s] de la Fayette is safe arrived in France, & found his Lady & family well.[4] From his letters, those of the Chev[alie][r] de la Luzerne, Count de Rochambeau & others to me dated between the middle & last of Feb[y], I think there will be no war in Europe this year, but some of the most intelligent of these writers are of opinion that the Emperial Court & Russia, will not suffer matters to remain tranquil much longer. The desire of the first to annex the Dutchy of Bavaria to its dominions in exchange for the Austrian possessions in the Netherlands, is very displeasing it seems, to the military powers, which added to other matters may kindle the flames of a general war.[5]

Few matters of domestic nature are worth the relation otherwise I might inform you, that the plan for improving & extending the navigation of this river [the Potomac] has met a favourable beginning. Tuesday last was the day appointed by Law for the subscribers to meet. 250 shares were required by law to constitute and incorporate the company; but, upon comparing the Books, it was found that between four & five hundred shares were subscribed. What has been done respecting the navigation of James River I know not—I fear little.[6]

This State did a handsome thing, & in a handsome manner for me; in each of these navigations they gave me, & my heirs forever, fifty shares; but as it is incompatible with my principles, & contrary to my declarations, I do not mean to accept of them. But how to refuse them, without incurring the charge of disrespect to the Country on the one hand, and an ostentatious display of disinterestedness on my part on the other, I am a little at a loss. Time & the good advice of my friends must aid me, as the Assembly will not meet till Octo[r], & made this gratuitous offer among, if not the last act of the last Session, as if they were determined I should not resolve what to do from the first impulse.[7] M[rs] Washington joins me in every good wish for you, & with sentiments of attachment & regard I am my D[r] sir y[r] aff[e] friend &[c]   G: WASHINGTON

Cy (Washington Papers: DLC).

1. For background on NG's censure of James Gunn for selling a horse belonging to the army—an act that ultimately led Gunn to challenge him to a duel—see above, Gunn's letter to NG of 23 February, NG's reply of the same date, and NG to Jackson, 28 February. In letters of 2 March, above, Gunn formally challenged NG to a duel and NG rejected the challenge.

2. In his letter to Washington of 25 April, above, NG reviewed his reasons for rejecting the findings of a court of inquiry, which in June 1782 had found Gunn's actions blameless. At the time of that inquiry, NG maintained that a precedent would have been established, had he upheld the court's findings, that would have been "productive of great mischief to the Army, and injury to the service." (NG to Benjamin Lincoln, 22 June 1782, above [vol.

11: 358]; the Findings of a Court of Inquiry and NG's Response, both dated 3 June 1782, are in ibid., pp. 286–87.)

3. The day before he wrote his letter of 25 April to Washington, NG commented on "the affairs of Banks" in a letter to Jeremiah Wadsworth. (NG to Wadsworth, 24 April, above) NG had seen Washington at Mount Vernon in November 1784. (NG to Carrington, 10 November 1784, above)

4. On Lafayette's return to France from a tour of America, see note at Lafayette to NG, 25 August 1784, above. Lafayette reported his safe arrival in a letter to Washington of 9 February. (Washington, *Papers*, Confederation Series, 2: 335–36; see also Lafayette's letter to NG of 9 February, above.)

5. In addition to Lafayette's letter of 9 February, Washington had received letters from La Luzerne on 15 February, and from Rochambeau on 24 February. (Washington, *Papers*, Confederation Series, 2: 335–36, 367–68, and 378–79) On the political situation in Europe, see above, Griffin Greene to NG, 2 November 1784, and Butler to NG, 23 December 1784.

6. According to the editors of his papers, Washington at this time was "the leader of a movement to form a public company for improving the navigation of the upper Potomac and linking it with the waters of the Ohio." (Washington, *Papers*, Confederation Series, 2: 86n) A bill authorizing the formation of the Potomac River Company was passed by the Virginia legislature in January 1785, as was one to establish the James River Company. At the Potomac Company's first meeting, which was held at Alexandria on 17 May, Washington was elected the organization's president. (Ibid., pp. 88–89n)

7. Washington had been notified of Virginia's gift of the shares to him in January. (Benjamin Harrison to Washington, 6 January, Washington, *Papers*, Confederation Series, 2: 256–57) As in the present letter to NG, he wrote to several other "friends and former associates expressing in agonizing terms his doubts about the propriety of his accepting the shares." In October, he formally relinquished them. (Ibid., p. 257n)

* * *

¶ **[FROM JOHN McQUEEN,** "Cottage" [Savannah, Ga.?], 23 May 1785.[1] Acknowledges NG's "agreeable favour" by Captain Pinder; is sorry that his own letter did not reach NG sooner.[2] NG's "reasons for not uniting in the loan just now are extremely good," and McQueen is "perfectly satisfyed," although it is "the opinion of some in Carolina that money may be obtained in Holland on the terms mentioned."[3] As Generals [Lachlan] McIntosh and [Anthony] Wayne, along with several others, have "come into the business," McQueen plans to sail "in about three Weeks."[4] He hopes to see the "Minister of Marine of France" and try to make "a very extensive contract for Live Oak Timber," to be delivered "at the Water side on Sappelo or any of the Islands southwardly." Thinks NG and "some other friends will benefit" from this voyage.[5] Although he is acquainted with, and has corresponded with, "the worthy Marquis LeFayett," who "acknowledged some obligations to me on his first arrival in America," McQueen is "fully persuaded" that a letter to Lafayette from NG "woud render me singular services." Asks NG to inform Lafayette that McQueen could "fulfill any contract that I might make for that kind of timber &ᶜ." McQueen would also welcome a "line of introduction to Doctʳ [Benjamin] Franklin or any other friend."[6] In an extended postscript, McQueen sends his regards to Judge [Aedanus] Burke, at whose house NG is reportedly staying.[7] Adds that "Sourby never has made his appearance in this quarter nor has he said a Word on the subject of Cumberland Island," Ga.[8] "Mʳ Pengree," who left "yesterday" after staying in Savannah for "eight days," is "delighted with the treatment he has rec[d] and acknowledges it all" to NG and Col. [Benjamin] Hawkins. Pengree would move "to this part of the country" if he did not expect NG to settle "on Cumberland. He is making a Settlement up S[t] Marys" River; McQueen finds him to be "a pleasing agreeable little fellow."[9] Osborne has been at Cumberland for "some time."[10] McQueen is "exceedingly" distressed by news from his wife that his son John "has an inflamation on his Liver." They are "at Bath drinking the Waters."[11] RCS (NcD) 3 pp.]

1. It appears from evidence in this letter that McQueen was probably in Savannah.

2. Neither letter mentioned here has been found.

3. In a letter to NG of 25 April, above, Nathaniel Pendleton reported that Pierce Butler had urged McQueen to travel to Europe and try to obtain a loan in Holland after putting together a group of investors. Pendleton wrote NG on 23 September, below, that McQueen was also going to Paris to present a gift of some 25,000 acres of land to the Comte D'Estaing from the state of Georgia in appreciation for his war services.

4. Wayne seems only to have considered the idea of entering into a partnership with McQueen. (Nelson, *Wayne*, p. 205) As noted at Morris to NG, 15 March, above, Wayne was unsuccessful in an attempt of his own to borrow working capital for his Georgia plantation from a Dutch firm. McQueen was still preparing to leave for Europe when Pendleton wrote NG on 23 September.

5. NG had also been trying to make a contract with the Marquis de Castries, the French naval minister, to supply timber for the French navy from his holdings on Cumberland Island. (NG to Marbois, 15 April; Marbois to NG, 18 May, both above, and NG to De Castries, 1 June, below) McQueen owned timberland on another Georgia sea island, Sapelo. In his letter of 25 April, Pendleton urged NG to consider joining with McQueen to seek the contract. Over the summer, however, Pendleton apparently changed his mind, for he cautioned NG in his letter of 23 September that McQueen's efforts in Paris could undercut NG's chances of success. Another friend of NG, Benjamin Hawkins, also expressed concerns about a possible union of interests between NG and McQueen. (See note at NG to Lafayette, 1 June, below.)

6. NG distanced himself from any involvement with McQueen in the letters of introduction that he wrote to Lafayette and Thomas Jefferson. (Both are below, dated 1 June.) As seen in Hawkins to NG, 25 June, below, McQueen was unhappy with NG's letter to Lafayette.

7. On Burke, see note at Flagg to NG, 17 October 1783, above.

8. "Sourby" may have been Henry Sonerby, "late of East Florida," whose petition to bring "slaves and effects into this State" had been granted by the Georgia Executive Council in December 1783, "till the meeting of the Legislature." (*Records of Georgia*, 2: 561)

9. Alexander Semple wrote to Gov. Samuel Elbert of Georgia on 18 May, requesting protection from "vagabonds" who were committing depredations along the border with East Florida. This letter was carried by "William Pengree Esq[r]," whose property, consisting "cheifly in Negroes & moveables," was threatened by the interlopers. Semple mentioned that Pengree was also carrying a letter of introduction that NG had written for him. (Lockey, *East Florida*, p. 544; the letter of introduction has not been found.)

10. See Henry Osborne to NG, 23 April, above.

11. On Bath, Va. (now West Va.) as a health resort, see above, vol. 11: 452n.

*   *   *

To Catharine Littlefield Greene

My dear Caty   Charleston [S.C.] May 25th 1785

We often find the pains and pleasures of human life are strangely jumbled together and that nothing is more common than to see people from mixed emotions discover joy and sorrow as the same thing. Nor is any thing more flattering than repeated proofs of affection from those we admire. And few things carry greater conviction of regard than the anxiety at seperation. Tranquility would alarm the heart and suggest what we would not wish to know. It is true anxiety is painful; but the cause in a great degree reconciles us to the thing. At some parts of your letter I was delighted. At others my foolish fondness took some alarm. I wish to see you happy and yet I am sure I should be misserable if I thought you could be so with out me. It is here we feel such a strong tide of mixt emotions springing from the same cause. We cannot see the object of our wishes suffer and not feel upon the occasion Nor can we hear they are happy when we are absent with out mortification and distress. I often suppress my own anxiety at our seperation for fear of wounding the sensibility of your heart and the delicasy of your Nature; but I cannot say but that I should be unhappy if I found you tranquil on the subject. I look forward to the moment of our Meeting with such fervor of affection that the agitations of the soul convulses the man [*illegible*][1]

I live in the great World when absent from you like a Monk in his Cell contemplating my future happiness. Those hours of Reverie afford me the only pleasing sensations which I enjoy. God grant they may be soon reallised by a short passage and happy Meeting.

I am just going into the Country. The heavy Rains have drowned me upwards of Seventy Acres of Rice. The Seasons seem to be at war with the happiness of this Country. I am still in hopes to get in a tolerable Crop. I expected to have planted not less than four hundred Acres of Corn Rice and Potatoes; but I am now a little apprehensive of falling some thing short.[2]

Most of the people of Charleston are gone into the Country. To night is the consort of St Cecelia, but my heart is too heavy to enjoy musick but of the soothing kind.[3] Capt Tom Shubrick is gone to England. Poor fellow, I fear he will never return.[4] Tell Colonel Ward to take a trip to [Carolina?]. Doctor Flagg is confident he will recover his health by it; and has written him a long letter on the subject.[5] Let him shake off old prejudices and try the experiment with out loss of time. The Doctor is quite the fond husband; but looks a little silly at times as if he felt a difficulty in reconciling present appearances with former sentiments.[6] Mr Bee is still in persuit of Mrs Shubrick; but with no better prospects of success.[7] Mrs Morris and Mrs Hambleton are delighted with their little pledges and are quite the Motherly Nurses.[8] Mrs Marshall is as full of warm wishes as ever but no body offers to cool the fire.[9] The family are all well [*one or more pages missing*]

AL (CtY). Incomplete.

1. NG, who had left CG in Newport, R.I., the previous January, traveled home in June, sailing from Charleston in the sloop *Charleston Packet* on the 15th and arriving in Newport on the 25th. (*South-Carolina Gazette and Public Advertiser*, 11–15 June; *Newport Mercury*, 25 June)

2. On NG's disappointing rice crop, see also his letters to George Gibbs of 3 February and to Nicholas Hoffman of 9 March, both above.

3. The St. Cecelia Society, the oldest musical society in America, has been called the "mainstay of Charleston's eighteenth-century musical life." The society was formed in 1762 by a group of " 'gentlemen amateurs,' " who were "supplemented by professional musicians engaged by the season." The organization had flourished during the 1770s, when "its concerts were affairs of great elegance and noteworthy musical interest." (Stanley Sadie, ed., *The New Grove Dictionary of Music and Musicians* [London: MacMillan Publishers, 1980], 4: 158–59)

4. NG's former aide Thomas Shubrick had been ill the previous summer. (NG to CG, 8 September 1784, above) He returned to South Carolina and, as seen above (vol. 9: 271n), lived another fifteen years.

5. NG's friend Samuel Ward, Jr., traveled to Virginia from Rhode Island that fall on NG's behalf. He wrote NG on 11 November, below, that his health was "greatly mended since I left home."

6. On Henry Collins Flagg's marriage, see note at NG to CG, 10 September 1784, above. In a letter to NG of 17 October 1783, above, Flagg had described himself as "truly the old batchelor."

7. Thomas Bee, a former delegate to Congress, was a lawyer in Charleston. His second wife had died in childbirth on 1 June 1784. Bee married Mrs. Susannah Bulline Shubrick in 1786. (*Biog. Directory of S.C. House*, 2: 69–70)

8. NG had written CG on 14 April, above, that "Mrs Morris has got a son." Ann-Barnett Elliott Morris was the wife of Lewis Morris, Jr. Their son, Lewis Morris, was born on 10 March. (*Biog. Directory of S.C. House*, 4: 413) "Mrs. Hambleton" was probably James Hamilton's wife, the former Elisabeth Harleston. (Forsyth to NG, 24 February 1784, above)

9. On "Mrs. Marshall," see Pendleton to NG, 30 January 1784, above.

To Catharine Littlefield Greene

My dear   Charleston [S.C.] May 29th 1785

Perry is arrivd and I expect we shall Sail in ten days or a fortnight. He is loaded with Corn and would have made a good freight but his Corn is a little damaged. However I am in hopes it will not hurt the sail very little.[1] I have just returned from the Country. Our prospects of getting in a good Crop of Rice is better than it was but it is too late in the Season to expect a great or even a good Crop. Tell Betsy Perry is well but he has such an aversion to writing that I dont beleive he will send a letter by this opportunity.[2] I will bring you a Fawn when I come and the Myrtle.[3] This is I suppose for Mrs [Sarah Pope] Redwood. I think I had something like a commision of this sort; but I have had too much perplexity to pay the common civilities of life much less those of gallantry. I will try to make it up by fine speeches; but here I have my doubts. I am but a bad hand at fine sayings and she a woman of too much penetration not to discover true from false coin. However she is but a woman, perhaps her vanity may help me out.[4] Mrs Washington is almost ready to lay in again. What think you of that? And laughs and chuckles at it as if it was the high Road to human felicity. She has a good heart and loves her husband dearly. They may truly be said to be a thriving Couple.[5]

We have just got the news of Mrs Goffs death. I was afraid of the ulcers in her throat. Poor woman her pains must have been greater than her pleasures. I suppose her husband will return here soon, as this event must render the place less agreeable to him.[6] Mrs Ned Rutledge looks like death[.] I have trying to prevail on her to take a trip to Newport; but she is so weded to her husband and Children that even the loss of health or the fears of death cannot seperate her.[7] Give my love to all about you and expect to see me shortly.[8] Yours   NG

ALS (MiU-C).

1. NG's younger brother Perry (b. 1749) had undoubtedly sailed the vessel from Rhode Island. For a biographical sketch, see above, vol. 1: 38n.

2. "Betsy" was Perry Greene's wife, the former Elizabeth Belcher. (Vol. 4: 203n, above)

3. By "Fawn," a yellowish-brown color, and "myrtle," a grayish-green one, NG most likely was referring to fabrics for clothing or for curtains, bed coverings, or other household furnishings that CG may have asked him to find. (See NG to CG, 25 May, above.)

4. On Sarah Pope Redwood, see NG to CG, 21 August 1784, above.

5. Jane Reily Elliott had married William Washington in April 1782; NG reported the birth of their first child in a letter to CG of 4 August 1783, above.

6. Rebecca Gough's death in Newport, R.I., was reported in the local newspaper on 7 May. She was the wife of "John Gough, Esquire, of South Carolina." The report noted that "during her residence at this place," Mrs. Gough had "merited every Mark of Esteem and Friendship from all, who were acquainted with her." Her funeral service was held at Trinity Church, Newport. (*Newport Mercury*, 7 May)

7. "Mrs. Ned Rutledge" was Henrietta Middleton Rutledge, the wife of Edward Rutledge. Although she may have "looked like death" at this time, she lived until 1792. (*Biog. Directory of S.C. House*, 2: 573)

8. As noted at the letter immediately above, NG returned to Newport, R.I., on 25 June.

*   *   *

¶ [FROM THE MARQUIS DE LAFAYETTE, Paris [May 1785?].[1] The Marquis de Castries thanks NG for his letters and will be pleased to "treat With You and Your friends, for the whole, or part of the Articles Mentionned in your letter—particularly masts, Yards, and lumber of a large size."[2] Castries requests an "Account" of what NG will furnish and NG's "proposals thereupon." Lafayette adds: "His determination I will afterwards forward to you with dispatch."[3] Lafayette will not "Set out" until 10 June;[4] a letter to him from NG has "been Announced in ten days" but has "not Yet Come to Hand."[5] NG must have received three letters from him, "pretty much the same."[6] Lafayette sends his "Best compliments" to Mr. and Mrs. Church.[7] Adds in a postscript: "I wish your Health may be Better and permit your travelling."[8] RCS (CtHi) 1 p.]

1. The exact date of this letter is not known, but as Lafayette mentioned that he would be leaving Paris on "10 June," the editors believe he may have written it sometime before the end of May.

2. NG's previous letters to Castries, the French naval minister, have not been found but were undoubtedly concerned with the possibility of the French government purchasing live oak for its navy from Cumberland Island, Ga. In the letter to Castries immediately below, NG made "some propositions for supplying the Navy of France with live oak" but did not include the specific information mentioned here. As seen above in Marbois to NG, 18 May, and below in NG to Foreste, 16 December, and NG to Castries [December 1785?], French officials were interested in purchasing live oak from NG.

3. If Lafayette forwarded Castries's "determination" to NG, the letter has not been found. Lafayette did write NG on 3 December, below, that Castries was interested in purchasing live oak from Cumberland Island on behalf of the French government. (See also NG to Castries, 1 June and [December 1785?], both below.)

4. Lafayette left Paris in June for Lyons "to promote American trade with the local manufacturers." (Idzerda, *Lafayette Papers*, 5: 331n)

5. This may have been NG's letter to Lafayette of 16 March, above.

6. Lafayette is known to have written to NG on 9 February, 16 March, and 16 April, all above.

7. On John Barker Church and his wife, the former Angelica Schuyler, see note at Carter [i.e., Church] to NG, 9 June 1783, above.

8. When he saw Lafayette in New York the previous December (see note at NG to Washington, 2 December 1784, above), NG may have expressed a fear that health problems could keep him from traveling to the South that winter. They did not.

*   *   *

To the Marquis de Castries

Sir   Charleston South Carolinia in America June 1st 1785

I take the liberty to Address your Excellency as well to thank you for your good offices in the sale of the Ship *Flora* in which I was interested[1] as to offer to your consideration some propositions for supplying the Navy of France with live oak. Perhaps the quality and value of this timber with you may not be suffic[i]ently known to impress its importance. Ships built with it have been known to run near forty years with little repairs and the timber still perfectly sound. I am not conversant enough with the expence and inconvenience of naval repairs to estimate the difference between this and common oak. It is certainly the most durable wood in service that has hitherto been discovered and the American Merchants are seeking it from all quarters to build with.

I am proprietor of part of Cumberland Island in the State of Georgia on which there is an immence quantity of this timber and of the best kind. I think its size is equal to the dementions for timber of the first rate line of battle Ships.[2]

The Island forms one part of the entrance into St Marys River which is of easy access and Twenty four feet water on the bar. Shipping the moment they enter the Harbour are perfectly Secure from all stress of weather. The banks of the Island and the debth of water in the harbour are well accomodated for loading a ship with the greatest convenience and dispach. The timber may be cut and got to the landing so as never to detain the Transports.[3] It will be necessary in order to have it cut to work without waste to have a surveyor to superintend the cutting with Moulds and instructions on the subject. Such a person being on the spot can always have the Timber ready for your orders. Should your Excellency think it a national object you shall have the timber on better terms than any set of private Merchants or any other power in Europe. In payment I will take bills for two thirds of the contract and one third in Rum brandy and coarse Woolen Goods. The last I propose as a conveni[enc]ey to his Majesty from the freight to lessen the expence of the transport service.[4]

I have the honor to be known to the Marquis de la Fyette [i.e., Lafayette] and the Chevileur de la Luserne [i.e., La Luzerne] who can inform your Excellency what degree of confidence you may repose in the information I give.[5] I have also had some convers ation with Monsieur La Foret [i.e., the Chevalier de la Foreste,] one of his Majestys Consuls for the Southern States who will give you a more particular history of the business.[6] I have the honor to be with the most profound respect Your Excellency's Most Obedient humble Servt NATH GREENE

ACyS (French Consular Correspondence: DLC).

1. As seen in Lafayette to NG, 9 February, above, the sale of the *Flora* to the French government had apparently been completed.

2. On NG's involvement in Cumberland Island, see note at Hyrne to Clay, 26 November 1783, above. For more about the timber there and its suitability for shipbuilding, see NG to Marbois, 15 April, above.

3. The harbor at the mouth of the St. Marys River was considered one of the best in North America. (See note at NG to Wadsworth, 24 April, above.)

4. On the possible interest of the French government in Cumberland Island and its timber, see Marbois to NG, 18 May, above; Castries to NG, 30 September; Lafayette to NG, 3 December, and Foreste to NG, 16 December, all below. The Marquis de Lafayette wrote NG on 3 December that Castries seemed "better disposed to purchase His naval Strores [i.e., stores] in America than ever He Had Been." No decision had been made by June 1786, however, when NG's death put an apparent end to this matter.

5. On Lafayette's assistance, see, for example, NG's letter to him of this date, below, and Lafayette's letter to NG of 3 December. La Luzerne was the former French minister to the United States.

6. See Foreste to NG, 16 December.

*   *   *

¶ [TO THOMAS JEFFERSON.[1] From Charleston, S.C., 1 June 1785. NG introduces John McQueen, "whose principal errand to Paris is to form a contract for live oak."[2] NG, who has previously written to Jefferson about the subject of live oak, recommends McQueen to Jefferson's "good Offices" but hopes "our propositions may not interfere with each other."[3] McQueen can give "a full history of the politicks of this Country." NG adds: "We are in anxious expectation to have the ultimate determination of the Emperor Joseph and the Court of France respecting the Dutch war."[4] ALS (MiU-C) 2 pp.]

1. Jefferson was the American minister to France. (*DAB*)

2. McQueen wrote NG on 23 May, above, that he was going to Paris to try to obtain a contract with the French navy for the timber that he owned on Sapelo Island, Ga. He asked NG to recommend him to the Marquis de Lafayette, adding that he would also be "glad of a line of introduction" to Benjamin Franklin "or any other friend." (See also NG to Lafayette, immediately below.) Jefferson received this letter on 3 September, but not from McQueen, who was still in the United States at that time. (See Jefferson to NG, 12 January 1786, and Pendleton to NG, 23 September 1785, both below.)

3. NG's previous correspondence with Jefferson on the subject of live oak has not been found. NG was trying to interest the French government in live oak from his holdings on Cumberland Island, Ga. (See NG to Marbois, 15 April, and Marbois to NG, 18 May, both above, and NG to Castries, this date, above.) On the "propositions" referred to here, see NG to Lafayette, immediately below. Jefferson replied to the present letter on 12 January 1786.

4. On the political situation in Europe, see Griffin Greene to NG, 2 November 1784, above.

¶ [TO THE MARQUIS DE LAFAYETTE. From Charleston, S.C., 1 June 1785. In a letter similar to the one immediately above, NG recommends John McQueen to Lafayette's "good offices" and explains the nature of McQueen's business in France.[1] Adds: "All I wish is that his propotitions may not interfere with those of mine which you promised to consult the Minister on last Winter and which has been since repeated by several of your Consuls."[2] ALS (Robert Goldman, 1979) 2 pp.]

1. See McQueen to NG, 23 May, above.

2. NG had been in correspondence with Lafayette about the possibility of selling live oak timber from Cumberland Island, Ga., to the French government. (See above, Lafayette's letters to NG of 16 March and [May 1785?].) The letter in which Lafayette "promised to consult the Minister"—the Marquis de Castries—has not been found, but Lafayette reported in his May letter to NG that Castries was "much Obliged to you for Your Communications, and Will with pleasure treat With You and Your friends." McQueen was traveling to France on personal business and on behalf of the state of Georgia. (McQueen to NG, 23 May; see also Pendleton to NG, 23 September, below.) As McQueen hoped to sell live oak to the French navy from Sapelo Island, Ga., Nathaniel Pendleton later worried that he might attempt to undercut NG's own negotiations with the French government. (Pendleton to NG, 23 September) Benjamin Hawkins wrote NG on 25 June, below, that McQueen thought NG had written the present letter "in a stile of indifference." Hawkins, too, expressed concern that McQueen's business in France "might in some way interfere with" NG's, and he encouraged NG either to "come on some agreement" with McQueen "or convince him (which is hardly possible) that the steps you have taken will have secured you the contract before he could arrive in France."

*   *   *

From James Hunter

Sir   Fredericksburg [Va.] 1 June 1785

I was so much hurt at your saying I was disposing of my Property whilst conveying it to you that I acknowledge, there was no Suffering I would not chearfully have submitted to, rather than have compleated the Mortgage. However I am very glad you are now undeciev'd. Mr Cooper may enjoy the Satisfaction of wishing to have done me an Injury towards you.¹

On advising with my Friends here, they recommend the giving up my Property in Portsmouth and this Town to obtain Relief from the Creditors, Mr Joseph Jones promised to see Col° [Edward] Carrington on the Subject, but the Col° having gone to Philadelphia, and not expected to Return until the 18th of this month, they did not meet. Mr Jones wish'd to acquaint him that he has resumed the Brewery, as I had not paid him, and it should be erased from the mortgage. He then wishd to prevail on him to accede to my Surrender, the other two Properties to the Creditors in general, who otherwise will involve me in Ruin by Confinement, as they are exasperated at my mortgaging to you.²

Mr Henry Banks, not only by Gazette but by Handbills has endeavoured to exculpate himself, and threw an Odium on me, the Letters from himself to his Brother which I have, and [those?] you left with Carrington I hope will allow me to prove him what he really is. His View I know is to get out of the State, and if so, we may give up all Thought of recovering the money left with him by [John?] Burnet. I wonder Forsyth has not been on, I have long heard of his coming, or would have wrote. He should bring Copies of J[ohn] Banks Letters to his Brother [i.e., Henry].³

Henry Banks is at present in Confinement and Keeps me here under a Writ of his against me for £20.000 altho I have not only press'd him by Letter, and thro' Mr Jones and others to appoint any one or two men to receive the Books & settle every Difference, yet nothing but a Publication would content him.⁴ My Friends advise me to procure Certificates from every Gentleman with whom the Company [i.e., Hunter, Banks & Company] have had Connections to prove to the world whether I have acted as became the Merchant^s Integrity, this is what Mr Banks cannot obtain, and I request Sir, that you, who have seen and Known so much of them and me will be so good as to furnish me with your Sentiments, as your Authority will have so much Weight. The stamping John Banks's Memory with the act of Forgery, will be weighed with you in the Scale of Equity when you oppose his Brothers Wishes to injure mine by the most false Aspersions. He has the Insolence to write me that he possess'd a Million of Acres, besides Officers Certificates & other paper Speculations which I hear are to large Amount, and says there is not a man he would sooner assist than myself, and the week after writes as you will see by the Prints.[5]

I have wrote to M[r] [Edward?] Penman to obtain me Certificates from those Merchants in Charleston [S.C.] who were acquainted with our Transactions, and I shall ever gratefully remember your Goodness to assist herein.

Tho' I am reduced to the most abject Poverty at present, depending on my Friends & Relations for my daily Bread, my Situation depriving me of every mode of subsisting by Trade yet I wish to retire from the World with the Good Name I ever endeavoured to Support.

My deceased Relation Left me £1000. clog'd with Conditions which I cannot accede to, indeed he has Claims nearly to that Amount upon H B & C[o] and altho' his whole fortune, was made from our Property, I expect never to receive or be benefitted one Shilling from the Estate. The World is all before me, and If I can only be exonerated from the heavy Claims around me by your acceding to this Surrender, I will labour the rest of my Days with Pleasure to Support my Family as I can.[6] I am very respectfully Sir Your mo. Ob Sr[t]   JAMES HUNTER

RCS (MiU-C).

1. In a letter to Robert Forsyth of 2 October 1784, above, NG had questioned Hunter's "intentions or integrity" in the sale of property in Portsmouth, Va., that he had pledged to NG as "counter security." (On the "counter security," see note at Skipwith to NG, 4 August 1784, above.) When or how NG became "undeciev'd" is not known. He replied to Hunter on 29 August, below: "I am sorry your Creditors impose so unreasonable a requisition on you as giving up my Mortgage."

2. On Edward Carrington's efforts to help NG obtain relief in Virginia from debts he had incurred on behalf of the late John Banks, Banks's former partners, including Hunter, Forsyth, and the late Ichabod Burnet; and Banks's brother and heir Henry, see above, NG to Carrington, 10 November 1784; NG to Henry Banks, after 11 November 1784; and Carrington to NG, 27 February and 23 March 1785.

3. In a lengthy notice in the *Virginia Gazette* of 27 May, Henry Banks denied that he was responsible for the debts of Hunter, Banks & Company and sought to "contradict an insinuation, of my having received from the effects and debts of the Company, considerable sums which have been appropriated to my own purposes." He alleged that Hunter and others formerly associated with the company—especially Isaac Smith and Preeson Bowdoin—were heavily indebted to him and had unscrupulously used him as a "cats paw" in their financial manipulations.

On the Banks brothers' letters that were now in Hunter's possession, see NG to Forsyth, 2 October 1784. On the bills of exchange, see also NG to Forsyth, 5 June, below. NG asked Forsyth in that letter to go to Virginia "as a piece of justice you owe me." Henry Banks, writing on 13 July, below, asked NG to go to Virginia with Forsyth, so "that by a general Investigation I might be able to prove my total Innocence in every step that I have taken." NG wrote Carrington on 29 September, below: "I did all I could to get Forsyth to Virginia but could not. I have laid a state of the whole matter relative to my engagements for that house before Congress and claim their indemnity should I finally suffer greatly in the business." (For NG's appeal to Congress, see his letter to Richard Henry Lee of 22 August, below.)

4. Banks was still in jail when he wrote NG on 13 July.

5. On Banks's land holdings, see his letters to NG of 2 September and 12 November, below, and Forsyth to NG, 18 June 1784, above. On Banks's writings against Hunter in the "Prints," see note 3, above.
6. NG replied to Hunter on 29 August.

To J[ames]. Strachan, J[ames]. Mackenzie & Company

Gentlemen   Charleston [S.C.] June 4ᵗʰ 1785
   I am a stranger to your house and am sorry to be reduced to the necessity of explaining some unhappy mistakes which have happened between the house of William Pearce & Company and my self. I sold them my Crop of Rice in Georgia. For which they agreed to pay sundry Accounts and give me a bill on your house for 800 Dollars. Long before the Crop was beat out they gave me the bills. But when the Crop was beat out, it fell considerable short of their expectation and short of the Amount of the bill & Accounts [by] Sixty or Seventy pounds. They then sent me a request to have the bills returned. But they [i.e., the bills] were gone before then and if they had not been gone they [i.e., the Pierce & Company] were not intitled to the bills but the ballance supposing no special contract had subsisted which was the case.[1] My own standing is secure in the business but as it is a house for whom I have a great esteem I should be sorry if any thing disagreeable should happen upon the occasion. I beg you will therefore honor the bills and if you suffer any inconvenience in the matter I will Settle it to your satisfaction. I beg leave to refer you to Capt Grant for further particulars.[2] I am Gentlemen Your Most Obedt humble Serᵗ   NATH GREENE

ADfS (MiU-C).
   1. For background, see above, NG to De Berdt, 3 and 13 April; Pierce & Company to NG, 8 April; Pierce to NG, 13 May; and NG to Pierce, 17 May. Pierce & Company wrote NG on 9 July, below, that they had drawn on him for £60 sterling.
   2. Strachan, Mackenzie & Company replied to NG on 30 July, below.

To William Semple[1]

Sir   Charleston [S.C.] June 4th 1785
   Your brother on Great Cumberland Island made a purchase of one quarter of my property in that Island, Little Cumberland and a tract I have on Crooked River on Crooked Creek for your house.[2] I wish to hear from you relative to the payments and manner of improving it. I think a most capital branch of business may be prosecuted there and I should like to join in the concern.[3] I mean to reside part of the year at the place my self.[4] I am going for Newport [R.I.] in a few days to which place please to direct your letters.[5] I am Sir with esteem Your Most Obedᵗ humble Serᵗ   NATH GREENE

ALS (PHi).

1. Semple was a Philadelphia merchant. (Eyre to NG, 7 March, above)

2. On William Semple's brother Alexander, see note at NG to Wadsworth, 8 March, above. For background on NG's involvement in Cumberland Island, Ga., see note at Hyrne to Clay, 26 November 1783, above. The circumstances of the purchase referred to here are not known. On the Crooked River, which is on the Georgia mainland, north of, and parallel to, the St. Marys River, see also NG to Marbois, 15 April, above.

3. Henry Osborne wrote NG from Cumberland Island on 30 August, below: "M[r] Semple at Philadelphia has been so much displeased with his brother's conduct here that he has suspended him so that I believe your bargain respecting the Island to be at an end."

4. NG did not visit Cumberland Island again, but his widow, Catharine, moved there with her second husband, Phineas Miller, in 1800 and lived there for the rest of her life. (Stegeman, *Caty*, pp. 173–210)

5. NG left Charleston on 15 June and arrived in Newport on 25 June. (See note at NG to CG, 25 May, above.)

To Robert Forsyth

Dear Sir   Charleston [S.C.] June 5th 1785.

I have got your letter with the inclosed copies of letters which passed between you and Mr. [E. John] Collette. They do not answer my expectation.[1] Greater part of the payments were made before Capt. [Erasmus] Gill made the promise. Such parts as were made afterwards I am in hopes we may secure. But pray how does Capt. Gill get off his promise relative to those payments?[2]

I am going for Newport [R.I.] in a few days.[3] It was my wish to have gone to Virginia with you but as you were not likely to be ready soon I thought I might as well go home.[4] However I hope this will not prevent your going and be assured it is for your interest to go as well as a piece of justice you owe me.[5] All the ballance due your house for the bills put into the hands of Henry Banks [by?] the old house of Hunter Banks & comp. in which are included Smith & Bodwain are accountable as Henry Banks acted for Smith & Bodwain and applyed your funds to the payment of their debts. Those gentlemen have been pushing Henry Banks to get all the property of the old house into their hands and have got a great deal. See them altogether and whatever you recover the whole will be answerable for. Smith & Bodwain are certainly good if none of the rest are.[6] But besides this business which is important there is all the matters in North Carolina which you alone can put into a train are going to ruin.[7] In addition to those considerations let my peculiar distressing situation have some weight with you. Your assurance that you had funds in your hands led me into security, and I hope you will not leave me longer in distress than is unavoidable.[8] You Hunter & Henry Banks perhaps may do much towards depositing such property as will induce Collette to give up my bond. Harris and Blackford [i.e., Blachford] I am in hopes we shall get clear of.[9] On inquiry I found you answerable for Mr. Queens [i.e., John McQueen's] debt and advised [Patrick] Carnes to see [Richard] Lushington and he is accordingly [secured?].[10]

If [John] Ferrie's lands are obtained for Collette whatever you deposit for my bonds will be given up. But as the recovery of those is an uncertain matter I wish you to make provision for any accident which may happen.[11] I am not so anxious for what you will do in the matter but for you to secure all you can from Hunter Henry Banks and Smith & Bodwain. Pursue the whole and I am confident you will get the greater part of the ballance due to your house.[12] Pray do not let trifles prevent your going. Yours aff. N. GREENE

Tr (GWG Transcript: CSmH).

1. Forsyth's letter has not been found. On the debt that NG owed to Collett and others as a result of his guarantee on behalf of the late John Banks, Forsyth, and others, see especially NG to Collett, 8 August 1784, above.

2. Gill's "promise" was probably the one referred to in Forsyth to NG, 18 June 1784, above.

3. As noted at his letter to CG of 25 May, above, NG left Charleston on 15 June and arrived in Newport on 25 June.

4. See Forsyth to NG, 22 April, above.

5. As noted at Hunter to NG, 1 June, above, Forsyth did not go to Virginia.

6. For background, see NG to Forsyth, 25 October 1784, above. (In that letter, NG referred to the firm as "Bradwine & Smith.") Henry Banks wrote NG on 5 August, below: "[Isaac] Smith[,] [Preeson] Bowdoin and [James] Hunter use every finess to draw from me my property in ord[er] that I may thus effect my enlargement." (See also Hunter to NG, 1 June.)

7. On the poor prospects for recovering anything of value from John Banks's estate in North Carolina, see Carrington to NG, 27 February and 23 March, above.

8. Forsyth's "assurance" to NG has not been found.

9. On the eventual settlement of the debts owed to Collett and the firm of Harris & Blachford, see notes at NG to Collett, 8 August 1784, and Pendleton to NG, 10 November 1784, above.

10. On the previously mortgaged slaves whom McQueen and Carnes had purchased from John Banks, see, for example, Pettit to NG, 26 July 1784, above. Lushington had been part of Banks's "Charleston speculation." (NG to Lushington, 28 August 1784, above)

11. See note at Forsyth to NG, 18 June 1784.

12. Forsyth's reply has not been found.

* * *

¶ [FROM THE MARQUIS DE LAFAYETTE, "Chavaniac in Auvergne," France, 12 June 1785. Discusses how "our children ought to be Educated."[1] Teaching them at home "Has an inconvenience," because they might be "Spoiled by the Complasency of Servants." A "school Education," on the other hand, has the "Advantages of Equality, and Concurrence," but contains "a grave danger of tempting the Morals." He adds: "Boys are very forward, and their Company particularly for the Younger ones may Be too instructive." Wishing to "Stear Between" these two options, he proposes [taking?] a house "near to a School," in a university setting, where the boys may "go to the University School, attend at the public lecture, play with the Boys in the proper homes and Return Home to

Do the work that Has Been given at School." During holidays, they could either "walk out of town with other Boys" or go to Lafayette's home, and if either takes sick, Lafayette would have them "attended by the Best phicisian in Paris." He will "conform to Every thing" that NG wishes, for NG will be separated from his son by a great distance.[2] NG has also asked him to hire "a French teacher and musician for the Young Ladies," but Lafayette is "to[o] ticklish" about the choice and will find it difficult to make a decision.[3]

On the situation in Europe, he reports that "The Dutch Arrangement is not quite fixed and it is debated Between three parties the State Holder's[,] the patriots which Borders upon Aristocrasy[,] and the New Raised Democratic party." He does not think "there can be any War this year," but the "present State of Europe Seems to be in a kind of ferment."[4] Lafayette has been visiting manufacturing towns, trying to bring French "merchants and Manufacturers into close Connections" with "American Houses" and "also to find out in what Manner [the French] may obtain favours for the trade of America."[5] Although he has recommended that Gouvion[6] "see Mons Pellitreau and Co[.,] as they are Connected" with NG's cousin [Griffin Greene], he cannot "obtain the order for a Cargoe of Masts and timber untill they Have answers Respecting the Experiments that are to be made in New England and Georgia about [the] woods." Adds: "It is already a Good thing they have Consented to Combat the prejudices which are so favorable to the North of Europe."[7] He hopes that "immediate" steps will be taken in the United States to "pay the public debts, to garrison the frontiers and form Magazines." He warns, though, that "if proper plans are not adopted, America will lack [a] great deal in the opinion of the world." Sends his regards to [James M.] Varnum, the Olney family, Col. [William] Washington, the Rutledge family, Gen. [William] Moultrie, and others. RCS (MiU-C) 4 pp. The manuscript is badly damaged.]

1. NG had agreed to send his son George Washington Greene to France to be educated with Lafayette's son. (Lafayette to NG, 16 April, above) Lafayette wrote Henry Knox on 11 May: "General Greene is So kind as to let me Have His Son to Be educated along with mine. I Cannot Express to You How Happy I am By this mark of his friendship." (Idzerda, *Lafayette Papers*, 5: 322)

2. George Washington Greene was sent to France to study with Lafayette's son in 1788, two years after NG's death. (Ibid., p. 304n)

3. The "Young Ladies" were presumably NG's daughters.

4. On the political situation in Europe, see Griffin Greene to NG, 2 November 1784, above.

5. Lafayette was visiting cities in the south of France, including Nîmes and Lyons. (Idzerda, *Lafayette Papers*, 5: xxv) His purpose was "to acquire some knowledge about our trade centers and our factories, with regard to the United States, and to mention to them the best American concerns, and the articles most in demand in this country [i.e., the United States?], so as to contribute my poor efforts to the extension of our trade with this continent [i.e., North America]." (Lafayette to Pierre-Samuel Du Pont de Nemours, 30 May, ibid., p. 327)

6. Jean-Baptiste de Gouvion had served as commandant of the Continental army's corps of engineers during the war. (Vol. 6: 478n, above) Lafayette asked him to "talk with the merchants of La Rochelle about trade with the United States and especially with the Indians" and also suggested that Gouvion be sent "to Dunkirk for the same purpose." (Lafayette to Du Pont de Nemours, 30 May, Idzerda, *Lafayette Papers*, 5: 327)

7. NG was hoping to sell timber to the French government from his holdings on

Cumberland Island, Ga. (See above, Lafayette to NG, [May 1785?], and NG to Castries, 1 June.) The Marquis de Castries, the French naval minister, was unwilling to sign a contract before he had seen samples. (See Pendleton to NG, 23 September, below.) Northern Europe apparently had been considered the best source of timber for shipbuilding.

*   *   *

From Edward Rutledge

[Charleston, S.C.] Sunday Night [before 13 June 1785][1]
I inclose you my dear Friend, the Will which you wished me this Morning to draw for you.[2] If it shall correspond with your Instructions, Sign, Seal it, in the presence of Three disinterested Witnesses.[3] If not, make the Alterations, & I will throw them into legal forms. It is one of the Wishes of my Heart that, you may live to see all the Objects of your Desires accomplished; & that the Happiness, of your private Life, may be as solid, as your public Life has been conspicuous, & beneficial. I hope with much Sincerity your better Half, for such she must be, whom the Divine Milton calls "God's Last, best Work," may be compensated for her many anxious Hours, in the participation of your Blessings.[4] I am my dear General truly yours   E: RUTLEDGE

RCS (NjP).
1. Rutledge informed NG in this letter that he was enclosing the will that NG had asked him to draw up "this morning." NG did not sign the will until 11 October, below, when he was about to leave Newport, R.I., with his family to settle on Mulberry Grove plantation, Ga. Although Rutledge is known to have visited Newport on occasion, no evidence has been found that he did so in 1785. It can therefore be presumed that NG asked to have the will drawn up sometime before he sailed to Newport from Charleston on 15 June. (See note at NG to CG, 25 May, above.) The last Sunday before NG's departure from Charleston was 12 June.
2. See NG's Will, signed 11 October.
3. As seen at ibid., the "disinterested Witnesses" were NG's brother-in-law, William Littlefield; Littlefield's wife, the former Elizabeth Brinley; and Phineas Miller, who had been hired in early October as a tutor for NG's children.
4. Rutledge undoubtedly referred here to a couplet from John Milton's *Paradise Lost*, book 5: "My fairest, my espoused, my latest found / Heaven's last best gift, my ever new delight."

*   *   *

¶ [FROM ROGER PARKER SAUNDERS, [Charleston, S.C.?], 22 June 1785. Hopes NG is "Safe arrivd at Rhode Island"; Saunders came "to Town" [i.e., Charleston] the day that NG sailed and thus missed seeing him.[1] He informs NG that Mr. [William] Price, "to whome D[r] Oliphant passed a Bond of yours is very pressing for the Money." Price has "[Thomas?] Fergusons Bond" and Saunders's "for It"; Saunders has told Price that he does not believe it can be paid "before the next Crop." Price "promises to wait if he is not pressed by others."[2] Ferguson has "never been paid" the £60 that is owed "for the 400

Bushels Corn" that NG obtained from him and "is now in great want of the Money."[3] RCS (MiU-C) 2 pp.]

1. As noted at NG to CG, 25 May, above, NG, who had been attending to business affairs in the South for several months, left Charleston on 15 June to sail home to Newport, R.I.

2. On Price, a merchant, see *Biog. Directory of S.C. House*, 3: 584. On the bond to pay for slaves purchased for NG from David Olyphant, see Pendleton to NG, 30 January 1784, above, and NG to Price, 12 August, below.

3. As seen above in NG to Telfair, 16 April, and Forsyth to NG, 22 April, NG had been trying to obtain corn for the feeding of slaves and others living on his Georgia plantation.

*   *   *

From Joseph del Pozo y Sucre[1]

My Dear Sir

From on board the Brigantine *Jesus, Maria, Joseph* 24th June 1785

That your Excell[y] may form a Judicious comparison, from the treatment you have experienced in S[t] Augustine in Florida,[2] and the unjust one I have received in Savanna that you may be pleased to form what opinion you may think proper on the matter, and have for that purpose inclosed the documents, which if Y[r] Exc[y] will have the patience to peruse, I am hopeful will meet your approbation, and so grievous, was a proceeding so vile, that their North Star was the Rapine of the Spanish Dollars they suspected I had without paying attention, to the Character respect and other Circumstances concurring in my person, if hereafter the Individuals of this Country should experience any coolness, among us, they will perceive they will be subject to a Reciprocity; Since I cannot pass over in Silence for my own honour, a transaction of such a Nature, nor by any means neglect to publish the same in the most lively expressions, in Justification of all Calumnies against me, which is the Chief object of this Letter.[3]

Your Excell[y] will see by the within documents, that I know how to distinguish those that Judge and think honorably, & consequently the Justice due to your Merit and on all occasions I will take a particular pleasure in obliging you; Your most affectionate & Sincere Servant and Friend. I Kiss your Hands   JOSEPH DEL POZO Y SUCRE

RCS (MiU-C). In Spanish; contemporary translation in the hand of David Montaigut. (See Montaigut to NG, 6 May 1786, below.)

1. One historian has speculated that Pozo may have been a Jesuit priest. (William Spence Robertson, *The Life of Miranda*, 2 vols. [Chapel Hill: University of North Carolina Press, 1929], 1: 167)

2. On NG's recent visit to East Florida, see NG to CG, 14 April, above.

3. The enclosures were letters to Gov. Samuel Elbert of Georgia and Vicente Manuel de Zéspedes, the governor of East Florida. (See Montaigut to NG, 6 May 1786.) In his letter to Zéspedes of 22 June, Pozo explained that, while in Savannah, he had been arrested, imprisoned, and fined in a matter involving a fugitive slave who was a sailor on his vessel. (MiU-C; in Spanish) NG received this correspondence in December, soon after he settled

in Georgia, but was unable to respond to it until he obtained a translation. (Montaigut to NG, 6 May 1786) A reply that NG drafted shortly before his death was apparently never sent. (The draft is below, dated after 6 May 1786.)

* * *

¶ [FROM BENJAMIN HAWKINS, Savannah, Ga., 25 June 1785. He arrived there three days after he left NG and has been waiting ever since for "the arrival of the Kings and Head-men of the Creeks:[1] some of whom are expected daily to arrive in town but not vested with sufficient power to adjust our differences[;] they were all on the way." He believes the "others have returned, and will wait the Treaty expected to be held, by the commissioners of the United States, according to the notification which they must have received. Had they arrived, the exhausted, deranged state of our Finances, would not have enabled us to feed them ten days without some extraordinary aid from the Merchants, who don't seem disposed to advance their money, but where they have certain prospects of gain, and the State they deem their worst debtor." Mr. [Peter] Bard and "some others" purchased 4,000 acres "far down on Crooked River on the south side," at the "sales of confiscated property in May"; Bard "immediately set out for that place" and has not returned. Hawkins believes that Bard took 500 pounds of goods with him "and has formed a trading scheme with the Indians."[2] Bryant, whom Hawkins and NG "saw at Cumberland, is to manage the business of the concern, and is a partner."[3] Hawkins has been told that "the lands on Cumberland where the forts stood, at the North and south end," were "vacant, and that Mr Ozborn [i.e., Henry Osborne] has entered them, in all near one thousand acres"; Osborne is also there now.[4] Major Lucas "and some other gentlemen" have recently "survey'd on the Great Satilla twenty thousand acres of the very best tide swamp," and Hawkins thinks the laws of Georgia will "support their titles."[5] Hawkins himself will be "too late to pick," but he intends "to have some" land; the "difficulty of procuring land warrants down the Country" will keep him from executing his plan "to the scope" he intended when he saw NG; before autumn sets in, "it will be impossible to continue in the swamps." Lucas informs him that "the lands are generally very fine and he will return to compleat the surveys next week." Hawkins will "follow the week after," and Lucas is "disposed to render me any service."[6] If Hawkins is healthy "in future," he plans to depend on his own "exertions" and to "bid adieu to the cursed Indian business."[7]

John McQueen has called on Hawkins and shown him NG's "letter of recommendation" to Lafayette; McQueen "do's not thank" NG for the letter, for he believes "it is in a stile of indifference." McQueen is now at Sapelo Island and is planning to go to France "early in the season." Hawkins has advised him "to go by Rhode-Island" because McQueen "might in some way interfere with your propositions to the French marine minister and I thought you might come on some agreement with him, or convince him (which is hardly possible) that the steps you have taken will have secured you the contract before he could arrive in France. You may count upon seeing him certainly."[8] Gen. [Anthony] Wayne is in Savannah and will "go to see, if not to speculate in, the Southern swamps." Hawkins thinks Wayne "and every body here, is unable to do much for want of warrants."[9] In a damaged portion of the letter, Hawkins discusses a conversation he had with the governor about the seizure of property by the state. "Some information" has recently been received from Indians that "the Spaniards have lately seized upon the persons and property of some hunters, and others & have refused to release either." He will not write anything more, as it would "put you to expense, of double postage for what would not be worth a farthing to you." RCS (NcD) 3 pp.]

1. Hawkins, who traveled with NG to Cumberland Island, Ga., and East Florida in March, had recently been appointed a commissioner to negotiate with the Creek Indians. (See NG to CG, 14 April, above.)

2. See Bard to NG, 8 May, above.

3. Bryant has not been identified.

4. Ft. St. Andrew was built by the British in 1737 at the northern end of Cumberland Island; Ft. William was completed three years later at the southern end. Neither fort was still standing at this time. (Bullard, *Cumberland Island*, pp. 31–38) On Osborne's involvement with Cumberland Island, see his letter to NG of 23 April, above.

5. John Lucas had served in the Georgia Continental line. (Heitman, *Register*) The Satilla River flows into St. Andrew Sound from the Georgia mainland, nearly opposite the northern end of Great Cumberland Island.

6. It is not known whether Hawkins acquired land on Cumberland Island.

7. As seen in the note at NG to CG, 14 April, Hawkins continued to serve as a commissioner to negotiate with the Indians.

8. See NG to Lafayette, 1 June, above. As noted there, NG was engaged in negotiations through Lafayette to sell live oak timber from Cumberland Island to the French navy. NG had also written directly to "the French Marine minister," the Marquis de Castries. (The letter is above, dated 1 June.) No evidence has been found that McQueen visited NG before sailing to France. (See, however, Pendleton to NG, 23 September, below.)

9. Wayne, like NG, had received a plantation on the Savannah River from the state of Georgia, and he, too, was confronting financial difficulties at this time. Through political contacts in the state, he was able to obtain from the Georgia legislature the grant of "a thousand-acre tract of land, named the Hazzard Patent, in southern Georgia at the head of navigation on the Satilla River." Wayne visited the property in July, and when he afterward complained to Gov. Samuel Elbert that the land was being "'nibbled at by surveyors,'" the Assembly subsequently "acted favorably to his plea." (Nelson, *Wayne*, p. 201)

¶ [FROM HOWSON, EDWARDS & COMPANY, London, 27 June 1785. They have NG's letters of 19 and 29 April [not found], "with the 1st and 2nd Bills drawn per Alex[ande]r Gillon on Messrs Lodowick Hovy & Son Merchts Amderdam," worth "£16.13s 4d Sterling." They have "Sent one of the Bills and it[']s Acceptd." They hope it will be "paid when due" the following August; it will be credited to Mr. Isaac Senter's account. They "immediately Ship'd" more goods to Senter, based on the "Good Character" that NG gave him.[1] RCS (MiU-C) 1 p.]

1. On Isaac Senter, see NG to Howson, Edwards & Company, 6 August 1784, above. No further information has been found about NG's dealings with this firm.

*   *   *

From Robert Morris

Dear Sir Philad[a] June 28th 1785

Your letter of the 20th May, enclosing an ordinance for encourageing Foreigners to lend Money &c came duely to hand,[1] but I am very sorry to inform you that M[r] [James?] Wilson & myself have this day received letters from Amsterdam which put an end to the expectation of Loans from that quarter, at least for so long as a War or the appearance of War shall exist.[2]

I dont know where the cause lies, but the[re] seems to be a more general Want of Money both in Europe & America than ever I knew, and every attempt at relief that I have heard of has proved abortive. If good Wishes would avail, your wants would soon be relieved. They are all I have to offer except the assurance that I am Dear Sir Your most Obedient & humble Servant ROB[T] MORRIS

RCS (CSmH).

1. The letter has not been found. In support of his efforts to obtain a loan in Europe, and in response to Morris's letter of 15 March, above, NG had presumably sent Morris a March 1784 act of the South Carolina legislature, allowing foreigners to charge interest at a rate of seven per cent per year on loans based on South Carolina real estate and to "prosecute suits" in the state's courts against borrowers who defaulted on their obligations. (*Statutes of S.C.*, 4: 642–43)

2. The Dutch firm of Wilhem & Jan Willink wrote NG on 8 July, below, that they were unable to consider the loan that NG had requested from them. (See also Morris to NG, 15 March, above, and NG's letter to the Willinks of 7 January 1786, below.) On the "appearance of War," see Griffin Greene to NG, 2 November 1784, above.

* * *

¶ [FROM CHARLES PETTIT, New York, 30 June 1785. NG has already "been informed of the Wreck of Col. [Clement] Biddle's Affairs."[1] Pettit is one of those who have been delegated to "save what we can from the wreck," and their attention has been drawn "to the Lands in this State near Kaatskill," in which NG and Biddle are tenants in common. Biddle "seems confident" that NG will "readily join us in making an entire Sale of the Whole," but they need to hear from NG before they "can safely act on that Plan." In the meantime, they are giving orders "to lay off the land in Lots of 200 to 300 Acres." These parcels will probably be sold at auction, as Biddle's estate must be liquidated "with all practicable Expedition." Pettit thinks they "will sell at a low Rate"—perhaps no "more than a dollar per Acre," although Biddle's "Ideas were raised to 20/. or upwards." If NG wants to "join in the sale," he should give a "special Power of Attorney" to someone. Pettit recommends "M[r] Adam Gilchrist," who formerly lived with Biddle, and who currently resides in New York. It would be better not to give the power of attorney to Pettit because of his "Trust in Col. Biddle's Estate."[2]

Pettit has been in New York "4 or 5 Weeks, studying Forms in the temporary School established by the U. States." He adds: "As yet I am but a Novice & like most Boys on first going to School, see so many Difficulties before me, that I wish myself at home again. We triffle away much Time, but luckily the Doors are not open to expose many of our Follies; I wish our Journals would testify more wisdom & System in our Decisions that I can perceive in them."[3] They have spent a long time "choosing a Minister for the Hague." Seven states favored Gov. [William] Livingston, but he declined. "The Friends of Gov[r] [John] Rutledge are offended, but he is again in Nomination without their apparent Approbation. Chancellor [Robert R.] Livingston is also named. On a former occasion he refused to be run for" that post, "tho' he wanted to be appointed as I am told, for London."[4] A "third Com[r] of the Treasury" is also needed, in addition to Mr. [Samuel] Osgood and Mr. Walter Livingston; "it is said it must be a Southern Gent[n]." Mr. [John Lewis] Gervais "was appointed & refused," and "M[r] [Nicholas] Eveleigh has been named & withdrawn."[5] The treasurer of Georgia, Mr. [Seth John] Cuthbert, "is named but not much known" about him. "He & M[r] A[rthur] Lee, in various attempts, have each had from 4 to 6 Votes but get no higher."[6] Pettit asks NG to suggest "a Name from the southward that is suitable."[7] Pettit has been told that his own name was "in nomination sometime ago" for the Treasury post, but he had previously served in the Quartermaster Department and does not live "far enough south, the Northern & Middle Regions having each one already." Had he been chosen, he believes he would have accepted, "if from no other Motive than to get clear of the Politicks of Penns[a]"; he has been "lugged in there" against his wishes and does not know "how to get out with honor, but in some such way as this."[8] He fears "the Event of the next Election," adding: "What would be flattering to some Minds, I shudder at the apprehension of—recent Examples enhance the Danger in my View." Pettit feels a "Desire for the Success of a particular Interest in that State, from various motives," but "would rather see their Measures conducted by an abler Pilot than my fears admit will be found."[9] He concludes: "I set out in Haste to give you but a few Lines on Business, but I have exceeded my own Views, in the Length to which I have run." RCS (MiU-C) 3 pp.]

1. See Pettit to NG, 23 March, above.

2. NG had already given Jeremiah Wadsworth a power of attorney to sell his "lands up the North [i.e., Hudson] River held with Colonel Biddle." (NG to Wadsworth, 24 April, above) On 12 October, below, NG gave Wadsworth a more specific power of attorney: "to divide with" Biddle "or the Commissioners appointed to settle his affairs, all our Landed Property, purchased of M[r] Abraham Lott, and held as Tenants in common upon the North River."

3. The "temporary School" was Congress, to which Pettit had been elected as a delegate from Pennsylvania in April. He took his seat there on 27 May. (JCC, 28: 397; Smith, Letters, 22: xxv)

4. Rutledge was eventually selected to be "minister plenipotentiary to the United Netherlands." (JCC, 29: 582)

5. On the earlier appointments of Osgood, Livingston, and Gervais to the Treasury posts, see note at Wadsworth to NG, 15 February, above.

6. Lee, a Virginian, was named to the third seat on the Board of Treasury. (JCC, 29: 582)

7. NG's reply has not been found.

8. Pettit served in Congress until 1787. (DAB)

9. On the Pennsylvania election of 1785, see Pettit to NG, 21 September and second letter of 20 January 1786, both below. As seen in a note at the first of those letters, Pettit's apprehensions were related to his candidacy for president of the state's executive council.

¶ [FROM DANIEL MCLANE, Charleston, S.C., 3 July 1785.[1] He has "connected" himself with Mr. David Hillhouse and has decided, with NG's permission, to go "to Cumberland Island for the purpose of making a settlement, and carrying on business, in the manner we talked of in this place, when you was here."[2] Will take "twenty or more white hands, with a ship carpenter for the purpose of cutting timber in the winter time, for it will be in the fall before Cap[t] Hopkins returns from Connecticut till then I cant leave our business here."[3] Hillhouse will "wait on" NG and receive "any instructions reletive to the place." Asks NG to give Hillhouse "an order to take possession of the Island" and "to advise me what part of the Island is the most eligible spot to fix on." Adds: "These particulars will be of consequence to me being a stranger there."[4] RCS (MiU-C) 2 pp.]

    1. McLane has not been identified.
    2. On Hillhouse, see his letter to NG of 19 July, below. NG presumably had talked with McLane and Hillhouse after his visit to Cumberland Island, Ga., that spring. (On the visit to Cumberland, see NG to CG, 14 April, above.)
    3. Hopkins commanded a cargo-carrying vessel for Wadsworth, Deane & Company (See Wadsworth to NG, 10 July and 5 September, both below.)
    4. Hillhouse wrote NG from New London, Conn., on 19 July, asking to visit NG at Newport, R.I., to deliver the present letter and receive instructions. NG's reply has not been found, but it is evident from Hillhouse's letter of 4 October, below, that NG did give him instructions about hiring workers to cut timber on Cumberland Island.

¶ [FROM JEREMIAH WADSWORTH, Hartford, Conn., 3 July 1785. He learned of NG's arrival at Newport, R.I., "by the News papers."[1] Had planned to be in New York and to have gone on to Newport when his "business there was finished," but "health & business" have prevented this. He will be in New York the following week and will stay there until he has concluded his "affairs with M[r] Church," who is to leave for England as soon as they finish.[2] Is not sure when he will see NG and wonders if NG is "going to the Southard."[3] Wadsworth promised CG that he would send his son [Daniel] to Newport, but the latter's "ill health" has kept him from going, and now, at his physicians' advice, the younger Wadsworth is "rideing up the Country."[4] Letters to Wadsworth should be directed to Mr. [Nathaniel] Shaler at New York. It has not been in Wadsworth's "power to take any measures to sell" NG's lands in New York or New Jersey, nor can he do so yet, as "it will be necessary to Visit each place."[5] In a postscript, he asks whether Griffin Greene "is comeing out"; the Dumoussays wrote him that Griffin was "to come out with M[r] [James] Price." Wadsworth concludes: "I rec[d] a letter dated at Versailles which says you will shortly be served with notice 'of Bills for £1000 Sterling being protested indorsed by you & this circumstance will not exalt your credit in this Country.'" The Dumoussays instructed Wadsworth "not to be uneasy" about the protest, "as it was a matter of course," but he is not "perfectly easy on this subject."[6] RCS (MiU-C) 3 pp.]

    1. NG reached Newport, R.I., from the South on 25 June. (NG to CG, 25 May, above)
    2. On Wadsworth's business affairs with John Barker Church, see Wadsworth to NG, 6 May, above.
    3. Wadsworth evidently wanted to know whether NG was planning to move to one of his plantations in the South. NG wrote him on 13 July, below, that he would "certainly" go south in the fall. Wadsworth postponed going to Newport several times during the summer and early fall for reasons of health. (See, for example, Wadsworth to NG, 5 and

11 September, both below.) It does not appear that NG saw Wadsworth again, although he did assign a power of attorney to Wadsworth during a visit to New York in August. (The power of attorney is below, dated 16 August.)

4. In a letter to NG of 10 July, below, Wadsworth reported that his son's health had improved.

5. For background, see NG's power of attorney to Wadsworth on 26 March, above. For a brief description of the properties, see Estimate of NG's Estate, before 9 January 1784, above. Wadsworth wrote NG on 28 July, below, that prospective buyers of the New Jersey property had decided it was too expensive. (See also NG to Wadsworth, 13 July, below.)

6. In regard to the French mercantile firm Dumoussay et Frères and the protested notes, see also Griffin Greene to NG, 14 November 1784, above, as well as Wadsworth to NG, 10 July, and NG to Wadsworth, 13 July, below. As seen in the two Wadsworth letters, Griffin Greene arrived in the United States from France about this time.

¶ [FROM AEDANUS BURKE, Charleston, S.C., 4 July [1785].[1] Introduces Mr. Abraham Wilkinson, a neighbor of his "in Broad-Street," a merchant "of the first buisiness, and a very sensible man." Wilkinson is traveling to Newport, R.I., with his wife, "a genteel welbred good woman," and plans to stay there until "the fall be over."[2] Nothing worth relating has happened in Charleston since NG left, except that "Huger has fought Pinckney at last. It is said that [Huger] was a stranger to all P[inckney]—said of him in the Court of Chancery and the people believe it. In the duel Huger behaved well—3 Pistols were fired—and Pinckney delivered his fire first every time at the other. P—y was wounded, confined only a few days." Burke adds: "You can't conceive how the people rejoice in Huger's behaviour & good fortune." Pinckney is "a man of great worth & abilities; a liberal generous fellow, wch is reason enough with a Yahoo, why he sh^d hate him in his hea[rt]."[3] Burke sends his respects to CG and wishes her and NG "ever[y] blessing & happiness." RCS (MiU-C) 2 pp.]

1. The year is not given, but the Huger-Pinckney duel referred to here took place in 1785. (Zahniser, *Pinckney*, p. 245)

2. Wilkinson and his "Family" reportedly arrived in Newport on the sloop *Dove* on 17 July. (*Newport Mercury*, 23 July)

3. According to a newspaper report, Charles C. Pinckney "was wounded in the thigh" in this duel, which was fought on or about 28 June. (*Newport Mercury*, 30 July) Daniel Huger, a plantation owner, had served in the South Carolina legislature and as a delegate to Congress. (*Biog. Directory of S.C. House*, 2: 340–41) In a letter to NG of 7 January 1784, above, Nathaniel Pendleton offered an uncomplimentary comment about Huger, who had recently separated from his wife. Pinckney, Huger's well-known opponent in the duel, had been a prominent Continental officer and an aide to Washington during the war. He would later serve as American minister to France and as the Federalist candidate for president in 1804 and 1808. (Ibid., pp. 525–27; *DAB*) Burke is said to have had "little sympathy for dissident demonstrators in the streets or for the lower orders unable or unwilling to recognize the requirements of the public interest. These he would refer to on occasion as 'Yahoos' and characterize their excesses as 'Yahooism.'" (Meleney, *Aedanus Burke*, p. 12)

*   *   *

To Governor Richard Caswell of North Carolina

Sir   Newport [R.I.] July 8ᵗʰ 1785

I take the Liberty of addressing you in behalf of the Family of Mʳ John Freebody of this Town.[1] I was intimately acquainted with the Father who is dead and feel a regard for his Children. He was one of the first Citizens of this Town in point of Fortune and supported a good moral Character through Life. His family has been educated with taste and delicacy and merits esteem and protection.[2] When the Enemy took possession of this Town in 1776 they fell under their power and their interest laying principally here they have been great sufferers.[3] When the Enemy evacuated this place the eldest Son of Mʳ Freebody happened to be upon Long Island and took the earliest oppertunity to return to his family and friends; but from the rage of party[,] objections were rais'd to his returning. His General Character and inoffensive conduct entitled him to a milder treatment; and nothing but the Spirit of the times can apologize for the difficulties he met with. The Legislature have taken full cognizance of the matter without finding the least imputation to his prejudice and admitted him to the full enjoyment of all his property and priviledges of a Citizen.[4] But it is said Nᵒ Carolina have confiscated a plantation belonging to him, his Brother and four Sisters and that the same is sold but the money not paid and the purchaser wil[ling] to relinquish the purchase upon the Legislat[ure] giving up his security. The object of this Letter is to solicit your Excellencys good offices in this business and to have it laid before the Legislature for their consideration.[5] I am sure it can never be their wish to oppress unfortunate Ladys who bear the best of reputations. I hope your Excellency and the Legislature will pardon the Liberty I have taken in this address and I shall feel myself under singular obligations for every kind of indulgence and justice that may be done the family. I have the honor to be with the highest respect your Excellencys most Obedient humble Servᵗ   NATH GREENE

ALS (Nc-Ar).

1. See Freebody to NG, after 2 July 1784, above.

2. John Freebody, Sr., who died in 1773, had been a leading resident of Newport. (Mason, *Annals of Trinity Church*, p. 156n)

3. The British occupation of Newport began in December 1776. (Vol. 1: 365–66n, above)

4. See note at Freebody to NG, after 2 July 1784.

5. Caswell later presented Freebody's request to the North Carolina General Assembly, which passed a resolution in January 1787 returning the confiscated estate to Freebody and his siblings. As part of the arrangement, Freebody was to reimburse the displaced owners for the cost of any improvements they had made to the property. (*NCSR*, 18: 382, 392, 443)

From Wilhem & Jan Willink

Sir   Amsterdam 8 July 1785
We have before us Your esteemed favour of 27 Apr by wh^ch we See you are determined to borrow from 2000 to 4000£ on your Plantation in the State of Georgia, and that you will Send the Necessary vouchers for the purpose.[1] We are Sorry to inform you of the impossibility to perform it at present. Since the Loans made Since our writing of 26 March 1784 are So extended and money become So scarce and [raisen?] in intrest & expences, that the Matters want to be postponed, more over none can be made before the Vouchers here are examined and approved and a stipulation is made when Shall be redeemed.[2] By a happy return of times we Shall early inform you of it and shall always rejoice to contribute to your & your Countrimen's prosperity & Satisfaction.[3]

If you or your friends find a conveniency in Shipping your produces hither, you may depend of our utmost exertions in the disposal to your best advantage.

A Contract for the oak & Cedar might be practicable, but it would not before the qualities were Seen & examined here. If you are disposed to Load a Ship with it and advice the terms on wh^ch you'll engage to deliver a quantity yearly, we Shall endeavour to bring this matter to a consistency ab^t Wh^ch we Shall expect to hear from you.[4] We remain respectfully sir Your most Hum^l Servt   WILHEM & JAN WILLINK

RCS (MiU-C).

1. NG's letter has not been found. For background, see above, Morris to NG, 15 March and 28 June. NG's plantation in Georgia was Mulberry Grove.

2. On the Willinks' letter of 26 March 1784, which was written to Robert Morris, see note at Morris to NG, 12 July 1784, above.

3. In a letter to the Willinks of 7 January 1786, below, NG again inquired about a loan and indicated that he was sending the requested documents. (See also Pendleton to NG, 23 September, below.)

4. See NG's letter to the Willinks of 7 January 1786. The "oak & Cedar" were from NG's holdings on Cumberland Island, Ga.

*   *   *

¶ [FROM WILLIAM PIERCE & COMPANY, Savannah, Ga., 9 July 1785. They have drawn on NG for "£60 sterling" and ask him "Please to honor it, and place the same to our joint Account."[1] RCS (MiU-C) 1 p.]

1. For background, see above, Pierce & Company to NG, 8 April; Pierce to NG, 13 May, and NG to Pierce, 17 May. NG's reply to the present letter has not been found. The London firm of Strachan, Mackenzie & Company wrote NG on 30 July, below, that they had been unable to honor his bill on Pierce & Company.

*   *   *

From William Blount

Dear Sir   Wilmington [N.C.] July 10th 1785

On my Way to this place I called at Kinston and the Governor show'd me a Letter that he had just received from you relative to the Administration on the Estate of John Banks.

I have immediately wrote you in answer to every Letter that I have ever recieved from you and by Letters recived [fro]m Charleston [S.C]. I have for some Time past daily expected the Pleasure of seeing you once more at Piney Grove or I should have wrote to you while at Charleston.[1] As yet I have not got into my Hands a Single Shillings worth of Banks's Property. I have several Suits depending from which I expect something will be got. I have no Papers with me here but fear the amount of the Property that will come to my Hands will not exceed one thousand dollars.[2] On my Return home I will write you very fully.[3] [Former] Governor [Alexander] Martin has delivered me Your Grant for the twenty five thousand Acres of Land.[4] I hope the information that you have heard respecting Genl Rutherfurd is ill grounded. I have not heard that it is true.[5] I shall attend the Indian Treaties in Georgia & S° Carolina in September & October and purpose to take my Seat in Congress in November.[6] With unfeigned Esteem I am, Your most Ob^t Servt

W^M BLOUNT

RCS (PHi).

1. NG's letter to Gov. Richard Caswell has not been found. On NG's efforts to gain restitution from the estate of John Banks in North Carolina, see, for example, his letters to Blount of 15, 24, and 26 October 1784 and Blount's to NG of 26 October 1784, all above. These letters and the present one are the only correspondence between them that has been found.

2. Edward Carrington wrote NG on 27 February, above, that Blount believed Banks's assets in North Carolina were "likely to be explained away to very little indeed."

3. If Blount wrote such a letter, it has not been found.

4. This was the land in present-day Tennessee that the North Carolina legislature had voted to give to NG three years earlier. (Alexander Martin to NG, 24 May 1782, above [vol. 11: 239–40 and n]) The deed, dated 1 March 1785, was signed by Martin, whose term as governor had since ended. (CtHi; Smith, *Letters*, 22: 412)

5. It is not known what information NG had obtained about Griffith Rutherford.

6. In November, commissioners appointed by Congress concluded treaties with Cherokee, Choctaw, and Chickasaw Indians at Hopewell, the plantation of Andrew Pickens in western South Carolina. Although Blount was not one of the commissioners, he did sign the Choctaw and Chickasaw treaties as a witness. (*JCC*, 30: 185–95; on the congressional appointments, see especially Mifflin to NG, 6 March 1784, and note at NG to CG, 14 April 1785, both above. For a discussion of Blount's land interests vis-à-vis the treaties, see Masterson, *Blount*, pp. 100–109.) Blount, one of six delegates elected by the North Carolina legislature in November 1784, did not take a seat in Congress until May 1786. (Smith, *Letters*, 22: xxiv; 23: xxiii)

*   *   *

¶ [FROM JEREMIAH WADSWORTH, Hartford, Conn., 10 July 1785. Has NG's letter of 1 July [not found]. Will leave the next day for New Haven, en route to New York, and will "inquire for the Tutor you want."[1] Since his last letter, Wadsworth has seen Mr. [James] Price, who told him that Griffin Greene has returned and that "the Bills were not paid or secured [to be?] paid out of the avails of the Ship." Before NG receives this letter, he will have seen Griffin Greene and will "know the particulars." The Dumoussays have not sent some "articles" that Wadsworth ordered, and they "make a poor apology for it"; he believes they do not "chuse" to give him credit. Is "sorry" to bring up "this disagreable subject," but NG will judge from his "own feelings" what Wadsworth's are.[2] Mrs. [Mehitable Russell] Wadsworth, "Daniel & Kitty" will accompany him to New York, and they may later "all come by Water to New Port."[3] Daniel's health is "mended by his last Journey," and Wadsworth is optimistic that he will recover, for his "Cough has left him & he is in pretty good Spirits."[4] Captains [Josiah?] Burnham and Hopkins are in Hartford; Wadsworth concurs with NG's opinion of the former.[5] RCS (CtHi) 2 pp.]

  1. On Wadsworth's help in finding a tutor for NG's children, see also his letter to NG of 5 September and NG's to him of 13 September, both below.

  2. See Wadsworth to NG, 3 July, above, and NG to Wadworth, immediately below. "The Ship" was the *Flora*, which Griffin Greene had sold before returning from France.

  3. Daniel and Catherine, or "Kitty," were two of Wadsworth's three children. (Destler, "Wadsworth," p. 3) On Wadsworth's purpose in going to New York, see his letter to NG of 3 July. The family did not go to Newport, R.I., because Mrs. Wadsworth "suffered so much in her journey by water" to New York that she did not want to make the trip. (Wadsworth to NG, 28 July, below)

  4. On Daniel Wadsworth's health, see Wadsworth to NG, 3 July.

  5. The letter in which NG gave his opinion of Burnham has not been found. On Hopkins, see also McLane to NG, 3 July, above.

*   *   *

To Jeremiah Wadsworth

Dear Sir   Newport [R.I.] July 13th 1785

   I am very sorry that you have farther occasion to be uneasy on account of the bills drew by Mr Griffin Greene.[1] He says that the goods for which the bills were originally given are actually paid for and that the house actually gave him a new credit for the goods he brought out with him before the bills was returned to them accepted. But after they returned from America accepted they did not choose to deliver them up; but keep them as a kind of additional security.[2] As the bills were given for the former advance and not for the present I think they ought not to have been held. For tho I might have made no objection to guaranteeing the new debt I should never have consented to their holding you responsible. However I am in hopes you will meet with no difficulty in the business. Mr Griffin Greene says if god spares his life he will certainly make payment which is not due until next February. And that you should run no risque I covered this Debt in a Mortgage to you before I left South Carolinia.[3]

I shall certainly go to the Southward this Fall and before I go I wish to give you the necessary transfer of the Stocks in the Barnea Dean Company [i.e., Barnabas Deane & Company].[4] And I wish also to consult and advise with you on many other matters. M[r] Thomas Smiths Son of New York, Has some inclination to purchace my Jersey Property. I offerd it to him for one thousand pounds Sterling. Please to consult him on the business.[5] I am glad to hear your Son is better and that your family are pretty well. Mrs Greene is in a bad state of health. The Children are all well. Yours Aff   N GREENE

ALS (CtY).
1. See above, Wadsworth to NG, 3 and 10 July.
2. As seen in ibid., the "house" was Dumoussay et Frères, a firm that Griffin Greene had dealt with in France.
3. For background on the disputed bills, see note at Griffin Greene to NG, 6 April 1784, above. According to Wadsworth's biographer, NG, at the time of his death, "still owed Wadsworth £2,000 for loans and £2,000 for the Griffin-Jacob Greene bills that he [Wadsworth] had endorsed. To secure these and other debts," NG "had signed but not delivered a mortgage to Wadsworth" on his South Carolina plantation, Boone's Barony. (Destler, "Wadsworth," p. 267)
4. Wadsworth sent papers for closing NG's affairs in the partnership on 5 September, below. (See also NG to Wadsworth, 7 September, and To Whom It May Concern, also 7 September, below.) NG and his family left Newport for the South in mid-October. (See note at Knox to NG, 27 October, below.)
5. Smith did not buy the property in New Jersey. (Wadsworth to NG, 28 July, below) As an executor of NG's estate, Wadsworth appears to have sold this property in 1788. (Wadsworth to Edward Rutledge, 16 November 1788, CtHi)

From Henry Banks

Sir   Richmond [Va.] July 13th 1785
    I have several times informed you that the Gentlemen for whom I made my assumpsits have sued me.[1] I am now in confinement and M[r] [James] Hunter shewing no inclination to see me.[2] Circumstanced as you are I think that yr personal attention alone can bring things square. Being determined to do no more Bussiness when I get released I shall probably leave this place and you of course may expect to find every obstruction thrown in y[r] way by the other party. I wish to my very soul that Maj[r] [Robert] Forsyth may come with you, that by a general Investigation I might be able to prove my total Innocence in every step that I have taken.
    Tis from you alone I expect sure Justice and fully perswade myself that it will be granted.[3]
    Be good eno[ugh] to inform me what is done with my Brothers Books and papers, and also forward to me those upon which you administred in [North] Carolina[,][4] as S B & H [i.e., Isaac Smith, Preeson Bowdoin, & James Hunter] refuse to make any Settlem[t] until I have them.[5] I am with great respect y[r] very ob Ser[t]   HENRY BANKS

RCS (MiU-C).

1. Only one previous letter from Banks to NG has been found: that of 7 October 1784, above. An assumpsit is a "contract (not under seal)" or a "suit for breach of such contract." (http://www.tiscali.co.uk/reference/dictionaries/difficultwords/data)

2. On Banks's "confinement," see also Hunter to NG, 1 June, above. Banks's situation had apparently not changed when he wrote NG on 5 August, below.

3. No reply has been found. Despite NG's urging, Forsyth did not go to Virginia to help settle the debts of his partnership with Banks's late brother John. (NG to Carrington, 29 September, below)

4. Banks alleged many years later that immediately after John Banks's death in North Carolina, NG "got every thing that he [i.e., John Banks] had, including money, bills, notes and evidences of debt; that Greene became immediately afterwards the administrator of Banks, and has rendered no account of his administration." (Banks, *Vindication*, p. 34) Banks also had "no hesitation in saying, that Greene converted every thing he got or could get, to his own uses and purposes, and destroyed every document which might militate against him and his deeds." (Ibid., p. 6)

5. According to Banks, this Fredericksburg firm was the predecessor of Hunter, [John] Banks & Company and was "half interested" in the latter partnership. (Banks, *Vindication*, pp. 10, 20)

*   *   *

¶ [FROM HENRY BANKS**, Richmond, Va., 15 July 1785. When he wrote NG "a few days since," he neglected to mention that "Mr [James] Hunter had advertised a Meeting of the Creditors of Hunter Banks & C° in[ten]ding to place the Books in their hands."[1] This will be "so great an injury" to his brother John's estate that Banks is "determined to withhold them, as Smith, Bowdoin & Hunter are by far the largest Debtors on those Books which tis their Wish to evade."[2] If NG were in Virginia "for a few weeks," they [i.e., Smith, Bowdoin & Hunter] "might be brought to a proper Understanding."[3] RCS (MiU-C) 1 p.]

1. Banks's previous letter is immediately above. In a notice in the *Virginia Gazette* of 9 July, Hunter, alleging that Banks had published an "illiberal insult on the delicacy of a Merchant's [i.e., Hunter's own] fame," called upon "such Gentlemen as are creditors to the late house of Hunter, Banks, & Co. to meet Mr. [Isaac] Smith, Mr. [Preeson] Bowdoin, and himself, at Fredericksburg, on the first of August next, when they will request them [i.e., the creditors] to choose one or more of their body to receive the Books and Papers of the Company into their hands, and prove [i.e., disprove] the veracity of Mr. Bank's publication." Banks's "publication"—in the *Virginia Gazette* of 14 May—is noted at Hunter to NG, 1 June, above.

2. On the firm of Smith, Bowdoin & Hunter, see also the note at the preceding letter.

3. No reply has been found.

¶ [FROM JEREMIAH WADSWORTH**, New York, 18 July 1785. He arrived there "yesterday," and "Mr Barna Gil" this day offered him "your Bond for Two hundred & fifty Guineas which he says is due." It was Gil's understanding that Wadsworth would probably "take it at a small discount," but Wadsworth told him he was "pushed for Money" because of "closeing with Mr [John Barker] Church & must in all this Month find a very large Sum." He promised to give Gil "a definitive answer in a day or two," however. If he thought NG wanted to have "this Bond taken up," Wadsworth would "get the Money and buy it for you as cheep as possible," but he is not sure of NG's wishes. He plans to be in New York for "a fortnight."[1] RCS (CtHi) 2 pp.; one or more pages missing]

1. This was presumably the bond for which Stephen Rapalje requested payment in a letter to NG of 25 September, below. Although he offered in that letter to take the amount due "out of" Wadsworth's store in New York if NG could not make payment, Rapalje later turned the bond over to the New York merchants Randall Son & Stewart. (Rapalje to NG, 27 October, below) NG wrote them on 12 March 1786, below, that payment would be "out of my power, until I can sell some of my landed property, or my plantations are more productive."

¶ [FROM DAVID HILLHOUSE, New London, Conn., 19 July 1785.[1] After NG left Charleston, S.C., Hillhouse and "Cap[t] M[c]Lane" decided to "take A part of the Island according to" NG's "proposal."[2] Hillhouse has McLane's letter to NG "on the subject" and will wait on NG anytime NG wishes.[3] He proposes going to Newport, R.I., the following week and would like to know "by the returning Post" if NG will be at home.[4] RCS (MiU-C) 1 p.]

1. Hillhouse (1756–1803), a native of Connecticut, moved to Georgia in 1786 or 1787 "to settle in the undeveloped mideast portion" of the state. After his death, his widow, the former Sarah Porter, became a prominent newspaper publisher. (*Dictionary of Georgia Biography*, 1: 455–56; Bruce P. Stark, William Brown, Jr., and John Espy, "Hillhouse Family Papers," finding aid, Yale University Archives)

2. Hillhouse and Daniel McLane had plans to create a settlement on Cumberland Island, Ga., and to provide workers to cut timber there. (See McLane to NG, 3 July, above, and Hillhouse to NG, 4 October, below.)

3. See McLane to NG, 3 July.

4. No letter from NG to Hillhouse has been found, and it is not known whether they met at Newport. It appears from Hillhouse's letter of 4 October, though, that NG gave him explicit instructions about hiring or purchasing a labor force for the island. It is not known whether Hillhouse carried out any of NG's directions or, indeed, if he and McLane ever took "part of the Island."

¶ [FROM DENNIS DE BERDT, London, 21 July 1785. He has received "several favors" from NG and has directed his answers to Rhode Island, as NG wished. "The Bill [for] £180 on Stra[c]han MacKenzie & Co is Noted & as they say not Likely to be paid."[1] The bill for "£116.13.4 [per Alexander] Gillon" on a Dutch firm "has met due honer."[2] RCS (MiU-C) 1 p.]

1. See NG to De Berdt, 9 March and 3 April, and NG to Strachan, Mackenzie & Company, 4 June, all above, as well as Strachan, Mackenzie & Company to NG, 30 July, below. Charles Pettit forwarded the present letter to NG, commenting that De Bert was "rather impatient" about this matter. (Pettit to NG, 21 September, below)

2. See also Howson, Edwards & Company to NG, 27 June, above.

*　　　*　　　*

To Samuel A. Otis

Sir   Newport [R.I.] July 24th 1785

Your letter of the 29th of April was inclosed to me by Col Henly and with it your account. I can hardly suppose you are serious in many of the charges.[1] Upon what principle can you suppose me answerable for [M[r]?] Pains expences.[2] You was a public Agent accountable to the public and only appointed by me. I only gave you such directions as the Treasury board gave me. If the public will not allow you those charges it is no fault of mine.[3] But in this you are subject to no greater hardships than I am. I have spent weeks and Months dancing attendance after the business without the least prospect of any allowance. And I was obliged to settle an account of upwards of two hundred thousand hard dollars for bills drawn for the Southern Army wherein I had not the least interest under heaven, and compelled to Account for every shilling without the least allowance for my expences altho I spent above five Weeks in Philadelphia on the business and [was] obliged to go there no less than three times on it.[4] In addition to this I now stand ingaged for the support of the Southern Army for more than I am worth in the World and if it finally falls upon me will reduce me and my family to begging and want.[5] No mans situation can be more cruel than Mine to be subject to private Misfortunes from public necessity. The Wines you purchased I am only one-third concerned in[;] Cox and Pettit the other two but what ever is right and just on this subject shall be done as soon as I have it in my power.[6]

Just as I was going to South Carolina last Winter I got a letter from you inclosing an account of the Ship Factor. I wrote you long since that Mr George Olney was equally concerned in that Vessel. I can but hope you have made some mistake in the Account[,] for to the best of my remembrance you wrote me there would be a ballance due to the Ship Factor. However M[r] Olney can tell more of this than I can, he having the papers.[7] On this subject we will take some measures to bring it to a close on my return from New York to which place I am going in a few days.[8] I am Sir with respect Your most Obed[t] humble Ser   NATH GREENE

ADfS (Ct).

1. Neither Otis's letter to NG of 29 April nor David Henley's, in which it was enclosed, has been found. (See, however, Otis to NG, 8 December 1783 and 21 December 1784, both above.) On his own and through the firms of Otis & Andrews and Otis & Henley, Otis had furnished uniforms and other supplies while NG was quartermaster general. Otis and his partner Henley had also had private business dealings with NG. (See above, vol. 2: 415–16n; vol. 4: 13n; vol. 6: 273.) On the "charges" referred to here, see note 3, below. As seen in the letter immediately below, Henley had recently presented drafts on NG, which NG had refused.

2. Nathaniel Paine had been in Philadelphia in September 1780 on business concerning Otis & Henley's accounts with the Quartermaster Department. (Charles Pettit to NG, 8 September 1780, above [vol. 6: 273])

3. Otis had served both as deputy quartermaster general in Boston and as an agent for the Clothing Department. (Vol. 2: 415n) On 15 April, in response to a petition from Otis, Congress empowered "the Commissioner for settling the accounts of the department of the clothier general" to "examine and settle the accounts of the late company of Otis and Andrews, of Samuel A. Otis, and of the late company of Otis & Henley, conformably to the resolves of Congress, as well in the department of the quartermaster general, as in that of the clothier general. And to the end that full justice may be done, between the said agents and the United States, touching the depreciation of monies, the said Commissioner is hereby instructed to receive from the Commissioner for settling the accounts of the

department of the Quarter master general, all such accounts, papers and vouchers as he may be possessed of, relative to the said agent's transactions with that department." (*JCC*, 28: 268) It appears from the present letter that some of the charges claimed in Otis's Quartermaster Department accounts had been disallowed.

4. NG's efforts to settle his accounts as Southern Army commander can be traced through his correspondence with Treasury comptroller James Milligan in this volume and in the notes at NG to Mifflin, 3 November 1783, above. Since the dissolution of the Southern Army in the early summer of 1783, NG had been in Philadelphia in October–November 1783 and again in June and November 1784. He asked to be reimbursed for the expenses of his stays there in letters to Milligan of 10 November and 7 December 1783 and 4 June 1784, all above.

5. For background on the claims against NG that had resulted from his guarantee of debts for Southern Army contractor John Banks and associates, see especially the notes at NG to Benjamin Lincoln, 19 December 1782, and Benjamin Harrison to NG, 24 December 1782, above (vol. 12: 308–9n, 341–42 and n), and NG's letter of 22 August, below, to the president of Congress, Richard Henry Lee.

6. John Cox and Charles Pettit, NG's assistant quartermasters general, had also been business partners of his. (As seen in his agreement with Pettit of 8 November 1783, above, NG relinquished his share in the partnership after the war.) Otis is known to have sent pipes of wine to NG on at least one occasion. (See above, Otis to NG, 21 May 1779, and NG to Otis, 17 September 1779 [vol. 4: 57, 393–94].) Pettit wrote NG on 8 September 1780 that in trying to settle Quartermaster Department accounts with Otis & Henley, he had found it difficult in some cases to distinguish their purchases for the public from those for "private account; some for yourself and some for Gent[lemen] of your family." (Vol. 6: 273)

7. Otis's letter enclosing his "account current" was presumably that of 21 December 1784. Although the "Ship Factor" was not mentioned in that letter, Otis probably charged NG ⅟₃₂ of the amount that had been owed to that person. In the fall of 1779, NG purchased half of Otis's ⅟₁₆ share in the privateer *Tartar*. (NG to Otis, 17 September 1779, above [vol. 4: 394]) Later, NG sold half of that investment to George Olney, with an agreement that Olney would share in the vessel's prize money. (Olney to NG, 6 January 1780, above [vol. 5: 244]; NG's letter to Otis about this matter has not been found.) After the *Tartar* was run aground and was stranded during the spring of 1780, Otis refused a request to pay prize money to Olney and argued that this was NG's responsibility. (Olney to NG, 26 October 1780, above [vol. 6: 435–36 and n])

8. No further correspondence between NG and Otis has been found. As seen in the letter immediately below, NG refused to accept drafts that Henley had presented against him.

To Nathaniel Russell

Sir   Newport [R.I.] July 24th 1785
    The drafts given upon me by Mr Henly I cannot accept. There is Money due them on my private Account I have no doubt; but there are charges in their Account to which I shall never agree.[1] They are charges of a public Nature and if the public will not pass them to their credit they cannot come against me for I gave them only such orders as were given me.[2] Such ballance as may be due from me on private Account I will strive to settle as soon as I can and in those Col [John] Cox and M^r [Charles] Pettit are equally concerned except in one charge for Moneys advanced Mr Story and these Gentlemen I expect to see in a few days.[3]

I will never involve my self farther for the Public being now under engagements for supplies for the Southern Army for more than I am worth and which should it finally fall on me will reduce me and my family to begary and want. And of all the Moneys due me from the public I cannot get a shilling.[4] As soon as I return from New York to which place I am going you shall hear farther from me on this subject. All that is just for me to do you may expect from me, so far as it is in my power.[5] I am Sir Your humble Ser   N GREENE

ADfS (MiU-C).

1. In regard to David Henley's drafts on NG, and NG's dispute with Henley and Samuel A. Otis over charges in his "private Account" with them, see the letter immediately above. It is not known when Russell, a Charleston, S.C., merchant, received the drafts.

2. As noted at ibid., NG had had both official and private dealings with Otis & Henley.

3. On the involvement of Cox and Pettit, see note at the letter immediately above. Nothing is known about the transaction involving Story, the former paymaster of the Quartermaster Department. As seen further in this letter, NG was planning to go to New York, but it is not known whether he dealt with this matter while he was there.

4. For background on the claims against NG that had resulted from his guarantee of debts for Southern Army contractor John Banks and associates, see especially the notes at NG to Benjamin Lincoln, 19 December 1782, and Benjamin Harrison to NG, 24 December 1782, above (vol. 12: 308–9n, 341–42 and n), and NG's letter of 22 August, below, to the president of Congress, Richard Henry Lee.

5. NG was in New York in early August. (NG to Gardoqui, 7 August, below) Nothing more has been found about the drafts that Henley sent to Russell or about NG's account with Otis & Henley.

                    *   *   *

¶ [FROM WANTON CASEY, Charleston, S.C., 25 July 1785.[1] Captain Fry, who arrived on the 18th, brought him NG's "very obliging Letter" [not found], enclosing several others for "Gentlemen here." Casey "immediately delivered them" and was "treated with every mark of attention, particularly by Gov[r] [William] Moultrie," with whom he dined "yesterday."[2] He is "sensible" of his "Obligations" to NG and lacks "words to express" his gratitude. As to the business he "came upon," nothing has "succeeded to" his "wishes or expectations," and his only remaining alternative is to "send the Ship after a Load of Salt"; he supposes it will sail "in a Week or 10 Days."[3] He intends to "take passage" with Fry, who will "sail soon for Rhode Island" and has "engaged some passengers among whom is Major [James] Hamilton."[4] Casey will send "three Water melons" to CG with Captain Dillingham, who is to sail the next day; would send more, but Dillingham "cant conveniently take them."[5] The melons "are mark'd with the Letter G." RCS (MiU-C) 2 pp.]

1. On Casey, a Rhode Islander, see also his letter to NG of 26 March 1784, above.

2. Capt. Thomas Fry's packet vessel, the *Diana*, reached Charleston from Newport, R.I., on 18 July. (*South-Carolina Gazette and Public Advertiser*, 19 July) The letter to Moultrie has not been found, nor is it known what other letters NG enclosed to Casey.

3. Nothing more is known about Casey's intended business in Charleston.

4. Fry sailed for Newport on 27 July. (*South-Carolina Gazette and Public Advertiser*, 2 August) In addition to Casey and Hamilton, the listed passengers included Isaac Macpherson and Col. Henry Hampton. (Ibid.) In a letter to NG of 23 August, below,

Robert Hazlehurst expressed regret that "Mr Casey^s stay in this City was not longer." Hamilton was in New York when he wrote NG on 5 October, below.

    5. Capt. E. Dillingham's sloop *William* was in Newport by 13 August. (*Newport Mercury*, 13 August)

¶ [**FROM JEREMIAH WADSWORTH**, New York, 28 July 1785. He was on his way to visit his wife and children at Lloyds Neck, Long Island,¹ when he received NG's letter of the 13th. Has now returned to New York and was informed "This Morning" that Mr. Smith and his brother, after consulting with Judge [William] Burnet, had decided that NG's farm was too expensive and that they could buy "much Cheeper" land adjoining it; Wadsworth believes "they never had a serious intention of buying" NG's property.² "Mrs [Mehitable Russell] Wadsworth suffered so much in her Journey by Water that she will not Venture by water again so that our New Port Journey must be given over"; Wadsworth will visit NG there as soon as possible after he returns to Hartford, Conn.³ RCS (CtHi) 2 pp.]

    1. "That July, Wadsworth brought his family to visit with John Lloyd, Jr., at Queens Village, Long Island, visiting there on weekends, assuring his wife how busy he was in the city." (Destler, "Wadsworth," p. 249)

    2. In his letter to Wadsworth of 13 July, above, NG, who had given him a power of attorney to sell his property near Newark, N.J., asked Wadsworth to consult with a son of Thomas Smith of New York, to whom NG had offered the property for "one thousand pounds Sterling." (See also the powers of attorney that NG assigned to Wadsworth on 26 March, above, and 16 August, below.)

    3. In a letter of 3 July, above, Wadsworth told NG that he hoped to travel to Newport, R.I., with his family. His own ill health kept him from going there before NG left in mid-October to settle in Georgia. (See below, Wadsworth to NG, 5, 11, and 17 September, and 2 October, as well as the note on NG's departure at Knox to NG, 27 October, below.)

¶ [**TO SILAS CASEY**.¹ From Newport, R.I., 30 July 1785. In "looking over" his papers, NG has found "an order" on Casey "for forty Dollars by Daniel Coggeshall on his way home" from New Castle, Del., in 1777. NG asks Casey to "discount it with Messers Jacob & Griffin Greene or settle it in some other way."² ALS (Thomas Casey Greene) 1 p.]

    1. On Casey, "a prominent East Greenwich [R.I.] merchant" and "litigious Yankee," see above, vol. 1: 62n.

    2. The order on Casey has not been found. Casey replied on 11 October, below, that he had paid the money "immediatly on Dan^{ls} arrival here."

¶ [**FROM J[AMES]. STRACHAN, J[AMES]. MACKENZIE & COMPANY**, London, 30 July 1785. They have NG's letter of 5 June and at "any other time" would have been pleased to comply with his request "in taking up William Pierce & C^{os} Bill" to him.¹ However, because of the "many and great Dissapointments" they have met, which they "feel Severely," they cannot "Indulge our Inclination to Oblidge you." RCS (MiU-C) 1 p.]

    1. See NG's draft of the letter to Strachan, Mackenzie & Company, dated 4 June, and Pierce & Company to NG, 9 July, both above.

¶ [**FROM HENRY BANKS**, Richmond, Va., 5 August 1785. He supposes that his "letters written for Charleston," S.C., have not reached NG. Their purpose was "to advise that the diferent persons to whom I unfortunately made assumpsits in behalf of my brother [John] had commenced Suit against me. [Isaac] Smith[, Preeson] Bowdoin and [James] Hunter use every finess to draw from me my property in ord[er] that I may thus effect my enlargement."[1] He does not know how far "such persecution may be carried" but believes that NG's "presence here would be of great Service to yourself and a Salve for me. Mr Hunter from his finesse and friends will palm upon the world the greatest Improbabilities and absolutely force me to do what I know is wrong."[2] Banks's financial prospects are "Superior to any thing that I can ever have to pay but without the Interposition of some one or my liberation[,] final Ruin may insue." He adds: "As my assumpsit to you in a great measure tended to injure me, Humanity I hope will tempt you to effect a Settlem^t of those acco^ts with S B & H which so much they wish to avoid."[3] RCS (MiU-C) 2 pp.]

1. The recent letters from Banks that have been found are those of 13 and 15 July, above. As seen there and in Hunter to NG, 1 June, above, Banks's creditors had succeeded in getting him placed under custody.

2. Hunter wrote NG on 30 September, below, that he, too, was "in Custody of this Court, overwhelm'd with Writs &c, many of which Banks advertises he has paid." (On Hunter's recent actions against Banks, see note at Banks to NG, 15 July.)

3. On Banks's "assumpsit" to NG, see note at his letter to NG of 7 October 1784, above. No reply to the present letter has been found. For further developments, see Banks to NG, 2 September, below.

¶ [TO DIEGO DE GARDOQUI.[1] From New York, 7 August 1785. NG recommends his cousin Griffin Greene, who "was introduced to you yesterday Morning in company with me," to Gardoqui's "good offices." Griffin Greene has a "plan of business in contemplation," and, if he pursues it, "will solicit your letters and countenance." NG hopes Gardoqui will "pardon the liberty" he has thus taken. "Nothing but a desire to serve a deserving young fellow would have induced me to have given your Excellency this trouble."[2] ALS (MiU-C) 2 pp.]

1. Gardoqui, the recently arrived Spanish chargé d'affaires, was to help negotiate the boundaries between the United States and Spanish-held territory. (*JCC*, 29: 567–69; Tanner, *Visit to St. Augustine*, p. 6) Helen H. Tanner has written that "Gardoqui's firm in Bilbao, Spain[,] had been the screen for secret dealings between Spain and the American colonies in the early years of the Revolution. American merchants took advantage of his presence in New York to press their demands for special trade concessions, and for a general commercial treaty with Spain." (Tanner, *Visit to St. Augustine*, p. 6)

2. Griffin Greene had recently returned from a lengthy stay in France on family business. (See Wadsworth to NG, 10 July, above.) On the "plan of business" that he wanted to discuss with Gardoqui, see NG's letter to Jacob Greene of 23 August, below. Later in 1785, Griffin was planning a transatlantic mercantile voyage. (Griffin Greene to NG, 22 December, below)

¶ [TO JAMES ABEEL.[1] From New York, 8 August 1785. NG has been "looking over the original letters to and from" Mr. Anthony Butler, who was in the Quartermaster Department under Gen. [Thomas] Mifflin. This correspondence relates to "a contract made for Camp Kettles and other Articles" with Mr. Samuel Ogden. NG has also been examining "a state of Mr Ogdens Account," relative to that agreement, and believes the manner in which Ogden "stated his account is just between him and the public[,] agreeable to the contract" made by Butler and taken up by Abeel.[2] ALS (RHi) 1 p.]

1. Abeel had been a deputy in the Quartermaster Department under NG. (Vol. 2: 314n, above)

2. Butler was the "agent for camp equipage" under Mifflin, NG's predecessor in the

Quartermaster Department. (Ibid., pp. 322, 323n) Ogden wrote to NG about his accounts on 29 February 1784, above.

¶ [FROM WILLIAM GOOCH, Boston, Mass., 10 August 1785.[1] Asks "what A man of my Age could do with Prudence with a Stock of five hund[d] Pound at Georg[i]a." Sees "nothing to Be done this way to aney Advantige." Hopes to hear from NG by "the very first Opertunity."[2] Sends "best regards" to CG. RCS (MiU-C) 1 p.]
1. The writer may have been related to the late John Gooch, on whom see Partridge to NG, 10 February 1784, above.
2. No reply has been found.

*   *   *

To William Price

Sir   New York Aug[t] 12th 1785

I was informed by Capt Roger Saunders that you was about to put my bond in suit given to Doctor Olliphant.[1] After telling you the circumstances I could not have expected to have been treated with such indelicasy nor should I have expected such an instance of unkindness from an Inhabitant of South Carolinia. It was my intention to pay you as soon as possible. I still mean it. The mode you adopt will not add but decrease my ability nor hasten the time of payment. As quick as my crop comes in I will discharge your bond. Until then I wish you to stay all process as it will be both useless and expensive[2]   N GREENE

ADfS (MiU-C).
1. See Saunders to NG, 22 June, above. The bond was for money originally owed to Dr. David Olyphant for slaves that Saunders purchased for NG. (Pendleton to NG, 30 January 1784, above)
2. See Price to NG, 1 February 1786, below.

*   *   *

¶ [FROM WILLIAM BURNET, Newark, N.J., 13 August 1785. Some "Mistakes & Inaccuracies" were discovered in both of the certificates "annexed by M[r] [Elias] Boudinot to the Papers," so the governor [William Livingston] "could not sign them." As Livingston's son "this Morning" brought them to Burnet and Boudinot, "without altering or sealing them," it was necessary to "send down to Elizabeth Town again for them." Burnet supposes that NG has been "uneasy & ready to conclude that we had forgot you but you see we had not"; he hopes the delay will not be "injurious." He has "this Moment" received the papers again and is immediately forwarding them to NG with his wife's son. He assures NG: "The mistakes were real owing to the Inattention of Mr Boudinot's Clerks & it was not owing to the Govern[rs] Caprice, that he did not seal the Papers at first."[1] Burnet concludes this letter "in great haste." RCS (MiU-C) 1 p.]
1. As seen in NG to Carrington, 29 September, below, Burnet sent NG a relinquishment of inheritance rights to lands on Cumberland Island, Ga. NG's claim to an undivided half

share of Cumberland Island lands derived from a 1783 indenture he had obtained from John Banks and Burnet's brother Ichabod, both of whom had since died. Without relinquishments, the inheritance rights of Banks's and Ichabod Burnet's heirs would have superseded NG's legal rights under the indenture. (See note at Hyrne to Clay, 26 November 1783, above.) John Banks's brother Henry gave up his "Right of Inheritance" to the Cumberland Island lands in November. (Ward to NG, 11 November, below)

¶ [POWER OF ATTORNEY TO JEREMIAH WADSWORTH. [New York], 16 August 1785.[1] NG grants Wadsworth a power of attorney to "grant bargain and sell, all or any the lands, messuages, houses, grounds, tenements, and hereditaments, situate lying and being, in the States of New York, and New Jersey, or either of them."[2] NG's signature is witnessed by A[lexander] Hamilton and Dirck Ten Broeck. DS (Ct) 2 pp.]

1. NG was still in New York at this time. (As noted at his letter to William Ellery of 23 August, below, he arrived home in Newport, R.I., on the 18th.)

2. This was the second of three such powers of attorney that NG gave to Wadsworth. (The others are dated 26 March, above, and 12 October, below.) On these properties, see Estimate of NG's Estate, before 9 January 1784, above.

¶ [FROM LEWIS MORRIS, JR., Charleston, S.C., 20 August 1785. He will write a "line or two" to send on NG's sloop, which, he understands, is to sail the next day.[1] Would have written sooner, but his "attention has been so confined to a sick family" that he has had to let many opportunities pass. Had planned to send a letter with Maj. [James] Hamilton, "but the account which I gave you of your crop was so flattering that I thought it best not to send it." Several of "my people led me into this error." Mr. Croskeys, "who must certainly know, says that your prospect is but tolerable and had I have represented it otherwise the deception might have proved injurious to yourself and consequently painful to me."[2] The season has been "fine" there since NG left, although some rain "would not be amiss," and it is Morris's understanding that the "crop in general is promising," in Georgia, as well as in South Carolina.[3] "Public affairs" are "in a very ticklish situation"; the next meeting of the legislature "will determine whether they are to be productive of good or evil. Money is very scarce—every body complains of the want of it. Great quantities have been shipped," and Morris believes that some "has been hoarded." Rice "is at a dull sale. No purchasers, except a Frenchman and a Spaniard and they pick where they please for twelve shillings and twelve and sixpence, and the rest is left on hand to go off in driblets. Paper money is much talked of and it is so promising to the schemes of many in this part of the Country as well as the upper that I fear we shall have it, or what is equally as bad, a suspension of justice." Morris has "nothing to do with politics or State affairs[,] but whatever is done," he must, as a citizen, "be involved in it." If the legislature could "keep up the credit of the special indents and for a time prohibit the importation of slaves, the evils complained of, might soon find a remedy." Morris believes that "to emit paper without funds to secure it, or faith to receive it would not only increase the confusion among ourselves, but make us the more contemptible abroad."[4] The "number of Carolinians at Newport" must make NG's "Society the more agreeable"; with the "assistance of Doctor Oliphant," who, Morris is told, is "as hearty and as young as ever," they must "frequently make a [corner?] club."[5] Morris sends his and his wife's "best respects" to NG and CG. RCS (CtY) 4 pp.]

1. Morris presumably referred to the *Charleston Packet*, in which the Greene family business had an interest. (NG to Hazlehurst, 26 June, above) As seen in the note at Smith to NG, 23 August, below, the vessel arrived in Charleston about 16 August. Although the date of its return voyage to Newport, R.I., has not been found, an advertisement in the *South-Carolina Gazette and Public Advertiser* of 18 August stated that the sloop would "sail positively on Sunday the 21st instant." It arrived in Newport by 10 September. (*Newport Mercury*, 10 September)

2. Hamilton had traveled north from Charleston in July. (Casey to NG, 25 July, above) John Croskeys assisted in the management of NG's South Carolina plantation, Boone's Barony. (Saunders to NG, 20 October 1783, above)

3. The returns on NG's rice crops were disappointing. (NG to Clarke, 23 November, below)

4. Historian Jerome Nadelhaft has written that when the South Carolina legislature met in a special session in September, it "faced a breakdown of law, order and the rules of commerce." (Nadelhaft, *Disorders of War*, p. 155) "Carolinians, who had amassed a postwar debt of more than £1,500,000 and had not paid off their prewar debts, contributed to England's economic woe; they were, in turn, affected. Threatened English houses pressured the merchants whom they had supplied, and the merchants passed the pressure on to their debtors. Trade suffered, and merchants and planters found themselves at odds, frequently in court." (Ibid., p. 157) When the legislature met in September, Gov. William Moultrie urged it not to "allow 'the power of the Law' to operate"—i.e., in the form of foreclosures—"for if it did the property of a large number of Carolinians would pass to aliens." (Ibid.) Moultrie advocated "modification" of the debtor laws, rather than "enforcement." (Nadelhaft, *Disorders of War*, p. 158) In their special session, the legislators "debated three important measures to relieve the state's economic ills, two of them specifically to aid debtors: prohibiting the slave trade, valuing property sold at public auction, and issuing paper money." (Ibid., p. 161) However, "Motions to prohibit the slave trade for three years were defeated twice, once by a close vote." (Ibid., p. 162) A bill to establish a "loan office to put in circulation £100,000 of paper money backed by property" did become law but was only partially successful in relieving the problems it was meant to address. (Ibid., pp. 163, 165–68) A "valuation act," which "regulated forced property sales," was also adopted. (Ibid., pp. 162–65) According to Nadelhaft, the laws enacted during that session favored wealthy, low country planter/debtors at the expense of poorer, "backcountry" citizens. (Ibid., p. 168)

5. Dr. David Olyphant, who had headed the Hospital Department in the South during the war, was a frequent visitor to Newport. In October 1785, he married Ann ("Nancy") Vernon of Newport and later settled there permanently. (See note at Saunders to NG, 3 December 1783, above.) On other South Carolinians who visited Newport at this time, see, for example, NG to CG, 21 August 1784, above, and the note at NG to Wadsworth, 23 August, below.) There was a "Corner Club" in Charleston at this time. (Meleney, *Aedanus Burke*, p. 85)

* * *

To Governor William Greene of Rhode Island

Sir [Newport, R.I., 22 August 1785][1]

I do my self the honor to inclose your Excellency a letter from Mr William Vassel, which I wish you to lay before the General Assembly.[2] If the facts he relates are justly stated his cause has some claim for Redress.[3] Power is often the Minister of injustice where people are agitated with public commotions but conviction and redress often follow when truth and reason prevail. I am too little acquainted with the business to form any opinion upon the question. Nor have I wish further than what concerns public justice and private right. But if Mr Vassels claim should be well founded it will do honor to the Assembly to consider it upon just principles. Perhaps it is impossible to restore him his property without the consent of the present possessor. All that the Assembly can do in that case is to offer a consideration and leave the parties to settle the rest. To do injustice to one in order to do justice to another will not lessen the evil. It appears to me the property is out of the reach of the Assembly and the only redress is a compensation. I wish the Legis[la]ture to grant the prayer of this petition to satisfy the Petitioner that it is not an act of power but a matter of right agreeable to the Law of Nations on which they have proceeded.[4] There are some things in Mr Vassels letter which would be in excusable upon another occasion but a mind oppressed with a sense of injustice will naturally complain in a tone of Reproach. Nor is he less wide of the Mark when he appeals to personal influence. Sensible how little this would avail him I have not presumed to enter upon the merits of the business; but I felt myself bound in honor to lay the matter before you Sir and submit the rest to your disposal. I should have done it at an earlier hour; but I thought a little delay might give a fairer opportunity for a more full and satisfactory investigation of the subject in question. I have the honor to be with great respect Your Excellencys Most Obedt humble Ser   NATH GREENE

ADfS (MiU-C).
    1. The date was taken from the docketing.
    2. Vassall had been introduced to NG in a letter from Joshua Upham of 10 May 1784, above. Vassall's letter to NG, which NG enclosed with the present letter, has not been found.
    3. On Vassall's situation, see ibid.
    4. William Greene's reply is below, dated 2 October.

To Richard Henry Lee,
President of the Continental Congress

Sir   Newport [R.I.] 22^d Augt 1785
    Misfortunes are more or less painful as they have been brought upon us by folly extravigance or impos'd by public necessity. Those of the latter kind may be distressing but cannot be dishonorable. I have long struggeled with difficulties in which I was involved while in Command to the Southward and which I should have laid before Congress at an earlier period but from a hope that I should extricate myself without their intervention. But as life is uncertain I should do great injustice to my family not to lay the matter before them and claim their indemnity,

should the precautions which I have taken prove insufficient for this purpose I will give them a history of the matter and leave the rest to their justice and the event of things.

The sufferings of the Southern Army in the Campaign's of Eighty One and Eighty Two for want of supplies of all kinds are known to all America. The inability of Congress to give effectual support at those periods need no explanation. In this situation without funds or public credit necessity compeled us to have recourse to many expedients to prevent a dissolution of the Army. In the spring of Eighty Two the Troops would have disbanded but from a seasonable supply of Cloathing got from Charlestown by the Gove'nor and Council of South Carolina.[1] Several hundred men had been as naked as they were born except a Clout about their middle for more than four months and the Enemy in force within four hours march of us all the time. Soon after this I got instructions from the War Office to get supplies of Cloathing in the best manner I could as there could be none sent from the Northward.[2] Mr John Banks one of the House of Hunter Banks and Company contracted to supply us. I advanced him a sum of money and gave him bills on Mr Morris for forty thousand dollars to secure the Cloathing. The whole of which was reported to the Secretary of War at the time.[3] Mr Banks's prospects for securing the Cloathing was with a set of Merchants in Charleston then in treaty with the Governor and Council of South Carolina for permission to remain with their Goods after the place should be evacuated and if the place should not be evacuated those Merchants were to contrive a plan for sending out the Cloathing for the Army.[4] Mr Banks in Writing of this transaction to his partners in Virginia and inclosing a number of the public bills, his letters being opened and the Circumstances not known it gave birth to a report that I held a Commercial connection with him, and this interpretation was more readily given to the affair from Mr Banks's hazarding a conjecture that it was probable I might. On this being communicated to me by the Governor of Virginia I took Mr Banks before the Chief Justice of South Carolina to make oath on the subject. A copy of his affidavit I enclose and have the original in keeping.[5] There are no transactions in life which are more vexatious than those which our Zeal to serve the public is made a subject of private accusation. It is no less mortifying to our pride than unfriendly to our Character. I despise popular prejudices and disdain vulgar suspicions. But least the Army might be tinctured with the rumours on the subject, and sap their confidence so essential to military operations, and the prospects of peace uncertain, I got General Wayne and Colo Carrington to look over the original papers, that the army might be convinced it was a public and not a private transaction, and such they found it. Their report has been made public.[6] Soon after the Enemy left Charleston the Inhabitants[,] who had been much harassed from the mode of subsisting the Troops[,] began to clamour against it. The discontent was so great as to give opposition in some cases and to threaten it in all. This rendered our collections difficult and precarious. Our Soldiers were soon reduced to the utmost distress and at times compeled from hunger to plunder the market in Charleston for support. I believe these are facts known to some of the members now on your floor. The universal cry was a contract for the subsistence of the Army; but such was the critical situation of our finance [that] the difficulty lay in finding persons of property to engage in the business. Application was made to almost every man of property and influence in the State. No one could be found and so scrupulous were the people at one period that no body would take bills on the financire except M[r] Banks and Company and they were the only persons that made any propositions for contracting and their conditions were high and their funds inadequate. The matter was refered to the General Assembly and their advice and assistance solicited upon the occasion. The General Assembly after making the necessary enquiry on the subject discoverd such a backwardness in the people to engage in a contract that they recommended our closing with the offer made by Banks and company even under all the disadvantages which it presented it self.[7] The difficulties which were foreseen were soon felt. The companies funds were inadequate, bills sold greatly under par and but few could be sold at any rate. Those funds which were in the hands of the company were tyed up by prior engagments and the Creditors insisted on further security before they would consent to their application for the support of the Army.[8] The repeal of the impost Law in South Carolina added another difficulty. My address on this subject gave Offence to the Assembly.[9] In this critical situation I had but a choice of difficulties, to turn the Army loose upon the Country or take the risque upon me of supporting the contractors. I chose the latter as the least evil. The sum I first engaged for was upwards of thirty Thousand pounds Sterln[g][,][10] but afterwards when public bills got into better credit I was obliged to give Occasional support by lodging bills to raise money upon, and this was attended with no small risque but happily with no loss. And that as little hazard might be run as possible in my engagments I made the company give an order for all the contract money and sums due on the Clothing department to be paid into the hands of those persons whose debts I had Guaranteed. The Order was given on M[r] [Charles] Pettit[,] the companies agent in Ph[i]ladelphia and one of the Creditors commissioned by the whole sent forward to receive it; and had it been complyed with, it would have discharged my engagments.[11] From this until my return to the Northward I was ignorant that those funds were diverted into other Channels. My indignation at the vulgar suspicions of my holding a conceirn with Banks and company impos'd a sort of silence on me which kept me ignorant of Mr Banks's villany until my arrival at Philadelphia. Mr Pettit then told me what had been done.[12] Alarm'd at the situation of the business I got Doctor [William] Burnet whose son [Ichabod] had been one of the company and was then deceased to send another of his sons [John] to Charleston to have deposits made from the companies funds for the security of those debts for which I stood engaged.[13] He went and the greater part was settled and I should have been discharged from the whole but from new Acts of Villany in Mr Banks.[14] Part of what now remains due is in dispute and I have a bond of indemnity and some mortgages for the rest. But after every precaution I have taken If I should suffer I hope Congress will indemnify me.[15] I have been much perplexed with the business [and] distress'd to the greatest degree in my private affairs; and have already traveled some thousand of miles upon it and am still involved in a Law suit and sundry other difficulties concerning the payments which have been made.

Thus have I given your Excellency a Short narrative of the origin and situation of this matter and have only to add on this subject that I never held any commercial connection with this company other than what concerned the public either directly or indirectly or ever received one farthing profit or emolument or the promise of any from them and my bond of indemnity expressly declares that I have no interest connection or conceirn in the debts for which I became bound all which I am willing to verify on Oath.

Another instance of private loss has attended my command which in many instances has been rendered more difficult and distressing than can be readily conceived. Baron Glusbeck an Officer created for special merit in the action at the Cowpens was in Charleston without mon[e]y or means to get to the Northward, and a foreigner and without credit. I had no money to advance him and indorsed his bills which returned upon my hands with damages and interest to the amount of near a thousand dollars which I have been obliged to borrow the money to settle and still owe it. My Public station impos'd this business upon me and altho' I would not have done it if I had known the fellow to have been as great an imposter as I have reason to believe him since, yet at the same time being commanding Officer I could not well refuse it.[16] I have the honor to be with Great respect your Excellencys most Obedient humble Servt NATH GREENE

LS (PCC, item 155, vol. 2: 710, DNA).

1. On the brief, clandestine trade for supplies with British merchants in Charleston, S.C., see above, Thomas Farr to NG, 10 February 1782, John Mathews to NG, 13 February 1782, and NG to Benjamin Lincoln, 9 March 1782. (Vol. 10: 347–48, 361–62 and n, 468)

2. See Lincoln to NG, 30 September 1782, above (vol. 11: 716–17).

3. See above, NG to Benjamin Lincoln, first letter of 11 November 1782 and 19 Decem-

ber 1782 (vol. 12: 168, 306, 308–9n), and NG to Robert Morris, 3 December 1782 (ibid., pp. 254–55). Lincoln was the secretary at war; Morris the superintendent of finance.

4. On Banks's plan to supply clothing to the Southern Army, see note at NG to Lincoln, 19 December 1782 (vol. 12: 308–9n). The merchants were British subjects who had requested and received permission to complete their business affairs in Charleston after the British army left the city. (Vol. 11: 519n, above)

5. The discovery of Banks's hint that NG might be considering a business connection with him was reported to NG by Gov. Benjamin Harrison of Virginia in a letter of 24 December 1782, above. (Vol. 12: 341–42) The resulting rumors and their consequences are noted at that letter. (Ibid., pp. 342–44n) Banks's statement denying that NG was personally involved in his business is above, dated 15 February 1783. (Vol. 12: 444–46)

6. See Statement of Gen. Anthony Wayne and Col. Edward Carrington, 15 February 1783, above (ibid., pp. 446–48).

7. The British evacuated Charleston on 14 December 1782. NG wrote Morris on 2 February 1783, above: "Ever since the Enemy have been gone we have been obliged to subsist our selves with the point of the bayonet. All the State Agents quitted the business the moment the enemy left Charles Town. Our Sufferings have been great, so much so, that the Troops have taken meat out of the Market by force in contempt of authority. This you may well suppose was no less alarming to the officers than the Citizens. Col Carrington has closed a contract with Mr Banks for the subsistence of the Troops at something less than eleven pence sterling per ration. This is the lowest it could be had as Not another Man or set of Men made an offer to enter into contract but Mr Banks." (Vol. 12: 404) On the provisions contract, see Carrington to NG, 18 February 1783 (vol. 12: 458–59 and n). On the advice from South Carolina officials, see ibid., p. 460n.

8. For a discussion of the financial difficulties that Banks encountered in trying to fulfill the terms of the provisions contract, see vol. 12: 309n.

9. It was NG's letter to Gov. Benjamin Guerard of 8 March 1783, above, that "gave Offence to the Assembly." (Vol. 12: 494–96) South Carolina's repeal of an earlier vote approving the federal impost proposal of 1781 is discussed at that letter. (Ibid., pp. 496–97n)

10. See Agreement between Hunter, Banks and Company and NG with Newcomen and Collett, 8 April 1783, above (vol. 12: 591 and n).

11. See above, Pettit to NG, 23 July 1783, and NG to Pettit, 29 July and 4 August 1783.

12. NG was in Philadelphia in October–November 1783. It appears from Banks's letter to him of 11 November 1783, above, that NG was concerned enough at that time to have written letters to Banks criticizing his business practices. It was while he was in Philadelphia that NG also decided to have the indenture he had obtained from Banks for an undivided half share of Cumberland Island, Ga., legally recorded in Georgia. (Hyrne to Clay, 26 November 1783, above)

13. On the death of Ichabod Burnet, see Flagg to NG, 17 October 1783, above. On John Burnet's efforts to settle debts that his brother had incurred as a partner of Banks, see, for example, Pettit to NG, 8 March 1784, 27 April 1784, and 6 May 1784, all above.

14. See Pettit to NG, 27 April 1784 and 10 June 1784, above.

15. On the debts still in dispute, see NG to Collett, 8 August 1784, and Pendleton to NG, 10 November 1784, both above. As seen in the notes at those letters, it was not until after the adoption of the United States Constitution—and years after NG's death—that Congress finally settled these obligations in favor of his estate. It does not appear that Congress took any action in regard to the present letter. On the "bond of indemnity" and mortgages, see NG's Statement of before 15 October, below.

16. On the issue involving Baron Glaubeck, see above, the note at NG to Washington, 29 August 1784, and such correspondence as NG to Morris, 3 June 1783; Joseph and William Russell to NG, 29 December 1783, and NG to La Caze & Mallet, 14 January 1784.

To William Ellery[1]

Sir   Newport [R.I.] Augt 23[d] 1785

Baron Stuben has made a visit to Newport. On our passage he has given me a history of his plans and prospects in life.[2] He says your Vote is the only obstruction to his obtaining a grant from Congress tho not equal to his former expectations yet will be very satisfactory.[3] Sensible of the delicasy of your situation I am at a loss how to address you on the subject. People will be apt to say Congress should be just before they are generous. But the question is whether this is an implied act of justice rather than a sense of generosity.[4] The Barons claims are high upon the score of merit. The ocenomy and order introduced into the Army from system and dicipline can hardly be too highly rated when we reflect how necessary they were to give a bias to our cause at particular periods. He who has contributed to an event in so imminent a degree has a claim to some thing more than justice.[5] He is the only remaining foreigner with whom we have to settle and if it were possible I should be happy if the manner could be made satisfactory. It is true many are suffering the greatest distress from a want of public justice, but so far as the Barons claims may interfere it can produce but little difference.[6]

N GREENE

ADfS (CtY).

1. Ellery was a Rhode Island delegate to Congress. (Smith, *Letters*, 22: xxvi)

2. The *Newport Mercury* of 20 August reported that NG, "accompanied by the Hon. Major-General The Baron de Steuben," arrived in Newport from New York the previous Thursday (18 August).

3. As noted in vol. 6: 426n, above, Steuben spent a great deal of time after the war lobbying Congress for compensation for his wartime service.

4. By the "delicasy" of the situation, NG referred to the fact that many American officers and troops had not yet received their own pay. NG was more explicit about that in the final sentence of this letter.

5. As noted above (vol. 5: 105n), Steuben's "rigorous program of drill" had established better discipline and order among the Continental army's troops in early 1778.

6. Steuben's account was finally settled in 1794, shortly before he died. (Vol. 6: 426n, above)

*   *   *

¶ [TO JACOB GREENE. From Newport, R.I., 23 August 1785. NG "left Griffin a little unwell in New York with a Slight Fever," which he hopes "will be of a Short Duration." NG would have stayed with him longer, but Griffin "would not consent."[1] NG reports that "Johnson came to New York, feigned himself Sick, relieved his Bondsmen and then ran off again as fast as possible."[2] Jacob's "Brandy will not sell in New York for more than half a Dollar. Griffin is trying to get it off. He purposes loading the Five Ships and going to Spain.[3] The Spanish Minister has given him Letters and Griffin intends if possible to get a Bill of him here to assist in Loading the Ships."[4] Griffin wants Jacob to send a note that is

now held "at [East?] Greenwich" to "Mr Cornelius Ray, Merchant, New York."[5]
NG sends his "Love to all your Friends." Tr (Foster Transcript: RHi) 1 p.]
    1. Griffin Greene, who had recently returned from France, soon made his way to
Newport, where he recuperated in NG's and CG's home. (NG to Wadsworth, 30 August,
below)
    2. This may have been Dr. Robert Johnston, who wrote to NG on 25 August, below.
    3. Griffin appears to have formed several plans during the late summer and fall of 1785
involving mercantile transactions between the United States and Europe. He sailed to
Charleston, S.C., in December, planning to load a cargo there for shipment to France or
Holland. (Griffin Greene to NG, 10 and 16 December, both below)
    4. See NG to Gardoqui, 7 August, above.
    5. On Ray, see his letter to NG of 21 September, below.

*   *   *

To William Shattuck[1]

Sir   Newport [R.I.] Augt 23[d] 1785
    M[r] [William] Crafts of Charles[t]on [S.C.] informed me that you had a
sett of bonds to which I subscribed as security given for the purchace of
Cumberland Island [Ga.].[2] I will acquaint you with some facts and then
leave you to act as you may think proper. While in command to the
Southward I was obliged to engage for large sums of Money for the
Contractors of the Army.[3] The sums were far more than all my property
is worth. Besides these[,] a considerable part of which remains unpaid[,]
I owe considerable sums of money on my own Account for which my
Southern property is under Mortgage.[4] If I get no relief for my public
engagements my family will be reduced to begary. I have by me now
about Eighteen hundred pounds in treasurers Notes on this State the
interest of which is paid Annually and upon which there can never be
any pretence for liquidation as they are taken in my own Name for
public service. I will give you these for the bonds you have in possession on the following terms for every two hundred pounds Sterling
three hundred pounds Lawful.[5] What ever remai[ns] due, I will give
you my own or other peoples obligations for there to the Northward.
I am going with my family to the Southward the first of October.[6] The
issue of my own affairs is uncertain; and I will tell you candidly that the
offer I make you affords you a better prospect of payment than will be in
my power to make you. After which you will act as you think proper. If
I had not been involved in heavy Debts for the public I could have
accomodated payment for all my other engagements; but it is now a
matter of great uncertainty. D[e]mands are now made upon me for
mor[e] than ten thousand Sterling. I wish to hear from you as soon as
possible as I shall [dis]pose of these Notes before I leave the State.[7] I am
Sir your most Obed[t] humble Se[r]   NATH GREENE

ADfS (MiU-C).

1. This letter was addressed to "Mr William Shattuck[,] Boston."

2. On the "security given," see note at Hyrne to Clay, 26 November 1783, above. If Crafts sent this information to NG, the letter has not been found.

3. For background, see NG to Lee, 22 August, above, and documents referred to there.

4. On the mortgage to which NG presumably referred here—on his South Carolina plantation, Boone's Barony—see his letter to Jeremiah Wadsworth of 13 July, above. NG also hoped to give a mortgage on his Georgia plantation in return for a loan he had requested from the Dutch firm of Wilhem & Jan Willink. (See, however, the Willinks' letter to him of 8 July, above.)

5. On NG's Rhode Island "treasurers Notes," see especially the note at William Greene to NG, 1 March 1784, and Littlefield to NG, 25 April 1785, both above.

6. NG and his family left Newport in mid-October to settle in Georgia. (See note at Knox to NG, 27 October, below.)

7. Shattuck did not accept NG's proposal. (Crafts to NG, 27 January 1786, below)

To Jeremiah Wadsworth

Dear Sir   Newport [R.I.] Augt 23^d 1785

My Children have all got the hooping Cough to such a degree that the Doctors advise me not to think of getting them innoculated.[1] This will confine me at home. I wish therefore if you can make it convenient that you would come here with the necessary papers to complete our settlement of the Barnea Dean stocks. I am anxious to settle the business to your satisfaction before I leave this Country. The sooner you can come the better.[2] The preparations for my Southern voyage will soon engross most of my time.[3] I will thank you to bring with you the other five hundred Dollars.[4] People knowing I am going away harass me to death for a number of little Debts.[5]

Bring Mrs [Mehitable Russell] Wadsworth or some of the Children with you. Newport is full of strangers from all parts. It may afford them an opportunity to get some agreeable acquaintances.[6]

I am anxious about a Tutor. Pray make all the enquiry you can on your Journey if you should not meet with any before.[7] I lament the want of one every day. Mr Flint gave me some reason to think his brother would be fond of such a place. If he is half equal to Royal nothing would please me better.[8] Yours affy   NATH GREENE

ALS (NIC).

1. NG evidently hoped to have his children immunized against smallpox before moving to Georgia. The inoculations were done in Georgia during the late winter of 1786. (NG to Knox, 12 March 1786, below) NG reported further on his children's illnesses and the death of his infant daughter in a letter to Wadsworth of 30 August, below.

2. As noted at previous correspondence between NG and Wadsworth, in July and August, Wadsworth was unable to travel to Newport before the Greenes moved to Georgia. Wadsworth sent papers for closing out NG's involvement in Barnabas Deane & Company with his letter to NG of 5 September, below.

3. NG was preparing to move his family to his Georgia plantation, Mulberry Grove. They left Newport in mid-October. (See note at Knox to NG, 27 October, below.)

4. NG again asked for "the other five hundred dollars" in a letter to Wadsworth of 30 August, below.

5. See, for example, Bently to NG, 1 September, below.

6. In his letter of 20 August, above, Lewis Morris, Jr., commented that NG must have been leading a busy social life because of the "number of [South] Carolinians" then at Newport.

7. Wadsworth tried to find a tutor for the Greene children. (Wadsworth to NG, 5 September)

8. On Abel Flint, a younger brother of NG's wartime colleague Royal Flint, see Wadsworth to NG, 17 September, below.

*   *   *

¶ [FROM ROBERT HAZLEHURST, Charleston, S.C., 23 August 1785. Acknowledges letters from NG of 29 June and 24 July [not found]. Regrets that "M[r] Casey[s] stay in this City was not longer," for "his acquaintance proved very agreable."[1] Charles "promises to pay faithfully a dollar & a half p[per] Week agreable to his engagement with you. If I find him neglectfull will sell him on such terms as shall appear most for your Interest."[2] There is little news to report; "Trade is extremely dull & will naturally remain so untill the new Crop comes to Market which at present has a very favorable appearence both in quantity & quality."[3] Hazlehurst believes, "from the benefit" that South Carolinians have experienced in going to Newport that summer, that "it will be much frequented for the future. Those that are now there write in high spirits, both to healthiness & the expence of living."[4] He will be pleased "to render you or your friends agreeable services in this place." RCS (MiU-C) 2 pp.]

1. See Wanton Casey to NG, 25 July, above.

2. Nothing more is known about the arrangement with Charles, apparently a slave of NG's who had been contracted out to work.

3. On economic conditions in South Carolina, see note at Morris to NG, 20 August, above. NG wrote Ethan Clarke on 23 November, below, that "the Crops are but light."

4. See note at Morris to NG, 20 August.

¶ [FROM ROBERT SMITH, Charleston, S.C., 23 August 1785. He received NG's letter [not found] "by Capt Channing," who delivered eighteen sheep to him. Encloses Channing's receipt for "the amount of what you paid." The sheep "are very good," and Smith offers his "best thanks for your kindness & the trouble you took in procuring" them.[1] RCS (MiU-C) 1 p.]

1. This may have been the Robert Smith (1732–1801) who was the first Episcopal bishop of South Carolina and a brother-in-law of NG's former aide Thomas Shubrick. Smith owned several properties in South Carolina, including Brabant plantation in St. Thomas & St. Dennis. (*Biog. Directory of S.C. House*, 3: 671–72) John Channing was captain of the sloop *Charleston Packet*, which arrived in the city about 16 August. In addition to sheep, the vessel's cargo included "Pine Boards, suitable for the inside work of a house, Onions, Mackarel, Cheese, Northward Rum, English Hay, Bricks, a few Maple Desks, and several elegant small ship Boats, Northward built." (*South-Carolina Gazette and Public Advertiser*, 16 and 18 August)

¶ [FROM DOCTOR ROBERT JOHNSTON, New York, 25 August 1785.[1] Johnston, who arrived in New York "a few hours" after NG left, is sorry he did not have "the pleasure of seeing" NG there.[2] He wrote NG "some time ago" about "a Charge of 758 17/90 Dol against me; a Bill drawn Augt 9th 1782 by you in my favour." Asks for "such information as" NG can give him about this.[3] Sends "respectfull Compliments" to CG. RCS (MiU-C) 2 pp.]

1. As seen by his letter to NG of 13 June 1782, above, Johnston, a physician, had been a purveyor for hospitals in the Southern Department. (Vol. 11: 324–25 and n)

2. NG must have left New York soon after he assigned a power of attorney to Jeremiah Wadsworth on 16 August. (See note at NG to Ellery, 23 August, above.)

3. The charge was probably for supplies purchased for the hospital department about that time. (See above, Ichabod Burnet's letter to Joseph Wragg of 4 August 1782, and Burnet to Robert Forsyth, 11 August 1782 [vol. 11: 486, 517].) Neither Johnston's earlier letter on this subject nor NG's reply has been found. (See, however, NG to Jacob Greene, 23 August, above.)

* * *

From the Reverend William Gordon

Dear General   Jamaica Plain [Mass.] Au't 27, 1785.

You will oblige me greatly by an answer to the following questions, upon the return of Mr. Mumford,[1] viz, was the proposal for Baron Steuben's attacking Kniphausen in the night, after the burning of Connecticut Farms [N.J.], on June the 6th; or after the engagement at Springfield on June the 23d? Had Gen'l Washington, the whole force included, on the 23d of June no more than 2500, or had he received between the 6th of June and that period any reinforcement? Was Gen'l Washington at Morris Town or at Short Hills on June the 23d? Was it upon Kniphausen's first advancing from Elizabeth Town that you advised Gen'l Washington to retreat under the feint of guarding the passes, or was the advice given or renewed when they advanced the second time June 23d? Did Gen'l Washington march at all, as the annual Register mentions *with the greater part of his army to secure West Point, etc.*, before the British advanced again toward Springfield on the 23d June?[2]

The readiness You have ever shewn to enable me to keep to the *exact* truth, encourages me thus to trespass upon your time. I know it will give you less pain to prevent my mistaking, than to read any of my mistakes in print. If the Baron is with you, make my respects acceptable to him,[3] and inform him I shall be glad of the Frenchman's name, whether nobleman or commoner, who encouraged his coming over and acquainted him with Mr. Beaumarchais being permitted to send us over military stores, for which Mr. Beaumarchais was to be debited and to account to the French ministry.[4] My best wishes attend You, your Lady and children, while you remain in these eastern states and when you remove to Georgia.[5] Your sincere friend and very humble Servant.

Have written to Mr. Hazard as proposed about Dr. [David] Ramsay's map of the Carolinas.[6]

Printed in *Proceedings of the Massachusetts Historical Society* 63 (1930): 515–16.

1. "Mr Mumford" may have been Edward Mumford (d. 1792), a Newport, R.I., merchant. (*Index of Obituaries in Boston Newspapers, 1704–1795* [Boston: G. K. Hall & Company, 1968], 2: 161) He evidently traveled between Boston and Newport, as Gordon seems to have asked him to carry letters and other material to and from NG. (See Gordon to NG, 12 September, below.) Gordon was writing a history of the Revolutionary War. (See his letter to NG of 31 January 1784, above.) He had visited NG in Newport in March 1784 to gather information. (NG to Knox, 25 March 1784, and Gordon to NG, 5 April 1784, both above) The questions in this letter pertained to American strategy and tactics in New Jersey in June 1780. (For information on the events referred to in this letter, see above, vol. 6: 38–39n.) As noted in vol. 12: 490n, above, the *Annual Register* was a British periodical that Gordon and Dr. David Ramsay both drew upon extensively in their histories of the war.

2. When he did not hear from NG, Gordon wrote a follow-up letter on 12 September, below. NG replied in a letter dated before 24 September, below.

3. Steuben, who had accompanied NG from New York, spent some time visiting the Greene family in Newport. (See NG to Ellery, 23 August, above.)

4. The name of the "Frenchman" who "encouraged" Steuben to come to the United States is not known. Pierre Augustin Caron (1732–99), who took the name "de Beaumarchais" in 1756, was a watchmaker who "had become accepted at [the French] court" and had demonstrated "a remarkable business talent." In 1776, with the aid of the French government, Beaumarchais created a "fictitious firm," Hortalez and Company, through which he channeled cash and supplies to the Americans during the war. (Boatner, *Encyc.*, p. 515; Beaumarchais is discussed in Boatner's entry for "Hortalez & Cie," ibid., pp. 515–18.)

5. NG and his family left Newport to settle in Georgia in mid-October. (See note at Knox to NG, 27 October, below.)

6. Ramsay, who had been an army physician, also served in the South Carolina legislature, on the state's executive council, and as a delegate to Congress during and after the war. His two-volume *History of the Revolution of South-Carolina from a British Colony to an Independent State* was published in 1785. (*Biog. Directory of S.C. House*, 3: 590–94; vol. 12: 490n, above) In his letter of 12 September, Gordon said he had asked Hazard to send the map to NG.

To James Hunter

Sir   Newport [R.I.] August 29th 1785

Your letter of June the first found me here a few days since. I imagine it went by the way of South Carolinia it was so long coming to hand.[1] I am sorry that Mr Henry Banks should Act so wicked as well as so foolish a part. It was certainly for both your interest to come to an amicable setttlement and he promised me most faithfully that he would do all that you could wish or desire; but promises with him I fear have but little force. The little I know of your Merchantile transactions in South Carolinia had all the appearance of candor and fair dealing. And these were the sentiments entertained of your conduct. I am sorry your Creditors impose so unreasonable a requisition on you as giving up my Mortgage. My whole property is involved in the consequences should my other resources fail. In this situation it is cruel in them to ask it. And the more so as this is not a debt in the order of business; but an Act of security.[2] I have the most flattering prospect of getting free from Harris & Blachfords demands and if Colletts attachment on [John] Ferrie[']s Lands take effect little will remain for me to pay. The Moment these are brought to issue and succeed, I will accede to your proposition. But if Harris & Blachford should obtain judgment against me and Colletts attachment fail I cannot relinquish the Mortgages as I have no other prospect for security.[3] However if I can indemnify my self in any other way I will do it, and return you the whole of your property. And at all events I will make a deduction from its product of five hundred pounds Sterling for the benefit of Mrs Hunter should necessity oblige me to avail my self of the Mortgages. But I am in great hopes the business will close more agreeable to all our wishes.[4]

In order to secure my self ultimately against loss, I have laid the Matter before Congress with John Banks's affidavit that I held no concern with the company directly or indirectly.[5] And I have a Certificate from [Robert] Forsyth to the same effect and wish for one from you.[6] Both Burnett [i.e., Ichabod Burnet] & Forsyth were in Philadelphia when I became bound for your house. The credit of the house being our only prospect of support for the Army and Mr Banks giving such strong assurances that no difficulty should result, together with the good opinion I had of you as a Merchant induced me to engage in the matter.[7] Inclosed I send you the Certificate you request; and a copy of Banks's affidavit.[8] I am Sir Your Most Obed^t humble Ser^t   NATH GREENE

ALS (RPB).
1. The present letter is a reply to Hunter's of 1 June, above.
2. NG referred to the debts he had guaranteed for John Banks, Hunter, and others as Southern Army contractors. (For background, see above, NG to Lee, 22 August, and documents referred to there.)
3. As seen in the notes at NG to E. John Collett, 8 August 1784, and Pendleton to NG, 10 November 1784, NG's obligations to Newcomen & Collett and Harris & Blachford were finally resolved by acts of Congress some years after NG's death.
4. See preceding note.
5. See NG to Lee, 22 August, and note 3, above. Banks's affidavit is above, dated 15 February 1783. (Vol. 12: 444–46)
6. In a statement dated 3 March 1785, Forsyth attested: "It having been insinuated by some, and propagated by others, that the honorable General Greene was concerned in the Charleston speculation, with John Banks and Company, and with the contract for the army, I do hereby certify, that the General was in no ways interested in either, with the said Copartnership." Forsyth's statement, which was submitted in support of CG's 1791 petition to Congress, seeking relief from the debts NG had guaranteed, is printed in Syrett, *Hamilton*, 10: 447; on the outcome, see note at NG to Collett, 8 August 1784. In another, undated statement that was submitted with CG's petition, James Taylor certified that Hunter had "made oath on the holy Evangelists, That he never considered" NG "either directly or indirectly concerned or interested in a purchase of goods, made by John Banks in Charleston, on the proper account and benefit of the following persons only, viz: John Banks, Robert Forsyth, Ichabod Burnet, John Ferrie, Robert Patton, and said James

Hunter; who further deposeth and saith, that he never heard, or ever understood, from either the abovementioned persons, either by letter or words, that General Greene was, any means concerned or interested in said purchase." (The statement is printed in Syrett, *Hamilton*, 10: 446–47.) As seen in Benjamin Harrison to NG, 24 December 1782, above, the rumors about NG's possible involvement with Banks and his partners had been drawn from hints found in an intercepted letter from Banks to Hunter. (Vol. 12: 341–42 and n)

7. See Agreement between Hunter, Banks and Company and NG with Newcomen and Collett, 8 April 1783, above (vol. 12: 591 and n). NG's aide Burnet and Forsyth, the Southern Army's commissary of purchases, had both left the army before then to enter partnerships with Banks.

8. As seen in his letter of 1 June, Hunter was seeking statements "to prove to the world whether I have acted as became the merchant^s Integrity." NG's "Certificate" has not been found. For the location of Banks's affidavit, see note 5, above. Hunter replied to NG on 30 September, below.

*   *   *

¶ [FROM THOMAS WOOSTER, New Haven, Conn., 29 August 1785.[1] He has heard that NG plans to move his family to Cumberland Island, Ga., "this Fall."[2] Having an inclination of his own "to visit that Country" and see if he could find a place where there is "a prospect of doing business to advantage," he would like to "accompany" NG there; asks for a reply. A Doctor Milne at New Haven, "who is a regular bred Physicia[n] at the Hospitals and Lectures in London," is also inclined "to settle in that Country, if he thought there woud be suffic[ient] encouragement"; Wooster asks NG for his opinion.[3] RCS (CtY) 2 pp.]

1. Wooster, son of Gen. David Wooster, had served as an aide to his father and as a captain in Webb's Additional Continental regiment during the war. The younger Wooster, a 1768 graduate of Yale College and father of seven, owned a store in New Haven but was "unsuccessful in business." He finally moved to New Orleans in 1791 but died the following year during a return voyage to New Haven. (Dexter, *Yale Graduates*, 3: 300–301; Heitman, *Register*)

2. NG was moving his family to his Georgia plantation, Mulberry Grove, and not to Cumberland Island. His reply, if any, to Wooster has not been found. Jeremiah Wadsworth wrote NG on 11 September, below, that Wooster was a "poor creature," who would "imbarrass you."

3. Dr. George Milne, a Scot, received a "D^r in Physic" degree from Yale at the college's September 1785 commencement. (Stiles, *Diary*, 3: 158n, 185)

*   *   *

To Jeremiah Wadsworth

Dear Col   Newport [R.I.] Aug 30th 1785

Since I wrote you last Tuesday I had the misfortune to loose my youngest Child with the throat distemper.[1] Mrs Greene is very poorly and my two little Girls very sick with the hooping Cough. Patty is so bad with it as to be dangerous.[2] Cousin Griffin is arrivd from New York and now lays sick with the fever at my house.[3] All these circumstances will prevent my going from home. I must beg you therefore to come to me as I am anxious to settle the Barnea Dean affair before I go South.[4] I am anxious for a Tutor You cannot oblige me more than in engaging me one. I shall not know what to do without one my Children are advancing in life so fast.[5] I will also thank you for the other five hundred Dollars.[6] Yours NATH GREENE

ALS (PHi).
1. NG wrote Wadsworth about his children's illnesses on 23 August, above. His infant daughter, Catharine, or "Caty," had most likely been born earlier in August. Neither the date of her birth nor that of her death has been firmly established, but an entry for 11 August in Dr. Isaac Senter's daybook indicates that NG was billed on that date for expenses relating to a birth in his household. (RHi) After her birth, the child had apparently been placed with Barbara Bently in East Greenwich. (See Bently to NG, 1 September, and Turner to NG, 5 September, both below.)
2. NG's other children, including Martha ("Patty"), who had been dangerously ill, recovered from the disease.
3. Griffin Greene had returned from France earlier in the summer. (NG to Wadsworth, 13 July, above)
4. Wadsworth sent the papers for closing NG's involvement in Barnabas Deane & Company with a letter to NG of 5 September, below.
5. As seen in ibid., Wadsworth tried to find a tutor for the Greene children.
6. On "the other five hundred Dollars," see also NG to Wadsworth, 23 August.

From Henry Osborne

Sir   Cumberland [Island, Ga.] 30th Aug[t] 1785
    I had not the honor of recieving your letter of the 9th June until the last day of July which is the only letter I ever had the pleasure of receiving from you.[1]
    Many of the refugees have come to this side S[t] Marys and settled on the Main.[2] M[r] Semple I think has not been as active as he ought in inducing people to settle on the Island. The idea of a Town is Passed nor do I beleive it now practicable to revive it.[3] M[r] Semple at Philadelphia has been so much displeased with his brother's conduct here that he has suspended him so that I believe your bargain respecting the Island to be at an end.[4]
    The British with Tonyn at their head behave more insolently than ever. Tonyn has sent several armed parties into this State and carried off people by force. I have colluded there Testamony but how far our Government will interfere I know not.[5] I have the Honor to be with due respect Sir Your Obd[t] Hb[le] Serv[t] H OSBORNE
    There was a large Franch Ship here three Days since for live Oake. The New Consul from Sav[a] was on board, he came on shore and ex[d] part of the Island. He was much pleased with the Oake but seemed displaced and dissapointed that no cargoe was ready for the Ship. She went for Sapalo.[6]

RCS (MiU-C).

1. The letter has not been found; Osborne had written to NG on 23 April, above, requesting directions for promoting settlement on Cumberland Island.

2. Although NG hoped to attract British refugees from East Florida to settle on Cumberland Island, Osborne had warned in his letter of 23 April that most of the prospective settlers were likely to leave for other British possessions unless measures were taken quickly to persuade them to stay. As Osborne indicated here, a number of refugees did move from East Florida to the Georgia side of the St. Marys River.

3. Alexander Semple, who kept a store on Cumberland Island, had apparently promised to purchase part of NG's share of Cumberland Island and to promote the settlement of British refugees there. (See NG to Wadsworth, 8 March, and NG to William Semple, 4 June, both above.)

4. Osborne referred here to William Semple of Philadelphia. (NG to William Semple, 4 June) On the "bargain," which NG had made with Alexander Semple, see preceding note.

5. On the Loyalist "banditti" who had been operating along the East Florida–Georgia border, see note at NG to CG, 14 April, above. Patrick Tonyn, the former British governor, was still in East Florida, supervising the evacuation of British subjects. (Ibid.)

6. On the French ship that stopped at Cumberland Island, see also Pendleton to NG, 23 September, below. The "New Consul from Sav[a]" [i.e., Savannah] was the Chevalier de la Foreste. (Marbois to NG, 18 May, above; see also Foreste to NG, 16 December, below.) John McQueen was hoping to sell timber from his holdings on Sapelo Island to the French government. (McQueen to NG, 23 May, above)

*   *   *

¶ [FROM BARBARA BENTLY, East Greenwich, R.I., 1 September 1785. Encloses "all the Bills Relating" to NG's "Daughter Katey Greene deceast[,] all but the Doctors who had Not Made out his but Said he would Make it out [and] send it as Soon as Posible."[1] The bills include £1.10 from Job Olney, Jr., for the coffin, 5s.5d. from Jacob and Griffin Greene, and Bently's "own" for £1.8.6. Abraham Greene also "has Some Demand for bidding to the funeral and ringing the Bell," but Bently has not yet been "been Able to get" it. RCS (MiU-C) 1 p.]

1. NG's and CG's infant daughter, Catharine, had died of "throat distemper" in late August. (NG to Wadsworth, 30 August, above) Bently may have been a wet nurse for the Greenes' two most recent babies. (See her letters to NG of 1 June 1784 and at the end of the June 1784 documents, both above.) Dr. Peter Turner sent his bill to NG on 5 September, below.

*   *   *

From Henry Banks

Sir   Richm[d] [Va.] Sep[r] 2. 1785

I have setled with Maj. Carns for the whole amo[t] of my Securityship by giving up Kentucky Lands to be valued.[1] I expect to arrange with the other demandants upon me in the same way this fall. Nothing will then rest upon me but the final Close of your Business; provided you will push your Securities and eventually decide upon the amo[t] I will use the same measures to y[our]self. Cumberland Island is represented to me as being exceedingly more valuable than £10,000 St^g. I should be glad if some plan was adopted of making the most of it, by disposing of the Timbe[r] and Cultivation for the purpose of whic[h] I would [invest?] £2500 in Negroes. Thus mig[ht] the Purchase money be paid by Instalm[ents] and further Secured upon the Negroes and as the Crops and Timber will bear a great annual Proportion towards payment I may be reimbursed for my heavy advances.[2]

I wish very much that you Would come to Virginia, that you w[ould] be both satisfied of my Innocence of things spoken to my prejudice and the readiness I ever have to do what is right.[3] I am your obe^t Ser

HENRY BANKS

RCS (MiU-C).

1. For background on the securityship in which Patrick Carnes was involved, see Saunders to NG, before 17 July 1784; Pettit to NG, 26 July 1784, and Penman to NG, 12 August 1784, all above. A few months earlier, Banks had announced in newspaper notices that he owned "Lands on the upper Waters of James River, and in different parts of the Western Country, which I wish to give to any person having an acknowledged demand against me, either for what they may be now valued by reputable men, or to give a security on them, to be sold in two years." (See, for example, *Virginia Gazette*, 27 May.)

2. NG derived his claim to an undivided half share of lands on Cumberland Island, Ga., from the indenture he had obtained from Banks's late brother John and the late Ichabod Burnet as security for guaranteeing a bond worth £10,000 for them. (Hyrne to Clay, 26 November 1783, above) Burnet's heirs had recently relinquished their rights of inheritance to the Cumberland Island land, but Henry Banks had resisted pressure to to do the same. (See above, William Burnet to NG, 13 August, and Edward Carrington to NG, 23 March.) On the island's resources and potential value, see NG to Marbois, 15 April, above.

3. NG's reply has not been found, but in a letter of 29 September, below, he asked Carrington "Please to write me whether Henry Banks will or will not give a relinquishment for Cumberland." NG did not go to Virginia but did send his friend Samuel Ward, Jr., to see Banks with a proposal that if "Banks will give a deed of relinquishment I will take the property for the sum I am engaged for on it. Or if Mr Banks will get my bonds up; and repay me the Money and interest already advanced on it I will give up the Mortgage immediately. It is in vain for Mr Banks to think of improving the property in the way he proposes. I shall never undertake it upon any such plan." (See below, NG's statement dated before 15 October, below.) Ward apparently did persuade Banks to give what Banks, in a letter to NG of 12 November, below, termed an "unequivocal Relinquishment" of "my Right of Inheritance to the lands purchased by my Brother and for the payment of which you stood bound." (See also Ward to NG, 11 November, below.) Some forty years later, in an unsuccessful memorial to Congress, Henry Banks would argue that the reimbursements that NG's estate received from Congress during the 1790s for the debts that NG had guaranteed for John Banks did "not exceed the losses which [John] Banks sustained on the contract for supplying the army with provisions, and that he [Henry Banks] is entitled, as representative as aforesaid, for all that Greene received, or might have received in consideration of the aforesaid administration, and likewise the interest held by Banks in Cumberland." (See Banks, *Vindication*, pp. 7–8; on the reimbursements by Congress, see notes at NG to Collett, 8 August 1784, and at Pendleton to NG, 10 November 1784, both above.)

From Barnabas Deane

[Dear] General   Hartford [Conn.] 4th Sepr 1785.
As the partnership of B. Deane & Cº Closed Last Decr, in which you was One Third Interested,[1] and the Sum for Transacting the Buisness being not fixed on, it may be pro[per] for me to Say what Sum I Expected for [my] Services; when I Entered on the Buisness I Gave up all my Private Trade & Confind my Self Entirely to the Companys Buisness. I have put them to no Expence for hir[ing] of a Clerk, or the keeping of a Horse wh[ich] was Necessary in Carrying on the Buisness.[2]

I Always Suppos'd that Two Hundred Pounds a Year would be a Reasonable Sum for my Services, (which would but Just Support me).

I Observe in the Calculation made for a Settlement with Col. [Jeremiah] Wadsworth & Your Self, that [my?] Services are Estimated at Abt One Hundred & [damaged] Pound a Year. I never mean to be uneasy with the Sum You & Col. Wadsworth [agreed?] On, You are Better Judges than my[self] the worth of Transacting the Buisness. If [after?] Consideration you Shall think the first [damaged] you have Affixed on Equal to the Services Done, I will make myself Content with it, Notwithstanding [m]y thinking on a Larger Sum.[3] I am Sorry our C[o]ncern was not more fortunate. I am with Esteem Dear Sir Yr Very Huml ser[vt]

B DEA[NE]

RCS (MiU-C).

1. Jeremiah Wadsworth, who bought out NG's share in the partnership at the end of 1784 (NG to Wadsworth, 29 December 1784, above), sent NG the papers for closing out his financial affairs on 5 September, below.

2. Deane had previously raised the issue of his compensation in letters to NG of 26 February 1784 and 30 March 1784, both above.

3. Wadsworth wrote NG on 5 September that he had "allowed Mr Deane One thousand pounds which he thinks little enough." NG appears to have tacitly agreed to that amount. (See NG's letter to Wadsworth and To Whom It May Concern, both 7 September, below.) As NG was a partner in the firm from April 1779 through December 1784—about 5.75 years (see note at Deane to NG, 5 January 1784, above)—the £1,000 for Deane's services amounted to a little less than £175 per year.

*   *   *

¶ [FROM DOCTOR PETER TURNER, East Greenwich, R.I., 5 September 1785.[1] Encloses his bill, which NG requested from "Mrs Bentley."[2] RCS (MiU-C). 1 p.]
1. On Turner, see note at his letter to NG of 31 May 1784, above.
2. The enclosure has not been found. Barbara Bently, who had collected several other bills related to the death of NG's infant daughter, Catharine, wrote NG on 1 September, above, that the doctor would send his "as Soon as Posible." Turner had undoubtedly been the attending physician at the time of Catharine's death.

*   *   *

From Jeremiah Wadsworth

My dear Sir   Hartford [Conn.] Septr 5th 1785
I received your favor of the 30th last Evening. I was then too much indisposed to think of comeing to New Port, the gloomy Picture of your
famaly did but increase my indisposition. I have been confined again to
my bed since I wrote you & have frequent attacks of Pain in ye Head &
limbs.[1]

I send this by Express with the Papers necessary for closeing [*damaged*] the Barnabas Dean[e] & Co concern.[2] You will see by the amounts
stated a difference from the former Estimate of £458.14.9 LM [i.e.,
Lawful Money][3] besides which their was several Small losses, to Wit, on
the £444.4.8 and £2500 in the hands of the Hopkins's Brig *Nicholas* &
Cargo. The latter is yet uncollected & at risk in St Criox. The Distillery
House cost more at ye time it was built, being in ye Wars than it is now
worth.[4] Some profit has arisen since the Estimate delivered so that at
present Mr Deane Estimates our Whole Stock to be worth Six thousand
Pounds,[5] but this includes the two last Voyages of the Brig^n [*blank*]
which have been performed at my Risk.[6] Nor is any interest or advance
allowed me for advances made for the Stills & Sundry other advances to
a large amount so that I believe the present mode of settlement is a just
one.[7] I have charged you no interest on the Nine hu[nd]re[d] poun[ds]
advanced in 1783.[8] If you find on examination that I have been mistaken
in my calculations I will alter them.[9] I have allowed Mr Deane One
thousand pounds which he thinks little enough but will abate the one
hundred if you think it just. He writes you.[10] I send you One hundred &
Twenty pounds nine Shillings and Eight pence in Money & my Bill on
Nat[haniel] Shaler at thirty days date for One hundred and fifteen
pounds L Money, these two Sums make the ballance to Wit—two hundred Eighty five pounds nine Shillings & Eight pence L.[11] I woud have
sent you the Ballance all in Cash but I am pressed for money, various
ways, and we have nothing that will command money. I am sorry to
hear Griffin Green is so unwell.[12] I am afraid for him, will it not be best
to have a Bill of Sale of these goods in N York in case of his death & Your
absence their might be some difficulties arise.[13] I have inserted in the Bill
of Sale for the Stock the Sum of Nine hundred & Sixty pounds Nine
Shillings & four pence[;] in the Quit claim deed eight hundred & twenty
pounds, the two Sums makeing the Ballance of Seventeen hundred &
Eighty pounds Nine Shillings & 4^d.[14]

At the approaching Commencement at New Haven I will get you a
tutor, but it will be Necessary to have your directions respecting a
Sallery. I suppose he is to be in your family, but write me particularly on
this Subject.[15] M^{rs} [Mehitable Russell] Wadsworth & all the family join
me in best wishes to your Selfe Mrs Greene & the Children. We hope ere

this the Children are better. We found when our children had the Hooping Cough [riding?] the best Medicine & Molasses & Water the best drink.[16] I hope to be able to come & see you Before You go to the Southward. When shall you sail.[17] The Deed must be Signed in pre-senc[e] of two Witness[e]s & acknowledged before a Justice of y[e] Peace or 2 men to make it Valid here.[18] I am dear Sir very sincerely & Affec-tionately Yours JERE WADSWORTH

RCS (MiU-C).

1. NG's letter to Wadsworth of 30 August is above. Wadsworth's most recent letter to him was presumably that of 28 July, above; as noted there, Wadsworth was unable to visit the Greenes before they left Newport, R.I., in October to live in Georgia.

2. NG had been anxious to obtain a final settlement of what Wadsworth owed him for his share in Barnabas Deane & Company. (See, for example, NG to Wadsworth, 30 August.) As seen in NG's letter to him, 29 December 1784, above, Wadsworth had purchased NG's share.

3. Deane wrote NG on 26 February 1784, above, that the value of the company's stock, which NG assumed from studying an earlier estimate to be about £7,000, was "as much Short of that Sum as the Am[t] of my Services & The debts Due from us." (The price of Deane's services is discussed elsewhere in this letter and at Deane to NG, 4 September, above.)

4. On the distillery, which was in Hartford, see also Wadsworth to NG, 6 May, above. As noted at his letter to NG of 16 November 1784, above, Wadsworth had advanced money to purchase the distilling equipment. According to historian Chester M. Destler, Deane & Company found it "difficult to exchange its new distillery's rum for horses for the French West Indies market." The company's lack of access to island markets was afterward resolved, however, through "governors' connivance, bribing customs officials, and smuggling"; Deane then was able to market the rum in exchange for "country produce for export to the islands" and "European goods, earning a profit larger than those of dry goods stores." (Destler, "Wadsworth," p. 258)

5. On the value of the stock, see also note 3, above, and Deane to NG, 4 September.

6. The brigantine was presumably the *Catherine*, which had been sent on trading voyages to Ireland. (Destler, "Wadsworth," p. 259)

7. On the advances for the stills, see note 4, above.

8. It is not clear whether the £900 included both company expenses and personal advances that Wadsworth had made for NG. (On the personal advances, see above, NG to Wadsworth, 21 April 1783 [vol. 12: 630], and Wadsworth to NG, 12–13 June 1783 and 26 July 1783.)

9. NG's reply is immediately below.

10. See Deane to NG, 4 September.

11. See also Shaler to NG, 20 September, below.

12. See NG to Wadsworth, 30 August.

13. The "goods in N York" were cargo that Griffin Greene had brought from France and for which he had received an advance. NG wrote Wadsworth on 13 July, above, that Griffin "says if god spares his life he will certainly make payment which is not due until next February. And that you should run no risque I covered this Debt in a Mortgage to you before I left South Carolina." (On the mortgage, see note at that letter.) NG wrote Wadsworth on 7 September that Griffin was "getting much better."

14. Neither document has been found. NG acknowledged receipt of £960.9.4 for his share of "the Stock in trade" on 7 September. (To Whom It May Concern, 7 September, be-low) The quitclaim was presumably for NG's share of property owned by the partnership.

15. The Yale College commencement was held on 14 September. (Stiles, *Diary*, 3: 184–85) As seen in his reply, immediately below, NG believed he had already found a tutor.

16. Several of NG's children had been ill with whooping cough. (NG to Wadsworth, 23 and 30 August)

17. See note 1, above.

18. Griffin Greene and William Littlefield, the witnesses to NG's receipt for his share of the company stock in trade, presumably also witnessed the signing of the deed. (To Whom It May Concern, 7 September)

To Jeremiah Wadsworth

My dear Sir   Newport [R.I.] Sept 7th 1785

I have just recievd the papers Accounts and Money by your Express. I will not detain your Express a moment to look into the settlement. The footing on which you have put it is generous and I dare say the state of it right.[1] I have signed and acknowledged the Deed and the conveyance of the stocks all which I hope will be found agreeable to your wishes.[2]

I am sorry to find your complaint still troublesome to you.[3] Since I left New York I have lost a Child and my eldest daughter is now very ill. Mrs Greene is very unwell but thinks her self a little neglected by you.[4] If you can make it convenient to pay her a visit it will make up for all past matters.[5] Griffin Greene is getting much better.[6] He has sold his Brandy and got part of the Money and the rest is soon expected. He intends to send the ship *Minerva* to Virginia to load with Tobacco; and wishes if you have any late price currents from Alexandria that you would be good enough to send him a copy. The kind assurances you made him on your leaving New York impresses him with a lively sense of gratitude. Any services you can render the house not to your own prejudice will add to my happiness.[7]

I expect to sail for Georgia in about four Weeks.[8] It would add to my happiness if you could take a quarter or half concern in Cumberland. My funds are unequal to so great a property. It is a triffle for you and the payments easy and I am certain you can not speculate on better prospects. I shall attend to the matter my self. Dont fail to write Church on the subject. If he and you would join me in the business it would make my heart as light as a feather.[9] Come and see us if you can and bring some of your family with you. We are in affliction but you will add to our comfort.[10] Tell Mr Dean I am perfectly satisfied with his conditions and should write him but dont wish to detain the Express.[11] Yours sincerely and affectionately   NATH GREENE

Miss Vernon is in the Country. I have lodged your Paquet with her Mother.[12]

NB I have got a Tutor therefore dont take any more trouble on the subject.[13]

ALS (CtY).

1. See Wadsworth to NG, 5 September, immediately above.

2. NG's receipt for "the conveyance of the stocks" is immediately below.

3. Wadsworth was troubled by "frequent attacks of Pain" in his "Head and Limbs." (Wadsworth to NG, 5 September)

4. NG wrote Wadsworth on 30 August, above, that his baby daughter, Catharine, had died and that his eldest daughter, "Patty," was very ill. CG and at least one other daughter had also been sick.

5. See note 9, below.

6. On Griffin Greene's illness, see NG to Wadsworth, 30 August, and Wadsworth to NG, immediately above.

7. Wadsworth replied on 11 September, below, that he was expecting to receive information from Virginia. On 17 September, below, he reported some prices on produce that he had received from Alexandria.

8. NG left for Georgia in mid-October. (See note at Knox to NG, 27 October, below.)

9. Wadsworth had written NG the previous spring that he would not be able to invest in Cumberland Island, Ga. (Wadsworth to NG, 10 April, above) In reply to the present letter, he reiterated that position but said he would try to interest his partner John Barker Church in an investment there. (Wadsworth to NG, 11 September)

10. As noted at his letter to NG of 28 July, above, Wadsworth was unable to visit NG and his family before they left Newport. The Greene family was "in affliction" because of the death of its youngest member. (Note 4, above)

11. See above, Wadsworth to NG, 5 September, and Barnabas Deane to NG, 4 September.

12. On Nancy Vernon, see Wadsworth to NG, 21 December 1783, above. Nothing is known about the "Paquet."

13. Wadsworth was helping to find a tutor for the Greene children. (Wadsworth to NG, 5 September) The person NG thought he had hired decided not to take the job. (Dow to NG, 9 September, below)

To Whom It May Concern

To all whom it may concern   [Newport, R.I., 7] September 1785[1]
Know Ye That I Nathaniel Greene of New Port in the State of Rhode Island For the Consideration of Nine hundred and Sixty pounds Nine shillings & four pence paid me by Jeremiah Wadsworth of Hart[ford] in the State of Connecticut, have bargained & Sold him the Said Jerem[ah] Wadsworth all my Right Title and interest in the Stock in trade which I have a right to have in the direction of Barnabas Deane & Co[.,][2] of which Company I the Said Nathanael Greene was one[,] Jeremiah Wadsworth & Barnabas Deane the two others[,] and we were equally concerned therein, my original Share of Said Stock was paid into the hands of y[e] Said Jeremiah Wadsworth in the Years AD 1779 and 1780, and his receipts given therefor to me and others for me by whom the Said Sums were paid.[3] I do hereby discharge the Said Wadsworth from all demands on acc[t] of Said receipts for Monies paid him or his agents in the Said Years AD 1779 and AD 1780. They all being for the original Stock aforesaid and my Share of y[e] Same.

I do by these presents confirm to him all my right title & interest therein & di[s]charge him from all future deman[d]s on the acc^t of Said Stock & Monies. In Witness whereof I have hereunto set my hand & Seal this [blank] day of September AD 1785.   NATH GREENE
Witness GRIFFIN GREENE
WILLIAM LITTLEFIELD

DS (CtY).
1. The date was determined from information in NG to Wadsworth, immediately above, and Wadsworth's reply of 11 September, below. NG was in Newport at this time.
2. For background, see above, NG to Wadsworth, 29 December 1784, and Wadsworth to NG, 5 September.
3. On the formation of the partnership, see Articles of Partnership between NG, Wadsworth, and Deane, 4 April 1779, above (vol. 3: 377–79 and n).

From Hendricus Dow[1]

Sir   Woodstock [Conn.] September 9th 1785
You doubtless remember my acceptance of your generous offer on the 3^d Ins^t as an encouragement for serving in your family as a private Instructor, & that I proposed to come to New-Port as soon as I should settle some business at Ashford which I supposed might be accomplished in a fortnight.[2] With pleasing reflections on my good fortune in having found a most eligible opportunity for going to the Southward, I returned to Ashford & without delay began to prepare for my Voyage, but an unforeseen accident has rendered my [purpose?] inconsistent with my Interest, &, I fear wholly impracticable.

My good Mother, to whom I am indebted for my Education, & who not long since with some reluctance consented to a proposal for seeking my fortune in the southern States on account of some late unfavourable occurrences in her affairs, & for several reasons, which I have not at present time to specify & which perhaps you have not leisure to hear, has forbid my departure & the prosecution of my wishes.[3]

Both on account of my own Interest & the obligation I am under to so great a patron of the Liberties of my country would I wish to serve you. But this timely notice of my circumstances I feel myself under obligation to send you, that you may not lose an opportunity of procuring for your family a more accomplished & worthy Preceptor[4] than, Sir, Your most obedient & most humble Servant   HENDRICUS DOW

RCS (MiU-C).
1. Dow (1761–1814), a 1784 graduate of Yale College, later became a student of theology and, eventually, a lawyer. (Dexter, *Yale Graduates*, 4: 336–37)
2. NG had been trying to find a tutor for his children. (NG to Wadsworth, 30 August, above) Neither his offer of the position nor Dow's acceptance has been found. As seen in his letter to Jeremiah Wadsworth of 7 September, above, NG knew by that date that Dow had agreed to his offer.

3. The "late unfavourable occurences" in Elizabeth Marsh Dow's affairs are not known. Her husband had died in 1772, when Hendricus Dow was about eleven years old. (Dexter, *Yale Graduates*, 4: 336)

4. NG received this letter on 13 September, one day before Wadsworth, had he known about it, could have tried to find another candidate for the job at the Yale College commencement. (See NG to Wadsworth, 13 September, below, as well as Wadsworth to NG, 5 September, above.) After Dow sent this letter, he apparently wrote to ask Dr. Ezra Stiles, the president of Yale, to try to find a tutor for NG's family. (NG to Wadsworth, 4 and 5 October, both below)

From Jeremiah Wadsworth

My dear Sir   Hartford [Conn.] Sept[r] 11 1785
I rec[d] your favor of the 7th incloseing y[e] Papers executed. I am exceedingly sorry for all your afflictions & wish my health was such that I cou'd come & see you. I am sorry M[rs] Greene is unwell[;] have wrote her herewith. I wou'd not miss seeing you & her before you go in any acc[t] but such is my health & such my business that I am not able to promise my selfe any thing.[1] I am lingering under a variety of complaints none very serious but combined they are formidable & tho they do not dispirit they disable me. I expect every moment to hear from Fitzgerald of Alexandria [Va.] when I do will communicate all y[e] intelligence to G G. & you may be assured I will do him every service in my power.[2]

I have written to M[r] Church largely on the subject of Cumberland Iseland and hope to have some good news from him as I see y[r] Island is become an object by y[e] British papers. But at present is impossible for me to take a concern in it as I am pressed for Money[;] however strange it may appear to you the truth is I am really imbarrassed and have several thousands to pay which I must raise by the first of October, & have no means but to sell goods at a loss, as borrow y[e] latter is impossible.[3] M[rs] [Mehitable Russell] Wadsworth joins me in affectionate complements to M[rs] Green y[r] Selfe & y[e] Children. I am d Sir your affect ser[t]

JERE WADSWORTH

[A] Number of people from Haddam [Conn.] want to buy your & Beckwells Land on y[e] North River. They will go & See it, but I cant describe its situation.[4]

Cap[t] Tho[mas] Wooster is comeing to New Port to make proposals to go with you to Cumberland Isel [i.e., Island.] He is a poor creature & will imbarrass you. I give you this hint least his plausibillity shou'd draw you in to give him incouragement to go. If you do you must Maintain him & his family & he will never do you any service. He must not go.[5]

RCS (MiU-C).

1. NG's letter of 5 September is above. Wadsworth's letter to CG has not been found. As noted at his letter of 28 July, above, Wadsworth was unable to visit the Greenes before they left Newport, R.I., to live in Georgia.

2. In his letter of 7 September, NG had asked Wadsworth to help Griffin Greene in a business venture.

3. NG had asked Wadsworth to invest in Cumberland Island, Ga., and to encourage John Barker Church to do so. (Ibid.)

4. NG had given Wadsworth powers of attorney on 26 March and 16 August, both above, to sell land that he owned near the North, or Hudson, River. He would give Wadsworth another such power of attorney on 12 October, below, just before his departure for the South. On this property, see Estimate of NG's Estate, before 9 January 1784, above. The land was not sold during NG's lifetime.

5. See Wooster to NG, 29 August, above.

*   *   *

¶ [FROM JOSEPH BROWN, London, 12 September 1785.[1] He "gave the utmost opposition to the late war," even though it was "fatal to my fortune" and cost him his "situation as a Wholsale dealer," in which he formerly earned almost £2000 a year. The reputation that NG "deservedly acquired" in the conflict "induced" Brown to "possess a good likeness" of him. Gen. [Joseph] Reed supplied him with "half length portraits" of NG and Washington,[2] and Brown "engaged one of our most Eminant artists to draw them at Whole-length"; Brown himself "sat for the deliniation of your Person." Assured that the drawings "would make good portraits," he "spared no expence to complete them."[3] He has sent a pair of the likenesses to Charles Thomson and has asked him to forward them to NG. Hopes "they will prove acceptable."[4] Has also "sent a pair of them dedicated to Congress & framed them in the best style I was capable of designing"; apologizes for not having framed the ones he sent to NG and Washington "in the same manner."[5] Adds: "America must ever look up to your Excellencys as instruments in the hand of providence who rescued her from the tyranny of a corrupt Government." He anticipates that "when the prints are seen on your Continent," there will be enough orders to compensate him for the cost of producing them. Brown takes "unspeakable pleasure in paying this tribute of respect to your distinguished merit—merit which has rendered you the admiration of the present Age & illustrious to posterity."[6] RCS (MiU-C) 3 pp.]

1. As seen in this letter, Brown was a London businessman.

2. NG's late friend and wartime colleague Reed had been in London from early 1784 until September of that year. (See Reed to NG, 12 February 1784, above.) The portraits that Brown used as models were by Charles Willson Peale. The English artist Thomas Stothard (1755–1834) made the drawings for Brown. (Washington, *Papers*, Confederation Series, 4: 84n) Stothard was considered "one of the most popular, prolific and successful artists of his time." (Ibid.; Turner, *Dictionary of Art*, 29: 731)

3. The noted engraver Valentine Green (1739–1813) executed the mezzotint engraving. (Turner, *Dictionary of Art*, 13: 614–15; Washington, *Papers*, Confederation Series, 4: 84n) Green's engravings of NG's and Washington's portraits are now in the possession of the National Portrait Gallery, Washington, D.C.

4. Charles Thomson, the secretary of Congress, wrote NG about the portraits on 2 December, below.

5. A letter that Brown wrote to Washington on 12 September has not been found. (Washington, *Papers*, Confederation Series, 3: 246) Washington replied on 30 May 1786, acknowledging receipt of the portraits and commenting that "the frames of these pictures are quite equal to my wishes, & you will please to accept my best acknowledgments of it;

& assurances that an apology for their being inferior to those sent to Congress, was altogether unnecessary." (Ibid., 4: 84) Washington wrote a friend on 25 November 1785: "I have never seen more than one picture of Genl Green, & that a mezzotinto print, sent to me a few days ago only, by the publisher a Mr Brown at No. 10 George Yard, Lombard street, London; taken it is said from a painting done at Philada." (Washington, *Papers*, Confederation Series, 3: 388)

6. NG received this letter, which was forwarded to him with Thomson's letter of 2 December, on 24 April 1786. (NG's reply to Thomson is below, dated 24 April 1786.)

¶ [FROM CALEB GIBBS, Boston, Mass., 12 September 1785. Before he left Newport, R.I., he intended to ask NG for "a Certificate of my being Aid de camp to you at the seige of Rhode Island and of my conduct during my stay in your [military] family and any other matter which comes within your knowledge of my conduct during my military life."[1] He asks for this now because NG is "about to leave this part of the Continent," and Gibbs may never see him again.[2] Washington gave him a certificate "when he left the Army," which "will be of service" to Gibbs "either in civil or military life."[3] Gibbs plans "soon to go to the eastward" and requests "an answer soon."[4] RCS (MH) 2 pp.]

1. Gibbs had been "captain of the commander in chief's guard." (Washington, *Papers*, Revolutionary War Series, 3: 449n) Nothing is known about his service with NG.

2. NG was preparing to move his family to Georgia; they left Newport, R.I., in mid-October. (See note at Knox to NG, 27 October, below.)

3. Washington's "certificate of service" for Gibbs was dated 1 December 1783. (Fitzpatrick, *GW*, 27: 253n)

4. As Gibbs did not mention the certificate in a letter to NG of 3 October, below, it is possible that NG had already sent him one.

*   *   *

From the Reverend William Gordon

Dear Sir   Jamaica Plain, [Mass.] Sep'r 12, 1785.

I have sent you by Mr. Mumford part of a map of New York and its environs, containing the portion of Long Island, whereon were our works; You will oblige me by marking out upon it, with a pencil or ink, the lines and fortifications and every thing else that may prove explanatory to the transactions that passed upon it. Whatever illustrations may be necessary be pleased to communicate in writing.[1] In a former letter I requested answers to the following queries,[2] viz.

Was the proposed night attack to be made by the Baron [Steuben], when [Baron] Kniphausen advanced the first time and burnt Connecticutt Farms [N.J.], or after the attack at Springfield Bridge?

Was Gen. Washington at Morris Town or at Short-Hills, when the last attack was made? Had he only 2500 the whole included at that period, or had he received any reinforcement after the enemy's fire [first] landing at Elizabeth Point making his number more than 2500?

Was the advice to retreat, and cover the necessity by pleading that it was to guard the heights, given upon the enemy's first coming out, or when they were advancing the second time toward Springfield?

Did he go or send any troops to the Highlands as the British historians say, after the landing of Kniphausen?[3]

The death of your child and the sickness in your family, of which I have been informed since writing them, may have prevented my receiving an answer. I sympathize with you under your exercises.[4]

Have requested Mr. Hazard to send you immediately a Map of the Carolinas executed for Dr. Ramsay's history, which he will do if he can procure one. Pray you to give me your opinion of it, and if it is good and will answer, to perfect it, where wanting, by marking scenes of action—the routes of the armies—and the places where they crossed rivers, etc., as I would make every thing as plain to the reader as possible.[5] I suspect that the Kings Mountain affair will be too *well* told in Dr. Ramsay.[6] Shall be glad to know, therefore, whether You are at a certainty as to Messrs. [William] Campbell, [Benjamin] Cleveland and [James] Williams's meeting by accident—whether they did not attack in three divisions, and in three different places, and whether when [Patrick] Ferguson drove one party, the other did not advance and attack him in flank or rear, so that he had it not in his power upon driving the one to push on and attempt a retreat; and whether you had it from Campbell himself or what other, that he found it exceeding difficult to prevail on his men to renew the attack.[7] The paper with which this is accompanied, I apprehend will be acceptable, but would not have it get into the public prints:[8] Have written in great haste but trust to your goodness to excuse it. With respects to Lady and family I remain your sincere friend and very humble servant.

Printed in *Proceedings of the Massachusetts Historical Society* 63 (1930): 517–19.

1. Gordon, who was writing a history of the war, had asked NG for his recollections of decisions and events related to various battles. (Gordon to NG, 27 August, above) NG's reply to the present letter is below, dated before 24 September.

2. Gordon was repeating questions he had asked in his letter of 27 August about events leading up to the battle of Springfield, N.J., in June 1780.

3. It is not known which British historians Gordon had in mind.

4. NG's infant daughter, Catharine, died in late August. (NG to Wadsworth, 30 August, above)

5. On David Ramsay's history of the war in the Carolinas, see also Gordon to NG, 27 August. NG did receive and mark the map of the Carolinas for Gordon. (Gordon to NG, 24 November, below)

6. Ramsay's account of the battle of Kings Mountain is reprinted in his *History of the American Revolution in Two Volumes*, ed. Lester H. Cohen (Indianapolis, Ind.: Liberty Classics, 1990), pp. 498–501.

7. See NG to Gordon, before 24 September.

8. The enclosure has not been found.

To Jeremiah Wadsworth

My dear friend   Newport [R.I.] Sept 13th 1785
    I wrote you by your Express that I had engaged a Tutor.[1] I have this
Moment got a letter from him informing me that he cannot go. I am
vexed with him to my soul; for I desird him not to ingage unless he
meant positively to go; for that I should write you to this effect; and he
most solemnly engaged, and now writes a great long detail of unforeseen accidents and new objections of his grand Mamma and the lord
knows what for an excuse.[2] My Children are suffering so much for want
of a good Tutor that I must beg you to engage me one on the best terms
you can. I was to give Dow thirty five guineas a year and board him free
of expence. The person engaging will have the use of a good Library[,]
live in my family and have charge only of my Children.[3] Do all you can
my dear friend to engage me a Tutor. It will distress me greatly not to
have one.[4] Mrs Greene is better and so is Patty.[5] Pray come and see us.
Mrs Greene says if you dont she shall never beleive you feel the same
sentiments for her as she for you.[6] Present me affectionately to your
family and all friends. Yours   NATH GREENE
    I write in the Post office and therefore take as it is, as the post is fast
going.

ALS (CtY).
    1. See NG to Wadsworth, 7 September, above.
    2. Hendricus Dow, who had agreed to serve as a tutor for the Greene children, wrote
NG on 9 September, above, reneging on his agreement.
    3. In his letter of 5 September, above, Wadsworth had asked about the salary that NG
proposed to pay.
    4. In ibid., Wadsworth had said that he would attend the commencement at Yale
College in mid-September and would try to hire a tutor there. He again offered to help
find a tutor in letters to NG of 17 September and 1 October, both below.
    5. NG's children had been ill with whooping cough. The youngest, Catharine, had died,
and NG's oldest daughter, Martha ("Patty"), was very ill. (NG to Wadsworth, 30 August,
above) On CG's health, see note at NG to Wadsworth, 11 September, above.
    6. In his letter of 17 September, Wadsworth apologized for not visiting the Greenes in
Newport. He did not see them before they left for Georgia in mid-October.

*   *   *

¶ [FROM JAMES PRICE, New York, 13 September 1785.[1] He was in Philadelphia "for Some time past" and did not receive NG's letter of 24 August [not
found] "til yesterday." Is "sorry that Some unforeseen disappointments" will
keep him from "entering into any engagements til May next." Expects "to
realize my present Stock" by then and will be "happy to engage in any concern
that may be to our mutual advantage."[2] RCS (MiU-C) 1 p.]
    1. Price had recently returned from France with NG's cousin Griffin Greene. (See above,
French & Nephew to NG, 23 April, and Wadsworth to NG, 3 and 10 July.)

2. It is not known what kind of business venture NG had proposed to Price. (See, however, NG to Wadsworth, 7 September, above.)

* * *

From Jeremiah Wadsworth

Dear Sir   Hartford [Conn.] Sept[r] 17[th] 1785

Your favor of the 13th reached me this Ev[en]ing. I will again look out for a Tutor, but y[e] best opportunity is lost (the commencement last Week at New Haven).[1]

I will send to the Wadsworths I mentioned to You.[2] Flint wou'd not go to Georgia. He was inquird of indeed he had been partly ingaged supposing he was to be at N Port but finding it was to Georgia he declined and I was glad As (you had wrote me You had one) I had no need to appologize.[3]

M[rs] Greene will do me y[e] justice to believe I have every sentiment of esteem & attachment And I will if possible come & see her but my health has been so very indifferent that I can not ride but a little. I was so much indisposed last Week at N Haven that I was oblidged to keep House when all y[e] World were abroad & amusing them selves.[4]

I am to day pretty well but have such a fixed indisposition that I hardly hope for a radical cure. I am d[r] Sir Sincerly Your friend

JERE WADSWORTH

M[r] Strong my Neighbor has been advised by [a] freind that one Robert Walls a young Man was sent from Savannah [Ga., 4?] Weeks since to New Port [R.I.] and from thence to come here. [As?] the time is long since elapsed since he ought to have Arrived[,] He thinks it probable he is at N Port & wishes inquiry to be made lest some accident may have happened to him.[5] I have rec[d] a letter from M[r] Fitzgerald about [7th?] Aug who says wheat is 5 / Tobacco 25 / Ham 28 / .[6]   JW.

RCS (CtHi).

1. See NG to Wadsworth, 13 September, above.

2. Wadsworth had heard that a young man named Decius Wadsworth, apparently a cousin, with whom he was not well acquainted, might be interested in the position. (Wadsworth to NG, 2 October, below)

3. In a letter of 23 August, above, NG had told Wadsworth that he was considering a younger brother of Royal Flint as tutor. According to a brief biographical sketch, Abel Flint, who graduated from Yale College in 1785, "excelled in scholarship, especially in Hebrew, and delivered an Hebrew oration at graduation." He was next a tutor at what is now Brown University before his ordination as a Congregational minister. (Dexter, *Yale Graduates*, 4: 404–5) Although NG wrote Wadsworth on 7 September, above, that he had hired a tutor, he learned soon afterward that this person had changed his mind. (Dow to NG, 9 September, above)

4. In his letters to Wadsworth of 7 and 13 September, NG had reported that CG felt neglected because of Wadsworth's failure to visit them. On Wadsworth's health prob-

lems, see his letters to NG of 5 and 11 September, both above. Wadsworth had been at New Haven a few days earlier for the Yale commencement.

5. Wadsworth asked about Walls again in his letter to NG of 2 October.

6. Fitzgerald was probably a business associate of Wadsworth. In his letter of 7 September, above, NG had asked Wadsworth to send any "price currents from Alexandria," Va., to his cousin Griffin Greene, who was planning a commercial voyage to Virginia. Wadsworth replied on 11 September that he had not yet heard from "Fitzgerald of Alexandria" but would forward the information as soon as he received it.

*   *   *

¶ [FROM HUGH WALLACE, Waterford [England?], 18 September 1785. Acknowledges a letter from NG, which was enclosed with one of 30 May from Wallace's friend Mr. Nicholas Hoffman.[1] Wallace is "sorry your Cropps proved so bad at Savanah [i.e., Savannah, Ga.] last year as to prevent your paying the Bill for £150 st[g] I paid for you, but that you would raise Money otherwise & pay it, which I shall expect as I did it to serve you."[2] Concerning "a Sum of Money" that NG's friends "Clark & Nightingale of Rhode Island paid a M[r] Wallace[,] a Navy Prisoner there," and for which they now hold NG accountable, Wallace remembers twice giving NG bills for $50 "to send [to] that Gentleman." He adds: "This is all the money Transactions I had there, so that there must be some mistake in this matter, which shall be settled when I know what the demand is, & they give you M[r] Wallace's Bill or rec[t] for the same."[3] Hugh Wallace is much in want of the £150; he reminds NG of "the great Loss I met with by my Estate being sold in America by the States, which hope I shall get some recompense for, from them, or from Goverment here, but at present it hurts me much."[4] He recently saw Maj. Pierce Butler and thinks "he is returned to America."[5] Wallace's wife is at Newark, N.J., "being turned out of her House at New York"; he hopes NG "can do her any Service," for "she has been cruelly treated."[6] RCS (NHi) 2 pp.]

1. The enclosure was most likely a copy of NG to Hoffman, 9 March, above, to which the present letter appears to be a reply.

2. See NG to Hoffman, 9 March, and Wallace's letter to NG of 1 July 1784, above.

3. Nothing more is known about this matter, which NG had mentioned in his letter to Hoffman of 9 March.

4. In his letter to NG of 1 July 1784, Wallace referred to his "Property b[e]ing confiscated and sold at New York & myself proscribed & banished from that Province." Hoffman, writing to NG on 4 October, below, acknowledged receipt of $200 "on your account" and inquired about "the Amount of the ⟨Bill you⟩ drew on M[r] Wallace."

5. On Pierce Butler's trip abroad, see his letter to NG of 23 December 1784, above. Butler arrived in Charleston, S.C., from London in December. (*South-Carolina Gazette and Public Advertiser*, 21 December)

6. NG's reply has not been found.

¶ [FROM NATHANIEL SHALER, New York, 20 September 1785. As requested in NG's letter to him of 12 September [not found], Shaler has "paid the Balance of Colo Wadsworths order to Capt Webster" and informed [Nicholas] Hoffman that he will pay him $200 "in a few Days" by NG's order.[1] RCS (MiU-C) 1 p.]

1. As part of the settlement of NG's partnership in Barnabas Deane & Company, Jeremiah Wadsworth had sent NG a bill on Shaler for £115 Lawful Money. (Wadsworth to NG, 5 September, above) NG presumably sent the bill to Shaler, with instructions to apply

it to certain debts that NG owed. Nothing is known about the payment to Webster. In a letter to NG of 4 October, below, Hoffman acknowledged receipt of $200 from Shaler "on your Account."

¶ [FROM CHARLES PETTIT, New York, 21 September 1785. He is forwarding a letter to NG from Mr. [Dennis] De Berdt. It "came under cover" to Pettit, who presumes that it reports "the noting & probability of Protest of the Bill you remitted for £180 Sterl^g and of Payment or Acceptance of the smaller bill of £116."[1] De Berdt was relying "on these Bills as an effective Remittance for Monies due to him before their Arrival" and is "rather impatient on the Occasion, especially as the London Merchants trading to America are really hard pushed on Account of the Disappointments they experience in Remittances." Because of this—and De Berdt's "Connection with Mr Reed's Family"[2]—Pettit is anxious "to replace the Money" as soon as possible, "especially as we shall yet owe him a farther Balance." They will pay interest to De Berdt "for the Delay," but that is "far short of a Compensation for the Shock it gives to Credit"; Pettit is sure that NG "will give it no unnecessary Delay."[3] Doctor Franklin's arrival in Philadelphia "seems to give general Joy," and no one has "more real occasion for rejoicing" than Pettit, as Franklin "will probably obtain by general Consent" an office for which Pettit was generally thought to be a candidate. Pettit "had obtained the Promise of divers of" his friends that they would not "permit my Name to be run, yet the Opposition, not being ascertained of this; would have issued plentiful Showers of Filth at & before the Election, which I hope will now be withheld."[4] Sends "Respectful Regards" to CG and "Love to George."[5] RCS (CtY) 2 pp.]

1. See De Berdt to NG, 21 July, above.

2. On De Berdt's connection with the family of Joseph Reed, Pettit's late brother-in-law, see note at Reed to NG, 12 February 1784, above.

3. The money was still owed to De Berdt when Pettit wrote NG on 20 January 1786. (See Pettit's first letter to NG of that date, below.)

4. Historian Robert Brunhouse has written that as the October election approached, "in the City of Philadelphia there was an unusual situation where both parties agreed unanimously on one man, Benjamin Franklin," who had returned from France "a month before election." Viewed as "the only man who could command the respect of both warring political factions," Franklin was elected president of the Pennsylvania Executive Council "by an almost unanimous vote" of that body. Much more maneuvering was involved in the election of a vice president, but Pettit's faction, the Radicals, or Constitutionalists, who had already succeeded in organizing the legislature by a narrow margin, were finally able to get agreement on Charles Biddle, "a mild Constitutionalist," for that post. (Brunhouse, *Pennsylvania*, pp. 176–79) According to Brunhouse, Pettit had been "the leading candidate of the Radicals" for the post of president before they learned of Franklin's availability. (Ibid., p. 177) Pettit later wrote NG that he was "absent & did not meddle" in the election, although he was "placed at the Head of the losing Ticket." (Pettit to NG, second letter of 20 January 1786, below) The legislature did reelect him a delegate to Congress, however. (Brunhouse, *Pennsylvania*, p. 179; see also Pettit to NG, second letter of 20 January 1786, below.)

5. "George" was NG's son George Washington Greene.

¶ [FROM CORNELIUS RAY, New York, 21 September 1785.[1] He has sent NG a dozen "Breakfas[t] Cups & Saucers" and "eight Hundred Dollars," as directed by Mr. Griffin Greene. Asks NG to advise Griffin Greene and "forward the inclosed Letter."[2] RCS (MiU-C) 1 p.]

1. Ray was a "prominent New York businessman." (Syrett, *Hamilton*, 3: 45n)
2. For background, see NG to Jacob Greene, 23 August, above. The enclosure has not been found.

*   *   *

From Nathaniel Pendleton

Dear General   Savannah [Ga.] Sept[r] 23[d] 1785.
    I imagine you have been much disappointed, and I can assure you not more so than I have been, that I have not been able to send you the appraisements of your Estate here. When I came to copy the Conveyance to send with the appraisements, I found there was a mistake in the number of acres. In the reciting part of the Deed it was found to be different from the descriptive part, and that there was a blank left relative to Morton Hall Tract, which might probably include the Land likely to be disputed. Thus Situated I determined to postpone sending you the Appraisements until I could get the Deed altered. I sent it back to M[r] [Samuel] Stirk to have it rightly made out; and to get it Executed, and I find it impossible to be done, unless I had sent expressly, to the commissioners, one of which lives in the Extreem part of the State one way, and the other to the other. I should by this opportunity have sent the Appraisements without the deed but the Governor and Council have been removed to Augusta ever since June, so that I cannot have the proper Testimonial before I send up there. One reason, too, which I confess has had some weight with me to damp my ardor in hastening them, was my not having heard from you relative to it, so that I thought it possible you might have declined the business, or postponed it.[1]
    M[r] M[c]Queen is preparing and will go to New York in two or three Weeks, and from there to England, or rather to France. By him I propose to send them to you, as it may be possible you may avail yourself of his going to send them.[2]
    About four or five Weeks ago, a frigate of the French Navy arrived off Tybee, which was sent here with Express Orders to go to Cumberland Island for a Sample of live oak timber for Ship building. The Consul was ordered to meet her here from Charleston [S.C.], & to proceed to Cumberland Island, there take 3000 feet, only on board, and proceed to Brest [France]. She came from the West Indias. The Captain was informed, here that there was no timber cut at Cumberland & therefore did not go there himself, with the Ship, but sent a boat and some Officers to examine the place, and to see if there was no timber cut. I understood this Vessel came to take your timber in Consequence of the Contract, and I suppose there must have been some misapprehension in the matter. Her orders were so pointed, that altho the Captain came only for a sample of the live oak timber, he would not take any other timber, but

from Cumberland Island, and went away without. I fear this circumstance will operate to your disadvantage, as there appeared no body on the Island to give any account, nor any timber cut, or cutting.[3]

M[r] M[c]Queen has been charged with a commission on the part of this State to Count D'Estaing, Which is to present him with the Conveyances from this State of 25,000 Acres of Land.[4] He intends proposing a plan Similar to yours for Supplying the French Navy with live Oak, and for the report of the Officers who called at Sapelo Island, it is probable the Report of this Captain will be in his favor. He had enough cut to load half a dozen Ships. M[c]Queen has hinted to me the advantage of a Union of your interest in France on this Business, and I suppose he will probably propose it to you. I confess it appears to me, that it would be a mutual benefit, to both parties, and by a proper coalition you might monopolize that trade, to the Exclusion of all others. You are however the best Judge of this; I only take the liberty to hint it to you, from the probability that otherwise you might mutually injure the Interests of each other in Striving to have a preference; if indeed you have not already established your Contract. M[c]Queen has had a great number of negroes employed on Sapelo, for a long time. He seems to bend his force, & fix his views more and more to improving it. I wish you could see each other, and compare your ideas, as I am convinced you would think with me, that it would be mutually beneficial to unite your interests.[5]

I[n] consequence of your Letter I Petitioned the Court, after having consulted the Cheif Justice, for direction how to proceed to forclose the mortgage you have of Cumberland which, the Court determined could not be done in the usual way by Bill in Chancery. Should I be able to get them in the morning before the Vessel sails I will send you Copies of the Petition & Resolution of the Court. But your observation is very just; for if their is no Equity, for you to foreclose, there is no Equity for them to redeem, and you are in Possession.[6]

M[r] Gibbons has been as good as his promise, and brought an action against you, for the disputed Lands of Morton Hall tract. I took the liberty to appear to the process, as I was informed M[r] [William?] Houstoun, on whom you depended principally, declined acting.[7] You will have it in your power in time to employ any body else, and I have been almost tempted to retain [James] Jackson, in your behalf. I have no particular liking to the man, but to a common Jury, he is taking. You cannot indeed be in danger of loosing but it may be well to omit nothing that can be done, by way of farther Security.[8]

I flatter myself with the strongest Expectations of seeing both yourself and family this fall.[9] You know I was rather inclined to bileous complaints in Carolina, and you will be surprised when I tell you, I have not lain down three hours with indisposition this summer and fall, nor taken one dose of medicine. I never was in higher health, any where. So is Pierce and his family, and Mrs Pendleton. Mrs Greene will tell you Who She is.[10]

We have lost our good friend Bard, who died in July with the Gravel. His family are well.[11] I hope you have enjoyed your usual health, and Philosophy, and that your little Cherubs, which I have formed so pretty in my imagination, are well.

That they and You may always be so, and be blessed with all sorts of felicity is the ardent prayer of Dr General Your Sincere friend

NATH^l PENDLETON

ALS (NcD).

1. Pendleton presumably was working on an "appraisement" of Mulberry Grove plantation in connection with the mortgage that NG hoped to give for that property. (See Pendleton to NG, 25 April, above.) Although the Dutch firm of Wilhem & Jan Willink had declined, at least temporarily, to offer NG a loan, they had suggested that he send "the Necessary vouchers." (Willinks to NG, 8 July, above) The commissioners were undoubtedly the Georgia officials who had purchased Mulberry Grove for NG. How Pendleton resolved the discrepancies in the property descriptions is not known, but NG appears to have sent the requested documents when he wrote to the Willinks on 7 January 1786, below. According to the Estimate of NG's Estate that the editors have tentatively dated at before 9 January 1784, above, Mulberry Grove contained "about two and twenty hundred acres and upwards."

2. On John McQueen's impending trip to France, see NG to Lafayette, 1 June, and Hawkins to NG, 24 June, both above.

3. Through correspondence with the Marquis de Barbé-Marbois, the French chargé d'affaires in Philadelphia, and with the Marquis de Lafayette and the Marquis de Castries, the French naval minister, NG had been trying to persuade the French government to purchase live oak from his holdings on Cumberland Island, Ga. (NG to Marbois, 15 April; NG to Castries, 1 June, and NG to Lafayette, 1 June, all above) Tybee Island is near Savannah. The Chevalier de la Foreste, the French consul for the southern states, wrote NG on 16 December, below, that his government was unlikely to enter into a contract without first seeing samples of the live oak from NG's holdings and that another vessel would probably be sent to Cumberland Island after NG was settled in Georgia. NG apparently wrote an apology to Castries about his failure to provide samples and, in a follow-up letter, urged him to send another vessel. (The follow-up letter is at the end of the December documents, below.)

4. On the Comte d'Estaing's role in the unsuccessful siege of British-held Savannah in 1779, see above, vol. 4: 366–67n.

5. See NG to Lafayette, 1 June, and Hawkins to NG, 24 June.

6. Neither NG's letter to Pendleton nor the copies of the court documents has been found. Court proceedings presumably were no longer required after Henry Banks relinquished his right of inheritance to Cumberland Island land. (See Ward to NG, 11 November, and Banks to NG, 12 November, both below.)

7. On William Houstoun, see NG to John Houstoun, 12 September 1784, above.

8. On the claim of William Gibbons, Sr., to part of the Mulberry Grove property, see NG's letter to him of 8 March, above.

9. NG and his family arrived in Georgia in November. (NG to Clarke, 23 November, below)

10. NG's former aide William Pierce, Jr., and his wife were Savannah residents. (Pierce to NG, [November 1785], below) Pendleton was married about this time to Susan Bard.

(See note at Pendleton to NG, 30 January 1784, above; *South-Carolina Gazette and Public Advertiser*, 6 October 1785.)

11. This was undoubtedly Peter Bard, whose will was probated 4 January 1786. Bard's widow, the former Anne Zubly, later married James Seagrove. ("The Will of Dr. John Joachim Zubly," ed. Charles G. Cordle, *Georgia Historical Quarterly* 22 [1938]: 387n)

To the Reverend William Gordon

Dear Sir   [Newport, R.I., before 24 September 1785][1]
The night attack proposed in a Council of War to be made upon the Troops under the command of General Kniphausen was while he lay at Connecticut Farms [N.J.] & towards the evening after he burnt that Viliage and the same Night he retreated back to Elizabeth Town.[2] He began his retreat about midnight just at the time our attack was to have commenced. The attack on Kniphausen was not moved in Council by Baron Steuben but he solicited a command upon the occasion.[3] After [Baron] Kniphausen retired back to Elizabeth Town it was that General Washington moved toward Kings Ferry [N.Y.] with the greater part of his force[,] leaving about 700 Men under my command at Springfield [N.J.]. The General with the rest of the Army marched as far as Pompton or near it and lay there at the time when Kniphausen made his attack upon me at that place. Part of the Troops under the command of Gen Washington returned to give me support but the Action was over and the Enemy again retired to Elizabeth Town long before they [i.e., the troops returning to help NG] got up. Our whole regular force at the time the Enemy came out to Connecticut Farms, did not exceed 2500 Men nor did we get any reinforcements for some time afterwards except Militia.[4]

The Action at Kings Mountain [S.C.] happened as follows: Major Fergason [i.e., Patrick Ferguson] moved up to the neighbourhood of the Mountains.[5] The three Militia Colonels who commanded in the Action collected their force in the different quarters where they lived and marching towards the Enemy accidentally Met and agreed upon a joint attack which was accordingly executed next day. Some dispute arose about the Right of command but it was finally agreed for [William] Cam[p]bell to take the command[6] who was with me in the battle of Guilford [Court House, N.C.] and gave me the Account of the difficulty bringing up the Militia to the charge after Fergason made his first Charge with fixed Bayonets. There is no doubt of the fact but I am going to live in that Country and do not wish to appear an Author upon the occasion. The Militia acted with spirit for undiciplined Troops but I believe there is little doubt if Fergason had continued his March after the first charge but that he would have made good his retreat, if not with the whole at least with a part of his Troops.[7]

I have marked the line of fortification upon Long Island [N.Y.] with a pencil.[8]

I thank you for your kind condolence⁹ And am dear Sir Your Most
Obed, humble Ser^t   NATH GREENE

ADfS (NjMoW).

1. The draft lacks a dateline. In his letter of 26 September, below, Gordon stated that he had received the present letter the previous Saturday, which was 24 September.

2. NG was replying here to questions that Gordon had posed in his letters of 27 August and 12 September, both above, about movements and strategies of the American army before the battle of Springfield in June 1780. On the battle, see above, NG to Washington, 24 June 1780 (vol. 6: 34–38 and n). For Gordon's narrative of these events, see his *History*, 3: 368–74.

3. Gordon described the Baron von Knyphausen's incursion to Connecticut Farms, N.J., and his retreat to Elizabeth Town in ibid., pp. 368–70. On those events, see also vol. 6: 9–11n, above. The proceedings of the council of war that Steuben attended are calendared in ibid., p. 7.

4. Gordon later wrote that Washington "marched with the greatest part of the army toward Pompton on the 21st, leaving about 700 men with the horse under the command of General Greene." Gordon included in his narrative several excerpts from NG's messages to Washington at that time concerning enemy movements. (Gordon, *History*, 3: 372) Gordon also used NG's information that the "whole regular force" of the American army "did not exceed two thousand five hundred men," and he wrote that Washington, after receiving word that the British meant to attack, "ordered a part of his troops to return and support Greene; but the action was over, and the enemy retreated before it could reach him." (Ibid., pp. 370, 372)

5. The action at Kings Mountain was the successful attack by American militia troops in October 1780 on an encampment of Loyalists commanded by Patrick Ferguson. (Vol. 6: 407–8 and n, above) Gordon described that action in his *History*, 3: 462–67.

6. In ibid., Gordon repeated NG's words almost verbatim: "Some dispute had arisen about the right of command; but it was finally agreed to give it to Campbell." (Gordon, *History*, 3: 464)

7. Gordon repeated NG's words that "the militia acted with spirit for undisciplined troops." (Gordon, *History*, 3: 466) He also echoed NG when he wrote: "The major [Ferguson] might have made good his retreat, if not with the whole, at least with a great part of his men, had he pursued his march immediately upon his charging and driving the first detachment; for tho the militia acted with spirit, it was with difficulty that they could be prevailed upon to renew their attack after being charged with the bayonet." (Ibid., p. 466) It is clear from the present letter that NG, who was about to settle on his plantation in Georgia, was concerned that any perceived slight upon the southern states' militia troops could have adverse consequences for him. Gordon replied that he made "it a rule not to produce my vouchers for the facts I relate, when it may lay them under difficulties." (Gordon to NG, 26 September) In his narrative, Gordon did not mention NG as a source for his comments about the battle. (On the battle of Guilford Court House, see above, NG to Samuel Huntington, 16 March 1781 [vol. 7: 433–35 and n].)

8. Gordon had sent a map of New York and Long Island to NG, asking him to mark "the lines and fortifications and everything else that may prove explanatory to the transactions" there. (Gordon to NG, 12 September)

9. Gordon had expressed his condolences for the death of NG's baby daughter, Catharine. (Ibid.)

*   *   *

¶ [FROM STEPHEN RAPALJE, New York, 25 September 1785. He is "exceedingly in want of the money" for NG's bond for 250 guineas.¹ Hopes this can be paid before NG leaves for the South; if not, Rapalje is willing to "take the amount" in goods from Col. [Jeremiah] Wadsworth's "Store kept here by Mess[rs] [Nathaniel] Shaler & Pebor." If NG cannot pay him at this time, Rapalje asks him "to mention the matter" to Wadsworth.[2] RCS (CtHi) 1 p.]

1. For background, see Wadsworth to NG, 18 July, above.
2. NG wrote to Wadsworth about this on 4 October, below. Rapalje wrote NG on 27 October, below, that he had sold the bond to "Mess[rs] Randall son & Stewarts."

*　　*　　*

From the Reverend William Gordon

Dear Sir　　　　　　　　　　　　　　Jamaica Plain [Mass.] Sep[r] 26. 1785

Your obliging letter, with the map [of] part of Long Island improved, were received on the saturday in good order.[1] Your information is such as I wished to receive. I make it a rule not to produce my vouchers for the facts I relate, when it may lay them under difficulties, so that you need not be under any apprehensions, of your being known to be an author as to any communications with which you may entrust me.[2]

Lest you should not receive D[r] Ramsay's map in time, or it should not answer upon inspection, have sent the maps of Virginia and Maryland, of North and S'h Carolina, on which I pray you, can you possibly find time, to mark your marches & countermarches, the same of Cornwallis's, the places where You, [Daniel] Morgan [Isaac] Huger & [Otho H.] Williams crossed the rivers, where battles were fought, & important matters transacted; and whatever else may tend to the illustration of the history of the war.[3] Let me hear, when you, your Lady and family mean to move to the south ward.[4] My best wishes will attend you; and I shall rejoice to hear, that you have tried and succeeded in the plan of admitting the negroes to the rights of copyholders, which if it could be once effected might possibly tend to their increasing so as to render further importations of them needless. Could you, by your example, prove instrumental in demolishing slavery and the importations of negroes, I should think you rendered the human species nearly as much service, as when you was fighting successfully against British attempts to reduce the white inhabitants of America to the hard condition of slaves.[5]

M[rs] Gordon unites in best respects, to Self Lady and family, with Your much obliged humble servant & sincere friend　　　　WILLIAM GORDON

Printed in *Proceedings of the Massachusetts Historical Society* 63 (1930): 520–21.

1. See NG to Gordon, before 24 September, above.
2. NG had asked Gordon not to cite him as a source of information he provided for Gordon's history of the Revolution. (Ibid.)
3. On David Ramsay's maps, see Gordon's letters to NG of 27 August and 12 September, both above. As seen in Gordon's letter to him of 24 November, below, NG responded to this request.
4. NG and his family left Newport, R.I., for Georgia in mid-October. (Note at Knox to NG, 27 October, below) Gordon acknowledged NG's reply, which has not been found, in his letter of 24 November.

5. Nothing more is known about a plan on NG's part to admit his slaves "to the rights of copyholders." (A copyhold is "a former tenure of land in England and Ireland by right of being recorded in the court of the manor" or "an estate held" in that manner. [*Webster's*])

To Edward Carrington

Dear Colonel   Newport [R.I.] Sept 29th 1785

I wrote you the 29th of April and inclosed you sundry papers relative to Hunters matters.[1] In that letter I desird you to settle for the Money I had of [James?] McCall a ballance due me on account of the Public bills. I wish to hear from you on the subject. But in addition to that I must beg you to retain so much of the public Money in your hands as will settle sundry outstanding bills against the Commisary and Hospital Departments in South Carolinia which I was threatened to be sued for last summer.[2] Only for having authorised the Persons to purchace for the Public in the same way you was authorised to provide for your Department.[3] There is nobody now to settle those accounts and I wish to have your funds by order of Congress appropriated as far as the demands are just to the payment of those Debts. I beg you will write me on the subject. But as far as respects my own ballance I must beg you the amount in your own hands until I can get an order for having it discounted. Please to write me whether Henry Banks will or will not give a relinquishment for Cumberland.[4] Burnett has given one. Inclosed is a copy.[5] I wish to hear from you on the subject of Hunters Mortgage.[6] I did all I could to get Forsyth to Virginia but could not.[7] I have laid a state of the whole matter relative to my engagements for that house [i.e., Hunter, Banks & Company] before Congress[8] and claim their indemnity should I finally suffer greatly in the business which I am in hopes I shall not if I free my self from Harris & Blachfords demands and [E. John] Collett[']s attachments succeeds on [John] Ferries Lands.[9] I am going for Georgia in a few days.[10] You will write to me there.[11] Mrs Greene desires her kind complements and good wishes for your health & happiness. I [am] dear Sir with esteem your Most Obedt humble Ser. NATH GREEN[E]

ADfS (MiU-C).

1. The letter of 29 April has not been found. On the legal work that Carrington was doing for NG in Virginia in regard to James Hunter's financial affairs and property, see, for example, his letter to NG of 23 March, above.

2. No specific reference to the threatened suit has been found. (See, however, Milligan to NG, 30 August 1784, above.)

3. Carrington had been the Southern Department's quartermaster general.

4. Banks did give the relinquishment. (See Banks to NG, 12 November, below.)

5. See William Burnet to NG, 13 August, above. The enclosure has not been found.

6. Concerning the mortgage that Hunter had given to NG, see NG to Robert Forsyth, 2 October 1784, and Hunter to NG, 1 June, both above.

7. See NG to Forsyth, 5 June, above.

8. See NG to Lee, 22 August, above.

9. As seen above in the notes at NG's letter to Collett of 8 August 1784, and at Pendleton to NG, 10 November 1784, the issues of Collett's and Harris & Blachford's claims against NG were not resolved until some years after NG's death.

10. NG and his family left Newport to settle in Georgia in mid-October. (See note at Knox to NG, 27 October, below.)

11. No further correspondence between Carrington and NG has been found.

*　　　*　　　*

¶ [FROM THE MARQUIS DE CASTRIES, Paris, 30 September 1785. He cannot yet reply positively to NG's "proposition" about supplying timber for the French government.[1] A French ship will gather samples of the timber, and if the wood is suitable, the French government would be very interested in doing business with NG.[2] RCS (MiU-C) 1 p. In French.]

1. See NG to Castries, 1 June, above.

2. On the unsuccessful attempt to obtain timber samples from Cumberland Island, Ga., see Pendleton to NG, 23 September, above. In a letter to NG of 16 December, below, the Chevalier de la Foreste reiterated that Castries was interested in doing business with NG but that the French government needed the samples before making a decision. NG's reply to Castries is near the end of the December documents, below.

*　　　*　　　*

From James Hunter

Sir　　　　　　　　　　　　　　　　　　Norfolk [Va.] 30 Septr 1785

I am honoured with your favour of 29 August this morning.[1] It found me in Custody of this Court, overwhelm'd with Writs &c, many of which [Henry] Banks advertises he has paid. I have no other Hope of Relief than from the insolvents Law, and I must avail myself thereof at once.[2] This measure will be speedily accomplish'd and releive me from a Fate that has wore every appearance of compleat Horror for many years.[3] I am much indebted to your Goodness for the Certificates, and am sorry you should have the Court Surmise, that the world imagined you, in a most distant manner Connected with Speculators. It carries with it so different an Idea of your general Estimation with mankind, that I should think your taking any Measures to refute so frivolous a Thought would only occasion a Supposition to arise, that there must be something in it.

I am highly sensible of your wishes for my Welfare, if it is in the Power of Man to bear the Misfortunes incident to Nature I think few have more Fortitude than myself. May you Sir never experience the Ingratitude of a Mankind which has ruined me. I am with most perfect Esteem Sir Your mo. Ob Serv[t]　　　　　　　　　　　JAMES HUNTER

RCS (MiU-C).

1. This letter is a reply to NG to Hunter, 29 August, above, and is the last correspondence between Hunter and NG that has been found.

2. On Henry Banks's "advertisements," see Hunter to NG, 1 June, above.

3. The outcome of this matter is not known.

To Jeremiah Wadsworth

Dear Sir   Newport [R.I.] Octob 1st 1785
Doctor Stiles has arrivd here and tells me he has engaged me a Tutor a
Mr Miller who is now at New Haven.[1] I have sent an Express for him as
we sail in ten days from this day.[2] The Express is to wait on Mr Miller
and if he will not agree to come to proceed on to Hartford to you and
I beg you to engage one on the best terms you can but to get me one at all
events. If Miller agrees to come as the Doctor [i.e., Stiles] says he will he
being authorised to settle all matters and to engage him positively,
I shall not want you to engage one; but if you have agreed for one to get
off on the best conditions you can. And what ever damages you are
obliged to give I will pay.[3] My case is peculiar and Mr Dowes disappointment has involved me in it.[4] Pardon the trouble I give you and
believe me yours most Affectionately   NATH GREENE
Will you come and see us or not.[5]

ALS (CtY).

1. Ezra Stiles, the president of Yale College, was an old friend of NG and had deep ties
to Newport, where he had been a Congregational minister for many years. (*DAB*) In
September 1785, after the Yale commencement, Stiles traveled to Newport. He arrived
there on 21 September and returned to New Haven, Conn., on 14 October. (Stiles, *Diary*, 3:
189) Stiles apparently was helping NG at the request of Yale alumnus Hendricus Dow,
who had reneged on an agreement to tutor NG's children. (Dow to NG, 9 September,
above; NG to Wadsworth, 5 October, below)

Stiles "engaged" Phineas Miller, a twenty-one-year-old Connecticut native who had
just graduated from Yale. (Dexter, *Yale Graduates*, 4: 430–31) Miller agreed to take the job
and was in Newport by 11 October, when he witnessed NG's Will on that date, below. In
addition to his duties as tutor to the Greene children, Miller also acted as NG's secretary,
helping him to organize his papers. NG wrote Samuel Ward, Jr., on 4 April 1786, below,
that Miller was a "great acquisition." NG, of course, did not fully realize what a "great
acquisition" Miller would turn out to be. Miller remained with the family after NG's
death in June 1786, helping to manage Mulberry Grove plantation and other business
affairs. He married CG in 1796. (Stegeman, *Caty*, pp. 169–70)

2. The Greenes sailed from Newport on 14 October and arrived in Savannah, Ga., at the
end of the month. (See note at Knox to NG, 27 October, below.)

3. As seen in note 1, above, Miller did agree to become the Greene children's tutor.
Wadsworth, however, did not receive this letter before he also found a tutor for them. (See
Wadsworth to NG, 2 and 3 October, both below.)

4. See Dow to NG, 9 September.

5. NG had written several times that he and CG were anxious for Wadsworth to visit
them before they left for Georgia. (See, for example, NG to Wadsworth, 7 and 13 September, both above.) Wadsworth wrote NG on 2 October that he hoped to visit them in the
South that winter.

From Catharine Ray Greene

Dear Freinds   [Warwick, R.I.?, 2 October 1785?]¹

I lament yr leaving us but Since tis your Determination Pray Heaven to grant you a Pleasant Passage health and Prosperity and every Blessing attend you and yours.² Do write us all oppertunities and Caty [i.e., CG] too. Do Caty Recolect all the good & Bad qualities of Fillis and if you think She will Sute me let Polly or Nancy know that they may write me[;] the one I have now is stife [i.e., stiff?] most every night with Cyder.³

Many thanks to you both for your Friendship and Politeness to Celia.⁴ When Yr Branches⁵ Come here Shall Return it as far as in my Power with true affection and Real Love Sub[s]cribe   C GREENE

RCS (RNR).

1. This undated note from CG's aunt Catharine Ray Greene was written on the back of her husband Gov. William Greene's letter to NG of 2 October, immediately below.

2. NG and his family were preparing to leave Rhode Island to settle on Mulberry Grove plantation, Ga. (See note at Knox to NG, 27 October, below.)

3. "Fillis" may have been a servant who was to be left behind when NG and his family left Rhode Island. It is possible that Catharine Ray Greene was referring in this sentence to Jacob Greene's daughter Polly, who sometimes stayed with NG and CG in Newport. (Jacob Greene to NG, 3 April 1784, above) Nancy may have been the Greenes' friend Nancy Vernon.

4. William and Catharine Ray Greene's daughter Celia was a cousin of CG. (Vol. 12: 266, above)

5. *OED* defines "branches" as children or descendants.

*   *   *

¶ [FROM GOVERNOR WILLIAM GREENE OF RHODE ISLAND, Warwick, R.I., 2 October 1785. Has received NG's of "this date" [not found] from NG's servant. Is sending five barrels of newly pressed "sider in exchange" for the wine. This includes one barrel that has been "boild and skim'd to prevent fermentation"; NG should let him know "if it continues sweet with a good body."¹ In regard to NG's and CG's impending departure, "We are exceeding unwilling to part with you but as interest makes it necessary submit with the hope that you and Family may hereafter make it convenient to return again to this State and spend the principle part of your Days."² They had hoped that NG and CG "could have made us another Viset but as your stay is so short cannot expect it." Wishes them "a safe Voyage and happiness." A letter from NG would "always be pleasing." Asks to be remembered to "Caty" and "your little flock too"; adds: "believe me to be your real Friend."³ Writes below his signature: "I laid your letter with Mr Vassel's respecting the Estate he mentions at Bristol before the Assembly who did not grant the favor wish'd for."⁴ Adds in a postscript that he is returning the wine with the cider and wants NG to pay for it with "as much Rice as you think proper."⁵ RCS (RNR) 2 pp.]

1. It appears from the last sentence of this calendar that NG was planning to take the cider with him to Georgia and that he had offered to exchange wine for it.

2. NG died the following June; CG never returned to Rhode Island to live.

3. On NG's and CG's relationships with the governor and his family, see note at William Greene to NG, 7 December 1783, above.

4. On William Vassall, see NG to William Greene, 22 August, above.

5. No further correspondence between NG and William Greene has been found.

*   *   *

From Jeremiah Wadsworth

Dear Sir   Hartford [Conn.] Octob 2. 1785

I rec^d yours of the 24 Just now.[1] I have sent to New Haven before for [Young?] Wadsworth, and expect him this Week When he shall come on to New Port. I am pleased with the Character given him by the tutors, but know Nothing of him my selfe.[2] My health is much better at present but I hope to be able to take your advise & come to ye Southward, in ye Winter. I am persuaded the advise is as good as it is disinterested, & shall certainly try to imbrace it.[3] I hear nothing from you respecting a Young Man from Savannah whose name is Robert Wals was to come here to live with our parson Strong.[4]

M^rs [Mehitable Russell] Wadsworth & ye Children join in affectionate Compliments to you & all yours. I am affectionately Yours

JERE WADSWORTH

I have a proposal from Biddles commissioners to divide your land from theirs as they will sell at all Hazards. Your power dont authorise me to divide it.[5]

RCS (CtHi).

1. In the letter of 24 September, which has not been found, NG had undoubtedly asked again for help in finding a tutor for his children. (See also NG to Wadsworth, 23 August and 7 and 13 September, all above.)

2. Wadsworth had not yet received NG's letter of 1 October, above, informing him that a tutor had been found. Wadsworth was proposing Decius Wadsworth, a cousin of his, who had just graduated from Yale College the month before. (Dexter, *Yale Graduates*, 4: 443–44) He wrote NG on 3 October, below, that he had never been "Wel[l] acquainted" with Decius Wadsworth but had now met him and offered him the job.

3. Wadsworth had been suffering from an undisclosed ailment. (See his letters to NG of 5 and 15 September, both above.) He was not able to visit NG in Georgia before NG's death in June 1786.

4. On Robert Walls, see Wadsworth to NG, 17 September, above.

5. NG had given Wadsworth a power of attorney to sell lands near the North, or Hudson, River that he held in common with the financially troubled Clement Biddle, but he had not specified a division of the property. (NG to Wadsworth, 24 April, above) NG gave Wadsworth more specific authority in another power of attorney, dated 12 October, below.

*   *   *

¶ [FROM JACOBUS VAN ZANDT, New York, 2 October 1785. When he saw NG in New York "last Spring," NG promised to send him the $2,000, with interest, "by the first oppertunity."[1] Since then, he has heard of NG being "in Town" but supposes that in the "hurry of business" NG forgot to call on him and make the payment.[2] As NG and his family are now "removed to S° Carolina,"[3] and it would be difficult to call on him there, Van Zandt asks NG "to remit" the money, which was a loan "to defray the exspence of Mrs Green from Morris Town, to her place of abode." Necessity urges him "to call on you with as much speed a[s] possiable." Adds beneath his signature: "The money was borrowed on yᵉ 10th June 1780, and you know what the depreciation was at that time."[4] RCS (MiU-C) 2 pp.]

1. "Last Spring" was most likely the spring of 1784, when NG stopped briefly in New York on his way home from Philadelphia to Newport, R.I. (NG to Steuben, 9 June 1784, above) The nature of NG's debt to Van Zandt is explained in the present letter.

2. NG had been in New York again in the fall of 1784 and in August 1785. (See, for example, NG to Gardoqui, 7 August, above.)

3. NG and his family left Newport to settle in Georgia on 14 October. (See note at Knox to NG, 27 October, below.)

4. After spending about six months with NG at the Continental army's winter camp at Morristown, N.J., CG left to return to Rhode Island on 10 June 1780. (Vol. 6: xlv, above) No correspondence at that time between NG and Van Zandt has been found, nor has NG's reply to the present letter.

*　　　*　　　*

From Caleb Gibbs

Dʳ Sir　　　　　　　　　　　　　　　　　　Boston [Mass.] Octʳ 3ᵈ 1785

Your sudden departure from Newport when I was last there, prevented my saying any thing to you respecting the loss I met with in the paper money I received of Mʳ Jacob Greene on your account in lieu of the gold I lent you.[1] When I mentioned the subject to you, the last Autumn at New York, you seemᵈ very willing to make me compensation, not only for the length of time I laid out of my money, but the loss on the paper.[2]

I cannot exactly say what the loss was, but the deprec[i]ation was so rapid at that period, it soon took a final leave of Circulation, and I verily beleive I had not parted with more than two thirds of the whole sum.

The present state of public securities (which is all I possess as property) being so very low, makes it necessary for me to live oeconomical, and to ask for Monies which are due me. You will I am persuaded agree with me in this Sentiment and pardon the liberty I have taken in mentioning this matter to you relying on you to transmit me the ballance by a safe conveyance previous to your departure from this country, as my necessities as I observed before make it necessary.[3]

Pray offer me in most respectful terms to Mʳˢ Greene, and May heavens best blessing attend you in all your arrangements. I have the honor to be With the greatest respect and Esteem Dear Sir Your most Obedient and very humble servant　　　　　　　　　　　　　C GIBBS

P.S. I should be glad to hear from you soon as convenient as I expect soon to go to the Eastern Country. The whole sum was

21. Guineas

4. Half Joes.[4]

RCS (MiU-C).

1. In a letter to NG of 12 September, above, Gibbs alluded to a visit he had made to Newport, R.I., but did not mention when it took place. The transaction that he referred to here may have been a loan that he made to NG in October 1780 to complete payment for a carriage for CG. NG wrote CG at that time that he was "afraid to call upon Griffin [Greene] and Jacob" to reimburse Gibbs, "for fear it should be inconvenient." (NG to CG, 7 October 1780, above [vol. 6: 351])

2. It is possible that NG stopped in New York on his way home from the South in the fall of 1784.

3. NG was about to move his family to his plantation in Georgia. (See note at Knox to NG, 27 October, below.)

4. The "Eastern Country" was presumably Maine. A "Half Joe" was a Portuguese gold coin worth about thirty-six shillings sterling. (*OED*) NG's reply to Gibbs has not been found.

* * *

¶ [FROM JEREMIAH WADSWORTH, Hartford, Conn., 3 October 1785. Since Wadsworth's letter to NG of the previous day, Decius Wadsworth "has arrived" and agreed "to come on" and see NG. He is willing to go to the South with NG's family, and Wadsworth has "promised him three guineas a Month to live in your family to be under your imediate protection." Decius Wadsworth's "Youth & inexperience of y[e] World are his, mine, and his fathers greatest objections. These are all removed by his being under your care & looking up to you as a parent." In a note below his signature, Wadsworth writes that he is "persuaded this is the very Person you want," although "I was never [Well?] acquainted with him."[1] RCS (CtHi) 1 p. The manuscript is damaged.]

1. In a letter to NG of 2 October, above, Wadsworth had suggested Decius Wadsworth, a recent Yale graduate, as a possible tutor for NG's children. As seen in NG's letters to Wadsworth of 1 October, above, and 4 October, below, NG had already hired Phineas Miller. Decius Wadsworth did travel to Newport, and NG expressed mortification to Wadsworth over not being able to hire him. (NG to Wadsworth, 5 October, below)

* * *

To Jeremiah Wadsworth

Dear Sir   Newport [R.I.] 4th October 1785.

Inclos'd I send you my Deed for the Property upon the North [i.e., Hudson] River. Please to dispose of it for me as soon as you can and on the best you can.[1] Inclos'd I send a Letter from M[r] Rappelyea.[2] If you will pay him in the way he proposes and it is agreeable I wish you would.[3] It will be more agreeable to be your debtor than his; and I am in hopes you will soon dispose of enough of my property to put you in Cash again.[4] If not I am in hopes to settle a part if not all from my present Crop.[5] I shall sail in Six or Eight days.[6] Write me often and particularly on receiving accounts from [John Barker] Church.[7] Some Gentlemen in Providence are disposed to take a Conceirn in Cumberland.[8] The matter is left uncertain for the present for particular reasons. I wrote you by Bliven relative to a Tutor that Doct[r] [Ezra] Stiles by the request of [Hendricus] Dow had engaged me one and if he came it was unnecessary for you to give yourself Any further trouble on the Subject; but if you should be under any engagments I would pay the damages.[9] Yours affectionately NATH GREENE

ALS (CtY).

1. NG gave Wadsworth the authority to sell this property in powers of attorney dated 26 March and 16 August, above, and 12 October, below. (See also NG to Wadsworth, 24 April, above.)

2. See Stephen Rapalje to NG, 25 September, above.

3. Rapalje had offered to take payment from NG in merchandise from Wadsworth's store in New York. (Ibid.) Wadsworth's reply has not been found. Rapalje wrote NG on 27 October, below, that he had sold NG's debt to another merchant.

4. Wadsworth wrote NG on 8 April 1786, below, that none of NG's northern property had been sold.

5. NG's "present Crop" of rice did not turn out well. (See NG to Clarke, 23 November, below.)

6. As seen in the note at Knox to NG of 27 October, below, NG and his family left Newport on 14 October to settle on his Georgia plantation.

7. Wadsworth's letter of 8 April 1786 is the only one of a later date to NG that has been found.

8. Nothing more is known about a possible interest of "Gentlemen in Providence," R.I., in investing in Cumberland Island, Ga.

9. On the tutor whom Stiles had helped to find, see NG to Wadsworth, 1 October, above. After receiving Wadsworth's letter of 2 October, above, NG wrote him again about this matter on 5 October, below.

From David Hillhouse

To Hon[ble] Nath[l] Green Esq[r]   Philadelphia Oct[r] 4th [17]85
    I arive safe on Thursday last, found servants very scarce & those Germans that was for sale had Wifes which cost the same price as men [*damaged*] they would be but little service to us unless it was in Farming or planting way. I could have Seven Men six Women & seven Children at £248.17.4 Currency 3 years one Gardner among them & one house joiner he would go for 2 years. Those men being unacquainted with our ax & having such Families that I dare not purchase them & unless you had other objects in View.[1] Col Eyers thought it not advisable but if you are of A differe[t] Opinion by Writing to Col: Eyers they doubtless may be had & sent to Charleston, at any time.[2] Being thus disapointed I have concluded to get five Men here. These with five I have agreed with in N England will all be ready to sail & take passage for Charleston on the 15th Instant of which I shall advise Cap[t] M[c]Lane that he may be prepar[d] for their conveyance [*damaged*] Island.[3]
    Head Carpenders was plenty & might be procur[d] on reasonable

terms but I have agre[d] with Cap[t] Ozburne for that purpose at the very extravagant price of 45 dollars per Month for six months. This I did entirely by advise of Co[l] Eyres who gives him A very high Character for the Business & thinks he will answer better than any other person at any price whatever. Cap[t] Ozburne says they can get from 30 to 50 feet Solid Timber p[r] day, thinks he can get 20 feet besides overseeing the others.[4]

I take passage on Wednesday for N Carolina. Shall Leave the care of geting & Shiping the hands from here with Col[o] Eyers to whom am under the greatest obligations for his assistance & attention.[5] My Comp[t] to M[rs] Green. Am Sir your Ob[t] and very Hum[bl] Ser[t]   DAVID HILLHOUSE

ALS (MiU-C).

1. Daniel McLane and Hillhouse were trying to find laborers to settle on Cumberland Island, Ga., in order to make NG's investment there productive. (McLane to NG, 3 July, and Hillhouse to NG, 19 July, both above) As Hillhouse had asked for directions in this matter, NG may have suggested immigrants arriving in Philadelphia as a source of affordable labor. As they would be cutting timber, it was essential that they be skilled in using axes.

2. Benjamin Eyre, who had been superintendent of the boat department during the war, owned a ship-building business in Philadelphia. (Vol. 4:196n, above) He had recently been advising NG on marketing timber from Cumberland Island. (Eyre to NG, 7 March and 14 May, both above) As seen in his letter to NG of 6 October, below, Eyre, at NG's behest, was also helping Hillhouse find workers for Cumberland Island.

3. Hillhouse had written to NG on 19 July, asking for instructions. He most likely called on NG in Newport, R.I., at that time, and may have hired some workers in Rhode Island or Connecticut before traveling to Philadelphia.

4. On Capt. Henry Osborne, see his letter to NG of 30 August, above.

5. Eyre discussed his attempts to hire laborers for Cumberland Island in his letter to NG of 6 October.

*   *   *

¶ [FROM NICHOLAS HOFFMAN, New York, 4 October 1785. Since having "the pleasure of s[e]eing" NG, Hoffman has received $200 from Mr. [Nathaniel] Shaler on NG's account.[1] He gives a "state" of the moneys he has received, including £99.5 from Charles Pinckney; £38 from Dr. [William] Burnet, and £80 from Shaler. From the total of £217.5.0, Hoffman deducts £14.11.6 for "Sundrys paid for you" on 3 July 1784, leaving a balance of £202.13.6. Asks what amount NG drew on Mr. Wallace.[2] Has been told that NG and his family "propose Sailing in a few days for" Charleston, S.C.[3] Wishes them "a pleasant and Agreeable Passage" and hopes to hear of their "Safe Arrivell." Will be "pleased in Executing" any "commands" NG may have. RCS (MiU-C) 1 p. The manuscript is damaged.]

1. NG had probably seen Hoffman during his visit to New York in August. (The letters that NG wrote while he was in New York include one to Diego de Gardoqui of 7 August, above.) On the money from Nathaniel Shaler, see Shaler to NG, 20 September, above.

2. For more about this matter, see Hugh Wallace to NG, 18 September, above. NG apparently replied to Hoffman on 10 October, but the letter has not been found. (Hoffman to NG, 20 October, below)

3. NG and his family left Newport, R.I., for Savannah, Ga., on 14 October. (See note at Knox to NG, 27 October, below.)

*   *   *

To Jeremiah Wadsworth

My dear Sir   Newport [R.I.] Octo 5th 1785
Your kindness and my own fears have involved me in one of the most embarrassing situations imaginable. Not recieving any letter from you last Week I concluded the difficulty of procuring a Tutor had baffled all your attempts. Doctor [Ezra] Stiles arrivd here and informed me that M[r] [Hendricus] Dow who first engaged had written to him to engage a Tutor to supply his place.[1] I told the Doctor I had written to you and that I would wait until fryday for an answer. After which if I got no intelligence I would embrace the offer of M[r] [Phineas] Miller. Fryday came and no letter arrivd. The time was so short the object so important and the consequences so disagreeable that I thought I had better run the risque of having two engaged and trust to your good Offices to accomodate the matter by some compensation for the disappointment.[2] But your industry exceeding my most sanguine expectations and success surpassing my fondest hopes causes me to regret my own impatience notwithstanding the pressing occasion. Young [Decius] Wadsworth is every thing I could wish him.[3] Miller appears cleaver and the generous contention between the two [as to] who should give way distressed me amazingly. Finally it was agreed between the two that M[r] Miller should stay and I confess I feel a regret in parting with either. I must beg you to apologize to the family and to insist upon refunding all the expences, which I have attempted here without success. I have none only to beg your pardon for the disagreeable dilemma in which I have placed you; and I must trust to your goodness and to my peculiar situation for your forgiveness.[4] I was very sorry when M[r] Wadsworth arrivd that I had sent the Express; and the more so as the young fellow was so much to my wishes. All that I can blame my self for except in being unfortunate was in not sending the Express by Hartford [Conn.] which would have remedied all the evils and put the busines[s] in a certain and easy train. But this never occured to me until M[r] Wadsworths arrival. M[r] Dow seems to be sent as an evil genius to involve me and my friends in a complicated scene of perplexities. I wish the devil had, had him before I ever heard of him.[5] If M[r] Wadsworth should wish to go to the Southward I have no doubt of getting him placed in some genteel; and agreeable family entirely to his wishes and I shall be always happy to serve him from the partiality I feel for him.[6] I wish you may make it convenient to Visit the Southern States this Winter. Nothing will give me more pleasure and if my embarassments do not oppress me too hard

I hope I shall have it in power to render your stay agreeable.[7] Present me to your family respectfully & affectionately   N GREENE
M[rs] Greene writes you.[8]

ALS (CtY).

1. NG had hired Dow to travel to Georgia with his family and act as tutor to his children, but Dow had later backed out of the agreement. (Dow to NG, 9 September, above) On Stiles's assistance in the matter, see NG to Wadsworth, 1 and 4 October, both above.

2. Friday was 30 September. NG wrote Wadsworth the next day that he had hired Miller.

3. Wadsworth, who had not yet received NG's letter of 1 October, wrote him on 2 October and 3 October, both above, that he had met with "Young Wadsworth" and was sending him to see NG at Newport.

4. Wadsworth's reply has not been found.

5. See note 1, above.

6. No evidence has been found of any further contact between Decius Wadsworth and NG.

7. In his letter of 2 October, Wadsworth had mentioned the possibility of visiting NG in Georgia that winter; he did not.

8. CG's letter to Wadsworth has not been found.

*   *   *

¶ [FROM JAMES HAMILTON, New York, 5 October 1785. He received NG's letter [not found] "respecting Cumberland" Island upon his arrival in New York; is "sorry I cannot answer it agreeable to your wishes, not having any further conversation about it with the parties conserned, only to tell, and you to have the refusal."[1] Hopes the "matter will be made agreable" to NG after Hamilton returns to South Carolina. His wife joins him in compliments to NG and CG.[2] RCS (MiU-C) 1 p.]

1. Hamilton had sailed from Charleston, S.C., at the end of July. (See Casey to NG, 25 July, above.) NG's letter "respecting Cumberland" may have been similar to others that he wrote to friends and acquaintances, offering an opportunity to invest in the Georgia island. (See, for example, NG to Butler, 9 September 1784; Butler to NG, 23 December 1784; Eyre to NG, 19 December 1784, and NG to Wadsworth, 3 February 1785, all above.)

2. As noted at Forsyth to NG, 24 February 1784, above, Hamilton, a former officer of the Pennsylvania Continental line, had married Mrs. Elisabeth Harleston, a South Carolinian. No further correspondence between Hamilton and NG has been found.

¶ [FROM BENJAMIN EYRE, Philadelphia, 6 October 1785. He received NG's letter [not found] from David Hillhouse.[1] They have "been on board of the Dutch ships but Cannot Get any to go to Georgia that are single. There is a gardenner, and a House Carpenter but they are both married." Eyre and Hillhouse think "the women would not suit you."[2] He will "keep a good lookout and go on board the first" ships that arrive and will "get [two]" for NG. If NG wants Eyre to contract with the two married men, he should inform him at once.[3] "Nothing more can be done with Sample & Kain here."[4] Eyre will send NG's hat by Captain Lawton.[5] "Times are very dul here."[6] He is "fiting out the *Alliance*," which "turns out a very good vessail."[7] RCS (MiU-C) 1 p.]

1. NG may have given the letter to Hillhouse when they met the previous summer. (See Hillhouse to NG, 19 July, above.)

2. As seen in Hillhouse to NG, 4 October, above, NG had undoubtedly asked Eyre to help Hillhouse find laborers to cut lumber and work his land on Cumberland Island, Ga.

3. NG's reply has not been found. Nor is it known if Eyre succeeded in finding laborers among the newly arrived immigrants in Philadelphia.

4. On Alexander Semple and Alexander Cain, see Eyre to NG, 7 March, and NG to William Semple, 4 June, above.

5. Captain S. Lawton of the *Newport Packet* arrived in Newport, R.I., from Philadelphia by 22 October. (*Newport Mercury*, 22 October)

6. Eyre presumably meant here that commerce was slow.

7. The *Alliance* had been a Continental navy frigate. (Vol. 11: 281n, above)

*　　*　　*

From Jacob Greene

Dear Sir

[East Greenwich, R.I.] Friday afternoon [before 8 October 1785][1]
As you are going Southward Soon I Should Wish to have a Settlement of our affairs before you go as it is uncertain When We Shall Meet again. I Spoke to Brother William [Greene] Some time ago. He told me there Was a going to be a General [*damaged*] Settlement then they Would Settle With me. I hear you have. I have never Seen him Since I have put my papers In Mr Maxwell [i.e., Adam Maxwell's] hands. He Will Wait on you when you Can attend to it. I have Wrote to the Rest of Brothers. You Will be So kind as to l[et] Mr Maxwell know When you Will be at Liesure.[2] My Best Wishes attend you, Sister [i.e., CG] and family. You[rs] affectionately   J. GREENE

RCS (MiU-C).
1. This letter bears only the dateline "Friday afternoon." Jacob, who lived in East Greenwich, wrote it shortly before NG and his family were to leave Rhode Island. As the last Friday before their 14 October departure was 7 October, Jacob undoubtedly wrote this letter before the 8th. (On the date that NG and his family sailed from Newport, see note at Knox to NG, 27 October, below.)

2. NG, his brothers, and their cousin Griffin Greene were partners in the family business, Jacob Greene & Company. Nothing is known about the general settlement to which Jacob referred. Nor is it known whether NG and Jacob met before NG left for the South. However, NG's letter to Griffin Greene of 8 January 1786, below, suggests that some kind of settlement was reached. No further correspondence between NG and Jacob Greene has been found.

*　　*　　*

From Christopher Greene

Dear Sir　　Potowomut [R.I.] Sunday Evening [before 10 October 1785][1]
I recived your letter by Ham, and observe you want me to Supply you with Some Cider and Potatoes.[2] I believe I Shall be able to Supply you from the farme, I wish you to let the Potatoes ly in the Ground, as long

as you Can any ways put it off, as they Grow now as fast as they have any time in the Season. The Cyder will be sent this week, your things at Nurse Benlys, Shall be Collected and Sent by Ham.[3] Your Books Brother B[ill] has Collected all that he Can find and will bring Down. Priestley on education is in my hands. I wish to keep it if agreeable, and I will Pay you for the Same. If not agreeable I will return it.[4] Mrs Greene has Sterns Sentamentle Journey, I wish to have it if agreeable as I have all the rest of his works unless it be his Journey.[5] If Sister Greene Concludes to let me have it Please to Send it by Brother Bill.[6] Please to Present my love to sisters [i.e., sister?] Greene, and accept my best wishes for your health and Happiness   CHRR GREENE

RCS (CtY).

1. This letter is docketed only "1785." It appears to have been written sometime in the days or weeks before NG's departure for the South on 14 October. The last Sunday before NG and his family sailed from Newport was 10 October.

2. NG's letter to his brother Christopher "by Ham," a family servant, has not been found.

3. On "the farme"—presumably NG's property in Westerly, R.I.—see Christopher Greene to NG, 26 March 1784, above. On "Nurse" Barbara Bently, see her letter to NG of 1 September, above.

4. "Bill" was Christopher's and NG's brother William Greene. Christopher may have referred here to Joseph Priestly's "Miscellaneous Observations relating to Education," originally published in 1778 and reprinted in 1780. (*DNB*)

5. Laurence Sterne was the author of one of NG's favorite books, *Tristram Shandy*. Sterne's *A Sentimental Journey*, an unfinished novel, was published in 1768, the year of his death. (*Columbia Encyc.*) On NG's affinity for Sterne, see above, vol. 1: 59n. One of NG's aides, Maj. John Clark, had asked to borrow a copy of *A Sentimental Journey* from NG in 1776. (Ibid., p. 342)

6. "Sister Greene" was undoubtedly CG. It is not known whether she returned the book.

NG's Will[1]

[Newport] Rhode Island, 11 October 1785

In the name of God Amen. I Nathaniel Greene late Major General in the Army of the United States of America do make and declare this to be my last and only will and Testament.

First. I give, devise and bequeath unto my much beloved Wife and to her Heirs Executors and Administrators my Carriages and Carriage Horses, and all the Plate and Furniture which we may have at the time of my death.[2]

Secondly. I give and bequeath all the rest of my property both real and personal to my Wife and Children to be divided equally amongst them to ⟨have and share alike; That is my Wife to have a share equal to one of my⟩ Children ⟨and if any of my Children⟩ should die before they come of Age, unmarried and without legal Issue It is my will and I direct that His, her, or their, share shall go to my Wife and surviving

Children to be divided among them as before said. And it is further my Will and I do hereby direct that should my Wife and Children all die without ever coming to the possession of my property that it be equally divided among my five Brothers, Namely Jacob, William, Elihu, Christopher, & Perry, after paying out the following Legacies. Fifteen hundred pounds to my cousin Griffin Greene, Five hundred pounds to Capt William Littlefield. One hundred Guineas to Mrs Phebe Sands and twenty five Guineas to each of the Children left by Mrs Paine.[3]

Thirdly. In case it should evidently appear for the benefit of my Children then I authorise my Executrix and executors to dispose of any part of the Estate hereby bequeathed or divised.

As I am convinced that the happiness of my Children will depend in an eminent degree on their education; it is my last will and earnest request to those to whose managment I have committed their estates that they will attend in a particular manner to the improvment of their understandings. As I hope my Sons will come forward and take an Active part in the Affairs of their Country; their education should be liberal. My Daughters should not be less suitable to their Station, and Circumstances. But above all things let their Morals be well attended to. To whatever changes of ⟨fortune they may be exposed they must be happy if their morals are⟩ pure. ⟨The smiles of fortune will⟩ afford but a temporary pleasure should their morals be otherwise.[4]

This advice if properly attended to will prove the best Legacy of a fond father.

I constitute and appoint my dear Wife my Executrix and my friend Colonel Jeremiah Wadsworth of Connecticut, and my friend Edwa⟨rd⟩ Rutledge Esqr of South Carolina my Executors to this my Will. Witness my hand and Seal at Newport this eleventh day of October 1785.

NATH GREENE

Signed Sealed Published and declared by the Testator as & for his last will & Testament. In the presence of us who in his presence and in that of ⟨each⟩ other have Subscribed our Names as Witness thereunto

WILLIAM GREENE

PHINEHAS MILLER

ELIZABETH LITTLEFIELD[5]

ACyS (CtHi). The text in angle brackets is from a Cy (RHi).

1. NG, who signed this document shortly before leaving Newport to settle his family on Mulberry Grove plantation in Georgia, could not have known how soon its provisions would have to be implemented. (He died in Georgia on 19 June 1786.) According to records in the Newport city clerk's office, the will was probated there on 16 September 1786. (Newport City Probate Book, 1: 423–24)

2. No inventory of NG's estate has been found.

3. Littlefield was CG's brother; Sands her sister. It appears that CG's other sister, Nancy Littlefield Paine, had died just recently. (See Senter Daybook, RHi.) It is not known how many children she left.

4. At the time of his death in June 1786, NG had five living children: George Washington Greene (1776–93), Martha ("Patty") Washington Greene (1777–1839), Cornelia Lott Greene (1778–1865), Nathanael Ray Greene (1780–1859), and Louisa Catharine Greene (1784–1831). (Clarke, *Greenes*, pp. 328–32) For more about their lives, see below, the Epilogue, at the end of the June 1786 documents.

5. On the witnesses, see note at Edward Rutledge to NG, [before 13 June?], above. As seen there, Rutledge had drafted the will.

*   *   *

¶ [FROM SILAS CASEY, Warwick, R.I., 11 October 1785. "Hurry of Business" has kept him from answering NG's letter of 30 July "respecting the money Dan*l* Coggeshall borrowed of you in the year 1777." Casey supposed that NG's brother Jacob "had long since" informed NG that Casey paid the money "immediatly on Dan*ls* arrivel here."[1] He finds among his memoranda that in 1775 he loaned NG "a camp Bed Sted & curtings"; asks NG to return them at his "convenence."[2] Wishes him "a Safe & quik passage."[3] RCS (MiU-C) 1 p.]

1. For background, see NG to Casey, 30 July, above.

2. Casey is known to have furnished supplies at that time to the Kentish Guards, of which NG was a member. (Vol. 1: 78n, above) NG's reply has not been found.

3. NG and his family left Newport on 14 October. (See note at Knox to NG, 27 October, below.)

*   *   *

¶ [POWER OF ATTORNEY TO JEREMIAH WADSWORTH.[1] From Newport, R.I., 12 October 1785. NG appoints Wadsworth his "Lawful Attorney" to "divide with Col*n* Clement Biddle of Philadelphia, or the Commissioners appointed to settle his affairs, all our Landed Property, purchased of M*r* Abraham Lott, and held as Tenants in common upon the North [i.e., Hudson] River, in the State of New-York."[2] As his attorney, Wadsworth has NG's "full & whole Strength, Power, and Authority in & about the Premises."[3] DS (CtY) 1 p.]

1. The witnesses to this document, which NG signed in the presence of John Handy Warden in Newport, were NG's brother-in-law William Littlefield and the recently hired tutor for NG's children, Phineas Miller.

2. For background, see Wadsworth to NG, 2 October, above. As seen by the note there, this was one of several powers of attorney that NG gave to Wadsworth for selling NG's property in New York and New Jersey. Biddle was in financial trouble at this time. (See, for example, Eyre to NG, 7 March, above.)

3. None of the New York or New Jersey properties had been sold when Wadsworth wrote NG on 8 April 1786, below.

*   *   *

Statement by NG

[Newport, R.I., before 14 October 1785][1]

Colonel Ward will deliver the Letter directed to Henry Banks with his own hands if possible; and inform M*r* Banks of the pains I have taken for a year past in trying to sell Cumberland Island and the other property Mortgaged to me for the amount of the Mortgage and have not been able to accomplish it altho it has been offerd in quarter shares to give every advantage in the sale of it. The Col will inform Mr Banks also that nothing will sell the property for the amount of the mortgage but freeing it from the encumbrance of the Mortgage by a deed of relinquishment. That if Mr Banks refuses this I intend to sue the Mortgage[,] sell the Premises for what they will fetch[,] and pro[s]ecute my bond of indemnity for the remainder.[2] I have John Banks's bond for ten thousand pound;[3] and as I know how to make Henry Banks responsible I shall not fail to do it providing he refuses a deed of relinquishment.[4] If Henry Banks will give a deed of relinquishment I will take the property for the sum I am engaged for on it. Or if Mr Banks will get my bonds up; and repay me the Money and interest already advanced on it I will give up the Mortgage immediately.[5] It is in vain for Mr Banks to think of improving the property in the way he proposes.[6] I shall never undertake it upon any such plan. I have been Sufficiently embarassed with the matter already. And besides which I can get the other half of the Island for a less sum than the amount of the Mortgage and the conditions of payment made agreeable. Col Ward will please to forward me a letter concerning the result and if he obtains the deed to have it forwarded by Post.[7]

ACy (RHi).

1. NG undoubtedly gave this document to his friend Samuel Ward, Jr., sometime before NG left Newport on 14 October to move his family to Georgia. It appears from Ward's letter of 11 November, below, that he had been in Virginia for as long as a month on the mission that NG gave him here.

2. The letter to Banks has not been found. For background on NG's efforts to get Henry Banks to relinquish his inheritance rights to a share of Cumberland Island, Ga., see especially Banks to NG, 2 September, and NG to Carrington, 29 September, both above. Ward wrote NG from Richmond on 11 November that he had delivered the letter to Banks and "danced a very regular attention upon him for a fortnight past[.] This morning I have got the deed signd and properly witnessd." In a letter of 12 November, below, Banks informed NG that he had given an "unequivocal Relinquishment" of his "Right of Inheritance to the lands purchased by my Brother [John Banks] and for the payment of which you stood bound."

3. In regard to the indenture from John Banks and Ichabod Burnet on which NG based his claim to an undivided half share of a large part of Cumberland Island, see note at Hyrne to Clay, 26 November 1783, above.

4. See note 2, above.

5. As noted at his letter to NG of 2 September, Banks asserted many years later that title to Cumberland Island should revert to him.

6. See ibid.

7. See Ward to NG, 11 November.

*   *   *

¶ [FROM NICHOLAS HOFFMAN, New York, 20 October 1785. Has NG's letter of 10 October [not found], asking for information about Clarke & Nightingale's bill.[1] Writes: "I can't give you any information relating [to] them, no

Such Bills has Ever come to our hands, or moneys recived from those Gentlemen." The only money they have received is mentioned in Hoffman's letter to NG of 4 October. NG informed Hoffman in his letter of 5 June [not found] that Major Eyre would pay "the Amount of a Cargo of live Oak, Cut on your Lands in Georgia by Capt Rogers Keane [i.e., Alexander Cain], of Phillide[lp]hia which you Expected would Amount to three Hundred Dollars[;] we have not receivd any Moneys from the Above Gentlemen, or heard from them, on the Subject."[2] Hoffman thanks NG for his "Kind offers of Service to our friends." The "Old Gentleman" will probably "spend the remainder of his days in Europe. His son Isaac proposes going to Canada."[3] Hoffman and his wife send their compliments to NG and CG. RCS (MiU-C) 2 pp.]

1. On Clarke & Nightingale, see NG to Hoffman, 9 March, above.

2. Benjamin Eyre had informed NG that Alexander Cain, in collusion with Alexander Semple, was cutting timber on NG's lands on Cumberland Island, Ga., and shipping it to Philadelphia. (Eyre to NG, 7 March, above) Although NG's reply to Eyre has not been found, it is clear from Eyre's to him of 14 May, above, that NG wanted to impound and sell the timber when it reached Philadelphia and have the proceeds sent to Hoffman.

3. Neither the "Old Gentleman" nor his son has been identified. No further correspondence between NG and Hoffman has been found.

*   *   *

From General Henry Knox, Secretary at War

New York 27 Octr 1785

I hope by this time my dear friend that you, Mrs Greene, and your little flock are safely housed at Mulberry Grove.[1] I sincerely wish you every joy that can animate an[d] chear human nature. I well know that you are disposed to view every event in the best lights—what a blessed talent compared with the grumbling churl who is enveloped in sorrows created by his own ill nature.

I crave a place in your memory and in return I assure you of a perpetual affection. It may not be worth much its true, but taken at its value. I request a line now and then informing me of the happiness of Mrs Greene and your little family.[2]

I have your two pieces of Cannon. The engraver is to set to work upon them immediately. As soon as they shall be finished they will be subject to your orders, as also the Standard, and the medal when it arrives which I expect soon.[3]

Should there be any service which I could render you and Mrs Greene, I pray you to command me without reserve. Mrs Knox joins me in affectionate regards to you and Mrs Greene. I am my dear Sir Your assured friend   H KNOX

RCS (NjMoHP).

1. The date of the Greenes' arrival at Mulberry Grove, Ga., is not known. NG and his family left Newport on 14 October. *The Newport Mercury* of 15 October contains a notice that "Yesterday sailed for Savannah in Georgia, the Sloop *Dove*, Capt. Phillips, with whom

went Passengers the Hon. Major-General Greene, his Lady and Family." A Charleston, S.C., paper reported that the *Dove*, with the Greene family aboard, arrived in Savannah on 30 October. (*South-Carolina Gazette and Public Advertiser*, 8 November) NG wrote Ethan Clarke on 23 November, below, that they had "arrivd" there some sixteen days after leaving Newport. The voyage itself was harrowing. (Ibid.) According to CG's biographers, the family first spent "several weeks" at the home of Nathaniel Pendleton in Savannah before taking up residence at Mulberry Grove. (Stegeman, *Caty*, p. 117)

2. NG replied to Knox on 12 March 1786, below.

3. In recognition of his wartime services, Congress had awarded NG two cannon, which were to be suitably engraved. (Thomson to NG, 18 October 1783, above) As noted at ibid., Knox was to oversee the engraving. Congress had earlier voted to present a gold medal and a British standard to NG in commemoration of the battle of Eutaw Springs. (Vol. 9: 519–20 and n, above; the medal is illustrated in ibid., pp. 520–21.) NG apparently did not receive any of these mementoes before his death.

*   *   *

¶ [FROM STEPHEN RAPALJE, New York, 27 October 1785. He had "to part with" NG's bond for 250 guineas "in payment to Messrs Randall son & Stewarts[,] Merchant here."[1] Hopes NG approves. "They are good men," and Rapalje did not think it would matter "whether the Bond was in their hands or mine."[2] RCS (MiU-C) 1 p.]

1. On the bond, see Wadsworth to NG, 18 July, and Rapalje to NG, 25 September, both above.

2. As seen in his letter to Randall Son & Stewart of 12 March 1786, below, NG was unable to comply with their request for payment.

*   *   *

From Samuel Ward, Jr.

Dear Genl   Richmond [Va.] 11th Novr 1785

I imbraced the first moment after my arrival at Richmond to deliver your Letter to M^r [Henry] Banks.[1] I have danced a very regular attention upon him for a fortnight past. This morning I have got the deed signd and properly witnessd.[2] There remains nothing now to be done but the getting an authentication under the great seal which I leave for Col^o Carrington to do and he will forward you the deed when that is done.[3] Mr Banks has not showed any reluctance to the transacting this business[;] my delays have arisen from the manners of the Country[;] their dignity will not permit them to do any thing without great formality & great consideration. I have had a thousand thoughts respecting your voyage, from the shortness of my own [I] think yours was not a long passage tho perhaps a rough one.[4] I find my health greatly mended since I left home. The weather for a month past has been warm the season uncommonly soft and mild. The feavers were almost intirely over when I arrivd[,] the yellow wearing off their faces very fast.[5] There is now as much health here as at any place I ever saw, and not a single inflammation of the breast or consumptive complaint in the country. I flatter myself I shall be able to pass the winter in Rhode Island and yet it would be no very great mortification or punishment to me to be obliged to make Mrs Greene a visit this winter—to have the sovereign pleasure of taking you by the hand and to kiss all your little folks pray do it for me. I give my best love to them All.[6]

The exact regimen I have prescribed myself for my health has prevented me from joining in the amusements of the season. I have been in but few families if in this situation I can judge of the manners of the People I think them a hundred years behind Us at the northward & there is more than that difference in the progress of the Arts. What does Mrs Greene think on this subject who sees so many things to esteem & to condemn among her northern friends.

The Assembly is sitting, they have been on the subject of trade but have made no conclusions. They are divided in sentiment, a few persons are for following the regulations of Boston entirely[,][7] others are for referring the regulation of trade wholly to Congress, and I am told some persons are for making a bargain with great Britain on the best terms they can. I think it is probable some temporary regulations will be made not materially different from their present system of duties imposts, and the Affair be referred [to Congress?]. As this plan will not [*damaged*] the shipping the present years [*damaged*] will give them an oppertunity to see the result of our negotiations in Europe. But away with politicks I know nothing about them. I have now only to request you to give my warmest regards to Mrs Greene with every good wish for her health and with every good wish for health and prosperity I am your friend s WARD

I thought I might as well write the sheet full as the postage will cost you no more. I thought you would wish the earliest advice on Banks affair.[8]

RCS (NjP).

1. For background, see NG's Statement dated before 14 October, above, and the note at Hyrne to Clay, 26 November 1783.

2. In the deed, which was signed at Richmond on this date, Henry Banks, as heir to his brother John, relinquished to NG his "equity of redemption" to property on Cumberland Island, Ga., and to "two several lots of Lands" in Brunswick, Ga. (The deed of relinquishment and related documents are recorded in the Office of the Clerk of Superior Court, Chatham County Courthouse, Savannah, Ga., Deed Book 1-C, pp. 389–99.) Banks wrote NG about the relinquishment on 12 November, below.

3. Edward Carrington's letter enclosing the deed has not been found.

4. NG's friend Ward had traveled to Virginia from Rhode Island to obtain the relinquishment from Banks. (NG's Statement, before 14 October) NG and his family left Rhode Island on 14 October to settle in Georgia. (See note at Knox to NG, 27 October, above.)

5. On Ward's health, see also NG to CG, 25 May, above. The "feavers" were probably malarial.

6. Ward was back in Rhode Island by mid-December. (Littlefield to NG, 16 December, below)

7. "At a meeting at Faneuil Hall on April 16, the merchants of Boston resolved to seek

the 'immediate interposition' of Congress for their relief, and to appeal to merchants throughout the states to work in behalf of augmenting the power of Congress to regulate trade." (Smith, *Letters*, 22: 369n)

8. NG replied to Ward on 4 April 1786, below.

* * *

¶ [FROM WELCOME ARNOLD, Providence, R.I., 12 November 1785. "The Bearer Mrs Eliza Pray" is Arnold's "Friend and the Wife of Mr Job Pray Merchant of Savannah." She has taken passage in a vessel "bound for Georgia, to her Husband." Mrs. Pray "is a person of a Very Slender Constitution." Arnold will be grateful for "Any Friendly offices" NG can offer her. RCS (MiU-C) 1 p.]

* * *

From Henry Banks

Sir   Richmond [Va.] Novr 12th 1785

Having relinquished my Right of Inheritance to the lands purchased by my Brother and for the payment of which you stood bound, you are left to act with the fullest Latitude therein.[1] The unequivocal Relinquishment which I made founded on the highest Sence of your Intention to do for the best in Behalf of my Brothers Estate, will prove to you that my first Intention was to place you secure in your agency therein, tho I still hope that those measures will be pursued which answer my fir[st] expectation and Wish.[2]

The lands which I hold in this Country have increased most rapidly in Value, so that if the appearance of Money had not been nearly banished from this Country I might have determined to discharge the Mortgage. Money will again soon find its way back and if the Georgia Lands remain unsold I shall [*damaged*] to relieve you, or if you could effect any purpose with my land in Kentucky or those on the uper part of the Ohio I shall most cheerfully give them up at a Valuation or secure the money thereon by a mortgage.[3]

I am too well perswaded of your wish to have the business brought to the most speedy close to repeat my own Solicitude therein so as to wish your neglecting any other Business more important, but when I remind you that while thus the prime of my life is spent in Idleness, While I am fully competent in property for all my Responsibilities, While I am ready to give that property for final release, while my Character is suffering and your own not unreflected on, I am sure that you will think it an object of Importance. You will if not now finally beleive me when I tell you that M^r [James] Hunter will throw every Opposition against settlement and that he has said things prejudic[ial to your?] Character. I wish nothing but a candid development of the whole of my Conduct, I think it [will?] do me honour, and have a confidence that you will when satisfied thereof be ready in confirming the propriety of my Measures.[4]

If you have any Regard for the feelings and Reputation of a young man, bring to the speediest issue those unhappy transactions.

[The only?] Barr to a Settlem[t] with [Smith, Bow]doin & Hunter is the want of the Books in North Carolina on which you administerd.[5] I hope you will direct them to the Hands of Col° [Edward] Carrington or some other Gentleman of whom you have knowledge & Confidence, without Nothing can be done and I may loose another year.[6]

I shall be exceedingly thankful for your Communications upon any thing which may lead to information in Setling with M[r] Hunter & Smith Bowdoin & Hunter.[7] I am sir Yr mo ob Ser   HENRY BANKS

RCS (MiU-C).

1. On Banks's relinquishment to NG, see also Ward to NG, 11 November, above. For background, see NG's Statement of before 14 October and the note at Hyrne to Clay, 26 November 1783, both above.

2. Years later, as seen by the note at his letter to NG of 2 September, above, Banks became more equivocal about the relinquishment.

3. Banks referred in this paragraph to the mortgage on an undivided half share of land on Cumberland Island, Ga., which NG had assumed by virtue of the unpaid indenture he had received from John Banks and Ichabod Burnet, both of whom were since deceased. (See note at Hyrne to Clay, 26 November 1783; on the relinquishment that NG had received from Burnet's heirs, see William Burnet to NG, 13 August, above.) Banks appears to have been expressing here a willingness to trade lands that he owned in Kentucky and along the Ohio River for NG's rights to Cumberland Island. He wrote NG on 13 January 1786, below: "I flatter myself that the Georgia lands will be sold to great advantage when all incumbrances" had been removed. NG, however, wrote Samuel Ward on 4 April 1786, below, that although the deed of relinquishment from Banks would "afford me the better opportunity of disposing of the Island to advantage," he was "so much prejudiced in favor of" Cumberland Island that he was "determined" to hold onto it, "as few are sensible of its value." NG and his heirs did retain their Cumberland Island holdings, and CG eventually settled there with her family.

4. On the legal maneuvering between Hunter and Banks, see especially Hunter to NG, 1 June and 30 September; NG to Hunter, 29 August, and Banks to NG, 13 and 15 July, 5 August, and 2 September, all above.

5. Banks had asked for these books in his letter to NG of 13 July, above. (On the firm of Smith, Bowdoin, & Hunter, see note at that letter and Banks to NG, 15 July.)

6. NG had not mentioned Banks's request in his letter to Carrington of 29 September, above.

7. NG's reply has not been found.

*   *   *

¶ [FROM WILLIAM LITTLEFIELD, Newport, R.I., 16 November 1785. According to a catalog extract, "Business matters—Gen. Greene's property in Rhode Island—Farm, house accounts, &c.,"[1] are the subjects of this letter. Littlefield "does not want to take care of *John* in the house owing to the old lady's uneasiness on account of her maids, Rose and Sylvia."[2] Extract printed in Stan V. Henkels, *Catalogue #1005* (1909), p. 18.]

1. On NG's farm in Westerly, R.I., see above, Christopher Greene to NG, 26 March 1784.
2. It appears from Robert Hazlehurst's letter to NG of 13 December, below, that John was a servant of NG's. The "old lady" was probably Littlefield's mother-in-law, Aliph Malbone Brinley. (See note at Littlefield to NG, 11 December, below.)

* * *

To Ethan Clarke

Dear Sir   Charleston [S.C.] Nov 23ᵈ 1785[1]

When news is scarce and little matters grow into importance some things attract the public notice which would otherwise lay buried in the bustle of life. From this circumstance it is possible the Southern papers may have announced to you our safe arrival in Georgia before this Letter comes to hand. We arrivd in sixteen days after we left Newport.[2] The passage was long and disagreeable, Catys sufferings inexpressible. Her fears magnified the smallest dangers into certain ruin. However we had two Gales in one of which we lost a man over board that were not pleasant and not altogether free from danger. Caty was so affrighted during their greatest violence as most to loose her senses. It was truly distressing to see her distress. The Children were a little sick at first but chearful all the rest of the voyage and far less troublesome than could have been imagined. We landed all safe without injury to passengers or property. Indeed every thing came much better than I expected that we brought on Deck. The Carriages were neither of them the least injured. It was happy for us we had not our horses as we must have thrown them over board to have quieted Catys fears if not from actual stress of weather. We found the house situation and out buildings more convenient and pleasing than we expected.[3] The prospect is delightful and the house Magnificent but very dirty. Nell was eight days mounted on a stage scowering the Cornishes and painted plaistering upon the sides of the Wall; and several more were spent on the Wainscoting and floors. When I left home the house began to look a little decent; but the glass is much broke. We have a Coach house & stables, a large out Kitchen and a Poultry house near fifty feet long & twenty wide parted for different kinds of Poultry with a Pigeon house on the top which will contain not less than a thousand Pigeons. Besides these there are several other buildings convenient for a family and among the rest a fine smoke house. The Garden is in ruins but there are still a great variety of shrubs and flowers in it. In the Poultry and the Garden Caty promises her self no small amusements and if they are not sufficiently interesting to give pleasure they may preserve her from disgust.[4] Mʳ Miller has begun his school and the children improve very fast. He is an exceeding cleaver lad.[5] Mrs Davis the housekeeper promises every thing we expected and after a little time I hope will find her self perfectly happy which I

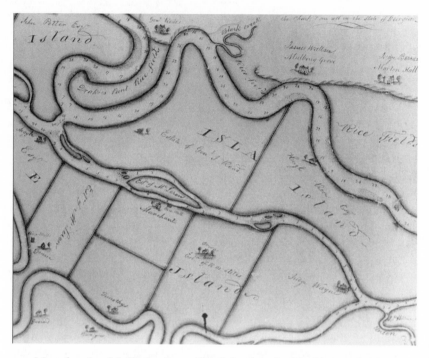

Map showing Mulberry Grove, Isla Island, and other Savannah River plantations; detail from Chart of Savannah River, *by John McKinnon, 1825*
(Georgia Historical Society)

imagine she is not in a scene so new.[6] I met with a great loss the third day after my arrival. The overseer set a Negroe to keep his Cattle from a body of Rice who very stupidly built a fire near it and set the whole in flames to the value of £200 Sterling. This is the more unfortunate as the Crops are but light.[7] My others matters are in a good train. Remember me to all friends Yours   NATH GREENE

ALS (MiU-C).
    1. NG apparently paid a brief visit to Charleston within a few weeks after his arrival in Georgia from Newport, R.I. (See Burke to NG, 27 November, below, and note at Knox to NG, 27 October, above.)
    2. The Greenes left Newport on 14 October and arrived in Savannah, Ga., on 30 October. (Note at Knox to NG, 27 October)
    3. Mulberry Grove plantation, the state of Georgia's gift to NG, had been confiscated from the estate of John Graham, a colonial lieutenant governor. (See Joseph Clay to NG, 6 August 1782, above [vol. 11: 494–95 and n].) It appears from NG's account here that the house may have been unoccupied since Graham's departure. (See, however, Saunders to NG, 27 November 1783, and NG to Saunders, 4 January 1784, both above.)
    4. According to her biographers, CG was in a precarious state of mental and physical health at this time. Depressed about the family's financial circumstances and the recent

death of her infant daughter, Catharine, she was also pregnant once again. (Stegeman, *Caty*, pp. 115–17)

5. Phineas Miller, the Greene children's recently hired tutor, had accompanied the family from Rhode Island. (See above, NG to Wadsworth, 1 October.) A Georgian who visited the Greenes soon after their arrival at Mulberry Grove described Miller as a young man "of amiable qualities, & a mathematical genius equal to any in the united states." (Isaac Briggs to Joseph Thomas, 23 November 1785, *Georgia Historical Quarterly* 12 [June 1928]: 181–82)

6. "Mrs. Davis," the housekeeper, was apparently from Rhode Island.

7. On NG's 1785 rice crops, see also Croskeys to NG, 16 February 1786, and NG to Knox, 12 March 1786, both below.

From the Reverend William Gordon

Dear Sir   Jamaica Plain [Mass.] Nov[r] 24, 1785.

I hope this will find you and your family safe and well in Georgia.[1] You have obliged me greatly by marking out, as you have done, upon the N. and S. Carolina map.[2] Have now sent you one of my proposals, for printing by subscription the History of the American Revolution, in four volumes.[3] After such experience of your friendship, I cannot doubt of your countenance, in promoting and hastening subscriptions, so far as it falls in your way, that so the work may be the sooner published, and with the embellishments mentioned in the proposals. Messrs. May & Hills, Merchants in Savannah do me the favour of receiving subscriptions on my behalf. With the sincerest regards to Self Lady and children, I remain with much esteem, Dear Sir, Your very humble servant and real friend

Printed in *Proceedings of the Massachusetts Historical Society* 63 (1930): 524.

1. On the Greenes' arrival in Georgia, see NG to Clarke, immediately above.

2. For background, see above, Gordon to NG, 27 August, 12 and 26 September.

3. The subscription proposal has not been found. As noted above, Gordon's four-volume history of the American Revolution was first published in London in 1788. (Vol. 10: 439n)

From Aedanus Burke

Dear General   Charleston [S.C.] 27th Novb[r] 1785

I was sorry that your short stay in our City deprived me of the pleasure I could well derive from a friendly tete a tete with you for many hours, as I had much to say to you.[1] Your advice particularly w[d] be of some consequence, about removing my property, Little as it is, from the Wateree River to that of Savanah [Ga.]; an object w[ch] I think of & resolve upon with much diffidence. I have some friends in Savanah who recommend it strongly. Others I have here whose opinion I value & approve of it.

I have to tell you that I am the Author of the *Salutary-hints*, except the whole of the 5th page, & part of the 6th down to the break; wch truly and honestly belongs to you.[2] I observe there is one whole sentence in page 4th every word of wch is yours, & in the order You wrote it;[3] and I must farther do you Justice; your judicious forceable observations on the Subject at large, enlarged & fited my mind for it, such as it is; so that in some sense you ought to father the whole of it, only that I have not done that Justice to the Subject, wch you well could bestow on it, if you took the trouble, and I speak without meaning any Compliment.[4] The production is hasty, and the pains it cost me to write it, was a trifle, compared with the difficulty I had to get it printed: so much afraid was every creature of offending the British. It put me in mind of a Conspiracy whenever I spoke of it, to any one. However as to my self, I w^{d} rather they should think me capable of working them mischief, then to have their friendship wch is brittle as their Glassware.[5] The B. are such a sett, I am not clear, but that their being afraid of any one, w^{d} procure him more of their good services, than any affection of theirs could; it w^{d} be geting a premium for insurance out of them.[6] With every wish for your welfare & happiness I remain dear Genl with sincere esteem Your most obd^{t} Servt AEDANUS BURKE

RCS (MiU-C).

1. It is not known when NG arrived in Charleston, or how long he was there, but his letter to Ethan Clarke of 23 November, above, places him in the city on that date. NG and his family had arrived in Savannah, Ga., from Newport, R.I., on 30 October, and they took up residence on nearby Mulberry Grove plantation sometime in November after a short stay in Savannah with Nathaniel Pendleton and his wife. (Ibid.; note at Knox to NG, 27 October, above; Stegeman, *Caty*, pp. 117–18)

2. Burke's pamphlet, *A few salutary hints, pointing out the policy and consequences of admitting British subjects to engross our trade and become our citizens; Addressed to those who either risqued or lost their all to bring about the Revolution*, was published in Charleston in 1785 and reprinted in New York in 1786. Burke wrote it under the same pseudonym, "Cassius," that he had used two years earlier in his critique of the Society of the Cincinnati. (See Flagg to NG, 17 October 1783, above.) In *A few salutary hints*, Burke warned South Carolinians that British merchants had seized an extraordinary amount of power by lending large sums of money to citizens who needed capital to restore their businesses and plantations after the war. He argued that although the British had been defeated militarily in the war, they could soon regain economic and even political ascendancy because many prominent residents were heavily in their debt. (For more about the pamphlet, see Meleney, *Aedanus Burke*, pp. 115–18.)

3. It appears that no copy of the original Charleston imprint of *A few salutary hints* survives. (Meleney, *Aedanus Burke*, p. 115n) The fifth page of the 1786 reprint could conceivably have "belonged" to NG, however, as it dealt with the problems of plantation owners who had borrowed capital and later suffered financial reverses from a poor return on their crops. According to the pamphlet, the British lenders "relied for payment on our crops of rice, indigo, and tobacco; their merchants well understood the advantages and disappointments of our trade, they knew the Carolina planter had no way under heaven to make payment, but by the produce of his crops." After the "seasons failed," the planters were under heavy obligation to their creditors, and the slaves whom the lenders had sold them "at 70 or 80 guineas" at the war's end "would not average three through-

out the country." Carolinians were thus becoming slaves to their British creditors, and "Carolina which cost the lives and blood of so many of her brave fellows, is no longer to be the country of those who fought for it; these, it seems, must be reduced to the condition of indigent vagabonds, or turn farmers of their own inheritance, and work them for their new masters." (*A few salutary hints*, p. 5) On the next page of the reprint, the author alleged that the merchants, to whom Americans had shown clemency by allowing them to stay and do business in South Carolina after the war, now constituted a "faction, to sow discontent and promote the views of the British ministry." (Ibid., p. 6)

4. On page 4 of the 1786 reprint, which is the second page of text, the author argued that the British had installed "a standing army of merchants, factors, clerks, agents and emissaries," who "monopolized our trade, speculated on our necessities, and holding out every object of temptation, plunged us into a debt which their depredations a little before, and our wants and distresses joined to their subtilty now, seduced us to contract." (*A few salutary hints*, p. 4) In a 1966 article, George C. Rogers, Jr., was the first historian to identify Burke, on the basis of the present letter to NG, as the author of *A few salutary hints*. Rogers observed that NG had "overextended his credit" in buying slaves for his plantations in South Carolina and Georgia, that his "principal creditors were British merchants," and that it would have been "natural" for NG "to have poured out his own feelings concerning British creditors and their agents to such a receptive listener as Burke." (George C. Rogers, Jr., "Aedanus Burke, Nathanael Greene, Anthony Wayne and the Merchants of Charleston," *SCHGM* 67 [April 1966]: 75–83)

5. The Charleston printers who published the pamphlet were Burd and Haswell. They placed an advertisement for *A few salutary hints* in the *Charleston Evening Gazette* of 14 November.

6. "The. B." were the British merchants. NG's reply to Burke has not been found. Burke stipulated in his will that his papers were to be burned after his death, and his biographer believes this request was honored, for no body of his personal papers has been found. (Meleney, *Aedanus Burke*, p. 2)

*   *   *

¶ [FROM WILLIAM PIERCE, JR., [Savannah, Ga.? November 1785].[1] Congratulates NG on "the arrival of yourself, and Family in Georgia."[2] His "business" has kept Pierce and his wife from "waiting on" the Greenes, but they offer their "particular respects" and ask that "when you come to Savannah, you will treat us and our House, with the freedom you would your own." Pierce's family is now "at Belmont," Ga., but will be in town "in a Week or two."[3] RCS (MiU-C) 1 p.]

1. A note, possibly docketing, on the cover of this letter reads "November 1785."
2. On the arrival of NG and his family in Georgia, see note at Knox to NG, 27 October, above.
3. Pierce, one of NG's former aides, was now a merchant, living in Savannah. (See, for example, his letter to NG of 24 September 1784, above.)

¶ [TO ROGER PARKER SAUNDERS. [From Mulberry Grove, Ga., after November 1785?].[1] NG has been examining "plantation Accounts" and thinks that his and Saunders's accounts may have been "blended in some instances at the different Stores for our plantations," especially in regard to nails. In two different accounts, quantities of nails are charged at a time when NG "had no building going on"; this "might be a mistake."[2] He has sent the bills to "Crosskees" [i.e., John Croskeys] and asks Saunders to look at them. "All the Articles" belonging to Mulberry Grove should be "delivered over to Croskeys," as NG does not wish to put Saunders "to farther trouble having already been too troublesome."³ Tr (PVfHi) 1 p.]

1. The typed transcript is dated only "1785." From its contents, the editors have inferred that NG was at his plantation in Georgia when this letter was written. He took up residence there sometime in November.

2. Saunders had been supervising plantation operations for NG, especially at Boone's Barony, S.C. (See note at Saunders to NG, 26 May 1783, above.)

3. Croskeys assisted in the management of Boone's Barony. (See Saunders to NG, 20 October 1783, above.)

¶ [FROM CHARLES THOMSON, New York, 2 December 1785. He has received "the enclosed letter" and a box for NG from Mr. [Joseph] Brown of London, which arrived on "the *Edward.*" According to Brown, the box contains "two prints, one of general Washington & the other of" NG.¹ If a ship were going "directly for Georgia," Thomson would "have hazarded sending the box by it"; but as there is none, he will wait for NG's "Orders."² He hopes "the climate of Georgia will correspond with your prospects & wishes." Is "confident that infant Government will derive great advantage from your becoming a citizen & inhabitant thereof." RCS (MiU-C) 1 p.]

1. See Brown to NG, 12 September, above.
2. NG replied to Thomson on 24 April 1786, below.

*   *   *

From the Marquis de Lafayette

My dear friend   Paris December the 3. 1785

Altho I do not much depend upon this Conveyance I must take every way to tell you that in my Last conference With Marechal de Castries the naval Minister, I found Him better disposed to purchase His naval Strores [i.e., stores] in America than ever He Had Been.¹ He tells me He will be particularly Happy to Make arrangements with one He So much Respects as général Greene but Wishes you first to Send a Small Cargoe, particularly of knees-crooked Timber, *Bois courbes de toutes Espece* [i.e., curved wood from all different kinds of trees] to any french port. I would prefer L'Orient or Rochefort, and particularly the Latter.² I insisted upon an *Engagement* ⟨he would⟩ purchase that cargoe but He says altho it is very probable, He Cannot engage to do it consistent With His principles.³ However, I think you may very Safely Send a Small quantity, and I wish you Will Have on Board a very Clever Capitain With orders to come immediately to me, and your *pleins pouvoirs* to treat on a Large Scale. Because the Wood Being once approuved of, I think you may enter into a Large Bargain,⁴ and in order to insure a Good Sale to your importation Back into America, I Would advise your Uniting With [Jeremiah] Wadsworth, our friend [James] McHenry and other Houses in the Several States, to Whom the Returning Vessels Should be directed. Your affectionate friend   LAFAYETTE

I am labouring to induce the Minister to take Your first Cargoe at all Events.[5]

RCS (Greene Papers: DLC). The text in angle brackets is from a copy at CtHi.

1. NG was trying to interest the French government in live oak timber from his holdings on Cumberland Island, Ga. Lafayette was helping him deal with French officials in this matter. (See, for example, NG's letters to the Marquis de Castries and Lafayette of 1 June, both above.)

2. A French naval vessel had recently visited Cumberland Island in an unsuccessful attempt to collect samples of the timber. (Pendleton to NG, 23 September, above) On "knees-crooked Timber," see note at Wadsworth to NG, 21 February, above.

3. Castries insisted on seeing samples of the timber before deciding whether to purchase it. (Foreste to NG, 16 December, below)

4. By "pleins pouvoir," Lafayette meant that the captain should have full powers to negotiate a contract.

5. Lafayette wrote NG again about this matter on 29 December, below. (See also NG's letter to Castries near the end of the December documents.) It does not appear that any samples were sent before NG's death in June 1786.

* * *

¶ [FROM WILLIAM R. DAVIE, Halifax, N.C., 4 December 1785. He has sent letters to NG "in every quarter of the Continent, and indeed it seems more difficult to get a letter to you now, than when you was surrounded by your enemies." NG "must remember" that at his "special instance," Davie "was in the service of the Continent" from 1 January to 1 June [1781] "or thereabouts, and that when we parted at Ninety Six, I rec^d no Certificate of these services."[1] Asks NG to "forward me one by post."[2] Davie concludes: "When I saw you last we thought of nothing but preserving our Country; our success has left us leisure to think of doing ourselves Justice." RCS (NcU) 1 p.]

1. Davie had served as a commissary with the Southern Army from January to June of 1781. (See biographical note and NG's letter of 11 December 1780, above, urging Davie to accept the post. [Vol. 6: 561–62 and n]) On the siege of the British post at Ninety-Six, S.C., see NG to Samuel Huntington, 20 June 1781, above. (Vol. 8: 419–22 and n)

2. If NG provided the certificate, it has not been found. Writing to NG on 23 April 1786, below, J. Cole Mountflorence enclosed a letter from Davie [not found] and commented that Davie was waiting for a reply.

¶ [FROM FRANCIS PHILLIP FATIO, [East Florida, 5 December 1785].[1] He has recently learned about NG's and his "Lady's safe arrival at Savannah," Ga., from "the Charleston [S.C.] newspapers." Takes "this first opportunity by our friend Mr [Henry] Osborne" to "congratulate you on the occasion" and to send "best respects," in which his wife and daughter share.[2] Is sending "a Box of Sweet Oranges from our Garden" to CG. Mr. Fleming also sends a box, and NG's family can judge "which are the best."[3] Fatio does not suppose that NG will visit Cumberland Island "during the winter" but has asked Osborne "to acquaint me in case you should travel to the Southward."[4] Fatio is going to his plantation at St. Johns "to overseer it in my son's absence."[5] RCS (MiU-C) 1 p.]

1. Fatio was a resident of East Florida. The date was taken from the docketing.

2. NG had met Fatio during his trip to East Florida earlier in the year. (See NG to

Zéspedes, 26 March, and Fatio to NG, 6 April, both above.) On Osborne, see his letter to NG of 23 April, above.

3. NG had stayed with George Fleming in East Florida in April. (See note at NG to Zéspedes, 26 March.)

4. NG did not "travel to the Southward" again.

5. Fatio owned a plantation at St. Johns, East Florida. (Fatio to NG, 6 April)

*   *   *

From Edward Fenwick

Sir   John's Island [S.C.] 5th Decemr 1785
    I am much concerned at being under the Necessity of giving you farther trouble respecting our late Agreement, but as it has been only partially complied with, I hope you will not take it amiss my again applying to you on that head.[1]
    Capt Wilmot (your Agent in the Bussiness) assured me at the time I treated with him that every Agreement of the sort you Made, would be implicitly complied with; It is true my Estate in Consequence of it, has been restored to me; but the right of Citizenship & being permitted to remain in the Country, where that Estate and all my nearest Relations are, has not been as yet granted.[2] These were the Motives which chiefly induced me to accede to your Proposals.[3] I must farther add that I have receivd late Accounts from England that all Monies due me by that Government for Cattle & other valuable Effects are struck off in Consequence of the Papers produced in my favor at the last Meeting of both Houses, and which I am willing if required to take my Oath of.[4] I must therefore entreat Sir, Your farther intrapositions in my behalf at the next sitting of the House.[5] And am Sir with the greatest Respect & Esteem yr most Obedt & hble servt   EDWD FENWICK

RCS (MiU-C).
    1. By "our late Agreement," Fenwick, a British officer who had provided intelligence to the Americans, referred to NG's promise to help him gain citizenship and recover his property from the South Carolina government after the war. (See NG to Guerard, 30 March 1784, 19 September 1784, and 4 February 1785, all above.) Fenwick's name had been taken off the confiscation list, but his citizenship had not yet been restored. (See notes at NG to Guerard, 19 September 1784 and 4 February 1785.)
    2. Capt. William Wilmot had enlisted Fenwick's assistance in return for NG's promise to intervene on Fenwick's behalf after the war. (See above, vol. 11: 180–81n, 545.)
    3. For NG's "Proposals" in regard to Fenwick, see "To Whom It May Concern," 14 August 1782, above (vol. 11: 545).
    4. Fenwick presumably referred to the submission of letters from NG to Gov. Benjamin Guerard to the South Carolina legislature in January 1785. These documents confirmed that Fenwick had acted as an American spy. (S.C., House of Representatives, *Journals, 1784–85*, p. 15)
    5. This letter was enclosed in one that Thomas Gadsden wrote to NG on 9 February 1786, below, commenting that the state senate had recently passed a resolution refusing to "receive any more Petitions from any Persons or Person banished from this State or either

of our Sister States." Fenwick, having rendered material aid to the American cause, thus found himself in the "disagreeable Situation" of being admitted to citizenship neither in his home state of South Carolina nor in England, where word of his contributions to the American cause had made him *persona non grata*. After receiving Gadsden's letter, NG wrote to Gov. William Moultrie on Fenwick's behalf. (The letter is below, dated 12 February 1786.) As noted at NG to Guerard, 19 September 1784, Fenwick's citizenship was restored in March 1786.

* * *

¶ [FROM THOMAS FARR,[1] Charleston, S.C., 10 December 1785. Introduces "Mr Jones a young Gentleman," who was a passenger on the vessel that brought Farr to Charleston from Philadelphia. Farr has a "good opinion" of Jones, who was recommended by "a very respectable Character."[2] Mrs. [Elizabeth Holmes] Farr joins in "our best respects to Mrs Greene and the rest of your Family, with best regards for yourself." In a note beneath his signature, Farr adds that "Doctor Olyphant with his Lady arrived yesterday from Rhode Island, in Mr Greene's Ship, after a tedious passage of 20 Days."[3] RCS (MiU-C) 1 p.]

1. Farr, a Charleston merchant who had been captured by the British and held prisoner, served several terms in the South Carolina legislature after the war. (Vol. 10: 178n, above)

2. "Mr. Jones" has not been identified.

3. Dr. David Olyphant, a South Carolinian, made frequent trips to Newport, R.I. (Morris to NG, 20 August, above) His "Lady" was his new wife, NG's and CG's friend Nancy Vernon, of Newport. (*South-Carolina Gazette and Public Advertiser*, 10 December) They arrived on the vessel *Bell*. (See Griffin Greene to NG, immediately below.)

* * *

From Griffin Greene

Dear Sir   Charles Town [S.C.] Decr 10 1785

I arived at this place, yesterday after a passage of 18 days, we have lost one third of our Stock, by bad wether. Your Horses are alive, but much chafed, altho I have used up 5 sheep Scins [i.e., skins] to prevent it, I shall let John have Hay, & Corn, to recrute them, before he sets out for Home.[1] On my arival, found your letter to me, with four inclosed to Gentlemen of this place, for which you have my hearty thanks.[2] I cannot at pressent inform you, what I shall do with the Ship, as soon as I come to a determination, will let you know.[3] I am sorry for your loss, & to ease you as much as in my powar, comply with your proposal. I paid Wm Littlefield 30£, in Cash, for which I have his Bills on you; this with my other acc^ts makes my acc^ts against you, amoun[t] to 310.1.5 so that their will be due me after deducting our Note, as you propose, [£]210.1.5 which you will please to forward me. Pray excuse my asking it, nothing but absolute nessety could Oblige me to do it.[4] My Lov[e] to Caty, I am very unhappy that I am not like to have the pleasure of seeing you both, whilst I am hear, I was in hopes something favorable would have turned up in your way, that would have put it in your powar, to have me come

& settle with you, to your & my advanta[ge] when ever that happens, let me know & I will come, pleas to write me & let me know all that is proper for me to be informed of,[5] I hope to be favoured with a letter from Couzin Caty.[6] I am your Friend.   GRIFFIN GREENE

RCS (CtY).

1. NG's cousin Griffin, who had returned from France the previous summer, was making a commercial voyage to the South. Although NG had written Jeremiah Wadsworth on 7 September, above, that Griffin intended to go to Virginia in the *Minerva* for a cargo of tobacco, Griffin seems to have changed his plans and taken a cargo to Charleston instead in the vessel *Bell*. (Hazlehurst & Company to NG, 16 January 1786, below) According to Casey Son & Greene's letter to NG of 26 October 1784, above, Griffin and Jacob Greene were "concerned in" the *Bell*, the commander of which, during the just-completed voyage from Newport, R.I., was a Captain Bentley of Rhode Island. (*South-Carolina Gazette and Public Advertiser*, 10 December) "John" was a servant of NG's. (See Hazlehurst to NG, 13 December, below, and Littlefield to NG, 16 November, above.) Griffin wrote NG on 22 December, below, that the horses were now "in a good way" and were being taken to Boone's Barony plantation by John. (See also Hazlehurst & Company to NG, 16 January 1786.)

2. NG's letter to Griffin, which was probably written sometime after the arrival of NG's family in the South, has not been found. NG apparently wrote letters of introduction for Griffin to Charleston merchants, but none has been found.

3. As seen by his subsequent letters to NG in December, Griffin planned to sail to Europe with a cargo from Charleston. (Griffin Greene to NG, 16 and 22 December; see also NG to Griffin Greene, 8 January 1786, all below.)

4. This was probably money that NG owed to Griffin after a settlement of his affairs with the Greene family business. (See Jacob Greene to NG, before 12 October, above, and NG to Griffin Greene, 8 January 1786.)

5. It does not appear that NG and Griffin saw each other while Griffin was in the South.

6. "Couzin Caty" was CG.

From William Littlefield

Dear General   Newport [R.I.] 11th Dec[r] 1785
    Permit me to congratulate you on your safe arival to Georgia. By an extract from a N. York paper we get a General account of your safety after a passuage of Sixteen days. How is M[rs] Greene and all the dear little Children after such a tedious Voyage.[1] I wrote you fully by Griffin who I hope has arrived safe before this.[2] Now comes on the cares of a family. M[rs] Littlefield is in bed with a fine Son and is as well as can possibly be expected. Betsy now begins to be anxious to get to House keeping and more anxious if possible for me to be doing some business, you know she has a large share of pride and I can add with pleasure as much oeconomy as I could wish her to have.[3] She has an aversion to living upon the Iseland. The thoughts of bringing up a family of Children there has determined us both against it. Was such an Idea to be suggested to the old Gentleman it would almost distract him. He has my promise not to live there before he consented and I dare not even think of it. He is now left without any of his Children with him except

Betsy.[4] Debby has gone to Pomfret [Conn.] since the death of her Uncle Godfrey Malbone and I imagine will not return soon if ever.[5] Fate therefore surmises to fix us here for the present and could I do business enough together with the proffits of my farm upon the Iseland to support us with decency should be perfectly happy. Our family will be small not by any means extravegant and a small income will suffice us.[6] I know too well my dear General your present embarrisments to ask or even wish any assistance from you; and could I possess myself of the monies due to me in Providence imediately could do without any; but the Gentlemen of the Bar has protracted the tryal & I cant get an Execution before June. The Law requires three months before the Sale of real Estate which will bring it to September before I can promise myself any thing from that quarter.[7] Perry remains undetermined about the Westerly farm[8] and the Sloop not ariv'd, had he accepted of your offer I should been glad to have purchased his & your parts of the Sloop & to try my fortune a while in that way. I could have made him payments easy to myself and advantagious to him.[9] But as that prospect appears to be doubtful what do you think of a Retail Store of Rum Shugar Molases Salt &[ca] and as soone as I am able to enter into the Flour Wheat & corn business, in the mean time to do as much at fishing as possible.[10] I must beg the favor of your opinion together with your good advice upon the Subject.[11] Betsy joines in love to the family, with every sentiment of esteem and respect I am Dear General your Sincere friend and humble Servant   W: LITTLEFIELD

N.B. Bridget is here & is over anxious to get to her mistress. Does M[rs] Greene still wish to have her?[12]

RCS (RNHi).

1. The *New-York Journal* of 1 December announced the safe arrival of the Greene family in Savannah, Ga. On the voyage from Newport, R.I., see also NG to Clarke, 23 November, above. Littlefield acknowledged a letter of that same date from NG [not found] on 16 December, below.

2. See Griffin Greene to NG, immediately above.

3. Littlefield's wife, the former Elizabeth ("Betsy") Brinley, had given birth to a son, Francis, on 7 December 1785. Francis died on 3 December 1787. (*Vital Records of Rhode Island*, 10: 511, 541)

4. The "Iseland" was Block Island, where CG's brother Littlefield had grown up; the "old gentleman" was undoubtedly Betsy Littlefield's father, Francis Brinley (1729–1816), who was a prominent member of the Newport mercantile community and owned a rope works there. ("Malbone Family Genealogy," RNHi, 1: 10; Hattendorf, *History of Trinity Church*, p. 374)

5. Deborah ("Debby") Brinley (1761–1846) was Betsy's older sister. Their uncle Godfrey Malbone, a prosperous Newport merchant who had moved to Connecticut during the war, died on 12 November 1785. As a brother of their mother (Aliph Malbone Brinley), and husband of their father's sister (the former Catherine Brinley), Malbone was the Brinley sisters' uncle both by blood and by marriage. ("Malbone Family Genealogy," RNHi, 1: 5, 6, 10, 11)

6. Littlefield owned a farm on Block Island. (Littlefield to NG, 22 March 1784, above)

7. No further information has been found about the "tryal."

8. On NG's farm in Westerly, R.I., see Christopher Greene to NG, 25 March 1784, and Burllinggame and Potter to NG, 30 March 1784, both above. Perry was NG's brother Perry Greene. Three months after NG's death, Jeremiah Wadsworth, one of his executors, visited the farm and reported that "it will want a considerable advance to save it from ruin. It has been & still is wretchedly managed." (Wadsworth to Edward Rutledge, 21 September 1786, CtHi)

9. The sloop in question may have been the *Charleston Packet*, in which NG owned an interest. (See notes at NG to Hazlehurst, 26 June 1784, above, and at Littlefield to NG, 16 December, below.)

10. No evidence has been found that Littlefield opened a store in Newport, such as he suggested here.

11. NG's reply has not been found, but a letter from Robert Hazlehurst & Company of 9 February 1786, below, indicates that NG did write to Littlefield about that time.

12. "Bridget," a Greene family servant, may have been left in Rhode Island because of illness. Dr. Isaac Senter, the family physician, had prescribed a treatment for her in September. (Senter Daybook, RHi). CG's wishes concerning her are not known.

*   *   *

¶ [FROM ROBERT HAZLEHURST, Charleston, S.C., 13 December 1785. Encloses two letters that "came in the Ship *Bell* who arrived last Thursday."[1] William Littlefield has sent two horses and NG's "servant John" in the vessel to Hazlehurst's "care."[2] The horses "are in a horrid condition in consequence of the severe Weather on the passage; one of them is so much bruised that John thinks it's rather doubtful if he will recover." Hazlehurst believes that it will survive, though.[3] NG will "no doubt advise immediately on receipt of this" letter what he wants Hazlehurst to do with the horses when they are "fit to Travel"; this will probably not be in less than "a couple Weeks."[4] He reports that the horses "are in a good Warm Stable & I have told John that he shall be supplyed with anything he thinks necessary to assist their recovery."[5] Sends "most Respectful Comp[ts]" to CG. Adds in a postscript: "No particular News stirring more than what the bearer can advise." RCS (MiU-C) 2 pp.]

1. NG's cousin Griffin Greene also arrived in Charleston on the *Bell*. (Griffin Greene to NG, 10 December, above)

2. On NG's "servant John," see also ibid. and Littlefield to NG, 16 November, above.

3. On the horses and their condition, see Griffin Greene to NG, 10 December.

4. In a letter to NG of 16 January 1786, below, Hazlehurst acknowledged that NG had sent him instructions concerning the horses.

5. As seen in Griffin Greene's letter to NG of 22 December, below, the horses did recover. In his letter of 16 January 1786, Hazlehurst informed NG that John was taking them to NG's "plantation at Parker's Ferry," S.C.

¶ [FROM WILLIAM LITTLEFIELD, [Newport, R.I., before 16 December 1785].[1] He longs to hear "particulars" of the Greene family's voyage south, "how the Children behaiv'd and if they all arrivd well."[2] His wife, Betsy, "joines in love to all the family"; Littlefield thinks she is writing to CG. He adds in a postscript: "One word upon Politics—the Genl Assembly has invested Congress with the whole powers of regulating trade Externally & internally and have adopted the requisitions & Resolutions of Congress respecting Lone [i.e., loan] office Certificates & all other Liquidated debts."[3] RCS (CtY) 1 p. One or more pages missing.]

1. Littlefield wrote NG on 16 December, below, acknowledging receipt of a letter from NG about the Greene family's recent voyage to Georgia—a subject he inquired about in this letter.

2. See Littlefield to NG, 16 December, below.

3. On earlier measures by Rhode Island relating to the power of Congress to regulate trade, see note at Pettit to NG, 23 March, above. In an October session, the Rhode Island legislature passed a slightly amended version of "An Act vesting Congress with the power of regulating foreign trade," as well as "An Act for raising and paying into the treasury of the United States, this state's proportion of three millions of dollars," as requested by Congress. (Bartlett, *Records of R.I.*, 10: 130, 145)

¶ [FROM GRIFFIN GREENE, Charleston, S.C., 16 December 1785. "Agreable to your request," Griffin informs NG that he intends to go to France, "either Bourdeaux or Rochforte."[1] He must "take goods" at his "own risk," because he cannot "obtain freight on acc[t] of British Ships having Meditiranian Passes and ou[r]s not having any." Finds it "heard [i.e., hard] that forren [i.e., foreign] Ships should have a prefference in our own portes."[2] He "lost 13 Cattle out of 41" that he brought from Rhode Island, and for the rest, which he put up "at Vandue," he could not "get an offer of ⅔ the first cost so that I have a most shocking prospect."[3] Hopes to leave Charleston in three weeks "at furthes[t]." Asks NG "to order goods or Bills to the amount due me." Is afraid he will not have "any property left" after he pays what he owes in France, "even to procure a load of Salt."[4] Has heard that a ship came "after a load of Timber & that she is returned without it";[5] if Griffin can be of any help with that or any other business in France, NG should "command" him. NG should send "Letters of cradit" for what is owed and can be "easy on acc[t] of any risk."[6] Griffin's "first letter" contains "the state of our acc[t]s."[7] Sends his "Love" to CG. RCS (MiU-C) 2 pp.]

1. Griffin had brought livestock to Charleston, planning to sell them there and proceed to Europe with a cargo of South Carolina goods. (Griffin Greene to NG, 10 December, above)

2. Griffin explained in a letter to NG of 22 December, below: "The British Ships have Medetiranian passes & I am subject to be taken by the Algereans so that I cannot get freight & am obliged to Load on my own acc[t] & Risk." (See also Jefferson to NG, 12 January 1786, below.)

3. In his letter to NG of 10 December, Griffin wrote that he had lost "one third of our Stock, by bad wether" during the voyage to Charleston.

4. On the money that NG owed to Griffin, see note at Griffin Greene to NG, 10 December.

5. On the French naval vessel that had been ordered to obtain samples of the timber from Cumberland Island, Ga., see Pendleton to NG, 23 September, above.

6. NG replied to this letter on 8 January 1786, below.

7. See Griffin Greene to NG, 10 December.

*   *   *

From the Chevalier de la Foreste[1]

Dear General New York December 16. 1785.

I have received your Favor of November last and I have forwarded your letters to Marshal de Castries an[d] Major G[al] delafayette.[2] The Marshal has received yours of the 1st of June last and answers to me that he has given orders for having a cargo of live oak upon which trials could be made in the King's dock yards and a resolution taken in consequence. He acquaints me that he writes to you in the same meaning.[3] But the unfortunate disappointement which the frigate *Les [Barbois?]* met with, will delay the conclusion of the business and I am aprehensive that the Minister will not order any Contract to be entered into without a previous trial of the qualities of the live oak. I expect he will send another frigate and your presence in Georgia will in that case prevent another disapointment.[4] You may depend, Dear General, upon my readiness to do any thing which may influence the Minister's determination, as I am convinced of the importance of the matter. I have been much flattered by your Congratulations upon the new favors conferred upon me by His Majesty.[5] I am with the greatest respect and esteem Dear General Your Most obedient humble servant

DE LA FORESTE

RCS (MiU-C).

1. Foreste received a commission from the king of France in the summer of 1785 to serve as French vice-consul at Savannah, Ga. It was soon decided, though, that as there was no French consul at Charleston, S.C., he should be based there instead. (*JCC*, 27: 597; *Records of Georgia*, 2: 639–40; S.C., House of Representatives, *Journals, 1784–85*, p. 15) In January 1786, Congress approved an appointment of Foreste as vice consul general in the United States, and he was subsequently based near Congress. (*JCC*, 30: 14–15)

2. NG's letter to Foreste of "November last" has not been found, nor has any letter NG may have written about that time to either the Marquis de Castries—the French naval minister—or the Marquis de Lafayette. NG's letter to Castries near the end of the December documents, below, was written as a follow-up to that November letter.

3. In his letter of 1 June, above, NG had proposed to Castries that the French government contract with him for timber from Cumberland Island, Ga. (See also Marbois to NG, 30 September, above.) Lafayette wrote NG on 29 December, below, apparently at the request of the French government, asking for specific samples of wood from Cumberland Island. He also asked in that letter that NG send a "Confidential Person with proper Powers to enter into a Contract."

4. The French navy had sent a frigate to Cumberland Island a few months earlier on an unsuccessful mission to collect timber samples. (Pendleton to NG, 23 September, above) In his November letter to Castries, NG had apparently apologized and explained the reasons for that mission's failure. In his December letter to Castries, NG promised that with "a few Months notice," he could prepare the samples that the French required.

5. The "new favors" can be deduced from note 1, above.

From William Littlefield

Dear General   Newport [R.I.] Dec[r] 16th 1785

Your kind fav[r] of the 23[d] Nov[r] [I] have this moment rec[d] by Cap[t] Easton. Nothing but the pleasure of your Society could add so much to my happiness as a Confirmation of your safe arrival and particularly to hear of the welfair of M[rs] Greene and the dear Little Children.[1]

I wrote you a few days ago by Cap[t] Channing mentioning that M[rs] [Elizabeth Brinley] Littlefield was safe in bed with a Son.[2] This is the

Ninth day and she is now setting up in her Chair and is perfectly well. I gave her your Letter to read and was obliged to take it from her before she had half finished. She regrets the Loss of your Society more than its possible for me to discribe. I deliver'd M^{rs} [Sarah Pope] Redwood your Letter and left her also in tears. We have no amusements of any kind this Winter. Assembly have been talked of but nothing done I fear they will end there. The old Spirit of Whig & Tory still exists which I imagine will frustrate the whole.[3] I shall call on Capt Easton for the Twelve Guineas and shall apropriate it towards the discharge of the Executions against Stephen Franklin if you have no objection.[4] I wrote you by Griffin [Greene] in what manner I have settled with the Heirs of the House which you liv'd in when hear, which I hope will be satisfactory to you.[5] Col^o Ward has arriv'd from Virginia and informes me that he has settled your busines[s] with [Henry] Banks agreeably to your wishes.[6] I wrote by Capt Channing that the Sloop had not arriv'd and I am sorry to say now that I fear she will never arrive hear again. She is Seiz^d at the Cape and its feard will be condemn'd; if so it must be attended with almost a total loss to the owners.[7] I shall pay particular attention to the contents of your Letter and will inform you respecting the Publick Securities before I offer them for sale and will wait your farther directions.[8] The Sloop will Sail in a few hours. All friends Generally well. Mrs Sands perfectly well.[9] I am Sincerely & affectionately with abundance of Love to Mrs Greene & the Children your Obd Servt WILLIAM LITTLEFIELD

RCS (CtY).

1. NG's letter to Littlefield of 23 November has not been found; on the Greenes' voyage from Newport to the South, see NG to Clarke, 23 November, above.

2. See Littlefield to NG, 11 December, above.

3. Historian Elaine Forman Crane has written that after the French army left Newport in 1781, the "curious mixture of whigs and tories was left to get on with each other as best they could." (Crane, *A Dependent People*, p. 157) In the postwar period, as restrictions on Loyalists were relaxed, Whig resentments undoubtedly resurfaced, but Crane believes that "as time went on, the former loyalists who trickled into town created little animosity and less furor." (Ibid., p. 159)

4. Nothing is known about this matter.

5. The letter to which Littlefield referred has not been found.

6. See Samuel Ward, Jr., to NG, 11 November, above.

7. This was presumably the sloop *Charleston Packet*, in which NG owned an interest. (See note at NG to Hazlehurst, 26 June 1784, above, and Littlefield's letter to NG of 11 December.) NG wrote Ethan Clarke on 6 April 1786, below, that Littlefield had informed him the "sloop *Charleston pacquet* is seized, sold and the house that chartered her wrecked."

8. Neither Littlefield's letter "respecting the Publick Securities" nor NG's "further directions" has been found.

9. Phebe Littlefield Sands was Littlefield's and CG's sister. (See note at NG to William Greene, 8 March 1784, above.)

*   *   *

¶ [FROM JOHN BOWMAN, Peachtree Santee, S.C., 21 December 1785. He understands that NG is "desirous of adding to your property upon Cumberland." Thinks "the Interest held by the heirs of the late M[r] Lynch" in property there will soon be sold; asks if NG is interested in purchasing it.[1] RCS (MiU-C) 1 p.]

    1. NG had been in communication with Bowman in September 1784 about their mutual holdings on Cumberland Island, Ga. (NG to Bowman, 10 September 1784, and Bowman to NG, 12 September 1784, both above) The prospective sellers were the heirs of Thomas Lynch (1727–1776), Bowman's father-in-law. (See note at NG to Bowman, 10 September 1784 and *Biog. Directory of S.C. House*, 2: 420–21.) No further correspondence between NG and Bowman has been found. The Lynch family continued to hold an interest in Cumberland Island until 1831. (Bullard, "Uneasy Legacy," p. 769)

*   *   *

From Griffin Greene

Dear General   Charlestown [S.C.] Dec[r] 22. 1785

    This is the third letter I have wrote you since my arivel hear.[1] Your Horses was very much hurt on our passage by the bad weather altho every possiable pains was taken to prevent it but they are now in a very good way & John will set out with them in a Short time. I have supplyed him with hay & Corn.[2] I have come to the worst market in the world nothing is don at selling only at Vandue & that for Cash so that goods sell for half the first cost. I took 41 Cattle from Rhode Island & Brought in only 28 alive & they will not sell for the first cost, so that you will see how I shall come out in this bussiness.[3] The British Ships have Medetiranian passes & I am subject to be taken by the Algereans so that I cannot get freight & am obliged to Load on my own acc[t] & Risk. This I fear w[ill] cause me to loose the freight as I dont expect produce will fetch much more than first cost.[4] I expect to go to Amsterdam hoping to find the best Price their if you or any of your friends have any freight for that place pray favour me with it, the risk is not much at this season of year, more in my Ship than in a British Ship.[5] I shall go to Sea in about three Weeks. I fear I shall not have enough to load my Ship with Salt after paying what I owe in France.[6] I have concluded to comply with your proposal & shall be very happy If you can make it convenient to furnish me with the ballance.[7] I feel my distresses & am not insensable of yours, but in this voyage depends my fate if I should not be able to load back even with Salt I am ruined. My Love to Caty & tel her I love her & never will forget her kind attention at Newport in my Sickness.[8] It is cruel to be so near you & not be able to come & see You,[9] but from a long sce[n]ario of misfortins [i.e., misfortunes] I am reconsiled to any fate. I am your friend   GRIFFIN GREENE

    P.S. Pray forward me Letters for Europe.

RCS (CtY).

1. See also Griffin Greene to NG, 10 and 16 December, both above.

2. See Griffin Greene to NG, 10 December.

3. Griffin also discussed this matter in his letter of 16 December.

4. On the difficulties that Griffin faced in undertaking a transatlantic commercial voyage, see also ibid.

5. Griffin had previously written NG that he intended to sail to France, "either Bourdeaux or Rochefort." (Griffin Greene to NG, 16 December) As he explained earlier in this letter, British vessels were less likely than American ones to be seized by Algerian pirates. (See also Jefferson to NG, 12 January 1786, below.) NG sent a letter to the Dutch firm of Wilhem & Jan Willink with Griffin. (The letter is below, dated 7 January 1786.)

6. On Griffin's debts in France, see also his letter to NG of 16 December.

7. See NG to Griffin Greene, 8 January 1786, below.

8. After his return from France the previous summer, Griffin had recuperated from an illness at NG's and CG's home in Newport, R.I. (NG to Wadsworth, 30 August, above)

9. NG replied on 8 January, below, that he could "illy" afford to visit Griffin in Charleston. They did not see each other again.

*   *   *

¶ [FROM EDWARD PENMAN, Charleston, S.C., 22 December 1785. NG must have been "misinformed" about there being any "Spare oxen" on the plantation of "the Revd Mr Simpson"; Penman is "greatly in want of oxen" himself.[1] He quotes from a letter of 4 November from his cousin [James Penman] that " 'Genl Green's proposals respecting Ship Timber are before Some of the most Capital Builders here, & as soon as I receive their Answer shall write him fully upon it.' "[2] RCS (MiU-C) 1 p.]

1. NG was undoubtedly trying to find oxen for Mulberry Grove plantation.

2. James Penman wrote NG from London on 9 February 1786, below, about prospects for selling ship timber in Europe.

¶ [FROM JOSEPH CLAY, [Savannah, Ga.?, before 23 December 1785?].[1] Mr. [James] Seagrove, who "was going out to see you this Morning," called on Clay "last night for a Receipt for the Amount of" NG's account. If NG needs a copy of the "Account of particulars" that was delivered to Mr. Gibbons, Clay will have one made out for him. The amount is "£25.0.10, which with the Interest from the end of the year brings it to £27.0.10."[2] Clay still is having trouble getting a "Settlement on Account of the 800 Dollars, Bills Exchange, short accounted for by Major Burnett" [i.e., Ichabod Burnet]. "Upon this principle," he writes, "I might have been chargeable with the whole sum paid him at least wth equal Justice. I paid him the Money by your Orders as per his Receipt a Copy of which you have."[3] Clay would be obliged if NG would write "to the Treasury board on the subject."[4] He is now writing a reply to a "Letter on the subject" from Mr. [John] Pierce;[5] has also sent the "Original receipt," which he "supposed wou'd have removed every objection nor can I conjecture on what Ground they can presume me liable for the Majors deficiency in Accounting for the Expenditure of that sum." RCS (PHi) 3 pp.]

1. The tentative date is based on Clay's reference here to a letter he was then writing to John Pierce, the paymaster general. That letter, dated 23 December, was written from Savannah. (WRMS, Misc. Ms. #22323, DNA; see also note 5, below.)

2. This may have been an account that NG had with Clay. (See NG to William Gibbons, Jr., 26 April, above.) Seagrove, who arrived in Charleston, S.C., from Rhode Island on the vessel *Bell* in early December, was apparently now in Savannah and is known to have been in contact with NG about this time. (See *South-Carolina Gazette and Public Advertiser,* 10 December; Seagrove to NG, [before 27 January 1786?], below.)

3. On "the 800 Dollars," see above, the note at Milligan to NG, 6 February, and NG's "Answers to the Auditor's Report," after 15 April.

4. No further correspondence about this matter has been found.

5. In his reply to a letter of 12 October from Pierce, Clay wrote that "as to the Bills, it was with great reluctance, & from necessity only," that he was "induced to make use of any of them, or rather their proceeds," on his "own Account, as they were appropriated principally for the purpose of procuring supplies." (Clay to Pierce, 23 December, WRMS, Misc. Ms. #22323, DNA)

¶ [FROM GODIN GUERARD, Prince William Parish, S.C., 26 December 1785.[1] He has bought "the Tract of Land upon Ilay [i.e., Isla] Island," which lies opposite to Mulberry Grove.[2] Has begun to clear the land "with a considerable Gang of hands" but may not be able to send more workers in time to "plant a full Crop." If NG has an "Overplus" of cleared land at Mulberry Grove, Guerard asks if he would consider renting it out; he will "wait on" NG the next time he is in Georgia.[3] RCS (MiU-C) 2 pp.]

1. Guerard was a son of the late John Guerard (1706–64), a South Carolina merchant. (*Biog. Directory of S.C. House,* 2: 297–98)

2. On Isla Island, see Saunders to NG, 27 November 1783, above.

3. It is not known whether NG rented any land to Guerard.

¶ [FROM WELCOME ARNOLD, Providence, R.I., 27 December 1785. Asks NG to "pay Messrs Thayer & Bartlett a bill of Exchange on London" for £82.18.4, equivalent to £111.17.10 in Rhode Island currency.[1] Cy (MiU-C) 1 p.]

1. See also Arnold to NG, 28 December, and Thayer & Bartlett to NG, 17 January 1786, both below.

¶ [FROM RICHARD CLAIBORNE, Richmond, Va., 27 December 1785. Asks for letters "to France, Holland and London," which may be of service to him, and which he trusts NG's "friendship will induce" him "to grant."[1] Claiborne has "pursued" a "Land business," accumulating some 300,000 acres, and now wishes to "make an adventure with part, either to sell—or form a Merchantile Establishment on the Credit of it." He has received letters from "General [Alexander] Spotswood and other Gentlemen, which do me much honor"; NG's letters would "increase that gratitude and attention which is due to such favors." NG should send the letters to Grays Inn, London, where Claiborne expects to be as of the "beginning of February." Any "commands" that NG may "honor" him with will be "faithfully executed."[2] Claiborne sends "best wishes and respects" to NG and CG. RCS (MiU-C) 1 p.]

1. On Claiborne, see note at NG's Journal entry for 6 September 1783, above.

2. It is not known whether NG wrote any letters on Claiborne's behalf.

¶ [FROM WELCOME ARNOLD, Providence, R.I., 28 December 1785. Encloses "an Account of the Several Small bills" that NG drew on him, to which Arnold has "added the fifty Guineas," bringing the total to £111.17.10. He has "drawn an order in favour of Messrs Thayer & Bartlett of Charleston payable in a bill of Exchange Drawn on London"; asks NG to "pay them."[1] RCS (MiU-C) 1 p.]

1. See also Arnold to NG, 27 December, above; Arnold to NG, 6 January 1786, and Thayer & Bartlett to NG, 17 January 1786, both below.

¶ [FROM WILLIAM HARRIS. Charleston, S.C., 28 December 1785. Mr. Mc-Queen asked Harris, his attorney, to find out whether NG still wants to sell his "part of Cumberland Island"; if so, Harris would "be obliged by a line" giving the terms.[1] He heard that NG was at Charleston and was "dissappointed" in not being able to see him there. RCS (MiU-C) 1 p.]

    1. John McQueen, who was traveling to France in the hope of selling shipbuilding timber from Sapelo Island, Ga., to the French government, was a former owner of the share of Cumberland Island property that NG now held (See NG to Lafayette, 1 June 1785; Hawkins to NG, 24 June 1785, and Pendleton to NG, 23 September 1785, as well as the note at Hyrne to Clay, 26 November 1783, all above.) Indeed, it was McQueen from whom Henry Banks and Ichabod Burnet had obtained the indenture for the Cumberland Island property that they had assigned to NG in August 1783. (See note at Hyrne to Clay, 26 November 1783.) NG's reply to Harris has not been found.

*   *   *

From the Marquis de Lafayette

My dear friend   Paris December the 29th 1785.

In consequence of the proposals you Have made some time ago, I am requested by the French Governement, to apply to you for an assortment of thousand Cubit feet of green oack ["By *green oack* I mean what is Called in America *live oack*, and is used there for Ship Building. But Have translated Litterally from the french—*chiren verd*"] in Knees, cut in your Cumberland island, and also for some pieces of new Cedar Wood ["The Red Cedar is what is commonly Used for the Upper works of Ships"], the Whole to be Sent to the harbour of Brest.[1]

As to the Price of the Cargoe We Cannot have it fixed at Such a distance, but this is an Experiment, and I very much wish the quality and cheapness of the Envoice may be Such as to encourage a Bargain with you upon a Very Large Scale which probably will take place immediately. I therefore would advise you to Send on Board the Vessel a Confidential Person With proper Powers to enter into a Contract with administration.[2] Most affectionately I am Your friend   LAFAYETTE

RCS (CtY). Notations in the margin of first page appear in brackets.

    1. NG had proposed "some time ago" to sell live oak timber from his holdings on Cumberland Island, Ga., to the French government. (See his letters to the Marquis de Barbé-Marbois, 15 April, and the Marquis de Castries, 1 June, both above.) Lafayette had been dealing with Castries, the French naval minister, on NG's behalf. (See, for example, Lafayette's letter to NG at the end of the May 1785 documents, above.) Lafayette had sent a similar letter to NG on 3 December, above, asking for samples, but the present letter appears to have a more official tone, as Lafayette mentioned here that he had been "requested by the French Government" to ask for the wood.

    2. No evidence has been found that NG had sent the samples by the time of his death the following June.

*   *   *

¶ [FROM NATHANIEL PENDLETON, [Savannah, Ga.], "Thursday" [before 30 December 1785].[1] He is "quite asshamed that the dray has not come Up to day," but "Simon is sick, and I have no body else to send with it." Pendleton has lost two "waggon horses," so the "rest are useless." If NG wants "the waggon and two horses," he may have them at his "own price, payable the first of May."[2] Pendleton has "four Negroe fellows," three of them "young, and Able," to "hire out." NG should let him know if he is interested. One of them "is a jobbing carpenter," and they all "can saw."[3] Hopes NG will "send for the dray, as I am really embarassed for want of servants." If NG prefers the wagon, he can have it "early next week." Pendleton has put NG's "Letters on their way" and is sending NG "one from Mr. [James] Seagrove" [not found], along with "Affectionate Compliments" to CG. RCS (MiU-C) 2 pp.]

1. The dateline gives only "Thursday"; the docketing reads "Dec[r] 1785." The last Thursday in December was the 29th. Pendleton was presumably writing from Savannah, where he lived.

2. In a letter at the end of the December documents, below, Pendleton wrote that he was sending NG's servant Ham with the dray.

3. It is not known whether NG contracted to hire these men.

¶ [TO THE MARQUIS DE CASTRIES. From [Mulberry Grove, Ga.? December 1785?].[1] NG wrote to Castries from Charleston "about a month since," conveying his "disappointment of the Frigate which came after live oak." Hopes his explanation there for "the cause of her failure" will "remove every unfavorable impression upon the occasion."[2] He has now moved his family "into this State" and plans to "reside upon Cumberland part of next season."[3] If Castries could give him "a few Months notice," NG could "have a Cargo of Lumber provided in readiness" and would see that "your commands" were "punctually executed."[4] If he had "had the least previous Notice," NG would have been able to "comply with your wishes" the previous summer, but he was "at the N⟨or⟩thward" when the vessel arrived, and it was "gone long before I heard of her particular errand."[5] Griffin Greene, from whom Castries purchased the *Flora*, will deliver this letter.[6] He is sailing to Amsterdam in a "fine Ship," which could be used to transport "a Load of live oak" from Cumberland Island, should Castries so wish. NG vouches for the quality of the timber and believes it could be of such value to the French navy that Castries would not want to "miss the opportunity of bringing it into use."[7] NG will be grateful for "Any services" Castries "may render M[r] Greene in this or in any other way." ADfS (MiU-C) 2 pp. The manuscript is damaged; text in angle brackets was taken from a GWG Transcript (CSmH).]

1. The approximate date is based on NG's statement here that he had written to Castries from Charleston, S.C., "about a month ago." NG is known to have been in Charleston in late November. (NG to Clarke, 23 November, above) Castries acknowledged receipt of that letter, which has not been found, in his to NG of 22 January 1786, below. NG was most likely at home, at Mulberry Grove.

2. On the French "Frigate which came after live oak" samples from NG's holdings on Cumberland Island, see Pendleton to NG, 23 September, above.

3. NG did not get back to Cumberland Island before his death the following June.

4. NG was hoping to contract with the French government to supply shipbuilding timber from his land on Cumberland Island. Castries was the French naval minister. (See NG to Castries, 1 June, above.)

5. See note 2, above. NG had been in Newport, R.I., at the time of the French vessel's visit to Cumberland Island.

6. In a letter to NG of 9 February, above, the Marquis de Lafayette reported that the sale of the frigate *Flora* to the French government had been completed. Griffin Greene, who had returned to the United States since then, was in Charleston at this time, preparing for a transatlantic voyage. (See Griffin Greene to NG, 16 and 22 December, both above.)

7. NG had not yet received Lafayette's letters of 3 and 29 December, above, reporting on the status of his dealings with Castries in this matter. No contract was concluded before NG's death.

¶ [FROM NATHANIEL PENDLETON, [Savannah, Ga.? December 1785].[1] He is sending "the dray by Ham." Would have sent "the Waggon, but one of the horses is lost."[2] When NG is there on Tuesday, "the day the Cincinnati meet," he "can see them and Determine."[3] Pendleton is "pestered to death with these Waggons & Negroes" and wishes them "well disposed of."[4] He must see NG before he "can draw the Mortgage" that NG mentions, "on account of the terms & Conditions of payment."[5] Sends love to CG "& the little ones." RCS (MiU-C) 1 p.]

1. This letter, which is docketed "Decr 1785," was undoubtedly written after Pendleton's letter dated before 30 December, above. Pendleton was probably in Savannah, where he lived.

2. Pendleton had asked NG to send someone for the dray because he did not have a servant available for the task. (Pendleton to NG, before 30 December) Ham was most likely a servant of NG's. (See NG to CG, 17 August 1784, above.)

3. The Georgia chapter of the Society of the Cincinnati, which was organized in August 1783, usually met in Savannah or Augusta. Gen. Lachlan McIntosh was its president. (Coleman, *Revolution in Georgia*, pp. 235–36) Pendleton most likely meant here that NG could see the wagons and horses referred to in the previous sentence. (See also Pendleton to NG, before 30 December.)

4. See ibid.

5. As seen in his letter to Wilhem & Jan Willink of 7 January 1786, below, NG was still hoping to obtain a mortgage on his Mulberry Grove plantation. (See also Morris to NG, 15 March, and the Willinks' letter to NG of 8 July, both above.)

¶ [AGREEMENT BETWEEN NG AND WILLIAM WILLIAMS. [Mulberry Grove, Ga., 5 January 1786].[1] NG hires Williams "to oversee his Plantation at Mulberry Grove" and will "give him for his own services, & for the services of six good field Negroes capable of doing each their tasks one hundred pounds [Ste]rling, & to keep him two Cows, & to have half the Pork raised from three sows & also to find him breadcorn, & to raise fowls to the halves for his own use, but none for sale." Williams promises "to discharge all the good offices which can be expected from a good Overseer, & to employ the hands committed to his care, both his own & others, to the best advantage for raising a good crop, to take care of the buildings & all his employers Property put under his direction. He is to find his own family Negroes, & keep two horses."[2] DS (ICN) 1 p.]

1. The place was determined from the contents; the date from a copy of this agreement at NjP. Williams has not been identified.

2. Julia Floyd Smith has written that "the qualities desired in an overseer were honesty, sobriety, and an understanding of the management of slaves." Overseers of rice plantations rarely stayed in the same job for an extended time, but moved instead from one plantation to another. Although Smith asserts that "the contract with the overseer enu-

merated the countless duties assigned to him and also expressed the attitude of the planter toward his slaves concerning care, health, and punishments," the present, brief agreement does not cover many specifics regarding NG's expectations. (Smith, *Slavery and Rice Culture*, p. 65 and n)

¶ [FROM WELCOME ARNOLD, [Providence, R.I.], 6 January 1786. Sends a duplicate of his letter to NG of 28 December 1785, adding that since writing that letter and "Drawing an order" in favor of Thayer & Bartlett for "£82.18.4 ½ S^{tg}," he has "found a mistake of £1.1.4 ½ S^{tg} Which make the amount £83.19.9 S^{tg}." Has therefore "drawn an order In favour of T[hayer] & Bartlett" for that amount and "desir^d them to retain the other order in their hands." Asks NG "to pay them by a Bill of Exchange drawn on London."[1] On the back of this letter is an undated, personal note to NG, in which Arnold writes that he has heard "you have Extricated your self from the person to Whom you became bound to serve your Friend by his taking the lands."[2] Arnold has also heard that CG "was exceedingly distressed" because of the weather during their voyage and that there had been "an accident of loos[ing] a man overboard."[3] Hopes "She is Cleverly Recovered, and Injoying every Temporal Blessing." Sends his and his wife's respects to her. RCS (CSmH) 2 pp.]

1. See Arnold to NG, 28 December 1785, above, and Thayer & Bartlett to NG, 17 January, below.

2. NG had not "Extricated" himself from the debts he had guaranteed for John Banks et al.

3. On the Greene family's voyage from Newport, R.I., to Savannah, Ga., see NG to Clarke, 23 November 1785, above.

*   *   *

To Wilhem & Jan Willink

Gentlemen   Savannah Georgia January 7th 1785 [i.e., 1786][1]

I wrote you in April last that I was still desirous to borrow a sum of Money for the imp[rove]ment of my property in this State ag[ree]ably to what Mr [Robert] Morris of Philadelp[hia] suggested to you in 1783.[2] In that lette[r] I told you I wanted to borrow from two to four thousand pound[s] and that I would soon forward the Documents for the security of the Money. If you are disposed to furnish the Money you will see by the documents which will accompany this letter th[at] the property is amply for the [Secu]rity of the sums requird. T[he] Negroes are estimated for a much less sum than I gave for them and paid a considerable part in cash. And the lands without the buildings and improvments are worth the Money estimated at and the buildings are very valuable and the improvements great.[3] I now live upon the place [i.e., Mulberry Grove plantation] and purpose to add greatly to both. I only mention this to convince you that I dont mean to take up money on the property by a false estimation and with a view of imposing a nominal property on you. If you wish for further satisfaction Comodore [Alexander] Gillon can inform you.[4] I shall make the necessary conveyances and deposit them in the hands of Mr Robert Hazlehurst of Charleston [S.C.] to take effect or otherwise as you may determin upon the business of the loan. Mr Hazlehurst is connected with Mr Morris and [is] a Gentleman of candor and integrity. If you have any other person in whom you can confide with greater confidence it will be equally agreeable to me.

I would not wish to have the Money for a shorter term than four Years or longer than Seven. One half the produce to be shiped for the discharge of the principal and interest and the ballance if any to be paid at the final period agreed on. You w[ill] please to signify your determin[a]tion as soon as possible. If you have any doubts on the subject I dont mean to press the business.[5] This letter will be deliverd you by Mr Griffin Greene a relation of mine. I beg leave to recommend him to the good officers of your house while at Amsterdam.[6] And if any thing can be done on the subject of live [oak] on which I wrote you last Ap[ril] he has a fine ship for freighting Lumber.[7] I am Gentlemen Your Most Obed^t humble Servt   NATH GREENE

ADfS (MiU-C).
1. The year was determined from the contents.
2. NG's April 1785 letter to the Dutch firm of Wilhem & Jan Willink has not been found. For background, see above, Morris to NG, 15 March 1785, and the Willinks' letter to NG of 8 July 1785.
3. The enclosures have not been found. (See, however, NG to Griffin Greene, immediately below, and Estimate of NG's Estate, before 9 January 1784, above.)
4. In the letter immediately below, NG wrote Griffin Greene, who was then in Charleston, preparing to sail to Amsterdam: "I have sent you a letter to Comodore Gillon who lives at Ashley Hill. He can give you the best Letters and the best advice. Ride out and see him."
5. The Willinks' reply has not been found, but Robert Morris advised NG in a letter of 28 January, below, that Americans could no longer expect to obtain credit in Holland.
6. See NG to Griffin Greene, immediately below.
7. See Griffin Greene to NG, 22 December 1785, above.

To Griffin Greene

My dear Sir   Mulberry Grove [Ga.] January 8th 1785 [i.e., 1786][1]
I am favored with your several letters with an account current and signifying your consent to the discount of your Note.[2] In your account there are two charges whic[h] are wrong. One is the [East] Greenwich [R.I.] Store account of £29.8.3. I had nothing at the Greenwich Store after settlement except the Articles enumerated in your Account the amount of which I have credited you for. The other charge of 29.8.3 was for articles before our settlement and included in it as you will see by a copy of the agreement. No account remained open between us but the Money Account between Jacob & me[,][3] a state of which I send you and in which you will see Jacob is credited for the discount with Kitt & Elihue.[4] You may rely on it that the account I now send you is just and

true in all its parts.[5] For the ballance I have sent you an order on Russel Jenkins & Company who I believe are my Factors. If they should not, find out who they are & shew them this letter and the order, and desire them to pay the Money. If it should so happen that I have not a sufficiency of Rice at market I have writ[t]en to M[r] Hazlehurst to advance you the Money and take the Rice or the Money from my factor as soon as it arrives which cannot be many days.[6] If I did not think this would reduce the matter of payment to a certainty I would come to Charleston rather than disappoint or delay you a moment notwithstanding I can but illy leave home. But I am in hopes you will have ready payment and so far as depends on me every thing to your wishes. It gives me pain to find you came to so bad a market. Had your passage been good your prospects would have been flattering. I can hear of no freighters in this quarter. On your arrival in Europe if you find you can make any thing by a freight of live oak I will further your wishes all in my power.[7] I have inclosed you some Letters; but my affairs are in too precarious a situation to enter upon farther engagements.[8] Should any accident attend me my family will be reduced to desperate circumstances. It distresses me that I cannot enter into all your views; but my situation is so critical that I am persuaded your feelings would revolt at my indiscretion to go into farther engagements in the present state of my affairs. Should kind fortune help me out of my difficulties nothing will add more to my happiness than to contribute to yours.

I send you some papers to be deliverd to Wilhem & Jan Willink Merchants in Amsterdam.[9] I believe it is a good house; but I have sent you a letter to Comodore [Alexander] Gillon who lives at Ashley Hill. He can give you the best Letters and the best advice. Ride out and see him.[10] The Letters to the Marquis de la Fyette and the Marshall de Castr[i]es you will have forwarded. I have recommended you to both of their good offices.[11] Let me hear from you upon all occasions and if in my power I will lay a foundation for a plan of business to the Southward.[12] God bless you and may kind fortune be more propitious than she has been. Persevere and faint not[.] An inflexible constancy will triumph over all difficulties and tho late yet at last will crown you with success. I am with esteem & affection Your sincere friend NATH GREENE

ALS (MiU-C).

1. The year was determined from the contents.

2. Griffin Greene had written to NG on 10, 16, and 22 December 1785, all above, and had mentioned his account with NG in the second of those letters.

3. On NG's settlement with Jacob Greene & Company, the family business, see Jacob Greene to NG, before 12 October 1785, above.

4. NG's letter to Jacob Greene has not been found. "Kitt" (i.e., Christopher) and Elihue Greene were NG's brothers.

5. The enclosure has not been found.

6. Russell, Jenkins & Company was a Charleston, S.C., factorage firm. (See their

advertisement in *South-Carolina Gazette and Public Advertiser*, 17 November 1785.) NG's order on them has not been found. Robert Hazlehurst wrote NG on 16 January, below, that he had learned from "Russell Jenkins & C° that there wi[ll] be a further parcel [of rice] down in a few days for the purpose of discharging y[our] acc^t with us & also a payment to M[r] Griffin Greene." (See also Hazlehurst & Company to NG, 9 February, below.)

7. For background, see NG's letter to the Marquis de Castries, near the end of the December 1785 documents.

8. In ibid. and the letter immediately above, NG had recommended Griffin Greene to Castries and the Dutch firm of Wilhem & Jan Willink. As seen in the present letter, NG also wrote to the Marquis de Lafayette on Griffin's behalf. Griffin was preparing for a transatlantic commercial voyage. (See his letters to NG of 16 and 22 December 1785.) He apparently sailed from Charleston on or about 10 February. (Hazlehurst & Company to NG, 9 February, below)

9. Except for the letter immediately above, these enclosures have not been found.

10. See also the letter immediately above.

11. NG's letter to Lafayette has not been found; on the others, see notes 5 and 6, above.

12. The present letter is the last one between NG and Griffin Greene that has been found.

From Thomas Jefferson

Dear Sir   Paris. Jan. 12. 1785 [i.e., 1786].[1]

Your favour of June 1 did not come to hand till the 3^d of September.[2] I immediately made enquiries on the subject of the frigate you had authorised your relation to sell to this government, and I found that he had long before that sold her to government, and sold her very well as I understood. I noted the price on the back of your letter, which I have since unfortunately mislaid so that I cannot at this moment state to you the price, but the Transaction is of so long standing that you cannot fail to have received advice of it.[3] I should without delay have given you this information but that I hoped constantly to be able to accompany it with information as to the live oak, which was another object of your letter. This, tho it has been pressed by Mr St John and also by the M. de la Fayette since his return from Berlin has been spun to a great length & at last they have only decided to send to you for samples of the wood. Letters on this subject from the M. de la fayette accompany this.[4]

Every thing in Europe is quiet, & promises quiet for at least a year to come.[5] We do not find it easy to make commercial arrangements in Europe. There is a want of confidence in us. This country has lately reduced the duties on American whale-oil to about a guinea & a half the ton, and I think they will take the greatest part of what we can furnish. I hope therefore that this branch of our commerce will resume it's activity. Portugal shews a disposition to court our trade; but this has for some time been discouraged by the hostilities of the pyratical states of Barbary. The Emperor of Maroces [i.e., Morocco] who had taken one of our vessels immediately consented to suspend hostilities, & ultimately gave up the vessel, cargo & crew. I think we shall be able to settle matters with him, but I am not sanguine as to the Algerines. They have taken two of our vessels, and I fear will ask such a tribute for a forbearance of their piracies as the U.S. would be unwilling to pay.[6] When this idea comes across my mind, my faculties are absolutely suspended between indignation & impotence. I think whatever sums we are obliged to pay for freedom of navigation in the European seas should be levied on the European commerce with us, by a separate impost, that these powers may see that they protect these enormities for their own loss.

I have the honour to be with sentiments of the most perfect esteem & respect Dear Sir your most obedient and most humble serv[t]

TH: JEFFERSON

RCS (PHi).

1. The year was determined from the contents.

2. See NG to Jefferson, 1 June 1785, above.

3. There is no mention of the frigate *Flora* or of NG's cousin Griffin Greene in ibid. In a letter of the same date, NG had thanked the Marquis de Castries for his role in the French government's purchase of the *Flora*. (NG to Castries, 1 June 1785, above; the Marquis de Lafayette reported the completion of the sale in his letter to NG of 9 February 1785, above.) In regard to Griffin Greene, Jefferson wrote David Howell on 27 January 1786, asking him to pass along to Griffin a memorial that Jefferson had received from a man complaining about his treatment as Griffin's servant in France. Jefferson added that Griffin could decide "whether either justice or generosity require him to do any thing in it; in which case I would offer myself to be the channel of communicating it to him [i.e., the former servant]. Having no acquaintance with Mr Greene, I take the liberty of solliciting you to inclose this paper to him with an explanation of the incident which has occasioned it." (Boyd, *Jefferson Papers*, 9: 233)

4. "St John" was Michel-Guillaume St. John de Crèvecoeur, the French consul in New York. (See his letter to NG of 30 November 1783, above.) The enclosures that Jefferson sent were most likely Lafayette's letters to NG of 3 and 29 December 1785, both above. In the second of those letters, Lafayette requested "an assortment of thousand Cubit feet of green oack."

5. For more about the recent political situation in Europe, see especially Griffin Greene to NG, 2 November 1784, and Pierce Butler to NG, 23 December 1784, both above.

6. Three American ships had been seized the previous July. The Moroccans released the one they had captured, but the two vessels taken off the coast of Portugal by "the Algerines" had been taken to Algiers, where the officers and crewmen were held captive under harsh conditions. (Boyd, *Jefferson Papers*, 8: 440–41, 555; on the negotiations for their release, see ibid., 9: 515–16, 614–22.)

From Henry Banks

Sir   Richmond [Va.] Jan[y] 13th 1786

In my last you were informed of M[r] Colletts being here which I expect has been communicated to you from himself.[1] I this day took up the Joint Bond of John Banks and self which was setled at £1050 to the Sixteenth day of Feb[y] last. All the papers relating to that transaction being in your hands I supposed the Communication necessary.[2] The

Assembly of Virginia having taken of[f?] the tax on patenting lands I have obtained Grants for a large quantity and am exceedingly desirous to make a tour to Europe to attempt a sale of them which can not be effected without my first arranging for all Debts that I may Owe. A Company is formed at Philadelphia for the purpose and I have subscribed 200,000 acres[;] the plan is extensive and liberal.[3]

The memorial which you have presented to Congress may be salutary to us both,[4] because I intend certainly at my going to New York to present one for the payment of the Vessels of Hunter Banks & C° from which probably something may be effected to answer both our Wishes.[5]

There is nothing which can extricate me from the Reputation of total Insolvency except your assistance and friendship, and that to be exerted no further than will tend to place your own affairs in the most eligable Way. I am so well assured of your Inclination herein That nothing but a Wish to destroy the Idea would make me so importunate.

I flatter myself that the Georgia lands will be sold to great advantage when all incumbrances are thus removed.[6] Believe me Sir that my every Wish is influenced by the most perfect desire of being extricated from those very disagreeable disputes and perplexities and of doing justice to you. The Honour of a line from you will be highly acceptable to Your mo H^l Ser[7]   HENRY BANKS

RCS (MiU-C).

1. There is no mention of E. John Collett in the most recent letter from Banks to NG that has been found. (Banks to NG, 12 November 1785, above) Nor has any recent letter from Collett to NG been found. (See the next note, however.)

2. It is not known what papers Banks referred to here. On the debts to Collett that NG had guaranteed for Henry Banks's late brother John and others, see especially the notes at NG to Collett, 8 August 1784, and NG to Lee, 22 August 1785, both above. Collett apparently refused to credit the payment he received from Henry Banks to that account, and he renewed his demands on NG soon afterward. (See below, Rutledge to NG, 20 May, and Collett's letters to NG of 6 and 24 March, 8 and 10 May, and 9 and 13 June.)

3. The Virginia legislature rescinded "the tax on patenting lands" during its October 1785 session. (Hening, *Statutes*, 12: 115) One historian has written that "after the Revolution, a significant number of merchants and other businessmen purchased huge tracts of wilderness land and labored strenuously to make their investments profitable." States began to put "millions of acres of unimproved land" on the market at this time in order to "reduce their indebtedness without increasing taxes," while merchants, finding trade to be less profitable than it had been during the war, began to view land speculation as potentially more lucrative. (Doerflinger, *A Vigorous Spirit of Enterprise*, p. 116) On Banks's use of frontier land holdings to pay his creditors, see especially his letter to NG of 2 September 1785, above.

4. See NG to Lee, 22 August 1785.

5. These may have been vessels that the firm used in privateering ventures during the war. (See, for example, PCC, item 196, vol. 10: 92, DNA.) It does not appear that Banks ever submitted a petition to the Continental Congress.

6. By "Georgia lands," Banks meant the lands—primarily on Cumberland Island—to which he had recently relinquished his rights of inheritance. (See Banks to NG, 12 November 1785, and the note at Hyrne to Clay, 26 November 1783, both above.) As noted

at his letter to NG of 2 September 1785, Banks tried several decades later to regain that property from NG's heirs.

7. No further correspondence between NG and Banks has been found.

*   *   *

¶ [FROM ROBERT HAZLEHURST & COMPANY, Charleston, S.C., 16 January 1786. They have NG's letter of 26 December 1785 [not found], with its "sundry" enclosures [not found], except the one for "M^r [John] Croskeys which we Su[ppose] you omitted."[1] Mr. Griffin Greene has undoubtedly informed NG about his situation with "the Ship *Bell* & the Cargo he brought in her."[2] As Hazlehurst & Company have not been introduced to him or received a letter of introduction for him, they cannot give "any information" about his business. "John" had left to take the horses to NG's South Carolina plantation [before?] they received NG's letters; the horses were apparently "recover'd so as to be able to perform the Journey."[3] Hazlehurst & Company are now sending NG thirty pounds of "good Co[ffee]" and "Six Pounds Hyson" tea, which they hope "will prove agreable"; the price is £13.12.6. Croskeys "has sent down a parcel of your Rice, but his orders were not to pay us any part thereof. We are however informed by Russell Jenkins & Co that there wi[ll] be a further parcel down in a few days for the purpose of discharging y[our] acc^t with us & also a payment to M[r] Griffin Greene."[4] There is "nothing new here worthy of communication." RCS (MiU-C) 2 pp. The manuscript is damaged.]

1. Croskeys assisted in the management of Boone's Barony, NG's South Carolina plantation. (Saunders to NG, 20 October 1783, above)

2. See Griffin Greene's letters to NG of 10, 16, and 22 December 1785, all above.

3. These were horses that Griffin Greene had brought with him from Rhode Island. (See his letters to NG of 10 and 22 December 1785, as well as Hazlehurst to NG, 13 December 1785, all above.)

4. On Russell, Jenkins & Company, see NG to Griffin Greene, 8 January, above. Hazlehurst & Company wrote NG again about this matter on 9 February, below.

¶ [FROM THAYER & BARTLETT, Charleston, S.C., 17 January 1786. This letter accompanies one from Welcome Arnold of Providence, R.I., who has sent them an order on NG for £82.18.4 ½.[1] They will remit this amount to Arnold's correspondents in London if it is agreeable to NG "to draw on some Person [in Lo]ndon in fav[our of]" a firm they name there "& forward us the same."[2] RCS (MiU-C) 1 p. The manuscript is damaged.]

1. See also Arnold to NG, 27 and 28 December 1785, both above. Arnold amended the sum in a letter to NG of 6 January, above.

2. NG's reply has not been found.

¶ [FROM HARY GRANT, Charleston, S.C., 18 January 1786.[1] He has just returned from several weeks at Georgetown and received NG's letter [not found]; hopes "this day to go & fullfill Your order if the things can be got in Town & will forward them in a few days."[2] NG's furniture has arrived from London, but Grant "cannot dispose of them for Cash but to a great Loss." Asks for directions.[3] RCS (MiU-C) 1 p.]

1. Grant, a merchant, was in partnership with James Simon of Beaufort, S.C., but appears to have been based in Charleston. (*Biog. Directory of S.C. House*, 3: 649; *Charleston Evening Gazette*, 29 June 1786) Grant and his wife had been among the passengers on the

vessel that carried NG from Charleston to Newport, R.I., the previous June. (*South-Carolina Gazette and Public Advertiser*, 11–15 June 1785)

2. For more about NG's order, see the letter immediately below.

3. NG's reply has not been found.

¶ [FROM HARY GRANT, Charleston, S.C., [20 January] 1786.[1] Encloses an invoice and bill of lading [not found] for "sundrys" shipped to NG on the schooner *Delight*.[2] The total cost for these articles is £13.7; they were "all purchest for ready money & at a Low advance[;] when Your Crop come to market the Cash will be very acceptable to me." Grant was unable to obtain a blacksmith's "Bellows in Town without taking the set of Tools with it"; as these articles "would be Usefull on the Plantation," he "agreed" to this and hopes NG "will approve."[3] He is sending "the mattress from London" but will wait for NG's directions regarding the furniture.[4] He and his wife would like to visit NG, but that is "impossible" at present. Encloses "the Inventory of the Articles in the Case N° 229" [not found]. RCS (MiU-C) 1 p.]

1. The date was taken from the docketing.

2. On the order that NG had sent to Grant, see also the letter immediately above. It appears from Grant's letter of 27 March, below, that NG was unable to comply with these terms.

3. NG did not approve of this purchase. (Grant to NG, 25 February, below)

4. As seen in the letter immediately above, the furniture had been sent from London. NG's reply has not been found.

* * *

From Count Thaddeus Kosciuszko

My dear General   Varsaw [Poland] 20 January 1786

It suprise me very much that, to this time, I have not one line from you,[1] I am alarmed, and my friendship for you puts Thousands disagreables thoughts into my head. Who knows, you maybe Sick, or dead, Good Generals as you pay the Same tribute to Dame Nature with the meanest Creature in this World, or perhaps you have forgot me as I am no more in your Country. Are we ought to Like only our Compatriots, not allowanc to be made for one [sett?] of Strangers; from your Philosophical turn of mind I would expect of enlarging the Limits of our affection contracted by prejudice and superstition towards the rest of mankind, and more. As for whom we have a Sincier Esteem, Let him be Turak or Polander, American or Japon. Do write me my Dear General of the Situation of your Contry because I heard many bad things; hoever When our King have asked me I gave him the best description I could. Writt me of your self of your family and of my friends. As to myself am in good health, Something richer, but very inhappy of the situation of my Country which I believe *nulla redemptio* and well as I am, so much am attached to your Country that I would Leave every thing behind, and would fly this very moment even in the Baloon to embrace you.

Could I obtain an honorable rank in your Country's Army. I am Dear General with Great Esteem your most Humble and most Ob[t] Ser[t]

COUNT KOSCIUSZKO

My respects to your Lady [and] to M[rs] Moris in Charstown [S.C.]. Tel her I propose to mary her, When hers Hosband dies and if he is in Life, which would be the most Surprising thing to Live So Long in that Country, my best Compliments to him.[2]

RCS (MiU-C).

1. This is the only letter between Kosciuszko and NG of later date than Kosciuszko's of 14 July 1784, above, that has been found.

2. "M[rs] Moris" was Lewis Morris, Jr.'s, wife, the former Ann-Barnett Elliott.

*   *   *

¶ [FROM CHARLES PETTIT, New York, 20 January 1786. He informed NG "last Summer," and thinks he also enclosed "a Letter from M[r] DeBerdt on the Subject," that "one of the Bills you transmitted to him on my Account for about £180 Sterling would probably be protested."[1] NG "then mentioned" that he believed "it would be paid in London, [not]withstanding the unpromising appearances I suggested to you."[2] Pettit recently has received two letters from his son [Andrew], "which shew [that] we have been disappointed in our Expectations." He gives brief extracts from the two letters, in the first of which, datelined Philadelphia, 19 December 1785, Andrew writes that a " 'M[r] Hawkins told me a few Days ago the Bill that was returned to Gen[l] Greene and which he told you there was a prospect of still being paid, was still unpaid, and M[r] DeBerdt wrote there was no probability that it would be paid.' " In the second letter, dated 16 January, Andrew asks if his father has " 'heard anything from Gen[l] Greene about the Bill he sent to M[r] DeBerdt which was returned?' " Hawkins "was a Clerk to M[r] DeBerdt & is now, or is to be, his Partner. His Business in this Country is to make Collections, in which he is industrious & importunate. We owe M[r] DeBerdt some Money, and I am really anxious on various Considerations to discharge it." Because of "various disappointments," the Pettits "have fallen in arrears in our Remittances in a Manner that hurts" Pettit's sensibility. He entreats NG "to have this Money replaced as early as possible, either in M[r] De Berdt's hands or ours, together with the Interest & Damages, which I doubt not you will recover from the Drawer of the Bill."[3] NG authorized Pettit to receive money from a Mr. Hooper for a horse "left in his Care"; this, "together with the Bills, you supposed would reimburse me for the Bills drawn on me by M[r] Saunders for your Use." Hooper has indicated to Pettit "that nothing was to be expected on that Account, for Reasons that he had given or would give to you."[4] Pettit concludes: "I need not repeat Expressions to convince you of my Necessities, nor can it be necessary to excite your Attention."[5] RCS (MiU-C) 2 pp.]

1. See Pettit to NG, 21 September 1785, and Dennis De Berdt to NG, 21 July 1785, both above.

2. NG's reply to Pettit's letter of 21 September 1785 has not been found.

3. NG's reply to the present letter has not been found. For more about this matter, see

William Pierce, Jr.'s, letter to NG near the end of the January 1786 documents. It is not known when or how the issue was finally resolved.

4. Neither NG's authorization to Pettit nor any correspondence with Hooper has been found. For background on the bills that Roger Parker Saunders drew on Pettit in the spring of 1784, see especially Saunders to NG, 29 May 1784, and Pettit to NG, 10 and 19 June 1784, and 26 July 1784, all above. Pettit wrote NG on 23 March 1785, above, that he hoped Saunders had "remitted the £300 Sterling to M^r DeBerdt in London either in Bills or in Rice, as I have relied much on it & shall be much hurt if it be not done." No later information about this matter has been found.

5. See note 3, above.

¶ [FROM CHARLES PETTIT, New York, 20 January 1786. He mentioned "a Matter of Business in a separate Letter," as NG "may have Occasion to shew it to others."[1] Discusses at length the problems involved in trying to get settlements of the accounts of former Quartermaster Department and other staff department officers.

"The Course of Depreciation so frequently overwhelmed and . unhinged the Rules established by Congress for the Settlement of Accounts that the different Commissioners are at great Loss for want of established Principles & Rules for their Government. Various Applications have been made to the Board of Treasury, to the Superintend^t of Finance [Robert Morris], while he was in Office, and to Congress, to establish such Principles & Rules as may be more easily & uniformly understood; but the Circumstances to be weighed & measured by such Rules are so various, numerous & heterogeneous, that they get lost in a maze of Difficulties whenever the Subject is entered upon and therefore cannot be brought to enter on any radical Measures, and it is with great Difficulty they [i.e., Congress?] are brought occasionally to form a Resolution of Expediency only; & when they do pass such a Resolution it is generally either of little Extent as to it's Object, or operative by a Reference to a train of former Resolutions occasionally passed on pressing Emergences, with limited and perhaps different Aspects. Hence every Commissioner is left too much to his own Discretion & Judgment in forming, as it were by Inference, the Rules by which he is to decide on various Matters that come before him. Some have Resolution enough to exercise this Discretionary Power so as to let few Obstacles impede their Progress. Others, more timid, or less inclined to dispatch the Business, boggle at many Things which the former pass pretty easily over, and shelter themselves behind the Letter, or a narrow Construction of some Act of Congress. The Comm^r for the Quarter Master's Department [William Denning], seems to be of the latter kind, tho' I believe a well meaning Man; but he is engaged in other Pursuits, being at this Time a sitting Member of the Assembly. The Com^r for the Commissary's Department makes better progress. He is more liberal in the Construction of his Powers, and attends to no other Business. I believe his Conduct is also more acceptable to his

Superiors as well as to the Accomptants. I have Reason to believe
the Plan will soon be altered so as to form one Office for the Accounts of the 5 Departments, which are now under 5 distinct Heads
acting independantly of each other."[2]

The last election in Pennsylvania "made considerable Changes in the Legisla-
ture. The Attack on the Bank [of North America] inflamed the Industry of M[r]
[Robert] Morris &c," and their party "made great Efforts throughout the State."[3]
For a time, "the Cry of Victory was on their side on a Supposition of a decided
Majority. The Choice of Speaker & Clerk first convinced them of their Mistake."[4]
Finance has become "the leading Object of Legislation," however, and it was
supposed that Morris's "masterly Talents in Finance would bear down all
Opposition" in that area. Pettit, who had been "placed at the Head of the losing
ticket," but was absent and did not participate in the election, later spoke with
Morris and concluded that the parties would cooperate on financial matters, "as
he agreed with me in the Objects to be accomplished & promised to adopt the
Means I had in view as far as his Judgment would permit on a candid Consideration of them. He framed his Plan so as to embrace the Objects I had proposed,
even more extensively than I had thought it prudent yet to aim at." But supposing he could thereby "draw in both Sides of the House, and enlist all the Public
Creditors in support of his Measures," Morris "made a bold Stroke to restore the
Bank by interweaving it into the Machine of the State in such Manner as to make
the latter dependant upon it; and, in order to accomodate the Revenues of the
State to Bank operations, he proposed such modes of raising Revenues as I
conceive are wholly inadmissible even under a british Constitution, much more
so under ours." Morris proposed doing away with "our ordinary mode of
Taxation on Land & Stock, *ad valorem,* and to lay on a Poll Tax of one Dollar P[er]
Head on Males fit to bear Arms, A Duty on Flour & Grain exported, The
Revenue of Excise to be trebled, and farmed out to the highest Bidder, and an
additional Impost on the Import of specified Articles, so high as in my opinion
would either introduce smuggling, or drive the Trade from our Ports to those of
our bordering Neighbours." Morris wrote to Pettit about his plan, asking his
opinion, and Pettit gave it to him "with Frankness & Candor"; Pettit also
helped his friends in the legislature as much as he "could at this Distance."
Morris's plan

> "was rejected by a large Majority (12 to 5) in the grand Committee of
> which he was Chairman, and another Plan reported to and adopted
> by the House, without any Aspect to the Bank, founded on the Rev-
> enues established last Year, and pursuing the same principles of
> funding then adopted, under a new modification to meet the Requi-
> sition of Congress, and extending the Plan to some other Objects
> which were last year in View but could not then be embraced. Bills
> were accordingly published for Consideration, one for complying
> with the Requisition of Congress, and another for paying to our
> own Citizens so much of our Quota of the contribution as is allowed
> to be discounted for Interest on the domestic Debt. This is done
> by opening a State Loan to receive in Certificates of certain Descrip-
> tions (Such as were admitted under the funding Act of last year) and

giving State Certificates on Interest in lieu of them. By which Means the State will be possessed of the original Continental Certificates & can discount the Interest on them at the Continental Loan Office according to the terms of the Requisition, & the State will then pay the Interest to it's Citizens in it's own Way & in such Money as it exacts from them in the Collection of Revenues. Mr Morris's plan proposed this mode of transferring the orig^l certificates also by a State Loan, but he made the Bank the Loan Officer for this Purpose, & the Treasurer for receiving all Revenues & making all Payments from the State: The Plan adopted does all by the ordinary State Officers & leaves the Bank unnoticed."[5]

Pettit believes that "by aiming at too much Mr Morris's Strength declined, and his opponents gained ground." Gen. [Anthony] Wayne and Gen. [Edward] Hand, "who were considered at least as warm if not able Partizans, resigned their Seats towards the Close of the Session."[6] "Another (tho' but a simple Vote) also resigned to avoid a Scrutiny on his Election, which it was supposed would not support him. Hands Place is supplied by one on the same Side, but the other two will afford contested Elections & the Success of the Parties is at least doubtful, tho' great Industry is used in Hopes of a more Successful Attempt to revive the Bank."[7]

If Pettit's "Passions were much engaged" in Pennsylvania party matters, he would "feel some Disgust at the Mode" of his re-election Congress. "While it was supposed Mr Morris & his Friends would have a Majority in the House, they affected to count on me for one of the Delegates. I thought it would look ill in me to refuse under their Choice when I had even left the House of Assembly to serve under the Choice of the other Side." After the House met, and the sides were found to be nearly balanced, conferences were held "to compound the choice in such manner as to afford some Gratification to both Parties." The "Republicans were more particular in expressing their wishes & Expectations that I should serve, than the others. I did not, it is true, wish to be outvoted, but I really wished to be left out of the Nomination & to remain at home to attend to my own Affairs." Pettit therefore "meddled no farther" than "to express this idea." In the Pettit election, however, "The Republicans left me out of their Ticket, and made a strenuous Exertion to carry an entire Set of their own. They succeeded in getting in one (Genl [Arthur] St Clair) by 34 out of 63 Votes, and afterwards, by a Manouvre, got in M^r [James] Wilson to the exclusion of D^r [David] Jackson, who, as I have been informed, was jockeyed out of one or two Votes which turned the Scale. Col. [John] Bayard & myself who were highest had but 39."[8]

Pettit does not know how "entertaining" NG will find "this History of Pennsylvania Politics," but "we are apt to think our Friends feel an Interest in what we are engaged in." It is perhaps "well for Mankind, especially in republican Governments, that there are such Dupes as me, who when they are called into the public Service engage in it with all their Might, and sometimes conceit they have the Weight of the State on their Shoulders." Pettit has been drawn into taking "a leading Part, and I have felt an Ambition as well as an Interest to continue till I get certain Points accomplished. The Restoration of Public Credit has been my principal Object." He sees it "thriving" more in Pennsylvania than in the other states and "cannot but flatter myself I have been of some use in the Business." He can "perceive the Example of our State operating in divers others, and even in Congress," and hopes "it's Influence will increase & raise up a spirit of Emulation in every State."

"Georgia will profit" by NG's residence there. "The State is young and the People but little informed of the Affairs of the Union, and of their Relationship to the federal Family. I hope much from the Information of M^r [Abraham] Baldwin who spent the last Summer in Congress & set out for Augusta in December. He is a Man of Learning and sterling good Sense." If NG is not acquainted with Baldwin, he has "a Pleasure to come."[9] Pettit asks NG for "a renewal of your Correspondence." He wants "to learn from you the State of Politics in your Country" and also feels "an Interest in the Welfare of your family and the Success of your Affairs."[10] Sends "respectful Remembrances to Mrs Greene, and my Affectionate Regards to George [Washington Greene]." RCS (MiU-C) 6 pp.]

1. See the letter immediately above.

2. The commissioner in charge of settling the commissaries' accounts was Jonathan Burrall. (Morris, *Papers*, 9: 947) In March 1786, Congress decided that "the settlement of the accounts of the said five departments be vested in one commissioner, to be appointed by Congress, and subject to the superintendence and controul of the board of treasury." (*JCC*, 30: 131) This act was amended in May to allow for two commissioners, one "for the quarter masters and commissary's departments," and the other for the "hospital, marine and cloathier's departments." Burrall (sometimes also spelled "Burral") was elected commissioner for settling the quartermaster and commissary accounts on 8 May. (Ibid., p. 239)

3. On the Bank of America, see note at Pettit to NG, 6 March 1784, above. The bank, whose state charter had been revoked by the legislature on 13 September 1785, "was forced to depend upon its federal charter and a charter granted by the state of Delaware. Not until it received a new charter from Pennsylvania in March 1787 was the bank's legitimacy assured." (Doerflinger, *A Vigorous Spirit of Enterprise*, pp. 300–301) For detailed discussions of the political events surrounding the repeal and eventual restoration of the charter, see Janet Wilson, "The Bank of North America and Pennsylvania Politics: 1781–1787," *PMHB* 66 (January 1942): 3–28, and Brunhouse, *Pennsylvania*, pp. 173–82.

4. The Republicans had supported George Clymer for speaker; he was defeated by Thomas Mifflin by four votes. The Radical candidate for clerk, Samuel Bryan, prevailed over the Republican, Peter Lloyd, by 33–30. (Brunhouse, *Pennsylvania*, p. 178) Robert Brunhouse has observed of the Radicals' success in winning these two posts that "these two successive blows dashed the hope which the Republicans had entertained." (Ibid.) For more about the results of the 1785 Pennsylvania election, see Pettit to NG, 21 September 1785, above.

5. On the contest between Pettit's plan and Morris's financial strategy, see Brunhouse, *Pennsylvania*, pp. 176–83. Pettit expressed his thoughts about Morris's "system" at greater length in a letter to James Hutchinson of 11 December 1785. (Smith, *Letters*, 23: 58–59)

6. Wayne, like NG, was faced with increasing financial difficulties at this time. (Nelson, *Wayne*, pp. 201–204) On his recent involvement in Pennsylvania politics, see note at Pettit to NG, 23 March 1785, above.

7. Brunhouse notes that "despite the significant number of Radicals in the [Pennsylvania legislature], the Bank did not give up the fight against the repeal of its charter." (Brunhouse, *Pennsylvania*, pp. 182–83) As seen in note 3, above, the bank's charter was not restored until 1787.

8. Pettit, who had been elected to Congress the previous spring, was reelected by the Pennsylvania legislature on 11 November 1785. (See Pettit to NG, 30 June 1785, above; Smith, *Letters*, 23: xxiv.) The voting for the four winning candidates was close, with John Bayard and Pettit each receiving thirty-nine votes; St. Clair, thirty-six, and William Henry, thirty-five. Brunhouse notes that "when the ballots were counted, it was discovered that sixty-eight had been cast although there were only sixty-seven members present." When a motion was made to elect a fifth delegate, "James Wilson received thirty-four ballots over his rival [David] Jackson who netted thirty-three." (Brunhouse, *Pennsylvania*, p. 179)

9. On Baldwin, see NG to Howard, 19 October 1783, above.

10. This letter and the one immediately above are the last correspondence between Pettit and NG that have been found.

¶ [FROM THE MARQUIS DE CASTRIES, Versailles, France, 22 January 1786. Acknowledges NG's letter of 23 [November 1785?] about the lumber from Georgia.[1] Thanks NG for his attention to this matter. The Marquis de Lafayette will inform NG about the king's intentions.[2] RCS (MiU-C) Text in French; translation by Alexandre Dauge Roth and George MacLeod. 1 p.]

1. NG's letter has not been found. The Chevalier de la Foreste wrote NG on 16 December 1785, above, however, that he had forwarded a letter to Castries for NG. (See also NG to Castries, near the end of the December 1785 documents.)

2. See Lafayette to NG, 29 December 1785, above.

¶ [FROM JOHN HIWILL, Savannah, Ga., 23 January 1786.[1] Transmits his "plan of operation on Wednesday Evening next" [not found].[2] RCS (MiU-C) 1 p.]

1. Hiwill has not been identified.

2. Nothing is known about this matter. By "Wednesday Evening next," Hiwill may have meant either 25 January or 1 February.

¶ [FROM JAMES SEAGROVE, [Savannah, Ga.?] "Thursday 1 Oclock" [before 27 January 1786?].[1] Since writing to NG "this morning," he has received NG's letter of "yesterday" [neither found].[2] Has delivered NG's letter for "Mr Gibbons" to "Maj^r [John?] Lucas," who is leaving for Augusta. As William Gibbons was "at the point of Death a few days since at A[u]gusta," NG should not count on him "for Corn" but should "ingage the first you can."[3] It is "truly unfortunate" that Seagrove did not know a boat was going NG's "way this Morning," as he could have sent NG's wine on it. Is sure that the price of "Salt must fall," as "Storeroom is not to be had." Considers himself "under infinite obligations to Mrs Green and the Lady's for their very polite attention"; when he is able, he will be "happy in paying my greatful respects." He will probably see NG the following day, as he is "partly engaged to attend Miss Turnbull." Sends his wishes for "the Lady's [i.e., CG's] better health." RCS (MiU-C) 1 p.]

1. A notation on the cover sheet reads: "Jany 1786." The last Thursday in the month was the 26th. It is possible that this letter was nearer in date to Joseph Clay's to NG of before 23 December 1785, above, than to late January. Seagrove's reference here to receiving NG's letter of "yesterday" suggests that he was not far from NG's Mulberry Grove plantation and was probably at Savannah. (See also Clay to NG, before 23 December 1785; as noted there, Seagrove had arrived in Charleston, S.C., in early December 1785.)

2. The present letter is the only one between Seagrove and NG of later date than Seagrove's of 23 February 1785, above, written from New York, that has been found. In that letter, Seagrove, to whom NG hoped to sell an interest in Cumberland Island, wrote that he would try to visit "Carolina and Georgia" soon. It is not known if he and NG discussed Cumberland Island or other commercial ventures at this time, as they had a

year earlier. As noted at his letter of 23 February 1785, Seagrove did establish himself in the Cumberland Island–St. Marys area. In 1788, some two years after NG's death, CG's brother, William Littlefield, appointed Seagrove and Jacob Weed "his 'lawful substitutes' because of the 'trespasses and other injuries' on Cumberland." (Bullard, *Cumberland Island*, p. 90)

3. It is not certain whether the Gibbons references here are to NG's lawyer William Gibbons, Jr., to Gibbons's father, William, Sr., who had disputed NG's title to part of the land at Mulberry Grove, or to both. (See NG to William Gibbons, Sr., 8 March 1785, above.) NG had been in touch with Gibbons, Jr., about corn the previous spring. (See NG's letter to him of 12 May 1785, above.) As seen in William Pierce, Jr.'s, letter to NG at the end of the January 1786 documents, below, NG was having trouble finding corn for Mulberry Grove plantation.

¶ **[FROM WILLIAM CRAFTS**, Charleston, S.C., 27 January 1786. "The very pressing calls of Mʳ Shattuck for monies due him in this Country" compel Crafts to ask NG "in the most serious manner" for "the payment of two years interest due on your bonds in his possession amounting to Twelve hundred & fifty Guineas."[1] Crafts assures NG "that nothing but the most pressing necessity shoud have induced me to trouble you at this time, being wel convinc'd of the difficulty of collecting payments." It will be "a particular favour," though, if NG can make "the whole or a partial payment." Asks for a reply.[2] RCS (MiU-C) 1 p.]

1. For background, see NG to William Shattuck, 23 August 1785, above.

2. NG's reply has not been found.

¶ **[FROM ROBERT MORRIS**, Philadelphia, 28 January 1786. NG's letter of 25 September 1785 [not found] has been "long unanswered," but as Morris "had paid Your draft in the Bank [of North America] and had no good News from Holland to Communicate it did not seem very material to write especially as my time has been very fully occupied."[1] The Pennsylvania legislature's "*worse* than foolish Conduct" in "attacking the Bank has given the Coup de Grace to American Credit in Holland."[2] NG can "no longer" have "any expectations from that quarter,"[3] and Morris believes "an assiduous application to the Cultivation and Improvement of your Estates will be the surest Means of relieving you from the Weight of your engagements." He wishes NG "Success in the pursuit and will try to wait your Convenience for the reimbursement of what is due to me, altho I feel most Sensibly in the course of my business the general Scarcity of Money which deranges my operations a good deal."[4] RCS (MiU-C) 2 pp.]

1. On the drafts that Morris had paid for NG, see above, NG to Morris, 13 November 1784. The Dutch firm of Wilhem & Jan Willink wrote NG on 8 July 1785, above, that they could not grant the loan that NG, with Morris's help, had requested from them.

2. On the Pennsylvania legislature and the Bank of North America, see Pettit to NG, second letter of 20 January, above.

3. In a letter to the Willinks of 7 January, above, NG had again inquired about a loan.

4. NG's indebtedness to Morris apparently included a bill that William Pierce & Company had drawn on Morris in NG's favor. (See the letter immediately below.) No further correspondence between NG and Morris has been found.

¶ **[FROM WILLIAM PIERCE, JR.**, [Savannah, Ga., January 1786].[1] He reports that the bill NG was "so unfortunate as to send Mʳ De Berdt has not met with the success I wished"; he had been led to believe it "would have been honored."[2] Pierce "took some pains to get it paid" after hearing from Mr. Grant, "notwithstanding I thought it unkind to send on the Bill without a Letter from us. Nothing could have induced us to draw a Bill for such a sum of Money but the prospect of getting 150 Bar^{ls} of Rice, by which we should have been enabled to make an handsome remittance, and be indulged with time to pay the balance."[3] The reason Pierce drew on Mr. [Robert] Morris in favor of NG was "the certain prospect of the Bills being paid." He is sorry this "is likely to be protested" but is "ready to make an imediate settlement" with NG "and remit for the balance."[4] If NG will call at his store, Pierce will show him "the correspondence that passe[d] between Messrs Strachan McKenzie & Co & myself on the subject of the Bill.[5] On a fair examination it will probably be found that there is some blame on both sides. All such disputes are better settled by the parties, than through the medium of a third person." RCS (MiU-C) 2 pp.]

1. The date was taken from the docketing. Pierce was based in Savannah.

2. On this matter, see also Pettit to NG, first letter of 20 January, as well as Pettit to NG, 21 September 1785, and Dennis De Berdt to NG, 21 July 1785, all above.

3. Hary Grant's involvement in the matter is not known; on the involvement of Pierce & Company—and on the shortfall in NG's 1784 rice crop—see Pierce to NG, 13 May 1785, and NG to Pierce, 17 May 1785, both above. It appears that NG sold his 1785 rice crop through another merchant. (Cumming to NG, 8 February, below)

4. It is not known when Pierce made this transaction. (See, however, Pierce & Company to NG, 9 July 1785, above.) Morris wrote NG on 28 January, immediately above, that he would "try to wait your Convenience for the reimbursement of what is due to me."

5. For background, see especially NG's letter to Strachan, Mackenzie & Company of 4 June 1785 and theirs to him of 30 July 1785, both above. As noted at NG to Pierce, 17 May 1785, problems related to the protested bill continued at least into the spring of 1786.

¶ [FROM WILLIAM PIERCE, JR., [Savannah, Ga., January 1786].[1] He finds it "impossible to engage Corn" at the price that NG stipulated, nor can he "get one of the Boats to take it up to your House." The price is "3/per Bushel," and although "Cash has been offered them, they will not take a farthing less."[2] He has "no fine Sheeting," but if he did, he would "send you up some patterns; such as Hamilton takes up with him is common, and I believe will be about 2/1 per yard."[3] NG's "account is made out, but Johnson is unfortunately in the Country, and it cannot possibly be got at" until he returns. Pierce concludes: "Sometime next Week M^{rs} [Charlotte Fenwick] Pierce and the Ladies will pay Mrs Greene a visit. I mean to accompany them."[4] RCS (MiU-C) 1 p.]

1. See note at the letter immediately above.

2. Pierce's firm had also found it difficult to buy corn for NG's plantation the previous spring. (See Pierce & Company to NG, 8 April 1785, above.)

3. NG and CG were undoubtedly furnishing their new home at Mulberry Grove. No further correspondence between Pierce and NG has been found. Hamilton was probably the Greenes' servant "Ham," or "Hambleton." (NG to CG, 17 August 1784, above; Cumming to NG, 9 June, below)

4. Nothing more is known about the proposed visit to Mulberry Grove.

¶ [FROM WILLIAM PRICE, Charleston, S.C., 1 February 1786. His creditors are "so clamarous for payment" that he must ask NG to discharge the "two Bonds due the 26 Novem 1784 & 1785 for £655.15.3 exclusive of Interest, or at least a handsome payment thereon."[1] Asks for immediate payment, "that I may be enabled to stop the repeated Duns at my Door, & in all probability several Writs against me should I not be able to make some part paym^t."[2] RCS (MiU-C) 1 p.]

1. On these bonds, which were owed for slave purchases, see note at NG to Price, 12 August 1785, above.
2. NG's reply has not been found.

*   *   *

From Aedanus Burke

Dear General   Charleston [S.C.] Feby 7th 1786

I was favored with a kind letter from y[ou] some time ago, & am thankful for your friendly opinion relating to my intended purchase near you.¹ I am off the notion [of] that place, Major [Pierce] Butler having advised me that it is not equal to the price asked, nor what some say of it. This however is not going to divert me from the determination of trying to get Lands in Georgia; They are cheaper, & of better quality, than any wh. finances like mine, can get in Carolina.² Nor do I care a farthing, what effect the removal of my little property may h^v as to my *politica[l] standing* here, I have seen a little of ups and dow[ns] in the fortune of other men, to shew me, On how sa[fe?] a foundation he builds his hopes, who relies on the opinion of a Y—o.³ Independance is my wish, & a little would amply content me. About 30 [workes?] on good lands with you, would be no bad thing, let me te[ll] you, my dear General; And any fall I might have here in consequence, would not break my bones; I shou[ld] come down as easy, as a Bear on the Wateree, [*damaged*] if very fat, and falling from the highest tree in the Swamp, wraps himself up & receives not the least injur[y] but if he happens to be thin & lean, he is dashed to pieces. With the warmest wishes for your good fortune & happiness, I am Dear Sir with great regard Yours

                                                   AEDANUS BURKE

RCS (MiU-C).
1. NG's letter, which has not been found, was undoubtedly a reply to Burke's of 27 November 1785, above.
2. No evidence has been found that Burke purchased land in Georgia.
3. Burke, a judge of the Court of Common Pleas and General Sessions in South Carolina, also served in the legislature and had been appointed in 1785 to "a three-year commission to revise and prepare a new digest of state laws." (*Biog. Directory of S.C. House*, 3: 105) "Y—o" was presumably "Yahoo." (See Burke to NG, 4 July 1785, above.)

*   *   *

¶ [**FROM RANDALL SON & STEWARTS**, New York, 7 February 1786. They enclose a copy of a letter they wrote to NG "this day" by a ship's captain "who sails this day."¹ In the copy, they state that they have received "in payment from Mr Stephen Rapalje of this City a Bond signd by [NG], John Banks, & Ichabod Burnet, in favor of John McQueen of the State of S^o Carolina for Two Hundred & Fifty British Guineas."² They allowed Rapalje "the full amo^t of the Bond with

Interest due, as he informd us you were to have pass'd through this City, the last fall; & that you had promised payment then."[3] They will be "much oblidg'd" if NG has it in his power to "remit us a Bill here," on some of his friends. If he cannot do so, but can send "any quantity of Rice" on the returning vessel, they will sell it for him without charging a commission and will apply the proceeds to the bond. If NG can now remit "the whole amount," they will deliver the bond to anyone he may name. On a separate sheet, "annexed" to the above, they add that if it is convenient for NG to ship rice from Charleston, S.C., there will be continual opportunities "from there for this place"; they will sell "whatever" amounts of rice NG may send them and will credit his account, free of commission.[4] RCS (MiU-C) 2 pp.]

1. The original letter has not been found.

2. For background on this debt, which was related to NG's acquisition of land on Cumberland Island, Ga., see note at Hyrne to Clay, 26 November 1783, above. Rapalje wrote NG on 27 October 1785, above, that he had turned the bond over to Randall Son & Stewarts.

3. NG and his family had sailed directly from Newport, R.I., to Savannah, Ga., the previous fall. (See note at Knox to NG, 27 October 1785, above.)

4. NG's reply is below, dated 12 March.

¶ [FROM THE CHEVALIER DE BRENAUT, St. Augustine, East Florida, 8 February 1786.[1] Thanks NG for introductions [not found] to the governor and Captain Howard "of this place."[2] He has "receivd every Civility possibele" from them. Was not able to conclude his "bussiness" there and is "just this moment Setting of for Cuba, and from thense" to Cap-Français.[3] RCS (MiU-C) 1 p.]

1. The writer of this letter has not been identified.

2. Vicente Manuel de Zéspedes, whom NG met during his visit there the previous spring, was the governor of East Florida. Charles Howard and Zéspedes both replied to NG on 11 February, below.

3. Cap-Français (now Cap-Haïtien) was on the northern coast of Hispaniola, in what is now Haiti.

*   *   *

From Thomas Cumming[1]

Sir   Savannah [Ga.] Feby 8. 1786

I do not recollect that I engaged to take your Rice at any particular price; we talked of eleven shill[gs] and of the payments; but I did not consider that any thing decided was said. Had I conceived that an agreement was made for your Rice, I shou'd not have made any difficulty in receiving it, altho' the Price might have been reduced. However I am willing to receive the Rice, as soon as you can conveniently send it down, at Eleven shillings p[er] C[ask]. I shall be glad you wou'd send it down as speedily as possible; this week if conven[t], if not, early next week.[2]

I am sorry there has been any misunderstanding between us, in this business. I am Sir Yr mo[t] Ob[t] Servant   THO. CUMMING

Whenever you have occasion for any thing out of my Store, it shall be furnished, on the terms I mentioned to you when you were in Savannah.[3]   T. C.

RCS (MiU-C).
1. As seen in the postscript to this letter, Cumming was a merchant.
2. NG, who had previously sold his rice from Mulberry Grove plantation through William Pierce & Company, presumably had spoken with Cumming about this matter. No earlier correspondence has been found.
3. It appears from Cumming's letters to NG of 21 February, 7 April, and later that he sold supplies and merchandise to NG on a regular basis.

*   *   *

¶ [FROM THOMAS WASHINGTON, Savannah, Ga., 8 February 1786.[1] Has just received NG's letter [not found] and would have "waited on you, E're this; but had some Business to transact." Will see NG "tomorrow, or next Morn[g] at Most." Asks, "if its Convenient[,] to delay the Answer Respect[g] the premises" until then, "as, if its In my power I mean to make the purchase and Enter into it, with Spirit."[2] Is going to "Carolina the last of the Week" and will be "happy to Execute" any commands NG may have for him there. RCS (MiU-C) 2 pp.]
1. Washington, the former owner of Hermitage plantation on the Savannah River, had been forced to sell it in September 1785. (Granger, *Savannah River Plantations*, p. 428)
2. It is not known what kind of "purchace" Washington had in mind. He wrote NG about cattle on 5 and 21 May, both below.

*   *   *

From Thomas Gadsden[1]

Sir   Charleston [S.C.] 9th Feb[y] 1786
The inclosed letter from M[r] [Edward] Fenwick to you, I have had in my Possession for several Months & wou[ld] Have sent it immediately on the Receipt of it;[2] but recollecting your Sentiments on the Subject the last time I had the Pleasure of seeing you, so exactly corresponding with my own; that I detained it till M[r] F. came to Town and then persuaded him to postpone sending it till the Meeting of the Assembly. Both Branches of our Legislature met a few days ago & I intended availing myself of the first oppertunity, to present a Petition to them in his favor, which I have been prevented doing by a sudden Resolution of the Senate, that they wou'd not receive any more Petitions from any Person or Persons banished from this State or either of our Sister States.[3] This unprecedented Resolve comeing so suddenly alarmed me amazingly & roused every feeling in behalf of my Friend. I immediately consulted General [John] Barnwell on his Situation, who advised me to trouble you on the Subject as the only certain Mode of his getting off the Banishment Law. He advised me to request of you to send a Memorial to the Legislature, stating in the strongest Terms the Agreement you

made with Mr Fenwick & your Promise of getting him restored in this his Native Country (as far as it lay in your Power,) on his complying on his Part with his Engagement with you.[4] Shoud I be so happy as to get any Paper of this kind from you, General Barnwell flatters me there will not be a doubt of his being allowed to Stay. Mr Fenwick is in a very disagreeable Situation shoud he be rejected in this Country. He has no Homes to go to. He cannot go to England. Major Butler who has lately arrived from London says they have stopped every thing from him there and his Name which was the first upon the Provincial List (and they woud have made ample Provision for him) was erased immediately on their hearing of the Circumstances which happened in this Country.[5]

I have no doubt but these Circumstances will induce you to say every thing in your Memorial or Letter to the Senate which you think will be of Service to him and shall be much obliged to you to dispatch the Bearer of this, who is sent Express as quick as you conveniently can.[6]

Mr Fenwick woud have wrote himself but has this Moment been informed by the Arrival of a Vessel from London of the Death of his Wife who died very suddenly.[7]

Mrs Gadsden[8] joins me in requesting to be rememberd to Mrs Green & beleave me to be with Esteem Sir Y^r very Hbl^e serv^t   THO^S GADSDEN

RCS (MiU-C).
1. Thomas Gadsden (1757–1791), a son of Christopher Gadsden, was a partner in the latter's mercantile firm. He had served in the South Carolina Continental line during the war and later was elected to several terms in the South Carolina General Assembly. He also served for a time as lieutenant governor, as had his father. (*Biog. Directory of S.C. House*, 3: 249–250; on Christopher Gadsden, see vol. 9: 469n, above.)
2. See Fenwick to NG, 5 December 1785, above.
3. The South Carolina Senate had passed a resolution on 8 February that "no Petition of a private Nature will be received after Saturday the 18th Instant." Two days later, the House informed the Senate that they had voted to "disagree" with this resolution. (See *Columbian Herald* [S.C.], 13 February, and "Special Supplement," 14 February.)
4. On Fenwick's "Engagement" with NG during the war, see NG to Guerard, 30 March 1784, 19 September 1784, and 4 February 1785, all above.
5. On Pierce Butler's recent trip to England, see NG's letter to him of 9 September 1784 and Butler's reply of 23 December 1784, both above.
6. NG wrote Gov. William Moultrie about Fenwick's situation on 12 February, below.
7. Fenwick's wife, Christiana, died in London on 20 November 1785. (Palmer, *Loyalists*, p. 268)
8. Gadsden's wife, Martha, was Fenwick's sister. (*Biog. Directory of S.C. House*, 2: 243)

*   *   *

¶ [FROM ROBERT HAZLEHURST & COMPANY, Charleston, S.C., 9 February 1786. NG's "favor" of 8 January [not found] was received on the 23rd. Mr. [John] Croskeys "has sent down" forty barrels of rice to Mr. Griffin Greene, "which amounted to £107.6.4. The sum therefore due him [i.e., Griffin Greene]

was £27 which we have paid & of course is at your debit in Account."[1] Croskeys sent another forty barrels of rice to Hazlehurst & Company, "the neat amount bein[g] £110.0.10 will be at your Credit when the Cash is received, which we expect will be to Morrow." They are sending NG "Garden Seeds the cost of which is £2.11.2," on the same vessel that carries this letter; peas are "scarce," or they would have sent more. CG's "easy Chair is likewise on board."[2] They have forwarded NG's letters for Capt. [William] Littlefield [not found] on a vessel to New York; the other enclosures were given to Griffin Greene, who "expects to sail to Morrow."[3] A ship's captain has given them an account of what he paid to a woman in Wilmington, N.C., for NG; "if agreeable we will repay it to him."[4] There is "nothing new of an extraordinary nature & for a knowledge of the proceedings of our Legislature we herewith send you a few of the last News Papers" [not found]. In a note below their signature, they add: "Rice is rather dull at 10/6" [per hundred weight?]. They think it may decline to 10/, the price it was at "10 days ago."[5] RCS (MiU-C) 3 pp.]

1. This rice was from Boone's Barony, NG's South Carolina plantation. On the money that NG owed to Griffin Greene, see also NG's letter of him of 8 January and Hazlehurst & Company to NG, 16 January, both above.

2. This may have been part of the furniture mentioned in Grant to NG, 18 and 20 January, both above.

3. The enclosures given to Griffin Greene, who was about to sail for Europe, may have included NG's letter to him of 8 January and NG's to Wilhem & Jan Willink of 7 January, above.

4. Nothing more is known about this matter.

5. Hazlehurst wrote NG on 25 March, below, that there was "no prospect of it's [i.e., the rice] advancing in Price."

¶ [FROM JAMES PENMAN, London, 9 February 1786. He delayed replying to NG's "obliging favour of the 12ᵗʰ June" [not found] until he could gather "full information" that would "enable you to judge with some degree of Certainty of the Value of the Ship Timber upon your Island and how far it would Answer your Expence in Shipping it for Europe."[1] Has not been able to find anyone "willing to Contract for receiving it upon the Spot." As he found "much difficulty in procuring Proper Information from the Public Offices," Penman approached "one of the First Ship Builders upon the River Thames, a Mʳ Barnard of Deptford," who contracts with the government "for Men of War" and "builds a Number of Ships for the East India Company."[2] He encloses Barnard's "Directions" and his "Scale of Dimensions for a Seventy four Gun Ship" [not found]. Penman has "discoverd by fatal experience That it will never Answer where you Pay superfluous Freight which you must do if shipped [in] a Rough State."[3] It will not be possible for NG to "convert" his "Timber to the most Advantage without the Aid of a sensible Ship Carpenter," but Penman supposes that NG could find one "from the Northward upon Tollerable easy Terms." He will be happy to provide any further information and wishes NG "Success in this Undertaking."[4] RCS (NcD) 2 pp.]

1. NG's letter to Penman of 12 June 1785 presumably concerned the possibility of Penman making contacts in England for selling NG's live oak and other timber from Cumberland Island, Ga. NG had asked about prices of timber in London in a letter to Dennis De Berdt of 9 March 1785, above.

2. NG may have wanted Penman to see whether the British government would be

interested in his timber for its navy. Since then, NG had had some success in convincing the French government to consider a contract for the timber. (Lafayette to NG, 3 and 27 December 1785, both above)

3. Penman meant that because of transportation costs, rough-cut timber could not be shipped to Europe profitably.

4. No further correspondence between Penman and NG has been found.

¶ [FROM CHARLES HOWARD,[1] St. Augustine, East Florida, 11 [February] 1786.[2] Is "highly honour'd" by NG's introduction for the Chevalier de Brenaut.[3] Has shown him "all the attention" due to such an eminent person. Brenaut sailed the previous day for Havana, "where if [cu]riosity is his only view, he will find an ample field to gratify it, but nothing else." RCS (MiU-C) 1 p.]

1. Charles ("Carlos") Howard was the Irish-born "secretary of the government" in East Florida. According to Joseph Lockey, he was "undoubtedly the most important official in the province," other than the governor and "possibly the treasurer." (Lockey, *East Florida*, pp. 34–35)

2. The month is illegible in the dateline, but as the Chevalier de Brenaut, the subject of this letter, wrote NG on 8 February, above, that he was leaving East Florida soon for Cuba, 11 February is the probable date.

3. See Brenaut to NG, 8 February.

¶ [FROM GOVERNOR VICENTE MANUEL DE ZÉSPEDES Y VELASCO OF EAST FLORIDA, [11 February 1786?].[1] Acknowledges NG's letter of introduction for the Chevalier de Brenaut, who sailed the previous day for Cuba.[2] RCS (MiU-C) 1 p. Text in Spanish. Translation by Phyllis and Avelino Gonzalez.]

1. The docketing appears to indicate a date of 11 January, but internal evidence and the letter immediately above suggest that 11 February is much more likely.

2. See above, Brenaut to NG, 8 February, and Howard to NG, this date.

*　　*　　*

To Governor William Moultrie of South Carolina[1]

Sir   Savannah [Ga.] Feb. 12th 1786

From my peculiar situation ⟨& from⟩ the nature of my engagements, ⟨I am reduced to⟩ the disagreeable alternative of forfeiting my promise or of addressing your Excellency once more upon the affairs of Mr. Fenwick.[2] Hard is my fate & cruel is the necessity. My feelings revolt at the business when I consider the light in which it may be taken. It is true I am not responsible for consequences, but private honor & public faith compel me to speak where I would wish to be silent. If my forward zeal in the hour of public calamity for the common safety of this Country, has led me into measures in this and other matters, which the sober season of tranquility cannot approve; I can only say that they cannot be more inconvenient to the public than they have been painful & distressing to me. The nature of my engage⟨ments⟩ in this business & the incidents attending the affair have all been stated in my former letters on this subject. To repeat them again I cannot think necessary upon this occasion. Mr. Fenwicks application at this moment originates in a resolution of the Honorable the Senate of the 8th of this instant, relative to banished persons. It is difficult for me to suppose him included in that resolution after the steps which have been taken in his favour. To grant him his property & not the right of injoying it, would be too personal to comport with the dignity of a Legislature. Nor can I consider his residence a matter of such importance.[3] However he may have offended; his attempts to restore himself, having placed him a pe⟨culiar⟩ situation, give him some claim to your pity ⟨& conside⟩ration. His losses & suffering in England, in matters of fortune, since this business took air, will no doubt have some weight in deciding upon the question.[4] I shall say no more than necessity obliges me & leave the event to the justice & humanity of the Legislature. If Mr. Fenwick should be included in that Resolve of the 8th which I am perswaded he is not, I must beg your Excellency to lay this letter before that honorable body & solicit their reconsideration of the matter.[5] I have the honor to be, with the most perfect respect Your Excellency's Most Obed[t] Humble Ser[t]

ADf (MiU-C). The text in angle brackets was taken from a Cy (ScCoAH).

1. Moultrie, the former Continental general, was elected governor of South Carolina in May 1785. (*Biog. Directory of S.C. House*, 2: 485–88)

2. NG had discussed the situation of Edward Fenwick, the former British officer who had spied for the Americans during the latter stages of the war, in letters that he wrote to Moultrie's predecessor, Gov. Benjamin Guerard, on 30 March 1784, 19 September 1784, and 4 February 1785, all above. The present letter was undoubtedly written in response to Fenwick's of 5 December 1785 and Thomas Gadsden's of 9 February, both above.

3. On the resolution to which NG referred, see Gadsden to NG, 9 February.

4. According to Gadsden, who was Fenwick's brother-in-law, Fenwick was denied any eligibility for income in England when it was learned that he had aided the Americans. (Ibid.)

5. As seen in the note at NG to Guerard, 19 September 1784, Fenwick's citizenship rights were restored in March 1786.

From John Croskeys

D[r] Sir   [Boone's Barony, S.C.] Feb. 16th 1786[1]

I received your Letter by Capt Saunders tho he did not Call he left the letter at the plantation.[2] I have Sent May with Mary To conduct hir the littel girl that Capt Sanders mention is but Small not more then Six or Seven years old the roads I understand is very bad So that I hant Sent the Litte[l] girl I think youe had beter Let hir Stay til warm weather Coms. Shold thear be any saver [i.e., safer] opertunety will Send hir. I have mor bad nuse To acquaint youe with. Youe had a fine younge feller died Last weake with the plureccy. I had Every thing done for hime that I cold do,[3] and the Crop fell much Shorter then I expected the new ground made but 125 barrels the old ground has beate[n out] 150 barrels & has a few more To beate. Most Every body has fell Short of thear expectation oing [i.e., owing] To late planting. M[r] [Thomas] Fer-

guson Expected upwards of 2000 barrels & dont make 1400 but we live in hopes of doing beter this yeare tho it threatins To be another weat Spells.[4] I have got a very good man at the nue ground now. He has a goodeel of wark done now with out much Trouble. The young wench that was under the doctors hands Seems To be intirely well. She has had no ale this 3 monts. The 2 old negros that I wanted to Sel I have never had an opertunity of Seling them the feller may I beleave will make a die he has ben Sick this 2 monts and Cant find what is the disorder but he has Some disorder he is So por he Cant scarse Walk. I have Sent down 40 barrels besides the 3 first parsels youe desird me To Send down have paid Tonno & Taylor and the freight of all that has gon down the man that I bought the Cattel of is very presing for his mony.[5] I Saw Capt [John] Blake in To[w]n the other day & told me he wantd Some mony from youe. The docter wants his 16 guineys,[6] M[r] [Joseph] Atkinson wants pay for the Seedrose, M[r] Ferguson wants pay for Cart & yoak. Irons the oversare [i.e., overseer] that is gon I was oblidge To pay 15 guineys out of my one [i.e., own] pocket. M[r] M[c]Cants is To move, he is moved his negro allready, he gets a plase at £20 per yeare I think it wont be of any advantage To youe To Let the plase. We Can keep a goodeel of backwater when tis not planted. I think To plant Corn thear as it will be muc handeer thear then at the river field as it will be more in my way.
I am D[r] Sir your hl Srt   JOHN CROSKEYS

RCS (MiU-C).
1. Croskeys was presumably writing from NG's South Carolina plantation, Boone's Barony, where he was the manager.
2. NG's letter to Croskeys has not been found. Roger Parker Saunders was overseeing the management of Boone's Barony in NG's absence. (See, for example, Saunders to NG, 26 May 1783, above.)
3. These were undoubtedly slaves on the plantation.
4. See Saunders to NG, 22 June 1785, above.
5. Nothing more is known about the purchase of the cattle.
6. This was presumably the doctor who had taken care of the slaves.

*   *   *

¶ [FROM THOMAS CUMMING, Savannah, Ga., 21 February 1786. "The negroes have been detained to day by the boat being on the beach"; it could not be "got of[f] untill the Tide raised." Cumming is sending "a Case Good Gin (three bottle wan[t][in]g)" and the "articles" that NG "left with DaCosta," including mattresses, an anvil, bellows, and other items listed "at foot" of the letter.[1] RCS (MiU-C) 1 p.]
1. Cumming was evidently forwarding items that NG had purchased from South Carolina merchant Hary Grant. (See above, Grant to NG, 18 and 20 January.)

¶ [FROM HARY GRANT, Charleston, S.C., 25 February 1786. Has NG's letter and is "sorry You did not aprove of my purchase of the Black Smiths Tools," which was "well indendid."[1] This letter will be "handed to" NG by "Mr. Price,"

from London, "My particular friend," who has business in Savannah, Ga. Grant recommends him to NG's "civilities."² Grant is "in treaty for a Capittall Garder [i.e., gardener?] just arrived from Scotland," for NG. RCS (MiU-C) 1 p.]
    1. NG's letter to Grant has not been found. On the blacksmith tools, see Grant to NG, 20 January, above.
    2. Nothing more is known about Price.

*   *   *

From Edward Rutledge

Dear General   [Charleston, S.C.?] 1 March 1786
    If you did not know that my Life is a Life of Hurry, & Bustle, you would think me a very Strange sort of a Genius, by my Silence; but the Weight of Business, Public, and Professional, is almost too much for me, as it leaves me scarcely any Leisure to discharge the Common offices of Friendship. However to the Point, We shall not have occasion for your Presence at the ensuing Court. [Michael J.] Harris, you know is the Person with whom the Affairs which respects that Concern was transacted;¹ & as he is in Europe it is necessary to obtain his Answ[er] to the Charges of your Bill. The Bill, or rather a Copy of it, has been transmitted to him, but his Answer is not yet come: as soon as it arrives I will transmit you a Copy of it.² Will you believe, you will because it is true, that Ferrie has not as yet put in his Answer. I have urged the Matter as much as possible, but hitherto without Effect. General Pinckney's Absence from Town, for a length of Time, & the long setting of the Assembly are the Excuses. However we shall adjourn in a few Days & you depend I will then obtain his Answer, tho' it be thro' the Medium of an Attachment. Indeed I do not think any Business will be done at March Court, the whole will stand over to June.³ Let Mʳˢ Greene however be consoled, for first or last I hope we shall free you of all your Difficulties. Mʳˢ [Henrietta Middleton] Rutledge desires to be affectionately remember'd to her, & offers her best Wishes for much Health & Happiness. She speaks very feelingly on the Subject, for her own Health is truly wretched.⁴ Be pleased to present me to her very respectfully & believe me to be my Dear General with much Esteem sincerely yours⁵

ED. RUTLEDGE

RCS (MH).
    1. For background on the firm of Harris & Blachford's claims against NG, see especially Pendleton to NG, 10 November 1784, above.
    2. NG was trying to keep Harris & Blachford from obtaining a judgment against him. (See NG to Hunter, 29 August 1785, and NG to Carrington, 29 December 1785, both above.) Neither the "Bill" nor Harris's "Answer" has been found.
    3. On the efforts to attach property belonging to John Ferrie, a former partner of the late John Banks, see especially Forsyth to NG, 18 June 1784, above. As seen there, Charles C. Pinckney was Ferrie's attorney. Ferrie's "Answer" has not been found. Rutledge wrote NG again about this matter on 20 May, below.

4. It appears from NG's letter to Henry Knox of 12 March, below, that CG was not experiencing good "Health & Happiness" at this time, either.

5. A note in NG's hand on this letter reads: "Answered 24ᵗʰ April." That letter has not been found.

* * *

¶ [FROM NATHANIEL RUSSELL, Charleston, S.C., 3 March 1786. He "did not intend to trouble" NG "on Business," but Capt. Robert Champlin, "who is Interested in the bond I recᵈ from you, knowing that it was due in Decʳ has d[rawn u]pon me, for £250. Stlᵍ & it is wholly out of my power to honour his bill unless you can let me have that Sum in part of your Bond, he is very pressing for his money."¹ Champlin is "fitting part of a Ship" to go to "the Coast of Africa."² RCS (MiU-C) 1 p.]

1. A total of 1,250 guineas had been due on NG's Cumberland Island, Ga., bonds in December 1785. (NG to Marbois, 15 April 1785, above)

2. NG's reply has not been found.

* * *

From E. John Collett

Sir Charleston [S.C.] 6 March 1786

I take the Liberty of Acquainting you with my arrival in this City, where I expected to have had the pleasure of meeting with you, but Mʳ [Nicholas?] Primerose informs me of your chief residence being in Georgia.¹ It would have give[n] me great Satisfaction and relief to have found it had been Convenient to you to have made me at least a partial payment, as I assure you I have been exceedingly distressed in having So Considerable a Capital locked up for So long a time, and I hope though you have not hitherto been able to assist me, yet that you have now made Such arrangements in my favor as will effectually relieve me, and enable me to make a Speedy remittance to Europe.²

You will oblige me Sir to inform me when I may expect the pleasure of Seeing you here, as I wish to make Such a disposition of my time as to return to England early in the Spring, and it will afford me the Sincerest gratification if we Can adopt Such Measures as will tend to give you [ease?] and every opportunity of Reimbursing yourself as I have not the most distant inclina[tion] of distressing you, or rendering you[r] present Situation more disagreeable than it must necessarily be of itself.³ I have the honor to be Sir Your most obᵗ hble Serᵗ E. Jℕᵒ COLLETT

RCS (MiU-C).

1. Primerose was Collett's attorney. (NG to Forsyth, 2 October 1784, above)

2. On Collett's financial claims against NG, see especially the notes at NG's letter to him of 8 August 1784, above. NG's hope that Henry Banks and other former partners of the late John Banks would relieve him of this debt turned out to be false. (See note at Henry Banks to NG, 13 January, above.) As noted at NG to Collett, 8 August 1784, NG signed new bonds for Collett just before he was taken fatally ill in June 1786.

3. Collett wrote NG again on 24 March, below, commenting that he had not received an answer to the present letter. A letter that NG wrote to Collett on the same date has not been found. (Collett to NG, 8 May, below)

*　　　*　　　*

¶ [FROM ROBERT FORSYTH, Augusta, Ga., 9 March 1786. "Mr. Walton"[1] hurried him so much the previous day that in "closing the letter" to NG "and M[r] Cummins,"[2] Forsyth "neglected to inclose the List handed with the Money by Capt. [Nathaniel] Pendleton."[3] Asks NG to "please now receive it." RCS (MiU-C) 1 p.]

1. This was probably Robert Walton, for whom NG provided a certificate on 11 March, immediately below.

2. Forsyth's letter of 8 March to NG and "Cummins"—probably Thomas Cumming—has not been found.

3. The enclosure, which is with this letter at MiU-C, was a list of money in various amounts and denominations, including "half Joes, Guineas, pistoles, Moisdores, french Guineas, Ducats, Dollars, and Doubloons."

¶ [CERTIFICATE FOR ROBERT WALTON. Mulberry Grove, Ga., 11 March 1786. NG certifies that Walton, "now of" Georgia, "furnished for the use of Col. [Henry] Lee's Legion in February 1781 sixteen horses valued at the time of delivery at 126000 weight of James River Tobacco or the value of it agreeable to the mode then adopted in the State of Virginia for ascertaining the price of horses furnished for public service." On 22 March [1781], "an order was given on the State of Virginia for payment which was protested by the Governor because it could not be allowed by Congress as part of the then requisition made on the State." The order has been returned to NG, who certifies that the money remains due to Walton. He also attests that "the horses were furnished at a most critical and interesting period of the Southern War," and further, that they were provided by Walton's "voluntary consent when others would not supply any but by impressment."[1] DS (PCC, item 42, vol. 8: 443, DNA) 1 p.]

1. Walton, then an "agent for the Georgia delegates to Congress," wrote NG on 19 April 1781, above (vol. 8: 122) that the Virginia legislature was refusing to pay him for the horses he had supplied. NG's reply to Walton is also above, dated 30 April 1781. (Vol. 8: 178) As seen in his letter to NG of 8 March 1785, above, Walton was still trying to obtain payment. The outcome of this matter is not known.

*　　　*　　　*

To General Henry Knox, Secretary at War

Dear Sir   Mulberry Grove [Ga.] March 12th 1786

I got your letter of October some little time past.[1] It was a long time on the way. I thank you for the polite attention you are paying to my public Trophies; but I have been so embarrassed and perplexed in my private affairs for a long time past which originated in the progress of the War that I have but little spirit or pleasure on such subjects.[2] My family is in distress and I am overwhelmed with difficulties and God knows when or where they will end. I work hard and live poor but I fear all this will not extricate me. I have met with some heavy losses this winter, I had fifty barrels of Rice burnt up and forty five sunk in Savannah Docks sent to market for sale. These losses add to my distresses greatly. My Crops failed owing to the wet season last year, and this deduction out of the little I made leave but a small support for my family.[3] Mrs Greene is just ready to lay in.[4] And the Children have just got out of the small pox by innoculation. They all had it very light.[5] Mrs Greene joins me in affectionate compliments to you and Mrs [Lucy Flucker] Knox. She is transformed from the gay Lady to the sober house wife.

This State has complied with all the Requisitions of Congress in the last Assembly except on the regulation of trade which I am confident will pass the next meeting.[6] The stupid policy which has prevaild in America since the peace I am of opinion makes Great Britain regret the close of the War. And I am not a little apprehensive she wants but a pretence to renew it. It is happy for us that we have Franc[e] for our guarantor or I fear we should make but a poor figure upon a second tryal.[7]

I never got any allowance for my back Rations from the year 1777. Be good enough to inform me how the Gen[l] Officers settled their accounts and whether any of them got any thing. And if they did whether I can and through what channel. And please to give me your opinion upon sending George to the Marquis de la Fyette agreeable to his request.[8] Let your answer be as candid as I trust your friendship is sincere.[9] Yours aff

NATH GREENE

ALS (GL-NHi).
1. See Knox to NG, 27 October 1785, above.
2. In ibid., Knox had discussed the engraved cannon, medal, and standard that Congress had voted to give NG in honor of his wartime services. (See also Thomson to NG, 15 October 1783, above.) NG's financial embarrassments were related to the debts he had guaranteed near the end of the war for John Banks et al. as army contractors. (See, for example, NG to Lee, 22 August 1785, above.)
3. On the rice that had been burned and "sunk," see also NG's letters to Ethan Clarke of 23 November 1785, above, and 6 April, below. NG similarly wrote Randall Son & Stewarts on 12 March, immediately below, that these losses from "the little crops I have made," together with the expenses of running the plantation, had left him with "little either for the support of my family or the payment of debts."
4. CG fell and went into premature labor in early April; the baby died soon afterward. (Stegeman, Caty, p. 121; see also NG to Clarke, 6 April, below.)
5. On the inoculation, see Brickell to NG, 29 March, below.
6. After several years of failing to adopt the federal impost proposal of 1783, the Georgia legislature approved most of that measure on 13 February 1786. (George R. Lamplugh, "Farewell to the Revolution: Georgia in 1785," Georgia Historical Quarterly 56 [1972]: 398–99)
7. By "stupid policy," NG presumably meant the failure to adopt a method for funding the federal debt.
8. The Marquis de Lafayette had proposed that NG send his son George Washington Greene to be educated in France. (Lafayette to NG, 12 June 1785, above)

Nathanael Greene Monument, Johnson Square, Savannah, Georgia
(*Reproduced from* The Remains of Major-General Nathanael Greene
[*Providence, R.I.: E. L. Freeman & Sons, 1903]*)

9. Knox wrote under the docketing of this letter: "This is the last letter I ever received from my truly beloved friend Gen[l] Greene."

To Randall Son & Stewarts

Gentlemen   Savannah River Mulberry Grove [Ga.] Mar. 12: 1786
    Your letter of the 7th Feb: is before me. It woud give me pleasure to take up my bond in your hands had I it in my power. At the time Mr Rapalje took it I told him the foundation & prospects I had of paying it & that if those failed I had no other certain resource.[1] My crops have failed & what adds to my misfortune I have lost ninety odd barrels of Rice by fire & Water this Season out of the little crops I have made.[2] These losses together with the plantation expences leave me little either for the support of my family or the payment of debts. Nothing woud give me greater pleasure [than] to comply with your wishes but the poverty of the Publick who owe me large sums & the scarcity of money will put it out of my power, until I can sell some of my landed property, or my plantations are more productive. And I have greater hopes this season than the last as I pay the most particular attention to the business myself. I beg my compliments to M[r] Randall and am Gentlemen Your most Obed[t] humble Serv[t3]   NATH GREENE

Cy (CtHi).
    1. For background, see Stephen Rapalje's letters to NG of 25 September and 27 October 1785, as well as Randall Son & Stewarts to NG, 7 February 1786, all above.
    2. On the losses of rice "by fire & Water," see also NG's letters to Ethan Clarke of 23 November 1785, above, and 6 April, below.
    3. No further correspondence between NG and Randall Son & Stewarts has been found.

*   *   *

¶ [TO RUSSELL, JENKINS & COMPANY.[1] From Savannah, Ga., 12 March 1786. NG asks them to pay "Mess[rs] Winthrop & Tod & Comp Nine pounds Sterling on sight" if they "are so much in cash from the Sales of Rice" sent to them "from the Plantation at Ponpon by M[r] Crosskies" [i.e., John Croskeys].[2] ALS (MiU-C) 1 p.]
    1. On this firm, see NG to Griffin Greene, 8 January, above.
    2. As seen in their letter to NG of 30 March, below, Winthrop, Tod & Winthrop was a Charleston, S.C., firm. As also seen there, Russell, Jenkins & Company declined to make this payment. "The Plantation at Ponpon" was Boone's Barony.

¶ [FROM THOMAS MORRIS, Charleston, S.C., 22 March 1786.[1] Introduces his brother, Benjamin Morris, who is visiting Georgia "with more thoughts of ultimately establishing Himself in the Commercial Line at Savannah." Thomas Morris knows of "no one in that Country" to whom he could better introduce his brother and "from whom he wou'd receive that candid information that He maybe wants." Hopes his brother will "always" prove "worthy" of NG's "countenance and civilities."[2] RCS (MiU-C) 1 p.]

1. Thomas Morris (d. 1829?), a Charleston merchant, was a son-in-law of Christopher Gadsden. (*Biog. Directory of S.C. House*, 4: 414–15)

2. It is not known whether Benjamin Morris established a business in Savannah.

¶ [FROM DOCTOR JOHN BRICKELL, 23 March 1786.[1] He has received a draft from Philadelphia for £22 to be paid to Mr. [Thomas] Cumming, who "will be satisfied" if NG "will give me an order upon him, as he owes you some money."[2] RCS (MiU-C) 1 p.]

1. Brickell was the Georgia physician who had recently inoculated members of NG's family. (See his letter to NG of 29 March, below.)

2. Brickell explained and apologized for this request in ibid.

*　　*　　*

From E. John Collett

Sir   Charleston [S.C.] 24 March 1786

I took the Liberty of addressing you on the 6th Instant p[er] post to Savannah, informing you of my arrival here, and begging to know what arrangements you are making in my favor, but I have hitherto not been honor'd with an answer.[1]

The anxiety of my Situation is Such as to induce me to trouble you again on the Business, & I dare flatter myself that on a personal interview Some mode may be adopted to ease your Situation, and relieve me, as I assure you I have no wish to add to your distresses by instituting a Suit, but on the Contrary have a Sincere inclination to give you every assistance in my power Compatible with my ultimate Safety.[2] I have the honor to be Sir Your mo obdᵗ hble Serᵗ   E. JNᵒ COLLETT

RCS (MiU-C).

1. Collett's letter of 6 March is above.

2. NG wrote to Collett on 24 March and 24 April, but the letters have not been found. (Collett to NG, 8 May, below) As noted at his letter to Collett of 8 August 1784, above, NG had just signed new bonds for Collett before he was taken fatally ill in mid-June 1786.

*　　*　　*

¶ [FROM ROBERT HAZLEHURST, Charleston, S.C., 25 March 1786. Acknowledges NG's letters of 8 and 14 March [not found] and sincerely feels "for your loss of the forty Five Barrels Rice at Savannah."[1] Adds: "Misfortune[s] really seem to attend you of late, but I flatter myself as you are now getting cleverly settled that there will be an end of them. I am sure no pains will be wanting on your side for that purpose both early & late, & whenever that is the case Fortune may be expected to smile, though she is a fickle Jade." He has delivered NG's "enclosures for the Gentlemen in this Town"[2] and has forwarded the one for Mr. [John] Croskeys [not found], writing him "at the same time that my opinion was he had best send the Rice as soon as convenient, for there is no prospect of it's advancing in Price. Whenever it comes the amount shall be appropriated as you desire, & whatever ballance remains in my hands afterwards, be subject to your orders. I am however of opinion it will be little or none if the quantity [of] Rice does not exceed Seventy Barrels."[3] Tells NG not to be concerned about a "Charge of Commission on any little matter of business which I transact for you"; NG is "extremely welcome to my trouble, at any rate untill you experience more favorable times." Hazlehurst will buy a good "Cellaret" if he finds one that is "cheap."[4] He is sending two barrels of flour, "the cost of which with Porterage &c, is £3.11/- to your debit. You have also a Hat, in a Box directed for you that came by M[r] Griffin Greene." Send his compliments to CG. RCS (MiU-C) 3 pp.]

1. On this loss, see also NG to Clarke, 6 April, below.

2. The enclosures probably included NG's letter to Russell, Jenkins & Company of 12 March, above. On the outcome of NG's request to that firm—and on Hazlehurst's involvement in the matter—see Winthrop, Tod & Winthrop to NG, 30 March, below.

3. On Croskeys and the rice from Boone's Barony plantation, see also Hazlehurst & Company's letters to NG of 16 January and 9 February, above, and 13 April, below. In the letter of 13 April, the firm reported that Croskeys had "only Forty Barrels upon hand instead of Seventy which you expected."

4. A cellarette is a sideboard with compartments, made to hold wine bottles. (*Webster's*)

¶ [FROM HARY GRANT, Charleston, S.C., 27 March 1786. "Few Men in this Country have felt more real Concern" for NG's "Loss" than Grant.[1] He will "allways feel Myself interested" and wishes NG good fortune. NG should have no "Uneasyness" over his "sm[al][l] debt with me."[2] He adds that it "affords me pleasure to serve You." RCS (MiU-C) 1 p.]

1. Grant may have referred here to NG's recent losses from his rice crop. (See NG to Clarke, 23 November 1785, above, and 6 April, below.)

2. Grant, a merchant, had supplied articles for NG's plantation. (See, for example, Grant to NG, 18 January, above.)

¶ [FROM DOCTOR JOHN BRICKELL, 29 March 1786. Encloses "the account," as NG's requested, and informs him that "People of fashion pay 5 guineas for inoculation: those whose circumstances are not elevated pay only 2."[1] Hopes the charges are "agreeable"; if not, "you may make any alterations you please." Adds: "The whole is such a trifle that I would rather loose it than give one moments dissatisfaction to General Greene." Had he not been "pushed for a remittance to be made to Philadelphia next Saturday," Brickell would not have "troubled the Gen[l] to settle it thro M[r] Cummins."[2] RCS (MiU-C) 1 p.]

1. Brickell was the physician who had recently inoculated NG's family. (See NG to Knox, 12 March, above.)

2. NG had an account with Thomas Cumming, a storekeeper in Savannah. (See Cumming to NG, 8 February, above.) On Brickell's request to recover the cost of NG's bill through Cumming, see Brickell to NG, 23 March, above. Another letter from Brickell is at the end of the March documents, below.

¶ [FROM WINTHROP, TOD & WINTHROP, Charleston, S.C., 30 March 1786. They wrote NG on the 28th that they had received "your Order on Mess[r] Russell & Jenkins in our favour for Nine pounds and that the Same was passed to the Credit of your Acco[t] with us."[1] However, they wrote this "in consequence of the application we made to those Gent[n] for the Money. Who assured us they would pay us the Amount in a few hours. And being persuaded from those Assurances we should receive it, we thought we could venture to write you they had paid us, but in a few hours after we Wrote you, we Called on them for the Money, and to our Surprise they replyed to us, that having looked into the State of your Acco[t] with them, They found no Ballance due you, and said it was inconven[ien]t to make any Advances for y[r] acco[t]." Winthrop, Tod & Winthrop next applied to Mr. [Robert] Hazlehurst [& Company], as NG directed, "but they could not make it Conven[ien]t to pay us. In this Situation the Matter Stands. You will therefore please to Observe that although we have given you a Receipt in full, yet we are Still without the Money."[2] RCS (MiU-C) 1 p.]

1. The letter referred to has not been found. For background, see NG to Russell, Jenkins & Company, 12 March, above.

2. Nothing more is known about this matter.

¶ [FROM DOCTOR JOHN BRICKELL, [March 1786].[1] Mr. [Thomas] Cumming has "an order on me for some rice." Asks if NG can "conveniently spare half a dozen barrels" and have them delivered to Cumming.[2] RCS (MiU-C) 1 p.]

1. The date was taken from the docketing.

2. On Brickell, Cumming, and NG, see also Brickell's letters to NG of 23 and 29 March, both above, and 11 April, below.

*   *   *

To Samuel Ward, Jr.

Dear Sir   Mulberry Grove [Ga.] April 4th 1786

I got your Letter from Virginia and the one you wrote me after your return home.[1] I thank you kindly for the Deed of relinquishment from Mr Henry Banks.[2] It will afford me the better opportunity of disposing of the Island to advantage; but I am so much prejudiced in favor of it, that I am determined to sell my property in South Carolinia and hold that[,] as few are sensible of its value.[3] M[r] Eustace who formerly had the vineyard in Virginia for making wine has lately been to Cumberland and says it is the first place upon the Continent which he has seen for raising Grapes for making wine and that he will undertake it on his own account if I will only grant him a few acres for tryal. It will be a most valuable property if it should be good for Wine independant of all the other staples.[4] How and where did you get the Idea of my having disengaged my self from my guarantee Bonds. I wish it was true but it is not. However the business is in a good train and I am under little apprehension of suffering. But it still hangs heavy upon my spirits as life and Lawsuits have uncertain issues.[5] Misfortunes have been hovering about me ever since my arrival. I had fifty barrels of Rice burnt soon after I came here and a little time ago I had forty five sunk and spoiled.[6] These two losses, the low price which Rice has sold for, and my Crops falling short more than one third in the first instance, has involved me in a disagreeable situation. And how to extricate my self I know not.[7]

Our situation here is pleasant and convenient. The house is large the

Garden extensive and elegant. The Trees shrubs and flowers are numerous and beautiful. There is a great variety of fruit Trees which add both to the pleasures of sight and taste. There are few situations to the Northward which have more natural beauties than this;[8] but I should value it more if I could spend the whole season on it. We go to Cumberland in July.[9] We are now engaged in planting and if no new misfortunes attack us we have a good prospect of a fine crop.

Mrs Greene got your letters and intended to answer them by this opportunity; but she fell down sprained her ancle and hurt her hip this Morning which will prevent her writing. This misfortune is the greater from her peculiar situation being under hourly apprehension of an event which her hopes and fears are constantly struggling with.[10] The Children have all had the smallpox by innoculation favorably, and the family are generally in good health.[11] The Children improve fast in reading and writing and you would be surprised to see the progress they have made in the grammer and Geography. Mr Miller is a great acquisition and I am not sorry Mr Dow disappointed me.[12] Remember us affectionately to the Governor and his Lady[,] Mrs Ward[,] Miss Celia and all the family.[13] Yours affectionately NATH GREENE

ALS (RHi).

1. Ward's letter of 11 November 1785 from Richmond, Va., is above; the one that he later wrote from Rhode Island has not been found.

2. On the deed of relinquishment from Henry Banks, see above, Ward to NG, 11 November 1785, and Banks to NG, 12 November 1785.

3. The "Island" was Cumberland Island, Ga. In the time before his death in June, NG does not appear to have made any further decision about either his holdings there or his South Carolina plantation, Boone's Barony.

4. Nothing more is known about Eustace and his idea for a vineyard on Cumberland Island.

5. E. John Collett, one of the holders of NG's "guarantee Bonds," was actively pursuing his claims against NG at this time. (See his letters to NG of 6 and 24 March, above.) It also appears that NG was hoping to disengage himself from at least part of this burden by means of a lawsuit in South Carolina. (Rutledge to NG, 1 March, above, and 20 May, below)

6. On these losses, see also NG's letters to Ethan Clarke of 23 November 1785, above, and 6 April, immediately below.

7. See Hazlehurst to NG, 25 March, above.

8. For more about the "natural beauties" of Mulberry Grove, see NG to Clarke, immediately below.

9. NG died in June, before he could make the trip to Cumberland Island.

10. On the outcome of the fall, see note at NG to Clarke, immediately below.

11. The children had been innoculated several weeks earlier. (NG to Knox, 12 March, and Brickell to NG, 29 March, both above)

12. On Phineas Miller, who had been hired as the Greene children's tutor, and Hendricus Dow, who had first accepted and then rejected the position, see especially NG to Wadsworth, 1 and 5 October 1785, and Dow to NG, 9 September 1785, all above.

13. Gov. William Greene's wife, Catharine Ray Greene, was CG's and Ward's aunt and

the mother of Ward's wife and first cousin, the former Phebe Greene. (See Vol. 1: 19n, above; *DAB*, 10: 437) Celia Greene was Phebe's sister. (Catharine Ray Greene to NG, 2 October 1785, above)

To Ethan Clarke

Dear Sir   Mulberry Grove [Ga.] April 6th 1786.
We got your and Mrs Clarkes letters about a fortnight since.[1] Mrs Greene sat down to give Mrs Clarkes an answer yesterday. After writing a few lines she had a call to the kitchen where she got a fall and sprained her ancle and hurt herself considerably. This accident will prevent her from finishing the letter.[2] It seemed to be a day of accidents. Mrs Davis's son got a kick from a horse soon after and had his upper lip cut through his jawbone from his nose downwards and the end of his nose split open.[3] This afforded me an opportunity of performing a capital piece of surgery by sewing it up. And I am in hopes it will not disfigure him greatly, but cannot pronounce positively it bled so freely as to render the operation difficult. Before we had got through this business, Patty fell down in a sort of fit, she had been running with Mr Miller after school and I fear over exercised.[4] It was a long time before we could recover her. Here we had a serious call for all our medical knowledge and I hardly know which is the greatest quack Mrs Greene or me. She [i.e., Patty] lay in a lifeless situation for two hours until I got a puke to operate which restored vital heat and activity to the circulating fluids. She seems to be pretty well over the matter this morning. Mrs Greene is confined to the bed or easy chair. The accident is the more unfortunate to her at this time from her peculiar situation. I wish the business was well over.[5] Had we Doctor Sentor at hand I should feel little anxiety.[6] The accidents of yesterday made me think of Job[']s Messengers. The family all well at noon and in the evening one half of it laid by the heels. However I am in hopes they will all soon be about again. Accidents and misfortunes are busy with us in almost every quarter. Just after my arrival here I had fifty barrels of rice burnt and a little time ago I had forty five sunk & spoiled which was sent to market.[7] And Capt Littlefield writes me the sloop *Charleston Paquet* is seized, sold, and the house that chartered her broke.[8] Here is a catalogue of misfortunes sufficient for the tryal of Jobs patience and Peters faith.[9]

This is a busy time with us, and I can afford but a small portion of time to write. We are planting. We have got upwards of sixty acres of corn planted and expect to plant 130 of rice. The garden is delightful. The fruit trees and flowering shrubs forms a pleasing variety. We have green peas almost fit to eat and as fine Lettice as you ever saw. The mocking birds serenades us evening and morning. The weather is mild and the vegitable Kingdom progressing to perfection. But it is a great deduction from the pleasures we should feel from the beauties and conveniences of the place that we are obliged to leave it before we shall have tasted of several kinds of fruit.[10] We have in the same orchard apples, pears, peaches, & apricots, nectarines, plumbs of different kinds, figs, pomegranates and oranges. And we have strawberries which measure three inches round. All these are cleaver, but the want of our friends to enjoy them with us renders them less interesting. Mrs Greene and all the children desire their affectionate compliments to you[,] Mrs Clarke[,] Polly & all the family.[11]

N. GREENE

Tr (GWG Transcript: CSmH).

1. Neither letter has been found. On Anna Ward Clarke, see note at Clarke to NG, 15 March 1785, above.

2. NG wrote Samuel Ward, Jr., on 4 April, immediately above, that CG hurt herself "this morning."

3. Mrs. Davis was the Greenes' housekeeper. (NG to Clarke, 23 November 1785, above)

4. Martha ("Patty") Greene was NG's eldest daughter, then nine years old. Phineas Miller was the children's tutor. Nothing more is known about this incident.

5. As a result of her fall, CG went into premature labor; the baby lived only a short while. (Stegeman, *Caty*, p. 121)

6. Dr. Isaac Senter of Newport, R.I., had been the Greene family physician. (See NG to Howson, Edwards & Company, 6 August 1784, above.)

7. On these incidents, see also NG to Clarke, 23 November 1785, and NG to Knox, 12 March, above.

8. See Littlefield to NG, 16 December 1785, above.

9. In the Bible, Job is remarkable for his patience, while Jesus's disciple Peter is renowned for his faith.

10. NG and his family were planning to leave for Cumberland Island in July. (NG to Ward, immediately above)

11. "Polly" was probably Clarke's six-year-old daughter, Anna Maria, who later married NG's son Nathanael Ray Greene. (See note at Clarke to NG, 15 March 1785.)

To Jeremiah Wadsworth

My dear Sir   Mulberry Grove [Ga.] April 6th 1786

I have been here near six Months and not a line from you.[1] Did I not hear of your being in health I should tremble for your safety. We talk and think of you often; but we almost begin to think without any retur[n]. It would mortify us to discover this to be the case; and if it is true in mercy to our feelings I hope you will keep it a secret. Mrs Greene would become a perfect misanthrope. If it was not for you and a few More she says, she should be almost ready to conclude that there was neither Merit or virtue in human Nature.[2] We live here in perfect retirement; but we are not free from misfortunes. Since I have been here, I have had two heavy losses. At one time I lost 50 barrels of Rice and at another 45. The first by fire, the last by water.[3] Fortune seems to lour upon me in what ever direction I move. It is said to be a long lane that has no turn. I should be happy to see a turn to this tide of misfortunes.

Mrs Greene expects to lay in every hour or she would write you; but she desires to be affectionately remembered to you.[4] Have you done any thing with my Jers[e]y plantation or the North River Lands. I wish them sold as early as you can get a good price for them either in cash or good security which I can exchange for my own.[5] Be so good as to let me hear from you.[6] Give my compliments to all your family and to Mr Trumbull. With esteem & affection I am dear Sir Your Most Obed humble Ser

NATH GREENE

ALS (Thomas Enoch Greene, 1993).

1. Wadsworth wrote NG on 8 April, below: "I have none of your favors since You left New Port," R.I.

2. CG, who had a close relationship with Wadsworth, had hoped for a visit from him before the Greenes left Newport the previous October. (See for example, NG to Wadsworth, 7 September 1785, above.)

3. On these incidents, see NG to Clarke, 23 November 1785, and NG to Knox, 12 March, both above.

4. Because of a recent fall, CG lost the child she had been expecting. (See note at NG to Clarke, 6 April, above.)

5. In powers of attorney dated 26 March 1785, 16 August 1785, and 12 October 1785, all above, NG had authorized Wadsworth to sell the lands he owned in New Jersey and near the Hudson River in New York. (On these properties, see also Estimate of NG's Estate, before 9 January 1784, above.) Wadsworth discussed the situation in his letter to NG of 8 April.

6. See ibid.

*   *   *

¶ [FROM THOMAS CUMMING, Savannah, Ga., 7 April 1786. He is unable to "get a piece of better Ozbgs" than the one "returned" and has sent it back. "Dowlas⁵" are "so extravagantly dear" that he only sent one piece.[1] Nor is he able to "send the Biscuit" for CG, but he has asked the "Baker to have a Keg ready to day," and it will be "sent up to morrow" by boat; there is "none to be had imported from the northward," and "those made here are nearly as good." In a postscript, Cumming notes a total bill of £2.9.2 for "Dowlas" and "2 bushels Allumsalt." RCS (MiU-C) 1 p.]

1. "Ozbgs" was presumably osnaburg, "a rough, coarse durable cotton fabric in plain weave made originally of flax and used in the gray [i.e., unbleached and undyed] for bagging," among other purposes; dowlas was a "coarse linen cloth." (*Webster's*)

*   *   *

From Catherine McLean[1]

Dear Sir   Retreat [Ga.] Thursday Night [before 7 April 1786?][2]

Your Freindly Letter handed me this Morning by Mr Millar (and for which I shall be ever gratefull) wou'd have been immediately answer'd but Company presend [i.e., present?], and the harey [i.e., hurry] and Bustle we are involv'd in, confuse my Ideas in such a manner, that I cannot now do it properly.[3]

The hint drop'd by you, Sir, was not unthought of by me. Dear bought and too fatal experience, long since convenc'd me of the unhappy truth of your too just Observation. From hence arose the Liberty I had before taken of having your Name inscribed in a power of Attorney with Major Cuthbert, Major Douglass and Mr Cole.[4] The first is a Gentleman of a fair Character, universally Esteem'd perfectly conversant in all matters of Business, and possesses a thorough Knowledge of the World, and Mankind in general. Of consequence in this State from his early exertions and steady attachment to the American Cause and from the public Offices he has fill'd with Honour.

Some twelve Months before M^r McLeans Death he wrote to his Freind and Correspondant Mr Jackson in London to engage some person to come to America, to assist him in settling his Affairs. One capable of manageing a most intricate, and long standing Business, and worthy of an implicit confidence, with whom he cou'd Live as a freind, as a Gentleman perfectly answering this description, he recommended Mr Cole who had received a Liberal Education, was Genteelly brought up, in the very Lap of Affluence, but by a Variety of accidents In which those in Business are ever liable, and which no human foresight cou'd prevent, He failed. From an innate principle of Honor he gave up his last Shillings to satisfy his just[?] Debts, Discharg'd them to a fraction and accepted Mr Jackson's offer. From those reasons I was induc'd to place the Management of my Affairs in his Hands. Hitherto Malice itself cou'd not impeach his conduct to an indefatigable industry he unites every possible disposition to oblige. He receives a Salary for transacting the Business, therefore he is in Duty, and I verily beleive, in inclination bound to do every thing for my Interest. Since he became resident in this Country, he has acquir'd the Esteem and Freindship of the best people in the State and thro' them, and his own Industry, he has plac'd himself in a road, by which I apprehend he will make himself a Competencys. He is now in Savannah and it wou'd have been a pleasing circumstance cou'd I have had the Opportunity before I depart, to introduce him to your knowledge, he has very particuarly expresd such a desire, from the Patronage and advice in those Affairs of mine which you may render him, shall I, Sir, remark to him, that it wou'd be well to call on you in his way to Augusta for which place he will proceed immediately after our departure. He is so well acquainted with the Business of this Estate, and can be so punctually servicable therein, that I have been more particular respecting him than the other Gentlemen. The Books, papers, Negroes, and Indigo Plantation &^ca are (by a power give him from Mr Clark, and myself some time ago) are in his possession and care. His attention thereto, will prevent your having any other trouble than may be necessary to know, that he pursues the most Judicious modes throughout those transactions. Give me leave, Sir to recommend him particularly to your Esteem, and I have the firmest belief he will evinc[e] a Worthyness of any Freindship bestow'd on him.[5]

M[r] Douglass for many years made a part of my Family, was brought up under M[r] M[c]Lean between them subsisted an entire Freindship and unlimited confidence. Such a one, as induc'd him with his last Breath, to recommend to M[r] Douglasses care and protection, his Widow, and Orphans which trust was in like Solemn manner accepted by him as yet the confidence has not been abus'd. Neither have I the smallest reason to think his Attachment ended with the Life of his Freind.

Those, Sir, are my reasons for placing the trust as I have done. I trust you will think them substantial ones. I can only add, if I am deceiv'd (which Heaven avert) that confidence is not to be plac'd in Man, and that Heaven form'd the whole World alike treacherous, and Faithless.

I am conscious that I ought first to have ask'd your permission, for the liberty I have taken, but convinc'd of your universally acknowledg'd Benevolence I was without a doubt but you wou'd forgive the freedom, and accept the trust for one *almost* Freindless, who entreats your protection under a thorough conviction, that proberty and Goodness never made vain offers of Freindship and that the large probity I leave cannot be misapplied under your Direction.

To M[rs] Greene, my Mother begs may be presented her affectionate Comp[ts] in which I most heartily join. May Heaven which ever gaurds [guards] the Good, have her in it's Holy Keeping; at all times particularly in her approaching hour of tribulation. Shall I presume so far on your Freindship as to conclude without one word of Apology, for trespassing so far on your Patience. Yes I will for to lengthen my Letter wou'd be to transgress in the very point for which I beg your forgiveness.[6] I therefore remain with every Sentiment of Respect and Esteem, Dear Sir, your most Oblig'd and mo. Obed[t] Serv[t] CATHERINE MCLEAN

RCS (MiU-C).

1. The writer was presumably the widow of Andrew McLean, who had owned estates along the Savannah River, including "Retreat," the plantation from which this letter was written. (Granger, *Savannah River Plantations*, pp. 406, 407)

2. McLean's reference in this letter to CG's "approaching hour of tribulation" suggests that the Thursday on which she wrote it may have been no later than 6 April. (See above NG to Ward, 4 April, and NG's letters of 6 April to Ethan Clarke and Jeremiah Wadsworth.)

3. NG's letter to McLean, which has not been found, may have been delivered by Phineas Miller, the Greene children's tutor.

4. Nothing is known about the power of attorney. Cuthbert was probably Maj. Alexander Cuthbert, who had served in Georgia Continental units. (Washington, *Papers,* Confederation Series, 1: 295n) In the next paragraph, McLean identified Cole, whose first name is not known, as an Englishman, hired by Andrew McLean to "assist him in settling his Affairs." Later in this letter, she also mentioned that her late husband had "brought up Douglass" and made him "a part of my Family." This person may have

been a son of Samuel Douglas, a Loyalist whose plantation, Blendon Hall, had been confiscated by the state and purchased by Andrew McLean. (Granger, *Savannah River Plantations*, p. 406)

5. The indigo plantation may have been the former Douglas property, Blendon Hall, where indigo was grown as an "agricultural experimentation." (Ibid.) Clark has not been identified, nor is it known if NG had any contact with Cole.

6. The editors chose to print this letter because it suggests some aspects of NG's brief life in Georgia that are not apparent in most of his other correspondence during this time. This is the only letter between McLean and NG that has been found.

From Jeremiah Wadsworth

My dear Sir   Hartford [Conn.] April 8 1786
    I have none of your favors since You left New Port.[1] In my last I advised you that their was no prospect of Sellling your Lands in the state of New York. This was in Jan[y] soon after which M[r] Cockburn who surveyed 2 Acres near it found a purchacer for a Small part of it the particulars of which Col [Charles] Pettit then at New York was to write you.[2] Yesterday I agreed with a Jonathan Smith of Hadam [i.e., Haddam, Conn.] to go to view the Small tract & if he likes it I am to procure him a deed from the other owners, but of a dozen who have been to view all have found other Lands in that Country more to their mind or have found such long credit from others as I coud not give. This circumstanc[e] forbids my being Sanguine that I shall sell. M[r] Cockburn gave hopes of finding purchasers when I was in New York in Febru[y] but I have heared nothing from him since. I do not know any thing about your Jersey Estate. Is their any body in possession, any rent to pay, who has the care of it, am I to look after it.[3]
    The letter herewith sent you came under Cover by the last post from New York the date of my letter from hear Dec[r] 7th.[4] I have better health than when you left this Country, but my old complaints hang on me.[5] Every thing federal has been neglected in this Country till the last of Winter their Seems now to be some hopes of a general impost & some System.[6] But the paper Money Spirit is growing fast & the desperation to pay of[f] all debts without mony is unn[e]cessary. Parsons has just returned from the Westward and is so charmed with that Country that he will I believe go their & carry with him many good inhabitants. I am anxious to hear from you & to know what you are doing, and how the Climatte suits you M[rs] Greene and the Children, to whom present my love. M[rs] [Mehitable Russell] Wadsworth & the Children join in every good wish.
    BD & C[o] [i.e., Barnabas Deane & Company] have met with loss of two thousand dollars by a Brigs geting in Saybrook Barr otherwise their affairs have been moderately prosperous.[7] I am dear sir very affectionately Yours   J WADSWORTH

RCS (MiU-C).

1. NG made a similar complaint in his letter to Wadsworth of 6 April, above.

2. NG had authorized Wadsworth to sell the lands he owned in New Jersey and near the Hudson River in New York in powers of attorney dated 26 March 1785, 16 August 1785, and 12 October 1785, all above. (On these properties, see also Estimate of NG's Estate, before 9 January 1784, above.) Wadsworth's January letter to NG has not been found. Nor is there any mention of this matter in the last two letters from Charles Pettit to NG that have been found. (Both letters are above, dated 20 January.)

3. No further correspondence between NG and Wadsworth has been found.

4. Neither letter has been found.

5. On Wadsworth's "old complaints," see, for example, his letter to NG of 11 September 1785, above.

6. As noted at Weedon to NG, 2 December 1783, above, the federal impost proposal of 1783 was never implemented.

7. Saybrook Bar is at the mouth of the Connecticut River.

*   *   *

¶ [FROM JAMES MILLER, Charleston, S.C., 10 April 1786.[1] Has NG's letter of 16 March [not found] and is "sorry" he cannot "comply with your terms relative to the wine you ordered." Miller does not "give a Credit in our own State" and is "determined to hold my property untill it will command Cash." RCS (MiU-C) 1 p.]

1. Miller was one of the British merchants who had petitioned to remain in Charleston after the war. (Rogers, *Evolution of a Federalist*, p. 100; S.C., House of Representatives, *Journals, 1783–84*, p. 187)

¶ [FROM DOCTOR JOHN BRICKELL, 11 April 1786. Is "obliged" to NG for the "order on M[r] [Thomas] Cumming"; will be "satisfied with whatever you will be pleased to allow."[1] RCS (MiU-C) 1 p.]

1. For background, see Brickell's letters to NG of 23 and 29 March and at the end of the March documents, all above.

¶ [FROM ROBERT HAZLEHURST & COMPANY, Charleston. S.C., 13 April 1786. They have not heard from NG since writing to him on 25 March. The present letter "serves to cover" one [not found] that they "receiv'd the day before yesterday from our mutual friend M[r] R[obert]: Morris."[1] NG has also received a copy [not found] of a letter from Mr. [John] Croskeys to Hazlehurst & Company, informing them that "he has only forty Barrels" of rice "upon hand instead of Seventy which you expected."[2] As this quantity is "so much less," NG must give "further instructions in regard to the proportion of payments you order'd us to make from your calculation on Seventy Barrels."[3] There is "nothing material at present here in respect to News." RCS (MiU-C) 2 pp.]

1. The letter from Morris has not been found.

2. For more about this matter, see Hazlehurst to NG, 25 March, above, and Hazlehurst & Company to NG, 20 May, below.

3. Hazlehurst & Company discussed NG's "instructions," which have not been found, in their letter to him of 20 May.

¶ [FROM THE CHEVALIER DE LA FORESTE, New York, 16 April 1786. Encloses "a letter from the Minister of the navy department," in answer to NG's of the previous November.[1] RCS (MiU-C) 1 p.]

1. See the Marquis de Castries's letter to NG of 22 January, above.

*   *   *

To Governor Edward Telfair of Georgia

Sir   Mulberry Grove Savannah River [Ga.] April 16ᵗʰ 1786

I have this moment got George Hanley Esquires letter enclosing me two orders of Council, one suspending the former assistant Judges of this County and the second appointing others in their places. I take the earliest opportunity of acquainting your Excellency that my own private affairs claim too great a proportion of my time to embark in any public business. You will therefore please to appoint some other person in my room and receive my acknowledgements for the honor done me.[1] I have the honor to be with great respect Your Excellency's most Obedᵗ Humble Serᵗ   NATH GREENE

LS (NcD).

1. The letter from Hanley, the secretary of the Georgia Executive Council, has not been found. Historian George Lamplugh has written that "animosity between tidewater and piedmont" in Georgia "came to a head in 1785–86," especially after the legislature voted in early 1786 to "remove the capital temporarily" from Savannah to Augusta. On 21 February, "ten local magistrates let themselves into the Savannah office of Secretary of State John Milton to search for local records, which they intended to retain in Chatham County." They "removed several books of conveyances, mortgages, deeds, grants, and wills and turned them over to the clerk of the county court." On 17 March, "the Council appointed three new assistant justices for Chatham, ordered them to demand the return of the records and delegated three upcountry lawyers" to "assist in this task." According to Lamplugh, this "strategy came a cropper" in April, "when the newly appointed Chatham justices resigned their commissions." (Lamplugh, *Politics on the Periphery,* pp. 51–52; see also "A Neglected Period of Georgia History," *Georgia Historical Quarterly* 2 [1918]: 201–24, and NG's letter to the Georgia Executive Council, immediately below.)

*   *   *

¶ [TO THE GEORGIA EXECUTIVE COUNCIL. From Mulberry Grove, Ga., 16 April 1786. In a letter similar to the one immediately above, NG declines an appointment to a judgeship because "it is totally incompatible with my situation in life to hold any public offices." ALS (MiU-C) 1 p.]

¶ [FROM DOCTOR JOHN IRVINE, Savannah, Ga., 20 April 1786.[1] He sends "herewith a phial of an Antispasmodic Julep" for CG. If her complaints return, "a small tablespoonfull" should be given "every other hour, or oftner as the Urgency may require." As he "would not wish by any means to nauseate her Stomach wᵗ Medicine, which at best is unpleasant," he has also sent "a box of Venice Treacle, let a fourth part of the Quantity sent be spread on a bit of Coarse linnen, & applied to the Region of the Navel, if the Complaint recurs wᵗ severity; which I sincerely hope will not happen."[2] RCS (CtY) 1 p.]

1. Irvine (d. 1809), a Scot, had established a practice in Georgia before the war. A Loyalist, he went to England during the conflict but returned to Georgia afterward and became one of the founders of the Georgia Medical Society. (Jones, *History of Savannah,* p. 437)

2. As seen in NG's letter to Samuel Ward, Jr., of 4 April, above, CG, who was near term in her pregnancy, had taken a bad fall. As noted at ibid., she went into premature labor, and the baby did not survive. It is not known if Irvine was prescribing therapies to try to alleviate postpartum symptoms.

¶ [FROM J. COLE MOUNTFLORENCE, Charleston, S.C., 23 April 1786.[1] He has "Kept the inclosed Letter till now, hoping to deliver it to" NG, who, he was led to believe, "would be here from Week to Week." As he is "returning to Halifax," N.C., soon, and as Col. [William R.] Davie asked him "to procure him an Answer,"[2] Mountflorence will "wait the Return of the Post from Savannah," Ga., in order to carry NG's letter to Davie. If NG has "any Commands for N° Carolina or Virginia," Mountflorence would be "happy" to "convey them."[3] RCS (MiU-C) 1 p.]

1. On Mountflorence, a North Carolinian, see above, vol. 9: 365n.

2. The enclosure, which has not been found, may have been a follow-up to Davie's letter to NG of 5 December 1785, above, asking for a certificate in regard to his service with the Southern Army.

3. No reply to Mountflorence or Davie has been found.

*   *   *

To Charles Thomson, Secretary of the Continental Congress

Dear Sir   Savannah River Mulberry Grove [Ga.] April 24th 1786

Your Letter with that of M[r] Browns was handed me a few days since. I live so retired that letters are often a long time coming to hand.[1] I will thank you to forward the letter to M[r] Brown which accompanies this; and I wish you to forward the Prints to me.[2]

I hope the Politicks of this State will please you better than they have done. The people begin to [be] more enlightened, and a more liberal policy to prevail. All the recommendations of Congress were adopted at the Meeting of the last Assembly excepting that respecting Trade and at the next Meeting in July I have no doubt of thats being adopted.[3] This State has been of little importance to the Union but its great increase of trade and population will soon place it among the first in the Confederation. If you can keep the Ship a float a few Years the Navigation will be less difficult. Many matters in Europe are a little alarming; but I hope they will all blow over.[4] I am dear Sir with esteem Your Most Obedient humble Servant   NATH GREENE

ALS (DLC).

1. See Thomson to NG, 2 December 1785, above.

2. NG's letter to Joseph Brown has not been found. (See, however, Brown to NG, 12 September 1785, above.) Thomson replied to NG on 5 June, below.

3. On Georgia and the federal impost proposal of 1783, see note at NG to Knox, 12 March, above.

4. NG may have been referring here to news such as Robert Morris had conveyed in his letter of 28 January, above.

*   *   *

¶ [FROM THOMAS CUMMING, Savannah, Ga., 24 April 1786. Has NG's letter of 22 April [not found]. As it would be "very expensive" to buy "new Sails for your Boat," Cumming has arranged with a sailmaker in Savannah to make a mainsail, foresail, and jib "out of old Ship Sails." This "will not cost more than one fourth what a new suit would"; NG should "send the Boat down and have the sails exactly fitted to her." A Mr. [Estane?] can advise as to "the best mode of getting the sails rigged, whether at home or in Savannah."[1] Cumming is "just setting out for Charleston," S.C., and will "take care to Execute" NG's "mem° for the fishing Seine." He will return in ten days. "Cast Nets" can be had "in town" at "seven Dollars each."[2] In an afternote, Cumming writes that NG's order for £6.7.3 in favor of "Mr Rogers" has been paid. RCS (MiU-C) 2 pp.]

1. In a letter of 24 May, below, Cumming referred to NG's "boat" as a "pettiauger." A petty auger was an "open flat-bottomed boat, generally two masted, carrying some thirty tons." (Vol. 3: xxxvii, above) On "[Estane?]," see also Cumming to NG, 27 May, below.

2. On the subject matter of this letter, see also Cumming to NG, 10, 15, and 24 May, all below.

¶ [FROM CHARLES DUPONT, 2 May 1786.[1] If NG will "send some person who may approve of such Cows" as Dupont has to sell, he "may have them on the terms" he mentioned, "but for Cash."[2] Asks if NG has written "for the young Collegian," and when "I may expect his arrival."[3] RCS (MiU-C) 1 p.]

1. Dupont, who lived in the Beaufort District of South Carolina and owned land elsewhere, served in the South Carolina legislature during and just after the war and also held local posts during the postwar period. (*Biog. Directory of S.C. House*, 3: 204–5)

2. See Dupont to NG, 3 June, below.

3. Nothing is known about this reference.

¶ [FROM THOMAS WASHINGTON, Greenwich, Ga., 5 May 1786.[1] He arrived there the previous day from "Carolina" but was not able to call on NG on his way. Encloses "Du Ponts letter."[2] Could not "get any Sheep." Hopes CG has gotten "better than when I was at Yr House."[3] Plans to call on NG "in a few days," but if NG should "Come down Sooner," Washington would "be hope[ful] to see" him. Washington has been told that Mr. Collett "is Com[in]g Round," perhaps "on business" with NG.[4] RCS (MiU-C) 2 pp.]

1. Greenwich was a Savannah River plantation near "the Hermitage," a confiscated estate that Washington had purchased in 1783. (Granger, *Savannah River Plantations*, pp. 428, 429)

2. See Charles Dupont to NG, immediately above.

3. On CG's recent health problems, see note at NG to Ward, 4 April, above. She did not recover immediately. (Stegeman, *Caty*, pp. 121–22)

4. See E. John Collett's letters to NG of 8 and 10 May, both below.

¶ [FROM DAVID MONTAIGUT, Savannah, Ga., 6 May 1786.[1] At NG's request, he sends translations of letters from Joseph del Pozo y Sucre to the governor of East Florida and to Samuel Elbert, "then" the governor of Georgia.[2] After NG has "perused and considered" these letters, Montaigut would "be glad to have them returned at your Conveniency." He also encloses a translation of Pozo's letter to NG, which accompanied the two others,[3] "the whole of which will give you a proper State of the matter." Sends his "best Respects to you and your Good Family." RCS (MiU-C) 1 p.]

1. Montaigut has not been identified.

2. Montaigut's translations of the letters to Vicente Manuel de Zéspedes, the governor of East Florida, and to Elbert have not been found. (Elbert was governor from January

1785 to January 1786.) The originals, in Spanish, are at MiU-C. (Pozo to Zéspedes, 22 June 1785, and Pozo to Elbert, 23 June 1785)

3. See Pozo to NG, 24 June 1785, above.

*   *   *

To Joseph del Pozo y Sucre

Sir   [Mulberry Grove, Ga., after 6 May 1786][1]
Your letter of the 24th of June dated on board the brigantine *Jesus Maria* was handed me in December last some little time after my arrival in this Country.[2] Not understanding the Spannish language it was a long time before I could get it interpreted.[3] I am no less grievd than Mortified at the outrage committed upon you in this State under an appearance of Law. The polite attention paid me at Augustine renders the contrast the more painful.[4] Individuals in free Governments have it but too much in their power sometimes to insult strangers under the sanction of Authority, which may be easily prevented under Governments where power is less in the hands of the people. It is much to be lamented that Political freedom gives a latitude which may invade the laws of hospitality and rules of good breeding. But I hope you will not hastily form the character of these States from the low Artifice and Maleovolence of a few. Nor can I persuade myself that an incident which originated in Avarice and was reprobated by the better order of people can ever influence the conduct of your Nation to treat with coolness those who have never offended and who entertain the highest sentiments of respect and esteem for them [*draft left unfinished*][5]

ADf (MiU-C).
1. The tentative date was determined from the contents and from Montaigut to NG, immediately above.
2. Pozo's letter of 24 June 1785 is above.
3. By "interpreted," NG meant "translated." (See ibid.)
4. On NG's visit to St. Augustine, East Florida, see his letter to CG of 14 April 1785, above.
5. A note on the draft in Phineas Miller's hand reads: "Part of a letter intended for an answer to that of Mr Joseph del Pozo y Sucre 1785."

From E. John Collett

Sir   Savannah [Ga.] 8th May 1786
A few days Since, I Was favor'd with both your Letters of ye 24 March & 24th April addressed to me in Charleston;[1] I am very Sensible Sir of the disagreeable Situation in which you are placed, & I assure you it is by no means my intention to add to your difficultys. On the Contrary it would give me the most Sincere pleasure to Congratulate you on a perfect deliverance from your Engagements on Banks's Account.[2] In order to

Effect So desirable an object, I will Consent to Extend to you any indulgence you can wish to ask, Consistent with my ultimate Safety.[3]

I am now in Savannah, where I Shall wait your answer, & will do myself the honor to attend any personal interview you will please appoint.[4] I am with Respect Sir Your most hble Sert   E. JN° COLLETT

RCS (MiU-C).

1. NG's letters have not been found. Collett had written to him from Charleston, S.C., on 6 and 24 March, both above.

2. On the guarantees that NG had provided for Collett on behalf of John Banks and others, see especially Agreement between Hunter, Banks and Company and NG with Newcomen and Collett, 8 April 1783 (vol. 12: 591 and n), the notes at NG to Collett, 8 August 1784, and NG to Lee, 22 August 1785, all above.)

3. As noted at ibid., NG signed new bonds for Collett just before he was taken fatally ill in mid-June.

4. Collett wrote NG again on 10 May, immediately below.

From E. John Collett

Sir   Savannah [Ga.] Wednesday Ev^g 10th May [17]86

I took the Liberty of addressing you on Monday last, informing you of my arrival here, & requesting you would be pleased to acquaint me when it would be Convenient to you to appoint a personal Interview.[1] But I rather apprehend my Letter miscarried, as the messenger by whom I forwarded it, returned again to Town, saying he had met one of your Servants on the Road and delivered it to him.

This Circumstance, and my not hearing from you, Occasions me to trouble you again, to request you will let me know when it [would?] be agreeable to you for us to meet.[2] I am with great respect Sir Your mo: hble Ser^t E. JN° COLLETT

RCS (MiU-C).

1. See Collett to NG, 8 May, immediately above.

2. NG apparently had a meeting with Collett shortly before writing Anthony Wayne on 14 May, below, that he had received "a summons of a serious and important nature to meet a Gentleman at Savannah to settle some affairs which for several years past has given me much pain and anxiety." (On the guarantees that NG had provided for Collett on behalf of John Banks and others, see especially Agreement between Hunter, Banks and Company and NG with Newcomen and Collett, 8 April 1783 [vol. 12: 591 and n], the notes at NG to Collett, 8 August 1784, and NG to Lee, 22 August 1785, all above.)

*   *   *

¶ [FROM THOMAS CUMMING, Savannah, Ga., 10 May 1786. Encloses "several Letters" that were delivered to him in Charleston, S.C. Cumming obtained a "Fishing Seine" for NG "with a great deal of difficulty" while he was there; it is "35 fathom in length" and should arrive in Savannah "in 2 or 3 days."[1] He found that "the late paper Emission is circulating in So Carolina, with great reputation"; believes, "from the unanimous determinations of the People," that "the

Credit of it will be well supported." This money is "rec^d equal to Gold and Silver in all payments, as well for Produce as in payment of Debts &c."² RCS (MiU-C) 2 pp.]

1. See also Cumming's letters to NG, 24 April, above, and 15 and 24 May, both below.

2. On the "late paper Emission" in South Carolina, see note at Morris to NG, 20 August 1785, above.

*   *   *

To General Anthony Wayne

Dear Sir   Mulberry Grove [Ga.] Sunday Morning [14 May 1786]¹
After we parted the other Evening I had a summons of a serious and important nature to meet a Gentleman at Savannah to settle some affairs which for several years past has given me much pain and anxiety.² Mrs Greene was desirous of taking a ride and went with me. I was so engaged in looking up Papers to make out an arrangement to close the business that I was going upon,³ that I entirely forgot to Mention to Mrs Greene that you was engaged to dine here that day. Nor did it occur to me That I ought to send you an apology until I had got a mile from home.⁴ I should have come back if I had been alone; but Mrs Greenes weak state was hardly equal to the fatigues of the Journey without returning.⁵ This determined me to go on and to trust to your good nature to excuse it. And as I knew it would make Mrs Greene very uneasy if she knew it I did not tell her of the engagement until we got home which was last Evening. She joins me in soliciting your company to spend the day with us that we may make some atonement for the disappointment which my negligence occasioned.⁶ I am dear Sir with esteem & affet Your Most O[bd^t] humble Ser   NATH GREENE

ALS (PHi).

1. The date was determined from the contents. The Sunday after NG received the "summons of a serious" nature that he referred to here (E. John Collett's letter of 10 May, above) was 14 May.

2. See ibid.

3. On "the business" referred to here, see especially Agreement between Hunter, Banks and Company and NG with Newcomen and Collett, 8 April 1783 (vol. 12: 591 and n), the notes at NG to Collett, 8 August 1784, and NG to Lee, 22 August 1785, all above.

4. Wayne had recently returned from Pennsylvania to his Savannah River plantation, Richmond. (Nelson, *Wayne*, p. 204; see also Pettit to NG, second letter of 20 January, above.)

5. CG had recently given birth to a child who did not survive. (See note at NG to Clarke, 6 April, above.)

6. Wayne's reply has not been found.

*   *   *

¶ [FROM THOMAS CUMMING, Savannah, Ga., 15 May 1786. He is "sorry" but cannot give "any positive assurance of paying" NG's debt of £30 to Mrs.

[Anne Zubly] Bard. Thinks NG's "Bill on Charleston" could be "easily negoci- ated," and if NG can "draw for the amount," Cumming will "chearfully En- deavour to obtain the money for it, so as to answer Mrs Bards purpose"; she will not leave Savannah until the 25th.[1] Cumming ordinarily would "chearfully advance you that or any other sum," but "Cash is so very scarce," and his own "Necessities so pressing," that it is impossible for him to do so. If he "had the Money, it wou'd be of no Consequence whether you owed me or not; as I should be at all times happy to serve you."[2] The bearer of this letter will deliver the "Fishing Seine"; the "Net is not quite finished" but "can be had any time after to morrow."[3] RCS (MiU-C) 2 pp.]

　　1. On Mrs. Bard, see note at Pendleton to NG, 23 September 1785, above. The nature of this debt is not known. (See, however, Peter Bard to NG, 9 March 1785, above.) As seen in Cumming's letter of 24 May, below, NG made arrangements for payment.

　　2. NG undoubtedly owed cash, or rice in lieu of cash, for items that Cumming had supplied to him in recent months. (See, for example, Cumming to NG, 8 February, above.) In a letter of 9 June, below, Cumming wrote that NG's "Account Current" was about £28 sterling, which would be "carried to your debt in new account."

　　3. On the "Fishing Seine" and net, see also Cumming to NG, 24 April and 10 May, above, and 24 May, below.

¶ [FROM WILLIAM LITTLEFIELD, Newport, R.I., 15 May 1786. He received the enclosed letter from Mr. Maxwell and is "at a loss how to Act in the matter. Have call'd on Mr Gibbs and he informs me that your orders to him was to deliver the boy one Suit of Cloaths and no more which he did imedeately." If NG is "to maintain the Boy," Littlefield believes he could do so for less expense "at your own House" than at Newport.[1] Maxwell "is very needy & the family has Subsisted for several months very much upon Charity."[2] Littlefield asks to be remembered "affectionately to Mrs G. and all the Children." RCS (CtY) 1 p.]

　　1. On Adam Maxwell, who had once been NG's tutor, see above, vol. 1: 14n. In the enclosed letter, dated 15 May, Maxwell wrote Littlefield that before NG left Newport, he "adopted" Maxwell's son "as one of his family & to be supported at his expence." According to Maxwell, NG left "Verbal orders with George Gibbs to supply and deliver such necessary clothing for the Boy untill he sent for him to Georgia in the spring." Maxwell added that NG had agreed to pay board for the child, who was also now in need of such articles of clothing as "a pair of Breeches & 2 pair of Overalls for summer, one pair Shoes & 2 pairs Summer Stockings." Maxwell asked Littlefield to go with his son to "Mr Gibb's Store" and order the necessary items, so that his son would "look like one whom Genl Greene has the care of." (MiU-C)

　　2. In a letter of 17 August 1784, above, NG had asked CG to "spare" part of a cask of rice to Maxwell. Nothing more is known about NG's relationship with the Maxwell family. Adam Maxwell died on 27 May 1786 at about fifty-two years of age. A newspaper account at that time described him as "for many years an eminent schoolmaster in this City." (*Newport Mercury*, 29 May)

¶ [FROM ROBERT HAZLEHURST & COMPANY, Charleston, S.C., 20 May 1786. They have NG's letter of 12 May [not found]. Mr. [John] Croskeys has sent them "Forty One Barrels Rice," which they "sold at 10/," giving NG a "Credit, say £107.14.2."[1] The rice was of "so indifferent" a quality "that it remained in Store Three Weeks before we cou'd meet a purchaser. Indeed if that article had not become scarce at Market, we apprehend it wou'd still have remained in our possession." They have "taken up" NG's note to James Jacks and will "pay Hary

Grant £40 whenever he calls for the same." The remaining balance "will go towards what you owe us being an equal proportion of what you wish'd us to pay to Mr Grant."² They are enclosing a letter from Mr. Rutledge, "in answer to the one you beg^d us to deliver him."³ NG's letter for Mr. Munro [not found] was given to him, "& he promised to furnish you with the Coffee & Sugar per this conveyance."⁴ They do not think they can obtain a cellarette "upon reasonable terms"; have been "offer'd an exceeding good one but the price is £26."⁵ They report that "Old Charles pays only One Dollar a Week, but that [is] tolerable punctual. It is our opinion that you had best not dispose of him untill you pay us a visit. For you may then probably fall upon some mode of making more by him than what he woud sell for, which we suppose wou'd be a mere triffle."⁶ Robert Hazlehurst sends "respectfull Comp^{ts}" to CG. RCS (MiU-C) 3 pp.]

1. The rice was from Boone's Barony, NG's South Carolina plantation. (See also Hazlehurst to NG, 25 March, and Hazlehurst & Company to NG, 13 April, both above.)

2. See Grant to NG, 18 and 20 January, both above. Nothing is known about the money that NG owed to Jacks, a Charleston merchant (*Charleston Evening Gazette*, 28 August 1786), or about NG's instructions in regard to Grant. Hazlehurst & Company wrote NG on 13 June, below, that they had paid Grant £40.5.11.

3. See Edward Rutledge to NG, immediately below.

4. See Daniel Munro to NG, 22 May, below.

5. On the cellarette, see Hazlehurst to NG, 25 March.

6. "Old Charles" was presumably a slave whom NG had put out to hire. NG apparently did not reply to this letter. (Hazlehurst & Company to NG, 13 June) Nor did he travel to Charleston again. In their letter of 13 June, which NG would not have received before he was taken fatally ill, the firm enclosed a copy of the present letter and asked him not to "draw any further Bills upon us."

*   *   *

From Edward Rutledge

Dear General   [Charleston, S.C.?] May 20th 1786

I received your Favor of the 13th Ins^t a day or two ago, thro' the Hands of M^r [Robert] Hazelhurst, & have thought a good deal on the Subject; but as he has just sent for this Letter, & says he must have it, in half an Hour, you must take my Sentiments as they arise, & marshal them in order like a good Officer, as you are.¹

There can be no Question with any Man of Common Sense, or Common Honesty in my opinion, whether the payment made in Virginia to Collett should be applied to the Credit of Hunter Banks & C°. It can be applied to no other Credit. It was their Money, purchased with their property, & specially stipulated by Banks to be paid on their Account in Virginia, all which Collett had Notice of. It was, & in any Court in the World would be considered to be a Fraud in him to apply the Property of one set of Gentlemen, to the Discharge of the Debts of another Set, & the colouring is stronger when this is done to the injury of an innocent Guarantee.²

The payment in Sugars is if possible stronger. When he received that payment he had not the most distant Idea, of applying otherwise than to the payment of Hunter Banks & C^{os} Bond.[3] I have before me *his* State of the Account.[4] In that he changes the Bond, casts the Interest & makes the Sum total—9188.3.4. Then he gives various Credits in wch Prioleau is included—2267.0.4 & strikes the Ballance of 6921.3.0. To this Ballance thus struck he adds the amount of a Note given, by a different House, & for a Debt not due at the Time Prioleau made the payment. Having once applied the payment he is precluded from carrying it to a different Account, unless there has been a manifest Error in the application. But here there is no Error; there would have been one had he applied it differently. Had he applied it to the Credit of a Debt not due, when there was one actually due, it would have been erronious unless he had been specially authorised. Because no Man has a Right to an anticipated payment; the Contract does not require it. The Laws do not sanction the Demand, & the Custom of our World is universally against it. I do not think your Case would be altered in Equity, by settling with Mr Collett, upon the above Plan. He has clearly a Claim upon you for something, That something can be ascertained (if he allows you the above Credits) without the Intervention of a Court of Law; & no Man's Case is ever made better, by paying thro' compulsion, what he was fairly & honestly bound to pay without. But to put it out of the way of Cavil, I would endeavour were I in your Situation to get [Robert] Forsyth's Sanction.[5]

[Charles C.] Pinckney has been trying for some time to draw [John] Ferrie's Answer, who indeed appears to be anxiously disposed to terminate the Suit.[6] But he has not yet finished it. As soon as he Shall have finished it, I'll send it. Dont come till you hear from me.[7] For I can't decide till I see it. It would have been done before, but unfortunately for you tho' fortunately for Miss Stead, Pinckney is courting & courting with Success.[8] M^{rs} [Henrietta Middleton] Rutledge is so declined, that I mean to pass three Months after June Court on your native Island.[9] But in sickness & in Health; she unites with me, in best Wishes for the Happiness of every part of your Family. Your affect^{te} Friend

ED. RUTLEDGE

RCS (MiU-C).

1. NG's letter to Rutledge, which has not been found, was obviously about E. John Collett's recent demands for the payment of debts that NG had guaranteed for John Banks et al. as army contractors. (Collett to NG, 8 and 10 May, above; see also the notes at NG to Collett, 8 August 1784, above.) Robert Hazlehurst & Company forwarded the present letter to NG with theirs of this date, immediately above.

2. Collett was pressing his demands on NG in spite of a settlement he had recently reached with Henry Banks, John Banks's heir. (See Henry Banks to NG, 13 January, above.)

3. On the bond, see also Agreement between Hunter, Banks and Company and NG with Newcomen and Collett, 8 April 1783 (vol. 12: 591 and n), and NG to Lee, 22 August 1785, both above.

4. Collett's "State of the Account" has not been found.
5. Collett apparently forwarded this letter—or a subsequent one from Rutledge that has not been found—to NG from Savannah, Ga., on 9 June, below, adding: "I shall wait your answer in Town." On the agreement that they reached a few days later, see note at NG to Collett, 8 August 1784.
6. See Rutledge to NG, 1 March, above.
7. This is the last letter between Rutledge and NG that has been found; NG died on 19 June.
8. Pinckney, whose first wife died in 1784, married Mary Stead in July 1786. (Edwards to NG, 8 June 1784, above; *Biog. Directory of S.C. House*, 2: 527)
9. On Mrs. Rutledge's health, see also NG to CG, 29 May 1785, above. The Rutledges sailed for Newport, R.I., on 27 June on the *Dove*, the same vessel that carried NG and his family to the South the previous fall. (*Charleston Evening Gazette*, 28 June)

* * *

¶ [FROM THOMAS WASHINGTON, Greenwich, Ga., 21 May 1786. Acknowledges NG's letter of the previous day. Is "truly sorry" he cannot "Send you The Request."[1] He will ask his "factor in Town To transfer some property of Mine in his Hands," and "if Possible Will procure that Sum." Washington has "a good assortm[t] of Dry goods" in the factor's "hands," which he obtained "to lift McQueens bonds for [Eastburgh?;][2] if any of them Will Answer the purpose of Cash You Shall Have any qau[ty] [i.e., quantity?] you Want." If the "Person you want it for" would "wait till the last of the Week," Washington "could procure Cash."[3] RCS (MiU-C) 2 pp.]
1. NG's request to Washington has not been found, but it is clear from this reply that NG had asked for help in paying a creditor.
2. Nothing is known about these bonds of John McQueen's.
3. No further correspondence about this matter has been found.

¶ [FROM DANIEL MUNRO, Charleston, 22 May 1786.[1] He has shipped fifty pounds of coffee "in Consequence of" NG's order [not found]. "Loaf sugar" is "exceedingly scarce" in Charleston, but Munro expects [Capt. Matthew] Strong to supply him with "about 500 lb." when Strong arrives from Philadelphia "in a Day or two."[2] Munro will then "send the Sugar by the first Opportunity for Savannah." RCS (MiU-C) 1 p.]
1. Munro was undoubtedly a merchant or storekeeper.
2. On NG's order, see also Hazlehurst & Company to NG, 20 May, above.

¶ [FROM THOMAS CUMMING, Savannah, Ga., 24 May 1786. Acknowledges receipt of NG's "draft on Mr [Robert] Hazlehurst for £20 St[erlin]g"; will pay that amount to Mrs Bard before she sails for New York.[1] Asks whether the sails for NG's "pettiauger," which are now ready, should be kept in Savannah until NG goes "Southward" or "sent up to Mulberry Grove."[2] RCS (MiU-C) 1 p.]
1. According to Cumming's letter to NG of 15 May, above, NG owed Bard £30, and she was planning to leave for New York on 25 May. Hazlehurst & Company wrote NG on 13 June, below: "You gave us no advice of your drawing this draft, but rather than dishonor shoud attend it caused our paying the amount." At the same time, they asked him not to "draw any further Bills upon us."
2. Cumming had made arrangements for the sails to be made several weeks earlier. (See Cumming to NG, 24 April, above) NG was planning to go to Cumberland Island in July.

(NG to Ward, 4 April, above) NG apparently replied to Cumming on 26 May, but the letter has not been found. (Cumming to NG, immediately below)

¶ [FROM THOMAS CUMMING, Savannah, Ga., 27 May 1786. Has NG's letter of 26 May.[1] Has been told that Mr. Estant "was taken away by force in a Vessel bound to Maryland, in consequence of a debt of his there." Cumming is not sure if this is true, but he heard "the Captain hint something of the kind several days ago."[2] If it is true, Cumming does not know what to do about the rigging of NG's "Pettiauger." The blacksmith "cannot get the irons ready before Monday." As Estant is gone, Cumming thinks "the Boat should be sent up now and return'd the first of next Week." He also reports that one supplier "has neither Blocks or Rope," but "they can be had at another place." Adds in a postscript that he has spoken with the captain of a "Vessel in port, who will rig the Boat as soon as the Irons are ready."[3] RCS (MiU-C) 1 p.]
  1. NG's letter, which has not been found, was presumably a reply to Cumming's of 24 May, immediately above.
  2. Cumming wrote NG on 24 April, above, that Estant would oversee the rigging of NG's boat.
  3. It is not known if the boat was successfully rigged or returned to Mulberry Grove before NG's death on 19 June.

¶ [TO PETER DEVEAUX.[1] From Mulberry Grove, Ga., 1 June 1786. NG needs "half a dozen bushels of Pease to plant" and would be obliged if Deveaux could supply him with "four five or six bushels." He can "exchange rough Rice for them or pay the Money." Asks when the "Season for the Sturgeon fishery" will be and whether Deveaux intends "to come and go agreeable to promise." CG "says you have long intervals between your Visits."[2] ALS[3] 1 p.]
  1. Deveaux owned a Savannah River plantation known as the Grange. (Granger, *Savannah River Plantations*, p. 221)
  2. This is the last letter written by NG that has been found. No reply has been found.
  3. This document was donated to the Greensboro [N.C.] Public Library in 1929. Its present location is not known.

¶ [FROM CHARLES DUPONT, 3 June 1786. The "very great Rains having overflowed" most of his "Pasture ground," he has had to "turn out the most" of his "Cattle into the Woods." As it will take "a few days to Collect them," he is sending NG's servant back and will "Send you the Cattle" on "Saturday next without fail."[1] RCS (MiU-C) 1 p.]
  1. Dupont had agreed to sell cattle for NG's plantation at Mulberry Grove. (See Dupont to NG, 2 May, and Thomas Washington to NG, 5 May, both above.) "Saturday next" was 10 June.

¶ [FROM CHARLES THOMSON, SECRETARY OF THE CONTINENTAL CONGRESS, New York, 5 June 1786. He has received NG's letter of 24 April and has taken "the first Opportunity of forwarding the box with the prints," on the "Schooner *Happy Return*"; a bill of lading [not found] is enclosed.[1] Thomson is "glad to hear that the politics of Georgia are taking a favorable turn and that a more enlightened and liberal policy begins to prevail." He hopes "it will continue, and that as the State increases in importance it will contribute to the utmost of its power and influence to give Weight & dignity to the Federal

Councils," for that is the "only means of preserving our internal peace and making Our [Country?] respectable in the Eyes of foreign Nations."² Df (DLC) 1 p.]
    1. See NG to Thomson, 24 April, above.
    2. See ibid.

*   *   *

From E. John Collett

Sir   Savannnah [Ga.] Friday Mornᵍ 9 June 1786
    The inclosed Letters were received by me this Morning from the Post Office, and as it is probable one of them may Contain Mʳ Rutledge's Opinion, I have taken the Liberty of forwarding them [p]er your own Servant from Mʳ [Nathaniel] Pendletons.
    I shall wait your answer in Town, which I hope will be Satisfactory, but Should Mʳ Rutledge not yet have wrote you, and you wish to have his advice in the Business, I will, in that case, leave Savannah on Sunday, So as to have the pleasure of Meeting you in Charleston on Wednesday or Thursday next.¹ I am with great respect Sir Your mo hble Serᵗ

                                                                E. JNᴼ COLLETT

RCS (MiU-C).
    1. The enclosures presumably included either Edward Rutledge's "Opinion" of 20 May, above, regarding NG's financial obligations to Collett, or a more recent letter from Rutledge that has not been found. (On the guarantees that NG had provided for Collett on behalf of John Banks and others, see especially Agreement between Hunter, Banks and Company and NG with Newcomen and Collett, 8 April 1783 [vol. 12: 591 and n], the notes at NG to Collett, 8 August 1784, and NG to Lee, 22 August 1785, all above.) Although he wrote here that he would leave Savannah on Sunday, 11 June, and meet NG in Charleston, S.C., the next week if NG still needed Rutledge's advice, Collett and NG did hold a final meeting at Pendleton's house in Savannah "on the Tuesday [13 June] before the death of General Greene." (See notes at NG to Collett, 8 August 1784, above; on the agreement they reached at that time, see ibid.) Collett wrote NG again on 13 June, below, presumably after that meeting. As seen there, they had also met on Monday, 12 June.

*   *   *

¶ [FROM THOMAS CUMMING, Savannah, Ga., 9 June 1786. He has "Exchanged the fourteen Dollars of cut money sent by Hambleton" and has "added Eight Dollars more to it." It would give him "pleasure" to advance a larger sum.¹ Encloses NG's "Account Current [not found]"; the balance due is £28.18.9 sterling, which is "carried to your debt in new account."² Cumming has just received a letter from Mr. [Robert] Hazlehurst "relative to the Live oak"; Hazlehurst is "not disposed to be interested in the Experiment." As NG is going to Charleston, S.C., he will be able to get Hazlehurst's "sentiments thereon fully."³ Sends "respectful Compliments" to CG and wishes NG "a very pleasant journey to Carolina."⁴ At the bottom of the letter, Cumming accounts for the "Cash sent by Hambleton," totaling £5.2.8. RCS (MiU-C) 2 pp.]
    1. The advance may have been for a trip to Charleston, S.C., that NG, as seen in this letter, was apparently planning to make. (See Collett to NG, immediately above.) "Ham-

bleton" was probably Ham, or Hamilton, a servant of NG's. (See NG to CG, 17 August 1784, and Pierce to NG, at the end of the January 1786 documents, both above.)

2. On this account, see, for example, Cumming to NG, 15 May, above.

3. In his letter, which has not been found, Hazlehurst probably indicated that he did not want to invest in NG's live oak timber holdings on Cumberland Island. (See also Hazlehurst & Company to NG, 13 June, below.) As seen by the note at the letter immediately above, NG did not go to Charleston.

4. See preceding note.

* * *

From E. John Collett

Sir   Savannah [Ga.] 13 June 1786

You will recieve herewith inclosed Copys of the Award & papers relating to the arbitration and also [a] Copy of the Account which you requested yesterday.[1]

On looking over the Conditional Bond this Morning I find no mention is made for the payment of the Interest provided the principal is recovered which must have been a mistake in Mr Pendletons drawing it out, as the Matter was well understood between us the Evening before.[2]

As no Convenient opportunity presents itself for my going to Charleston till towards the end of the Week, I will thank you to give me a Memorandum of the different Property which you wish to dispose of in the Northern States, with the lowest price to each, and if on my going thither this Summer, I should approve of the whole or any part thereof, I will do myself the pleasure of informing you.[3]

I omitted yesterday to put you in Mind of the order drawn by Mr Campbell for the amount of the Express which I paid to him in Petersburg [Va.],[4] and as I shall be in want of a little pocket Money before I leave Savannah, I will thank you Sir to give me an order on M^r [Thomas] Cumming or any Gentleman who does your Business here, for the amount—Ten pounds Virg^a Money or £7.10 Sterling.[5] I am with Respect Sir Your mo. hble Ser^t E. JN^o COLLETT

RCS (MiU-C).

1. This letter was undoubtedly written after a meeting between NG and Collett at Nathaniel Pendleton's house earlier on this date. (See note at Collett to NG, 9 June, above.) The enclosures have not been found.

2. On the bonds that had been signed that morning—valued at "about six thousand pounds sterling, payable at different periods"—see note at NG to Collett, 8 August 1784, above. For background, see especially Agreement between Hunter, Banks and Company and NG with Newcomen and Collett, 8 April 1783 (vol. 12: 591 and n), the notes at NG to Collett, 8 August 1784, and NG to Lee, 22 August 1785, all above. In the last of those letters, NG had unsuccessfully sought help from Congress with the unpaid debts he had guaranteed for John Banks et al. as army contractors. Collett, writing first from Charleston, S.C., and then from Savannah, had been pressing NG for a settlement for more than two months before this meeting. (See Collett to NG, 6 and 24 March, 8 and 10 May, and 9 June, all above.)

3. NG had apparently offered his unsold lands in the North to Collett as part of the settlement. (On these holdings, see Estimate of NG's Estate, before 9 January 1784, above.) In making the settlement, NG may have hoped that his southern properties—especially Mulberry Grove plantation, Ga., where he now lived; Boone's Barony plantation, S.C., and his undivided half share of a large part of Cumberland Island, Ga.—would become increasingly profitable and valuable and that they would enable him, by one means or another, to pay off not only his obligation to Collett, but also the large debt that he still owed to the firm of Harris & Blachford for other guarantees to Banks et al. (On the debt to Harris and Blachford, see especially Pendleton to NG, 10 November 1784, and NG to Lee, 22 August 1785, above.) Nothing is known with any certainty about NG's state of mind after meeting with Collett—if he felt a sense of relief, for example, that a decision, however much he had hoped to avoid it, had finally been reached in this particular matter, or if his obligations may have now seemed even more burdensome than before. Whatever his feelings may have been, he became fatally ill soon after returning home from Savannah and died on 19 June. (See Epilogue, below.) The financial affairs of his estate would take some time to resolve, but in the case of the guaranteed debts, Congress eventually did grant relief to CG. (See notes at NG to Collett, 8 August 1784, and Pendleton to NG, 10 November 1784.)

4. On James Campbel, a Virginia attorney employed by Collett, see NG to Forsyth, 25 October 1784, above. Collett had recently obtained a settlement in Virginia from John Banks's heir, Henry Banks, but was apparently unwilling to credit it against the guarantee that NG had given to John Banks et al. (See above, Henry Banks to NG, 13 January, and Rutledge to NG, 20 May.)

5. It is not known whether NG saw this letter before he left Savannah to return home.

From Robert Hazlehurst & Company

Dear Sir   Charleston [S.C.] 13th June 1786
Annex'd is [a] Copy of our last respects dated the 20th Ult° since which we are without your favours.[1]

We have paid Hary Grant £40.5.11, this money for your Account, & we have also paid your draft in favor of Thomas Cumming for £20.

After this we beg you will not draw any further Bills upon us, for it will not be convenient, our entering into further advances, as we have occasion for all the Cash we can raise, I shall continue in the same situation during the summer.

You gave us no advices of your drawing this draft, but rather than dishonor shou'd attend it caused our paying the amount.[2] With great respect & esteem we are Dear sir Your Affe frds & Servts[3]

ROBT HAZLEHURST & Cº

RCS (MiU-C).

1. Hazlehurst & Company's letter of 20 May is above.

2. "This draft" was presumably the one on Cumming. (See Cumming to NG, 24 May, above.)

3. This letter, the last in the series, cannot have reached NG before he was taken fatally ill on his way home from Savannah, Ga., to Mulberry Grove plantation the next day. (See note at Collett to NG, 13 June, immediately above, and the Epilogue, immediately below.)

Epilogue

The best account of NG's final days is in the second volume of William Johnson's 1822 biography of NG. (Johnson, *Greene*, 2: 419–21) George Washington Greene drew heavily on Johnson's account of NG's death in his three-volume work about his grandfather, which was first published in 1867–71, and added some details that may have been passed down in family lore. (Greene, *Greene*, 3: 532–36)

Shortly before he was fatally stricken, NG met with one of his creditors, E. John Collett, in Savannah, Ga. Collett had been seeking payment for some time for debts that NG had guaranteed for John Banks et al. as contractors to the Southern Army. (See above, Collett to NG, 9 and 13 June, as well as the notes at NG to Collett, 8 August 1784.) Accompanied by CG, NG went to Savannah on Monday, 12 June 1786, and met with Collett at the home of Nathaniel Pendleton that day and again on Tuesday, 13 June. (See ibid.) In the sessions with Collett, NG, who had tried unsuccessfully to obtain relief from those debts from Congress the previous year, agreed to sign new bonds for the payment of what he owed Collett. (See notes at NG to Collett, 8 August 1784, and NG to Lee, 22 August 1785, above.)

According to Johnson, on their way home after the meetings with Collett, NG and CG stopped to visit William Gibbons, and the two men are said to have "walked into the rice-field together, to view the progress of Mr. Gibbon's crop" under a sun that was "intensely hot." (Johnson, *Greene*, 2: 419, see also Greene, *Greene*, 3: 532–33.) After leaving Gibbons's plantation, NG "complained of a pain of the head." This continued the next day, "but not in any alarming degree." On the day after that, however, "the pain increased greatly, particularly over the eyes and the forehead appeared inflamed and swollen." Pendleton came to Mulberry Grove "on a visit" that day and was alarmed at NG's "obvious depression of spirits, and reluctance to join in conversation." Pendleton alerted the family to his concerns, and Dr. John Brickell was called. (Johnson, *Greene*, 2: 419) Brickell "took a little blood, and administered some ordinary prescriptions," but the swelling continued, and another physician, Dr. Donald MacLeod, was "called into consultation." MacLeod decided "to blister the temples, and take blood freely." This, however, "proved too late; the head had swollen greatly, and the patient sunk into a total stupor, from which he never revived." (Johnson, *Greene*, 2: 419–20) MacLeod wrote a note to NG's close neighbor and wartime colleague Anthony Wayne, who had recently returned to his own Savannah River plantation: "Gen Greene, I am distress'd to inform you is just about closing the chapter of life. As you may wish to be here at the unhappy moment, I thought it a duty to inform you. Mrs Greene's Situation is not to be described." (PHi; the letter is erroneously

*Equestrian statue of Nathanael Greene, by Henry Kirke Brown (1877),
Stanton Park, Washington, D.C.*
(Library of Congress)

docketed "2 July 1786"; see also Nelson, *Wayne*, p. 204.) Wayne came to Mulberry Grove and sat by the bedside of his comatose friend, who died early in the morning of Monday, 19 June. Wayne relayed the news to Col. James Jackson at Savannah: "My dear friend General Greene is no more. He departed this morning at six o'clock A.M. He was great as a soldier, greater as a citizen, immaculate as a friend. His corpse will be at Major Pendleton's this night the funeral from thence in the evening. The honors, the greatest honors of war are due his remains. You, as a soldier will take the proper order on this melancholy affair. Pardon this scrawl; my feelings are but too much affected because I have seen a great and good man die." (Printed in Greene, *Greene*, 3: 534)

The cause of NG's death has never been determined with any certainty and will probably never be known. Popular lore held that he died of "sunstroke," brought on by walking in Gibbons's rice fields during the heat of the day. Johnson commented: "The disease to which he fell a victim, has generally been pronounced, a case of phrenitis produced by the action of the sun, commonly termed, *a stroke of the sun*. Whether the inflamed and swollen forehead, and the gradual extension of the swelling, may not seem to indicate some other cause, will rest with the skilful in medical practice, to decide." (Johnson, *Greene*, 2: 422n) NG had certainly been under enormous stress for some time before his death, because of the mounting financial pressures, but Jeremiah Wadsworth wrote Washington several months afterward that he understood NG, "just before his death, or rather before he fell sick," to have been

> "in better Spirits than he had ever been before, since his arriveing with his family in Georgia—as he had good prospects of geting clear of his troubles with the crediters of Banks & Co. and a Contract with the French Nation for Timber was so nearly compleated as to promise him sufficient funds for all his other purposes. Mr [Phineas] Miller . . . assures me the General was in good Spirits and that he is persuaded he died of a fever in the Head which might have been removed if the Physicians had understood his disorder[;] he had for some time before had an inflamation in one Eye—which was almost done away, when he was Sezed at table with a Violent pain in his Eye & Head which forced him to retire, a fever ensued the Symptoms increased and a few days put an end to his existance. I am my selfe persuaded that something of the apperplectick kind was the cause of his death as I was informed that the day after one of the important actions to the Southward he was taken suddenly with a disorder in the head which deprived him of sence & motion for some time and those about him best Skilled in the healing art—pronounced it an appoplexy." (Wadsworth to Washington, 1 October 1786, Washington, *Papers*, Confederation

Series, 4: 283; nothing is known about an "apperplectick" occur-
rence during NG's southern campaign such as Wadsworth alluded to here.)

On Tuesday, 20 June, NG's body was brought by boat to Savannah,
where it was met by the Chatham County "militia, representatives of
the municipality, members of the Society of the Cincinnati, and many
persons in private and official life." It was carried to Pendleton's house
"on Bay Street next to the corner of Barnard street." (*Remains of General
Greene*, p. 83; Greene, *Greene*, 3: 534) The *Charleston Evening Gazette* of 26
June reported that "the melancholy ac[c]ount of his death was made
known by the discharge of minute guns from Fort Wayne; the shipping
in the harbour had their colours half masted; the shops and stores in the
town were shut; and every class of citizens, suspending their ordinary
occupations, united in giving testimonies of the deepest sorrow." The
funeral procession, which began about five P.M., moved from "the Pendleton house to the Colonial cemetery, belonging to Christ's Church,"
an Anglican church. (*Remains of General Greene*, p. 83; Greene, *Greene*, 3:
535) NG's grandson George Washington Greene recounts that the light
infantry, with reversed arms, conducted the body

> "to the left of the regiment, then filed off, right and left, to the front
> of the battalion. The dragoons took their places on the flanks of the
> coffin. The march began; the artillery in the Fort firing minute
> guns as the long line advanced, and the band playing a solemn
> dirge. The muffled drums gave forth a sound of woe. When they
> had reached the burial-ground where a vault had been hastily
> opened, the regiment filed off to right and left, resting on their
> arms, with faces turned inwards, till the coffin and pall bearers
> and long train of mourning citizens had passed through. There
> was a solemn pause as the Hon. William Stevens, in the absence of
> a clergyman, took his stand by the head of the coffin, and with
> tremulous voice read the funeral service of the Church of England.
> Then the body was placed in the vault, the files closed, and march-
> ing up to the right of the vault, gave three general discharges; the
> artillery fired thirteen rounds, and with trailed arms all slowly and
> silently withdrew." (Greene, *Greene*, 3: 535; the "Regimental Or-
> ders" for the funeral procession are reprinted in *Remains of General
> Greene*, pp. 193–94.)

After the interment, members of the Georgia chapter of the Society of
the Cincinnati repaired to the "coffee-house," where they voted a motion "that as a token of the high respect and veneration in which this
society hold the memory of their late illustrious brother, Major General

Greene, deceased, George Washington Greene, his eldest son, be admitted a member of this society, to take his seat on his arriving at the age of 18 years." (*Charleston Evening Gazette*, 26 June; as seen later in this Epilogue, the "eldest son" died at age eighteen.)

The *Charleston Evening Gazette* commented at this time that "in giving the decorous part of a great man's life . . . no little difficulty frequently arises in doing justice to honorable actions in such a manner as to avoid luxuriant panegyric; but in the history of this brave man the human materials were so excellently forged & suited, as to form in the altogether something like humanity's ornament and pride. In a public capacity he may be justly stiled, the 'political saviour of the southern states.' " The newspaper account concluded: "in private life the General was courteous, affable, and accomplished; in sentiment, exceedingly liberal, ever judging with candor of those who differed in opinion with himself; exhibiting that generosity of conduct, that universal philanthropy which are ever the distinguished characteristic of great minds." (*Charleston Evening Gazette*, 23 June)

Responses to NG's untimely death were immediate and heartfelt. On 11 July, Henry Lee, Jr., wrote Washington from New York, where he was a Virginia delegate to Congress: "Universal grief reigns here. How hard the fate of the U States, to loose such a son in the middle of life— irreparable loss. But he is gone, I am incapable to say more." (Smith, *Letters*, 23: 394) The Marquis de Lafayette wrote Thomas Jefferson, the American minister to France, that he had received the "Sad, and so much to Be lamented Account of the death of our friend General Greene" in a "late letter of a private Nature" from Gen. Henry Knox. "It is a Great loss for the United states to which He Has Been an Useful servant, and I May add a Great Ornament. I Have personally lost a friend, and Heartily Mourn for Him." (Boyd, *Jefferson Papers*, 10: 311) NG was a "Great and Good Friend," wrote Lafayette in an October 1786 letter to Washington. (Washington, *Papers*, Confederation Series, 4: 312) Knox commented to his former commander-in-chief that "the death of our common & invaluable friend genl Greene, has been too melancholy and affecting a theme to write upon." (Ibid., p. 302) Washington, too, lamented the loss of his trusted wartime lieutenant in several letters during the summer and fall of 1786. It was "with very sincere regret" that he received the news of NG's death, he wrote Lee in July. (Washington, *Papers*, Confederation Series, 4: 171) To the Comte de Rochambeau, Washington expressed the feelings of many: "The Public, as well as [NG's] family & friends, has met with a severe loss. He was a great & good man indeed." (Ibid., p. 180)

Three years after NG's death, Alexander Hamilton delivered a Fourth of July "Eulogium on the late Major General Greene" to the New York chapter of the Society of the Cincinnati. He paid tribute in it to NG's character and accomplishments while at the same time regretting the brevity of NG's life and the loss of his talents in shaping the new nation. "From you who knew and loved him, I fear not the imputation of flattery or enthusiasm when I indulge an expectation that the *name* of *Greene* will at once awaken in your minds the images of whatever is noble and estimable in human nature," Hamilton asserted in introducing his remarks. "For as high as this great man stood in the estimation of his Country, the whole extent of his worth was little known." He continued: "As a man the virtues of Greene are admitted; as a patriot he holds a place in the foremost rank; as a statesman he is praised; as a soldier he is admired. But in the two last characters especially in the last but one his reputation falls far below his desert. It required a longer life and still greater opportunities to have enabled him to exhibit in full day the vast, I had almost said the enormous powers of his mind. The termination of the American war not too soon for his wishes nor for the welfare of his country, but too soon for his glory, put an end to his military career. The sudden termination of his life cut him off from those scenes, which the progress of a new immense and unsettled empire could not fail to open to the complete exertion of that universal and pervading genius, which qualified him not less for the senate, than for the field." ("Eulogy on Nathanael Greene," 4 July 1789, Syrett, *Hamilton*, 5: 347) Hamilton offered a detailed tribute to NG's "perseverance, courage, enterprise and resource" in his southern command and lamented the loss of "this consumate General, this brave soldier, this discerning statesman, this steady patriot, this virtuous citizen, this amiable man." (Ibid., pp. 357, 359)

In Savannah, the location of NG's burial site later became a mystery, as no marker had been erected. As early as 1820, the city council appointed a committee to determine the site, but the resulting report was "partial, unsatisfactory, and inconclusive." During the nineteenth century, "tradition, ever unreliable, invented several theories as to the disposition of General Greene's body." (*Remains of General Greene*, pp. 31–32) One was that "his remains had been deposited in the vault" of John Graham, the former owner of Mulberry Grove, and had later been removed by one of Graham's descendants, while another conjecture held that a "certain [unmarked] mound, near the corner of Oglethorpe avenue and Bull street, covered the remains of General Greene." According to yet another theory, NG's body had been removed by his family to Cumberland Island. (Ibid., pp. 32–33) While the burial site remained unknown, the city of Savannah in 1829 completed an obelisk in Johnson Square that now bears the inscription: "Major-General Nathanael Greene[,] born in Rhode Island 1742[,] died in Georgia 1786. Soldier, patriot, and friend of Washington. This shaft has been reared by the people of Savannah in honor of his great services to the American

Revolution." (*Remains of General Greene*, p. 133) In March 1825, Lafayette, then visiting the United States, laid the cornerstone for this monument, which originally honored both NG and Gen. Casimir Pulaski. (Ibid., pp. 135–36n)

When the Rhode Island Society of the Cincinnati, with the assistance of prominent residents of Savannah, undertook another search for NG's burial site around the turn of the twentieth century, the "Jones" vault in Savannah's Colonial Park Cemetery was opened and searched. This was the burial place of Noble Wimberly Jones (d. 1805), a speaker of the Georgia Assembly and delegate to the Continental Congress, and members of his family. In one corner of the vault, workmen found a skeleton among the fragments of a coffin. A "silver gilt" coffin plate that was found with the bones was inscribed "1786," with the letters "ael" and "reene" also visible. Three metal buttons, engraved with eagles, were found among the bones; these would have belonged to the uniform of a major general in the Continental army. Cleaning of the coffin plate later revealed NG's full name, date of death, and age. Near NG's remains were those of "a male person, probably eighteen or nineteen years of age," which were subsequently presumed to be those of NG's son George Washington Greene, who died in 1793. (*Remains of General Greene*, pp. 39–42, 120) The two sets of remains were removed from the Jones vault and were reinterred on 14 November 1902 under the obelisk in Johnson Square. A tablet in Colonial Park Cemetery now marks the site where the remains were found. (*Remains of General Greene*, pp. 123–79)

CG lived at Mulberry Grove for a number of years after NG's death. In the summer of 1786, she returned for a visit to Newport, R.I., where NG's will (dated 11 October 1785, above) was probated in September. (See *Newport Mercury*, 28 August 1786; Washington, *Papers*, Confederation Series, 4: 283.) While trying to settle NG's financial affairs, she made additional trips to the North before finally obtaining the relief that NG had sought from Congress for the debts he had guaranteed on behalf of Banks et al. (See above, the notes at NG to Collett, 8 August 1784, and at Pendleton to NG, 10 November 1784.) Phineas Miller, the Greene children's tutor, helped her in managing the plantation. Legend has it that CG assisted Eli Whitney, who stayed at Mulberry Grove for a time in 1792–93, in the invention of the cotton gin. CG and Miller were married in 1796 and in 1800 left Mulberry Grove to settle on Cumberland Island, where they spent the rest of their lives. Miller died in 1806; Catharine in 1814. (Stegeman, *Caty*, pp. 125–210)

As seen in the notes at his will, 11 October 1785, NG was survived by five children. The eldest, George Washington Greene, who was eleven when his father died, was sent to France in 1788 to pursue his studies under Lafayette's guidance. (Idzerda, *Lafayette Papers*, 5: 304n) Soon after his return to America in 1793, George died in a canoeing accident on the Savannah River at age eighteen. (Stegeman, *Caty*, p. 162) Martha ("Patty"), the oldest daughter, was educated at the Moravian School in Bethlehem, Pa., and was married first to John Corliss Nightingale of Providence in 1795. After his death, she married Dr. Henry Edmund Turner, son of Dr. Peter Turner of East Greenwich, R.I. Martha, four of whose children lived to adulthood, died in 1839. (Clarke, *Greenes*, pp. 328–29) Cornelia Lott Greene was also educated at the Moravian School. She married Peyton Skipwith of Tennessee in 1802. He died six years later, and in 1810 she married her first cousin Edward Brinley Littlefield, son of her uncle William Littlefield. Cornelia had three children with Skipwith; of six other children that she had with Littlefield, only one lived to adulthood. (Clarke, *Greenes*, pp. 329–31) Nathanael Ray Greene, who was six when his father died, grew up at Mulberry Grove and on Cumberland Island. In 1808 he married Anna Maria Clarke, daughter of NG's Newport friend Ethan Clarke. (Anna's mother was a daughter of Samuel Ward, Sr., a former governor of Rhode Island, and a sister of NG's longtime friend Samuel Ward, Jr.) Nathanael Ray, who divided his time in later years between Rhode Island and Georgia, was the father of historian George Washington Greene (b. 1811). (Clarke, *Greenes*, pp. 331–32; *DAB*) Louisa Catharine Greene, who was only two years old when NG died, was married on Cumberland Island in 1814 to James Shaw, "a Scottish gentleman many years her senior." (Stegeman, *Caty*, p. 208) They had several children, but apparently none was still living when Louisa Catharine died in 1831. (Clarke, *Greenes*, p. 332; for brief biographical sketches of CG, her children, and their spouses, see also "Biographical Appendix," *Georgia Historical Quarterly* 54 [1970]: 263–75.)

On 11 July 1786, three weeks after NG's death, Congress resolved to erect a monument to his memory at "the seat of the federal government." (*JCC*, 30: 395) A congressional committee consisting of three of NG's longtime friends and colleagues—Henry Lee, Jr., Charles Pettit, and Edward Carrington—recommended the following inscription in a report given on 8 August: "Sacred to the Memory of Nathaniel Greene, Esqr, a native of the State of Rhode Island, who died on the 19th of June, 1786, late Major general in the service of the United States, and commander of their army in the Southern department. The United States in Congress Assembled in honor of his patriotism, valour and ability, have erected this Monument." (Ibid., 31: 504) It was not until 1877, however, that an equestrian statue of NG, by Henry Kirke Brown, was placed in Washington's Stanton Park. (*Remains of General Greene*, p. 175) Another statue of NG, also by Brown, was furnished by the state of Rhode Island in 1870 for the National Hall of Statuary in the Capitol at Washington. (Ibid., p. 204) Rhode Island also honored him in 1931 with a statue that stands outside the State House in Providence. With the completion of this thirteen-volume series of his papers, the editors hope they have also helped to erect a fitting memorial to a "great and good man," whose important role in the winning of American independence was much better known to his contemporaries than it has been in more recent times.

ADDENDA

Documents Found since the Publication
of Earlier Volumes in the Series

To Moses Brown[1]

Esteemed Friend   Coventry [R.I.] November 26th 1770
I take the freedom to make application to you to get some necessary
information relative to the rumour of a Spanish war. I want to be
inform'd whether the report be probable or groundless.[2] For haveing
been very closely confined in attending my father in his illness and at
his death (of which misfortune I suppose you have been acquainted
with),[3] I have not had opportunity to get such intelligence with respect
to that report as the Circumstances of our business seems to require, for
haveing three Vessles at Sea if the report be true should think proper to
make some insureance but if it is without foundation should not incline
to make any. Therefore please to inform me agreeable to my request and
give me such further intelligence as you may think is requisite for me to
know, all which I shall esteem and consider as a particular mark of your
friendship and will greatfully acknowledge the favor. I am with the
greatest respect your Sincere friend.   NATHANAEL GREENE JUN
PS Our Vessels are gone to the Islands.[4]

ALS (RHi).
1. Moses Brown was the youngest of four brothers who built a modest family business
into a commercial and industrial empire. NG's family did much business with the
Browns. (Hedges, *Browns*)
2. The report was "groundless."
3. Nathanael Greene, Sr., died on 16 November 1770. On his death, see note at NG to
Samuel Ward, Jr., 5 March 1771, above (vol. 1: 20–21).
4. By "the Islands," NG presumably meant the West Indies.

To Moses Brown

Esteemed Friend   Coventry [R.I.] April 9th 1771
I think it my duty to acquaint you of the measures pursuing in Our
Town. As I consider you and a few others the Body from whence all the
different branches of politicks have their rise and Support[,] I say as I
consider you in that point of light I should be wanting in duty not to let
you know what Changes and alterations are planning out in Coventry. I
do not mean that I am under any fixt Obbligation to give you intel-

ligence, But upon A supposition of your being a true Friend to the Real interest of this Colony and a Zealous supporter of Our Happy Constitutional principles in which point of light I ever Considered you, I say upon that Consideration I should be Remiss not to give you timely information of all matters that were likely to Concern Civill polity or the well being of this Goverment, and in an especial manner where I thought you would be likely to adopt any plan to Obviate their Schemes[.] I know not for what reason but there is the greatest Opposition forming against Judge [Stephen] Potter['']s ensuing Election that I ever saw in my Life against any Representative[.] His conduct and mind hath been almost Uniformly the Same in Publick measures Except the Affair of your Bridge and they have not the least Objection to my going again if I will not Support the Judges Ensuing Election so Zealously[.][1] We recievd from your Company Last year a very Seasonable Supply towards the Securing and Effecting Our Election[.] That and the promotion of the Prox of Governor [Joseph] Wanton, was what induced You and Others to Accomodate us as you did[.] I am very Confident that Our Natural interest amongst the people Last year would have obtaind Our Election without any Assistance But that Lessens not the Obligation on our part nor diminishes your good intentions towards us[.] Permit me to Solicit your assistance for the Judge again providing you think him Worthy. I declare I almost blush to think what I am writing but when I consider I am not Petitioning for my Self but for a common Friend to a Certain party I am emboldined to pursue the track. But nevertheless was I not Concious that the Judge would do his Town and the Goverment better Services than any Other person in it I would not be so Strongly Attached to this interest, as to oppose any Man the better sort of people thought worthy by their Suffrage to Represent them in the General Assembly[.][2] I am in great haste therefore must put a period to the Effusion of Ink and Submit it to your prudence not doubting but you'l do the thing that is most Advisable. I am with much regard your friend.   NATH GREENE JR

ALS (Joseph Rubinfine, 1994).

1. When the first volume in this series was published in 1976, the editors had not found conclusive evidence that NG was the "Nathaniel Greene" or "Nathaniel Greene, Jr." who represented Coventry in the Rhode Island legislature during the early 1770s. (See above, vol. 1: xvi–xviii.) This letter strongly suggests that the person in question was indeed NG. "Nathaniel Greene" represented Coventry in the May 1770 session of the legislature, as did "Nathaniel Greene, Jr." in May 1771, May 1772, May 1775, and probably also in 1774. (Bartlett, *Records of R.I.*, 7: 12, 26, 44; see also ibid., pp. 262, 268.) In the December 1774 session, "Nathaniel Greene, Jr." was named to a committee "to revise the militia laws of this colony." (Ibid., p. 262) "The Affair of your Bridge" undoubtedly concerned a petition in 1770 for a lottery to raise $400 for repairs to "the great bridge" over the Pawtucket River, between the towns of Smithfield and Cumberland, which "is so out of repair, that it is almost impassable." The lottery was granted. (Ibid., p. 21)

2. On Potter and NG, see vol. 1: 6n, above. Potter, who had been one of the two deputies that Coventry sent to the legislature in 1770, was apparently defeated in the 1771 election. (Bartlett, *Records of R.I.*, 7: 4, 12, 26) As seen in the preceding note, NG was elected again that year.

To Nicholas Brown and Company

Gentlemen   July 17, 1772

Cousin Griffin Greene desired me to write you in his name for fear you should grow impatient at his delay, and he fears to make any farther excuses, lest you should think they were imaginary and not real, and therefore applyed to me to inform you of his present situation and the cause of your irons not being sent sooner.

We have furnished him with some piggs [i.e., pig iron] and shall supply him with more soon, he has now got and will have very soon [*illegible*] enough to make 4 tons of iron which he intends for you but you must exercise patience for you cannot have it speedy.[1] His bellows that answers tolerably well for refining will not answer for drawing the iron. Therefore, he is obliged to get a new pair of bellows and he intends to make them of wood, it may be sometime before they'd be done, but so soon as they are done, you may depend & believe upon the same quantity of iron. He made some trial to draw out a quantity of iron with these bellows for you, but they wanted stocks to such a d[eg]ree that I advised him to stop, until he got things in better order not doubting but you'd rest satisfied, when informed how matters were. I am your assured friend   NATHANAEL GREENE, JR.

Tr (RPJCB).
1. A month later, the Greene family's forge in Coventry, R.I., was destroyed by fire. (See Petition to the Rhode Island General Assembly, before 20 August 1772, above [vol. 1: 35–36].)

To Thomas Arnold[1]

Friend Thomas   Fulling Mill [Coventry, R.I.] March 28 1774

I recivd yours of the 14 of this Instant after my return from Providence. With regard to the subject of Matrimony, I can only say farther, if you'l hear not Moses [i.e., Moses Brown?] upon the hill, nor the prophets of Smithfield [R.I.], neither will you me.[2] I forgot to ask what play was agoing to be Acted, please to send me the play by Mr Greene, that I may have the perusal of it. Send my books by Mr Greene also. I detain Mr [James M.] Varnum & Mr Greene whilst I write this scrawl therefore excuse the haste. I am your Assured friend.   N GREENE JR

My regards to Joseph.

ALS (RHi).

1. On Arnold, see above, vol. 1: 21n.

2. As seen at ibid., Arnold, "one of NG's closest friends," was "the only guest outside the family who was invited to NG's wedding" to Catharine Littlefield in July 1774.

*　　　　*　　　　*

¶ [PETITION OF THE BRIGADE SURGEONS, [1 March–5 June 1776].[1] The surgeons of the "several" regiments in NG's brigade "Humbly" observe that, "animated with patriotism and a desire to render themselves useful," they sacrificed the "Ease and Comforts of Domestic Life" and joined the army "when Our bleeding Country was first called to Arms, by the Invasion of our Unnatural and Cruel Enemies." They joined in order to "attend their freinds and Neighbours thro' the Fatigue and perils of the Camp and Bloody feild, And by the healing Art to Administer releif, Comfort, and health to the sick and Wounded." Believing that the "scene would be Short," they did not concern themselves with the "pecuniary recompence." They remind NG that "Physick is a Study, that requires much time, labour, and Application," and they have spent "much of the Prime of Life, and some of us the whole of our Patrimony in acquiring this knowledge." They "are now in the meredian of Life" and have left "Extensive practice[s] in the Country," which are "liable to fall into the hands of others," to serve their country. Also, many of them have families who depend upon their "daily earnings." The surgeons have done their best to discharge their duties, and they "flatter themselves" that they have merited NG's "approbation." Moreover, "notwithstanding the Excellent provission made by the Contenent for the supply of the General Hospital," and the "skill and Knowledge" of the doctors who serve there, yet "for a greater part of the time, the Patients under our Care have been more numerous than those sent to the general Hospital, which has rendered our service Constant and severe." The petitioners now "find it Impossible Even with the Utmost frugallity and Oeconemy to live in Charecter as Gentlemen and reserve any thing for the support of their Familys out of their present pay." They therefore ask that NG "represent their Aggreived State" to the commander in chief and ask him to "lay the same" before Congress or take "such other measures" as will "be most Expedient."[2] Signed by surgeons Joseph Joslyn, Elisha Story, and Samuel Tenny, and surgeon's mate Martin Herrick. D (WRMS, Misc. Records 231–22, #30, DNA) 2 pp.]

1. The petition is undated. The span of dates is taken from the facts that Martin Herrick, one of the petitioners, did not become a surgeon's mate until 1 March 1776, and that Congress raised the pay of brigade surgeons on 5 June 1776. (See next note.)

2. No evidence has been found that NG addressed Washington in regard to this petition or that Washington presented the surgeons' case to Congress, but on 5 June 1776 Congress "augmented the pay of regimental surgeons to $33⅓ per month." (*JCC*, 5: 419)

¶ [TO AN UNKNOWN PERSON. From "Headquarters Amboy, N.J.," 15 October 1776. Announces the appointment of Col. Clement Biddle as a "Volunteer Aid de Camp" to NG.[1] Catalog excerpt (*The Collector* #863 [1979]) 1 p.]

1. On Biddle, see above, vol. 1: 310–11n.

*　　　　*　　　　*

From Governor William Livingston of New Jersey

Sir   Elizabeth Town [N.J.] 24 Oc^r 1776

Your Favour of the 22^d Instant, I received last Evening;[1] and should comply with your request with the greatest alacrity, was I clear that the ordering the Battalion of Militia to assist in erecting Magazines was properly within my Province. I presume you mean a new Battalion not at present in Service because any Regiment now on Duty is subject to General [Hugh] Mercer[']s orders, who can consequently station them in any part of this State where he conceives them most useful. And as to a new Battalion, no Law or ordinance of any of our Conventions (the present Legislature not having passed the Militia Bill brought in the last Session) has made provision to enable the Governor to call out the Militia;[2] but they are to turn out monthly as they do at present. By the old Law indeed which is not repealed by our present Constitution, the Governor as Commander in Chief, may order out the whole military force of this State to repel an actual Invasion, but the Business for which you request them seems to be of a very different Nature. Again if they are to be considered [truly?] as the Militia of this State, and to be paid by it, while employed in erecting Magazines for the Benefit of the United States, it will not be relished by our Legislature. If by the United States, it may be questionable how far the Congress will conceive themselves obliged to pay a Battalion raised at the request of one of their Generals without their Concurrence. I conceive therefore that the requisition ought to come from Congress, or at least from General Washington; and in that Case I would submit it to a Quorum of my Privy Council and take their Directions in the matter.[3] I flatter myself Sir your Candour will excuse my stating the above Difficulties, which does not proceed from any Inclination to retard the Service (which I hope no man has more at heart) but from a desire to keep within the verge of my own Duty; & not to administer any Cause of Complaint to the particular State which I have the honor to represent. I am with great Esteem Sir Your most humble & most obedient Ser^t

ADf (MHi).

1. NG's letter has not been found. NG was at Fort Lee, N.J., by 24 October 1776 and was planning to establish magazines of arms and supplies in anticipation of the Continental army's retreat through New Jersey.

2. Livingston had sought such an ordinance from his legislature in a speech on 11 September 1776; the Assembly adjourned on 8 October without passing the requested measure. (Livingston, *Papers*, 1: 172n)

3. No such request has been found from either Washington or Congress.

To General James Ewing[1]

Sir   At Bougarts Tavern [N.J.] Decem 19. 1776[2]
I am directed by his Excellency General Washington to desire you to send down to Meconkea ferry, sixteen Durham Boats & four flats.[3] Youl send them down as soon as possible. Send them under the care and direction of some good faithful Officer. I am Sir your most obedient & very humble Servant   NATHANAEL GREENE

ALS (MWiW-C).

1. The recipient's name is not given, but it was undoubtedly Ewing, a Pennsylvania militia general whom Washington had placed in command of the militia units on the upper Delaware River. (Washington to Ewing, 12 December 1776, Washington, *Papers, Revolutionary War Series*, 7: 306–7)

2. Bogart's Tavern, at the intersection of present-day routes 263 and 413 in Buckingham Township, Pa., is currently known as the General Greene Inn.

3. The boats were to be used to ferry the army across the Delaware River as part of Washington's plan to attack the German garrison at Trenton, N.J. McKonkey's Ferry (now Washington Crossing, Pa.) was about nine miles up the river from Trenton. Durham boats were shallow-draft vessels, forty to sixty feet long and eight feet wide, which had been developed to carry iron ore.

To Catharine Littlefield Greene

Morristown [N.J.] Feb[r]uary 1, 1777
This will be handed you by one whom you will be glad to see. He comes home on the recruiting service, but more particularly to be with you until you are in Bed.[1] I have all along flatterd my self with the hopes of coming home a few weeks this Winter, but the Enemy are determind to rob me of that happiness.

My dear I wish to be with you in the hour of Affliction.[2] Remember my Soul hovers about you in distress and tho incapable of giveing relief would gladly share your pains. You must make a Substitute of your brother who will chearfully do you every service in his power. He is a good Naturd tender Hearted lad, but Education has had a great share in rendering him unfit for the fatigues of the Army. However I am in hopes time and a farther Acquaintance with human life and Mankind, he will get the better of all those little difficulties.

Pray has your brother Simon ever sent you your Negro Boy?[3] I fear he has not, as you say there is no body with you. Let nothing be wanting that will be necessary to contribute to your ease and comfort, during your sickness. I wish you a safe and happy time, a fine Daughter Or a lovely *Son*. Billy will tell every thing about the Army, where we are and what about. Major Blodget had orders, was to call on and receive your orders.[4]

I wrote for a few Shirts, Stockings, Stocks &c, which if convenient should be glad to receive at the Majors return.[5]

I lodge at one Mr Hoffmans, a very good Naturd *doubtful* Gentleman. He has a charming Wife, a great lover of the Clergy.[6] Major Clarke one of my Aid de Camps, is Eternally perplexing her with doubts and difficulties by dark hints and oblique insinnuations respecting the purity of the Manners and principles of the Church of England.[7]

My love to all friends—to my little Son.[8] Write me every Opportunity. You need not be much afraid of the Enemy. They dare not stir upon the main, besides they will soon be obligd to recall all their force from Newport to New Jersey to hold their ground here.[9] In haste I am Affe[c]tionably yours   N GREENE

ALS (MiU-C).

1. CG's brother William Littlefield was a captain in the newly formed Rhode Island brigade. (See note at NG to CG, 20 May 1777, above [vol. 2: 86n].) By "in Bed," NG meant until his then-pregnant wife delivered.

2. CG's "Affliction" was her pregnancy. She gave birth to a daughter, Martha Washington Greene, in mid-March 1777.

3. The "Negro Boy" was undoubtedly a house servant of CG. Simon Littlefield, a brother of CG, lived on Block Island, R.I.

4. Maj. William Blodgett, an aide to NG and a Rhode Island native, had apparently gone home for a visit.

5. NG's letter requesting the clothing has not been found.

6. On businessman Nicholas Hoffman, see also his letter to NG of 7 April 1784, above. As noted there, Hoffman "fled to the British in New York" soon after NG stayed in his home. Sarah Ogden Hoffman, his wife, was the daughter of a Loyalist sympathizer. She was paroled in January 1778, "after placing a security of one thousand dollars for spreading a rumor that the British were about to invade" New Jersey, and was later charged with escaping to New York with £1000 that had been forfeited to the state. (Thayer, *Morris County*, p. 194; on Mrs. Hoffman, see also Livingston, *Papers*, 5: 523–24.)

7. Maj. John Clark, Jr., was the aide referred to here.

8. NG's son, George Washington Greene, was then about one year old.

9. The British did not evacuate Newport, R.I., until October 1779.

To Colonel Joseph Trumbull[1]

Dr Sir   Camp near Philadelphia Nov 17, 1777

Please to transmit me an account of the rations I have drawn since July twelve months and also the sums of money drawn since that time. Let the rations be made out in substance not in value.[2]

We cannot rout the enemy from Philadelphia yet. Fort Mifflin after the most obstinate defence ever made by such a garrison was evacuated Night before last.[3] We are still in hopes to render General Howes situation so restless in the city as to determine him to leave it before the close of the campaign.[4]

The Successes of the Northern Army is all glorious.[5] We have strove but in vain. This Army is the great Devil that we have to contend with. Our troops are good, but there is not enough of em. I wish all the States had as nearly filld their Regiments as Conecticut.

The Comisary department has been distressing since you left it; and I fear upon the present plan, will grow worse and worse.[6] The publick has been the worst informd with regard to the operations here that ever a people was, from every publication I have seen.

Make my Complements agreeable to Mrs [Amelia Dyer] Trumbull and beleive me to be with sinsere regard your most Obedient & very humble Servt N GREENE

ALS (CtHi). The letter is addressed to "Col Jonathan Trumbull [Jr.?] in Connecticut." The contents, however, clearly establish that it was written to Joseph Trumbull (1737–78), another son of Gov. Jonathan Trumbull of Connecticut.

1. Before his resignation during the summer of 1777, Trumbull had served as commissary general. (Heitman, *Register*)

2. The account, if Trumbull sent it, has not been found. On or about 10 November 1777, the general officers of Washington's army had met and produced a report that recommended increasing the monetary value of the daily ration. (See General Officers to Washington, 10 November 1777, above [vol. 2: 193–94].)

3. On the decision to evacuate Ft. Mifflin, which stood on Mud Island in the Delaware River, see NG to Washington, 14 November 1777, above (vol. 2: 197–98 and n). Most observers agree that the three-week defense of the fort in the face of increasingly heavy bombardment by the British had been gallant.

4. Washington's army was not able to force the British under Gen. Sir Robert Howe to evacuate Philadelphia during 1777.

5. NG was referring to the capture of the army of Gen. John Burgoyne at Saratoga, N.Y., by the American forces commanded by Gen. Horatio Gates.

6. In the spring of 1777, Congress reorganized the Commissary Department by creating two commissaries general, one of purchases and the other of issues. Trumbull was offered the former post but declined it on the grounds that the new scheme, under which deputy commissaries were appointed by, and responsible to, Congress, would be unworkable. As NG noted here, the new system did not work well, and Congress reestablished the previous system on 14 April 1778. (Risch, *Supplying*, pp. 169–73; *DAB*)

To Colonel Clement Biddle

Dr Col

Head Quarters [Springfield Meeting House, Pa.]
Feb 14th [1778] half past three[1]

I receivd two Letters from you within an hour past. I am very sorry to find so small a collection of Waggons.[2] Search the country through and through. Mount your pressing parties on Horses for expeditions sake. Harden your heart, and dispatch business as fast as possible.[3] I have got many parties out collecting Waggons, Horses, Cattle, Hogs & Sheep. The Waggons I shall forward to you as fast as they come in. We have made considerable collection of Horses, and I think it will be best to send them to Camp, to Night, that as many Waggons may be riged out as possible, to come on for forage.

I think I shall move from this position to Night or tomorrow morning[.] We are in the midst of a d——d nest of Tories and as we are in the neighbourhood of the Enemy a change of position becomes necessary for security sake.[4] I am with great respect your most obed[t] Serv[t]

N GREENE

ALS (Catherine Barnes, 2002).

1. The year was taken from a GWG transcript (CSmH) and is consistent with the contents of the letter.

2. In a letter to Washington of 15 February 1778, above (vol. 2: 285), NG wrote that Biddle had collected "but a few Waggons. The Inhabitants conceal them."

3. Despite his encouragement in this letter, NG wrote Washington again on 15 February, at 8 P.M., that Biddle had "but a poor prospect of geting Waggons" and requested that Washington send some from camp. (Vol. 2: 286, above) As seen in NG to Biddle, 19 February, immediately below, the foraging was being done to feed the army, and Biddle did find supplies of food and forage to send to the troops.

4. In his first letter to Washington of 15 February, NG wrote that Biddle also complained about the "disaffection of the people." On 15 February, NG moved his headquarters to Providence Meeting House, Pa. (See NG to Washington, second letter of 15 February 1778, above [vol. 2: 286].)

To Colonel Clement Biddle

[Providence Meeting House, Pa.]

Dr Sir   Thursday Evening 8 oClock [19 February 1778][1]

Your favor this moment was deleverd me.[2] I am glad to hear such a number of Waggons was loaded to day. General Wayne wrote me a few hours since that there was great quantities of Hay between Marcus Hook and Willmington.[3]

By Letters from Camp I find the cry for provisions still continues; but I am in hopes it is not so great as it was.[4]

Agreeable to your advice I will send down another party to Marcus Hook in the morning and if necessary will give them orders to continue there all Night.

I purpose to move in the morning. I wish to know where the best position will be to coopperate with your designs. I have given Orders for the troops to be in readiness to march by ten in the morning.

Col Lawrence wrote me last night that Col Lurteloh expected 300 Waggons from Lancaster.[5] Pray has he advertized you of this circumstance?

The Quakers are very angry, youl certainly be read out of Meeting, and called an Apostate.[6] Yours   N GREENE

ALS (PPIn).

1. This letter is dated simply "Thursday Evening." The date assigned by the editors, 19 February, was derived from the contents. The place was taken from other of NG's letters during this time.

2. Biddle's letter to NG has not been found.

3. On Gen. Anthony Wayne's foraging expedition, see note at Washington to NG, 12 February 1778, and NG to Washington, 20 February 1778, both above (vol. 2: 282n; 292).

4. By "Camp," NG referred to the Continental army's encampment at Valley Forge, Pa. The letters to NG discussing the continued need for food in the army have not been found.

5. The letter to NG from Col. John Laurens, an aide to Washington, has not been found. Col. Henry Lutterloh was the acting quartermaster general of the army. On 20 February 1778, above, NG wrote Washington: "We want nothing but Waggons to make a grand forage." (Vol. 2: 292)

6. Biddle, like NG, had grown up as a member of the Society of Friends. He had been disowned in 1775 for "studying to learn the art of war." It is not known if any additional action was taken against him at this time, but in 1781 Biddle became one of the founding members of the "Free Quakers," who retained most of the core beliefs of Quakerism but did away with disownment and excommunication and held that forcible resistance against warlike invasion was laudable. (Charles Wetherill, *History of The Religious Society of Friends Called by Some The Free Quakers, in the City of Philadelphia* [Philadelphia, 1894], found on the Quaker Writings Home Page)

*   *   *

¶ [FROM GENERAL PETER MUHLENBERG, [Camp, Valley Forge, Pa., 9 April 1778.][1] Washington wants him to move the cloth in the "Virginia Store" to Lancaster, Pa.[2] Muhlenberg will send it off "to Morrow," when the tailors who have been selected for "making it up" are to leave, if he can get wagons.[3] Catalog extract (Dodd, Mead & Company, *Autographs and Manuscripts, Catalogue No. 55* [December 1899], p. 57)]

1. The date was taken from the catalog description; the place was derived from the contents.

2. By "Virginia Store," Muhlenberg meant the supply depot of the Virginia Continental line at Valley Forge.

3. By "making it up," Muhlenberg meant turning the cloth into clothing for the troops. NG's reply has not been found.

*   *   *

To Colonel Ephraim Bowen[1]

Camp at Valley Forge [Pa.], June 3, 1778

"You are hereby appointed Deputy Quarter-Master-General, of army of U.S., for state of Rhode Island and Providence Plantations[,][2] and you are authorised to contract for and purchase within the said district, all such Wagons and horses as shall be needed, to be purchased within said state for use of army and transport of stores, or shall be directed by Quarter-Master Greene, or his assistants, of all conditions in District and gradually to perform all things necessary to be done and performed by a Deputy Quarter-Master-General within said state; you are to appoint so many assistants and clerks for conducting said business as you find from time to time necessary, paying them a reasonable compensation for services and being careful to keep none in pay longer than shall be necessary, and for your own trouble and expense in the premised, you shall receive pay at rate of $75.00 per month and 6 rations per day together with a commission at rate of 1 o/o (per cent) on all your necessary disbursements in Department. Given under my hand, in Camp at Valley Forge, June 3, 1778

NATHANAEL GREENE, QUARTER-MASTER-GENERAL"

Tr (Typescript: R-Ar).

1. On Bowen, see above, vol. 3: 23n.

2. Bowen had originally been appointed to this post by Gen. Thomas Mifflin, NG's predecessor as quartermaster general. He continued to serve as deputy quartermaster for Rhode Island "throughout NG's tenure." (Ibid.)

*   *   *

¶ [FROM JOSEPH REED, "Mr Henrys," 9 June 1778. Congress has appointed "the General [i.e., Washington], Mr. Dana," and Reed a committee to help "arrange the Army."[1] Because of this appointment, Reed has postponed his return home. He supposes that NG will receive "some Direction to quarter" Dana and him, "but as you are pretty thick at Moore Hall I will relieve you from the Incumbrance of self and Servant for the present by remaining at Mr. Henry's." Asks for "some Oats or other Grain for my Horses as we are very destitute."[2] Printed in Smith, *Letters*, 10: 61]

1. On 4 June, Congress directed that its resolutions concerning the reorganization of the army, enacted on 25 May, be sent to Washington, who, "with the advice and assistance of the honble. Joseph Reed And Francis Dana, Esq^s or either of them, is hereby directed and empowered to proceed in arranging the same according to the said resolutions." (*JCC*, 11: 570)

2. During the winter and spring of 1778, Moore Hall, near Valley Forge, Pa., had served as the residence and meeting place for the congressional Committee at Camp, of which Reed had been a member. Moore Hall was about two miles from Washington's head-quarters. (Smith, *Letters*, 9: 61n) On 13 June, Reed wrote from "Major Henry's" to Clement Biddle, the commissary general of forage, asking for grain for his horses because none was available on "this [i.e., the east] Side of Schuykill" River. He added: "I wrote a day or two ago to Genl Green on this Head not recollecting that I should have applied to you—but none being then in Camp I had only his Promis to supply me as soon as it arrived." (MH)

*   *   *

To Nehemiah Hubbard

Sir   Camp Valley Forge [Pa.] June 12th 1778

Your's of the 25th May & 5th of June are recieved.[1]

Mr Bingham is to account with me for the purchases he has made, any monies you may have furnished him with shall be replaced immediately.[2]

I hope you will spare no pains in getting Col^o Lamb's Ready to March agreeable to the instructions I gave you in my former Letters on that subject.[3]

I am glad Col^o Hay calls on you for I am sure he has too much upon his hands for any one man to execute seasonably.[4] You will give him all the aid in your power from time to time as he shall make application & mutually assist each other in council, information & execution of public business.

You will purchase for Col° Sheldon as many horses as he may want for the dragoon service & discharge all proper bills that fall properly within the QMG department.[5] You will be very particular in keeping proper vouchers to support the charges.

In your next Letter enclose me a return of the number of Assistants you have appointed & the conditions on which they are engaged.[6] You will pay particular attention to the Instructions I first gave you that was, not to keep any Assistants or Clerks on pay, longer than the service actually demands it.[7] I do not wish you to be deficient in the necessary aid; but to be very careful not to keep any on the pay lists that are not requisite to transact the public business. Useless Agents only serve to prey upon the vitals of the Continental funds[,] eat up our national wealth & give disgust to the Inhabitants who see them supported at the public expence without rendering any considerable services for their Wages.

The great number of Stores comeing on from the Eastward will render it necessary that the Post at Danbury have a large supply of teams, for the purpose of forwarding them. I am Sir Your humble Servant   NATH GREENE

LS (Robert F. Batchelder, 1996).

1. Neither letter has been found.

2. Ozias Bingham was an assistant deputy quartermaster employed by Hubbard, the deputy quartermaster for Connecticut. In a summary of purchases made by Quartermaster Department employees, dated 9 January 1779, Bingham is listed as having spent $10,000. (Vol. 3: 156, above)

3. Col. John Lamb commanded the Second Continental Artillery Regiment. NG's instructions are in his letter to Hubbard of 15 May 1778, above (vol. 2: 390).

4. Udny Hay was deputy quartermaster for the lower part of New York state. (Vol. 2: 371n, above)

5. Elisha Sheldon commanded the Connecticut Light Horse regiment. (Heitman, *Register*)

6. In his letter of 27 June, Hubbard assured NG that he would send the returns. (Vol. 2: 48, above)

7. NG's instructions to Hubbard have not been found, but those contained in his letter of appointment as deputy quartermaster to John Davis, dated 23 March 1778, above, were probably similar. (Vol. 2: 320)

To Joseph Webb

Sir   Camp at Kaykayatte [i.e., Kakiat, N.Y.] July 14 1778

On the receipt of this you will cease makeing Portmanteaus or Valeeses. We think we have a sufficiency for the demand of this Campaign. I receivd a Letter from you some time past but whether it was answerd I cannot recollect, and I am seperated from my papers on the march which prevents my reduceing of it to a certainty.[1] You will please to forward us an account of your disbursements; and let the Portmanteaus &c. be sent to M[r] Nehemiah Hubbard DQMG at Hartford.

The particulars of the Battle of Monmouth and the Enemys march through the Jerseys, you see in the Papers.[2]

We are now crossing the North [i.e., Hudson] River, the left Wing of the Army crosses to day at Kings ferry, the right to morrow & the second line next day.

There is a French fleet consisting of 12 Sail of the Line & 4 frigates, off Sandy Hook—*Mischief thou art on foot now let it work.*[3] A French frigate of 36 Guns sunk an English Sloop of 20 Guns near the Capes of Delaware a few days since.[4] Great Britain & France will soon be by the Ears. Things are ripening fast in Europe for a general war. British pride stands upon a slippery foundation and bids fair to meet with a very great fall.

The Parliamentiary Propositions for a reconciliation with the United States are truly farcical; and as such the Congress have treated them.[5]

My best respects to your and M[r] Deans family and all others of my acquaintance at Weathersfield.[6] I am Sir your humble Servant.

NATH GREENE

ALS (Charles Hamilton Galleries, Inc., 1982).

1. Neither Webb's letter to NG nor NG's reply has been found.

2. For more on the battle of Monmouth (28 June 1778) and the march of the British army commanded by Sir Henry Clinton through New Jersey, see NG to Jacob Greene, 2 July 1778, above. (Vol. 4: 449–52 and n)

3. NG was roughly paraphrasing from William Shakespeare's *Julius Caesar*. The actual lines are: "Now let it work! Mischief, thou art afoot; Take thou what course thou wilt!" (*Julius Caesar*, act iii, scene 2)

4. On 8 July 1778, the twenty-eight gun British frigate *Mermaid* was forced ashore by French vessels near Sinepuxent, Md. The captain of the *Mermaid* reported that he had formally surrendered to an unnamed American privateer captain. (James Hawker to Viscount Howe, 29 July 1778, UkLPR, Admiralty 1/1904)

5. A special commission sent from England, often called the Carlisle Commission, proposed terms of reconciliation in a letter to Congress of 9 June. As these proposals stopped short of offering Americans their independence, Congress completely rejected "propositions so derogatory to the honor of an Independent Nation." (Henry Laurens to the Carlisle Commissioners, 17 June 1778, Smith, *Letters*, 10: 122–23)

6. NG was sending his respects to Barnabas Deane and other friends in Wethersfield, Conn., which was the home of his close friend Col. Jeremiah Wadsworth, the commissary general of purchases. In April 1779, Deane, Wadsworth, and NG became business partners in the firm of Barnabas Deane & Company. (See note at NG to Wadsworth, 26 July 1783, above.)

Bill of Expences[1]

1775	Nathanael Greene Gen[l]	Do
June 12	To 2 pare of Stocking had of Perry[2]	8. 0
	To a Mehogane Desk & Book Case had of Thomas Spencer	[£]15. 6. 0
July 17	To Cash paid your Wifes Expences down to the Camp	1. 1. 0
1776	To W[m] Arnold Act[3]	3. 0
Jan[y] 6	To 1 Y[d] of Lawn	9. 0
	To E[zer] Wall Act	3. 8.11
	To godds Wall had Mathewson for your Cloase	8. 6

1775
August 7   To 7 ⅛ Yds. Of Calico at 6/9 per yd £ 2..8..1

To 3/11 Yd of hollon[4]	2/	
To 1 Lawn Apron	7/	3. 2. 1
To 10 doz of Whale bone	5/	

the [a]bove articles Del[d] to Nancy Littlefield[5]

To 1 Silk Handkerchief & 4 yds Shoe binding	4. 3
To 1 hare Comb	6
To ¼ Yards of fusten[6]	2. 9¾
To 1 ¼ Yds of Muslin	4.11¼
To 1 pocket hankerchif & 1[oz] of garlick thred	2. 6
To 1 peace of wide Tape & Skane of Silk	1. 5
To ⅜ yds of Muslen	1. 9
To 2 ½ yds of flourd Sarge [i.e., flowered serge]	7. 6

1776
May 31

To 1[oz] Thred	1. 0
To 8 ¾ yds of Calico at 6/	2.12. 6
To 6 Skains of Silk	4. 6
To 1 Chare of Welcom Arnold[7]	4.13. 0
Nov 4 To Cash paid for Stockens & Cambrick	5.17. 6
To 1 Pare of Shoe to your Wife	6. 0
To Cash Paid Granny Arnold	1. 4. 0
To Paul Greene Act	2. 6
To Cash Paid for Medisons for your Wife	7. 6
To 2 Hankerchiefs	4. 0
To Cash Paid for Nussing [i.e., Nursing] your Wife	2.13. 5
To 2 ¾ Yds of Striped Hollon	7. 9
To 4 ¼ Yds of homespun Checks	15. 3
To 2 Skains of English Thred	4

1776	To 14 yds of Worsted greset[8] at 5/	3.10. 0
Nov. 4	To Sundry good your Wife had of Welcom	
Cont.	Arnold	1. 6. 0
	To Sundry good your Wife had of Tilling-	
	harst[9]	13. 5. 3
	To 1 Skaine of Couler[d] Thred	2
	To Cash paid your Wifes Expences to Camp	5. 6. 0
	To Cash paid for Dictionary & gloves &	
	Shoes	1. 1. 0
	To Cash paid for Ruffels for Child	2. 0
	To Cash paid Widow [Sumford?] makeing	
	your Wifes Polane	12. 0
	To 1 pare of Shoes for Washington[10]	4. 6
	To the Sum you are to Charged with that You	
	had over your Proportion in the Division	
	of the Real Estate[11]	300. 0. 0
	To Sundrys as p[r] Act Drawn out Brought	194.10. 0
	forward	
	To 1 hat for Washington	6
	To 1 pallet Bedsted	1. 4
	To 1 Bedlock	1.10
	To 40[oz] of gees feathers at 2/	4. 0
	To Paid for Spinning toe[12]	6
	To 3 Quarts of molasses	2
	To 3 Yards of Tocloath	6
	To 4 ½ Yds of fine linnen	1. 2
	To Cash paid for Sundrys for your [wife?] in	
	Boston	9
	To James Greene Shoe Act	16
	To Cash Sent to Boston to make Silver Cups	7. 4
	To Cash paid for Making Silver Cups	3.18
	To 41[w] of Beef	17
	To 100[w] Salt Pork	3. 6
	To 62[w] Sugar	2. 6
	To 2 ¼[w] of Beeswax	5
	To 3 ½[w] of Cotton at 3/	9
	To 9 ¼ of Flax	9
	To 22[w] of Sugar	16
	To 1 Peck of Salt	4
	To 5[w] of Codfish paid for Spinning	1.10
	To 6 pare of Linnen Stocking at 9/6	2.17. 0
	To 3 large linnen hankerchiefs	12. 0
	To 3 Yds of Calico	18. 0
	To 3 yds of gingham	1. 0. 3
	To 1 Black Silk handkirchefs	6. 0

1776	To 2 Cotten [Romoll?] Handkerchiefs	5. 0
Nov. 4	To 1 Checkd linnen handkerchief	2. 3
Cont.	To 3 Bandanner handkerchiefs	1.10. 0
	To 1 Spotted Linnen hankercheif	4. 6
	To 2 & 9/16 yds Striped Cotten	7.10
	To 4 ½ Yds of Calico at 10/	2. 5. 0
	To 4 linnen Caps	9. 4
	To 3/5 Yds of Blue Calico	12. 9
	To 2 Stampt linnen handkercheifs	12. 0
	To 3 half foannasses [furnaces?]	7. 4. 0
	To 7 ½ Yds of Garden Satting	4.10. 0
	To Blue great Coat	1. 5. 0
	To Molly Spinks Act ·	3. 2. 2
	To 1 linnen & 1 Check'd Shirt	11. 0
	To 1 pare of Shoes & 2 Worsted Caps	16. 6
	To 1 Clock	13.10. 0
	To John Caseys[13] Act	1.14.10
	To Sylvester Greene[14] Act	2.11. 8
	To 48 ½ʷ of Beef	16. 2
	To 36ʷ of Flour	9. 0
	To 3 ½ Yds of linnen of Sam Buffon	1. 1. 0
	To paid Spencer Merrel ac't	3. 9
	To paid Stephen Potter[15] for Dressing Cloath	14. 3
	To Paid Gideon Mumford[16] Act	9. 9. 0
	To Doctor Joslin[17] Act	1. 8.10
	To 41 Yards & ⅝ fine Hollon of John Reynold[18]	18.15. 0

D (Swann Galleries, 1982?).

1. This account is docketed "Bill of Expences for from 1775." No terminal date is given, but the reference in the account to the settlement of the estate of Nathanael Greene, Sr., which was begun in April 1778 but not completed until 1779, means that some items listed here dated from at least as late as 1779. As the individuals who can be identified were from Rhode Island, it is likely that this account was prepared by someone associated with Jacob Greene & Company, which handled NG's financial affairs in the state.

2. This was probably NG's brother Perry Greene.

3. William Arnold was a member of the Kentish Guards with NG. (Vol. 1: 69, 72, above) "Act" is the abbreviation for account in this document.

4. This is a misspelling of holland, a fabric made of linen or cotton, often glazed, and used for children's clothing, window shades, and upholstery. (OED)

5. Nancy Littlefield was CG's sister.

6. This is a misspelling of fustian, a kind of coarse, sturdy cloth. (OED)

7. Welcome Arnold was a Providence, R.I., merchant. (See vol. 1: 54n, above, and NG's correspondence with him in the present volume.)

8. This is presumably a misspelling of grisette, an inexpensive gray fabric. (OED)

9. This may have been Nicholas P. Tillinghast, a Newport merchant. (See vol. 9: 523n, above.)

10. Undoubtedly, this was George Washington Greene, NG's son.

11. On the division of the estate of NG's father, see Division of the Estate of Nathanael Greene, Sr., 10 June 1779, above. (Vol. 4: 136)

12. This is a misspelling of tow, a coarse, broken flax or hemp fiber prepared for spinning. (*OED*)

13. The Casey family lived in East Greenwich. Several Caseys had served in the Kentish Guards with NG. (Vol. 1: 62, above)

14. Sylvester Greene had served in the Kentish Guards with NG. (Vol. 1: 62, above)

15. For more on Stephen Potter, see above, vol. 1: 6n, and NG's letter to Moses Brown of 9 April 1771, in this, the Addenda section.

16. Gideon Mumford, a merchant from East Greenwich, had served in the Kentish Guards with NG. (Vol. 1: 77n, above)

17. Dr. Joseph Joslyn had been the Greenes' family physician. (Vol. 1: 187, above)

18. John Reynolds was also a member of the Kentish Guards. (Vol. 1: 72, above)

To Colonel Ephraim Bowen

D[r] Sir   Coventry [R.I.] Sept 29th 1778

M[rs] Greene will be exceedingly oblige[d] to you to get a good Stove made for her. She wishes it to be lind with Tin. The sooner you can get it done the greater will be the obligation[.] If you have any safe conveyance please to forward it.

I hope you have sent off all the Horses agreeable to the conversation you and I had the other day. The censorious Times will require double diligence to save yourself from reproach and there are not a few who wish to find you trip[p]ing.

My best regards to your good Lady [Sally Angell Bowen], Your Cousin & his Lady.[1] I am with Sentiments of regard your most Obed[t] humble Ser[v]   N GREENE

Facsimile in The Rendells, Inc., *Catalog* #164 (1983).

1. NG may have been referring here to Bowen's older stepbrother, Jabez Bowen, who was the lieutenant governor of Rhode Island, and his wife, Sarah Brown Bowen.

*   *   *

¶ [FROM ABRAHAM LOTT, Beverwyck, N.J., 24 October 1778. He has not written before because he did not know NG's whereabouts after "the raising of the Blockade at Rhode Island."[1] By NG's letter of 19 October, which he received two days ago, Lott discovered that NG had returned to Fredericksburgh [N.Y.], and he could not "let slip the favorable conveyance" to reply.[2] Col. [William Smith] Livingston and others gave Lott "an account of the Rhode Island Expedition" and "the concurring circumstances, which were the Causes of its miscarriage."[3] Most people fault the Comte d'Estaing for leaving Newport "so precipitately" and blame him for the expedition's "failure." Lott, too, believes d'Estaing "moved off rather sooner than he need have done, and that we Should have taken the place, and made the whole Garrison Prisoners of war, with the whole of the Enemies Stores, if he had remained but 24 hours longer before the place." Had the allies captured Newport, the British army in New York would have also "fallen," and Britain would have been forced to make peace "on such Terms as we should dictate. It is therefore not to be wondered at that some people are a little vociferous, against Monsr Le Compte d'Estaing." Lott is "greatly Obliged" to "Genl & Mrs Hancock" for remembering him.[4] They showed him "the greatest marks of Attention" when he was in Boston, and he ranks them "among the most virtuous Citizens. It is true they live high," but Lott does not believe they are "Tinctured With the prevailing vices of the Town" that NG mentioned, and which Lott also witnessed. In fact, Lott went so far as to remark to some friends there that he expected "to find a pious Religious set of people," but found instead that "very little remains of it amongst them. A Sad foreboding this, that in times of danger and universal distress, *vice* instead of *virtue* should prevail, and Especially among a people formerly highly esteemed for their Moral, as well as Religious professions." He prays that "God may not in his great displeasure punish this Land for these growing Abominations, but may turn the hearts of all its Inhabitants to do what is truely praise worthy, and Acceptable to him." Mrs. Livingston is "perfectly recovered," and Lott hopes to see her "here" soon.[5] "Col^o Bill" [i.e., William Livingston] has sent in his resignation, which Lott hopes will be accepted for the sake of Livingston's wife.[6] Lott and Livingston expect to go to Philadelphia "Next Monday" for a short visit. He congratulates NG on the birth of another daughter and is "proud" that NG plans to name her after Lott's daughter Cornelia.[7] Sends compliments to CG "upon her happy delivery" and hopes the "the Child may live & be a comfort to you both." Mrs. Livingston recently delivered a son, "who for his age is a promising lad."[8] NG cannot doubt Lott's wish to meet him in New York soon. Lott has received information that indicates the British are planning to evacuate the city. He assumes they will stay there "as long as they possibly can," but he hopes he is mistaken in this. As Washington's army moved from White Plains "shortly" after Lott left camp, and as they have not settled in any "fixed place" since then, he has not sent his hemp. If he sends it to Fishkill, he wonders if there will be "empty return waggons to Boston" that could carry it there. He also asks when he should send it.[9] Mrs. [Gertrude Coeyman] Lott and family send their respects. RC (ScCMu) 3 pp.]

1. The French naval blockade of Rhode [i.e., Aquidneck] Island ended 21 August 1778, but American land forces did not finally leave until 31 August. (Vol. 3: 480–86; 499–504, above)

2. NG's letter to Lott of 19 October 1778 has not been found.

3. Col. William Smith Livingston, Lott's son-in-law, had been wounded in the battle of Rhode Island. (Vol. 3: 10n, above)

4. John Hancock, the former president of Congress, had commanded 5,000 Massachusetts militia troops in the battle of Rhode Island. He and his wife, the former Dorothy Quincy, were known for the "ostentatious display" of their wealth. (*DAB*)

5. Lott's daughter Catherine was married to William Smith Livingston. (Vol. 3: 10n, above)

6. As seen at Livingston's letter to NG of 23 October 1778, above, his resignation was accepted by Washington. (Vol. 3: 10)

7. NG's and CG's third child, Cornelia Lott Greene, was born 23 September 1778. (Vol. 3: 55n, above)

8. Lott wrote NG on 23 December 1778, above, that his new grandson had recently died. (Vol. 3: 124)

9. NG's reply has not been found.

¶ [MAJOR ICHABOD BURNET TO COLONEL JEREMIAH WADSWORTH. [From Fredericksburg, N.Y.], 14 November 1778.[1] Sends an extract from a letter to NG from Mr. [Nehemiah] Hubbard, so that Wadsworth can give the "necessary Orders" for loading the wagons with flour. In the excerpted paragraph, Hubbard writes that "the Govenour" [Jonathan Trumbull of Connecticut] has asked him for "150 Teams to transport the Baggage of the Convention troops from Enfield to Sharon."[2] Hubbard will obtain the wagons and order them to "bring back loads of Flour to this post."[3] ALS (CtHi) 1 p.]

1. The location was taken from other of NG's letters of this date.

2. The excerpted letter from Hubbard, the deputy quartermaster of Connecticut, has not been found. On the movement through Connecticut of the Convention army—the captured troops of Gen. John Burgoyne—see note at NG to James Davenport, 9 November 1778, above (vol. 3: 52n).

3. Hubbard was stationed at Hartford, Conn. As seen in NG's letter to him of 14 November 1778, above (vol. 3: 69), the flour was for the army of Gen. Horatio Gates.

¶ [FROM BARTHOLOMEW VON HEER, "Sommersett County," N.J., 11 December 1778. The "Storming Wether" is preventing his command from changing quarters.[1] "All the Inhabitants in this Naborhood would by where [i.e., be very] glad, to have my Troops i[n] Winter Quarters with them, if only Forage could by provided sufficient for my Troops." He has remained at Somerset Court House for five days, awaiting directions as to where to winter; NG promised to get those directions from Washington. If von Heer's men are to relocate, he asks that NG find them quarters where they can "provide" for themselves. While his command has been "hir," their horses have been on "half Allownce." Asks NG to have the forage master at "Blockenind" [i.e., Pluckemin?] provide forage so that the horses can get their "full Allownce"; otherwise, they will "suffer." He must remain at Somerset Court House for at least "this Day and to morrow," because the Raritan River is too high to cross.[2] RCS (Joseph Rubinfine, 1999) 2 pp.]

1. Von Heer commanded the maréchaussée, or mounted provosts, from June 1778, when they were established, until 1783. (See above, vol. 2: 427.)

2. NG's reply has not been found, but in January 1779, von Heer's command was stationed at Millstone, N.J. (See his letter to NG of 24 January 1779, above [vol. 3: 179].)

*   *   *

To Major Robert Forsyth

Dear Sir   Philadelphia January 31[,] 1779

We have some prospect of seting out for Camp to morrow or next day.[1] Mrs Greens Horses is unfit for use one of them being almost blind with a disorder in the Eyes cald the Hooks. Please to send me forward the little Bays.[2]

There is some News from the West Indies not altogether to our likeing, the particulars you will see in the Papers tomorrow.[3] Yours

NATH GREENE

ALS (Thomas E. Baker, 1992).

1. NG was still in Philadelphia on 4 February 1779, when he wrote to Joseph Reed, the president of the Pennsylvania Council. (Vol. 3: 208, above)

2. In his reply of 3 February 1779, Forsyth wrote that "faithful old John comes with his Bays in very good order." (Ibid., p. 207)

3. The *Pennsylvania Journal and Weekly Advertiser* reported on 3 February 1779 that British forces had captured the island of St. Lucia on 20 December 1778.

To Major Richard Claiborne

Sir   [Philadelphia, between 3 January and 9 February 1779][1]

I have your favor of the 3ᵈ.[2] I cannot conceive that the Captains of Artificers can have any occasion for Horses and therefore will not furnish or forage any except those that acts as superintands.

Whenever the nature of their duty renders a saddle Horse necessary, on application they shall have one; but to keep Horses for them to ride about the Country in persuit of idle amusements is what I cannot consent to. There is not [*damaged*] objection of their being unnecessary; but the difficulty and expence of supporting the Horses in Camp which cannot be dispensed with, and to add to this burden, useless Horses will be both impolotick and unjust. I am Sir Your humble Serᵗ NATH GREENE

ALS (PCC, item 173, vol. 2: 21, DNA).

1. The date, which is not given, is conjectured from the pen used, the style of writing, and the letter's placement in the PCC, as well as from the facts that the contents show that Claiborne was then in camp, serving as an aide to NG, and that NG was away from the army. From this evidence, the editors believe the letter was written between 3 January and 9 February 1779, while NG was in Philadelphia.

2. Claiborne's letter has not been found.

Memorandum Relating to the New Establishment of the Army[1]

[Middlebrook, N.J., 10 March 1779?][2]

9 I think 16 feet is too great an interval between the Platoons; the Camp will be too extended; half the distance is sufficent.[3]

Will it not be best to have a company of Pioneers to each Battallion to carry all the Axes, Picks & Shovels.

14 The quarter master

15 quarter master General

16 No alarm should be given unless the danger is great.

14 This seems to be the quarter masters duty but as he must apply to the Adj [i.e., adjutant] for the party, will it not be as well to stand as it does.

15 This seems to be the quarter master Generals duty; but for the same reason that a Regimental adj is more proper than the quarter master, The adj General is more Suitable than the quarter master General.[4]

18 This examination should take place three times a week at least.

19 3 Shirts 2 pair stockings—2 Numer Less

D (MiU-C).

1. This appears to be a memorandum commenting on what became chapters 14 through 18 of Baron von Steuben's regulations for the army. Chapter 14 concerns the march of the army; Chapter 15, the disposition of the army's baggage on the march; Chapter 16, the laying out of a camp; Chapter 17, the manner of entering camp; Chapter 18, necessary regulations for preserving order and cleanliness in camp, and inspection of the men and their equipment. As Steuben's rough draft has not been found, it is not possible to compare NG's numbering of the sections with his. It appears, though, that there was some alteration in the numbering between the draft and the final, printed version of the regulations. (Joseph Riling, *Baron Von Steuben and His Regulations, containing a facsimile of the Original Regulations for the Order and Discipline of the Troops of the United States* [Philadelphia: Ray Riling Arms Books Company, 1966])

2. The docketing, in a hand other than NG's, gives a date of 27 August 1779. However, Washington, Gen. Arthur St. Clair, and Lord Stirling all commented on Steuben's proposed regulations on 10 or 11 March 1779. (Steuben Microfilm) Believing that NG would have reviewed the proposed regulations at about the same time, the editors have posited the above date for the memorandum. The place was taken from other of NG's letters at this time.

3. The final regulations kept a distance of sixteen feet between platoons.

4. The comments labelled "14" and "15" may have related to regulations concerning the army on the march. In the printed version of his regulations, Steuben did have the quartermaster general give the order of march and the brigade quartermasters the right to regulate the arrangement of the pioneers on the march. NG's observations concerning the quartermasters and adjutants do not appear to correspond to any section of the final regulations.

*   *   *

¶ [**FROM JOHN KING**, Rutland, Mass., 12 June 1779. "Presuming on a casual Acquaintance," from their having lived in the same house during the spring of 1776,[1] and relying on NG's "generosity of Sentiment," King is "induced to trespass" on NG's good nature "at this busy Season" by sending this letter. He is a conductor of stores in the British artillery service. He was ordered to join a detachment in Georgia, but en route his ship and several others were "captured by the Continental Frigates *Warren* &cᵃ."[2] After landing in Boston on 23 April, King and the other prisoners were marched to Rutland and "quarter'd with the Inhabitants on signing Parole." Purchasing "Clothes & Necessaries" to enable him "to bear the scorching beams of a torrid Sun" reduced his "humble Purse to its last Guinea." He lost most of those clothes when captured and has been forced to sell the rest to cover his expenses since his arrival in Rutland; consequently, he is like a "naked, starving Lazarus." He has written to friends in New York for money, but the journey is so "prolix and precarious," and his necessity so "laconic & pressing," that he "must inevitably starve if some Guardian Angel doth not extend an helping Hand." He hopes, therefore, that NG, from "his benevolence & the high Regard oft express'd" for King's "dearest Friend Mʳ Abrᵐ Livingston," will grant him "a Parole to go to New York" so that he can arrange to be exchanged.[3] "If there is no Impropriety in such an Indulgence," NG will "confer infinite Obligations" on King with a "favourable" reply to this "earnest Request."[4] Hopes NG may be "crown'd with Health and Laurels." RCS (ScCMu) 3 pp.]

1. During the spring of 1776, NG was on Long Island, N.Y. (See above, vol. 1: 211–90.)

2. On 17 April, the Continental Navy vessels *Warren, Queen of France,* and *Ranger* captured seven vessels from a convoy carrying passengers and supplies from New York to Georgia. (Vol. 3: 431n, above)

3. Abraham Livingston was a New York merchant before he relocated to South Carolina, where he became the Continental agent. (Vol. 3: 134n, above)

4. NG's reply has not been found.

*   *   *

To Colonel Charles Pettit

To Mr. Petit.   [New Windsor, N.Y., 13 July 1779][1]

The congress are mistaken if they suppose I wrote either under the influence of passion or prejudice.[2] I wrote what I thought, and I think what I wrote. It is no small misfortune, that that body are too little acquainted with the nature of the business of the staff, to distinguish between evils incident and inseparable from it, and those which originate from neglect or any other improper cause.[3] Designing men, who dislike the system or the agents employed in it, have nothing more to do, to ruin the one or destroy the other, than to employ a few secret emissaries to instil poison and jealousies into the people. This being worked up into a ferment, and the congress ignorant of the cause, they fall upon measures to remedy the evil that only serve to add new difficulties. They who do not support measures from their usefulness, will ever be the sport of designing men. It is astonishing, how easily the honest and well-meaning, are duped too, into the most destructive measures, by the secret artifices of a few. In a government like ours, how cautious ought legislators to be in crediting evil reports to the prejudice of their servants; and how careful to examine their actions before a judgment is formed, or a decision takes place! How much the reverse of this has been the policy of congress in several instances!

I will venture to pronounce, we shall ever be in confusion and distress while popular frenzy takes the lead in administration, instead of just measures founded in maxims of sound policy.

Have not the tories a power to render us odious to one another? Cannot they create jealousies concerning the designs of the army? How easily can they brand the fairest characters as violators of public trust! Nothing is easier than to set such measures in operation; and distrust and deep-rooted prejudices, with perhaps violent ⟨measures against the suspected, are the consequences.

A *bad system* and *abuse of trust* are popular subjects. Change your system and remove delinquents, is their cry. This must be done to satisfy the people, whether any more useful system can be substituted, or better men be found to serve in the department or not. The object of administration seems to be, not whether business be well done, but whether individuals gain by it; not whether better men or better systems can be adopted, but whether a change is a popular measure. Unfortunate people! to be the sport of every wind and tide of passion and prejudice. I have said very little to any body in support of the system, or in justification of those employed in the department. But I am confident, fatal experience will soon convince the world that there can be no change for the better. The constitution of the department, or the extent of its business, appears to be little known to congress. Therefore, the monies expended in it, are in amount both alarming and inexplicable to them. It is evident they know nothing of the nature of the business from their manner of inquiry. Neither have they any idea of the difficulties incident to it. I enclose you a copy of what I wrote to congress, by which you will see I shall consider myself a volunteer after your resignation, and determine to get out of the business as soon as possible, without giving my enemies an advantage over me from the manner in which I leave the department.[4] This precaution may be necessary for you to attend to. I entered this department upon the express condition of your acting with me; the moment you quit, I shall think myself at liberty also.[5] There are few men with whom I would be concerned in business like this. Men are difficult to be found whose capacity, knowledge of business, temper and integrity can be relied on. And to be connected with men deficient in either, or to form connexions at haphazard, is a risk that I will not run. I am willing to make any reasonable⟩ sacrifice, but I will not expose my character and fortune to certain ruin. As soon as you announce your resignation formally to me, I shall send in mine. But at the same time, I mean to offer my services as a volunteer, but will not be answerable for monies spent in the department, or for the supplies that may be wanted. I have found it very difficult to support myself with our united exertions. What is to be expected, therefore, when two principal branches are lopped off?

I like you[r] address to congress, and would cheerfully have signed it, if it had been only to awaken their attention to the state of the department. I am far from being displeased with your resignation.[6] I think you have just cause, and would be wanting to yourself were you to continue in office. This circumstance will open a door through which I can escape out of the department, which both my wishes and interest lead to. It is now in a tolerable state. I am not certain it would be in my power to continue it so with our whole exertions; and, therefore, it may be a happy circumstance in the end, that we have an opportunity of quitting it when in a tolerable condition. [*one or more pages missing*]

Tr (GWG Transcript: CSmH). The text in angle brackets was taken from Johnson, *Greene*, 1: 137–38.

1. The transcript is dated 13 January 1780, but the contents clearly establish that this letter was written in July 1779. The place was taken from other of NG's letters at the time.

2. NG was referring to his letter of 24 June 1779 to John Jay, the president of Congress. (Vol. 4: 179, above) For Congress's reaction, see the notes at ibid.

3. A special committee of Congress was then investigating the activities of the employees of the quartermaster and commissary departments. NG saw the appointment and activities of this committee as a witch hunt, directed at him and his department. (See notes at The Committee for Superintending the Staff Departments to NG, 7 June 1779, above [vol. 4: 126], and the introduction to that volume, pp. xv–xvi.)

4. NG was referring to the last paragraph of his letter to Jay of 24 June.

5. On the circumstances surrounding NG's acceptance of the post of quartermaster general and of the appointment of Pettit and John Cox as his assistants, see above, vol. 2: 307–311n.

6. On the "resignation" of Pettit and Cox, see vol. 4: 180–83n. As seen there, they had threatened to resign in a letter to Congress of 7 July 1779. (PCC, item 192, p. 241, DNA)

To Colonel Thomas Chase

Sir   New Windsor [N.Y.] July 19th 1779

I have yours of the 25th and 1st of July.[1]

Mr Brewer returns loaded with Money which I hope will enable you to pay your debts and bring your Accounts to a close. This I wish you to effect as soon as possible as I think it is more than brobable [i.e., probable] there will be a general revolution in the Department.[2]

If Continental Measures and Continental property are of so little consideration with the different States that they cannot be supported or protected[,] One may venture to predict the period of the dissolution of our Union is not far distant. It is really matter of surprise and concern to see what little attention the general interest has paid to it by particular States. This policy is big with every evil and will either sooner or later prove fatal to our connection if pursued.[3]

I have laid the matter respecting the Barracks before the Congress[4] but as it will take sometime to procure a decision thereon, I wish you to settle some conditions of a[n] agreement between the proprietors and the public respecting the use of the ground until the Congress shall decide upon the question. This is the only mode you have left for saving the Barracks from total ruin; for its evidedent [i.e., evident] Legislation will not interfere. I am sir your humble Ser^t   NATH GREENE

This is an object of some importance and may lead to consequences perhaps not at present conceived of. I wish you to consult with some of the first Charactors in Boston respecting the mode and conditions of the contract and pursue their advice.

ALS (Joseph Rubinfine, 1998).

1. Chase's letter of 25 June 1779 to NG has not been found; that of 1 July 1779 is above, vol. 4: 195.

2. NG was referring to the reorganization of the Quartermaster Department approved

by Congress on 9 July 1779. (See Congressional Resolution of 9 July 1779, vol. 4: 234 and n, above.)

3. The reference here was to the demolition of a Continental barracks in Charlestown, Mass., by the private owner of the land on which it had stood and the refusal of the state of Massachusetts to intervene. Chase reported on the incident in his letter to NG of 1 July 1779.

4. See NG to John Jay, 14 July 1779, above (vol. 4: 228). On Congress's response, see note at ibid.

＊　　　＊　　　＊

¶ [TO COLONEL UDNY HAY. From New Windsor, N.Y., 22 July 1779. NG sends him a copy of an act of Congress.[1] LS (Scott A. Winslow, 1998) 1 p.]

1. The enclosure was presumably a copy of a resolution of 9 July 1779 concerning the Quartermaster Department. (See Congressional Resolution of 9 July 1779, above [vol. 4: 234 and n].)

＊　　　＊　　　＊

From William Duer[1]

Rhnybeck [i.e., Rhinebeck, N.Y.], Aug. 27th, 1779

"The Spirit of Enterprise so eminently displayed by our Army at Stoney Point, and on the late occasion at Paulas' Hooks (for the Communication of which receive my Thanks) cannot fail to intimidate our Enemies, whilst it gives heartfelt Joy to every true American.[2] I flatter myself that the Conviction which this must impress of the Point of Discipline to which the Troops are arrived, and the late Signal Success of our Allies the French, will bring to reason a Nation hitherto too haughty; and confident of success, to listen to the mild Voice of Peace.[3]

"I sincerely wish it not only for the sake of human Nature, but because I am afraid from the present political Complexion of our affairs, that the several Constitutions which the different States have formed with so much wisdom, and care, may be subverted, and that after a severe Contention, and the most horrid Anarchy, the Liberty for which so many have struggled both in Council and the Field, may become a Victim to our own factious Dissentions—You see I venture to breath the Spirit of Peace even to a Soldier not being yet a Convert to the Doctrine, which some have sedulously endeavored to inculcate, that in that Character the Idea of a Citizen of America has been lost."

Extract (Anderson Galleries, *Catalogue #1213* [March 1916], p. 17).

1. Duer was a former delegate to Congress from New York. His wife, "Lady Kitty" Alexander Duer, the daughter of NG's friend and fellow Continental officer Lord Stirling, was a friend of CG. (*DAB*; vol. 2: 86n, above)

2. On the capture of the British posts at Stony Point, N.Y., and Paulus Hook, N.J., see above, NG to John Cox, 17 July 1779 (vol. 4: 236–37 and n), and NG to CG, 23 August 1779 (ibid., pp. 333, 334n).

3. A French squadron commanded by the Comte d'Estaing had captured the West Indian islands of St. Vincent on 17 June 1779 and Grenada on 4 July 1779, and d'Estaing had also defeated a British fleet commanded by Lord John Byron near Grenada on 6 July 1779. (Boatner, *Encyc.*, p. 1185)

*　　*　　*

¶ [FROM ABRAHAM LOTT, Morristown, N.J., 18 September 1779. His failure to reply to NG's letter of 25 August [not found] was due to "Indisposition, and not to inattention." He describes his seizure by a "hot Nervous fever" and discusses his recovery. Is still in a "state of convelescence" but has recovered enough "to pay a visit to Mʳˢ [Gertrude Coeyman] Lott & Mʳˢ Livingston, now at Colᵒ Abeel's, where the latter expects momently to be brought to bed, and upon which Account her Mother Attends her."[1] The food at NG's quarters would be "perfectly Agreable" to Lott and "Mʳ Beverhoudt," and they would certainly pay a visit if those quarters were "more Accesable to Gouty feet & Limbs," but as Beverhoudt "would make but a poor figure in the rough Grounds" that NG occupies, they have "thought it most prudent" to postpone their visit until NG gets to "a more hospitable Country."[2] They both wish to "see the works at West Point, which After the labor expended thereon," must be "very formidable." Lott is greatly concerned over "the Indisposition of Mʳˢ Greene & the Two Children." If "Beverhoudt & family" had not arrived, he would have taken "very peculiar pleasure" in having CG spend the summer with his family, particularly because he believes she would thereby "have escaped the disorder she labors under."[3] For now, he can "only wish," but "hereafter" he may be able to "carry those wishes to effect." He sincerely hopes that she will "benefit from her Journey to the Eastward" and that NG will confirm Lott's wishes.[4]

NG's report about the arrival of Adm. [Marriot] Arbuthnot "has proved true," but "from Every information" Lott has received "from the other side of the Water, the Reinforcement he has brought will not create much new trouble to you."[5] Indeed, if the Report "about Compt D'Estaing's coming on this Coast with a formidable fleet and Armament proves true," Lott hopes "we may Kidnap Sʳ Henry & the admiral in New York."[6] His "wishes in this respect are extravagent," but he hopes "they are Not Altogether Chimerical. Certain it is that their completion is desireable, and more particularly So to the poor New York Refugees," among whom he includes himself. The British retreat "from before Charlestown must in its consequences operate as a Defeat, and in the Eyes of the Neutral European powers, appear much more disgraceful."[7] Adds: "Would it not be a clever thing if Compte D'Estaing took their Whole fleet & army in Georgia? Such a thing is not improbable; nay it is founded in Sound reason that he should make a Sweep of that weak part of the British possessions before he Attempts their more Strong holds in and about New York."[8] American "Exploits" against Stony Point and Paulus Hook are "glorious & will not only rank the Conductors thereof high in the Annals of American fame, but hold them up to all the powers of Europe, as the bravest of men, who have executed Arduous tasks with less bloodshed than any undertakings of the same Natures we have Any Accounts of; and it will also convince Britain that she has no Poltroons to contend with, but with a people Virtuous & who dare to risque every thing in defence of their much injured rights and priveledges[.]"[9] Gen. [John] Sullivan's "Success" will "teach the Savages, and their more Savage Allies And leaders" that they should live "upon friendly terms with the united States of America."[10] Heretofore, they have "always been Accustomed to carry fire & devastation with them in all their Warfare"; now, they "experience the effects thereof thence and hereafter will be cautious in how they Injure our out Settlers" in the future, "as they find they are not out of the reach of the Arms of America." The Penobscot expedition has "failed to the great damage of the Eastern Trade"; Lott is "sincerely Sorry" for this, "but perhaps good may come out of Evil."[11] The "Eastern States were so intent upon Navigation and making money that way, that they Almost forgot the Army. This Stroke may remind them of their Duty, and annimate them more to assist in the General Cause." Lott hopes, at least, that "this may be the case." He is "much Obliged" to NG for the "friendly hint about Col° Livingston, & So is" Livingston. Lott is sure that Livingston will benefit from NG's "advice," but he believes "there is much more Smoke than fire[;] the few articles he has had out are very trifling; yet it is imprudent in him to let even This Little leak out & make a Noise."[12] Lott sends respects from Mrs. Lott, Mrs. Livingston, and "Col° Abeel's family." RCS (ScCMu) 4 pp.]

1. Lott's daughter Catherine Lott Livingston gave birth to a daughter on 19 September 1779. (Vol. 4: 458n, above) James Abeel, the deputy quartermaster in charge of purchasing camp equipage, was a friend of both Lott and NG. (Vol. 2: 314n, above)

2. Lott and his family, who were refugees from New York City, were living in a small house at Beverwyck, the estate of Lucas Von Beverhoudt. (Vol. 3: 125n, above)

3. In a letter to Lott of 4 October 1779, above, NG reported that CG was feeling better. (Vol. 4: 458) As seen in NG's letter to CG of 30 August 1779, above (vol. 4: 343), it was NG's son, George Washington Greene, and younger daughter, Cornelia Lott Greene, who had been ill. Both recovered. Lott would not have been able to entertain CG, as Beverhoudt and his family had returned and were living in the main house at Beverwyck.

4. CG, who had been in Rhode Island, accompanied NG's brother Jacob to Newburyport, Mass., in September to see Jacob's daughter Polly. (See Jacob Greene to NG, 21 September 1779, above [vol. 4: 402].)

5. Arbuthnot left England with a fleet of 215 vessels on 25 May 1779. He did not reach New York until 25 August. His fleet brought only half the number of troops that had been promised to Sir Henry Clinton, and most of them were suffering from a virulent fever, which had killed a hundred men during the voyage and would soon infect the New York garrison. (Mackesy, *War*, p. 261; Willcox, *Clinton*, pp. 283–84)

6. The reports were true. The Comte d'Estaing's fleet had returned to American waters from the West Indies on 21 July 1779. Although his orders were to sail back to France after securing French possessions in the West Indies, d'Estaing had proceeded to the Georgia coast and would begin a siege of Savannah on 23 September. Washington hoped that d'Estaing would come north to join in an assault on New York, but d'Estaing had no intention of doing so. (See note at Jabez Bowen to NG, 6 September 1779, above [vol. 4: 365].) "S[r] Henry" was the British commander, Sir Henry Clinton; "the admiral" was probably Adm. John Byron.

7. A small British force commanded by Gen. Augustine Prevost had turned back from Charleston, S.C., on 12 May 1779. (Vol. 4: 105 and n, above) As Prevost's move against the South Carolina low country succeeded in its purpose of keeping an American force commanded by Gen. Benjamin Lincoln from invading Georgia, it is difficult to construe the British retreat as a great victory for the Americans. (See Boatner, *Encyc.*, pp. 214–15, 1034–36.)

8. D'Estaing did attack the British force at Savannah. For an account of this unsuccessful operation, see note at Jabez Bowen to NG, 6 September 1779, above. (Vol. 4: 365)

9. For more about the capture of the posts at Stony Point, N.Y., and Paulus Hook, N.J., by American forces commanded by Gen. Anthony Wayne and Maj. Henry Lee, respectively, see NG to John Cox, 17 July 1779, and NG to CG, 23 August 1779, both above. (Vol. 4: 236, 333)

10. On Gen. John Sullivan's expedition against the Iroquois nation, see Headnote on the Sullivan Expedition, above (vol. 4: 22–27).

11. On the unsuccessful expedition against the British post at Penobscot, in present-day Maine, see Samuel A. Otis to NG, 30 August 1779, above (vol. 4: 347).

12. William Smith Livingston was Lott's son-in-law. On 4 September 1779, NG wrote CG that Livingston had "made a great deal of money in driving a trade not altogether allowable." (Vol. 4: 363, above; see also Livingston to NG, 16 September 1779, [ibid., p. 388].)

¶ [FROM COLONEL CLEMENT BIDDLE, New Windsor, N.Y., 21 October 1779. Encloses a letter from his brother concerning "the want of money in my Department."[1] This is "so alarming" that Biddle requests NG's "particular Attention to it." Without an "immediate" infusion of "at least Two millions," the army will lack grain if it takes the field, and Biddle will be unable to form the "necessary magazines for winter." With the exception of the agents in Providence, R.I., the "Eastern purchasers" on whom he depends, as well as those in New York, are all without money. NG must help him obtain "that sum as soon as possible."[2] In a postscript, Biddle reports that he has ordered "returns of persons employd to be made to the board of war," and a copy sent to NG, "without delay."[3] RCS (Joseph Rubinfine, 1998) 1 p.]

1. Owen Biddle's letter concerning the lack of money in the Forage Department has not been found.

2. In a letter of 6 November 1779 to Assistant Quartermaster Charles Pettit, who was responsible for obtaining funds for the department from Congress, NG made a pointed appeal for money, especially for the "Eastern," or New England, agents. (Vol. 4: 20–21, above)

3. On the returns demanded by the Board of War, see Benjamin Stoddert to NG, 3 December 1779, above. (Vol. 5: 145 and n) NG again asked Biddle for a return on 24 December 1779, above. (Ibid., p. 203)

¶ [FROM COLONEL CLEMENT BIDDLE, [Morristown, N.J.], "Monday Noon" [3 January 1780].[1] He has just received a letter from Gen. [Anthony] Wayne, requesting forage for twenty horses. Asks where Wayne and his aides, a ˙ party of five, will be quartered. RCS (Joseph Rubinfine, 1998) 1 p.]

1. The date was taken from the docketing; the place from NG's and the army's whereabouts at this time.

¶ [TO GEORGE WASHINGTON. From Camp, Tappan, N.Y., 12 August 1780. There are fifty-eight "private property teams" now serving with the army. The "new regulation," however, mandates that no wagon and team belonging to military or staff officers be kept in service.[1] "These are all under this predicament." Their owners ask either to have the teams "discharged" or to be paid for their teams' "future service." To move, the army requires at least eighty wagons, and the total does not include the "great number" needed in the commissary and forage departments; those, if discharged, will "add so much to the distress of the service." Moreover, the wagons belonging to the staff officers are all driven by "private waggoners," and if they withdraw their wagons and teams, the army will have to find fifty-eight teamsters. The "People" are "anxious to get their teams out of service," but NG does not want to let them go, "under present circumstances," without getting Washington's "direction therein, es[peci]ally as we are now impressing from the country [to?] keep up the necessary transportation." He needs an "immediate answer" because "the people are waiting."[2] LS (Washington Papers: DLC) 2 pp.]

1. In its reorganization of the Quartermaster Department of 15 July 1780, Congress directed that "no military or staff officer shall own, or in any manner be interested in any boat, shallop, waggon or other carriage, horse or team, employed on hire or contract, in the service of the United States, on pain of forfeiting a sum equal to that which shall have become due for the service of such boat, shallop, waggon, or other carriage, horse or team, during the whole time they shall have been so employed; and for a second offence such officer shall be dismissed from the service." (*JCC*, 17: 632–33)

2. In his reply of the same date, Washington instructed NG to retain the teams and to assure the owners that they would be paid. He added that he expected NG to take steps to replace the teams as quickly as possible. (Vol. 6: 208, above)

* * *

From Colonel Josias Carvil Hall[1]

Dear Sir   Baltimore Town [Md.] Dec[r] the 15th [1780][2]

I am directed by the Ladies of Baltimore Town to address you 600 Shirts for the use of the Maryland Soldiers. They will have as many more soon which will be disposed of any way which shall be thought most advisable[.] They complain that they are yet to be informed whether those already contributed have been disposed of according to their Intentions & request you will favor them with a Line acknowledging the Receipt of these.[3]

M[r] Rob[t] Smith writes from the Havana that the armament destined against Pensecola suffered much in the late Hurricane[;] Four of the seven men of war returned dismasted. The Admiral remained in a Frigate to collect his scattered Fleet. The Gen[l] also remains with intent to take post somewhere westward of the Mobile if he can not collect troops enough to attempt Pensicola. It is feared many of the Transports are wholly lost in which case they must give up their intended expedition & content themselves with breaking up the Island of Providence[.][4] I suppose Gov[r] [Thomas Sim] Lee & Gen[l] [Mordecai] Gist will officially inform you of State of our military Preparations or at least as I can not give you much satisfaction on that head I will leave it to them. I am with the greatest Respect & personal esteem y[rs]   JO CARVIL HALL

RCS (MiU-C).

1. Hall (1756–1814) had commanded the Fourth Maryland Continental Regiment since December 1776. (Heitman, *Register*) He was declared a supernumerary on 1 January 1781 and retired from the service, but it appears that he tried unsuccessfully to appeal his supernumerary status. (Richard Potts to Samuel Hughes, 24 July 1781, Smith, *Letters*, 17: 441 and n)

2. The year was taken from the docketing.

3. As seen at Mordecai Gist to NG, 14 February 1781, above, the artillery company that was transporting the shirts to the Southern Army from Baltimore was detained in Virginia. (Vol. 7: 228n) The idea of Maryland women providing shirts for NG's troops from that state seems to have originated with Washington, who had written to Mary Digges Lee, the governor's wife, on 11 October, thanking her for the "patriotic exertions of the Ladies of Maryland in favor of the Army" and recommending that any money they might collect be used to purchase shirts and stocks for the troops of the Southern Army. (Fitzpatrick, *GW*, 20: 168) It is not known whether NG responded to Hall's request.

4. On 18 October 1780, two days after it sailed from Havana, a fleet convoying the Spanish force that was to have attacked British-held Pensacola, West Florida, encountered a hurricane. Badly damaged, it was forced to return to Havana, but this did not end the plans of the governor general of Louisiana, Bernardo de Gálvez. In February 1781, he led a smaller invasion force against Pensacola and succeeded in capturing that post on 10 May 1781. (J. Barton Starr, *Tories, Dons, and Rebels: The American Revolution in British West Florida* [Gainesville: University of Florida, 1976], pp. 193–95, 211)

*   *   *

¶ [FROM COLONEL JOHN GREEN, 11 [January] 1781.[1] Sends a return [not found] of the "detachment sent from Virginia" under his command.[2] He is "about Twenty five miles from Camp" but has been detained for at least a day by "extream" rain, and a rise in "the waters" may delay him longer. His men need rest and time to clean themselves and their arms. He plans to "halt within about ten or twelve miles of camp" to await NG's orders. RCS (MiU-C) 1 p.]

1. The letter is dated "December 11ᵗʰ 1781," but other letters at the time clearly demonstrate that it was written in January. No place is given, but it appears from what Green wrote here that he was near Colston's Mill, N.C.

2. Green's detachment numbered about 400 men. (See Baron Steuben to NG, 15 December 1780, above [vol. 6: 584].)

*   *   *

From Colonel Charles Pettit

Philadelphia 13ᵗʰ Febʸ. 1781

I am now, my dear sir, to acknowledge the receipt of your two favours by General Duportail & Major Giles; the latter came to hand a day or two before the other.[1] We can hardly enough extol the bravery and good conduct of General Morgan and the little corps of heroes under his command.[2] Nor are we unmindful of the merit & skill of the General who has made so happy a disposition of his small resources as to baffle and impede the approach of an enemy with a force so much superior to his. We flatter ourselves with the expectation of something brilliant in a few days from your left; but it must be brilliant indeed to outshine what has happened on your right.[3] We chimney corner soldiers do not always judge rightly of actions in the field, but we must nevertheless be allowed, or at least we take the liberty, to utter our opinions on all that happen which have enough in them of either good or ill to draw attention. We now give the palm clearly to Genˡ Morgan on a supposition that the action of the Cowpens, in point of real bravery, generalship in action, and good soldiership, excels all that have happened, taking all circumstances into view, that of Stoney point not excepted.[4] I need not descant on the particular merits of each nor draw those parts into comparison which are most worthy of notice; neither shall I now enquire whether this piece of success was aided by the ill conduct of the enemy. It is enough that the victory was complete, and atchieved in the open field by inferior numbers labouring under many other disadvantages, over the chosen troops of a boasting enemy. Could we know that you were in a condition to follow up the blow and avail yourself properly of the advantages such a victory ought to give you, our joy would be supreme. But the chilling reflection of your real situation is mortifying to the friends of America in proportion to their knowledge of it, and strikes your personal friends with additional chagrin. Be not, however, discouraged. If you persevere and succeed your glory will be the greater. If you fail of the success we wish, you will hardly fall short of what we have a right to expect. From these considerations some consolation may be drawn, hard as it is to be reduced to such resources for it. The eyes and expectations not only of America, but of Europe are upon you. Your military character, though it has less to lose than some others in the world, from being less known than it deserves, has the extensive field of fame before it; and though you may meet with impediments and difficulties which may require more than common fortitude and common skill to withstand and surmount them, there is yet a chance of your triumphing over them. The war in America depends not solely on the circumstances arising within it. A lucky turn elsewhere may weaken the enemy, or strengthen our hands in a manner that may occasion a favourable change & turn the tide in our favour.

The traitor who has lately with so much success, and with shameful want of molestation on our part, impeded the reinforcements & supplies which would otherwise have come to you, we have reason to believe is recalled from Chesapeak.[5] The Storm which happened some weeks since has done more damage to the enemy's fleet at Gardner's Island than we at first imagined. I have it from a member of Congress today that the *Culloden* is entirely lost & but 17 of the crew saved, a frigate also lost; a 90 Gun ship blown out to sea dismasted, and one or two other ships of the line dismasted, beside other damage less conspicuous.[6] This leaves a superiority in favour of the fleet of our ally, and it is whispered, but I have no certainty of it, that a few ships are detached from R. Island. The supposition is that they are gone to Chesapeak. If they should catch Mr Arnold there, it would be a clever stroke.[7] These, however, are but flattering suggestions of what *may* happen, and I have no solid authority for the supposition. I take it for granted however that on these probabilities the Enemy's force will be recalled from Chesapeak; but you will know more of the matter before this reaches you.[8]

I believe I have heretofore mentioned to you the arrangements going forward respecting the great branches of business, and that M[r] Livingston & M[r] Lee were in nomination for the choice of Minister for foreign affairs. No election has yet been made, and perhaps may not be speedily.[9] As Financier, Governor Johnston, Rob[t] Morris, George Bryan & John Gibson have been put in nomination.[10] A friend of yours was sounded on this subject & at his request his name has been kept out of sight.[11] The two first I hear have declared off. M[r] G. will probably get but the vote of the one who named him. For the War Department Gen[l] Gates, Gen[l] Sullivan, M[r] Peters, Col. Pickering & Col. Scammell have been talked on, & I believe put in nomination.[12] For Minister of marine S[r] James Jay is making interest.[13] Your friend has also been asked for his name on this occasion, but he does not choose it should run for either tho' he were sure it would succeed.

The Jersey line made but a poor hand of their attempt to revolt; but about 150 came into the measure; they were soon suppressed, 2 of them executed & the rest pardoned.[14]

You will excuse the shortness of this, if such an appology be necessary—as writing by Candle light under a cold which gives me a disordered head, is not pleasant. If matter and occasion offers before I find an opportunity of conveyance I will begin again.

RC (ScCMu). The letter, which is not signed, is docketed "Col Pettit," and the contents support this attribution.

1. Neither letter has been found. Louis le Bégue de Presle Duportail, the chief engineer of the Continental army, who had been captured in the surrender of Charleston, S.C., had been exchanged in late 1780. Edward Giles had served as Gen. Daniel Morgan's aide-de-camp and had carried the dispatches announcing Morgan's victory in the battle of Cowpens to Congress. Duportail left NG's camp in South Carolina on or about 13 January 1781; Giles on 25 January. (See NG to Washington, 13 January 1781, and NG to Giles, 25 January 1781, both above [vol. 7: 113, 193].)

2. As seen further along in this letter, Pettit was referring to Morgan's victory at Cowpens, on which see Morgan to NG, 19 January 1781, above. (Vol. 7: 152–61)

3. NG's "left" was the area between the Pee Dee River and the South Carolina coast. Pettit undoubtedly referred here to an operation against Georgetown, S.C., by Col. Henry Lee, Jr., and Gen. Francis Marion. The attack there took place on 25 January 1781, but NG would not have known its results when he wrote the letters that Pettit mentioned at the beginning of this letter. This operation was only partially successful. (See Lee to NG, second letter of 25 January 1781, above [vol. 7: 197].)

4. On the capture of the British post at Stony Point, N.Y., by an American force led by Gen. Anthony Wayne, see NG to John Cox, 17 July 1779, above. (Vol. 4: 236–39)

5. Pettit referred here to the invasion of tidewater Virginia by Gen. Benedict Arnold. For more about Arnold's successful drive up the James River, which did cut NG's line of supplies from the North, see Baron Steuben to NG, 8 January 1781, above. (Vol. 7: 76–81)

6. After receiving intelligence that a French squadron would be sailing from Rhode Island, Adm. Samuel Graves dispatched a three-ship squadron from New York to intercept it. On 22 January 1781, the British vessels were hit by a hurricane off Long Island. The seventy-four gun *Culloden* was driven ashore and destroyed, but its crew escaped un-

harmed. The seventy-four gun *Bedford* survived, but only because its crew dismasted the vessel. The third ship, the sixty-four gun *America*, disappeared and was feared lost for a time. It had been blown south to Virginia, however, and returned to New York in early February, badly damaged and in need of major repairs. (Clinton, *American Rebellion*, p. 250n)

7. After the British disaster, the French admiral at Newport, R.I., the Chevalier Destouches, sent a squadron to the Chesapeake at Washington's urging. The three frigates and one ship of the line drew more water than the British ships supporting Arnold, and, unable to operate effectively, soon returned to Newport. Their only success was the capture of a forty-four gun British warship along the way. (W. M. James, *The British Navy in Adversity: A Study of the War of American Independence* [London: Longmans, Green and Co., 1926], p. 270)

8. The British force in Virginia was not recalled.

9. Pettit's letter discussing the reorganization that Congress had undertaken has not been found. The new arrangements, which had begun with the appointment of committees in May and August 1780, resulted in the establishment of the office of secretary of foreign affairs on 10 January 1781 and of the offices of superintendent of finance, secretary at war, and secretary of marine on 7 February. (*JCC*, 19: 42–44, 71, 123–24, 126–28) Robert R. Livingston, a delegate to Congress from New York, and Arthur Lee, a delegate from Virginia and former American commissioner to France, were nominated for the foreign affairs post on 17 January 1781, but the election, which Livingston won, was not held until 10 August of that year. (*JCC*, 19: 65; 21: 851–52)

10. Thomas Johnson had been governor of Maryland from March 1777 to November 1779; in 1780–81, he was a member of the Maryland legislature and was elected a delegate to Congress but did not attend. (*DAB*; Smith, *Letters*, 16: xix) George Bryan was a justice of the Pennsylvania Supreme Court and former vice-president of that state's Supreme Executive Council. (*DAB*) John Gibson was a former auditor general and member of the Board of Treasury. He had been embroiled in controversy since soon after his election to the latter post in November 1779, when Francis Hopkinson, the treasurer of loans, charged him and the other commissioners with operating in an arbitrary and capricious manner. (Morris, *Papers*, 1: 269n; *JCC*, 18: 1091–92) Robert Morris, who was then a delegate from Pennsylvania, was elected superintendent of finance on 20 February. (Morris, *Papers*, 1: 5)

11. This "friend" was presumably Petitt's brother-in-law Joseph Reed, who was then president of the Pennsylvania Supreme Executive Council.

12. Gen. Horatio Gates, a former president of the Board of War, had been NG's predecessor as commander of the Southern Department. (*DAB*) John Sullivan, a former Continental major general, was a delegate to Congress from New Hampshire. (*DAB*; Smith, *Letters*, 16: xxi) Richard Peters had been secretary to, and member of, the Continental Board of War. Timothy Pickering, NG's successor as quartermaster general, had also been a member of that board, and Col. Alexander Scammell had served as adjutant general of the Continental army from 5 January 1778 until 1 January 1781, when he resigned to assume command of the First New Hampshire Continental Regiment. (*DAB*) Unable to reach an agreement on any of these candidates, Congress voted on 28 February to postpone a decision. (*JCC*. 19: 205–6) When an election was finally held on 30 October 1781, Gen. Benjamin Lincoln was named secretary at war. (*JCC*, 21: 1087; Joseph Reed to NG, 1 November 1781, above [vol. 9: 510–516])

13. Sir James Jay, a brother of John Jay, was a New York physician who had lived in England from 1762 to 1778. At the time of this letter, he was a member of the New York Senate. (Morris, *Papers*, 1: 115) The marine post was offered to Gen. Alexander McDougall, but he declined, and the duties of the office were then assigned to Morris, the superintendent of finance, who exercised them for the duration of his term. (Ibid., p. 4n)

14. On the mutiny in the New Jersey Continental line, see Washington to NG, 2 February 1781, above. (Vol. 7: 240 and n)

*   *   *

¶ [FROM COLONEL WILLIAM WASHINGTON, "Dennis Logan's," N.C., 11:30 A.M., [14 March 1781].[1] The enemy marched at sunrise toward Deep River without beating their drums.[2] Washington will move "down on their Right & Camp." RCS (MiU-C) 1 p.]

1. The date was determined from the contents and another letter that Washington wrote to NG on 14 March 1781, above, repeating and amplifying the information he reported here. (Vol. 7: 431)
2. This was Lord Cornwallis's army.

*   *   *

From Governor Abner Nash of North Carolina

Dear Sir   Warren County [N.C.] May 7. 1781
I had the honour to receive y[r] fav[r] dated the 21. april & have no doubt y[r] operations ag[t] the Enemys post in S[o] Carolina will eventually have the most Happy Effects.[1] At the same time I am to acq[t] y[o] that L[d] Cornwallis sensible of his inability (as I suppose) to face you has marched in ful force into the Heart of this State[.] They crossed Tar River at Lemons's Ferry yesterday but to what perticular part they may be bound I cannot say.[2] I suppose & believe their plan must be by distressing this state to call y[r] attention off from S[o] Carolina, & indeed sir I have little to say for the militia force of this State. I have been using every endeavour to draw the people out to Oppose the progress of the Enemy—as yet without Effect. They turn out badly and for the present it appears that the state must be over run & perhaps ruined unless you save us. Our new recruits are ready, but there is a want of good conduct in collecting them together. I hope for the pleasure of hearing from y[o] & am wth the highest respect & Esteem D[r] sir Y[r] ob serv[t]   A NASH

RCS (ScCMU).
1. NG's letter of 21 April 1781 to Nash has not been found; the Southern Army was operating against the British post at Camden, S.C., at that time. (Volume 8, above)
2. Cornwallis's army was en route to Virginia. After crossing the Tar River at Lemon's Ferry, the British troops marched in a northeasterly direction and reached Halifax, N.C., on 12 May 1781. A few days later, they crossed into Virginia, joining with the force commanded by Gen. Benedict Arnold at Petersburg on 20 May. (See Vol. 7: 225n and 269n, above.)

From General Robert Lawson

D[r] General   Pr[ince]. Edward [Va.] May 14th 1781.
You have no doubt expected the Militia from this State before this.[1] In the first place they have in general manifested an uncommon reluctance in marching to your Army—arising I apprehend from two causes—first

the season of the Year, & secondly the lengthy march into a hot & disagreeable Country, the Climate of which they entertain horrid ideas of. From the movements of Cornwallis & Phillips, it appears certain that they mean to make this State the scene of the Southern War this Campaign.[2] The Executive impress'd with this idea, have order'd me to stay here, together with such militia order'd to join you, & who have not actually march'd.[3] I have reason to imagine that there are now at Salisbury upwards of 500 Men. Col° Cocke who was in G[i] [Edward] Stevens Brigade is order'd by me to that place.[4]

I have no doubt but that you'll direct your course this way, should Cornwallis move into this State, which seems not to be doubted at present. Should the Event prove otherwise, the Militia first order'd will join you with all possible dispatch.

I must beg you'll do me the honor in the mean time, of giving me such orders as you may see cause, which shall be obey'd with alacrity.

The Marquiss is on the North side of James River, with the whole of the Troops collected in this State.[5] The Enemy are on the South Side, at liberty to go where they please, & are doing all possible injury to the unfortunate & defenceless Inhabitants who fall in their way. Indeed I cannot avoid expressing my ardent wish, that you were with your Troops in this State. I am confident it would change the face of things greatly in our favor—and it is not only mine, but the ⟨anxious wish of Virg[a] that this should be the case. The Enemy have already done us⟩ inexpressible Injury, by burning our Tobacco, & taking & destroying our Magazines of provisions collected at different places on James & Appomatox Rivers.

The Militia are order'd to the amount of About 1000 to rendezvous at the Court House of this County; to join the Marquiss in opposing the progress of the Enemy in this State, or to march to you as exigencies may require. I beg again your particular instructions,[6] and have the honor to be with the highest respect, Sir, Your most obed[t] humble Serv[t]

RO: LAWSON

RCS (ScCMu). The text in angle brackets is from a typed Tr at ScCMu.

1. As seen in his letter to Gov. Thomas Jefferson of 1 April 1781, and in Baron Steuben's to NG of 30 March 1781, both above, NG had expected a detachment of 2,000 Virginia militiaman, who were to be called into service to replace the state's militia troops who had left the Southern Army after the battle of Guilford Court House. (Vol. 7: 17–18; 14–16)

2. Lord Cornwallis had begun marching his army toward Virginia from Wilmington, N.C., on 25 April 1781. On 20 May, at Petersburg, Va., he joined forces with an army that had been commanded by Gen. William Phillips before Phillips's death from typhoid on 13 May. (See note at Marquis de Lafayette to NG, 3 May 1781, above [vol. 7: 196–97].)

3. These orders are in a letter from Jefferson to Lawson of 8 May 1781. (Boyd, *Jefferson Papers*, 5: 613; see also Jefferson to NG, 30 March 1781, above [vol. 8: 13–14].)

4. This officer was probably Col. Nathaniel Cocke of the Halifax County militia. On 15 May 1781, Col. James Read reported that there were 300 Virginia militiamen at Salisbury, N.C. (See Read to NG, 15 May 1781, above [vol. 8: 266–67].) It appears that these men joined NG, but many of them claimed that they had already completed their

terms of service by escorting British prisoners in Virginia; NG sent them home. (See Robert Wooding to NG, 10 August 1781, above [vol. 9: 163].) Those who stayed with NG's army were commanded by Majors John Ward and Alexander Rose. (See Ward to NG, 8 July 1781, and NG to Rose, 23 July 1781, both above [vol. 8: 511; vol. 9: 65].)

5. On 15 May 1781, the Marquis de Lafayette was at Wilton's, just north of the James River. (Lafayette to Anthony Wayne, 15 May, Idzerda, *Lafayette Papers*, 4: 102) In a letter to NG of 18 May 1781, Lafayette estimated that he had about 2,200 men, including 1,200 militia, serving with him. (Vol. 6: 281–82)

6. NG replied to Lawson on 26 June 1781, above. (Vol. 6: 466)

*   *   *

¶ [**FROM COLONEL CHARLES PETTIT**, Philadelphia, 2 November 1781. It was not until "some days" after Maj. [William] Pierce arrived in Philadelphia that Pettit received NG's letter of 17 September, because Pierce had "packed [it] up with his eastern letters."[1] Not being acquainted with Pierce, Pettit feared he would "lose the opportunity of getting that information about you which a tete á tete only can give." After receiving NG's letter, though, he "sought and obtained an acquaintance" with Pierce, which has been "pleasing." Pettit is sorry that Pierce could not spend more "time with my family," both "on account of his own merit, as from the regard you express for him." Congratulates NG on "your series of successes amidst the series of complicated difficulties," and especially for the "arduous affair at Eutaw."[2] Pettit will say no more about this, allowing "less firmly attached friends" and "the world at large" to praise the merit of NG and his "band of Heroes"—which they do "unsparingly." He finds himself "so much interested" in NG's situation that he seems to be NG's "representative" there, but modesty obliges him to "say no more" than that he receives the praise "with grateful complacence." If there were "any doubtful points, or any clouds or shades arising which would obscure the brilliancy of" NG's conduct, it would be Pettit's duty to dispel them, "but nothing of the sort appears." In fact, he can truthfully, and with great satisfaction, say "that no campaign or series of actions during the war has obtained more universal approbation & applause than those in the Carolinas during the last twelve months. May your Laurels never fade!"

Pierce will bring seven shirts and stocks to NG. Maj. [Ichabod] Burnet also planned to send on "a hat with some other articles" for NG, but Pettit is not sure if Burnet did so, for he has not seen or heard from him since Pierce's arrival. Pettit fears that Burnet's "health has failed him, or that some other cause not known when he went from here, detains him."[3] When Burnet left Philadelphia, he gave Pettit "some bills of Exch^e" and asked him to "sell a few to raise a little ready money for Cap^n Swan & some other purposes; afterwards he desired me to sell more," which Pettit did until the total sold reached $20,000.[4] "For certain reasons," Burnet did not want him to inform "the Treasury" that he had these bills. Their sale, however, "brought it to the knowledge of the Financier" [Robert Morris], who met with Pettit and asked him not to sell any more of them. Pettit did not tell the Financier the amount of the bills he held, "but left him to suppose it was about 20,000 Dollars."[5] Adds: "The money is yet chiefly unappropriated. They sold from 5/ to 5/3 the dollar. If the money is to be turned over to the Treasury, which may be the case if they undertake to furnish the supplies Major Burnet is in pursuit of, I shall try hard to get payment out of it for our Iron contract & for some contingent expences of Office I have been obliged to make advances for since my supplies of cash failed. This, however must be as circumstances will admit."[6]

Pettit has heard rumors that CG is "on the way hither." In his opinion, which is "strongly corroborated" by NG's "friends from the southward, & those in this Town," she should "proceed no farther." If he can convince CG to remain, Pettit and his family will happily entertain her "as long as we can make this Town agreeable to her," for they have "house-room to spare her." If CG "should determine to proceed," however, they "will endeavour to accommodate her in it." In either case, Pettit will provide her with whatever amount of money "she shall choose to take."[7] While NG remains outside Charleston, "Carolina must be an inconvenient residence for her without taking into consideration the unavoidable difficulties and inconveniences of the Journey, which are dreadful in idea, & must be worse in practice for a lady." If NG is able to "crown" his "career of success" by taking Charleston, he may, "like Alexander, mourn that" he has "nothing more to conquer—and in that case you will, of course as I take it, come to the northward."[8]

Pettit is writing "in haste." Supposing that he had "the week before" him to write, he "put off the business" until "this morning," when he learned that Pierce is leaving at 1 or 2 [P.M.], which "hour is at hand."[9] Despite this deadline, he will add "a word or two on our concerns." He previously informed NG that he had "bargained away the ⅛th of the Ship *Revolution*, the principal part of the paymᵗ was in meadow lots—the residue not yet recᵈ."[10] The ship was captured a few days later, though, "so that what we got was so much saved." Another of their investments, the ship *Congress*, sent in a prize that earned its owners some £2000.[11] After that capture, the *Congress* put into Cap-Français, where it contracted a debt of some £2000 before going on a "cruize intending to send in Prizes to pay the debt."[12] Near Charleston, it encountered the *Savage*, a sloop of war nearly its own size and mounting sixteen six-pound guns and four four-pounders. The *Congress* captured it after "an obstinate engagement which obliged her to proceed homewards." En route, the *Savage* was retaken by the frigate *Solebay*, so the *Congress* returned "emptyhanded & a good deal mauled."[13] At a meeting of the owners, a large majority decided that "privateering was become ineligible" and that the *Congress* should be sent on a trading voyage. Its "debt in the West Indies must be paid & no way could be found but by sending the ship to do it." The *Congress* "will sail in a few days for the Havanna," and from there it will go to Amsterdam and return "with such property as she creates for the Owners & a Freight of dry goods." The "meadow lots being an useless kind of property to us, & wanting much expence to put them in order," Pettit "bartered them away for 1/32ᵈ of the ship *Congress*; which I intended should be on our compʸ account." However, [John] Cox has "declined taking a farther intᵗ in the ship, though he would not consent to sell our original 1/16ᵗʰ." Pettit, therefore, asked him "to elect for you as to the new purchase—he declined it. We therefore decided the matter by lot," which gave NG, if he agrees to take it, "this farther concern—that is instead of 1/3ᵈ of a sixteenth," one-third of three thirty-seconds. The additional share will cost

"£500—that is valuing the ship at £16000 subject to the debt abroad & the new outfit." Asks for NG's "determination." The *Congress* can carry about 1,900 barrels of flour, but it will take only about half of that amount on the voyage to Havana. "From thence to Europe from ¼ to ½ of the sugars as may happen; & from Amsterdam hither about 10 per Cent in dry goods if the war should continue." The *Congress* "equals our expectations in point of sailing, that is, beats every thing; but carries too little [armament] for her size & force." For now, Cox declines taking out insurance on their firm's original share of one-sixteenth of the vessel, but Pettit intends to insure the additional one thirty-second share, "especially if it rests all on me." Asks if NG wants any insurance. "The prin[cipal] will be about 40 per C^t round."[14]

The "Iron Works have finished their blast." The "prospect of peace" makes Pettit "doubtful Work is moving forward on the forge," which should be operational in two months or less. Pettit finds the iron business "heavy & requiring so much attention & skill (on which the profits entirely depend) & the difficulties so great of getting proper hands & seeing that every thing draws right" that he is strongly tempted "to sell out—if can be done." If he could find someone who understood the business and would make it his own, Pettit would "gladly keep a concern," but he is "not sufficiently skilled" himself "to make it either your interest or mine to bestow the trouble it requires to keep it going extensively. Yet it is an estate I have an attachment to; & my mind recoils at the serious thought of parting with it.[15] Fearing that he may be "too late" with this letter, he must "cut it short." As Mr. [Joseph] Reed is writing to NG, Pettit "can with the more ease avoid political subjects."[16] He ends by affirming his strong "affection" for NG. RCS (ScCMu) 4 pp.]

1. NG's letter of 17 September 1781 to Pettit has not been found. The "eastern letters" would have been those intended for correspondents in New York and New England.

2. On the battle of Eutaw Springs, see NG to Thomas McKean, 11 September 1781, above (vol. 9: 328–38).

3. In a letter to NG of 24 October 1781, Pierce reported that Burnet, who had traveled north to try to recover his health, had gone to his home in New Jersey. Burnet returned to Philadelphia on 4 November. (See Pettit to NG, 4 November 1781, above [vol. 9: 526].)

4. As seen in Burnet's letter to NG of 20 August 1781, above (vol. 9: 210), Capt. John Swan of the Third Continental Regiment of Light Dragoons had gone to Philadelphia to buy equipment for the cavalry regiments serving with NG.

5. For more about the bills of exchange, see Burnet to NG, 6 November 1781, and Morris to NG, 7 November 1781, both above. (Vol. 9: 538, 544)

6. The "Iron contract" was for cannon produced for the American government by the Batsto Iron Works, which was owned by a partnership consisting of NG, Pettit, and John Cox. Pettit discussed its operations further along in this letter. The "contingent expences of office" were money that was owed to NG and Pettit for their services as quartermaster general and assistant quartermaster general respectively.

7. CG was on her way to join NG. She arrived in Philadelphia in December 1781 and, despite Pettit's efforts to dissuade her from going farther, left there in January 1782. She reached NG's camp in South Carolina on 25 March 1782. (See Pettit to NG, 14 December 1781; Burnet to NG, 5 February 1781, and Burnet to Pettit, 12 April 1782, all above. [Vol. 10: 55, 317; vol. 11: 38])

8. Pettit referred here to Alexander the Great.

9. As seen in Pettit to NG, 4 November 1781, Pierce was detained in Philadelphia for several days after his intended departure date. (Vol. 9: 526)

10. The sale of the *Revolution* is discussed in Pettit's letter to NG of 23 August 1781, above (vol. 9: 229–30).

11. In his letter of 23 August, Pettit wrote that the share of the partnership of NG, Pettit, and Cox in that prize was £150. (Ibid., p. 230)

12. Cap-Français was in what is now Haiti.

13. For an account of the engagement between the *Congress* and the Royal Navy sloop of war *Savage*, taken from the report of the *Savage*'s captain, see Gardner W. Allen, *A Naval History of the American Revolution*, 2 vols. (Boston and New York: Houghton Mifflin Company, 1913), 2: 565–67. According to Allen, George Geddes commanded the *Congress*.

14. In a letter to Pettit of 29 August 1782, above, NG announced that he was "perfectly satisfied in being further interested in the *Congress*" and that he approved of all of Pettit's business decisions concerning their investments. (Vol. 11: 595)

15. A short time later, Pettit found a potential buyer for the Batsto Iron Works, but that person, Joseph Ball, was unable to complete the purchase, and the deal fell through. In 1784, Pettit decided to take over management of the furnace. (See Pettit to NG, 14 December 1781 [vol. 10:55], 19 August 1782 [vol. 11: 561], and 13 March 1784, all above.)

16. See Joseph Reed to NG, 1 November 1781, above (vol. 9: 510). As noted above, Pierce did not leave as planned, so Pettit was able to continue this letter to NG on 4 November 1781. (Vol. 9: 526–28)

¶ [TO COLONEL ROBERT HERIOT. From Headquarters [High Hills of Santee, S.C.], 7 November 1781. NG has received Heriot's letter of 30 October and is "much Obliged" for the wine that Heriot has "been so good as to procure."[1] Is sending a wagon to bring it to camp. Asks if Heriot can also send "a hogshead of Spirit, or good Rum, which at present we want exceedingly."[2] ALS (ScU) 2 pp.]

1. The letter from Heriot, a South Carolina militia officer, planter, and merchant at Georgetown, S.C., has not been found. (On Heriot, see *Biog. Directory of S.C. House*, 3: 331–32.)

2. Heriot wrote NG on 12 November 1781, above, that he had sent wine, rum, a cask of porter, and cheese. (Vol. 9: 567)

¶ [FROM CAPTAIN PETER JAQUETT, Light Infantry Camp [near Johns Island, S.C.], 23 January [1782].[1] He is "at a loss" to know how "to act concerning M[r] [John] Vaughan's Appointment in the present muster"; asks for "directions." Based on assurances from the "Governor [Caesar Rodney] and Council" that he would receive an appointment in the Delaware Continental Regiment, Vaughan accompanied the regiment when it marched from Delaware in April 1780. By order of Gen. [Horatio] Gates in October 1780, he became an ensign in Jaquett's company, and by NG's order in February 1781, he joined Capt. [Robert] Kirkwood's company. Vaughan, who "has been very attentive to duty ever Since his first appointment," received "an unfortunate wound" in the battle of Guilford Court House and "will never perfectly recover." However, "from the last intelligence from Delaware," Jaquett has learned that there is "no Probability" that Vaughan will be commissioned. Vaughan, who carries this letter, will await NG's directions as to how Jaquett should proceed.[2] RCS (MiU-C) 1 p.]

1. The year was determined from the contents and from NG's reply, written by his aide Nathaniel Pendleton, which is above, dated 24 January 1782. (Vol. 10: 253)

2. NG decided that Vaughan was "undoubtedly entitled to his rank" and ordered that his commission date from October 1780. (Ibid.)

¶ [FROM CHARLES FREER, Johns Island, S.C., 6 February 1782.[1] A person from Charleston whom he met "Last evening" told Freer "there was nothing new. The Fireing was scaleing of Guns."[2] According to another person, "there was a large Fleet (of Russians)" off Charleston bar. Freer will investigate.[3] RCS (MiU-C) 1 p.]

1. Freer had served as a captain in the South Carolina militia in 1775–76. (Moss, *S.C. Patriots*)

2. In "scaleing their guns," the British were firing their artillery pieces to remove rust or "scale" from the inside of the barrels.

3. This report was not true.

*   *   *

From General Benjamin Lincoln, Secretary at War

[Philadelphia, 1783][1]

While the Maryland Artillery continues to serve with the southern Army as Artillery, I think they shoud be command[ed] by their own Officers, whose feeling must be wounded shoud another line of conduct be adopted. Yet I do not conceive that there wou'd be either injustice or impropriety in placing those companies with the Virginia artillery, under the same field Officers.[2]

Memorandum (Gist Papers: MdHi). The text above was obviously extracted from a longer letter, which has not been found. NG had it sent to Gen. Mordecai Gist, the commander of the Maryland troops of the Southern Army. The document is docketed "Abstract of a letter from the Sec^r at War to Gen Greene respecting the Maryland Artillery 1783."

1. As seen in the source note, this letter is docketed 1783. It was presumably written early in the year, as NG had referred the issue of the Maryland artillery to Lincoln in a letter of 8 October 1782, above. (Vol. 12: 43–45)

2. NG discussed the issue in some detail in ibid. Field officers were those at or above the rank of major.

INDEX

Index abbreviations
ADQM—Assistant Deputy
    Quartermaster
CG—Catharine Littlefield Greene
DQM—Deputy Quartermaster
GW—George Washington
NG—Nathanael Greene
QM—Quartermaster
SoArmy—Southern Army

A

Abeel, James, 252n, 560 and n, 732, 733
and n; *letter to*, 560; *biog. note*, vol. 2:
314n
Accounts and account books: NG and
public, x, 17 and n, 46, 49 and n, 77, 78n,
83n, 119 and n, 165, 166n, 169, 170n,
173–75 and n, 176 and n, 177–78 and n,
197–98, 199n, 200n, 201, 203 and n, 221
and n, 227–28, 230n, 241 and n, 247–48
and n, 248, 249n, 252 and n, 258–59 and
n, 259, 260n, 263, 269n, 276, 284, 286 and
n, 288, 308, 321 and n, 385 and n, 397–98
and n, 399–400 and n, 428n, 444–45,
449–50 and n, 477, 478n, 500–501, 512,
555–56, 557–58 and n, 600, 637, 638n,
669, 671, 719, 730; of staff departments
and personnel, 7n, 12, 17–19 and n, 33,
46, 49 and n, 53 and n, 70–71, 79 and n,
90, 91n, 119 and n, 165, 170n, 173–75
and n, 178n, 181 and n, 204 and n, 205n,
227, 230n, 235n, 242, 251–52 and n, 264–
65 and n, 286 and n, 308, 309n, 326 and
n, 399–400 and n, 415, 416n, 428n, 435,
436n, 440 and n, 444, 445, 477, 478n,
555–56, 557, 558n, 560 and n, 600 and n,
651–52, 654n, 717, 718n; SoArmy and, 17
and n, 17–19 and n, 33 and n, 77, 78n, 90,
169, 170n, 176 and n, 227–28, 229–30n,
239, 241 and n, 449–50, 451n, 471 and n,
500, 556, 557n, 637, 638n; of J. Banks et
al., 55 and n, 58–59 and n, 77, 227–28,
229–30n, 250n, 302–3, 304n, 310 and n,
319 and n, 327, 330–31 and n, 331–32n,
332, 355–56, 365n, 375, 378–79, 391,
392n, 402–3 and n, 409–10, 426n, 427
and n, 449–50, 451n, 461–62, 500–501,
535, 538–39, 553, 554 and n, 620 and n;
of superintendent of finance's office, 77,
78n; of army suppliers, 151 and n, 500,

555–56 and n; for NG's private ex-
penses, 162–63 and n, 320, 321 and n,
334–35 and n, 340–41 and n, 345, 346,
648, 678, 689 and n, 694; comptroller
and, 169, 170n, 177–78 and n; C. Pettit's
public, 227–28, 229–30n, 239, 257 and n,
308, 309n; R. P. Saunders and, 356, 357n,
625; of W. Pierce & Company, 523
Actors, 492, 496n
Adams, John, 167n, 316, 352n, 384n
Adams, Mr., 517
Adams, Peter, 18, 19n
Adams (brig), 20n
Adjutants, 46, 166n, 178n, 234n, 726
Admiralty, 451n
ADQMs. *See* DQMs and ADQMs
Africa, 284n
African Americans. *See* Antislavery; Slavery / slave trade; Slaves
Agents, 7 and n, 59, 79, 154, 164, 252n,
254n, 322, 522n, 560n, 568n, 668n
Aide(s)-de-camp: NG's former, xii, 5–6
and n, 6, 7n, 8–9 and n, 9, 23–24 and n,
35, 36n, 40–41 and n, 43, 48, 50–51, 61–
62 and n, 66–68 and n, 69n, 70n, 71, 74n,
80 and n, 83, 84, 85, 95 and n, 97 and n,
99 and n, 101n, 102–3 and n, 106, 111,
115, 124, 132, 133n, 135, 136n, 138–39,
142n, 143–44 and n, 144–45n, 146, 147,
148n, 150 and n, 159 and n, 160 and n,
162, 183n, 197–99 and n, 200, 218 and n,
231–33 and n, 234–35 and n, 235–36 and
n, 244, 258, 295 and n, 323n, 336–37 and
n, 348–49 and n, 349–51 and n, 357n,
358–59, 382n, 387, 388, 393n, 396–97 and
n, 397–98 and n, 407 and n, 408–9 and n,
423–25 and n, 500, 502n, 507n, 513–15
and n, 516 and n, 521 and n, 528n, 529,
530n, 534n, 562, 563n, 572n, 579n, 594–
96 and n, 617n, 625 and n, 640 and n, 641
and n, 656–57, 668 and n, 694 and n, 695
and n, 697n; NG's (during war), 21n,
169, 170n, 176, 178 and n, 197, 199n, 203,
227, 228, 229–30n, 241, 258, 259, 288,
337n, 385n, 407, 408–9, 500, 501, 588 and
n, 637, 710, 712, 713 and n, 742–43, 744n;
A. Wayne's, 49n, 467n, 735; GW's, 122
and n, 178n, 188n, 285n, 293n, 548n,
588n; Congress and, 218 and n;
R. Howe's, 272n; British, 309n; Lafayette's, 353n; D. Morgan's, 738n

313–14 and n, 332, 333n, 398, 399n, 417,
419, 433 and n, 433–34, 438–39, 446, 492,
496n, 506, 520 and n, 552, 553n, 581,
582n, 593, 629, 630n, 633 and n, 636,
637n, 643–44 and n, 648, 661–62; and
Flora, 27–28, 32–33, 132 and n, 133n, 240
and n, 283–84 and n, 284n, 287, 288n,
313–14 and n, 329, 346–47 and n, 398,
399n, 438–39, 492, 506, 507n, 520 and n,
532, 640, 645, 646n; Lafayette and, 29,
118, 240, 274–75 and n, 287, 288n, 313,
314n, 329 and n, 379, 380n, 398, 452 and
n, 531–32 and n, 533n, 596n, 626–27 and
n; and taxes, 43, 179–80 and n, 182 and
n, 358; and his army and QM department pay and subsistence, 83n, 173–75
and n, 221 and n, 252 and n, 263, 269n,
271 and n, 277, 446 and n, 512, 570; British merchants and, 119–20, 132, 133n,
240 and n, 284n, 312, 313n, 319, 341 and
n, 365, 366n, 406–7 and n, 428 and n,
428–29n, 433–34, 471–72 and n, 480,
481n, 484–85 and n, 521 and n, 522, 523–
24n, 537 and n, 544, 550n, 555 and n, 559
and n, 592, 593 and n, 642, 648, 650,
651n, 656–57 and n; European merchants and, 132 and n, 446, 446n, 504
and n, 547, 548n, 550; and merchants in
East Florida, 135, 136n, 161–62 and n,
182–83n, 371n; Penmans and, 135, 136n,
161–62 and n, 182 and n, 198, 199, 200n,
200–201 and n, 215 and n, 235, 236n,
503–4, 637 and n, 662 and n; W. Pierce,
Jr. / Pierce's partnerships and, 138–39,
332n, 336–37 and n, 381, 382n, 436, 502n,
515–16 and n, 521 and n, 522–23 and n,
524n, 537, 559, 656–57 and n, 657 and n;
H. Pendleton and, 142 and n, 240, 668
and n; W. Gibbons Jr. and, 161, 193n,
336, 337n, 381–82 and n, 393, 436, 502n,
515–16 and n, 519–20 and n, 655, 656n;
and servants' expenses, 162–63 and n,
188, 410; and travel expenses, 169, 170n,
176 and n, 177–78 and n, 197–98, 199n,
203n, 215 and n, 239, 283–84, 288, 289n,
321 and n, 385 and n, 410, 477, 556, 604–
5 and n; and northern properties, 179–
80 and n, 220–21 and n, 277–78 and n,
281, 459, 460n, 466 and n, 480, 481n, 483
and n, 506, 507n, 511–12, 513n, 519 and
n, 545, 546n, 547, 548n, 553 and n, 559
and n, 586, 587n, 604 and n, 606, 607n,
611, 612n, 614 and n, 620, 631, 632n, 678
and n, 681, 682n, 695, 696n; and mortgages and indentures, 183 and n, 198,
365n, 388, 389n, 390, 393, 426n, 443n,
447, 474, 478n, 503–4, 505–6, 507n, 513–
15 and n, 552, 553n, 561 and n, 567,

568n, 570, 571n, 574, 578–79 and n, 582n,
594, 595, 596n, 614–15 and n, 619, 620n,
641 and n, 642–43 and n; Philadelphia
merchants and, 195 and n, 213 and n,
224 and n, 263–64, 321n, 332, 333n, 355,
440 and n, 468 and n, 522 and n, 537,
538n; R.I. merchants and, 195 and n, 205,
213 and n, 216, 224, 277 and n, 278 and
n, 318, 365–66 and n, 414, 415n, 473, 474
and n, 544, 559 and n, 614 and n, 638,
642, 643, 648, 689 and n; C. Biddle and,
202, 203 and n, 221n, 256–57 and n, 321
and n, 322n, 480, 481n, 483 and n, 493,
506, 507n, 545, 546n, 604 and n, 614 and
n; Jacob Greene and, 205, 239, 277 and n,
283–84 and n, 338, 339, 345 and n, 446,
474, 605, 606n, 611 and n, 614, 643, 644n;
estate of, 209n, 219–21 and n, 221–22,
317, 332n, 352n, 367–69n, 377–78n, 397n,
400n, 425n, 426n, 507n, 553n, 568n, 575–
76n, 579n, 612–13 and n, 632n, 656n,
703n; estimate of estate of, 219–21 and
n, 221–22, 317, 352n; R. Forsyth and,
249–50 and n, 307–8, 330–31 and n, 376,
377n, 402–3 and n, 461, 462n, 500–501,
502n, 503 and n, 535, 536n, 538–39 and
n, 553, 554n, 600; and sloop *Charleston
Packet*, 250 and n, 338 and n, 339, 376n,
562, 563n, 676; Gov. W. Greene and, 256
and n, 268; G. Gibbs and, 264n, 377,
378n and n, 446 and n, 689 and n; W. Littlefield and, 277, 278, 446, 629, 635 and
n, 689 and n; Christopher Greene and,
277; S. Ward Jr. and, 278, 614–15 and n,
617–18 and n, 635; N.Y. merchants and,
289 and n, 301 and n, 341n, 341 and n,
346, 437, 473 and n, 522, 554–55 and n,
590, 591n, 592 and n, 593, 594n, 598–99
and n, 604–5 and n, 606, 608 and n, 615–
16, 617, 658–69 and n, 671 and n; E. Edwards and, 310 and n, 327, 332, 333,
334n; H. Banks and, 366, 402 and n,
403n, 403–5 and n, 422 and n, 427 and n,
461, 514–15 and n, 553, 554n, 554 and n,
559–60 and n, 578–79 and n, 596n, 600
and n, 614–15 and n, 619–20 and n, 635;
J. McQueen and, 377, 378n, 402n, 514,
515n, 527, 528n, 595, 658–59 and n;
S. Vernon and, 377, 378, 378n; W. Gibbons Sr., and, 381, 520 and n, 595, 596n,
656n; P. Carnes and, 402n, 410, 476–77,
478n; J. Seagrove and, 447, 448n, 452,
454, 457–58 and n, 493n, 499n, 655; Ga.
merchants and, 472n, 488 and n, 516 and
n, 521 and n, 522–23 and n, 524n, 559,
656–57 and n, 657 and n, 659–60 and n,
665 and n, 668 and n, 672, 673 and n,
674, 678, 682, 684–85 and n, 687–88,

688–89, 692 and n, 693 and n, 694 and n, 695, 696; and ideas for trade, 485–86, 487n; I. Senter and, 512; J. Clay and, 515–16 and n; Conn. tanner and, 516–17 and n; Boston merchants and, 555–56 and n, 557–58 and n; and privateer *Tartar*, 556, 557n; boat belonging to, 684–85 and n, 692, 693. *See also* Bonds (personal), NG and; Credit, NG and
—Family matters: and CG, ix–x, 54, 55n, 71, 72–73, 74–75n, 76, 81, 83 and n, 86–87, 91, 92–93 and n, 98 and n, 143, 144n, 147, 163 and n, 164, 196, 203, 210n, 215 and n, 231–33n, 248, 249n, 252, 253n, 264n, 266, 271, 276, 277n, 284 and n, 293n, 294, 295, 296n, 297, 298 and n, 299, 308, 311, 312n, 328, 339, 339n, 348 and n, 374, 376–77 and n, 386–87 and n, 391–92 and n, 405n, 428, 455n, 465, 474n, 483n, 489–93 and n, 493, 506, 511–12, 513n, 528–29 and n, 529–30 and n, 530–31 and n, 553, 590, 603, 605 and n, 606n, 612–13, 621, 634, 641, 669, 669 and n, 675, 677–78, 683, 688 and n, 693, 697n, 710n, 712–13 and n, 725, 743, 744n; and children, ix–x, 76, 92, 164, 167n, 186 and n, 196, 256n, 257 and n, 273 and n, 276, 321 and n, 322, 328, 334–35 and n, 335n, 340–41, 345, 369, 374, 387, 474 and n, 493, 501–2 and n, 539–40 and n, 552 and n, 553, 571 and n, 576, 577n, 578, 580 and n, 581–82, 583 and n, 584n, 590 and n, 593 and n, 596, 603, 612–13, 614n, 618, 621, 622–23n, 634, 641, 669 and n, 675, 676, 700–701n, 703–4n, 713, 721, 724 and n, 732, 733n; and deaths of children, x, 576, 577n, 578 and n, 580n, 583, 589 and n, 590n, 622–23n, 669n, 677n, 683n, 703n, 704n; and expenses, x, 72, 73n, 74n, 83 and n, 85 and n, 92–93 and n, 142 and n, 229n, 239, 257 and n, 263–64 and n, 266, 267n, 268, 297, 298n, 308, 318, 320, 321 and n, 332, 333n, 334–35 and n, 339 and n, 340–41 and n, 345, 346, 374, 387, 428, 590, 604–5 and n, 606n, 648, 662 and n, 678, 682, 689 and n, 690, 692, 720–22 and n; and move to Ga., x, xi, 44n, 91n, 167n, 249n, 263n, 348n, 353n, 520n, 541n, 553n, 559n, 570, 571 and n, 572n, 573, 574n, 576n, 590n, 591, 595, 596n, 597, 598n, 599 and n, 600, 603 and n, 605 and n, 606, 607n, 608, 609n, 611 and n, 614 and n, 615n, 616 and n, 617, 618n, 621–22 and n, 623, 625, 626, 627, 630, 632, 634, 640, 642, 678n, 681, 692n; and Mulberry Grove plantation, x, xi, 44n, 91n, 488n, 621–22 and n, 674–75, 676–77, 677–78, 683, 688, 692, 693, 696n, 697–99n, 703n,

704n; and cousin Griffin Greene, xi, 26 and n, 26–28 and n, 28–29 and n, 32 and n, 32–33, 34, 132 and n, 132–33 and n, 239, 240 and n, 277 and n, 283, 284n, 287, 288n, 313–14 and n, 332, 333n, 346–47 and n, 370, 380n, 398, 399n, 400–401 and n, 417, 418n, 418–21 and n, 429–31, 433 and n, 433–34, 438–39 and n, 446, 492, 496n, 506, 520 and n, 547, 548n, 552, 553n, 569–70, 576, 577n, 578, 581, 582n, 583, 586, 593, 606n, 613, 629–30 and n, 633 and n, 636, 637n, 640, 641n, 643–44 and n, 648 and n, 661–62, 673, 709; and children's health, 6, 511, 576, 577n, 581–82, 583, 584n, 589, 590, 621, 669 and n, 672n, 676, 677n; NG on, 27, 35–36, 85, 92, 161, 164, 253, 254n, 280, 387, 391, 590, 613, 621, 676–77, 677–78; and brother Jacob, 34–36 and n, 54–56 and n, 159n, 185–86 and n, 218 and n, 277 and n, 283–84 and n, 321, 328 and n, 329 and n, 338, 339, 345 and n, 346–47 and n, 370 and n, 386n, 446, 512, 569–70, 578, 605, 606n, 611 and n, 613, 614, 643, 644n; and housing in Newport, 35, 185n, 328, 329n, 512, 517, 635; and other siblings and Greene relatives, 35–36 and n, 37n, 147, 150n, 203 and n, 218, 219n, 277–78 and n, 283, 284n, 345, 372–73 and n, 374 and n, 375, 376 and n, 474, 530, 531n, 603 and n, 611 and n, 611–12 and n, 613, 643; and tutors, 167n, 387, 388n, 475, 476n, 501–2 and n, 541n, 552 and n, 571, 577 and n, 581, 583 and n, 584n, 585 and n, 590 and n, 591 and n, 602 and n, 604 and n, 606 and n, 607, 609, 610n, 621, 623n, 675, 676, 680n, 703n; and home in Coventry, R.I., 210n; and W. Littlefield, 217, 273 and n, 277, 375n, 446, 511–12, 513n, 613, 614n, 620, 629, 630–31 and n, 632, 633n, 634–35 and n, 662, 676, 689 and n, 712; and household furnishings, 593, 612, 648, 649, 662 and n, 673, 690; in NG's will, 612–13
—Opinions, military: of his services, xiii, 44–45, 161, 276; on desertions and mutiny, 4, 9, 10n, 11–12, 19–20, 37, 48, 56, 60; on supply and supply-department matters, 5, 20, 22, 46, 58–59, 668, 714, 717–18, 723, 726, 730 and n; on preparations for troops' departures, 14, 22–23, 37, 44, 47–48, 56, 58, 60; on Continental army, 36, 96; on his army's achievements, 44–45; on plundering, 45; on pay and subsistence matters, 46, 49, 50, 53, 54, 58, 137–38, 221, 258–59, 569; on departures of his troops, 59, 75; on his former spies, 64, 448, 663–64; of various

547, 548n, 550 and n, 554–55 and n, 555
and n, 555–56 and n, 557–58 and n, 558–
59n, 559 and n, 565, 567n, 572, 572 and
n, 574–75, 590, 591n, 592 and n, 593 and
n, 594n, 598–99 and n, 604–5 and n, 606,
608 and n, 614 and n, 615–16, 630n, 632
and n, 637 and n, 638, 642–43, 644 and n,
645n, 648 and n, 649 and n, 650, 651n,
656 and n, 656–57 and n, 658–59 and n,
659–60 and n, 661–62 and n, 665 and n,
666, 668 and n, 671, 671 and n, 672–73
and n, 673 and n, 673–74, 678, 682, 684–
85 and n, 687–88, 688–89, 689 and n,
689–90 and n, 692 and n, 693 and n, 694
and n, 695 and n, 696 and n; and N.C.,
7n, 111n, 136n, 139 and n, 163, 406n,
410n; Philadelphia and, 7n, 154, 162, 195
and n, 205, 206, 213 and n, 213–14 and n,
224 and n, 257 and n, 263–64, 266, 275
and n, 321, 332, 333n, 345, 355, 360–61,
362n, 394n, 417, 421n, 432n, 440 and n,
452, 454, 458, 459n, 467, 468 and n, 480,
482n, 485, 505, 518, 519n, 537, 538n, 577,
578n; of Savannah and Ga., 8–9 and
n, 23–24, 51, 138–39, 331, 332n, 336–37,
388, 393, 396–97 and n, 399 and n, 400n,
423–24, 458n, 488 and n, 489n, 502n,
515–16 and n, 518, 519n, 521 and n, 522–
23 and n, 524n, 543, 550 and n, 559, 623,
625n, 656–57 and n, 657 and n, 659–60
and n, 665 and n, 668 and n, 672, 673 and
n, 673–74, 678, 682, 684–85 and n, 687–
88, 688–89, 692 and n, 693 and n, 694
and n, 695, 696; Havana and, 9, 23, 24n,
84, 85n, 145, 146, 148n, 150 and n, 232,
244, 303, 456–58 and n, 459, 467, 468n,
477, 485–86, 488n, 509 and n; in Va., 16,
28, 96, 250n, 303, 304n, 330, 331n, 365n,
411 and n, 535, 586; Loyalist, 16n, 136n,
147, 149–50n, 289n, 351n, 592 and n; of
N.Y., 16n, 209n, 251–52 and n, 262, 289
and n, 328, 341 and n, 346, 362n, 437,
457–58, 459, 460 and n, 466 and n, 467,
473 and n, 493n, 499n, 554–55 and n,
570, 581, 590, 592 and n, 593, 594n, 604–5
and n, 607, 608 and n, 615–16, 617, 658–
59 and n, 671 and n; and West Indies, 24,
25n, 87, 118n; European, 27, 132, 132 and
n, 243, 275, 398, 417–18n, 419, 420, 433,
438n, 446, 446n, 503 and n, 540 and n,
544, 547, 548n, 550, 552, 555, 644; of
Boston and Mass., 71n, 138–39 and n,
204 and n, 234n, 284n, 291, 326, 346, 418,
419, 440, 522 and n, 555–56 and n, 557–
58 and n, 570, 571n, 618 and n, 656 and
n; A. Pettit as, 87; and economic conditions, 118n, 132, 163, 360–61, 362n, 406,
434, 452, 458, 459, 459n, 460 and n, 467,

468, 474, 480, 486, 492–93, 511, 517, 518,
518n, 522 and n, 550, 559, 563n, 618 and
n, 633 and n, 647n; British, 119–20, 132,
133n, 154, 184–85, 240 and n, 242, 243,
283–84 and n, 290 and n, 296n, 312,
313n, 318, 319, 324n, 331n, 351n, 365–66
and n, 377, 378, 406–7 and n, 428 and n,
428–29n, 433–34, 471–72 and n, 480,
481n, 484–85 and n, 488, 521 and n, 522
and n, 523–24n, 537 and n, 544, 550n,
559 and n, 563n, 592, 593 and n, 624n,
638, 648, 650, 651n, 662; in St. Augustine
and East Florida, 136n, 161–62, 458,
459n, 486, 508–9; of Newport and R.I.,
195 and n, 205 and n, 213 and n, 214 and
n, 216, 224, 241 and n, 249n, 251, 256,
263, 263n, 275n, 277, 278, 320, 365–66
and n, 378n, 407, 414, 415n, 418, 428 and
n, 437, 473, 474 and n, 482n, 511, 513n,
517, 518n, 544, 558 and n, 559 and n, 572,
574n, 598–99 and n, 614 and n, 615–16,
631n, 638, 642, 643, 648, 689 and n, 723n;
and GW, 206 and n; of Hartford and
Conn., 217–18 and n, 251 and n, 445, 517
and n, 518n, 576n; and soldier's pay,
261–62; of Baltimore, 345; J. Seagrove as,
447, 448n, 452, 454, 457–58 and n, 459,
467, 468n, 499n; and Cumberland Island, 470, 471n, 472n, 518, 519n, 537,
577, 578n; dispute involving, 522 and n;
and land speculation, 647n. See also
Banks, John; Deane, Barnabas; Greene,
Griffin; Greene, Jacob & Company; Pettit, Charles; Pierce, William, Jr.; Wadsworth, Jeremiah
Mercier, John D., 451n
Mermaid, H. M. S., 719 and n
Merrel, Spencer, 722
Merriweather, James, 4, 9, 11, 12n, 21n
Mexico, 484n, 491, 507n, 508, 509 and n
Middleton, Arthur, 49n, 93, 94n
Middletown, Conn., 300n
Mifflin, Thomas: *letters to*, 169, 178, 258,
280; *letters from*, 254, 274; *biog. note*, vol.
1: 234n; and W. Mifflin, 158n; as presi-
dent of Congress, 169, 170n; and NG,
169–70 and n, 254 and n, 274, 280; and
Pa. politics, 178n, 654n; as QM general,
178n, 560 and n, 717n; and GW, 188n;
and Indian commissioners, 274, 280,
289n. See also Congress
Mifflin, Warner, 155–58 and n; *letter from*,
155; *letter to*, 191
Milan, Italy, 167 and n
Militia, American, 307n, 589, 597, 598n. *See
also militias of particular states*
Militia, Loyalist, 12n, 154n, 200, 201n,
202n, 280 and n, 347 and n, 598n

and n, 369 and n, 515–16 and n, 521 and n, 523, 524n, 562, 563n, 622, 625–26 and n, 641 and n, 648 and n, 661–62 and n, 664–65 and n, 671 and n, 672–73 and n, 682, 689
Owen, James B., 244n
Owen, John, 319n
Oxen, 10, 25, 43, 277, 381, 637

P

Paca, William, 126, 127 and n, 128n, 130, 138 and n, 166 and n; *letters to*, 130, 166; *letter from*, 138
Paine, Nancy Littlefield, 613 and n
Paine, Nathaniel, 555, 556n
Paint, 136n
Paper, 79, 148n
Paris: J. Wadsworth and, 74, 208 and n, 398; money coined at, 213n; Welles family and, 246n; T. Kosciuszko and, 355; merchants of, 398, 419, 433, 547, 548n, 552; Griffin Greene and, 400, 401 and n, 419, 420, 433, 438–39; J. McQueen and, 528n, 533, 534n; Lafayette and, 531–32 and n
Parker, Alexander, 50
Parker, Daniel, 5, 16n
Parker, Daniel & Company, 5, 6n, 15, 16n, 132n
Parole, 727
Parsons, Mr., 681
Partridge, Samuel: *letter from*, 242
Paschke, Frederick, 94–95
Passaic River, 220, 460n, 483, 506
Passes and passports, 139n
Pasture, 43
Patton, Robert, 411 and n, 422, 423n, 427, 461–62, 477, 478n, 575n
Paulus Hook, N.J., 107 and n, 732, 733n
Pawling's Mills, Pa., 159n
Pawtucket River, 708 and n
Pay and subsistence: of delegates to Congress, 7n, 186 and n, 203; of army officers and staff department personnel, 12, 14n, 18–19 and n, 19n, 31, 32n, 33, 41, 46, 49 and n, 50 and n, 53 and n, 54, 58, 59n, 70, 77, 78 and n, 79, 86, 88, 90, 91n, 112, 136–37 and n, 137–38 and n, 165, 166n, 172 and n, 173–75 and n, 181 and n, 204, 205n, 207 and n, 260 and n, 261–62, 264–65 and n, 273n, 286 and n, 299, 300n, 311, 355n, 378–79, 415, 416n, 435, 436n, 444, 445, 487n, 710 and n, 716; cavalry troops and, 13, 14n, 19, 62, 63n; officers' retirement, 31, 32n, 50 and n, 299, 300n, 306, 311, 312n, 438n; NG and matters concerning, 38–39 and n, 39–40 and n, 46, 49 and n, 50, 53 and n, 54, 60, 61n,

77, 78 and n, 95, 112, 169, 170n, 172 and n, 173–74, 175n, 207 and n, 221 and n, 241 and n, 247–48 and n, 252 and n, 258–59 and n, 269n, 271 and n, 276, 435, 436n, 444, 445, 446 and n; Congress and, 41, 53 and n, 54, 55n, 76, 78 and n, 130n, 136–37 and n, 137–38 and n, 169, 170n, 172 and n, 173n, 204, 205n, 241 and n, 258–59 and n, 263, 415, 416n, 435, 436n, 444, 445, 710n, 711; R. Morris and matters concerning, 41, 53–54n, 77, 78 and n, 130n, 138 and n, 207 and n, 316, 318n; advances of, 50, 58, 59n, 130n; certificates for, 53, 327, 328n, 339, 361–62, 371, 372n, 480–81 and n, 535; of matross, 60, 61n; depreciation of, 61, 63n, 204, 205n, 252n, 264, 265n, 269n, 271, 273n, 435, 436n; of Va. line, 61, 63n; states and, 61–62, 63n, 204, 221 and n, 252 and n, 260 and n, 261–62 and n, 262n, 263, 264, 269n, 273n, 276, 415, 437, 438n, 446 and n, 481 and n; grievances concerning, 76; of Pa. line, 76, 88; of Md. line, 130n; GW's army and, 132n; B. Lincoln and matters concerning, 138 and n, 172n, 173n; of clerk for NG, 168–69 and n; GW and matters concerning, 173n; for preparing digest of S.C. laws, 236, 237n; of wounded soldier, 260 and n, 261–62 and n; of impost officials, 263; of Spanish troops, 486; of plantation overseer, 515–16, 641 and n; Baron Steuben and, 569 and n; militia and, 711
Paymasters: J. Clay as, 6, 7n, 170n, 451n, 500, 637, 638n; J. S. Dart as, 13, 18, 19 and n, 19n, 49, 59n, 135, 136n, 162 and n, 169, 170n, 176, 197–98, 199, 201, 261n, 450, 450 and n, 451n, 477, 500; and SoArmy accounts, 13, 17 and n, 49, 58, 90, 169, 170n, 176 and n, 229n, 449–50 and n, 451n, 500, 637, 638n; and GW's army, 18, 19; and pay proposal, 41; J. Pierce as, 104–5 and n, 286 and n, 409n, 637 and n, 638n; of QM department, 181 and n, 204n, 444; certificates of, 327, 328n; J. Story as, 558n
Peace: treaties of, 28, 29n, 31n, 37, 38n, 40, 47 and n, 48, 49n, 102, 103n, 110 and n, 132, 136n, 177, 186, 364n; comments and opinions concerning, 31, 44–45, 58, 110, 118 and n, 129, 139, 154, 177, 204, 209, 210, 723, 731; economic effects of, 72, 102, 103n, 132, 164, 240; proposals concerning, 719 and n
Peaches, 677
Peale, Charles Willson, 587n
Pears, 677
Peas, 10, 676, 693